Lifespan Development

Accepted by
CP
20801

95293049
c-3
np

Lifespan Development

A TOPICAL APPROACH

Janina M. Jolley
Clarion University of Pennsylvania

Mark L. Mitchell
Clarion University of Pennsylvania

Madison Dubuque, IA Guilford, CT Chicago Toronto London
Caracas Mexico City Buenos Aires Madrid Bogota Sydney

Book Team

Executive Publisher *Edgar J. Laube*
Acquisitions Editor *Steven Yetter*
Project Editor *Ted Underhill*
Proofreading Coordinator *Carrie Barker*
Photo Editor *Rose Deluhery*
Permissions Coordinator *Karen L. Storlie*
Production Manager *Beth Kundert*
Production/Costing Manager *Sherry Padden*
Production/Imaging and Media Development Manager *Linda Meehan Avenarius*
Visuals/Design Freelance Specialist *Mary L. Christianson*
Marketing Manager *Carla Aspelmeier*
Copywriter *Jennifer Smith*

Basal Text *10/12 Times Roman*
Display Type *Futura Book*
Typesetting System *Macintosh™ QuarkXPress™*
Paper Stock *50# Mirror Matte*

Vice President of Production and Business Development *Vickie Putman*
Vice President of Sales and Marketing *Bob McLaughlin*
Vice President of Business Development *Russ Domeyer*
Director of Marketing *John Finn*

A Times Mirror Company

The credits section for this book begins on page 509 and is considered an extension of the copyright page.

Cover and interior designs by Maureen McCutcheon Design

Cover image by Claude Monet, *The Artist's Garden at Vétheuil* (detail), Ailsa Mellon Bruce Collection © 1995 Board of Trustees, National Gallery of Art, Washington.

Line art rendered by Precision Graphics, unless noted otherwise.

Freelance Permission Editor Karen Dorman

Copyedited by Cindy Peck; proofread by Ann M. Kelly

Production by Michelle Campbell

Copyright © 1996 Times Mirror Higher Education Group, Inc.
All rights reserved

Library of Congress Catalog Card Number: 95–76283

ISBN 0–697–12981–0

No part of this publication may be reproduced, stored in a retrieval system, or transmitted, in any form or by any means, electronic, mechanical, photocopying, recording, or otherwise, without the prior written permission of the publisher.

Printed in the United States of America by Times Mirror Higher Education Group, Inc., 2460 Kerper Boulevard, Dubuque, IA 52001

10 9 8 7 6 5 4 3 2 1

To Neal Jolley and Zoë Kibbe

BRIEF CONTENTS

CONTENTS

CHAPTER 8
SELF- AND MORAL DEVELOPMENT 252

CHAPTER 9
ATTACHMENT 284

CHAPTER 10
LOVE AND FRIENDSHIPS 312

CHAPTER 11
THE FAMILY 336

Issue in Focus

Research in Focus

Theory in Focus

PREFACE

We wrote this book to help students think like developmental psychologists. Specifically, we want students who read this book to:

- Critically examine claims about the nature and causes of development;
- Have a clear understanding of the major issues in developmental psychology—from nature/nurture to the effects of day care; and
- To understand what developmental psychologists have learned—and what they still need to learn—about the development of memory, intelligence, attachment, and other developmental issues.

To reach these goals, we decided to write a readable, topical text. We decided on a topical/chronological approach for the same reason that professors often organize their lectures around topics (such as moral development, cognitive development, and attachment): the topical/chronological approach allows us to discuss lifespan theories and processes in an organized, coherent way rather than in bits and pieces.

We decided to make the text as easy to read and learn from as possible because there are already many topically organized handbooks, edited volumes, and texts that are suitable for graduate students and advanced undergraduates. To make the text readable, we used a simple, straightforward writing style and focused on explaining major concepts rather than bombarding students with one "factoid" after another. To help students organize, retain, and think about what they read, we have included self-check questions, summary tables, diagrams, focus boxes, and key terms.

If our experiences with this material are any indication, we have succeeded. We hope that your students will benefit as much from using this text as ours have.

Supplementary Materials

Brown & Benchmark Publishers has gathered a group of talented individuals with many years of experience in teaching lifespan development to create supplementary materials that will assist instructors and students who use this text. The supplements are designed to make it as easy as possible to customize the entire package for the unique needs of professors and their students.

An ***INSTRUCTOR'S MANUAL*** has been prepared by the authors of ***Lifespan Development: A Topical Approach.*** Each chapter of the manual includes a summary outline, learning objectives, key terms, sample lectures, classroom/student activities, questions for review and discussion, overhead transparency masters, and lists of supplemental readings.

The *Instructor's Manual* includes a comprehensive ***Test Item File*** consisting of over 1,000 items. Each item is referenced to its related learning objective and text page and is classified as factual, conceptual, or applied based on the first three levels of Benjamin Bloom's taxonomy.

The questions in the *Test Item File* are available on *MicroTest III*, a powerful but easy-to-use test-generating program by Chariot Software Group. *MicroTest* is available for DOS, Windows, and Macintosh. With *MicroTest,* you can easily select questions from the *Test Item File* and print a test and an answer key. You can customize questions, headings, and instructions; you can add or import questions of your own; and you can print your test in a choice of fonts if your printer supports them. You can obtain a copy of *MicroTest III* by contacting your local Brown & Benchmark Sales Representative or by phoning Educational Resources at 800–338–5371.

The ***Brown & Benchmark Developmental Psychology Transparency/Slide Set*** consists of 100 newly developed acetate transparencies or slides. These full-color illustrations include graphics from various outside sources. Created by Lynne Blesz-Vestal, these transparencies were expressly designed to provide comprehensive coverage of all major topic areas generally covered in developmental psychology. A comprehensive annotated guide provides a brief description for each transparency and helpful suggestions for use in the classroom.

A large selection of **Videotapes,** including *Seasons of Life,* and *Childhood,* is also available to instructors, based on the number of textbooks ordered from Brown & Benchmark Publishers by your bookstore.

The ***Human Development Interactive Videodisc Set*** produced by Roger Ray of Rollins College, brings lifespan development to life with instant access to over 30 brief video segments from the highly acclaimed *Seasons of Life* series. The 2-disc set can be used alone for selecting and sequencing excerpts, or in tandem with a Macintosh computer to add interactive commentary capability, as well as extra video and search options. Consult your Brown & Benchmark Sales Representative for details.

The AIDS Booklet, 3e, by Frank D. Cox of Santa Barbara City College, is a brief but comprehensive introduction to the Acquired Immune Deficiency Syndrome which is caused by HIV (Human Immunodeficiency Virus) and related viruses.

The Critical Thinker, written by Richard Mayer and Fiona Goodchild of the University of California, Santa Barbara, uses excerpts from introductory psychology textbooks to show students how to think critically about psychology. Either this or the AIDS booklet is available at no charge to first-year adopters of our textbook or can be purchased separately.

B&B CourseKits™

B&B CourseKits™ are course-specific collections of for sale educational materials custom packaged for maximum convenience and value. CourseKits offer you the flexibility of customizing and combining Brown & Benchmark course materials (B&B CourseKits™, Annual Editions®, Taking Sides®, etc.) with your own or other material. Each CourseKit contains two or more instructor-selected items conveniently packaged and priced for your students. For more information on B&B CourseKits™, please contact your local Brown & Benchmark representative.

Annual Editions® Magazines, newspapers, and journals of the public press play an important role in providing current, first-rate, relevant educational information. If in your lifespan development course you are interested in exposing your students to a wide range of current, well-balanced, carefully selected articles from some of the most important magazines, newspapers, and journals published today, you may want to consider *Annual Editions: Human Development, Annual Editions: Aging,* or *Annual Editions: Death, Dying, & Bereavement,* published by the Dushkin Publishing Group, a unit of Brown & Benchmark Publishers. Each *Annual Editions* contains articles on topics related to the latest research and thinking in lifespan development. *Annual Editions* is updated on an annual basis, and there are a number of features designed to make it particularly useful, including a topic guide, an annotated table of contents, and unit overviews. For the professor using *Annual Editions* in the classroom, an Instructor's Resource Guide with test questions is available. Consult your Brown & Benchmark sales representative for more details.

CourseMedia™ As educational needs and methods change, Brown & Benchmark adds innovative, contemporary student materials for the computer, audio, and video devices of the 1990s and beyond. These include the following:

- Stand-alone materials
- Study guides
- Software simulations
- Tutorials
- Exercises

CourseMedia™ also includes instructional aids you can use to enhance lectures and discussions, such as:

- Videos
- Level I and III videodiscs
- CD-ROMs

CourseWorks CourseWorks (formerly Kinko's CourseWorks in the U.S.) is the Brown & Benchmark custom publishing service. With its own printing and distribution facility, CourseWorks gives you the flexibility to add current material to your course at any time. CourseWorks provides you with a unique set of options, including:

- Customizing Brown & Benchmark CourseBooks
- Publishing your own material
- Including any previously published material for which we can secure permissions
- Adding photos
- Performing copyediting
- Creating custom covers

A ***Customized Transparency Program*** is available to adopters based on the number of textbooks ordered. Consult your Brown & Benchmark Representative for ordering policies.

Acknowledgments

The inspiration for writing *Lifespan Development: A Topical Approach* took only a few hours to germinate. However, actually writing the text took years of diligence, toil, and care. If it had not been for the support of our publisher, friends, and family, we could not have met this challenge.

To our publisher, Brown & Benchmark, we offer our appreciation for their support and encouragement. Specifically, we wish to thank our editor, Steven Yetter; developmental editor, Ted Underhill, production editors, Gloria Schiesl and Michelle Campbell; visuals/design freelance specialist, Mary Christianson; permissions coordinator, Karen Dorman; photo editor, Rose Deluhery; and copy editor, Cindy Peck for their hard work and vision. We also thank Michael Lange for asking us to join the Brown & Benchmark team and for his support during the first drafts of *Lifespan Development.*

In addition to thanking the team at Brown & Benchmark, we would like to thank three groups of dedicated reviewers whose valuable comments have greatly enhanced the quality of *Lifespan Development.* First, we would like to thank the dedicated professors who made helpful comments and shared their insights with us:

Thomas Andre, *Iowa State University*
Martha M. Ellis, *Collin County Community College*
John Gibbs, *Ohio State University*
Gayle Y. Iwamasa, *Ball State University*
Vivian Jenkins, *University of Southern Illinois*
Daniel K. Lapsley, *Brandon University*
Alice LoCicero, *Lesley College*
Stuart I. Offenbach, *Purdue University*
William Panak, *Iowa State University*

Second, we would like to thank two journalists, Robert Tremblay and K. Lee Howard for reviewing various drafts of *Lifespan Development: A Topical Approach.* Bob and Lee's comments made the text's reading level and content more accessible to student readers. Third, we wish to thank Professor Edward Caropreso for his comments and insights.

Finally, we offer our gratitude to our family and friends for believing in us and providing us with moral support over the many years of this project.

Lifespan Development

1

Chapter

Developmental Psychology: Issues and Methods

We laugh, we cry, we are born, we die,
Who will riddle me the how and the why?

ALFRED LORD TENNYSON

Chapter Overview

This chapter introduces the broad field of lifespan developmental psychology. In this chapter, you will learn how developmental psychologists try to describe, predict, and explain the psychological changes people go through during their voyage from "womb to tomb." You will see that in trying to describe, predict, and explain development, developmental psychologists address important, practical, and controversial issues. Finally, you will learn how developmental psychologists try to gather accurate and unbiased information about these issues.

What Is Lifespan Developmental Psychology?

Lifespan developmental psychology is the *scientific* study of how people grow and change from conception to the moment of death. If you ponder this definition, you will realize that lifespan developmental psychology is a vast and complex field. Imagine trying to describe, predict, and explain all the physical, social, and cognitive changes that you have undergone since your mother's ovum united with your father's sperm!

Describing Development

Trying to accomplish just one of these goals—*describing* who you are today and how you have changed over the years—is a monumental task. To formulate accurate descriptions, developmental psychologists draw not only on their own research but also on the work of anthropologists, biologists, sociologists, and specialists from every field of psychology (see table 1.1).

What has been the result of these efforts to describe development? By accurately describing the similarities and differences among age groups, developmental psychologists have challenged inaccurate, age-based stereotypes. As you will see throughout this text, having an accurate picture of different age groups is of immense practical value. For example, information gathered by developmental psychologists has helped grandparents better relate to their grandchildren, parents better relate to their children, and college students better relate to their siblings, parents, and grandparents.

In addition to helping people better relate to one another, developmental psychologists aid teachers, medical professionals, and sales representatives. Imagine a school teacher who doesn't know how children think, a nurse working with terminal patients who doesn't understand the dying process, or a sales representative trying to sell a product to a particular age group without knowing how different age groups behave. No wonder most nursing programs, most teacher education programs, and many MBA programs require their students to take developmental psychology (see table 1.2).

Table 1.1

Developmental Questions from Different Fields and Areas of Psychology

Field or Area	Developmental Questions
Anthropology	Is development the same in all cultures?
Biology	How do genes influence development?
Clinical psychology	Why are some people more susceptible to mental illness than other people?
Industrial psychology	What role does job satisfaction play in adult development?
Intelligence	Are declines in intelligence in old age substantial? Can these declines be reversed?
Linguistics and psycholinguistics	Are children better than adults at learning languages?
Memory	Why are adults able to remember more than children?
Perception	How does our ability to perceive the world change with age?
Personality	How does personality change over the lifespan?
Physiological psychology	How do brain development and hormonal changes affect psychological development?
Social psychology	How do parents and peers shape values? What affects sex-role development?
Sociology	Do different social groups experience the same patterns of development?

Predicting Development

Describing development paves the way for *predicting* development. For example, if you know how 7-year-olds think compared to 2-year-olds, then you can predict what changes a 2-year-old's thinking will undergo by the time she turns 8. Similarly, knowing the changes people undergo as they age may help you predict your own future. Certainly, specifying precisely what changes people undergo as they age is a considerable improvement over just stating "people change as they age." However, there are three problems with age-based predictions.

First, people tend to pay too much attention to age differences and not enough attention to similarities. For example, from what you have read in the popular press, you may think that there are enormous age-based differences in intelligence between 50-year-olds and 60-year-olds. However, many studies fail to find differences. Even when age differences are found, the differences are often quite small (Baltes, 1993; Baltes & Staudinger, 1993).

Second, some parents take age predictions too seriously. If their child isn't walking, talking, or adding at the "right" age, they believe their child is lagging behind developmentally. What these parents should consider is that for most things, there is not an *ideal* age, but rather an *average* age. Furthermore, they should realize that this average age is hardly typical. Indeed, about half of the children will reach a specific developmental level before the average age and half will reach the level after that age. Consequently, most children will not reach a given level of development at the average age.

Table 1.2

Relevance of Developmental Psychology to Various Professions

Profession	Developmental Questions
Adoption counselor	What kind of people would be the most effective parents for a particular child?
Advertiser	How can I produce ads that appeal to different age groups?
Counseling psychologist	What key issues do people struggle with at different times in their life? How does a normal __-year-old behave? What problems will people "grow out" of?
Judge	Should an elderly person be made a ward of the court? Would a child be better off with her mother or father? Should a juvenile offender be treated like an adult? What factors may encourage a criminal to reform?
Lawyer	To what extent can children's testimony be trusted?
Manager	What should our retirement policy be?
Nurse	What explanations can a child understand? How should babies be treated? What special considerations should be taken in treating an elderly person? a teenager? How do people cope with and understand death?
Physician	What are the effects of certain genetic abnormalities (for example, Down syndrome)? To what extent can children's accounts of illness or abuse be believed? To what extent is a medical problem caused by aging or illness? Is the failure of an infant to thrive due to psychological or to physical problems?
Social worker	What makes a family unsuitable for rearing children?
Teacher	How do children learn? Is a child developmentally delayed? What educational materials should be introduced at what age? What factors, at this age, will contribute to lifelong learning? What social tasks are important for a child to master at this age?

Third, chronological age is not the only predictor of development. If it were, then everyone of the same age would be at the same developmental level. However, people who are the same age are not necessarily at the same developmental level. Thus, if we want to predict what a girl would be like in two years, we need to know not only her age, but facts about her family, her health, the kinds of learning experiences she is getting, and her level of physical development (for example, whether she has reached puberty yet). These other variables are not as easy to measure as age, but they must be measured if we are to accurately predict development.

Normative social events are nonbiological events that most people in a given culture experience at the same time. In the United States, high school graduation is a normative social event. What might be some effects of graduating unusually early or late, or of dropping out of high school?

Explaining Development

If age alone is not enough to help us predict developmental changes, it is even more inadequate for *explaining why* people develop the way they do. Knowing that people change with age doesn't tell us why they change. That is, age alone does not cause people to change. Instead, people change because certain events tend to happen to them as they age. According to Mavis Hetherington and Ross Parke (1993), as people age, they encounter three major kinds of events: (1) normative age-graded events, (2) nonnormative events, and (3) cohort or historical events.

Normative Age-Graded Events

Normative age-graded events are events that most people (normally) experience at about the same age. Consequently, when developmental changes seem to be tied to age, we can attribute these changes to normative age-related events. These causes of development can be divided into two types: normative maturational and normative social events.

Normative Maturational Events **Normative maturational events** are biological events that most people experience at about the same age. As you can see from table 1.3, common normative maturational events include teething, being ready to walk, the hormonal changes of puberty and menopause, the rapid development of the brain between infancy and adulthood, and physical aging. Normative maturational events are the same regardless of culture and serve to make people similar. For example, almost everyone walks and talks at about the same age. In chapter 4, and throughout this book, you'll see numerous examples of how physical development affects psychological development.

Table 1.3

Examples of Types of Events Affecting Development

Normative Maturational Events	Nonnormative Events	Normative Social Events	Historical Events
Teething	Job promotion	Entering kindergarten	Wars
Walking	Divorce	Dating	Civil rights movement
Puberty	Losing job	Graduating from high school	Economic depressions
Menopause	Winning the lottery	Marriage	Natural disasters
Physical aging	Late parenthood	Parenthood	Famines
Wrinkling	Early widowhood	Entering workforce	Droughts
Diminished vision	Study abroad	Children leaving home	Assassination of a national leader
Diminished strength	Cancer	Death of parents	Introduction of cable television
	Early puberty	Grandparenthood	Acts of terrorism
	Going to a private school	Retirement	Challenger disaster
	Multiple sclerosis		Riots
	Alzheimer's disease		

Normative Social Events Nonbiological events that most people in a given culture experience at about the same age are called **normative social events.** Going to first-grade, dating, graduating from high school, marriage, entering the workforce, parenting, retirement, and grandparenting are all normative social events for many Americans (see table 1.3). However, because a culture's norms determine which social events are normative, different cultures will have different normative social events. For example, going to high school is normative for some cultures, but not for others. In fact, having a transition period between childhood and adulthood, what we call adolescence, is not normative in all cultures.

Although normative social events may be different for different cultures, all cultures have normative social events and most people will experience role changes based on social expectations. As Ravenna Helson and Abigail Stewart (1994) have found, these role changes often result in personality changes. Thus, some changes we associate with age can be tied to changes in social roles.

Nonnormative Events

Nonnormative events are unexpected events that either don't happen to most people or happen at an unusual age. For example, getting Alzheimer's disease would be a nonnormative event because it is unusual for people to get it. Becoming a widow at 17 would be a nonnormative event because the death of the spouse occurred at an unusually young age.

As table 1.3 shows, nonnormative events can be biological, as in the case of cancer, or social, as in the case of divorce. Nonnormative events, whether biological or social, push people in new directions of development and are responsible for many of the differences between individuals.

Cohort or Historical Events

A **cohort** is a group of people who are born at about the same time and who share common historical experiences. Thus, **cohort or historical events** are those that affect a specific group of people who share a common time in history. For example, the cohort born in the United States in the late 1970s shared the experience of watching the Persian Gulf War on television. The experience of viewing live warfare, occurring thousands of miles away, while sitting in one's living room was a novel event that may make the 1970s cohort different from all previous cohorts who did not grow up watching live warfare on television (Beasom & Krauss, 1992).

Thus, cohort or historical events affect a society, changing—at least momentarily—what is and isn't normative, as well as what is or isn't nonnormative. Most people would readily recognize the developmental importance of certain sensational historical events, such as wars and famines. But the effects of many historical events on development are usually not obvious until we compare one cohort—people who were born about the same time and who experienced the same slice of history—with another cohort. Whether we compare cohorts informally (as a relative may have done by telling you "When I was your age . . .") or whether we compare cohorts more objectively, it is hard to escape the conclusion that people are partly products of their times (see box 1.1).

Difficulty of Explaining Development

If you think about all the possible normative age-related events, nonnormative events, and cohort or historical events that could affect development and then you contemplate

Box 1.1

ISSUE in FOCUS

Cohort Differences

Memories of a Virgin Prom Queen

Driving to the library on a beautiful spring day, I spotted the huge black-and-white store sign: "Free Condoms with Prom Tux Rentals," the sign advertised, propped next to three grinning mannequins in penguin suits.

That's just great, I thought. At least no one will get pregnant or AIDS on the most sacred of all high school nights. On the other hand, does this mean sex is automatically part of the evening's champagne and lobster, Le Grand Entrance into a fancy hotel ballroom, and that tearful Last Dance?

What is wrong with this picture?

My own prom was a 1960s stomach-churning, clammy-handed evening of "Will he like my dress?" "Will my girlfriend be there?" and "Will my hair friz during our slow dance?" I don't remember condoms being part of the tuxedo kit.

I do remember my boyfriend looking dashing in an ensemble of shimmering satin lapels, swishy tails, and a crisply pleated white shirt with pearl buttons. His waist was swathed in a passionate purple cummerbund. I was flattered by how much effort he had made to please me.

When I first ushered him into the living room for Mother's approval, I remember wishing we could just skip the prom and spend the evening somewhere alone. He looked too handsome just for dancing.

But my mother's reminder of our strict curfew quickly dampened our 17-year-old ardor, even though I was secretly pleased she didn't mind letting him know that we had "rules" at our house.

And so we did what thousands of prom nighters before us had done: dined on rubbery lobster, danced, laughed and flirted until it hurt, drank too much warm, watery beer, and picked at cold scrambled eggs at the 2 A.M. breakfast, under the watchful eye of my boyfriend's parents.

Too soon, prom night was over, my curfew up. Home before 3, or you're grounded, Mother had warned. We did make out in his dad's Olds for a few minutes out front of my house.

The smell of the car's leather seats, his English Leather, and The Association crooning *Never My Love* are with me 24 years later. That night I felt beautiful, desirable and—is "safe" the right word?

Safe, because kissing was the limit, and he knew kissing was the limit, and it was all OK. There was no discussion about going further.

He didn't ask, I didn't have to answer, and we were free, in an old-fashioned kind of way, to enjoy our innocent and glamorous prom night.

And so when next June rolls around, I'll be thinking about that condom sign at my neighborhood tux shop. I imagine a crowd of too-cool high school studs, laughing nervously like Beavis and Butt-head in their spiffy tuxedos, condoms tucked away in their designer wallets.

At the prom, their girlfriends will know they have condoms ready, the guys will know they know . . . and a lot of questions are going to get asked, a lot of feelings and futures are going to be hurt, and I wonder: Will kids wish the whole condom issue had never come up?

For some, it will be still the most glamorous and memorable evening of the high school year. For others, maybe not.

Source: Spence, S. L. (1994, April 18). Letter to the editor. *USA TODAY.*

trying to prove the effects of each event, you can see that explaining development is even more difficult than describing or predicting development. Certainly, describing what you are like now is easier than trying to explain *why* you are the way you are.

Value of Explaining Development

Partly because explaining development is so challenging, people find it fascinating. They argue about such issues as whether marriage makes one more mature, whether retirement is a blessing or a curse, whether a person would be strengthened or devastated by the death of a spouse, and whether a strict parenting style is the best way to rear children.

Another reason people are fascinated with explaining development is that explanation may lead to control: If we know what events cause development, we may be able to control development. If we know why one person developed into a criminal whereas another developed into a solid citizen, why one individual became a

Box 1.2

SELF-CHECK

A. Match each of the following research questions with its psychological goal.

a. description or prediction

b. explanation

____ 1. Are more intelligent people more moral?

____ 2. How do friendships change over time?

____ 3. Why do women's colleges produce a greater proportion of successful women than co-ed colleges?

____ 4. Are children who participate in Head Start more likely to go to college?

____ 5. Why do some people adjust better to widowhood than others?

B. Match each of the following life events with the type of event it is.

a. normative maturational

b. normative social

c. nonnormative

d. historical

____ 1. heart attack

____ 2. retirement

____ 3. economic depression

____ 4. puberty

____ 5. promotion to division manager at age 24

____ 6. war

____ 7. teenage pregnancy

____ 8. menopause

____ 9. high school graduation

____ 10. winning the lottery

____ 11. marriage

Please turn to the end of this chapter to check your answers before going on to the next section.

genius whereas another became a person of low intelligence, or why one elderly individual is an active elderly person whereas another is senile, then we may be able to maximize the chances that most people will reach their full potential. Thus, the facts that developmental psychologists discover could help you better direct your own development and help society better direct the development of its members by telling us the best ways to rehabilitate crack babies, run schools, find friends and mates, rear children, plan retirement, and live happily during retirement.

Controversies in Developmental Psychology

When you realize how relevant, complex, and broad developmental psychology is and then consider how many people think they are experts in development (after all, they see themselves develop, they know how to rear children, etc.), you should not be surprised to learn that, on many issues in developmental psychology, people disagree. In fact, as you shall see, people disagree not only about the causes of development, but even about the course of development (see table 1.4).

What Is the Course of Development?

Describing the course of development would seem to be simple and without controversy. It is not. Two questions are deceptively complex and important: (1) To what extent do we change as we age? (2) If we do change significantly, do we change gradually or suddenly? Two major developmental controversies have grown as researchers have attempted to answer these questions. These controversies are stability versus change and continuity versus discontinuity.

Stability Versus Change

People who disagree about the extent to which we change as we age are involved in the **stability versus change** debate. Those on the change side of the debate believe that people will change considerably (for example, Miller & C'deBaca, 1994), whereas those on the stability side argue that people change little (for example, Costa & McCrae, 1994). Thus, you might expect that compared to change advocates, stability advocates would favor longer prison terms ("once a criminal, always a criminal"), be more supportive of societies that determine a person's occupational future by age 10 (for instance, the former USSR), believe that Head Start would have lifelong effects, and favor moving the retirement age to 70.

However, the two sides would not totally disagree on these issues because even those on the stability side of the debate would, for the most part, admit that people change. Similarly, most change advocates acknowledge some stability during much of the lifespan. Thus, the debate is not about whether or not change occurs, but about how much change occurs and when (Heatherton & Nichols, 1994). People generally have assumed that childhood is a period of fast change, and adulthood—except for later adulthood—a

Table 1.4

Controversial Issues Confronting Developmental Psychologists

- Do preschool achievers "burn out"?
- Should students attend school year-round?
- Is self-esteem overrated?
- Can morality be taught?
- What are the effects of watching television?
- What are the effects of day care?
- What are the effects of being an only child?
- What are the effects of divorce on children? On parents? On grandparents?
- How should children be reared?
- What is the best way to discipline a child?
- Should a child be taught to be bilingual?
- What happens if little boys play with dolls?
- What are the effects of playing with toy weapons?
- What are the effects of drugs such as nicotine and alcohol on fetal development?
- What are the cognitive abilities of a fetus?
- What are the effects of abortion on the mother? On the father?
- What are the effects of cross-racial adoption?
- At what age do job skills decline?
- Are nursing homes harmful?

period of relative stability (Bloom, 1964; James, 1890/1981). For example, a common argument is that 50 percent of intellectual development is completed by the age of 4 (Salkind, 1985). Similarly, Freud proposes few changes in male development after age 14 (Hall & Lindzey, 1978).

Recently, these commonly accepted notions have been challenged by investigators who have found that both intelligence and personality may change significantly during the adult years. For example, John Nesselroade (Nesselroade, 1994; Nesselroade & Boker, 1994) argues that researchers often falsely dismiss change in people's test scores as measurement error. However, as you will see in future chapters, the debate is far from settled (Caspi & Herbener, 1990; Heatherton & Nichols, 1994).

Continuity Versus Discontinuity

If we do change, how do we change? This is the question argued by those in the **continuity versus discontinuity** debate. People taking the *continuity* position think of development as analogous to going up an escalator: It's a gradual, step by step, continuous process, whereby each new event or change builds on earlier experiences (Hetherington & Parke, 1993). There are no dramatic shifts. Because change is so gradual, a person's behavior after a small change can be viewed as a simple extension of their behavior immediately before they made the change (Baltes & Reese, 1984). If we apply the continuity view to children's cognitive development, we would argue that children's thinking simply becomes more and more logical as they age: Its basic quality does not change.

People taking the *discontinuity* position, or **stage theory** approach, on the other hand, tend to see development as occurring in abrupt spurts followed by plateaus, with the spurts often tied to maturational events such as rapid brain growth. That is, we stay in one stage for a while and then move to a qualitatively different stage. Qualitative changes in our brain allow us to think or act in a different way than we could before, just as qualitative changes in a caterpillar's body cause it to move from the caterpillar to the butterfly stage. For example, Piaget—a stage theorist who you'll be introduced to in chapter 2—believes that the *quality* of our thinking changes as we progress from one cognitive stage to the next. Adult thinking is not simply more logical than children's thinking; it's a different *kind* of thinking (see figure 1.1).

Most people find the discontinuity, or stage theorists', view intuitively appealing. Many believe that childhood and adolescence are periods of rapid, dramatic psychological changes that can be tied to abrupt physical changes. To support this belief, almost any parent can cite cases in which a child seemed to show very little progress for months and then suddenly seemed to make an enormous change almost overnight. For example, an infant may not speak a word the first 2 1/2 years of life, but once speaking may use complete sentences and become a loquacious toddler.

Continuity advocates account for these cases by arguing, quite cleverly, that the change has been a slow and steady process, but we don't notice it until it is expressed in a very visible behavior. People often see a "sudden" change because they didn't notice the gradual changes. The casual passerby sees sudden, dramatic changes in a building, but time-lapse photography reveals a series of gradual transformations. Similarly, a relative you see only once a year may think you've suddenly changed ("My, how you've grown" or "You dropped a lot of weight fast, didn't you?"), but to you the changes have been painfully slow and steady. In other words, continuity advocates claim that what, at first glance, looks like sudden, discontinuous change would look like steady, continuous change on closer, more constant, and more objective inspection. Thus, the child who seems to have learned language in a discontinuous manner may have been practicing the words in her head for months before actually speaking. If we had paid closer attention or if we had been better able to measure her thinking, we would have discovered that she was gradually acquiring words, even though she didn't feel compelled to speak them.

Figure 1.1

Discontinuous Versus Continuous Development

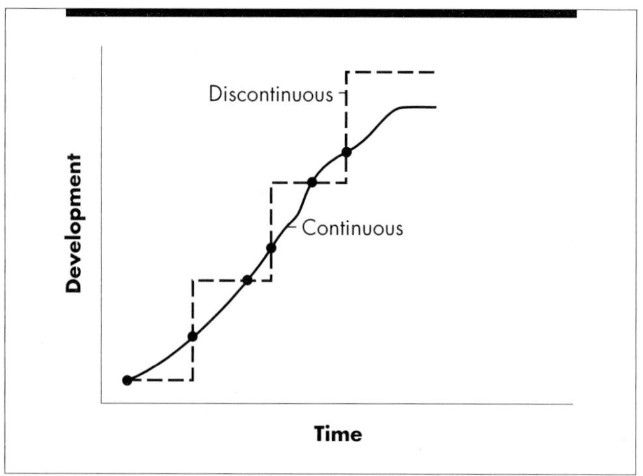

Note: If measurements are taken only at the dots, both continuous and discontinuous models will fit the data.

As Robert Siegler (1994) points out, developmental psychologists will not be able to solve the continuity-discontinuity debate as long as they continue to take "snapshots" of development. What we need, according to Siegler, is for researchers to spend the time and effort to get "videotapes" of development. By intensively observing individuals throughout the entire period of change—what Siegler calls the **microgenetic method**—we will be able to map the course of development (Siegler & Crowley, 1991).

What Are the Causes of Development?

Arguments about the course of development are mild compared to arguments about the causes of development. Trying to answer the questions "Why have you become the person you are today?" "What forces would cause you to change?" and "What should a parent do to rear happy, sweet, productive, active, and moral children?" is almost a sure way to start a heated discussion. Four developmental controversies have been debated to explain the causes of development: nature versus nurture, maturation versus learning, free will versus determinism, and individuality versus universality.

Nature Versus Nurture

Perhaps no issue has stimulated more arguments through the years than the **nature versus nurture** debate, the argument about whether heredity or environment is more important. In various forms, you hear this argument everywhere. Are criminals born dishonest or are they products of their environment? Is intelligence inherited or is it the result of one's upbringing? What about musical ability? Athletic ability? Leadership ability?

Many nature-nurture arguments arise from discussing personal political philosophy (Angoff, 1988). If the alcoholic, gambler, or the problem child is born that way, then parents are not to blame and social programs to rehabilitate them would be a waste of money. If people's problems are entirely due to their genes, we should spend money on developing chemical treatments, genetic treatments, and perhaps programs designed to ensure selective breeding.

Is athletic ability inherited or is it the result of upbringing? The nature versus nurture debate is one of the hottest controversies in developmental psychology.

On the other hand, if people's problems are due to their environments, we should not rely on technological answers but instead provide social programs to help troubled people. Similarly, if all differences between women and men are inborn, we should just accept them. If, however, some of these differences, such as women more often doing poorly in math, are due to the environment, we should change the environment. These changes might involve changing how parents treat their daughters, how television characterizes women, or how math instructors teach their classes. Thus, a person who believes that criminals should be rehabilitated, that the poor suffer primarily from lack of opportunities, and that schools and parents are artificially limiting women's potentials would tend to be a nurturist (Feather, 1985).

On the other hand, a person who believes that murderers should be executed, that the poor are often the genetically inferior, and that biological differences between men's and women's brains account for the differences between the genders would tend to be a naturist. Examine your own political philosophy. Consider such problems as crime, the urban poor, and the more than 25 million adults in the United States who are functionally illiterate (Schultz & Schultz, 1990). For those problems that you think are due to inherited differences between people, do you favor doing nothing or looking for technological answers? For those problems you think are due to living in an impoverished environment, do you favor more money being spent on social programs?

Maturation Versus Learning

When we relate the nature-nurture debate to development, we are usually talking about the **maturation versus**

learning debate, a question of whether development results from biological changes (maturation) or from learning from the environment. Put another way, does development unfold according to a preprogrammed genetic code or is development being programmed and reprogrammed by the environment? Some examples of specific maturation-learning questions include these:

1. Do children acquire the ability to determine how far away objects are because their bodies and brains have matured or do they acquire depth perception through practice and interaction with the environment?
2. Are fears learned or the product of brain development?
3. At puberty, boys begin to outperform girls in math. Is this difference the result of our society treating boys and girls differently as they reach puberty or is this the product of changes in the brain that occur at puberty?
4. Is a child misbehaving and inattentive in class because her brain hasn't developed to the point where she can attend or because she is being rewarded for misbehavior?

In addressing each of these questions, nurturists would emphasize the role of learning. Instead of focusing on biological processes regulated by heredity, they would focus on learning from practice and experience. Accordingly, they would argue that one's personal timetable was not mapped out before leaving the womb. Instead, an extreme nurturist would argue that if we fully understood the effects of nurture, we could program a person's development after birth, making virtually anything possible. An extreme nurturist would argue that if we knew enough about learning, we could teach anyone to be a genius and even train the child of two clumsy parents to be a world-class gymnast.

As you may already suspect, many behaviors require both maturation and learning. Human beings need to be biologically ready to learn. Before an infant can learn to talk, his brain and vocal apparatus must be sufficiently mature. Likewise, both biological readiness and experience are necessary before an infant can become attached to her parents, start to walk, or become toilet-trained. Therefore, few developmental psychologists are extreme nurturists or extreme naturists. Instead of asking, for each of the four questions, "are the changes due to maturation *or* learning?" they ask "are the changes due more to maturation or more to learning?"

Despite this important refinement to the nature-nurture question, the answers you get to the four maturation versus learning questions will depend not only on the specific behavior or ability being discussed but also on whom you ask. Naturists argue that the impact of maturation on development has been underestimated and maturation's impact will be fully revealed only when scientists do more thorough biological research. They also point out that one's genes can determine one's environment. For example, parents who give a child a great deal of attention may do so because their child demands it. Therefore, if you find that children who receive more attention are smarter, you cannot conclude that giving children more attention raises their intelligence. It may well be that more intelligent children demand more attention.

Nurturists counter by saying that developmental psychologists have focused their attention on the parts of the lifespan most affected by maturation. Developmental psychologists have intensively studied age periods accompanied by rapid physical change (e.g., birth, early childhood, adolescence, and old age). However, developmental psychologists have all but ignored parts of the lifespan not accompanied by dramatic physical changes, such as young adulthood and middle age. According to nurturists, when developmental psychologists overcome this "maturation bias," we will more fully understand the impact of learning on development. We will examine this issue in depth in chapter 3, but for a preview of some of the issues, see table 1.5.

In addition to disagreeing about the extent to which nature influences us, people also disagree about *how* nature influences us. What is human nature? In the next sections, we will discuss two major debates about human nature: the active versus passive debate and the individuality versus universality debate.

Free Will Versus Determinism (Active Versus Passive)

The **free will versus determinism** debate boils down to a dispute as to whether we actively create our own environment (free will) or whether we passively and predictably react to events that happen to us (determinism). Advocates of free will claim we take an active role in our own development, seeking out and organizing our experiences. Advocates of determinism claim that we are passive machines that are molded by the environment like an artist molds a piece of clay. Do you think your destiny is the result of how you were "programmed" by your environment? Or do you think that you had a role in your destiny? In other words, are you a passive learner of habits or an active explorer and discoverer of rules?

The position you take on this issue has important practical implications. For example, if children are basically passive sponges, then schools should be places where children are drilled on information so they will absorb it. If, however, people are active participants in their own development, schools should be places where children are allowed to explore and discover things on their own.

Individuality Versus Universality

Historically, most developmental psychologists have focused on discovering universal truths that apply to everyone, regardless of culture or experience (Plomin, 1990). This emphasis on the universality of human development is evident in the popularity of stage theories such as those proposed by

Table 1.5

Debate: Will Future Research Reveal that Nature or Nurture Is More Important?

The Nature Position	The Nurture Position
As Americans, we are biased toward believing in environmental influences and assuming that everyone is equal. Earlier research was guided by this incorrect belief, but future research will not be.	Past research has been biased by a "nature" view. For example, most research has focused on periods of rapid biological change and ignored most of the lifespan (adulthood) where biological changes are minimal and where environment may have a large effect.
We are increasing our knowledge of the brain and learning how to look for genes that affect development. As a result, we will be able to unravel the previously undiscoverable effects of nature.	We are improving our ability to accurately describe an individual's environment. As a result, we will be able to find environmental effects we were unable to discover before.
We have assumed that genes have the greatest impact in early life. However, genes could be activated at any age. Future research may find that genes are responsible for many developmental changes now assumed to be due to environment.	Stability has been assumed to be due to nature, but research may find that some stability is due to nurture.
Our nature causes us to change, leave, or create our environment.	The environment affects how genes are expressed.

Sigmund Freud, Erik Erikson, and Jean Piaget. As you will see in chapter 2, such stage theories propose that because maturation is the major driving force in human development, and that all people mature in the same sequence and at about the same rate, all human beings acquire certain abilities or go through similar crises at about the same time. Developmental psychology's emphasis on universality is also evident in the kinds of statistics we commonly use to describe people. For example, we usually calculate averages so that we can describe what the average person is like at a given age.

Although universality has been the orientation of most developmental psychologists, the debate of **individuality versus universality** has been started anew in recent years as the study of individual differences has gained popularity. This interest in individual differences has come primarily from two sources. First, cross-cultural psychologists have stressed that people reared in different cultures will develop differently (Wade, 1993). Second, the study of **behavioral genetics,** a discipline concerned with the influence of heredity on behavior and development, has contributed to the debate. Behavioral geneticists, such as Robert Plomin (1990), have stressed that our genetic differences may cause differences in development. In their efforts to find genetic bases for development, behavioral geneticists have also found evidence for environmental bases for individual differences. For example, they found that genetically identical twins sometimes develop in different ways. In later chapters, you will see how Plomin and other behavioral geneticists use twin and family studies to discover how nature and nurture influence such traits as intelligence and mental health.

Controversies in Developmental Psychology: Concluding Comments

As you have seen, there are several core controversies about the course and causes of development. In one form or another, these controversies are hotly debated by virtually everyone (see table 1.6). Where a society sides on these controversies affects whether a society:

provides certain social programs (for example, Head Start, Elder Hostel),

puts resources into education,

values being a "good" parent,

tries to rehabilitate criminals,

determines whether an individual will be a professional or an unskilled laborer while the individual is still in childhood,

tries to develop adults' potential,

supports equality for women,

respects the elderly for their abilities,

accepts "not being in love" as a rationale for divorce, and

enforces strict punishments on people who break laws.

Even on those rare occasions when the developmental psychologist's work does not relate to the *general* issues of development such as nature versus nurture or stability versus change, the developmental psychologist is not necessarily safe from controversy. For example, the work of developmental psychologists has implications for how the elderly should be cared for, how morality should be taught, whether couples should stay together "for the sake of the children," whether pornography should be illegal, and how a child should be told about a parent's death. Because developmental psychologists deal with so many relevant, personal, emotional, and political issues, studying these issues in an unbiased way is possible only by properly applying scientific research methods.

Scientific Research

Research methods, when properly applied, allow us to study controversial issues in an unbiased way because they produce observable evidence that either supports or refutes a particular claim. If one scientist doubts another scientist's evidence, she can examine that evidence or replicate the

Table 1.6

Core Controversial Issues

Issue	Basic Positions	Assumptions and Implications
Stability versus change	1. Human behavior is relatively stable through the lifespan.	Behavior is due almost entirely to inherited characteristics. The study of lifespan development is irrelevant since people don't change throughout the lifespan. People's futures can be determined at an early age. We should give long prison terms to juvenile delinquents. Retirement age should be increased since elderly workers are basically the same as younger workers.
	2. After a period of rapid change, behavior remains stable until old age.	Development is largely governed by early maturational processes. The study of adult development is unnecessary since adults do not change. Since adults do not change, investing in adult education or in the rehabilitation of criminals is wasteful.
	3. Human behavior changes throughout the lifespan.	Experience plays a large role in development. However, some psychologists, such as Erikson, believe that development is governed by maturational events throughout the lifespan. Supporters believe that it is valuable to study lifespan developmental psychology.
Continuity versus discontinuity	1. Development occurs gradually.	Development occurs in quantitative rather than qualitative ways. Changes are refinements or extensions of old ways rather than being entirely new ways. Children simply know *less* and think *less* than adults.
	2. Development involves making abrupt changes from one stage to another qualitatively different stage.	Development is due to qualitative changes, which are often caused by maturational events. Children think in ways that are *different* from adults.
Nature versus nurture	1. Heredity determines who we are.	Being a "good" parent is not particularly important, and technological solutions, such as drugs and genetic engineering, should be used to solve social problems. Differences between ethnic groups in school achievement are inherited.
	2. Environment—not genes—determines development.	Parenting and education are very important jobs. Social programs should be used to solve developmental problems. Differences between ethnic groups in school achievement are due to social conditions.
Maturation versus learning	1. Development is the product of biological maturation.	Certain concepts should be taught to children only when they are *biologically ready* to learn those concepts. Differences in the psychological development of men and women are due to hormonal changes. Little development occurs during early and middle adulthood.
	2. Development is the product of experience.	People can learn virtually anything at any age. Differences in the psychological development of men and women are due to their being treated differently, especially as they approach puberty. Many developmental changes can occur during early and middle adulthood. Women have to learn to be good parents.
Free will versus determinism	1. Development consists of people reacting to events.	Society should take credit or blame for an individual's actions. Learning by rote and by flash cards is a good idea. If a crisis (divorce, death of a loved one, abuse) befalls a person, the person can only suffer and be devastated. The drug addict is a victim of society.
	2. People play an active role in their own development.	People should take credit or blame for their own actions. Students should be allowed to discover principles on their own. How one reacts to a crisis is up to the individual. The drug addict chooses to be an addict.
Individuality versus universality	1. Development is a product of the interaction between genes and experience.	People develop differently from one another because of differences in their genes and their environments. Therefore, we should use longitudinal designs to closely follow each individual's unique course of development, and we should look for developmental differences between individuals and cultures.
	2. Development is governed by universal maturational/environmental events.	We share so many genes and common experiences that everyone's development follows basically the same course. Thus, there is little need to do cross-cultural research or to look for genetic differences between individuals. Because everyone's development follows the same pattern, nothing is lost when researchers ignore an individual's behavior and simply look at the group's average.

Box 1.3

SELF-CHECK

Identify the controversies represented by each of the following statements. Then identify which side of the controversies each statement represents. (A given statement may reflect more than one controversy.)

Controversies

nature versus nurture
passive versus active
individuality versus universality
stability versus change
continuity versus discontinuity
maturation versus learning

Situations and Beliefs

1. "Children should go to school as early as possible."
2. "An embryo is a person."
3. "All people are alike."
4. "Early identification and educational tracking of low-ability individuals are realistic ways of preparing such people for their future."
5. "Intelligence can be learned."
6. "Divorce and other crises have inevitable and often insurmountable negative effects on their victims."
7. "We should support Head Start and government aid to poor women with dependent children."
8. "No two people develop in the same way."
9. "Schools should help children discover principles rather than learn facts."
10. "A depressed mother kills her newborn. The jury concludes that postpartum depression is a biological event beyond her control. Hence the jury decides that the mother should not be punished."
11. "Prejudice is innate."
12. "We can choose how we react to crises."
13. "Children learn best through drills and rote learning."
14. "The death penalty may deter people from committing crimes."
15. "The retirement age should be increased."

Please turn to the end of this chapter to check your answers before going on to the next section.

study to "see for herself." As you'll see, the public nature of scientific research not only allows scientists to obtain unbiased information, but also to build on one another's successes and failures.

Science Avoids Bias

The goal of science is **objectivity,** or the extent to which research is unbiased and free of personal interpretations. The basic idea behind the scientific method is that we should bravely test our assumptions, rather than simply presume that those assumptions are correct. By collecting observable evidence, we can see whether or not our ideas are accurate. Ideally, we should change our assumptions if the evidence doesn't support them.

But suppose we were so biased that we did the study incorrectly or reported our results inaccurately? Our biases would be revealed because researchers are expected to publish articles that describe their research study in enough detail that other scientists can replicate it. Thus, if someone who does not share our bias doesn't believe the results of our study, they can rely on the **replicability** of the study, or the extent to which its results can be repeated under similar conditions to produce the same results. If they don't get the same results, our bias would be revealed. Thus, one advantage of publishing research is that other scientists can check the individual scientist's work.

Science Progresses

Another advantage of publishing research is that scientists get to build on each other's work. This is useful because science often progresses through trial and error. Typically, one person has a **hypothesis,** an idea that can be objectively tested to see if it is right or wrong. For example, Harry Harlow (1958) hypothesized that infants form attachments to their mothers because the mother fulfills the infant's primitive needs. Research hypotheses, such as Harlow's, may come from the researcher's intuition, from reactions to someone else's research, or from the researcher's views about what a theory would predict in a certain situation. Harlow's hypothesis was based on his knowledge of drive theories. At that time, drive theories assumed that all human behavior stems from attempts to satisfy primitive biological drives, such as the hunger drive. Therefore, Harlow reasoned that a baby becomes attached to its mother because the baby associates her with the reduction of hunger and the pleasures of eating.

Once a hypothesis is formed, the researcher tests it to find out if it is right or wrong. If the hypothesis is wrong, the researcher abandons or modifies it. As you'll read in chapter 9, Harlow's original hypothesis was wrong. The mother's provision of food was not enough for the infant to form an emotional attachment to her. In a study where Harlow separated newborn rhesus monkeys from their mothers and gave them a choice of a wire mesh "surrogate" mother equipped with a bottle or a terry cloth surrogate mother, the infant monkeys chose to spend most of their time with the soft terry cloth mother. Apparently, contact comfort was more important than food to the formation of the infant's attachment to the mother.

Once some form of the hypothesis is supported, other scientists may test the revised hypothesis. If the revised hypothesis is supported, the hypothesis may be considered a *fact*. Largely because of Harlow's work, most psychologists accept as fact that infants, as well as all people, need contact comfort.

Once a series of facts have been discovered, a scientist may try to tie these facts together into a **theory,** a set of rules that explains a broad range of findings and suggests other hypotheses that could be tested. Scientists then conduct research on that theory to test and refine it. After much work, a more accurate theory is formed. As a result of researchers and theorists building on each other's work and insights, science accumulates knowledge and comes closer and closer to knowing the truth. As you will see in chapter 9, there are now several theories of attachment, which have stimulated much research and greatly enhanced our understanding of how infants and children become attached to their caregivers.

Understanding and Judging Developmental Research

We have argued that by properly applying research methods, developmental psychologists can provide you with accurate information. Accurate information may help you be a better parent, understand your parents better, or improve the quality of your relationships. Therefore, you should know enough about research that you can benefit from recent research discoveries.

You should also know enough about research that you are not misled by poorly conceived or improperly conducted research. Unfortunately, many bad research studies are published in books, newspapers, and popular magazines (see box 1.6 for an example of bad research).

The rest of the chapter will help you to understand and evaluate research studies. Specifically, we'll help you answer the two basic questions you should ask of every study: (1) Did the researchers accurately measure the particular aspect of development they were concerned with (for example, intelligence or moral reasoning)? and (2) Are the researchers' conclusions about the course or cause of development valid?

Measuring Behavior and Concepts

Before you can accept a researcher's conclusions about how or why a particular aspect of behavior develops, you must first find out whether the researcher has a good measure of that behavior. For example, before you accept a researcher's claim about how moral reasoning changes over the course of the lifespan or about what causes people to advance to a higher moral level, you must first determine whether the researcher has a valid measure of "level of moral reasoning." But how can you judge whether a measure has **validity,** or whether it measures what it claims to measure?

Qualities of a Good Measure

A valid measure should be unbiased, reliable, and should make justifiable inferences. To be unbiased, the measure should be **objectively scored,** that is, a person's score should not be affected by who does the scoring. In other words, if you take an intelligence test, you don't expect the score you get to be determined by who "grades" it. You would know that something was wrong if one scorer reported that your IQ was 118 and another scorer, looking at the same results, said your IQ was 158.

In addition to being objectively scored, an unbiased measure should be **standardized,** or administered in the same way every time. Thus, regardless of your race, sex, or social class, you should get the same instructions and the same amount of time to take the test. This standardization should reduce the effect of any biases the researcher may have.

Objective scoring and standardization not only decrease the measure's vulnerability to bias, but they also contribute to **reliability,** or the ability of the measure to produce the same results from one day to the next. If your IQ were measured by a reliable test, the score you get today would be similar to the one you would get if you were to retake the test next week. Your score would not be affected by random fluctuations due to lack of standardization, objectivity, or other chance changes (such as having a bad day). Measures must be reliable because changes in scores should be due to real developmental changes rather than to a measure that produces inconsistent scores.

A valid measure must be unbiased. It should be reliable. However, there is more to validity than having an unbiased measure that produces scores for a research participant that are consistent and stable. A valid measure must also make accurate inferences from behavior.

In contrast to assessing objectivity, standardization, and reliability, determining whether a measure is making correct inferences from behavior is difficult. You can easily tell whether or not a measure is objective. For example, if an investigator measures moral development by asking people to write an essay that the investigator then arbitrarily scores, the measure is subjective. On the other hand, if the investigator uses a multiple-choice test that is computer-scored, the measure is objective. Standardization is also simple to establish. Just ask whether the same procedures are followed each time. Likewise, reliability is easy to assess. Simply find out if research participants get similar scores when they are retested.

But how do you determine whether the inferences made by the measure are correct? It is tempting to believe that a measure titled "The Moral Development Scale" that is constructed by a Ph.D. at a prestigious university must be valid. However, it is easy to make invalid inferences from behavior. What we infer to be an ability problem may actually be a motivational problem (and vice versa), and what we believe to be a psychological problem may instead be a physical problem (and vice versa). Imagine the problems of trying to infer complex mental states such as love, morality, creativity, intelligence, wisdom, and self-esteem. Then, imagine how difficult it would be to measure these traits in infants. Because of the difficulty of measuring traits, you should always question claims of people who purport to have valid measures of such things. Specifically, you should ask three questions: (1) Do the inferences the measure makes follow from logic or theory? (Rotter, 1990); (2) Is there any research evidence that supports the measure's validity? and (3) How could the researcher's inferences be wrong?

Common Kinds of Measures

To prepare you to question the objectivity and validity of specific measures, we are going to critique the most commonly used general measurement strategies: observation, interviews, questionnaires, tests, and scientific instruments.

Observation Like most everyone else, developmental psychologists watch others. However, the developmental psychologists' scientific observations differ from casual observations in at least two ways. First, these observations are **systematic.** Specific behaviors are looked for and immediately recorded. Developmental psychologists don't rely on their memory of events. In fact, they may videotape research participants so that others can recheck the accuracy of their initial observations. Second, observations are as objective as possible: Behavior is recorded, not interpreted or labeled. Skilled observers don't label behavior with subjective terms such as *lazy, frightened,* or *excited.* What one person interprets as *lazy,* another may interpret as *relaxed* or *efficient.* Although we may all agree that a person is not performing a given task, we might have very different interpretations of the reasons for that behavior: *stupid, shy, terrified, lack of confidence, overconfidence, lazy, rebellious, deaf,* or *ill.* Who is to say which observer is right? All

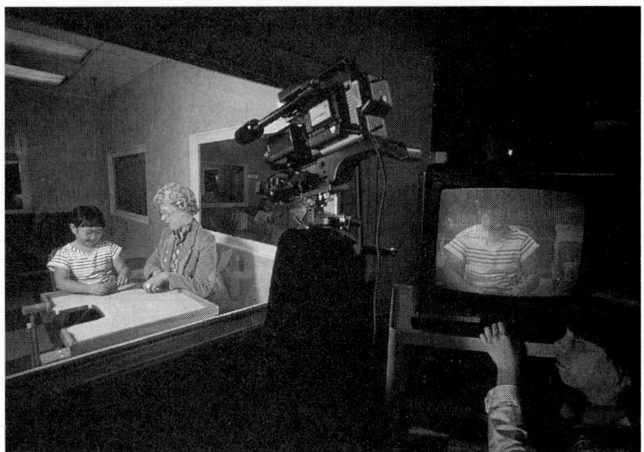

Developmental psychologists often rely on videotape to help them make systematic observations.

we can say is that some of the observers must be wrong or that the reason for the person's behavior is some combination of these elements.

To prevent observers from interpreting behavior, observers should be trained to separate facts (observations) from opinions (subjective interpretations). Then, to verify that the training worked, two observers should watch the same videotape of the research participant. If both observers, without consulting one another, report the same observations, we can be relatively confident that their observations are free of subjective interpretations and biases that would ruin their objectivity.

When properly executed, observation accurately tells us what a person did. However, scientists often try, at some point, to go beyond describing behavior to interpreting what the person was thinking while doing that behavior. These interpretations may not be valid. For example, if an observer notes that 1-year-olds do not attend to objects when she covers the object with a cloth, can she conclude that those 1-year-olds think the object no longer exists? Such a conclusion could be questioned. After all, the infants may simply stop looking because they have limited attention spans.

Yet, despite the problems with observation, it is the method of choice when studying social behavior. Furthermore, it is the only method we can use when studying 2-month-old infants and others who cannot tell us what they are thinking (see box 1.4).

Interviews, Questionnaires, and Tests Although observation is sometimes the only way to obtain information from an infant, older children and adults can be questioned. Asking questions is quicker and easier than observing people. Furthermore, whereas observation is limited to watching existing behavior, questioning allows a more detailed exploration of people's thoughts, feelings, and opinions as well as reports of their past behaviors and plans for future behaviors.

Box 1.4

RESEARCH in FOCUS

Telling Us More Than They Can Say

A major challenge for developmental psychologists who study infants is to accurately infer from an infant's behavior what the infant does and does not know. Because infants haven't learned language, they cannot answer questions such as: "Do you have depth perception?" "Do you think objects exist when they're out of sight?" "Do you recognize your mom's voice?" However, developmental psychologists have devised clever ways to get some tentative answers to these questions.

For example, if we want to know whether an infant likes something, we can use several techniques. We can see if the child will turn his head to look at the stimulus, we can measure how long the child will look at the stimulus, and we can see if the baby will suck a pacifier to make the stimulus appear.

To tell whether infants can see the difference between two patterns, we take advantage of the fact that people pay less attention to a stimulus they have seen repeatedly. Thus, if we show the same stimulus repeatedly, even infants will start paying less attention to it.

If an infant can tell the difference between a new and an old stimulus, the infant will pay more attention to the new stimulus. If, on the other hand, the infant cannot tell the difference, the infant will not pay more attention to the new stimulus than to the old. How do we know the infant is paying more attention to the new stimulus? We can time how long he or she looks in the direction of the stimulus. In addition, we can monitor the infant's heart rate, blood pressure, and brain waves to determine if the infant is more aroused by the new stimulus.

There are several ways to ask questions. The least scientific method is the **unstructured interview,** or simply asking whatever questions come to mind.

Unstructured interviews are, by definition, unstandardized. Consequently, unstructured interviews also lack replicability. Scientists can't repeat the observations because they don't know in what order the original researcher asked the questions. In fact, in many cases, they don't even know what questions the original investigator asked.

Many unstructured interviews also lack objectivity because answers are either not recorded or recorded so inaccurately that no one knows what the research participant actually said. Often, to trust the unstructured interview is to trust the interviewer's memory of what research participants said.

In addition to being deficient in standardization and objectivity, the unstructured interview's validity is threatened by the same problem that threatens all question-asking methods: What people say is not always true (see table 1.7). People may give answers they think will help the researcher; they may give answers they think will make themselves look good; sometimes their memory isn't accurate; often they don't know why they did what they did; sometimes they make up something if they don't know the answer; and sometimes they simply want to have fun with the researcher.

Although also vulnerable to self-report and memory biases, the **structured interview** avoids most of the objectivity and replicability problems that plague the unstructured interview. In the structured interview, a questionnaire is prepared and the researcher reads the questionnaire to the research participant. The structured interview has two major advantages over the unstructured interview. First, because the structured interview is standardized and because answers tend to be objectively recorded, other researchers can repeat the study if they are skeptical about the original study's results. Second, researchers can evaluate the quality of the questions. For instance, researchers can see whether the questions led the respondents to the "right" answer (for example, "You do like this nursing home, don't you?") or whether the questions were too complicated for respondents to understand.

Although the structured interview allows other scientists to detect possible threats to validity because of the interviewer's way of phrasing questions, it does not allow them to assess bias due to nonverbal behavior. For example, the researcher may have influenced the research participants' answers through nonverbal cues such as nodding his head during desired answers and frowning during unwelcome answers.

Partly because of the problems of nonverbal bias and the difficulty of standardizing nonverbal behavior, many researchers prefer the **questionnaire method** to the interview method. Rather than reading the questions to the research participants, as in the structured interview method, researchers simply give the written questionnaire to the research participants and have them complete it by themselves. The questionnaire also has the advantage that people's responses are made anonymously, thus encouraging respondents to be more honest and open than they might be in an interview. However, even these precautions do not guarantee that research participants will answer

Table 1.7

Strengths and Weaknesses of Popular Measures

Measures	Strengths	Weaknesses
Unstructured interview/projective tests	May provide some insights Better for assessing thoughts than behavior	Not replicable Interviewer bias likely Self-report bias
Structured interview	Replicable Fairly objective Better for assessing thoughts than behavior	Interviewer bias possible Self-report bias
Questionnaire	Inexpensive Replicable Objective Better for assessing thoughts than behavior	Self-report bias
Standardized tests	Replicable Objective* Some checks on self-report bias Better for assessing thoughts than behavior	Validity not guaranteed Self-report bias possible
Observation	Useful for assessing physical and social development	Objectivity difficult Hard to assess thoughts
Instruments	Replicable Objective Unbiased Better for interpreting behavior than thought	None—but validity should still be questioned

*Standardized tests are objective if fixed-alternative objective questions, such as multiple-choice questions are used, or a scoring key is strictly adhered to. If open-ended (essay-type) questions are asked and answers are subjectively scored, objectivity is questionable.

honestly. Furthermore, as with all question-asking methods, even if research participants answer to the best of their abilities, their memories or impressions may be wrong.

A more formalized version of the questionnaire, designed to reduce the effects of self-report biases, is the standardized **psychological test.** Although psychological tests are often used to measure abilities, these questionnaires have been developed for many other aspects of behavior, from leadership ability to anxiety level. You probably remember taking several different types of psychological tests in school and at work.

Perhaps the best way to understand the value of standardized psychological tests is to contrast them with projective tests. With projective tests, research participants look at an inkblot or a photograph and then tell a story about what they see. Projective tests are more like unstructured interviews than they are like standardized tests. Projective tests are often not standardized, not objective, not reliable, and not valid. Standardized psychological tests, on the other hand are standardized, objective, and reliable. Almost the only similarity between projective tests and standardized tests is that, in both cases, the meaning of the research participants' responses is arguable. In the case of a projective test, people may question whether it is valid to interpret research participants' responses in terms of Freudian theory. In the case of standardized tests, we can argue about what an individual's score really means. For example, what does a score on an IQ test really mean? Thus, although most scientists would agree that IQ tests provide objective information, some would argue that these tests do *not* provide valid data.

Scientific Instruments In addition to watching and listening to people, scientists can use machines to objectively record people's behavior. Computers and other devices don't have biases, usually don't lose their concentration, and sometimes provide a permanent, objective record of behavior.

Although machines provide objective, unbiased, and replicable information about what people do, be prepared to question people who interpret this information. For example, if a scientist says his shock machine measures aggression, you should ask: "Is pressing a button on a 'shock machine' to supposedly deliver a shock to a stranger really a valid measure of aggression?" Perhaps it is really a measure of compliance. Similarly, just because a machine accurately measures brain waves, do not take it on faith that these brain waves signify intelligence, impulsivity, or emotionality.

Box 1.5

SELF-CHECK

What are the limitations associated with each of the following measuring techniques? Some techniques have more than one limitation.

Measuring Technique

1. observation
2. unstructured interview
3. structured interview
4. questionnaires
5. tests
6. scientific instruments

Limitations

a. low replicability
b. self-report bias
c. not standardized
d. lack of objectivity
e. interviewer bias
f. participant's behavior may be misinterpreted

Please turn to the end of this chapter to check your answers before going on to the next section.

Summary of Measures As you have seen, measurement is an important part of any developmental research study. Tables 1.7 and 1.8 will help you evaluate the strengths and weaknesses of a measure as you attempt to determine the quality of a research study.

Research Designs

Although evaluating the quality of measures is important, good measures alone do not guarantee sound research. For instance, the use of a standardized personality test does not guarantee that a study will yield valid or useful results. Measures are only one part of the **research design.** The researcher's general strategy about who to test under what conditions will determine how useful the result will be. When evaluating a researcher's strategy, you should ask two questions:

1. Did the researchers choose the right design for the particular question they were trying to answer?
2. Did the researchers correctly use that design?

Criteria for Choosing

Ideally, the choice of research design should depend on three factors:

1. Whether the researcher wants to *describe* development, *predict* development, or *explain the causes* of developmental changes (see table 1.9);
2. Whether the researcher is concerned with generalizing the study's results to other groups, situations, or places; and
3. Whether the design allows the researcher to use the best measures available.

Table 1.8

What to Ask When Judging a Measure: A Validity Checklist

Were the measurements *unbiased?*

___ Was it administered in the same, standard way to each participant?

___ Were observers "blind" (unaware of the research hypothesis)?

___ Was it objectively scored?

Is the measure *reliable?*

___ Is there evidence that the subjects would get the same scores if they were retested?

___ Are there any reasons to suspect that the measure would not produce stable, consistent scores? (Is the scoring subjective? Is the administration poorly standardized? Does the measure reflect temporary changes in subjects' mood?)

Are the researchers *accurately interpreting* the behavior?

___ Does the interpretation follow from sound logic or theory?

___ Is there evidence that the measure is valid? (Does it correlate with other measures of the concept? Do high and low scorers differ in ways that are consistent with how people who are different on the concept should differ?)

___ Could participants' self-reports be inaccurate (because of lying, forgetting, or not knowing)?

___ Could the participants' behavior have some other meaning?

Table 1.9

Difference Between the Goals of Description, Prediction, and Explanation

Description	Prediction	Explanation
What math skills does a 7-year-old learn?	Will a child be ready to learn math next year?	What causes a person to be able to understand complex math?
Is a person developmentally delayed?	Is a person likely to be developmentally delayed?	What causes a person to be developmentally delayed?
What percentage of 5th-grade students are extremely prejudiced?	What factors predict whether an individual will be prejudiced?	What do parents do that causes their children to be less prejudiced?
What are the characteristics of a hyperactive child?	What factors in a person's childhood will tend to predict whether they will be hyperactive? Are hyperactive children successful adults?	What causes hyperactivity?
What is a person's intelligence?	What will that person's intelligence be in the future?	How can the person's intelligence be increased—or rate of intellectual decline be decreased?
Does this individual have Alzheimer's disease?	Will this individual develop Alzheimer's disease?	What causes Alzheimer's disease?

Descriptive Relationships Versus Causal Relationships If researchers want to describe or predict development, they need to know only what variables are related to developmental changes. For example, Len Lecci and his colleagues (Lecci, Okun, & Karoly, 1994) found that people who have more life regrets (goals that they wish they had pursued) tend to be less happy than those with fewer regrets. This research describes a relationship between regrets and happiness. However, it does not explain why regrets and happiness are related. There are at least three sets of possible explanations for why regrets and happiness are statistically associated:

1. Life regrets cause unhappiness.
2. Unhappiness causes one to remember and dwell on lost opportunities.
3. Regrets and unhappiness are side effects of some other factor. That is, they have no influence on each other, but they are both influenced by some third factor. In this case, many different third factors could lead to both life regrets and unhappiness. For example, low intelligence, the tendency to procrastinate, alcoholism, unemployment, or personal tragedy could lead to both life regrets and unhappiness.

To describe or predict behavior requires only that research finds a relationship among variables. But explaining behavior requires showing which variables causes which. So you should not be surprised to find that a research design that successfully describes or predicts developmental changes may not effectively explain why a certain developmental change occurred (and vice versa, see table 1.10). Thus, if researcher A wants to describe the behavior of children who watch television and researcher B wants to determine whether watching television *causes* violence, both might use the same measure, but they should definitely use different research designs.

Generalizability If the goal is description or prediction, the researcher should use a descriptive design, whereas if the goal is to make causal statements, the researcher should use an experimental design. But how should a researcher seeking to describe development choose among the various descriptive designs? How should a researcher attempting to explain development choose among the various causal designs?

An important consideration in choosing the right design is **generalizability,** the degree to which the researcher wants the study's results to apply to people and settings other than those in the study. Usually, designs that allow the researcher to study a large and representative sample of individuals in natural, real-life situations are going to produce results that generalize to a greater extent than designs that force researchers to study few people in an artificial setting.

Appropriate Measures Finally, researchers should choose designs that allow them to use appropriate measures (see table 1.11). For instance, surveys only allow researchers to ask people questions. Since question-asking will often be an inappropriate means of getting information about physical or perceptual development, a researcher would not use that design to study infants' perceptual and physical development.

Table 1.10

How Designs Compare on Generalizability and Meeting the Goals of Developmental Psychology

Design	Goals	Generalizability
Case study	Description and prediction	Low
Lab observation	Description and prediction	Moderate*
Naturalistic observation	Description and prediction	High*
Survey	Description and prediction	High*
Cross-sectional	Description and prediction	Moderate*
Longitudinal	Description and prediction	Moderate*
Longitudinal sequence	Description and prediction	High*
Lab experiment	Explanation	Moderate*
Field experiment	Explanation	High*

*If based on a random sample of the appropriate group of people.

Types of Designs

Now that you know the three most important criteria for choosing a design, you are ready to critically examine the most common research designs. You will start with *descriptive designs.* Then, you will see how these descriptive designs are modified to track down age-related changes in *age-specific designs.* Finally, you will learn about the only designs that allow you to explain *why* certain developmental changes occur—*experimental designs.*

Descriptive Designs By definition, all **descriptive designs** allow researchers to describe the relationships among variables. Descriptive designs differ from each other primarily in terms of what measures they employ and how likely they are to provide generalizable results. In the next few sections, we will examine the most popular descriptive designs: the case study, survey, naturalistic observation, and lab observation.

The Case Study The potential and limitations of descriptive methods are epitomized by the **case study,** an in-depth study of a single person. The study may involve observing, interviewing, testing, or electronically monitoring the research participant.

How do researchers decide who will be the research participant of a case study? Sometimes, the research participant is chosen because she has experienced some unusual nonnormative events. For instance, Genie (Curtiss, 1977; Pines, 1981; Rymer, 1993) was chosen as a case study research participant because she had been almost completely cut off from human contact for the first 13 years of her life. Since few individuals have that kind of upbringing, Genie was studied intensively. Scientists wanted to know the effect of a deprived environment on development. One interesting and sad thing they discovered was that Genie never learned to use language normally.

If you didn't know that the case study is a descriptive rather than a causal design, you might be tempted to agree with someone who concluded that the study proved that deprivation causes language impairment. But don't leap to this conclusion—and don't let others get away with leaping to such conclusions. Nobody knows that isolation caused Genie's problems. Other factors may have caused her language impairment. She may have been born with a brain defect or she may have lost her ability to speak normally as a result of abuse, malnutrition, or some other cause. In short, like all descriptive designs, case studies do not allow us to state that one factor causes another.

However, case studies may allow researchers to say that one factor *doesn't always* cause another. For example, *if* Genie had been able to speak normally, we could say that isolation *doesn't always* cause individuals to permanently lose their language abilities. Note, however, that even if Genie had been able to learn to talk normally, no responsible psychologist would say "isolating children causes no permanent harm to language development." Instead, psychologists could say only that isolation doesn't harm language abilities in *all* cases. Psychologists couldn't predict that isolation would usually lead to permanent damage because they couldn't know whether Genie's reaction to isolation was the typical case or the exceptional case. Trying to generalize from one case to everyone is risky.

Nevertheless, some investigators do generalize from a single case. Sometimes, they claim that the individual they are studying is so typical and ordinary that the results would surely generalize to the average person. Other investigators may claim that the process they are studying is biologically based and so fundamental that every healthy human being will develop in the same way. Beware of such claims. After all, how do we know that someone is typical? A "typical" person may just be a convenient person to study (for example, the researcher's closest relative). If we study only one person, how do we know that a process is the same in *all* healthy humans?

In summary, when you read about a case study, be very cautious about leaping to conclusions. No matter how

Table 1.11

A Checklist of Which Measures Are Typically Used for Which Research Designs

	Possible Measuring Techniques				
Design	**Interview**	**Questionnaire**	**Tests**	**Observation**	**Instruments**
Case study	X	X	X	X	X
Survey	X	X	X		
Naturalistic observation				X	X
Lab observation				X	X
Lab experiments	X	X	X	X	X
Field experiments	X	X		X	X

interesting the case of the mass murderer or the child prodigy is, cause-effect statements or generalizations cannot be made from case studies. That is, the case study fails both as a causal design and as a descriptive design. People's gullibility for case studies is responsible for many myths and stereotypes. Some of these include the following myths: most adults go through a midlife crisis, all woman suffer from "empty-nest syndrome" when their children leave home, teens are the unhappiest age group, cohabitation reduces the incidence of divorce, most married people have affairs, most marriages are miserable, work causes unhappiness, and that African Americans have low self-esteem. Despite such misconceptions, case studies do provide opportunities to study once-in-a-lifetime events, and they may stimulate hypotheses that can be tested using other methods. For example, if we think a certain course of development is typical because we have observed it in one case, we could find out whether it was indeed typical by using lab observation, naturalistic observation, or a survey.

Survey Research Because **survey** research, unlike the case study, involves studying *many* people, survey results often have greater generalizability than results from a case study. But not always. Before you can determine to whom the results apply, you need to know who responded to the survey. For example, a researcher may be studying widows in Chicago (e.g., Lopata, 1975, 1988; Morycz, 1992). Before jumping to the conclusion that these results generalize to all widows, you should first ask whether the sample fairly represents the limited population studied. If the researcher surveyed every widow in Chicago, her results obviously apply to Chicago widows. However, she probably didn't question every widow in Chicago. Instead, she probably questioned a sample of those widows. The question that must be asked is: Are the people in her sample typical of Chicago widows? If the sample is composed of widows who go to the researcher's church, the answer is probably "no." If the sample is composed of widows who answered a newspaper advertisement, the answer is probably "no." In fact, you should usually assume that the sample is *not* a fair, representative sample no matter how large it is, unless the researcher used **random sampling,** a system whereby everyone in the designated group has an equal chance of being surveyed.

Unfortunately, many people, especially nonpsychologists such as newspaper reporters and book authors, do not use random sampling. Their results are therefore probably biased. This bias often explains conflicting poll results. For example, one survey study may report that most people are happily married, while another may report that most people are unhappily married (see box 1.6). Which should you believe? The one that used random sampling rather than convenience sampling. In **convenience sampling,** researchers haphazardly survey people who were convenient, such as those who call in with their opinions or those who belong to the researcher's civic club.

Once you have determined that the researcher obtained a representative sample of her designated group, you still have to be wary of generalizing the results to other groups. Even though her results apply to Chicago widows, the results may not be generalized to the small-town widow (Jolley, 1979). Furthermore, as you learned in the section about questionnaires, you should be wary of self-report bias. Specifically, try to look at the questions asked and determine whether any of the questions were *leading,* or phrased to produce (lead the person to) a certain answer, such as "You miss your husband, don't you?"

When properly conducted, surveys can provide interesting and timely information that will help us describe and predict development. For example, surveys can tell us how children view death, what percentage of adolescents are using steroids, how many adults are having

Box 1.6

RESEARCH in FOCUS

How to Make Millions by Doing Bad Research

Popular authors, such as Shere Hite, can become rich by writing books based on shoddy research. Scientists are critical of such poorly conducted research because the results can be misleading. In Hite's case, her results were almost completely the opposite of what numerous studies have shown to be true. For example, she claimed, among other things, that 98 percent of women want to make basic changes in their love relationships, 95 percent are being emotionally and psychologically harassed by the men they love, and 70 percent of those women married for more than 5 years are having affairs. Yet, the 1987 Harris poll of 3,000 people found 89 percent of married couples claiming that their relationship with their partner is satisfying.

Where did Shere Hite go wrong?

1. *Poor sample harms generalizability.* A poor sample was one important research flaw. Although Hite's sample was large, it was not random or representative because her survey was sent only to women's groups and fewer than 1 in 20 questionnaires was returned, possibly because the questionnaire contained 127 essay questions.
2. *Bad questions lead to bad answers.* A second mistake in the research design was that Hite asked one type of question when she asked about women's mothers and a different type of question when she asked about women's fathers. For example, she asked whether respondents feared their fathers, but not whether they feared their mothers; she asked whether respondents wanted to spend time with their mothers, but not whether they wanted to spend time with their fathers. Given that she asked questions about fathers and mothers that differed, it is not surprising that respondents' comments about their fathers were different from their comments about their mothers.
3. *Coding was subjective.* Another major flaw in Hite's research was her subjective interpretation of the respondent's comments. We don't know if respondents' comments about their fathers differed from their comments about their mothers. We don't know because the only thing we have is that Hite coded, or interpreted, their "father responses" differently from their "mother responses." Did she code them differently because they were different, or merely because Hite interpreted them differently? That is, was Hite objective?

   Scientists doubt that Hite's interpretations were objective for several reasons:

   a. Objectively coding 127 essay questions is difficult.
   b. She had no training in objectively coding responses.
   c. She showed no evidence of being objective as reflected by her failure to use blind techniques in which the survey participant and person scoring the responses is unaware of the hypothesis.
   d. She failed to set up a scoring key for the essays.
   e. She did not show that her ratings correlated well with that of other trained raters; thus she provided no evidence that she was objective.

Source: Streitfeld, D. (1988). Shere Hite and the trouble with numbers. *Chance, 1,* 26–31.

midlife crises, and how the elderly feel about their lives. However, you should be aware of two limitations of the survey method.

First, like the case study and all descriptive methods, surveys do not allow researchers to make cause-effect statements. A survey researcher can say that widows are more depressed than marrieds, but she can't say that widowhood causes depression. Widows may differ from marrieds in many ways that may contribute to both their widowed status and to their depressed state. That is, the same poverty, stress, or health condition that led to a spouse's death may afflict the widow, causing depression.

Do not make the mistake of thinking that the researcher can make cause-effect statements if she asks people, "Why did you . . . ?" If someone asks widows why they are depressed, their answer may or may not be accurate. Some depressed people know why they are depressed, but some do not. As a classic study demonstrated (Nisbett & Wilson, 1977), people often do not know why they do things. Indeed, several studies have found that participants may claim that a treatment helped them when the treatment actually hindered their development (Finckenauer, 1979; Laurence, as cited by Adler, 1990).

The fact that people's answers do not always reflect truth brings us to the second problem with survey methods.

Survey research is an *indirect* method of describing behavior because researchers are asking people what they did or what they think. Such answers may be inaccurate for a variety of reasons: people may not know why they did what they did, they may have forgotten what they did, or they may be telling us what they think we want to hear. Admittedly, researchers may increase the accuracy of survey results by not asking people *why* they did something, by not placing unreasonable demands on people's memories, and by not asking questions that lead respondents to the desired answer. But regardless of what the researchers do, the results will still not be free of bias. Sudman and Bradburn (1982) have shown that even minor changes in question wording affect survey results. Similarly, Krosnick and Schuman (1988) have shown that merely changing the order in which questions are asked can greatly affect responses, even when the questions concern controversial topics, such as abortion.

Naturalistic Observation Because people may inaccurately report their own behavior, some researchers don't like to rely on self-reports. Instead, they prefer to observe people's behavior for themselves. One way of doing this is **naturalistic observation,** or observing organisms in their natural environment. Developmental psychologists have used naturalistic observation to study both aggression and helping behaviors in nursery school children (Eisenberg-Berg, 1979), to uncover the daily routines of the elderly, and to study how parents and children interact.

Although naturalistic observation has the flexibility of the survey technique without the problems of self-report biases, it is not free of problems. One of the problems is observer bias. Perhaps the easiest way to understand how observer bias can mar the objectivity of an observational study is to observe another person's behavior for just 5 minutes. Write down everything the person does during that time and you will face two challenges.

First, you'll be tempted to make subjective inferences about that person's mood, emotions, and intentions. That is, even though you can see only behavior, you'll interpret that behavior and try to read motives and emotions into that behavior. The trouble is that your personal interpretation might be very different from another observer's interpretation. When we read motives and emotions into behavior, others may not see what we see. Consequently, observations are no longer objective.

Second, because of the lack of a systematic way of recording behavior and because many behaviors may occur in a short space of time, you may be unable to record everything you would like to record. Thus, what you record may be very different from what another person records. Fortunately, both of these sources of observer biases can be reduced by training the observers to report only certain behaviors, rather than their interpretations of those behaviors.

If the researcher has taken steps to reduce observer bias, the next thing to look for is who was observed. Because observation may be time-consuming, it is tempting to observe only a few individuals. If only a few people are observed, the study may have no more generalizability than a case study. If, on the other hand, the researcher observes a random sample of the larger group being studied, naturalistic observation studies can have tremendous generalizability. The random sampling allows generalization to a larger group of people and the naturalistic setting allows generalization to other real-life settings.

Thus, when properly conducted, a naturalistic observation study has generalizability to a population (by observing a large random sample of people), generalizability to real-life settings (by observing behavior in real-life settings), and objectivity (by training raters to report specific behaviors instead of their interpretations of behaviors). However, even a properly conducted naturalistic observation study has four limitations.

1. As with all descriptive designs, such a study does not allow the researcher to make causal statements. Behavior is observed, but not its causes.
2. As with all observational methods, naturalistic observation is not well-suited to studying unobservable events such as thoughts and feelings. Although in certain cases observation can be used to study thoughts, it is best suited for studying observable events such as physical development and social behavior.
3. Even when studying behavior in a naturalistic setting, the observer may not see people acting as they normally would. For example, the research subjects may act unnaturally if the observer is visible. This is especially true if the observer (in trying to be sure that her observations are objective and accurate) is carrying around a clipboard, check sheet, or a video camera. If, on the other hand, the observer goes out of her way not to be noticed by the participants (so they will act naturally), the researcher may be unable to accurately observe and record their behavior.
4. The behaviors the researcher wants to observe may not happen very often in a naturalistic setting. Like a police detective on stakeout, the researcher may have to wait hours for the behavior to occur one time. By that time, the observers may be so bored that they miss it.

Laboratory Observation The researcher can observe research participants more easily and accurately by moving them into the laboratory and observing them. By using **laboratory observation,** the researcher can calmly and unobtrusively monitor participants from behind a one-way mirror, rather than running after participants or hiding from them. Rather than relying on memory or split-second judgments, the researcher can review videotapes of the participants' behaviors. Rather than waiting for the critical behavior to occur, the researcher can set up the lab so that desired behaviors are more likely to occur. For example, if the researcher wants to observe play, the researcher can clear the lab of everything except for a few toys.

When evaluating lab **observation** studies, realize that the increased accuracy of observation in the lab may be offset by lack of generalizability. Two factors weaken the ability of lab observation studies to provide generalizable results.

First, observed behavior may be less natural in a lab setting. That is, research participants' behavior may not be typical of their ordinary, day-to-day behavior, but rather only of their behavior when they are in a lab. However, behavior in the lab is not always artificial. If researchers are studying physical development or studying naive infants, the artificiality of the lab probably does not interfere with generalizability.

Second, the results may not be generalizable because only a few participants were observed or because the research participants are volunteers. Research participants who volunteer for a study by answering an advertisement are probably not representative of the general public because most people don't respond to these advertisements. As with the survey, ask the question: "Are the people being studied a representative sample of the population I am interested in—or are they representative of some other sample, such as children of professors?"

In addition, to these two problems, lab observation studies are vulnerable to most of the same pitfalls as naturalistic observation studies. Thus, regardless of whether a researcher uses lab observation or naturalistic observation, always determine whether behavior was systematically and objectively recorded. Be especially wary of observational researchers who label behavior with interpretive terms such as (*moody, greedy,* or *protective*) or who claim to "see" what people are thinking or perceiving. Finally, remember that just like naturalistic observational researchers, lab observational researchers should not make causal statements.

Conclusions About Descriptive Designs Any of the research techniques we have discussed can be useful for determining whether or not two factors are related. The key is to measure two variables (for example, television viewing and violent acts) and then compute a **correlation coefficient,** a statistic that tells you the extent to which two factors are related. Correlation coefficients range from −1 to +1. The sign of the correlation coefficient (positive versus negative) tells you the direction of the relationship.

Positive correlations between two variables mean that when one factor is high, the other tends to be high (for example, height and weight). Put another way, when one variable is low, the other tends to be low as well. Thus, a positive correlation between television viewing and violence would mean that the more television someone watched, the more violent acts they would perform. In other words, the less television watched, the fewer violent acts performed.

Laboratory observation is easier and can be more accurate than natural observation. However, lab observations may not be as generalizable.

Negative correlations, on the other hand, mean that when one factor is low, the other tends to be high (for example, happiness and depression). Thus, a negative correlation between television viewing and violence would mean that as television viewing increases, the number of aggressive acts committed decreases.

Note, however, that the sign of the correlation coefficient doesn't tell you anything about the strength of the relationship between two variables. The strength of the relationship is indicated by how far the correlation is away from zero. A zero correlation means no relationship, so it makes sense that the farther away the correlation is from no relationship, the stronger the relationship. Therefore, to find the strength of the relationship, cover up the sign. Then, the larger the number, the stronger the relationship. Thus, a correlation of −.8 indicates a much stronger relationship than a correlation of +.4. To better understand these concepts, let's go back to our television viewing and violence example.

A positive correlation of +.2 would indicate that television viewing and violence were slightly related, a correlation of +.5 that they were moderately related, and a correlation of +1.00 would mean that they were perfectly related—if you knew how much television someone watched, you could predict, with 100 percent accuracy, how many violent acts they performed. For example, you would know that the child watching the *least* TV would be the *least* violent and that the child watching the *most* TV would be the *most* violent.

Similarly, a negative correlation of −.2 would indicate that viewing and violence were slightly related, a correlation of −.5 that they were moderately related, and a correlation of −1.00 that they were perfectly related—if you knew how much television a person has watched, you could predict, with 100 percent accuracy, how many violent acts they performed. For example, you would know that the child watching the *least* TV would be the *most* violent and that the child watching the *most* TV would be the *least* violent.

Because human behavior and development are rarely controlled by a single factor, perfect relationships are rare. Consequently, few correlations between variables studied by developmental psychologists come close to either +1 or −1. Indeed, most of those correlations are closer to 0 (which indicates no relationship) than to either +1 or −1.

Because descriptive designs can provide data that can be used to compute correlation coefficients, descriptive designs are often called **correlational designs.** If the proper measures are used and a large, representative sample of people studied, correlational designs can tell us how closely two factors are related. Therefore, correlational information can be useful for describing or predicting development. However, these designs cannot tell us *why* the factors are related (see box 1.7). These designs are not useful for telling us what *causes* certain developmental changes.

Age-Specific Designs

Although developmental psychologists are interested in using case studies, surveys, naturalistic observation, and lab observation to describe the relationship between events and developmental changes, they are also interested in **age-specific designs,** research designs that are used to describe and predict how we change with age. Therefore, developmental psychologists often adapt conventional descriptive designs to compare different age groups. More specifically, most conventional descriptive designs can be incorporated into any one of three basic kinds of age-specific designs: *cross-sectional designs, longitudinal designs,* and *sequential designs.*

Cross-Sectional Design

The **cross-sectional design** compares people of one age group with people of at least one other age group (see figure 1.2). For example, in a controversial early study, David Wechsler (1972) contrasted the raw IQ scores of adults from age groups ranging from age 20 to 90. He found that older groups had lower scores on many subscales. These findings supported his notion that the "decline of mental ability with age is part of the general senescent process of the organism as a whole" (p. 30).

Figure 1.2

Examples of Longitudinal and Cross-Sectional Designs

The longitudinal study comes from retesting the same cohort every seven years. Thus, the cohort born in 1951 would be tested when they are 25, 32, and 39 (see bottom row). The cross-sectional study comes from testing several different cohorts at the same time. Thus, the 1990 cross-sectional study depicted here (in the right-hand column) studied a cohort born in 1916 whose members were 74 years old in 1990, a cohort born in 1923 whose members were 67 in 1990, a cohort born in 1930 whose members were 60 years in 1990, and so forth.

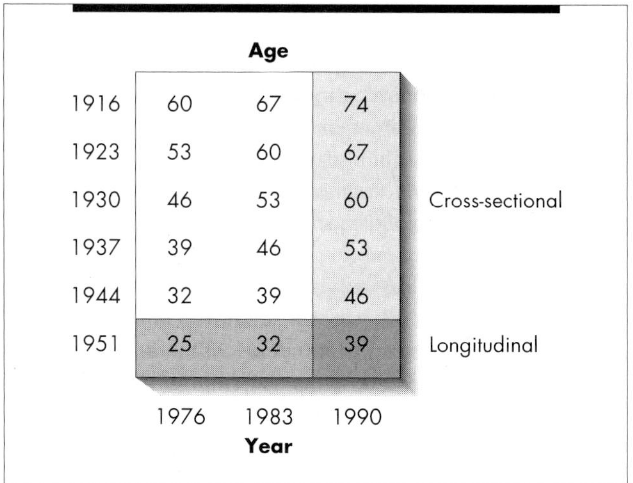

However, because the groups differed in terms of many factors besides age, we disagree with Wechsler's conclusions. One can't assume that age is responsible for the differences in IQ scores. Indeed, the IQ differences may well be due to the **cohort effect,** the effect of belonging to different generations that have different histories. In considering Wechsler's study, you may have asked yourself: "Aren't there enormous differences between the historical and cultural experiences of the 20-year-olds and the 90-year-olds?" The 20-year-olds probably had the benefit of better schooling, more experience with standardized tests, more motivation to do well on tests, and greater familiarity with the kinds of information and questions asked in the more recently developed intelligence tests (Schaie, 1986, 1994). Thus, even under ideal conditions, a cross-sectional study can't establish which differences are the product of biological aging and which are the product of different experiences.

Besides the cohort effect, many cross-sectional studies are affected by sampling bias because neither the sample of older adults nor the sample of younger adults is a representative sample (Schaie, 1986, 1994). For example, if a university researcher pays participants to be in a study, the researcher's young adult group may be college students whereas the older adult group may be poverty-stricken members of the community (Poon, 1985). Consequently, differences between the "young" and "old" group could just as easily be labeled differences between the "middle-class" and "poor" or "educated" and "uneducated."

Because cross-sectional researchers do not test and retest the same individuals, they cannot conclusively determine whether individuals change as they age. You

Box 1.7

RESEARCH in FOCUS

Why Correlations Don't Establish Causality

Three Ways to Look at a Relationship

Correlational findings do not allow researchers to make causal inferences. The danger of erroneously making causal inferences from correlational findings is illustrated by early work on the serious mental disorder called **autism,** a disorder originating in childhood in which the individual is noncommunicative and withdrawn. Scientists discovered that parents of autistic babies spend less time holding their babies than parents of normal babies. Many people leapt to the conclusion that the autistic child's parents were to blame for the infant's condition. Parents of autistic children not only had to live with the autistic child, but with the guilt and shame of others telling them that it was their fault.

From what you now know about correlational research, you realize that correlations don't prove causality. More specifically, as box figure 1.7A illustrates, parents' holding behavior may not cause autism. Instead of holding behavior causing autism, it might be the other way around: Autism might cause the parents to hold their child less. Alternatively, there may be no direct connection between autism and parental holding behavior. Rather, the two may be indirectly related only because of some third factor. For example, some kind of stress (poverty or low-level lead poisoning, for instance) might cause the child's autism and also cause the parents to have less time or energy to hold their child.

Which of the three possibilities is the truth? Researchers now know that autism causes the parents' holding behavior. Parents of autistic children start out holding their child as much as parents of normal children. However, since autistic children hate to be held, whereas normal children love to be held, parents of autistic infants are soon holding their child less than parents of normal children. Thus, the guilt and shame that parents of autistic children suffered in the past was unwarranted. Unfortunately, even today, some people are ignorant of this fact and continue to cruelly and erroneously blame the parents of autistic infants for "not holding them enough when they were little."

Box Figure 1.7A

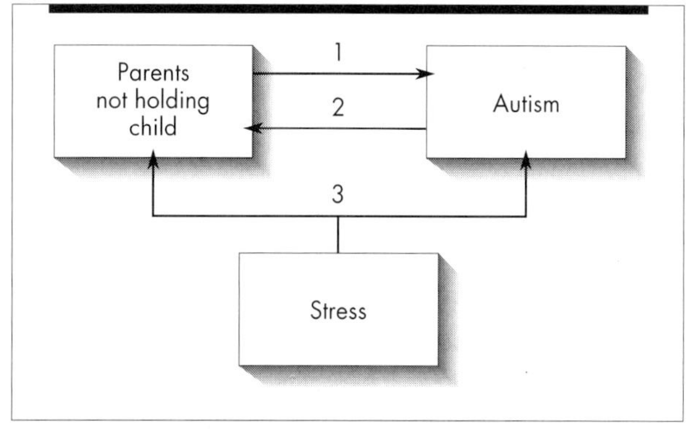

may wonder why developmental psychologists use cross-sectional designs given the difficulty of avoiding sampling bias and the impossibility of avoiding cohort effects. The main reason is that cross-sectional designs provide a relatively inexpensive and quick way to compare different age groups. However, there are alternatives to cross-sectional designs.

Longitudinal Designs The major alternative to the cross-sectional study is the **longitudinal design.** As you can see in figure 1.2, a longitudinal study follows one group of people over a period of time. Longitudinal designs provide information on how individuals change over time, thereby overcoming one of the major limitations of the cross-sectional design. Thus, when the results of longitudinal studies conflict with results from cross-sectional studies, people tend to believe the longitudinal studies. As an example, look at Cunningham and Owens' (1983) longitudinal comparisons of people as they age which, in direct contradiction to Wechsler (1972), show that people retain their intellectual abilities well into their sixties. Whose results do you think more closely reflect the truth?

If you said the longitudinal study, don't be too sure. Despite the fact that the longitudinal study was time-consuming and expensive to conduct, it is not as perfect as it first appears. Certainly, it describes the extent to which each individual's scores changed. But it doesn't determine that those changes were due to aging. Perhaps the longitudinal study failed to find decreases in IQ over the lifespan because research participants remembered test items, became more comfortable in the testing situation, or learned how to take tests. Or, it may be that the

Box 1.8

SELF-CHECK

1. What advantages does laboratory observation have over naturalistic observation?
2. What one advantage do surveys and observational studies have over case studies? What one big disadvantage do they share with case studies?
3. An advice columnist asks people to participate in a survey about their marriages. Of those who write in, 80 percent are unhappy because their spouses don't listen to them. What can the advice columnist *not* conclude? Why?
4. What problems are there with surveying adolescents about their drug use?
5. Rufus finds a correlation of +2.00 between intelligence and television viewing. What would you say to Rufus?
6. Having irregular eye movements while reading is correlated with reading problems. What does this correlation suggest? What is another possibility?
7. If the number of television sets in a household correlates +.3 with intelligence, what would that mean? What if the number of television sets correlated −.3 with intelligence?
8. A researcher wants to know what percentage of adults go through midlife crises. What design would be most appropriate?
9. A researcher watches children play with toys in her lab. She sees many fights. What kind of design is being used? Will she be able to tell people what causes the children to fight? Why or why not?
10. A defense attorney points out that his client, a convicted murderer, had a terrible childhood. What design is being employed? What conclusions is the attorney trying to make us draw? Why would these conclusions not be scientifically valid from this evidence?
11. A person from a disadvantaged group becomes successful. He argues that because he did it on his own, no member of a disadvantaged group needs any government help. Why might his conclusion be invalid?

Please turn to the end of this chapter to check your answers before going on to the next section.

measuring instrument itself changed. Perhaps the investigators are using a different and easier IQ test than they did 50 years ago.

Alternatively, a historical trend that would lead to higher scores, such as getting better nutrition and health care than when they were younger, may be counteracting the effects of deterioration due to aging. Last, but not least, the results may be due to **attrition,** or the dropping out of research participants due to death, loss of interest, or loss of contact. You can't reasonably assume that there are no differences between the kinds of people who remain in a study and the kinds of people who drop out (Schaie, 1994). At least two reasons can explain why the dropouts are more likely to exhibit declines in IQ than those who stayed in. First, the dropouts may have dropped out due to forgetfulness. Second, and especially common when studying an elderly sample, the dropouts are probably in poorer health and as a result may be at greater risk of suffering some biological deterioration.

In conclusion, attrition creates serious problems in interpreting longitudinal studies. If the researcher compares the people who stay in the study with the original group, the researcher is comparing apples and oranges with oranges. That is, the researcher is comparing a larger group with a biased sample of itself. If, on the other hand, the researcher looks only at the people who stayed in the study until its completion, results are based on a select group of people. Consequently, claiming that the results generalize to all elderly people would be extremely risky.

Sequential Designs You have seen that the results of longitudinal studies may be contaminated by attrition, historical trends, changes in tests, or subjects getting used to testing procedures. You have seen that cross-sectional designs may be contaminated by cohort effects. To overcome the individual limitations of each of these designs, K. Warner Schaie (1965, 1977, 1986, 1994) proposed a series of hybrid designs that he calls **sequential designs.** By combining longitudinal and cross-sectional designs, the sequential design may allow developmental psychologists to separate cohort effects from age effects (Baltes, Reese, & Nesselroade, 1988; Viken, Rose, Kaprio, & Koskenuvo, 1994).

To understand the basic principles behind these designs, let's take a look at one, the **longitudinal sequence design** (Baltes, Reese, & Nesselroade, 1988). As you can see from figure 1.3, in a longitudinal sequence design, the researcher begins with a cross-sectional study. Then, the researcher retests these same research participants at some later time, thereby adding a longitudinal aspect to the study. If an age effect is found for both the cross-sectional and longitudinal aspects of the study, the researcher can be relatively confident that there is a true age change. However, if

Figure 1.3

Examples of a Longitudinal Sequence Design

Time 1 (Age in 1990)	Time 2 (Age in 1997)
60	67
53	60
46	53
39	46
32	39

the age effect is found in only one aspect, the result is less certain. For example, if the age effect is found only for the cross-sectional aspect, the age-related differences may not be due to aging, but to differences between cohorts.

Schaie (1994) attempted to use the longitudinal sequence to disentangle the effects of age and IQ. His first step, which he and his colleagues performed in 1956, was to do a cross-sectional study in which he gave intelligence tests to a group of people ranging in age from 22 to 70. Then, in 1963, 1970, 1977, 1984, and in 1991, all those who could be located were tested again, thereby adding a longitudinal aspect to the study. The cross-sectional aspect of the study replicated the typical pattern of decline during the adult years: scores on the verbal abilities subscale peaked at age 32, followed by steady decline. However, the longitudinal part of the study told a different story. Scores on the verbal abilities scale increased until about age 60. After age 60, there was only a small decline.

So, what is the effect of age on IQ? We can't say because even the longitudinal sequence design is still only a correlational design. However, our best guess would be that cohort effects account for declines in IQ scores during early and middle adulthood and that aging, at least until age 55, does not cause declines in IQ scores.

Conclusions About Age-Specific Designs As you have seen, tracking the effects of age is difficult. Cross-sectional designs may yield different results from longitudinal designs, and even sequential designs should not be completely trusted. The problem is that age-specific designs are correlational designs, and as you learned in the previous section, correlational designs cannot prove that age or any other variable has caused a given effect.

Different research designs yield different findings on the IQ of older adults. Based on sequential designs, it appears that aging doesn't usually cause an IQ decline until at least age 55.

Experimental Designs

As suggested by the fact that many designs fail to establish causality, proving that one variable causes a developmental change is a difficult feat. To establish causality, a researcher must not only demonstrate the change occurs *after* the factor is introduced, but also show that no other factor could account for the change. Fortunately, however, there are two types of **experimental designs,** or research designs that reveal causal relationships between variables. The **lab experiment** and the **field experiment** can both demonstrate causality.

The Lab Experiment In the simplest case, the lab experiment consists of two groups of research participants: the *experimental group,* which receives some kind of treatment, and the *control group,* a comparison group that doesn't receive the treatment. For example, in a study of the effects of nutrition on longevity, the experimental group would get a special diet, whereas the control group would eat a normal diet. In this study, diet would be the **independent variable** because it varies between groups, independently of the research participants' wishes. The key, of course, is to make sure that the two groups are very similar before introducing the independent variable. The way to do this is by **random assignment,** or determining which research participant is in which group by flipping a coin (head = experimental, tails = control), rolling a die, or using some other random process. Random assignment gives each research participant an equal chance of being put in either group. Consequently, it would be very unlikely that such groups would differ greatly or systematically on any single variable, whether that variable is age, race, gender, IQ, or whatever, until after the independent variable was introduced.

Once research participants have been assigned to a group, they should be treated identically except that the control group doesn't receive the independent variable. If, in the nutrition study, the group getting the special diet received more attention than the group getting the normal diet, that attention would be a **confound,** a factor that is unintentionally manipulated and that might account for effects attributed to the independent variable. Assuming that there are no confounds, the next step is to measure and record *all* research participants' scores on the **dependent variable,** the behavior or characteristic that the researcher predicts will be influenced by the independent variable. In this case, the dependent variable is how long each research participant lives. You hope that longevity will depend on diet, and you know longevity depends on the individual's genes and experiences.

Once the research participants' scores are collected on the dependent variable, these scores are analyzed using a test of statistical significance. Basically, such tests describe how likely it is that the differences between the control and experimental group are due to chance. If the results are **statistically significant,** they are unlikely to be due to chance. The fact that one group lived longer than the other is probably *not* a coincidence. Therefore, we could be relatively confident that if the study were done again on a similar group of research participants, the basic pattern of results would be the same. In other words, a statistically significant difference between groups tells us that the groups differ not because of chance, but because of the treatment. Thus, if the research participants in the special diet group lived longer than those in the normal diet group, and this difference was statistically significant, we could say that the diet increased longevity. If, on the other hand, the results were not statistically significant, we would not be able to determine whether one group's increased longevity was due to chance or due to the diet. In other words, nonsignificant results are inconclusive.

Actual lab experiments show that putting rats on strict diets does increase their longevity (McCay & Maynard, 1939; Ross 1972, 1978). These results suggest that if people would eat much less than they normally eat, they would live longer and healthier lives. But do results of lab rat studies generalize to humans? Similarly, do results of laboratory experiments on the effects of televised violence generalize to real-life behavior? Just as with lab observation, one possible problem is that research participants may change their behavior because they know they are being observed.

Certainly, you should question the generalizability of laboratory research. However, the generalizability of lab experiments is often impressive (Banaji & Crowder, 1989) and few would argue that lab experiments are without value. To give but two examples: Lab experiments have shown that training can increase the IQ scores of the elderly (Schaie, 1988, 1994) and that writing about problems in adjusting to college speeds up freshmen's adjustment to college (Pennebaker, Colder, & Sharp, 1990). However, despite the power of lab experiments, some researchers believe that the artificiality of the lab and the sampling problems of relying on volunteer research participants limit the lab experiment's usefulness.

Field Experiments To overcome the limits of lab experiments while maintaining their advantage in making causal statements, some experimenters turn to **field experiments,** studies in which research participants are randomly assigned to either the experimental or the control group in a real-world, rather than a lab, setting. To illustrate, let's look at a classic study that could have been used in a recent court case (see box 1.9).

In a field experiment, Marshall Klaus and his colleagues (1972) examined the effects of early mother-child interaction on bonding. Specifically, they determined, on the basis of random assignment, that one group of mothers (the experimental group) would get an extra 16 hours of contact with their babies soon after birth, whereas the control group was not given this extra time.

One month later, the two groups were observed again. Klaus and his associates found that the experimental group soothed their infants more, fondled them more, and engaged in more eye contact with their infants than the control group did with their infants.

Since these differences were statistically significant, Klaus and his associates concluded that his independent variable (early mother-child interactions) has an effect on several dependent variables (soothing, fondling, and eye contact). He could safely make these conclusions because he did the one thing necessary to make his study an experiment—he used random assignment. Because he used a field setting, he can be more comfortable in generalizing his results to real life.

However, because he tested only the effects of first-day interaction on bonding at 1 month of age, his results apply only to first-day interactions and bonding at 1 month. In other words, it would be extremely careless to conclude that these results mean that if mothers don't spend enormous amounts of time with their infant, bonding will be permanently weakened. Moreover, it would be wrong. Goldberg (1983) showed that the effects of early attention on bonding wear off before the infant is 2 months old.

Conclusions About Experimental Designs When properly used, field and lab experiments are powerful tools for demonstrating that a given factor causes a certain effect. However, as with any research, results can be biased unless proper precautions are taken (see table 1.12). For example, in both the lab and the field, researchers may unconsciously interact with research participants in a way that biases their participants' behavior. Experimenters may also unconsciously record or interpret behavior in a biased manner. Furthermore, research participants can also bias results. That is, if

Box 1.9

ISSUE in FOCUS

In a Bind Over Bonding

Two new mothers who almost left a suburban hospital in 1993 with the wrong babies say the hospital deprived them of sharing their newborns' first hours.

Officials at Fitzgerald Mercy Hospital, outside of Philadelphia, discovered their error by checking wristbands on mother and child. They switched the babies back to their biological parents before anyone left the hospital.

But the parents of the two babies contend in Common Pleas Court lawsuits that they endured "emotional pain and suffering grief, and mental anguish" as well as "deprivation of . . . affection and bonding with their newborn child."

1. If you were the parents' attorneys, what scientific evidence would you present to support the parents' claims? Why?
2. If you were the hospital's attorneys, what scientific evidence would you present to refute the parents' claims? Why?

SOURCE: AP *The Derrick,* April 8, 1994.

research participants know—or think they know—the hypothesis, they may change their behaviors to comply with the researcher's hypothesis. A safeguard against both of these problems is to use the **double-blind technique,** a research method in which both the person collecting the data and the research participant are uninformed (blind) as to whether the research participant is in the control or in the experimental group.

Given the fact that experiments allow researchers to make causal statements and researchers can do experiments in the lab or in the field, you may be surprised to learn that many developmental psychologists don't do experiments. Why?

The answer to this question lies in the fact that to do an experiment, you must be able to randomly assign research participants to get differing amounts of the independent variable. Age, the central variable in much developmental research, cannot be randomly assigned. No matter how much we want to, we can't alter a person's age. We cannot randomly assign people to be 2 years old or 100 years old.

Similarly, variables such as race, gender, personality, and intelligence cannot be independent variables because they cannot be randomly assigned. Furthermore, even when it's possible to randomly assign a treatment, it may be unethical to do so. Thus, whereas we could randomly assign children to be either isolated like Genie was (experimental group) or to have a normal childhood (control group), we shouldn't and we wouldn't. Such an experiment would be unethical, immoral, and illegal. Finally, even when it is both possible and ethical to randomly assign research participants to a certain condition, there may be practical obstacles that can't be overcome.

To give but one example, Lovaas (1987) wanted to do an experiment to see whether a new treatment could help victims of autism. However, parents wouldn't cooperate because nobody wanted to have their child in the control group. Parents wanted their child to get the experimental treatment. Consequently, rather than using random assignment, he had to bow to the parents' wishes that treatment be given on a "first come, first served" basis. Although you can certainly understand the parents' feelings, the effect of their demands is that we can't be sure that Lovaas' treatment is working.

Despite the fact that it may often be impossible, impractical, or unethical to do experiments, the ideal of making groups equivalent by random assignment is something many investigators emulate. To approximate

Table 1.12

False Conclusions from Research: How to Spot Them

Are researchers saying that one factor influences another? If so,

___ Did they use an experimental design?

___ Did they properly execute that design? (Did they randomly assign participants to groups? Did they do tests of statistical significance to determine whether their treatment had an effect?)

Are researchers implying that their results apply to most people? If so,

___ Did they test enough people?

___ Is their sample representative of the general population?

___ Did their participants adequately represent minorities?

___ Did they use random sampling to get their participants?

Are researchers claiming to measure some abstract concept such as intelligence, personality, moral development, or self-actualization? If so,

___ Was their measure scored objectively?

___ Was the measure reliable?

___ Is there any evidence that the measure is valid?

___ What other meaning could participants' behaviors have?

Box 1.10

SELF-CHECK

1. If a researcher wants to know whether day care improves social development, what design should the researcher use?
2. A doctor notes that teenagers who have acne eat pizza and junk food. The doctor concludes that pizza and junk food cause acne. Why might the doctor's conclusions be wrong? What should the doctor have done differently to determine if there is a causal relationship?
3. What design should a researcher use if she wants to know what patients in a nursing home do? What if she wants to know whether giving patients more responsibilities improves their mental functioning?
4. What is the difference between naturalistic observation and field experiments? What is the difference between laboratory observation and laboratory experiments?
5. What is an advantage of field experiments over lab experiments? Naturalistic observation over laboratory observation?
6. You want to study the effects of being reared bilingual. What design would you use? Why?
7. What are the major age-related designs, and what are the major advantages and disadvantages associated with each?
8. What is the difference between random sampling and random assignment?

Please turn to the end of this chapter to check your answers.

random assignment, some researchers match research participants on critical variables when doing cross-sectional studies (for example, making sure the different groups have the same amount of education) or when comparing people who have had different life experiences, such as comparing widows with married women (for instance, making sure both groups have the same social class or health status). As you will see in chapter 3, some investigators use the ultimate in matching by comparing identical twins.

CONCLUSIONS

In this chapter, you were introduced to the emerging field of lifespan developmental psychology. You saw that developmental psychology is a vast field in which vastly different people holding vastly different ideas using vastly different methods study vastly different issues and age groups. Yet, despite their differences, developmental psychologists are united in their shared belief in the scientific method. They believe that by checking their opinions against fact, truth can be grasped.

We hope that you share the developmental psychologist's curiosity and cautious optimism. Specifically, although there may be no easy, absolute, all-or-none correct position on the controversial issues, we trust you will critically examine the facts that you will learn in the following chapters and use those facts to develop an informed opinion on the issues. In short, we want you to value facts, not just for their own sake, but for the purpose of seeing the "big picture." After all, as you'll see in chapter 2, developmental psychologists do not live by facts alone.

SUMMARY

1. Lifespan developmental psychology is the scientific study of how we grow and change from the point of conception to the moment of death. The main goals are to describe, predict, and explain development.
2. To achieve the goals of description, prediction, and explanation, developmental psychologists look not only at how we change as we age, but also at how we are affected by three major kinds of events: normative age-graded events (normative maturational and normative social), nonnormative events, and cohort or historical events.
3. Normative maturational events are biological growth processes that permit changes in behavior.
4. Normative social events are nonbiological events that most people experience at about the same age.

5. Nonnormative events are unexpected events that neither happen to everyone nor follow a preset schedule.
6. Cohort or historical events are events that change what is considered normative or nonnormative.
7. The microgenetic method allows researchers to intensely study the period of change and may help them to answer the continuity/discontinuity problem.
8. The behavioral genetic movement has led to insights on both the nature-nurture issue and the individuality-universality issue.
9. The major developmental controversies are stability versus change, continuity versus discontinuity, nature versus nurture, maturation versus learning, free will versus determinism, and individuality versus universality. One's position on these issues is often related to one's political philosophy.
10. To get answers to the broad, complex, controversial, and emotional questions that face them, developmental psychologists rely on the scientific method.
11. The main advantages of the scientific method are that it is objective, self-correcting, and that it allows scientists to build on each other's work.
12. Good science begins with good measures. Good measures are objective, replicable, and valid.
13. The most common measuring techniques are observation, interviews, questionnaires, tests, and scientific instruments.
14. When observation is systematically recorded and focuses only on the actual behavior observed, it can provide objective information about what people are doing.
15. In terms of replicability, objectivity, and reducing self-report biases, structured interviews and questionnaires are better than both unstructured interviews and projective tests.
16. Realize that the validity of any measure can be questioned.
17. Research designs differ in terms of the measures they use, the generalizability of their findings, and the extent to which cause-effect statements can be made based on their results.
18. There are two main components of generalizability: (1) extending the results to people who weren't in the study and (2) extending the results to real-life situations.
19. If subjects are a random sample of a larger group, the researcher can generalize the results to that larger group. However, many researchers don't use random samples.
20. If the behavior of participants is measured in a lab, the results may not generalize to real life. Thus, some researchers prefer to measure behavior in a natural setting.
21. None of the descriptive designs (case studies, surveys, naturalistic observation, and laboratory observation) can be used to make cause-effect statements. However, if questionnaires, interviews, or observations are used to measure the dependent variable in a lab or field experiment, causal statements can be made.
22. The relationship a researcher finds between age and a certain factor may depend on which age-specific design the researcher uses. A very imperfect general rule is that sequential designs should be trusted more than longitudinal designs which, in turn, should be trusted more than cross-sectional designs.
23. Both lab experiments and field experiments allow researchers to make cause-effect statements because both use random assignment. Field experiments can have more generalizability than lab experiments for the same reason that naturalistic observation can have more generalizability than lab observation.
24. Three major factors restrict the use of experiments: (1) some factors, such as age, can't be randomly assigned; (2) some factors, such as stress or diet, shouldn't be randomly assigned; and (3) some factors, such as wealth or education, are difficult to randomly assign.

KEY TERMS

age-specific designs 26
attrition 28
autism 27
behavioral genetics 12
case study 21
cohort 6
cohort effect 26
cohort or historical events 6
confound 30
continuity versus discontinuity 9
convenience sampling 22
correlation coefficient 25
correlational design 26
cross-sectional design 26
dependent variable 30

descriptive design 21
double-blind technique 31
experimental design 29
field experiment 30
free will versus determinism 11
generalizability 20
historical events 6
hypothesis 14
independent variable 29
individuality versus universality 12
lab experiment 29
laboratory observation 24
lifespan developmental psychology 4
longitudinal design 27
longitudinal sequence design 28
maturation versus learning 10
microgenetic method 10
naturalistic observation 24
nature versus nurture 10
negative correlation 25
nonnormative events 6
normative age-graded events 5
normative maturational events 5
normative social events 6
objectively scored 15
objectivity 14
observation 25
positive correlation 25
psychological test 18
questionnaire method 17
random assignment 29
random sampling 22
reliability 15
replicability 14
research design 19
sequential designs 28
stability versus change 8
stage theory 9
standardized 15
statistically significant 30
structured interview 17
survey 22
systematic 16
theory 15
unstructured interview 17
validity 15

SELF-CHECK ANSWERS

BOX 1.2

Part A: **1.** a; **2.** a; **3.** b; **4.** a; **5.** b.

Part B: **1.** c; **2.** b; **3.** d; **4.** a; **5.** c; **6.** d; **7.** c; **8.** a; **9.** b; **10.** c; **11.** b.

BOX 1.3

1. Nurture, learning, universality; **2.** nature; **3.** universality; **4.** stability, nature, continuity; **5.** nurture; **6.** passive, change; **7.** nurture, learning, and change; **8.** individuality; **9.** active; **10.** nature, passive; **11.** nature; **12.** active; **13.** passive; **14.** learning; **15.** stability.

BOX 1.5

1. f; **2.** a, b, c, d, e, f; **3.** b, e, f; **4.** b, f; **5.** b, f; **6.** f.

BOX 1.8

1. Easier to objectively record behavior and to ensure that relevant behaviors occur.
2. More generalizability. All have inability to make causal statements.
3. Can't conclude that lack of listening causes marital problems because can't determine causality with a survey. Can't conclude that 80 percent of marriages are unhappy because the research probably has sampling bias.
4. Self-report biases and can't determine causes of drug use.
5. Since correlation coefficients can range from only −1 to +1, Rufus has made a calculation error.
6. Eye problems cause reading problems and so money should be spent to rectify eye problems. However, being unable to read may cause the irregular eye movements.
7. People living in houses with an above-average number of television sets tend to have slightly higher IQs than people living in houses with a below-average number of TV sets. If the correlation is −.3, people living in houses with an above-average number of television sets tend to have slightly lower IQs than people living in houses with a below-average number of TV sets. In neither case can we make any statements about why this relationship exists.
8. Survey method.
9. Lab observation. No, because she is using a descriptive, not a causal, design.
10. Case study. The environment caused this behavior. Can't make causal conclusions from a case study design.
11. He is drawing his conclusion from a case study. This individual's experience may be atypical and not generalizable.

BOX 1.10

1. Field experiment, randomly assigning people on waiting list for day care to either get day care or stay on waiting list.
2. Perhaps all teenagers eat pizza and junk food. Do an experiment where some patients get special diet and others are randomly assigned to control group that eats a typical junk food diet.
3. Naturalistic observation. She could conduct a field experiment.
4. In field experiments, random assignment is used and causal statements can be made. In lab experiments, random assignment is used and causal statements can be made.
5. Field experiments may have more generalizability. Naturalistic observations may have more generalizability.

6. Ideally, field experiments are used when you want to make causal statements.
7. Cross-sectional, longitudinal, and sequential. *Cross-sectional advantages:* inexpensive, quick. *Cross-sectional disadvantages:* "age" effects may really be due to a cohort effect or to sampling bias, and causality cannot be determined. *Longitudinal advantages:* provides information on how a group of people changes over time. *Longitudinal disadvantages:* age-related changes may really be due to attrition, changes in the measuring instrument, or participants getting used to the testing procedures; lack of generalizability to other cohorts; can't determine causality; and it is time consuming. *Sequential advantages:* may be able to separate cohort effects from age effects. *Sequential limitations:* can't determine causality and very time consuming.
8. The key difference is between "assignment" and "sample." When a research participant is assigned, he is put in a condition. He may be assigned to an advisor, the experimental group, detention, etc. In contrast to assigning him to a different group or condition, sampling from groups involves measuring the participant because he is already a member of a certain group. Once you understand the difference between "assignment to" and "sampling from," the difference between random assignment and random sampling will be less confusing. In random sampling, we want to know about a group, but we don't want to measure every single person in the group. Therefore, we take a random sample, which gives every group member an equal chance of being selected. If our random sample is large enough, it will give us a fair, representative sample of the larger group. Myers (1992) likens it to randomly scooping out 1,500 beans from a giant barrel containing 60 million white beans completely mixed with 40 million green beans. The random sample should contain roughly 60 percent white beans. In random assignment, we try to *create* two groups that are equal to each other by randomly putting people into either an experimental or control group. That is, because of random assignment, the groups should be equal before the treatment is introduced. Therefore, if they differ significantly after the treatment is introduced, we assume that the treatment made them different.

Chapter

Theories of Human Development

There is nothing so practical as a good theory.

Kurt Lewin

Chapter Overview

Developmental psychologists use research to obtain facts. To make sense of these facts, they turn to theory. To determine whether the theory makes sense, developmental psychologists look for facts that either support or disconfirm the theory. By checking theories against facts, theories evolve or die.

In this chapter, you will get an overview of six theories of development that help us understand personality development, social development, and cognitive development. To make the best use of these theories, realize that theories provide a point of view. This fact has three implications.

First, just as it may be useful to look at the same event from several people's points of view, it may be useful to look at one aspect of development from the perspective of several different theories. Second, just as you shouldn't commit yourself to one point of view without knowing the facts, you should not commit yourself to a certain theory without checking out the facts. In later chapters, you will be better able to see how well these theories fit the facts. In many cases, you will see how well these theories have evolved to cope with troublesome facts and fierce competitors. Third, just as you tend to like a point of view that agrees with your own, you may like one theory because it agrees with your point of view. Realize, however, that a theory is not correct merely because it reflects your own position on philosophical issues.

THE CHARACTERISTICS OF A SCIENTIFIC THEORY

If you should not judge a theory based on whether you like it, how should you judge the quality of a theory? According to many experts, theories should be judged on their ability to provide a new perspective, their internal consistency, the extent to which they are consistent with the facts, and their ability to stimulate research.

A major purpose of a theory is to *provide a new perspective.* Ideally, this perspective differs from commonsense views and hence can broaden our understanding (Boneau, 1994). Thus, the same theory that a narrow-minded person rejects because "it doesn't make (common) sense," a scientist may love because it offers a new view of reality. Scientists realize that there is a difference between echoing common sense and being correct. The history of science is full of examples of ideas that are now accepted, but were rejected or laughed at when they were initially introduced. Perhaps the most famous example of a controversial theory becoming accepted was Darwin's theory of evolution. Darwin was condemned and ridiculed for his theory of evolution. Now, of course, we realize that the controversial nature of his theory was not a weakness, but a strength. Because it was controversial, people paid attention to it and were forced to think about themselves in a new way. Regarding humans as related to animals has deepened our understanding of human nature and development.

However, a theory must be more than controversial. The ravings of a lunatic might be controversial, but they wouldn't make up the meat of a scientific theory. A theory must also seem to capture the truth. Skeptics would question the truth of the lunatic's theory on two grounds. First, skeptics would point out that the lunatic's theory lacks **internal consistency:** It contradicts itself. If the theory's "story" is inconsistent, it can't be accurate. Second, opponents would also attack the accuracy of the lunatic's theory by pointing out that it is not supported by research.

In response to these attacks, theories either change or perish. As a result, theories that survive tend to be more internally consistent and more consistent with research findings than commonsense notions.

A scientific theory should not only be internally consistent and be consistent with the facts, but it should also be both broad and **parsimonious.** In other words, a scientific theory should explain a broad range of events (Boneau, 1994) while relying on only a few principles. Theories having these two qualities find the common thread that links thousands of otherwise unrelated facts. Without theories that summarize a wide range of phenomena with a few principles, we might be so overwhelmed by facts that we would lose the forest for the trees. Obviously, in a field as vast as developmental psychology, broad yet parsimonious theories are very popular with students: Remembering a few general principles is easier than memorizing numerous facts.

In addition to summarizing many facts with a few general rules, a good theory should make specific predictions. The ability to make specific predictions is of practical value: If you need help, would you rather get vague hints or specific advice? Making specific predictions is also of scientific value because specific predictions can be tested, thus enabling scientists to refute or refine inaccurate theories.

Finally, a good theory has **heuristic value:** It is a source of hypotheses. Good theories build on existing knowledge because they stimulate psychologists to generate testable hypotheses. If these hypotheses are later supported by research, our understanding of human development is expanded and enriched. As you might expect, theories that are controversial, logically consistent, consistent with facts, broad, parsimonious, and make specific predictions tend to have heuristic value.

Box 2.1

SELF-CHECK

1. Why do scientists value parsimony? Do you think an accurate theory of development can be parsimonious?
2. Do you see a conflict between breadth and parsimony?
3. What advantages do you see to stating a theory in formal mathematical terms?
4. What two criteria do you think have the most effect on whether a theory has heuristic value?

Please turn to the end of this chapter to check your answers.

THEORIES OF DEVELOPMENT

Now that you understand what the ideal theory tries to do, you are ready to begin to judge how well theories of development meet this ideal. Although you will have to wait for future chapters to more fully judge how well these theories fit the facts, you will be able to make some preliminary judgments. For example, you will see that none of these theories have the breadth that an ideal theory would have. That is, none of them are so broad that they try to explain *all* of development. Instead, they usually focus on only one aspect of development. For instance, Piaget's theory focuses on cognitive development, whereas Freud's focuses on personality development.

Although you will be able to make some preliminary judgments about these theories, please keep the following facts in mind:

1. Each of these theories will be covered in greater depth in future chapters.
2. Theories that don't agree with common sense aren't necessarily wrong. Without such theories, we'd never

Box 2.2

THEORY in FOCUS

Are You a Freudian?

Freud is well known for holding unpopular views. However, certain aspects of his theory are quite acceptable to many people. Thus, even though some students argue that they completely disagree with Freud, we doubt that this is really the case. To find out where you stand, answer the following questions.

1. Do you think that childhood experiences affect later adult personality?
2. Do you think that young children put everything in their mouth?
3. Do you think that there are times when people don't really know why they did something?
4. Do you think that, around ages 5 through 7, little boys suddenly decide that they want to be just like their father?
5. Do you think little boys dream of marrying someone just like their mother?
6. Do you think that very young children have no conscience?
7. Do you think people occasionally forget unpleasant or embarrassing events?
8. Do you think that, for many humans, sex is an important drive?
9. Do you believe in the theory of evolution?
10. Do you think humans experience a struggle between their animal urges and society's demand for civilized, controlled, polite behavior?

Note: A Freudian would answer "yes" to all of these questions. However, we should point out that agreeing with all these positions does not necessarily make you a Freudian.

progress beyond common sense. That's why scientists like theories that provide a new worldview.

3. Even a theory that is wrong may be very valuable. For example, although Newton's theory of physics has been disproven, engineers use Newton's principles to build bridges and buildings. Similarly, a theory of developmental psychology does not have to be 100 percent accurate to help people be better parents, teachers, and citizens. Instead of perfection, a valuable theory only needs to be more accurate than common sense.

Psychoanalytic View

At the dawn of the twentieth century, a remarkable theory emerged that explained human development as the product of a struggle between nature and socialization. Freud's **psychoanalytic theory** was the first comprehensive theory to emphasize the role of unconscious processes and instinctual drives in shaping human development.

Sigmund Freud's Psychoanalytic Theory

Sigmund Freud was not only the father of psychoanalysis, but he was also an important contributor to modern developmental psychology. Even developmental psychologists who reject Freud's theory tend to applaud his accomplishments: popularizing the idea that early childhood experiences have consequences for our later development ("The child is the father of the man"); observing that children learn by identifying with their parents; and relating Darwin's theory of evolution to developmental psychology. Consequently, even though you may not be one of Freud's devoted followers, you may agree with many of Freud's basic assumptions. (To find out the extent to which you agree with Freud, see box 2.2.)

Basic Assumptions Perhaps the best way to begin to understand Freud's theory is to realize that his theory is closely linked to Darwin's theory of evolution. Freud's (1915) attempt to link Darwin's theory of evolution to psychology is obvious in his assumption about what motivates our behavior. Freud believed that our behavior, like that of all other animals, is largely an attempt to satisfy biological needs. These biological needs are so powerful because the survival of the species depends on satisfying these needs. For example, if people don't eat or don't have sex, they will die before having offspring. In other words, people who did not have those powerful survival drives died out, whereas those who did have powerful survival drives gave birth to offspring who inherited those strong survival drives. Consequently, much of our behavior involves satisfying primitive, animalistic **instinctual drives.**

To satisfy our instinctual drives, we rely on psychic energy. Freud postulated that each of us has a constant amount of psychic energy that is always available. How we use this energy is determined by our biological needs, level of maturation, experience, and our current environment.

Three major sources of psychic energy are the instincts of eros, ego, and thanatos. **Eros instincts** are those related to procreation and the preservation of the species. At the core of eros is a special kind of psychic energy called **libido,** or sexual energy. It is this sexual energy that governs much of development by exciting the specific part of our body that corresponds with our maturational stage.

Whereas eros is concerned with the preservation of the species, **ego instincts** are related to the preservation of the individual. Needs for food, water, elimination, and escape from pain are examples of ego instincts.

Late in his career, Freud proposed another type of instinct that focuses on death and destruction. Death instincts, or **thanatos,** are at the root of all hostile and destructive activities, from looting to suicide.

Although instinctual drives are important, the major theme in Freud's theory was **unconscious motivation.** To Freud, the mind is like an iceberg—mostly hidden. What we are conscious of is only the tip of that iceberg. Below the calm surface of our conscious awareness is an active, dynamic, turbulent unconscious that contains most of our thoughts and memories. Although these unconscious thoughts are hidden from our conscious mind, Freud believed that they have an enormous influence on our behavior. Much of the unconscious is created as the result of conflicts between different structures of our personalities.

The Structure of the Personality In the psychoanalytic view, the human mind is organized into three components—the id, ego, and superego. The first part of the personality, the **id,** is present at birth. The id is the instinctual component from our animal (evolutionary) past that operates on the **pleasure principle:** It seeks pleasure through the immediate gratification of instinctual desires (usually physical urges for food, water, warmth, or sex), regardless of the long-term consequences. However, the id's desire for pleasure is hampered by its ignorance of reality—the id is unaware that the fulfillment of its needs is dependent on external events. The only way the id knows to get things is to wish for them. Because wishing doesn't make it so, the id eventually realizes that its urges cannot be satisfied by internal events such as fantasizing, but requires external events. Someone, or something, has to make things happen in the external world if the infant is to have her urges fulfilled. A caregiver must provide a breast or bottle to satisfy hunger, a blanket for warmth, a soft voice to be soothed. This awareness of external events becomes associated with a portion of the id energy and makes possible the infant's later realization that she can cause external events. This realization marks the birth of the **ego,** the rational component of personality.

The ego is like an executive secretary/servant to the id. It plans and implements actions that will fulfill the id's desires. The problem is that a child with only an id and an ego knows what he wants and knows how to get it, but doesn't appreciate that desires should be met through socially approved means. The young child's conduct code is to do what will satisfy his instinctual desires without getting into trouble. Eventually, however, the child internalizes the parents' rules, adopting the parents' values and morals as his own, thereby forming the **superego.**

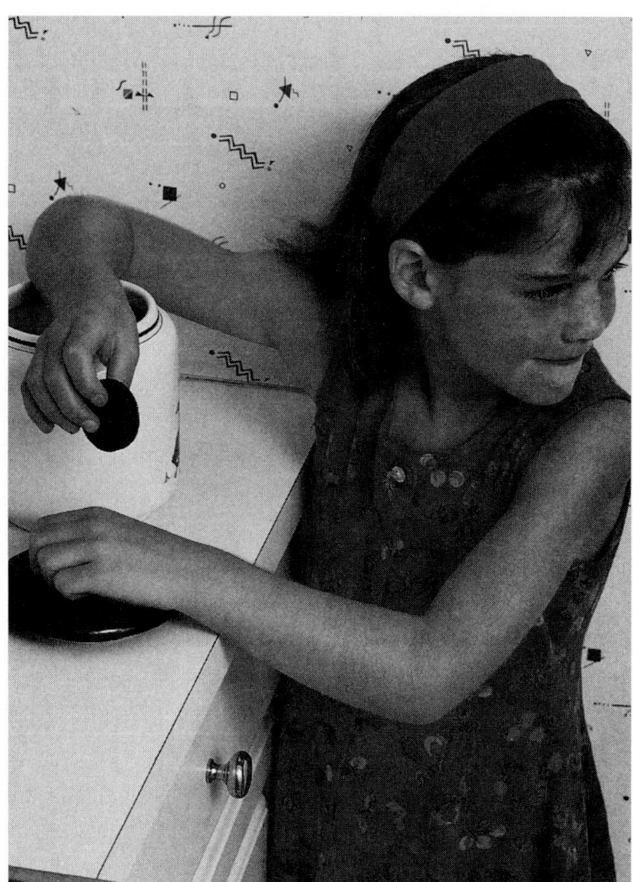

According to Freud, before children internalize their parents' values and morals and develop their superego, their goal is only to satisfy the desires of the id as quickly as possible without getting into trouble.

As you can imagine, the id and superego are often in conflict. The id seeks immediate gratification of its desires for food, aggression, and sex, while the superego seeks morally perfect behavior. It is up to the ego to resolve these conflicts. Often the ego's solution is to stall the id until those needs can be gratified in a socially acceptable manner. For example, the ego may suggest that sex be delayed until marriage or that a person buy her own lunch rather than stealing it from someone else's plate.

But what if the id's needs can't be gratified in a socially acceptable manner? If the consequences aren't too great, sometimes the ego will decide to do the socially inappropriate action. Often, however, the ego will deal with the problem by **repression,** pushing the id's needs out of consciousness into the unconscious. Unfortunately, although repressed thoughts are gone from the conscious mind, they are not destroyed. Instead, they are banished to the unconscious where they can cause anxiety as they continue their struggle to enter consciousness. Thus, an apparently long-forgotten incident from childhood can continue to hinder an adult's development.

Table 2.1
Freud's Stages of Personality Development

Ages	Freud's Stages/Periods
0–1	Oral
1–3	Anal
3–6	Phallic
6–12	Latency period
12–onward	Genital

Stages of Development In addition to theorizing about the structure of personality, Freud was the first psychologist to propose a stage theory of development (see table 2.1). Specifically, he proposed that all children learn to relate to the world as they progress through four biologically determined stages. At each stage, libidinal (sexual) energy is focused on a specific part of the body, affecting how the infant or child relates to the world. The child's progress at each stage will have a lasting affect on adult personality.

The **oral stage** begins at birth and lasts about a year. During the first year of life, infants get great enjoyment from objects associated with the mouth, such as breasts, food, and other oral activities (sucking, eating, and biting). During the oral stage, the child is almost completely dependent on the mother or caregiver. If the mother takes good care of the infant by feeding him when he is hungry, the child learns that he can depend on and trust others. However, if the infant's oral needs are not met during this stage, the individual may become fixated (stuck) in this stage. This **oral fixation** may result in an adult who is preoccupied with such oral traits as excessive eating, drinking, talking, or biting sarcasm.

If a child's oral needs are satisfactorily met, she will enter the **anal stage** during the second year of life. The focus of this stage is getting pleasure from eliminating and retaining feces. Not coincidentally, parents often introduce toilet training at this time. Toilet training is the first time the child must learn to postpone a powerful natural urge and, in some ways, is the first real opportunity for the child to actively cooperate with his parents. How the parents go about toilet training (kind, but firm versus harsh and punitive) and the toddler's ability to master it (some parents start toilet training before the child is physically able) has far-reaching consequences. For example, if a child is slow to master toilet training, the child may have low self-esteem. Furthermore, a negative toilet-training experience may lead to **anal fixation.** Anal fixation is commonly expressed in two forms, the anal expulsive and the anal retentive personalities. The **anal expulsive** is sloppy, rude, and likely to throw tantrums, whereas the **anal retentive** is typically stingy and preoccupied with cleanliness and orderliness.

Freud believed that boys must resolve the Oedipus complex, their desire to sexually possess their mothers, to successfully complete the phallic stage of development.

Those children who successfully work through the challenges of the anal stage enter the **phallic stage** (approximately ages 3 to 5). Children in the phallic stage are preoccupied with sexual anatomy, especially the anatomy of the opposite sex (playing doctor is common in this age group). They derive pleasure through their genitals by discovering masturbation. During the phallic stage, boys develop superegos by resolving the Oedipus complex. Girls develop superegos by resolving the Electra complex (Freud, 1940, p. 99).

The **Oedipus complex** is the boy's desire to sexually possess his mother and his jealousy of the chief rival for mom's affections—dad. Although the wish to possess the mother physically and psychologically is unrealistic, the boy pursues these desires and is eventually forced to confront his father over who is the primary recipient of the mother's attention. This confrontation leads to the boy's fear that his father will punish him (possibly through castration) for his incestuous behavior. To overcome this **castration anxiety,** the young boy gives up his sexual wishes for his mother and identifies with his rival father. Later, as an adult, he will marry someone like his mother.

The young boy's identification with his father has two powerful and noticeable consequences. First, he changes from "mommy's boy" to "daddy's boy." Thus, by identifying with his father, he assumes a masculine sex-role identity. Second, he internalizes his father's values and morals, thus developing a superego. As you may have noted, before this age, children can be extremely cruel when unsupervised by adults. But now, under ordinary circumstances, boys enter the **latency period,** a time when they behave (at least compared to how they were before) like cub scouts: kind, obedient, and cheerful. Of course, unsatisfactory resolution of the Oedipus complex may lead to a delay or even a failure to develop the superego, which may, in turn, lead to juvenile delinquency.

Freud was not as explicit about how girls develop their feminine sex-role identities and superego. Indeed, Freud admitted that there was much about female psychology that he did not know. Nevertheless, he speculated that the young girl's **Electra complex** has some similarities to the young boy's Oedipal complex. In both cases, the child wants to possess the parent of the opposite sex and has some antagonism toward their rival—the same sex parent. However, many psychoanalysts believe that the Oedipal (or Electra) complex is much more complicated for girls than for boys. Rather than experience castration anxiety, the young girl experiences anxiety because she has already lost her penis. This sense of loss escalates into penis envy. Eventually, through a mechanism that Freud did not spell out, the Electra complex is resolved when the girl channels her desire for a penis into identification with her mother.

Freud believed that females had inferior sex-role development and weaker superegos than males because they did not experience castration anxiety. He argued that the intense fear of castration was the only thing strong enough to motivate complete identification with the same-sexed parent.

The latency period lasts from about age 6 until puberty. During this period, children try to avoid sexual desires through repression and avoid sexual relationships by avoiding the opposite sex. Thus, in almost any fourth-grade class, we see that the children have segregated themselves by gender (although research shows that segregation occurs as early as preschool, Maccoby, 1988).

With the onset of puberty, sexuality reemerges during the final phase, the **genital stage.** This time around, however, sex is not directed toward the parent of the opposite sex. Instead, sexuality is more appropriately focused on opposite-sex peers. Also, unlike the phallic stage, individuals in the genital stage are not interested in their own selfish pleasure. Rather, according to Freud, a person who has reached the genital stage is interested in having sex with one, and only one, other person and the focus of the sexual relationship is on giving the other person pleasure and on having children.

For Freud, a strong believer in Darwin's theory of evolution, love is necessary in the genital stage for the survival of the human species. For our species to survive, parents must not only have children, but those children must live into adulthood. Without love, parents wouldn't stay together. Without both a mother and father, the stone-age child's chances of survival to adulthood would have been slim.

Evaluation of Freud's Theory As shown in table 2.2, Freud's theory meets at least two criteria of a good scientific theory: providing a new perspective and having breadth.

Freud provided a remarkable new perspective on human behavior. Rather than see us as rational, nonsexual beings, Freud depicted us as largely irrational animals, driven by unconscious sexual urges (Stricker, 1994).

Freud's theory is also quite broad. One index of its breadth is that Freud's theory is quoted by scholars in such fields as sociology, art, English, and history, as well as in psychology. As you will see in later chapters, followers of Freud have contributed theories of personality development as well as theories of social development (Bowlby, 1992).

At one level, his theory is parsimonious: one principle—the unconscious—explains all. At a deeper level, however, Freud's theory involves many principles. According to Freud's defenders, numerous principles are needed because humans are complex.

Critics charge that Freud's theory fails to make specific, testable predictions. One obstacle to testability is that Freud's concepts (such as the id and the unconscious) are hard to measure objectively. Another problem is that the theory is so vague that it can be used to make contradictory predictions. For example, strict toilet training could lead to neatness *or* messiness. The theory's vagueness has also lead to questions about both its internal consistency and its heuristic potential. Skeptics ask: Is it consistent to say that strict toilet training can lead to neatness or messiness? How does a researcher test this two-sided hypothesis?

Because of its perceived lack of heuristic value, Freud's theory has not been intensively researched. This is unfortunate because research may have helped to refine the theory. The research that has been conducted provides mixed support for his theory. For example, his concepts of the unconscious and of repression have received some research support, whereas his concept of the Oedipal complex has not (Hall & Lindzey, 1978).

Nevertheless, Freud deserves credit for telling us what he believed to be the truth, rather than telling us what we wanted to hear. Thus, rather than telling us how wonderful and rational we are, Freud told us what he saw—a human nature that was inherently selfish and hedonistic, being dominated by sexual and brutally aggressive animal-like instincts.

Similarly, rather than telling us that the right environment could easily temper our animal nature, Freud claimed that most of our behavior was an attempt to satisfy biological motives that promoted personal and

Table 2.2

Critique of Freud's Psychoanalytic Theory

Does Freud's Theory Meet the Criteria of a Scientific Theory?

Criteria	**Rating**
1. Provides a new perspective	High
2. Is internally consistent	Low
3. Is consistent with facts	Moderate
4. Has breadth	High
5. Has parsimony	Moderate
6. Makes specific predictions	Low
7. Has heuristic value	Moderate

How Freud Stands on the Controversies

1. Human development is affected more by *nature.*
2. People *passively respond to maturational events.*
3. Development occurs in abrupt, *discontinuous* stages.
4. Behavioral characteristics are *stable* after early childhood.
5. All humans develop according to *universal,* maturationally determined stages.

species survival. Furthermore, even though he believed that the content of the psychosexual stages was influenced by culture, he believed that the physical focus, timing, and inevitability of the stages were determined by maturational forces. Thus, Freud was a naturist.

Like most naturists, Freud believed in the discontinuity of development. That is, he believed that development occurred in abrupt, biologically determined stages. In fact, Freud was the first contemporary psychologist to propose a stage theory of development. Also like most naturists, Freud believed that personality was stable for most of the human lifespan. Indeed, he believed that the male personality was set by the time the boy entered latency (about age 6). This extreme position on the stability side of the stability versus change debate is controversial. Few contemporary developmental psychologists would agree that personality is set by such an early age. However, most would agree that the early years are an important influence on later development.

Finally, since Freud believed that development was governed by biological processes common to all members of our species, he viewed development as universal. In short, on most issues, Freud is like most naturists.

Where Freud departs from most naturists is on the passive versus active issue. Instead of holding the typical naturist view that we are actively involved in our own development, Freud viewed us as passive victims of our instinctual urges.

Box 2.3

SELF-CHECK

Part A

Indicate whether each of the following statements is true or false.

1. Freud emphasized the importance of childhood experiences on adult development.
2. Freud stressed the importance of conscious thought processes.
3. The ego dominates the id.
4. The ego is concerned with morality.
5. According to Freud, castration anxiety is very important for the development of the superego.
6. Research unequivocally supports Freud's notion that, as a result of the repression of sexual urges during the latency stages, children segregate themselves by gender.
7. Freud's theory is broad.
8. Freud thought that personality was relatively stable throughout adulthood.
9. Freud was a naturist.
10. Freud thought we could choose our own course of development.

Part B

Answer the following questions.

11. Give at least one example of how Freud's theory is tied to Darwin's theory of evolution.
12. List Freud's psychosexual stages of development in the order in which they occur.

Please turn to the end of this chapter to check your answers.

As you have seen from our brief overview, Freud is probably one of the most misunderstood theorists in psychology. But even when people understand parts of his theory, they often reject it because they don't like it or it makes them feel uncomfortable and anxious. For example, some people reject his notions of infantile sexuality without even considering the evidence. Although no theory in developmental psychology is totally correct, we must separate our own prejudices from justified criticism. Realize that Freud himself wished that parts of his theory were untrue, but he felt that he had to be bold enough to go where the evidence led him. Furthermore, realize that Freud was an innovative theorist who was constantly rethinking and revising his position. If Freud were alive today, his theory would probably be different. To get an idea of what Freud's theory might look like today, let's look at the work of one of his disciples.

Erik Erikson's Psychosocial Theory

Among the many students who studied under Freud was an artist and high school graduate named Erik Erikson. Despite not being formally trained as a psychologist, Erik Erikson became one of Freud's most influential disciples.

Basic Assumptions Although Erikson owes much of his theory to Freud, he differs from Freud on several issues. First, whereas Freud was on the stability side of the stability versus change issue (recall that with Freud, development essentially ceased before adulthood), Erikson was on the change side. Thus, Erikson expanded Freud's stage theory to encompass the entire lifespan. Second, whereas Freud was an extreme naturist, Erikson was receptive to the nurture position. Consequently, whereas Freud's stages revolve around ways of dealing with biological instincts, Erikson's **psychosocial stages** center on culture and on how each of us solves eight psychosocial (personal and social) tasks. However, before you conclude that Erikson was a nurturist, keep in mind that the time at which a person enters each of his psychosocial stages is determined by maturation. Thus, although Erikson emphasized the role of nurture more than Freud, he was still very much a naturist. Table 2.3 shows how Erikson's stages coincide with Freud's.

Finally, Erikson thought human nature was kinder and more active than Freud did. That is, rather than viewing humans as passive slaves to their instinctual drives, Erikson saw people as basically good and as actively struggling to achieve positive developmental outcomes. Thus, whereas the ego in Freud's theory is primarily limited to a fire-fighting role (that is, mediating conflicts between the id and superego), the ego in Erikson's theory actively strives for growth.

Stages of Development As you can see from table 2.3, Erikson's first five stages parallel Freud's. As you can also see from the table, Erikson (1963, 1968) believed that the task of the **oral-sensory stage** infant (0 to 1 year) is to resolve the issue of basic **trust versus mistrust.** As infants, we decide whether or not the world can be trusted. We learn whether others are predictable and whether they will help us when we need it. Since our first and most important encounters with the world are with our parents, the infant-parent bond is central to the outcome of this crisis. If a secure bond is formed, then we learn to trust the world; if a weak bond is formed, then we will not trust it. Erikson believed that the quality of this first bond between infant and parent laid the groundwork for all future relationships. Thus, the present quality of your relationships with your friends and family may still be affected by how responsive your parents were to your needs when you were an infant.

Erikson's second task, **autonomy versus shame and doubt** characterizes the **muscular-anal stage.** During the second year of life, autonomy (independence) is fostered in us because of biological maturation. Specifically, the development of our sphincter muscles helps us retain and eliminate our feces at will; skeletal, nervous system, and muscle development give us the ability to walk, develop eye-hand coordination, and talk. Thus, the level of physical maturation attained during the muscular-anal stage challenges children to define and discover how much control they have over their own behavior. If children are provided the opportunity to test their limits and exert independence, they will develop a sense of autonomy.

Put another way, if children are *not* given the opportunity to test their limits, they never learn that they can effectively control their own bodies, much less exert some control over their environment. The child who fails to learn autonomy will grow into an adult filled with self-doubt and low self-esteem. Consequently, during this stage, there are two ways to be a bad parent. First, the parent may be overprotective. Overprotectiveness may save the child from some accidents, but prevents the child from testing limits and meeting challenges. Thus, the nurturant parenting style that facilitated development during the first year of life may be harmful if it is continued during the second year of life. Second, the parent may be too restrictive. Being too restrictive prevents children from feeling that they have control over their environment. However, Erikson did not mean that parents should let their children run wild. Parents must set boundaries if children are to become socialized. The balancing act parents must achieve is getting their children to conform to social expectations without devastating their children's wills.

During the **locomotor-genital stage** (4 to 5 years), children work through the task of **initiative versus guilt.** A child who learns initiative can make plans, set goals, and attain them. A crisis occurs when we realize that not all our goals can be attained, especially the Oedipal ones. When we discover that social taboos prohibit us from possessing one parent and rivaling the other, we internalize society's morals and values. The result is the superego—the source of all guilt. Although socialized behavior requires a superego, the superego suppresses initiative. Consequently, Erikson viewed the development of the superego as one of life's major tragedies (Crain, 1992).

The **latency stage** (6 to 11 years) is marked by the quest for **industry versus inferiority.** Between the ages of 5 and 12, we acquire important cognitive and social skills. We learn to do work that is valued by society, to possess "steady attention and persevering diligence" (Erikson, 1950, p. 259), and to work and play with our peers. Unfortunately, depending on how we respond to the inevitable failures we will have, we may leave this stage feeling inadequate and inferior. How we respond to failure depends not only on how our parents, teachers, and peers treat us, but on how we feel about ourselves. If we left the muscular-anal and locomotor-genital stages with feelings of shame and guilt, chances are we will leave the latency stage with

Table 2.3

A Comparison Between Freud's and Erikson's Stages

Ages	Freud's Stages	Erikson's Stages	Erikson's Psychosocial Conflict
0–1	Oral	Oral-sensory	Basic trust versus mistrust
1–3	Anal	Muscular-anal	Autonomy (independence) versus shame and doubt
3–6	Phallic	Locomotor-genital	Initiative (having a sense of purpose) versus guilt
6–11	Latency	Latency	Industry (feeling capable) versus inferiority
11–18	Genital	Puberty and adolescence	Identity (sense of self) versus role confusion
18–45		Young adulthood	Intimacy (committed love) versus isolation
45–65		Adulthood	Generativity (creating or caring for others) versus stagnation
65+		Maturity	Integrity (pride in accomplishments) versus despair

feelings of inferiority. If we have feelings of autonomy and initiative, we will probably take occasional failures in stride, seeing them as opportunities to learn and grow. As the ancient Japanese proverb states, "Fall down five, get up six."

The task of the **puberty** and **adolescence** stage (ages 11 to 18) is **identity versus role confusion.** The task of identity formation (knowing who we are) is a lifelong task. However, during adolescence this task is especially prominent because of dramatic physical, social, and cognitive changes. Physically, we change in so many ways that we may bare little resemblance to the child we were a few months before. Socially, we are torn (Are we who our peers think we are or are we who our parents think we are?) and confused—especially if our peers seem to be changing their minds about who we are. Cognitively, we are capable of thinking more abstractly. Our new ability to think abstractly has at least four consequences for the identity versus role confusion crisis.

1. Because we can reason more abstractly, we may be embarrassed by the simplicity and inconsistency of some of our earlier beliefs, values, and ideals. Thus, we may have trouble accepting ourselves.
2. Because we are able to think hypothetically, we may try out different roles and values. Finding a role that "fits" can be exciting, but trying on numerous roles and not being sure that any certain one is "definitely you" can be confusing and overwhelming.
3. Because we can think about abstract events such as the future, we are keenly aware of the demands that the future will place on us. We may feel pressed to change so that we can measure up to the challenges that we imagine we will face as adults.
4. We are now, for the first time, able to come up with our own answer (rather than echoing our parents' or our peers' answers) to the question "Who am I?" Thus, we are free to find ourselves and to develop a sense of inner continuity with what we were before and what we will become. However, there is a cost to this freedom to develop an enduring sense of identity. We may fail. If we fail, we suffer role confusion and we may feel "lost."

Because Erikson believed that development occurred throughout the lifespan, he divided adult development into three stages: Young adulthood, adulthood, and maturity. During **young adulthood** (ages 18 to 45), we confront the crisis of **intimacy versus isolation.** We discover whether we are capable of sharing ourselves with another. Like Freud's genital stage, this crisis is resolved when we can be committed to a relationship. Specifically, intimacy is the product of mutual warmth, understanding, trust, love, and mature devotion.

Before we can develop intimacy, we must first know who we are (identity) and be secure in our relationship with the world. (Then, all we need to do is to find the right partner!) If we have learned to mistrust the world, to feel insecure about our role in life, then intimacy will not be achieved. We will live in emotional, if not physical, isolation. As you can see, Erikson's description of intimacy versus isolation, gives some insights into why some people may be right when they say "I'm not ready for a steady relationship" or why some people may be very wrong if they think that getting married will solve their problems and remove their inadequacies.

Adulthood (ages 45 to 65) marks the midlife crisis of **generativity versus stagnation.** Generativity includes the

To resolve the identity versus role confusion conflict postulated by Erikson, adolescents may try on numerous roles or values until they find one that fits.

creation and care of children (the next generation) as well as the creation of products and ideas through work. The task of generativity is to grow, to produce, and to contribute to the benefit of future generations. If we fail to create, we fall into stagnation. That is, we may get stuck in a comfortable, but selfish and unproductive rut.

Maturity (ages 65 and up) is marked by the crisis of **integrity versus despair.** During our final years, most of us will look back on our lives and evaluate how worthwhile it was. If our life review results in a sense of satisfaction, we will spend those years with a sense of integrity. A highly successful resolution to this conflict is epitomized in the song "I Did It My Way," where the singer "about to face the final curtain" admits to having a few regrets ("but too few to mention") and is happy to have lived life "my way."

However, if we feel that our lives were not worthwhile, that we didn't live the life we should have or that life didn't give us our share of opportunities, then we will spend our final years in despair—bitter, remorseful, incomplete, empty, dissatisfied, and filled with regrets. Presumably, people who spend their adulthood in stagnation will spend their maturity in despair.

Box 2.4

SELF-CHECK

1. What similarities are there between Freud's and Erikson's theories?
2. What are the major differences?
3. Erikson's theory provides a less novel perspective than Freud's. Is this good or bad?

Please turn to the end of this chapter to check your answers.

Evaluation of Erikson's Theory Erikson's theory is intuitively appealing. But is it a good theory? As you can see from table 2.4, Erikson's theory receives moderate to high marks on six of the seven criteria on which theories are judged.

As we have emphasized, Erikson's theory adheres to most of Freud's premises (Green, 1989). However, Erikson did differ with Freud on three core issues: (1) Erikson thought that the conscious ego was more powerful and important than Freud did; (2) Erikson thought social forces such as peers, work roles, and society were more important than Freud did; and (3) Erikson put more emphasis on development continuing through adulthood. Because all these changes are consistent with the optimistic, nurture-oriented American spirit, we give Erikson's theory only a moderate rating for "provides a new perspective."

Although Erikson's theory has no obvious contradictions, Erikson's reliance on psychoanalytic principles (which rate low on internal consistency) warrants a moderate score on internal consistency. Furthermore, Erikson's theory is sometimes inconsistent with the facts. For example, his theory states that before intimacy can be achieved, a person must attain an identity. Yet, research demonstrates that women often solve their identity and intimacy crises simultaneously (Gilligan, 1982). Similarly, Erikson's theory indicates that all people experience a midlife crisis (generativity versus stagnation), yet research fails to demonstrate a universal crisis during adulthood (Vaillant, 1977; Costa & McCrae, 1980, 1990, 1994).

Erikson's theory has breadth and is moderately parsimonious, but it does not make specific predictions. Researchers who study emotional and social development find that Erikson accurately describes many of the central issues of life in his eight psychosocial stages. However, he does not adequately address the causes of development. For example, "What kinds of experiences lead to the resolution of a specific psychosocial conflict?" "How does the resolution of one psychosocial stage influence the outcomes of later psychosocial crises?" Erikson acknowledges his general vagueness. He once said, "I came to psychology from art, which may explain, if not justify, the fact that the reader will find me painting contexts and backgrounds where he would rather have me point to facts and concepts" (Erikson, 1950, p. 17).

Because Erikson's theory does not make specific predictions, its heuristic value is limited. Consequently, his theory has not been extensively tested. Yet, as you will see in later chapters, some research has been done (for example, Ryff & Heinecke, 1983; Whitbourne & Tesch, 1985), and other theorists have expanded on Erikson's ideas (for example, Franz & White, 1985; Marcia, 1976).

On the issues (see table 2.4), Erikson departs significantly from Freud. Whereas Freud depicts human nature as hedonistic and animalistic, Erikson views human nature as basically good. Specifically, Erikson dwells less on the development of neuroses and more on the development of a healthy personality. Rather than concentrate on our irrational, sexual instincts, Erikson emphasized the rational, adaptive side of human nature.

Erikson also differs with Freud on the nature-nurture issue. Whereas, Freud was a naturist, Erikson was more of a nurturist. Erikson believed that people actively struggle to resolve *social* conflicts and personal dilemmas as they progress through his eight stages of psychosocial development.

As stage theorists, both Freud and Erikson believed that development is discontinuous and universal. However, Freud believed that development was stable (for males) after resolution of the Oedipus complex, whereas Erikson viewed development as a lifelong process.

Table 2.4

Critique of Erikson's Psychosocial Theory

Does Erikson's Theory Meet the Criteria of a Scientific Theory?

Criteria	Rating
1. Provides a new perspective	Low
2. Is internally consistent	Moderate
3. Is consistent with facts	Moderate
4. Has breadth	High
5. Has parsimony	Moderate
6. Makes specific predictions	Low
7. Has heuristic value	Moderate

How Erikson Stands on the Controversies

1. Human development is affected more by *nature* (however, he did stress nurture more than Freud).
2. People are *actively involved in their own development.*
3. Development occurs in abrupt, *discontinuous* stages.
4. Behavioral characteristics may *change* throughout the lifespan.
5. All people develop according to *universal,* maturationally determined stages.

The Learning Perspective

You have seen that Freud's theory was attacked both for overemphasizing the role of nature as well as for taking an extreme stability position. You saw how Erikson's revision of Freud's theory addressed these criticisms. Some, however, believe that rather than revise Freud's theory, an entirely different approach—the behaviorist approach—is needed.

The behaviorist approach has been fruitful. Indeed, much of what we know about human development stems from research by "behavioral" or learning theorists.[1] For example, by observing how children react to various environmental influences, learning theorists have begun to understand how and why children form emotional attachments to others, adopt sex roles, become interested in school, learn to abide by moral rules, and form friendships.

Basic Assumptions

Rather than trying to guess what's in someone's unconscious mind, **behaviorists** focus on observable behavior. According to behaviorists, just as focusing on the behavior of objects has made physics a powerful science, focusing on the behavior of humans and animals will make psychology a powerful science.

Despite this apparently objective attitude, behaviorists do hold philosophical positions. For example, rather than believing that we inherit a human nature, early followers of **behaviorism** believed that we are born a blank slate, inheriting only the ability to learn from our environment. Consequently, development is almost entirely the result of learning. In other words, nurture, not nature, determines whether we become shy or outgoing; lazy or hardworking; a baker, banker, or candlestick maker.

If development is the result of learning from the environment, then understanding how we learn from our environment is essential to understanding development. Therefore, the next sections focus on three ways that we learn from our environment: classical conditioning, operant conditioning, and modeling.

Classical Conditioning

During the seventeenth and eighteenth centuries, British philosophers John Locke and David Hume argued that

[1] Skinner (1950) claims that operant conditioning is not a theory.

learning occurs through **association,** the assumption that we naturally associate events that occur in sequence. In the late nineteenth and early twentieth centuries, this idea of association formed the cornerstone of Ivan Pavlov's (1927/1960) work in classical conditioning.

Pavlov's work on learning arose almost by accident. Originally, he was studying a simple reflex, the production of saliva in dogs. His basic procedure was to make a surgical opening in a dog's cheek and then place a tube that collected saliva from the dog's salivary gland into a glass beaker. By measuring how much saliva was in the beaker, Pavlov could determine how much the dog salivated. Thus, when he put meat powder in the dog's mouth, he could measure the extent to which the meat powder automatically increased salivation.

One day, however, Pavlov realized a problem with this research. He realized that, after a dog had been brought to the lab a number of times, the dog would begin to salivate *before* the meat powder was placed in its mouth. The sight or smell of the food, the sight of the dish that it was kept in, even the footsteps of the lab assistant who administered the powder, were sufficient to stimulate the production of saliva. Clearly, the dog was not born producing saliva to the sound of a human footstep. The animal had learned a "conditional" reflex (the reflex occurs only for animals that have been exposed to certain conditions). This insight became the basis for classical conditioning.

In the early part of the twentieth century, John B. Watson became fascinated with Pavlov's demonstration that reflexes could be learned. Watson proposed that all behavior, human as well as that of other animals, could be explained in terms of this classical conditioning. In the classical conditioning situations that most concern developmental psychologists, people learn to associate a **neutral stimulus** (one that doesn't elicit any emotional reaction) with a second stimulus that always (unconditionally) elicits an emotional response. The classic case is what happened to Little Albert when he was in the care of Dr. Watson (Watson & Rayner, 1920). Before Watson even met Little Albert, Watson knew that a loud noise would scare Albert. Watson knew this because every infant with good hearing is afraid of loud noises (Izard, 1978; Sroufe, 1979). Because the fear reaction to a loud noise is innate and thus not learned (not conditioned), the loud noise is an **unconditioned stimulus,** and the fear in reaction to the noise is an **unconditioned response.**

What Watson was unsure about is how Little Albert would respond to a white rat. So, he presented Little Albert with a white rat and found out that, although Albert seemed interested in the rat, Albert showed no strong emotional reaction to it. Consequently, Watson concluded that, for Albert, the rat was a neutral stimulus.

But Watson didn't want the rat to remain a neutral stimulus. Watson wanted little Albert to learn to fear the rat. In other words, Watson wanted to *condition* Albert so that the rat no longer was a neutral stimulus, but instead became a **conditioned stimulus** that elicited the **conditioned response** of fear.

To condition Albert, Watson presented the rat and then had his lab assistant make a loud noise. The loud noise startled and scared Albert. After numerous pairings of the rat with the loud noise, Albert eventually became conditioned: If he saw only the rat, he became afraid. Watson had succeeded in turning the rat into a conditioned stimulus that elicited the conditioned response of fear. In other words, Watson had shown that fear could be learned through **classical conditioning,** a type of learning in which a neutral stimulus, after being paired with an unconditioned stimulus, begins to trigger a response similar to that normally triggered by the unconditioned stimulus (see box 2.5).

The Little Albert demonstration shows how a single traumatic event can create strong fear. It shows that we learn classically conditioned responses even when we don't try to and even when we don't want to. Further studies have demonstrated that these conditioned responses do not merely fade over time: One bad experience may mar us for life.

On the positive side, research has shown how to reverse the unwanted effects of classical conditioning (see box 2.6). Just as we learned our fears and dislikes, we can *un*learn them through **extinction.** In extinction, the conditioned response fades when a conditioned stimulus is *not* followed by an unconditioned stimulus. That is, facing things that scare us without suffering bad results will eventually reduce those fears. In addition, we now know that classical conditioning is not only responsible for some of our negative emotional reactions, but also for many of our positive emotional reactions. For example, although classical conditioning may have caused you to hate liver and fear snakes, it may also have caused you to love rock music, pizza, and the color red. Thus, classical conditioning has not only increased the number of things you dislike, but also the number of things you like. Finally, classical conditioning enhances our uniqueness—because of different experiences, we don't all have identical likes and dislikes. Imagine a world where no one thought tofu tasted better than hamburger, everyone wanted to marry tall brunettes, and everyone's favorite color was white!

Although classical conditioning explains many of our involuntary, automatic emotional reactions, it does not explain how we learn voluntary, willful actions. It cannot explain how we learn such active and complex skills as talking, using tools, playing racquetball, or programming a computer (Crain, 1992). When we master such skills, we are not simply reacting to stimuli. Instead, we engage in a great deal of active, voluntary, trial-and-error behavior, discovering what works best. Learning theorists attribute these deliberate actions to operant conditioning.

Box 2.5

THEORY in FOCUS

Classical Conditioning Flow Chart

Although the idea behind classical conditioning is fairly simple, the terminology can be confusing. For example, how do you know whether a given event is (a) a conditioned stimulus, (b) a conditioned response, (c) an unconditioned stimulus, or (d) an unconditioned response?

If you have trouble keeping these four terms straight, the flow chart below can help you. For example, suppose you were told that Mary almost drowned in the ocean and so she is now afraid of the ocean. Furthermore, suppose you were asked to determine whether her fear of the ocean was a conditioned response, a conditioned stimulus, an unconditioned response, or an unconditioned stimulus. Using the chart can help you answer that question.

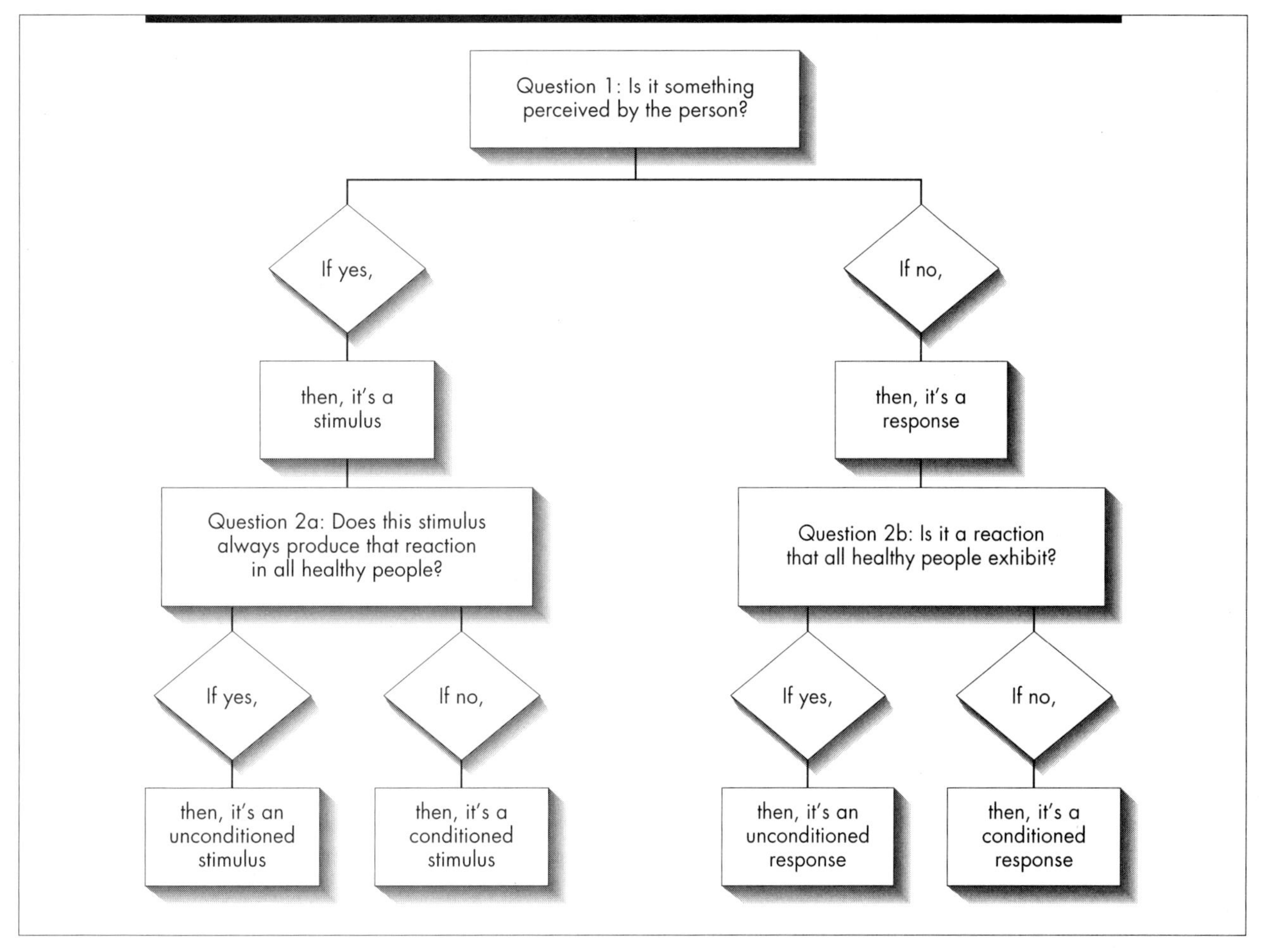

Operant Conditioning

Through **operant conditioning,** we learn what to do and what not to do. Specifically, we tend to repeat behaviors that are rewarded, and we tend not to repeat acts that are not rewarded. We can be reinforced (rewarded) in two ways.

First, we can be reinforced when we receive a desirable stimulus after we have emitted the "correct" behavior. In that case, we have received **positive reinforcement,** a rewarding stimulus, such as attention, money, or food, which, when presented after a response, strengthens the response.

Second, we can be reinforced for a behavior if doing that behavior "turns off" an unpleasant stimulus. In real life, there are many examples of people repeating the behavior that puts an end to the unpleasantness. Parents will pick up a crying baby to stop it from crying; you'll get up to turn off a buzzing alarm clock; and a child may clean up

Box 2.6

RESEARCH in FOCUS

Using Classical Conditioning to Overcome Fears

During the 1920s and 1930s, one of Watson's colleagues, Mary Cover Jones (1924), first applied the principles of classical conditioning to help children overcome fears. In a procedure called direct conditioning, she helped a young boy, Peter, overcome his fear of furry animals. Below is an excerpt that Watson copied from Jones' casebook:

> Peter was an active, eager child of approximately 3 years of age. The child was well adjusted to ordinary life situations except for his fear [sic] organization. He was afraid of white rats, rabbits, fur coats, feathers, cotton wool, frogs, fish and mechanical toys. From the descriptions of his fears you might well think that Peter was merely Albert B . . . grown up. Only you must remember that Peter's fears were "home grown," not experimentally produced as were Albert's. Peter's fears though were much more pronounced. (Watson, 1928, p. 62)

When a rat was brought into the room, Peter screamed and fell on his back. Jones sat Peter in a high chair, and as he was about to begin his lunch, a caged rabbit was brought into the room and placed about 12 feet from Peter. Care was taken not to disturb Peter's eating. The next day the rabbit was brought a little closer, and on succeeding days the same routine was followed, taking care not to arouse Peter's fear. Finally, the rabbit could be placed on Peter's table and Peter ate with one hand and petted the rabbit with the other hand. Peter's fears of cotton wool, a fur coat, and feathers were also found to have been eliminated, and his reactions to a rat and other animals greatly diminished (Hothersall, 1990).

1. What type of study is this? (see chapter 1)
2. Do you think the results of this study can be generalized to other children with fears? Why or why not?
3. What would be the advantages of having a control group for this study? How should the control group be treated?
4. How would you measure Peter's fear?
5. Which of the following positions does the study support: (a) nature or nurture? (b) stability or change?

Please turn to the end of this chapter to check your answers.

her room to quiet a nagging parent. In all these cases, behavior (picking up the baby, getting out of bed, cleaning the room) has been increased through **negative reinforcement,** the strengthening of a response by withdrawing an aversive stimulus after the response is emitted.

Thus far, we have talked about why we behave in certain ways. But there's another question that may be just as important: Why *don't* we behave in certain ways? The two basic answers to this question are extinction and punishment.

In extinction, the behavior is no longer reinforced. Since reinforcement fuels behavior, removing reinforcement causes the behavior to die out. The worker who does not get paid for putting in extra hours will stop putting in extra hours. The "class clown" who no longer gets attention for cutting up will stop acting up—especially if there is another behavior that *will* get attention.

In punishment, a bad outcome occurs after the person does the "wrong" behavior. The objective is to stamp out the undesired behavior. Thus, spanking a child, "grounding" teenagers, and fining or imprisoning adults are all attempts to stop "bad" behavior.

Note that the only thing that negative reinforcement and punishment have in common is that both involve unpleasant stimuli (see figure 2.1 and table 2.5). Negative reinforcers are unpleasant events that occur before, and until, the "right" behavior is performed, and they increase the likelihood of that behavior. **Punishment,** on the other hand, occurs after the "wrong" behavior occurs and is designed to decrease or stamp out that "bad" behavior. Thus, a father who nags his daughter until she cleans up her room is using negative reinforcement; a father who nags his daughter for having stayed out too late is using punishment. A grandmother who makes you feel guilty so that you go to see her to relieve your guilt is using negative reinforcement; a grandmother who makes you feel guilty for past sins is using punishment.

Operant conditioning researchers have shown us that one simple principle—the results of our past actions determine our future actions—can account for a great deal of development. But this principle cannot account for development caused by maturation and heredity. Furthermore, it cannot account for development caused by observing, imitating, and modeling others.

Figure 2.1

Reinforcement Versus Punishment

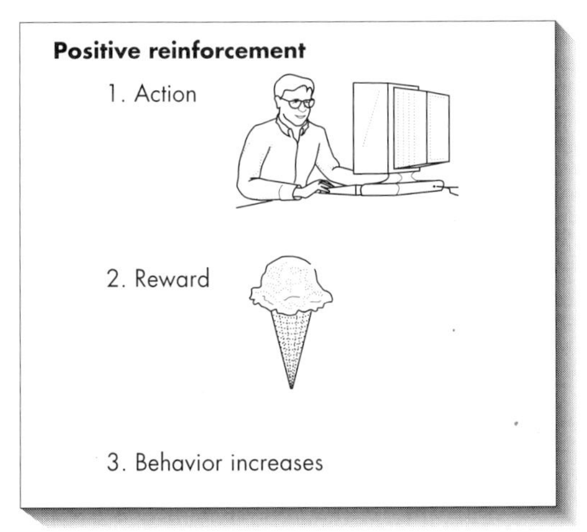

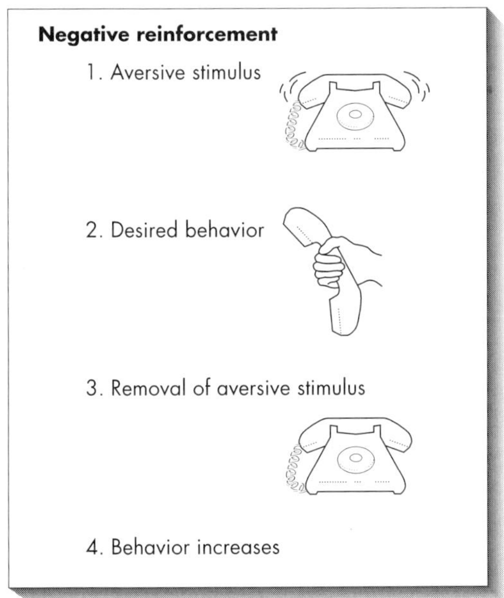

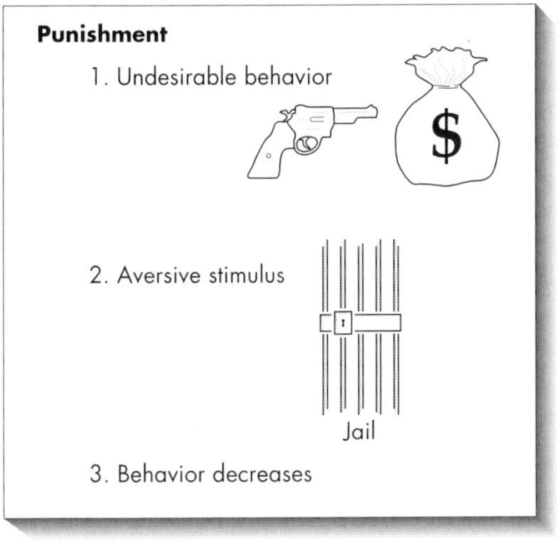

Social Learning Theory

To account for both our ability to learn from personal experience and from the experiences of models, Bandura (1962) developed **social learning theory.** According to social learning theory, we learn from many types of models. Some things are learned through direct observation. For example, when you enter a new situation, such as your first college class, you watch how other people behave and pattern your actions after theirs. Other things are learned through **symbolic models** such as verbal instruction, television, or written matter. As you study this book, you are learning through symbolic modeling.

Modeling, in all its various forms, plays an enormous role in development. From your parents, you may learn to walk, talk, smile, express anger, pray, vote for a certain political party, and view women as equal to men; from your peers, you may learn how to play by their rules so you'll be socially accepted; from your grandparents, you may learn how to act when you are old (see box 2.7); from television, you may learn just about anything—from aggressive acts to what car to buy (Eron, 1987). Imagine how long it would take to learn all the things you already know if you had to learn them solely through the consequences of your actions!

The concept of imitation is an ancient one, but Bandura has increased our appreciation of its importance. He has shown how models can influence a wide range of behavior and has given us a better understanding of how the social environment changes behavior. In his more recent theorizing, Bandura, (1986, 1989a, 1989b) further distinguishes himself from traditional learning theorists by proposing a cognitive behaviorism that emphasizes our ability to actively *think* about ourselves and the world. This emphasis is represented in Bandura's concepts of forethought and self-regulatory mechanisms.

Forethought **Forethought** is the ability to predict likely outcomes of actions. As adults, forethought is integral to much of our behavior. When your alarm went off this morning, you may have contemplated the possible consequences of sleeping in (perhaps missing class, missing breakfast, or being late for work). Based on those possible consequences, you either got up or slept in. Similarly, when you were deciding on whether to go to college, you probably weighed the consequences of different decisions.

For most of us, our ability to predict outcomes of actions improves with experience. Thus, as a newborn, you did not possess forethought. However, by interacting with your environment, you gradually learned that your actions do have consequences. This knowledge gives you the power to actively choose what will happen to you.

Self-Regulatory Mechanisms When considering what will happen to you, you look not only at expected external

Box 2.7

THEORY in FOCUS

Learning to Act Old

Ellen Langer (1983) investigated the effects of early exposure to the elderly on how people behave when they grow old. She interviewed 39 elderly residents of old-age homes in Boston about whether they had a grandparent living in the home when they were young children. If they had, the grandparent, though old to the child, was still relatively young—presenting an image of an aging adult as alert and active. Langer reasoned that this image would become the child's idea of aging and would influence that person's behavior when he or she became old.

Langer's expectations were confirmed. Independent judges, blind to her reasoning, rated the residents who had lived with a grandparent as more alert and active than those who hadn't. Presumably, this latter group learned about aging in the typically negative fashion that emphasizes debilitating effects. The positive conception of aging gained by people who had lived with a grandparent was strong enough to withstand both a lifetime of varied experience and the dulling effects of the institutions they currently lived in.

1. Which theory best explains these results? Why?
2. What kind of study is this?
3. What alternative explanations are there for these results? (*Hint:* How might a naturist explain the results?)
4. Which of the following positions does the study support: nature or nurture, stability or change?

Please turn to the end of this chapter to check your answers.

Table 2.5

Similarities and Differences Between Negative Reinforcement and Punishment

	Negative Reinforcement	Punishment
Similarities	Unpleasant stimulus involved	Unpleasant stimulus involved
Differences	Unpleasantness comes *before* desired behavior	Unpleasantness comes *after* undesired behavior
	Increases desired behavior	*Decreases* undesired behavior

(outside) rewards, but at whether you will reach your own internal goals. That is, rather than just considering praise, rewards, and criticisms from others, you give yourself praise and criticism, depending on whether your actions violate or match your own internal standards. In Bandura's terms, you use **self-regulatory mechanisms** to monitor your own behavior.

Where do internal goals come from? One source is from internalizing standards set by parents. However, children do not automatically accept parental standards. For example, older children are more likely to internalize standards than younger children, and children who respect their parents and see their parents behave in a consistent manner are more likely to internalize parental standards than those whose parents are neither respected nor consistent. However, even the standards of a beloved, consistent parent will not be automatically internalized. For example, if parents extravagantly reward their children for finger painting, the children will decide that they are painting for external rather than internal rewards. That is, the children will decide that they are finger painting for the reward (money) rather than because they like it.

According to social learning theorists, our expectations are partly determined by the goals we have internalized. These goals are based on our past experiences and beliefs about our own self-efficacy. What might this fallen sprinter's goal for the next time be?

Box 2.8

SELF-CHECK

PART A

Answer the following questions.

1. Little Stella cries when told to take a nap. Soon, her parents stop making her take naps. How would Skinner describe Stella's case? What would he advise the parents to do?
2. Little Smedley cries until his parents read him a bedtime story. Smedley's parents always end up reading him a story. How would Skinner describe Smedley's situation? What would he advise the parents to do?
3. According to Skinner, would giving a child a dollar for every hour she studied be a good idea? Do you agree? Why or why not?
4. Sam and Priscilla are engaged. To ensure a long, happy marriage, their parents offer to give Sam and Priscilla $1,000 on their first anniversary, $2,000 on their second, and so on. According to Skinner, is this a good idea? According to Bandura, is this a good idea?

PART B

Indicate whether each of the following statements is true or false.

5. Punishment and negative reinforcement are the same thing.
6. Bandura, like all behaviorists, views humans as passive and ignores thoughts.

Please turn to the end of this chapter to check your answers.

Even if children internalize their parents' general standards, the extent to which the children carry out these goals may be less than what the parent desires because the level at which standards are set depends on **self-efficacy,** the degree to which we think we can be effective in a given situation. If we don't believe we will be effective, we tend to set low goals. Because our level of self-efficacy depends on whether we have been successful in the past, Bandura would agree with the adage "Nothing succeeds like success."

Evaluation of the Learning Perspective

As both advocates and critics of learning theory agree, learning theory meets all of the criteria of a scientific theory. It provides a new perspective: humans as learning machines, programmed by their environment. Learning theory is internally consistent and consistent with the facts. Learning theory also has breadth and parsimony. Much of human behavior can be explained by the concepts of classical conditioning, reinforcement, and modeling. Finally, learning theorists make specific predictions and test their hypotheses in tightly controlled experiments to provide objective evidence for the suspected causes of development. Consequently, learning theory has heuristic value.

If learning theory meets all the criteria of a good scientific theory, then why don't all developmental psychologists adopt the learning view? A major reason is that many people don't agree with the learning theorists' positions on the philosophical issues. Specifically, some critics believe that in trying to explain human behavior as being exclusively due to a few simple principles, behaviorists have made two mistakes: (1) they have ignored the effect of nature, and (2) they have ignored nonbehavioral aspects of development, such as physical development and cognitive development.

Critics object to the behaviorist's extreme nurture position not only because it overlooks the impact of genetics and biological maturation on development, but also because it leads to three other positions that many naturists find objectionable. First, because people are the product of their experience, behaviorists assume that human nature is neither good nor bad. Second, because people are the product of their experiences and experience continues as long as we live, behaviorists assume that development is continuous and that people therefore have the capacity to change throughout the lifespan. Third, because we are the product of our experience, and each of us has different experiences, human development is characterized by individual differences rather than universal patterns (see table 2.6).

In addition to feeling that learning theorists overemphasize the environment's importance, many critics object to *traditional* learning theory's view that we are organisms that passively react to the environment. Skinner and Watson paint us as creatures who are always passive actors in the theater of life—responding to what happens to us, repeating behaviors for which we are reinforced, and avoiding behaviors for which we are punished. It is unlikely, however, that our minds are so narrow that we can make only the simplest of associations. Many developmental psychologists believe that instead of passively learning from experience, we actively seek out and try to make sense of our experiences.

Table 2.6

Critique of the Learning Perspective

Does the Learning Perspective Meet the Criteria of a Scientific Theory?

Criteria	Rating
1. Provides a new perspective	High
2. Is internally consistent	High
3. Is consistent with facts	High
4. Has breadth	High
5. Has parsimony	High
6. Makes specific predictions	High
7. Has heuristic value	High

How the Learning Theorists Stand on the Controversies

1. Human development is affected more by *nurture.*
2. Traditional learning theory maintains that people *passively respond to environmental events.* Social learning theory proposes that people may *actively* choose those environmental events.
3. Development occurs steadily and *gradually.*
4. Behavioral characteristics may *change* throughout the lifespan.
5. *Individual differences* in development are the rule.

In conclusion, many of the strongest objections against learning theories are leveled against caricatures, or at least outdated, versions of behaviorism (Kimble, 1992). For example, Bandura's version of behaviorism postulates that people are active—they set goals, make plans, reflect on their behavior, and interpret situations (Maddux, 1994). However, even some of those who understand modern behaviorism believe that it does not pay enough attention to (1) how biological events shape development and (2) how thought develops.

To compensate for these limitations of the behavioral approach, some developmental psychologists think that it needs to be supplemented with another viewpoint. Still others believe that the behavioral approach needs to be replaced by another viewpoint. For many developmental psychologists, the approach that complements—or, in some cases, competes with behaviorism—is the cognitive structuralist view.

The Cognitive Structural View

Cognitive structuralists strongly disagree with traditional behaviorists on at least three issues. First, whereas behaviorists only study behavior, cognitive structuralists study thought. Second, whereas traditional behaviorists believe that we are products of our environment, supporters of **cognitive structuralism** believe that our development is largely influenced by biological maturation. Thus, a strict behaviorist would say that, with the right instruction, any second grader could do advanced algebra. On the other hand, the cognitive structuralist would argue that the average second grader cannot learn advanced algebra because the child is not biologically ready. Third, whereas traditional behaviorists view us as passive, cognitive structuralists view us as active. Contrary to the traditional behaviorist view that we need to be rewarded to learn, cognitive structuralists believe that we naturally want to learn. We are not robots waiting to be programmed by drill and rote memorization to learn certain responses. Instead, we are active explorers trying to discover universal rules. Because we actively interpret information, flooding children with information that they are not ready for will not produce the desired effect. They will not be able to interpret the information, and they will ignore information that they cannot interpret.

You now know the core assumptions held by cognitive structuralists. But what is the cognitive structuralist approach? The cognitive structuralist approach is the view that changes in intellectual development result from changes in mental structures. In other words, as we restructure the way we mentally represent the world, our views of the world become more sophisticated and developed. The most prominent, general, and comprehensive of these cognitive structuralist theories—and the most prominent theory in developmental psychology (Beilin, 1992) is Jean Piaget's.

As you will learn in chapter 6, Piaget (pronounced "Pea-ah-zhay") believed that thinking—like eating—is a "basic life function" that helps us adapt to our environment (Piaget, 1970). Thus, just as our body transforms the food we eat and fits it into our bodily structures (such as bones, muscles, and blood), our mind transforms information and fits it into our mental structures. Piaget called these mental structures **schemata,** or organized, coherent categories of information.

Once we form a schema (*schema* is the singular of *schemata*), we want to use that structure to understand the world. When we were babies, we had the schema of putting things in our mouth. We fed that schema by putting everything possible in our mouth. When we were a little older, we learned the schema of counting. We fed that schema by counting everything we saw—sometimes to the irritation of our parents. In college, some students learn the schema of "defense mechanisms." They then fit an incredible amount of their peers' behavior into that category—often to the irritation of their friends. The process of understanding the world by fitting it into our preexisting schemes is called **assimilation.**

You may have to accommodate your schema of "winter sports" to assimilate snow golf.

The problem with assimilation is that if one's schema is incomplete or inaccurate, that person's understanding of the world will be inaccurate. The person who uses the television schema to understand a computer is missing something. Similarly, the person who can view African Americans only in terms of a stereotyped schema is missing out. Likewise, the baby who sucks a bottle the same exact way that he sucked his mother's breast may go hungry. Consequently, in the child's quest to assimilate the world, he may engage in **accommodation,** or revising existing schemes or adding new schemes. An infant learns to suck a one-hole bottle differently than a three-hole bottle. By revising his schemes (accommodation), the child is more able to assimilate. In other words, by making oneself more compatible with the world out there (accommodation), a person is better able to take in the world (assimilation). Thus, assimilation and accommodation often occur together.

Even when assimilation and accommodation don't occur simultaneously, assimilation eventually requires some accommodation because if you keep adding information to a schema, you'll eventually have to restructure it (just as if you eat a great deal, your body will have to change). To illustrate, think of your initial exposure to developmental psychology. At first, your notion of developmental psychology was very global. Perhaps you thought of it as a bunch of scientists videotaping infants or as doctors who treat children with psychological problems. However, after finding out about the different areas studied by developmental psychologists (such as moral behavior and retirement, for example), you revised your notions of developmental psychology. More specifically, rather than merely incorporating this information into your preexisting global view of developmental psychology, you restructured (accommodated) your schemes to create several categories for developmental psychology.

The motivation for changing our existing schemes is **equilibration,** our need to resolve contradiction. Piaget thought equilibration was as necessary for survival, as automatic, and as biologically driven as **homeostasis,** the body's need to maintain an internal balance. Just as your body will sweat when your temperature is out of balance (too hot), Piaget believed that if you are cognitively *disequilibrated* (exposed to something you don't understand), you will actively seek information to help you revise your cognitive structures so that you can regain equilibration.

Many people try to take advantage of the equilibration principle by deliberately disequilibrating you. A professor may try to disequilibrate you by giving you some information that, given your current schemes, seems inconsistent or confusing. The professor then hopes that because you should be motivated to equilibrate yourself, you will accommodate (reorganize) your knowledge in a way that will allow you to make sense of the new information. As a result, you will not just learn information, but you will also develop cognitively. Similarly, some feminists believe that having people see women behave in nontraditional ways will disequilibrate people and that people will equilibrate by revising their stereotyped views of women.

Stages of Development

Unlike some cognitive structuralists, Piaget believes that the cognitive changes that occur in us as we develop are as abrupt and dramatic as the changes that occur as a caterpillar changes into a butterfly. As you read about the four stages of cognitive development (sensorimotor, preoperational, concrete operations, and formal operations), note that the main thing that happens is *not* that people learn more information as they progress from one stage to the next, but that they develop a different *way* of thinking (see table 2.7).

In the first stage, the **sensorimotor stage** (ages 0 to 2), the child is developing a very basic understanding of how the physical world works and how one's body works. Learning is through direct physical experience with objects.

Table 2.7

Piaget's Stages of Cognitive Development

Stage	Description	Age
Sensorimotor	The infant learns about the relationships between motor actions (moving an arm) and sensory experiences (feeling the arm hit the floor). Because the child does not use words or visual images to think about the world, the child is concerned primarily with whatever sensory experiences he or she is having at the moment.	Birth to 2 years
Preoperational	The child begins to represent the world with words and images that reflect increased symbolic thinking. Consequently, a child can think about the past and future, although such thinking is often not logical.	2 to 7 years
Concrete operations	The child can reason logically about concrete events and can mentally reverse sequences. The child can predict what would logically come next (if you pour water from this wide glass into this thin tall glass, what will happen?), as well as reason backward (if adding 5 + 2 = 7, then subtracting 2 from 7 will get you ____?).	7 to 11 years
Formal operations	The adolescent reasons in more abstract, systematic, and adult-like ways.	11 to 15 years

During this stage, infants learn about such things as gravity (when things are dropped, they fall). Near the end of this stage, Piaget believed that children learn **object permanence,** the belief that objects continue to exist even when they can't be seen. If an infant has not attained object permanence, doing magic tricks for the child is easy. Just cover a ball with a cloth, and the ball has vanished. The infant thinks the ball no longer exists. Then, take the ball out from under the cloth and the ball has magically reappeared. Perhaps this lack of object permanence is why such games as peek-a-boo seem so exciting to infants at this age.

Piaget believed that a child reaches the **preoperational stage** (2 to 7 years) once the child has grasped the idea of object permanence and can use **symbolic thought,** using mental symbols such as words to refer to objects. Although the preoperational child can use words, she *cannot* use words and other symbols well enough to think *logically* through the consequences of doing a physical action—unless the child has seen that action performed before. For example, if you ask a preoperational child to solve a simple word problem such as, "Pretend you have three apples. How many would you have if you gave me one?" she could not solve it. However, if you actually gave her three apples and then asked for one, she probably could come up with the number of remaining apples, provided she could count that high. Thus, like the sensorimotor child, the child at the preoperational stage learns best by doing. In fact, the term *preoperational* means "before" (*pre*) being able to do mental **operations,** actions performed mentally, rather than physically. In other words, the preoperational child cannot mentally transform information in a logical way.

Perhaps the best way to understand preoperational thought is to contrast it with thought at the next highest stage, the **concrete operations stage** (7 to 11+ years). As the term *concrete operations* suggests, the concrete operational child can perform operations—mental manipulations of physical objects that are *reversible* (for example, you get from B to A by retracing the steps that took you from A to B).

Since operations are mental manipulations, you should not be surprised to know that the only way a preoperational 3-year-old can count to five is by counting concrete objects such as her fingers, whereas a concrete operational child can count to five in her head without any objects being physically present. Similarly, a preoperational child could know that 8 + 4 = 12, but finds that of no value in trying to figure out the answer to "What's 12 – 4?" The concrete operational child, on the other hand, can reverse operations and thus grasps the notion that subtraction is the opposite of addition. Because children first start thinking logically about physical objects during the concrete operational stage, this stage is also when children first start doubting Santa Claus, realizing the impossibility of his being everywhere at once (Fehr, 1976).

By age 11 or 12, some children will enter the **formal operations stage.** Formal operations refers to the ability to perform mental operations on operations, what Piaget calls **second-order operations.** People who enter this cognitive stage of development have shifted from thinking about the actual to thinking about the possible. They can think about hypothetical topics such as the future, the meaning of life, and the process for testing scientific

Box 2.9

SELF-CHECK

1. Would Piaget believe in the value of a course in lifespan development?
2. A child is always putting things in her mouth. How would Piaget's explanation for this behavior differ from Freud's?
3. Children tend to be better at following rules after the age of six. How would Freud explain this? How would Bandura explain this? How would Piaget explain this?
4. Would Piaget agree with the statement, "Children will learn when they are ready"? Why or why not? Would Skinner agree with Piaget? Why or why not?
5. What is the difference between assimilation and accommodation?
6. According to Piaget, what are the four stages of cognitive development that people go through?
7. What is the main characteristic of formal operational thought?

Please turn to the end of this chapter to check your answers.

hypotheses. In other words, the major characteristic of this stage is the ability to think about *abstract* ideas in a systematic and logical way.

Evaluation of Piaget's Theory

Piaget's theory has had a powerful impact on our conception of human development. Psychologists, educators, and the general public have adopted many of his ideas about how children think. But is this wide adoption of his theory merited? Although we will take up this question in greater depth in chapter 6, you can already come to certain conclusions.

Even on the basis of this preliminary overview of the theory, you can tell that Piaget's theory meets at least six of the seven criteria of a scientific theory. Most notably, he provided us with a new perspective. Specifically, he was the first popular developmental theorist to stress that children are active, adaptive creatures whose thought processes are very different from those of adults.

Piaget's theory is internally consistent and largely consistent with the facts. However, as you will see in chapter 6, research does contradict some of Piaget's assertions. For example, Piaget's research strategy led him to underestimate the thinking abilities of young children in at least two ways. First, he tried to find out what children think by asking them. This technique is fine for adults. However, since young children have limited language abilities, they may know more than they can tell. Indeed, Rochel Gelman (1972, 1978) found that when linguistic limitations are compensated for, young children often demonstrate higher cognitive skills than Piaget predicted. Second, some of Piaget's tasks were unfamiliar and artificial. Research has shown that children think in a more sophisticated way about familiar tasks (Cohen, 1983).

Piaget's theory has breadth and parsimony. His concepts of equilibration, assimilation, and accommodation explain much of cognitive development. However, many criticize him for not defining or operationalizing these three concepts precisely. For example, David Klahr (1982, p. 85) asks: "For 40 years we have had assimilation and accommodation . . . What are they? How do they do their thing? What is it after all this time, we know no more about them than when they first sprung on the scene?" Piaget's vagueness about these core concepts results in a lack of specific predictions about the exact mechanisms of development. However, the theory rates high in heuristic value because of the wealth of research it has stimulated (see table 2.8).

Piaget's theory reflects his strong naturist position. As befits a naturist, Piaget explained development in terms of four universal and maturationally determined stages. That is, movement through the stages is due to equilibration—our inherited tendency to accommodate and assimilate information into schemes. Also consistent with his naturist leanings is his belief that children are actively involved in their learning process. Piaget frequently emphasized children's "innate" curiosity and their need to learn.

The Humanistic View

Like the cognitive structuralists, humanists stress the role of nature and the individual's ability to be active in his or her own development. In fact, this emphasis on the individual's active nature is part of the reason humanism describes itself as "The Third Force." More specifically, humanism considers itself "The Third Force" because it emerged as a rebellion against the two then-existing forces in psychology: (1) behaviorism, which, according to humanists, looked at people as *passive* machines, ignoring people's humanity; and (2) psychoanalysis, which humanists regarded as portraying human nature as evil and as *passive*.

You know what the rebels are against, but what are they for? Humanists share four premises: (1) subjective experience is important; (2) free will and creativity are important determinants of one's personality; (3) all people inherit a tendency to be the best they can be; and (4) psychological research should be relevant to human experience (Buhler & Allen, 1972). In the next two sections, we will discuss the two most influential spokespersons for these premises: Abraham Maslow and Carl Rogers.

Table 2.8

Critique of Piaget's Cognitive Structural Theory

Does Piaget's Theory Meet the Criteria of a Scientific Theory?

Criteria	Rating
1. Provides a new perspective	High
2. Is internally consistent	High
3. Is consistent with facts	Moderate
4. Has breadth	High
5. Has parsimony	High
6. Makes specific predictions	Moderate
7. Has heuristic value	High

How Piaget Stands on the Controversies

1. Human development is affected more by *nature*.
2. People are *actively* involved in their own development.
3. Development occurs in abrupt *discontinuous* stages.
4. Behavioral characteristics are *stable* after about age 16.
5. All people develop according to *universal*, maturationally determined stages.

Abraham Maslow's Theory of Self-Actualization

Maslow is often called the spiritual father of humanistic psychology. Not only did he help "The Third Force" gain academic respectability, but he also popularized the humanistic movement.

Basic Assumptions In popularizing the movement, Maslow introduced the general public to the concept of **self-actualization,** "the full use and exploitation of talents, capacities, potentials, etc." (1970, p. 150). He felt that just as a rose seed has an inborn tendency to become a beautiful rose and just as an acorn has an inborn tendency to become a mighty oak, people have an inborn tendency to become self-actualized.

To study self-actualization, Maslow looked at the lives, values, and attitudes of people he considered to be healthy and creative. By carefully examining the lives of 18 of these people (9 contemporaries and 9 historical figures, including Abraham Lincoln, Thomas Jefferson, Albert Einstein, Eleanor Roosevelt, and Jane Addams), he arrived at 15 basic characteristics possessed by self-actualizers (1970, pp. 153–172):

1. More efficient perception of reality and more comfortable relations with it;
2. Acceptance (of self, others, nature);
3. Spontaneity, simplicity, naturalness;
4. Problem centered, as opposed to being ego-centered;
5. The quality of detachment, the need for privacy;
6. Autonomy, independence of culture and environment;
7. Continued freshness of appreciation;
8. Mystic and peak experiences;
9. *Gemeinschaftsgefuhl* (the feeling of kinship with others);
10. Deeper and more profound interpersonal relations;
11. A democratic character structure;
12. Discrimination between means and ends, between good and evil;
13. Philosophical, unhostile sense of humor;
14. Self-actualizing creativeness; and
15. Resistance to enculturation, transcendence of any particular culture.

Maslow stressed that, despite having these 15 characteristics, the self-actualizers he studied were far from perfect. Their commitment to their chosen work and values sometimes led them to be ruthless, and they often put their work before the needs and feelings of friends and family. Thus, not surprisingly, self-actualizers, like other mortals, suffer guilt, anxiety, sadness, and conflict. Yet, as imperfect as self-actualizers are, Maslow thought that they come as close as humans can come to perfection.

Although the vast majority of people will fail to become self-actualized, most will get a glimpse of self-actualization by having what Maslow called **peak experiences,** an especially joyous and exciting moment. Peak experiences are often triggered by intense feelings of love, exposure to art or music, or experiencing the overwhelming beauty of nature. Although most of us have had peak experiences on a number of occasions, the most powerful peak experiences are rare. These are the magic moments of ecstasy portrayed by poets and the religious rapture of deep mystical experiences. The highest peaks are described by Maslow as "feelings of limitless horizons opening up the vision, the feeling of being simultaneously more powerful and also more helpless than one ever was before, the feeling of great ecstasy and wonder and awe, the loss of placing in time and space . . ." (Maslow, 1970, p. 164). Maslow describes such an experience when he kissed his soon-to-be wife for the first time.

Hierarchy of Needs If most people have peak experiences and have an inborn tendency toward self-actualization, why are so few people self-actualized? Maslow explained the dearth of self-actualized people by saying that self-actualization is but one human need. For this one need to drive the individual, more basic needs must be met first. If basic needs, such as the need for food, safety, love, and

According to Maslow, the overwhelming beauty of nature can trigger a peak experience, a brief glimpse of self-actualization.

Figure 2.2

Maslow's Hierarchy of Needs

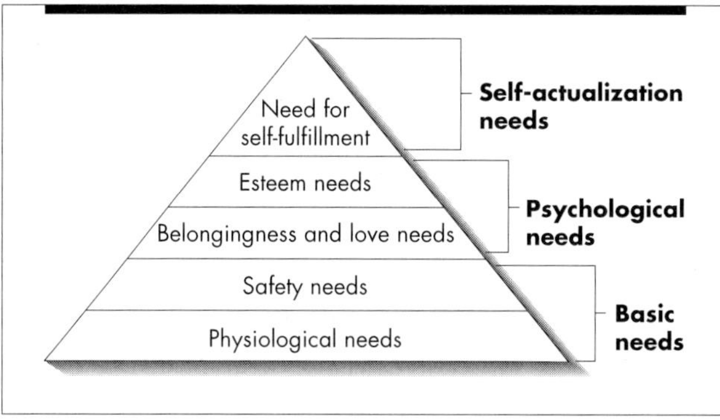

self-respect are not met, the person will not strive for self-actualization. In fact, severe deprivation of food, warmth, or love can lead to death or to neurosis and psychological maladjustment. Once these basic needs are met, people will strive to meet their needs to develop their potential. But until lower-level needs are met, people will not aspire to growth. For example, the starving person usually doesn't think of writing the best poem, rather she thinks of food.

You now understand the basic idea behind Maslow's **hierarchy of needs:** Higher level needs aren't influential until lower-level needs have been met. To get a more detailed understanding of the need hierarchy, look at figure 2.2. After viewing figure 2.2, you'll be able to answer such questions as: What needs have to be met before a person will be concerned about security? about status? about love?

Evaluation of Maslow's Theory Maslow rates high on four of the seven criteria on which scientific theories are judged. He gets very high marks for providing a new perspective, that of exploring the positive dimensions of human experience.

He also gets high marks for internal consistency. However, his theory isn't consistent with the facts. There is little evidence that there are five basic needs and that we fulfill lower needs first (Alderfer, 1972). Even Maslow's own research provides only weak support for the theory because Maslow's research was "exploratory." Maslow was the first to acknowledge the limits of his research:

> It's just that I haven't got the time to do careful experiments myself. They take too long, in view of the years that I have left and the extent of what I want to do. (Maslow, 1972, pp. 66–67)

Maslow's theory has breadth and parsimony (he explains all development in terms of his hierarchy of needs). However, Maslow doesn't make predictions about what variables are necessary for a person to progress up the ladder of needs. Perhaps because of this lack of specific, testable predictions, little research has been directed at testing his theory (see table 2.9).

Carl Rogers' Theory of Self-Concept

Like Maslow, Carl Rogers was a leader and pioneer in the field of humanistic psychology. Like Maslow, Rogers

Box 2.10

SELF-CHECK

1. Can Maslow's theory explain anorexia nervosa (self-starvation)? What about compulsive gambling?
2. How, according to Maslow, would poverty stunt development?
3. How would the model explain why wealthy and respected people get divorced?
4. How might Maslow interpret a successful businessperson's "midlife crisis"?
5. At what level of the pyramid (see figure 2.2) would a person's behavior be most predictable by behavioristic principles? Least?
6. Do you think that being loved is more important to most people than having good self-esteem? What would Erikson say? What would Maslow say?
7. Does Maslow's hierarchy suggest that it would be better to grow up in a poor, but affectionate family, or in a rich, but cold family? Why?

Please turn to the end of this chapter to check your answers.

Table 2.9

Critique of Maslow's Self-Actualization Theory

Does Maslow's Theory Meet the Criteria of a Scientific Theory?

Criteria	Rating
1. Provides a new perspective	High
2. Is internally consistent	High
3. Is consistent with facts	Low
4. Has breadth	High
5. Has parsimony	High
6. Makes specific predictions	Low
7. Has heuristic value	Low

How Maslow Stands on the Controversies

1. Human development is affected more by *nature.*
2. People are *actively* involved in their own development.
3. Development occurs in abrupt *discontinuous* stages.
4. Behavioral characteristics may *change* throughout the human lifespan.
5. *Individual differences* in development are the rule.

emphasized the importance of self-actualization. But perhaps Rogers' most significant contribution to developmental personality theory is his work on self-concept.

Basic Assumptions Rogers found that his clients talked about wanting to be their "true self" or their "real self." Consequently, Rogers began investigating the **self,** our beliefs about who we are. The self enables you to answer such questions as: What do you stand for? What do you believe in? Are you good or bad? industrious or lazy?

Rogers felt that the answers to these questions were established in childhood. Whether you feel yourself to be good or bad probably depends on how your parents treated you. The same is true for whether you think you're industrious or lazy: If your parents always called you lazy, you probably think you are lazy. Furthermore, if your parents emphasized that there is a big difference between who you are and who you ought to be, you will have a poor self-image.

What you think you believe in is also influenced by your parents because, when you were a child, parents put **"conditions of worth"** on you: You were of worth (value) when you did things they approved of (agreed with them, loved your younger sister) and worthless when you did things they disapproved of (hitting your sister). Because you valued your parents' approval, you disowned thoughts and feelings that they disapproved of. Thus, if you had the thought "Sometimes, I wish Grandma were dead," you would disown that thought. In other words, you tried to be what others wanted you to be rather than who you were. If you kept trying to live up to what others want you to be, you would lose touch with who you really were. In Rogers' terminology, denying your thoughts and feelings will cause your picture of yourself to become **incongruent** with who you really are.

As you might expect, the person who becomes estranged from herself by denying her true feelings is doomed to be unhappy. Specifically, incongruence leads to confusion, tension, anxiety, maladjustment, vulnerability, defensiveness, and threats.

What can be done to reduce incongruence? One solution is to place a person in the nonthreatening relationship with a therapist. The therapist, rather than putting conditions of worth on the client, would give the client **unconditional positive regard.** In other words, the therapist accepts the person, regardless of what the client thinks or feels. The warm and accepting counselor provides an atmosphere where the client's true self is free to come out. Consequently, congruence may be achieved.

Once a friend or therapist has helped you achieve congruence, you can maintain congruence by staying open to your thoughts and experiences. If you continue to accept yourself for who you are, you will be free to follow your inborn tendency to self-actualize. Because you are making decisions that are right for you, rather than decisions that are right for the imaginary person that some people want you to be, your continued growth as a person will be guaranteed.

Evaluation of Rogers' Theory Rogers' self theory is scientifically more sound than Maslow's self-actualization theory. Rogers receives moderate or high ratings on all seven criteria. Rogers provided a new perspective, that of emphasizing the self-concept, the development of which we will discuss in chapter 11.

In terms of accuracy, Rogers' theory is internally consistent. Furthermore, Rogers has provided considerably more research support for his position than Maslow did.

The main criticism of Rogers can be leveled against all humanistic psychologists: Neither he nor any other humanist has been able to prove that we have an inborn desire to strive toward self-actualization. Therefore, he receives a moderate rating for being consistent with the facts.

Rogers' theory has breadth and is moderately parsimonious (see table 2.10). Although he was more research-oriented than Maslow, Rogers' theory is often vague about the causes of development and has generated only a modest amount of research. Consequently, the theory has not had enormous heuristic value. Nevertheless, it, like the other theories we have discussed, has had a positive impact on how children are reared (see box 2.11).

On the philosophical issues, Rogers usually agrees with his fellow humanist, Maslow. Like Maslow, Rogers is a naturist. Both believe that we are inherently good: It is society

Box 2.11

THEORY in FOCUS

Implications of Theories for Child Rearing

Our assumptions about the world affect how we act. In the seventeenth century, Descartes dissected animals without anesthesia and was amused by their screams. Was he sadistic? To answer this question, let's examine how you would react if a teddy bear yelped when you sat on it. You might be surprised. You might wonder how the manufacturer made the bear emit such a life-like response, but you would not believe the teddy bear was in real pain. You might sit on it again to hear the squeak. Are you sadistic? No, because you know teddy bears can't feel pain. Similarly, Descartes wasn't sadistic because he "knew" that animals couldn't feel pain (Schultz & Schultz, 1990).

Throughout history, parents have brutalized their children (Aries, 1962). Children have been used as sex aids, beaten severely, taken to public hangings, wakened in the middle of the night by a person in a menacing costume who threatened to come back and kill them if they didn't obey their parents, and infants have been wrapped in swaddling clothing (clothing wrapped so tightly that the child can't move and becomes black and blue). Like Descartes, these parents were not sadists. They were "normal" parents who did not know they were doing anything wrong. As some have said, "Almost every parent does the best they know how."

Developmental theorists have reduced ignorance and corrected many popular misconceptions, thereby paving the way for more humane treatment of children. Freud, in his psychoanalytic theory, pointed out that what happens to children will affect their adult development. Although you probably accept this belief without question, prior to Freud, many people believed that there was no relationship between childhood and adulthood. Childhood and adulthood were two entirely different phases, just as the caterpillar and the butterfly stage are different phases. Consequently, any mental harm done to the child would not have lasting effects and was therefore permissible. Freud's theory repudiated this assumption. He pointed out that childhood traumas (such as using children as sex aids) could leave lasting scars. Furthermore, Freud warned that overly strict or harsh treatment may produce a conforming child, but a neurotic adult.

Erikson, like Freud, emphasized that children need to be cared for if they are to grow up to be well-adjusted adults. Like Freud, Erikson stressed that parents should be very responsive to the child's needs and wants during the first year of life. Like Freud, Erikson felt that parents should not be overly harsh or restrictive. Perhaps his theory's most important contribution to child rearing was to help people understand that the "terrible two's" are a normal part of development and that parents should not try to beat the 2-year-old into submission, but rather appreciate and encourage their 2-year-old's strides toward independence.

Traditional learning theorists promoted more humane child rearing in two ways. First, they stressed that rewards are a more effective way to get children to behave than punishments. Second, they helped people realize that parents are often rewarding bad behavior with attention and extinguishing good behavior by ignoring it.

Later, social learning theorists, such as Bandura, stressed that parents are able to exert more control by setting a good example (being good models) than by telling children to behave in a certain way. Consequently, some parents have quit their own bad habits (smoking, drinking, cursing, and procrastinating) in order to help their children. In addition, Bandura's recent work on self-efficacy also supports Erikson's belief that parents must allow children opportunities to explore their abilities and to succeed on their own.

Humanism counters the historical image of children being evil creatures that must be subdued, restrained, or threatened. Not only do humanists stress that children are good, but they also encourage parents to respect their child's individuality.

Continued

that causes us to deviate from our natural path toward self-actualization. Like Maslow, Rogers believes that we are actively involved in our own development and that we have the capacity to change throughout our lifespan.

The issue that separates Rogers from Maslow is whether development is characterized by continuity or discontinuity. Maslow endorses the view that development is discontinuous as a result of rapid "peak experiences" or jumping to the next stage in the pyramid. Rogers, on the other hand, holds that development is a continuous process of becoming more and more congruent.

Box 2.11

THEORY in FOCUS

Concluded

Finally, Piaget's cognitive structuralist theory emphasizes that children will learn if they are allowed to explore on their own at their own rate. Thus, activities that were considered frivolous and unnecessary several hundred years ago are now regarded as vital for development. Piaget would frown at swaddling clothing and overly restrictive parenting because he believed that children learn by actively exploring their world. He would despise the use of child labor because, as he wrote, "play is the work of the child." Even today, many parents benefit, and many more would benefit, by realizing that, for many things, children are willing learners when they are developmentally ready. Pushing children to learn before they are mentally ready results in frustration, resentment, lowered self-esteem, and perhaps even a stunting of the child's natural curiosity and willingness to learn.

In short, although these theories have many differences, they all encourage more humane treatment of children. All of these theories would advise against using harsh punishment or threats of violence as a characteristic way of dealing with one's child, and virtually all would oppose swaddling clothing or overly restricting one's child.

Table 2.10

Critique of Rogers' Self Theory

Does Rogers' Theory Meet the Criteria of a Scientific Theory?

Criteria	Rating
1. Provides a new perspective	High
2. Is internally consistent	High
3. Is consistent with facts	Moderate
4. Has breadth	High
5. Has parsimony	High
6. Makes specific predictions	Moderate
7. Has heuristic value	Low

How Rogers Stands on the Controversies

1. Human development is affected more by *nature*.
2. People are *actively* involved in their own development.
3. Development occurs *gradually*, in a step-like fashion.
4. Behavioral characteristics may *change* throughout the lifespan.
5. *Individual differences* in development are the rule.

Box 2.12

SELF-CHECK

1. Combined, the developmental theories give us better insight into child rearing. But what problems might arise from being devoted exclusively to one, and only one, of the theories?
2. How does Rogers' idea of the self differ from Freud's view of the ego? Freud and Erikson both believed that the superego created problems for the individual. To what extent would Rogers agree? Why?
3. Are "conditions of worth" just another way of saying that we are reinforced for some behaviors and not others? What does Rogers think is wrong with conditions of worth? What do you think would be the behaviorists' response?
4. Why, according to Bandura, do children not accept as part of their self-concept, the ideals their parents try to impart to them?
5. How do Maslow and Rogers differ in their views of the course of development? How do they differ in their views of factors preventing the individual to becoming self-actualized?
6. An individual feels he cannot do well in college. How would Rogers handle this situation? How would it differ from Bandura's approach?

Please turn to the end of this chapter to check your answers.

Table 2.11

Do the Major Theories Meet the Criteria of a Scientific Theory?

Criteria	Psychoanalytic (Freud)	Psychosocial (Erikson)	Learning	Cognitive Structural
1. Provides a new perspective	High	Low	High	High
2. Is internally consistent	Low	Moderate	High	High
3. Is consistent with the facts	Moderate	Moderate	High	Moderate
4. Has breadth	High	High	High	High
5. Has parsimony	Moderate	Moderate	High	High
6. Makes specific predictions	Low	Low	High	Moderate
7. Has heuristic value	Moderate	Moderate	High	High
Criteria	**Humanism (Maslow)**	**Humanism (Rogers)**	**Common sense**	
1. Provides a new perspective	High	High	No	
2. Is internally consistent	High	High	No	
3. Is consistent with facts	Low	Moderate	Low	
4. Has breadth	High	High	High	
5. Has parsimony	High	High	Low	
6. Makes specific predictions	Low	Moderate	Low	
7. Has heuristic value	Low	Low	Low	

Table 2.12

How the Theorists Stand on the Controversies

Controversies	Psychoanalytic (Freud)	Psychosocial (Erikson)	Learning	Cognitive Structural
Nature versus nurture	Nature	Nature	Nurture	Nature
Active versus passive	Passive	Active	Passive[1]	Nature[2]
Continuity versus discontinuity	Discontinuity	Discontinuity	Continuity	Discontinuity
Stability versus change	Stability	Change	Change	Stability
Individual differences versus universality	Universality	Universality	Individual differences	Universality
Controversies	**Humanism (Maslow)**	**Humanism (Rogers)**	**Common sense**	
Nature versus nurture	Nature	Nature	Either	
Active versus passive	Active	Active	Either	
Continuity versus discontinuity	Discontinuity	Continuity	Either	
Stability versus change	Change	Change	Either	
Individual differences versus universality	?	?	Either	

[1] However, Bandura's social learning theory portrays humans as more active than Watson's or Skinner's theories.
[2] Although often called an interactionist, Piaget stresses the role of biologically determined stages.

Conclusions

In this chapter, you have learned about the characteristics of a good scientific theory and about the philosophical issues that divide developmental theories. You then studied six theories of human development, determined their stance on the philosophical issues, and evaluated them based on their scientific merit (for a review, see tables 2.11 and 2.12). As you read the rest of this book, you will learn more about these theories, learn more about the facts that relate to their philosophical positions, and learn more about the facts that relate to their predictions. Thus, the theories that you favor today may not be the ones you will favor after studying this book.

Summary

1. Not only should the ideal theory be specific, parsimonious, broad, and consistent with known facts, but it should also provide a new perspective and have heuristic value.
2. Freud popularized the idea that early childhood experiences affect later development.
3. According to the psychoanalytic view, the human mind is organized into three components: the id, ego, and superego.
4. The Freudian psychoanalytic view traces psychosexual development through four *biologically* determined stages: the oral, anal, phallic, and genital stages.
5. Erik Erikson expanded Freud's stage theory to encompass the entire lifespan and to include the effects of culture on development. In addition, Erikson believed the ego was not merely a servant to the id, but had its own wants.
6. Traditional behaviorists believe that development is the result of events in the environment.
7. Classical conditioning occurs when a previously neutral environmental event is associated with an environmental event that already elicits a reaction. Classical conditioning plays a big role in emotional reactions.
8. Operant conditioning occurs when a person makes a connection between a voluntary action and an environmental outcome.
9. Social learning theory accounts for both our ability to learn from personal experience and from the experience of models.
10. Cognitive structuralists, such as Jean Piaget, focus on the active thought processes that enable people to understand and organize their perceptions.
11. Piaget believed that we try to fit information into cognitive structures called schemes. Information that we can digest into existing schemes is assimilated. Information that can be absorbed only if we slightly modify our existing schemes is accommodated. Equilibration, the need to fit as much information into organized schemes as possible, helps maintain balance between assimilation and accommodation.
12. Piaget proposed four qualitatively different stages of cognitive development: sensorimotor, preoperational, concrete operations, and formal operations.
13. Humanists share four premises: subjective experience is important; free will and creativity are important determinants of one's personality; all people inherit a tendency to be the best they can be; and psychological research should be relevant to human experience.

Key Terms

accommodation 55
adulthood 45
anal expulsive 41
anal fixation 41
anal retentive 41
anal stage 41
assimilation 54
association 48
autonomy versus shame and doubt 44
behaviorism 47
behaviorists 47
castration anxiety 41
classical conditioning 48
cognitive structuralism 54
concrete operations stage 56
conditioned response 48
conditioned stimulus 48
conditions of worth 60
ego 40
ego instincts 40

Electra complex 42
equilibration 55
eros instincts 39
extinction 48
forethought 51
formal operations stage 56
generativity versus stagnation 45
genital stage 42
heuristic value 38
hierarchy of needs 59
homeostasis 55
id 40
identity versus role confusion 45
incongruent 60
industry versus inferiority 44
initiative versus guilt 44
instinctual drives 39
integrity versus despair 46
internal consistency 38
intimacy versus isolation 45
latency period (Freud) 42
latency stage (Erikson) 44
libido 39
locomotor-genital stage 44
maturity 46
modeling 51
muscular-anal stage 44
negative reinforcement 50
neutral stimulus 48
object permanence 56
Oedipus complex 41
operant conditioning 49
operations 56
oral fixation 41
oral-sensory stage 44
oral stage 41
parsimonious 38
peak experiences 58
phallic stage 41
pleasure principle 40
positive reinforcement 49
preoperational stage 56
psychoanalytic theory 39
psychosocial stages 44
puberty 45
punishment 50
repression 40
schemata 54
second-order operations 56
self 60
self-actualization 58
self-efficacy 53
self-regulatory mechanisms 52
sensorimotor stage 55
social learning theory 51
superego 40
symbolic models 51
symbolic thought 56
thanatos 40
trust versus mistrust 44
unconditional positive regard 60
unconditioned response 48
unconditioned stimulus 48
unconscious motivation 40
young adulthood 45

Self-Check Answers

Box 2.1

1. One role of science is to make the world understandable. Finding a few principles that summarize the essence of a field is one way of making a field more understandable; however, it is possible that development may be so complex that a parsimonious theory would be inaccurate.
2. Breadth and parsimony do not necessarily conflict. Ideally, a theory should have both. However, it may be easier to have a broad theory that is *not* parsimonious.
3. A mathematical statement of a theory should be internally consistent and have the advantage of making clear, specific predictions.
4. Theories that provide a new perspective and make specific predictions are probably the ones that stimulate the most research (have the most heuristic value). Their new perspective gets people interested in testing them, and their specific predictions make testing possible.

Box 2.3

Part A:

1. True.
2. False. Freud emphasized the importance of the unconscious.
3. False. The ego is like an executive secretary/servant to the id.
4. False. The superego, not the ego, is concerned with morality.
5. True (for males).
6. False. Sex segregation occurs before the latency stage.
7. True.
8. True.
9. True.
10. False.

Part B:

11. Freud believed that we inherited an animalistic nature (the id); that, because of their evolutionary value, we have strong instinctual drives such as sex; that our animal nature struggled against society's rules; and that the genital stage set the stage for a family that would provide for the survival of their children.
12. Oral, anal, phallic, and genital.

Box 2.4

1. Both believe in unconscious process and in stages. Their views on the first 11 years of life are similar.
2. a. Erikson places more emphasis on the conscious ego (as exemplified by his belief that forming an identity is very important).

b. Erikson places more emphasis on social (nurture) factors as reflected by his focus on psychosocial conflicts
   c. Erikson includes adult development, thus his is the first lifespan developmental theory.
3. A disadvantage is that it means that Erikson's theory does not provide a unique perspective. On the other hand, if it is more accurate, then accuracy would more than compensate for its failing to provide a unique perspective. However, realize that just because Erikson's theory is more consistent with common sense does not necessarily make it more accurate.

Box 2.6

1. Case study.
2. Yes, if you believe the laws of learning, like the laws of gravity, apply to everyone.
   No, because one shouldn't generalize without a large, representative sample.
3. A control group would allow us to rule out the possibility that Peter simply "outgrew" his fear. The control group should be treated similarly to the treatment group in all respects except for the treatment. Therefore, the control group might be talked to about the value of bravery.
4. Increases in heart rate, self-report of fear, loudness of screaming when the rabbit was presented, and how close he would get to the rabbit are all possibilities.
5. a. Nurture.
   b. Change.

Box 2.7

1. Bandura's theory, because it claims we learn from models.
2. Correlational
3. Because it is correlational, it is risky to assume that exposure to models causes the residents to be more active. As a naturist would point out, it could be that grandparents who lived in the home were more alert and active than grandparents who did not live in the home (especially since some who were not living in the home were dead). The residents inheriting these genes would tend to be more active and alert. It could also be that families who brought the grandparent into the home were more caring, sociable, or energetic than those who did not. Any of these characteristics could have influenced the behavior of the nursing home residents.
4. Nurture; stability.

Box 2.8

Part A:

1. Stella has punished her parents for telling her to take a nap. Stella's parents should not reward Stella for crying. Otherwise, she may cry whenever her parents do something she disapproves of. Instead, her parents should try to extinguish the crying by ignoring it.
2. Smedley is using negative reinforcement to increase his parents' "bedtime story-reading behavior." The parents could ignore the crying to extinguish it.
3. Skinner would say it was a good idea because reinforcement increases behavior. You might disagree because (as Bandura would predict) the child would realize that he was studying because it was work he got paid for, not because he personally valued learning or achievement.
4. According to Skinner, this offer would encourage a long (but not necessarily happy) marriage by rewarding length (but not happiness) of marriage. Bandura would argue that this is a bad idea because the couple may think that they are staying together for extrinsic reasons (the money) rather than intrinsic reasons (love).

Part B: **5.** False. **6.** False.

Box 2.9

1. No, since we reach formal operations, the final stage of development, around age 11. Yes, because we are always assimilating and accommodating.
2. Piaget might say that the child is trying to assimilate the object via a sucking schema. Freud might say that the child can express sexual energy only through the mouth. Thus, whereas Piaget focuses on the way the child at the sensorimotor stage understands the world, Freud focuses on how the child at the oral stage releases sexual tension.
3. Freud would explain this as the result of the development of the superego, which occurs after the Oedipal complex is resolved. That is, the child internalizes the parent's rules to avoid coming into a dangerous conflict with the parent. Bandura might explain it in terms of children having more models (parents and peers), more experience with models, more ability to model, and having increased feelings of self-efficacy about being able to control their own behavior. Piaget would explain it in terms of entering the concrete operations stage, during which children are first able to understand rules.
4. Yes. Piaget believes that maturation drives development. Skinner would disagree, believing that nurture is essential. According to Skinner, without rewards, no school learning would take place. Conversely, with enough drill, practice, and reward, anything can be learned at almost any age.
5. Assimilation is the addition of information that fits one's existing views; accommodation is the change of existing views to fit new information.
6. Sensorimotor, preoperational, concrete operations, and formal operations.
7. Abstract, logical thought.

Box 2.10

1. No. Desire for food is a first-level need. Gambling would be hard to explain, but might reflect a need for status. However, even this explanation would not explain why a person would continue gambling even after gambling caused the breakup of the gambler's family.
2. Poverty would limit people to focusing only on lower-level needs.
3. Their marriages weren't allowing them to reach self-actualization. Or, they had reached self-actualization—self-actualizers often have strained interpersonal relationships.
4. He would interpret it as a search for self-actualization.
5. People at the lower levels of the pyramid (especially level 1) would fit the behavioristic model fairly well. People who are self-actualized, however, would behave in ways that would not be predicted by behaviorism.

6. Erikson says that people need to know who they are before they can have true intimacy in their relationships. Maslow says that until belongingness needs are met, status is not important.
7. Because your lower-level needs will be met more quickly, Maslow might predict that you would be better off in a rich, but cold family.

Box 2.12

1. You would be looking at things from only one perspective. Thus, you might miss out on insights that would be gained by looking at things from other viewpoints.
2. The self is not a servant to the id or a mere mediator of conflicts between the id and superego. Instead, it is a powerful, positive force for growth. Rogers would agree that bowing to standards imposed by others could hinder development.
3. "Conditions of worth" may also mean that we are punished for "unacceptable" behavior. Rogers claims that "conditions of worth" may cause people to try to be something they aren't. Behaviorists would argue that since people aren't born to be a particular way, they cannot be reinforced to behave in a way that is against their nature. However, punishment should be avoided whenever possible.
4. Children reject a principle their parents are encouraging because the parents don't consistently model the behavior, or because the children don't respect the parents, or because the parents are pushing the principle so hard that it is clearly the parent's value and not the child's.
5. Maslow believed that development is more discontinuous. Whereas Maslow believed that unsatisfied needs prevent self-actualized needs from being expressed, Rogers believed that "conditions of worth" prevent people from knowing their true selves, thereby blocking self-actualization.
6. Rogers would give the student unconditional regard that might help him decide whether he really wanted to go to college and that might help his self-esteem. Bandura would try to boost the student's self-efficacy, probably by having him succeed on some academic task.

3

Chapter

Genes and Environment

A mind is neither in pre-established coordination with reality nor molded from without. Rather, through a lengthy series of interchanges between the individual and environment, the coordination is gradually achieved.

HEINZ WERNER, 1957

Chapter Overview

How do we develop into the people we are? Not very long ago, people asked this question somewhat differently. Specifically, they asked: "Are we the product of a genetic program *or* have we been programmed by our environment?" However, we now know that we are the products of both nature *and* nurture. Consequently, today's experts go beyond asking whether people are the product of nature or nurture to asking the question that we will address in this chapter: How do genes and the environment interact to determine development?

YOUR BIOLOGICAL HERITAGE

It is very difficult to determine the effect of heredity by looking only at your present behavior because your present behavior has been affected by the environment. Recognizing this fact, researchers turned to studying newborn babies. However, studying newborns is not a perfect way to isolate the effect of heredity. Even if you had been studied the second you were born, your genetic program had already been influenced, perhaps dramatically so, by living about nine months in a unique environment: your mother's body. Therefore, if we want to find a time when you were influenced only by your genes, we would have to go back to the moment of your conception.

Conception

The process of conception is an odyssey beyond imagination. For most people, this odyssey begins when their mother's ovaries released an **ovum,** a ripe egg. Whether in the throes of passion or during a calculated attempt to conceive ("According to the thermometer, today's the day"), their father ejaculated about 300 million sperm into their mother. Of those millions of sperm, fewer than 20,000 reached the ovum alive.

The first of the sperm to reach the egg found it surrounded by a protective barrier. They tried to penetrate this barrier by releasing a digestive enzyme that ate through the ovum's protective coating. One sperm got in first, and the ovum immediately became impregnable to all other suitors.

Through this union of a single sperm with a single egg, a **zygote** was created. But how would this one-celled zygote develop into a human being? How could a single cell contain your biological heritage—a heritage that would strongly influence what you would look like, how smart you would be, how quickly you would learn to walk, how you would age, and even how you would die? How could this lone cell contain the information to make you unique? To answer these questions, you must understand the genetic code.

The Genetic Code

The vast amount of information constituting a genetic blueprint for development is carried in the 23 chromosomes you received from your mother's ovum and the 23 chromosomes you received from your father's sperm. **Chromosomes** are strands of DNA in the nuclei of cells that occur in pairs and carry genetic information. **DNA, or deoxyribonucleic acid,** is a complex molecule running the length of each chromosome that forms the genetic code. Along the length of each DNA molecule, are strung thousands of **genes,** the units of hereditary transmission. Since each gene contains a specific piece of information, the zygote that formed you contained an immense amount of information—enough to fill thousands of 1,000-page books (see box 3.1).

By taking advantage of some of its vast amount of information, the zygote created an exact copy of itself, using a process of cell division called **mitosis** (see figure 3.1). In mitosis a cell duplicates its 46 chromosomes, then divides in half to form two distinct cells. If this exact copy splits again on its own, then an identical twin develops. However, for most of us, this exact copy becomes our second cell. As mitosis continues, the two-celled organism changed to a four-celled organism to an eight-celled organism. Mitosis continued so that by the time you were born, you consisted of billions of cells.

Although all these billions of cells could be traced to that original zygote, all these cells were not identical copies of the first. Some cells became muscle, others became skin, and so forth. How could one cell create so many different cells? To understand how, imagine that we make three copies of a computer disk full of different programs. Then, we put the copies in three identical computers. In the first computer, we load the word processing package. In the second, we load the calculator program. In the third, we load the video game program. Naive users may perceive three different machines: a word processor, a calculator, and an arcade game. However, the only real difference is in which programs are activated. In a similar way, different cells, being copies of the original zygote, do not differ so much in what genes they have, but in which of their genetic programs are activated. Depending on which genes are activated, the cell becomes a muscle, skin, or brain cell. Thus, if the wrong genes were activated, almost anything would have been possible—from eyes turning to bone to the brain developing a tumor. Fortunately, the wrong genes are rarely activated because activation is not left up to chance. Instead, the genes are activated depending on where the cell is located and what surrounds it.

A single-celled zygote could therefore contain enough information to direct the creation of an infant. But how does the genetic program allow for siblings to differ from one another? After all, every normal zygote has 23 pairs of chromosomes. Furthermore, if everybody gets one member of each pair from their mother and the other member of each pair from their father, why don't family members look and act more alike? You'd think that at least some children from the same parents would be identical. Yet, no two zygotes are alike. (As we mentioned earlier, identical twins are alike because they come from the same zygote. Hence, identical twins are called **monozygotic** because *mono* means one).

To emphasize that no two zygotes are alike, realize that you share only about half your genes with each of your brothers and sisters—and this is true even if one of your siblings is your fraternal twin or **dizygotic** twin, a twin who comes from a second (*di* means two), entirely different zygote. Furthermore, realize that your mother and father could have produced more than

Figure 3.1

Mitosis Versus Meiosis

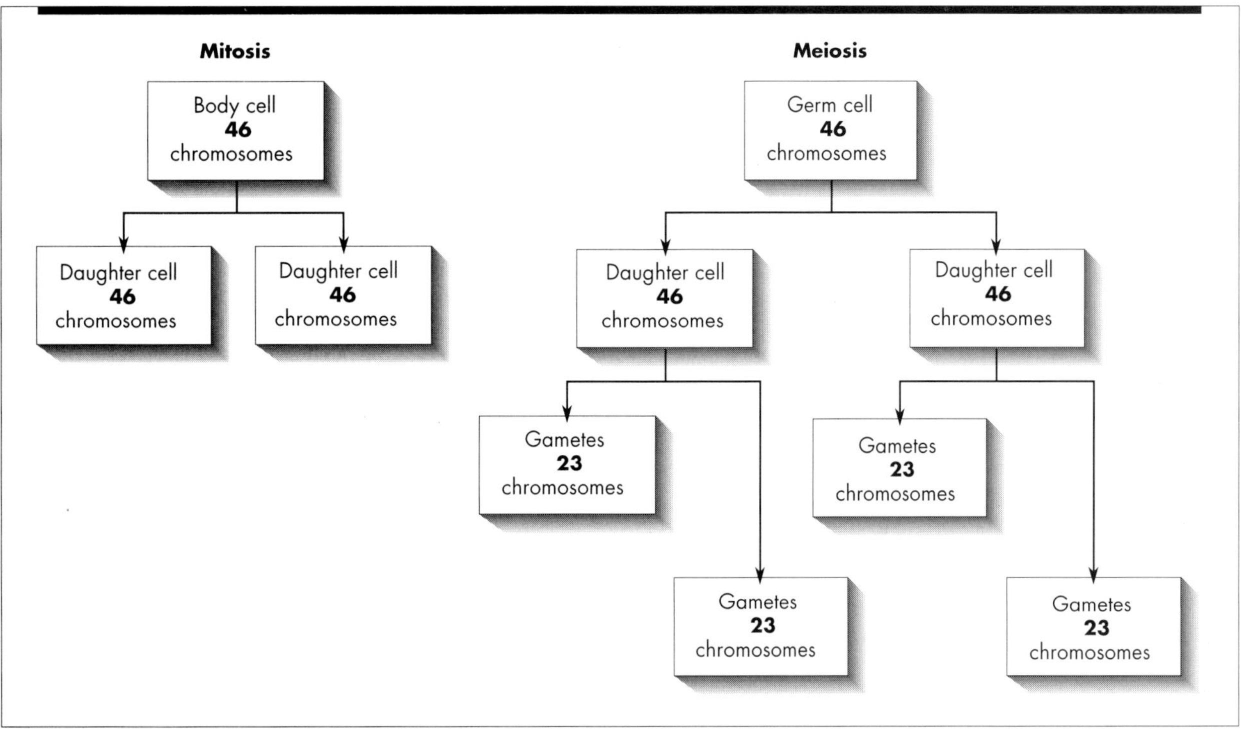

64,000,000,000,000 different zygotes. Thus, even if your mother and father had 64 trillion children together (and we know that's inconceivable), it is possible that none of those children would share your biological heritage. In fact, it's even possible that none of them would share each *other's* biological heritage. Each could be genetically unique. So, you aren't one in a million, you are one in 64 trillion!

With each parent contributing half of his or her genetic heritage to each zygote, how is it possible that the same parents could create so many different zygotes? To understand how this is possible, you need to realize that new cells are created in two different ways. Earlier in this chapter, you learned that most human cells are produced through the process of mitosis. In mitosis, a cell duplicates its genetic material and then divides in half. The result is two identical cells, each with 46 chromosomes. However, human sex cells are produced in a different way. Specifically, sex cells are produced through **meiosis.**

Meiosis does not result in two identical cells, each with 46 chromosomes. Instead, as you can see in figure 3.1, in meiosis, sex cells are formed in the testes or ovaries by converting a germ cell that has 46 chromosomes (23 pairs) into four **gametes** (sex cells) that each have 23 unpaired chromosomes.

As developmental psychology students, it is not vital to remember that meiosis results in four gametes. But it is vital to realize that two things happen during meiosis that ensure genetic variability.

First, early in meiosis, as a chromosome pair splits apart, they may, on some occasions, exchange genes, a process called **genetic reshuffling** or crossing-over. To picture genetic reshuffling, imagine one member of the chromosome pair as a slice of bread covered with peanut butter and the other member as a slice of bread covered with jelly. You then make a sandwich by pairing the two slices. If you separated the pair of slices, some of the jelly might stick to the peanut butter side and some of the peanut butter might stick to the jelly side. Because some of the peanut butter and some of the jelly have switched places, both original bread slices have been changed. In a similar way, genetic reshuffling alters both members of the original chromosome pair. Instead of having one member that is an exact copy of the chromosome obtained from the father (a bread slice with pure peanut butter) and an exact copy of the chromosome obtained from the mother (a bread slice with pure jelly), the chromosome obtained from the father now has been altered so it has one or two genes from the chromosome inherited from the mother (there's a little jelly on the peanut butter) and the chromosome obtained from the mother now has one or two genes from the chromosome

Box 3.1

RESEARCH in FOCUS

A Closer Look at the Chromosome

Researchers have unlocked many of the secrets of the genetic code. They have found that chromosomes are made up of strands of DNA, which in turn, is made up of thousands of genes. Genes, in turn, are made up of a string of thousands of molecules called **nucleotides** (see box figure 3.1A). Consequently, saying that your genetic program consists of only 46 chromosomes may be misleading since those 46 chromosomes are made up of 3 billion nucleotides that may contain 10 trillion bits of information.

Although we could talk about each of these 3 trillion nucleotides, most people refer to genes as the basic unit of heredity because genes carry information that influences or determines a specific trait. At the molecular level, a gene is any segment of a DNA molecule that is capable of producing a specific protein molecule. Following a blueprint laid down by the genes, DNA directs the synthesis of proteins—the basic building blocks of life. The kind of protein that will be built depends on the order in which nucleotides are sequenced along the "spine" of the DNA molecule. This sequencing is like a genetic Morse code. But rather than dots and dashes, your genetic code uses four nucleotides to spell out all the instructions your body needs for manufacturing proteins. As you can see from the box figure 3.1B, all four nucleotides are composed of sugar and phosphates. They differ from each other only in terms of what chemicals—adenine (A), thymine (T), cytosine (C), and guanine (G)—connect the sugar groups to each other. As you can also see from the box figure 3.1B, three nucleotides make up a genetic "word" and a gene is a sentence of these three-"letter" words. Note that even one mistake in the thousand-nucleotide-long code could spell disaster.

Continued

originally inherited from the father (a little peanut butter on the jelly). Thus, genetic reshuffling is one way that nature ensures genetic variety.

The second—and most important—source of genetic variability happens later in meiosis, after the pairs have split up. At that time, there is some chromosome shuffling, as one member of the chromosome pairs goes to one side of the cell and its partner goes to the other side of the cell. Then, the cell divides in the middle, leaving two sex cells, each with 23 chromosomes. The important point to realize is that, from your father's 23 pairs of chromosomes, one sperm doesn't get either the first member of every pair or the second member of every pair. A sperm might get the first member of the first chromosome pair, the second member of the second pair, the first member of the third pair, the first member of the fourth pair, the second member of the fifth pair, and so on.

Put another way, the first chromosome that one of your father's sperm cells received might be from your paternal grandfather, the second from your paternal grandmother, and the third from your paternal grandfather. Since any pattern of splitting up the 23 chromosome pairs is possible, there are at least 8 million (2 to the 23rd power) different ways that you could get half of your father's genetic material (see box 3.2).

Combining Chromosomes

How was your father's and mother's genetic information combined? The first step was for the 23 chromosomes from your mother and the 23 chromosomes from your father to pair up. For the first 22 pairs of chromosomes, each member of a pair always has a similar shape to the other so the members of the pairs match up well. However, this is not the case with the 23rd pair of chromosomes, the so-called sex chromosomes.

As with all chromosome pairs, your mother and father each contributed one chromosome to the 23rd pair. Your mother gave you an X-shaped chromosome, your father gave you either an X-shaped chromosome or a Y-shaped chromosome (see box 3.3). If your father contributed a Y, then you are probably a male (XY); if he contributed an X, then you are a female (XX). Note that the father, not the mother, determines the child's gender. Unfortunately, many people don't understand this. In China, both men and women blame the mother for the gender of the child: Men beat their wives for giving birth to a daughter, and some wives commit suicide out of shame of giving birth to a daughter. Even in Western society, we have a long tradition of talking about whether a wife met the obligation of "bearing her husband a son." (Henry the Eighth "lost" several wives through divorce and murder because they gave him only daughters, even though these daughters were the result of his X chromosomes.)[1]

[1]It should not surprise you to learn that saying the child's gender is entirely due to the male may be an oversimplification. Characteristics of the mother may affect whether X sperm or Y sperm are most likely to reach and penetrate the ovum.

Box 3.1

RESEARCH in FOCUS

Concluded

Box Figure 3.1A

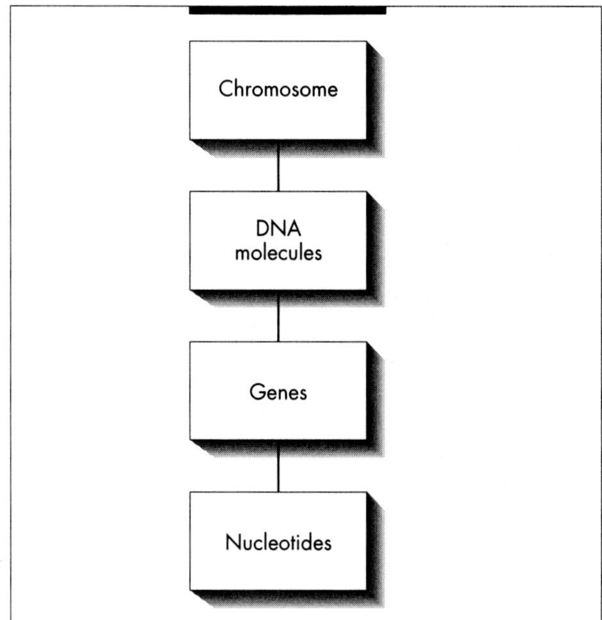

Box Figure 3.1B

DNA Molecule.

Watson-Crick structure of DNA molecule. Note that each side of the DNA molecule consists of alternating sugar and phosphate groups. Each sugar group is united to the sugar group opposite it by a pair of nitrogenous bases—adenine-thymine or thymine-adenine and cytosine-guanine or guanine-cytosine. Differences in the sequences of base pairs establish the identity of the many different kinds of DNA.

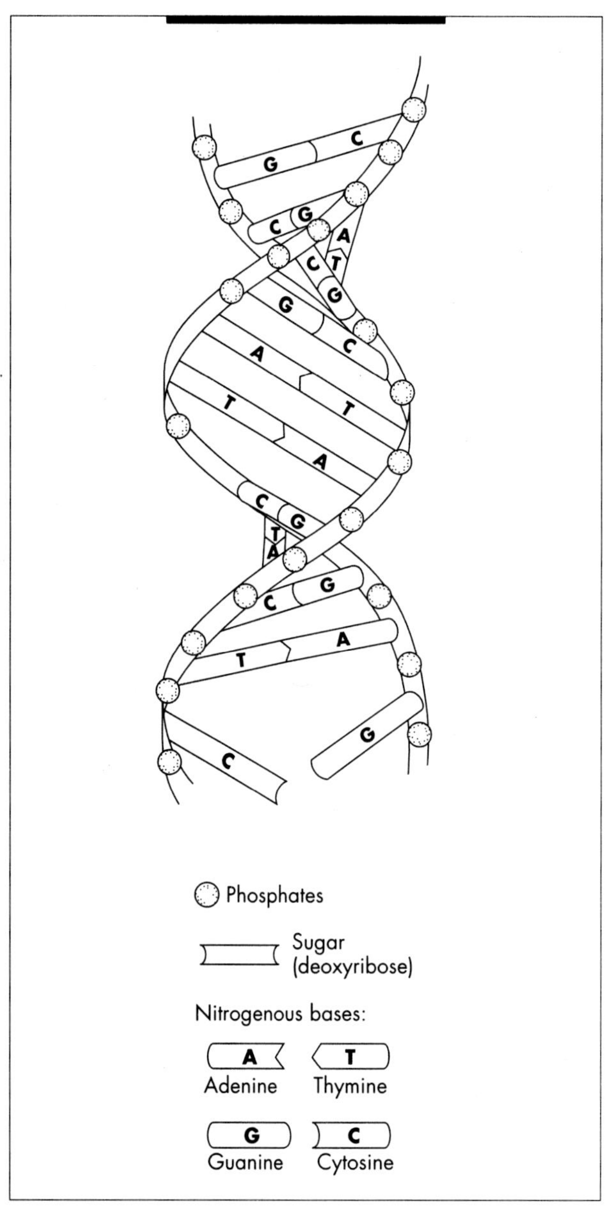

Box 3.2

RESEARCH in FOCUS

How Meiosis Is Like Tossing Coins

When you flip a coin, there are two equally likely possibilities: heads or tails. Similarly, when a given chromosome pair splits up during meiosis, there are two equally likely possibilities[1]: the sex cell (sperm or ovum) will get either the chromosome inherited from the individual's mother or the chromosome inherited from the individual's father. Thus, if humans had only one pair of chromosomes, your father would produce only two kinds of sperm, and your mother would produce only two kinds of ova. Since your mother would produce only two kinds of ova and your father only two kinds of sperm, together your parents would only be able to create four (2 × 2) different genetic combinations. Thus, if they had five children, at least two of them would be genetically identical!

But what if humans had 2 pairs of chromosomes? Then, the situation would be like flipping 2 coins: there would be 4 equally likely combinations. Since each parent would produce 4 different kinds of sex cells, together the parents could create 16 (4 × 4) different kinds of zygotes. In reality, humans have 23 pairs of chromosomes. Consequently, each parent isn't limited to producing 2 (2 to the first power) kinds of sex cells, as they would if humans had

Box Figure 3.2A

The Possibilities When Flipping One Coin

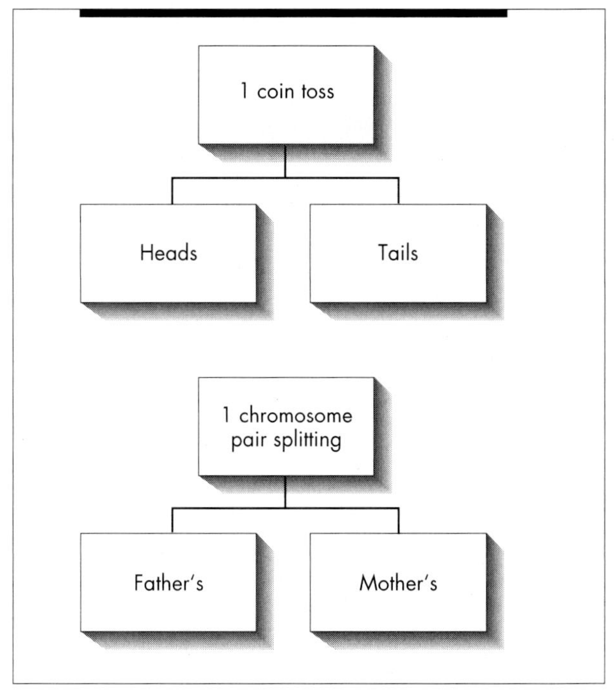

[1]For the sake of this example, we are ignoring the possibility of genetic reshuffling.

Continued

Combining Genes

Although different combinations of the 23rd pair of chromosomes (the so-called sex chromosomes) results in different genders, the main purpose of chromosomes pairing off is so that genes can pair off. Genes are chemical units that contain instructions for producing or influencing a specific trait. Every gene has its own address or **locus,** a specific location on a specific chromosome. To combine genetic information, then, the first step was for the chromosomes from your father and mother to pair off so that their loci matched up. Since chromosomes pair off so that genes match up, almost no human characteristics are affected by a single gene. Most must be controlled by at least a *pair* of genes. To be more precise, for each locus, there are two **alleles,** or specific forms of the gene. For instance, at the locus that determines the amount of hair people have on their legs, you might get two different kinds of alleles: a hairy legs allele from your father and a nonhairy allele from your mother. These alleles represent, for leg hair, your **genotype,** or genetic makeup. (To help keep genetic terminology straight, consult table 3.1.)

But what is your **phenotype,** how your genes are actually expressed? In other words, what do your legs actually look like? Predicting how hairy your legs would be from your genotype would have been simple if both your alleles for that trait had been **homozygous,** the same. That is, if both alleles were hairy, you would tend to be hairy; if both were not hairy, you would tend not to be hairy. But in our example, the alleles were **heterozygous,** or different. What happens when alleles are heterozygous?

Dominance and Recessiveness Thanks to the work of the nineteenth-century geneticist, Gregor Mendel, we can both understand and predict what will happen when alleles are heterozygous. Mendel's work began by

Box 3.2

RESEARCH in FOCUS

Concluded

just one pair of chromosomes) or even 4 different kinds of sex cells (2 to the second power), as they would if humans had two pairs of chromosomes, but 8 million (2 to the 23rd power). In other words, the number of possible combinations of sex cells each parent could produce is equal to the number of different possible combinations of heads and tails you could get from flipping 23 separate coins. Thus, together your mother and father would be capable of producing 64 trillion (8 million × 8 million) different zygotes—even without genetic reshuffling.

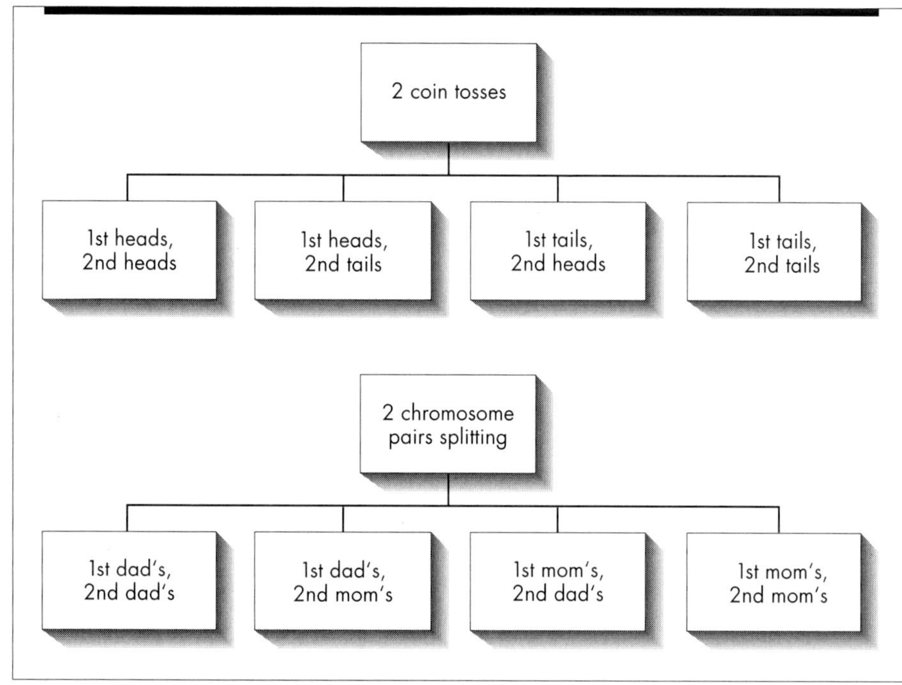

Box Figure 3.2B

The Possibilities When Flipping Two Coins

breeding pea plants that had been tall for generations with pea plants that had been short for generations. He found that all these hybrids turned out to be tall. The **dominant allele** in this case is for tallness. In other words, if present, the tall alleles were always expressed (that is, they dominated). The dwarf form of the gene, or **recessive allele,** receded into the background and was not expressed when paired with a dominant gene.

But what happened to the nonexpressed dwarf alleles? Were these recessive genes destroyed? The answer to this question became clear when Mendel bred his tall hybrids with one another. He found that one fourth of the offspring were short. Furthermore, when he bred these short offspring with one another, he *always* ended up with short offspring. Consequently, Mendel concluded that the dwarf allele had not been destroyed; it had just not expressed itself in the tall allele's presence.

As with sweet peas, when humans inherit heterozygous genes, the dominant version of the gene is expressed as the phenotype. Also as with the sweet peas, although the recessive allele lies dormant for this generation, its information may be passed on to future generations. Thus, two parents could be very similar to one another, yet, like the two tall, hybrid pea plants, give birth to a child who does not resemble either of them. This child may, however, strongly resemble one or more of the grandparents. Partly because of recessive traits, certain characteristics, such as grandmother's dimples or grandfather's blue eyes, may skip a generation. (See table 3.2 for a list of common dominant and recessive traits.)

Polygenic Traits Many people quickly grasp the idea of recessive and dominant traits. They understand that if both parents exhibit a dominant trait, the parents may be heterozygous for that trait, and so the child may not exhibit

Box 3.3

RESEARCH in FOCUS

Why Males Are Responsible for the Child's Gender

Genetically, what makes a male, is having an X and a Y chromosome. The Y chromosome must come from the father because, as you can see below, women's ova have only X chromosomes. Men, on the other hand, can produce two different kinds of sperm, X sperm and Y sperm.

1. What percentage of male and female offspring does this arrangement seem to assure? Why?
2. How could a society produce deviations from these percentages?
3. What do you think would be the effects of significant deviations from these percentages?
4. Why do you think male children have been more valued than female children?
5. Do you think parents should choose the gender of their child? Why or why not?

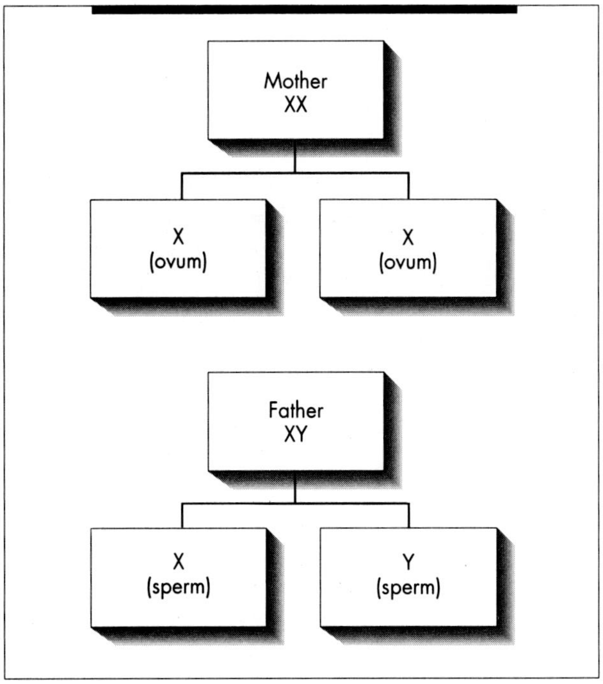

Mother
XX

X (ovum) | X (ovum)

Father
XY

X (sperm) | Y (sperm)

Please turn to the end of this chapter to check your answers.

that trait. Consequently, they are not shocked when two dimpled parents have a child who has no dimples. Furthermore, many people understand that if both parents exhibit a recessive trait, then both parents are homozygous for that trait. Therefore, the child will be homozygous for that trait and will exhibit that trait. Two nondimpled parents will almost always have children who are also nondimpled.

Some people not only understand the idea of recessive and dominant traits, but try to apply this knowledge. For example, if they exhibit a trait carried by recessive genes and they are particularly proud of that trait, they try to choose a mate who also exhibits that trait. In fact, we have known blue-eyed people who refused to marry anyone who didn't have blue eyes because they wanted blue-eyed children. However, many efforts at determining or predicting the characteristics of one's children are unsuccessful because most characteristics are **polygenic,** or influenced by many genes. For example, an individual's phenotype for such traits as intelligence and even eye color are the result of several different genes working together.

Genetic Defects

It may be fortunate that people cannot always choose a mate who will give them children with the desired characteristics, especially if these "good" characteristics, such as blue eyes, are only good because of an arbitrary whim of some segment of society. On the other hand, it may be unfortunate that people do not consider genetics when breeding because not all chromosomal and genetic combinations are ideal. In fact, one out of every seven babies in the United States is born with an obvious **congenital defect,** or birth defect (Apgar & Beck, 1974). Although some congenital defects are caused by environmental agents such as maternal use of drugs, many were inherited (Kopp & Kaler, 1989).

As you can see from looking at the inherited defects listed in table 3.3, most defects are produced by recessive genes. The tragedy of these recessive traits is that often neither the mother nor the father has the defect, yet they may unknowingly pass the gene on to their offspring. In a few of these cases, if the parents had known the risk, they would have chosen to be childless.

If a gene for a defect is dominant, at least one of the would-be parents usually knows there is a risk of passing that defect on because one of the parents has the defect. However, a few dominant defects are passed on because parents don't know they possess the trait until after they have conceived. One of the most tragic of these defects is **Huntington's chorea,** a gradual deterioration of the

Table 3.1

Common Terms Used in Genetics

Term	Definition
Allele	The specific form of a gene. Alternate forms of a gene at a given locus. For example, for the leg hair gene, there are at least two alleles: hairy leg allele, nonhairy leg allele.
Dominant alleles	An allele is dominant if it is always expressed when it is present.
Gene	A unit of instruction for producing a protein. A gene may determine or influence a specific trait. Different forms of a gene are called alleles, and people often use the terms *allele* and *gene* interchangeably.
Gene pairs	Since chromosomes pair off, even traits determined by a single gene are really controlled by a pair of genes, one obtained from one's mother, the other, from one's father. Gene pairs could also be called pairs of alleles.
Genotype	Genetic makeup. Differs from phenotype in that some of the genes (alleles) may not be expressed because they are recessive.
Locus	The place on a chromosome where a specific gene (allele) is located.
Meiosis	A process of cell division, resulting in a parent cell producing four offspring that each have half of the parent cell's genetic material. Thus, whereas the parent cell may have 46 chromosomes (23 pairs), the cells produced by meiosis would have only 23 chromosomes. Meiosis is used only for producing sperm and egg cells.
Mitosis	A process of cell division, resulting in a parent cell producing two offspring that each have an exact copy of the parent cell's genetic material. Thus, if the parent cell has 46 chromosomes (23 pairs), the cells produced by mitosis would also have 46 chromosomes.
Phenotype	The characteristics the individual actually exhibits. Because of the effect of the environment and the nature of recessive and dominant traits, an individual's phenotype (exhibited traits) may or may not coincide with the individual's genotype.
Recessive alleles	Recessive alleles do not express themselves if they are paired with a dominant form of the gene (allele).

Table 3.2

Common Dominant and Recessive Traits

Dominant Traits	Recessive Traits
Brown eyes	Blue eyes
Kinky hair	Wavy, straight hair
Normal hearing	Congenital deafness
Lack of pattern baldness	Pattern baldness
Dark hair	Light hair
Color vision	Color blindness
Poison ivy immunity	Poison ivy susceptibility
Presence of melanin	Albinism—lack of melanin
Double jointedness	Normal joints
Thick lips	Thin lips
Roman nose	Straight nose
Cheek dimples	No dimples
Extra, fused or short digits	Normal digits
Farsightedness	Myopia (nearsightedness)
Normal blood clotting	Hemophilia
Normal blood cells	Sickle-cell anemia
Normal metabolism	Phenylketonuria
Normal physiology	Tay-Sachs disease
Huntington's chorea	Normal brain and body maturation
Facial dimples	No facial dimples
Tongue roller	Nonroller
Bent little finger	Straight little finger
Mid-digital hair	No mid-digital hair
Widow's peak	Straight hair line
Can't bend thumb backward by more than 45 degrees	Hitchhiker's thumb
Big toe shorter than second toe	Big toe substantially bigger than second toe

nervous system resulting in the progressive decline of physical and mental abilities. Because Huntington's chorea usually strikes after the age of 40 (Thompson & Thompson, 1986), carriers frequently pass the trait on before they realize the risk. Now, because of a recent breakthrough, people can be tested for the rare Huntington's chorea allele that we know has its locus on chromosome 4. People who believe that they may be carriers can find out before the disease strikes and before they decide to have children. However, many of those who are at risk don't want to take the test. For some, an uncertain future may be easier to live with than a known death sentence.

If you were at risk, would you want to know whether or not you had the allele? On the one hand, learning that you didn't have the allele would release you from worrying about Huntington's. Even learning that you did have it might help you plan your life and decide whether to have children. On the other hand, knowing that you had the

SELF-CHECK

1. What is the difference between an allele and a gene?
2. What is the difference between a genotype and a phenotype?
3. What is the significance of the fact that each gene has a locus? *Hint:* Would dominance and recessiveness be relevant if genes did not have loci?
4. What is the difference between meiosis and mitosis?
5. What would happen to the number of chromosomes humans have if sex cells (sperm and ova) reproduced by mitosis?
6. What is the difference between heterozygous and homozygous?
7. If a person is homozygous, will their phenotype reflect their genotype? Why or why not?
8. If a person is heterozygous, will their phenotype reflect their genotype? Why or why not?
9. Why are the most deadly genetic defects recessive?
10. Arrange the following in order of complexity: nucleotides, chromosomes, genes, DNA molecules.
11. What is the difference between monozygotic and dizygotic twins?
12. Why might it be theoretically possible to take a live skin cell from an individual, and from that single cell, clone a genetic duplicate of the person?
13. Which is a more important source of genetic variability—genetic reshuffling or "chromosome shuffling"?
14. Who determines the child's gender? Why?
15. "To know what the child will look like, don't look at the parents, look at the grandparents." Why might this statement have some validity?
16. What would happen if extraversion was controlled by a single gene and that gene only had two alleles—shy and outgoing—and shy was the dominant allele?

Please turn to the end of this chapter to check your answers.

Singer Arlo Guthrie has decided not to be tested to see if he carries the allele for Huntington's chorea, the disease that killed his father, Woody Guthrie. What would you decide in his situation?

allele would also make you dread the inevitable decline of your mental andphysical abilities. Furthermore, it would make you feel even more responsible if you had a child who carried the allele.

Sex-Linked Defects

Usually, if you exhibit a recessive defect, you received a gene for that defect from both your mother *and* from your father. However, this rule does not hold for **sex-linked defects,** defects that are the result of genes that appear on the X chromosome, but not on the Y. If a male receives a recessive allele for a sex-linked defect on his X chromosome (the chromosome he received from his mother), his phenotype will express that trait because there is no allele on his Y chromosome to counteract the defect. If a female, on the other hand, receives a recessive gene for a sex-linked defect on one of her two X chromosomes, she will not necessarily have the defect. If her matching allele on the other X chromosome is dominant for normal development, her phenotype will not express the defective trait. However, she may be a carrier for the defect, passing it on to future generations. Partly because of sex-linked defects, the odds of having an inherited defect are greater for men than women.

Table 3.3

Descriptions of Major Recessive Hereditary Defects

Defect	Description
Cystic fibrosis	A fatal disease that occurs about 1 in 1,000 births. The child lacks an enzyme that stops mucus from obstructing the lungs and digestive tract. Few people who inherit this condition survive beyond adolescence. Over 10 million Americans are carriers who can transmit the gene for cystic fibrosis to their offspring.
Diabetes mellitus	The person is unable to metabolize sugar properly because the body does not produce enough insulin. If untreated, diabetes is usually fatal. However, the disease can be controlled by taking insulin and restricting one's diet. Diabetes usually appears in late adulthood, although as many as 1 child in every 2,500 is diabetic. The locus for a rare form of the disease is located on chromosome 11.
Hemo-chromatosis	The person suffers from iron poisoning because the small intestine absorbs much more iron than the body needs. Symptoms usually don't occur until the person is in his or her 40s. Because the symptoms resemble arthritis, diabetes, and cirrhosis, hemochromatosis is often misdiagnosed as one of these other conditions. Consequently, the disease is perceived as rare although it may actually be one of the most common genetic disorders.
Hemophilia	A condition sometimes called "bleeder's disease." The child lacks a substance that causes the blood to clot. Consequently, the child could bleed to death if scraped, bruised, or cut. The locus for both types of this disease is on the X chromosome.
Muscular dystrophy (MD)	There are more than ten forms of this genetic disease, which attacks the muscles. As the disease progresses, the individual becomes unable to walk and may gradually lose most or all motor capabilities. Occasionally MD causes death. Becker's MD and Duchenne's muscular dystrophy are both located on the X chromosome. About 1 in 4,000 males will develop Duchenne's disease; more than 100,000 Americans have inherited some form of MD.
Phenyl-ketonuria (PKU)	The child lacks an enzyme necessary to digest foods (including milk) that contain the amino acid phenylalanine. If this condition is not detected and the child is not placed on a diet of milk substitutes, phenylpyruvic acid will accumulate in the body and attack the developing nervous system. Long-term effects of untreated PKU are hyperactivity and severe mental retardation. PKU occurs in 1 of every 10,000 Caucasian births and is much less frequent among people of African or Asian heritage.
Sickle-cell anemia	A blood disorder found in people of African heritage where the red blood cells have a peculiar flattened shape (normal red blood cells are spherical). The sickle-shaped red blood cells are fragile and so they clog small blood vessels. The blocked circulation kills off tissue, thereby leading to pneumonia, rheumatism, heart disease, and kidney failure.
Tay-Sachs (infantile amaurotic idiocy)	A degenerative disease of the nervous system that always kills its victims, usually by their third birthday. It primarily affects Jewish children of Eastern European ancestry. Approximately 1 in 30 American Jews is a carrier.
Thalassemia	An anemia related to sickle-cell, but found in people of Mediterranean origin.

A common sex-linked trait is color blindness. The recessive gene for color blindness is carried on the X chromosome. Since it is recessive, if a female receives the color-blind allele from only one parent, she will not suffer from color blindness. On the other hand, a male who gets the allele will express the trait because it's his only allele for that trait: his Y chromosome doesn't have the gene. Consequently, men are at least five times more likely to be color blind than women.

A sex-linked defect that has attracted a great deal of recent attention is the **fragile X syndrome,** so-called because a certain part of the X chromosome tends to break during preparation of cell cultures. Some experts believe that the fragile X chromosome may be the second leading chromosomal cause of mental retardation (Barnes, 1989; Nussbaum & Ledbetter, 1986). For men, having a weakness in their one and only X chromosome usually results in retardation. For women, the effect of having one weak X chromosome is not as dramatic because women have two X chromosomes (Nussbaum & Ledbetter, 1986; Opitz & Sutherland, 1984). Consequently, the fragile X syndrome may be the reason men are more likely to suffer from mild retardation than women.

Mental retardation and color blindness are not the only sex-linked traits. As you can see from table 3.4, several genetic problems are more likely to afflict men than women.

Detection and Prevention of Inherited Disorders Can anything be done to prevent inherited defects? Although scientists are optimistic that they will soon be able to repair or alter unwanted genes, often the only thing that can be done is for carriers to abstain from reproduction. However, not reproducing has its costs: the world might be deprived of another Jonas Salk or Mother Teresa.

Box 3.5

RESEARCH in FOCUS

Passing on Dominant Defect Versus Passing on Recessive Defect

As you have seen, for almost all genes, one allele comes from the father and one from the mother. Since both parents got an allele from each of their parents, they each have two alleles for the trait. Consequently, there are four (2 × 2) possible gene pairs their child could receive. Therefore, for genes that have only two alleles, the child has a one in four chance of inheriting any given combination. This fact is important in estimating the risks of birth defects. For example, let's assume that "D" is the dominant defective gene and "n" is the recessive normal gene. In this situation, if one parent has the defect, then that parent carries either a Dn or a DD combination.

Box Table 3.5A

Mother is heterozygous for the defect

		Ova	
		D	**n**
Sperm	n	nD **defect**	nn **no defect**
	n	nD defect	nn no defect

= Half (2/4) with defect
Half (2/4) without it

Box Table 3.5B

Mother is homozygous for the defect

		Ova	
		D	**D**
Sperm	n	nD **defect**	nD **defect**
	n	nD defect	nD defect

= All have defect

Continued

What should prospective parents do? One thing parents might consider is genetic counseling. A genetic counselor can determine whether one or both potential parents are carriers and then calculate the probabilities of passing on the gene (see box 3.5). Based on knowing the probabilities of passing on the gene and the severity of the disorder, the couple can make an informed decision about what to do. If the probability of a defect is relatively low, people may decide to play the odds. If the probability is high, they may decide not to gamble. Indeed, in some communities of Hasidic Jews, couples are screened before arranged marriages to avoid pairing a man and woman who each carry an allele for the fatal Tay-Sachs disease.

Before conception, modern science can let prospective parents know the odds of producing a defective fetus. Soon after conception, modern technological procedures such as amniocentesis and chorionic villi biopsy can let couples know whether or not their fetus has a genetic defect. However, both of these technological procedures are controversial and both may occasionally lead to miscarriages (Butter, 1993).

In **amniocentesis,** a needle is inserted into the amniotic sac that surrounds the fetus, and fluid is removed. This fluid contains skin cells that have been sloughed off by the fetus. By examining these cells, more than 75 chromosomal and metabolic disorders can be detected (Fuchs & Cederquist, 1978). However, there are two drawbacks to amniocentesis. First, although the technique is relatively safe, it may lead to miscarriages in up to 1 percent of all cases. Second, it can be performed only between the 14th and the

Box 3.5

RESEARCH in FOCUS

Concluded

As you can see from box table 3.5A, if the parent with the dominant defect (in this case, the mother) is heterozygous for that trait, the odds of the child having the defect are 50 percent (assuming the other parent does not also have the defect).

If, however, the parent with the defect (in this case, the mother) is homozygous for the particular dominant defect, then the chances of the offspring having the trait are 100 percent.

By extending this logic to all possible cases, we can construct the following table:

Box Table 3.5C

Probability Child Will Have Defect

	Defect Is Dominant	Defect Is Recessive
Both parents are homozygous for defect.	100%	100%
Both parents are homozygous for normal gene.	0%	0%
Both parents are heterozygous.	75%	25% (but there's a 75% chance that the child will either have it or be a carrier)
One parent is homozygous for the normal gene; one is homozygous for defect.	100%	0% (but there's a 100% chance that the child will be a carrier)
One parent is homozygous for the normal gene, but the other is heterozygous.	50%	0% (but there's a 50% chance that the child will be a carrier).
One parent is homozygous for defect; the other is heterozygous.	100%	50% (but there's a 100% chance that the child will either have the defect or be a carrier)

Table 3.4

Descriptions of Major Sex-Linked Hereditary Defects

Defect	Description
Becker's muscular dystrophy and Duchenne's muscular dystrophy	Both are genetic diseases that attack the muscles.
Bipolar disorder	The person is susceptible to excessive mood swings.
Cleft palate	The child is born with a groove in the roof of the mouth.
Diabetes insipidus	The person suffers intense thirst and urinates excessively because the body fails to produce enough antidiuretic hormone.
Hemophilia A & B	Both are characterized by excessive bleeding.
Parkinsonism	A disease that strikes late in life. It begins with muscular tremors or shaking. As the disease progresses, weakness, paralysis, and death are possible.
Retinitis pigmentosa	A leading cause of blindness.

16th week of pregnancy. Usually, it takes another two weeks to get the test results, leaving little time to consider terminating the pregnancy if an abnormality is found. For this reason, more people are turning to **chorionic villi biopsy,** a more risky procedure (it may induce miscarriages in as many as 5 percent of all cases) that permits testing as early as the eighth week after conception (Begley, Carey, & Katz, 1984). A catheter is inserted through the mother's cervix into the **chorion,** a membrane that provides nourishment to the fetus. As the fetus grows, some cells are sloughed off and can be found in the chorion. Once the fetal cells are extracted from the chorion, the fetal cells can be tested for the same abnormalities as in amniocentesis.

If the results of these tests show that the fetus is free of genetic defects, this technology has given parents some peace of mind. But what if an abnormality is found? Moral, religious, and personal beliefs often conflict with harsh reality. If you found out you were the parent of a defective fetus, what would you do—prepare to receive a defective child into your home, terminate the pregnancy, or plan to put the baby up for adoption? Box 3.6 addresses this issue in greater depth.

In addition to testing for genetic defects, prenatal genetic testing can also determine the sex of the fetus. Like many technological advances, genetic testing has proven to be a double-edged sword. Many people feel that knowing the sex of their child before it's born would help them prepare. For example, they would know what color of clothes to buy or what color to paint the nursery. On the other hand, some people plan to have only one child, and a few of these people want to ensure that the child is the preferred sex, usually male. If the fetus is female, the woman may abort, and try again, until she conceives a male. Although this may seem to be a shocking new development, female infanticide has been common throughout the history of our species. From ancient Sparta to modern day China, parents have killed their daughters while treasuring their sons.

Chromosomal Defects

Thus far, we have discussed congenital defects, such as diabetes, muscular dystrophy, and sickle-cell anemia, that are the result of getting "bad" genes from one's parents. However, not all congenital defects are the result of defective genes. Some inherited defects are due to chromosomal abnormalities, most of which result from faulty meiosis producing faulty sperm or eggs.

Down Syndrome

Most chromosomal abnormalities are fatal, preventing the embryo from surviving past the first trimester (Elseth & Baumgardner, 1984). However, some chromosomal abnormalities are not so immediately life-threatening. The most common of these is **Down syndrome,** a condition characterized by mild mental retardation, a cheerful disposition, and a distinctive physical appearance. People with Down syndrome have almond-shaped eyes with eyefolds, round heads with a sloping forehead, webbed fingers and toes, a thick tongue, dental abnormalities, and a flat-footed walk (see figure 3.2). There are two major types of Down syndrome: (1) translocation of chromosome 21, and (2) nondisjunction of chromosome 21 (Magenis, Overton, Chamberlin, Brady, & Lorrien, 1977).

Figure 3.2

Down Syndrome Child

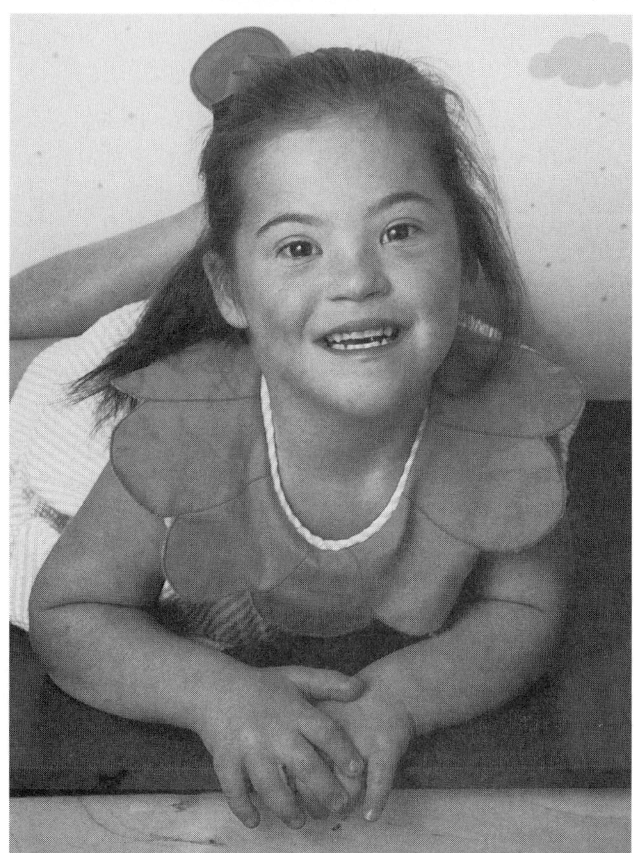

In **translocation,** part or all of one of the 21st chromosomes is in the wrong location. Instead of pairing off with the other 21st chromosome, it has attached to another chromosome pair (usually to chromosome 14). Thus, although the person has the normal number of chromosomes (46), the chromosomes aren't in the right location. Instead of having 23 pairs of chromosomes, the individual has one trio of chromosomes (usually a pair of chromosome 14s combined with part or all of a 21); one lone 21st chromosome; and 21 normal chromosome pairs.

In **nondisjunction,** by far the most common form of Down syndrome, the person has an extra 21st chromosome because one of the parent's 21st chromosome pairs fails to split apart during meiosis (see figure 3.3). With one parent contributing two 21st chromosomes and the other contributing one, the child ends up, not with a pair of 21st

Box 3.6

ISSUE in FOCUS

Thinking It Through: The Risk of Passing on a Genetic Defect

1. Suppose one of the siblings of the person you were to marry had the following conditions, but your prospective spouse did not. If you two had a child, what would be the probability of the child having that condition? For the purposes of this exercise, assume your prospective spouse is heterozygous for the trait if the defect is recessive. Assume that you are heterozygous for the trait if the defect is recessive and runs in your family.
2. If the defective trait is dominant and your prospective spouse does not have the trait, what must your prospective spouse's genotype be? If the defective trait is dominant and you do not have the trait, what must your genotype be? Is this true even if the trait runs in your family?
3. If your prospective spouse's sibling has Tay-Sach's, what must the genotype of your prospective spouse's parents be?
4. In general, when it comes to your own offspring, would it be better if the genetic problem afflicting your prospective spouse's sibling were dominant or recessive? Why?
5. If someone you loved had a family history of a genetic problem, would that stop you from marrying that person? Why? If it would, what defects and what level of risk for those defects, would you consider unacceptable?
6. If your spouse had a family history of a genetic problem, would that stop you from having children with that person? Why? If so, what defects and what level of risk for those defects, would you consider unacceptable? Would you consider adoption? Why or why not?
7. Under what circumstances, if any, would you consider amniocentesis or chorionic villi sampling? Why?
8. Just under 50 percent of people who find out through amniocentesis or chorionic villi sampling that the fetus is defective abort the fetus. What would you do in similar circumstances? Why? What arguments would people who disagree with your position make?
9. Could you put a child with a serious genetic defect up for adoption? Why or why not?

Please turn to the end of this chapter to check your answers.

Box Table 3.6

Condition	Is the Defect Recessive or Dominant?	Does It Run in Your Family?	Approximate Odds of First Child Having Trait
Cystic fibrosis			
Diabetes			
Hemophilia			
Huntington's chorea			
MD			
PKU			
Sickle-cell			
Tay-Sachs			

chromosomes, but with *trisomy 21*, three (*tri* means "three") 21st chromosomes. As you might expect, people suffering from nondisjunction have 47 chromosomes, rather than the normal 46.

We don't know the cause of nondisjunction. However, we do know that babies born to older mothers, especially mothers over 40, are much more likely to have this form of Down syndrome than are babies born to younger mothers. One hypothesis is that as the mother's ova age, the risk of abnormalities increases (the mother's ova are as old as she is). However, some research suggests that 25 percent of Down syndrome can be attributed to defective sperm (Magenis et al., 1977). Thus, it has been argued that babies with older mothers also tend to have older fathers and that older fathers are more likely than younger fathers to produce defective sperm.

Table 3.5

Sex Chromosome Abnormalities

Sex Chromosomes	Description
Klinefelter's syndrome—XXY	These men may look "feminine" because they have developed breasts and a broad-hipped female figure. These men are sterile. Psychologically, they are often impulsive and have below average intelligence.
Supermale syndrome—XYY (YYYY . . .)	These men tend to have persistent acne and are below average in intelligence.
Turner's syndrome—XO	These women may not have ovaries. If they have ovaries, their ovaries are underdeveloped. Consequently, they are unable to menstruate or ovulate. In addition, their breasts also tend to be underdeveloped. The skin on their neck is webbed. They tend to have around normal intelligence, but they have trouble with spatial tasks and handwriting.
Poly-X syndrome—XXX	These women appear to be normal. That is, they have normal secondary sexual development. Furthermore, they may be of normal intelligence. However, they often have poor verbal skills and a poor short-term memory.

Figure 3.3

Karotype of Down Syndrome

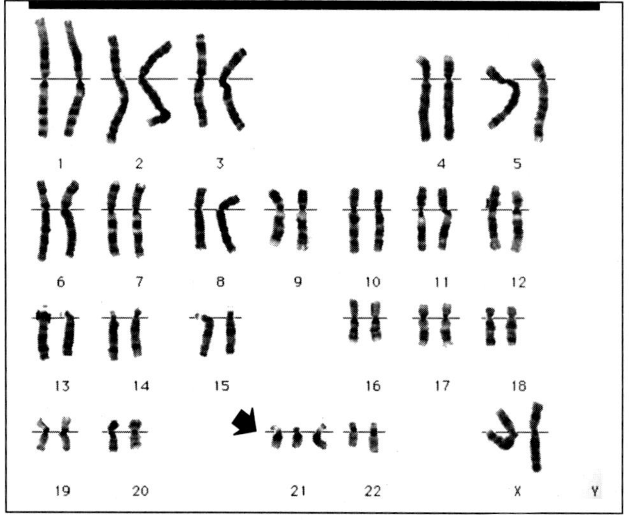

Sex Chromosome Abnormalities

Down syndrome is the only form of chromosomal abnormality involving the first 22 chromosomes in which the individual survives through infancy with any regularity. However, most chromosomal abnormalities concerning the 23rd chromosome—the sex chromosomes—do not threaten the individual's survival. In fact, some women with an extra X chromosome (XXX) and many males with an extra Y (XYY) live normal lives. However, some sex chromosomal abnormalities, such as (XO) severely increase the risk of fetal death, and some (XXY) tend to cause sterility and mental retardation. For more information about sex chromosome abnormalities, see table 3.5.

Genes Beyond Conception

The role of genes starts, but by no means ends, at conception. As you've seen in the case of Huntington's chorea and as you'll see in the next chapter, genes play a major role in physical development throughout life. For example, genes influence when a person reaches puberty, when a man starts to go bald, and when a woman begins menopause. Genes even play a role in death because most cells are genetically programmed to divide about 50 times—rapid aging and death may occur when this genetic program runs out.

The influence of genes is not limited to physical development. Psychological factors such as intelligence and personality are also strongly linked to the genetic program. In fact, as you can see from box 3.8, some people believe that genes play a strong role in how individuals and societies behave. However, most people would *not* say that genes cause certain psychological traits. Rather, most would argue that the interaction of genes and the environment produce these traits.

One of the first people to point out that genes interact with the environment at a wide variety of levels was Donald Hebb (1966). As you can see from table 3.6, Hebb felt that genes interacted with the chemical and the physical environment to affect development.

Hebb also realized that *when* things happen to you is almost as important as *whether* they happen to you. To emphasize this point, developmental psychologists have coined the term **sensitive period** to describe a period during which a certain skill or characteristic is most influenced by environmental events. How long is a sensitive period? When is the sensitive period? The time during which the environment is critical depends on the skill or characteristic. For example, the sensitive period

Box 3.7

SELF-CHECK

1. If a person has a defect that is carried by a dominant gene, how could you tell whether the person is heterozygous or homozygous for that trait? (*Hint:* What would be the characteristics of the person's parents?)
2. Both members of a couple have a genetic defect. Their first child is due in 7 months. For the sake of the child, would it be better if the defect was recessive or dominant? Why?
3. Neither member of a couple has a particular genetic defect. However, that defect does run in both their families. Their first child is due in 7 months. For the sake of that child, would it be better if the defect was recessive or dominant? Why?
4. A woman has a recessive genetic defect. She would like to have a child. Therefore, she wants to go to a sperm bank where they can identify a donor who is homozygous for the dominant, normal form of the allele. Do you think she should be allowed to do this? Why or why not?
5. Why are the deadliest genetic defects recessive?
6. What would happen to the Huntington's chorea allele if the onset of Huntington's was at birth rather than much later in life?
7. Why are men more likely than women to be color blind? to be mentally retarded?
8. Which is the riskier procedure: amniocentesis or chorionic villi biopsy? Why do some people opt for the riskier procedure?
9. Early research found that XYY males were more likely to be in jail than XY males. On this basis, it was concluded that the XYY male tended to be more aggressive. Now, it appears that this conclusion was incorrect. Why was this conclusion incorrect? (*Hint:* look at other characteristics of the supermale syndrome.)
10. Which is the most common form of Down syndrome? How do the two forms differ?
11. Older mothers are more likely to give birth to babies suffering from nondisjunction. What explanations can you offer for this fact?

Please turn to the end of this chapter to check your answers.

for acquiring a first language is between age 2 and the onset of puberty (Johnson & Newport, 1989; Lenneberg, 1967), whereas the sensitive period for sex-role assignment is reported to be during the first 18 months (Money & Annecillo, 1987; Money & Erhardt, 1973).

Table 3.6

Hebb's Model Versus More Simplified Views

Oversimplified model (the view many held before Hebb): Development is the product of genes.

Hebb's model: Development is the product of genes and their *interactions* with:

- Chemicals in the prenatal environment (alcohol, nicotine, thalidomide);
- Chemicals in the postnatal environment (lead, steroids, zinc, iron, protein);
- Sensory stable factors (things everyone is exposed to, such as language and a nurturant caregiver); and
- Sensory variable factors (things that not everyone is exposed to, such as different peer groups and educational opportunities).

We do not mean to imply, however, that all sensitive periods occur after birth. Perhaps the most important set of sensitive periods is before birth when our bodies are most susceptible to damage from drugs and diseases.

Chemical Influences on Development

Our bodies rely on absorbing chemicals from the outside environment in order to grow and sustain physical functions. Although many chemicals are beneficial, our bodies can also be harmed by many chemical agents. Hebb categorized these chemical agents into those that influence prenatal development and those that influence postnatal development.

Prenatal Influences: Teratogens

During the transformation of a zygote into a newborn baby, many things can alter its genetic course. Substances that may alter the genetic course are called **teratogens,** literally "monster makers." Teratogens often work by creating **mutations,** chemical changes in the genetic code that lead to changes in the genotype. The precise outcome of these mutations depends on both the developmental stage of the fetus and the teratogenic agent. As a rough but convenient way of categorizing fetal development, people often break fetal development into three trimesters, a three-month period of pregnancy. As you will see, the general rule is that fetuses are most susceptible to teratogens during the first trimester. There are four categories of teratogens: diseases, drugs, maternal malnutrition, and radiation (see table 3.7 for a summary).

Diseases

Most maternal diseases have their greatest impact between the 3rd and 12th week after conception (see figure 3.4). If a mother contracts a disease *after* the first trimester, there

Box 3.8

THEORY in FOCUS

Sociobiology

Many people believe that evolution and heredity have played major roles in determining human physical characteristics. Sociobiologists take evolution and heredity one step farther. Specifically, they believe that evolution and heredity have shaped human psychological characteristics and human societies.

Most people accept the idea that inherited psychological traits play a role in some animal societies. The complex, social behaviors of ant and bee colonies, of wolf packs, and of migrating animals such as birds and whales are commonly accepted examples of genes that influence social behavior.

But isn't human social behavior different? Sociobiologists argue that human social behavior isn't that different from the social behavior of other animals. To support this claim, they make two points. First, according to evolution, we evolved from lower animals. Consequently, we share some basic similarities to them. Second, nonhuman animals exhibit some humanlike characteristics, such as sacrificing for the good of the group, being territorial, adopting orphaned children, having sex roles, and engaging in warfare.

But do we really inherit social behavior? Sociobiologists argue that we do, and they cite as evidence certain cultural universals, or things that are done in every culture studied. For example, all cultures have taboos against incest. Some sociobiologists also claim that all societies are territorial and that all engage in aggressive acts. If people living in widely different environments all share certain common characteristics, then these commonalties may be due to inherited predispositions.

Sociobiologists would say that we inherit these tendencies for the same reason the baby giraffe inherits a long neck: it aids the survival of the species. Due to natural selection, maladaptive behaviors and traits were killed off, whereas adaptive behaviors were passed on. Thus, because incest often leads to defective genetic combinations, we are programmed to make incest taboo. Similarly, because the aggressive and territorial survived and killed off the peaceful and nonterritorial, aggressive and territorial genes survived and were passed on.

Although it might be easy to understand how natural selection would encourage people to be aggressive, what about other traits, such as altruism or helping others? Shouldn't you only be concerned about your own survival? Why bother to help others? Sociobiologists point out that if you help someone, that person will be more likely to help you out when you're in trouble. Thus, altruism may not be as unselfish as you might think. Furthermore, sociobiologists argue that you are most likely to help out someone who is genetically related to you. For instance, you would probably be more likely to help your niece than to help a total stranger. By helping people who are genetically similar to you, you ensure that your genes survive—and according to sociobiology, getting your genes to survive is what life is all about. Thus, according to sociobiologists, a parent who dies saving her two children from a fire, was selfishly ensuring that her genes would survive. Although she wasn't conscious of it, she was doing precisely what natural selection had programmed her to do.

But if our behavior is so strongly influenced by genes, where are those genes? Sociobiologists argue that genetic predispositions are not contained on any single gene, but are polygenic. Thus, tracking down the genes that cause these behaviors would be extremely difficult.

As you might expect, sociobiology is not without its critics. Many people feel it overestimates the role of nature and ignores the role of nurture. A substantial number of people feel that sociobiology, by arguing that we just do what comes naturally, provides a justification for racism and sexism in our society. Whatever the truth about sociobiology, one thing is certain: it has stimulated a lot of debate.

1. Do you think it is accurate to say that both ants and humans engage in altruism? Why or why not?
2. Do you accept the argument that since all societies engage in a certain practice, it must be part of human nature? What would a behaviorist say?
3. Do you believe that warfare, aggression, and territoriality are all cultural universals?
4. Do you think there is such a thing as human nature or do you agree with Locke's idea of humans being blank slates? Do you think we have predispositions? Do you think we have instincts? Why?
5. "Genes only make proteins; they cannot map out behavior." How might a sociobiologist respond to such a statement?

Please turn to the end of this chapter to check your answers.

Table 3.7

Adverse Prenatal Influences: Common Teratogens

Agent	Possible Outcomes
Diseases	
Acquired Immune Deficiency Syndrome (AIDS)	May cause child to be born with AIDS, eventually resulting in the child's death.
Influenza (flu)	May retard intellectual development, and some evidence suggests that it may increase the chances of the child developing schizophrenia.
Mumps and polio	May retard intellectual development.
Rubella (German measles)	May cause heart disease, cataracts, deafness, and mental retardation.
Syphilis	May kill fetus or cause bone, liver, and brain damage (if not treated before the end of the first trimester).
Toxemia	This condition, which may result in premature birth and anoxia (oxygen deprivation), results when poisons created in the mother's body poison the fetus. An infection could be responsible for the poisoning or the mother's own waste products may poison the inter-uterine environment.
Toxoplasmosis	Can lead to prenatal blindness and serious brain damage.
Drugs	
Accutane	Expectant mothers using this acne medication were 26 times more likely to have a child with serious birth defects.
Alcohol	Fetal alcohol syndrome.
Antibiotics	Cataracts, retarded skeletal growth, premature delivery.
Anticonvulsants	Heart problems, cleft palate.
Aspirin	Retarded growth, miscarriage.
Cocaine	Miscarriage, brain damage, sluggishness, poor attention span.
Codeine, morphine, and methadone	Addicted baby, withdrawal symptoms (fever, tremors, convulsions, breathing problems, intestinal disturbance).
Hallucinogens	Spontaneous abortions, behavioral abnormalities.
Insulin and tolbutamide	Death.
Nicotine	Deficiencies in physical growth and development, may be involved in hyperactivity; linked to increased chances of spontaneous abortion and chronic respiratory problems.
Sex hormones	Heart malformations, spontaneous abortion, and may cause a genetically XX female infant to look like a male.
Thalidomide	Abnormalities in arms and legs.
Pollution (carbon monoxide, lead, and mercury)	Mental retardation.
Maternal malnutrition	Low birth-weight, increased chances of mental retardation, lower IQs, attention deficits, rickets, epilepsy, cerebral palsy.
Radiation	
X-rays	Miscarriage, defect in central nervous system, mental retardation.
Nuclear radiation	Dislocated hips, malformed eyes, heart disease, leukemia, mental retardation.
Other environmental causes	
Anoxia (oxygen deprivation)	Epilepsy, mental retardation, behavior disorders, poor attention span, hyperactivity.

Figure 3.4

Sensitive Periods in Prenatal Development. The greatest danger of major structural defects caused by teratogens is in the early weeks of the embryonic period, represented by the darkest bars.

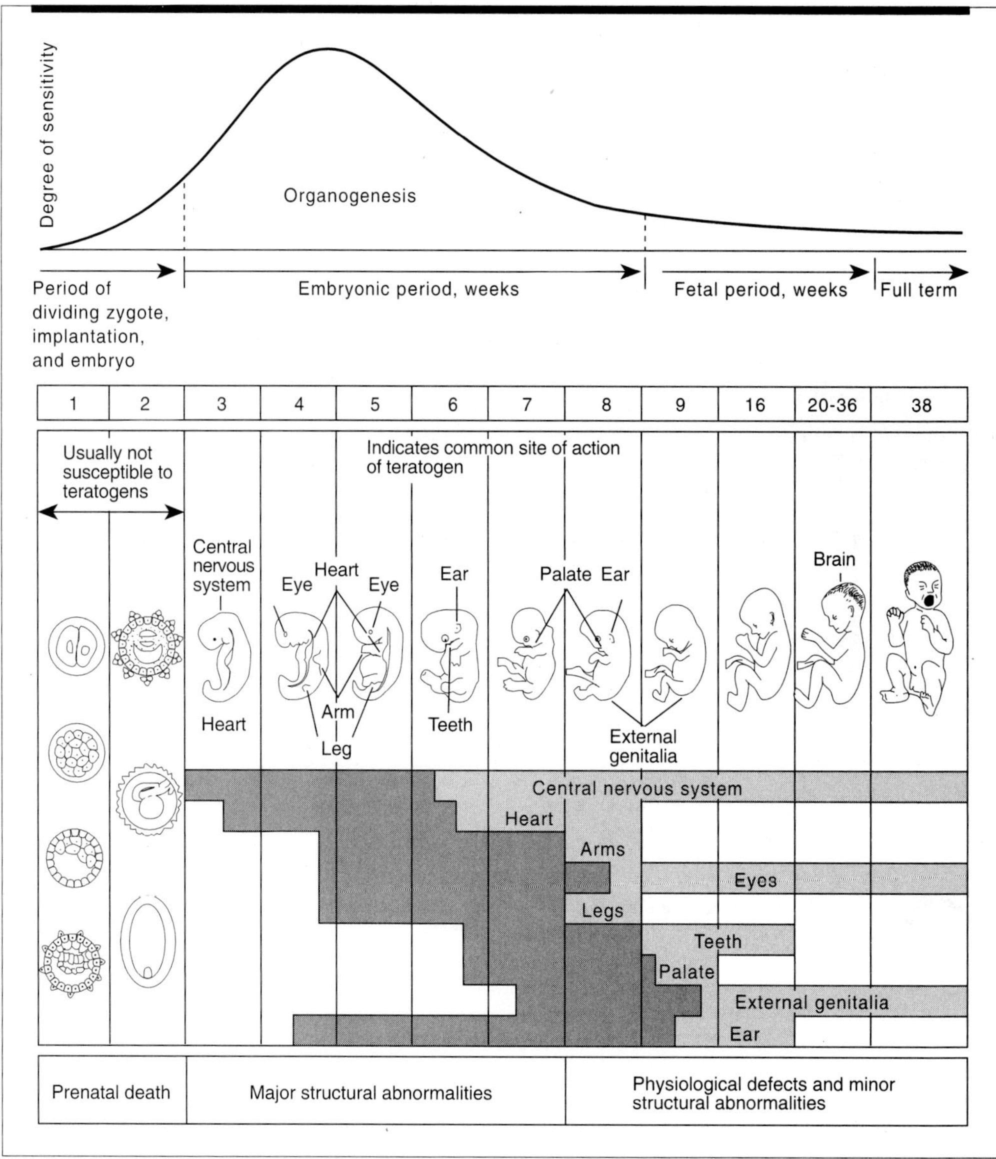

is a good chance her fetus will not be harmed. For example, if a mother contracts rubella (German measles) during the first trimester, her baby will probably be born with heart abnormalities, cataracts, or deafness. If she contracts rubella during the second or third trimester, it is likely her fetus will be unharmed.

Two notable exceptions to the safer-after-the-first-trimester rule are the fetus's vulnerability to autoimmune deficiency syndrome (AIDS) and syphilis. If a mother contracts AIDS at any point in her pregnancy and she gives birth to a live baby, there is a substantial risk that the baby will be born with AIDS. A fetus is most susceptible to syphilis after the first trimester because the disease cannot pass the placenta barrier until then. If an infected mother does not get treatment before the second trimester, her fetus may die or suffer from liver, bone, or blood diseases.

When thinking about rubella, AIDS, syphilis, or the other common teratogenic diseases listed in table 3.7, keep two facts in mind. First, many of these diseases can be prevented. For example, women can be inoculated against rubella, the mumps, and polio. Unfortunately, however, one in seven married women in the United States have not been inoculated against rubella. Second, it's unfortunate that the embryo is most vulnerable during the first trimester because many women don't realize they are pregnant until the second trimester. Thus, many women, thinking they are only taking a slight risk with their own health, unwittingly put their embryo at risk.

Drugs

Perhaps the best advice for women who plan to conceive or are currently pregnant is to refrain from all drugs, including one of America's favorites: alcohol. Alcohol consumption can sometimes lead to fetal alcohol syndrome (FAS).

Figure 3.5

Child with Fetal Alcohol Syndrome

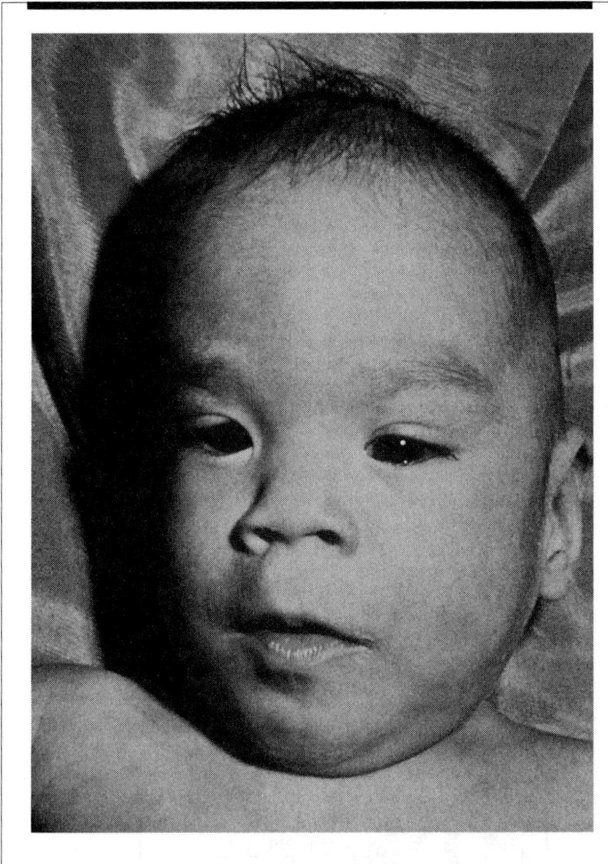

Physically, an individual afflicted by FAS has abnormal facial characteristics such as widely spaced eyes, short nose, short eyelid slits, and abnormal jaw protrusion (Streissguth, 1976) (see figure 3.5). In addition, the typical FAS newborn is smaller than the average baby and remains significantly shorter and lighter than its peers throughout life.

Psychologically, a person suffering from FAS may have mild to moderate mental retardation. Even with an enriched environment, most FAS children have depressed IQs.

Not surprisingly, the more a mother drinks, the more likely the child is to suffer from FAS. It has been estimated that 33 to 43 percent of infants born to alcoholics suffer from FAS (Stressiguth, Landesman-Dwyer, Martin, & Smith, 1980). However, no one who drinks is completely safe. Just a few drinks a week can, in rare cases, lead to FAS.

Moderate drinking is most risky during the last few months of pregnancy, when, as figure 3.4 shows, brain development is proceeding at a rapid rate (Aaronson & MacNee, 1989).

In conclusion, alcohol and pregnancy do not mix. To underscore this point, consider the following facts (Barr, Streissguth, Darby, & Sampson, 1990):

1. The March of Dimes estimates that, each year, 50,000 babies have alcohol-related birth defects.
2. The United States Health and Human Services Department reports that fetal exposure to alcohol is a leading cause of mental retardation.
3. Even moderate prenatal exposure to alcohol is linked to lower IQ scores and poorer motor performance.
4. Some of the problems that have been attributed to maternal caffeine use may actually be due to alcohol (Streissguth et al., 1989).

Maternal Malnutrition

Not only can the genetic program be derailed by what a mother consumes, but also by what she doesn't consume. If the mother, and thus the fetus, is severely malnourished, the newborn will have a low birth weight and may suffer from one or more of the following: mental retardation, rickets, epilepsy, and cerebral palsy.

Unfortunately, even when malnutrition isn't severe enough to result in mental retardation, it may still hamper the child's mental development. Thus, in poverty-stricken areas where mothers either don't have access to or don't know about proper nutrition, children are doubly disadvantaged. Not only are they handicapped by their deprived postnatal environment, but because of their deprived prenatal environment, they may be ill-equipped to rise above their circumstances (Lozoff, 1989). Clearly, if we are to create equal opportunities for all people, maternal malnutrition must be conquered.

Radiation

In addition to disease, drugs, and malnutrition, pregnant women must worry about radiation. Because of the dangers of radiation to the fetus, before a woman is x-rayed, she should be asked if there is any possibility that she could be pregnant. Radiation from an X ray could severely damage a fetus or, in some cases, kill it. Even if a fetus survives exposure to large doses of radiation during the first trimester, it will usually be born mentally retarded with observable defects in its central nervous system.

We are not saying that any exposure to radiation is deadly. Some radiation occurs naturally in our soil and our food. Most of the time, naturally occurring radiation is not a major threat to developing fetuses. However, exposure to unnatural sources of radiation, such as industrial-grade plutonium, used in the manufacture of nuclear warheads and reactors, or radioactive fallout from nuclear explosions, is dangerous.

Much of our knowledge about the impact of radioactive fallout comes from studies conducted after the United States dropped a nuclear bomb on Hiroshima at the end of World War II (Neel & Schull, 1956; Schull & Neel, 1958). Pregnant women who were near the explosion later gave birth to children with one or more of the following defects: dislocated hips, malformed eyes, abnormal hearts, leukemia, and mental retardation.

Box 3.9

ISSUE in FOCUS

What a Pregnant Woman Should Not Do

In the past 9 months, how many of these substances have you used or been exposed to? Check all that apply.

Products

___ alcohol
___ marijuana
___ cocaine
___ heroin or methadone
___ thorazine
___ valium
___ tobacco
___ hormones or steroids
___ over-the-counter drugs
___ acne medications like accutane or tetracycline
___ antacids
___ aspirin
___ large doses of fat soluble vitamins, such as a, d, and e
___ artificial sweeteners
___ artificial coloring in food
___ meat cooked with charcoal, meat cooked "rare," or meat preserved with nitrates

Environmental Pollutants

___ polluted air
___ ionizing radiation
___ virus-caused diseases
___ drinking polluted water

Activities

___ engaging in sex with someone who has VD or AIDS
___ cleaning kitty litter
___ using pesticides
___ working with or using chemicals that contain lead such as paint strippers, pesticides, oven cleaners, ceramics

If an expectant mother wanted to do everything possible to reduce the chances of birth defects, she would avoid *all* of the above during pregnancy. What percentage of women do you think avoid all of these threats? Do you think it is realistic to require women to avoid all of these threats? Should women be prosecuted for exposing themselves to these threats while pregnant? Should women be denied employment in jobs that require exposure to these threats? What assistance, if any, should the government give to help pregnant women avoid these threats?

More recently, there has been great concern over the 1986 meltdown of Russia's nuclear reactor in Chernobyl. Scientists are closely monitoring the impact of nuclear fallout from that explosion on subsequent births.

Conclusions About Common Teratogens

The remarkable thing about most teratogens is that they are avoidable. Many babies born with defects may have been born normal if their mothers had only taken proper precautions. The problem is that many people don't realize the risks to their child when they take a pill, have a couple of drinks, smoke cigarettes, or do many other things that our society considers acceptable or even "normal." Not thinking, not knowing, and not caring are probably the three most common causes of birth defects. But before you condemn mothers whose children have birth defects, try the quiz in box 3.9. You may find that being responsibly pregnant would entail a dramatic shift in your lifestyle.

Chemical Effects on Postnatal Development

Thus far, we have described how exposure to chemicals in the womb can affect development. But what about the effects of exposure to chemicals after birth? Although many drugs tend to have less effect if exposure is after the first trimester, most of the things that can affect prenatal development can also affect development after birth. Pollution, drugs, radiation, and hazardous materials may cause changes in the genes, thereby causing changes in health, behavior, and appearance. In fact, many of the causes of biological aging are linked to things in the environment that produce genetic mutations. That is, exposure to sun, lead, cigarettes, alcohol, certain drugs, pollution, a nutrition-poor diet, and polyunsaturated fats may not only cause damage by altering body chemistry and damaging cells, but may also accelerate the aging process by increasing genetic mutations (Rosenfeld, 1985).

Worldwide, the most serious postnatal chemical threats to reaching one's genetic potential is undernutrition in the forms of protein deficiency and iron deficiency. Experts

Table 3.8

Postnatal Chemical and Biological Threats

Agent	Possible Outcomes
Chemical	
Aspirin	Exposure to it as an infant may result in bleeding. Exposure to it before age 13 may cause Reyes Syndrome (which may result in fever, vomiting, and coma).
Carbon monoxide	Brain damage, death.
Cocaine	Death.
Honey	In young children, it has been known to cause death.
Iron deficiency	Anemia, decreased mental and motor abilities, shorter attention spans.
Lead poisoning	Decreases in mental functioning.
Mercury poisoning	Retardation, death.
Steroids	Shrinking of the testes, aggressive behavior, acne, sleep disturbances, damage to heart and liver.
Tranquilizers	May cause newborns to die from respiratory distress syndrome (the infant stops breathing).
Zinc deficiency	Impaired physical growth, sluggishness, apathy.
Diseases	
Anemia	Sluggishness, irritability, impaired mental and motor abilities.
Meningitis	Retardation, blindness, deafness, death.

estimate that 40 to 60 percent of all children suffer from undernutrition, usually involving protein deficiency (Galler, 1984). Such undernutrition, especially when it happens during the first years of life, may irreversibly damage mental development. If children have been malnourished during their first few years of life, a good diet later on may sometimes help them catch up in terms of physical development, but will not allow them to catch up in terms of mental development (Lozoff, 1989). Experts also estimate that 20 percent of all children suffer from iron deficiency. Infants suffering from iron deficiency tend to have lower mental and motor test scores. As with protein deficiency, getting a good diet after the first year is *not* enough to compensate for iron deprivation during infancy (Lozoff, 1989).

Another serious postnatal threat is lead poisoning. Lead poisoning may affect nearly 17 percent of the world's children, resulting in decreases in mental abilities. Even in the United States, 16 percent of children show high lead levels in their blood. This is a serious problem because children exposed to lead are not only less coordinated, but also four times more likely to be mentally retarded, six times more likely to have a reading disability, and seven times more likely to fail to graduate from high school.

In the United States, there is also concern about steroids. Some experts estimate that from 6 to 10 percent of all American teenage males are using steroids. Steroids can increase muscle strength, but may also damage the liver, heart, kidneys, and sex organs as well as cause adverse psychological effects.

We have mentioned only the most common chemicals that can adversely affect development (see table 3.8 for a more inclusive list). But keep in mind that not all chemicals are harmful. Remember, we are made of chemicals. We eat chemicals, breathe chemicals, and excrete chemicals. Chemicals, in the form of good nutrition, good air, and clean water, are vital for physical growth and psychological well-being. Chemicals, in the form of prescription drugs, may be able to reverse some of the negative effects of aging. For example, the drug etidronate reverses much of the loss of bone that is the main symptom of osteoporosis, a disease that affects almost 20 million Americans. Similarly, estrogen can be used to counteract some of the adverse effects of menopause. Thus, the key is not to avoid all chemicals, but to realize the long-term effects of exposure to selected chemicals.

Sensory Stable and Sensory Variable Factors

Of course, the chemical environment is just one aspect of postnatal environments. As you learned in chapter 2, several theorists, most notably the behaviorists, emphasized the role of the social environment on development. In fact, as Hebb recognized, a person's genetic program interacts with two different kinds of nonchemical, environmental events: sensory stable factors and sensory variable factors.

One category of chemical that can adversely affect development after birth is steroids. Some experts estimate that 6 to 10 percent of U.S. male teens are risking damage to their liver, hearts, kidneys, and sex organs in trade for more muscle strength.

Sensory Stable Factors

Hebb believed that one reason we tend to underestimate the degree of interaction between the environment and the genetic program is because of **sensory stable factors,** those things in the environment that all members of the species encounter. We tend to assume that because almost every member of the species does a certain behavior, the behavior was rigidly preprogrammed by heredity. However, part of the reason all members behave the same way is because they share certain common experiences. By varying these sensory stable factors, we can see whether behavior really is so rigidly preprogrammed. In many cases, we find that the genetic program is more accommodating to changes in the environment than people originally thought. That is, the universality of certain behaviors is often due to sensory stable factors.

The power that sensory stable factors play in universal behaviors is clearly seen in **imprinting,** the tendency of young animals to learn to approach and associate with a parent or other role model. Through imprinting, certain animals form attachments to their caregivers within hours of being born. For example, young geese and ducklings often form attachments to the first moving object they see. Within hours of birth, the young bird will follow that object anywhere. And later, when it matures, it will try to mate with that object or something closely resembling it. In the wild, the first thing a baby fowl usually sees is its mother. Therefore, most baby fowl imprint to their own kind and later mate with their own kind.

But what if the first thing the baby fowl sees is not its mother, but a human? As Konrad Lorenz (1935) discovered, ducklings will imprint to humans. Not only will the young ducklings follow humans around, but, when they grow up, they may also try to mate with humans. Lorenz "discovered" this fact one day when he fell asleep on the lawn. He awoke to find that a male duck he had imprinted was stuffing worms into Lorenz's mouth—as any proper male courting a female would.

Fortunately, most young fowl don't see inquisitive scientists during their first hours. Instead, their almost universal, stable, early experience is seeing a moving adult fowl. This stable experience combined with their genetic programming causes them to imprint on their own species.

As you will see in chapter 9, some psychologists (for example, Bowlby, 1980) argue that babies attach to their caregiver in much the same way as fowl imprint to their parents. Just as the fowl enjoyed the universal early contact with a moving fowl, most babies enjoy the almost universal early experience of having a caregiver who spends long periods of time with them during their early years. Based on that intense contact, infants become *attached* to their caregivers. As an infant, you cried to make them come to you and you squirmed around to maintain eye contact. Later, you got upset when they would leave you for the evening. Of course, there were several differences between you and your fine-feathered friends. You demanded more than the mere presence of another person; you wanted that person to reliably care for you. Furthermore, whereas the sensitive period for the duck to form an attachment was during the first three days of life (if the duckling first sees his mother four days after birth, he will flee from her), the sensitive period for you did not begin until you were about six months old. Finally, unlike the duck, you were capable of forming strong attachments to more than one person. Yet, for all these differences, you did seem programmed to form attachments (see table 3.9).

Just as you are programmed to form attachments, you are also programmed to learn language. Almost all humans are exposed to language throughout their lives. That is, exposure to language is a sensory stable factor. However, as you read in chapter 1, one poor girl was not exposed to language during her early years. As a result, she was unable to ever master language. To read more about her unfortunate life, read box 3.10.

Table 3.9

Comparing Attachment and Imprinting

Criteria	Imprinting	Attachment
Timing of the sensitive period	The sensitive period is during the first 3 days of life.	The sensitive period does not begin until the infant is about 6 months old.
	Animals can imprint on one, and only one, target.	Humans are capable of being attached to several individuals.
Required behaviors of successful target	To be the target of imprinting, the only things a parent has to do are to (1) be present during the sensitive period and (2) move.	To be the target of attachment, a caregiver must be *responsive* to the infant.
Required physical appearance of successful target	To be the target of imprinting, appearance doesn't matter. Indeed, ducklings have attached to people and even to a beer bottle.	Humans seem to innately show favoritism for human faces and may even show favoritism for attractive human faces (Langlois, Roggman, & Riser-Danner, 1990).

Sensory Variable Factors

Although some human experiences are universal, most are not. Thus, Hebb labeled the most common environmental events affecting our development as **sensory variable factors.** A sensory variable factor is anything in the environment that is not universal to all members of a species.

A useful way of looking at how sensory variable factors interact with a person's genetic program is in terms of **range of reaction.** Rather than rigidly fixing behavior or ability, genes set boundaries on the range of one's behavior or ability (Gottesman, 1963). For example, the amount of air you blow into a balloon affects how big it will be, but the maximum size of the balloon was set at the factory. In a similar fashion, the environment can determine where in the range of reaction you fall, but the boundaries of the range are determined by heredity. Thus, you did not inherit a single IQ, but rather a range of IQs.

How broad will the range of reaction be? Depending on the trait, the reaction range may be extremely broad or rather narrow. The reaction ranges for personality and intelligence are fairly broad, whereas the reaction ranges for height and eye color are fairly narrow. In other words, sensory variable factors play a large role for some traits, but a very limited role for others.

Just as the reaction range is useful for emphasizing the influence sensory variable factors can have on certain traits, another term is useful for emphasizing the limits of sensory variable factors. That term, which is almost the opposite of reaction range, is **canalization,** or the degree to which genes limit actual behavior or expressed potential (Waddington, 1966). Traits that the environment can readily modify, such as personality, intelligence, and temperament, are not highly canalized. Walking, babbling, and eye color, on the other hand, are hard to modify and are thus highly canalized.

The age at which you start to walk is highly canalized, or affected by your genetic makeup. However, environment can interact with genes to speed up your timetable or slow it down.

To illustrate just how highly canalized walking is, consider the research of Wayne Dennis (1940) on Hopi Indian children. Hopi custom is to wrap a newborn in a blanket and tightly bind the baby to a plank of wood referred to as a cradleboard. The baby is kept there for nine months, with few moments of freedom. One outcome of this practice is to limit the baby's opportunity to practice the movements needed to walk. Dennis contrasted those babies raised on cradleboards with babies raised by Hopi mothers who had abandoned the cradleboard custom. These babies had more freedom of movement and therefore the opportunity to make movements used in walking. The surprising outcome of Dennis' study is that the two groups of babies started to walk at about the same time. The restrictive environment of the cradleboard was not strong enough to deviate these babies from their genetic plan.

Box 3.10

ISSUE in FOCUS

Genie: The Experience of a Wild Child

Few humans have grown up without any real contact with other human beings. One such child was found in California when a partially blind 50-year-old woman arrived in a welfare office with her 13-year-old daughter asking for directions to the office for services for the blind. The instant the eligibility worker saw the daughter, "Genie," she called her supervisor. The supervisor agreed that something was wrong with the girl. During a visit to the girl's home, the supervisor convinced the mother that Genie should be taken to the Los Angeles Children's Hospital for tests. Later, both parents were charged with willful abuse.

Why were people alarmed when they saw Genie? When she arrived in the welfare office, this 13-year-old girl could not stand erect or speak; she could only whimper. She was a pitiful, malformed, incontinent, unsocialized, and severely malnourished creature. She weighed only 59 pounds and was 54 inches tall. She was unable to straighten out her limbs, could not chew, and spent much of her time spitting. Because of her constant spitting, her clothing reeked.

Genie was not toilet trained and she had a ring of hard callus around her buttocks. She showed no signs that she could perceive heat or cold. On the Vineland Maturity scale, she scored at the level of a 1-year-old. She could recognize only about 20 words and could only say "Stopit" and "Nomore."

Her problems were quite understandable in view of how she was reared. She had been isolated in a small room and had not been spoken to by her parents since infancy. That is, from the age of 20 months, until she was 13 1/2 Genie lived in nearly total isolation. Naked and restrained by a harness that her father had fashioned, she was left to sit on her potty seat day after day. She could move only her hands and feet. She had nothing to do. At night, when she was not forgotten, she was put into a sort of straitjacket and caged in a crib that had wire-mesh sides and an overhead cover. She was often hungry.

If she made any noise, her father beat her. He never spoke to her. Instead he barked and growled at her. The task of taking care of Genie fell to her older brother. Following his father's instructions, he never talked to Genie and fed her hurriedly and in silence.

At the hospital, they tried to help Genie. But working with Genie was not easy. When she became excited or agitated, she urinated on the floor. Yet, Genie was human. She delighted in discovering the world. She loved outings and enjoyed examining the meats and plastic containers in grocery stores.

Continued

However, Dennis (1960) later found that even the highly canalized behavior of walking can be delayed by experience. Specifically, when studying neglected, institutionalized Iranian orphans, he found that only 15 percent of the 3- to 4-year-olds could walk. Other researchers have found that not only can the environment delay the onset of walking, but it can also speed it up, probably by strengthening the relevant muscles. For example, Thelen and Fisher (1982) found that infants in cultures where babies are encouraged to spend more time upright tend to walk sooner than infants in cultures where children spend much more time lying down. As further evidence that strengthening relevant muscles can accelerate walking, Zelazo (1976) experimentally demonstrated that having infants exercise the stepping reflex causes them to walk about two months earlier than they normally would.

The Ecology of Human Development

Not all behaviors are as dependent on physical growth, strength, and maturation as walking is. Some behaviors and characteristics are less canalized and thus more dependent on sensory variable factors. For example, although you inherited part of your personality and basic temperament, your present personality is also, at least partly, the result of experience (Plomin, 1989, 1993; Rose et al., 1988). Similarly, although you inherited an intellectual potential, environmental factors have played a role in determining how much of that potential you have realized.

Just as taking a close look at the components of heredity—genes and chromosomes—has helped us understand the impact of heredity on highly canalized traits, taking a close look at people's environments will help us to accurately assess the impact of environmental events on more malleable, less canalized traits.

Box 3.10

ISSUE in FOCUS

Continued

After several months of therapy, Genie learned to recognize many words. Eventually, she learned to speak in three-word utterances. However, unlike normal children, Genie never learned how to ask a question and didn't understand much about grammar. Her speech development was very slow. Although she showed that some language can be acquired after the sensitive period for language acquisition, her case suggests that not learning language until after the sensitive period may severely limit the level of acquisition.

When Genie's brain patterns were examined, the data showed that Genie used her *right* hemisphere for both language and nonlanguage functions (99 percent of all right handed people use their *left* hemisphere for language). Her left hemisphere was functionally dead. Perhaps this finding explains why Genie was remarkably good at tasks that typically involve the right hemisphere (for example, spatial tasks), but poor in those requiring the left. For example, on the Mooney Faces Test, which requires subjects to distinguish real from "false" faces in which features are misplaced and to point out several features of the face, Genie's performance was the highest reported in the literature for either child or adult.

Through her several years of rehabilitation, Genie made considerable progress. Her IQ increased from 38 in 1971 to 74 in 1977. However, she made less progress on activities primarily governed by the left hemisphere, including language.

Obviously, Genie has many problems besides her lack of syntax and her dependence on the right hemisphere of her brain. During her formative years, she was malnourished, abused, unloved, and deprived of all toys and companionship. Consequently, she is strange in many ways.

In 1978, Genie's mother became her legal guardian. During all the years of Genie's rehabilitation, her mother had also received help from the staff at Children's Hospital. An eye operation restored her sight, and a social worker tried to improve her behavior toward Genie. Shortly after Genie's mother was named guardian, she astounded the therapists and researchers who had worked with Genie by filing suit against the hospital on behalf of herself and Genie charging that they had disclosed private and confidential information concerning Genie and her mother for "prestige and profit" and had subjected Genie to "unreasonable and outrageous" testing.

Sources: Pines, M. (September 1981). The civilizing of Genie, *Psychology Today,* 28–34. Rymer, R. (1993) *Genie.* New York: HarperPerennial.

Continued

The first step to understanding and examining people's environments is to realize that humans don't face simply one environment. Rather, individuals are affected by many different, yet interrelated environments. A useful model for considering the complex and varied environments that affect human life is Urie Bronfenbrenner's (1979, 1989, 1993) *human ecology model.*

Bronfenbrenner's approach is also known as the **ecological systems approach** because he sees development as a dynamic process involving an interaction between the individual and several, interconnected environmental systems. A **system** is the interplay between two or more environments. In his theoretical model, he describes four systems for human experience: the microsystem, the mesosystem, the exosystem, and the macrosystem (see figure 3.6).

Your **microsystem** corresponds to your immediate environment. The current microsystem contains your current physical setting (for example, dorm room, library, or home) and the people and experiences found in that setting. Thus, your microsystem not only contains the physical and material aspects of your immediate environment, but also other people, complete with their "distinctive characteristics of temperament, personality, and systems of belief" (Bronfenbrenner, 1989, p. 227).

Because your immediate environment frequently changes, you live in several microsystems. The people and experiences of your home, school, work, church, and neighborhood represent the variety of microsystems you live in.

The interplay between two or more of your microsystems (for example, the relations between your home and school) defines the second level of your environment—your **mesosystem.** By coining the term *mesosystem,* Bronfenbrenner draws attention to three facts. First, people vary in the number of different microsystems they experience. For example, a nursing home resident may experience very few microsystems, whereas a working parent may interact with many microsystems in the course of a single day. Second, what happens in one microsystem may affect

Box 3.10

SELF-CHECK

Concluded

1. One explanation for Genie's problems is that the sensitive period for learning language is somewhere between 1 and 13 years of age. That is, if we do not learn language by age 13, we cannot learn it because we have missed the sensitive period. However, since this is a case study, other explanations may account for Genie's language deficits. Can you think of any?
2. In spite of the fact that Genie's mother was an accomplice for 13 years to abusing Genie, Genie's mother was appointed legal guardian. Judges rarely take an abused child away from the parents. What does this tell you about our society's assumptions about the nature versus nurture issue?
3. If Genie's mother had been the abuser and her father the accomplice, would the court have given the father custody of Genie? Why? (*Hint:* Our society may hold one position on the active versus passive issue when it pertains to men, another for women.)
4. How much more progress do you think Genie will make? What does your answer reveal about your assumptions about the stability versus change and continuity versus discontinuity debates discussed in chapters 1 and 2?
5. Do you think Genie should be encouraged or discouraged from having children? To what extent would you encourage or discourage her? Why? (You may want to talk about your assumptions about nature and nurture and the difference between phenotype and genotype.)

Please turn to the end of this chapter to check your answers.

Box 3.11

SELF-CHECK

1. Give two examples of genes influencing traits or behavior after conception.
2. Why might the same drug have different effects depending on when the individual was exposed to it? How does your answer relate to the concept of sensitive periods?
3. In general, during which trimester is the unborn most vulnerable to teratogens? During which trimester is brain or nervous system damage most likely?
4. Why is it difficult to pin down the effects of nicotine and caffeine on the unborn?
5. Why do you think some heavy drinkers end up with children who have no symptoms of FAS whereas some people who have very few drinks during pregnancy end up with an FAS child?
6. What research technique was used to estimate the effects of nuclear radiation on the unborn? What problems are there with this technique? Despite the weaknesses of this technique, the conclusions have been generally accepted. Why?
7. What are the leading postnatal chemical threats?
8. To what extent can a good diet during late childhood make up for malnutrition during the first year or two of life?
9. What are the similarities and differences between imprinting and attachment? sensory stable factors and sensory variable factors?
10. A group of nursing home residents are put on a weight-lifting program. Would this be an example of a sensory stable or a sensory variable factor?
11. If a trait is strongly influenced by the environment, what can be said about the trait's reaction range? about the degree to which the trait is canalized? the trait's heritability?
12. What is a sensitive period? What evidence supports the idea of a sensitive period for language?
13. What evidence can you present to support the notion that even physical and motor development are affected by the environment?

Please turn to the end of this chapter to check your answers.

Figure 3.6

Bronfenbrenner's Human Ecology Model

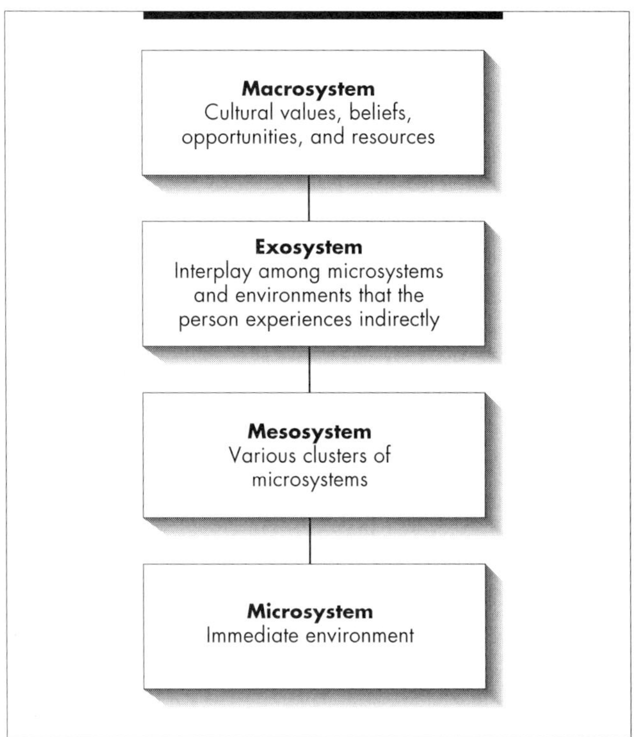

another. For instance, events at home may affect events at school. Third, people vary in terms of the degree of conflict that exists among their microsystems. Devoted parents may have conflicts between their family microsystem and their work microsystem, and religious individuals may have conflicts between their work microsystem and their church microsystem.

The study of mesosystems has proved useful in studying ethnic differences. For example, Laurence Steinberg (1992) and his associates studied ethnic differences in school achievement. In a study comparing Asian Americans, African Americans, Hispanic Americans, and European Americans, they found that individual microsystems were not useful in predicting school achievement. Rather, the interplay of microsystems (that is, the mesosystem) was important. Specifically, Steinberg found that European American youngsters benefited from the combination of *authoritative parenting* (a parenting style characterized by good communication and freedom within reasonable limits) and peer support for achievement. Hispanics, on the other hand, suffered from a combination of parental *authoritarianism* (a highly restrictive and often hostile parenting style characterized by one-sided communication and directives, rather than discussion and dialogue) and low peer support. Finally, for Asian American students,

The curriculum offerings in your major may be decided by a faculty committee that does not include students. Such a committee system would be a part of your exosystem that affects you indirectly by deciding what classes will be available for you.

the benefit of peer support for academic excellence offsets the negative consequences of authoritarian parenting.

The idea that we are affected by the interplay of several environments is also relevant to Bronfenbrenner's third system, the **exosystem.** Whereas your mesosystem contains two or more environments that you directly experience, your exosystem contains at least one environment that you experience indirectly (that is, you aren't in that environment). Thus, an exosystem is like a mesosystem in that it consists of the interplay between two or more environments. However, unlike the mesosystem, at least one of these environments is not directly experienced by you. Instead, the environment is experienced by another person and it affects you indirectly when you come in contact with that person. For a child, an exosystem may contain his parents' workplace. A child usually does not directly experience a parent's workplace; however, the workplace may affect the child's home environment. For example, work-related travel and stress level may influence the home. Thus, the interplay between a parent's workplace and the child's home environment forms an exosystem.

Bronfenbrenner stresses that we have little or no control over these environments that indirectly affect us. A single parent has little or no control over the affordability of quality child care. A young child has virtually no control over whether his parents are employed. As with many exosystem events, each of these events (quality child care, parental employment) has the potential to markedly change the developmental path. For the young child, his parents' employment may make the difference between growing up in a ghetto sparse in opportunity or a middle-class neighborhood rich in opportunity. For the single parent, the availability of affordable day care may determine whether she remains employed or goes on welfare to stay home and care for her offspring.

The **macrosystem** is the fourth level of environment, representing the values, beliefs, opportunities, and resources of one's culture. Garbarino (1982) compares the macrosystem to a blueprint. Your blueprint contains the assumptions, expectations, and values of your culture. This blueprint tells you how men and women are supposed to act, how children are supposed to be reared, how you are supposed to act toward people of a color other than your own, and what the social hierarchy is. Although you may not agree with all of the values of your macrosystem, those values still played a role in molding you into the person you are today.

The extent to which these values play a role is a matter for debate. For example, some argued that the Los Angeles riots of 1992 reflected a macrosystem failure. Specifically, according to Vice president Quayle, the 1992 Los Angeles riots reflected a lack of commitment to "family values." According to others, however, the problem was due to an exosystem that deprived the Watts community of economic opportunity and hope. Clearly, more research is needed to explore the effects of our different environments. Nevertheless, Bronfenbrenner's model provides a useful starting place from which to think about and explore the impact of the environment.

Assessing Hereditary and Environmental Influences

By taking a detailed look at the genetic and environmental forces that mold you, you have seen that your development has been influenced by genes *and* their interactions with the prenatal chemical environment, the postnatal chemical environment, sensory stable factors, sensory variable factors, and Bronfenbrenner's different systems (microsystems, mesosystems, exosystems, and macrosystems). Yet, people are not satisfied with merely knowing that they are a product of nature and nurture. They always seem to want to know how much of a certain trait is due to nature and how much is due to nurture. The ideal way to answer these queries would be to separate the two. However, heredity and environment are inseparable. The environment determines whether and to what extent your genetic program is activated, and your genetic program determines how much you can be influenced by your environment. Put more simply, you cannot exist without an environment or without inheriting a nervous system.

Because nature and nurture cannot be separated in a meaningful way, the goal is to determine "the degree, intensity, and nature of the constraint exerted by biology" (Gould, 1983). In other words, the developmental psychologist's task is to determine a trait's **heritability quotient**—a number expressing the degree to which differences between people in a population are due to genes.

The problem is that the heritability quotient of a trait depends on two factors completely unrelated to the effect of genes: (1) how much variability there is in the population's gene pool and (2) how much variability there is in the environment. For example, the population of Hawaii has high genetic variability because the population includes people of many different races (genetic backgrounds). A socialistic country such as Sweden has less environmental variability than a capitalistic country such as the United States because the economic structure of a socialistic country distributes resources more equally.

In comparisons of people with very different heredities, but similar environments, the heritability quotient will be high. For example, if you study the height of U.S. citizens, you'll find that heredity plays a very large role because we come from diverse gene pools and most of us are well fed. On the other hand, if you compare people with similar heredities, but dissimilar environments on a trait such as height, heritability will be much lower. Thus, if you study the height of Ethiopians, you'll find that environment plays a larger role than heredity because they are fairly homogeneous in terms of genes, but differ greatly in terms of how well nourished they are. Because a trait's heritability quotient depends on what group is studied, calculating heritability quotients hasn't been tremendously successful in answering the nature-nurture question. Fortunately, other approaches, such as within-species comparisons, selective breeding, kinship studies, and twin studies have proved more fruitful.

Within-Species Comparisons

One way to look for the effects of heredity is to look for behaviors that are performed by every member of a species. For example, language, walking, and living in social groups seem to be universal human behaviors. Furthermore, sociobiologists (for example, Buss 1991; Wilson, 1975) have argued that certain aspects of the macrosystem, such as encouraging territoriality, preparing for warfare, and putting males in dominant roles, are universals. As you might imagine, determining the universality of a behavior is not easy. But even once we have established that the behavior really occurs in all cultures and in all individuals, we must take care to ensure that the reason for the behavior's universality isn't due to sensory stable factors—universal similarities in their environments. For example, naturists might argue that forming societies is inborn whereas nurturists might say that forming societies is simply an adaptive response to sensory stable factors. Does the behavior owe its universality to some genes that we all share? Or does it owe its universality to the fact that all environments reward it? Often, we cannot tell.

Occasionally, however, we can determine that a universal behavior is innate. For example, all baby humans babble. A nurturist would want to argue that babies learn to babble because they are exposed to a sensory stable factor—seeing and hearing other humans talk. However, the naturists point out that since even children who are both blind and deaf babble, babbling must be inherited.

Selective Breeding

Another way to determine whether a trait is inherited is to use selective breeding. In **selective breeding,** researchers first mate animals that share a desired trait (ability to run mazes quickly, so-called "maze-bright" rats). Then, they only mate the few offspring that clearly evidenced the trait (the fastest maze runners) and breed them with one another. The researchers continue doing this for several generations. If they can successfully breed animals that have a given trait, the trait obviously has a substantial genetic component (McClearn, 1993). Using selective breeding, psychologists have bred maze-bright rats (Tryon, 1940), fast race horses, extremely attached Australian shepherds, aggressive pit bulls, and acrobatic Siamese cats.

If selective breeding has been so successful, why hasn't it been used with humans? To some extent, most people voluntarily engage in some form of selective breeding because people tend to mate and marry others who are similar to themselves in race, education, and intelligence. However, most people would not support formal attempts to institute selective breeding. Sperm banks are extremely controversial and no current laws exist to force or even encourage sterilization. To many people, there are few words uglier than **genocide,** the deliberate and systematic destruction of a racial, political, or cultural group to get rid of certain genes.

From a purely scientific point of view, there are two reasons to oppose extreme forms of selective breeding. First, for the survival of the species, genetic variability is important. A trait that is harmful in one environment may be helpful in another (Gould, 1983). Thus, with selective breeding, we might wipe out a trait necessary for the future survival of the species. Second, since important human traits are polygenic (influenced by many genes), selective breeding would be extremely difficult. The most reliable way of successfully breeding these polygenic traits would be through inbreeding. Unfortunately, in addition to magnifying genetic strengths, inbreeding can magnify genetic weaknesses. For example, consider the history of certain royal families in which members mated with close relatives. Their inbreeding allowed recessive genetic defects to be expressed, resulting in having a high percentage of children who suffered from hemophilia, mental retardation, and other genetic defects.

Kinship Studies

Perhaps the most commonly used method to examine the effects of heredity is to conduct a **kinship study,** an investigation in which the researcher compares similarities and differences among family members. But a question arises when researchers find that family members sharing the same roof share the same traits: Are the family members similar because they share similar genes or because they share a similar environment?

Psychologists have used two major strategies to deal with this question. The first strategy takes advantage of the fact that household members sometimes differ in terms of their *kinship,* the degree to which they are related and thus are likely to share common genes. Within a household, kinship can range from a maximum of 1.00 in the case of identical twins (who come from the same zygote) to 0.00 in the case of adopted children who are neither biologically related with other children in the home nor with their adopted parents. However, most kinship quotients within a nuclear family, such as the kinship among biological siblings (unless they are monozygotic twins), between a child and the biological mother, and between a child and the biological father, are 0.50. If a trait is inherited, then the degree to which household members share a common trait should increase as their kinship quotient increases. Thus, brothers and sisters should be more similar to each other (kinship quotient = 0.5) than half-brothers (kinship quotient = 0.25).

Unfortunately, this approach is based on a questionable assumption that all household members share the same environment. In reality, all members have different experiences and the degree to which they share the same experiences may increase as kinship increases. For instance, stepchildren may interact more with their natural parent than with their stepparent; parents may expect their natural children to be more similar to themselves than their adopted children—and may act on these expectations, creating different environments for each.

As we have seen, there's a strong possibility that the more related two people are, the more similar their environments. Consequently, investigators have difficulty determining whether similarities in traits are due to similarities in environment or similarities in heredity.

To reduce the problem that more related individuals may have more related environments, Suomi (1987) has studied monkeys. He finds that almost at birth, children of shy monkeys are more fearful and that such monkeys tend to remain shy during their early years, regardless of how they are reared. Thus, his results suggest that shyness in monkeys is inherited.

Other investigators try to deal with the possibility that kinship may be related to environment by comparing related people who were reared apart from each other. For example, they might compare two sisters who were adopted by different families. Or they might compare an adopted child with her biological mother. Similarities would provide evidence for the importance of heredity.

Even more ambitious researchers make comparisons that will allow them to further disentangle the effects of nature and nurture. For example, they might make all of the following comparisons:

1. Looking at the similarities between sisters who have been adopted by the same family (to estimate the combined effects of heredity *plus* shared environment);

Table 3.10

Average Correlation Coefficients for Intelligence Test Scores from 100 Kinship Studies

Relationship	Kinship Quotient (how related the people are)	Correlations when Reared Together	Correlations when Reared Apart
Unrelated persons	0.00	+ 0.23	−0.01
Foster parent/child	0.00	+0.24	——
Biological parent/child	0.50	+0.42	+0.24
Siblings	0.50	+0.47	+0.24
Dizygotic twins	0.50	+0.60	——
Monozygotic twins	1.00	+0.86	+0.72

Source: Adapted from T. J. Bouchard, Jr. and M. McGue, "Familial Studies of Intelligence: A Review" in *Science*, 212: 1055, 1981.

Note: "1.0" is a perfect relationship. "0" means there is no relationship.

To try to separate the effects of nature from nurture, researchers compare indentical twins with fraternal twins.

2. Looking at the similarities between sisters who have been adopted by different families (to estimate the effects of heredity);
3. Seeing if adopted sisters living together are more similar than adopted sisters living apart (to estimate the effect of a shared environment); and
4. Seeing if adopted sisters are more similar to each other than they are to the other members of their adopted family (to estimate the effects of heredity).

To see the power of this technique, consider table 3.10. The table summarizes the findings of 100 studies that examined the kinship and intelligence scores of more than 100,000 pairs of individuals (Erlenmeyer-Kimling & Jarvik, 1963; Bouchard & McGue, 1981; McGue, Bouchard, Iacono, & Lykken, 1993). As you can see, identical twins were most similar in terms of IQ, and unrelated individuals were least similar. Thus, the table provides strong evidence that intelligence is influenced by heredity.

Twin Studies

The most popular kind of kinship studies involve twins. Ironically, if researchers merely study identical twins reared together, they are more apt to establish that environment has a role than that heredity has a role. Why? Any similarity between the twins could be due to *either* similar genes or to similar environments, but any differences *must* be due to differences in environment. Thus, if a nurturist finds a strong similarity between identical twins reared together, she can argue that the similarities between the twins *may* be due to the environment and that any differences between the twins *must* be due to the environment. For example, Baker and Daniels (1990) found that identical twins differ in terms of depression and psychological well-being. Thus, they knew these differences had to be due to differences in the twins' environments. In attempting to pin down the specific environmental causes of these differences, Baker and Daniels found evidence that differential parental treatment seems to play a role.

Finding a strong relationship between traits of identical twins reared apart provides stronger evidence for the role of heredity. However, remember that nurturists emphasize that anything less than a perfect relationship shows some environmental influence over the trait. Furthermore, nurturists argue that environmental similarities have not been eliminated: twins reared apart may be reared by similar families because adoption agencies used to try to find foster parents who matched the natural parents in terms of ethnic background and intelligence.

Two bits of evidence support the idea that similarities between twins reared apart may be largely due to

Box 3.12

SELF-CHECK

1. Rank the following environments from least to most complex: macrosystem, microsystem, mesosystem, and exosystem.
2. Does the individual have more control over the mesosystem or the exosystem? Why?
3. Assume that you are a member of an oppressed minority group. Which environmental system (macrosystem, microsystem, mesosystem, or exosystem) would you devote most of your energy to try to change? Why?
4. Cross-cultural research allows a good chance to look at the effects of which of Bronfenbrenner's environments?
5. Working mothers may experience conflicts between which of Bronfenbrenner's environments?
6. Similarities between twins would be most impressive if they were reared in different ______ systems.
7. If a society treats all their children alike, will the heritability of traits appear to be high? Will traits appear to be highly canalized? Why? Will sensory variable factors be plentiful in that culture?
8. If a trait has a wide reaction range, is it strongly affected by the environment? Is it highly canalized?
9. If we look at the IQs of people who share very similar genes, but experience very different environments, the heritability quotient for IQ in that population will be ______ . If, on the other hand, we look at the IQs of people who come from distinctly different genetic backgrounds and who experience a common environment, the heritability quotient for IQ in that group will be ______ .
10. What difficulties are there with drawing conclusions from within-species comparisons?
11. Do you think results from selective breeding studies with animals can be generalized to humans? Why?
12. What is the advantage of comparing two siblings who were adopted by different families over simply comparing two siblings living together?
13. According to heritability quotients, who is more genetically similar: two dizygotic twins, a brother and sister, or a son and mother?
14. An investigator gives four groups a personality test: monozygotic twins, dizygotic twins, non-twin siblings living together, and unrelated, adopted children living together.
    a. Which group will have the highest correlation? the lowest?
    b. The investigator subtracts the correlation between adopted, unrelated siblings from the correlation between related siblings. Why?
    c. The investigator subtracts the correlation between dizygotic twin pairs from the correlation between monozygotic twin pairs. Why?
    d. If genetics is the only factor affecting personality similarity, which result (the one obtained in *b* or the one obtained in *c*) should be higher? Why? (*Hint:* calculate the kinship quotients).
15. Given that most IQ tests stress vocabulary, can you come up with a nurture explanation for why identical twins score more similarly than fraternal twins on the vocabulary composite test?
16. Does the fact that most IQ tests are timed tests suggest that these correlations may be due to something other than intelligence?
17. If you wanted to prove that environment affects psychological traits, what kind of twin study would you do? Why?

Please turn to the end of this chapter to check your answers.

sharing similar environments. First, recent studies comparing twins reared apart find a smaller relationship between twins' IQs than do older studies. This finding is baffling—until one realizes that adoption agencies are spending less effort than they once did on matching children to parents. Thus, it may be that the older studies are comparing twins who share highly similar environments, whereas recent studies are comparing twins reared in less similar environments (Loehlin, Willerman, & Horn, 1988). Second, Bronfenbrenner has found that the degree of similarity between twins reared apart is high when twins lived in similar exo- and macrosystems. However, the similarity between twins reared apart is dramatically less when the twins live in different exo- and macrosystems (Bronfenbrenner, 1986).

Perhaps the twin studies that make the most convincing argument for nature are those that compare identical (monozygotic) and fraternal (dizygotic) twin pairs. A nurturist can argue that identical twins are more alike than siblings because, unlike other siblings, identical twins are the same age. Because they share the same birthday, they share many of the same experiences both inside and outside of the womb. However, since, like identical twins, fraternal twins share the same birthday, it is difficult for a nurturist to explain why identical twins are more alike than fraternal twins.

The clever nurturist might argue that the similarities are based on physical similarities and expectations. People expect identical twins to be alike. Furthermore, identical twins look alike and appearance affects how people are treated. Finally, identical twins are closer to each other and thus influence each other more than fraternal twins do. However, even these ingenious explanations do not *always* work when comparing fraternal and identical twins because there are some twins who everyone believed to be identical, but when genetic tests were performed, the twins turned out to be fraternal! A nurturist would have a very difficult time explaining why true identical twins were more similar to each other than fraternal twins who everyone had assumed were identical.

What do studies comparing fraternal twins with identical twins tell us? As you saw in table 3.10, identical twins have more similar IQs than fraternal twins. Numerous other studies (see Loehlin & Nichols, 1976) show that identical twins are also more similar than fraternal twins on several other cognitive tests. These studies suggest that intelligence is, to a measurable extent, inherited. If intelligence is strongly influenced by heredity, what about other psychological traits?

Auke Tellegen and others (Tellegen, Lykken, Bouchard, Wilcox, Segal, & Rowe, 1988) compared identical and fraternal twins reared together and identical and fraternal twins reared apart on several personality variables. He found that identical twins reared apart since birth were *more* similar to one another than fraternal twins reared together, at least in terms of confidence, self-esteem, resistance to stress, leadership, and obedience. Tellegen interprets these results as showing that personality is strongly influenced by heredity.

Heritability Across the Lifespan

The studies we have discussed suggest that personality—in childhood—is strongly influenced by heredity. However, these studies do not tell us much about the effects of heredity on adult personality because less than 3 percent of the participants were over 21.

Although you might think that heritability would be the same for adults as for children, this is not necessarily the case. Nurturists argue that the environment may have more of an effect in adulthood. They argue that adults live in more varied environments than children and that adults are less influenced by such heredity-propelled forces as maturation.

Naturists, on the other hand, argue that people create their own environments (Scarr & McCartney, 1983). As adults, we may be more able to create, control, and select our own environments. As adults, the inherited aspects of our personality—those factors that influence our environment—have freer rein. Thus, naturists argue that heritability might increase in adulthood.

You have heard the argument. What does recent research have to say about this debate? McGue and his colleagues (1993) analyzed the data from several studies that included adult twins. These studies reveal that heritability quotients for IQ actually increase from 51 percent during childhood to 80 percent in adulthood. Thus, genetic factors become more important in determining cognitive differences between people during the adult years than during childhood.

If genetic factors become increasingly important for cognitive development, what about personality development? Nathan Brody (1994) reports that most of the available data do not provide clear evidence for genetic influences on personality change after childhood.

To illustrate the basic findings of the work reviewed by Brody, consider a recent cross-sequential study. Richard Viken and his colleagues (1994) studied the heritability of neuroticism and extraversion in 15,000 Finnish twins aged 18 to 53. Although they found that genetic factors (heritability) were significant between ages 18 and 53, heritability quotients did decrease. For example, for both men and women, heritability quotients for extraversion decreased from 0.52 for young adults (aged 18 to 23) to 0.41 for adults aged 42 to 53. The major drop occurred during the late teens and late twenties. An additional small drop occurred during the forties. Viken and his colleagues (1994) also found that heritability for neuroticism decreases during the late teens and late twenties, but then remains stable.

Throughout adulthood, heritability seemed more important for maintaining personality stability than for personality change. However, although Viken and his associates show a decreasing role for genetics in personality development (change) during the adult years, we cannot say that genetic factors are not important—they are. Viken's findings merely suggest that they become less important with age. Furthermore, their study relied on self-report data (a self-administered personality inventory). Brody (1994), as well as Viken's research group, caution that self-report measures may not be sensitive enough to tap aspects of personality that may change. Thus, although there is little evidence that genetic factors play a significant role in adult personality change, it is premature to conclude that genetics are not important.

Conclusions

Twin studies and recently developed research techniques have led to progress in understanding the roles of nature and nurture. However, we will probably never be able to completely disentangle the two. The environment affects genes and genes affect the environment.

Even before you were conceived, your environment affected your genetic heritage. The environment brought your parents together. Put another way, if your parents had lived in entirely different environments, they would never have met and their genes would have never been combined. After your parents met, the vaginal and uterine environment played a role in determining whether you received an X chromosome from your father (making you female) or a Y chromosome (making you male). For example, acidic vaginal and uterine environments are more likely to kill sperm cells having the Y chromosome than to kill X sperms (Rorvick & Shettles, 1970).

After conception, the prenatal environment may end the genetic program if viruses or malnutrition cause the fetus to die. Occasionally, the prenatal environment permanently alters the genetic program, as is apparently the case with *diethylstilbestrol (DES),* a synthetic estrogen that acts like testosterone once in the brain. This synthetic hormone was given to pregnant women in the 1950s to prevent miscarriage. Later, the drug was banned because the daughters of these women had an abnormally high incidence of cancer. Now, research suggests that all future female descendants of these women—granddaughters, great granddaughters, and so on—may also be prone to have cancer (Cook, 1987). On a more positive note, the right environment can weaken or reverse the effects of a genetic defect. For example, with a proper diet, individuals with PKU can live normal lives.

The genetic program affects the environment. Mothers may form opinions of the neonate even before it is born based on its activity level in the womb. After it is born, its gender, physical attractiveness, and irritability will affect how it is treated. In addition, it is clear that most healthy children are born already programmed to manipulate certain sensory stable factors in the environment (such as a caring parent). Furthermore, some research suggests that children may create the environments that match their genetic predispositions. For example, an inherently social child may seek out social situations or elicit social behaviors from others, thereby either finding or creating a highly social environment. Similarly, intelligent children appear to demand intellectual stimulation (Plomin, 1986, 1993; Scarr & McCartney, 1983). In addition, an individual's personality seems to determine what levels of favorable and adverse life events that person will experience (Headey & Wearing, 1989).

Even when our genetic program doesn't alter the environment, it may alter how we are influenced by the environment. For example, for highly canalized behaviors, such as walking, the environment plays a very small role. Conversely, some genetic heritages are more vulnerable to fetal alcohol syndrome than others (Kopp & Kaler, 1989); and some people seem more genetically predisposed than others to react to environmental stress by developing bipolar disorder (Shum, Morton, & Rice, 1992).

Because heredity and environment are usually inseparable, it's hard to determine what their separate roles are. Thus, some have focused—and the rest of this book will focus—on how genes and environmental systems affect us, rather than debating their relative contributions. But despite the difficulties of disentangling the effects of heredity and environment, researchers have made progress in estimating the roles of nature and nurture. The major conclusion from their recent work is that genes play a larger role than we previously believed. Some have viewed these discoveries with woe, believing that little can be done about heredity: How can we cure shyness or criminal behavior if these traits are inherited?

Yet, we can be optimistic about treating "inherited" problems for two reasons. First, few behaviors—and no psychological problems—are completely dominated by genes. For example, even though schizophrenia is presented as an inherited mental illness, half of all people whose identical twin has schizophrenia will not suffer from the disease. Similarly, even though shyness (Daniels & Plomin, 1985) and autism seem to be inherited, both problems can be modified by changing the environment (Brodt & Zimbardo, 1981; Landers, 1987; Suomi, 1987). Even the effects of Down syndrome can be significantly modified through an enriched environment (Turkington, 1987). Second, we may eventually learn not only what traits are inherited, but what genes control specific traits and how to modify those genes or develop a drug that turns off the defective allele. However, this will take some time—our genetic code may be the product of the precise sequencing of approximately 3 billion nucleotides, only 10 million of which have been mapped (Dworetzky, 1987).

SUMMARY

1. We are a product of the interaction between nature and nurture.
2. A zygote is formed through the union of a sperm and ovum. The sperm and ovum each contribute 23 chromosomes.
3. A person's genetic information is carried on 46 chromosomes made up of strands of DNA. Thousands of genes are strung along each chromosome.
4. Through mitosis, the single-celled zygote divides into the billions of specialized cells that comprise each of us.

5. The information for a specific trait has a locus (location on a specific chromosome). At each locus, there are usually two alleles, one from each parent.
6. Whereas one's genotype is one's genetic makeup, one's phenotype is how the genes are actually expressed. One's phenotype is determined by gene dominance and environmental influences.
7. Most traits are polygenic, or due to the interaction of several genes.
8. The 23rd chromosome of the sperm determines gender. Specifically, an X sperm produces a female, a Y sperm produces a male.
9. Congenital defects may be inherited or may be due to teratogens.
10. Most inherited defects are recessive.
11. The tragedy of defects caused by teratogens is that they are often avoidable.
12. Sensory stable factors are those things in the environment that all members of the species encounter.
13. A sensory variable factor is anything in the environment that is *not* universal to all members of the species. How much of an impact they have on development depends on how strongly a given trait is canalized. A highly canalized trait has a high heritability and a narrow reaction range.
14. Bronfenbrenner's human ecology model views development as a dynamic process involving an interaction between the individual and the environment. Development occurs within four contexts of experience: the microsystem, mesosystem, exosystem, and macrosystem.
15. Most of the chemicals that have prenatal effects can also have postnatal effects.
16. To help separate the effects of nature and nurture, developmental psychologists use four major research strategies: within-species comparisons, selective breeding, kinship studies, and twin studies.

KEY TERMS

alleles 74
amniocentesis 80
canalization 93
chorion 82
chorionic villi biopsy 82
chromosomes 70
congenital defect 76
dizygotic 70
DNA 70
dominant allele 75
Down syndrome 82
ecological systems approach 95
exosystem 97
fragile X syndrome 79
gametes 71
genes 70
genetic reshuffling 71
genocide 99
genotype 74
heritability quotient 98
heterozygous 74
homozygous 74
Huntington's chorea 76
imprinting 92
kinship study 99
locus 74
macrosystem 98
meiosis 71
mesosystem 95
microsystem 95
mitosis 70
monozygotic 70
mutations 85
nondisjunction 82
nucleotides 72
ovum 70
phenotype 74
polygenic 76
range of reaction 93
recessive allele 75
selective breeding 99
sensitive period 84
sensory stable factors 92
sensory variable factors 93
sex-linked defects 78
system 95
teratogens 85
translocation 82
zygote 70

SELF-CHECK ANSWERS

BOX 3.3

1. 50 percent male and 50 percent female because the father produces two kinds of sperm and each should be equally likely. Thus, just as in flipping a coin, when two possibilities are each equally likely, the chance of each outcome is 50 percent.
2. Selectively killing or aborting one gender or by encouraging sex practices that would give either the X sperm or the Y sperm an advantage in getting to the ovum. The killing of girl children has been practiced in some cultures throughout history, and breeding practices that favor either the X sperm (if a female is wanted) or a Y sperm (if a male is wanted) have been used in cattle breeding for decades.

3–5. Answers will vary because these issues are matters of opinion. The key to good answers to these questions is to give reasons for your opinions.

BOX 3.4

1. The different forms a gene can take are called the alleles of that gene. For example, the gene controlling leg hair comes in at least two types—a hairy leg allele and a nonhairy leg allele. Often, however, the terms *gene* and *allele* are used interchangeably.
2. Genotype is one's genetic makeup. It may differ from phenotype (actual characteristics) because not all genes will be expressed.
3. The locus for a gene is a place where the allele of that gene from the father interacts with the allele of that gene from the mother. Without a locus, genetic information could not be efficiently combined. The alleles from the mother's genes would almost never encounter the corresponding alleles from the father. Since alleles would not be matched up with each other, the issue of which is dominant would be irrelevant.
4. Mitosis results in two cells, the second of which is an exact copy of the parent cell. Meiosis also starts with a single cell, but results in four cells—none of which are identical to the original cell. Instead of consisting of pairs of chromosomes, each of these cells consists of unpaired chromosomes. Thus, each has half the genetic information of normal cells. Meiosis is useful for producing sex cells (which will combine with another sex cell that also has half the normal amount of genetic information to produce a cell that has the normal amount of genetic information and the normal number of paired chromosomes), whereas mitosis is useful for creating cells necessary for growth or for replacement of dead cells.
5. Each generation would have twice as many chromosomes as the previous generation. For example, if your grandparents each had 46 chromosomes, your parents would have 92 chromosomes; you would have 184 chromosomes; your children would have 368; and your grandchildren would have 736 chromosomes. Soon, there would be no room in the cells for all these chromosomes. Thus, although it might seem nice to inherit all your family's genetic material, such an inheritance would be impractical—not to mention the difficulties of combining all this information to arrive at a phenotype.
6. Heterozygous means that, for a given gene, the person has two different forms of the alleles. Homozygous means that, for a given gene, the person inherited two identical forms of the allele. Thus, an individual who was heterozygous for hairy legs would have a hairy leg allele and a nonhairy leg allele, whereas a homozygous individual would have either two hairy leg alleles or two nonhairy leg alleles.
7. Generally, their phenotype will match their genotype because both alleles are sending the same information. However, environmental events can prevent genes from being expressed.
8. No, their phenotype will often not match their genotype because a recessive gene will not be expressed.
9. If these defects were dominant, the individual would die before being able to reproduce. However, since they are recessive, the person can carry them and, if they mate with someone else who also carries a recessive gene for the defect, they may pass it on to their children.
10. Chromosomes are most complex, followed by DNA molecules, then genes, and then nucleotides (see box figure 3.1a).
11. Monozygotic twins are identical twins (coming from the same zygote). Dizygotic twins (fraternal twins), on the other hand, come from two different zygotes. They are no more alike, from a genetic standpoint, than most brothers and sisters.
12. In theory, all your basic cells are the result of mitosis from the original zygote. Thus, cells from normal tissue contain all that original information; they simply do not activate all those programs. For cloning to occur, someone would have to find a way to activate all those programs.
13. "Chromosome shuffling" is a more important source of genetic variability because (1) it happens every time mitosis occurs; and (2) by itself, it makes it possible for one couple to have the potential to conceive any one of 64 trillion possible offspring.
14. The father determines the child's gender because he is the one who contributes either an X sperm (making the child female) or a Y sperm (making the child male). The mother always contributes an X ovum (because the mother, by virtue of being female is XX).
15. In one sense, the child's genes come from the grandparents. Put another way, the parents' genes come from the child's grandparents. Thus, looking at the grandparents may give you some ideas about what recessive traits that are not expressed in the parents' phenotypes may still exist in the

Box Table 3.6

Condition	Is the Defect Recessive or Dominant?	Does It Run in Your Family?	Approximate Odds of First Child Having Trait
Cystic fibrosis	Recessive		If it does not run in your family, then zero. If it runs in your family, then 25%.
Diabetes	Recessive		If it does not run in your family, then zero. If it runs in your family, then 25%.
Hemophilia	Recessive		If it does not run in your family, then zero. If it runs in your family, then 25%.
Huntington's chorea	Dominant		If it does not run in your family, then zero. If you have it, then 50% to 100%.
MD	Recessive		If it does not run in your family, then zero. If it runs in your family, then 25%.
PKU	Recessive		If it does not run in your family, then zero. If it runs in your family, then 25%.
Sickle-cell	Recessive		If it does not run in your family, then zero. If it runs in your family, then 25%.
Tay-Sachs	Recessive		If it does not run in your family, then zero. If it runs in your family, then 25%.

parents' genotypes. Thus, if the two parents are brown-eyed but both sets of grandparents have blue eyes, then there is a reasonable chance that the child will have blue eyes.

16. There would only be two types of people (as far as phenotypes are concerned)—shy people and outgoing people. Note that if two outgoing people had children, those children would always be outgoing. On the other hand, sometimes, two shy people would have an outgoing child. The key to predicting what would happen when one or both of the parents is shy is to find out about the couple's parents (the child's grandparents). For example, if one of the parents came from a long line of shy people, that parent would probably be homozygous for the shy allele. Consequently, all that person's children would be shy, regardless of who he or she married. However, if one of the couple's parents was outgoing, then that member of the couple is heterozygous, and therefore is capable of having outgoing offspring. Specifically, if a heterozygous shy person mates with an outgoing person, there is a 50 percent chance that their first child will be outgoing. If, on the other hand, a heterozygous shy person mates with another heterozygous shy person, there is a 25 percent chance that their first child will be born outgoing.

Box 3.6

1. See box table 3.6, page 83.
2. If the defective trait is dominant and your prospective spouse does not have the trait, your prospective spouse must be homozygous for the normal form of the allele. The same would be true of you—unless we are dealing with a gene that is activated later in life, as is the case with Huntington's chorea. This is true even if the trait runs in your family.
3. Both of your spouse's parents would have to be heterozygous for Tay Sachs. Both would have to contribute the defective, recessive allele for the sibling to have Tay Sachs. Neither can be homozygous for Tay Sachs because they would have died before reaching middle childhood.
4. It would be better if it were dominant because your spouse would not carry the gene. Consequently, your children would not have the defect (unless you had the defect).

5–9. Answers will vary because these issues are matters of opinion.

Box 3.7

1. If one of the person's parents does not have the defect, then the person is heterozygous for the defect. If both parents had the defect, then the chances are more than 25 percent that the person is homozygous. Looking at both sets of grandparents would give you a better idea of the correct odds.
2. It would be better if the defect was dominant. If it is recessive, then the child has a 100 percent chance of inheriting the defect. If it is dominant, the odds might be as low as 75 percent.
3. It would be better if the defect were dominant. In that case, the child will not get the defect (since neither parent has it).
4. Answers will vary because this issue is a matter of opinion.

5. If these defects were dominant, people would die before they were able to mate. Consequently, the deadly form of the allele would not be passed on to future generations.
6. The Huntington's chorea allele would not be passed on and would thus become "extinct."
7. Color blindness is a recessive gene carried on the X chromosome; it is not carried on the Y chromosome. Thus, for a woman to be color blind, she must inherit the color-blind allele from both parents. However, if a man inherits one color-blind allele from his mother, he will be color blind. Similarly, if a woman inherits one fragile X chromosome, it is not a serious problem as long as her other X chromosome is normal. For men, however, if they receive a fragile X chromosome, that's the only X chromosome they have.
8. Chorionic villi biopsy seems to be riskier to the fetus. However, because it can be done earlier in pregnancy, some people use it instead of amniocentesis.
9. XYY males tend to be less intelligent. Thus, when they commit crimes, they are more likely to get caught. Hence, even though they are more likely to go to jail, they are not necessarily more violent.
10. The most common form of Down syndrome is nondisjunction. In nondisjunction, the problem is due to a defect in one of the parent's sex cells. This defect, due to faulty meiosis, creates a sex cell that contains not one, but two 21st chromosomes. Consequently, when it joins with the other parent's sex cell, the zygote has three (rather than 2) 21st chromosomes. In translocation, there is a problem when the two sex cells combine their genetic material. Instead of the two 21st chromosomes pairing off, one of them attaches to the wrong set of chromosomes.
11. One possibility is that the mother's eggs deteriorate over time. Another possibility is that older mothers mate with older fathers who, because of their age, may have more defective sperm. We can also not rule out the possibility that older women may be more likely to have been exposed to some environmental agent that may damage the ova (such as radiation or drugs).

Box 3.8

1. Answers will vary because this issue is a matter of opinion. However, you could certainly argue that ants really aren't capable of showing concern for others in the same ways humans can.
2. A behaviorist might counter that certain behaviors are reinforced by all existing environments.
3. They seem to be.
4. Answers will vary because this issue is a matter of opinion. However, we do not seem to have rigidly preprogrammed instincts the way some primitive animals have. But, given cultural universals, we may have some predispositions.
5. The animal research shows that genes can control behavior in animals.

Box 3.10

1. Since this is a case study, we do not know whether Genie would have still had trouble with language even if she had been spoken to during her early years. It may be that she was born with brain damage or that malnutrition caused her language deficits. In addition, we should be wary of generalizing from one individual to all of humanity.
2. There appears to be an assumption that mothers are naturally good parents to their own children—even when there is evidence to the contrary.
3. Probably not. The mother was ultimately not charged with any crimes, probably because she was viewed as a passive victim of the tyrannical father. Society would be more reluctant to accept the view that the father could be a passive victim of the mother's whims. In our society, men are seen as active (whether as heroes, corporate leaders, or villains), whereas women are often seen as passive (whether as "groupies," executive assistants, or codependents).

4–5. Answers will vary because these issues are matters of opinion.

Box 3.11

1. The onset of puberty, the onset of menopause, the onset of Huntington's chorea, being ready to walk, and being ready to talk are all examples of genes influencing people after conception.
2. If the drug that causes cell damage is introduced during the sensitive period for brain development, retardation may result. However, if that same drug is introduced when the sensitive period is past, little or no damage may occur.
3. The unborn is most susceptible to teratogens during the first trimester. Because the brain and central nervous system develop most rapidly during the third trimester, brain damage, if it occurs, is most likely to occur during this period.
4. Smokers differ from nonsmokers in a variety of ways. They not only smoke more, but they also drink more alcohol and consume more caffeine. In many cases, it is hard to determine whether an effect is due to exposure to nicotine or caffeine or to some other factor.
5. Fetal alcohol syndrome depends not only on whether the mother drinks, but also on *when* she drinks as well as the infant's genetic vulnerability to this syndrome.
6. The case study was used to estimate the effects of nuclear radiation on the unborn. The case study is not a good research method because it is hard to generalize from a poor and limited sample and because it usually does not allow us to make cause-effect conclusions. However, in this case, many people were affected; there was a solid, biological basis for explaining how radiation could have such affects; and there were no reasonable alternatives for the rapid rise in defects.
7. Leading postnatal threats are lead poisoning and the lack of such chemicals as proteins and iron.
8. A good diet during late childhood can help make up for malnutrition in early childhood in terms of height and weight. However, it cannot completely make up for losses in intelligence.
9. For a detailed examination of the differences between attachment and imprinting, see table 3.9. Sensory stable factors are events in the environment that almost everyone is exposed to (hearing language), whereas as sensory variable factors are environmental events that are *not* common to everyone (going to college, having your particular mother and father).

10. It's a sensory variable factor because not all elderly people go on weight-lifting programs.
11. A trait that is strongly influenced by the environment has a broad reaction range, is not highly canalized and is probably low in heritability.
12. A sensitive period is a time during which biological events are such that the organism is ready to develop in a certain way. Furthermore, if the organism does not get the necessary stimulation and environmental support during this time, development in that area will be limited or nonexistent. For example, the case of Genie suggests that the sensitive period for learning language ends before age 14—if we don't learn language by then, we will have a very difficult time learning language because the time period during which our brain was ready to learn language has expired.
13. Having children exercise the stepping reflex causes them to walk about two months earlier than they normally would.

Box 3.12

1. Microsystem, mesosystem, exosystem, and macrosystem.
2. The individual has more control over the mesosystem because, in contrast to the exosystem, we do experience it directly.
3. This is a matter of opinion. You have the most control over your microsystem, but it is the macrosystem that is at the root of your problems. Thus, depending on how ambitious you are, you might try to make changes at the macrosystem level (changing society's values), or you might work on an exosystem (the parent branch of the company you work for, the board of trustees at your school), or you might work on components of your mesosystem (your peers, your immediate workplace).
4. Cross-cultural research gives us insight into a powerful environmental system that we may tend to ignore—the macrosystem.
5. Working mothers may experience conflicts at the mesosystem level. That is, their roles as parent and as worker may conflict. They may also experience some conflict at the macrosystem level if societal norms and values oppose letting women work. Furthermore, inadequate transportation or day care may present some exosystem conflicts.
6. Similarities between twins would be most impressive if the twins were reared in different macrosystems.
7. The heritability of traits will appear to be high and traits will appear to be highly canalized for one simple reason: the sensory variable factors are being limited. If environmental events are held constant, then any differences between individuals would have to be due to heredity. Note that this does not mean that environmental factors cannot and do not play a role in development. It only means that, in this culture, differences between individuals are hard to trace to environmental events because everyone is being exposed to roughly the same environmental events. Thus, similarities among individuals may be due to the environment, but these similarities are not measured by the heritability quotient. As you may recall, the heritability quotient only tries to determine the extent to which heredity makes people differ.
8. If a trait has a wide reaction range, it is strongly affected by the environment. Consequently, it is *not* highly canalized.
9. If we look at the IQs of people who share very similar genes, but experience very different environments, the heritability quotient for IQ in that population will be *low*. If, on the other hand, we look at the IQs of people from distinctly different genetic backgrounds and who experience a common environment, the heritability quotient for IQ in that group will be *high*.
10. It is hard to prove that a behavior is universal. However, even once that is done, we cannot say that the universality is due to genes that we all share. It could be due to similarities between our environments.
11. Answers will vary because this issue is a matter of opinion. Clearly, we are making an inference when we generalize from animals to humans. People who argue that we can generalize would point to the theory of evolution as providing a rationale for generalizing from animals to humans and would point to instances where results from animals held true for humans. People who argue that we cannot generalize would say that there are qualitative differences between us and the other animals and would point to cases where results from animals did not generalize to humans.
12. Comparing two siblings who were reared apart results in a "purer" (but by no means pure) index of the effect of heredity, whereas if we only compare two siblings reared together, we don't have any idea about whether the similarities are due to heredity or sharing a common family environment.
13. All have the same heritability quotient—0.50.
14. a. Monozygotic twins should have the highest correlation; the unrelated, adopted children should have the lowest. b. By subtracting the similarity between two unrelated siblings living in the same household from the similarity between two related siblings, the investigator is trying to estimate the effect of heredity that is unbiased by the fact that the related siblings live together. Note that this strategy may work in subtracting environmental effects caused by events that all family members experience. However, if related family members are treated more similarly and have a more similar environment than unrelated family members, then this estimate would overestimate the role of heredity. c. If the investigator looked only at similarities between identical twins, the correlations would reflect the effect of both heredity and sharing the same family environment. By subtracting the correlations obtained for fraternal twins, the investigator has controlled—to some extent—for the effect of living in a similar environment. However, if identical twins are treated more similarly than fraternal twins, then the estimate will still overestimate the effects of heredity.
d. Both should be the same because the difference in genetic

similarity in both cases is 0.50 (0.50 – 0 = 0.50 for comparing siblings to unrelated persons; 1.00 – 0.50 = 0.50 for comparing identical twins to fraternal twins).

15. Identical twins may talk to each other more than fraternal twins or they may be more likely to take the same classes.

16. It's possible that identical twins may share some ability that is not directly related to classical definitions of intelligence. For example, they may work, read, and move at the same rate of speed or they may react to time pressure in the same way.

17. You would use identical twins because any differences—any correlation less than 1.00—would be strong evidence of the effect of environment. Furthermore, you might be able to claim that similarities were due to sharing a common environment. Therefore, no matter what you found, it would provide evidence for the effect of environment.

Chapter

Physical Development

Whatever is formed for long duration
arrives slowly to its maturity.
SAMUEL JOHNSON

Chapter Overview

Each of us began as a single cell. As adults, we now have more than 100 billion cells in our brain alone. How was this physical transformation accomplished? What changes lie in store for us in the years to come? In this chapter, we will address these and other questions about physical development.

One reason we will be discussing physical development is that physical development is interesting in its own right. For example, many parents are delighted by their infants' rapid physical growth and some are obsessed by their own gradual physical decline. Similarly, many of us are interested in knowing if our physical development is determined entirely by heredity or if there are things we can do to optimize our physical development.

Another, more important, reason that we will be discussing physical development is that physical development affects psychological development. Thus, in this chapter we will address such questions as:

What are the psychological effects of reaching puberty at 12? at 16?

What steps can be taken to minimize the negative physical aspects of aging?

What are the psychological effects of menopause?

What can be done to reduce the chances of becoming senile in old age?

Prenatal Physical Development

Physical development begins at conception. At that instant, a single sperm cell fertilizes an ovum (egg). Although this fertilized egg is only one cell, it contains a genetic blueprint to build an entire body. If the blueprint is accurate and all goes well, this single cell will develop into a fully functioning infant in about 9 months (average gestation is 38 weeks post ovulation) (Blackburn & Loper, 1992).

Because so many changes occur during these 9 months, it would be confusing to talk about **gestation** (the time between conception and delivery) as a single period. Therefore, to more clearly communicate the massive changes that occur during gestation, developmental psychologists divide it into three periods: the period of the zygote, the period of the embryo, and the period of the fetus (see figure 4.1).

Figure 4.1

The Periods of Prenatal Development

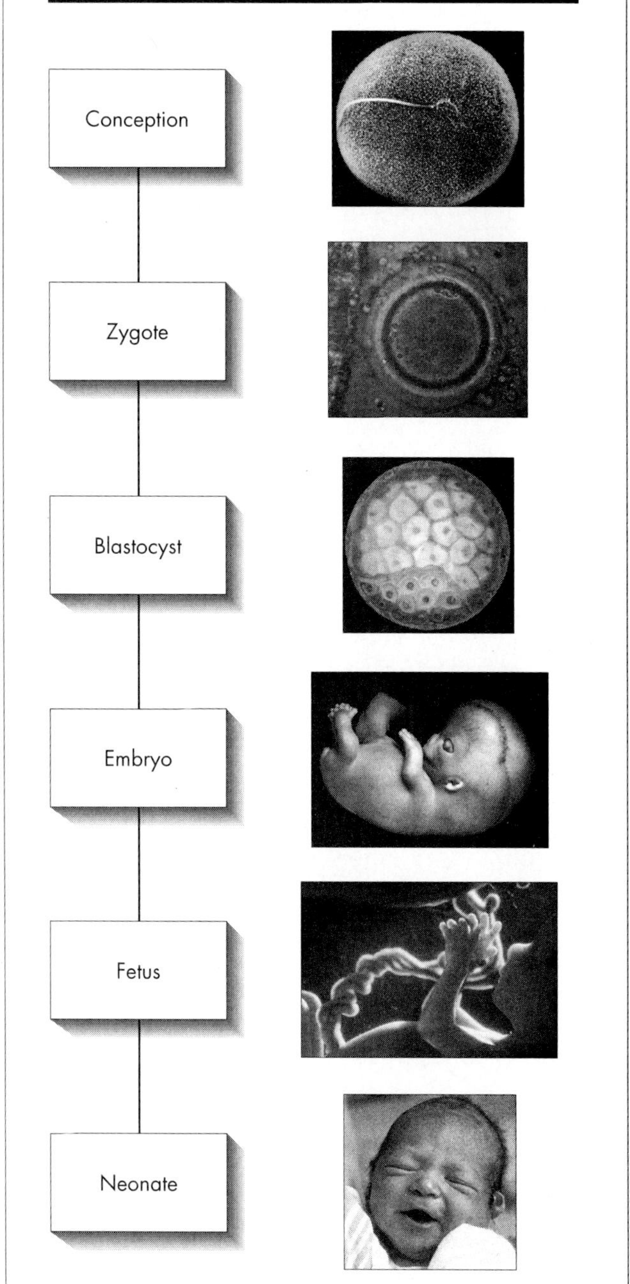

The Period of the Zygote: The First 2 Weeks of Life

During the first period, the **period of the zygote,** the zygote journeys through the fallopian tube (which is as thin as a hair) to the uterus. During its 6- to 10-day journey to the uterus, the zygote multiplies rapidly. Within 7 days, the one-celled fertilized egg has become a 100- to 150-cell, ball-like structure called a **blastocyst.**

As you can see in figure 4.2, the blastocyst has two layers of cells. The inner layer, the **embryoblast,** will develop into the embryo—and eventually into a person. The outer layer, the **trophoblast,** will become the placenta, the umbilical cord, and the amnion. In other words, the trophoblast will become the embryo's life-support system.

As the blastocyst nears the uterus, two things happen that will allow it to get nourishment from its mother. First, the blastocyst forms small, burr-like tentacles called tendrils. Second, the mother's uterus becomes engorged with blood so that the uterus can nourish and sustain a developing embryo. Thus, by the time the blastocyst enters the uterus, everything is ready for implantation.

Implantation occurs when the tendrils tap the mother's blood supply by burrowing into the uterine wall, an action that is critical for two reasons. First, it allows the blastocyst to take in vital nourishment from the mother's blood. Second, it allows the blastocyst to secrete the hormone human chorionic gonadotrophin (HCG) into the mother's blood supply. HCG signals the brain and pituitary gland to continue sending luteinizing hormone (LH) to stop the mother from menstruating (Blackburn & Loper, 1992; Moore, 1982). If the blastocyst, which is smaller than the eraser on the top of a pencil, did not secrete HCG, the blastocyst might be swept out of the woman's body with her monthly menstrual flow.

The release of HCG makes early pregnancy detection possible. Although a woman may suspect that she is pregnant when she skips a period, skipping a period is only indirect and imperfect evidence that HCG has been released. If she wants to know whether she is pregnant, she should get direct evidence that she is producing HCG by testing her blood or urine for its presence. She can test her urine by either going to a physician or by using a do-it-yourself pregnancy test.

Figure 4.2

Blastocyst

The embryoblast will become the embryo. The trophoblast will become the embryo's support system.

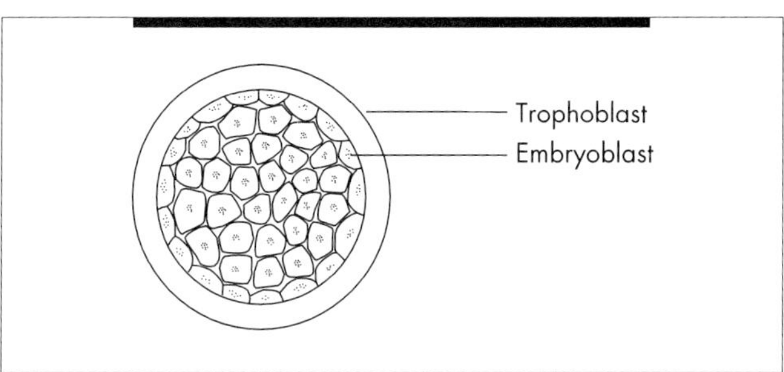

Figure 4.3

The Position of the Fetus Relative to the Placenta, Umbilical Cord, and Amniotic Sac

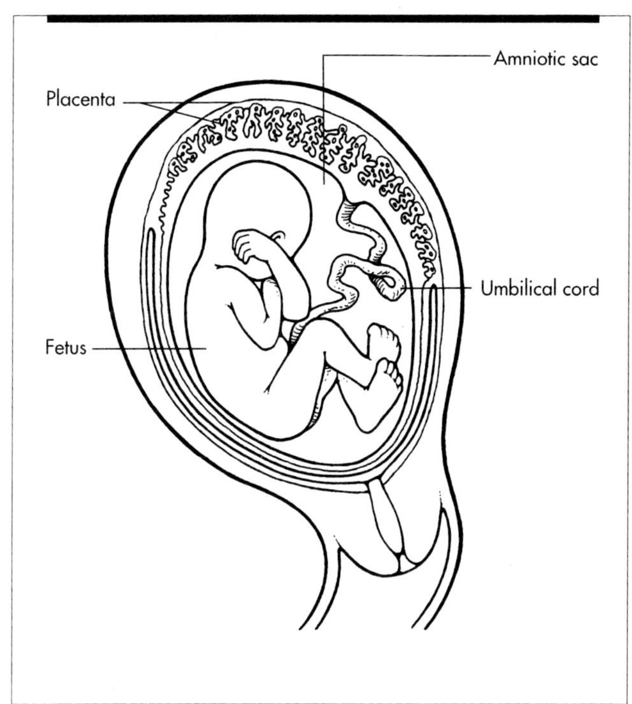

We should emphasize that these techniques for early pregnancy detection work only if there has been successful implantation. That is, they do not detect conception itself. This is an important point because conception does not always result in implantation. Indeed, half of all zygotes *never* implant in the uterus (Blackburn & Loper, 1992; Roberts & Lowe, 1975). Even those zygotes that do implant in the uterus may implant in a place that does not give them adequate, stable, and sustained access to the mother's blood supply. Partly because of these problems in implantation, only one out of four zygotes survive to birth (Diamond, 1986).

What is responsible for the high percentage of unsuccessful implantations? It would seem logical that implantation problems could be due to a defect in the uterus. However, implantation problems are rarely due to such defects: most women can accept implanted zygotes. Indeed, postmenopausal women—even those in their sixties—can give birth if they are implanted with a fertilized egg (Versci, Gholami, Panci, & Caffa, 1993). Instead, implantation problems usually result from one of two causes.

First, the fallopian tube may be clogged. Since the zygote can't reach the uterus, uterus implantation is impossible. If implantation occurs in the fallopian tube, a tubal pregnancy may result. Tubal pregnancies are life threatening to the mother because, as the embryo grows, it causes the fallopian tube to rupture. Without emergency surgery, the mother may bleed to death. Surgery not only terminates the pregnancy, but often results in the loss of a fallopian tube, making a subsequent pregnancy more difficult. The second major reason for implantation problems is that the zygote has severe genetic defects and it dies before reaching the uterus.

For the zygotes that do successfully implant, the period of the zygote ends about 2 weeks after conception. During these first 2 weeks of life, the successful blastocyst has accomplished some remarkable feats. It has grown from a single-celled organism into an organism containing more than 100 cells, and it has become linked to its mother's blood supply. Despite these accomplishments, the blastocyst is very unimpressive looking: It is only a small blister on the uterine lining (Apgar & Beck, 1974).

The Period of the Embryo: From 2 Weeks Through 2 Months

During the **period of the embryo,** the trophoblast (outer layer) develops into the placenta, umbilical cord, and amniotic sac (see figures 4.2 and 4.3). The tendrils that burrowed into the lining of the uterus thicken and become the **placenta,** an organ in which small blood vessels from the mother and the embryo intertwine to take nutrients and oxygen to the embryo and to remove wastes from the embryo's bloodstream.

The embryo (and later the fetus) is joined to the placenta at the abdomen by the **umbilical cord,** a structure containing two arteries and one vein that transport blood between the embryo and placenta. Although the mother's bloodstream exchanges material with her offspring's in the placenta, their blood never mixes. A membrane separates the mother's and embryo's blood vessels, allowing some substances to pass through, while blocking others. Unfortunately, as you learned in chapter 3, certain harmful drugs, such as insulin, alcohol, and cocaine, and certain diseases, such as AIDS and rubella, can be transferred along this route.

Figure 4.4

Cephalocaudal and Proximodistal Development

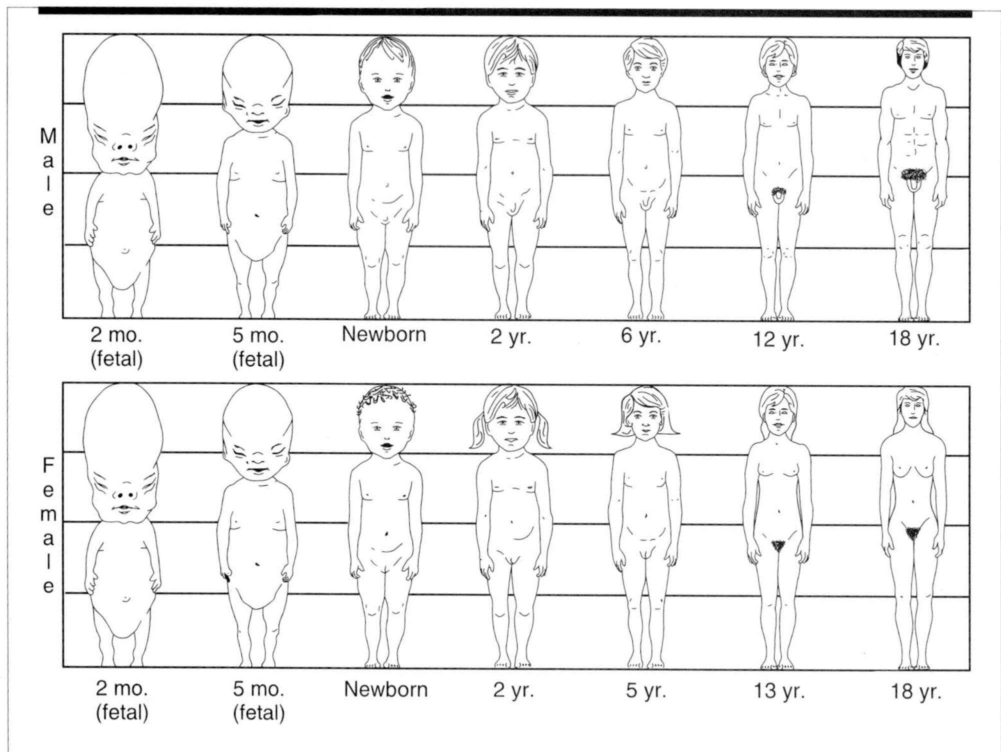

The final part of the trophoblast is the **amniotic sac,** a watertight bag that surrounds the embryo and contains amniotic fluid. By floating in the amniotic fluid, the embryo is cushioned from injury and maintained at a constant, warm temperature.

Protected by the amniotic sac and nourished by the placenta, the embryo grows rapidly. By the end of this period, the embryo will be recognizable as human (see figure 4.1). From the time of conception until the end of the second month, the baby's size will increase 2 million percent (Hetherington & Park, 1993). At no other period of development will the individual experience such rapid growth (Apgar & Beck, 1974).

Although the rapid growth is impressive, the most dramatic changes during the period of the embryo involve the development of vital organs and physiological systems. From the original single layer of cells that was the blastocyst, all the organs, glands, muscles, bones, and major systems develop.

Describing the timing of all the changes that occur during the six-week period of the embryo is difficult. Fortunately, however, embryonic development—as well as fetal and infant physical development—seems to proceed according to two fundamental principles: cephalocaudal and proximodistal.

Cephalocaudal[1] development refers to the fact that physical development usually starts at the head and then moves down the body until it reaches the toes. As you can see in figure 4.4, development proceeds *downward* from head to toe (top to bottom). In accordance with the cephalocaudal sequence, the head is the first part of the embryo to develop.

The principle of **proximodistal** development refers to the fact that development usually occurs in the middle of the body before it occurs in the periphery. In figure 4.4, you can see that development proceeds from the center of the body and then radiates *outward* toward the extremities. In accordance with the proximodistal sequence, the inner organs develop first, then the arms and legs, and finally the hands and fingers.

To more precisely specify the timeline of embryonic development, the head, central nervous system, heart, and inner organs (except the genitals) start developing during the first two weeks of the embryo period. Next, the arms, legs, hands, and feet grow (Moore, 1982).

By the end of the embryonic period, several miraculous events have occurred. The embryo's gender is established. (For a detailed explanation about how sex differentiation occurs, see box 4.1.) The embryo's tiny heart starts to beat, pulsing blood through its circulatory system. The brain now exerts dominance over the embryo's other developing systems, causing muscles to contract, and signaling the endocrine system to secrete hormones.

The embryo's liver manufactures red blood cells; its eyes, nose, ears, and mouth are formed; and its arms, legs, toes, fingers, and external genitalia are delineated. By the eighth week after conception, the embryo weighs just 1/30 of an ounce, yet it has all the parts and organs of a human. It is now a fetus.

[1] The term *cephalocaudal* literally means "head to tail." However, in human development, it denotes head to toe development.

Box 4.1

ISSUE in FOCUS

Prenatal Sex Differentiation

Gonads are the organs that produce sex cells (ova or sperm) and sex hormones. In the sixth week of gestation, both XX and XY embryos develop the indifferent gonad, a cluster of cells that could potentially become either the male gonads (testes) or the female gonads (ovaries). In addition, all embryos have primitive forms of both the male *and* female sex structures (that is, the Wolffian and Müllerian structures). The Wolffian structure is a primitive form of the epididymis, vas deferens, and seminal vesicles (see Figure 4.13). The Müllerian structure is the precursor to the fallopian tubes, uterus, and upper vagina. Although the embryo's genotype will predispose it to develop as either a female or male, the embryo at this stage has the potential to become either sex.

In the normal female embryo, the gonads develop into the ovaries and the Müllerian structure develops into the fallopian tubes, uterus, and the upper portion of the vagina. The Wolffian structure naturally withers away as the Müllerian structure develops.

Male sex differentiation is more complicated. Possessing the gene, testis determining factor on the Y chromosome (Page et al., 1987), is only the first step in male sex differentiation. Unless, three events occur, the embryo will develop as a female, or have female sex characteristics. Consequently, some biologists go so far as to say all fetuses start out female and that male sex differentiation is a deviation from the female plan (Bleier, 1984).

First, for an XY embryo to develop into a normal male, the Y chromosome must release a protein that stimulates the indifferent gonad to develop into the testes. If this protein is not released, then the XY embryo will develop into a female.

Second, the placenta, the organ that nourishes and sustains the fetus, must successfully stimulate the testes of the male (XY) embryo to produce testosterone. Testosterone, in turn, stimulates the development of the Wolffian structure into the male reproductive structures. (The placenta sends similar messages to female fetuses but because XX fetuses don't have testes, they don't produce sufficient amounts of male sex hormone to deviate from the initial female plan).

Third, to become a normal male, the female genital tract must degenerate. The female (Müllerian) structure will degenerate only if the XY embryo's testes produce a hormone specially designed for that purpose, the Müllerian regression factor (MRF). The release of MRF in a male embryo causes the Müllerian structure to be absorbed.

In short, the male embryo is masculinized by testosterone and defeminized by MRF. If a male embryo fails to secrete male sex hormones or lacks receptors for the male hormones, then the embryo may mature into a girl or possess some female sex characteristics (such as fallopian tubes).

The Period of the Fetus: 3 to 9 Months

The final phase of prenatal development, the **period of the fetus,** lasts from the third month until birth. During this stage, the organs and physiological systems mature to the point that the fetus can survive in the outside world.

Starting in the third month, the bones partially harden, muscles develop, and the external genitalia become recognizable as male or female. Around the end of the fourth month, the mother will feel her baby move for the first time, and the fetal heartbeat can be heard with a stethoscope.

At about five months, basic reflexes necessary for early survival outside the uterus appear. Sucking, swallowing, hiccuping appear, along with the less vital **Babinski reflex,** the fanning of the toes in response to stroking the bottom of the foot. During the fifth and sixth months, the nails begin to harden, the skin thickens, sweat glands form, and eyebrows, eyelashes, and scalp hair sprout. In addition, a soft, down-like hair called **lanugo** covers the baby's body. (Most fetuses shed their lanugo before they are born.)

By six months, the eyes have developed and the fetus can open and close them. Somewhere around the 24th and 25th week of gestation,[2] the fetus reaches the **age of viability,** the point when the organs and physiological systems of most fetuses are mature enough for the fetus to survive outside the womb (see figure 4.5).

[2] As technology develops, fetuses will be able to survive at younger and younger ages. If the age of viability is defined as the point at which the fetus has any chance of survival, then the age of viability can be as early as 20 weeks.

Figure 4.5

Survival as a Function of Gestational Age

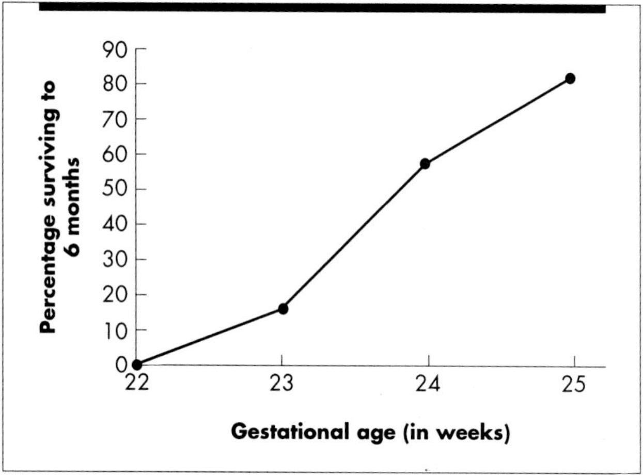

Source: November 26, 1993, *New England Journal of Medicine.*

A major reason that most infants born before this time do not survive is because their bodies don't produce enough **surfactin,** a liquid that allows the lungs to transfer oxygen from the air into the blood. Without enough surfactin, air sacs in the infants' lungs collapse, and they die from **respiratory distress syndrome.** Fortunately, recent medical advances in manufacturing surfactin (such as the drug Exosurf) may decrease the incidence of respiratory distress syndrome deaths, as may technological advances that would allow young infants to do what they did while in the womb—"breathe" liquids that contain oxygen, rather than breathing air (Horbar, Wright, Soll, Wright, Fanaroff, & Korones, 1993).

Summary of Prenatal Development

In this section, you learned about the three periods of prenatal development. During the first phase, the period of the zygote, the ovum is fertilized and the blastocyst journeys from the fallopian tube to the uterus. Implantation marks the beginning of the period of the embryo. During the period of the embryo, the major organ systems emerge and start to carry out their functions. During the period of the fetus, the organs and physiological systems mature to the point that the fetus can survive outside the uterus.

Birth

Sometime around the ninth month after conception, the fetus is ready to be born. The mother's uterus starts having contractions and expels a brand new baby. The actual birth process takes place in three distinct phases (see figure 4.6).

The first and longest phase is **effacement and dilation,** a period marked by the thinning (effacement) and enlargement (dilation) of the cervix. That is, as the cervix stretches, it gets thinner (just as a rubber band gets thinner as it is stretched). This stretching, called dilation, allows the cervix to get big enough for the baby to pass through. For many first-time mothers, effacement and dilatation may be a 12- to 15-hour ordeal. Fortunately, this phase is usually much shorter (only 6 to 8 hours) for subsequent deliveries.

Figure 4.6

The Position of the Fetus at Birth

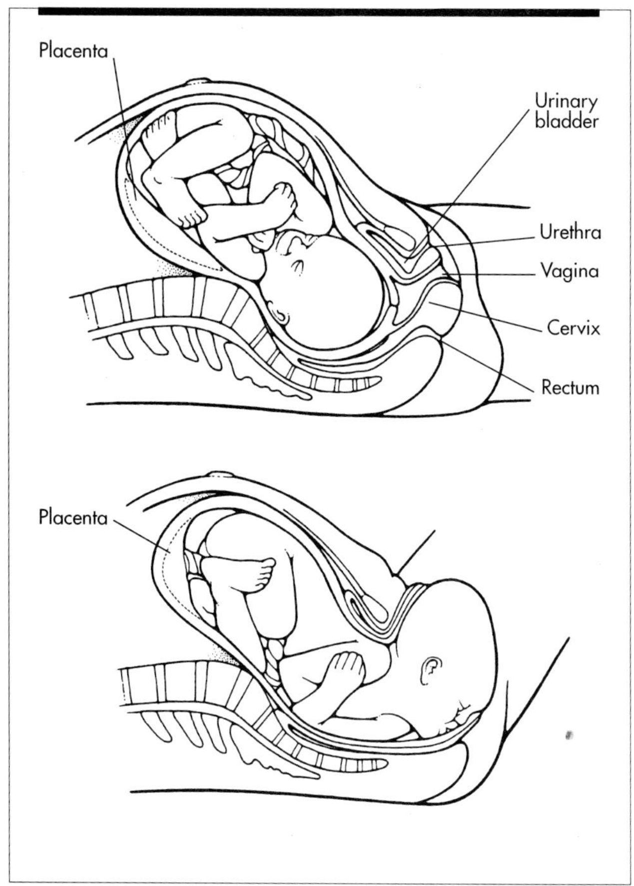

The second phase is **expulsion of the fetus,** the actual delivery of the baby. Once the cervix has dilated to about 10 centimeters, the mother is actively trying to push the baby out through the birth canal (vagina). This is usually quite painful and lasts about 90 minutes for a first delivery and 45 minutes for subsequent births.

The third phase is **expulsion of the afterbirth.** A few minutes after delivery, the mother's body expels the placenta and other fetal membranes (i.e., the afterbirth).

The Effects of Birth on the Neonate

The birth experience is a difficult experience not only for the mother but also for the baby. Imagine having your head and body shoved through a tube substantially smaller than

Box 4.2

SELF-CHECK

PART A
Indicate whether each of the following statements is true or false.

1. Most zygotes successfully implant in the uterus.
2. The two-month-old embryo weighs more than half a pound.
3. The embryo has soft bones.
4. Four months after conception, the fetus has reached the age of viability.

PART B
Answer the following questions.

5. Put the following periods of prenatal development in the correct order: embryo, fetus, and zygote.
6. How soon after conception can pregnancy be detected?
7. During the period of the embryo, which develops first—legs or feet? Head or neck?
8. What is the purpose of the amniotic sac? The purpose of the placenta?
9. Babies seem to have big heads. What principle does this exemplify?

you are. No matter what angle you try, the only way to get through is for the bones in your skull to compress so that your head comes out somewhat pointed and your body is bruised and battered. You may look the worse for wear, until the bones in your head slide back into place and your body assumes a normal color. Fortunately, most babies survive the birthing experience just fine. However, if the labor is long and the birth canal narrow, the potential for permanent harm is real. The power and force of a mother's contraction may break her baby's bones or even crush her baby's skull.

A **neonate** (newborn) may also be damaged during delivery if the physician uses forceps to change the angle of the baby's head or to pull the baby out. The extent of damage depends on the location where the forceps were placed and the amount of pressure exerted to extract the baby. Forceps casualties include cerebral palsy (motor damage), mental retardation, blindness, and deafness. The use of forceps was quite common in the days when most women were anesthetized during delivery. Because a woman was unconscious, she couldn't help push her baby out, so forceps were usually necessary to remove the baby (hence the procedure was often referred to as the "knock 'em out and drag 'em out" technique). Today, most babies are born to conscious mothers, and the need for forceps has been greatly diminished.

But, what about difficult deliveries? Suppose a baby is positioned incorrectly (see figure 4.6) to pass through the birth canal? Or, what if the mother's birth canal can't accommodate the baby? Fortunately, physicians save many high-risk babies from extreme physical trauma by delivering them through **Cesarean section,** an operation in which the baby is removed through the walls of the abdomen and uterus.

About 25 percent of all deliveries in the United States are through Cesarean (Taffel et al., 1991). However, even the Cesarean procedure has risks. Although a Cesarean-delivered infant is not battered, the newborn risks receiving some brain damage from oxygen poisoning because it is exposed to oxygen too fast. Recently, researchers have argued that physicians are too eager to perform Cesarean sections because they wish to avoid malpractice lawsuits (Localio et al., 1993; Masters, Johnson, & Kolodny, 1985). Indeed, some experts believe that fewer than 15 percent of all births should be by Cesarean section (Sperling, 1990).

Assessing Neonatal Health

Because of the potential for trauma during birth, the possibility of congenital defects, and the dangers associated with a baby being born before its organ systems are mature enough to sustain life outside the womb, a newborn's health status should be assessed directly following birth and monitored closely thereafter. If a problem is detected, special medical care should be provided to help the newborn survive.

For many years, the **Apgar Scale** (Apgar & Beck, 1974), has been used to assess the health of newborns (see table 4.1). At 1 minute and 5 minutes after birth, a physician or nurse gives the newborn a rating of 0, 1, or 2 on each of five dimensions: heart rate, respiratory effort, muscle tone, body color, and reflex irritability. A high score of 7 to 10 indicates that the newborn's condition is good, a score of 5 may suggest some developmental difficulties, and a score of 3 or less indicates that the infant will probably die.

Table 4.1

The Apgar Scale

	Score		
	0	**1**	**2**
Heart rate	Absent	Slow—less than 100 beats per minute	Fast—100 to 140 beats per minute
Respiratory effort	No breathing for more than one minute	Irregular and slow	Good breathing with normal crying
Muscle tone	Limp and flaccid	Weak, inactive, but some flexion of extremities	Strong, active motion
Body color	Blue and pale	Body pink, but extremities blue	Entire body pink
Reflex irritability	No response	Grimace	Coughing, sneezing, and crying

Source: From Virginia Apgar, "A Proposal for a New Method of Evaluation of the Newborn Infant" in *Current Researches in Anesthesia and Analgesia*, 32: 260–267, 1953.

Whereas the Apgar Scale is used to assess difficulties immediately following birth, the Brazelton Neonatal Behavioral Assessment Scale (NBAS) (Brazelton, 1973, 1984, 1988; Brazelton, Nugent, & Lester, 1987) is used to assess long-term neurological health. On the third day following birth, an examiner rates the newborn on 26 categories (see table 4.2). Then, the neonate is assessed on the same dimensions several days later.

A low score on the NBAS indicates brain damage. If an infant scores below average, parents are encouraged to go through Brazelton training, an enrichment program that trains parents to stimulate their infant's development.

Preterm and Low Birth-Weight Infants

Some babies receive low scores on the Apgar and Brazelton Scales because they were born too early. That is, rather than being a normal full-term infant who has a gestation period of 38 to 42 weeks, some infants are **preterm,** having a gestation period of less than 38 weeks.

Other babies receive low scores on the Apgar and Brazelton Scales because they aren't physically mature enough at birth. For example, whereas the average newborn weighs 7 1/2 pounds, about 7 percent of all newborns are **low birth-weight** infants who weigh less than 5 pounds.

As one might expect, many children who were born too early are not physically mature enough at birth. For example, most preterm infants are also low birth-weight infants. However, note that not all low birth-weight infants are preterm. Some low birth-weight infants have a normal gestational period. Infants who are small for their gestational age are most commonly called **small for date.**

To assess whether a small-for-date or preterm baby is at high risk, physicians determine whether the neonate has reached a sufficient level of physical maturity. For example, physically immature infants often have **lanugo** (fine downy hair) and a thick coating of **vernix** (a lanolin-like substance) on their faces and bodies. Their nipples may not be visible, and an immature male's testicles may not have descended into his scrotum. As most of these infants mature, the lanugo and vernix will disappear, nipples will develop, and the testicles will descend.

More crucial than the neonate's appearance, however, is whether reflexes such as breathing and sucking are present. If these reflexes are not present, the neonate will not survive without special equipment to help him breathe, maintain a constant temperature, and sustain nourishment. Even with special equipment, the neonate may not survive. In North America, about 60 percent of the infants born three months early and about 20 percent of the infants born one month early suffer from respiratory distress syndrome. Respiratory distress syndrome is responsible for about half of all newborn deaths in the United States (Behrman & Vaughan, 1983).

If the preterm infant does not succumb to respiratory distress syndrome, chances are fairly good that the infant will develop the reflexes necessary to support life. In fact, the neurological development of a short-gestation infant usually continues at about the same rate as if the infant were still in the womb (Kopp, 1983, 1987; Kopp & Kaler, 1989). For example, suppose an infant was born after a gestation period of 32 weeks. Then, 8 weeks after being born, he or she would show the same level of brain development as a 40-week unborn fetus.

Table 4.2

The 26 Categories on the Brazelton Neonatal Behavioral Assessment Scale

1. Response decrement to repeated visual stimuli
2. Response decrement to rattle
3. Response decrement to bell
4. Response decrement to pinprick
5. Orienting response to inanimate visual stimuli
6. Orienting response to inanimate auditory stimuli
7. Orienting response to animate visual stimuli—examiner's face
8. Orienting response to animate auditory stimuli—examiner's voice
9. Orienting response to animate visual and auditory stimuli
10. Quality and duration of alert periods
11. General muscle tone—in resting and in response to being handled, passive and active
12. Motor activity
13. Traction responses as he or she is pulled to sit
14. Cuddliness—responses to being cuddled by examiner
15. Defensive movements—reactions to a cloth over his or her face
16. Consolability with intervention by examiner
17. Peak of excitement and capacity to control self
18. Rapidity of buildup of crying state
19. Irritability during examination
20. General assessment of kind and degree of activity
21. Tremulousness
22. Amount of starting
23. Lability of skin color—measuring autonomic lability
24. Lability of states during entire examination
25. Self-quieting activity—attempts to console self and control state
26. Hand-to-mouth activity

From *Cultural Perspectives in Child Development* by Wagner and Stevenson. Copyright © 1982 W. H. Freeman and Company. Used with permission.

Causes of Low Birth-Weight and Preterm Infants

Researchers have identified several factors that may contribute to low birth-weight and preterm infants (Kramer, 1987). This research reveals that at-risk infants are most likely to be born to mothers who have any of the following characteristics:

- Have bad health,
- Are too thin,
- Smoke during pregnancy,
- Have not had good prenatal care,
- Live in high-crime neighborhoods,
- Belong to a minority group,
- Are teenagers,
- Have had many pregnancies, and
- Have previously had miscarriages, low birth-weight, or preterm infants.

All of these risk factors are associated with poverty. Thus, low birth-weight and preterm births are most common among the poor. For example, among healthy, economically comfortable, white women between 20 and 30 years of age, about 3 percent of all births are low birth-weight. In contrast, economically distressed, ethnic teenagers have rates that are sometimes three times higher (Hilts, 1991; Institute of Medicine, 1985). Consequently, because of the increase in poverty in the United States in recent years, the percentage of low birth-weight infants has been increasing.

Researchers make at least two general suggestions for what can be done to decrease the number of low birth-weight and preterm infants. First, women who are pregnant need better nutrition and medical care. It is especially important for mothers to gain between 24 to 28 pounds during pregnancy (Jonaitis, 1988). Gaining this weight corresponds to eating about 150 more calories per day during the first trimester and about 350 extra calories during the second and third trimesters. More important than gaining weight is sound nutrition before and during pregnancy. Physicians recommend a diet rich in vitamins and minerals, and they will usually prescribe vitamin supplements.

The second suggestion for decreasing the number of low birth-weight infants is that pregnant women should not smoke. Toxic agents contained in tobacco, such as nicotine, carbon monoxide, and cyanide, interfere with the supply of blood to the fetus. Consequently, the fetus is deprived of essential nutrients and oxygen (Maidman, 1988). The major effect of these toxic agents is that fetuses exposed to them do not grow adequately and are considerably smaller at birth than babies born to nonsmokers.

Long-Term Outcomes for Preterm and Low Birth-Weight Infants

If our society fails to prevent low birth-weight infants, what happens? Fortunately, disaster is avoidable. In recent years, advances in medical technology, skill, and knowledge have increased the number of low birth-weight infants who survive infancy. These advances have also decreased the chances for long-term negative developmental outcomes. Most low birth-weight infants develop normally or have mild to moderate dysfunctions (Beckwith & Parmelee, 1986; Cohen & Parmelee, 1983). There is even

Box 4.3

SELF-CHECK

Answer the following questions and fill in the blanks where indicated.

1. Some clinical psychologists and psychiatrists believe that people who suffer birth trauma are more susceptible to suicide. If this is true,
   a. Which of the following positions would this finding support—nature or nurture? stability or change? active or passive?
   b. This finding would have the greatest appeal to which one of the following theorists? Freud, Maslow, Piaget, or Skinner?
   c. Are there other explanations for the conclusion that "birth trauma causes a person to be unhappy and to commit suicide"?
2. Apgar scores will probably be higher ___________ after birth.
   a. 1 minute
   b. 5 minutes
3. "Good" scores on the Apgar would range from _____ to _____.
4. A baby is pink, shows no reflex irritability, actively squirms, has irregular and slow breathing, and has a heart rate of 120 beats per minute. What would be the baby's Apgar score?
5. What test assesses a newborn's reactivity to the environment?
6. A baby weighs 4.5 pounds at birth. It is clearly a ___________ infant. How could you determine whether it was a preterm baby or a small-for-date baby?
7. If a baby is preterm and has no breathing or sucking reflexes, can it develop those reflexes? Why do many preterm infants die?
8. What can be done to reduce the number of preterm and low birth-weight infants? What are the costs and benefits of such an approach?

Please turn to the end of this chapter to check your answers.

some hope for cocaine babies (Chasnoff, Griffith, MacGregor, Dirkes, & Burns, 1989; James & Coles, 1991).

Unfortunately, this technology is expensive and imperfect. It costs almost $160,000 to save the life of just one very small premature infant (Young & Stevenson, 1990). Furthermore, about 12 to 16 percent of the smallest low birth-weight infants and about 6 to 8 percent of the larger low birth-weight infants will be seriously handicapped (Kopp & Kaler, 1989). The most severe cognitive deficits appear among those who come from unstable and impoverished backgrounds (Milham et al., 1983).

The Developing Brain

Although low birth-weight infants who get poor care after birth are at the highest risk, low birth-weight infants may continue to have cognitive deficits even when they receive good nutrition after they are born. In all too many cases, they catch up physically, but not mentally. That is, they may reach normal height and weight, but their brain development—and consequently their cognitive development—never catches up.

There are at least two reasons why many "early" interventions have a limited effect on brain development. First, many of these interventions start well after the child is born. For example, Head Start originally focused on children who were 4 years old or older. Second, even those that start right after birth may be too late because, consistent with the cephalocaudal principle, the normal newborn's brain is substantially more developed than the rest of the body.

Before a child is born, she already has all the neurons she will ever have. In fact, the brain of an eight-month human fetus has two to three times *more* nerve cells than an adult brain (McAuliffe, 1985). The brain loses a tremendous number of brain cells right before birth and during childhood (Kandel, 1981).

Despite this loss of brain cells, the brain does develop and grow after the eighth month of prenatal development. One reason the brain develops and gains weight during early childhood is the explosive growth of connections (synapses) from one brain cell to another. These synapses are necessary to perform such human activities as walking, talking, and advanced thinking.

Although synapses grow throughout life, most of the growth of synapses occurs during the first five years of life (Bower, 1994). To better visualize this fact—and to clearly see the cephalocaudal principle in action—let's contrast brain development with body development. As you can see in figure 4.7, when children are born, their bodies weigh only about 5 percent of what their adult bodies will. In contrast, their brains are already 25 percent of adult weight. By age 2, their brains have blossomed to about 75 percent of adult weight while their bodies lag behind at a meager 20 percent. By about their fifth birthday, their

Figure 4.7

Brain and Body Development

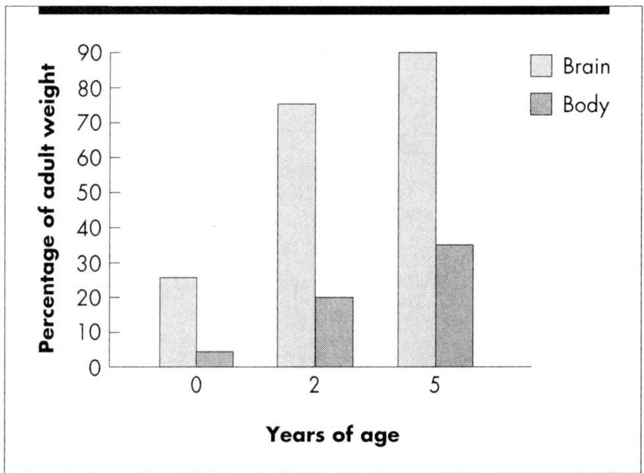

Figure 4.8

The Neuron

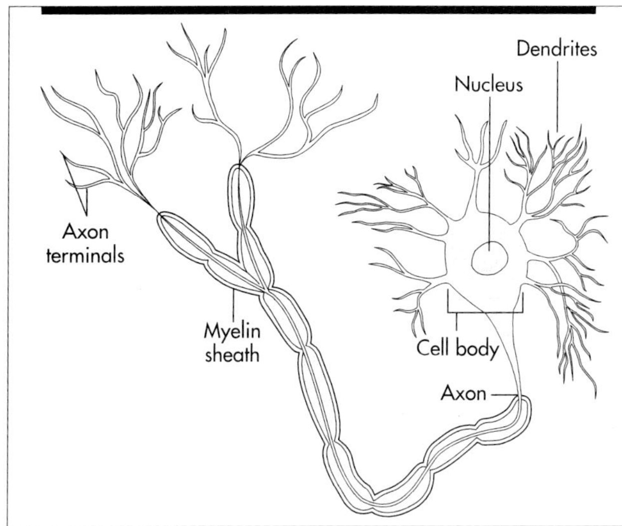

brains have achieved 90 percent of adult brain weight, whereas five years later, at age 10, their bodies will weigh only about 50 percent of their adult weight.

Why does the brain grow so quickly relative to the rest of the body? The main reason may be that it plays a major role in orchestrating the development of the rest of the body. In harmony with the endocrine system, the brain sends messages to the rest of the body, signaling it to grow and develop. To help you understand how the brain executes its role, let's review the major structures and organization of the central nervous system.

Neurons

The basic unit of the nervous system is the **neuron,** a nerve cell (see figure 4.8). The function of most neurons is to receive and transmit neural impulses to the other neurons. During prenatal development, the body manufactures about 250,000 neurons a minute (Cowan, 1979) and reaches a total of about 100 billion neurons (Hubel, 1979) at the time of birth. Birth marks the end of neuronal production. In other words, at birth each person has all the neurons that he or she will have for life.

Interestingly enough, much of the brain's weight is not from neurons, but from **glial cells** (from the Greek "glue") that nurture and protect the neurons. As the brain cells develop, glial cells produce **myelin,** a waxy substance, that forms a sheath around some of the neurons. Myelin speeds up the rate of neural transmission (just as putting insulation around a bare wire improves electrical transmission), thereby improving communication between neurons. Consequently, diseases that destroy myelin, such as multiple sclerosis and syphilis, impair neural communication. Furthermore, because myelin is so important to effective neural communication, many maturational changes correspond with **myelination,** the process of neurons being coated with myelin.

Motor development (the development of muscular coordination), for example, is linked to myelination. Since myelination of neurons proceeds according to both the cephalocaudal and the proximodistal principles, the sophistication of a person's motor activities also proceeds according to these principles. In accordance with the cephalocaudal principle, a baby is able to lift his head, then his chest. In accordance with the proximodistal principle, the baby is able to develop control over his arms before his hands. Later, after further myelination, he is able to reach out and grab objects with his hands, then sit, crawl, stand, walk, run, and skip.

Just as myelination of neurons in the body promotes motor development, myelination of neurons in the brain promotes language and cognitive development. For example, the acquisition of language coincides with the myelination of specific parts of the brain. In addition, increased cognitive abilities during adolescence coincide with the myelination of the **reticular formation,** the part of the brain responsible for attention.

Organization of the Brain

To better understand the effect of myelination on different parts of the brain, and to better understand brain development, you need to understand how the brain is organized. As you can see by looking at figure 4.9, the brain is organized into three distinct areas: the hindbrain, midbrain, and forebrain. From an evolutionary standpoint, the **hindbrain** is the most primitive part of the brain. It is also the most necessary for survival. The hindbrain governs such necessary functions as breathing, heart rhythms, and body temperature, as well as reflexes, movement, balance, coordination, attention, and sleep. In addition to regulating basic

Figure 4.9

The Brain

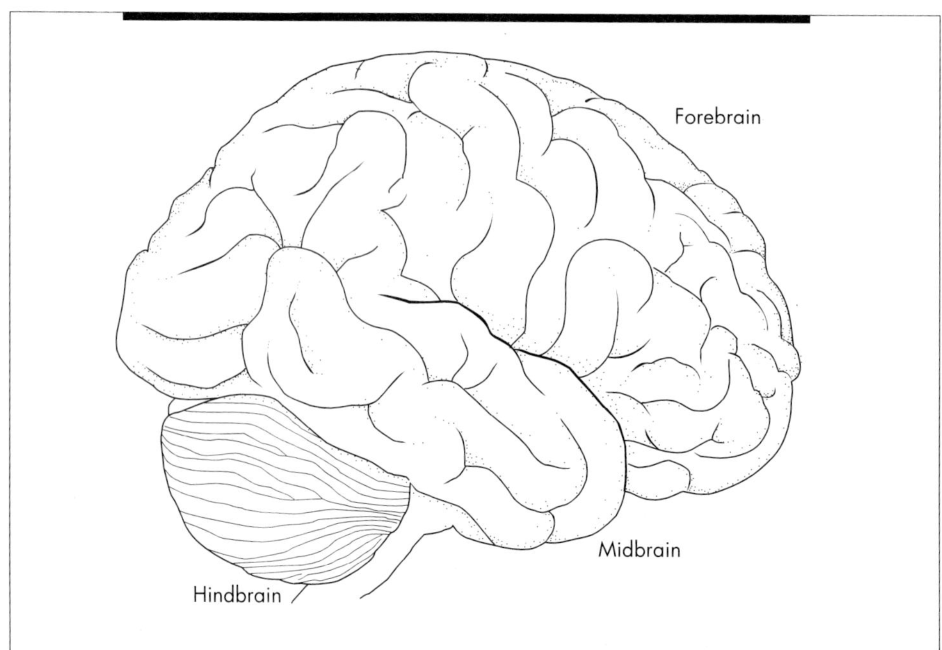

body functions, the hindbrain contains the neural pathways that connect the left side of the body with the right side of the brain, and the right side of the body with the left side of the brain.

Defects or injury to the hindbrain can be fatal. For example, if an infant has an immature hindbrain, the child may "forget" to breathe, resulting in **Sudden Infant Death Syndrome (SIDS).** SIDS is a leading cause of death in infants between 2 weeks and 1 year of age (Lipsitt, 1979).

Next oldest on the evolutionary scale is the midbrain. The **midbrain** serves as a relay station for almost all of the information coming in and out of the cerebral hemispheres. It relays to the higher cognitive centers what the rest of the body needs and relays to the rest of the body what to do to meet those needs.

Several structures in the midbrain form the **limbic system,** which plays a major role in emotions. Indeed, Jerome Kagan (1989) believes that emotional temperament, as well as a person's level of shyness, are the result of the particular limbic system that he or she inherited. The limbic system also plays a role in primitive urges like hunger, thirst, lust, and aggression. If the id is part of the brain, then the id is the limbic system. Malfunctions in the limbic system may lead to insatiable desire—or the lack of desire—for food, sex, or some other primitive need.

The newest part of the brain, in an evolutionary sense, is the **forebrain.** The forebrain is comprised of two halves called the two cerebral hemispheres. Although the cerebral hemispheres are not absolutely necessary for survival, they separate humans from all other animals because they control our highest intellectual functions. The forebrain is the center of creativity and inhibitions, our plans for the future and our abilities to implement them. The forebrain is what allows us to learn, speak, read, have thoughts, and realize dreams. In addition to being the center of thought, the forebrain dictates many of the body's actions. Furthermore, it inhibits the limbic system, sometimes by blocking emotions. Consequently, as the forebrain develops, the ability to plan increases, as does the ability to keep the limbic system's short-term emotional impulses under control.

To better understand how these three centers operate, think of a small company consisting of an executive officer (forebrain), a middle manager (midbrain), a foreman (hindbrain), and the workers (the rest of the nervous system). The hindbrain takes care of the moment-to-moment details necessary for the body to survive. It sends orders to the workers in the rest of the nervous system and responds to simple requests from these workers. Its decisions are limited to reflexes that adjust and regulate basic body functions and movements.

The midbrain doesn't deal with the mundane tasks of second-to-second survival. Rather, it deals with the task of day-to-day survival by meeting the body's basic needs for food, water, and sex and dealing with threats from the immediate environment.

The forebrain is concerned with the big, long-term picture. Not only does it want to ensure moment-to-moment and day-to-day survival, it wants to ensure future survival. Part of that survival is to learn about the environment and how to function within it.

Like most companies, the forebrain, midbrain, hindbrain, and the rest of the nervous system share a common goal—survival of the person or animal. And like most companies, communication occurs between the different levels of operation. Information sent up the ladder is usually for the purpose of informing and consulting. Information sent down the ladder is usually in the form of an order. Thus, the hindbrain informs the higher centers when there is a problem in temperature regulation. The forebrain gives orders to take measures that remedy the problem.

Cerebral Lateralization

Perhaps it would be more accurate to say that at least one of the two forebrains gives orders to take measures that remedy the problem. We say this because the two sides of the forebrain perform different functions. This tendency for the left and right cerebral hemispheres to carry out different functions is called **lateralization.**

Even before birth, the two cerebral hemispheres have different functions. The right cerebral hemisphere controls the left side of the body; the left cerebral hemisphere controls the right side of the body. As the cerebral cortex matures, lateralization increases as certain areas of each cerebral hemisphere begin to specialize in specific mental abilities. The left hemisphere is usually responsible for language, math, and speech; and the right hemisphere is usually responsible for tasks that involve interpreting visual and spatial information or information about people's emotional states. The two hemispheres not only process different kinds of information, but they process information in different ways. The left hemisphere processes information analytically and sequentially, while the right processes information simultaneously as a whole. To oversimplify, the left brain uses more step-by-step, logical reasoning whereas the right brain is more intuitive. (Some left-handed people are the mirror image of this pattern.) By the time most of us reach adulthood, this division of labor (lateralization of function) is pronounced.

Although the two hemispheres have specific skills, they do not operate in isolation. They are connected by a bridge of neurons, called the **corpus callosum,** that allows the two cerebral hemispheres to communicate freely. This is fortunate because human thought and creativity rely on the integration of right- and left-brain abilities. As Levy (1985) demonstrated, even the simple task of reading a story involves the integration of both hemispheres—the left to understand the words and their meaning, the right to appreciate the humor, emotional content, and imagery.

Laterality and Plasticity

The lateralization of the forebrain is important in brain development and the acquisition of necessary human skills. However, when brain cells become specialized in specific tasks they lose their **plasticity,** or capacity to work on other tasks. Because plasticity decreases with age, children who suffer brain damage are much more likely to recover physically and psychologically than adults. For example, children (up to age 8) who suffer damage to the speech area of their left hemisphere will often have no permanent speech impairment because their right hemisphere takes over. This is rarely the case for adults. Adults usually suffer permanent impairment because their brains have lost plasticity. One tragic consequence of this loss of plasticity is a poor prognosis for many adult stroke victims.

Laterality and Gender

Studies have pointed to two general abilities on which men and women differ. On the average, females show higher verbal ability than males, but lower spatial and math abilities. Although this difference is not great, and certainly couldn't be used to predict differences between a given man and woman, the difference in average scores between groups of men and groups of women is remarkably consistent. Can this difference be tied to differences in hemispheric specialization?

Brain research has far to go before this question is answered. However, we do know that men's brains are more lateralized than women's brains. Verbal and spatial abilities appear to be more widely distributed in both hemispheres for women, whereas they appear more rigidly segregated in men—verbal on the left, spatial on the right (Bloom, Lazerson, & Hofstander, 1985). The reason that women may be able to use both hemispheres more than men is because women's corpus callosums are bigger than men's (Hines, 1982). For this reason, women may be more likely to recover from brain damage. Similarly, women's advantage over men in verbal fluency may be due to the fact that women use both hemispheres for language.

Laterality and Reading

What happens if laterality fails to develop? Considerable evidence suggests that some cases of **dyslexia,** a reading disorder unrelated to intelligence, are caused by a defect in laterality development (Corballis, 1983). Some dyslexics have a hard time integrating information from different hemispheres. For example, when blindfolded and allowed to briefly hold an object in their left hand, dyslexics may have trouble picking out that object from a collection of objects if they have to pick it out with their right hand. Furthermore, many dyslexics tend to be able to read better if they cover one eye than if they use both eyes. Because many dyslexics have trouble integrating information received from different sides of the body (information that goes to different hemispheres), some experts feel that their problem is located in the corpus callosum (the bridge between hemispheres).

We should not lead you to believe that experts agree on the cause of dyslexia. Some experts believe the problem may be due to an inability to break down words into their component syllables and letters. This inability may stem from reading with the right brain (which recognizes only overall patterns and shapes of words) rather than with the left brain (which can break things down into parts). However, the inability to break down words into component parts may be due to the inability to sound the word out—dyslexics have

Figure 4.10

The Endocrine System

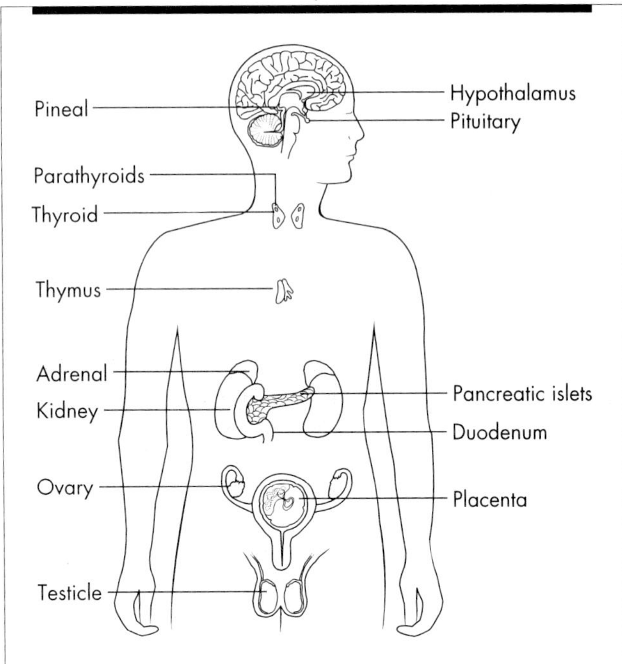

Figure 4.11

Acromegaly

difficulty integrating visual and auditory information. For example, dyslexics have trouble matching written words or letters to the sound of the word or letter (Vandershaf, 1987). Other experts argue that there are numerous types of dyslexia. Clearly, scientists do not yet agree on the exact nature of the dyslexic's problem.

The Endocrine System

Brain development is important not only because it affects mental development, but also because it regulates physical development. The brain orchestrates behavior and development in close association with the endocrine system (see figure 4.10). The endocrine system influences development by secreting **hormones—**potent chemical substances that regulate organs—into the bloodstream. Each hormone causes a specific reaction in the body. One might stimulate growth, another sperm production, and another might increase heart rate.

The **pituitary gland** is the "master gland" because its hormones stimulate the release of hormones from all other glands. As you can see in figure 4.10, the pituitary is a small pea-sized gland located at the base of the brain. As you will see in the next section, the pituitary, under the direction of the hypothalamus (a part of the brain's limbic system), initiates all the physical changes we associate with development.

The Developing Body

One of the hormones secreted by the pituitary is **growth hormone (GH),** which is responsible for the gains in weight and height associated with physical maturation. Growth hormone brings about physical growth by stimulating protein synthesis and causing the body's cells to divide. Not enough growth hormone during childhood results in **pituitary dwarfism,** a condition in which the person's body proportions appear normal, but the person is extremely small in stature. On the other hand, too much growth hormone during childhood results in **giantism,** a condition in which the person's body proportions appear normal, but their stature is enormous.

Normally, the amount of growth hormone produced by the pituitary tapers off during adolescence and our bodies stop growing (see box 4.4). However, sometimes a person starts to produce too much growth hormone during adulthood causing **acromegaly** to develop. As you can see from the photographs in figure 4.11, someone suffering from acromegaly will experience thickening of the tissues of the skin, nose, eyelids, and lips.

Box 4.4

ISSUE in FOCUS

Steroids and Sports

A current controversy exists over the use of synthetic forms of hormones, that is, steroids. Professional as well as amateur athletes have taken steroids to improve their athletic performance. From football players to female body builders, people have ingested synthetic forms of testosterone to help them build muscle. The pervasiveness of this trend is underscored by a 1989 NIH report claiming that 10 percent of high school males use steroids.

Although steroids can help athletes "bulk-up," steroids also damage vital organs such as the heart muscle and can lead to aggressive outbursts. Recently, another hormone, human growth hormone (HGH), has been synthesized. From the viewpoint of an ambitious athlete or parent of an athlete, human growth hormone has two advantages. First, HGH is hard to detect with drug tests. Second, HGH can increase not only strength, but also size. However, HGH users sometimes suffer severe side effects, such as acromegaly, high blood pressure, and heart failure. The power and side effects of steroids lead to some important ethical questions, such as these:

1. Do you think parents or coaches should be allowed to give children steroids? If not, what should be the penalty for giving children steroids?
2. Should children be allowed to decide whether they want steroids? Should adults be able to use steroids? Why? If not, what penalties would you impose on violators?
3. Do people have the right to "be the best they can be" in the short run, regardless of long-term risks?
4. Suppose HGH had these potential side effects, but reduced physical signs of aging. Should 60-year-olds be able to take HGH? What about 80-year-olds?
5. Suppose a drug was developed that had the same side effects as steroids and did for mental strength what steroids do for physical strength. Would the demand for the drug be as high as the demand for steroids? Should people be allowed to take such a drug? Why or why not?

The Sequence of Physical Growth

The effect of growth hormone is noticeable soon after birth. At birth, most neonates weigh between 6 and 9 pounds. Growth hormone stimulates such rapid growth that, by their second birthday, most children have gained 20 pounds (roughly four times their birth weight) and have reached half of their adult height. From age 2 until puberty, gains in height average of 2 to 3 inches per year, and weight gains are about 6 to 7 pounds a year. (Unfortunately, as you can see from box 4.5, some children gain much more weight than that.)

Accompanying these gains in height and weight are skeletal and muscular changes. At birth, most of a newborn's bones are soft, flexible, and resistant to breaks (a great advantage to anyone who wants to maximize the odds of surviving a trip through the birth canal). However, tasks such as sitting, standing, and walking can't be learned until these bones harden and become less flexible. During childhood new bones develop in the wrists and ankles that give children the control and coordination needed to tie their shoes, write, climb, and ride a bicycle.

In accordance with the cephalocaudal principle, the first bones to grow and harden are in the skull, and the last bones to harden are in the legs. Usually, the hardening of leg bones isn't complete until the late teens. (Consequently, some teenage weight lifters have needed surgery to correct the problem of developing muscles that are too strong for their leg bones.)

At the same time the skeletal system is growing, the muscles are also developing. However, whereas people develop new bone cells throughout life, they are born with all the muscle cells they will ever have. Rather than gain muscle cells, development is marked by the replacement of water in the muscle cells by salts and protein. Following the cephalocaudal principle, the first muscles to develop are in the head and neck, followed by the muscles in the trunk, arms, and legs. Thus, a baby can lift her head before she can sit up, and she can sit up before she can walk.

Both skeletal and muscular development are very gradual until **puberty,** the time of sexual maturation. With the onset of puberty, a surge of growth hormone triggers a growth spurt of about two years (see figures 4.12 and 4.13). Whereas physical development during childhood occurs in cephalocaudal and proximodistal directions, during the adolescent growth spurt, development occurs in the opposite directions. Legs grow to their full length before arms, and hands and feet reach their full size before arms and legs (Katchadorian, 1977). This reverse of normal body proportions may temporarily cause teenagers in the middle of this spurt to look gangly and awkward.

The first sign of the growth spurt is an increase in weight. Fat accumulates especially on the pubescent's thighs, arms, buttocks, and abdomen. An increase in height soon follows this weight gain, burning up some of the fat, and redistributing the rest. About one year after the gain in

Box 4.5

RESEARCH in FOCUS

Obesity

CONSEQUENCES OF OBESITY

Obesity affects both physical and psychological health. Physically, being overweight increases one's risk for heart diseases and diabetes. Psychologically, being overweight is linked to poor self-esteem (Raudenbush & Zellner, 1994). One reason that being overweight may be linked to low self-esteem is that discrimination against overweight people is pervasive and socially acceptable (Crandall, 1994). Indeed, overweight children are more likely to be teased, more likely to be excluded from peer groups, and more likely to be chosen last when children are picking teams. As adolescents, they will date less and be less likely to be admitted to a prestigious college. Once in college, their own parents will spend less money on them than on their slimmer siblings. Finally, in the job market, overweight people face discrimination. In short, overweight people are not treated fairly (Buckmaster & Brownell, 1988; Crandall, 1994; Myers, 1992).

OBESITY THROUGHOUT THE LIFESPAN

Because obesity can cause so much pain, experts have been searching for ways to prevent and cure obesity. Keys to successful prevention and cure come from understanding weight gain over the lifespan.

Contrary to what you might expect, obese infants do not always become obese adults. Indeed, 3 out of 4 heavy infants will be normal weight at age 21. However, if the child is overweight around age 4, the odds of being overweight as an adult increase tremendously. One reason for this is that the number of fat cells in the body is established early in life. Thus, if you are overweight as a child, you will have more fat cells than other people, even people who become overweight as adults. You can still lose weight, but you must do so by shrinking those fat cells. Keeping those fat cells shrunk is difficult (it's as if you have a "fat memory"). Consequently, 86 percent of overweight boys and 80 percent of overweight girls become overweight adults (Hetherington & Parke, 1993).

Unfortunately, people can gain weight at any time. Indeed, ages 25 to 34 are a prime time for getting fat. Becoming less physically active and drinking beer (which causes the body to burn up fat more slowly than normal) causes men to get bigger waists and to develop jowls and women to gain weight around their hips and stomachs. Women are especially likely to gain weight during this period, partly because having a child tends to add about 10 pounds per pregnancy.

George Blackburn (Hellmich, 1992) reports that ages 35 to 50 seem to be a good time for losing weight. Indeed, David Williamson (Hellmich, 1992) found that people in their forties are more likely than any other group to be dieting. After age 55, people's weight usually decreases.

NATURE OR NURTURE?

We have looked at when weight gain occurs, but what causes weight gain? Despite the fact that being overweight in early infancy does not predict being overweight in adulthood, naturists make a strong case for genetic factors. They argue that, at around age 4, there is a critical period for obesity. This argument is supported by the fact that the number of fat cells are determined fairly early in life. More convincingly, they show that infants of two

Continued

height and weight, the muscles grow. Although the growth spurt is similar for both boys and girls, the two sexes perceive it quite differently: Girls see these gains as getting fatter, whereas boys see the gains as getting stronger and more muscular.

There is considerable variation in when individual children experience the growth spurt. Thus, knowing that the average age for girls is 10 1/2 and 13 for boys (Tanner, 1981) is not that helpful in predicting the onset of an individual child's growth spurt. For example, even though the average for girls is 10 1/2, a girl may start as early as 7 1/2 years or as late as 12.

Surprisingly, the timing of the growth spurt seems to have implications for math ability. For some reason, children who mature later than the average age tend to have better spatial ability than early maturers (Waber, 1977).

Not surprisingly, the exact timing of the growth spurt has implications both for how other people treat the emerging adolescent as well as for the adolescent's self-perceptions. Generally, an early-maturing boy is held in high esteem and tends to have high self-esteem, whereas an early-maturing girl is an outcast and has low self-esteem. Conversely, males are distressed to be slow maturing,

RESEARCH in FOCUS

Concluded

obese parents have a greater sweet tooth than infants born of two parents of normal weight (Milstein, 1980). This is a convincing bit of evidence because (1) a sweet tooth in infancy predicts obesity at age 3 and (2) children of two obese parents are much more likely to be obese than children of two normal-weight parents (Winnick, 1974).

In addition to showing that obesity runs in families, researchers have shown that at least one reason that obesity runs in families is genetic. For example, adopted children and biological parents' weights are correlated, but adopted children's weights are **not** correlated with the weights of their adoptive parents (Stunkard, Sorenson, Hanis, Teasdale, Chakraboryty, Schull, & Schulsinger, 1986). Furthermore, if one identical twin is overweight, then the other twin is likely to be overweight—and this relationship is twice as strong as the relationship found in pairs of fraternal twins (Stunkard, Foch, & Schulsinger, 1986). Finally, even when identical twins are reared apart, the weight of one twin corresponds closely with the weight of the other twin (Bouchard, Lykken, Segal, & Wilcox, 1986).

Nurturists point out that the naturists' evidence does not conclusively exclude the role of the environment. Indeed, the fact that many twin pairs consist of one overweight twin and one average-weight twin shows that the environment has a role. Similarly, the fact that fat cells are determined at an early age does not mean that heredity determines the number of fat cells. What parents feed their children—not heredity—may determine the number of fat cells. In some people's minds, the case for fat cells being determined by early feeding patterns rather than heredity is strengthened by the fact that there is very little relationship between obesity in early infancy and obesity in adulthood.

WHAT CAN BE DONE?

Although the evidence supports the idea that nature is more important than nurture, obesity is not completely determined by nature. By controlling our activity level and eating habits, we can lose weight.

Clearly, the research suggests that we should try to establish good eating habits at an early age. The most effective programs for preventing obesity in childhood focus on teaching both parents and children (Hetherington & Parke, 1993). The focus on parents is not surprising given that parents of obese children prompted 2.3 times as much eating as parents of normal-weight children (Klesges et al., 1986).

These weight-control programs use many techniques that would be applauded by traditional behaviorists. For example, the techniques include having children become aware of cues in the environment that cause them to snack, teaching children to eat more slowly, rewarding exercising, keeping junk food out of the house, and encouraging children not to eat while watching television.

Successful programs, however, also use techniques that fall beyond the scope of traditional behaviorism. For example, they teach clients to eat only when they are hungry rather than when they are aroused. With young children, it is especially important not to use a purely behavioral approach. That is, if parents are very obvious in rewarding the eating of healthy foods ("if you eat your spinach, you can have dessert"), children will learn that parents don't expect them to like healthy foods. A more effective approach is to introduce young children to vegetables by letting children dunk their vegetables into a tasty dip (Turkington, 1992).

whereas girls are often pleased that they are slow maturing. Fortunately, however, once late-maturing males and early-maturing females reach adulthood, they seem to benefit from their tumultuous adolescence (see box 4.6).

Both sexes not only gain in height and weight during the growth spurt, but experience dramatic increases in strength. The increases in skeletal and muscular mass are greater for males than females because of the male sex hormone, **testosterone,** secreted by the testes (Tanner, 1978). Thus, by the mid twenties, skeletal and muscle weight accounts for 40 percent of the body weight of an average man, but only for 24 percent of the weight of the average woman (Marshall, 1977).

Testosterone may also decrease men's body fat. Whereas 25 to 28 percent of the average female body is fat, only 19 to 23 percent of the average male's is. However, men are more likely to suffer from weight-related health problems such as heart disease. Men are probably more vulnerable because their fat is typically concentrated in the stomach (near vital organs), whereas women's fat is typically concentrated on their hips or buttocks.

Figure 4.12

Average Age and Duration of Male and Female Spurts in Height

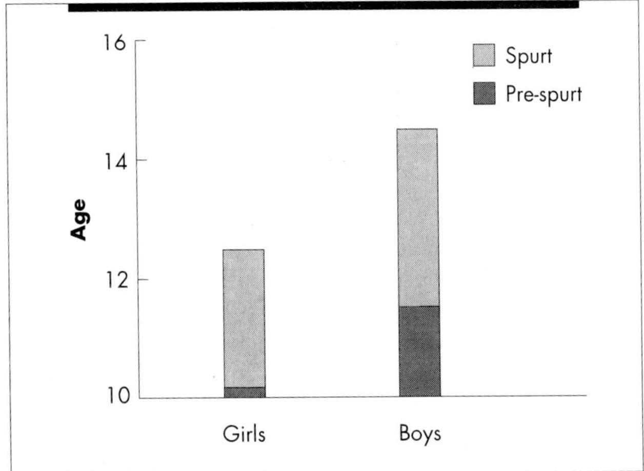

Figure 4.13

Average Age and Duration of Male and Female Spurts in Weight

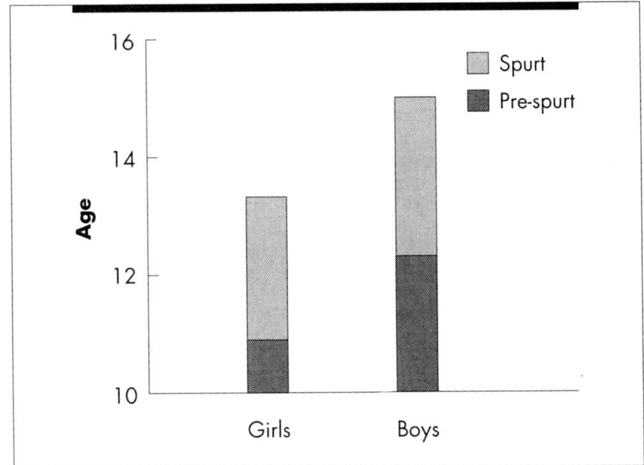

Sexual Development

Although the adolescent growth spurt is a sign of puberty, the most important feature of puberty is the maturation of primary and secondary sex characteristics. **Primary sex characteristics** are the reproductive organs. **Secondary sex characteristics** are the nonreproductive sex traits such as breasts and pubic hair. Like physical growth, sexual maturation is also governed by the pituitary gland. In the next two sections, you will see how the pituitary orchestrates sexual development and function.

The Male Genital Tract

At the onset of puberty, the male reproductive glands, the **testicles,** grow. This causes the enlargement of the **scrotum,** the skin sack housing the testicles. In most males, the left testicle hangs slightly lower than the right, creating the illusion that one testicle is larger than the other. However, both testicles are about the same size. The scrotum is designed to maintain the optimal temperature for sperm production and to protect the testicles from injury. Thus, in cold weather or when a male feels threatened, the scrotum contracts, pulling the testicles nearer the body for additional warmth or protection. Conversely, in warm weather, the scrotum relaxes, moving the testicles away from the body so that they remain cool enough for sperm production (see figure 4.14).

Sperm production starts when follicle-stimulating hormone from the pituitary stimulates the testicles. The sperm is transported to the seminal vesicles for storage via the **vas deferens.** In the seminal vesicles, the sperm are protected and maintained in a protective fluid called **semen,** the fluid that is ejaculated during orgasm.

Table 4.3

Male Sequence of Puberty

Event	Average Age of Onset
Follicle-stimulating hormone signals testicles to increase production of testosterone.	10
Testicles and scrotum grow larger.	11
Pubic hair sprouts.	12
Penis growth starts.	12.5
First ejaculation.	13
Weight spurt starts.	13
Height spurt peaks.	14
Muscle and organ growth peaks.	14.5
Voice lowers.	15
Facial hair appears.	16
Final pubic-hair pattern.	18

The Process of Male Sexual Maturation Male sex development is dictated by a class of hormones called **androgens** (literally, "man-makers"). The most influential androgen, testosterone, is produced by the testicles. As shown in table 4.3, around the age of 11, testosterone stimulates the enlargement of the testicles, scrotum, and the growth of the seminal tubules. Shortly after the testicles begin to develop, pubic hair sprouts. At about age 12 1/2, the penis rapidly grows and reaches its full size at around age 15. The male

Box 4.6

ISSUE in FOCUS

Early Versus Late Maturation

The age at which a child reaches puberty seems to have important short-term and long-term psychological consequences—especially if the child is a boy (e.g., Jones & Musson, 1958; Faust, 1977; Clausen, 1975; Simmons, Blyth, Van Cleave, & Bush, 1979). Box Table 4.6 summarizes the basic differences between early and late maturers. As you look at the chart, keep in mind that whereas the differences between early- and late-maturing boys tend to be sizable and consistent, the differences between late- and early-maturing girls are often small and inconsistent.

1. Why do you think the timing of puberty seems to have more impact on boys than girls?
2. Why, in the short run, is it better to be an early-maturing male, but bad to be an early-maturing female?
3. Early-maturing women and late-maturing men seem to be worse off in the short run, but better off in the long run. Why do you think that is the case?

Box Table 4.6

The Effects of Early Versus Late Maturation

Early-Maturing Female	**Late-Maturing Female**
Short-term correlates	
Rated less socially desirable	Rated more socially desirable
Rated less poised	Rated more poised
Less involved in school activities	More involved in school activities
Feels conspicuous	Fits in with peers
More parental restrictions	Fewer parental restrictions
More parental conflict	Less parental conflict
Dates earlier	Dates later
More social stress	Less social stress
More anxiety	Less anxiety
Less outgoing	More outgoing
Long-term correlates	
Better problem-solving skills	Poorer problem-solving skills
Better coping skills	Poorer coping skills
Early-Maturing Male	**Late-Maturing Male**
Short-term correlates	
Physical superiority	Physical inferiority
Rated more relaxed	Rated less relaxed
Rated good-natured	Attention-seeking
More popular	Less popular
Self-controlled	Impulsive
Not too talkative	Talkative
Long-term correlates	
More conforming	Less conforming
Intolerant of ambiguity	More tolerant of ambiguity
Less flexible	More flexible
Overcontrolled	Uninhibited
Less expressive	Expressive
Lacks curiosity	Curious

Figure 4.14

The Male Genital Tract

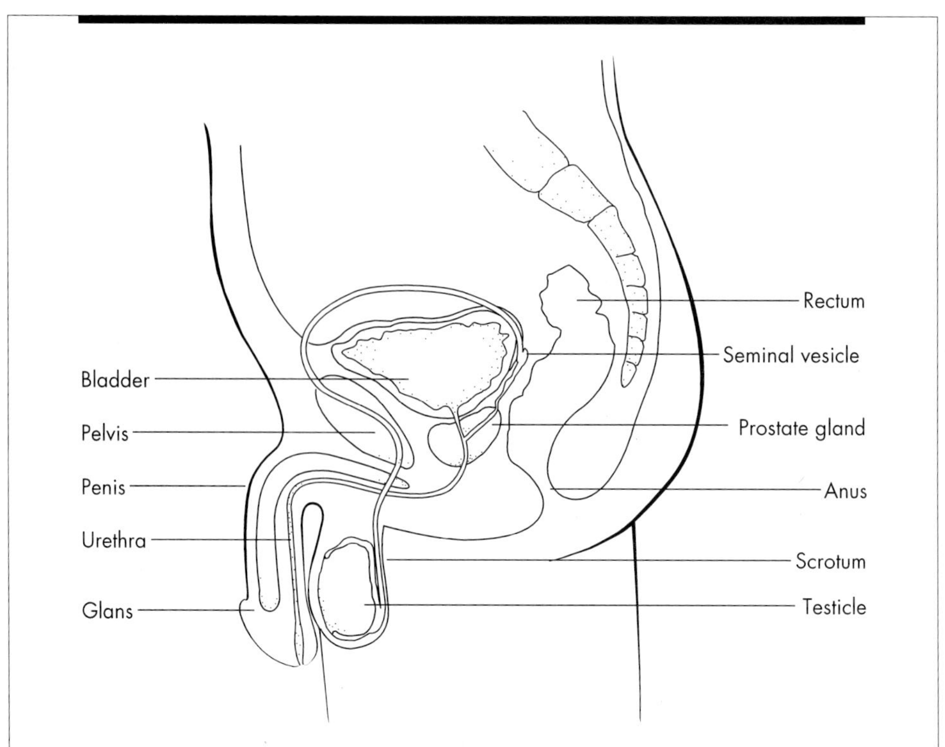

landmark of puberty is his first ejaculation at about age 13. He is now capable of fathering (but not necessarily caring for) a child (Blackburn & Loper, 1992).

After reaching sexual maturity, the male voice will lower due to thickening of the vocal chords. About one year after their voice has lowered, most men will grow facial and body hair. However, some may not grow facial and body hair until their late teens or early twenties. Despite this variation in the development of secondary sexual characteristics, the development of the primary sexual characteristics is usually completed by the teens. Perhaps because sexual development is usually completed in the teens, sexual orientation is usually established during the teens. For example, whereas 26 percent of 12-year-olds are unsure of their sexual orientation, only 5 percent of 18-year-olds are unsure (Remafedi, Resnick, Blum, & Harris 1992).

The Female Genital Tract

The **clitoris** (see figure 4.15) is a female's primary sexual organ. Like the penis, the clitoris is composed of a tissue capable of erection. During sexual arousal, blood rushes into the genital tissue, causing the clitoris and surrounding tissues to swell. Stimulation of an erect clitoris may result in **orgasm,** intense pleasure caused by sexual stimulation.

Near the clitoris is the **urethra,** the tube that carries urine from the bladder. Surrounding both the urethra and clitoris are the **labia:** folds of tissue protecting the genital area. In back of the urethra is the **vagina:** the pathway through which a baby passes from the uterus to the outside world, and the opening in which a man normally inserts his penis during intercourse.

The **cervix** is the pathway between the vagina and the **uterus,** the hollow organ where the embryo is implanted and develops. Above the uterus are the fallopian tubes followed by the ovaries. Within the **ovaries,** are stored the oocytes (immature sex cells). Specifically, oocytes are contained in fluid-filled spaces called ovarian **follicles.** These follicles provide the nourishment and support necessary for an oocyte to ripen into an **ovum,** or mature sex cell. The ripened ovum will travel from its follicle inside an ovary to the uterus via a **fallopian tube.**

The Process of Female Sexual Maturation Whereas androgens stimulate male sexual development, follicle-stimulating hormone and estrogen stimulate female sexual development. When a girl is about 9 years old, her pituitary gland releases follicle-stimulating hormone. **Follicle-stimulating hormone (FSH)** signals the ovaries to produce the female sex hormone **estrogen.** In turn, estrogen produces a myriad of changes, transforming the girl into a woman. Specifically, both the uterus and vagina grow larger and acquire thicker walls. The uterus also develops a set of powerful muscles for housing any future fetuses and pushing them out during labor. Although these internal changes are the most important for reproductive function, they are not as noticeable as the external ones. The dramatic addition of secondary sex characteristics herald the emerging woman to the world.

Estrogen causes the hips to broaden and the waist to become narrower. Estrogen also redistributes and increases the size of fatty deposits, especially under the breasts. For

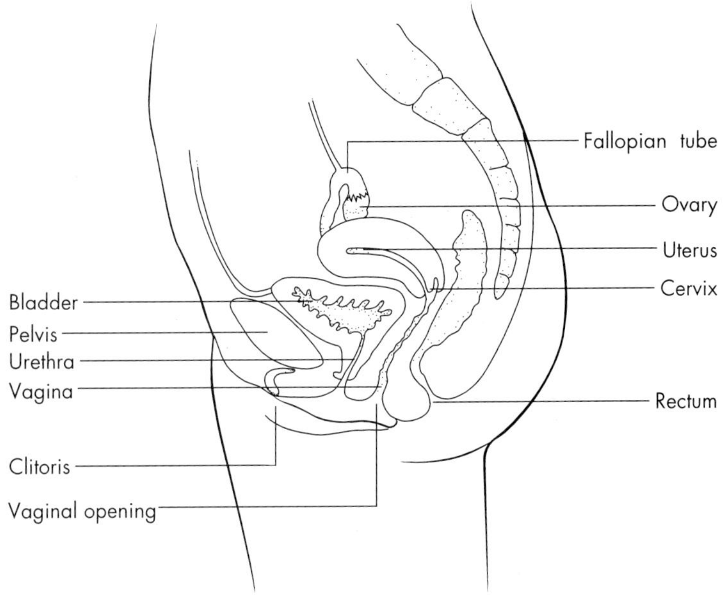

Figure 4.15

The Female Genital Tract

many, the budding of their breasts is the first external sign that puberty has begun. Pubic hair sprouts before or during breast development, followed about two years later by the growth of hair under the arms. Menstruation starts about two years after the breasts bud (see table 4.4) (Blackburn & Loper, 1992).

The first menstrual period, called **menarche,** is a memorable event for most women. Women recall it with such mixed emotions as excitement, pride, apprehension, and embarrassment (Greif & Ulman, 1982; Woods, Dery, & Most, 1983). Girls who understand what menarche is and know what to expect are more likely to perceive their first menstrual period as a positive experience. If, on the other hand, a girl does not understand what menarche is, the experience can be quite unpleasant. Indeed, some psychoanalytic theorists argue that if a woman is unprepared for the changes of puberty, she may develop **anorexia nervosa,** or self starvation. The anorexic can starve herself to the point that menstruation stops, thereby retarding the transformations of puberty. Some cognitively oriented behaviorists disagree, arguing that anorexia is an adolescent's attempt to exert control over her life. Such adolescents wish to escape the control of overprotective parents, yet remain the center of their parents' attention.

Table 4.4

Female Sequence of Puberty

Event	Average Age of Onset
Follicle-stimulating hormone signals ovaries to increase production of estrogen and progesterone.	9
Internal sex organs begin to grow larger.	9.5
Breasts bud.	10
Pubic hair sprouts.	11
Weight spurt starts.	11.5
Height spurt peaks.	12
Muscle and organ growth peaks and hips become visibly larger.	12.5
Menarche.	12.5
First ovulation.	13.5
Final pubic-hair pattern.	15
Full breast growth.	16

Secular Trend There is great variation in pubertal timing among both female and male adolescents. Many perfectly normal adolescents will lag three years behind or ahead of the average ages shown in tables 4.3 and 4.4. Furthermore, many adolescents will deviate from the sequence of events listed in these tables. For example, some females may sprout pubic hair before their breasts bud.

Many factors, such as genetics, nutrition, and health, can explain individual differences in pubertal timing. The importance of nutrition, health, and other environmental factors are highlighted when we compare the average age of puberty for contemporary adolescents against previous generations. A female born in the United States this year will probably start her first menstrual period before her

13th birthday. However, her great-grandmother, born in 1910, started her first period when she was 14. Girls living in Europe during the nineteenth century didn't enter menarche until they were 15 1/2 to 17 1/2 (Malina, 1979). Males have followed a similar pattern.

Children not only grow up faster than they did in the previous century, but they are about an inch taller and several pounds heavier. These gains in development are referred to as a **secular trend.** Probable causes of this secular trend are improved nutrition and medical care, as well as improved environmental circumstances, reduced family size, and the fact that the genes for height are dominant over genes for shortness (Malina, 1979; Tanner, 1978).

Motor Development

In addition to affecting sexual development, physical development affects motor development. To grasp the importance of motor development, try to imagine what you were like the day you were born. It must have been like awakening in an alien world. Nothing you felt, touched, saw, heard, or smelled made sense. You not only had to learn the objects and sounds of the world, you had to learn how to coordinate your body's movements with the world's gravity, patterns, and rhythms. At first, your actions and movements were random (like the first time you played a video game or backed a trailer). Slowly, as you discovered your physical capacities in relation to this environment, you gained control and learned to integrate your movements with the objects of this world.

Fortunately, when you entered this world you had a repertoire of reflexes that helped ensure your survival (see table 4.5). That is, you had reflexes that allowed you to protect yourself, explore the world, and get food.

To protect yourself, you reflexively blinked when a gust of air hit your face and you withdrew your foot from any painful stimulus. You also protected yourself through the **Moro reflex**—if you felt yourself falling or heard a loud noise, you flailed your arms. (Although we do not recommend it, you have probably seen people let their baby think she is falling to observe the Moro reflex.)

A reflex that aided you in exploring the world was the **grasping reflex.** That is, when something was placed in your hand, you grabbed onto it.

Finally, you were well prepared to be breast fed. To locate food, you had the **rooting reflex**—when your cheek was gently stroked, you turned your head to face that object. Thus, if the object was your mother's breast or a bottle, the rooting reflex got you closer to a situation where you could effectively use your **sucking reflex**—the reflex to suck anything that is placed in your mouth. Although you knew little about the ways of the world, your reflexes were evidence of your potential to master it.

As you gained experience and as your brain matured, you learned to control your body and to deliberately move your arms and legs. As you gained control of your body, you lost those reflexes no longer needed for survival (for example, crying, sucking, and smiling reflexes). However, those reflexes necessary for long-term survival persisted. Thus, as an adult you still have reflexes for coughing, sneezing, blinking, and yawning.

Remarkably, this transition from random, reflexive movement to organized, deliberate actions followed the two rules of Gesell's principle of developmental direction. First, mastery of your body progressed from head-to-toe (cephalocaudal). You could lift your head before you could walk. Second, mastery of your body progressed from the center of your body to the extremities (proximodistal). You gained control over your legs before your toes; your shoulders before your fingers. Consequently, when you first waved to your family, you didn't move your wrist or fingers, you moved only your shoulder.

Similarly, as you can see from figure 4.16 (Shirley, 1933) and table 4.6, developing the ability to walk proceeds in accordance with the proximodistal and cephalocaudal principles. If motor skills are governed by the same principles that govern physical growth, is motor development solely a function of maturation?

Arnold Gesell (1952), who discovered the principles of cephalocaudal and proximodistal development, thought so. However, Gesell erred in being too much of a naturist. Motor development depends on *both* maturation *and* practice. Practice can speed up motor development. For example, as we described in chapter 3, practice can make children walk earlier than they normally would.

Not only can practice speed up motor development, but it can also change the course of development. For instance, by age 1, most children show a preference for using either their right or left hand. This preference usually is a sign that one of the cerebral hemispheres is becoming dominant. Left alone, children will continue to develop dexterity in their dominant hand. However, in the past, many children who showed a preference for their left hand were forced to use their right hand instead. Although most contemporary experts advise against this practice, clearly hand dominance can be altered by practice.

Once cerebral dominance emerges, children can hold an object with one hand and manipulate that object with the other. By their first birthday, most have taken their first steps. Walking opens up a whole new world to the toddler, a world full of independence and new dangers. By age 2, most children can run, jump, climb stairs, kick a ball, turn the pages of a book, and draw with crayons.

As they mature, children become more coordinated and master more difficult skills. At age 3, most children get great pleasure from running. They delight in their ability to make quick starts and stops and turn sharp corners. By age 5 or 6, they are climbing, throwing, skipping, and balancing. By age 7, most can ride a bicycle. By 9, they are ready for team sports, and by 10, they can catch a fly ball (Sahler & McAnamey, 1981).

Table 4.5

The Neonate's Reflex Repertoire

If You	Then the Baby's
Tap the bridge of the nose, shine a bright light suddenly into the eyes, clap hands about 18 inches from the infant's head, touch the white of the eye with cotton	Eyes close tightly.
Make a sudden contact or noise	Head drops backward, neck extends, arms and legs fling outward and back sharply (Moro reflex).
Extend forearms at elbow	Arms flex briskly.
Lightly prick soles of feet	Knee and foot flex.
Stand infant; press foot to bed	Feet step.
Pull baby to sit	Eyes snap open, shoulders tense. Baby tries unsuccessfully to right head (China doll reflex).
Pull baby on tummy on flat surface	Head turns to side and lifts. Baby crawls, lifts self with arms.
Support chest on water surface	Arms and legs "swim."
Place baby on back and turn head to side	Body arches away from face and side; arm on face side extends, leg draws up, other arm flexes (tonic neck reflex).
Stroke foot or hand on top	Limb withdraws, arches, returns to grasp.
Stroke palm or sole at base of digits	Limb grasps.
Stroke outside of sole	Toes spread, large toe sticks up.
Tap upper lips sharply	Lips protrude.
Stroke cheek or mouth	Mouth roots; head turns, and tongue moves toward stroking object; mouth sucks.
Stroke cheek or palm	Mouth roots; arms flexes; hand goes to open mouth.
Place an object over nose and mouth	Mouth works vigorously; head twists; arms fling across face.
Stroke leg, upper part of body	Opposite leg or hand crosses to push your hand away; withdraws.
Rotate baby to side	Head turns, eyes precede direction of rotation.
Suspend by legs	Body curls to upside-down ball, legs extend, arms drop into straight line; neck arches backward.

From *The First Twelve Months of Life*, 1973, by the Princeton Center for Infancy and Early Childhood. Frank Caplan (General Ed.). Copyright © 1971, 1972, 1973 by Edcom Systems, Inc. Published by Bantam Books, a division of Bantam Doubleday Dell Publishing Group, Inc. All rights reserved.

With adolescence comes an initial period of awkwardness caused by rapid and uneven muscle and skeletal growth. However, this initial awkwardness is followed by a progressive increase in power, speed, and skill that will continue until about age 30. Because of the growth-stimulating actions of the male sex hormone testosterone, most males experience greater gains in power and speed than females do. However, females usually have superior manual dexterity. For example, evidence suggests that women are better sharpshooters than men because their trigger fingers are steadier. For similar reasons, it has been argued that women would make better surgeons.

The Developing Senses

Not only does maturation change the body's capacities to manipulate the environment, but it also changes the ability to sense and perceive the world. In this section we will explore the development of the major senses, including vision, hearing, taste, smell, and touch.

Vision

Development of the eye begins around the fourth week of gestation (Acredolo & Hake, 1982). By 7 months of gestation, the visual pathway is anatomically complete and functional. It contains all the structures shown in

Figure 4.16

Motor Development

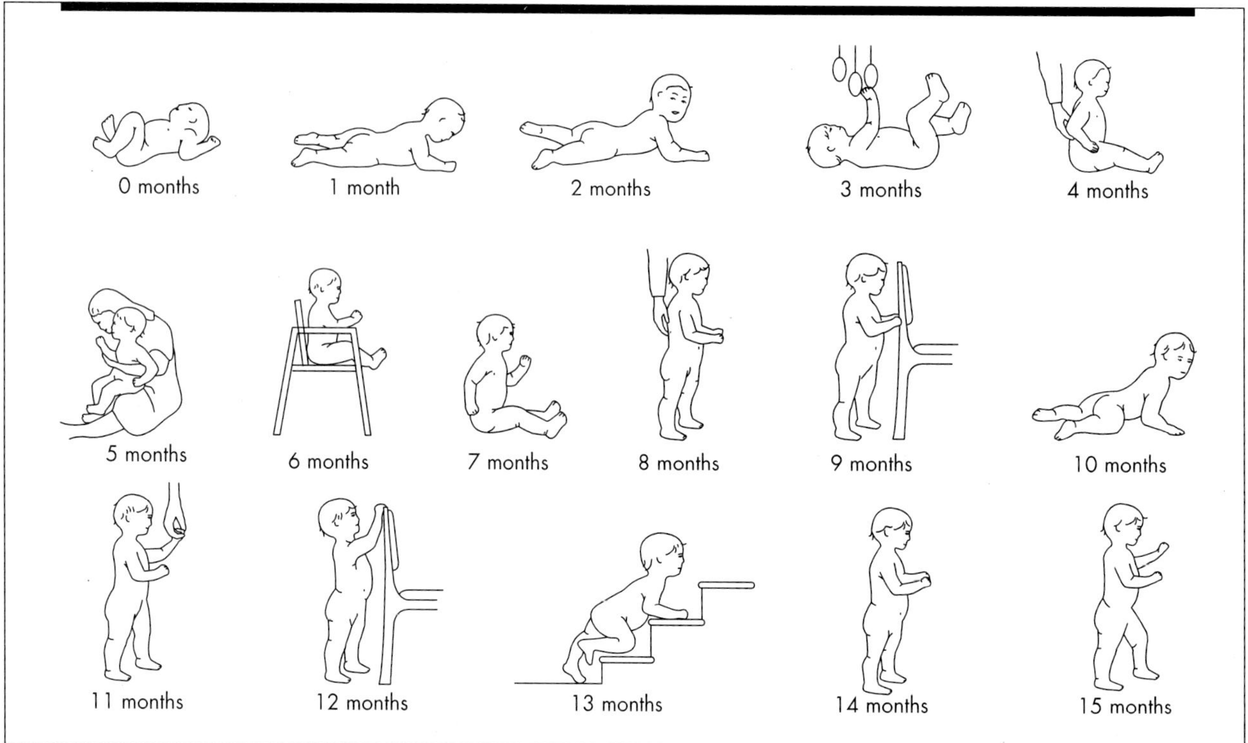

Table 4.6

Age Norms (in Months) for Important Motor Milestones

Skill	Month When 50% of Infants Have Mastered the Skill	Month When 90% of Infants Have Mastered the Skill
Lifts head 90 degrees while lying on stomach	2.2	3.2
Rolls over	2.8	4.2
Sits propped up	2.9	4.7
Sits without support	5.5	7.8
Stands holding on	5.8	10.0
Walks holding on	9.2	12.7
Stands alone momentarily	9.8	13.0
Stands well alone	11.5	13.9
Walks well	12.1	14.3
Walks up steps	17.0	22.0
Kicks ball forward	20.0	24.0

figure 4.17, including the cornea, lens, pupil, iris, and retina. The **cornea** is a transparent membrane that covers and protects the eyeball. The **iris** is the colored part of the eye that blocks light from entering the pupil (eye color is really the iris color). The **pupil** is the dark area, in the center of your eye, that dilates and constricts to vary the amount of light that enters your eye. The **lens** focuses the light onto the **retina** where the receptor cells that convert light into neural activity are located.

Although the eye may be anatomically complete at 7 months of gestation, the visual system takes several years to mature. In fact, in the late 1950s, we still believed that neonates were born blind. However, thanks to the pioneering work of Robert Fantz (1958, 1961), we now know that newborns have limited visual ability.

Figure 4.17

The Eye

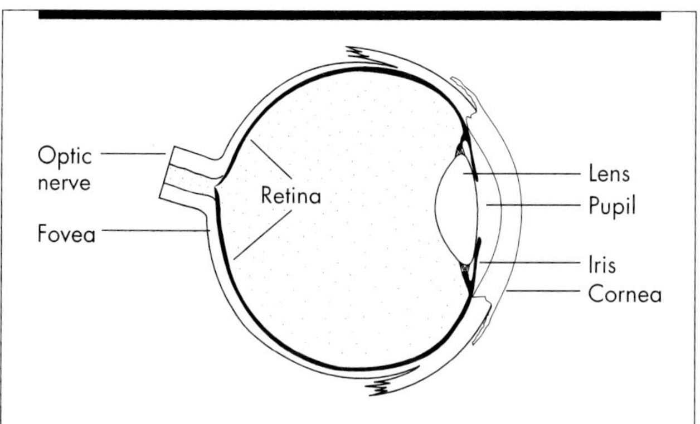

To test newborn's visual acuity, Fantz constructed a "looking chamber" (see figure 4.18). Infants were placed on their backs. Two visual patterns were suspended about 10 inches above their eyes. The researcher looked through a peephole to observe and record where the infant was looking. The researcher could tell what the infant was looking at because the image was reflected in the infant's eyes. This permitted the researcher to assess how long the infant looked at each pattern.

Fantz found that newborn's look longer at striped patterns than at a solid gray patch. The fact that newborns show a visual preference demonstrates that not only can newborns see, but they can also discriminate between dissimilar objects.

Although newborns can see, they can't see very well because of problems in focusing. One focusing problem is caused by the inability of the newborn's lenses to **accommodate,** or adjust to focus on objects at different distances. The newborn's eyes maintain a fixed focus at about 19 centimeters (just shy of 1 foot) (White, 1971). Anything closer than 19 centimeters or farther than 19 centimeters is blurred. In time, the lenses will start accommodating so the baby can focus on any object.

A second focusing problem is caused by the fact that there isn't enough distance between the front and back of the newborn's eyes. Just as a magnifying glass lens must be a certain distance away from a piece of paper if you are to focus the sun's rays on it, the lens of the eye must be a certain distance from the retina to focus light on it. Because the lens is too close to the retina, the infant's visual acuity during the first month of life is somewhere between 20/200 and 20/800 (Banks & Salapatek, 1983). In other words, at 20 feet, the infant can see what the average adult can see at 200 to 800 feet. Fortunately, as the eyes mature, the distance between the front of the eyes and the back of their eyes increases. This improves visual acuity. By the end of the first year, most infants can see as well as an adult (Aslin, 1987; Banks & Salapatek, 1983). That is, they have 20/20 vision.

Figure 4.18

Fantz's Looking Chamber

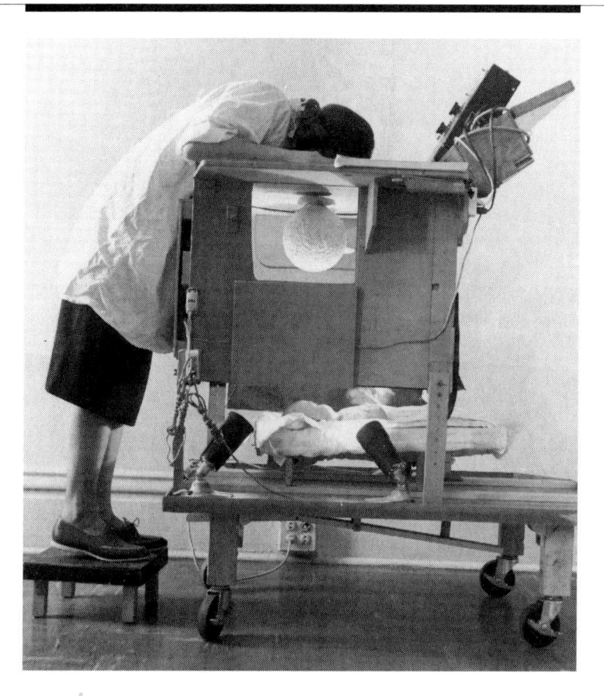

Depth Perception

By the time a baby can crawl, he can judge distances with a fair amount of accuracy because he has developed **depth perception.** We know about infant's depth perception abilities because of studies using a "visual cliff."

In visual cliff studies, researchers put infants on a slightly raised glass runway suspended about 3 feet above the floor. As you can see in figure 4.19, on one side of the runway, a checkerboard pattern is right underneath the glass plate so that the surface appears solid. On the other side of the runway, the checkerboard pattern is nearly 3 feet below the glass plate. This side gives the illusion of a sudden drop—a visual cliff. In an experiment with human babies aged 6- to 14-months, Gibson and Walk (1960) found that only three of 36 infants could be coaxed to the "deep" side of the cliff by their mother's calls. The remaining 33 had developed depth perception and weren't about to jump off a cliff, even for the love of mom.

But do infants have depth perception before the age of 6 months? Apparently, they do. More recent studies suggest that depth perception is present at 4 months of age (Aslin, 1987; Aslin & Smith, 1988; Campos et al., 1978).

Person Perception

Babies quickly develop person perception, or the ability to recognize other human faces. When looking at a face, 1-month-olds tend to concentrate on the edges, focusing on the chin and hairline (Maurer & Salapatek, 1977). By

Figure 4.19

The Visual Cliff

2 months, they scan the features of the face, with a special emphasis on the eyes (Hainline, 1978). Also at 2 months they can tell the difference between a human face and a face-like configuration (Maurer & Barrera, 1981). And, as infants grow older, they increasingly favor looking at faces over other objects. For example, Haith, Berman, and Moore (1977) studied babies' attention to the reflections of faces over a 45-second period. They found that babies who were 3- to 5-weeks-old fixated on the face only 22 percent of the time, 7-week-old infants 88 percent, and 9- to 11-month-old infants 90 percent of the time.

As babies grow older, they also become more sensitive to **biological motion,** or the patterns of human locomotion. For example, you can easily determine if someone is walking normally or walking with a limp. Indeed, you can probably determine with some accuracy whether a person is old or young, man or woman, just from their walk.

Studies by Robert Fox and Cynthia McDaniel (1982) show that the ability to distinguish patterns of human locomotion develop at a very young age. They observed whether 2-, 4-, and 6-month-old infants tended to look at a pattern of randomly moving dots or a pattern of dots that simulated a person running in place. Two-month-old infants showed no preference. In contrast, the 4- and 6-month-old infants demonstrated a definite preference for the pattern of biological motion.

Hearing

Hearing is the fetus's first perceptual link to the outside world. Not only can the fetus hear the sounds of amniotic fluid sloshing about and the mother's heartbeat, it can hear the muffled sounds of the external world as well. It hears what its mother and the humans nearby say (it doesn't understand it). It hears the music played. It hears the television. In fact, midway through pregnancy, a fetus will jump in a startled reaction to loud noises (for example, a door slamming).

At 6 months, the fetus can be tested for deafness by applying a tone-producing vibrator to the mother's abdomen and monitoring changes in fetal heartbeat. And it may recognize what it hears. For example, in one intriguing study, 16 pregnant women read Dr. Seuss's story, *The Cat in the Hat,* to their fetuses during the last two weeks of pregnancy. When the babies were born, they had a choice of sucking on two nipples. The first produced a recording of their mothers reading the Seuss story. Sucking on the other nipple produced a recording of their mother reading *The King, the Mice, and the Cheese.* Which nipple did the newborns prefer to suck on? The *Cat in the Hat* (DeCasper & Spence, 1986, 1991).

The human ear is well developed at birth. Only modest gains in sensitivity and responsiveness will be made during the ensuing years. In fact, as we will see when we examine language development, a baby can distinguish differences between certain verbal sounds that an adult can't. Although a developing child's hearing does improve to some extent, the major concern is to avoid damaging the ear through exposure to excessive noise or physical force (for example, boxing or slapping the ears).

Taste

Infants explore much of the world by putting virtually anything and everything in their mouths. In a way, the mouth is a good tool for exploring because the mouth is one of the body's most sensitive areas. The mouth is not only sensitive to taste, but to pain, pressure, and temperature.

Although a person has taste buds throughout the mouth, the highest concentration is on the tongue. Taste buds are sensitive to four basic sensations: bitterness, saltiness, sourness, and sweetness.

Taste buds start to work the moment they are stimulated. Because fetuses open their mouths and swallow amniotic fluid by the 10th week after conception (Humphrey, 1978), some scientists assume that the fetus can taste (Acredolo & Hake, 1982). We know that newborns can taste because they prefer sweetness over other tastes. They definitely don't like sour or bitter flavors. This preference for sweetness persists throughout childhood. Thus, it's a myth that children, if left to their own devices would choose a balanced diet. Only in adolescence or adulthood do some (but by no means all) people learn to enjoy other flavors as much as sweets.

Smell

Smell and taste are closely linked. You probably can remember as a child plugging your nose to blunt the taste of a horrible-tasting food or medicine. You probably also remember your mouth watering in response to the delicious smells of fresh baked bread or frying bacon. Much of the enjoyment we receive from food comes through our sense of smell.

Research on infants' sense of smell has been scant. What little research there is suggests that newborns are sensitive to and show definite preferences for specific odors. For example, Steiner (1979) found that newborns made negative and positive facial expressions in response to various odors.

Touch

Touch consists of several senses: heat, cold, pain, and pressure. One's sense of touch is stimulated when an external stimulus either causes body hairs to move or deforms the skin. These changes activate nerve endings in the skin that communicate information to the brain about the encounter.

Touch is well developed in a newborn as evidenced through the neonate's many reflexes. For example, if you prick the bottom of a newborn's foot, she will withdraw it.

Physical and Motor Changes

You have seen how, relatively early in life, maturation contributes to physical growth, sexual development, motor development, and sensory-perceptual development. For most of us, physical development is completed during early adulthood. During our thirties, it becomes evident that our bodies have begun the slow process of **aging,** the progressive cellular and bodily deterioration that culminates in death. Outward signs of aging become noticeable by the time we are in our thirties. However, our bodies have been aging since before birth. For example, during fetal development a fetus's fingers are fused until a hormone signals the tissue that connects the fingers to die. Similarly, you may recall the massive death of neurons that occurs during the final month of fetal development. Thus, we don't suddenly start aging when we enter our thirties; however, the lack of growth and physical development makes aging and deterioration more noticeable.

Why Do We Age?

No one knows what causes aging. However, biologists have several interesting ideas (see box 4.8). For example, some biologists believe that we age and eventually die because our cells have a **limited division potential** (Hayflick, 1977, 1987, 1992). Specifically, our cells can divide only 50 times. Hayflick and his colleagues discovered the 50-divisions limit by studying cultured human embryonic cells. They argue that when we run out of cell divisions, we run out of the cells necessary to sustain life. Cell division is necessary to replace cells destroyed by injury or everyday wear. In fact, every 7 years all the cells in your body, except nerve and muscle cells, are replaced.

Another group of biologists (for example, Wilson, 1974) believes aging can be explained by the **wear and tear theory of aging,** the idea that genetic damage is caused by the accumulation of environmental insults. Just as teratogens can alter our DNA before we are born, environmental pollutants, such as radiation and chemicals, alter our genetic code throughout our lives. The result is physical aging.

Still another theory attributes aging to the breakdown of our immune system. Because of genetic changes in our cells, our immune system begins to perceive our body's own cells as "foreign" and tries to destroy these cells. According to the **autoimmune theory of aging,** such autoimmune responses increase as we age, making us more vulnerable to disease and stress.

No matter what the cause of aging, all of us who survive into adulthood will age. What can we expect as we progress through our adult years? In the next few sections, we will discuss the major signs of physical aging.

The Aging Process

Fifty percent of us will reach our full height by early adulthood. By the age of 70, most of us will shrink 1 to 2 inches because of changes in our posture and the compression of bones in our spinal column. With increasing age, many women and some men are concerned about the ravaging effects of **osteoporosis,** the decalcification of the bones resulting in a collapse of the skeletal system. In both sexes, the distance between the bottom of the nose and chin will decrease as a result of changes in teeth, bone, muscles, and connective tissue.

Most people will probably reach their maximum strength by age 30, followed by a slow and steady decline. During the course of the adult lifespan, most lose 30 to 40 percent of their strength (Fiatarone et al., 1990). This loss in strength is primarily due to losing muscle. William Evans and Irwin Rosenberg (1991) report that adult Americans tend to lose 6.6 pounds of muscle with each decade of life. This loss increases after age 45. Most adults notice that as they age, most of the muscle weakening will occur in the back and leg muscles, leading to a greater chance of injury from lifting heavy objects. By middle age, most of us will have difficulty sustaining great muscular effort and will have to learn to pace ourselves. Our reflexes and reaction times will slow, especially with disuse, and our manual dexterity will decrease steadily after the age of 33.

Box 4.7

SELF-CHECK

Indicate whether each of the following statements is true or false.

1. A newborn has more neurons than a 10-year-old does.
2. A newborn has more synapses than a 10-year-old.
3. It is easier for a low birth-weight child to catch up in terms of height than in terms of intelligence.
4. By age 5, the brain is 90 percent of its adult weight.
5. The brain plays a role in directing physical development.

Answer the following questions and fill in the blanks where indicated.

6. Why is myelination correlated with developmental changes?
7. If a child and an adult suffer an injury to their ____________ brains, their language abilities will suffer. However, because they have more p____________, the ____________ will recover more fully than the ____________. Will men or women recover more fully from such injuries? Why?
8. Why is the corpus callosum implicated in dyslexia?
9. Why is the pituitary gland called the "master gland"? What influences it?
10. What has to happen before a newborn can walk?
11. What two kinds of cells are not replaced throughout the lifespan?
12. Why do adolescents, during their growth spurt, *look* awkward?
13. At what ages, might we expect girls to be taller than boys?
14. Distinguish between primary and secondary sexual characteristics.
15. Injury to the testes at age 11 would have what effect?
16. The secular trend seems to be due to genes and ____________, especially since anorexia nervosa can retard ____________.
17. How does learning to walk follow Gesell's principles?
18. How did Robert Fantz determine that newborns can see?
19. Why is growth of a newborn's eyes necessary for improving visual acuity?
20. How did the visual cliff study show that infants perceived depth? Do the results mean infants are born with depth perception?
21. What would a skeptical scientist want to know about the *Cat in the Hat* study?

Please turn to the end of this chapter to check your answers.

As you can see in figure 4.20, with age, there will also be a tendency to gain weight and body fat. In part, the weight gain is due to loss of muscle. Muscles burn calories. Thus, when we lose muscle, we burn fewer calories. However, most people tend to continue to eat the same amount. The excess calories will be converted into fat, and fat redistributes through the body. Men tend to accumulate fat in the stomach; women accumulate it on the hips and thighs. After age 55, weight tends to stabilize or decline. However, muscle loss continues. Since muscle loss is harmful, some researchers have experimented with giving men in their fifties testosterone. Not surprisingly, men given testosterone developed larger muscles, better strength, and lower cholesterol levels (Sih, 1994).

Figure 4.20

Percentage of Body Fat by Age and Gender

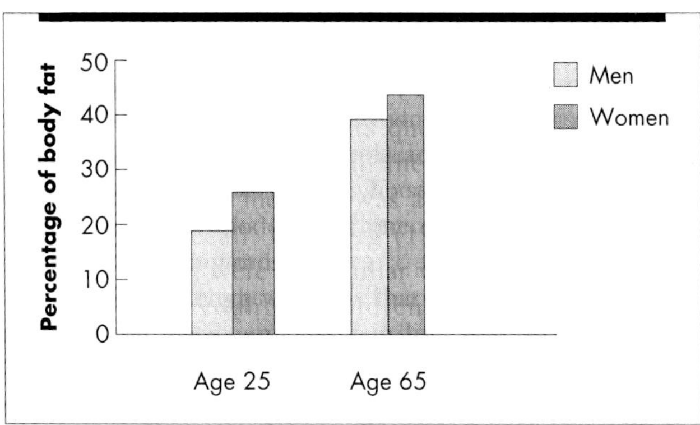

Box 4.8

THEORY in FOCUS

Biological Theories of Aging

In their quest to unlock the secret of physical aging, biologists have proposed several theories. The following summary describes five biological theories of aging.

Wear and tear theory (Wilson, 1974; Marchalonis, Schluter, Wilson, Yocum, Boyer, & Kay, 1993). Like a machine, the body simply wears out after a certain amount of use. Thus, aging is the result of cellular damage caused by everyday use and the accumulation of environmental insults. The body tries to replace cells that are lost to such "wear and tear." However, cells found in many tissues (for example, the heart, nervous system, liver, and skin) cannot replace themselves. Aging and death result, in part, from the accumulation of cell loss in such tissues.

Autoimmune theory (Walford, 1969). Aging occurs because the body's immune system loses its ability to correctly distinguish between the body's own cells and foreign proteins, bacteria, and viruses. Thus, the immune system may fail to attack foreign threats, as well as create antibodies that destroy the body's own healthy cells.

Cross-linkage theory (Bjorksten, 1974). Aging is the consequence of changes in collagen, an important connective tissue found in most organ systems. As people age, changes in collagen lead to the wrinkling of their skin; loss of elasticity in blood vessels, skin, muscle tissue, the lens of the eyes, and other organs; and slows the rate at which wounds heal. Changes in collagen also cause people's noses and ears to grow larger during adulthood.

Free radical theory (Harman, 1968, 1993). Aging is caused by free radicals, highly reactive chemical compounds that contain an unpaired electron. Free radicals are produced when oxygen is used inside the cell. If the free radical encounters an antioxidant, such as vitamin E, the unpaired electron will be neutralized. However, if the electron is not neutralized, it will seek to steal an electron from the cell's molecules by smashing against the molecules. Damage to these molecules results in cross-linking of connective tissue, DNA mutations, and changes in protein behaviors.

Cellular aging theory (Hayflick, 1977; 1992). Aging occurs when cells lose their capacity to replicate. Embryo cells grown in culture, undergo about 50 doublings before death of the cell strain.

As people age, their skin will lose its elasticity, largely due to accumulated sun damage (Kligman, Grove, & Balin, 1985; Montagna & Carlisle, 1979), and wrinkles will appear. Skin sometimes takes on the crisscrossed look of parchment (Rossman, 1977). With age, there will be a greater chance of developing warts on the face, scalp, and torso. Small blood vessels frequently break, appearing as tiny black-and-blue marks. Age spots (liver spots) appear as brown areas of pigmentation.

Aging also causes the death of heart and liver cells, making these organs less efficient. Thus, older people may not be able to run as far as they used to and may not be able to take the same level of medications they once did. Indeed, because the liver becomes less efficient at ridding the body of toxins, a drug dosage that is appropriate at age 70 may be dangerous at age 80.

Diet and Exercise

Fortunately, proper diet and exercise can retard many of the physical changes associated with aging (Jenkins, 1978). Thus, athletes such as Nolan Ryan and Kareem Abdul Jabbar have performed at world-class standards in their forties, and Satchel Paige and Gordie Howe excelled in professional sports well into their fifties. A 60-year-old who follows a regular exercise program and indulges in a proper diet can still beat an out-of-shape 20-year-old on the tennis court. One study, found that people in late adulthood who participated in the Senior Olympics—an athletic competition for older adults—had a greater capacity for physical exertion than some young adults. In addition, Evans and Rosenberg (1991) found that 90-year-olds who were put on a consistent exercise program, could increase their muscle mass by 15 to 20 percent and increase their strength by 200 to 300 percent in only 8 weeks.

Research also shows that the reaction times of active older people in their sixties and seventies are faster than the reaction times of nonathletic younger people in their twenties (Spirduso & Clifford, 1978). The rule with aging seems to be, "What you don't use, you lose."

Staying in shape not only helps maintain your exercise capacity and reaction time, but it may extend your life. An

8-year longitudinal study of more than 17,000 men and women found that sedentary individuals were more than twice as likely to die during the 8-year period than those who were moderately fit (Blair, Kohl, Paffenbarger, Clark, Cooper, & Gibbons, 1989).

Illness and Impairment

The probability of contracting a chronic disease or illness increases as we age (Palmore, 1981). About two out of every five people aged 65 to 75 have some physical impairment (Riley & Foner, 1968). The majority of people age 80 or older have at least one chronic impairment. The four most prevalent conditions afflicting the elderly are arthritis (38 percent), hearing deficit (20 percent), visual deficit (20 percent), and heart condition (20 percent). Elderly women are more likely to suffer from arthritis, hypertension, and visual impairment, whereas elderly men are more likely to have hearing problems.

The Aging Brain

The loss of neurons is an inevitable fact of life. As you read earlier, neuron death starts before you are born. There is much debate about the actual rate of loss, and many people are critical of the staining and sampling techniques of researchers who give estimates (Bondareff, 1985). However, a common estimate is that during most of your adult life you will lose about 10,000 neurons a day. While this may seem like a lot, it only adds up to a loss of 5 to 10 percent of your neurons by the age of 75. Is this loss significant? Probably not. Recent studies suggest that, neuronal loss is often compensated for by the plasticity of the remaining neurons and by the creation of more synapses (Coleman, 1986; Curcio, Buell, & Coleman, 1982). However, a few people do lose enough neurons to have what experts call chronic brain disorder.

When former U.S. President Ronald Reagan announced in 1994 that he suffered from Alzheimer's disease, national attention was drawn to this condition.

Chronic Brain Disorders

What many people call senility, experts call chronic brain disorders. In elderly patients, there are two common types of chronic brain disorders: senile dementia and multi-infarct dementia (strokes). Both conditions begin with occasional moments of disorientation and mild symptoms of either depression or anxiety. Both become gradually more severe and are eventually accompanied by **dementia,** a general loss of intellectual abilities. In addition, victims may become emotionally volatile and act in socially inappropriate ways (Schaie & Willis, 1991b).

Although senile dementia and multi-infarct dementia share similar symptoms, they are different diseases—as autopsy results have clearly demonstrated. The brain of a person suffering from senile dementia is shrunken and atrophied, covered with patches **(plaques),** looks rusted, and is filled with tiny twisted tubes **(neurofibrillary tangles)** (Nuland, 1994; Terry and Wisniewski, 1975). We don't know why this transformation occurs, but the effect is devastating.

The cause of multi-infarct dementia is a series of small strokes brought on by **arteriosclerosis—**hardening of the arteries. Smoking, a high fat diet, lack of exercise, and a genetic predisposition are all possible culprits.

Alzheimer's Although chronic brain disorders are most common in people over age 70, other forms of dementia occur in middle-aged adults. **Alzheimer's disease** attacks people as young as 40 and afflicts about 100,000 people a year. The disease is named for Alois Alzheimer, who described the peculiar afflictions of one of his patients in the early 1900s. The patient, a 50-year-old man with no previous health problems, had begun to experience profound loss of current and recent memory and had become disoriented. His symptoms steadily increased, followed by severe depression, hallucinations, and paranoid delusions. Shortly before his death, the patient had full-blown dementia, "the progressive loss of all mental functions, including the ability to speak, to form abstractions, and even to carry on basic daily acts such as eating, dressing, and excreting" (Bloom et al., 1985, pp. 276–278).

Alzheimer's is a form of senile dementia, usually associated with old age, that affects an estimated 4.4 million

Americans. Although Alzheimer's strikes, on the average, at age 69, the disease may strike people in their forties as well.[3] Like senile dementia, Alzheimer's is characterized by brain atrophy, plaques, and neurofibrillary tangles. The progressive decline into dementia and death lasts 10 or 20 years. A related disorder, Alzheimer-type senile dementia strikes older people. Victims of Alzheimer-type senile dementia have only a few years to live.

What causes Alzheimer's disease and Alzheimer-type senile dementia? Until recently, Alzheimer's was as much a mystery to researchers as it was to its befuddled victims. Now, researchers have some of the pieces to the Alzheimer's puzzle. We know that some people inherit Alzheimer's. For example, Allen Roses (1990) has found a common defect in chromosome 19 among people suffering from late-onset familial Alzheimer's. We also know some of the environmental events that are associated with Alzheimer's and Alzheimer-type senile dementia. Specifically, we know that Alzheimer's patients have an abnormally high concentration of aluminum in their brains (Perl, Gajducek, & Garruto, 1982), that smokers are more than twice as likely to develop Alzheimer-type dementia than nonsmokers, that thin women are at high risk, and that people who are college educated and have jobs that require high-level mental skills are less likely to get Alzheimer-type dementia (Stern et al., 1994). But, as yet, we don't know why smoking is related to Alzheimer-type senile dementia, why high aluminum concentrations are found in the brains of Alzheimer's patients, why thin women are at higher risk, and why people with college educations and professional jobs are less likely to get Alzheimer's.

Summary and Conclusions About Brain Changes Although the likelihood of dementia increases with age, it is not a part of normal aging. Most people will die with more than 90 percent of their neurons intact. Thus, most of us will suffer no dramatic brain-related cognitive decline or personality changes as we age. This is especially true if the aging person does not accept negative stereotypes about aging (Levy & Langer, 1994).

Reproductive Changes

Throughout their lives, most men and women maintain interest in sex. However, the reproductive organs in both genders degenerate with age, decreasing or eliminating their ability to reproduce. These changes are probably caused by a decline in the production of neurotransmitters that stimulate the hypothalamus to signal the pituitary to release sex hormones (Aiken, 1989).

Reproductive Changes in Women

Between the ages of 50 and 51, the average female enters **menopause,** the cessation of a women's menstrual cycle and the end of female fertility (Blackburn & Loper, 1992; Treloar, 1981). Two key age-related changes terminate a woman's ability to reproduce (Harman & Talbert, 1985). First, the aging of oocytes (eggs) destroys the necessary genetic material. Second, deterioration of the uterus makes the implantation of a blastocyst unlikely.

Changes in the reproductive system have additional effects. For example, when the ovaries wither, estrogen decreases. Lack of estrogen increases the chance of osteoporosis and some forms of cancer. Lack of estrogen also makes the skin lose thickness and fluid (thus causing the skin to look older); makes breasts flatten and sag; lowers the voice; and may result in growth of facial hair. Lack of estrogen may also lead to a lack of natural lubrication during intercourse.

Although these changes may sound undesirable, many women perceive these changes positively. That is, many women regard menopause as a time of sexual liberation because they no longer have to worry about getting pregnant. In fact, Rena Wing and Karen Matthews (Elias, 1990) found that postmenopausal women, whether or not they took hormones, had better mental health than premenopausal women. Furthermore, many of the negative physical effects of menopause can be blunted through hormone therapy. Even without hormone therapy, cracking, bleeding, and pain from intercourse can be avoided by using artificial lubricants.

Reproductive Changes in Men

Most men produce sperm until they die. Many 60- and 70-year-old men are quite capable of fathering children. However, as men age, they produce less testosterone. Consequently, older men produce fewer sperm, ejaculate with less force, and have fewer and less stable erections than in their youth. Therefore, the probability of impregnating a woman decreases with age. The good news for aging lovers is that premature ejaculation, the great fear of the younger male, is rarely a problem. Sexual partners often enjoy the increased control and endurance of a mature male.

As with women, hormonal changes that affect reproduction also affect other parts of the body. Specifically, with a slight decrease in testosterone, most male bodies lose muscle and some hair. In addition, there is a tendency to develop breasts and for men's voices to become higher.

Sexuality and Aging

Although age-related changes in the reproductive organs may diminish or eliminate one's ability to reproduce, aging does not signal the end of sexuality. As will be discussed in chapter 11, many elderly people continue to enjoy an active and satisfying sex life.

[3] Alzheimer's originally was used to describe a dementia that afflicted middle-age adults.

Summary of Physical Changes

In this section you have gained an appreciation for the physical changes that accompany aging. Although there are many hypotheses for why we age, scientists have yet to determine the exact causes and mechanisms of aging. However, we do know what physical changes you can expect as your body ages. The good news is that although all of us may expect losses in physical strength and capacity, the rate of decline can be slowed through exercise and proper diet.

Sensory Changes

During the adult years, our sensory organs gradually deteriorate. Although there are dramatic individual differences in both the timing and degree of impairment, sensory decline is a universal feature of the aging process. In this section, we will briefly summarize the major changes in each sensory system.

The Aging Eye

A number of biological changes occur in the visual system during the adult years. As you age, the lenses of your eyes continue to grow. They become harder and less flexible, making accommodation (focusing) more difficult. The lens also becomes less transparent, taking on a yellow tinge. This yellowing of the lens has two outcomes. First, since you are, in effect, wearing yellow sunglasses, your perceptions have a yellow haze to them. Second, you don't get as much light to your retina as you did when you were younger. As a result, older people require more light than younger people to see fine detail, such as the print in phone books.

By the time you're 70, your lenses may be so clouded that most of the light entering your eye is blocked before it can reach your retina. This condition is referred to as **cataracts,** and afflicts 20 to 25 percent of 70-year-olds (Corso, 1981). Cataracts may be treated by using lasers that destroy the impurities in the lens or by replacing the natural lens with an artificial lens.

Not only do the lenses get hard and cloudy, the pupils become smaller with age (Kline & Schieber, 1985). Thus, night vision is often severely impaired because of the combined effects of smaller pupils limiting the amount of light entering the eye and opaque lenses blocking the meager light that does get in.

In addition to having poor night vision, people also have difficulty adapting to changes in illumination as they age. The ability to adapt is weakest when it is dark. Thus, "most stairway falls taken by older people occur on the top step, precisely where the person typically descends from a window-lit hallway into the darker stairwell" (Myers, 1990a).

Because they have poor night vision and they are not good at adjusting to changes in lighting (such as those caused by the glare of bright headlights, going from a well-lit street to a dark road, or going from reading the dash to looking at the road), many elderly people should not drive at night. Yet, giving up the privilege of driving is difficult for many elderly people because they are giving up some of their independence.

Eye muscles also may become less effective with age. For example, many middle-aged people have difficulty looking up without raising their heads. The combined effect of changes in eye muscles, the lens, and pupil may result in poorer depth perception.

A final visual problem that increases with age is destruction or malfunction of cells in the retina. Often this is the result of diseases that restrict blood flow to the retina, such as diabetes (the leading cause of blindness in the United States) or **glaucoma** (high pressure in the eye causing hardening of the eye and damage to the internal structures of the eye). Any retinal loss affects vision directly because the retina is where the rods and cones, the cells that convert light into nerve impulses, are located.

We can't say when a particular person will suffer from these age-related problems. Some people still have excellent vision at 70. Others have cataracts when they're 30. Some of this variation is genetically determined, some of it is induced through experiences. For example, people who stare directly at the sun, especially during an eclipse, have a great chance of damaging their eyes because of the destructive effects of ultraviolet rays.

Hearing

With age, some hearing loss is almost inevitable. Hearing difficulties progress at about the same rate as vision problems. For both senses, the number of people with impairments increases around the age of 40 and shows a sharp increase after 60 (Schaie & Willis, 1991). About 15 percent of those over 65 are legally deaf. Most hearing impairments associated with aging are caused by damage to the **cochlea,** the primary neural receptor of hearing. The most common source of cochlear damage is exposure to loud or continuous noise. Table 4.7 lists several culprits, including power tools, cars, compact cassette or disc players, stereos, drums, and human voices. It's important to remember that damage from these things is cumulative. What you do to your ears today may not show up until you're 60.

Hearing loss is usually greater for high frequency sounds (Corso, 1977). For instance, a person with a hearing problem is more likely to hear a bass than a soprano, a man's voice more than a woman's. Also, hearing loss is usually greater for men than for women. Finally, hearing loss presents the greatest problem under what are called **masking conditions,** situations in which a sound may be hidden (masked) by surrounding sounds. Because of masking, trying to hear someone talk at a party, on a busy street, or over the sound of an air conditioner, may be futile.

Losing your hearing can lead to social isolation. You not only fail to hear what is said to you, but less is said to

Table 4.7

Effects of Events on Hearing Loss

Decibels	Example	Damage
160	Shot gun blast	Any exposure causes hearing loss.
150	Jet	
140	Rock band at close range	
130	Alarm sirens at close range	Prolonged exposure causes hearing loss.
120	Loud thunder, stereo headset at full volume	
110	Jackhammer	
100	Subway train, power mower	
90	Bus, motorcycle, snowmobile, loud home stereo, blender, heavy traffic	
DAMAGE STARTS		
80	Busy street corner	None
70	Normal car	None
60	Normal conversation	None
50	Quiet car	None
40	Quiet office or room	None
30	None	None
20	Whisper	None
10	None	None
0	Threshold of hearing	None

Source: Adapted from D. Coon, *Introduction to Psychology: Exploration and Application*, 4th edition, West, 1986.

you because people tire of talking with you. People dislike having to constantly repeat themselves and become very impatient when asked to repeat themselves.

From reading this section on hearing, we hope you will learn two simple, but practical, rules. First, when talking to an elderly person, don't get angry if you're asked to repeat yourself. Instead, speak loudly (but don't shout or scream), at not too high or too low a pitch, in a place where there are few background noises that might mask your message. Second, avoid unnecessary exposure to loud noises. As we have suggested, hearing loss can often be prevented by avoiding noise. In fact, in some cultures, it is rare to find an old person with significant hearing loss because it is rare for a person to be exposed to loud or continuous noise.

Taste

Taste sensitivity is at its best between ages 18 and 50. Thus, as you may have noticed, adults can discriminate between more flavors than children. After 50, taste sensitivity declines, especially for the sensations of saltiness and sweetness. It is not entirely clear why this decrement occurs because taste buds regenerate throughout the lifespan. Regardless of the cause, these changes rob the elderly of subtle flavors and may encourage poor dietary habits. Just when people should be restricting salt and sugar to ward off cardiovascular problems and diabetes, they tend to add more salt and more sugar just to make food taste like it did in their forties.

Smell

We don't know whether the sense of smell changes over the lifespan. Some research suggests a decline with age. However, much research fails to demonstrate a decline. What we do know is that people can impair both the sense of smell and taste by smoking.

Touch

Evidence for age changes in touch is inconclusive. However, many elderly people do suffer from circulatory or neurological disorders that deaden the sensation of touch, especially in the arms and legs.

Conclusions

In this chapter, we gave you an overview of the important physical changes that occur from conception to old age. As you will see in future chapters, physical changes may be related to (1) the rapid growth of mental and social abilities from infancy to young adulthood, (2) the stability of those abilities during most of adulthood, and (3) the decline of those abilities during late adulthood. As you will also see, almost all discontinuous, qualitative changes in intellectual and social development can be traced to discontinuous, qualitative physical changes, such as spurts in brain growth or the production of hormones.

In terms of intellectual development, you have seen that brain changes are associated with the abilities to learn to talk and to concentrate. If research on the brain continues at its present pace, scientists will soon be able to show that specific brain changes cause certain intellectual changes. To give you an idea of the kinds of findings that may soon emerge, Thatcher, Walker, and Giudice (1987) found that the brain undergoes major growth spurts that *may* be the cause of the four stages of development described by Piaget.

In terms of social development, bodily changes affect how people view themselves and how they are viewed by

Box 4.9

SELF-CHECK

1. Which biological theory of aging best explains neural and muscular aging?
2. How much strength do most people lose between ages 30 and 60?
3. How can the effects of physical aging on muscle strength, reaction time, and life expectancy be reduced?
4. Do most older adults have chronic brain disorders? What causes multi-infarct dementia?
5. What is the main distinction between senile dementia and multi-infarct dementia?
6. Some people once recommended that older people shouldn't cook with aluminum pots. Why, do you think, this turned out to be useless advice?
7. Even when we control for neuron loss, some older people seem to suffer fewer declines in mental sharpness than others. These people tend to be those who stay active and involved. Can you generate a physiological explanation for their success?
8. What changes end a woman's fertility?
9. Why should many elderly people avoid night driving?
10. When conversing with an elderly person who has poor hearing, what two things should you keep in mind?

Please turn to the end of this chapter to check your answers.

others. For instance, as a boy goes through puberty, he is treated more like a man than as a boy; as a child becomes capable of walking, more demands are placed on her.

Certainly, as you will see in future chapters, physical changes play an important role in understanding development. But how can you remember the bewildering number of physical changes that occur throughout the lifespan? You might start by remembering four general principles. First, physical development usually proceeds from head to toe (cephalocaudal) and from the center of the body to the extremities (proximodistal). Second, although there are marked differences between the physical development of men and women, these differences are primarily due to testosterone. In the periods during which males have little testosterone—at the beginning of life and near its end—men and women are extremely similar. Third, sensory and physical abilities tend to improve after birth and decline near death, but severe decline of any kind is not inevitable. Usually, a good environment can reduce the extent of decline. Fourth, as people age and learn, their neurons become more specialized. The cost of this specialization is that plasticity is lost. This loss of plasticity may account for adults apparently being worse than young children at (1) recovering from brain damage and (2) learning language.

SUMMARY

1. Physical development begins at conception when a single sperm fertilizes an ovum.
2. Human gestation takes about 9 months.
3. Prenatal development occurs in three major periods: the period of the zygote, the period of the embryo, and the period of the fetus.
4. The period of the zygote marks the zygote's journey from the fallopian tube to the uterus and includes its implantation in the uterine wall.
5. Only about 25 percent of all zygotes successfully implant.
6. During the period of the embryo, the trophoblast develops into the placenta, umbilical cord, and amniotic sac.
7. By the end of the period of the embryo, all the organs, glands, muscles, bones, and major systems have begun to develop.
8. Throughout prenatal development, physical growth adheres to Gesell's cephalocaudal (head-to-toe) and proximodistal (center-out) principles.
9. Fetuses can hear, feel, see, and perceive.
10. The three phases of birth are (1) effacement and dilation, (2) expulsion of the fetus, and (3) expulsion of the afterbirth.
11. Birth is physically taxing and potentially dangerous for the emerging fetus. Permanent damage is probable during difficult births and with the use of forceps.

12. Poverty, poor nutrition and medical care, teenage pregnancy, and exposure to teratogens are related to low birth-weight and preterm infants.
13. The brain is central to all physical and psychological functions.
14. The basic unit of the nervous system is the neuron, which receives and transmits neural impulses.
15. Myelination of the neurons is linked to important maturational changes.
16. The three areas of the brain are the hindbrain (regulates basic body functions), the midbrain (the seat of emotions and primitive urges), and the forebrain (higher intellectual functions).
17. In most people, the left hemisphere processes language, math, and speech analytically and in a sequential fashion. The right hemisphere processes visual, spatial, and emotional information.
18. Verbal and spatial abilities are more widely distributed in both hemispheres in women, whereas as men's cerebral hemispheres are more rigidly segregated.
19. Dyslexia may be caused by a defect in cerebral lateralization.
20. The pituitary gland is the "master gland" of the endocrine system because its secretions stimulate the release of hormones from all other glands.
21. Throughout childhood, motor development is dependent on the maturation of the nervous system and practice.
22. During childhood, muscle and skeletal development occur gradually until the growth spurt marking the onset of puberty.
23. The timing of puberty has different consequences for boys and girls. Early-maturing boys and late-maturing girls seem to have an initial advantage. However, later in life, the late-maturing male and early-maturing female are psychologically healthier.
24. The endocrine system stimulates the development of primary and secondary sex characteristics.
25. The secular trend refers to the fact that the children in modern cultures reach puberty at a younger age than children of earlier generations.
26. The major structures of the eye are the cornea, iris, pupil, lens, and retina.
27. Vision is best during middle childhood and adolescence.
28. As babies mature, they become more sensitive to social stimuli and biological motion.
29. Physical and motor decline begin in the thirties. Those who do not exercise and eat a nutritionally poor diet decline more dramatically and at a faster rate.
30. Menopause heralds the end of a woman's reproductive years. Men can often produce sperm until their death.
31. Although you may lose 10 percent of your neurons by the time you are 70, you should experience little cognitive decline if you are otherwise healthy.
32. Dementia (chronic brain disorder, Alzheimer's disease) is not a part of normal aging.
33. During the adult years, everyone's vision deteriorates as their lenses become more opaque, the pupils become smaller, and the eye muscles weaken. Additional damage to the eye may be caused by the destruction or malfunction of cells in the retina.
34. Most hearing loss is avoidable.
35. Hearing loss is greater for higher frequency sounds and presents its greatest problem under masking conditions.
36. Taste sensitivity is at its best between the ages of 18 and 50.
37. Evidence for age changes in smell and touch are inconclusive.

KEY TERMS

accommodate 135
acromegaly 124
afterbirth 116
age of viability 115
aging 137
Alzheimer's disease 140
amniotic sac 114
androgens 128
anorexia nervosa 131
Apgar scale 117
arteriosclerosis 140
autoimmune theory of aging 137
Babinski reflex 115
biological motion 136
blastocyst 112
cataracts 142
cephalocaudal 114
cervix 130
Cesarean section 117
clitoris 130
cochlea 142

cornea 134
corpus callosum 123
dementia 140
depth perception 135
dyslexia 123
effacement and dilation 116
embryoblast 112
estrogen 130
expulsion of the afterbirth 116
expulsion of the fetus 116
fallopian tube 130
follicles 130
follicle-stimulating hormone (FSH) 130
forebrain 122
gestation 112
giantism 124
glaucoma 142
glial cell 121
grasping reflex 132
growth hormone (GH) 124
hindbrain 121
hormones 124
iris 134
labia 130
lanugo 115
lateralization 123
lens 134
limbic system 122
limited division potential 137
low birth-weight 118
masking conditions 142
menarche 131
menopause 141
midbrain 122
Moro reflex 132
myelin 121
myelination 121
neonate 117
neurofibrillary tangles 140
neuron 121
orgasm 130
osteoporosis 137
ovaries 130
ovum 130
period of the embryo 113
period of the fetus 115
period of the zygote 112
pituitary dwarfism 124
pituitary gland 124
placenta 113
plaques 140
plasticity 123
preterm 118
primary sex characteristics 128
proximodistal 114
puberty 125
pupil 134
respiratory distress syndrome 116
reticular formation 121
retina 134
rooting reflex 132
scrotum 128
secondary sex characteristics 128
secular trend 132
semen 128
small for date 118
sucking reflex 132
Sudden Infant Death Syndrome (SIDS) 122
surfactin 116
testicles 128
testosterone 127
trophoblast 112
umbilical cord 113
urethra 130
uterus 130
vagina 130
vas deferens 128
vernix 118
wear and tear theory of aging 137

Self-Check Answers

Box 4.2

Part A: **1.** False. **2.** False. **3.** True. **4.** False.

Part B: **5.** Zygote, embryo, fetus; **6.** Two weeks; **7.** Legs (proximodistal), head (cephalocaudal); **8.** Amniotic sac (protection), placenta (nourishment); **9.** Cephalocaudal development.

Box 4.3

1. a. Nurture, stability, passive; b. Freud; c. People who have difficult births may differ from people who do not in many ways. Mothers who have difficult births may be less experienced parents, more ambivalent about having a child, have poorer prenatal care, have lower incomes, and have more health problems. Any one of these factors could account for the statistical relationship between birth trauma and suicide.
2. b.
3. 7 to 10.
4. 7.
5. Brazelton Neonatal Behavioral Assessment Scale (NBAS)
6. Low birth-weight; preterm infants may have lanugo and vernix, their nipples may not be visible, and boys' testicles may not have descended.
7. If the child is kept alive long enough, he or she will develop those reflexes. Many preterm infants die from respiratory distress syndrome caused by a lack of surfactin.

8. We need to reduce the number of teenagers giving birth and we need to make sure mothers are healthy during their entire pregnancy. Paying for medical care and meals for expectant mothers costs money, but it costs much less than taking care of preterm infants.

Box 4.4

Answers will vary because these issues are matters of opinion.

Box 4.6

1. One possibility is that male peers place more emphasis on physical maturity than female peers do. Another possibility is that, whereas physical maturity has primarily positive effects for males, the effects of physical maturity are mixed for females. Thus, the negative effects of being considered less socially desirable by same-sex peers may be balanced by having more interactions with the opposite sex.
2. Feminists might argue that, as a sexist society, we will value people more as they come to look more like a man, whereas we will value people less as they come to look more like a woman. There are, however, other possibilities.
3. One possibility is that both early-maturing females and late-maturing males learn from adversity. One thing they might learn from adversity is not to place too much emphasis on superficial physical characteristics. Another possibility is that, by virtue of being less popular, they are not as influenced by their peers. As a result, they may develop more independence and self-reliance.

Box 4.7

1. True. **2.** False. **3.** True. **4.** True. **5.** True.
6. Myelination speeds up the rate of neural transmission.
7. Left; plasticity, child, adult. Women will recover more fully because their brains are less lateralized.
8. The corpus callosum is the bridge that helps the two hemispheres communicate. Some evidence suggests that dyslexics have difficulty integrating information from their two hemispheres.
9. The pituitary produces hormones that stimulate the secretion of hormones from other glands. It is influenced by the hypothalamus, a part of the brain's limbic system.
10. The bones in the legs and ankles must harden and become less flexible. In addition, the leg muscles must get stronger.
11. Muscle cells and neurons.
12. They do not develop according to the cephalocaudal principles (legs grow before arms) and they do not develop according to the proximodistal principle (their hands reach full size before their arms).
13. Between 10 1/2 and 13
14. Primary sexual characteristics are vital for sexual reproduction. Secondary characteristics are traits that are associated with gender, but are not essential for reproduction (development of breasts, growth of pubic hair, for example).
15. The scrotum would not grow and more importantly, sperm production would not occur.
16. Nutrition, menstruation.
17. Infants are able to lift their head, sit up, and crawl before they could walk. Thus, motor development progressed in a cephalocaudal manner.
18. He showed that the newborns looked longer at some patterns than at others.
19. For the lens to be able to focus light on the retina, the lens must be far enough away from the retina.
20. Children avoided the part of the glass plate that had a "visual cliff." This does not mean that infants are born with depth perception because the infants studied were already several months old and were already crawling.
21. Do most babies prefer *The Cat in the Hat?* (There was no control group.) Were mothers more animated when they read the Seuss story? (After all, they had so much practice reading it that they shouldn't be stumbling over the words.)

Box 4.9

1. The wear and tear theory.
2. 30–40 percent.
3. By exercise.
4. No. Strokes that are brought on by hardening of the arteries cause multi-infarct dementia.
5. Senile dementia is characterized by brain atrophy, plaques, and neurofibrillary tangles. The brains of people suffering from multi-infarct dementia do not have these characteristics. Rather, multi-infarct dementia is caused by a series of small strokes brought on by arteriosclerosis.
6. Alzheimer's patients have an abnormally high concentration of aluminum in their brains. The aluminum in the brain could be a side effect, rather than a cause, of Alzheimer's.
7. When people stay active, the neurons that remain may form more synapses.
8. Deterioration of the uterus makes implantation unlikely, and the oocytes (eggs) deteriorate with age.
9. Yellowing of the lens and smaller pupils allow less light to get into the eye and the smaller pupils and make the lens less able to adapt to changes in lighting.
10. Speak in a loud, medium-pitched voice and try to talk when (or where) background noises are not prominent.

Chapter

Learning and Memory Throughout the Lifespan

Life is a series of experiences, each one of which makes us bigger, even though sometimes it is hard to realize this.

Henry Ford

Chapter Overview

You entered this world knowing virtually nothing. Like an alien who wakes up in a foreign world, you looked without comprehension; heard without understanding; touched, tasted, and smelled a world that you couldn't fathom. You didn't even know the difference between yourself and the rest of the world. But you rapidly learned. Today, you are continuing to learn about the world and about what is and isn't important to you. Before you die, you will have learned more than 500 times as much information as is contained in the *Encyclopedia Britannica* (Hunt, 1982).

Your learning hasn't been limited to declarative knowledge, facts you can state (declare), for example, "humans are mammals" and "my birthday is August 26." You have also picked up considerable procedural knowledge, knowing how to do things (what procedures to follow) and learning how events are connected. In other words, you not only "know that" many things are true, but you also "know how" to do many things.

Developmental psychologists are interested in your rapid learning of information for two major reasons. First, just as genes and physical maturation are the mechanisms through which nature influences your development, learning and memory are the mechanisms by which nurture influences your development. In other words, if the environment changes you, it is because you have learned from your environment. Second, developmental psychologists are interested in how and why your ability to learn changes throughout the lifespan. For example, they might ask: How does the memory of a 14-year-old differ from that of a 26-year-old? Are the differences due to maturation or experience?

In this chapter, we will study two aspects of learning and memory (Petri & Mishkin, 1994). We will begin by discussing the traditional, behavioral models of learning. We will emphasize how learning theory is useful for describing how we learn certain primitive types of procedural knowledge. For example, you will see how people learn that two events are

associated (going to the dentist is associated with feeling pain) or that certain behaviors produce certain effects (whining gets you what you want). Such learning, which may involve lower centers of the brain (Tulving, 1985), probably comprises most of the learning done by young children. However, such learning is not limited to childhood. We continue to passively make simple associations throughout the lifespan.

We will conclude this chapter by discussing the information-processing approach, which emphasizes that learning and remembering declarative knowledge does not always involve simple associations. Instead, it may involve several stages or levels of processing information. As you will see, this approach, by virtue of breaking memory down into several different processes, has allowed scientists to specify precisely how the mind changes as people age. That is, rather than just making general statements about the mind, scientists can pinpoint which processes change and which do not. As we'll see, by pinpointing where processing breaks down and by knowing what strategies for processing information work, we can help people of all ages improve their ability to remember.

Figure 5.1

Classical Conditioning

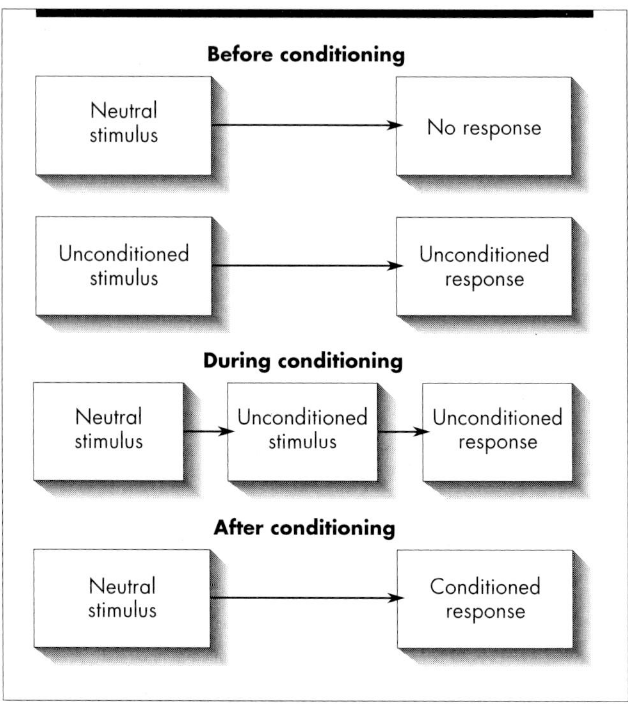

Behavioral Models of Learning

Long before the information-processing approach, behaviorists investigated how animals and people acquire certain primitive kinds of procedural knowledge. For example, behaviorists studied how organisms learn which events follow one another and how organisms learn which behaviors lead to getting the best outcomes. Such simple learning is vitally important during infants' early years for at least three reasons: (1) they need to learn some simple things, such as how to move their legs so they can walk; (2) their brains are not well developed, so sophisticated abstract learning is not possible; and (3) they are unable to learn through language.

Although the acquisition of primitive procedural knowledge is one of the most important tasks of infancy, we should point out that this acquisition can and does occur throughout the lifespan. Consequently, it is important to discuss the most popular paradigms for investigating the most primitive aspects of procedural memory: classical conditioning, operant conditioning, and social learning.

Classical Conditioning

As you may recall from chapter 2, Ivan Pavlov, through his experiments on dogs, discovered classical conditioning and many of its laws. In these experiments, he showed that a dog would learn to salivate at the sight of the person who fed it (Pavlov, 1927/1960). When **classical conditioning** occurs in humans, a person learns to respond in a certain way to a previously neutral stimulus because that stimulus has been associated with another meaningful stimulus (see figure 5.1). In other words, the stimulus becomes a signal that another stimulus is coming. For example, a baby may associate his baby bottle with a meaningful stimulus—food. Consequently, when he sees his baby bottle (stimulus), he becomes happier (response).

As we pointed out in chapter 2, this conditioning occurs automatically and involuntarily. Thus, a girl may become nervous at the sight of a pool because she nearly drowned in a pool a few years ago. She may wish that she were not afraid; she may act as if she is not afraid; but she will *feel* afraid.

As you can see from these examples, classical conditioning plays a large role in emotional responses. Our likes, dislikes, and fears are largely the result of classical conditioning. Yet, some people are unaware of classical conditioning and most underestimate its effects. Indeed, it was not until John Watson and Rosalie Rayner (1920) induced a fear of rats in Little Albert (by having an assistant make a loud noise whenever Albert saw the rat) that people recognized that fears could be the result of conditioning.

How could people be unaware of classical conditioning, the factor that governs many of their emotional reactions? The reason is that people often don't remember the incident where they were conditioned. For example, you may not remember learning to fear lightning or what made you hate liver. But even if you remembered every single classical conditioning experience you had, you may underestimate its effects unless you fully appreciate two basic principles of classical conditioning: (1) Conditioning is not forgotten, and (2) conditioning is not limited to the originally neutral stimulus; instead, it generalizes to stimuli that resemble that stimulus.

Because conditioning is not forgotten, we rarely outgrow our dislikes or fears. A traumatic event early in childhood may, unless dealt with through therapy, last a lifetime. Because classical conditioning generalizes, its effects extend far beyond the original conditioning situation. For example, a daughter abused by her father may learn to fear not only her father, but to fear all men.

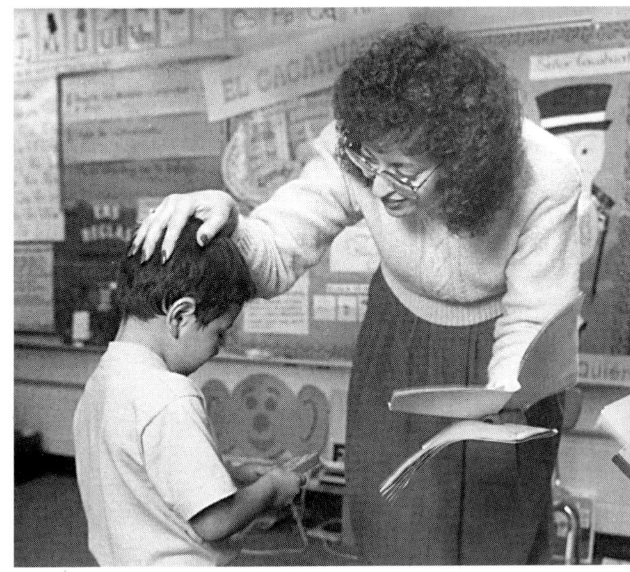

Teachers, parents, executives, and others often benefit from reminders to reward "good" or desired behavior when they see it rather than just noticing undesired behavior.

Operant Conditioning

In contrast to classical conditioning, **operant conditioning** involves learning a connection between a response and an outcome (Skinner, 1938). As you learned in chapter 2, one common outcome is **positive reinforcement,** a reward. People engage in all kinds of undesirable behavior for positive reinforcement. For example, a child whines because when he whines, his parents give him what he wants; a teenager sells drugs to get money; and a student may come to class late to get attention.

Only two things aren't obvious about positive reinforcement. First, people fail to realize that we will repeat actions that bring us good consequences. Parents, teachers, and executives benefit greatly from having psychologists tell them to "reward good behavior." How often have you seen a child ignored for behaving, but rewarded for misbehaving? Even in some mental hospitals, nurses reward patients exhibiting unhealthy behavior by giving them more attention than patients displaying healthy behavior. Second, good behavior should not be reinforced every single time it occurs. If behavior is rewarded only part of the time, people will continue that behavior long after the rewards stop (Nye, 1992). To illustrate, imagine that Tommy is rewarded every time he brushes his teeth and Suzy is rewarded about once for every five times she brushes her teeth. Then, their parents stop rewarding Tommy and Suzy. Who will stop tooth-brushing first? Tommy will stop first because he is more likely to realize that the rules for getting rewards have changed.

Clearly, behaviors that are rewarded only part of the time are behaviors that last. If people did only those behaviors for which they were always rewarded, however, people wouldn't do much. Thus, partial reinforcement is responsible for many of our good habits. Unfortunately, however, the powerful effect of partial reinforcement is also responsible for many bad habits. For example, suppose that both Suzy and Tommy cry in the supermarket until they get their favorite candy. Tommy's parents always give into this ploy, whereas Suzy's parents give in only occasionally. Both parents, on the advice of a psychologist, decide never to give in again. Which child will stop these crying episodes first? Tommy.

In addition to doing things for positive reinforcement, people do things for **negative reinforcement,** the removal of an unpleasant stimulus. We turn on air conditioners to escape a sultry environment; we put on our seat belts to terminate the seat belt buzzer; people take aspirin to stop pain; adolescents clean up their rooms so their parents will stop nagging them; little children cry "uncle" so their arms will stop hurting, and parents "give in" to stop their 2-year-old's whining.

As you may have noted, negative reinforcement and positive reinforcement are very similar. Both are reinforcements; therefore both increase behavior. Both reinforce behavior by rewarding behavior. They simply use different forms of rewarding. Positive reinforcement rewards by adding a pleasant stimulus; negative reinforcement rewards by taking away an unpleasant stimulus. Thus, just as a positive number involves adding something and a negative number involves taking something away, positive reinforcement means adding something and negative reinforcement means taking something away.

Although negative reinforcement, like positive reinforcement, increases behavior, positive, rather than negative, reinforcement is more effective. For example, when you use positive reinforcement on a friend, you both win.

Table 5.1

Operant Conditioning: How Behavior Is Determined by Its Consequences

Behavior Performed	Consequence of Behavior	What Person Will Do in the Future
Child nags parents about wanting a candy bar.	Positive reinforcement—child obtains the desired candy.	Repeat the behavior—child will nag in the future.
Parents buy child a candy bar.	Negative reinforcement—parents' get a break from the child's nagging.	Repeat the behavior—parents will give in next time the child nags.
Child nags parents about wanting a candy bar.	Extinction—parents ignore nagging, don't buy candy bar.	Child will eventually stop nagging.
Child nags parents about wanting a candy bar.	Punishment—parents yell at child or send child to the car.	Child will be less likely to nag for candy bar in the future.

You get her to do what you want—and she wants to do it. When you use negative reinforcement, she is doing the desired behavior only to stop your unpleasantness. Eventually, she may come to realize that she is actually rewarding you for being unpleasant! Therefore, she may wise up and decide to stop *your* unpleasant behavior by using either extinction or punishment.

In **extinction,** your friend would simply ignore your unpleasant behavior. Since your demands were no longer being rewarded, you might stop misbehaving. (For instance, as shown in table 5.1, a parent being nagged by her child about a candy bar might ignore the child, as if nothing were happening.)

If your friend used punishment to prevent your behavior, on the other hand, you might be in real trouble. Instead of ignoring your whining, she might try to stop your whining by hitting you. Obviously, such punishment has serious drawbacks in stopping behavior. It makes the person being punished feel angry or anxious; and it doesn't tell that person what *to* do—only what *not* to do. Children, in particular, sometimes suffer because parental punishment is excessive. Physical punishment produces not only physical scars, but also psychological scars that may result in hating or fearing one's parents.

But what should parents do if a child is misbehaving? Sometimes, parents can get the child to stop misbehaving by simply ignoring the bad behavior or by distracting the child with another task. If punishment is necessary, the undesired behavior should be punished immediately. Waiting weakens the link between the bad behavior and the punishment and encourages the child to find ways to talk his way out of being punished. Parents should explain why they are punishing the child; otherwise the child may think he is being punished only because the parent is in a bad mood. In addition, parents should explain what the child should have done instead ("Paint on this paper, not on the walls"). Finally, parents can consider using time-out procedures, such as making the child sit quietly in a chair in his room for a length of time (usually the same number of minutes as the child's age), rather than physical punishment.

Differences Between Classical and Operant Conditioning

You have seen that classical conditioning plays a large role in our emotional responses to stimuli, whereas operant conditioning plays a large role in what behaviors we choose to do. The two forms of learning also differ in that operantly conditioned responses are strongest when rewards follow responses only some of the time, whereas classically conditioned responses are strongest when the previously neutral stimuli are consistently paired with the meaningful stimuli. For a summary of the differences and similarities between operant and classical conditioning, see figure 5.2.

Similarities Between Operant and Classical Conditioning

We could dwell on the differences between operant (voluntary, active behavior that changes the environment) and classical (involuntary, passive behavior that simply reacts to the environment) behavior. However, we'd prefer to emphasize their similarities (see figure 5.2).

In both forms of learning, simple connections are made between stimuli and responses. We continue to make these simple connections throughout our lives. Thus, our lives are constantly being molded by our experiences.

Both forms of learning can be extinguished. For operant conditioning, extinction occurs when the behavior is not reinforced. Thus, an elderly person who has been active his entire life may, in a nonreinforcing environment such as an unresponsive nursing home, become idle. In other words lifelong habits may be extinguished. For classical conditioning, extinction means presenting the previously neutral stimulus, but not following it with the innately meaningful stimulus. By changing the connection between the two stimuli, the subject learns that the first stimulus does not always signal that the second stimulus will soon be present (Rescorla, 1988). For example, if a dog learns to salivate to a bell because the bell has always been followed by meat powder, the salivation can be extinguished by presenting the bell alone (without meat

Figure 5.2

Similarities and Differences Between Classical and Operant Conditioning

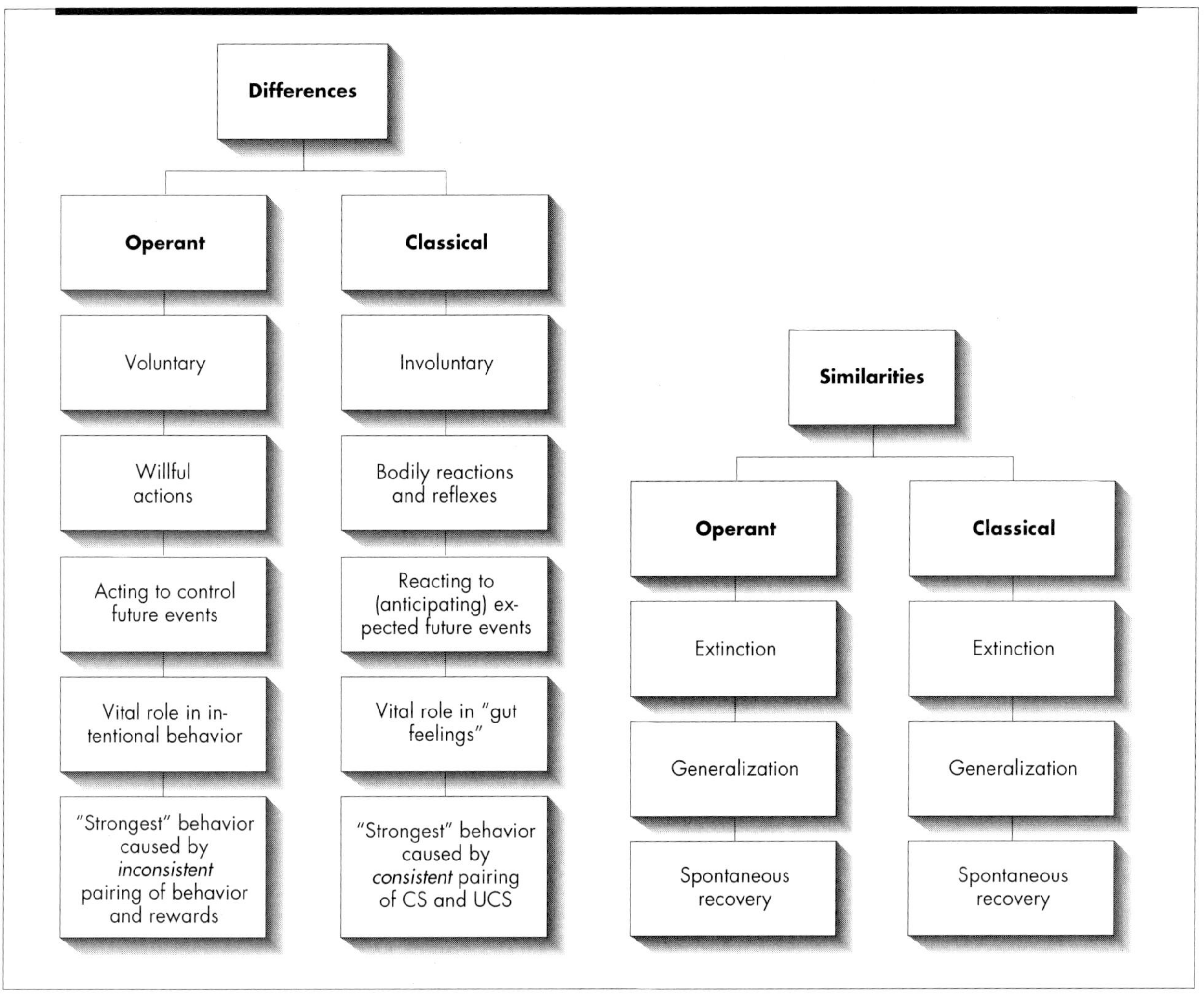

powder) numerous times. By similar pairing of a feared stimulus with a stimulus that is not frightening, lifelong fears can be extinguished (Bouton, 1994).

In both operant and classical conditioning, **spontaneous recovery** may occur. In these cases, the response reappears after it has been extinguished (Bouton, 1994). Thus, a person may seem to regress, either by going back to old habits (operant conditioning) or old fears (classical conditioning).

In both operant and classical conditioning, there is **generalization,** a situation in which a response learned in one setting may be elicited in a similar setting. To take an example from operant conditioning, we may behave toward a teacher we have never seen before just as we behaved toward the teacher with whom we are most familiar. To take an example from classical conditioning, Little Albert became afraid of not only white rats, but of beards, fur coats, and rabbits. Partly because of the Little Albert study, Dollard and Miller (1950) theorized that early childhood experiences may have tremendous weight because children are likely to not only learn through operant and classical conditioning, but to overgeneralize what they learn.

Finally, as we have already suggested, both forms of learning appear very early in development. Newborns can be classically conditioned (Stamps & Porges, 1975) and operantly conditioned (Sameroff, 1968). Researchers use this fact to find out what newborns can see, hear, or remember. For example, researchers might reward a baby if the baby kicks when she sees a certain picture. After the baby is conditioned, the researcher can move the picture

Box 5.1

ISSUE in FOCUS

Are Schools Using Too Much Positive Reinforcement?

There is growing concern that we are overusing positive reinforcement in our school systems, especially in the early elementary school grades. Specifically, by relying so heavily on positive reinforcement, we may be stunting children's natural curiosity. Many followers of Jean Piaget believe that if children are allowed to actively explore their world, their natural curiosity will propel them to learn as much as they can, given their state of brain development. Trying to push children by offering rewards for achieving things children are not biologically ready to learn can only lead to frustration. This frustration can impair children's desire to learn.

Failure is not the only factor that can reduce a child's natural curiosity. Even success may weaken a child's interest in learning. That is, a child getting rewards for learning may fall victim to the **overjustification effect,** the effect of determining that the justification (reason) for an action must be due to outside forces (in this case, the reward) rather than to a person's wanting to do it (Bandura, 1986; Lepper & Greene, 1979). In other words, by giving too many rewards for performance, a teacher may turn play into work. For example, Bandura and his colleagues found that children enjoyed finger painting less if they were paid for finger painting. Thus, by placing emphasis on rewards such as grades and gold stars, we may decrease the child's natural curiosity and interest in learning. Without realizing it, we may be replacing learning for learning's sake with learning for grades and monetary rewards.

farther away. If the baby can see the picture, she will kick. If the baby can't see the picture, she won't kick. Similarly, the researcher could wait a month and present the picture. If the baby remembers that kicking in the presence of the picture brings a reward, she will kick.

The fact that newborns can be operantly conditioned is helpful to researchers who are trying to find out what the non-talking infant knows. However, since newborns are very limited in what behaviors they can perform, only simple behaviors, such as sucking, can be operantly conditioned. Fortunately, as infants gain more voluntary control over their bodies, more kinds of operant behaviors (leg kicks, hand shakes) can be conditioned (Lipsitt, 1982). In addition, as infants grow older, they become faster and better learners. For example, Hill, Borovsky, and Rovee-Collier (1988) found that 6-month-olds learned a certain operant response (kicking) three times faster than 3-month-olds and remembered it twice as long.

As a result of rapidly developing new behaviors and becoming faster learners, young children rapidly increase their ability to make simple associations. Thus, by early childhood, classical and operant conditioning are powerful tools that parents and teachers can use to direct development. However, as box 5.1 points out, these tools can be misused.

Social Learning Theory

Classical and operant conditioning can explain much of our behavior. Whereas our gut-level emotional reactions are often the result of classical conditioning, many of our actions are the result of how we have been reinforced by parents, peers, and life. However, as you learned in chapter 2, not all of our actions are the result of reinforcement from our environment.

As social learning theorists emphasize, we may act as we do because of how others were reinforced, a process called *vicarious reinforcement* (Bandura, 1982b). Consequently, if you see that others are punished for a certain behavior, you'll learn that behavior, but be unlikely to imitate it. On the other hand, if others are rewarded for a certain behavior (aggression), you will tend to model or imitate, that behavior. You are particularly likely to model people that you respect. Perhaps because of **modeling,** we see that many behaviors—from aggression to cigarette smoking to accents—run in families (Eron & Huesmann, 1987).

To anyone who has heard a little boy say he wants to grow up to be just like Dad or has seen infants mimic parent's facial expressions, observational learning is not a surprising phenomenon. Few people are shocked to learn that monkeys aren't the only ones who see and then do. It seems we all know that modeling is one reason parents' actions speak louder than words.

Yet, even though we know that modeling is a powerful phenomenon that begins early in life, few people seem to apply this knowledge. How many parents pay proper attention to their children's playmates? How many in our society fully appreciate the value of minorities having successful role models? How many of us realize that watching televised violence increases our own tendency to be violent (Eron, 1982; Eron & Huesmann, 1987)? How many parents spank a child while saying, "That will teach you to hit your

Box 5.2

SELF-CHECK

1. What is the difference between declarative knowledge and procedural knowledge?
2. How does classical conditioning differ from operant conditioning?
3. How are classical and operant conditioning similar?
4. Compare and contrast negative reinforcement and punishment.
5. How could social learning theory account for a person's memory getting worse during old age?

Please turn to the end of this chapter to check your answers.

little sister"? How many people do you know who complain about "kids these days," yet model the wrong behavior or fail to act in the warm, nurturant, and competent way that would make them effective models?

INFORMATION PROCESSING

As you study this chapter, your main goal is to acquire declarative knowledge. Specifically, you are trying to place information in **semantic memory,** a memory of concepts and meanings. You will do this much more efficiently than a 6-year-old would. To understand why you are more efficient, let's look at what is involved in information processing. To succeed in storing information in semantic memory, you must process the text's information at several levels, each "deeper" than the next. You begin with the most superficial level, the **sensory level,** sensing these splotches of black print on white pages. After your eyes have sensed these ink marks, your mind must consciously pay **attention** to the ink marks. Then **perception,** or your organization and interpretation of the words as letters and words, occurs (Klatzky & Forest, 1984). Next, you must actively make an association between the text's information with other things that you know. Indeed, a key to succeeding in this course is having the ability to reach deep into memory and pull out either a personal experience or a previously learned concept that relates to what you are reading. In this way, you'll make the material meaningful—and meaningful information is relatively easy to remember.

Yet, making new information meaningful by associating it with old memories is not enough to ensure that you will remember the information in this chapter. You must also retrieve the information from your memory. The key to retrieval is **organization.** Unless the information in your brain is well organized, you will have trouble locating it when you need it (for example, during an exam over the material).

Sensation and Perception: The First Steps of Processing

You intuitively understand the importance of studying memory. You realize that if you lost your memories, you would not be the same person. Not only would you be robbed of your past, but you would also be robbed of your very sense of self. Your memories are part of your uniqueness.

But why study sensation and perception? Aren't those processes the same for everyone? No, as the following story reveals:

> A group of Hindus were exhibiting an elephant in a dark room. Because the room was too dark to permit the people to see the elephant, they all felt it with their hands. One felt its trunk, and declared that the beast resembled a water pipe; another felt its ear, and said it must be a large fan; another its leg, and thought it must be a pillar; another felt its back, and declared the beast must be like a great throne. According to the part which each felt, he gave a different description of the animal.
>
> WHINFIELD, 1975, P. 217

This simple story has great significance for any student of learning. First, like the Hindus in the dark room, there is much of reality to which we are blind. We cannot hear many sounds, we cannot see many light waves. Our senses detect only a sliver of reality. Second, reality, like the elephant, is too large for any one person to grasp. Each person selectively attends to the part of reality that she or he can hold on to. Third, even though each person perceives only a few scraps of reality, almost everyone is convinced that they know what the whole story is (Kussin & Wrightsman, 1985). Just as each Hindu observer would be upset at anyone who even suggested that his view of the elephant was incorrect or incomplete, many people are upset at the mere suggestion that their view of reality is not correct. Imagine telling an opinionated person that her views were not firmly based in reality, but rather were largely products of her own mind, only loosely associated to the few fragments of reality she had chosen to perceive!

Because each of us lives in our own subjective reality, with our own sensations and perceptions, we all perceive the world differently. You've observed countless instances where two people were at the same place at the same time, but weren't sharing the same experience. You've seen people disagree about the movie they saw together, the dinner they had together, the argument they had together.

Since we learn from experience and since perception affects our experiences, perception obviously affects what we learn and remember. Consequently, developmental psychologists are interested in perception.

Sensation: The Raw Material of Perception

As you learned in chapter 4, the cornerstone of perception is **sensation,** the raw sensory information received through our sense organs. John Locke, the famous seventeenth-century philosopher, explained that all knowledge comes through the senses. Locke may have overstated the case when he argued that we are born a blank slate on which experience etches our abilities, thoughts, and desires. However, without our senses, we are blind to the world of experience. Without our senses, we learn nothing—the slate remains blank. In short, we must experience the world before we can learn from it.

We don't learn from much of what happens around us because we don't sense it. Your inability to hear the high pitch made by a dog whistle only hints at the hidden universe of stimuli that exists beyond your awareness. At this moment, you are being bombarded by countless radio waves, X rays, microwaves, infrared and ultraviolet light, and a wide range of pressure (sound) waves. Yet, you are oblivious to all but a fraction of the stimulation around you because your sense organs aren't sensitive to them.

To describe the limits of our sense organs, psychologists use the word **threshold,** the level of stimulation required before the presence of a stimulus can be detected. The two types of thresholds essential to our discussion are absolute threshold and difference threshold.

The **absolute threshold** is absolutely the lowest level of stimulation that can be detected. For example, humans can just barely see a candle flame 30 miles away on a clear, dark night; barely taste 1 teaspoon of sugar in 2 gallons of water; barely feel a bee's wing falling on your cheek from a distance of 1 centimeter (Galanter, 1962). However, as we age, our absolute threshold for stimuli probably changes as our hearing and eyesight diminish.

The **difference threshold** is the smallest difference between two stimuli that can be detected. The size of the difference threshold (also called the "just noticeable difference") varies among individuals. For example, whereas some people have "perfect pitch" and can distinguish between different musical notes, others are "tone deaf" and can't make these fine musical distinctions. Such differences in thresholds help explain why two people observing the same phenomenon have different experiences. For example, if a person with "perfect pitch" and a tone deaf person attended a concert together, they would not share the same experiences.

Perception

Differences in sensation are not the only reasons that two people may experience the same event differently. Even if two people had the same sensations, they would differ in how they turned these sensations into meaningful perceptions of the world. For example, because of differences in their motives and past experiences, different individuals may interpret the same events in very different ways. Furthermore, as illustrated by the story about the Hindus and the elephant, people will often pay attention to different things. Realize that, of the numerous things that are above the absolute threshold, people perceive only a select few. Because attention is so selective and because people interpret things differently, your perception of a lecture may be vastly different from that of the person who sits next to you. As a result, students often find looking at each other's notes illuminating.

Even though you and a friend may be exposed to the same sensory stimuli, for example, watching the same movie, you may each perceive it differently.

Memories

Many people wonder how sensations and perceptions become memories. You may be surprised to find out that all your sensations, even those that are not consciously perceived, enter a memory. If a sensation is paid attention to (consciously perceived), it goes from that first memory to a second memory. If that experience is then made meaningful, the experience may go on to a third memory, where it will be permanently stored. In the next few sections, we will discuss the properties of these three types of memories, how their properties affect our lives, and how these properties change through the lifespan.

Sensory Memory

Almost as soon as you sense information, the information enters sensory memory. Since **sensory memory** momentarily

Figure 5.3

Probing the Sensory Register

Subjects were shown an array of letters for a fraction of a second. They then heard a high, medium, or low tone that signaled them to report the letters in the first, second, or third row, respectively. People usually reported three out of four letters in a row accurately.

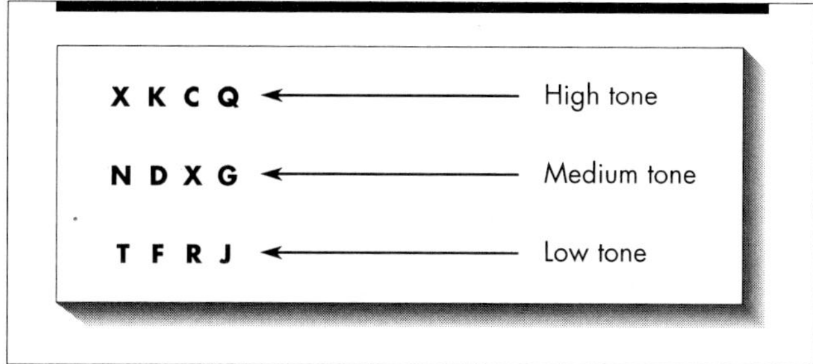

holds everything that you sense, sensory memory is enormous. Yet, because the vast majority of what gets into sensory memory quickly fades without a trace, you may be unaware that you have a sensory memory. But you do. In fact, you have several sensory memories—one for each sense.

George Sperling (1960) was the first to prove that we have sensory memories. Specifically, Sperling showed that we each have an **iconic memory,** a visual sensory memory. Prior to Sperling's work, people didn't realize they had an iconic memory because such memories are so brief, usually lasting only fractions of a second. For example, if a grid of 12 letters were flashed in front of you for just a second (see figure 5.3), you would have that entire grid in visual sensory memory. But before you could read off even four of those letters from your memory of that grid, the memory would have faded.

Because sensory memory for hearing (**echoic memory**) lasts far longer than iconic memory (2 seconds as compared to 1/2 of a second), most people are more aware of their echoic memory than they are of their iconic memory. To appreciate echoic memory, imagine a little answering machine in your head. This machine records all noises your ears pick up, whether or not you're "home" (paying attention). However, the answering machine has a very short tape (about 2 seconds). Therefore, messages are constantly being recorded over.

Owning this answering machine allows you to play back a sentence that you initially didn't pay attention to. Thus, if a teacher says to a daydreaming student, "Are you paying attention, Ms. Williams?" Ms. Williams may be able to respond, "Yes, I am paying attention."

How can Ms. Williams do this when she really wasn't paying attention? First, when she hears her name, she comes out of her daze. She knows it's a call she wants to take. Then, she replays the mentally tape-recorded message (or listens to the mental echo) and hears "paying attention, Ms. Williams?"

Short-Term Memory

Ms. Williams' lack of attention illustrates a second reason that people may be unaware of their sensory memories: only a small fraction of the information entering sensory memory enters consciousness. You are highly selective about what you pay attention to and filter out most things. Once you pay attention to the information, it enters **short-term memory (STM)).**

The Limited Size of Short-Term Memory Your attention must be selective because short-term memory is small (Cowan, Wood, & Borne, 1994). If it were infinitely large, you could pay attention to everything at the same time. However, short-term memory can't hold much information. Specifically, most people's short-term memories are limited to holding somewhere between seven plus or minus two chunks (five to nine chunks). A **chunk** is a meaningful unit of information. Put another way, a chunk is any set of items learned as a group. For example, *CUT* is three letters, but it is also one set of items learned as a group (one meaningful unit). Thus *CUT* is one chunk. *TCU,* on the other hand, is also three letters. However, *TCU* would be three chunks for most people, especially for those unfamiliar with ***T***exas ***C***hristian ***U***niversity (TCU).

The fact that short-term memory is limited to seven plus or minus two chunks severely limits our thinking. As cognitive psychologists say, our small short-term memory limits our capacity to process information. To further emphasize that the characteristics of short-term memory (especially its limitations) influence our thinking, some cognitive psychologists refer to short-term memory as **working memory** because that's where we think about information and do mental "work."

Often, our limited capacity forces us to oversimplify the world. Because we don't have room in working memory for all the different shades of gray, we tend to see the world in black and white. We are sometimes able to attend to a few salient differences between situations, problems, or people, but incapable of attending to all the key differences. Often, the result is that we stereotype situations, problems, or people. For example, when meeting with a group of people, we may focus on their salient physical characteristics (gender, race, age, height), but fail to process other important characteristics (each individual's personality). We may also form chunks from the information that fit our stereotypes and fail to process information that is not relevant to the stereotype (Hastie, 1980).

The limitations of working memory affect not only perception and memory, but also decision making. Because working memory is limited, we don't consider all our options and all the possible consequences when we make a decision (Miller, 1956; Simon, 1980). The limits imposed on us by our limited short-term memory are evident in a wide variety of decisions, from the most important to the everyday (Simon, 1980). For instance, despite

Figure 5.4

Effects of Small Versus Large STM Capacity on Decision Making

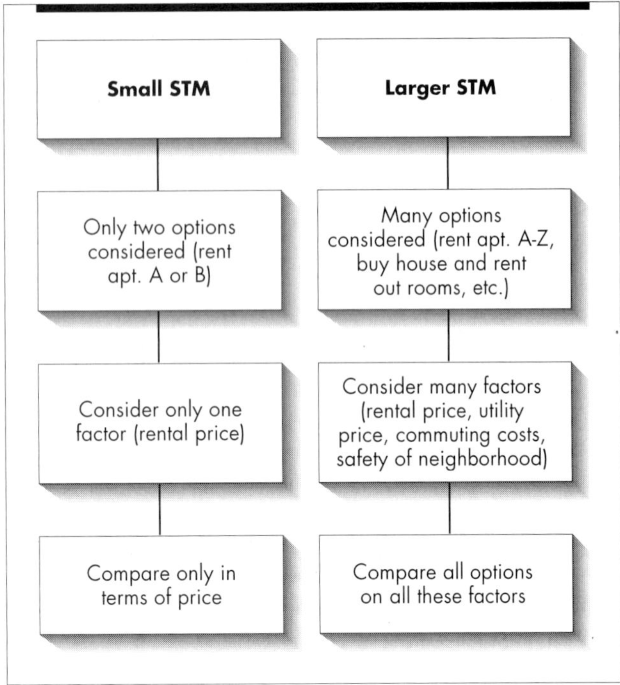

the importance of electing the right person for President and despite having several months to think about it, most people base their vote for President on only one piece of information (Herstein, 1981). Despite having numerous options and asking the question almost daily ("What are we having for dinner?"), most Americans vary their dinner around eight basic menus within a given year. For a closer look at how the limits of STM affect our decision making, see figure 5.4.

No doubt the limit of seven plus or minus two chunks of information restricts our STM in countless other ways—from the number of digits in a phone number, to the number of main characters on a successful TV show, to the number of notes on a musical scale, to the number of wonders of the world, to how we decide what to do on Friday night (Miller, 1956). We'll probably never completely realize the degree to which we are shackled by our limited STM.

As you have seen, the fact that the size of short-term memory is limited impedes our ability to think about and process information. Therefore, people have wondered if there might be some way to overcome this limitation by increasing STM's size. Although there's no way to increase the number of chunks we can hold, we can increase the size of those chunks. Rather than holding seven small chunks of information, we can hold seven large chunks of information. The process of putting together pieces of information to form or increase the size of a memory chunk is called **chunking.**

What determines whether we chunk information? The degree to which we group a great deal of information into a few meaningful units depends on how mentally active we are and how familiar we are with the material. Because chunking involves actively finding connections between bits of information, it's not surprising that we chunk more when we are alert and healthy than when we are tired and sick. Similarly, it's easier to find links between bits of information if the material is already somewhat familiar so that any relationships between the bits are clearer. Thus, if you read the assigned chapter before your professor lectures on it, you should have no trouble with her "going too fast" because your familiarity with the material allows you to chunk what she's saying. On the other hand, your friend who didn't read the chapter may think the professor is going too fast. Since your friend is less able to chunk, his short-term memory capacity is quickly overloaded. As you will learn later in this chapter, these two factors—(1) the degree to which you are mentally active and (2) the degree to which you are experienced with certain information—change as you age.

The Limited Duration of Short-Term Memory Because of the limited size of short-term memory, few items get into STM. Because of the limited duration of short-term memory, the information that does get in, doesn't stay long. Information in short-term memory can't last more than 30 seconds unless it is rehearsed (Peterson & Peterson, 1959).

Adults can rehearse information in two ways: maintenance rehearsal and elaborative rehearsal. In **maintenance rehearsal,** the information is repeated for the purpose of being maintained in short-term memory. The information isn't being processed more deeply; it's simply being repeated. Maintenance rehearsal is like saying the information silently to yourself.

The last time you looked up a number in the phone book and walked to the phone and dialed the number, you used maintenance rehearsal. Many times when you take notes, you use maintenance rehearsal because you want to hold information in memory just long enough to write it down. You hope to make it meaningful later, when you have time to think about and study your notes.

The problem with maintenance rehearsal is that it maintains information only in short-term memory. It doesn't effectively transfer the information into permanent memory. Thus, soon after you stop maintenance rehearsal, the information is lost. Unfortunately, many "D" students don't realize the ineffectiveness of maintenance rehearsal. Consequently, they spend hours repeating key terms, only to fail exams. If you don't believe the research that repeating information over and over is ineffective (Glenberg, Smith, & Green, 1977), try to draw a penny from memory. Most people are remarkably inaccurate, even though they've seen pennies thousands of times (Nickerson & Adams, 1979).

Figure 5.5

The Stages of Memory

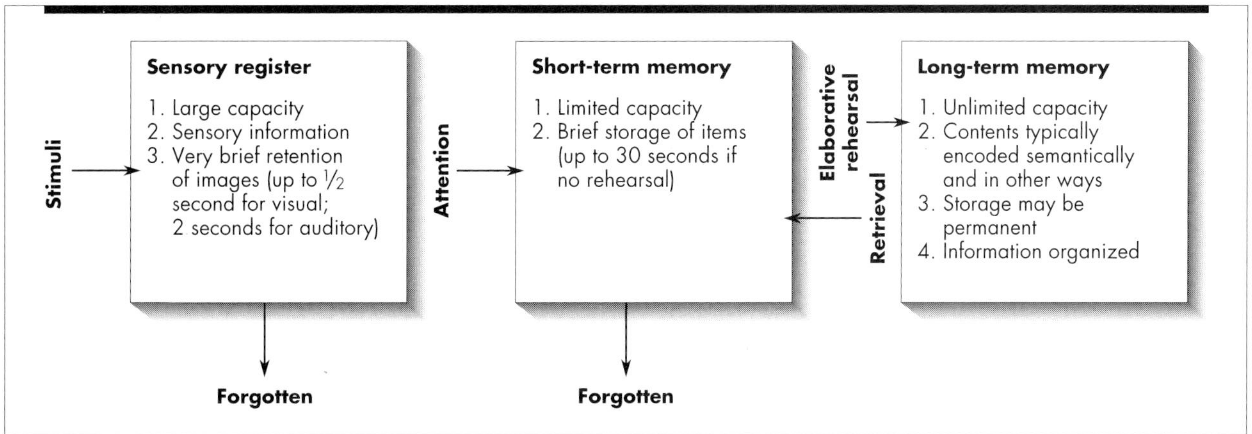

Long-Term Memory

If repeating or exposing yourself to information repeatedly doesn't help you remember, how can you get information into permanent memory? The answer to this question becomes obvious once you understand long-term memory. **Long-term memory (LTM)** is a place where meaningful information lives—and where meaningless information is discouraged from trespassing (see figure 5.5). For example, the grocery store clerk will not remember all the prices he rings up, the cab driver won't remember all the boring conversations she had.

Encoding To emphasize that long-term memory is a place where meaningful information is stored, consider how difficult it is to remember information that is not meaningful. For instance, imagine trying to remember information like the following: *drocvytljourenvzoOpuflkjrouldj vh3hbjlaxmfowahg-hfguir097-540sdpjfzgoiztjga.*

On the other hand, meaningful information is much easier to remember. This is especially true when the information is conveyed in an organized way, as in the following sentence: "I'm responsible for the spaceship Challenger blowing up," confessed an engineer.

Because meaningfulness is essential to memory, everyone can remember the last sentence, whereas few can recall the meaningless sequence of numbers and letters. In other words, for long-term memory, **encoding**—getting information into memory—is easier when information is meaningful. But if meaning is the key to memory, why do some people have better memories than others? The trick to having a better than average memory is to make information that may not immediately seem meaningful, become meaningful. Technically, the best way to get information into long-term memory is to use **elaborative rehearsal,** making the material meaningful by thinking about it and relating it to other things that you know (Craik & Watkins, 1973).

How can you make information meaningful? How can you breathe life into the lifeless pages of a chemistry book? Admittedly, making some courses and texts seem meaningful will tax your creativity. Yet, you will generally be able to remember enough to pass any course if you ask questions of the material, such as:

How is this information similar to what I already know?

How is this different from what I already know?

What examples of this concept can I give?

How can I use this information?

Retrieval Once information gets into long-term memory, it stays there. You may not always be able to retrieve it, but it's there. Information you can't retrieve to answer fill-in-the-blank questions, for example, reveals its presence by being on the "tip of your tongue" or by helping you recognize the right answer on a multiple-choice version of the same test. Information that is so hard to get at that it can't even help you on a multiple-choice test reveals itself in the fact that you can relearn the information in much less time than you learned it the first time. Like many things, memorizing is much easier the second time around. Thus, concepts you "forgot" after the general psychology final (for instance, classical conditioning), are concepts you can quickly relearn when you encounter them in advanced courses.

Being able to recognize and quickly relearn "forgotten" facts shows that information isn't forgotten, but merely hard to find. Thus, the view that memory traces, like photographs, fade over time is no longer accepted. Almost everyone realizes that we can remember certain events that happened long ago better than we can recall yesterday's lunch. Even people suffering from dementia often have wonderful memories of events in their youth.

Figure 5.6

The Two Forms of Interference

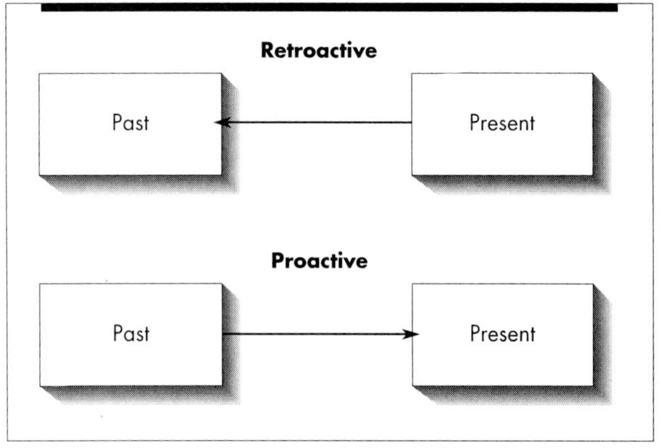

Trying to retrieve one article from a disorganized mass is more difficult than using organization to help locate it. Organization can also help you retrieve information from your long-term memory.

But if long-term memories don't fade over time, why are many older memories hard to find? For the same reason some people have trouble finding things in their purses or in their rooms—with so many things in a *disorganized* storage space, it's hard to get at the one particular thing you want.

How, specifically, does irrelevant information stored in long-term memory impede **retrieval**, the process of finding information you have in memory? Irrelevant memories can interfere with your ability to find the memory you want in two ways: proactive interference and retroactive interference (see figure 5.6).

In **proactive interference,** information you learned some time ago interferes with your memory for something you learned more recently. For example, suppose you have some misconceptions about developmental psychology. Then, in this course, you're taught information that corrects those misconceptions. What happens when you're tested over the new information? You search your memory for the correct information, but you may recall your previous misconceptions instead.

Some of our students have reported embarrassing cases where they called their new boyfriend by their old boyfriend's name. Such a mistake is simply a case of proactive interference. However, convincing the new boyfriend of this is not that simple!

In **retroactive interference,** new memories interfere with your ability to recall old memories. If you've moved a great deal, you may experience retroactive interference when you try to recall the phone numbers for the last three places you lived. Some students believe in avoiding retroactive interference. Thus, if they have a psychology test tomorrow afternoon, the last subject they study tonight is psychology. Then, tomorrow, they will skip their morning classes. In this way, they hope to avoid acquiring any (irrelevant) new memories that might interfere with their memories of psychology. A drawback to this strategy is that the grades in their morning classes may suffer.

Organization One reason that avoiding irrelevant information may improve exam scores is that it is easier to organize a little information than to organize a lot of information. But if you have a lot of information, must "irrelevant" information interfere with your search for the "relevant" information? Or, can you have a lot of information and still retrieve it? Fortunately, if you know where to look, you shouldn't be distracted by irrelevant information, no matter how much of it there is.

The dictionary and a good library are both examples of how you can have a great deal of information without interference—if the information is organized. Because the words in the dictionary are in alphabetical order, you can easily find the one word you want. Because a good library is organized and contains a catalog of its holdings, you can easily locate the one book you need.

To appreciate how a well-organized system can help you deal effectively with large amounts of information, realize that people don't say, "Could you give me a 25,000-word dictionary? It will take me too long to find the word I'm looking for in this 50,000-word dictionary." However, if the words in the dictionary weren't organized, size would matter. Smaller would be better.

Whether we're talking about dictionaries, libraries, offices, or memories, the key to accessing what you need from any large storage system is to have a good filing system. We all know this. We laugh at the person who can never find things in her office because she just shoves things in drawers. We're appalled by stories of librarians who just throw books into the library, without bothering to correctly catalog, mark, and shelve them. Yet, people routinely cram information into their memory without any inkling of how they are going to retrieve it (see box 5.3). Don't be one of those people. Don't dump information into your long-term memory the way some people cram things into a drawer. Instead, file it away. To reiterate: before putting information into LTM, catalog and organize it, so you'll have a way to retrieve it.

Box 5.3

RESEARCH in FOCUS

The Evils of Cramming

1. Cramming is often maintenance rehearsal, rather then elaborative rehearsal.
2. Even when information is encoded into LTM, there may be no way to retrieve it because no retrieval cues were memorized.
3. If cramming involves staying up late at night before the test, during the test you may be too tired to energetically search for and retrieve the memorized information.
4. Evidence suggests that you will learn to hate material that you cram into memory, whereas you will learn to like material you periodically review.

The first step to organizing information is to understand the structure of the information you have and to see the relationships among the different pieces of information. Thus, before you read a chapter, you might skim it to understand how the chapter is organized. After you read it, you might outline it. Or, you might draw charts or diagrams to help visualize the relationships between the different bits of information—a strategy that experts have found extremely effective (Dubois, 1987). (For other strategies that experts have found effective, see box 5.4).

If you have not systematically organized your memory, one salient retrieval cue you can use is to think about what was happening when you learned the information—for example, where you were or what mood you were in (Smith, 1980). For this reason, police may try to help witnesses remember key events by returning them to the scene of a crime.

Some psychologists have found that both your state of mind when you learned the information (mood cues) and the place where you learned it (environmental cues) are effective retrieval cues (Bower, 1981). Apparently, we automatically file events by when they happened or how we were feeling when they happened. Bower and Mayer (1989) report that the effect of mood cues is different from environmental cues. With environmental cues, the match is between the environment at encoding and the environment at retrieval. In contrast, the match for mood is between the mood at retrieval and the emotional tone of the material itself, not the mood at encoding. Consequently, you will remember better when tested under the same conditions as when you originally learned the material. Put another way, sometimes, the facts you need for a test are not stored as organized concepts in semantic memory but rather are stored in **episodic memory,** a memory of personal events or episodes stored by when or where the event occurred ("The time the professor brought the child to class . . .") As figure 5.7 illustrates, although episodic memory is different from semantic memory, it is part of declarative memory (Tulving, 1993).

Figure 5.7

Types of Long-Term Memory

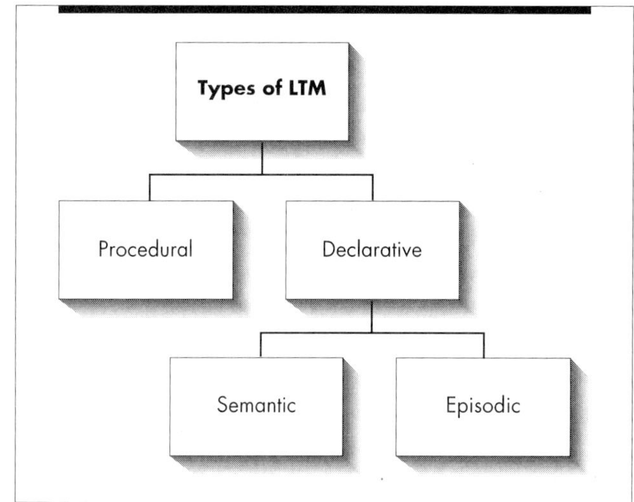

Reconstruction In spite of good organization, people will make some memory mistakes because even the best memories are not verbatim videotape recordings of what happened (Kilhlstrom 1994). On the contrary, the best memorizers memorize least. They memorize only the key pieces, the critical facts, the gist, the essence.

Why are good memorizers so selective about what they choose to memorize, even though long-term memory's capacity is virtually infinite? Although long-term memory is a gigantic pit, to fill the pit you have to use short-term memory—a very small shovel. Furthermore, good memorizers don't want to fill up their memories with unnecessary, repetitive, useless information that could cause interference.

If good memorizers memorize only selective bits of an incident, why does it seem as if they've memorized the whole thing? When trying to remember something, good

Box 5.4

ISSUE in FOCUS

Effective Memory Strategies

Most of us don't make the best use of our memories. In this box, you'll get to see how well you use your memory. First, read the following table and judge whether you are more likely to use the strategies adopted by good memorizers or by the poor memorizers. Then, you can determine to what extent you take advantage of the wide number of effective memory strategies that are available to you.

GOOD VERSUS POOR MEMORIZERS: WHICH ARE YOU?

Good Memorizers	Poor Memorizers
Pay close attention.	Don't pay attention and don't take responsibility for paying attention.
Identify critical facts.	Don't know relevant from irrelevant facts.
Focus on main points.	Try to remember word for word.
Understand and then memorize.	Memorize only.
Actively and creatively try to find meaning in facts.	Practice passive rote memorization and repetition of facts.
Understand how information is organized. Understand that information follows outlines and that examples support main points.	Don't understand how facts are organized.
Rely on inferences to reconstruct facts.	Try to memorize word for word.
Try to remember facts and retrieval cues.	Don't think about retrieval cues.
Test themselves to see if they have memorized the information.	Don't monitor (check) their memory.

EFFECTIVE MEMORY STRATEGIES

Place a checkmark by the memory strategies you use.

Selective encoding
- underline selectively
- distinguish between important and unimportant points
- summarize main points

Elaboration
- imagery
- mnemonics
- metaphor
- analogy
- paraphrase in your own words
- encode using more than one strategy

Organization
- understand how information is organized
- choose appropriate and effective retrieval cues
- be aware that related items may cue memory
- reorganize information so new material better relates to your prior knowledge

External representation
- notes
- conceptual maps
- charts
- diagrams
- tables
- graphs
- outlines

Monitoring
- testing yourself
- seeing where you are making mistakes and correcting errors

memorizers transform this "bare bones" version into "the whole story." How? In the same way archaeologists reconstruct a dinosaur from a few pieces of bone—by making inferences. Just as archaeologists make inferences based on bones and their knowledge of the world, the good memorizer takes the few original memories and uses clues to reconstruct the rest (just as good students underline only the few key words that will help them reconstruct the entire page).

Because memories are reconstructions, the ability to make good inferences is vital to accurate memory. This is one reason experts have good memories—they are more likely to make the correct inferences. For example, a

The reason a big fish seems to keep growing in fishing tales may be because most memories are actually reconstructed from selective pieces of information.

knowledgeable baseball fan knows that with two out, the batter didn't deliberately ground into a double play or hit a sacrifice fly; a novice fan wouldn't have this knowledge (Chiesi, Spilich, & Voss, 1979).

But what if your inference rules change between the time you learned the information and the time you recall it? Then, your recollection may be inaccurate (Spiro, 1980). For example, Snyder and Uranowitz (1978) had students read a case history of "Betty K." One week later, some students were told that Betty was now living with a lesbian partner, a second group was told that she was living with a heterosexual partner, and a third group was told nothing more about Betty's lifestyle. Then, all the students' memories for the original case history were tested by questions like the following: "In high school, Betty (1) went steady; (2) dated many men; (3) occasionally dated men; (4) never went out with men; (5) no information provided." Students who were told about Betty's moving in with a lesbian reconstructed the case history as having reported that Betty never went out with men, whereas those who were told that Betty had moved in with a heterosexual tended to reconstruct the case history as having reported that Betty dated or went steady. Thus, the students put together their memories of Betty K.'s case history differently, depending on whether the rule they were using was to recreate their memory of a "lesbian" or a "straight" person's life history. Because changing one's reconstruction rule may change one's reconstruction of an old memory, a middle-aged union member might remember starting to drink when he was 21 (actually, it was when he was 18, the drinking age back then) and voting for Jimmy Carter (he really voted for Reagan, but can't imagine that he would have voted for somebody so anti-union).

An actual example of how biased reconstruction rules have biased many older people's memories comes from the research of Cathy McFarland and her associates (1992). Specifically, they looked at how people's assumptions about how skills change with age affect their memory. They found that if an older person thought that a skill decreased with age, their memory was that they were much better at that skill when they were younger. Conversely, for skills that people commonly assume increase with age, older people remembered themselves as having much less of that skill when they were younger. These memories were inaccurate: These skills do not increase or decrease with age.

As you have seen, the fact that "remembering is like writing a book, not like reading a book" (Bartlett, 1932, p. 213) means that we can't always trust our memories of childhood. As you can see from box 5.6, this fact is important to consider when evaluating the "false memory" debate.

How Memory Changes over the Lifespan

Now that you understand how memory works, you're ready to see how memory changes over the lifespan. As you may already suspect, the basic "hardware" of memory (sensory memory, short-term memory, and long-term memory) doesn't change significantly during most of the lifespan. However, the "software" of memory does change. With age, our ability to pay attention changes; our rules for reconstructing memories may change; the kinds of strategies we employ may change (for example, increasing our use of elaborative rehearsal); and the kinds of cues that we find useful and meaningful may change.

Infancy Through Childhood

To determine how children's memories develop, we must be able to measure their memories. However, determining what infants and young children remember is difficult. Infants can't speak; therefore they can't tell us what they remember (Thomas, Lykins, Letterman, Whitaker, Martin, Graham, & Pittman, 1994). Even with preschoolers, measuring memory is difficult. Is the child making mistakes because she can't remember or because she isn't paying attention or isn't following instructions? Clearly, children's inability or unwillingness to respond in an ideal manner makes it hard to assess the accuracy of their memories.

Box 5.5

SELF-CHECK

Indicate whether each of the following statements is true or false.

1. Our attention is extremely selective.
2. Sensory memory for hearing lasts 7 seconds.

Answer the following questions.

3. Why are developmental psychologists so interested in the information-processing approach?
4. What is the difference between the absolute threshold and the difference threshold?
5. How do sensory and short-term memory differ?
6. How do maintenance and elaborative rehearsal differ?
7. Give an example of interference. What can be done to avoid it?
8. What is the difference between episodic and semantic memory? What is their relationship to declarative memory?
9. Why aren't children good at reconstruction? Could this deficit ever lead to their having a better memory for an incident than adults?

Please turn to the end of this chapter to check your answers.

Despite the tendency for children to "tell" less than they know, researchers have found that children have impressive sensory, short-term, and long-term memories—as you'll see in the next few sections.

Sensory Memory

Information gets into the adult's sensory memory merely as a result of the adult's sensory system detecting the stimulus. Information gets into a child's sensory memory the same way. The only difference is that young children aren't as quick as adults at getting information into sensory memory. Specifically, children need to look at an object about .14 seconds before a visual image develops in sensory memory, whereas adults can form the mental picture after looking at an object for a mere .10 seconds (Hoving, Spencer, Robb, & Schulte, 1978).

Size Just like the adult's sensory memory, a child's sensory memory is large. In fact, the sensory memory of a 5-year-old is just as large as the sensory memory of an adult (Morrison, Holmes & Haith, 1974). Experts believe that children under the age of 5 have equally large sensory memories; however, the sensory memories of such young children haven't been measured.

Duration In addition to matching adults in size of sensory memory, children can also hold information in sensory memory just as long as adults. Specifically, most children and adults hold information in visual sensory memory for less than a second.

Short-Term Memory

Once information in sensory memory is attended to, it moves into short-term memory (STM). Since adults have more control over what they pay attention to than young children do, adults have more control over what gets into short-term memory. But do adults have larger short-term memories?

Size Case (1972) tried to answer this question by reading numbers to children and asking them to repeat the numbers in numerical order, from highest to lowest. He found that 6-year-olds could repeat only two numbers at a time, 8-year-olds could repeat three numbers, and 10-year-olds could repeat four numbers. The finding that children's short-term memory grows with age is consistent with Alfred Binet's observations in the early 1900s. In fact, digit span memory was used as an item on Binet and Simon's original intelligence test. Specifically, the more digits a child could repeat, the higher his or her mental age would tend to be.

As impressive as Binet's and Case's findings are, they do not prove that raw short-term memory capacity increases with age. Perhaps because older children are more familiar with numbers, they are better at chunking and ordering numbers. In other words, what appears to be a larger short-term memory capacity is really the result of better chunking of numerical information.

This idea that increases in short-term memory capacity are due, not to increases in raw short-term memory capacity, but to gaining more experience with information (and thus being better able to chunk that information), is fascinating. But how can it be tested? Two ingenious studies have tried to get around the problem of adults being more experienced than children. In the first study, Michelene Chi (1978) found some stimuli that were more familiar to children than to adults. Specifically, she found 10-year-olds who were members of a chess club and compared them to non-chess-playing adults on a chess reproduction task.

Box 5.6

RESEARCH in FOCUS

Accuracy of Childhood Memories

Some of the earliest and most influential developmental theorists have questioned the accuracy of childhood memories. Freud finally decided that many of his adult client's memories of being sexually abused as children were inaccurate. Piaget reported that he had a vivid childhood memory of being kidnapped, a memory that he later found was completely false. This suggests that some of our memories of early childhood may be based on hearing parents or others tell us about what we did.

Experimental evidence also suggests that childhood memories may be inaccurate. For example, Elizabeth Loftus (1979) has done a series of studies showing that memories are often reconstructions. Furthermore, by asking questions that sneak in misinformation, we can actually change a person's memory. To show how asking questions that contained misinformation could sabotage the original memory, Loftus asked certain subjects, "How fast was the car going when it passed the red farmhouse?" This question served to sneak in misinformation: there was no red farmhouse. However, this question caused subjects to remember seeing a red farmhouse. Indeed, on the average, subjects who have been misled are *more* confident about their incorrect recall than individuals who have not been misled and are thus recalling correct information.

More recently, Loftus (1992, 1993, 1994) has induced entirely new false memories in people. For example, she may convince them that they went to the hospital for a minor operation when they were four. These memories are so strong that people often continue to believe the false memory, even after Loftus tells them that the memory has been implanted.

Working with children, Stephen Ceci (1994) finds that memories can be implanted in young children. Indeed, 3- to 4-year-olds are more suggestible than 5- to 6-year-olds. As with Loftus' work, he finds that some children can't be convinced that the memory was implanted. Interestingly, Ceci also reports that adults, even professional psychiatrists, are very bad at determining which child is reporting a true memory and which child is reporting a false one.

Despite this theorizing and research, in recent years, we have been urged to "believe the children" in all accusations of child abuse. For example, investigators have listened seriously to accusations that a teacher made them eat a boiled baby. But perhaps more fantastic, preschool teacher, Kelly Michaels, was accused of raping and assaulting children with knives, forks, spoons, and Lego® blocks; playing piano in the nude; making children eat her feces and drink her urine; and licking peanut butter off the children's genitals. Yet, during her tenure at the school, no adult—no teacher, administrator, or visitor to the school—noticed anything unusual. Nor did any child mention anything bad about her behavior. Indeed, even after questioning by a suspicious social worker, children initially denied being victimized. However, the social worker, by being insistent, ended up with statements from the entire student body saying they were sexually abused. Children told of being forced to stick a sword up Kelly's rectum, of being turned into a mouse during a plane trip, of seeing her penis, and of being abused, with other children, inside a tractor. Despite the absurdity of these accusations, Kelly Michaels was convicted of child abuse.

1. In these examples, what problems were created by using an unstructured interview? What problems do you see with giving a child a knife and an anatomically correct doll and asking children to show where they were poked?
2. What self-report biases might be stronger in children than in adults? What interviewer biases might be stronger when dealing with children?
3. One "expert" suggested to parents that nightmares, bed-wetting, masturbation, and changes in behavior were symptoms of sexual abuse. What questions would you have of someone making such a statement?
4. According to one mother, her daughter's behavior changed several months after Kelly Michaels quit the center. The mother's analysis was, "My daughter was all over my husband. She had turned into a little 5-year-old whore!"
   a. What scientific principles is the mother violating?
   b. The mother claims this behavior started only after parents were told to look for signs of abuse (long after Kelly Michaels had quit the center). What questions does this raise?
5. If a child said that nothing happened, an "expert" explained that the denial proved that abuse had taken place. From a scientific view, what is the problem with the expert's explanation?

Please turn to the end of this chapter to check your answers.

Supporting the idea that experience is the important factor, the 10-year-olds had better short-term memory for where chess pieces were located. Since some people might argue that the results simply showed that certain children are smarter than certain adults, Chi tested both groups with stimuli that adults had more experience with (numbers). With numbers, the adults had better short-term memories. In the second study, Case, Kurland, and Goldberg (1982) tried to rule out the effects of experience by employing a task that was unfamiliar to both children and adults—repeating numbers in a foreign language. Children performed as well as adults.

At first glance, the results from both of these studies are surprising. We all know from our experiences with children that their short-term memories aren't as good as ours. The key is that there's a difference between "raw" short-term memory capacity and the ability to make the best use of that capacity.

There are at least three ways in which children don't use their short-term memory capacity as well as adults do. First, children aren't as good as adults at chunking. That is, they lack our ability to skillfully pack material into short-term memory. Second, children's short-term memory capacity may be drained by tasks that adults do automatically and that don't drain adults' STM capacity. If you remember the first time you tried to drive or type, a great deal of conscious effort (STM capacity) was involved. But now, those processes are more automatic and they take less conscious effort. Third, children don't have the adult's skill at controlling what gets into short-term memory. Because they are poor at filtering out irrelevant information, a lot of irrelevant information finds its way into STM, often at the expense of relevant information (Bargones & Werner, 1994; Enns, 1990).

Attention Why are children more likely than adults to pay attention to the wrong things? Whereas adults can ignore irrelevant stimuli, young children are prisoners of the object's **physical salience** (how intense or noticeable it is). For example, children can't ignore bright lights and loud noises as well as adults.

Why are adults better able to tune out irrelevant stimuli? One reason may be that everything is new to the young child, whereas to the adult, most things are familiar and thus less distracting. Therefore, even though newborns can learn to become less aroused by familiar stimuli **(habituation),** young children do not have the experience with stimuli that adults do. Another reason may be that adults are better at knowing what things are important and deserving of attention. Another reason may be that brain development helps adults do a better job of paying attention.

Whatever the reason, adults are more intelligently selective about what gets into STM. This fact is obvious to anyone who has observed an infant. Infants are always getting distracted, sometimes even in the middle of nursing.

As Piaget pointed out, the inability to tune out irrelevant stimuli limits the preoperational child's problem-solving abilities. For example, if you show a 4-year-old two rows of coins, both containing five coins, the child will say the row that is longer has more coins. He fails because he doesn't ignore the irrelevant dimension (length). Researchers have found that on many tasks, if children are told what to attend to, their performance improves dramatically. Fortunately, as children age, they naturally become less distracted by irrelevant information. Thus, an 8-year-old could easily compare a short row of five coins with a long row of five coins and determine that the two rows have the same number of coins.

The skill of attending to relevant information and ignoring irrelevant information, **selective encoding,** continues to develop throughout much of the lifespan. In high school, students must know what is important and what is irrelevant to solve word problems. In college, success depends largely on realizing what's important ("What are the main points of the lecture?") and what isn't. Beyond college, experts in any given field know what things about the situation can be ignored. For example, the clinical psychologist knows which characteristics of the patient or her life can be ignored and which are of utmost importance; the teacher knows which errors are simply the result of carelessness and which indicate deficits in understanding; and more experienced physicians are, in many cases, dramatically more accurate than younger physicians at making correct diagnoses (Mayer, 1992). Such expertise clearly does not occur immediately, but develops after years of experience.

Chunking Certainly, children waste raw short-term memory power by attending to useless information. But they squander their short-term memory capacity in other ways as well. Perhaps just as wasteful is their failure to chunk information.

If you understand what goes on when you chunk information, you'll appreciate why children don't chunk. One way to chunk information is to see a relationship among the items. Thus, you could chunk the numbers 1, 2, 4, 8, 16, 32, once you realized that each number is twice as large as the previous number. However, to chunk this way, you have to know basic arithmetic, a skill most young children have not acquired.

The other way to chunk is by associating the new information with a piece of information already contained in long-term memory. For example, if you were given the digits *1776,* you would code it as the year the United States was founded, rather than as four separate digits.

To use either method of chunking, you have to rely on information that is already in long-term memory. Simply put, although you chunk familiar information (like this phrase), you can't chunk unfamiliar information (like *qzxcbrrvt edcujm mkyh*). Consequently, one reason children may fail to chunk is because almost everything is relatively unfamiliar to them. However, even when information is familiar, children will often *not* chunk information until they reach the stage of concrete operations. Only after children have reached Piaget's concrete operations stage (around age 7), do they begin to automatically apply general, logical rules to organize, classify, and categorize information (Flavell, 1985).

Until children learn to chunk information, they will not be able to store much in short-term memory. As an example of the power of chunking, consider the college student, S. F. At first, if S. F. read a series of digits he could repeat (remember) only six digits at a time. But after years of practice, he was able to remember more than 70 digits.

Although few of us can remember 70 digits, we have all developed impressive chunking strategies. For example, imagine a first-grader reading a first-grade book. Her entire short-term memory capacity is consumed by the three words, "See Spot run!" You, on the other hand, can chunk the letters into words easily, an ability that has been honed by hours of practice and reading over 20 million words.

Automatic Processing In addition to chunking the letters into words (and perhaps even the words into phrases), you can also process the letters and the punctuation automatically, almost effortlessly. As a result of chunking and automatic processing, you may be able to keep the entire content of a children's book in your short-term memory.

With practice, children will automate the task of reading. Then, since the process of reading is not taking up as much memory capacity, children will be able to keep more of what they have read in STM and will have more room in STM to think about what they are reading.

Similarly, once children automate the task of adding numbers, they can do more advanced math problems. Before they have automated that task, teaching word problems or how to solve algebraic equations may be futile because even simple computations exhaust STM capacity, leaving no room for processing the reasoning behind these procedures.

Duration Children can keep unrehearsed information in short-term memory as long as adults (20 seconds). However, young children are unlikely to rehearse information at all (Conrad, 1972). Although it is true that, by first grade, children can be taught to rehearse, they won't rehearse on their own until about fourth grade. Consequently, adults usually keep important information in short-term memory longer than young children because, unlike young children, adults rehearse.

Retrieval Not only are adults better at rehearsing information in STM, they're also better at retrieving information from STM. Keating and Bobbit (1978) found that, for the average child, the speed of scanning STM increases between ages 9 and 17. We should note, however, that retrieval speed for mentally gifted children did not increase after age 9.

Children's Short-Term Memory: A Summary Although experts have not reached a firm consensus on the matter (Case, 1985; Kail, 1988; Pascual-Leone, 1985), the child's short-term memory may have the same capacity (seven plus or minus two chunks) and duration as adults. However, children don't use this capacity efficiently. Too often, they don't pay attention to relevant information, they don't rehearse, and they don't chunk information. In short, they either don't have or don't use strategies that make good use of STM. As you'll see, children's failure to use memory strategies also limits their use of long-term memory.

Long-Term Memory

One of the first questions about children's long-term memory is: When do children first have a LTM? Answering this question is a challenge. Obviously, we can't ask a 2-month-old baby what she remembers from yesterday. Even with older children, assessing memory is a problem because children don't seem to know what "remember" or "forget" means. When told to remember something, children won't attend to it any more closely than when they're not so instructed.

To get around the problem that children may remember, but be unable to tell us what they remember, psychologists have relied on **recognition tests,** methods of determining whether children recognize what they have seen before. From research on children's recognition ability, psychologists have concluded that even infants have impressive memory abilities.

Newborns, even those born prematurely, prefer to look at objects they have not seen before. This indicates that they recognize the "old" objects (Werner & Siqueland, 1978). Two-month-olds prefer a new object over an old object even when two weeks have elapsed since their last exposure to the old object (Frantz, Fagan, & Miranda, 1975).

Perhaps infants' most impressive and most useful memory feat is their ability to distinguish between familiar faces at an early age (Walton & Bower, 1993). Fagan (1992) found that 5-month-old infants could recognize familiar and unfamiliar faces. Fagan reports that 5-month-olds are so good at recognizing faces that they can recognize a photograph of a person after being allowed to study the actual person for several minutes. Although 5-month-olds can recognize faces, they cannot distinguish between complex visual patterns until they are about 9-months-old (Rose, 1981).

By the time children are 2 1/2 years old, they demonstrate impressive recognition abilities. In fact, Perlmutter and Lange (1978) found that, on certain tasks, 2-year-olds' recognition abilities equaled adults' recall. It should be noted, however, that Perlmutter and Lange's tests weren't

One important memory skill for infants is recognizing faces. By five months of age, babies can recognize faces from photos.

fair to adults. They gave adults a difficult essay test ("Tell me all you know"), while giving the children a simple true-false test ("Have you seen this before?"). Obviously, when 2 1/2-year-olds compete against adults, they need all the help they can get. But by age 4, children can sometimes compete fairly well with adults (Brown & Scott, 1971). For example, with an easy task, and only a 25-second delay, 4-year-olds demonstrated 100 percent accuracy.

Development of Strategies Despite research touting children's memories, children don't remember information as well as adults. For example, very few 20-month-olds can remember a novel event for more than a year (Boyer, Barron, & Farrar, 1994). Children don't remember much because they don't know how to use their memories. Nothing is wrong with their storage capacity (that is, "hardware"), but children haven't learned the memory strategies ("software") that will let them take full advantage of their memories.

According to Zinchenko (1983), infants don't have any "software." Specifically, during the first two years of life, memory is totally involuntary. Infants exercise no control over what they remember. Unlike adults, they don't actively commit information to memory.

Attention What "software" do young children lack? The most obvious is their inability to pay attention (Cook & Odom, 1992; Odom, et al., 1975). If children don't pay attention, the information won't get into short-term memory. If information doesn't get into short-term memory, then it can't get into long-term memory. Surprisingly, young children don't realize that the longer they pay attention to something, the more likely it is that they'll remember it. However, as Pat Miller and her colleagues have shown, if young children are helped to attend only to the relevant information, they remember it as much as older children (DeMarie-Dreblow & Miller, 1988; Miller, Woody-Ramsey, & Aloise, 1991; Woody-Ramsey & Miller, 1988).

To emphasize the degree to which attention may account for age differences in memory, consider the results of a study conducted by Pat Miller and Michael Weiss (1981). In that study, young children remembered less task-relevant information than older children. However, young children recalled more task-irrelevant information than older children.

Rehearsal Failure to rehearse also contributes to poor memories in children. Before age 5, most children are unable to rehearse (Flavell, 1985). However, most 4-year-olds would not perceive their inability to rehearse as a serious problem. About half of all 4-year-olds grossly overestimate how much they can recall (Flavell, Friedrichs, & Hoyt, 1970). Even by age 5, 30 percent claim they never forget (Kreutzer, Leonard, & Flavell, 1975). With such good memories, why bother to rehearse?

Children's claims about forgetting points out that young children have almost no **metamemory,** knowledge of how their memory works. Fortunately, however, their metamemory improves with age until middle adulthood, at which time metamemory seems to neither increase or decrease. With increased matamemory, comes better use of strategies. As you can see from figure 5.8, the progression of using strategies follows a fairly predictable pattern. The development of rehearsal fits this pattern nicely.

By age 5, most children can rehearse. But they don't. In fact, children younger then 7 rarely rehearse. Why? Is it because rehearsal doesn't help them recall? No. Five-year-olds learn information better if made to rehearse (Flavell, 1970), as do many learning disabled children (Torgeson & Goldman, 1977).

Why do children start using rehearsal after the age of 7? School may be the reason. School places more demands on children's memories and probably makes children more aware of their memories' limitations. Consequently, older children have learned to use rehearsal to study and test themselves over class material (Flavell, Friedrichs, & Hoyt, 1970). Teachers can also encourage children to use

Fixgure 5.8

The Predictable Progression in the Development and Use of Memory Strategies

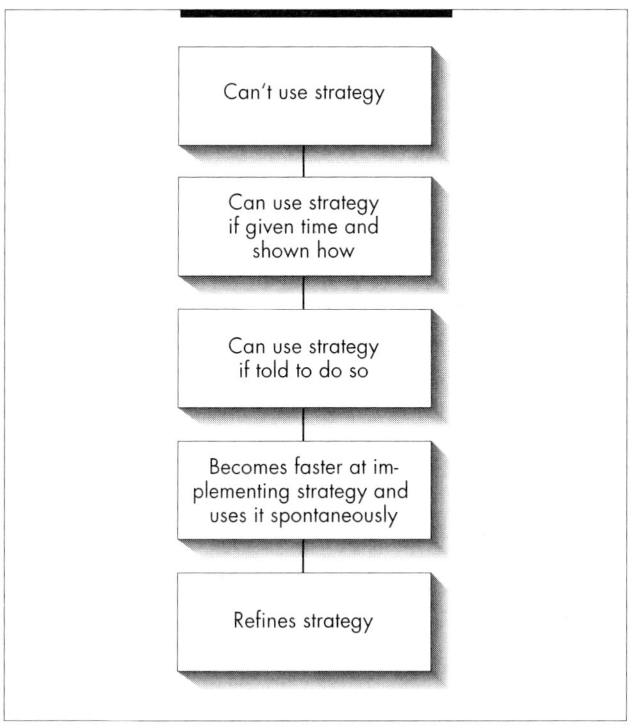

rehearsal by (1) encouraging them to use a rehearsal strategy (Kennedy & Miller, 1976) and (2) telling them when the strategy is useful (Pressley, Forest-Pressley, Elliot-Faust, & Miller, 1985).

Once a child starts to spontaneously rehearse, the next step for improving memory is to improve the quality of rehearsal. To demonstrate that the quality of rehearsal affects memory, Ornstein, Naus, and Liberty (1975) asked sixth-graders to rehearse like second-graders, and second-graders to rehearse like sixth-graders. Specifically, when given a list of words (for example, *peanut, rock, tar*), the sixth-graders had to rehearse each item in isolation. That is, they had to repeat the first word they heard several times; then when they heard the next word, they had to repeat that word, and only that word, over and over again. Thus, their rehearsal pattern was: *peanut, peanut, peanut,* then *rock, rock, rock,* then *tar, tar, tar.* The second-graders, on the other hand, had to engage in cumulative rehearsal, where they rehearsed all the words they heard to that point (for example, *peanut, rock, tar, peanut, rock, tar*). As the researchers predicted, the second-graders remembered the words as well as a typical sixth-grader would, whereas the sixth-graders remembered the words as poorly as a typical second-grader.

Improving the quality of spontaneous rehearsal is difficult. Ornstein's second graders only had to make a simple change in their rehearsal pattern—from rehearsal in isolation to cumulative rehearsal. Although changing from rehearsing in isolation to cumulative rehearsal dramatically increased recall and seemed easy to do, getting second-graders to use cumulative rehearsal strategies on their own is difficult.

Elaborative Rehearsal If getting 7-year-olds to engage in cumulative rehearsal is difficult, getting them to engage in more sophisticated rehearsal strategies, such as elaborative rehearsal, is almost impossible. The jump from rote repetition to actively making material meaningful is great. One indicator of the difference between the two types of rehearsal is that while most 8-year-olds use maintenance rehearsal, only 47 percent of all 10-year-olds use elaborative rehearsal (Pressley & Levin, 1977). However, the jump from rote to elaborative rehearsal can be made once the child has enough experience with the world and becomes aware of the effectiveness of relating new information to previously learned information.

Although young children don't use elaborative rehearsal, even 4-year-olds can benefit from elaborations made up by someone else. As children grow older, they develop greater proficiency at elaborative rehearsal, as shown by two facts. First, whereas younger children benefit most from elaboration provided by someone else (Turnure, Buium, & Thurlow, 1976), older children benefit most from elaborations they make up themselves (Reese, 1977). Second, by age 14, 94 percent claim to use elaborative rehearsal (Pressley & Levin, 1977).

Why is elaborative rehearsal one of the last strategies that children develop? One possibility centers on the obvious fact that, to relate new information to "old" (information already in memory), children need to have old information. In other words, young children don't have the knowledge (old information) to elaborate with. Unlike adults, they are just beginning to develop organized mental structures on which to hang (relate) the information. Therefore, all they can do is use rote repetition. We can all empathize with this situation. When we are exposed to information that is so new and unfamiliar that we can't relate any of our experiences to it, we probably don't use elaborative rehearsal either.

Organization Related to their failing to make information meaningful, children often fail to organize information. Extremely young children (before age 1) do not have a sense of self or a sense of time, so they can't organize information around events and times, such as "When I was one and we went on that vacation . . ." In other words, they may be unable to have an episodic memory.

In terms of semantic memory, even slightly older children (2-to 8-year-olds) fail to notice when information fits nicely into categories. For instance, they might not see that the following list contains words from three categories: *hat, suit, tie, dog, cat, hamster, red, blue, green.* An adult would automatically develop retrieval cues, "I need to remember three clothing articles, three family pets, and three colors," but a young child would not. Thus, whereas even 2-year-olds can use categories to improve recall *if the categories are pointed out to them* (and the categories are ones that the child understands), children under age 8 tend not to use categories spontaneously unless the words are highly associated (such as *mommy, daddy, baby*).

Even though children under 8 usually don't use categories, they can be trained to do so. In fact, children as young as 5 can learn organizational strategies (Moely, Olson, Halwes, & Flavell, 1969). However, their categories may be of poorer quality than those of older children (Moely, 1977). An exciting application of this work has been that teaching about categories and organization can greatly help some learning disabled children (Rabinowitz & Chi, 1987).

Reconstruction Rules Although some "software," such as organization, can be taught, children's memories are necessarily limited until their thinking develops to the point that they can take advantage of reconstruction. Until then, they can't approach the memory of a good adult memorizer because good memorizers rely on thinking almost as much as memorizing. Adults can memorize only a few key details of an event, but even years after the event, take those few details, combine them with logic and general knowledge of how the world works, and arrive at a reasonably accurate reconstruction of what happened. Young children (under age 5), however, have a limited knowledge of how the world works and rarely make logical inferences (Paris, 1978). Thus, they are unable to take advantage of reconstruction (Markman, 1979).

Piaget was one of the first to dramatically illustrate the importance of the development of thinking on memory. In one study, Piaget and Inhelder (1973) showed children a group of sticks that were arranged in order from shortest to longest. Then, they had children try to remember how the sticks were arranged. Children who were tested 6 to 8 months after seeing the arranged sticks did better than children who were tested minutes after seeing the arranged sticks! Piaget and Inhelder's explanation, later supported by research done by Liben (1975), was that during the ensuing months children developed a better understanding of ordering. Consequently, they were able to use that principle to reconstruct what they had seen.

Children's Long-Term Memory: A Summary We have seen that children do not tap the potential of their long-term memories. Perhaps this is why we have trouble remembering our early childhood experiences (see box 5.7). However, by age 6 or 7, most children start using strategies that enable them to better use their memories. With age, children use strategies more frequently, and they develop better strategies. They begin by repeating (rehearsing) information, then they organize information (around age 10), and finally they learn how to make the information meaningful (around age 13). Their progress at rehearsing, organizing, and elaborating information follows a fairly predictable sequence. At first, they can't use the strategy at all. Then, they can use the strategy, but they typically don't. It is at this point that teachers and parents, by encouraging children to employ a strategy, can help children learn. Finally, children are able to use strategies on their own (see table 5.2 for a review of how children's memories and strategies develop).

Age is not the only factor that improves children's memories. Coaching, practice, and experience can all improve children's memories. For example, Ratner (1984) found that how often mothers questioned their 3-year-olds about what happened in the past, predicted how good the children's memory was at age 4. Practicing recall improved recall. Lindberg (1980) found that when younger children were as familiar with a subject as older children were, younger children remembered just as much as their "elders." Apparently, experience with a field, be it baseball or psychology, makes one more likely to use elaborative rehearsal and more likely to make inferences. Finally, as you have seen in the cases of organization and rehearsal, coaching can help children develop more effective strategies and thereby remember better.

Table 5.2

Long-Term Memory Landmarks

Age	Memory Landmark
Birth	Recognizes mother's voice and novel objects.
5 months	Recognizes faces.
9 months	Recognizes patterns.
2 years	Child's recall of list improves when told that the list is made up of certain categories. Respectable performance on recognition tasks.
4 years	Good recognition task performance. May not understand that memory is fallible. Can't do elaborative rehearsal. Can benefit by rehearsing elaborations made by others. Doesn't use reconstruction.
5 years	Can be trained to use categories to organize material. Very little spontaneous rehearsal. Can reconstruct.
6 years	Learns that paying attention improves memory.
7 years	Uses rote rehearsal spontaneously.
11 years	Uses cumulative rehearsal spontaneously. Is increasing efforts to organize information.
14 years	Uses elaborative rehearsal frequently. May underline and summarize information.

Box 5.7

THEORY in FOCUS

Infantile Amnesia

One of the great mysteries of memory is why we don't remember our first two to three years of life. Freud, who brought the phenomenon to the attention of psychologists, dubbed this forgetting **infantile amnesia** (Freud, 1938). Since Freud, investigators have documented that infantile amnesia exists (Waldfogel, 1948), but the cause for this is still hotly debated. The most common explanations are that the memories were not encoded into long-term memory; that the memories were repressed; that they were encoded in a way that the adult mind can't reconstruct; that the context has changed; and that the memories disappeared as a result of a rapid decrease in the number of synapses in the brain.

Some have argued that infantile amnesia isn't due to forgetting, but to never having remembered anything in the first place. Because infants probably don't rehearse and certainly don't use elaborative rehearsal, perhaps information never gets into their permanent memories. If infants don't store anything in permanent memory, it would explain why we can't recall infant memories—even under hypnosis. Under hypnosis, adults usually don't recall actual events that happened before they were 1 or 2. Instead, they may recall a story they heard when they were 5 or 6 about what they did when they were younger. (In fact, many of your "childhood memories" aren't from direct, personal experience, but from hearing your parents talk about you having that experience). One of the most interesting examples of this fact comes from the famous developmental psychologist, Jean Piaget. He vividly remembered being kidnapped. He could even "see" his attacker. Then, one day, his former nanny wrote the family. She had found religion and was confessing her sins. One of those sins was making up a story about Jean being kidnapped so that she would get a reward.

The hypnosis data dispels Freud's idea that infantile amnesia is due to repression, unconsciously wanting to forget those early years. If memories were unconsciously repressed, hypnosis should bring them to the surface. However, just because hypnosis can't recover the memories, doesn't mean the memories never existed. In fact, we know that some memories did exist. We know because Nelson and his colleagues (Nelson & Ross, 1980) have established that there have been instances of 2-year-olds remembering events a year or more after those events occurred.

Where did the memories go? We know it isn't simply the passage of time. Centenarians can remember things that happened when they were 6, so why can't an 18-year-old remember what happened when she was 2?

One set of possibilities revolves around the idea that infantile amnesia results from the adult mind working differently than the infant's mind. For example, the adult might not be able to reconstruct a memory from bits and pieces left by the child (White & Pillemer, 1979). Or, it may be that children have memorized things visually rather than in words. Or, it may be that children didn't file their memories according to when things happened, the way adults do. Thus, for adults, "last week" or "1995" or "What I did yesterday" might be retrieval cues, but these same cues would be worthless for a young child. In support of these ideas, Sheffield & Hudson (1994) showed that toddlers can remember tasks that they learned during a session weeks earlier if they are properly cued. The proper cue was not verbal. Instead, the cue was having them do other tasks that they did during that session. Thus, it appears that the memory for the tasks were linked together.

Unfortunately, these explanations are incomplete. Although these hypotheses might explain why children can't remember what happened *before* they were *2* years old, they can't explain why children can't remember anything that happened to them before the age of *3* years (other than memories of sights, smells, touches, and tastes): 2- to 6-year-olds seem to recall information in ways similar to adults (Hudson & Nelson, 1983).

Another related set of explanations comes from the idea that the right cue is needed to unlock childhood memories. Cues might be available if everything was exactly the same as it was when children learned the information (Tulving, 1972). However, the child's world changes dramatically after the age of 2. Furthermore, even if the world were the same, adults would perceive it differently. Short infants have a dog's-eye view of the world; adults see the world from a much greater height. In support of this hypothesis, Neisser and his graduate students (1984) have done studies suggesting that looking at the world from a much shorter height aids recall of childhood memories.

Finally, some researchers believe that infantile amnesia is the result of a massive reorganization of the central nervous system. Between birth and age 2, synapses are gained at a rapid rate, but are then lost. Adolescents have only about half the number of synapses they had at age 2 (Spear, 1984). It is perhaps possible that childhood memories disappear with those synapses.

Box 5.8

SELF-CHECK

Indicate whether each of the following statements is true or false.

1. Children's performance on a digit span task increases with age.
2. Children's raw STM capacity increases with age.
3. Most 10-year-olds use elaborative rehearsal.
4. Two-year-olds can use categories to improve recall.
5. Children under the age of 8 will rarely use categories as cues to help recall.

Answer the following questions.

6. Is sensory memory marked by stability or by change from the period from age 5 to adulthood?
7. Describe the key differences in how adults and children use their STM.
8. How do we know that infants have a long-term memory?
9. Describe the progression in the development of employing memory strategies.
10. Characterize the quality of a 4-year-old's metamemory.
11. What normative social event may be responsible for a 7-year-old using rehearsal more frequently and effectively than a 5-year-old?
12. What is infantile amnesia? Discuss four explanations for it and tell which are likely and which are unlikely.
13. What facts about the course of development of recognition memory suggest the impact of nature?
14. What can be done to improve a child's memory?

Please turn to the end of this chapter to check your answers.

Memory Through Adulthood

Through most of adulthood, the basic "hardware" of memory (sensory memory, short-term memory, and long-term memory capacity) doesn't change dramatically. However, memory "software" may improve, thereby improving our ability to use our hardware. Such improvements seem most likely if we or others put more demands on our memories, as is the case when we take college courses (Poon, 1985; Ratner et al., 1987; Zivian & Darjes, 1983).

In early adulthood, memory improves in our area of expertise. Thus, baseball fans develop better memories for baseball games, and physicians develop better memories for patients' problems (Spilich et al., 1979). This indepth, highly organized knowledge of a particular subject area appears to be the reason that experts are better problem solvers than novices (Bedard & Chi, 1992; Mayer, 1992). Furthermore, this highly developed memory for one's area of expertise may even last into old age (Friedman-Erickson, Hamilton, Hawkins, Rudisill, & Lorence, 1994).

But is there a point at which memory declines significantly? After all, everyone can name some older people who have poor memories. The existence of elderly people with deficient memories raises at least three important questions. Are these people typical of the elderly or atypical? For those with deficits, are the deficits in sensory, short-term, or long-term memory? Finally, can the deficits be corrected?

Answering these questions is not as easy as you might think. Even research addressing the simple question, "Do young adults have better memories than the elderly?" encounters several problems.

The first problem is the result of a sampling bias. Typically, researchers compare young college students with elderly people who have never been to college. A study by Ratner et al. (1987) found that although young college students did better than the elderly on memory tasks, young noncollege students and retirees did *not* differ. Schaie (1979) found similar results. Furthermore, Bowles and Poon (1985) and Taub (1979) have found few memory differences between the elderly and young adults when both samples have a high vocabulary level.

A second problem is that the elderly might not be as motivated to perform a mindless, artificial, laboratory rote memorization task as college students are. Evidence that motivation may be a factor comes from several sources. First, whenever the elderly do better than college students, the elderly are said to be more motivated (Poon & Schaffer, 1982). If the elderly's superior recall performance can be explained by saying that they were more motivated on the particular task, then why can't we say that when college students do better that the college students were more motivated? Second, Ratner et al. (1987) found that college students studied harder and longer than retirees. Third, the biggest differences between college students and elderly adults' recall comes from studies that involve meaningless tasks, such as memorizing

One reason studies have found a better memory performance in younger people may be sampling bias. Young adult college students were compared with elderly people who had never been to college. What might be the result of testing elderly professors?

nonsense syllables. Fourth, when recall is tested for real-world events, such as those reported in newspapers, the elderly do as well as young adults (Poon, 1985). Fifth, if prodded or coached, differences between age groups can usually be eliminated, weakened, or even reversed. Sixth, the elderly tend to perform poorer on rote recall of details, but not on recall of main ideas (Gilbert & Levee, 1971; Meyer, Rice, Knight, & Jensen, 1979; Zelinski, Gilewski, & Thompson, 1980).

The seventh and final problem with comparing the elderly with young adults is that any memory differences might be due to differences in health. Even if most elderly adult subjects remembered slightly more words than the younger adult subjects, two elderly adults in ill health could score so poorly that they could pull down the average score for the elderly subjects below the average for young adult subjects.

Now that you've been warned that (1) the research about age differences in memory may only reflect differences in motivation to work for the experimenter and that (2) studies showing age declines don't mean that all elderly people show declines, you're ready to look at what age difference research has found.

Sensory Memory

As we have already mentioned, information goes from the senses to sensory memory. In light of sensory deficits that the elderly experience, you might expect that their sensory memory would be vastly inferior to that of younger adults. However, under testing conditions that minimize the effect of differential sensory abilities, there is little difference between the young adult's and the elderly's visual sensory memory (Botwinick, 1978).

Short-Term Memory

The elderly who are in good health can hold practically as much information in short-term memory as young adults (Botwinick, 1984; Craik, 1977; Salthouse, 1985). In other words, the seven plus or minus two rule holds for the elderly as well as for adults and children (see figure 5.9). However, compared to young adults, the elderly are slower at retrieving information from short-term memory. That is, when they read the list "cat, cucumber, cracker, curt, clip, cop, cello," both the elderly and young adults will correctly answer "yes" to the question: "Was the cracker on the list I just read you?" However, the elderly will be slower to say "yes" than the young adults.

Although adults of all ages may appear to be equally effective at encoding information when simple tasks are involved, significant age differences emerge when more demanding short-term memory tasks are required. For example, what happens when young and old adults are asked to complete a task that requires them to simultaneously encode and transform information? In a series of five experiments, Timothy Salthouse and Eric Skovronek (1992) answered this question by using a computer-administered version of a cube comparison test. In the test, participants are shown two different three-dimensional cubes. Participants can clearly see three faces on each cube. On each of the faces, there is a letter (for example, *a, c, f*). The orientation of these letters varies. Some are right-side up, some are upside down, and some are on their sides. Young and old adults were asked to determine whether the two cubes were essentially the same, except that one had been rotated. Answering this question is very difficult and for most people involves considerable mental processing. Specifically, to solve these problems, a person must simultaneously encode and transform information (by mentally rotating the visual image of one or both cubes).

Figure 5.9

How STM Capacity Changes During Adulthood

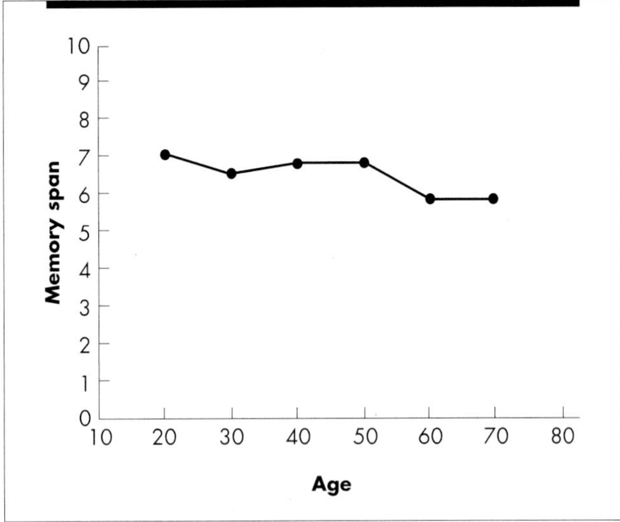

Salthouse and Skovronek (1992) found that young and old adults were equal in their ability to temporarily hold untransformed information in their short-term memories. However, when presented with the complex cube task, the elderly were less accurate than the younger adults. These results are consistent with the view that increased age may be associated with a decreased ability to transform or abstract information while preserving the products of earlier processing.

Finally, some elderly fail to actively suppress irrelevant information (Connely & Hasher, 1993; Kane, Hasher, Stoltzfus, Zacks, & Connelly, 1994; Rogers, 1993). Consequently, information that the elderly would like to ignore enters short-term memory, limiting the amount of room available to process relevant information. This reduced ability to tune out distractions may cause the elderly problems on tasks where they have to divide their attention, such as when they are driving and talking at the same time.

In conclusion, the elderly experience some declines in the ability to use short-term memory. These declines are most apparent when the elderly are doing complex tasks in an unfamiliar environment. However, if the elderly are doing a familiar task in a distraction-free environment, their performance may be equal or superior to that of younger people. For example, Timothy Salthouse (1985) found that experienced older typists typed as fast as younger typists.

Long-Term Memory

Do the elderly have poorer long-term memories than the rest of us? Admittedly, older adults report more memory failures than younger adults (Hultsch, Hertzog, & Dixon, 1987). But do they report more failures because they have more failures or because they remember failures better than other adults? They may be more aware of their failures because the elderly take memory failures more seriously than younger adults. When the elderly forget, they become distressed ("I'm losing it."), whereas when younger adults forget, they reason that they are "under stress" or "preoccupied with an important problem" (Cavanaugh, Gardy, & Perlmutter, 1983; Zarit, Cole, & Guider, 1981).

In real-life situations, the elderly tend to remember as well as, if not better than, younger adults. Poon and Schaffer (1982) found that older adults were more likely to remember to call a certain number every few weeks than young adults. When asked to recall important, newsworthy events, older adults performed equal to younger adults for items about the recent past and better than young people for items about the distant past (Poon, Fozard, Pualshock, & Thomas, 1979). Perhaps we should say that the elderly's memories weren't as bad as the young adults' memories for remote events, since both groups recalled fewer events from the remote past than from the recent past. Contrary to some stereotypes, the elderly's memory for long ago events is worse than their recall for recent events (Erber, 1981).

In contrast to studies of memory for real-life events, lab studies suggest that the elderly have poorer memories than young adults. As you can see in figure 5.10, some lab studies suggest that the elderly's memories bear some similarities to children's memories.

However, even the lab studies point to some unexpected strengths of memory in old age. For example, some would expect the elderly, because of all the knowledge they have in memory, to be more vulnerable to interference, and thus to forget faster than younger adults. However, the elderly don't forget faster than younger adults (Poon & Fozard, 1980).

Furthermore, lab studies do not reveal a storage problem with the elderly's long-term memory. It seems that memories can last a lifetime. In fact, Bahrick and his colleagues (Bahrick, Bahrick, & Wittlinger, 1975; Bahrick, 1984) found that, even 35 years after graduating, people were still very good at recognizing pictures of former high school classmates.

The elderly do perform poorly (in lab tasks) in acquiring information and rapidly retrieving information from long-term memory. They don't organize the information psychologists give them (Eysenck, 1977). Thus, the more elaborative rehearsal required by the material, the worse they do (Eysenck, 1974). Conversely, if tested by a method that doesn't require them to organize or think of retrieval cues (such as recognition or cued recall), the elderly's performance is very similar to that of younger adults (Hultsch, 1975). Furthermore, the elderly benefit from being given cues when first exposed to the material. For example, the elderly will remember more if they are told what categories (for example, *colors, states,* and *farm animals*) words in a list will fit into prior to being shown the list (for example, *red, blue, green, Arkansas, Nebraska, Utah, cow, pig,* and *chicken*).

Figure 5.10

How Recall, Spontaneous Organization, and Speed of Processing Change Over the Lifespan

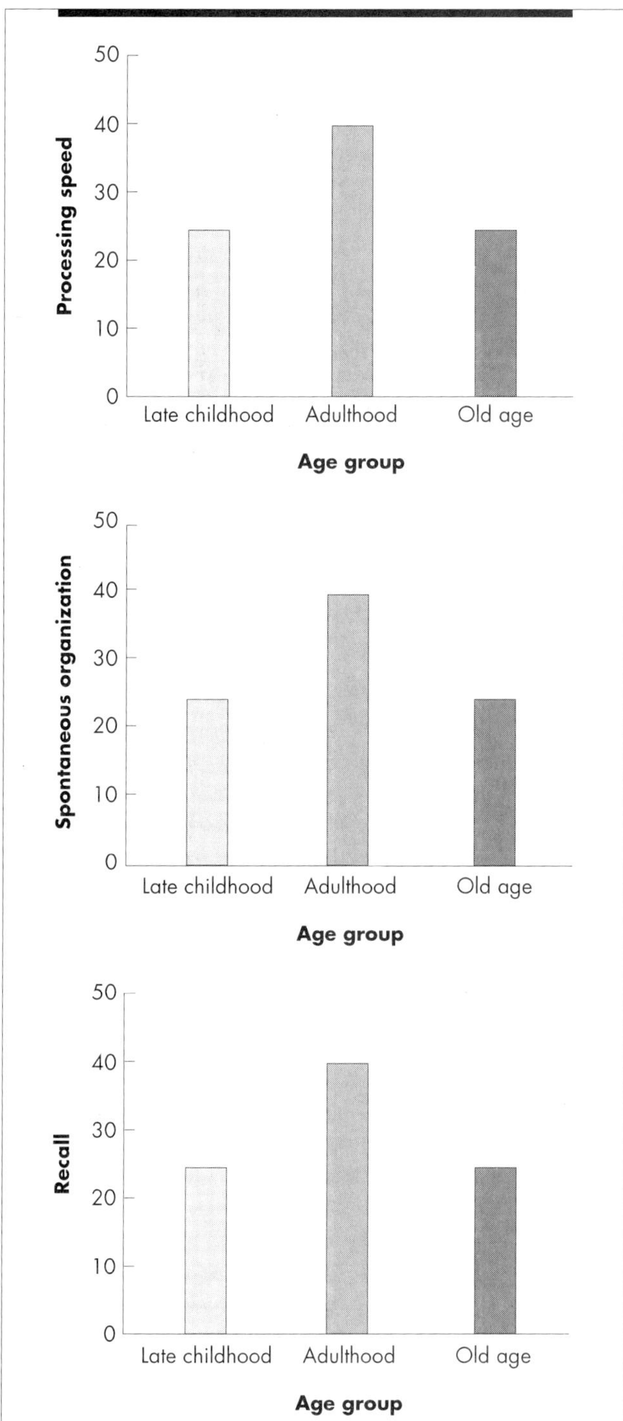

Table 5.3

Situations in Which Elderly Do Well on Memory Tasks Versus Situations in Which They Tend to Do Poorly

Elderly Do Well When	Elderly Do Poorly When
Familiar stimuli are used (vocabulary words they are familiar with).	Unfamiliar stimuli are used (difficult vocabulary, nonsense syllables).
The task is natural (summarize a newspaper article).	The task is artificial (remember a list of words).
They are tested on main points.	They are tested on details.
They are not timed or rushed.	They are rushed.
They are told to use memory strategies.	They are told not to use memory strategies.
They take recognition tests.	They take recall tests.

As the previous example shows, the elderly don't automatically organize the information researchers give them. However, do not conclude that the elderly cannot organize information. The elderly can organize information if they are told to do so (Smith, 1980). Furthermore, they will tend to organize information if the material is familiar and meaningful to them (Hultsch & Dixon, 1983).

Because the elderly have the ability to organize information, we suspect that they are simply not motivated to organize in most lab studies. Their attitude toward the boring lab tasks may be similar to that exhibited by Sherlock Holmes. When Watson informed Holmes of something Holmes hadn't known, Holmes said, "Now that I know, I'll do my best to forget it." This attitude would explain the elderly's poor performance on dull memorization tasks, their good performance on familiar tasks, and their great ability to remember important main points, but not details.

Memory Interventions

As table 5.3 shows, under certain conditions, older adults will tend to perform as well as younger adults on memory tasks. Yet, as you have probably observed, some ostensibly healthy older adults have memory problems. What can be done to help them? Many things have been tried, but few have proven successful. Lack of the neural transmitter acetylcholine has been suspected as a source of memory problems. For example, Drachman (1978) found that a drug that blocks the effects of acetylcholine can cause young adults to show memory deficits resembling senility. Consequently, researchers have tried giving the elderly a drug—physiostigmine—that would increase how well the brain used acetylcholine. Results have been disappointing. Others have suspected that depression causes deficits in the elderly's memory. Unfortunately, efforts to restore memory by using antidepressants have not succeeded either.

Some investigators have tried a nonmedical approach—teaching and encouraging the elderly to use memory strategies. Although elderly subjects initially showed great improvements, the improvements didn't last for the simple reason that subjects stopped using those strategies (Poon & Schaffer, 1982). Thus, it appears that, for some elderly people, memory problems may be due to not using strategies rather than to any physiological deterioration. However, as you will see in the next section, some elderly suffer enormous lapses for strictly biological reasons.

Biological Threats to Memory

Health problems that accompany aging can impair memory directly and indirectly. Because memory is an active process requiring attention, elaborative rehearsal, and retrieval, any ailment that prevents a person from focusing mental energy will indirectly impair memory. Thus, a wide range of ailments, from aches and pains to heart disease, can weaken a person's memory ability. However, the physical problems that most directly affect memory are the **dementias,** abnormal conditions involving deterioration of the brain leading to the loss of mental ability.

The longer people live, the greater their chances of suffering from dementia. Dementia occurring after age 65 is called **senile dementia.** But even though 80-year-olds are twice as likely to be senile than 60-year-olds, only about 20 percent of people over 80 are senile. To restate an important point, 80 percent of the people over 80 are *not* senile.

As you learned in chapter 4, one common form of dementia is senile dementia of the Alzheimer's type, that is, **Alzheimer's disease.** By robbing people of both their long-term and short-term memories, Alzheimer's disease dramatizes how important memory is. In advanced stages of the disease, Alzheimer's patients may not recognize their own family members and are constantly confused.

Memory Through Adulthood: Conclusions

Alzheimer's disease dramatizes the importance of memory. Without long-term memory, we have no past. Without short-term memory, we have no present. Therefore, the development of memory is an important part of development.

From early adulthood to mid-adulthood, significant improvements in memory for knowledge related to our profession (such as medical knowledge for physicians and selling strategies for salespeople) allow us to process job-related information in an increasingly efficient and expert way (Mayer, 1992; Sujan, Sujan, & Bettman, 1988). Improvements in our knowledge probably affect other aspects of our lives as well. For example, Cooke (1991) found that expert mothers had significantly richer knowledge structures than novices.

By the time we are 69, there will be measurable decreases in our memory for where we learned new information and from whom (Schacter, Osowiecki, Kaszniak, Kihlstrom, & Valdiserri, 1994) and for how quickly we can access visual memories (Dror & Kosslyn, 1994) and process unfamiliar information. However, by taking advantage of the fact that we are very familiar with much of our environment (Rogers, 1993) and by using memory strategies, we can usually minimize any weaknesses due to normal physiological breakdowns (Schaie, 1994). Thus, not surprisingly, people who have jobs or educational experiences that challenged them to use memory strategies and people who have tried to keep mentally active are likely to have good memories in old age (Muir & Kennedy, 1994). In other words, most of you will be blessed with good memories throughout your lifespan.

But what about Alzheimer's disease? You can take comfort in two facts. First, Alzheimer's is less likely to strike college-educated people. Second, Alzheimer's typically strikes late in life. Consequently, if researchers can find some way to delay its onset by just a few years, almost everyone will die before they suffer from it. Given

Box 5.9

SELF-CHECK

1. What methodological problems might cause studies to inaccurately reflect the memory changes that accompany aging? In what ways can even accurate results be misleading?
2. Compare and contrast late childhood, adulthood, and old age in terms of processing speed, spontaneous organization, and recall performance.
3. An elderly person tells you that the elderly have poorer memories than younger people because the elderly are more vulnerable to interference. Why does this explanation make sense? Is it accurate?
4. Describe three techniques used to improve the elderly's memories. Then, evaluate their effectiveness.

Please turn to the end of this chapter to check your answers.

this fact and the intense efforts researchers are making to understand and prevent Alzheimer's disease, it's possible that nobody reading this book will suffer from it.

Conclusions

To a large extent, you are the sum of your knowledge and your actions. Your knowledge is largely a function of your experiences and those of your models. Specifically, because of classical conditioning, you may know how to react to a familiar stimulus, and because of operant conditioning, you may know how to act in a familiar situation. In a situation you've never experienced, you may know how to behave because you've observed someone else successfully cope with those situations. Because these three kinds of learning occur throughout the lifespan, the exciting implication of the simple, but powerful, principles of classical, operant, and observational learning is that a person's behavior can be dramatically changed at any age.

Just as your procedural knowledge can expand at any point in your lifespan, so too can your declarative knowledge. In fact, as you age, you have more knowledge and experience that you can apply to any given situation. Therefore, as you age, it should be easier for you to engage in elaborative rehearsal. Perhaps this is why all our colleagues say that older students do much better in school than their "college-age" counterparts. Even in very old age, a knowledge of how to use memory (metamemory) can offset most decreases in natural ability to memorize. However, there is one kind of learning where it may pay to be young. That kind of learning is, as you'll see in the next chapter, language learning.

Summary

1. Classical conditioning is responsible for many of our emotional reactions.
2. People often repeat behaviors that have been reinforced.
3. Punishment has serious side effects.
4. Newborns can be classically and operantly conditioned. Researchers use this fact to study what newborns sense and like.
5. Social learning theorists emphasize the fact that we often learn from models.
6. Since what is remembered depends on what is sensed and perceived, problems in sensation or perception may be misdiagnosed as memory problems.
7. The "hardware" of memory are sensory memory, short-term memory, and long-term memory. The basic capacities of these memories do not change substantially throughout most of the lifespan.
8. Short-term memory's capacity is limited to seven plus or minus two chunks of information. However, the size of a chunk is not limited. As we become more familiar with a certain kind of material (be it psychology or chess), we are able to form larger chunks.
9. In general, children's memories are better than most people think. Even 2-month-olds exhibit long-term memory.
10. It is not clear whether children have a smaller short-term memory than adults. But clearly, they don't use strategies that would allow them to make better use of STM, such as chunking and rehearsal, as well as adults do.
11. Children slowly learn the strategies necessary to get information in and out of long-term memory: elaborative rehearsal, organization, and reconstruction. Up to a point, the more memory demands placed on a child, the faster the child will learn these strategies.
12. Children's ability to use a strategy seems to go through three stages: (1) being unable to use the strategy; (2) being able to use the strategy when told to and shown how to; and (3) using the strategy on their own.
13. Some learning disabled children can benefit greatly from instruction in rehearsal and organization.
14. Adults often memorize only the essential details and then make inferences to reconstruct the rest of what happened. Young children can't do this because their thinking has not progressed to the point where they can make logical inferences.
15. Most people greatly overestimate the difference between the memory abilities of elderly adults and the memory abilities of young adults. Contrary to popular stereotypes, when health, motivation, and education level are controlled for, usually only one substantial difference exists between the two groups—the elderly are slower to retrieve information from both short-term and long-term memory than young adults.
16. Many of the memory problems suffered by the elderly are due to their choosing not to use memory strategies.
17. A minority of elderly suffer from dementias. When a dementia occurs after 65, it's called senile dementia. One common senile dementia is Alzheimer's disease.
18. Although nobody knows the cause of Alzheimer's, scientists are optimistic that they will soon find a way to delay the onset of this dreaded disease.

Key Terms

absolute threshold 156
Alzheimer's disease 176
attention 155
chunk 157
chunking 158
classical conditioning 150
declarative knowledge 149
dementia 176
difference threshold 156
echoic memory 157
elaborative rehearsal 159
encoding 159
episodic memory 161
extinction 152
generalization 153
habituation 166
iconic memory 157
infantile amnesia 171
information-processing approach 150
long-term memory (LTM) 159
maintenance rehearsal 158
metamemory 168
modeling 154
negative reinforcement 151
operant conditioning 151
organization 155
overjustification effect 154
perception 155
physical salience 166
positive reinforcement 151
proactive interference 160
procedural knowledge 149
recognition tests 167
retrieval 160
retroactive interference 160
selective encoding 166
semantic memory 155
senile dementia 176
sensation 156
sensory level 155
sensory memory 156
short-term memory (STM) 157
spontaneous recovery 153
threshold 156
working memory 157

Self-Check Answers

Box 5.2

1. Declarative knowledge consists of facts that can be stated ("knowing that"). Procedural knowledge consists of things you know how to do (dance, play tennis, take notes, etc.) as well as your nonverbal knowledge of rules about how the world works (what gets rewards, what will happen next).
2. Classical conditioning occurs automatically and involuntarily; involves learning to respond in a certain way to a previously neutral stimulus because that stimulus has been associated with another already meaningful stimulus; is important for emotional reactions; and is strengthened by consistent pairing of the CS and UCS.
3. Both operant and classical conditioning are simple forms of learning that appear very early in development. In addition, both are subject to extinction, generalization, and spontaneous recovery.
4. Both negative reinforcement and punishment involve an unpleasant stimulus. However, with negative reinforcement, the goal is to increase, rather than decrease, behavior. Furthermore, with negative reinforcement, the unpleasantness stops once the person does the "right" behavior. With punishment, on the other hand, the unpleasantness starts once the person does the "wrong" behavior.
5. An individual might have "learned" through modeling other elderly persons with memory deficits that all elderly people have memory problems. When this individual aged and started to forget things, she might assume that her forgetting is an inevitable memory problem. Her belief might result in a self-fulfilling prophecy. That is, her memory might in fact deteriorate because she expects it to and therefore doesn't try to prevent that deterioration by using memory improvement strategies.

Box 5.5

1. True.
2. False—echoic memory lasts about 2 seconds.
3. Developmental psychologists from Piaget onward have sought to identify the mechanisms of cognitive development. A complete answer to what cognitive development is and how it proceeds would begin with a thorough understanding of the parts of the mind. The information-processing perspective allows an analysis of the *specific* individual components of processing and how each of them changes with age.
4. The absolute threshold is the lowest level of stimulation that can be detected. The difference threshold is the smallest difference in stimulation that can be detected.
5. Short-term memory differs from sensory memory in that STM is smaller (it can hold only 5 to 9 chunks), lasts longer (up to 30 seconds), is where thinking occurs, and requires attention to get information into it.

6. Maintenance rehearsal involves rote repetition and serves only to keep (maintain) information in short-term memory. Elaborative rehearsal involves elaborating on the material by relating it to other things that are known. Once the information is made meaningful, the process of elaborative rehearsal facilitates the moving of the information into long-term memory.
7. One good example of interference is trying to keep retroactive and proactive interference straight. Interference is a problem, especially when a person knows many similar terms or has had many similar experiences. However, one way of reducing interference is to organize material.
8. A memory of personal events or episodes is an episodic memory ("I remember driving to school and seeing . . ."). A memory of concepts and facts is a semantic memory ("I know that the Supreme Court ruled that the tomato is a vegetable.") Both semantic and episodic memories are parts of declarative memory.
9. Children would be less likely to use reconstruction because they do not know enough about how the world works to form the inferences needed for reconstruction to work correctly. In some cases, this might make their memories more accurate than an adult's because children might recall what they actually saw rather than a reconstruction of an incident.

Box 5.6

1. The questions the investigator asks determine the answers the investigator obtains. With an unstructured interview, we don't know that children were asked to show where they were poked. Such a question is clearly leading—it assumes the child was poked.
2. Children may be more likely to give an answer that will get them approval or attention. Because children have poor verbal skills, interviewers may be more likely to ask leading questions.
3. Do molested children exhibit these symptoms to a greater degree than normal children?
4. (a) The mother's description of her daughter's behavior was not objective. (b) The parents' expectations may be causing the unusual behavior or may be causing the parents to interpret the behavior as unusual.
5. Evidence will not change the expert's opinion. No matter what the child says, the expert will argue that the child's statement proves abuse.

Box 5.8

1. True.
2. False.
3. False.
4. True.
5. True.
6. Sensory memory's size and duration seems to be stable from age 5 to adulthood.
7. Adults are better at paying attention to relevant information (thus more of it gets into their STM). Once information is in STM, adults are better at chunking the information, better at rehearsing it, and faster at retrieving it.
8. They prefer new objects to objects they have seen before.
9. They progress from not being able to use the strategy, to being able to use the strategy if given time and shown how to use it, to being able to use the strategy if told to use it, to using the strategy on their own, to refining the strategy.
10. A 4-year-old's metamemory (knowledge about how their own memory works) is very poor. They think their memory is much better than it is, they don't realize that attention helps memory, and they don't know anything about the value of rehearsal.
11. Entering school.
12. Infantile amnesia, the inability to remember what happened before the age of 3, is probably not caused by repression of those memories or that those memories were never formed. The most likely explanations are that we lose the cues that access those memories or that memories got lost due to reorganization in the brain.
13. We are much faster at recognizing faces (at 5 months) than patterns (at 9 months). One explanation is that it is more adaptive for the species to inherit the ability to recognize friendly, familiar faces.
14. Children's memory can be improved by quizzing them often about what happened in the past and coaching them about the use of cues, rehearsal, and attention.

Box 5.9

1. Getting a fair sample of both young and elderly, motivating both groups equally, and controlling for health are key methodological problems that must be overcome to accurately determine what memory changes accompany aging. Accurate results could still be misleading because an average decline with age may be a very small decline or may be due to a few individuals declining dramatically.
2. In terms of processing speed, spontaneous organization, and recall, the elderly may be closer in proficiency to late childhood than to early- or mid-adulthood.
3. Because the elderly have more information in long-term memory, one might think that they would be more vulnerable to interference. There is, after all, more "wrong" information to bump into. However, research suggests that the elderly do not have more interference-related forgetting than young adults.
4. To improve the elderly's memory, researchers have (1) used antidepressants, (2) tried drugs that will improve the brain's ability to use a neurotransmitter involved in memory, and (3) encouraged the elderly to use memory strategies. None of these strategies was tremendously successful, but memory training worked until the elderly stopped using those strategies.

Chapter

The Development of Intelligence and Cognition

It is not enough to have a good mind; the main thing is to use it well.

DESCARTES

Chapter Overview

Perhaps no topic in developmental psychology generates more intense controversies than intelligence. Not the least of these controversies is: What is the best way to study the development of intelligence? In this chapter, we will examine three approaches: the traditional psychometric approach, the cognitive developmental approach, and the systems approach.

We will start by exploring the psychometric approach, the traditional IQ test approach. Unlike many other approaches to human development, the psychometric approach is concerned more with individual differences than with describing universal patterns of development. Thus, whereas Piaget discusses universal stages of cognitive development, the psychometric approach focuses on individual IQ scores (Sternberg, 1988).

The psychometric approach is useful for addressing such developmental controversies as: Is intelligence mostly due to genes or to environment? What, if anything, can be done to increase a person's intelligence? Does a person's intelligence quotient (IQ) remain relatively constant from birth until death? Studying the psychometric approach is also useful for developing insights into what IQ is. That is, by examining the psychometric approach, you'll learn why IQ tests were developed; what IQ tests are like; how to interpret an IQ score; how IQ scores relate to performance on other tasks; and, perhaps most important, what IQ tests do *not* measure.

Next, we will see how Piaget's cognitive developmental approach grew out of the IQ testing movement. Like the intelligence testing approach, the cognitive developmental approach recognizes that logical thinking changes as we evolve from infant to adult. However, whereas intelligence tests measure these changes solely in terms of older children answering more questions correctly than younger children, the focus of Piaget's cognitive developmental approach is on describing how the *quality* of children's thinking changes as they grow older.

Finally, we will pursue a promising new trend that challenges conventional notions of intelligence—the systems approach, the view that the intelligence measured by traditional IQ tests, as well as the mathematical, logical intelligence emphasized in Piaget's theory, does not include several other kinds of intelligence that each of us

possesses. If nothing else, the systems approach reminds us that a person who does poorly on conventional measures of "intelligence" may nevertheless have other types of intelligence. Ideally, the systems approach will stimulate useful discoveries about how our varied mental abilities develop. For example, the systems approach may lead to new ways of identifying children's special talents, to ways of fully developing these special talents, as well as to ways of redesigning schools so that all children, by developing all their abilities, become more well-rounded.

The Psychometric Approach

Before we can study the development of intelligence, we must be able to define and measure intelligence. Unfortunately, defining and measuring intelligence is difficult and controversial—even though almost everyone agrees that we all have a *general* mental capacity that determines how we think and solve problems. Indeed, people are so comfortable with the idea of intelligence that they are constantly judging each other's intelligence—and they're not very generous in their assessments (Sternberg, 1982). Even though we often subjectively "measure" other people's intelligence, the goal of many researchers is to develop an objective, accurate measure of intelligence. This is the challenge of the psychometric approach to intelligence—to measure (*metric* means "measure") mental (*psycho* means "mind") intelligence.

Sir Francis Galton

The psychometric approach began with the nineteenth-century British scientist Sir Francis Galton, a member of British aristocracy who advocated **eugenics,** the selective breeding of humans for desired traits. Galton's vision of eugenics was inspired by his cousin Charles Darwin, who argued that nature selects successful traits through "the survival of the fittest." Galton believed that if we sped up the process of evolution by making sure the fittest reproduced most, a super race of humans would evolve.

Of course, those who accept eugenics believe that important human traits, such as intelligence, are inherited. Galton did, and he collected evidence to support this belief. For example, he found that height and academic achievement often ran in families. To Galton, the fact that these traits ran in families was proof that height and academic achievement were inherited. As you might expect from the son of wealthy, eminent parents (and someone related to Charles Darwin), Galton ignored the possibility that all the social, cultural, and economic advantages afforded the British aristocracy might have something to do with academic achievement running in affluent families (Fancher, 1993).

Having convinced himself that superior traits are inherited, Galton knew that he wanted people with superior traits to breed (and those with inferior traits to have no children). To do this, he needed to know who had these superior traits, but at the time there was no way of measuring those traits. So, Galton set out to invent a way.

Galton's belief in inheritability and his obsession with quantifying human superiority can be seen in his many attempts at measuring intelligence. He tried to measure intelligence by measuring such different things as head size, reaction time, sensory acuity, muscular power, and body proportions (Galton, 1869). Apparently, Galton was not alone in his obsession with measuring human traits: More than 10,000 visitors to London's 1884 International Exposition *paid* to have Galton assess these alleged "intellectual strengths."

Despite his efforts, Galton failed in his attempt to predict intellectual superiority. "Superior" people scored no better on his tests than less superior people, and Galton's various tests failed to correlate with one another. Yet, his efforts were not totally wasted because he helped stimulate the idea that mental capacities could be measured.

Alfred Binet

Once Galton had persuaded people that intelligence could be measured, the next step was to actually measure it. But before this step could be taken, two things had to happen. First, there had to be a need for intelligence tests, a need strong enough to pay for the time and research it would take to develop such a test. Second, someone had to be clever enough to devise such a test.

The need arose in the late 1880s after the French government passed a law requiring all children to attend school (Hothersall, 1990). One result of this law was that more children had a hard time keeping up in their regular classes. Consequently, people started asking the question: "What should be done with such children?"

What should be done with children who were not learning depends on why the children were not learning. If children were not learning because they did not have the mental ability to keep up, they should be put in a special class. However, not all of the children who were performing poorly lacked the ability to learn. Many did not have the opportunity to learn. For example, a child might be doing poorly in the sixth grade because her previous teachers did a poor job of teaching basic skills such as reading and multiplication. Similarly, a child from a disadvantaged background might have learned incorrect grammar and habits at home. Thus, the question of what to do with children who were doing poorly in school became the question: "How can we accurately determine who is unable to learn from normal instruction?"

Figure 6.1

The Normal Curve

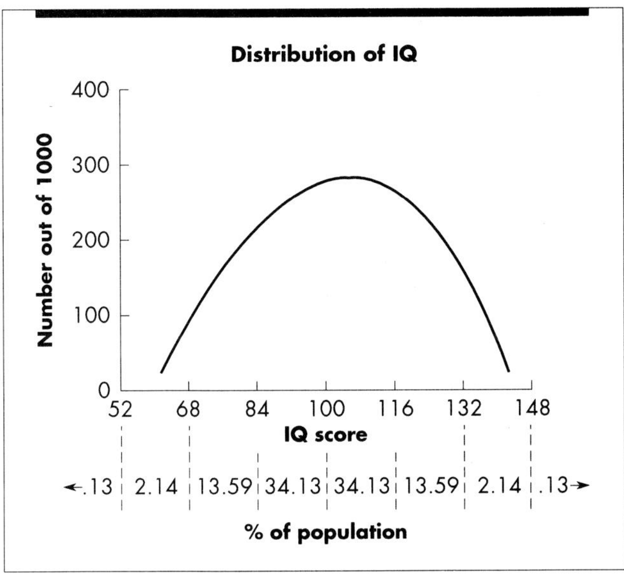

One misuse of intelligence tests was to screen out potential immigrants to the United States who had "undesirably" low scores.

Table 6.2

Common IQ Classifications

IQ	Classification	Percent of Population
148+	Genius	0.13%
139–147	Very superior	1%
120–138	Superior	11%
110–119	High average	18%
90–109	Average	46%
80–89	Low average	15%
70–79	Borderline	6%
< 70	Mentally retarded	3%

Source: From D. Wechsler, *The Measurement and Appraisal of Adult Intelligence*, 4th edition, Williams & Wilkins, Baltimore, 1958.

Fortunately, in 1937, Terman revised the test to overcome these two problems. With Terman's 1937 revision, developmental psychologists could test children as young as age 2. Furthermore, Terman made the test more useful for longitudinal research by creating two versions of his test.

Galton's Dream Revisited

Terman, like Galton, was committed to eugenics. Also like Galton, Terman believed that massive intelligence testing was the key to an effective eugenics program. Thus, Terman argued that people should be tested to "take account of the inequalities of children in original endowment" and measure their "vocational fitness" (Terman, 1916). His racist views of intelligence are evident in the following quote:

> [retardation is] . . . very, very common among Spanish-Indian and Mexican families of the Southwest and also among Negroes. Their dullness seems to be racial.
>
> . . . There is no possibility at present of convincing society that they should not be allowed to reproduce, although from a eugenic point of view they constitute a grave problem because of their unusually prolific breeding. (Terman, 1916, pp. 91–92)

Terman's dream was to use intelligence tests to "bring tens of thousands of . . . high-grade defectives [individuals with low IQs] under the surveillance and protection of society. This will ultimately result in curtailing the reproduction of feeble-mindedness and in the elimination of an enormous amount of crime, pauperism, and industrial inefficiency" (p. 7).

Goddard, Yerkes: Eugenics Continued

Two men—Henry Goddard and Robert Yerkes—would quickly make Terman's dream of massive intelligence testing a reality. Strangely enough, both men would do this by taking advantage of U.S. foreign policy—The Immigration Restriction Act of 1882 and America's involvement in World War I.

Henry Goddard was active (along with Alexander Graham Bell) in trying to improve American society by encouraging the sterilization of "feeble-minded" individuals. In addition to the "threat" of feeble-minded individuals already living in the United States, he was aware of another source of "defective" genes—immigrants. Congress was already aware of this threat, having passed the Immigration Restriction Act of 1882, which forbade entry of individuals with well below normal intelligence into the United States.

Box 6.1

SELF-CHECK

1. For a eugenics program to be successful, what two conditions must be met?
2. On what basis were Galton's tests considered to be objective measures? Why were his tests rejected?
3. How was the motivation for creating Binet's test different from the motivation for creating Galton's?
4. Binet included "familiar items" in his test. What general type of question would be a familiar item? What was Binet's rationale for using such items?
5. Why was the Stanford-Binet more useful to developmental psychologists than Binet's original tests?
6. If a 10-year-old child has a mental age of 12, what is the child's IQ?
7. Why was the 1937 revision of the Stanford-Binet more useful to developmental psychologists than the original Stanford-Binet?

Please turn to the end of this chapter to check your answers.

At the time, however, there was no way to assess whether someone had low intelligence. In 1913 and 1914, Goddard and his assistants tested European immigrants as they first entered the United States through Ellis Island. Immigrants with unacceptably low intelligence test scores were turned away. Due to Goddard's efforts, deportations of immigrants more than tripled.

Fewer than three years later, Robert Yerkes, a Harvard psychologist, spent two weeks at Goddard's institute developing tests that could be given to World War I army recruits. Just as Goddard used testing to decide who was mentally unfit for U.S. citizenship, Yerkes used testing to decide who was mentally unfit for the U.S. Army.

Both Yerkes and Goddard found that people of Northern European descent scored higher on intelligence tests than people of other descents. Both Yerkes and Goddard interpreted their findings as evidence of the superiority of Anglo-Saxons. Like Galton, both Yerkes and Goddard ignored environmental factors such as prior schooling. However, unlike Galton, Yerkes and Goddard also disregarded the influence of cultural background. For example, Yerkes and Goddard ignored the fact that people from non-English-speaking countries and from different cultural backgrounds would be at a disadvantage. Thus, Yerkes and Goddard's test penalized immigrants who couldn't answer such questions as "What is Crisco?" and "Who is Christy Matthewson?" (a baseball player).

Although Goddard's and Yerkes' racist position enjoyed some popular support (leading to the highly restrictive immigration law of 1924 and laws authorizing eugenic sterilization in 27 states), it was an embarrassment to the field of psychology and to test developers. Ultimately, Terman acknowledged that IQ was more than innate ability—that education, cultural values, and other experiences also affected scores.

The Wechsler Tests of General Ability

The Stanford-Binet was revised again in 1986 (Thorndike, Hagen, & Sattler, 1986) and is still used to test mental ability today. However, it is no longer the most commonly used intelligence test. The most commonly used intelligence tests are the Wechslers (Lubin et al., 1984). Like the Stanford-Binet, each of the Wechsler tests is individually administered and yields a score for general intelligence, that is, an IQ. However, the Wechsler tests are more informative than the Stanford-Binet because they have a nonverbal (performance) part, as well as a verbal part, and the tests give a score for each part. (To see how performance and verbal items differ for the Wechsler test aimed at adults, look at table 6.3).

One advantage of the Wechsler tests yielding both a verbal and performance score is that differences between a person's two scores can provide valuable information. For example, a child with a low verbal score but a high performance score may be innately intelligent, but may be victimized by a language barrier, a bad school, or an impoverished home environment. On the other hand, a child who does well on the verbal scale—but poorly on the performance scale—may have some coordination problem or some damage to the right side of the brain.

Thus far, we have discussed the Wechsler as if it is a single test. However, a test that would be appropriate for testing a child's intelligence would be inappropriate for testing an adult's intelligence. The questions would seem childish and the tasks silly. The converse is also true. It would be inappropriate to give a preschooler a test that adults would find appropriate. Therefore, the Wechsler is actually three tests, each targeted for a specific age group: the **Wechsler Adult Intelligence Scale (WAIS)** for adults (see table 6.3), the **Wechsler Intelligence Scale for Children (WISC)** for school-age children; and the **Wechsler Preschool and Primary Scale of Intelligence (WPPSI)** for preschoolers.

Table 6.3

Sample Items from Wechsler's Adult Intelligence Scale (WAIS)

Source: Adapted from D. Wechsler, *Manual for the Wechsler Adult Intelligence Scale—Revised,* Psychological Corporation, New York, 1981.

Scale	Skill Measured	Example
Verbal		
General Information:	Knowledge of well-known facts	Why are dark clothes warmer than light-colored clothes?
Similarities: Asks in what way certain objects or concepts are similar.	Abstract thinking	How are an apple and a peach similar?
Arithmetic Reasoning: Word problems.	Arithmetic reasoning	A coat that normally sells for $60 is reduced by 15 percent during a sale. What is the price of the coat during the sale?
Vocabulary:	Word knowledge	Define *tirade.*
Comprehension:	Tests practical information and ability to evaluate past experience	Explain this saying: "Shallow brooks are noisy." What is the advantage of keeping money in a bank?
Digit Span: Presents a series of numbers orally and instructs the person to repeat them forward or in reverse order.	Short-term memory	I'm going to read you some numbers and I want you to repeat them back to me in order. Ready? 2-7-5-8-6-2-5-8-4
Performance		
Digit Symbol: A timed task in which numbers must be associated with printed images of various shapes.	Speed of learning and writing	
Picture Completion: The missing part of an incompletely drawn picture must be identified and named.	Visual alertness and visual memory	
Picture Arrangement: A series of comic-strip pictures must be arranged in the right order to tell a story.	Understanding of social situations	
Block Design: Pictured designs must be copied with blocks.	Ability to perceive and analyze patterns	
Object Assembly: Puzzle pieces must be assembled to form a complete object.	Ability to deal with part-whole relationships	

Infant Intelligence Tests

Although suitable for preschoolers, neither the WPPSI nor the Stanford-Binet is appropriate for testing infants or toddlers. Both tests require much more verbal fluency and a greater attention span than the typical 2-year-old toddler has—and much, much, more verbal fluency and ability to pay attention than a typical infant has. Consequently, researchers who want to examine infant intelligence must look beyond the Binet and the Wechsler.

One of the first "intelligence" tests for infants and toddlers was developed by Arnold Gesell, a Yale University pediatrician. During the 1920s and 1930s, Gesell and his colleagues studied hundreds of middle-class infants and toddlers, charting the sequence and timing of numerous developmental events. These norms were the foundation of the **Gesell Developmental Schedules** (Gesell & Amatruda, 1947), a series of tests designed to evaluate a child's progress in four areas: (1) motor development (such as grasping a cube and throwing a ball), (2) adaptive behavior (such as reaching for a desired object), (3) language development, and (4) personal-social behavior.

Because Gesell's Developmental Schedules assessed more domains of development than traditional intelligence tests, Gesell gave each child a **developmental quotient (DQ)** instead of an IQ. A DQ of 100 means that a child passed most of the problems listed at a level appropriate for his or her age group. A DQ over 100 signifies a child with accelerated development, and a child with a DQ lower than 100 is performing below average.

Today, the **Bayley Scales of Infant Development** (Bayley, 1969) are more widely used than the Gesell. The Bayley is designed for infants aged 2 to 30 months. It contains three subscales: (1) the *Motor* scale, (2) the *Mental* scale (for example, adaptive behaviors), and (3) the *Infant Behavioral Record* (rating of the child's behavior on such dimensions as goal-directedness, fearfulness, and social responsivity). Like the Gesell, a DQ is computed by comparing the number of items a given child successfully completes with the average number of items that same-aged children successfully complete.

Infant tests are useful for diagnosing neurological deficits and mental retardation—even when these conditions are mild and hard to detect through standard medical or neurological examinations (Escalona, 1968; Honzik, 1976). Moreover, Linda Siegel (1981) reports that it is possible to predict which children are likely to be developmentally delayed at age 2 (as indicated by DQ of less than 85) from their score on the Bayley Mental Development subtest at age 4 months. Siegel also found that children's earlier performances on the Bayley scale were positively correlated with scores on standardized tests of language development at age 2. In sum, infant scales predict a child's future performance on assessments of those particular skills and abilities (such as motor ability and language) that the infant tests are designed to evaluate.

Despite these successes, infant intelligence scales are criticized because they are poor predictors of later IQ scores (Honzik, 1983; McCall, 1983; Rubin & Balow, 1979). Furthermore, the younger the child, the lower the correlation between DQ and IQ (Anderson, 1939; Honzik, 1976).

Why are infant scales poor predictors of later IQ? Perhaps infant scales fail to predict later intelligence because intellectual abilities change during early childhood. For example, McCall (1983) believes that environmental factors do not have much of an effect in early infancy, but do have an effect in later infancy. Once environmental factors "kick in," intelligence will change. However, if infant scales can't predict later intelligence because intelligence changes so much, then no measure of infant behavior would predict later intelligence. Such is not the case. If we measure the degree and speed at which 9-month-old infants are more responsive to unfamiliar stimuli, this measure will correlate significantly with their scores on childhood IQ tests (Bornstein, 1985; DiLalla, Thompson, Plomin, Phillips, Fagan, Haith, Cyphers, & Fulker, 1990; Fagan & Singer, 1983; Weinberg, 1989).

Another reason that DQ correlates poorly with IQ is that the infant and adult tests tap different abilities. If the tests tap different abilities, comparing them would be like comparing apples and oranges. We know that the infant scales measure sensory, motor, language, and social skills, but what skills do IQ tests tap?

The answer to this question is a matter of debate. As you may recall, Binet felt that his test tapped a wide variety of skills necessary to succeed in school. However, he did not provide any evidence for this impression. More than 10 years after Binet's death, Charles Spearman (1927) used sophisticated statistical techniques to argue that the test measured a general factor (which was later called Spearman's "g"). His argument was based on the fact that people who tended to answer one type of question correctly (math problems) also tended to answer other types of questions correctly (verbal problems). Spearman's argument that "g" measured a general, inborn ability to learn was so convincing that it contributed to the practice of tracking; a practice in which students are assigned on the basis of IQ scores to either vocational education programs that would prepare them for blue-collar jobs or to broader, more challenging programs that would prepare them for professional jobs (Gould, 1981).

Not everyone, however, accepted Spearman's conclusions. Indeed, many people argued that, if there really is a "g" factor, the correspondence between how people did on one type of item and how they did on another type of item should be higher than it is. Consequently, they argued that IQ tests did not measure one general ability, but measured several different abilities. For example, Louis Thurstone (1938) initially thought that Spearman's "g" was really composed of nine different abilities. Soon thereafter, Thurstone decided that Spearman's "g" was composed of seven factors.

Not everyone, however, agreed with Thurstone's seven-factor model (see table 6.4). Indeed, Thurstone himself later decided only five of those factors were important (1938). For a time, one of the most influential researchers in the field of intelligence and aging, Warner Schaie accepted this five-factor model (Schaie, 1958). Then, two influential researchers, John Horn and Raymond Cattell (1967), decided that Thurstone's seven abilities really reduced down to two abilities. As you will see, research based on tests of the two abilities identified by Horn and Cattell comes to different conclusions than Schaie about how intelligence changes with age.

You might find it troubling that the experts disagree about the number of abilities that intelligence tests measure. However, there are two reasons why these differences are not troubling to developmental psychologists. First, despite their differences, all of these experts would agree that IQ tests measure different abilities than infant scales. Thus, they would all agree that one reason for the low correlation between infant scales and IQ tests is that the tests measure different abilities. Second, because of their differences, the experts provide different insights about how intelligence changes with age—as you soon will see.

Is IQ a Stable Characteristic?

When intelligence testing first became widespread, it was assumed that intelligence increased with age. Thus, a child would be more intelligent at age 8 than she was at 6.

Table 6.4

Different Views About the Number of Abilities Measured by Intelligence Tests

Thurstone	Schaie	Horn & Cattell	Spearman
Verbal meaning	Verbal meaning	Crystallized intelligence	
Numerical reasoning	Numerical reasoning		
Spatial intelligence	Spatial intelligence		"g"
Inductive reasoning	Inductive reasoning	Fluid intelligence	
Word fluency	Word fluency		
Perceptual speed	(Schaie sometimes uses perceptual speed)		
Associative memory			

Table 6.5

Correlations of IQs Measured During Early and Middle Childhood with IQs at Ages 10 and 18

Age of Child	Correlation with IQ at Age 10	Correlation with IQ at Age 18
4	.66	.42
6	.76	.61
8	.88	.70
10	—	.76
12	.87	.76

Source: From M. P. Honzik, J. W. McFarlane, and L. Allen, "Stability of Mental Test Performance Between 2 and 18 years" in *Journal of Experimental Education*, 17:309–324, 1948.

However, it was also assumed that the rate at which a person's intelligence increased was extremely consistent. Consequently, it was assumed that IQ was a stable characteristic. A person with an IQ of 110 at age 6 should have an IQ of 110 at age 66. In the next two sections, we will examine this assumption. We will begin by seeing whether IQ is stable during childhood.

Stability of IQ During Childhood

What does the evidence show about the stability of IQ? Some of the earliest evidence comes from a longitudinal study of more than 250 children (Honzik, Macfarlane, & Allen, 1948). In that study, the results of which are summarized in table 6.5, children were given IQ tests every two years from the time they were 6 until they were 18. As you can see from table 6.5, a child's IQ in middle childhood is a reasonably good predictor of that child's IQ in adolescence. Thus, there is some evidence of stability.

However, as you also can see by looking at table 6.5, there is some evidence of change. For example, the correlation between IQs measured at ages 8 and 10 (.88) is greater than the correlation between IQs measured at ages 6 and 10 (.76), or at ages 8 and 18 (.70). Consequently, there is some change in IQ over time.

In fact, when individual profiles are examined, we find that many children show wide variations in their IQ scores over the course of childhood. For example, Robert McCall and his associates (McCall, Applebaum, & Hogarty, 1973) looked at IQ scores of 140 children who had taken intelligence tests from age 2 1/2 to age 17. Their findings were remarkable. More than half of these individuals displayed wide fluctuations in IQ over time, and the average range of variation in their IQ scores was 28.5 points! One child in seven varied at least 40 points. In fact, changes of 70 points are not unheard of (Hindley & Owen, 1978).

In short, IQ is reasonably stable for some children, yet very unstable for others. These findings indicate that an IQ score is not an indication of one's absolute inborn potential for learning or intellectual capacity. If it were, the intellectual profiles of virtually all children would be highly stable, showing only minor variations due to errors of measurement.

If IQ does not represent one's inborn intellectual ability, what does it represent? Today, many experts believe, as Binet did, that an IQ score is merely an estimate of a person's intellectual performance at one particular time—an estimate that may or may not be a good indication of that person's intellectual capabilities.

Causes of Instability in Children's IQ Scores

The fact that IQs can increase or decrease suggests that the environment may play a crucial role in determining intellectual performance. Indeed, the authors of the California Longitudinal Study were intrigued to find that the children whose IQ scores fluctuated the most were those from unstable home environments—that is, children whose life experiences also had fluctuated, from periods of happiness to times of turmoil (Honzik et al., 1948).

The investigators were also intrigued by two findings suggesting that sex-role socialization appears to affect IQ scores. The first of the findings was that more boys than girls had long-term gains in IQ. Admittedly, rather than being due to boys being socialized differently from girls, this finding could be due to boys' brains maturing differently from girls'. However, the second finding is more supportive of the nurture view: The girls who were most likely to show increases in IQ were the girls who had developed interests in masculine activities (McCall et al., 1973).

If uncontrolled events can alter IQ scores, can planned interventions have an effect? The answer seems to be

Head Start and daycare programs can increase children's IQ scores temporarily. The reasons the effects aren't lasting are a source of debate.

"yes." As Binet showed in the early 1900s (Gould, 1981) and others from Reuven Feuerstein (1980) to investigators studying programs like Head Start (Zigler & Styfco, 1994), parent education, and day care (Ramey & Haskins, 1981) have shown, planned educational programs can increase children's IQ scores. Furthermore, adoption into achievement-oriented, middle-class families appears to increase IQ scores (Scarr & Weinberg, 1983; Schiff et al., 1982).

Unfortunately, however, many of the positive effects of these programs seem to fade over time. For example, the IQ gains in Head Start tend to disappear after a couple of years. Nurturists argue that the gains diminish because, after the training ends, the environmental factors that were depressing IQ, such as poverty, still remain. In addition, some nurturists argue that the training is not intensive and extensive enough. That is, more effort needs to be made to train the parents and more effort needs to be made to train children how to think.

We will cite two studies that support the nurturist position. First, the IQ gains from the Carolina Abecedarian Project, which provided educational day care 8 hours a day, 5 days a week, 50 weeks a year from infancy to age 5 as well as parental education and school help until age 8, showed stable IQ gains 4 to 7 years later (Campbell & Ramey, 1994). Second, lasting increases in IQ have been produced by Feuerstein's training, which involves teaching students strategies about how to think about the world. Indeed, not only do the gains last, but students continue to gain IQ points.

Naturists, on the other hand, argue that the effects of training wear out because the person's natural intelligence eventually shows through. In support of this position, Robert Plomin (Fulker, DeFries, & Plomin, 1988; Plomin, 1993) finds that the correlation between a child's IQ and the child's adopted parents' IQ decreases with age whereas the correlation between the IQ of the child and his or her biological parents increases with age.

Stability of IQ During Adulthood

We have discussed the stability of IQ scores during childhood, but what about adulthood? Do IQ scores remain stable throughout our adult lives?

From ages 18 to 40, IQ scores are fairly stable. However, some people show significant gains, whereas others show significant losses. Furthermore, according to longitudinal studies, most people improve their ability to correctly answer certain kinds of IQ questions (Schaie, 1994). For example, as people get older, their performance on vocabulary-type items often improves.

When the relationship between aging and WAIS scores is investigated with cross-sectional studies, a fairly consistent pattern emerges. Both verbal and performance scores peak early (verbal scores by the mid-twenties, performance scores by the late teens). Once scores peak, there are declines in both subscales with increasing age.

These age-related declines are typically small on the verbal scale and more pronounced on the performance scale, a phenomenon termed the **classic aging pattern** (see figure 6.2). If we examine how aging affects the various individual verbal and performance subtests, we get a more detailed look at the classic aging pattern. Specifically, we find that, among the verbal scales, most of the subtests show very little change over time. However, substantial decrements are found on *all* of the performance scales. The net effect of the classic aging pattern is that the older the person is, the worse he or she performs on IQ tests.

Although cross-sectional studies (studies that compare a group of young adults with a group of older adults) suggest that IQ declines substantially with age, realize that cross-sectional studies are flawed. They tend to overstate the extent of age-related declines in WAIS scores because, as you learned in chapter 1, cross-sectional studies do not control for cohort effects. For example, older adults may be at a disadvantage on the WAIS because their generation had less education, lower quality education, and less familiarity with test taking than more recent generations. Furthermore, items on current tests emphasize facts and skills that are emphasized in today's schools rather than facts and skills that were emphasized in schools 40 years ago.

Because of the problems with cross-sectional studies, many researchers prefer to use longitudinal studies (following a group of people and retesting them at periodic intervals) to investigate the relationship between aging and

Figure 6.2

WAIS Classic Aging Pattern

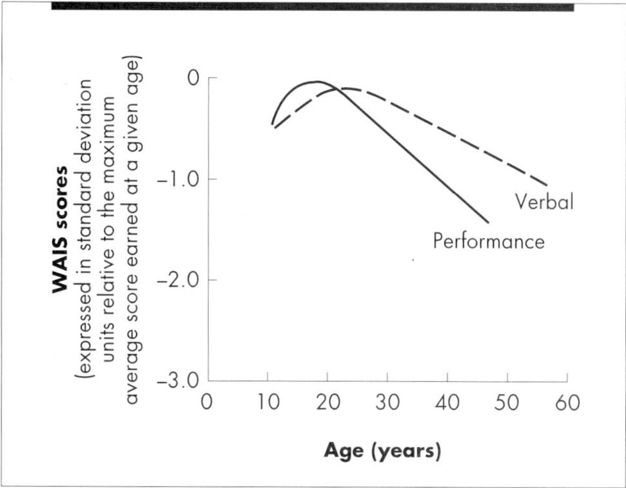

intelligence. But although the longitudinal approach has some advantages over the cross-sectional approach, the longitudinal approach is not perfect.

Indeed, two flaws with the longitudinal approach may cause longitudinal studies to understate the extent of age-related declines in WAIS scores. First, over the course of a longitudinal study, participants may become more familiar with being tested and become more familiar with test items. Second, over the course of the study, less capable participants tend to drop out.

Both of these factors may, in the later years of the study, artificially inflate the group's average IQ. Perhaps for these reasons, the declines reported by longitudinal studies tend to be small. In fact, some longitudinal studies even report modest increases in WAIS scores with increasing age, at least on the verbal scale (see Botwinick & Siegler, 1980; Schaie, 1994). For example, Hertzog and Schaie (1988) found evidence that intelligence increased during early adulthood, was stable during middle age, and started to decline around age 56.

You have seen that longitudinal methods paint an optimistic picture of the effects of aging on IQ, whereas cross-sectional methods paint a more pessimistic picture. Which picture is more accurate? That's a matter of debate.

Among those taking the optimistic view are Paul Baltes and Warner Schaie (1976; Schaie, 1994; Schaie & Baltes, 1977), who conclude that the assumption of a universal decline in intelligence with increasing age is a myth. Their conclusion is based on four arguments.

First, Baltes and Schaie argue that the declines reported in cross-sectional studies are due to cohort differences. That is, recent generations have better education (only 38 percent of the people in 1940 graduated from high school) and better test-taking skills. In addition, younger people's school learning is more recent and more relevant to the items asked on modern intelligence tests. Consequently, differences between the younger, well-educated group and the older, less educated group are not due to age, but to education and other factors. In other words, you could argue that IQ tests are culturally biased against older adults. In support of this position, several longitudinal studies show a high degree of stability of IQ scores (Owens, 1953; Schaie, 1994; Schwartzman et al., 1987).

Second, Baltes and Schaie argue that even when a difference is due to age, the difference often can be attributed to a physical reason. For example, older people do more poorly on timed tests. This decrease in speed may be due to declines in physical ability rather than to a decline in mental ability. In addition, older people may do more poorly on tests because they have trouble seeing the diagrams and making out the words. In support of this position, Pokin, Schaie, and Krauss (1983) found that by making the print on tests larger, elderly people scored significantly higher.

Third, Baltes and Schaie argue that age-related declines are *not universal.* IQ declines occur in varying degrees for different people. Some people are greatly affected, some are not. For example, declines in IQ are often small to nonexistent for elderly who are in good health (Schaie, 1982) and nearly 30 percent of 80-year-old volunteers do as well as adults in their prime (Powell & Whitla, 1994). In addition, those who experience declines may experience declines in some abilities, but not in others. Thus, the effects of age on test performance, rather than being consistent, are extremely inconsistent.

Fourth, Baltes and Schaie argue for **plasticity theory,** the belief that declines in test performance associated with age can be largely reversed. In fact, Baltes and Schaie find that giving older people just five hours of training can dramatically improve their IQ scores.

However, not all theorists share Baltes' and Schaie's optimism. For example, Horn and Donaldson (1976) contend that all the *unflawed* research shows that IQ declines significantly as we age. In other words, Horn and Donaldson attribute IQ declines to aging rather than to cohort differences and do not regard age-related declines as reversible through training. As you can see from box 6.2, some elderly people would agree with Horn and Donaldson that intellectual abilities really do decline with age.

Fluid Versus Crystallized Intelligence As you can see from reading box 6.2, Donald Hebb believes in two basic kinds of intelligence. These two kinds, first identified by Horn and Cattell (1967), are called fluid and crystallized.

Fluid intelligence, which represents our capacity to use new and unique kinds of thinking to solve unfamiliar problems, is determined mostly through heredity. It is what people mean when they refer to "raw, inborn intelligence." Interestingly, Binet's "novel" items would measure fluid intelligence. More specifically, items that tap fluid intelligence involve having people find the pattern in a set of

Box 6.2

ISSUE in FOCUS

Reminiscences of a Prominent Psychologist

D. O. Hebb, a noted psychologist in the field of learning and perception, retired in 1977. Hebb found that on reaching his sixties and seventies, he retained his addiction to difficult crossword puzzles, which draw primarily on previously acquired information (crystallized intelligence). But he gradually lost interest in solving mathematical brain teasers, which require the juggling of new ideas (fluid intelligence). As Hebb put it: "I'm not quite senile, not yet. I can keep up appearances, and there are points on which I can still outtalk younger colleagues. But—between you and me, privately—the picture is one of slow, inevitable loss of cognitive capacity" (Hebb, 1978, p. 23).

1. Could Hebb be wrong? How?
2. Are the losses he describes inevitable?
3. Do you agree with the idea that mathematical brain teasers require fluid intelligence, whereas crossword puzzles require crystallized intelligence?

numbers, learn the meaning of a made-up word from seeing it in several sentences, or write down as many words as they can that start with the letter *e*.

Crystallized intelligence, on the other hand, is what some people would call expertise and is similar to what some call wisdom (Baltes & Staudinger, 1993). It is factual knowledge acquired through education and experience, and it is useful for solving familiar problems. Thus, Binet's "familiar" items would tap crystallized intelligence. More specifically, items that measure crystallized intelligence could include items that asked people to define vocabulary words or do math problems.

According to logic, as well as to Hebb's own experience, age should have different effects on these two different intelligences. Recall that crystallized intelligence reflects our accumulated store of what we have learned from experience. As we age, we have more experiences and thus more opportunities to learn from experience. Therefore, crystallized intelligence is likely to remain relatively stable or even increase as we grow older.

Fluid intelligence, on the other hand, is a more innate capacity that requires an efficient brain and nervous system. Since our physiological capacities are known to degenerate with increasing age, a corresponding decline in fluid intelligence is to be expected (Horn & Donaldson, 1980). Thus, to reiterate, crystallized intelligence should remain stable or even increase with advancing years, whereas fluid intelligence should decline during adulthood.

What support is there for this prediction? One piece of evidence comes from the WAIS—if one interprets the verbal score as a measure of crystallized intelligence and the performance score as a measure of fluid intelligence. Interpreted in this way, the classic aging pattern supports the prediction. That is, WAIS verbal scores (crystallized intelligence?) decline less with age than performance scores (fluid intelligence?).

Some experts believe that fluid intelligence, such as the ability to work at "mind teaser" puzzles, declines with advanced age.

Another piece of evidence comes from Schaie's Seattle Longitudinal Study (Schaie, 1994). The evidence from this study should be weighted heavily because of its use of a sequential design. As you will recall from chapter 1, sequential designs avoid many of the weaknesses of cross-sectional and longitudinal designs. Warner Schaie began his study in 1956 with a cross-sectional study. Since 1956, he has added new cross-sectional and longitudinal cohorts every seven years.

Schaie's study is also important because it goes beyond looking at overall IQ scores. Instead, Schaie adapted a version of Thurstone's test so that he could look at the five aspects of intelligence that he believes are measured by intelligence tests:

1. *Verbal meaning:* vocabulary.
2. *Numerical reasoning:* basic math.

3. *Reasoning:* the ability to see a pattern in a series (for example, 2, 4, 6).
4. *Spatial intelligence:* the ability to visualize what a figure would look like if it were rotated.
5. *Word fluency:* the ability to come up with words quickly. Might be measured by giving a person two minutes to write down as many words as he can that start with the letter *b*.

If we consider verbal meaning (vocabulary) and numerical reasoning (basic math) to be measures of crystallized intelligence, we would expect them to increase with age. Consistent with this hypothesis, 67-year-olds are superior to 25-year-olds in verbal meaning and mathematical ability. If we view inductive reasoning, word fluency, and spatial ability as measures of fluid intelligence, they should decline the most with age. Consistent with this hypothesis, 80-year-olds are poorest of any other age group on these three scales.

More direct support for the prediction comes from research using specially designed tests of fluid and crystallized intelligence. These studies find that fluid intelligence declines and crystallized intelligence increases as we grow older (for example, Cunningham et al., 1975; Hayslip & Sterns, 1979; Horn & Cattell, 1967; Kausler & Puckett, 1980). Thus, it may be that declines in fluid intelligence are often compensated for by gains in crystallized intelligence.

Box 6.3

SELF-CHECK

1. What are the two types of items used in the Wechsler? How do they correspond to the items used by Binet and Simon?
2. Why aren't infant intelligence tests good predictors of performance on later IQ tests?
3. Why do people use infant intelligence tests?
4. Describe the classic aging pattern. Indicate whether each of the following statements is true or false.
5. Research on children's IQ provides evidence for both stability and change in intelligence during childhood.
6. Research on children's IQ provides some evidence for the effect of nurture on intelligence.
7. Age-related declines in intellectual abilities are universal.
8. Crystallized intelligence declines faster than fluid intelligence.

Please turn to the end of this chapter to check your answers.

Conclusions About the Psychometric Approach

Although not all the founders of intelligence tests had the most admirable of intentions, most were geniuses who valued objective, scientific, statistical evidence. Indeed, Galton's insistence on correlating his tests with achievement and with one another led him to admit that his tests did not measure intelligence. Similarly, Terman looked at the data and was forced to conclude that the environment had some effect on intelligence.

The psychometric approach has proved valuable. Thanks to it, we know that:

- IQ is fairly, but not completely, stable over the lifespan.
- Firstborns and children from small families are most likely to be intelligent.
- The quality of the home environment correlates with the child's IQ.
- IQ is influenced by nurture, as reflected by the fact that identical twins may have different IQs.
- IQ is influenced by nature (Pederson, Plomin, Nesselroade, & McClearn, 1992). The impact of nature is revealed by high correlations between the IQs of identical twins, by the high correlations between the IQs of parents and their children, and by the high correlation between an adopted child's IQ score and the IQ score of the biological mother (Bouchard et al., 1990).
- Declines in IQ in late adulthood are not universal. People in poor health, people who are not college educated, and people who do not have intellectually challenging jobs or hobbies are most likely to suffer losses.
- Intelligence tests tap some general mental ability, as reflected by the fact that IQ tests correlate with brain activity, choice reaction time, and success in school. They are also the best overall predictor of job performance that we have (Ree & Earles, 1993).
- Environmental interventions, such as Head Start, adoption, and day care can increase IQ scores (Feuerstein, 1980; Ramey & Haskins, 1981; Scarr & Weinberg, 1983; Zigler & Styfco, 1994).

But there is much that the psychometric approach, with all its statistics, does not tell us. It does not tell us *how* intelligent people think differently from less intelligent people. It tells us only that older children get more questions right than younger children! It does not tell us *how* thinking changes as our mental age increases.

If everyone interested in intelligence pursued the psychometric approach, we would never know how people think. Fortunately, there was a brilliant nonpsychologist working in Binet's lab, a person who hated numbers and statistics. This person's job was to find out which questions older children got right more often than younger children. But what he was really interested in doing was finding out *why* younger children got those questions wrong. What were they thinking? By following his interests rather than his assigned job, Jean Piaget became not just another lab worker, but the founder of the most popular view of cognitive development.[2]

JEAN PIAGET'S VIEW OF COGNITIVE DEVELOPMENT

As you learned in chapter 2, Jean Piaget's **cognitive developmental theory** is commonly regarded as the most influential and controversial theory in developmental psychology. It emerged during the 1920s as the first serious challenger to behaviorism. Today, Piaget's theory of cognitive development has no rival in scope and depth (Beilin, 1992).

But Piaget is reported to have once said, "To the extent that there are Piagetians, to that extent I have failed" (Elkind, 1982). If Piaget's theory is the most influential theory in developmental psychology, why was he opposed to "Piagetians"? Because scientific groupies are likely to perpetuate dogma—the bane of the scientific method. Dogma clouds the discovery of truth not only by impairing scientific vision, but by impeding change. Piaget was against dogma and for revising theory. That is, just as a child's vision of reality is transformed over time, so too was Piaget's vision of cognitive development transformed over time. Indeed, Piaget's theory was under revision throughout his lifetime.

Core Concepts

Although Piaget was continually revising his theory, most of the core concepts did not change. Indeed, most of the core concepts that he introduced in the 1920s were still the crux of this theory when he died in 1980 (Beilin, 1992).

Most of these core concepts reflect the fact that Piaget started his career as a biologist. (In fact, by age 14, he was a world-recognized authority on snails.) That is, during most of his career, Piaget emphasized the role of biology. For example, he believed that thinking (intelligence) is a "basic life function" that helps us adapt to our environment (Piaget, 1952). Also, as would be expected from someone with a biological background, Piaget defined psychological development as an *inborn,* spontaneous process that continually adds, modifies, and reorganizes the individual's (psychological) structures (Piaget, 1970).

Vygotsky's theory and, to some extent Piaget's, emphasizes that older children who are slightly higher in cognitive development can teach a younger child to think at the higher level more quickly than they might on their own.

Having defined development, Piaget's next task was to explain why, when, and how development occurs. Let us first address the "why" question: Why do we add to, modify, and reorganize our mental structures? Initially, Piaget suggested that there were four causes of cognitive development: social interaction, experience, maturation, and the process of equilibration (Piaget, 1970).

Social Interaction

In the 1920s, despite his biological emphasis, Piaget emphasized the role of *social interaction* in stimulating the development of thought and language. Specifically, Piaget stressed that when children interact with other children, this social interaction prods cognitive development. Conflicts and arguments with other children force the child to examine his own views of the world relative to the views of others (Flavell, 1963). Therefore, Piaget argued that, rather than have a teacher guide a child through a problem, the child may be helped much more by working through the problem with a peer who is only slightly above him in developmental level.

During the 1930s, Piaget deemphasized the role of social interaction. Instead of viewing cognitive development as an outcome of social interaction, he came to view social interaction and cognitive development as both being outcomes of the same thing: biological maturation. Interestingly, although Piaget dismissed the importance of social interaction for cognitive development long ago, United

[2] Contrary to myth, Binet also emphasized qualitative differences over quantitative differences. Indeed, there is some possibility that Piaget's key ideas came from Binet (Siegler, 1992).

States educators are now starting to place a heavy emphasis on the importance of social interaction in cognitive development (see box 6.4).

Experience

Like the behaviorists, Piaget recognized that experience can affect cognitive development. However, in contrast to the classical behaviorists' notion that people learn by *passively reacting* to stimuli in their environment, Piaget asserted that each of us is *actively involved* in acquiring knowledge from experience. We want to understand the world; we want to build a mental model of it. Consequently, rather than have children learn by drill and repetition, Piagetians feel we learn best when we're allowed to explore our environment. Active involvement, whether by physical manipulation of objects in the environment (playing ball) or mental manipulation of environmental objects (problem solving), is a natural and effective way to learn. As Piaget was fond of saying, "Play is the work of the child."

Maturation

What can you learn from playing or experimenting with the world? According to Piaget, learning is limited by one's level of **maturation,** biological development. As befits his biological background, Piaget believed that changes in the way we think about the world can occur only after changes have occurred in the brain. For example, Piaget would argue that there is no point in teaching addition and subtraction to a child younger than 6. Similarly, Piaget would claim that there is no point in teaching abstract concepts to children who have not yet reached adolescence.

Recent research supports Piaget's belief that biological maturation is important for cognitive development. As you may recall from chapter 4, the rate of maturation for an individual's nervous system partially regulates cognitive growth. The myelination of axons in the brain is accompanied by such dramatic cognitive events as language development and abstract reasoning. Furthermore, spurts in brain maturation occur at the ages that Piaget thought they would—at ages coinciding with rapid cognitive development.

Equilibration

Maturation is not the only biological force for cognitive development. We also have an inborn need to adapt to our environment. To adapt, we form mental structures that, ideally, parallel the structure of the real world. These organized mental structures are called **schemata** (singular is **schema**).

Once we have formed a schema, we use that mental structure to understand the world, to organize all our experiences within the framework of that mental structure. For example, when we were young, we had the schema of putting things in our mouth. We fed that schema by putting everything possible in our mouth. When we were a little older, we learned the schema of counting. We fed that schema by counting everything we saw (much to the irritation of our parents). The process of understanding the world by fitting it into our schemas is called **assimilation.**

Figure 6.3

The Value of Accommodation

Dennis assimilates but fails to accommodate.
DENNIS THE MENACE® used by permission of Hank Ketcham and © by North America Syndicate.

"NOW MARGARET'S *REALLY* GONNA BE A KNOW-IT-ALL. HER DAD JUST GOT A ***FACTS*** MACHINE!"

The problem with assimilation is that if a child's schemata are incomplete or inaccurate, her understanding of the world will be inaccurate. The child who uses the schema for television to understand a computer is missing something. Similarly, the child who sucks a bottle the same way that he sucked his mother's breast may go hungry (see figure 6.3). Consequently, in the child's quest to assimilate the world, he may engage in **accommodation** by revising existing schematas or adding new schemata.

Modifying their mental structures (accommodation) allows children to better adapt to the environment. Thus, infants learn to suck a one-hole bottle differently from a three-hole bottle and to distinguish the end of a rattle from a thumb. By revising their schemas (accommodation), infants are more able to assimilate. Thus, assimilation and accommodation often occur together.

Even when assimilation and accommodation don't occur simultaneously, assimilation eventually requires some accommodation because the addition of information to a schema will force the restructuring of that mental category. To illustrate, think of your initial exposure to developmental

Box 6.4

THEORY in FOCUS

Lev Vygotsky's Theory of Cognitive Development

Russian psychologist Lev Semmenovich Vygotsky's (1896–1934) theory of cognitive development has enjoyed recent popularity among American educators. Like his contemporary, Jean Piaget, Vygotsky believed that development was due to the interplay between nature and nurture (Crain, 1992). However, Vygotsky is best known for his ideas about how social factors—such as culture and the people with whom we associate—can develop our thinking (Wertsch & Tulviste, 1992).

To emphasize that thinking does not originate within the individual, Vygotsky tried to avoid using the word *thinking*. Instead, he preferred the term **inner speech.** The term *inner speech* emphasizes that, like outer speech, inner speech is learned from others.

As evidence that thinking (inner speech) is largely an internalization of other people's thinking, Vygotsky points to children's early speech. At age 3, children use *egocentric speech* by talking aloud to themselves. What are they saying? They are saying many of the things that have been said to them: "No! That's bad" or "Brush your teeth." That is, they are internalizing what other people have said and are using this to plan and direct their own actions. According to Vygotsky, children gradually internalize their speech and no longer need to talk aloud to themselves. Nevertheless, their inner speech still reflects internalized social processes.

To this point, we have seen that Vygotsky believes that cognitive development results when people internalize aspects of the social environment. Thus, a child who has a low level of interaction with other people or who comes from a primitive culture, probably will not develop a high level of sophisticated, analytical, scientific thinking. In other words, because people develop by internalizing their social environment, it is important to provide an appropriately stimulating social environment.

What is an appropriately stimulating social environment? Obviously, such an environment should help raise a child above his current level of development to his potential level of development for his age. But how do we know what the child's potential is?

Vygotsky addressed these questions with his concept of the **zone of proximal development.** This zone refers to the gap between the child's current level of skills and what the child's skill level could—with proper instruction—soon be. Specifically, the zone refers to the gap between a child's ability to solve problems independently and the ability to solve problems with the help of a tutor (Vygotsky, 1978). To emphasize that classroom instruction should focus more on the level of potential development than the level of actual development, Vygotsky used the following example:

> Imagine that we have examined two children and have determined that the mental age of both is seven years. This means that both children solve tasks accessible to seven-year-olds. However, when we attempt to push these children further in carrying out the tests, there turns out to be an essential difference between them. With the help of leading questions, examples, and demonstrations, one of them easily solves test items taken from two years above the child's level of [actual] development. The other solves test items that are only a half-year above his or her level of [actual] development. (Vygotsky, 1956, pp. 446–447)

Thus, educators need to not only assess what has been learned, but also to determine what is in the process of "coming into being." By taking into account the zone of proximal development, we can promote cognitive development.

Vygotsky's ideas have been the focus of such teaching intervention programs as "reciprocal teaching" (Wertsch & Tulviste, 1992). In reciprocal teaching, children of different cognitive abilities are paired. By interacting with children who function at a slightly higher cognitive level, it is believed that less advanced children will develop more quickly.

psychology. At first, your notion of developmental psychology was very global. Perhaps you thought of it as a bunch of scientists videotaping infants or as doctors who treat children with psychological problems. However, because of this course, you expanded on that vague notion. For example, you added the fact that there were several areas of developmental psychology. Rather than just incorporating this new information into your preexisting global view of developmental psychology, you restructured (accommodated) your view of developmental psychology by creating several categories to represent developmental psychology (see figure 6.4). Similarly, your original schema of a given minority

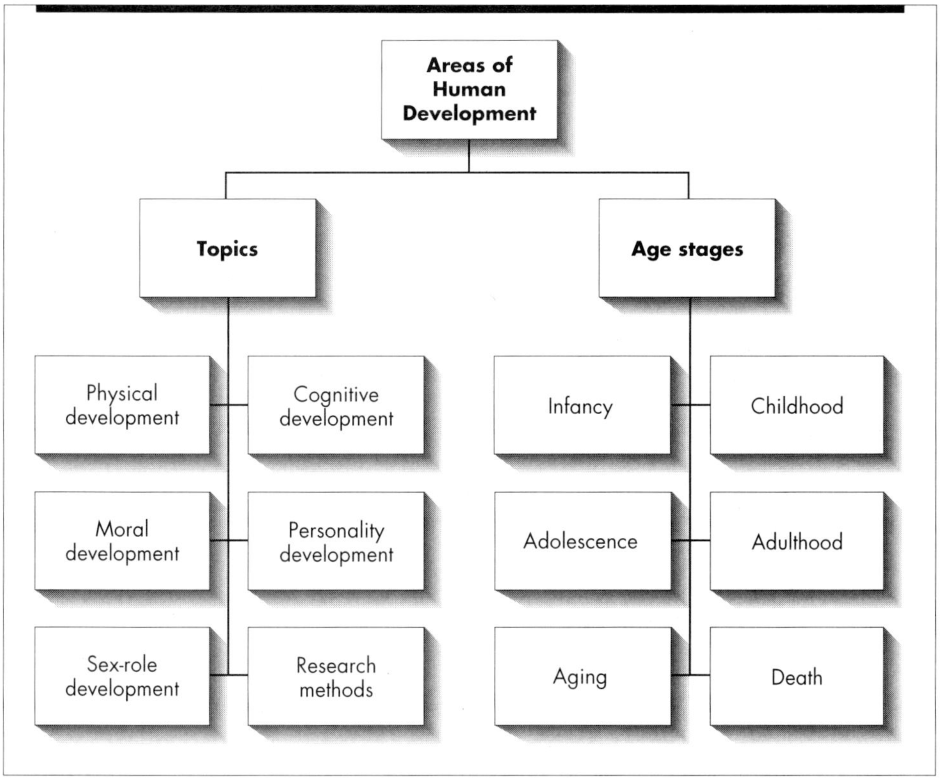

Areas of Human Development

Topics: Physical development; Cognitive development; Moral development; Personality development; Sex-role development; Research methods

Age stages: Infancy; Childhood; Adolescence; Adulthood; Aging; Death

Figure 6.4

Different Categories of Developmental Psychology

group (such as African Americans, women, AIDS victims) may have been very limited. However, as you assimilated more individuals into your schema, you were forced to accommodate. For example, as you learned of mothers, babies, young children, and respected athletes who had AIDS, your schema of AIDS victims was revised.

According to Piaget, assimilation and accommodation, whether they happen together or separately, do not happen by chance. Instead, we are *driven* to assimilate as well as to accommodate. Piaget termed this drive to fit everything into schemata **equilibration.**

As you learned in chapter 2, Piaget thought equilibration was analogous to **homeostasis.** In homeostasis, the body preserves its physical structures, such as the brain, by making adjustments to the outside world. For example, on a warm day, the body sweats to keep body temperature from going much above 98.6 degrees. In equilibration, we preserve our mental structures by making mental adjustments to the outside world. Hence, Piaget believed that if we are *disequilibrated* by something we don't understand, we will actively revise our cognitive structures so that we can regain equilibration. In short, he believed that once we are aware that there is a contradiction between reality and our schemata, we will resolve this cognitive conflict by revising our schematas (accommodation).

Summary of Piaget's Core Concepts

In sum, Piaget believed that biological processes play a strong role in cognitive development. The biological process of maturation determines when cognitive development can occur. The biological process of equilibration motivates people to actively explore the world. Specifically, equilibration motivates people to (1) *assimilate* by fitting new experiences into their existing views of the world and to (2) *accommodate* by changing their views to fit new experiences.

Now that you are familiar with Piaget's answer to the question: "Why does cognitive development occur?" let's turn to his answers to the questions of "how" and "when" cognitive development occurs. We will start by addressing the question: "What kinds of changes do our schemata undergo?"

The Stages

The kinds of changes that occur, according to Piaget, are as sharp and dramatic as the changes that occur as a caterpillar changes into a butterfly. As we go through the four stages of cognitive development (sensorimotor, preoperational, concrete operations, and formal operations), the main thing that happens is *not* that we learn more information, but that we develop a *different way* of thinking.

Sensorimotor (Ages 0 to 2)

The central task of your first 18 months is to form schemata of the physical world. To understand the importance of developing these schematas, realize that when you were born you did not even know who you were, much less comprehend the world around you. Your hand was just as much (or as little) a part of you as the mobile dangling above your crib. Everything swirled together in one undifferentiated kaleidoscope of sensation.

Box 6.5

SELF-CHECK

Indicate whether each of the following statements is true or false.

1. Piaget finished revising his theory in 1970.
2. Piaget hoped that there would be many ardent disciples of his theory.
3. Piaget's theory has a strong "nature" orientation.
4. Piaget eventually decided that increased social interaction and increased cognitive development were just by-products of maturation.
5. Piaget's latest view of the impact of social interaction on cognitive development is now shared by virtually everyone.

Answer the following questions.

6. How does Piaget's view of the importance of experience differ from that of traditional behaviorists?
7. Compare and contrast the processes of assimilation and accommodation.

Please turn to the end of this chapter to check your answers.

Through experience, you learned to identify the parts of your body as "me" and the objects and people in the world as "not me." You then not only had to form concepts (schemata) for the objects in your world, but you had to begin to understand the relationships among these objects and yourself. Because you were born without language and without preconceptions about this world, you had to explore the world through your senses and physical actions. Therefore, Piaget called the first stage of cognitive development the **sensorimotor stage.**

Circular Reactions Imagine how primitive a newborn's thinking must be. The newborn has no words and almost no experience of the world beyond the womb. All the newborn has are some reflexes and its five senses. How can the newborn begin to understand this unfamiliar world? Although he can look, touch, smell, taste, and hear, nothing makes sense. Nothing is connected.

One morning, while lying in his crib, the newborn flails about and something (his thumb) touches his mouth. He opens his mouth and sucks his thumb. Thumbsucking feels good. However, the thumb comes out. In an attempt to have that good feeling again, the newborn flails his arms wildly. However, his hands just hit his face and fall away. The newborn can't catch his hand because his whole body moves when he flails his arms: The newborn has not yet differentiated the movement of his arms from the movement of his entire body. In Piaget's terminology, the newborn has not yet made the accommodations necessary to assimilate his hand to the sucking schema (Crain, 1992).

Figure 6.5

Circular Reactions

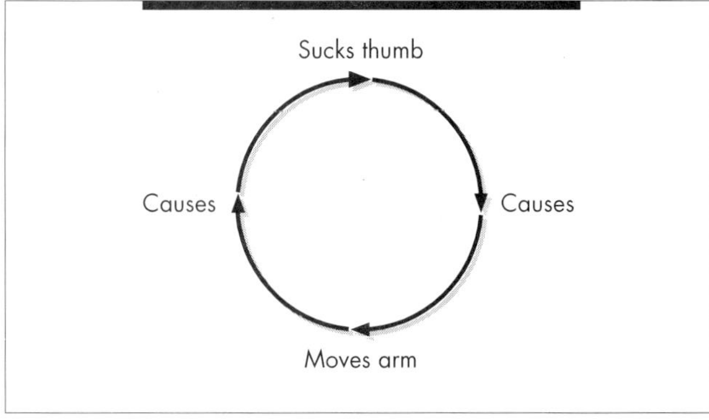

Later, after repeated failures, his thumb again finds its way into his mouth. Eventually, the infant forms a connection between moving his arms and the pleasure of sucking his thumb. That is, he eventually assimilates his hand into his sucking schema. This process of fitting two previously unrelated schemata into a common schema is called a **circular reaction.** It is accommodation in its earliest form (see figure 6.5).

At first, circular reactions involve coordinating different parts of the body (such as hand and mouth). Later, circular reactions help babies coordinate their actions with events in the external environment. For example, Piaget's daughter Anna kicked her legs and caused the dolls dangling above her crib to move. She gazed at the dolls for a moment, then kicked again, and watched the dolls move again. Anna had formed a schema connecting her movement (kicking) with an event in the environment (dolls moving). Through this type of coordination, children begin to actively construct their concepts of the world. Through the process of these trial-and-error circular reactions, children accomplish the developmental tasks of the sensorimotor stage—the formation of rudimentary concepts of space, causality, and object permanence.

Spatial Relationships Anna probably learned about spatial relationships by forming schemas connecting her movement with events in the environment. For example, suppose that there was a teddy bear in Anna's crib. She reaches, misses, and then reaches again. At last, she makes contact. She brings it toward her and snuggles with it. As she brings it toward her, the teddy bear appears to grow in size. Gradually, one reach at a time, she learned about spatial dimensions, such as distance (depth perception) and size.

Causality Suppose Anna becomes afraid and cries. Someone enters her sensory realm, picks her up, holds her, and makes a soothing sound. Later, Anna wakes up. She begins to cry again because she is hungry. The caretaker magically appears and feeds and cuddles with her. The caretaker disappears. Eventually, Anna learns that crying makes the caretaker appear. Consequently, she learns to deliberately cry. More importantly, she learns that she can make things happen. That is, through the process of circular reactions, she has leaned a rudimentary notion of causality.

Object Permanence Anna has learned that she can make her caretakers appear. But what happens when her caretakers are not holding, feeding, or playing with her? At first, she believed that her caretakers—as well as all other objects—existed only when she could sense them. When objects were out of sight, they were out of the world; they no longer existed. Eventually, as the world became more predictable and understandable, Anna began to believe that her caretakers existed even when she didn't see them. Still later she learned that other objects might exist even when she didn't see, taste, touch, smell, or hear them. Piaget termed this insight—that people and things exist even when they cannot be sensed—**object permanence.**

Summary of the Sensorimotor Stage In summary, you were born an uncoordinated, uncomprehending organism. By first exploring the world through sensing and moving, and then later forming connections between bodily and external schemata (circular reactions), you achieved the objectives of the sensorimotor stage: developing object permanence and rudimentary notions of space and causality.

Preoperational Thought (Ages 2 to 7)

A child is said to have reached the **preoperational stage** once she has grasped the idea of object permanence and can engage in **symbolic thought,** the use of mental symbols, such as words, to refer to objects. However, the preoperational child cannot use words and other symbols well enough to think through the *logical* consequences of doing a physical action—unless she has seen that action performed before. Thus, like the sensorimotor child, the child at the preoperational stage learns best by doing. In fact, the term *preoperational* means "before" (pre) being able to do mental **operations,** an action performed mentally, rather than physically.

To reiterate, although preoperational children use language, they do not use it in the same way adults do. For example, preoperational children engage in **nominal realism,** the belief that the object's name is a real part or characteristic of the object. In other words, young children believe that (1) the name for an object is part of the object (just like the object's color, size, shape, or weight), that (2) the object or person cannot be called anything else, and that (3) no other thing may go by the same name. For example, if a child had a schema for rope, and someone else insists on calling a rope "twine," the preoperational child will insist that the rope cannot be called twine because "it is rope." In other words, to a preoperational child, "A rose by any other name would *not* smell as sweet."

Despite the problem of nominal realism, the preoperational child's ability to use language helps social and cognitive development. Language brings the preschooler's social interaction up to a higher level. Consider how you would explain to someone that you need to use the toilet without using words or any other symbol (for example, a drawing) to convey your need. How could you do it? Even if you found a way, it would not be nearly as efficient and accurate as stating, "I need to go to the bathroom."

The acquisition of symbolic thought not only makes it easier to communicate with others, but it opens a whole new world of thought. Although your high school English teacher may have been wrong when he said, "You don't really understand something until you can put it into words," you know that writing and talking about a subject help you better understand things and often leads to new insights.

Magical Thought Preoperational children use symbolic thought for more than thinking and interacting with reality. Symbolic thought also pervades their play and their dreams. Thus, preoperational children play "make-believe" and may even have an imaginary playmate. In addition, children start having nightmares at about the same time they begin to use mental symbols. Piaget believed that the images in dreams symbolize their anxieties and experiences from waking life. Through symbols, children represent their fears in the form of bad dreams and monsters under the bed.

However, unlike adults who know that dreams are not reality, Piaget believed that young children engage in **magical thought.** That is, they often do not distinguish between the concrete world and the world of imagination. Piaget claimed that children not only mistake dreams for reality, but they also believe their waking imagination. This contributes to **animistic thought** in which a person attributes life to inanimate objects. Animistic thought is exemplified by children's belief that the sun follows them, that rocks have feelings, that their teddy bear "feels sad," and that the family minivan misbehaves.

Another reflection of the preoperational child's tendency toward unscientific thinking is that young children believe in **phenomenalistic causality.** In other words, children believe that if two things occur together, one caused the other. For example, if you raise the blinds in the morning, and the sun has risen, the preoperational child believes that raising the blinds causes the sun to rise. Note that what characterizes phenomenalistic causality is its magical quality. As adults, we have learned to be skeptical about magic. We prefer scientific, physical explanations for events. Thus, we question anyone who claims to be able to make the sun rise by lifting the blinds. Similarly, we ask a magician "How did you do it?" because we assume that magic doesn't really exist. However, young children ask no such questions because they view the world as a magical place.

Egocentric Thought Although the world seems like a magical place to preoperational children, the world may seem less magical than it did when they were in the sensorimotor stage. Early in the sensorimotor stage, babies fail to physically differentiate themselves from the rest of the world. Consequently, if another person vanishes from sight, the sensorimotor child seems to believe that the other person no longer exists.

All preoperational children, on the other hand, realize that others are *physically* separate and independent from themselves. That is, every preoperational child knows that other people have an existence that does not depend on whether the child is thinking about them. However, preoperational children have not learned that others are *psychologically* independent from themselves. Specifically, preschoolers have not learned that other people's thoughts and perceptions are also separate from their own. In other words, preoperational children engage in **egocentric thought** because they are unable to perceive things from another person's point of view. Preoperational children assume you hear what they hear, see what they see, and know what they know. Because of their egocentrism, preoperational children omit key details when talking to you.

Preoperational egocentrism also explains why children do things that seem selfish. Because they think everyone knows what they know and sees what they see, preschoolers block your view when watching television, speak to you while you're talking on the phone, and have trouble adjusting to other people's schedules for what and when things should be done.

Concrete Operations (Ages 7 to 11)

Perhaps the best way to understand preoperational thought is to contrast it with thought at the next highest stage—the stage that most children in the United States enter before they are 7 years old—the **concrete operations stage.** As the name suggests, the concrete operational child can perform operations, but only on physical objects. Operations are *mental, logical* manipulations of objects that are *reversible*. In other words, by retracing the steps that took you from A to B, you can mentally go from B back to A.

Since operations are mental manipulations, you should not be surprised to know that the only way a preoperational 3-year-old can count to five is by counting actual objects such as his fingers. In contrast, a concrete operational child can count to five in her head without any objects being physically present. It also should not surprise you that a preoperational child, unable to reverse operations, could know that 8 + 4 = 12, but find that of no value in trying to figure out the answer to "what's 12 – 4?" The concrete operational child, of course, can easily grasp the notion of subtraction being the reverse of addition.

Since operations are logical, you shouldn't be surprised that preoperational children have little difficulty believing in Santa Claus. However, because children can first start thinking logically about physical objects during the concrete operational stage, this stage is when children first start doubting Santa Claus. They can now realize the logical impossibility of him being everywhere at once (Fehr, 1976).

Quantitative Thought The concrete operations stage also marks the beginning of quantitative thought. Before this stage, children can deal only with quantitative dimensions in a qualitative way. For example, if he had three boxes of different sizes, a preoperational child might call the largest box "Daddy," the second largest "Mommy," and the smallest "Baby." In contrast, the concrete operational child will deal with differences in size in quantifiable ways, for example, "largest, smallest" or "this one is 4 inches taller than that one." In Piaget's terminology, only when a child reaches concrete operations can she engage in **seriation** by arranging objects in a logical order.

Conservation The ability to quantify different aspects of objects makes conservation possible. **Conservation** is the recognition that quantity is a constant characteristic of certain objects.

To understand conservation, consider Piaget's classic conservation of mass demonstration (see box figure 6.6C). You present a child with two balls of clay of equal mass and ask the child, "Are they the same?" If the child disagrees, you add or take away clay from a ball until he agrees that they are equal. Next, you tell the child, "Watch this." You then roll one of the balls into the shape of a sausage and ask the child, "Now are they the same?" A preoperational child typically answers, "No, this one is larger because it is longer," or "No, this one is larger because it is fatter." The concrete operations child, on the other hand, realizes that only the shape has changed, not the amount. Therefore, she answers, "Yes, they are the same."

Next, the researcher rolls the sausage back into a ball and asks the preoperational child, "Now, are they the same?" He answers, "Yes." Note that the preoperational child fails to conserve mass merely because an irrelevant dimension (shape) is altered, whereas the concrete operational child knows that the amount has *not* been altered. She has conserved mass.

Box 6.6

RESEARCH in FOCUS

Examples of Conservation Tasks

Box Figure 6.6A

Conservation of Number

The concrete operational child realizes that although one row of beads is now longer than the other, each row still has the same number of beads.

Show child two rows of beads of equal number and length.

Spread the beads in one of the rows.

Box Figure 6.6B

Conservation of Volume

The concrete operational child realizes that although the water level in one glass is now higher, both glasses have the same amount of water.

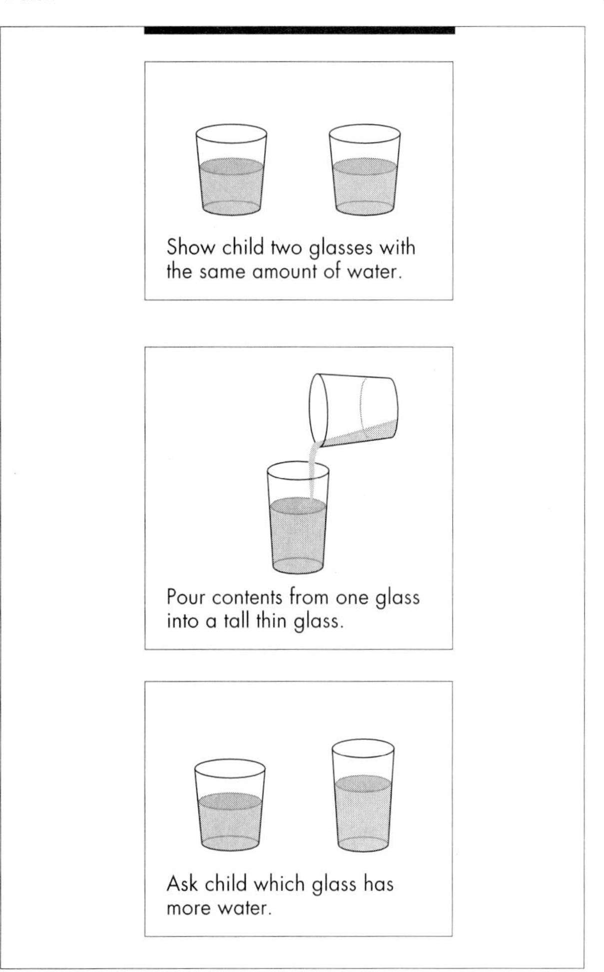

Box Figure 6.6C

Conservation of Mass

The concrete operational child realizes that although one piece of clay is now longer and thinner, both pieces of clay still have the same amount of clay.

Conservation of mass involves the following understandings:

1. That actions can be reversed,
2. That changes in one dimension can be compensated for by changes in another dimension, and
3. That logical thought, rather than what is observed, should be relied on and trusted.

Since conservation of mass involves such advanced reasoning, it should not surprise you that concrete operational children also conserve many other dimensions of objects, including volume, number, and area (see box 6.6).

In addition to solving conservation tasks, concrete operational children can solve **class inclusion problems.** To solve class inclusion problems, the child must understand that a specific set of objects (such as Siamese cats) is also a subset of a more general category (that is, all cats).

In the typical class inclusion task, a child is shown five brown buttons and four black buttons. The child is then asked: "Are there more brown buttons or more buttons?" The preoperational child answers that there are more brown buttons. He doesn't understand that brown buttons can be both a class in their own right as well as a part of the more general class of "all buttons." Put another way, he doesn't understand that an object can be included in more than one class. Thus, just as the preoperational child's egocentrism reveals the inability to see more than one viewpoint (his own) and his failures on conservation tasks reveal the inability to attend to more than one dimension, class inclusion tasks also reveal the preoperational child's inability to attend to two dimensions at once.

Because preoperational children aren't good at considering more than one factor at a time, they have difficulty comparing things. Furthermore, because they have trouble thinking of more than one thing at a time, they tend to think in absolute terms. To the preoperational child, things are either black or white—things are not blacker or whiter than some other alternative.

People who have achieved concrete operations, on the other hand, can realize that things are relative. They can also attend to several dimensions at the same time. Furthermore, they can analyze things and break down problems into steps. As you can see, concrete operational thought is relatively sophisticated. In fact, even people who reach the stage beyond concrete operations often prefer to think at the level of concrete operations. Furthermore, most people (60 to 70 percent of Americans) remain in concrete operations throughout their life (Neimark, 1975, 1979).

Formal Operations (Ages 12 Through Adult)

By age 11 or 12, some children will go beyond concrete operations and reach the **formal operational stage.** People who enter this cognitive stage of development have shifted from thinking about the actual to thinking about the possible. More technically, formal operations refers to the ability to perform mental operations on operations, what Piaget calls **second-order operations.** In other words, abstract thought is a major characteristic of this stage. Piaget emphasized two kinds of abstract thinking performed in formal operations: metathought and propositional logic.

Metathought **Metathought** is thinking about thinking. People in formal operations analyze their own thought processes. For example, they may question whether their thinking is logical and rational; they may ask what assumptions they are making; and they may wonder if there is another way to think about a problem. You may have found that in writing or talking about a situation, you have engaged in metathought. You may have realized your logic was fuzzy, your assumptions questionable, or your definition of a problem limited.

Propositional Logic **Propositional logic** is the kind of formal logic you would learn in a logic class. In a test of propositional logic, you might be given two or more hypothetical statements (propositions). Then, you would be asked what conclusions could be logically drawn by combining the statements. For example, you might be given two hypothetical propositions: (1) "All toads have teddy bears" and (2) "George is a toad." Then, you would be expected to logically conclude that "George has a teddy bear."

Piaget believed that propositional logic was necessary for scientific reasoning. The need for a scientist to have at least some kinds of propositional logic seems evident from Piaget's "colorless liquid task." If you were to go through this task, a researcher would present you with four beakers of colorless liquid marked *1, 2, 3,* and *4,* and a fifth beaker of colorless liquid labeled *g.* You would be told that by dropping *g* into a certain combination of the liquids contained in beakers *1, 2, 3,* and *4,* you can produce a yellow liquid. Your task is to find that particular combination.

People who have reached formal operations go about solving this task systematically. For example, they may try *1* and *g,* then *2* and *g,* then *3* and *g,* then *4* and *g.* Next, they try *1, 2,* and *g,* then 1, 3, and *g,* then *1, 4* and *g.* Next, they try *2, 3,* and *g,* then *2, 4,* and *g.* By pursuing the problem in a systematic way, they soon discover the necessary combination of solutions (usually *1, 3,* and *g*). People who have not reached formal operations try to solve the problem randomly. They try one combination, then they try some unrelated combination. Because their approach is unsystematic, they may repeat a combination they already tried. Furthermore, unless they are lucky (or try for a long, long time), they fail to find the solution.

Behavioral Changes During Formal Operations This newly developed ability to use abstract thought may cause profound changes in an adolescent. Specifically, as compared to when they were at concrete operations, the adolescent at formal operations may (1) have a better ability to

SELF-CHECK

Indicate whether each of the following statements is true or false.

1. According to Piaget, the primary change in thinking is that we gradually refine our way of thinking as we learn more information.
2. The preoperational stage lasts until age 9.
3. Babies are born with the knowledge of object permanence.
4. Once a child develops language, thinking becomes much more logical.
5. A preoperational child can think through the physical consequences of throwing a jar against a window.
6. Preoperational children realize that a name is just an arbitrary label that we give to objects.
7. "My doll feels sad" is an example of animistic thought.
8. Preoperational children seem to be able to think about several things at a time.

Answer the following questions.

9. According to Piaget, what are "operations"?
10. How does solving the conservation task show that a child can use operations?
11. Why are class inclusion problems difficult for preoperational children?

Please turn to the end of the chapter to check your answers.

People who have reached Piaget's formal operations stage are able to find the solution to the "colorless liquid task" much more efficiently than people still functioning at concrete operations.

understand figures of speech, (2) have an expanded sense of time and space, and (3) be more conscious of two sets of abstract, hypothetical events: ideals and possibilities.

Figures of Speech Whereas concrete operational children take things literally, people at formal operations don't. For example, people at formal operations understand figures of speech, such as *metaphors* ("He is the rock of my life") and *similes* ("Her mind works *like* a computer"). A person at concrete operations might argue that "he is not a rock" and that "her mind is not a computer." Because understanding figures of speech requires abstract thought, questions that require people to show that they understand figures of speech appear frequently on college entrance exams.

Time and Space Formal operational thought is revealed not only by being able to think about words in a more sophisticated and abstract way, but also by thinking about time and space in a more abstract way. Specifically, Piaget claimed that people in formal operations have an *expanded concept of time and space*. Because many adolescents have just acquired this expanded concept of time and space, they are likely to enjoy thinking and talking about their newfound visions of these concepts. Thus, you may remember a time during your adolescence when you contemplated the nature of infinity and your place in it—realizing you were just a sneeze in the scope of creation. Our students commonly report that when they were in their early teens, they wondered whether the nucleus of an atom was really a sun and its electrons were planets of another universe.

Ideals and Possibilities Although reaching formal operations opens the mind to the world of possibilities and ideals, it also introduces new frustrations. Adolescents who have recently acquired formal operational thought can now envision their perfect world. However, they are often disillusioned when their world, parent, or religion doesn't measure up to their vision of perfection. Whereas they previously accepted authority and rules, adolescents now question authority and rules. Their parents hear remarks such as, "Why is it that way? That's a dumb rule. If that's the reason for the rule, then how come . . . ?" Rules and authority are not the only things adolescents question. They also question themselves and wonder what they could and should become.

Summary of Formal Operations In summary, formal operational thought is characterized by the ability to perform operations on operations (second-order thought). This opens the mental world to metathought, propositional thought, expanded concepts of time and space, metaphors and similes, as well as ideals and hypothetical possibilities. However, the ability to think about hypothetical events may also lead the adolescent to disillusionment, rebellion, and to an identity crisis.

Critique of Piaget's Theory

Piaget's theory is the best known and most widely accepted theory of cognitive development. Almost every public school teacher has studied and been influenced by Piaget. For example, most teachers believe that children learn best when they are actively involved in doing something rather than when they are listening to lectures or doing drills. Furthermore, many schools wait to teach certain things until the age at which most children are, according to Piaget, ready. For example, algebra is rarely taught to children before the age of 12 (the beginning of formal operations), and some school systems have even recommended that children wait until they are age 7 to start school (the beginning of concrete operations).

Although Piaget's theory has been influential, it is not without its critics. Piaget's theory has been attacked on several grounds including his failure to

1. Explain the causes of cognitive development,
2. Use research methods that prevent bias and accurately assess the abilities of young children,
3. Show that there really are universal, qualitatively different *stages* of thinking,
4. Explain why some children do not enter the stages at the ages Piaget said they would, and
5. Account for cognitive development beyond adolescence.

Inadequate Explanation of the Causes of Development

Many people criticize Piaget for not clearly indicating how children move from one stage of intellect to the next (Siegler, 1994). After considering the issue, Piaget (1970) concluded that the maturation of the brain and the nervous system interact with the child's experiences to promote cognitive growth.

Presumably, children are always assimilating new experiences and accommodating to those experiences, thereby reorganizing their schemata into increasingly complex mental structures. Maturation influences intellectual development by affecting the ways children can act on objects and events, which in turn will determine what they learn from their experiences. As children continue to construct and reorganize their cognitive schemata, they will eventually think about old information in new ways and begin the gradual transition from one stage of thinking to the next.

This vague explanation of cognitive growth raises more questions than it answers. For example, what maturational changes are necessary before children can progress from one stage to the next? What kinds of experiences must a child have before she will construct mental symbols, understand cognitive operations, or begin to operate on ideas and think about hypotheticals?

Because the theory does not answer these types of questions, many researchers have come to view Piaget's theory as an elaborate description of cognitive development that has little, if any, explanatory value (Brainerd, 1978). In fact, because the theory is so vague about the causes of development, some neo-Piagetians (for example, Case, 1985; Klahr, 1984; Siegler, 1986) have supplemented Piaget's theory with a more specific approach—the information-processing approach we discussed in chapter 5.

To his critics, Piaget's inability to precisely explain the causes of development was a serious flaw. To Piaget, it was not. As a biologist, Piaget had thrived on describing the characteristics of animals; as a psychologist, he thrived on describing cognitive development. Americans urged him to explain cognitive development because such knowledge (unlike knowledge about snails) could be used for a practical goal—to speed up development. But Piaget had little interest in accelerating development. In fact, he called the question about how to apply his theory "The American Question," presumably because only Americans were interested in such nonsense (see box 6.8). Piaget was satisfied with giving us a description of cognitive development, a window to the child's world.

Although Piaget was not very specific about the causes of cognitive development, his theory is more specific about the causes of cognitive development than most (Siegler, 1994). Piaget did emphasize that maturation drives cognitive development and that accommodation is spurred by disequilibration. Let's see whether the research supports these claims.

The Role of Nature As you learned in chapter 4, spurts in the growth of the brain occur at ages corresponding to Piaget's four stages. However, it is not clear how these brain changes lead to increased cognitive capacity. Ideally, changes in the brain would lead to an increase in short-term memory capacity. This increase in short-term memory capacity (working memory) could explain why older

Box 6.8

ISSUE in FOCUS

Accelerating Cognitive Development

Piaget was not interested in accelerating cognitive development. He felt cognitive development would occur when the child was biologically ready. In fact, at one time Piaget claimed that cognitive development *couldn't* be accelerated. However, we know that is not the case. Cross-cultural research suggests that Western education speeds up cognitive development by one or two years. Piaget eventually concluded that giving children opportunities to practice Piagetian tasks and teaching children what to attend to *would* accelerate development. In addition, one of Piaget's most prominent students, Barbel Inhelder, found that setting up situations in which children's schemata were in conflict would sometimes result in changes in development. That is, because they realized that their schemas were inadequate, children would try to establish new ones. As the equilibration principle would predict, Inhelder noted that the children who were most confused showed the greatest increases in development.

History is full of examples of parents who successfully strove to make their children geniuses, but at the cost of the child's mental health. Such efforts are probably misguided, especially in light of the tiny relationship between intelligence and success. As Bloom (1985) has discovered, motivation is much more important than ability for success. In his study of how successful people were reared, Bloom found that successful people's parents provide these types of support:

1. Encouraged (but didn't push) them to pursue whatever field these children were interested in,
2. Provided them with one-on-one instruction at an early age, and
3. Continually hired more expert and more demanding instructors.

children can think in more complex ways than younger children. However, as you learned in chapter 5, there is little evidence that maturation increases short-term memory capacity (Case, 1985).

The Role of Nurture You have seen that the evidence does not clearly support Piaget's idea that brain maturation drives cognitive development. But does the evidence clearly contradict Piaget's idea that environment alone is not very important? Contrary to Piaget, two environmental events—education and culture—can affect one's stage of development. For example, contrary to Piaget's maturational view, Gelman (1972) has been able to use training to take children to the next stage of cognitive development. Similarly, Renner (1976) has been able to train college students to reach formal operations. In addition, in some cultures, nobody reaches formal operations (Neimark, 1975).

The Role of Disequilibration Admittedly, Piaget does acknowledge that nurture has some role in cognitive development. Specifically, he thought that cognitive development occurred when people were disequilibrated. That is, he thought that accommodation would occur because people would seek equilibration. However, the evidence does not support this position. Gelman (1982) taught children to do Piagetian tasks by modeling and reinforcement, not by disequilibrating them. Similarly, Siegler (1994) found that shifts in strategies usually occurred when children were working on simple problems, rather than on difficult, challenging, disequilibrating ones. Furthermore, Siegler found that changes in strategies often followed successful attempts at using old strategies.

Inadequate Research Methods Piaget has also been criticized for the "unscientific" way in which he got the information that formed the basis of his theory. Rather than use traditional, scientific research methods known for their objectivity and ability to reduce bias, Piaget used the "discovery method." That is, rather than use controlled methods so that each child was asked the same questions, he used a semi-structured interview technique in which children were presented with the same series of tasks, but were not necessarily asked the same questions. This lack of standardization could have biased the results and conclusions of his research. Supporters of his method (for example, Beilin, 1992) believe that Piaget's use of the discovery technique is justified because it produced insights that traditional methods may not have yielded.

Partly because of his research methods, Piaget may have underestimated the thinking abilities of young children. For example, when slightly different tasks or wordings are used, young children often show more sophisticated reasoning (and less egocentrism) than Piaget gave them credit for. To cite just one example, recall that egocentrism is supposed to persist through age 6. According to Piaget, 4-year-olds believe that everyone thinks like they do and sees the world as they do. However, 4-year-olds seem to have the ability to understand other people's perspectives, as reflected by the fact that they adapt their speech and vocabulary, depending on whether they are speaking to a 2-year-old or to an adult. Thus, contrary to Piaget's theory, 4-year-olds can take their listener into account (Masangkay et al., 1974).

How serious are these criticisms of Piaget's methodology? Perhaps the best way to evaluate these criticisms is to see whether researchers using different methodologies have come to different conclusions. Therefore, we will now examine the extent to which the findings of post-Piagetian researchers fit with Piaget's four stages of development.

Sensorimotor Stage In general, research supports Piaget's claims about the sensorimotor period. The infant seems to start out with an isolated set of reflexes, but soon develops some fairly complex and coordinated schemata. Thus, the infant who could only flail his arms soon learns to put his thumb in his mouth, then learns to play with toys (and food) in a repetitive way, and then explores new ways to play with toys. This development proceeds in a predictable sequence.

On the surface, the development of object permanence seems to proceed in the predictable sequence outlined by Piaget. At first, infants seem to act as if an object that disappears no longer exists. Later, infants will search for an object that has disappeared, but they may search for it in the wrong place. For example, they may see you hide it in a drawer, but they may look for it on top of a table on the other side of the room—where they found the object last time. Or, you can hide an object in your left hand and move it to your right hand and they will act as though the object has to be in your left hand—where they saw it last (Bower, 1982).

As impressive as these demonstrations are, they don't tell us what the child actually thinks. The infant may know where to look, but be too impulsive to look there. Or, infants may just have a short attention span. In support of these alternative explanations, infants go right to the object if allowed to hunt for it immediately after it disappears (Bower, 1982; Gelman & Greeno, 1988). In addition, Renee Baillargeon and her colleagues (Baillargeon, 1993, 1994; Baillargeon & Graber, 1988) find that even very young infants seem to be surprised when an object disappears. For example, Baillargeon has infants watch a model train go behind a wall. Sometimes, the train reappears on the other side of the wall; sometimes, it does not. Then, Baillargeon raises the wall to reveal an empty set of tracks. If infants have seen the train pass through on the other side of the wall, they briefly glance at the tracks. If, however, infants have not seen the train pass through to the other side, they stare for some time at the empty tracks.

Preoperational Thought You have seen that Piaget underestimated the abilities of young infants. How accurate was he with preoperational children?

Piaget's general conclusions are basically correct: As almost any parent will tell you, preoperational children think differently from adults and from infants. Unlike infants, they can use language to think about the past and the future. However, unlike older children, preoperational children do not think logically. Trying to use logic on a preoperational child can be frustrating! Also, as Piaget pointed out, preoperational children have trouble with conservation tasks because of their inability to attend to two dimensions at once (Case, 1985; Pascual-Leone, 1970). In addition, preoperational children are egocentric. As John Flavell (1993) has shown, part of the reason preoperational children may be egocentric is that 3-year-olds can't understand the concept that beliefs are different from reality. In other words, 3-year-olds don't think that they—or others—can have false beliefs. Thus, if they have a certain belief about something, others must have that same belief.

However, Piaget again underestimated children. As we mentioned earlier, preoperational children sometimes show less egocentrism than Piaget thought (Flavell, Everett, Croft, & Flavell, 1981). In addition, Rochel Gelman (1972) has shown that young children can, under some circumstances, do conservation tasks. Furthermore, Judy DeLoache (1994) has shown that, under the right conditions, young children can think of an object in two ways. For example, 3-year-olds can see "little Snoopy's room" as both "little Snoopy's room" and as a small-scale model of "big Snoopy's room."

Concrete Operations In general, research supports the idea that concrete operational children think more logically than younger children, but not as abstractly or hypothetically as older children. However, Piaget thought that, during concrete operations, all children would acquire certain skills in a certain order. Such is not the case (Case, 1985; Kuhn, 1988). For example, some children may master conservation of volume before conservation of number, whereas others may master conservation of number before conservation of volume (Tomlinson-Keasey, Eisert, Kahle, Hardy-Brown, & Keasey, 1979).

Formal Operations Research supports, for the most part, Piaget's assertion that older children are more able to think systematically and logically about abstract events. For example, older children are more likely than younger children to be able to answer the following question: "If *P* is true, *Q* is not true. *P* is true. What can we say about *Q*?"

However, Piaget was too optimistic about how early formal operations developed. For example, in one study of 80 children, ages 11 to 18, only two got all the Piagetian tasks correct (Martorano, 1977). Only 25 percent of all

Piaget may have been too optimistic about how early people develop formal operations. Only half of all college students are thinking at the formal operations level.

first-year college students are at formal operations (McKinnon & Renner, 1971) and only 50 percent of all college students have reached formal operations (McKinnon, 1976).

Are There Really Universal Stages?

Thus far, we have discussed cognitive development as if there were distinct stages that *everyone* goes through. However, as we have hinted, some critics question whether we all experience cognitive development in abrupt, qualitatively different stages (Brainerd, 1978; Bray et al., 1994; Broughton, 1984; Flavell, 1982; Siegler, 1994). These critics argue that a child does not suddenly learn a group of general thinking skills that he or she can easily apply to a wide range of situations.

As you will see, critics of the stage approach make three major arguments. First, they argue that the ability to think logically about some problems does not mean that one has developed the ability to think logically about *all* problems. Second, they argue that thinking at one age is not completely different from thinking at other ages. Third, they argue that, as children move to the next stage, they do not suddenly learn an entire group of thinking skills.

Domain Specificity Whereas Piaget believed that thinking ability was a general ability, we now know that it is domain specific. That is, people who can think brilliantly about their field (domain) of expertise cannot think as abstractly about problems dealing with situations outside their area of expertise. For example, political science majors may think in formal operational terms about political problems, but not about physics problems; whereas physics majors may think in formal operational terms about physics problems, but not about political science problems (DeLisi & Staudt, 1980). Similarly, Feldman (1986) found that child prodigies operate at formal operations in their area of specialization, but at average (usually concrete operations) levels in other areas.

Nonqualitative Path of Development Two lines of evidence run counter to Piaget's idea that children at one stage of development think completely differently from children at another level of development. The first bit of evidence comes from the vast number of research studies that have attempted to see whether training programs can teach preoperational children to do well on conservation tasks.

According to Piaget, preoperational children lack the cognitive structures necessary to solve conservation problems. That is, as the name of the stage suggests, preoperational children do *not* have the cognitive structures necessary to think in terms of operations. Put another way, if Piaget were a strict stage theorist, he might argue that preoperational children can't be trained to think in terms of operations for essentially the same reason a caterpillar can't be trained to fly—both lack the necessary structures. Yet, training studies show that preoperational children can learn to use operations. Specifically, study after study has shown that preoperational children can learn to master conservation tasks (for example, Gelman, 1982). Consequently, some critics believe that the training studies deliver a devastating blow to Piaget's theory.

The second line of evidence against the idea that thinking is qualitatively different at each stage comes from research that intensively studies children who are near the boundary of a stage. For example, 5-year-olds (who are preoperational) often fail conservation tasks. However, other 5-year-olds sometimes succeed at these concrete operational tasks. On some occasions, they may be wrong in a conservation of number task because they look only at the length of the row of coins. However, on other occasions, they may be right, because they use better strategies (counting the number of coins in each row or pairing each coin in one row with a coin in the other row). It is hard to know what they will do on any given occasion (Siegler, 1994).

Learning Groups of Skills Finally, as we mentioned earlier, children will often be at a higher level on one skill than on another (supposedly related) skill. That is, research shows that it may be months or even years before a 6-year-old who can seriate and conserve number (and thus should be at concrete operations) will be able to pass other concrete operational tests such as class inclusion or conservation of volume (Tomlinson-Keasey, Eisert, Kahle, Hardy-Brown, & Keasey, 1979).

Based on these research findings, many felt that a core assumption of Piaget's theory had been disproven. However, in a thorough analysis of Piaget's writings, Chapman (1988) concluded that Piaget never intended that a child should progress uniformly through each stage. Such synchrony in development was to be more an exception than the rule (Beilin, 1992).

Timing of Development

Even if there are stages, critics of Piaget's theory point out that many children do not enter Piaget's stages at the ages he has described. Indeed, not only do many children *not* enter formal operations at age 12, but most people *never* enter formal operations. For example, only 30 to 40 percent of adults in the United States function at formal operations. Furthermore, in some societies (for example, preliterate societies with little or no formal schooling), no one can solve Piaget's formal operational problems (Dasen, 1977; Dasen & Heron, 1981).

In response to the fact that some people reach the stages at ages different from what Piaget's theory says they should, Piaget's supporters counter that Piaget placed little importance on age and that he never intended the loose age perimeters identified with his stages to serve as age norms. Piaget opposed the notion that reaching a certain age guaranteed a corresponding level of cognitive development.

In response to criticisms that most people never reach formal operations, Piagetians counter that the fact that some adolescents achieve formal reasoning is evidence that this fourth stage exists. The existence of a formal operations stage does not require that all adolescents and adults must think this way, just that it is possible.

Development Beyond Adolescence

Whereas some have argued that Piaget goes too far by proposing that we all reach formal operations, others argue that he didn't go far enough (Arlin, 1975; Commons et al., 1982; Labouvie-Vief, 1985). That is, they do not believe that cognitive development ends at formal operations.

Their first argument is that cognitive development proceeds past mid-adolescence. For example, at the beginning of college, students often look for facts. Then, college students realize that not all questions have factual answers and therefore we must rely on opinions. At first, college students interpret this to mean that all opinions are equally valid. Later, college students realize that some opinions are better (more supported by evidence and logic) than others. In adulthood, we not only become more expert in solving familiar problems (as you learned in chapter 5), but we also learn to be more sophisticated in dealing with real-life problems. For example, we learn to consider more and more points of view and we learn how to organize our lives.

In response to this first attack, Piagetians would point out that Piaget did not believe that cognitive development ends in adolescence. Especially in his later writings, Piaget emphasized that cognitive development is a lifelong process. If he had lived longer, he might have more fully developed this idea.

The second attack is that formal operational thinking is limited. It is useful for scoring high on IQ tests and solving certain problems in logic class, but it has limited value for real-life problem solving. In real life, problems are not clear-cut and solutions are not absolutely right or wrong. Adolescents and others who are limited to formal operational thought often find that their idealistic thinking gets them in trouble. Therefore, there must be something beyond formal operational thought.

Patricia Arlin (1975, 1977, 1983) was one of the earliest to argue that some people's thinking develops beyond formal operational thought. She characterizes formal operational thought as a *problem-solving* stage characteristic of how bright adolescents and adults solve problems that other people give to them.

She argues that truly creative thinkers transcend formal thought. Thus, people like Albert Einstein and Marie Curie operated at a higher stage of thinking in which they were able to rethink and reorganize existing knowledge and then *ask* crucial questions and define new problems. Arlin calls this stage the **problem-finding stage.**

Since then, Labouvie-Vief (1985) also has argued that adult thinking transcends formal operational thought. In addition to considering the rules of logic, the wise adult decision maker must understand people, practical constraints, and cultural constraints.

How would Piagetians react to these attacks? Piagetians would concede that Piaget's theory does not account for creative thinking, "street smarts," or wisdom (Beilin, 1992). Thus, they would admit that Piaget's theory is not a theory about the development of *all* types of thought. Instead, it is only a theory about the development of *logical* thought. Piagetians would then argue that, as a theory of logical thought, Piaget's theory is correct—formal operational thought is as sophisticated as people's logical thinking abilities get. Since nobody has proven that humans develop a more sophisticated form of logical thinking than formal operations, Piagetians can be fairly comfortable with their argument that formal operations is the most developed form of logical thought (Beilin, 1992).

Systems Theorizing

To this point, our discussion of the development of intelligence has focused on one kind of intelligence: the analytic, logical ability that Binet wanted to measure because this ability helped students do well in school. Because other IQ tests followed in Binet's footsteps, our description of how IQ changes through the lifespan was a description of how analytic, logical ability changes throughout the lifespan. Likewise, because Piaget began by trying to discover *why* younger children couldn't correctly answer some of Binet's intelligence test questions, Piaget's theory deals only with the development of analytic, logical ability.

Recently, system theorists have suggested that there is more to intelligence than analytic, logical ability. In this section, we will look at two system theories: Robert Sternberg's triarchic theory of intelligence (1985, 1988) and Howard Gardner's (1983, 1993) theory of multiple intelligences.

Sternberg's Triarchic Theory

According to Sternberg's (1985) **triarchic theory** of intelligence, there are three kinds of intelligence: componential (analytic), experiential (creative), and contextual (practical intelligence). The last two of these intelligences are not directly related to analytic, logical ability, nor to conventional notions of intelligence.

Componential: Analytic Thinking

One kind of thinking—**componential intelligence**—does fit our conventional notion of intelligence. People who score high on componential tests do well on intelligence tests and in school. In other words, componential intelligence refers to the ability to use memory and to reason analytically. More specifically, componential intelligence involves three types of processes: knowledge acquisition, executive, and performance.

As the name suggests, **knowledge acquisition components** are used to acquire information and to represent information mentally. Basically, knowledge acquisition processes are learning strategies. As you may recall from chapter 5, effective learning strategies include such things as paying attention to relevant information (and ignoring irrelevant information) as well as making connections between newly learned information and information already stored in memory (effective elaborative rehearsal).

Your knowledge acquisition components are of little use in problem solving unless their actions are coordinated and directed. The aptly named **executive components** processes manage your knowledge acquisition components. For example, the executive plans what to do (deciding what the problem is, what steps are involved, and figuring out how much time and energy should be spent on each step). In addition, executive processes check to see if the plan was properly carried out. Thus, the more planning and reflection you do, the more you are involving executive processes.

Although Sternberg advocates that people should involve their "executives," the strategy can be carried out only by the "workers" (the performance components). The **performance components** include many abilities, such as being able to add, being able to reason logically, and being able to read the problem. These abilities are important and are primarily what conventional IQ tests measure. That is, conventional IQ tests do not extensively test the ability to plan (executive processes) or learn (knowledge acquisition components), but rather they test the ability to quickly and accurately perform fairly simple mathematical and reasoning tasks.

To appreciate how the three processes (knowledge acquisition components, executive components, and performance components) work together, imagine an 11th-grader taking a math test. As she works on the first problem, her executive processes determine a strategy. The executive processes decide which formula applies. Once she's decided on the formula and which numbers go in which slots in the formula, her performance components do the actual adding and multiplying. After the performance processes have obtained the answer, the executive processes again come to the forefront. They try to evaluate the answer ("That can't be right, it's way too big. I'd better do it over" or "The teacher said the math would be so simple we wouldn't need a calculator, but to get the answer, I have to figure out the square root of 161. Something must be wrong"). Of course, to get the right answer, the student not only needs to employ her executive and performance processes, but she also needs to have learned the material earlier (employing her knowledge acquisition processes).

One exciting aspect of breaking down performance into these parts is that instead of saying to a child "You're slow" or "You got these questions wrong," teachers and counselors can look at where the child went wrong. Does he lack basic calculation skills (performance processes) or does he tend to adopt the wrong strategy (executive processes)?

If the child lacks the basic skill, we can design practice problems to isolate that particular skill. Even if the child has the skill, we can give him extensive practice and feedback on that skill so that he can do the skill automatically. By automatizing these subtasks, the child will be free to devote his mind to checking the work, to thinking about what he is learning, and to developing strategies (Glaser & Bassok, 1989).

If the child lacks the general strategy, this can also be taught. Thus, it may be that we can teach intelligence. This hope is more than a pipe dream. Research by a variety of people (Mayer, 1984; Siegler, 1986; Sternberg & Ketron, 1982) all suggest that, to some extent, intelligence can be taught.

Beyond child development, these findings also have implications for adult development. As you can see, there are at least two ways in which adults could become smarter in their domain of expertise (Ericsson & Charness, 1994). First, through experience, they could automatize some of the performance components of a task. Second, through experience, they could learn certain strategies that would help them perform the task better.

Experiential: Creative, Synthetic Thinking

Whereas traditional IQ tests and traditional schools emphasize the ability to break problems down into steps and solve them using step-by-step reasoning (componential intelligence), Sternberg feels that an even more valuable kind of intelligence is **experiential intelligence.** Sternberg defines it as the ability to have insight, to see the big picture, to see old problems in new ways, and to apply old solutions to new problems.

A student with a high experiential intelligence may not do well on multiple-choice tests, but may ask the best

Automatization of some tasks that require only componential thinking may free us up to develop and use more of what Sternberg calls experiential intelligence, or insight and creativity in thought.

questions and make the most interesting observations in class. In addition, a student with experiential intelligence may do well on essay questions because—rather than regurgitating facts from the book—the student may put information together in new ways, thereby arriving at intriguing insights. As computers become more and more adept at using logical reasoning, the ability to think creatively, to use what we know in new situations, and to think about things in new ways may become more valuable. Even today, Sternberg laments that (componentially) intelligent people are a dime a dozen, but that creative brilliance is rare.

Measuring experiential intelligence is difficult, but Sternberg proposes two tactics. First, since experiential intelligence involves applying old knowledge to new situations, you can directly test it by having people solve novel problems. Care must be taken, however, to ensure that the problem is neither too novel nor too familiar. The problem should not be unlike anything the test takers have ever encountered because they should be able to rely on some previous experience to solve it. But the problem should not be too familiar because the test takers should use some insight and creativity.

The second tactic for measuring experiential intelligence is based on Sternberg's assumption that insightful people are able to apply old knowledge to new problems partly because they can use old knowledge and strategies quickly and easily. Hence, he measures **automatization,** how quickly a process that is, at first, consciously controlled (such as driving a stick-shift car) becomes automatic. To use automatization to measure experiential intelligence, he first has a person repeat a relatively simple task several times. Then, he measures two things. First, he measures how many times the person has to repeat the task before processing speeds up. This is a measure of how *quickly* a person benefits from experience. Second, he measures how much processing speeds up with practice. This is a measure of *how much* the person benefits from experience.

Presumably, older adults would take longer to automatize tasks. However, in one's area of expertise, any loss in automatization speed could be offset by having had more opportunities to automatize the task. In addition, with age, one has more old knowledge to apply to a task. Thus, creativity could increase throughout the lifespan.

Practical/Contextual: Adaptive (Playing the Game) Thinking

In addition to componential and experiential intelligence, Sternberg posits a third kind of intelligence: practical/contextual. **Contextual intelligence** is similar to what people call real-world intelligence, practical intelligence, cleverness, or "street smarts." People with high contextual intelligence seem to know how to get what they want. Sternberg argues that some people who score low on IQ tests designed to measure academic intelligence are very high in practical (contextual) intelligence. Therefore, Sternberg believes we need tests specifically designed to measure practical intelligence. He measures practical intelligence in two ways.

First, he looks at how people apply standard information-processing aspects of intelligence to practical situations. For example, do people recognize logical errors in advertisements? Can they plan a route to a number of stores in the shortest amount of time? Can they apply the knowledge they learned in a general psychology class to a real-life problem?

Second, Sternberg measures **tacit knowledge,** the unspoken rules that help us adapt or get ahead. An item measuring tacit knowledge might ask a person to pretend that he is in his second year in a specific job and has too much work to do in the time allotted him. Then, he gets a list of activities that he could pursue in the next three weeks, noting that he doesn't have time to accomplish everything. His task is to prioritize the list. The closer his ranking of activities matches how his bosses would rank those activities, the better he understands the unwritten rules of business.

Another way of seeing how well people have learned unwritten rules of real life is to show pictures of two people and then ask "Which of these two people is the boss?" Or, a person might look at pictures of couples and be asked "Which couples are boyfriend/girlfriend and which couples are strangers?"

You have seen that Sternberg believes that an important part of practical intelligence is knowing the real world's unwritten rules. If people do not know the rules of the environment, they cannot adapt to that environment. Thus, the questions that require identifying what tasks are most important and those that require figuring out the relationship between two people from a photo both tap an important ability—the ability to adapt to the environment.

However, Sternberg believes that practical intelligence extends beyond the ability to adapt to an environment. Specifically, practical intelligence includes at least three abilities: (1) the ability to adapt to the existing environment; (2) the ability to find and live in the right environment for one's personality; and (3) the ability to modify the environment to make it more compatible with one's needs. According to Sternberg (1988), "a smart person knows not only when to stay and to try to adapt herself, but also when to get out. But the best answer to a problem of adjustment is not always either adaptation or selection. It might be shaping: in other words, changing the environment to suit you" (p. 11).

As we mentioned earlier, practical intelligence increases during adulthood. Adults learn how to prioritize and manage the multiple demands of adulthood (earning a living, paying bills, shopping, planning meals, maintaining a house or apartment, child rearing, accommodating one's partner). Adults learn the unwritten rules in their relationships and in their place of business. Adults learn that a perfectly logical solution is not always the most practical one. Adults realize that there aren't always right answers, that different people have different values, that backup plans are sometimes necessary, and that it is often wise to think through the implications of a variety of scenarios before acting (Baltes & Staudinger, 1993). Thus, it should not be surprising to learn that, in some tests of wisdom, the elderly score higher than the young (Baltes & Staudinger, 1993).

Gardner believes that schools tend to place too much emphasis on linguistic and spatial-mathematical intelligence. Not enough attention is given to developing other forms of intelligence, like the bodily-kinesthetic intelligence used in basketball.

Howard Gardner's Multiple Intelligences

Whereas Sternberg is satisfied with three kinds of intelligence (componential, experiential, and contextual), Howard Gardner believes that there are at least seven kinds of intelligence: logical-mathematical, linguistic, spatial, musical, bodily-kinesthetic, interpersonal, and intrapersonal.

As the name implies, **logical-mathematical intelligence** includes logical and mathematical thinking. In addition, logical-mathematical intelligence also includes scientific thinking. Gardner (1993) believes it is logical-mathematical intelligence—and only logical-mathematical intelligence—that Piaget's theory covers.

Linguistic intelligence is the ability to use words. The verbal section of the SAT is designed to measure linguistic intelligence, as are many of the verbal subscales of most intelligence tests.

Both linguistic and logical-mathematical ability are important to our society. Most of our schools strive to increase only these two abilities. The tests our society uses to measure "intelligence" and to determine admission to school tap only these two abilities.

Although linguistic and logical-mathematical abilities are important, Gardner believes that our society's emphasis on these two intelligences is unfortunate because it causes us to ignore five other *equally important* intelligences. As a result, children are pushed to develop abilities they may not have and are not encouraged to develop abilities that they do have.

Note that in his attack on standard intelligence tests, Gardner has much in common with Sternberg. However, Gardner's conception of intelligence is broader than Sternberg's. For example, Sternberg's view does not incorporate spatial, musical, and bodily-kinesthetic intelligences in his model.

Spatial intelligence is the ability to form a mental model of a spatial world and to be able to maneuver and operate using that model. Architects, engineers, sculptors, and painters are examples of people who need high levels of spatial intelligence.

Musical intelligence is clearly evident in people such as Mozart, Billy Holiday, Beverly Sills, Ella Fitzgerald, and Billy Joel. The Suzuki violin program attempts to develop young children's musical intelligence.

Bodily-kinesthetic intelligence is the ability to skillfully coordinate the body's movements to achieve a given objective. Successful dancers, athletes, surgeons, and crafts people all have a high level of bodily-kinesthetic intelligence.

Interpersonal intelligence is the ability to understand other people—what motivates them, how they work, and how to work cooperatively with them. Successful salespeople, managers, politicians, teachers, clinicians, and religious leaders benefit from high interpersonal intelligence. Interpersonal intelligence would seem to be an important aspect of Sternberg's contextual intelligence.

Box 6.9

SELF-CHECK

Answer the following questions.

1. How do thought and behavior change as a child enters formal operations? What are the potentially negative consequences of these changes?
2. How does propositional logic differ from metathought?
3. Why do some people object to Piaget's research methods?
4. What evidence is there that preoperational children are not as egocentric as Piaget claimed?

Indicate whether each of the following statements is true or false.

5. The notion that children develop by abruptly moving through qualitatively different stages has been supported by research.
6. Most people enter formal operations around age 12.
7. Piaget believed that cognitive development stopped at adolescence.
8. Piagetians believe that Piaget's theory encompasses the development of all types of thought.
9. Piaget has been accused of being vague about what causes cognitive development.

In the blanks, write the letter of the description that best matches the name or term.

10. ___ Sternberg
11. ___ Gardner
12. ___ Componential intelligence
13. ___ Metacomponents
14. ___ Experiential intelligence
15. ___ Contextual intelligence
16. ___ Tacit knowledge
17. ___ Linguistic intelligence
18. ___ Bodily-kinesthetic intelligence
19. ___ Interpersonal intelligence

a. "street smarts"
b. tapped by SAT verbal score
c. seven intelligences
d. a skilled politician is high on this
e. triarchic theory
f. measured by traditional IQ tests
g. Michael Jordan may be #1 on this
h. unwritten rules
i. strategies for solving problems
j. creativity

Intrapersonal intelligence, on the other hand, is the ability to know oneself and to use this self-knowledge effectively. A person with high intrapersonal intelligence knows her strengths and limitations, knows why she does things, and is not her own worst enemy.

In short, by redefining intelligence, Gardner has posed new challenges to schools and developmental psychologists. Specifically, we must learn how to (1) help all children develop a minimal level of competence in each of these seven abilities and (2) identify which abilities each child is naturally blessed with and then find ways to help each child achieve "genius" in those areas.

INTELLIGENCE IN PERSPECTIVE

As you have seen, intelligence can be defined in many different ways. The bottom line is that intelligence is what the test maker decides it is. For Galton, intelligence was the ability to react quickly to stimuli and to tell the difference between similar tones, lights, and odors. (James Bond with his lightning quick reflexes and ability to taste differences between wines would have done very well.) Why was that intelligence? Galton reasoned that smarter people learn more from experience because they are better able to react to experience and better able to detect subtle differences in experience. However, Galton abandoned those tests because they failed to correlate with his ultimate criterion of intelligence: success in school.

To Binet, intelligence was nothing more than the ability to do well in school. He was hired to develop a test that would predict school success and that's what he did. He used two basic kinds of tasks: familiar tasks (such as defining the words *airplane, hat,* and *river*) and novel tasks ("fold this square piece of paper to make a triangle"). Wechsler's IQ tests are also in this mold, with the verbal subscales involving familiar tasks (which may assess crystallized intelligence) and the performance subscales involving novel tasks (which may assess fluid intelligence).

According to Sternberg, there are three intelligences: componential, experiential, and contextual. Gardner describes seven types of intelligence. Thurstone also identifies seven intelligences, but his seven are different from Gardner's. Guilford claims there are 120 intelligences.

What is the truth? The truth is that humans probably have many different abilities. Which and how many abilities we want to identify as types of intelligence is ultimately up to our society and its test constructors. Because people seem to agree that there is more than one type of intelligence, but would probably be overwhelmed by more than seven, we think that, for the immediate future, there will be between two and seven kinds of intelligence.

Is the debate over different theories of intelligence pointless? No, the debate itself is useful, if for no other reason than it accentuates what Binet always claimed: that intelligence is an arbitrary and limited concept. Furthermore, the debate continues to stimulate more research and thought about the nature of human abilities and of wisdom (Baltes & Staudinger, 1993; Frederiksen, 1986). This research and theorizing should pay off in finding better, more accurate ways to measure, develop, and tap human potential.

SUMMARY

1. The psychometric approach focuses on measuring intelligence, which it has traditionally defined as those logical and analytical abilities that facilitate success in school.
2. Like Binet, many modern psychometricians measure intelligence through both verbal tasks (which may tap what the person already has learned) and performance tasks (which are often considered "purer" measures of what the person can learn).
3. Unlike Binet's test, modern intelligence tests produce an IQ score. An IQ score describes how a person performed on the test relative to other people in the same age group. Most people's IQs are between 84 and 116.
4. Although some early intelligence test makers did not have extremely noble motives and even though some early intelligence tests were flawed, modern intelligence tests have some validity. For example, compared to people with low IQs, people with high IQs tend to be more successful in school and more successful in jobs that require complex thinking. Nevertheless, traditional intelligence tests measure a limited range of abilities.
5. Although early intelligence testers overestimated heredity's role, heredity does play a role in intelligence.
6. Although IQ is, on the average, fairly stable from ages 6 to 60, it is not stable for everyone. For many individuals, IQ changes tremendously during childhood.
7. In later adulthood, IQ declines. Experts disagree as to whether these declines are reversible and preventable. They agree, however, that the declines are greater on performance tasks than on verbal tasks. Thus, even if the declines aren't preventable, gains in crystallized intelligence may offset losses in fluid intelligence.
8. Infant tests of intelligence do not tap the same abilities that child and adult IQ tests do. Nevertheless, such tests provide some evidence that intelligence is stable and can be useful in diagnosing problems in development.
9. By looking at changes in the number of problems we can solve as we get older, the psychometric approach has established that IQ is fairly stable over the lifespan, that IQ is strongly influenced by nature, and that the speed of solving certain problems tends to decrease in later adulthood.
10. Rather than looking at changes in the number of problems we can solve as we get older, Jean Piaget looked at what children were thinking when they solved problems.
11. Piaget believed that we naturally want to explore and understand the world. In other words, because of equilibration, we are driven to assimilate and accommodate the world.
12. Piaget proposed four stages of cognitive development: sensorimotor, preoperations, concrete operations, and formal operations.
13. From birth until about age 2, children are in the sensorimotor stage. During this time, they learn how to relate to their bodies and to the world.
14. When a child develops object permanence and symbolic thought (usually at about age 2), he has entered the preoperational stage. Children at preoperations (usually ages 2 through 7) are egocentric and engage in magical thinking (animistic thought and phenomenalistic causality). Preoperational children also have difficulty attending to two dimensions at once and they often attend to irrelevant dimensions. As a result, they do poorly on conservation and class inclusion tasks. Finally, preoperational children fail to predict the logical consequences of actions.
15. Concrete operational children (ages 7 to 12) can think logically about physical (concrete) events. Most people do not advance beyond concrete operational thinking.
16. According to Piaget, most children reach formal operations by age 12. People in formal operations can apply logic to abstract ideas. They also have an expanded concept of time and space, don't take things literally, see new possibilities, and examine their own thinking. Formal operations may pave the way for adolescent rebellion and role confusion.

17. Piaget has had an enormous impact on parents, teachers, schools, society, and psychology.
18. Piaget has been criticized for using less than completely standardized research methods, underestimating the intelligence of young children, overestimating the intelligence of adolescents and adults, failing to account for adult cognitive development, and failing to specify precise *causes* of development. In addition, his notion of qualitatively different stages has been questioned.
19. Systems theorists define intelligence more broadly than conventional psychometricians do. For example, Gardner believes that—in addition to the logical and linguistic skills measured by conventional IQ tests—intelligence includes such things as the ability to understand others, the ability to understand oneself, musical ability, bodily-kinesthetic ability, and spatial ability. Gardner's work should stimulate experts to devise ways that will help people develop all of their intelligences.
20. Sternberg proposes three different kinds of intelligence: componential (analytical), experiential (creative), and contextual (practical). Not only is Sternberg trying to measure these abilities, but he is also working on ways to help people develop and improve their "intelligences."

KEY TERMS

accommodation 195
animistic thought 199
assimilation 195
automatization 210
Bayley Scales of Infant Development 188
bodily-kinesthetic intelligence 211
chronological age 183
circular reaction 198
classic aging pattern 190
class inclusion problems 202
cognitive developmental theory 194
componential intelligence 209
concrete operations stage 200
conservation 200
contextual intelligence 210
crystallized intelligence 192
developmental quotient (DQ) 187
egocentric thought 200
equilibration 197
eugenics 182
executive components 209
experiential intelligence 209
fluid intelligence 191
formal operational stage 202
Gesell Developmental Schedules 187
homeostasis 197
inner speech 196
intelligence quotient (IQ) 183
interpersonal intelligence 211
intrapersonal intelligence 212
knowledge acquisition components 209
linguistic intelligence 211
logical-mathematical intelligence 211
magical thought 199
maturation 195
mental age 183
metathought 202
musical intelligence 211
nominal realism 199
object permanence 199
operations 199
performance components 209
phenomenalistic causality 199
plasticity theory 191
preoperational stage 199
problem-finding stage 208
propositional logic 202
psychometric approach 181
schema 195
schemata 195
second-order operations 202
sensorimotor stage 198
seriation 200
spatial intelligence 211
Stanford-Binet 183
symbolic thought 199
systems approach 181
tacit knowledge 210
triarchic theory 209
Wechsler Adult Intelligence Scale (WAIS) 186
Wechsler Intelligence Scale for Children (WISC) 186
Wechsler Preschool and Primary Scale of Intelligence (WPPSI) 186
zone of proximal development 196

Self-Check Answers

Box 6.1

1. Desired traits must be inheritable, and there must be a way to identify who has the desired traits. **2.** Head size, reaction time, etc. can be measured objectively. The problem was that the measures did not correlate with other measures of intelligence or with each other. **3.** Galton was trying to find a mechanism that made eugenics possible. Binet was trying to solve a practical problem of identifying who could and who could not learn from conventional classroom teaching. **4.** One type of familiar item would involve defining vocabulary words. Binet could justify these questions on two grounds. First, because all French schools were supposed to have the same curriculum, items from the second-grade curriculum should be familiar to all third-graders. Second, past performance is a good predictor of future performance. **5.** The Stanford-Binet could be used to study not only children, but adults as well. Thus, with Terman's development of the Stanford-Binet, developmental psychologists could, for the first time, examine the stability of intelligence through the lifespan. **6.** 120 (because $12/10 \times 100 = 120$). **7.** The revised Stanford-Binet could be used with children younger than age 5 and could therefore be used to find out about the development of intelligence in early childhood. Because there were two forms of the test, longitudinal research that involved retesting people over time could be done without giving people the same test each time.

Box 6.3

1. Performance items, which are similar to Binet's unfamiliar items, and verbal items, which are similar to Binet's unfamiliar items. **2.** There are at least two possibilities why scales of infant development do not correlate highly with scores on IQ tests. First, the scales measure very different abilities than those measured on IQ tests. Second, whereas intelligence during infancy may be determined by biology, intelligence in childhood may be affected by both environment and biology. For example, once a child learns language, the child can learn more from his or her parents. **3.** Infant intelligence scales, like the Bayley, are used because they can be used for children who do not have the vocabulary or attention span to take traditional IQ tests; they can diagnose neurological problems or retardation; and they predict language development. **4.** Verbal scores peak in the mid-twenties and then slowly decline; scores on the performance scales peak in the late teens and then decline at a faster rate. **5.** True **6.** True **7.** False **8.** False

Box 6.5

1. False **2.** False **3.** True **4.** True **5.** False **6.** Traditional behaviorists believed that because people are passively programmed by experience, cognitive development is simply the result of getting enough experience (through drills, lectures, etc.). Piaget believed that people want to actively create a model of reality. Thus, they should be allowed to explore the world rather than being passively exposed to lectures and drills. Furthermore, maturation limits what can be learned, so children should not be taught a skill until they are biologically ready to learn it. **7.** Both processes are driven by equilibration—the drive to fit everything into mental structures. Assimilation involves fitting experiences into existing mental structures. Accommodation involves changing existing mental structures to fit experience. Assimilation and accommodation often occur simultaneously. That is, just as putting another item into a trash bag may alter the shape of the bag, assimilating an item into a cognitive structure may alter that structure.

Box 6.7

1. False **2.** False **3.** False **4.** False **5.** False, unless the child has seen someone throw a jar against a window before. **6.** False **7.** True **8.** False, if they could, they would probably not be fooled by conservation tasks or class inclusion problems. **9.** Operations are mental, logical manipulations that are reversible. **10.** To solve the conservation task, the child must be able to mentally reverse the physical manipulation that made the two objects appear dissimilar. **11.** Preoperational children have trouble thinking about more than one thing at a time. Class inclusion problems require the child to be able to think about two things at once. Specifically, they must be able to think of an object as belonging both to (1) a subclass as well as to (2) a more general class.

Box 6.9

1. In the formal operations stage, the child is able to understand figures of speech, has an expanded sense of time and space, and is more conscious of ideals and possibilities. In addition, the child is able to engage in metathought and propositional logic. The "down side" of these changes is that adolescents may see themselves and life as meaningless; they may be overwhelmed by the possibilities of what they could become; and they may be frustrated with themselves and others who fail to live up to their ideals. Thus, disillusionment, rebellion, and an identity crisis may result from entering the formal operations stage. **2.** Propositional logic is the ability to apply the rules of deductive logic. Metathought, on the other hand, is the ability to cross-examine and reflect on one's own thinking. In Sternberg's terminology, metathought would be an executive process whereas propositional logic would be a performance component. **3.** Unlike the ideal scientific research method, which uses rigid controls to reduce human bias, Piaget used a less controlled method—the discovery method. Part of this method involved using the semi-structured interview, which allows the investigator to arbitrarily ask different questions to different subjects. By varying the questions asked, Piaget may have biased the answers he received. **4.** When Piaget's tasks are modified, preoperational children often show that they can take other people's points of view. In addition, comparing how 4-year-olds talk to adults versus how they talk to 2-year-olds shows that 4-year-olds can take their listener into account. **5.** False **6.** False **7.** False **8.** False **9.** True **10.** Sternberg—e. triarchic theory **11.** Gardner—c. seven intelligences **12.** Componential intelligence—f. measured by traditional IQ tests **13.** Metacomponents—i. strategies for solving problems **14.** Experiential intelligence—j. creativity **15.** Contextual intelligence—a. "street smarts" **16.** Tacit knowledge—h. unwritten rules **17.** Linguistic intelligence—b. tapped by SAT verbal score **18.** Bodily-kinesthetic intelligence—g. Michael Jordan may be #1 on this **19.** Interpersonal intelligence—d. a skilled politician is high on this

7

Chapter

Language Development

The mystery of language was revealed to me. . . .
Everything had a name, and each name gave birth to a new thought.

HELEN KELLER

Chapter Overview

For the first time in her life, Jane speaks. Her parents beam. In the next few months, Jane's parents will have much to smile about. With a speed that would put most adults to shame, Jane will learn a new language. In a couple of years, her vocabulary will grow from one word to thousands—and vocabulary growth may be the least impressive aspect of her language learning. In addition to learning vocabulary, Jane will learn thousands of language rules. Admittedly, Jane's parents probably don't have an inkling of all that she is learning. They're just happy that, because Jane can now speak, they can learn more about what their daughter is thinking. Perhaps just as important, because Jane can now understand language, her parents have new ways of teaching and disciplining her. They don't have to deal with the question: "How do you control a child who doesn't know what 'no' means?"

This chapter will help you appreciate the developmental importance of language acquisition and change. You'll first learn what language is. You'll understand that language is more than words. How much more? So much more that there's an entire field devoted to the study of language: linguistics.

Once you understand what language is, we'll describe how language develops. Until recently, almost all research on language development centered on childhood (Gleason, 1985; Kemper, 1992). Even today, our knowledge about language development during the adult years is quite limited. Therefore, our coverage of language development in this chapter will focus more on childhood than on adulthood and old age.

After we've described the sequence of language development, we'll try to explain how people learn language. Past theorists thought humans were preprogrammed to learn language. Other theorists thought that language learning was simply a result of living in an environment that rewards people who use language. Today, most theorists focus on the interaction between nature and nurture. Even though most psycholinguists agree that both nature and nurture are necessary, they disagree considerably over the exact mechanisms of

language acquisition (Rice & Schiefelbush, 1989). Because there is so much controversy, we will survey only the most established theories.

Once you understand the major theories of language development, we'll address the controversial question: "What is the relationship between the development of language and the development of thought?" There are three basic views concerning this issue.

One view is that thought shapes or influences language. According to that view, Jane's language development will have to wait until her mental abilities have developed. Conversely, the second view holds that language helps children think more effectively. Language influences or shapes thought. Therefore, language development (or the lack of language development) will influence a child's cognitive development. The third view is that there is no connection between thought and language. Language can develop without thought developing, and thought can develop without language. People believe that the two are connected only because people express many of their thoughts through language.

What Is Language?

Before we can discuss the development of language, we must know what language is. **Language** is a structured system of symbols that have socially agreed upon meanings. These symbols may be sounds (as in the case of speech), written symbols (as in the case of reading and writing), or gestures (as in the case of sign language). Although there is research on both the acquisition of written language and on the acquisition of American Sign Language, most developmental research has focused on the acquisition of spoken language. Therefore, this chapter will focus primarily on the development of spoken language.

Since ancient times, people have claimed that language is what sets humans above all other animals. Although recent research suggests that other animals do communicate through sounds and gestures, there is little evidence that any of these communication systems approach the complexity of human language (Gleason, 1985).

Although language is a form of communication, not all forms of communication qualify as language. Language is distinguished by several properties. Some of these distinct properties are **functional properties,** things that only human language has the ability to do. Others are **structural properties,** complex rules that govern the way sounds and words can be put together. We will begin by discussing the functional properties that make human language unique.

The Functional Properties of Language

What can human language do that animal communication can't? Perhaps nobody has spent more effort addressing this question than Stuart Altmann (1967). Building on the work of Charles Hockett (1960), Altmann concluded that, unlike animal communication, human language has the functional properties of displaced reference, productivity, prevarication, pragmatics.

Displaced reference is the ability to refer to objects and events that are not physically present. This includes referring to things in the past and future, as well as communicating about things removed from our sensory realm. Perhaps it is language that allows children to go beyond the sensorimotor stage.

As far as we know, most animal communication is about the here and now. For example, our dog barks to scare off potential intruders who are within his sensory realm (on the sidewalk outside our living room window). Our cat purrs to express pleasure at being stroked. Although most animal communication is in response to the present, some animals are capable of displaced reference. For example, Gould (1982) discovered that honeybees perform a specific dance to tell other bees where they have discovered food (see box 7.1).

Productivity (also called generativity) is the capacity to produce novel messages. Human language systems are so high in productivity that most human utterances are novel. Some of these creative utterances are admired by lovers of poetry and literature. Others are not. For example, a 3-year-old might say, "I goed to school," or "I like cat more than Daddy," statements that the child has probably not heard before. Although people of all ages are constantly making original and novel statements, this originality and novelty are not characteristic of communication systems used by most other animals.

Prevarication is the ability to lie. As you know, human language systems lend themselves easily to prevarication. Perhaps human languages lend themselves to lying because they include negations, such as *no, not, nein,* and *nyet.* At least two bits of evidence support the idea that being able to use negatives (an ability that does not develop immediately) is vital for developing the ability to lie. First, humans start lying as soon as they develop the ability to properly use negations such as *no* and *not.* Second, even apes will lie if they are taught to use negatives. For example, Lucy, a chimpanzee who lived in an Oklahoma home, was taught a primitive form of sign language (Temerlin, 1975). She was not reliably toilet-trained. When asked if she defecated on the carpet, she would promptly deny the allegation by signing "No." If asked who was responsible, Lucy would implicate an innocent human by pointing or signing the human's name.

The final functional property of human language we will discuss is **pragmatics,** the use of language to affect the

Box 7.1

THEORY in FOCUS

Do Animals Have Language?

Developmental psychologists have long been intrigued by the question: "Do animals have language?" If the answer to this question is "yes," then (1) language development may be a relatively simple process explainable strictly in terms of simple laws of learning, and (2) animal research could be very useful in understanding how human language develops.

But do animals have language? Admittedly, animals can communicate. A bee can tell other bees where to go for food; a cat's meow can signal its need for attention; and a dog's growl can let people know their company isn't wanted. But the fact that animals can communicate does not mean that animals have language. Language is more than communication. Specifically, language has at least four characteristics (Brown, 1973).

First, language is *learned.* Genetically programmed dances (like the bee's dance) and genetically programmed vocalizations such as mating calls and alarm calls are not considered language. Consequently, even though some apes have at least 32 cries, including different alarms depending on whether the predator is an eagle, a leopard, or a snake, these cries are not language.

Second, language has *semanticity,* that is, its symbols arbitrarily represent ideas, events, or objects. For example, the assignment of the morpheme "rose" to roses is arbitrary. We call a rose a rose because that's what we've been taught. If we had been taught that the rose was called a "muffin" or an "ort" or a "sock," we'd call it by that name. In other words, unlike paintings, our language is not *iconic,* looking like or resembling what it refers to. The bee's dance, on the other hand, is not language because it is iconic and it therefore lacks semanticity. Specifically, the bee shows the direction of the honey by dancing in that direction. Similarly, your pet's communication lacks semanticity. You know only that your cat is meowing for attention (rather than food or to get outside) because he's rubbing up against you; you know your dog wants your food only because she's looking at your food.

Third, language is capable of *displacement,* referring to things that aren't currently in the immediate area. That is, in true language, people can talk about the distant past and the future, as well as about events that are occurring in places they have never been. The bee lacks displacement because it can't talk about last week's food or next month's food. It can talk only about the nectar it just found. Similarly, ape warning cries occur only in reaction to the current presence of an enemy in the immediate area.

Fourth, language is *productive,* capable of producing new utterances by recombining symbols to form meanings never heard of before. You've probably heard children say things they never have heard before. By recombining words, each of us can say things we've never heard before. We may even be able to say things that nobody has ever said before, such as: "My term paper is late because a genetically altered cockroach, roughly the size of a poodle, escaped from the biology lab and took several megabytes out of my computer." The bee, on the other hand, is limited to communicating about where food is. Most animals seem limited to emitting the same cries, barks, and songs that all members of their species produce and to produce these sounds in the same sequence as every other member of their species does.

If animals don't have a language, can they be taught a language? That is, can they be taught to acquire a system of learned symbols and combine these symbols according to rules? Several attempts have been made to teach language to chimpanzees, the animal most genetically similar to human beings. The first attempt, in 1931, was with the chimpanzee Gua. Gua never babbled and never learned to say a single English word. In the 1940s, another chimpanzee, Viki, after much effort, learned four words. Viki showed researchers that chimps simply have a hard time making the muscle movements required in speech. For example, for Viki to pronounce a *p* sound, she had to hold her lips together with her fingers.

Researchers have tried several tactics to get around the "speech barrier." In 1966, a chimpanzee named Washoe was taught American Sign Language (ASL). Washoe did learn 130 different signs. Furthermore, she learned to generalize. That is, if she saw someone wearing a kind of hat she had never seen before, she would use the sign for "hat" to describe what the person was wearing. However, Washoe never learned **syntax**, word order. In the 1980s, another chimp, "Nim Chimpsky" also learned sign language. Like Washoe, Nim didn't seem to understand the importance of word order and rarely got beyond two- to three-word phrases. Furthermore, videotapes of Nim suggested that he

Continued

Box 7.1

THEORY in FOCUS

Concluded

basically repeated what his trainers told him or responded to what his trainers cued him to do. In short, chimpanzees seem to be able to learn operant responses, whether those responses are pulling a lever or making the sign that their trainer wants.

Although the consensus is that animals can't learn language, animals can learn words. Even household pets know what some words mean ("sit," "no," "walk"). Chimpanzees are even able to string words together into phrases. However, these phrases are not constructed according to grammatical rules. The words in the phrases are either haphazardly ordered ("now food want") or exact repeats of what the chimps were taught. Put another way, chimps show neither any evidence of syntax nor of having combined words in creative ways to express new ideas. Not only does a chimp's word use fail to show syntax and productivity, but it also lacks displacement. Indeed, a chimp's use of language, especially spontaneous language, is almost exclusively limited to making requests or demands. Lastly, chimps do not use abstract words such as *freedom* or engage in *metalanguage,* speaking about language itself.

Despite the fact that teaching chimps language has been a failure, we have learned some important things through this noble failure. Perhaps the most important thing is how remarkable our own ability to master language is. Five facts emphasize how uniquely human our ability and desire to learn language is:

1. Whereas animals are reluctant language learners, humans are eager to learn language. In fact, whereas teaching words to an animal requires a great deal of modeling and reinforcement, children who are not taught a language will sometimes invent their own.
2. Whereas animals learn language slowly, humans learn quickly. Indeed, some children who watched animals undergo sign language training picked up sign language before the animals did.
3. Whereas animals do not learn syntax, children do.
4. Whereas animals do not show productivity, children do.
5. Whereas animals do not have parts of the brain dedicated to language, humans do. Indeed, almost as soon as they are born, infants show that they prefer to process language in their left brain.

behavior, knowledge, or attitude of another (Austin, 1962; Searle, 1969, 1975). The pragmatic, social function of most animal communication is limited to greeting or warning. For example, our cat greets us by running to us while meowing, then rubbing against our legs and purring. Then, she hisses at the dog to warn him not to approach her.

Human language, on the other hand, is used to communicate more than greetings and warnings. As table 7.1 shows, we can also use language to convey our beliefs, to try to make another do something for us, to commit ourselves to an action, to express our feelings, and to change things. Perhaps more important, language enables us to communicate complex ideas to each other and to pass on knowledge from one generation to the next.

Because of the pragmatic function of language, children need to learn many rules about how to use language effectively in social situations. For example, children must develop the ability to adapt their speech to fit their listeners and the situation. By now, you have developed considerable sophistication in adjusting your speech to make it more effective. For instance, the way you would talk in a job interview is probably more formal than the way you

Table 7.1

Categories of Speech Acts

Representatives	Speaker conveys his or her belief that a certain proposition is true (for example, assertion that dogs are smarter than cats).
Directives	Speaker attempts to get the listener to do something (for example, ordering, commanding, begging, requesting).
Commissives	Speaker commits himself or herself to a future action (for example, promises, vows, contracts).
Expressives	Speaker expresses his or her psychological state (for example, apologizes, welcomes, expresses thanks, expresses feelings).
Declarations	Speaker's words bring about a change or a new state of affairs (for example, "You're fired").

Note. From I. Brown, Jr., "Language Acquisition: Linguistic Structure and Rule-Governed Behavior" in *The Functions of Language and Cognition,* edited by G. J. Whitehurst and B. J. Zimmerman. Copyright © 1979, New York: Academic Press, New York. Reprinted by permission.

talk with your family and friends. Similarly, if you were speaking to a 3-year-old, you probably would select different words than if you were speaking to an adult.

In addition to adjusting our words to the context and audience, we need to learn the pragmatic rules that govern how we start a conversation (Farb, 1975). Although you may not have given it much conscious thought, there are strict rules about how to start a conversation. Indeed, as table 7.2 shows, there are only six "acceptable" ways to open a conversation. Of course, once the conversation starts, there are complex pragmatic rules that must be followed to maintain the conversation.

The Structural Properties of Language

As we have discussed, people cannot effectively communicate without knowing certain pragmatic rules. However, before they can use pragmatic rules, they must be able to apply the structural rules of language. Thus, to effectively communicate, speakers must be able to apply **grammar,** the structural rules of language.

These structural rules are so complex that no adult can list them all. Yet, all normal children master language's four structural properties:

1. **Phonological rules:** rules governing which sounds are part of the language and which sounds can be put together.
2. **Morphological rules:** rules governing whether a group of sounds is a word (vocabulary rules).
3. **Syntactic rules:** rules governing the order in which words can be put together to make meaningful sentences.
4. **Semantic rules:** rules determining what a statement means.

As we mentioned earlier, no one can list all of these rules of grammar. But if they can't be listed, then how can we say that we know them? To show that you know something about each of the four types of structural rules, realize that:

1. You know that "pzk," and "qr" are not plausible sound combinations (phonological rule).
2. When describing someone cute, you use the term *adorable,* rather than *ableador* (morphological rule).
3. You know that "Why I not can?" is in the wrong word order (syntactic rule).
4. You immediately recognize that the statement "I am blue" has more than one meaning, depending on the context (semantic rule).

Phonological Rules

Every language is based on a set of sounds. Therefore, the first step toward language acquisition is to master the basic sounds used in language: phonemes. **Phonemes** are distinctive sounds that can be combined to create a word.

Table 7.2

Rules for Opening a Conversation

1. *Request information, services, or goods.*

    Do you have the time?

    Please pass the salt.

    Could I borrow a match?

2. *Request a social response.*

    I've never seen it rain so hard, have you?

    This sure is a long line! I wonder how long we'll have to wait.

3. *Offer information.*

    Did you hear about the robbery last night?

    You seem to be lost.

4. *Express an emotion such as anger, pain, joy, as a strategy to solicit a comment from the listener.*

    Ouch!

    Look at this!

5. *Stereotyped statements such as greetings, apologies, thanks, and so on.*

    Hello.

    I'm sorry.

    Thanks a lot.

6. *A substitute statement to avoid a conversation about a subject the speaker anticipates the listener will introduce.* An example would be a water-cooler meeting between a boss and subordinate; the boss anticipates a conversation about a raise, so she hurriedly speaks first and uses an avoidance opener:

    The traffic sure was heavy this morning.

Source: From P. Farb, *Word Play: What Happens When People Talk,* Alfred A. Knopf, New York, 1975, pages 96–97.

For example, the *c,* the *a,* and the *n* sounds can be put together to say *can.* English has about 40 phonemes; other languages have anywhere from 20 to 80 phonemes. When adults try to learn a second language, they often fail to master the phonemes of that language. As a result, adults sometimes gain more respect for the young child's ability to recognize and speak the phonemes of the native tongue.

Morphological Rules

Once children learn to produce and recognize phonemes, they must master morphological rules that govern how words are formed. All words consist of one or more **morphemes,** the smallest units of speech that carry meaning. For example, the word *desire* represents a single morpheme; *desirable* contains two morphemes; the stem *desire* and the morpheme *-able.* The morpheme *-able* tells us that the word is not an action verb, but rather a descriptive adjective. Other morphemes could be added to *desirable* by adding the prefix *un-* to create *undesirable,* and by tagging the suffix *-ness* to make *undesirableness.*

Morphological rules govern the order in which morphemes may appear within a word. For example, in English it is not permissible to say *desirableun.* Rather, morphological rules ensure that such negative markers such as *un* and *non* must be prefixes that come before the stem (for example, *un*desirable) rather than suffixes.

Semantic Rules

Semantic rules govern the meaning of words. Each word is really just an arbitrary symbol for an idea, event, or object. We call a rose a rose because that's what we've been taught. If we had been taught that a rose was called an "ort," we'd call it an ort.

The meaning of individual words is called **lexical meaning.** Learning the meaning of words is essential for communication, but difficult. Mastering the meaning of words is more complex than learning the one-to-one correspondence between specific sounds and specific objects or events in our environment. A child must learn that some words refer to only one object (for example, [my] *mother*), whereas other words refer to a class of objects (*cats*). The meaning of other words depends on the context. For example, the meaning of *that, there,* and *it* depends on other elements in the sentence. Depending on the context, *it* could be a toy, a whale, or a taco.

Denotative and Connotative Meanings To make things even more difficult, words have at least two kinds of meaning: denotative and connotative (Osgood, 1963). **Denotation** is the concrete, specific dictionary meaning of a word. For example, an actual pig (a sexually immature domestic swine) is the concrete, direct meaning of the word *pig.*

Connotation refers to the implied or emotional meaning of a word. For instance, *night club* and *saloon* have similar denotations but different connotations (see table 7.3 for more examples).

Table 7.3

Words with Similar Denotations, but Different Connotations

Cheap	Thrifty
Advisor	Mentor
Plump	Fat
Stubborn	Determined
Conforming	Cooperative
Assertive	Pushy
Spontaneous	Impulsive
Youthful	Immature
Nonconforming	Disobedient
Concerned	Nosy
Elderly	Old
Transition	Crisis
Free spirit	Brat
Self-assured	Cocky
Weak	Feeble
Tired	Haggard
Pretty	Gorgeous
Open-minded	Indecisive

Syntactic Rules: Word Order

Learning the meaning of words is an impressive task. Yet, even lower animals can learn the meaning of a few words. What nonhuman animals cannot learn is **syntax,**[1] the rules governing how words can be put together to form meaningful sentences. In other words, syntax focuses primarily on how word order affects meaning.

Developing a sophisticated knowledge of syntax is essential because (1) most word combinations produce meaningless garbage (for example, "combinations garbage produce word meaningless most") and (2) even meaningful combinations may not express what the child wants to say (for example, "The pig ate the wolf" does not mean the same thing as "The wolf ate the pig").

To emphasize that language is more than a collection of individual words, some linguists distinguish between lexical meanings and syntactic meanings. As you learned earlier, lexical meanings refer to the dictionary definitions of individual words. **Syntactic meanings** (also called *propositional meanings*), on the other hand, refer to the meanings that words and phrases take on when they become parts of sentences.

Noam Chomsky (1957) pioneered the study of syntactic meanings. In fact, all theories of syntactic meaning since 1957 have been based on Chomsky's theory (Pinker, 1994; Rayner & Pollastsek, 1989).

Clearly, a key to understanding syntactic meaning (the meanings that words and phrases take on when they become parts of sentences) is to analyze sentence structure. Chomsky and other experts on syntactic meanings analyze

[1]When some psycholinguists use the term *grammar,* they really mean syntax. However, in this chapter we will use *syntax* to refer to the rules governing word order and we will use *grammar* to refer to all the structural rules of language, including phonology, morphology, semantics, and syntax.

sentence structure using **immediate constituent analysis**—a linguistic technique that captures the hierarchical organization of sentences (Bloomfield, 1933; Singer, 1990). As you can see in figure 7.1, in such an analysis, a sentence is first subdivided into its major parts: (1) a noun phrase, and (2) a verb phrase. Then each subpart is further divided to the level of the individual word.

By studying the hierarchical organization of sentences, developmental psycholinguists have discovered the sequence of syntactic development. They have mapped children's progress in learning how to put words together in the right way. They have even gained some insights into how children are able to accomplish the amazing feat of creating and applying complex syntactical rules—without ever being told about these rules. Table 7.4 provides a summary of the properties of language we've discussed in this section.

Figure 7.1

Immediate Constituent Analysis—Surface Versus Deep Structure

(a) According to phrase structure rules, we can view this sentence (abbreviated as S) as two phrases—a noun phrase (NP) and a verb phrase (VP). The NP can be further divided into an article (art), an adjective (adj), and a noun (N). Similarly, the VP can be segmented into an adverb phrase (adv) consisting of a preposition (prep) and a pronoun (pro), preceded by an auxiliary (aux) and a verb (v). This diagram illustrates the categorization of each word as a specific part of speech in the surface structure of the sentence. Notice that this sentence is passive—the subject *car* is being acted upon. (b) As you can see in this figure, we can rearrange the passive sentence to make it an active sentence. A deep structure view of the same sentence shows the relationship between the subject and object in a different manner. Although the surface structure in (a) reveals the arrangement of a passive sentence, the sentence can be rearranged in (b) to show an active sentence, whereby the subject, *she* acts upon the object, *car*.

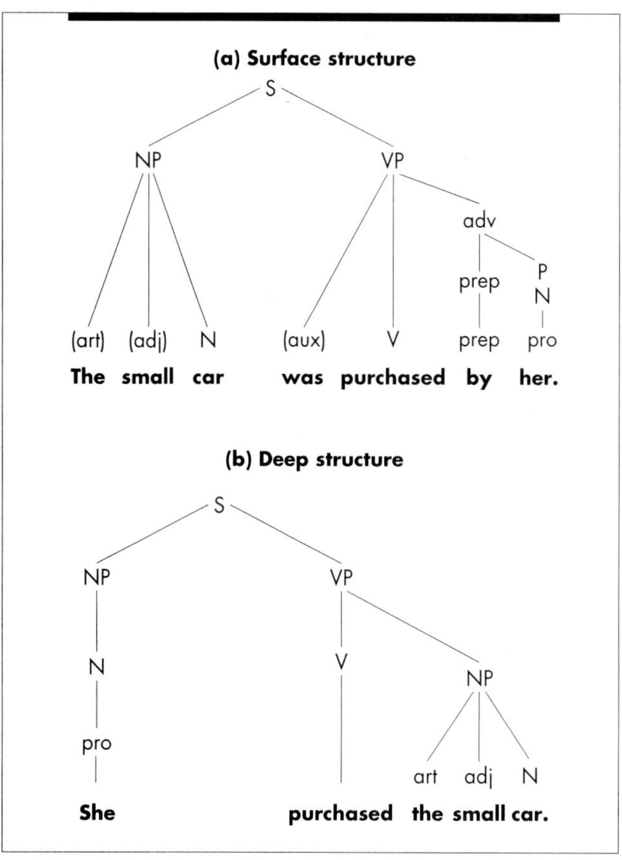

The Acquisition of Language

Although most developmental psycholinguists have focused on the language skills acquired during infancy and childhood, recent work has shown that language is a dynamic process that changes throughout the lifespan. In this section, you will study language development from before birth through old age. We will trace this development through the two periods of language acquisition—the prelinguistic and linguistic periods.

The Prelinguistic Period (Ages 0 to 1)

The **prelinguistic period** begins at birth and ends at about age 1 with the onset of patterned speech. Thus, infants in the prelinguistic period are not able to speak, nor are they able to understand speech. Yet, although a newborn is unable to speak or understand language, she already has acquired several abilities necessary for language development. As you learned in chapter 4, the human ear is well developed before birth. Not only can the fetus hear amniotic fluid sloshing about and the mother's heartbeat, it can hear the muffled sounds of the external world. It hears what its mother says. It hears the music played. It hears the television. In fact, midway through pregnancy, a fetus will jump in a startled reaction to loud noises. This ability to hear will facilitate the development of language comprehension, the **receptive function** of language, and the ability to produce language, the **productive function** of language.

Prelinguistic Development of the Receptive Function

Although newborns do not understand language, they do process it. In fact, infants are born with a special sensitivity to speech. Two-day-old infants can tell the difference between their mother's voice and an unfamiliar voice. From a very early age, infants can also distinguish speech sounds from other sounds in their environment such as dog barks, clanging pots and pans, and music (DeCasper, 1990; Hutt et al., 1968). Furthermore, several studies indicate that cerebral specialization for speech occurs at a very young age, probably before birth (DeCasper, 1990; Molfese, 1985). Specifically, newborns show the adult pattern of processing speech in the left hemisphere and other sounds in the right hemisphere. For instance, Dennis Molfese (1985) found that speech stimulates infants' left cerebral hemisphere, whereas the right hemisphere responds to

Table 7.4

Summary Table: The Different Properties of Language

Functional Properties
Displaced reference: the ability to refer to objects and events that are not physically present.
Productivity: the capacity to produce novel messages.
Prevarication: the ability to lie.
Pragmatics: the ability to influence others.
Structural Properties
Phonological rules: rules governing sound combinations.
Morphological rules: rules governing the formation of words.
Syntactic rules: rules governing the arrangement of words in sentences.
Semantic rules: rules determining the meaning of language.

music. Similarly, Anthony DeCasper (1990) exposed 24 newborns to the sound of either a heartbeat or a woman speaking. The newborns were able to choose which ear would hear the sound by varying the frequency at which they sucked a pacifier. Newborns chose to hear speech in the right ear and the heartbeat in the left ear. (The right ear corresponds to the left cerebral hemisphere and the left ear to the right hemisphere.) Because newborns have limited postbirth language experience, DeCasper's findings suggest that processing speech differently from other environmental sounds originates before birth.

Young infants not only distinguish speech sounds from non-speech sounds, they can distinguish between several phonemes. For example, Peter Eimas (1976, 1982) used sucking rate to test whether 1-month-old infants could tell the difference between phonemes. Infants not only equaled adults in their ability to distinguish among many of the phonemes used in their culture (for example, "ma," "na," "dah," and "gah"), but could also do something many adults can't—perceive differences between phonemes not used in their culture. However, infants quickly lose this ability to distinguish between phonemes not used in their culture's language (Eimas, 1982).

Perhaps related to infants' ability to distinguish among phonemes is their ability to distinguish between different spoken passages. In chapter 4, you learned about *The Cat in the Hat* study (DeCasper & Spence, 1986) in which a stranger either read a passage that the infant's mother had repeatedly read aloud during the last two weeks of pregnancy or the stranger read a different passage. Fetuses preferred to hear the passage that their mother had read to them during their last two weeks of fetal development.

Box 7.2

SELF-CHECK

1. How does human language differ from animal communication?
2. How do children and apes differ in terms of the way that they learn language?
3. When apes are "taught" language, how does their use of language differ from human use of language?
4. The phrase "Help sir you?" violates what rules?
5. The phrase "I like qrpzk" violates which rules?
6. The phrase "The child is lazy and active in" violates what type of rule?
7. How do the words *cooperative, agreeable,* and *conforming* compare to each other in terms of (a) denotative meaning and (b) connotative meaning?

Please turn to the end of this chapter to check your answers.

Although we have emphasized the impressive prelinguistic abilities of young infants, we should also note infants' limitations. For example, although infants can distinguish among many phonemes, not until the end of their second year will they be able to hear *all* the distinctions that their language requires (deVilliers & deVilliers, 1979). For instance, most 3-month-old infants cannot tell the difference between "sa" and "za" (Eilers, Wilson, & Moore, 1977).

Prelinguistic Development of the Productive Function

Just as infants are born with the capacity to perceive speech sounds, they are also born with the ability to produce sounds. Kaplan and Kaplan (1971) have identified three stages of prelinguistic sound production: (1) crying, which begins at birth, (2) cooing and other vocalizations, which start at the end of the first month, (3) and babbling, starting around six months of age. Although the age at which individual children achieve these abilities varies, the order of language development is universal across all language cultures (Atkinson, McWhinney, & Stoel, 1970).

Crying Pragmatics begin to develop as soon as a baby starts **crying.** Although Jane's first cries may be spontaneous and random, they soon become a deliberate attempt to establish human contact and interaction. Indeed, "It is the sound of the cry that parents listen to determine what the infant needs. Parents tune in to this channel to learn to

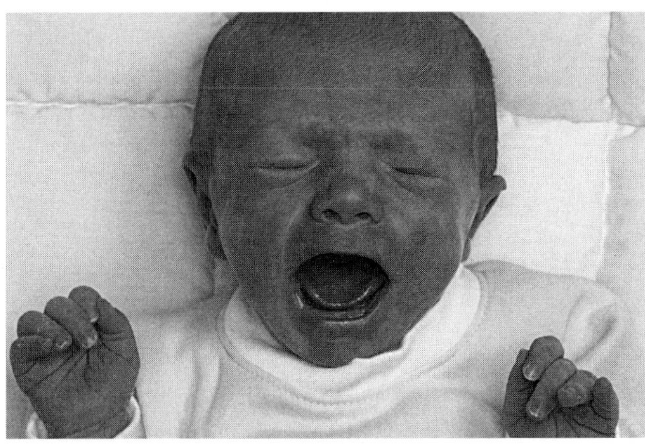

Crying is an infant's first pragmatic communication and the first step to developing language ability.

understand what their infant is trying to say . . . and to establish the foundation of a communication system" (Lester & Boukydis, 1985; Roberts, 1987).

What are infants trying to communicate by crying? Most often, they cry because they are hungry. They also cry to communicate that they feel pain, shock, fear, fatigue, cold, overstimulated, want attention, desire physical contact, or dislike being undressed (Leach, 1989).

Crying does more than communicate the baby's needs. It also helps speech development by providing babies with an awareness of their lips, tongue, palate, jaw, and voice (Roberts, 1987).

Cooing The next step in speech development—**cooing**—occurs between one and two months of age. At that time, babies begin producing coos, an array of vowel-like sounds, produced by repeating over and over again such vowels sounds as "aaaah" and "ooo" (Reich, 1986). These coos closely resemble the sounds made by pigeons and doves. Babies seem to coo when they are content. For example, babies commonly coo after feeding or when they are awake and dry. For this reason, coos are sometimes called "happy sounds."

Like crying, the onset of cooing is biologically determined and does not depend on the environment. Thus, deaf children start cooing at the same age as children who can hear (Lenneberg et al., 1965).

Furthermore, the evolution of cooing also depends on biological maturation rather than on environmental stimulation. Thus, between two and six months, the coos of both deaf and hearing children become more varied. Specifically, whereas early cooing involves only the easy-to-pronounce vowel sounds, later cooing involves both vowels and consonants (Reich, 1986).

Babbling Infants' speech continues to evolve so that they soon progress beyond the cooing stage. Thus, by the time they are 6 months old, most infants are in the **babbling** stage, a period in which infants produce a greater number of clearly articulated vowels and consonants than they did in the cooing stage, produce these distinct sounds in a seemingly random mix, and begin to imitate adult intonation patterns (Delack, 1976; deVilliers & deVilliers, 1979; Kaplan & Kaplan, 1971; Tonkova-Yampol'skaya, 1969).

At almost any restaurant, you can easily pick out a child who is about to progress beyond the babbling stage. Just find a table where at least two adults and an 8- to 12-month-old baby are seated together. Typically, the two adults are engrossed in conversation, ignoring the baby. Soon, the baby "enters" the conversation. What the baby says does not reflect what the adults are saying, but the baby's intonation pattern does reflect the adults'. Put another way, the baby's speech has the same rhythm as the adults'—only the sounds have been changed.

Although babbling, in its advanced stages, may mimic the intonation of adult speech, it is not simply the imitation of adult speech. This fact is demonstrated in four major ways. First, babbling includes phonemes not present in the language used by people in an infant's household. In fact, most infants produce almost all the phonemes used in any human language. Second, if you listened to tape recordings of 6-month-old infants born to families of various nationalities, you would not be able to distinguish the babbling of a French infant from the babbling of Peruvian, German, or Canadian infants. Third, some sounds that are common in adult language are present in early babbling (for example, "g," "k," and "h"), but these sounds are not present in later babbling (Lepold, 1953). Fourth, and most convincingly, even deaf infants babble (Fromkin & Rodman, 1983).

Why do babies babble? As in the case of crying, babbling has a very pragmatic function. When babies imitate the rhythm of adult speech, they are trying to get attention and be included in social interaction. In some cases, babbling may be an attempt to communicate a specific message. For example, when infants want a toy, food, or some other object, they often babble as they reach for or point toward the desired object.

In addition to babbling for pragmatic reasons, babies also babble when they are excited (Menyuk, 1971). Furthermore, babies may babble for the sheer pleasure of producing sounds and exercising the vocal tract. That is, evolution may have made babbling enjoyable so that infants would develop speech.

Whatever the reasons for babbling, it does evolve into speech. Gradually, babbling infants begin to selectively produce those sounds that they hear others produce and stop producing phonemes that aren't contained in the language spoken in their household. By about 10 months of age, an infant's babbling resembles the language spoken in his or her household (Gleitman, 1987). (Table 7.5 summarizes the stages of the prelinguistic period.)

Figure 7.2

Stages of Language Acquisition

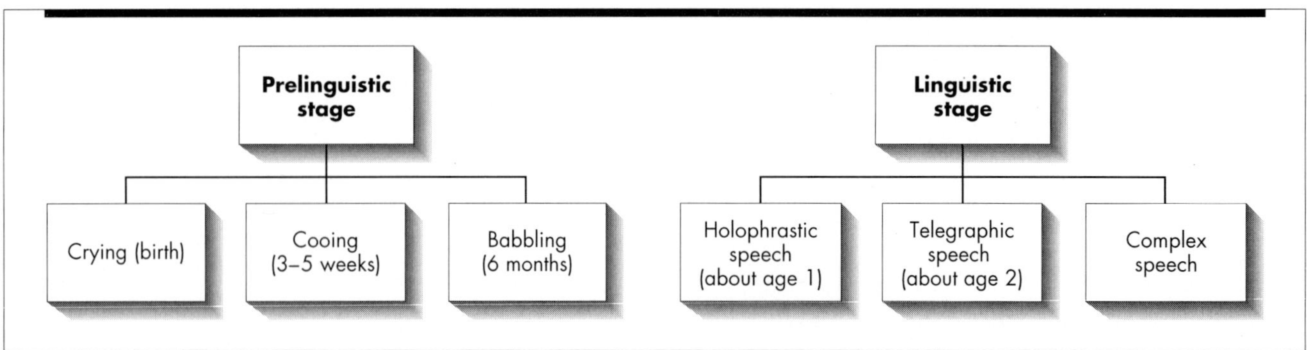

Table 7.5

Summary of the Prelinguistic Period

Stage	Age of Onset	Function
Crying	Birth	Pragmatic: Establishes human contact and gets others to make baby feel better.
Cooing	1 to 2 months	Pragmatic: Encourages others to interact with the baby. Also, expresses contentment.
Babbling	by 6 months	Pragmatic: Encourages social interaction and communicates specific needs. In addition, babbling allows the baby to express excitement and to exercise the vocal tract.

The Linguistic Period (Age 1 Onward)

Even though babbling babies may not be saying words, they often understand certain words. That is, research suggests that babies can comprehend words before they speak their first word (Molfese, 1985). However, experts have traditionally decided that the **linguistic period** of language development begins when a baby speaks his or her first word.

Because of this definition, the linguistic period usually begins sometime around the toddler's first birthday. At about one year of age, most toddlers begin to replace their babbling with **patterned speech,** that is, meaningful speech.

The first word marks the beginning of a stage that will last the rest of the person's life. However, although the linguistic period lasts a lifetime, the greatest growth in language development will occur early in the lifespan. As we shall see, the linguistic period is punctuated by three dramatic periods of growth: the holophrastic period, the telegraphic period, and the beginning of complex speech (see figure 7.2).

Holophrastic Speech: The One-Word Stage

Most children speak their first word when they are about 1 year old. The exact age at which a child will speak this first word, however, varies from infant to infant. There are many reasons why one child will speak before another. For example, because girls are biologically more mature than boys, they tend to speak earlier than boys.

Usually, the exact age at which a child speaks his or her first word is not very important. One reason for this is, as we mentioned earlier, that children can often understand words before they can produce them. Thus, although this first spoken word is observable evidence of the child's realization that sounds have meaning, one child may be producing this evidence whereas another—equally advanced—may be holding back on this evidence.

Another reason that people should not take the exact age at which the first word is spoken too seriously is that this age is hard to objectively determine. This is true because children's first words usually contain one syllable—"da"—and can be hard to distinguish from babbling. Indeed, family members are often the only people able to understand these first "words" and must translate them for outsiders. Fortunately, with practice, infants can produce sounds that conform more and more to the words spoken by those with whom they interact.

One reason that children's first words are hard to understand is that they have not yet mastered the sounds (phonological rules) of their native language. Ironically, even though the babbling sounds they produced during their first year contained many phonemes, it will take several years before they can both hear and produce all the phonemes of their native language (Prather, Hedrick, & Kern, 1975; Reich, 1986). Specifically, the children won't be able to clearly hear the difference between all the phonemes of their native language until they are almost 3 years old, and they will not be able to properly pronounce all their language's phonemes until they are about 4 years old.

If a child's poor pronunciation makes it difficult to make out what she is trying to say, realize that the child is probably saying the name of an object. Typically, a child's first words refer to things that move or can be played with, rather than to objects that are stationary. For example, a young child is more likely to say *ball* or *plane* than *chair* or *sofa* (Nelson, 1973).

Another tip to understanding what very young children are saying is to realize that they are in the holophrastic stage, a stage at which they use one word to convey the information usually contained in a whole phrase or sentence. An example, of **holophrastic speech** would be if Jane exclaimed, "Cookie!" This holophrase means, "I want you to give me that cookie." Similarly, Jane might say, "Plane!" to mean "Look at that plane up there."

In addition to using one word to represent an entire phrase, children in the holophrastic stage often will use **overextension,** that is, the use of a single word to mean many different things. For example, young children will often use the word *Daddy* to refer to all adult men, and *doggie* to refer to all four-legged animals, from cats to cows. Overextension is so common that almost one third of a child's words will be overextended during the holophrastic stage (Nelson & Nelson, 1978).

Psycholinguists stress that overextension should not be dismissed as a silly mistake. Instead, "It seems entirely reasonable for the child to use an available word to represent different but related objects—it is almost as if the child were reasoning 'I know about dogs, that thing is not a dog. I don't know what to call it, but it is like a dog' . . ." (Bloom, 1976, p. 23).

In addition to overextension, children may use **underextension,** that is, the use of a single word in a highly restricted and individualistic way. For example, a child may use the word *Mommy* to refer to only his or her mother. No other woman can be a Mommy.

Combining Words: The Beginning of Syntax

Holophrastic speech is still common between 18 and 20 months of age. Yet, by this time, most children are also beginning to use two-word utterances. Initially, there are noticeable pauses between the words of the phrase. For example, the child may say "Ball" (pause) "gone" (Bloom, 1973).

By the time the child is age 2, he or she probably will be using two-word combinations on a regular basis. This two-word stage heralds the beginning of the child's ability to use sentences and to understand syntax (word order).

Stages Based on Mean Length of Utterance (MLU)

Once children begin combining words, chronological age is a poor predictor of language development. Two children of the same age may differ dramatically in their ability to put words together to form sentences and phrases. To objectively measure these differences in language development, Roger Brown (1973, 1986) developed a measure called the **mean length of utterance (MLU).** As the name suggests, the longer the length of a child's typical phrase, the bigger the MLU. More specifically, as you can see in table 7.6, the MLU is obtained by taking a sample of a child's statements and then calculating the average number of morphemes in those statements.

By comparing a child's MLU at different ages, one can chart the child's language development. In fact, as a result of mapping the MLU scores in three children (whom he referred to as Adam, Eve, and Sarah), Roger Brown (1973, 1986) was able to define five stages of syntactic development.

Table 7.6

Selected Rules for Calculating Roger Brown's Mean Length of Utterance (MLU)

1. Tape record and then transcribe the child's utterances (utterances are phrases or sentences).
2. Take a random sample of 100 of these utterances.
3. Count the number of morphemes. However, do not count the following as morphemes.
   a. Don't count "fillers" like "mm" or "oh" as morphemes.
   b. If a child stutters several times before finally saying the word, don't count each stutter as a morpheme. That is, count the word only once.
   c. Don't give the child credit for every morpheme in compound words (such as *see-saw, pocketbook, birthday,* etc.), in proper names (*Mr. Robert Smith*), and ritualized duplications (*choo-choo, night-night, quack-quack*). Instead, treat compound words, proper names, and ritualized duplications as being composed of only a single morpheme.
   d. Score *doggie, mommie,* etc. as being only one morpheme long. Admittedly, some would argue that *doggie* is two morphemes: *dog* + *ie* (a morpheme indicating that the object is small). However, Brown argues that most young children call all dogs—no matter how large—*doggie.* Therefore, children are not using the *ie* ending as a morpheme to change the meaning of *dog.* Instead, the children are just saying *doggie* and *mommy* to mean the same thing as the single morphemes *dog* and *mom.* Therefore, children should get credit for only one morpheme instead of for two.
   e. Credit only one morpheme for expressions such as the following: *gonna, wanna, halfta,* etc.
4. Divide the total number of morphemes by 100 (the total number of utterances that you scored) to get the MLU.

Source: Adapted from R. Brown, *A First Language: The Early Stages,* Harvard Paperback, Cambridge, Mass., 1973, page 54.

Stage 1 (MLU 1.0 to 2.0): The Telegraphic Stage In Brown's first stage, children use **telegraphic speech.** In other words, they rarely use plural endings, nouns, articles (such as *the, an, a*), or verb endings. Thus, their speech sounds like the abbreviated speech of a telegram. Typical statements include: "Mommy go," "Throw ball," "Good baby," or "All gone."

Because stage 1 is often characterized by two-word phrases, some might naively believe that stage 1 linguistic development is not much more complex than the one-word speech of the holophrastic period. However, stage 1 is far superior to the holophrastic period because children now have syntax: they are combining words. Like adult language, most of their "sentences" are structured with the subject first, then the verb, and then the object (for example, "I want Pepsi!").

Stage 2 (MLU 2.0 to 2.5) During Brown's second stage, children learn general syntactic rules, such as how to use articles and prepositions (such as *in, on*). As a result, their speech becomes less telegraphic. That is, rather than say "ball floor," they may say "A ball is on the floor."

In addition, children learn the regular past tense form of many verbs. That is, they know they can change a verb from present tense to the past tense by adding *-ed* to the end of the verb. Indeed, they are so good at applying this rule that they apply it even to unfamiliar verbs. For example, if you asked a stage 2 child what the past tense of *wug* was, he would say *wugged*. However, their skill at applying this general rule to every verb gets them into trouble because many verbs (the so-called irregular verbs) do not conform to these rules. Thus, children say *breaked* instead of *broke, eated* instead of *ate,* and so on.

The practice of applying a general rule to every situation—even to words that are exceptions to the rule—is called **overregularization.** Some parents become unnecessarily concerned about overregularization. For example, parents may be upset when their child who—at an earlier age—correctly said "I went," "I ate," "feet," and "mice" suddenly starts saying "I broked," "I eated," "foots," and "mouses." Such parents often say, "He never heard that around here." But that's exactly the point. The child is progressing from merely repeating what he has heard to applying rules to language. Thus, ironically, the increase in errors shows progress because the child is showing that he understands that language has rules.

Another advance that occurs during stage 2 is that children learn to use **grammatical morphemes,** modifiers that allow language to more specifically and accurately represent what the person really means. For example, sometime during their third year, most children produce their first grammatical morpheme when they add an *s* to nouns to make them plural, or use *in* and *on* to signify location (Pinker, 1994).

By keeping detailed records of Adam, Eve, and Sarah's mastery of 14 grammatical morphemes, Roger Brown (1973, 1986) found that all three children acquired morphemes in the same order. The order in which the 14 morphemes are learned is listed in table 7.7.

As you can see from that table, the children first acquired the present progressive verb form—"I playing," "I running," "I eating." Next they acquired the prepositions *in* and *on* (both are spatial concepts), followed by the plural ending /s/.

Irregular past tense endings are mastered next—"I came," "It broke," "I ate." Then, they acquired possessive inflection ("Dad's car") on through contractible progressive auxiliaries ("I'm"). Based on his detailed observations of Adam, Eve, and Sarah, Brown concluded that all children acquire these morphemes in the same order.

Stage 3 (MLU 2.5 to 3.0) As children learn to produce longer sentences, not only do they produce more complex sentences, but they also produce more types of sentences. For example, in stage 3, children are able to ask questions and to use negation.

Negation Use of negative morphemes in language is called **negation.** Negative morphemes include words such as *no* and *not,* prefixes such as *un-* (unhappy), *dis-* (disappear), and *non-*, the suffix *-n't* (*can't, don't*), and words associated with negative constructions such as *hardly* and *any*.

Negations are used to express rejection, nonexistence, and denial (Bloom, 1970; Brown, 1973). Children express rejection even before they speak their first word. For example, it is common for a 9-month-old baby to cry when handed to a stranger and to continue crying until she is returned to her caregiver. Once children enter the holophrastic period, they usually express rejection with the simple word *no*. Later, they add *no* to affirmative statements to express rejection ("no go"), nonexistence ("no pocket"), and denial ("no dirty").

Even though young children can use the word *no,* they have trouble following instructions that include negative morphemes. Thus, on being told "Don't pick the cat up by the tail," the child may pick the cat up by the tail. The parent's immediate reaction is often anger at the child for willfully disobeying. However, the problem may simply be that the child doesn't comprehend the negative morpheme. Thus, it is usually better to tell the young child what you *do* want ("Pick the cat up with both arms under her belly") than to request what you don't want.

If being able to hear and understand negative statements is difficult, being able to speak grammatically correct negative statements is even more so. For example, one day Ursula Bellugi (1967), an associate of Roger Brown, was talking to Adam. Adam announced that he had a watch. When Ursula said that she did not think that Adam owned a watch, Adam insisted that he did. Specifically, he responded, "What do you think I am, a no boy with no watch?" Clearly, Adam knew something about negation. However, his concept of how to construct a negative sentence was at odds with the adult form.

Despite the challenges of constructing negative sentences, by the time children reach Brown's third stage of

Morpheme	Meaning Expressed or Presupposed	Examples
1. Present progressive: *-ing*	Ongoing process	I walk*ing*.
2. Preposition: *in*	Containment	*In* basket.
3. Preposition: *on*	Support	*On* floor.
4. Plural: *-'s*	Number	Two balls.
5. Past irregular:[a] *went*	Earlierness[b]	It *broke*.
6. Possessive: *-'s*	Possession	Adam*'s* ball.
7. Uncontractible copula:[c] *are* vs. *was*	Number (singular or plural); past or present	*Was* that a dog?
8. Articles: *the, a*	Specific-nonspecific	That *a* book. That *the* book.
9. Past regular: *-ed*	Earlierness	Adam *walked*.
10. Third person regular: *-s*	Number; earlierness	He walk*s*.
11. Third person irregular: *has, does*	Number; earlierness	He *does*. She *has*.
12. Uncontractible auxiliary be: *is, were*	Temporary duration; number, earlierness	This *is* going.
13. Contractible copula be: *-'s*	Number; earlierness	That*'s* a book.
14. Contractible auxiliary be:[d] *-'s, -'re, m*	Temporary duration; number, earlierness	I'm walking.

Table 7.7

Grammatical Morphemes in Customary Order of Acquisition

[a]Formation of past tense by means other than *-ed*. For example, "Dad *went* to the store."

[b]Denotes understanding that an action or state may occur before the time of utterance.

[c]Use of the verb *to be* as a main verb without contraction. For example, "I am hungry."

[d]Use of the verb *to be* as a main verb with contraction. For example, "I'm hungry."

Source: From H. H. Clark and E. V. Clark, *Psychology and Language: An Introduction to Psycholinguistics*, Harcourt, Brace, Jovanovich, New York, 1977.

Expressing and understanding negation is an important part of Brown's third stage of language acquisition.

syntactical development, they have learned to place a negative in the correct order in a sentence ("I will not eat that" rather than "I not will eat that"). Indeed, they can even use double negatives. For example, they can say, "No, don't untie my shoes!"

Asking Questions At first, children ask questions simply by raising the pitch of their voices at the end of a statement ("You like this?") rather than by changing word order ("Do you like this?") (deVilliers & deVilliers, 1979).

When children enter their third year, they begin to master interrogatives, that is, the ***wh-* questions.** Most often, this first question is some variation of "What's that?" ("whatsat," "whatssit," "whatsit," "whaddes," or "whatisdes") (deVilliers & deVilliers, 1979). As you can see, children first learn the phrase "whatsat" as one word. Then, they break it down into "What that is?" Eventually, they learn to invert subject and verb ("What is that?") (Klima & Bellugi, 1966).

The *wh-* questions are generated in the following order—where? what? who? why? when? Notice that the first three questions refer to location (where), objects (what), and agents (who). Only later do children master the cognitively more complex questions about causality (why) and time (when).

Stages 4 and 5: Complex Syntactic Constructions As we have seen, preschool children have learned many syntactical rules, including regular verb tenses, regular plurals, negation, and questions. However, it is not until children are 7 to 8 years old that they begin to approach the syntactic ability of adults.

As you may recall, prior to age 7, children engage in overregularization (see table 7.8 for a summary). However, around age 7, children learn the exceptions to syntactical rules. For example, they learn the correct past tenses of irregular verbs (*saw, gone, went*) and the correct plurals for irregular nouns (*sheep, geese*). Interestingly, in Alzheimer's patients, these last learned verb forms and plurals are the first to be forgotten (Ullman, 1994).

In addition to learning exceptions to grammatical rules, 7- to 8-year-olds use more complex syntactical structures (deVilliers & deVilliers, 1979). For example, they begin to use simple passive sentences ("Mary was kissed"). In addition, they use more *tag questions* (such as "Pepper looks tired, *doesn't she?*" or "You're pleased, *aren't you?*"). Furthermore, children become more sophisticated in how they use personal pronouns. Thus, rather than say "Her and him went," they are more likely to say "They went" (Dale, 1976).

Semantic Development

Children's progress in developing the ability to use longer and more complex statements is both dramatic and impressive. However, this progress can happen only after the child has made impressive, but less dramatic, progress in developing a vocabulary.

The fact that having a good working vocabulary is a prerequisite for using complex syntax is most obvious early on in life. For the first 10 months, children usually don't use any words. Then, about age 1, they speak their first word. For the next few months, vocabulary growth is slow, with children learning literally one word at a time (Reich, 1986). Thus, at 18 months (six months after the first word), the average child has a speaking vocabulary of only about 50 words. Fortunately, speaking vocabulary growth picks up speed so that by the time children are age 2 (six months after their 50th word), they can produce about 200 words. This rapid growth in spoken vocabulary is commonly called the **vocabulary spurt** or *naming explosion* (Benedict, 1979; Bloom, 1973; Woodward, Markman, & Fitzsimmons, 1994). The child's speaking vocabulary continues to grow rapidly. Consequently, most 6-year-olds can produce between 8,000 and 14,000 words (Carey & Bartlett, 1978; Lenneberg, 1967).

Actually, knowledge of what words mean progresses faster than we described because children usually understand a word before they speak it. For example, children typically know what their first word means about three months before they actually speak it. Furthermore, the gap between the time a child knows a word and the time she speaks it actually gets bigger before it gets smaller. For instance, H. Benedict (1979) found that children can comprehend their first 50 words approximately five months before they produce them.

Table 7.8

Slobin's Four Phases of Grammatical Application

Phase	How Grammatical Rules Are Applied	Example
1	Rules are not applied.	
2	Child memorizes words (such as forms of irregular verbs) but is not applying rules.	May say "It broke," but cannot create the past tense form of an unfamiliar irregular verb.
3	Child is forming grammatical rules and making errors because of overregularization: applying rules to irregular words.	May say "It breaked" or "My foots hurt."
4	Child knows rules and learns exceptions to the general grammatical rules.	Uses proper adult language most of the time.

Note. Adapted from "Cognitive Prerequisites for the Development of Grammar" by D. I. Slobin, 1973. In C. A. Ferguson and D. I. Slobin (Eds.), *Studies of Child Language Development*, New York: Holt, Rinehart, & Winston.

Phonological Development

Part of the reason for the gap between understanding and speaking is that the child has trouble producing certain sounds. The difficulties of producing sounds make it more likely that the child will speak vowel sounds and words like *dada* sooner than the child will say *mother*. The difficulty in producing the right sounds is partly because certain muscles aren't developed enough. The difficulty is also partly due to lack of practice and experience. To get a sense of children's difficulties, consider an African dialect that uses tongue clicks as a phoneme. How hard would it be to learn to click as you spoke?

The School Years

By the time most children enter kindergarten, they have a vocabulary of 8,000 to 14,000 words and have mastered most of the basic forms of grammar (Gleason, 1985). Yet,

Box 7.3

SELF-CHECK

Indicate whether each of the following statements is true or false.

1. By adolescence, language development has stopped.
2. The onset of cooing, the evolution of cooing, and the onset of babbling are biologically determined.
3. Children deal with syntax almost as soon as they can speak.
4. By age 2, children have mastered the art of saying "no."
5. By age 6, children approach adult levels of grammatical sophistication.

Answer the following questions.

6. What evidence suggests that newborns are genetically preprogrammed to learn language?
7. What evidence points to a possible role for nurture in the development of language?
8. What are the names and ages of onset of the three prelinguistic stages?
9. What are the names and ages of onset of the three major linguistic stages?
10. What is overextension?
11. What is the MLU and why is it useful?
12. What is overregularization? What should parents do if they find their child engaging in overregularization?

Please turn to the end of this chapter to check your answers.

their language development is far from complete. During the school years, children will master more complex rules of language as well as learn written language.

Gains in Semantic Awareness During grade school, children will also make significant gains in vocabulary and become more aware of the hierarchical relationships among words. That is, they will understand that a spotted dog is a Dalmatian, which is a kind of domesticated canine, which is a mammal, which is a kind of animal, which is a living organism.

During the school years, children also begin to make linguistic inferences. In other words, their understanding of a series of words may go beyond the actual words stated. For example, consider this statement: "Jimmy was very hungry. When his mother came home, the cake was all gone." A child may infer from the statement that Jimmy ate the cake. By age 10, most children can synthesize information to make accurate inferences—even when the pieces of information they need to put together have been separated by several sentences (Johnson & Smith, 1981).

At the same time children learn to synthesize information, they develop the ability to appreciate the hidden meaning of sentences (Ackerman, 1982, 1986). For example, if a 10-year-old girl enters her house covered with mud, and her father remarks, "My, what a lovely lady," the girl probably will detect the father's sarcasm.

During grade school, children become more aware of the hierarchical relationships among words. They may know their dog belongs to the pet group, which is just one kind of domesticated animal, for example.

Gains in Metalinguistic Abilities The main reason children can make linguistic inferences is that they are developing **metalinguistic skill,** the ability to think and talk about language. Children with metalinguistic awareness consciously understand that language is an arbitrary and rule-bound system. They know that words are made up of separate sounds, they know what a word is, and they know what a sentence is.

Table 7.9 maps out the skills necessary for metalinguistic awareness. As you can see, metalinguistic abilities usually emerge after age 5, well after children are proficient producers of sounds and sentences (Bullinger & Chatillon, 1983; Clark, 1978).

Table 7.9

Skills and Awareness of Language

1 1/2 to 2 Years

1. Ability to monitor one's own ongoing utterances.

   Prerequisite to:

   a. Spontaneously repairing one's utterances for grammar and understanding,

   b. Practicing sounds, words, and sentences, and

   c. Adjusting one's speech to different listeners.

3 to 4 Years

2. Ability to check the result of one's utterance.

   Prerequisite to:

   a. Checking whether the listener has understood. If not, repairing or trying again,

   b. Commenting explicitly on own utterances and on those of others, and

   c. Correcting others.

3. Ability to test reality.

   Prerequisite to:

   a. Deciding whether a word or sentence "works" in furthering listener understanding.

4. Deliberately attempting to learn language.

   Prerequisite to:

   a. Practicing new sounds, words, and sentences, and

   b. Practicing speech styles of different roles.

School Age

5. Predict the consequences of using particular forms (inflections, words, phrases, sentences).

   Prerequisite to:

   a. Applying appropriate inflections to "new" words,

   b. Judging utterances as appropriate for a specific listener or setting, and

   c. Correcting word order and wording in sentences judged as "wrong."

6. Reflect on the product of an utterance (structure independent of use).

   Prerequisite to:

   a. Identifying specific linguistic units (sounds, syllables, words, sentences),

   b. Providing definitions of words,

   c. Constructing puns, riddles, or other forms of humor, and

   d. Explaining why some sentences are possible and how to interpret them.

Source: Adapted from E.V. Clark, "Awareness of Language: Some Evidence from What Children Say and Do" in *The Child's Conception of Language*, edited by A. Sinclair, R. Jarvella, and W. Levelt, Springer-Verlag, New York, 1978.

Peter and Jill deVilliers (1979) found that children under age 5 do not understand that words are made up of separate sounds. That is, these children cannot answer questions such as, "What is the first sound in your name?" and "If you take the "s" sound off *scream*, what's left?" Furthermore, preschool children usually don't understand that words are arbitrarily connected to meaning. For example, a preschooler might think that a cat is called a cat because it meows, not because some people arbitrarily decided to call it a cat.

As we have suggested, metalinguistic awareness includes several different types of abilities (see table 7.10). These include the recognition that:

1. Speech sounds (such as /c/) are different from other environmental sounds (such as sneeze),
2. Only some speech sounds create actual words (*cat* is a word, but not *caz*),
3. Words are arbitrarily related to their referent (dogs could have been called *radishes*),
4. Words must occur in a certain order ("Feed the cat," not "Cat the feed"), and
5. Certain combinations are nonsensical, even though the order is correct ("Eat the fruit," but not "Eat the sofa.").

Several studies have provided information about when children begin to develop metalinguistic skills. For example, the deVilliers (1972, 1979) investigated children's abilities to judge and alter word order in active sentences. Children were asked to teach a puppet how to speak correctly by talking to the puppet and correcting its language. Part of the time, the puppet used proper word order (for example, "Pat the dog"). At other times, the puppet spoke in reverse order ("Dog the pat"), or in a nonsensical fashion ("Drink the chair"). The children indicated whether the puppet was right or wrong and then were required to help the puppet say it the "right way."

The deVilliers' puppet research revealed two important points. First, the better the children's ability to correctly speak and understand complex sentences, the better they were at both detecting the puppet's errors and explaining grammatical rules to the puppet. In short, the better and more experienced the children were at using a rule, the more likely it was that they could explain that rule (deVilliers & deVilliers, 1992). Second, children were able to use certain grammatical rules in their own speech well before they were able to explain those rules to the puppet. Thus, it appears that use of the rule leads to awareness of the rule, rather than awareness of the rule leading to use of the rule.

In another study of children's metalinguistic development, John Flavell and his colleagues (Flavell, 1981; Flavell, Speer, Green, & August, 1981) instructed both kindergartners and second-graders to construct a building

Table 7.10

Abilities Included in Metalinguistic Awareness

Type of Awareness	Ability	Item Used to Test Ability
Component sounds	The ability to identify the distinct sounds contained in a given word.	Take the "a" sound off the word *address*.
Word-meaning correspondence	The appreciation that words are arbitrarily connected to meaning.	Could you call a rose an apple and an apple a rose?
Rules of grammar and semantics	The ability to reflect on the grammatical rules of language.	Which is correct, "I went to the store" or "Me went to the store"?
Ambiguity	The knowledge that the meaning of certain words, phrases, or sentences may vary depending on the context:	
	(1) Double meaning (lexical ambiguity).	Give two meanings for the words *glasses, stick,* and *ruler*.
	(2) Surface-structure ambiguity.	Give two meanings for the sentence, "Fat cats and dogs."
	(3) Deep-structure ambiguity.	Give two meanings for the sentence, "The shooting of the soldiers was terrible."

out of blocks by following tape-recorded instructions. The tape recording was made by a child. In some places, the recorded instructions left out important steps. At other places, the recorded instructions contained unfamiliar words and inconsistencies. Both the kindergartners and second-graders responded to these poor instructions by looking puzzled and by replaying the instructions. Yet, when the children were asked about the instructions, the second-graders were more likely than the kindergartners to complain of problems with the instructions. One explanation for this finding is that the second-graders had a better idea of what good instructions should be like.

This child may be in stage 1 of Chall's proposed stages of reading development, learning to encode single words.

Mastering the Written Word

In our complex society, learning language is more than learning to speak and understand spoken language. Language development also requires the abilities to read and write. We will begin discussing the development of reading by describing Jeanne Chall's stages of reading development.

Reading Jeanne Chall (1983) proposes a prereading stage followed by five stages of reading development. In the prereading stage, children learn letter and number discrimination, recognition, and visual scanning, as well as the rudiments of reading. For example, they learn their "a, b, c's" and can recognize their own name.

When children are about 6-years-old, most enter Chall's first stage of reading. In stage 1, they learn to encode single words to understand simple stories. Because they are now able to pay closer attention, they improve their ability to discriminate among letters, and reading comprehension skills begin to develop.

Near the middle of the second grade, children enter stage 2. Their reading of individual letters becomes more fluent, and so more attention can be directed toward understanding the meaning of what is read.

Around the time they enter fourth grade, most children enter stage 3. Stage 3 marks a major turning point in reading.

Box 7.4

RESEARCH in FOCUS

Learning How to Read

Illiteracy is a serious concern—and no wonder. In the United States

- 24 million American adults are functionally illiterate (Schultz & Schultz, 1990).
- One-fifth of all school children are functionally illiterate.
- Of the 1992 high school graduates, at least 700,000 were unable to read (*USA Today,* 1992).
- Most businesses say that many of their workers have poor reading and writing skills (Schultz & Schultz, 1990).

The high illiteracy in the United States is especially disconcerting because the educational establishment has taken several steps to try to improve literacy. Two of the most prominent of these steps are educational television shows such as "Sesame Street" and the whole-language method.

In the *whole-language method,* children read interesting stories and write their own stories. The main idea is to make reading a meaningful experience. In this sense, it is consistent with Piaget's view that children need to construct their own categories and their own reality rather than being drilled on basics. Another important and related belief is that children do not have to be drilled on what each letter represents because children can use the context to guess the meaning of unfamiliar words. For example, the child reading, "No use crying over ___________ milk" could guess that the missing word was *spilled.*

Ironically some experts blame the whole-language method for our high illiteracy rate. They point out that a key assumption of the whole-language method—that children will correctly guess the meaning of unfamiliar words—is completely wrong. In fact, children are very poor (right less than 25 percent of the time) at guessing words from context (Perfetti & Roth, 1981). Furthermore, research finds that poor readers, not good readers, try to guess words from context (Perfetti & Roth, 1981; Stanovich, 1980). Consequently, many experts argue that we should go back to the old way of teaching reading—phonics.

Phonics involves learning to "sound out" words. Proponents of phonics point out that language revolves around sounds (Chall, 1967). The task of reading is to translate printed words into speech sounds. Phonics does this by teaching about the sounds associated with letters or letter combinations that make up words. Put another way, children have to be able to decode the phonemes before they can understand the morphemes.

With enough drill and practice, readers learn to decode phonemes quickly and automatically.

Continued

During this stage, children move from focusing on the individual meaning of each word to actually understanding fairly complex material. Attention is now well under the reader's control, and scanning rates improves steadily.

By the time most children reach high school, they are in stage 4. By this time, lower-level reading processes such as scanning and understanding basic phonological rules are established. Because most adolescents no longer have to spend energy sounding out words, they can direct their attention to sophisticated comprehension skills such as inference and the recognition of different viewpoints. For example, a student in a high school psychology class might read a chapter on personality theories and recognize that Freud had a more negative view of human nature than Maslow.

In college, some readers enter stage 5. Stage 5 reading incorporates the synthesis of new knowledge with one's own conceptual integration, critical judgment, and new thinking. For example, a student in a developmental psychology class might discover that there are several similarities between Freud's psychosexual theory and Piaget's cognitive structural theory, or critically evaluate a theory based on empirical evidence.

The ability to read is a skill many of us take for granted. However, despite much progress, *illiteracy,* or the inability to read or write, is still a major problem in the United States (see box 7.4).

Writing Because reading and writing both involve the written word, many of the same things that help us develop the ability to read also help us develop the ability to write. Thus, according to Maryanne Wolf and David Dickinson (1985), learning to write is not something that we learn in second grade. Instead, learning to write begins in infancy with our first baby book. We continue to learn as a result of parents, siblings, and caretakers, who read and tell stories, recite the alphabet, and unconsciously give us tools to

Box 7.4

RESEARCH in FOCUS

Concluded

Consequently, readers can focus their attention on the meaning of the passage or on weaknesses in the writer's arguments. Most studies suggest that the phonics approach is superior to the whole-language approach for learning how to read. However, whole-language advocates argue that there should be better, long-term studies of the developmental impact of reading programs. For example, they believe that the whole-language program might do better than phonics on measures that tap the total number of books a person reads in his lifetime and the extent to which a person's thinking is influenced by what he reads.

By now, you can understand why some experts object to the very popular whole-language method. However, you probably don't understand why some experts also object to the very popular "Sesame Street." After all, "Sesame Street" uses a phonics-type approach to introduce children to the sounds of the different letters. So what objections could people possibly have about "Sesame Street"?

One objection is that an important reading skill is attention span and "Sesame Street," like most television shows, does not help increase children's attention span. Second, reading involves identifying main ideas in a passage (Hall, 1989). "Sesame Street," with its short segments that deal with very few ideas at a time, does not challenge children to develop the ability to abstract the key ideas. Third, reading involves drawing inferences from what is read (Beck & McKeown, 1986; Bransford & Johnson, 1972). Since haphazard, chaotic, unpredictable, and nonsensical events are the norm on "Sesame Street" (these gimmicks capture children's attention), there is no opportunity for children to develop the ability to draw logical inferences. Fourth, a key aspect of reading is monitoring one's own performance (Brown, Armbruster, & Baker, 1986). That is, asking, "Did I understand that? Does this make sense?" Critics argue that a child who asked those questions while watching "Sesame Street" would be extremely confused.

You have seen that there is controversy about the whole-language method and that there is controversy about "Sesame Street." Is there anything that reading experts agree on? Yes. To promote a child's reading, most experts would agree that:

- Children should not be allowed to watch more than six hours of television a day.
- Parents should read aloud to their children.
- Children should see adults read.
- There should be at least 15 minutes a day of silent reading time.
- Surround children with books.
- Let children have their own books.

develop models of both reading and writing. Gradually, we learn that (1) words are written by people and that (2) books are full of words and tell stories (Sulzby, 1982).

These stories help us in at least two ways. First, they help us learn to use language in a more decontextualized manner—that is, to talk explicitly about events outside the immediate context (Heath, 1982; Scollon & Scollon, 1979). Second, these stories stimulate us to create our own make-believe tales (Rubin & Wolf, 1979).

Language Development During Adulthood

Psycholinguists used to assume that language development was complete by age 5 (McNeill, 1970). That is, they believed that once the critical period of the preschool years had passed, the only development that occurred was mere elaboration of what had already been established. For example, vocabulary would continue to grow.

Recently, however, this stability position has been challenged on two fronts. First, researchers have shown that people experience changes in all aspects of language throughout their lives (Kemper, 1992; Owens, 1984; Rice & Schiefelbush, 1989). Second, psychologists have pointed out that although people's use of grammar may not change dramatically, the way they use language to meet their goals may change considerably. Put another way, once the preschool years are past, the goal of developmental psycholinguists is "not so much a better understanding of how language is structured, but a better understanding of how language is used, not so much what language is, as what language is for" (Hymes, 1972).

In the next few sections, we will see what progress has been made in illuminating the changes that occur in how we use language as we progress from childhood to old age. Unfortunately, that progress has been limited because, until recently, most research in this area was confined to

Box 7.5

SELF-CHECK

Indicate whether each of the following statements is true or false.

1. At age 18 months, most children can understand only about 50 words.
2. By age 8, children are able to make inferences and understand hidden meanings of sentences.
3. Children under age 5 have very little metalinguistic skill.
4. Children become consciously aware of a grammatical rule and they articulate it; then they start to use that rule.

Answer the following question.

5. What are the main events that lead to improved reading comprehension?

Please turn to the end of this chapter to check your answers.

Figure 7.3

Parts of the Brain Associated with Language-Related Activities

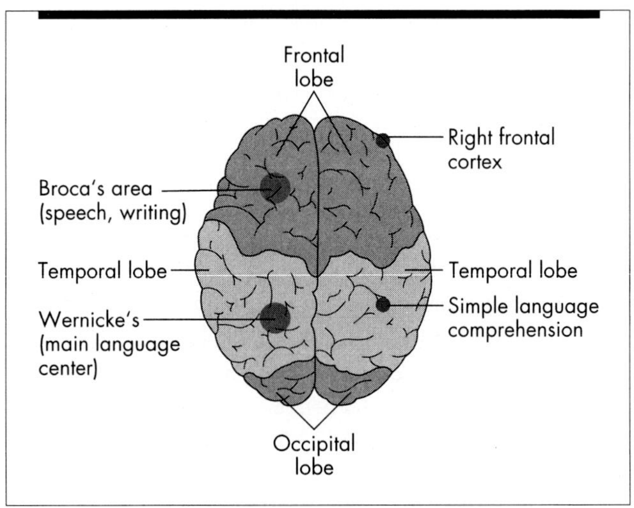

studies of individuals who had experienced brain damage. Fortunately, the future looks more promising because preliminary research has begun in at least five areas of language development during adulthood: brain lateralization, lexicon, discourse, comprehension, and metalinguistic skills (Obler and Albert, 1985).

Brain Lateralization

In 1975, Brown and Jaffee observed that the effect of a certain brain lesion was *not* the same for all victims. Instead, some people suffering damage to the "language centers" on the left side of the brain experienced little permanent damage, whereas others suffered severe and permanent loss of language. One important factor determining the effect of the wound was the person's age. Generally, the older the person was, the more likely language ability would be permanently impaired.

Why were older people's language abilities more debilitated by damage to part of the left brain? Brown and Jaffee offered two possible explanations: (1) language organization within the left hemisphere changes across the lifespan, or (2) the relative degree of left-hemisphere responsibility for language increases across the lifespan.

There is no direct evidence for the idea that language organization *within* the left hemisphere changes across the lifespan. Nevertheless, there is some indirect evidence. Perhaps the most important evidence comes from research on **aphasia,** a language disorder involving damage to the language centers of the brain.

To help you understand the significance of the aphasia evidence, we will briefly define and differentiate between the two major types of aphasia: Wernicke's and Broca's. The two types are associated with damage to different parts of the brain (see figure 7.3) and have distinctly different characteristics. **Broca's aphasia** is characterized by a break in neural transmission between the frontal lobes and the vocal musculature. Broca aphasics know what they want to say (that is, they've retained their semantic abilities) but, when they try to speak, their words come out in the wrong order. That is, their syntax is severely impaired. People with **Wernicke's-type aphasia,** on the other hand, do not understand speech. Thus, although Wernicke's-type aphasia victims may be able to speak fluently, and at times grammatically, they don't understand the words they produce. In short, whereas Broca's aphasics have trouble *producing* language, Wernicke-type aphasics have trouble *understanding* language.

The reason it is important to realize that the two types of aphasia are caused by damage to different parts of the brain is that these two kinds of aphasia are prominent at different ages. Specifically, aphasia linked to Wernicke's area—fluent aphasia of the Wernicke's-type—is more prominent in adults over 60, whereas nonfluent Broca's-type aphasia is more prevalent in people in their fifties.

Why do these problems occur at different ages? Many psycholinguists (for example, Cornell, Fromkin, & Mauner, 1993; Obler et al., 1978) argue that this correlation may indicate changes in brain organization as one gets older. Perhaps the same brain damage that causes Broca's aphasia at a young age may—because of changes in the brain's organization—cause Wernicke's aphasia at an older age.

Further support for the hypothesis that language organization within the left hemisphere changes across the lifespan comes from the work of Harry Whitaker (1980). He proposed that language becomes more automatizes (automatic) with increased use, and that automatization is caused by changes in how the left hemisphere works. In a cross-sectional study of 30-, 50-, 60-, and 70-year-olds, Obler and Albert (1985) found support for Whitaker's notion that language becomes more automatized with age. Specifically, Obler and Albert (1985) found that despite the fact that people generally do things more slowly as they get older, older people do not need more time than younger people to recite number sequences. From this finding, they conclude that (1) language becomes more automatized with age and that (2) this automatization must be linked to brain functions. Admittedly, Obler and Albert (1985) are making some risky inferences. Indeed, even they concede that their hypothesis hasn't been directly tested. However, with recent advances in the technology of observing changes in brain functioning, their hypothesis may soon be tested.

But what of Brown and Jaffee's other hypothesis—that the relative degree of left-hemisphere responsibility increases across the lifespan? In contrast to being unable to find any direct evidence to support—or refute—Brown and Jaffee's first hypothesis, there is the opposite problem with their second hypothesis. That is, there are findings that support—and findings that refute—the hypothesis that the left hemisphere becomes more responsible for language as we get older. Given the conflicting research findings, Obler and Albert (1985) tentatively conclude that the degree of lateralization does not change with age.

Lexicon

Lexicon refers to the individual dictionary that each of us uses. It contains all the words we use and the underlying definitions of each. Our lexicon is always changing. Some words are added, some words are deleted, and some definitions are revised. For example, your definition of "school" has changed dramatically from when you were a preschooler.

As we mentioned earlier, it had traditionally been assumed that lexicon was the only skill that changed after basic grammar had been established (Owens, 1984). Consequently, psycholinguists have researched lexical skills in adults more than any other language ability.

Some of their research verifies commonsense notions. For example, as people get older, they forget the names of things more often (see, for example, Borod, Goodglass, & Kaplan, 1980; Burke, MacKay, Worthley, & Wade, 1991; Kaplan, Goodglass, & Weintraub, 1976). Furthermore, in a cross-sectional study of 30- and 70-year-olds, Loraine Obler and her colleagues found that 70-year-olds were less able to accurately name objects and actions by the correct nouns and verbs (Nicholas, Obler, Albert, & Goodglass, 1985; Obler, Albert, & Goodglass, 1981).

Language abilities change as we age. This may be because we rely more on our left brain hemisphere for language. Other reasons for changes in language ability may include fewer opportunities to use language skills and declines in hearing.

In terms of the ability to give accurate definitions of words, Obler found there were no significant differences between young adult subjects (on the average, 18.4 years) and older adult subjects (average age 70.6 years). However, the elderly may use language less efficiently. The tendency to give multiword definitions of words increases between the ages of 30 and 40, levels off until age 70, and then accelerates after the age of 70. In addition, older people take longer to start to pronounce their answers, and their answers take more time to complete (Balota & Duchek, 1988). As box 7.6 shows, this slowing down can have negative consequences for how others view the elderly.

Why are people over 70 slower to come up with definitions and more likely to come up with multiword definitions? One possibility is that this inefficiency in using language is simply a reflection of a less efficient memory system (Kemper, 1992). To understand how memory might "slow down," realize that when a piece of information is stored in memory, that piece of information is not isolated. Instead, pathways are formed between that information and similar pieces of information. These connections are called association pathways because they form connections (associations) between related concepts. When a specific concept is activated in one's memory, this activation is spread along the associative pathways to related concepts in that memory. Thus, this **spreading activation** gives the person access to memory areas related to the concept that was initially remembered. For example, reading about people over 70 years old may trigger memories about one's grandparents.

If age differences in spreading activation could be demonstrated, it could explain why older adults give more elaborate definitions, take longer to start pronouncing their answers, and take longer to complete their answers. However, the research on age differences in spreading activation

Box 7.6

ISSUE in FOCUS

Elderspeak

People commonly regard the elderly as less competent than younger adults. These negative expectations are reflected in stereotypes that the elderly are less competent communicators (Kemper, 1992). These stereotypes result in what Ryan, Giles, and Henwood (1986) call the *communication predicament of aging*. Specifically, the negative expectations held by others and the elderly themselves create a

> vicious cycle in which the changes of aging (e.g., physical appearance, voice quality, hearing difficulties, slowness of movement, loss of role) elicit interpretations from others of diminished competence; and these inferences then lead to constraining conditions in which the older person has less opportunity to communicate effectively . . . diminished self-esteem and withdrawal from social interactions . . . [and further] physiological, psychological, and social declines (pp. 16–17).

One manifestation of the communication predicament of aging is that other people tend to speak to the elderly in a type of babytalk called *elderspeak* (Snow & Ferguson, 1977). For example, Caporael and her colleagues (Caporael, 1981; Caporael & Culbertson, 1986; Caporael, Lucaszewski, & Culbertson, 1983) studied the attitudes of people who care for institutionalized elderly adults. They found that these caregivers believe that older adults wish to be addressed in a simplified register with exaggerated pitch and intonation. Caregivers assume that elderspeak will improve the attention and comprehension of elderly adults. However, elderly adults often regard elderspeak as demeaning and disrespectful (Coupland & Coupland, 1990).

does not overwhelmingly support the hypothesis that spreading activation is slower with adults. On the one hand, some researchers report significant age differences in the spreading activation patterns of adults (see Bowles & Poon, 1985; Howard, Shaw, & Heisey, 1986; Petros, Zehr, & Chabot, 1983). On the other hand, several other studies fail to uncover such age differences (see Balota & Duchek, 1988; Burke, White, & Diaz, 1987; Cerella & Fozard, 1984). The studies that fail to find age differences in spreading activation tend to agree with Balota & Duchek (1988), who concluded that although the input and output processes are slowed with age, "the basic retrieval mechanism of spreading activation is spared by age."

More research is needed to explain why short-term memory becomes less efficient with age and how this is linked to changes in language. Although we don't fully understand the mechanisms for memory changes, we do know that slower long-term and short-term memory retrieval, failure to use memory strategies, and poorer attention correspond to a decrease in language complexity for the elderly. This decrease in language complexity can be seen in research on discourse and comprehension.

Discourse

Discourse is the ability to communicate thoughts verbally. When asked to tell a story or write a description of a picture, adults will vary on the elaborateness of their description. Cross-sectional data of 30- to 80-year-olds reveals a U-shaped curve (Obler, 1980; Obler & Albert, 1985).[2] Specifically, both the younger and older groups used more elaborate speech, whereas the 50-year-olds' speech tended to be brief. When asked to write, the 50-year-olds often produced incomplete sentences, such as "woman washing dishes." The more elaborate speech of the younger and older groups was characterized by more repetition, redundancy, metalinguistic comments (for example, "Now, what was I saying?"), and personalizations.

Although older adults and younger adults both use elaborate speech, the speech of older adults is less complex and fluent than that of younger adults. For example, Walker et al. (Walker, Hardiman, Hedrick, & Holbrook, 1981; Walker, Roberts, & Hedrick, 1988) compared speech samples of college-aged adults with adults ages 60 to 91. The older adults used shorter sentences with fewer clauses, made more revisions as they spoke, and used interjections more often.

Comprehension of Spoken Language

A major problem in assessing comprehension of spoken language is that hearing tends to decrease with age. Therefore, whenever reading the results of a study on the relationship of aging to comprehension of spoken language,

[2]This U-shaped pattern is sometimes used as evidence for the *regression hypothesis*, which claims that language deterioration is the reverse of language acquisition (Kemper, 1992).

consider the possibility that the results may really reflect a hearing—rather than a comprehension—problem.

To determine the degree to which differences on a speech comprehension test may really reflect differences in hearing ability, some researchers give the tests under two conditions: noisy conditions and quiet conditions. If older subjects do as well as younger subjects in the quiet conditions but much worse in the noisy conditions, then researchers know that the differences reflect differences in hearing ability rather than differences in comprehension (Obler & Albert, 1985).

Using this strategy, Nickerson, Green, Stevens, and Kalikow (1975) studied 19 young subjects (ages 15 to 21) and 22 old subjects (ages 60 to 87) with good hearing on a speech-perception-in-noise task. Specifically, the researchers had subjects write down the last words of each sentence they heard. Half of the sentences had last words that were highly predictable (for example, a rose bush has prickly *thorns*). The other half had last words that were difficult to predict (for example, the boy can't talk about the *thorns)*. Surprisingly, younger and older subjects were *equal* in their reliance on context. In other words, both younger and older subjects were better able to remember the last word when it was highly predictable (a rose with prickly thorns) than when the word was not highly predictable (the boy can't talk about thorns).

Despite this similarity between younger and older adults, one series of studies suggests that older adults don't comprehend verbal information the same way that younger people do (Obusek & Warren, 1973; Warren, 1961; Warren & Warren, 1966). These studies examine a fascinating illusion called the verbal-transformation effect. The verbal-transformation effect is produced by having people listen to a short tape recording of a single syllable being repeated over and over. For example, we might have people listen to the syllable *tress* being played over and over. Amazingly, people do not simply hear the syllable over and over. Instead, they transform that single syllable into several words.

Obusek and Warren report age-related changes in both the frequency and quality of the transformations reported. The oldest adults reported the fewest transformations. In other words, they made fewer mistakes in hearing the syllable. In addition, older adults report real words (for example, *stress*) whereas younger adults also report nonwords that conform to English word constraints (for example, *estre*). Children report nonwords that could not exist in English (for example, *sress*).

Obler and Albert (1985) point out how nicely these findings illustrate the various ways we may label the performance of the elderly: "Are we to call the elderly rigid or realistic? Working from common sense or working with limited imagination or creativity?" (p. 468).

Metalinguistic Skills

Metalinguistic skills continue to change during adulthood. Common tests of metalinguistic knowledge are (1) asking subjects to generate a list of items, (2) measuring how quickly and accurately a person can do the Stroop task, (3) generating morphological antonyms, (for example, "What is the opposite of *conscious?*"), and (4) reciting the months of the year backwards.

List Generation List generation is measured by counting the number of correct items given in a specified period of time, usually 60 seconds. Two forms of this task are widely used. In the first, people are asked to list anything they can think of that belongs to a broad semantic category. For example, they might be asked to "Name as many animals as you can." In the second type of task, people are asked to list by phonological/orthographic properties. That is, they might be asked to "Name as many words as you can think of that begin with the letter *r*. To solve both types of tasks, the participant must recognize the similarities among words.

It has been reported that the elderly are slightly but consistently slower than younger adults on both types of list-generation tasks (Lezak, 1976). However, because the elderly are more often affected by time constraints, it could be argued that elderly subjects would generate just as many words as younger subjects if given more time. For this reason, Obler & Albert (1985) measured the number of words generated over two periods of time—60 and 90 seconds. Contrary to Lezak's research, in the task of listing as many words as possible that had a certain first letter, no age-related reductions in ability were found for either time period. However, on the animal listing task, there were significant age-related reductions for both time periods. These findings suggest that time constraints do not account for age-related declines in list generation. Instead, the findings suggest that age-related declines in spreading activation between related concepts may hamper the elderly's ability to retrieve words belonging to the same conceptual category.

The Stroop Task Obler and Albert also report age declines on the Stroop task. The **Stroop Task** (Stroop, 1935) requires people to read words as quickly as possible. The words are blue, black, red, green, and brown. The task is challenging because the ink colors are different from the color described by the word. For example, you might see the word *green* written in yellow ink (see figure 7.4). In a study comparing 30-, 50-, 60-, and 70-year-olds, it was found that subjects got faster and more accurate until about age 60, when subjects became slower to respond and made more errors (MacLeod, 1992). These results suggest that above age 60, words (learned organizations of letters) become less powerful perceptual units relative to color (unlearned perceptual units).

Morphological Antonyms and Backward Recitation of Months Morphological antonym tasks (for example, "What is the opposite of *visible?*") require people to understand the relationship between words. In contrast, reciting the months of the year backwards requires subjects to

Figure 7.4

An Example of the Stroop Task

Figure 7.5

Metalinguistic Performance on Morphological Antonyms Test

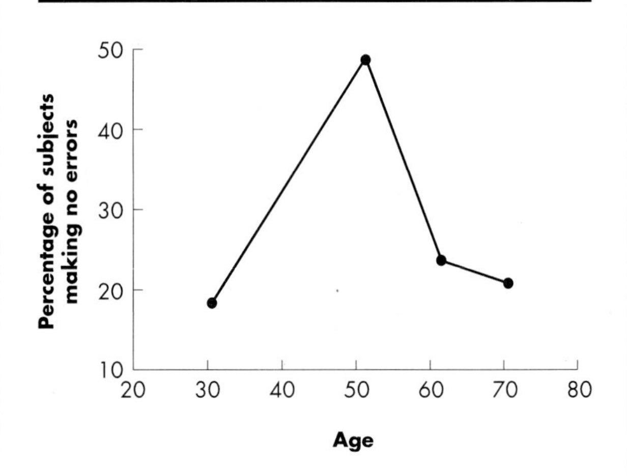

organize and reorganize words. On both types of tasks, Obler and Albert (1985) found an inverted U-curve for males (see figure 7.5). Specifically, on the morphological antonyms task, the 50-year-olds scored highest and the 30- and 70-year-olds both scored poorly. For reciting months of the year backwards, the 30- and 70-year-olds again took the longest to respond. However, instead of the 50-year-olds, it was the 60-year-olds who performed best. What all this means is uncertain.

Conclusions About Age-Related Changes in Language Use

As was the case with the morphological antonyms task, several studies reported in this section clearly indicate that age differences occur on a variety of language tasks. Also, as was the case with the morphological antonyms task, the significance of these differences is much less certain. However, the challenge for future research is quite clear.

First, unlike current research, future research cannot afford to rely on tasks (such as the Stroop task and the verbal transformation effect) that are fascinating in their own right, but not well connected to language ability. Instead, future research will have to concentrate more on tasks that tap metalinguistic skills and linguistic abilities.

Second, unlike current research, future research cannot afford to rely so heavily on cross-sectional studies. Because current findings are based almost exclusively on cross-sectional studies, the age differences could reflect a cohort effect rather than a true age effect. For example, the age differences may simply reflect differences in how the different generations were educated. Therefore, future research must include longitudinal and sequential designs that will supplement the existing cross-sectional studies.

Third, future research must go beyond speculating about age-related changes in the brain. Instead, future research must use sophisticated, brain-imaging techniques to determine whether these age-related differences are due to actual physical changes in an aging brain.

In short, we know little about language development across the lifespan. Researchers are just starting to investigate this area. However, with the help of energetic and creative researchers (one of whom might be you), we will soon know much more.

Theories of Language Acquisition

We have discussed how individuals' use of language changes as they get older. Now we will turn our attention to *why* these changes occur. In the 1950s, people used to debate whether language was learned by imitation and reinforcement (Skinner, 1957) or whether language learning was an inborn ability (Chomsky, 1959). Today, almost everyone agrees that both nurture and nature play important roles in language acquisition. What people now argue about is whether nature or nurture is more important. Therefore, let's turn to the research to learn about the merits of the learning and biological models for language acquisition.

Learning Theory

Behaviorists, such as B. F. Skinner (1957), support the **learning theory** of language acquisition, the belief that language, like any other behavior, is learned through association, imitation, and reinforcement. Thus, a Skinnerian would say that toddlers learn to *associate* the objects, people, and events in their life with words. They accomplish this by *imitating* the words and syntax of other people. When they master a new word or phrase, they are *reinforced* by others with smiles, hugs, and praise. In addition, when they make an error in word usage, they are corrected.

The behaviorists' position seems a reasonable explanation for much of language acquisition—until we observe children learning to speak. One of the first things observers notice is that children use words in ways they have never heard before. Therefore, the acquisition of syntax must involve more than mere imitation. Parents are constantly

Box 7.7

SELF-CHECK

Indicate whether each of the following statements is true or false.

1. Language development (other than vocabulary) is complete by age 12.
2. With age, the brain becomes more specialized so that the left hemisphere (as opposed to the right hemisphere) becomes even more involved in processing language.
3. Eighty-year-olds give less elaborate descriptions of a picture than other groups, and their descriptions will more often include incomplete sentences.
4. Older adults show a more sophisticated response to the verbal-transformation effect than younger adults do.
5. The poorer performance of older adults on speech comprehension tasks may sometimes be due to problems with the elderly's hearing.
6. Because list-generation tasks are timed, the elderly's poorer performance on these tasks may simply reflect the fact that the elderly are generally slower and react poorly to timed tests.
7. Research based on the Stroop task suggests that, words (being extremely well-learned organizations of letters) are more powerful perceptual units for the elderly than they are for younger adults.
8. We now have a fairly good understanding of language development through the lifespan, thanks to the use of (1) tasks that tap key linguistic and metalinguistic abilities, (2) longitudinal research designs, and (3) studies that use brain-imaging techniques to specifically pinpoint the exact nature of the changes in the brain that accompany aging.

Answer the following questions.

9. What evidence suggests that language organization within the brain changes with age?
10. How do older adults' abilities to define words differ from those of younger adults?

Please turn to the end of this chapter to check your answers.

amazed at the new word combinations their children create. For example, in a recent class assignment, one of our students reported the following conversation with a 3 1/2-year-old girl:

> **STUDENT:**
> *"That's a very pretty hat you have on. I really like the colors."*
> **GIRL:**
> *"They're more betterful than my other hats."*

Simple imitation cannot account for this creativity. Furthermore, research suggests that although children may learn individual words through imitation, children do *not* learn syntax through imitation.

Another problem with the learning theory explanation of language learning is that parents do not always reinforce children for grammatically correct utterances. For example, little Mary is not likely to be rewarded for the grammatically correct, but socially unacceptable phrase, "Mommy, I drew on the living room walls with my crayons." However, when she says "Mommy, me wuvs you," she is likely to be hugged for this socially acceptable—but grammatically incorrect—phrase.

As this example suggests, parents are more likely to correct the child for factual errors (for example, "Mommy is a boy") than for grammatical errors (deVilliers & deVilliers, 1980). Admittedly, about a third of the time, adults do respond to children's grammatical errors (Bohannon & Stanowicz, 1988). However, that means that about two thirds of the time adults ignore children's grammatical errors.

Why don't parents correct grammar more frequently? One reason is that many parents do not know when the child has made a mistake. After all, no one knows all the rules of grammar. However, the most important reason may be that correction is futile. Children simply do not seem to learn from being corrected.

If children don't learn from correction, what do children learn by verbally interacting with their parents? The evidence is correlational, but suggestive. For example, Alison Clarke-Stewart (1973) showed that children whose mothers talked to them a great deal had larger vocabularies at the age of 17 months than children whose mothers were less talkative. More convincingly, other investigators have found that parents who frequently encourage conversations by asking questions, making requests, and issuing commands that invite verbal responses have children who (compared with children from similar backgrounds whose parents are less communicative) (1) produce longer utterances during the preschool years; (2) recognize more letters and numbers by age 6; and (3) score higher on tests of reading

Children whose parents talk to them frequently seem to gain language proficiency more quickly than those whose parents are quieter. Is this proof that environment, or nurture, has a stronger effect on language development than genetics, or nature?

proficiency in the second grade (Harris, Jones, Brookes, & Grant, 1986; Norman-Jackson, 1982; Price, Hess, & Dickson, 1981). Furthermore, other studies have found that the more a mother uses complex sentences when talking to her child, the earlier and more rapidly her child will learn to speak in complex sentences (Clarke-Stewart & Hevery, 1981; Gleitman, Newport, & Gleitman, 1984).

Although the results of these studies make a persuasive case that parents' speech affects children's speech, that case is not watertight. That is, there are other explanations for these findings. For example, perhaps bright children elicit more sophisticated comments from their parents than do less gifted children. Or, perhaps verbal parents tend to pass these verbal genes to their children. However, from reviewing experimental studies of children undergoing speech therapy, we can point to at least one conclusively proven, positive effect of parental interaction: Children undergoing speech therapy show greater gains when their parents are taught how to interact verbally with their children (McDade & Varnedoe, 1987).

How People Talk to Young Children

Whereas experts suspect that adults influence children's speech, it is common knowledge that children influence adults' speech. For example, if you've ever talked to a baby, you may have found yourself using "baby talk." That is, rather than use the complex, long sentences you speak when conversing with other adults, you have used what developmental psychologists call **motherese.**

Researchers have intensely studied motherese. For example, Gelman and Shatz (1977) found that both adults and older siblings speak to young children slowly, in high-pitched voices, and with an emphasis on key words. Motherese usually takes the form of questions ("More milk?"), commands ("Sit down"), or simple statements that are repeated over and over in an attempt to attract the child's attention ("Daddy loves his little girl").

Adults change the level of their motherese to fit the child. For instance, one study recorded the voices of 20 adult strangers as they talked with a 2-year-old boy. Whenever the boy indicated he didn't understand a statement made by an adult, the adult made the next sentence shorter and simpler (Bohannon & Marquis, 1977). Furthermore, additional studies reveal that as a child's language becomes more complex, mothers usually increase the complexity and length of their sentences (Newport, Gleitman, & Gleitman, 1977; Philips, 1973). Finally, we should note that motherese never completely goes down to the child's level: Whenever adults speak to children, the adult's language is still slightly more complex than the child's.

In conclusion, children and parents influence each other's speech. The effects of children on parents' speech are obvious and can be easily explained in terms of imitation, reinforcement, and correction. The effects of parents on children's speech are not as obvious and *cannot* be as easily explained in these terms. Admittedly, imitation, reinforcement, and correction may account for the acquisition of individual words and phrases and may play a role in helping children develop the ability to properly use grammar. However, imitation, reinforcement, and correction cannot completely account for children's acquisition of the rules of grammar.

The Biological Model

Nativists are thoroughly convinced that learning theory cannot come close to explaining how children learn language. To support this position, they argue that children do not have (1) the *opportunity* to learn from corrections or (2) the *ability* to learn from corrections.

According to nativists, children do not have the opportunity to learn from corrections because (a) parents usually let grammatical errors slide; (b) even when parents tell a child that a statement is incorrect, the parents rarely actually model the correct way of making the statement; and (c) parents rarely tell the child what underlying rule was violated.

According to nativists, children do not seem to be able to learn from corrections. That is, even when a parent models the right form, the child often will be unable to repeat what the parent said. Indeed, when asked to repeat the parent's corrected version ("Don't say 'I goed home,' say

'I went home,' okay?"), the child may say "I goed home. That's what I said." Yet, despite the lack of true correction and the ineffectiveness of correction, children somehow discover the complex system of rules that underlies language.

According to supporters of the **biological model,** such as Noam Chomsky (1959, 1968, 1980) and David McNeill (1970), children are able to master these rules because they are genetically programmed to do so. That is, rather than being predisposed to imitate specific phrases, children are predisposed to learn the underlying structure of the language. By figuring out the structure of their language, children gain the ability to combine words in an infinite number of ways.

Nativists such as Chomsky and McNeil are called **structuralists**[3] because they believe that children learn the structure of language. That is, Chomsky and McNeil believe children are born to learn the underlying structural *rules* that govern language. Specifically, children are born to learn two types of rules that every language follows—substantive universals and formal universals.

Substantive universals are rules that relate to a specific element, such as rules related to the use of nouns or verbs. For example, the rules governing the use of the verb *to be* (such as in I *am,* you *are,* she *is*) represent the application of a substantive universal. In comparison, **formal universals** are general rules that relate to linguistic forms (for example, active sentences such as "Feed the cat").

According to Chomsky and his followers, the reason language development is similar even among people who speak different languages is that we all inherit the ability to discover substantive and formal universals. That is, because language acquisition is governed by innate forces, Japanese and Nigerian children acquire language in the same way. To further support the idea that language development is tied to biological development, Lenneberg (1967) points out that language acquisition in children is consistently correlated with motor development. Finally, numerous experts have pointed out an even more persuasive bit of evidence that ties language development to biological development: Our ability to learn language correlates with the myelination of neurons in the brain's speech centers.

Language Acquisition Device

We have presented evidence suggesting that biology plays a strong role in language development. But how powerful is the effect of nature? In the seventh century B.C., an Egyptian Pharaoh named Psammetichus I, performed a study based on the assumption that biology was extremely important to language learning. The pharaoh believed that language was innate, and that in time, each of us would develop language as we matured. However, the pharaoh reasoned that the innate language we are all born with is altered because of our early interaction with other people and their language. In an attempt to discover what the innate language was, Psammetichus isolated two infants at birth from all but the most minimal human contact to see which language would naturally emerge. Would it be Egyptian (Psammetichus's personal favorite), Greek, Hebrew, or Sanskrit? Unfortunately, these infants died from lack of social contact well before they uttered their first word.

Unlike the Pharaoh, Chomsky and other structuralists do not argue that we are born with the knowledge of a certain language. Instead, they believe we are born to learn the structural rules that underlie whatever language we are exposed to. Noam Chomsky attributes this natural ability to acquire language to a structure in the brain that he calls the **language acquisition device (LAD).**

Evidence of Language Functions in the Brain

Although no one has uncovered the actual brain structure corresponding to LAD, Chomsky's general premise that the brain is prewired for language acquisition has some support. For example, we know that certain areas of the brain, such as Broca's area and Wernicke's area, specialize in language development and production. We also know that, unlike most of the parts of the brain, the region called Wernicke's area (see figure 7.3) is not the same size on the left side of the brain as it is on the right side. Instead, it is larger on the left (language) side of the brain. Furthermore, we know this difference is innate because even fetuses show this difference (Damasio & Geschwind, 1984).

Additional evidence supporting Chomsky's biological model is found in studies that demonstrate a critical period for optimal language learning. Miller (1981) concludes that this critical period encompasses the years between birth and age 6. The case of Genie (see chapter 3), the girl who spent her childhood shackled in a small bedroom and who could develop only very primitive language abilities, certainly supports this view. Further evidence of biological influence is the fact that all languages share similar characteristics despite vast cultural differences in the learning environment. Specifically, Lenneberg (1967) notes that all languages have these characteristics:

1. Structured in accordance with principles of human cognition,
2. Constrained by rules of phonology, grammar, and semantics,

[3]Despite having the same name, these linguistic structuralists have nothing to do with the early psychologists who followed Wilhelm Wundt.

Box 7.8

SELF-CHECK

Indicate whether each of the following statements is true or false.

1. The behavioristic approach proposes that language, like other behaviors, is acquired through imitation and reinforcement.
2. The behavioristic approach explains language development better than any other approach.
3. Parents fail to correct grammatical mistakes about two-thirds of the time.
4. There is conclusive evidence that parents who talk more to their child and ask more questions of their child cause their child to have well-developed verbal abilities.
5. Motherese can be explained in terms of behavioristic principles.
6. The typical child has the ability and the opportunity to learn from adults who point out errors the child is making in his or her speech.
7. The location of the LAD has been identified.

Answer the following questions.

8. What prevents parents from correcting all of their child's grammatical mistakes?
9. Why is Chomsky considered a structuralist?
10. As opposed to the behaviorists, Chomsky believes that nature plays a vital role in language development. What evidence is there that supports a nature position?

Please turn to the end of the chapter to check your answers.

3. Governed by social rules that govern the use of language, and
4. Capable of being learned by any normal human.

Indeed, even deaf children, deprived of the opportunity for imitation and verbal reinforcement, develop a form of gestural language (Feldman, Goldin-Meadow, & Gleitman, 1978).

Language Development and Cognitive Development

Historically, the issue of whether nature or nurture plays a greater role in language development has been fiercely debated. In more recent years, however, one of the most hotly debated topics among developmental psycholinguists is the relationship between the development of language and the development of thinking. The controversy boils down to this question: Do we develop language independently of other cognitive abilities, or is there a significant relationship between the development of language and thought? As you might imagine, there are people on all sides of this controversy. Specifically, there are strong supporters of each of the following three positions:

1. There is no connection between language development and cognitive development.
2. Cognitive development leads to language development.
3. Language development leads to cognitive development.

The Non-Interactionist Position

Chomsky has argued that language is basically independent of thought (Piatelli-Palmarini, 1980). He believes that we are born with a language acquisition device. Because of LAD, all we need is maturation and minimal exposure to speech for language to unfold. As some parents have said, "Just because they can talk, you expect they can think—and that's not the case." However, other scholars give more importance to interaction of language and cognitive abilities.

Piagetians: Cognition Causes Language

Perhaps the most notable of these scholars are the Piagetians. Piaget (1967) and his followers (Bates, 1976; Cromer, 1974; Furth, 1966; MacNamara, 1972, 1987) believe that we develop the ability to use language as a result of being able to verbally express our nonlinguistic knowledge. That is, our language development is a reflection of our cognitive development (Kemper, 1992). Put another way, language development is an effect—not a cause—of cognitive development.

To explain how language grows out of our non-language abilities, Piagetians point to evidence that linguistic abilities "map onto" previously established cognitive categories. For example, a child will first gain the nonlinguistic concepts of "action" and "concrete object." Later, the child will acquire the parallel linguistic concepts of "verb" and "noun."

In a sense, the Piagetians hold two positions. First, like Chomsky, they argue that language development does not lead to cognitive development. Second, unlike Chomsky, they argue that cognitive development determines language acquisition.

Box 7.9

THEORY in FOCUS

Using Cognitive Principles to Accelerate Language Development

Can we use cognitive learning principles to accelerate language development? William Fowler and Amy Swenson (1979) have conducted a series of important experiments on this very question. Their approach assumes that language acquisition is a product of cognitive learning rather than a result of biological maturation or simple operant conditioning. Children are taught by parents to learn a series of abstract language rules in a standard sequence. Numerous teaching techniques are used, including having parents model specific words, engage in language play with their infants, and look at books together. Fowler and Swenson found rapid gains in the speed of language acquisition in the training group compared with a control group. Even more impressive is their finding that the training works for parents of various educational and linguistic backgrounds (for example, English, Italian, Chinese).

Sinclair-de-Zwart (1969) tested Piaget's hypothesis that language development does not promote cognitive growth by teaching 4-, 5-, and 6-year-olds the correct meaning of the words *more* and *less*. Next, she tested whether this new linguistic ability would increase the children's performance on a cognitive task requiring a conceptual understanding of quantity. She found that her "language therapy" had little effect. Her findings suggest that language development does not facilitate thought.

Additional evidence for Piaget's position that language development does not promote cognitive development was found in studies of deaf children. For example, Furth (1966) studied the cognitive development of deaf children who did not have language. He found that their cognitive development paralleled that of hearing children. Furth interpreted his finding as meaning that cognitive growth occurs independently of language.

It is not enough for Piagetians to show that language development does *not* lead to cognitive development. They must also show that the opposite idea *is* true—that cognitive development promotes language development (Langer, 1981; Sinclair 1971). To this end, MacNamara (1972) argues that infants first develop concepts. They then try to understand the meaning of words spoken to them through their association with these concepts. "The infant uses meaning as a clue to language, rather than language as a clue to meaning" (p. 1). The findings that young children overextend and underextend words supports the conclusion that it is children's own concepts—not what words they have had an opportunity to learn—that determine whether they use a wide or narrow range of words to describe an object. Because Piagetians believe that cognitive development influences language development, some cognitive theorists have actually tried to use cognitive principles to accelerate language development (see box 7.9).

Critics of the "cognitive development causes language development approach" say that such cognitive theories oversimplify the complex relationship between language and thought. For example, critics point out that—contrary to the cognitive view—there is not a perfect correspondence between linguistic and nonlinguistic forms of knowledge. Therefore, cognitive theorists are wrong when they try to explain all linguistic concepts by saying that those linguistic concepts map directly onto nonlinguistic ones. To illustrate that linguistic concepts do not always map onto nonlinguistic ones, Maratos and Chalkley (1980) attack the notion that the use of verbs—a linguistic concept—directly maps onto actions—a nonlinguistic concept. They start by pointing out that many verbs, such as *know* and *love,* do not refer to physical actions. Then, they point out that, like some verbs, certain adjectives, such as *reckless,* refer to how people act. Finally, Maratos and Chalkley (1980) point out that, in a nonlinguistic sense, it would seem that *reckless* is more like the physical actions described by verbs such as *run* or *jump* than it is like the passive, unchanging state described by adjectives such as *red* or *big*. Thus, Maratos and Chalkley (1980) make a convincing case that the mastery of a concept such as a "verb" or "adjective" cannot be accounted for merely by stating that it grows out of—and maps directly onto—a nonlinguistic category, such as from a concept that we might label "physical actions."

Another attack on the cognitive viewpoint comes from researchers who study how children apply specific linguistic rules. As you know, children learn certain linguistic rules about grammatical acceptability. They quickly learn that "Put the hat on," "put it on," and "put on the hat" are grammatically acceptable, but "put on it" is not (Rice, 1982). Although the cognitive theory can explain how a child learns the meaning of these

Figure 7.6

Vygotsky's Schema for the Development of Language and Thought

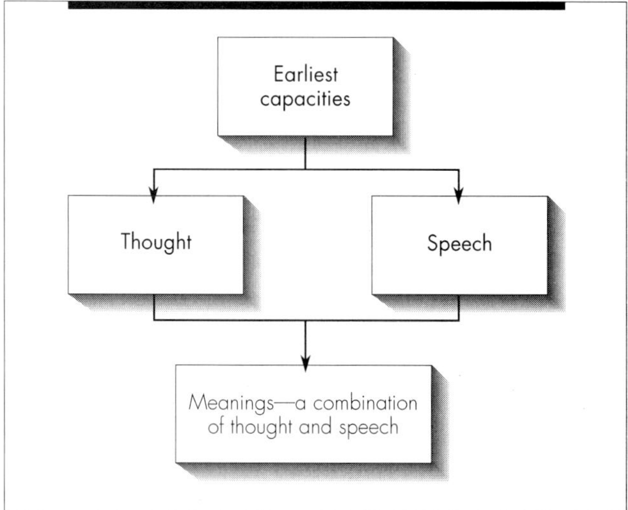

sentences, it cannot explain how children learn the formal linguistic rule that tells them which sentences are grammatically correct (Cromer, 1981). That is, a child cannot map language onto nonlinguistic, physical, real-world concepts that parallel the intricate and complex rules of grammar.

Language Stimulates Cognition

In response to these criticisms, many have backed off the strong cognitive hypothesis that cognition causes language development. A few have even reversed their position. That is, instead of contending that cognitive development leads to language development, they agree with the position advocated by Lev Vygotsky and Benjamin Whorf: That certain linguistic advances may promote cognitive development (Kemper, 1992).

Lev Vygotsky

Russian psychologist Lev Vygotsky (1934/1986) believed that language provides a more powerful medium for representing abstract experience than imagery and mental operations. He pointed out that language develops more quickly than mental operations. For example, a 3-year-old who is already forming complex sentences with abstract clauses is only starting to think about the nonlinguistic, physical world in preoperational terms. Furthermore, language, at least early in development, is more flexible than thought. This 3-year-old's language shows great flexibility and creativity, whereas her cognitive operations are limited and inflexible.

Vygotsky holds that language and cognition initially develop along separate pathways. However, later speech and thought are united, resulting in more complex forms of speech and thought (see figure 7.6).

The beginnings of this unification of thought and speech are illustrated by **inner speech,** in which a child uses language as an aid in reasoning. Inner speech differs from external (social) speech because it is internalized, highly abbreviated, and consists mostly of predicates, rather than subjects. Thus, whereas a child might say to others, "I'm running through the house" (external speech), the child might say to himself "running." To use Vygotsky's words:

> Inner speech is not the interior aspect of external speech—it is a function in itself. It still remains speech, i.e., thought connected with words. But while in external speech thought is embedded in words, in inner speech words die as they bring forth thought. Inner speech is to a large extent thinking in pure word meanings. It is a dynamic, shifting, unstable thing, fluttering between word and thought, the two more or less stable, more or less firmly delineated components of verbal thought. (p. 149)

In sum, Vygotsky says that language and thought are inextricably bound together, although not identical. The activity of thinking depends on internal and overt speech and develops as a result of interpersonal experience. That is, through listening to others, the young child learns to think. Through language, the child is told what strategies to use and when to use them. Young children's imitation of others' thinking is often obvious because the child thinks out loud. With older children, this thinking occurs mentally and silently. However, regardless of age, a person's thinking can be elevated to a new level by talking to a more skilled thinker. For example, suppose a person cannot solve a particular problem by himself. The problem is just a little beyond his current level of thinking ability. If a more skilled partner offers hints and demonstrations that help the person solve the problem, the person's thinking ability will improve.

Benjamin Whorf

Benjamin Whorf (1956) also believed that language affects thought. Taking from the writings of Sapir (1921), Whorf proposed two interrelated hypotheses about the relation between language and thought: linguistic determinism and linguistic relativity.

Linguistic determinism states that the structure of language determines all other forms of perception and thinking. Its corollary is the **linguistic relativity hypothesis,** often called the Whorfian hypothesis. The **Whorfian hypothesis** states that the structures of a particular language influence the thinking process of the native speakers of that language. In other words, a person's entire way of thinking depends on the grammar of his native tongue.

Box 7.10

SELF-CHECK

Indicate whether each of the following statements is true or false.

1. The evidence supports the idea that language and thought develop independently.
2. According to Vygotsky, young children's language is more sophisticated than their thought.
3. The evidence supports Whorf's linguistic relativity hypothesis.

Answer the following questions.

4. What evidence is there that language development does not lead to cognitive development?
5. What is the evidence against the idea that language concepts "map onto" already existing nonlinguistic, cognitive concepts?
6. How does inner speech differ from outer speech?

Please turn to the end of this chapter to check your answers.

Is the Whorfian hypothesis correct? Is it really true that if we don't have a word for something, we can't conceive of that thing? In support of Whorf's linguistic hypothesis, some evidence suggests that people who have many words for a concept (for instance, the Hanunoo people of the Philippines have 92 words for rice) are able to make finer discriminations among members of that concept than people who have only one word. Since all rice is the same to the authors, we have no doubt that the average Hanunoo would beat us in any contest that involved identifying or sorting different kinds of rice. But it would be irresponsible to say that the Hanunoo can make these discriminations because of their language. In addition to having more words for rice, they have much more experience with rice than we do. It may be that their experiences have affected their language, rather than their language affecting their experience.

One interesting study that argued *against* the idea that language affects perception was done by Eleanor Rosch (1973). She studied the Dani, a people in New Guinea, who have only two words for color—dark and light. She presented them with some colors and made up names for each color. Which color names did they have the easiest time remembering? The basic colors: red, yellow, green, blue, brown, purple, pink, orange, and gray. Her finding indicates that the Dani had these categories, even before they had words for them. Her results also account for an interesting set of findings: Languages that have only three words for color have words that stand for black, white, and red. Languages that have only six words for colors have words that stand for black, white, red, yellow, green, and blue. Languages that have seven words for colors have words representing black, white, red, yellow, green, blue, and brown. Furthermore, if you ask anyone who has a word for red to point to the shade that best represents red, people from all over the world will point to the same shade. Taken together, this evidence overwhelmingly pushes the view that perception shapes language. Thus, Whorf's extreme position—that language determines perception—was wrong.

CONCLUSIONS

Research suggests that infants are born with the biologically based capacity to learn language. However, actual language is not innate because its emergence depends on the child's verbal interaction with his or her caregiver. The behaviorists' learning principles may explain why an infant acquires a specific language, whereas Chomsky's theory explains why children learn the rules of grammar so easily.

The relationship between thought and language is not totally understood. On the one hand, we know that language is not necessary for thought. In 1964, Furth studied deaf children who had no language at all. (Their parents thought that teaching them sign language might prevent them from learning English). These children did very well on thinking tasks and showed no cognitive deficits. Even people with language often think visually or nonverbally. In fact, Albert Einstein is reported to have come up with his theory of relativity years before he could put it into words. We also know that language does not determine thought: Whorf's linguistic relativity hypothesis is wrong.

But can language influence thought? Some humanists think that language is one of the things that makes us human. It lets us share ideas and realize when we're being irrational. Conceivably, an inferior language (such as the language used in government reports or the language suggested by George Orwell in his book *1984*) could dehumanize us. Some feminists think that certain aspects of our language, such as sexist language, already cause us to think about women in nonhuman ways. Although these ideas are intuitively appealing, research has yet to demonstrate that they are correct.

SUMMARY

1. Language consists of phonemes (the sounds of language), and grammar (the rules of language). Grammar is composed of semantics, syntax, and pragmatics. Therefore, learning language involves learning the sounds of the language, the meanings of individual words, rules about how to combine words (word order), and learning how to strategically use language to influence and get along with others.
2. Unlike animal communication, human language allows us to talk about things that aren't physically present (displacement), encourages us to say things that we have never heard anyone else ever say (productivity), requires us to not only say the right words but also to say them in the right order (rules of syntax). In addition, unlike animal communication, humans must learn language. We are not born with it, and our words are so arbitrarily tied to what they represent that we cannot intuitively figure out what a word in a foreign language means.
3. Morphemes are the most basic unit of meaning.
4. Denotation refers to the concrete, dictionary meaning of words, whereas connotation refers to the emotional meanings of words.
5. Surface structure is the actual words produced, whereas deep structure is the meaning behind words.
6. Different surface structures may be produced by using the rules of transformational grammar.
7. The ability to produce sounds represents the productive function of language, whereas the receptive function is the ability to understand speech.
8. During the prelinguistic period, children go through three language steps: crying, cooing, and babbling.
9. During the linguistic period, children progress from holophrastic speech to telegraphic speech to grammatically correct speech to complex speech.
10. During the holophrastic stage, children overextend and underextend speech.
11. Between ages 2 and 5, children begin to use grammatical morphemes, acquire semantical rules, learn to use negation, and learn how to ask questions.
12. By the time most children enter kindergarten, they have a vocabulary of about 8,000 words.
13. Between ages 5 and 8, children make significant gains in syntactical and semantical awareness, and acquire metalinguistic abilities.
14. Language is usually centered in the left cerebral hemisphere. Damage to the language centers of the brain may result in either Wernicke's-type aphasia or Broca's aphasia.
15. Lexicon is the individual dictionary each person uses. As compared to younger adults, the elderly tend to forget names more often, use more multiword definitions, and take longer to answer questions.
16. Decrements in spreading activation may explain why the elderly have greater difficulty generating lists of conceptually related words.
17. With age, words become less powerful perceptual units relative to colors.
18. Learning theorists, such as Skinner, believe that language is learned in the same way any other behavior is learned, whereas nativists believe the ability to learn the grammar of language is inborn.
19. Noam Chomsky attributes our natural ability to acquire language to a hypothetical structure in the brain called the Language Acquisition Device (LAD).
20. One of the most hotly debated topics among developmental psycholinguists is whether language development helps cognitive development or whether cognitive development promotes language development or whether there is no connection between the two.
21. Piagetians hold that cognition causes language, whereas Vygotsky and Whorf believe that language causes cognition.
22. Research suggests that we are born with the biologically based capacity to learn language, but require verbal interaction for language to develop.

Key Terms

aphasia 236
babbling 225
biological model 243
Broca's aphasia 236
connotation 222
cooing 225
crying 224
denotation 222
discourse 238
displaced reference 218
formal universals 243
functional properties 218
grammar 221
grammatical morphemes 228
holophrastic speech 227
immediate constituent analysis 223
inner speech 246
language 218
language acquisition device (LAD) 243
learning theory 240
lexical meaning 222
lexicon 237
linguistic determinism 246
linguistic period 226
linguistic relativity hypothesis 246
linguistics 217
mean length of utterance (MLU) 227
metalinguistic skill 231
morphemes 221
morphological rules 221
motherese 242
negation 228
overextension 227
overregularization 228
patterned speech 226
phonemes 221
phonological rules 221
pragmatics 218
prelinguistic period 223
prevarication 218
productive function 223
productivity 218
receptive function 223
semantic rules 222
spreading activation 237
Stroop Task 239
structuralists 243
structural properties 218
substantive universals 243
syntactic meanings 222
syntactic rules 221
syntax 222
telegraphic speech 227
underextension 227
vocabulary spurt 230
Wernicke's-type aphasia 236
Whorfian hypothesis 246
wh- questions 229

Self-Check Answers

Box 7.2

1. Several properties distinguish human language from other forms of communication. These include functional properties, such as the ability to refer to things that are not physically present (displaced reference), the ability to say things that have never been said before (productivity), the ability to lie (prevarication), and the ability to use language in sophisticated ways to change both ourselves and our social world (pragmatics). In addition, language is distinguished by structural properties such as phonological rules, morphological rules, syntactic rules, and semantic rules. Finally, human language also differs from animal communication in that it has *semanticity,* or the fact that the names for ideas and objects are entirely arbitrary.
2. Unlike other animals, humans have a part of the brain devoted to learning language. Consequently, compared to animals, humans are much more eager language learners, are much faster learners, and don't need as much modeling and reinforcement to learn language.
3. Humans clearly learn syntax and clearly demonstrate productivity. Animals don't appear to learn syntax or demonstrate productivity. Furthermore, only humans seem to engage in *metalanguage,* talking about language.
4. "Help sir you?" is a violation of a syntactic rule. The word order is incorrect.
5. "I like qrpzk" violates both phonological and morphological rules.
6. "The child is lazy and activein." Violates morphological rules—the word *activein* should be *inactive.*
7. *Cooperative, agreeable,* and *conforming* have similar denotative meanings, but different connotative meanings.

Box 7.3

1. False. Language development occurs throughout the lifespan.
2. True. We know this because deaf children and normal-hearing children do not differ at these stages.
3. False. Children initially enter the holophrastic stage where they use one word to stand for an entire phrase. It is not until about a year after they speak their first word that they start combining words.
4. False. Admittedly, children learn to express rejection and to say "no" at any early age. However, mastering the grammar of negative statements is difficult and is not accomplished in the first two years of life.
5. False. Children usually don't reach this level until they are 7 or 8. Until then, they don't use passive sentences, they don't use "tag" questions, they misuse personal pronouns (using *him* when they should say *he* and vice versa), and they overregularize both irregular verbs ("I *goed*") and nouns (*sheeps*).
6. Newborns can distinguish speech sounds from other sounds, they process speech in the left hemisphere, they prefer to process speech in their right ear, and they can detect some subtle differences between phonemes.
7. The newborn's impressive abilities may result from what the child heard before being born. For example, DeCasper's work suggests that fetuses have some memory of what they heard during the two weeks prior to birth. In addition, there are limits to the newborn's ability to distinguish among phonemes. Specifically, children cannot distinguish among all the phonemes of their native tongue until almost the third year of life.
8. Crying (which starts at birth), cooing (starts around one month), and babbling (starts around six months).
9. The holophrastic period, which begins around age 1 with the child's first word; the telegraphic period, which begins around age 2; and the complex speech period, which begins around age 8.
10. Overextension is the use of a word to stand for a more general concept than it does. For example, the word *doggie* might be used to stand for any four-legged mammal.
11. MLU is the mean length of utterance. The longer the average length of an utterance, the more morphemes a child is combining. Therefore, the longer the MLU, the more complex the child's syntax is likely to be. The MLU is preferable to just knowing a child's age because, whereas children of the same age may have very different levels of syntax, children of the same MLU tend to have similar level of syntax.
12. Overregularization is a form of overgeneralization. Specifically, it involves applying regular forms to words that don't follow the general rules (so-called "irregular" words). For example, saying "I goed" instead of "I went." Parents should not be distressed at this because it is a normal phase of language development. The child is discovering and applying grammatical rules. The child will learn the exceptions to these rules soon enough, but the first step is to learn the rules.

Box 7.5

1. False. At age 18 months, most children can speak only about 50 words. They can understand substantially more. In fact, most could understand 50 words as early as age 13 months. Part of the reason for the lag between understanding and speaking is that the child lacks muscle control and practice in producing certain sounds.
2. False. These abilities are not usually evident until age 10.
3. True
4. False. Children use the rule before they can express the rule.
5. As the ability to automatically sound out individual words increases and the reader can devote more attention to understanding the main ideas, reading comprehension improves.

Box 7.7

1. False. Metalinguistic skill development occurs throughout adulthood.
2. False. The evidence does not clearly support this position.
3. False. The statement is true of 50-year-olds.
4. True.
5. True.
6. False.
7. False.
8. False!
9. First, the type of language disorder a person is likely to have depends on the person's age. Wernicke's-type aphasia, characterized by the inability to understand language is more prevalent in people above age 60. Broca's aphasia, characterized by a problem in correctly producing speech, is more prevalent in the 50 to 59 age group. Second, the older a person is, the more serious the language impairment caused by a wound to the left side of the brain.
10. Older subjects are less accurate, give longer definitions (both in number of words and length of definition), and take longer to start giving their definition.

Box 7.8

1. True.
2. False.
3. True.
4. False. Admittedly, parents who have more sophisticated interactions with their children end up with children who are more verbally advanced. However, verbal children may elicit more speech from their parents or may have inherited verbal abilities from their more verbal parents.
5. True.
6. False.
7. False. There is no direct evidence of a specific part of the brain labeled the language acquisition device. However, we know that parts of the left brain, especially Wernicke's area, are—even before birth—devoted to using language.
8. Parents do not recognize all grammatical mistakes, they cannot always clearly explain the grammatical rule that has been violated, and children do not seem to learn from most corrections.

9. He believes that children are born preprogrammed to learn the underlying structural rules (the grammar) of language.
10. Even though cultures differ, countries differ, and languages differ, language development proceeds in the same way in all countries. In addition, language development is tied to both motor development and to myelination of neurons in the brain's speech centers. Finally, there seems to be a critical period for language development (if a child has not learned a language by age 6, the child will never master any language).

Box 7.10

1. False—the evidence is inconclusive.
2. True. Young children's language is more creative and flexible than their thinking.
3. False. For example, one study showed that the number of words a person has for color does not affect her ability to discriminate among different colors.
4. Teaching children the correct meanings of the words *more* and *less* did not improve children's performance on a task requiring a conceptual understanding of quantity. In addition, deaf children who did not have language showed the same level of cognitive development as hearing children.
5. First, there is a serious problem with the idea that children first learn the concept of "verb" by thinking of verbs in terms of a concept they have already learned—"physical actions." The problem is that not all verbs relate to physical actions (for example, *know, love*). Furthermore, some adjectives (such as *reckless*) would seem to relate to physical actions more than some verbs. Second, many of the complex, arbitrary, grammatical rules have no counterpart in physical reality.
6. Inner speech is more telegraphic and less grammatical. It involves verbs more than nouns.

Chapter

Self- and Moral Development

It's not only the most difficult thing to know one's self,
but the most inconvenient.
JOSH BILLINGS

Chapter Overview

Normal development in most Western societies requires that each of us establish our own separate, individual identities while also respecting other people's viewpoints. As you know, reaching these two goals is not easy. In high school, you knew people who were going through an identity crisis. Because they were so unsure of who they were, their friends and parents may have been very worried about them. Even today, you probably know someone who seems "lost" because he or she has a poorly developed sense of self. Certainly, you see almost daily news reports about the alleged misconduct of some public figure or the actions of someone who has lost self-control and harmed another person or property.

In this chapter, you will learn how most people are able to develop both a sense of self and a sense of morality. After discussing how individuals develop an understanding of themselves, we will discuss how people develop the ability to understand others. Then, we will discuss the development of moral reasoning. Finally, we will discuss the gap between moral reasoning and moral action.

Figure 8.1

William James's View of the Self

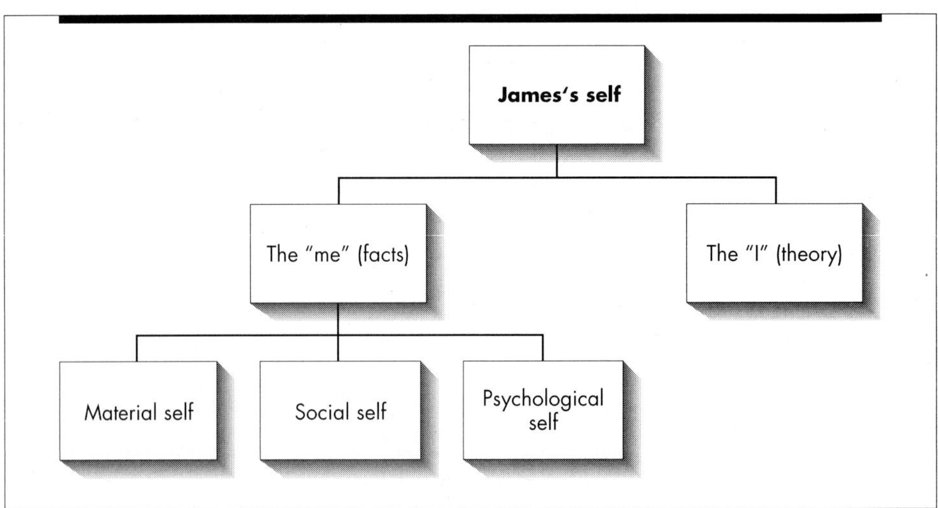

The Self

What is the self? If you reflect for a moment, you realize that the self is a broad and multifaceted concept. To have a sense of **self,** a person must not only know who and what she is, she must know what she is not. Self-knowledge incorporates "everything that one knows about one's own experience in the world as an individual, about one's unique position and status in the social order, about one's personal characteristics, and about one's identity over time (past, present, future), and place" (Damon, 1983, p. 11).

As you can see, describing the self and categorizing all its elements is a difficult task. William James (1892/1961) was the first psychologist to try to define all the aspects of self. He started by dividing the self into two major components: the "me" and the "I" (see figure 8.1).

The **"me"** contains all that can be known about the self and has three parts: the material self, the social self, and the psychological self. The **material self** is composed of all one's physical possessions—from a stereo to one's body. Thus, the individual who works out at the health club is enhancing and preserving his material self at least as much as one who waxes his BMW.

People who are focused on their material self are also often concerned (as are most people) with the **social self,** one's social identity, social behavior, and reputation. James noted that since the social self is how we are known by others and since each person perceives us and interacts with us differently, we may have many social selves—a different one for each person we know.

Although people who might be considered rich and superficial would supposedly have a well-developed material self (they own quality possessions) and social selves (they know how others perceive them), such people may be accused of having a poorly developed **psychological self,** spiritual self. That is, according to the stereotype, such superficial people would not have beliefs, ambitions, and goals that are independent of the material and social self. Research suggests that such individuals would be unhappy (Kasser & Ryan, 1993; Myers, 1992).

Whereas the *me* represents a collection of raw data about oneself, the **"I"** represents a theorist who interprets and organizes those data, weaving them into a few consistent themes. For example, the "I" organizes your experiences so that you see a continuity to your existence. Because of the "I," you probably see yourself as basically the same person as you were two years ago (although perhaps older and wiser). Indeed, it would be upsetting for most of us to be told that we had "really changed" and no longer resembled our old self. (Thus, wives sometimes attack their husbands by saying, "You're not the man I married" or "The man I married would never . . .")

The "I" also decides what experiences are relevant to one's self-concept and how they are relevant (Damon, 1983). For example, suppose you're driving and you get into an accident. What does this experience mean? Does it mean you are a bad driver? An unstable person? Or, does it have nothing whatsoever to do with your self-concept ("Accidents happen" or, "The other guy was a lousy driver").

Although James's version of the self is not universally accepted, almost every theorist's view of the self reflects James's influence. For example, Cooley (1922) and Mead (1934) believed that the self was James's social self—no more and no less. They argued that it is through others that we know ourselves. Think about this. Isn't your opinion of yourself very similar to what other people think you are? If everyone changed their opinion of you, would your self-concept change? Such a hypothesis would most certainly follow from social interactionist theories we discussed in chapter 6, such as Lev Vygotsky's (1934/1986) theory. However, researchers have yet to answer this question.

More recent theorists (Brown, 1965; Kelly, 1955; Epstein, 1983) view the self as being very similar to James's "I." Specifically, they focused on the idea that the self is a theory. According to Epstein (1983), the self-theory organizes our experiences in a way that both allows

Figure 8.2

Different Views of How the Self Develops

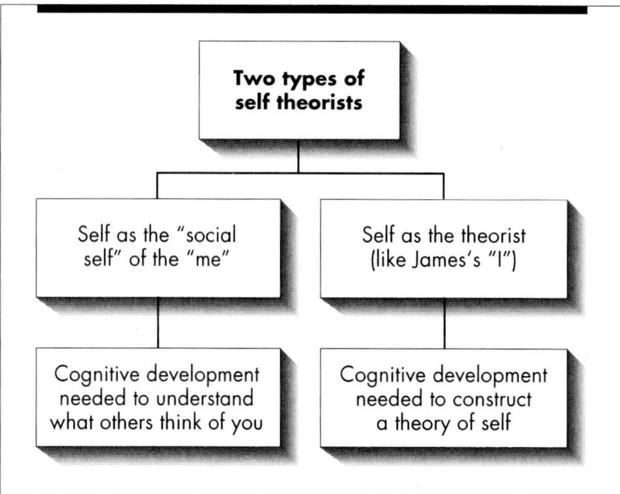

us to feel good about ourselves and allows us to predict our own behavior. Others, such as Greenwald (1980), argue that the self operates primarily to help us feel good about ourselves, even when that involves distortion and self-deception. In other words, Greenwald considers the self to be more of a biased historian than a theorist.

Changes in Self-Knowledge

No matter how we conceive of the self, we realize that its development depends on cognitive development (see figure 8.2). If we see the self as Cooley and Mead did, we realize that the development of the self must wait until the person can consider others' points of view. If we view the self as a theory, we realize that the sophistication of a person's self-theory depends on that person's level of reasoning. Therefore, in the next section, we will take a closer look at the relationship between cognitive development and self-knowledge.

Infancy

As Piaget emphasized, our capacity for reasoning at birth is fairly primitive. At birth, infants do not perceive a difference between themselves and the rest of the world. Everything is one—one global, undifferentiated, unified whole. In the sensorimotor stage, infants learn that they are separate from the rest of the physical world and learn about their physical self. Clearly, we must learn that we are different from the rest of the world before we can develop a self-theory.

When do infants first realize that their physical self is unique and relatively stable from day to day? Infants, of course, can't answer that question because they can't talk. However, developmental psychologists discovered a clever way to get infants to reveal the answer to that question.

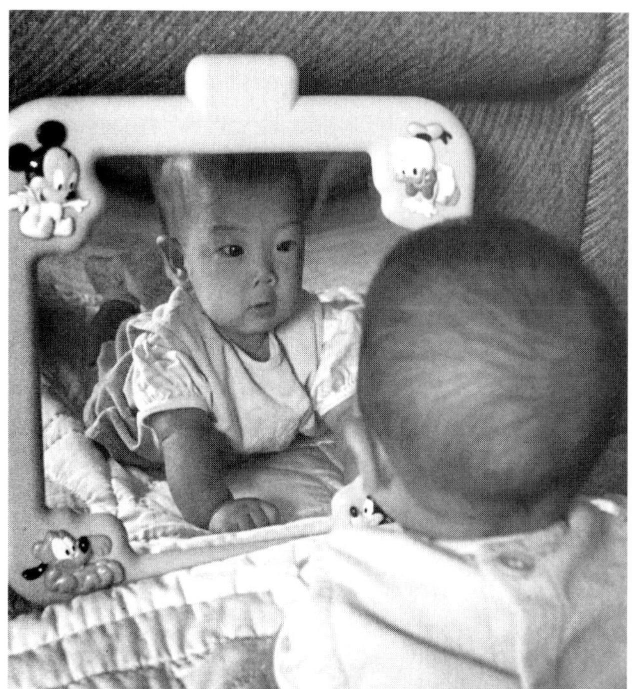

Infants do not develop a sense of themselves or recognize their image in a mirror until the second year of life.

To understand how developmental psychologists get infants to answer the question, realize that another way of stating the question is to ask, "When do infants first realize that the face in the mirror is their own?" To understand how developmental psychologists answered that question, imagine that you woke up one morning, looked in the bathroom mirror, and saw a bright red smudge on your nose. What would you do? Because you recognize that it is your nose that has the smudge, you probably would touch your nose and try to find out what the stuff is. But, what if you didn't know that the reflection was of your nose? What if you thought it was a picture of someone else? Would you still touch your nose? Probably not.

Using this reasoning, several investigators put a bright spot of red rouge on babies' noses and then observed how infants reacted when looking at their own reflection in a mirror (Bertenthal & Fischer, 1978; Lewis & Brooks-Gunn, 1979). Children under one year of age don't touch their noses (Lewis & Brooks-Gunn, 1979); therefore, we infer that they don't recognize themselves. One-year-olds seem to believe the reflection is another child and may touch the reflection or try to look behind the mirror to find this other child. However, sometime during the second year of life, most children learn to recognize their own image. By about 18 months, they will point to pictures of themselves when their names are called (Damon & Hart, 1982). By age 2, almost all children give evidence of self-recognition when they gaze at their reflection in a mirror.

In conclusion, most people assume that an infant's first recognition of her physical self (usually around age 2) marks the beginning of the "me-self." However, many related questions about how the self develops are still unanswered. For example, nobody knows exactly how this initial self-recognition develops into the complex network of cognitions, emotions, motives, values, and behaviors composing the individual's self-concept (Harter, 1983).

Early Childhood: Development of the Material Self

Starting around age 2, children acquire two important and related abilities that will affect their self-concept: language and preoperational thought. Gaining the ability to use and understand such symbols as words, pictures, gestures, and numbers has a profound impact on the development of self. With the advent of symbolic thought, children can store their experiences. That is, they can express their experiences and incorporate them into their self-theories.

Children can also use language to express their individuality. A common way of defining oneself is to show that one is not like everybody else and that one's wishes are different from the wishes of one's parents. Consequently, during the "terrible two's," one of the most frequently spoken words by children is *"NO!"*

Language also lets parents and peers tell a child what they think of him or her ("smart," "bad boy," or "good girl"). Despite children's egocentrism at this age, children often take these messages to heart. Unfortunately, at this age, children have difficulty understanding that they can still be good people even though they engage in unacceptable behaviors. Thus, being yelled at for breaking something (especially if abusive language is used) may make them feel bad about themselves.

Whether verbal attacks have a lasting effect is a matter of debate. On the one hand, Erikson (1963) felt that being criticized for one's failures at this age could have permanent effects. Specifically, he felt that failing to successfully resolve the autonomy versus doubt and shame crisis would make one less able to deal with other crises. On the other hand, no toddler has a stable sense of self. Until around age 6, children believe that they and objects in the world can undergo magical transformations (such as change gender or species). Therefore, it would seem that even if they viewed themselves as bad, they wouldn't see themselves as being permanently "bad." Clearly, since we don't know for sure that criticism is relatively harmless, parents should avoid unnecessary or severe criticism.

In addition to influencing the degree to which the child likes him or herself, the ability to use language also influences the development of gender identity. At about the age of 2 1/2 to 3, most children can identify themselves as a "boy" or "girl" (Brooks-Gunn & Lewis, 1982). At about age 5 or 6, most boys believe they will always be boys and most girls believe that they will always be girls (Marcus & Overton, 1978; Slaby & Frey, 1975). By age 3 1/2, most children know what traits each gender has and by age 5, they know which toys, clothing, and occupations are "male" and which are "female" (Deaux & Lewis, 1984). Our 5-year-old niece even "knows" which Saturday morning cartoon shows are "male" and which are "female." Furthermore, for many young children, there are no exceptions to these gender-based rules. There are no male nurses and no female physicians—even if one's own mother is a physician! Consequently, at an early age, children may be limiting their definition of self based on their gender.

Language is not the only way children learn about themselves. As Piaget pointed out, during early childhood, toddlers continually explore their physical world through play: toying with the boundaries between self and other, between real and fantasy, and between order, freedom, and chaos (Gardner, 1982). This play is not frivolous. It is essential because it is the child's vehicle for understanding the world.

Especially essential to development of self is the child's imaginative play, where he or she tries on the roles of others—police officer, doctor, nurse, mommy, daddy, teacher, baby. Role playing helps children explore options and explore their potential roles in society. Children learn to relate the behaviors and states of others with their own. By labeling traits as good and bad, happy and sad, old and young, children define who they are—and who they are not.

For the preschooler, these self-definitions are usually not evaluative. That is, they do not describe themselves by saying "I'm good" or "I'm bad." Instead, the self-definitions focus on physical attributes ("I'm a girl. I have brown hair and freckles"), possessions ("I have a turtle"), or preferred activities ("I like to eat"). In other words, these self-definitions focus on the material self.

Robert Selman was one of the first investigators to realize that children's self-definitions emphasize the material self (Selman, 1980; Yeates & Selman, 1989). He investigated how children understand themselves and others by asking children to solve interpersonal dilemmas. The "Mike dilemma" that follows is one such dilemma (Selman, 1980):

> Eight-year-old Tom is trying to decide what to buy his friend, Mike, for a birthday present. By chance, he meets Mike on the street and learns that Mike is extremely upset because his dog, Pepper, has been lost for two weeks. In fact, Mike is so upset that he tells Tom, "I miss Pepper so much that I never want to look at another dog again." Tom goes off, only to pass a store with a sale on puppies. Only two are left, and these will soon be gone. (p. 94)

Selman then asked whether Tom should buy Mike a puppy. Follow-up questions probed a number of psychological issues surrounding the perspectives of self and other.

Selman found that young children have **physicalistic conceptions of self.** That is, they fail to distinguish between inner psychological experience and outward behavior. That is, they think that what people say and do accurately reflects what people really think. Consequently,

Figure 8.3

The Effects of Preoperational Thought on Development of Self

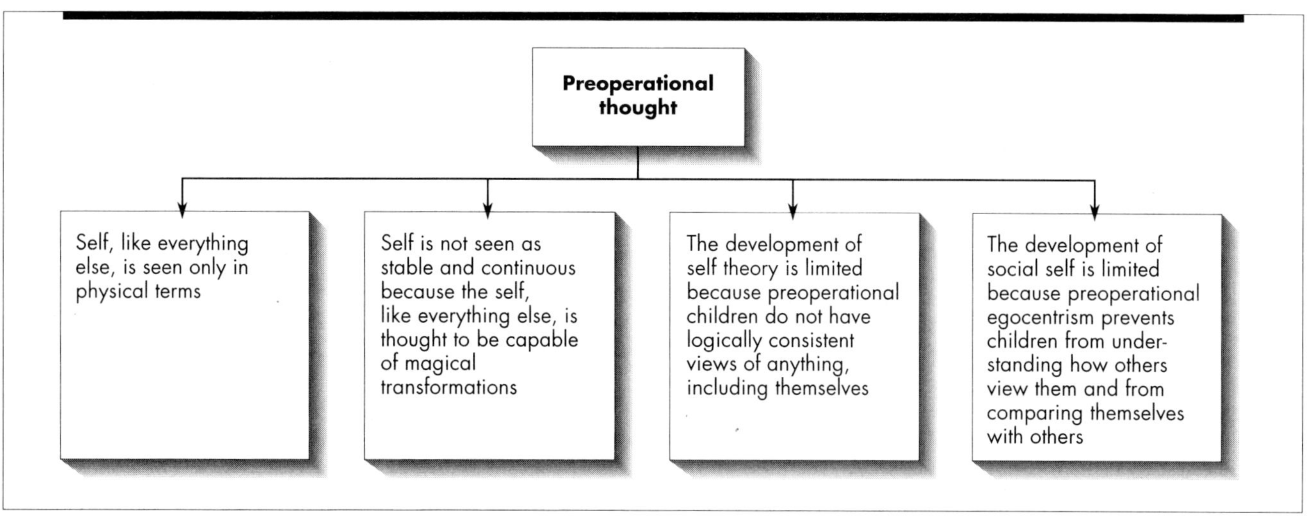

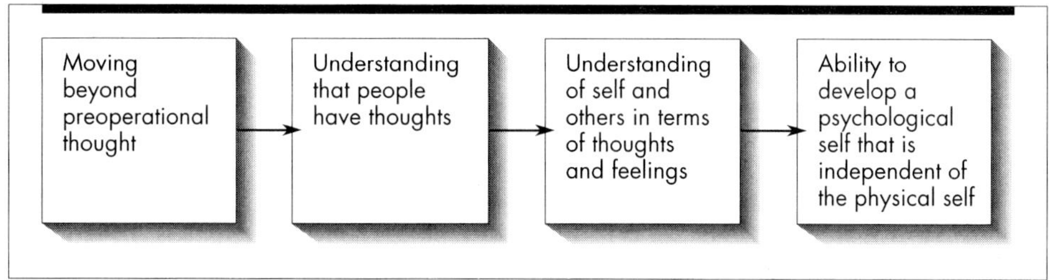

Figure 8.4

How Moving Beyond Preoperational Thought Influences the Development of the Psychological Self

when confronted with the Mike dilemma, these children will deny that a person's statements and behavior can be distinguished from the person's feelings: "If I say that I don't want a puppy ever again, then I really don't ever want one." Because the child is unaware of psychological experience apart from overt physical attributes or acts, it's evident that the child views the self only in physical terms.

The physicalistic concept of self is just one of many aspects of self that is shaped by the young child's preoperational level of thinking (see figure 8.3). As we already mentioned, the child's preoperational-level belief in magical transformations (the belief that tomorrow, they may change their gender) interferes with developing a stable, continuing, enduring sense of self. In addition, since preoperational thought is not logical thought, children in the stage of preoperational thought do not feel compelled to construct a logically consistent view of themselves. Behaving in contradictory ways does not bother them. Finally, preoperational egocentrism prevents them from developing a social self as they do not compare themselves with others and they do not understand how others view them. Thus, you should not be surprised that when they leave preoperational thought (around age 6), dramatic changes in self occur.

Later Childhood

Between the ages of 5 and 7, two related changes occur. Both of these changes have profound effects on how children view themselves. First, children enter concrete operational thought (see figure 8.4). As a result, they are able to think about the world and themselves in a more logical and more analytic way. That is, they are able to think about more than one variable at a time; are able to make finer distinctions; are able to understand that things are relative; are less likely to think in terms of strict stereotypes and absolutes; are able to understand others' viewpoints; and are able to compare themselves to others.

Second, they begin school. School entry also means entry into a broader social world. This broader social world combined with accelerated cognitive development helps children better understand the viewpoints and experiences of others. They are exposed to new roles. No longer are they simply family members, but they are also members of society.

As a result of both moving out of egocentrism and being exposed to a broader social world, children realize that there are differences between inner and outer states. By age 8, they realize that there can be discrepancies between psychological and physical experience. For example, when 8-year-olds read Selman's story about Mike, they realize that Mike might really want another puppy (psychological

Figure 8.5

Forces on Young Children (Ages 7 to 9) Contributing to the Development of a Social Self

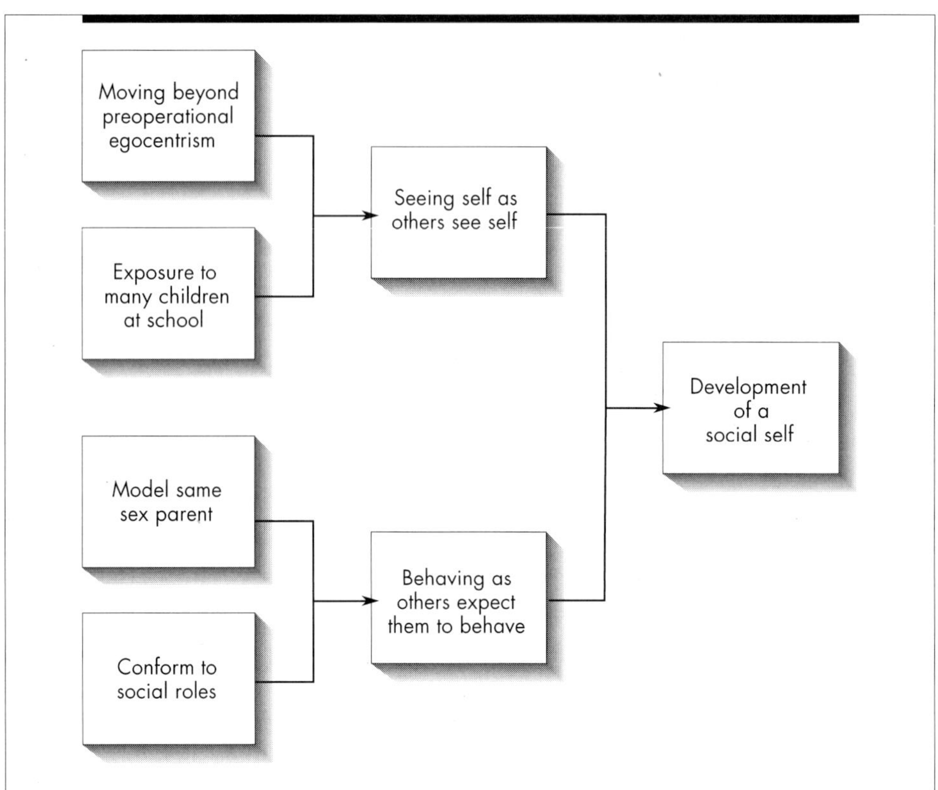

experience) even though he claims he doesn't (physical [behavioral] experience). Not coincidentally, around age 7 or 8, children begin to define their "true self" in terms of subjective inner states (beliefs, emotions, hopes) rather than material outer states (pets owned, people they live with, physical appearance). In James's terms, this increased awareness of one's own thoughts and emotions would represent development of the psychological self.

Middle childhood is also a time when the social self emerges. Children's self-descriptions now emphasize how they differ from others (McGuire & Padawer-Singer, 1976). For instance, the tallest boy in the class will describe himself as tall, whereas the only person from out of state will incorporate that fact into her self-description. Furthermore, as Erikson pointed out, concerns with one's competencies relative to others is a primary concern (for example, I can throw a baseball further than anyone else in my class). Finally, at this stage, children model their same-sex parent and accept the roles that others have assigned them (see figure 8.5).

In adolescence, peers become more important in helping a person develop a sense of self.

Adolescence

The tremendous physical, social, and cognitive changes that occur during the teenage years have dramatic changes on adolescents' self-concepts. Physical changes alter not only the material self, but the social and psychological self as well. Hormonal changes force teens to come to terms with themselves as sexual beings and often cause self-esteem to be affected by how well they are accepted by the opposite sex (and this acceptance depends largely on what one's body looks like). Furthermore, as teens start to look like adults, they start being treated more like adults and start to think of themselves as adults. As a prospective adult, teens look more and more to peers and less and less to parents for developing a sense of self. As prospective adults, they also place increasing importance on making their own decisions and striving toward their own long-term goals. Thus, whereas a preteen will probably work almost equally hard on subjects she dislikes and likes because that's what others expect her to do, teenagers won't. The teenager may say, "If I don't like a subject, I won't do anything in the subject . . . on the other hand, in subjects I do like, my science and mathematics, I really work" (Secord & Peevers, 1974, p. 139).

During adolescence, both the bodily changes and the new role of the peer group are very visible. However, we should not overlook another dramatic, if less visible, influence on the adolescent's self—cognitive development.

During adolescence, many people achieve formal operations. For the first time, they are able to think about hypothetical possibilities. For the first time, they are able to think abstractly. As a result, they (1) are keenly aware that they will soon be adults, (2) realize there are many possible people they could become, and (3) can think abstractly enough to form a self-theory that gives continuity to their life despite all the changes that have occurred in their material, social, and psychological selves and despite the fact that their parents see them as one person, whereas peers see them as a different person. In short, consistent with Erikson's view of adolescence as a time of identity crisis (see chapter 2), teenagers seem to respond to the dramatic changes going on by constructing an integrated personality theory to describe their motives, feelings, and thoughts (Damon & Hart, 1982; Harter, 1983).

The ability to develop a sophisticated self-theory does not mean that teenagers act in a consistent manner. Developing such a self-theory often involves trying on different roles to see how they fit. Consequently, one day, they may be politically conservative; the next day, they may be liberal. To add to this inconsistency, adolescents do not always act in accord with their idealized self-images. For example, they may view themselves as being morally good (Damon, 1984) and caring about social justice, yet treat members of oppressed groups (women, Hispanics, African Americans) with contempt.

In conclusion, an important task of adolescence is developing an identity. Having a great deal of leisure time as well as having advanced to formal operations, allows them to develop a self-theory that gives some sense of continuity (in spite of the dramatic physiological, social, and cognitive changes in their lives), consistency (in spite of behaving one way around parents and another way around peers), and a sense of uniqueness and individuality (in spite of frequently being forced to conform to either the peer group or one's parents). As a result, most adolescents present a more organized, complex, and abstract view of themselves than children can (see figure 8.6).

Adulthood

Although adolescents make significant strides toward developing a self-theory that incorporates their past, present, and future, the development of self doesn't stop at adolescence. Instead, as Erikson (1959) has argued, the self continues to change and develop throughout adulthood. In other words, as people age, their views of themselves continue to become more complex, incorporate more roles, and involve more descriptions of motives, values, intentions, and other internal psychological states. The self expands as the individual takes on an increasing number of roles: spouse, parent, employee, member of the community, and eventually, citizen of the world.

Perhaps because the self can change in so many ways and for so many reasons, a number of theories have been developed to explain development of the self throughout the lifespan. Although the theories tend to focus on different forces for adult development, they fall into two basic categories.

First, there are stage theories. Lifespan **stage theories** argue that certain changes can occur only at certain ages. For example, a stage theorist might say that true intimacy can happen only during adulthood. In addition, lifespan stage theories usually suggest that if people master the particular challenge at each age-related stage, they will enjoy bliss and contentment when they reach the final stage of development.

Second, there are "continuous" theories. "Continuous" theories do not propose any magic years for facing particular challenges or for achieving personal growth. Instead, the "continuous" theories emphasize that adult development is the result of lifespan processes that continue to operate during the 50+ years of the life called adulthood.

Lifespan Stage Theories

Two of the most popular stage theories are Erik Erikson's theory of psychosocial development and Jane Loevinger's (1966, 1976) theory of ego development. As you learned in chapter 2, Erikson focuses on three major crises in adulthood: (1) determining whether to share oneself with another; (2) deciding whether to be productive and give to both the next generation and society as a whole or to "look out for number 1"; and (3) determining whether one's life was worthwhile (see table 8.1).

Like Erikson, Loevinger developed a lifespan stage theory (see table 8.2). According to Loevinger, most junior high students and some adults are at the **conformist stage,** where they are concerned with obeying rules, maintaining appearances, and conforming to their group's (clique's) standards.

During adolescence, many people reach the stage where they will remain for the rest of their lives: the **conscientious stage.** People in the conscientious stage have internalized many of society's rules. They are not following rules because they are concerned with what other people think. Instead, they are following certain rules because they believe and accept those rules. Consequently, when they violate these rules, they feel guilty. We do not mean to imply that they are complete "prisoners" to all of society's rules. They aren't. In some cases, they choose which rules of society to follow and which to ignore.

Figure 8.6

Physical and Cognitive Changes that Occur During Adolescence and Promote Change in the Self

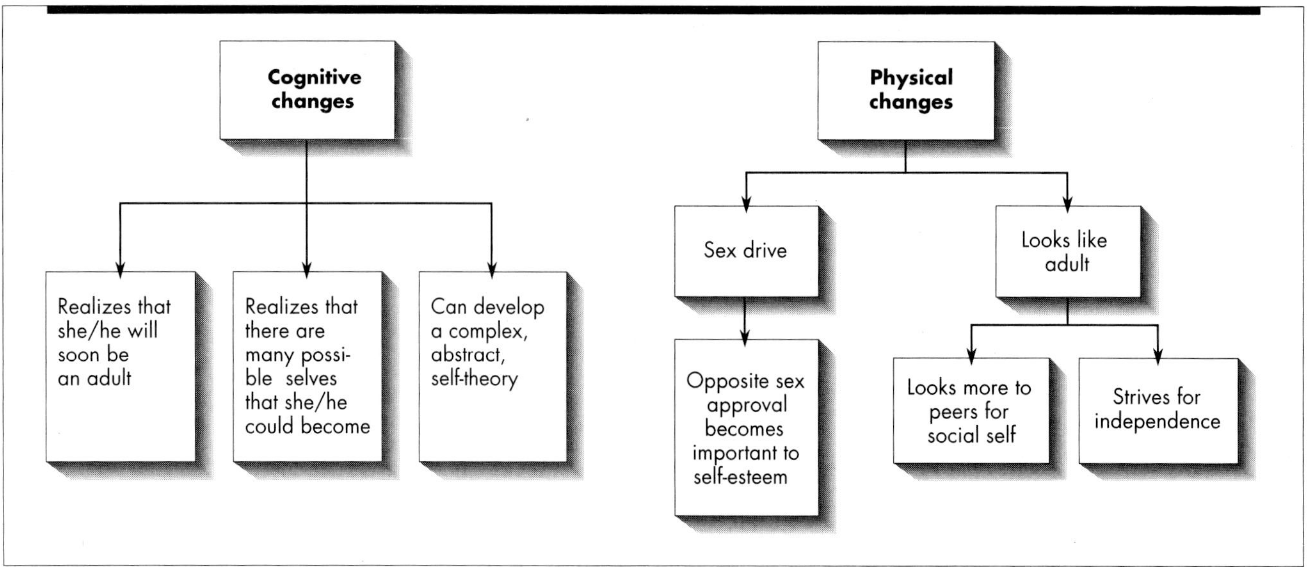

Box 8.1

SELF-CHECK

PART A

Indicate whether each of the following statements is true or false.

1. At birth, infants have a primitive sense of self.
2. By age 2, children have a social self.
3. Before age 4, most children either don't know their gender or believe that their gender may change.

PART B

Answer the following questions.

4. What are two reasons that most theorists believe that cognitive development is a prerequisite for developing a sense of self?
5. How does preoperational thought limit young children's sense of self?
6. What are two main forces that affect the development of the social self between the ages of 5 and 7?
7. What are several important effects of formal operational reasoning on the development of adolescent self-concept?

Please turn to the end of this chapter to check your answers.

Table 8.1

Erikson's Psychosocial Model of Personality Development

Years	Stage	Crisis
0 to 1	Oral-Sensory	Trust versus Mistrust
1 to 3	Muscular-Anal	Autonomy versus Shame or Doubt
3 to 6	Locomotor-Genital	Initiative versus Guilt
6 to 11	Latency	Industry versus Inferiority
11 to 18	Puberty and Adolescence	Identity versus Role Confusion
18 to 45	Young Adulthood	Intimacy versus Isolation
45 to 65	Adulthood	Generativity versus Stagnation
65+	Maturity	Ego-integrity versus Despair

The point is that they are extremely loyal to those rules they have accepted. Unfortunately, there is a dark side to their devotion to such rules. The dark side is that they will condemn anyone who disagrees with their views. You probably know someone who is at the conscientious stage and rejects you because of your religious or political beliefs. In fact, most people never transcend the conscientious stage. Few of us are tolerant of people who completely disagree with us. Most of us think our society's way is the best way. However, a few people will transcend the conscientious stage. Those few will reach

Stage	Who Reaches This Stage	Characteristic Attitudes/Behaviors
Conformist Stage	Many pre-adolescents	Doing what the clique wants.
Conscientious Stage	Many adolescents	Believing in society's rules and disapproving of people who don't share those beliefs.
Autonomous Stage	A few adults	Believing in society's rules, but also accepting of people with different values.
Integrated Stage	Very few adults	Having a consistent philosophy of self, but also cherishing people who have different philosophies.

Table 8.2

Loevinger's Lifespan Stage Theory

the autonomous stage and, of those few, some will even make it to the last stage—the integrated stage.

In the **autonomous stage,** people are fully aware of the range of choices available and can tolerate—rather than condemn—people whose choices differ from their own. They recognize that their beliefs are a function of their own upbringing and personality. Therefore, they can appreciate that since others have different personalities, developmental histories, and needs, other people may have beliefs that differ from one's own. For the most part, people in the autonomous stage exhibit a "live and let live" philosophy.

Those who develop beyond the autonomous stage reach the ultimate stage of ego development—becoming an integrated person. Those at the **integrated stage** can reconcile their own inner conflicts, remain at peace with what they are, recognize and accept what they cannot attain, and cherish—rather than merely tolerate—other people for their individuality. Put another way, the goal of the integrated person is to create an environment that would allow all people to express their individuality and fulfill their potential.

Not surprisingly, Loevinger had difficulty describing exactly what an integrated person was. She felt, however, that an integrated person would be fairly similar to what Abraham Maslow called a self-actualized person.

Box 8.2

SELF-CHECK

PART A

Indicate whether each of the following statements is true or false.

1. Erikson's theory has extensive research support.
2. A person at the conscientious stage will do whatever the peer group wants him or her to do, even if it's against the law.
3. A person at the conscientious stage conscientiously follows all of society's rules.
4. Most adults reach the autonomous stage.
5. People at the autonomous stage generate their own rules, independent of society (that is, they are autonomous).
6. There are clear-cut, objective guidelines for determining if someone has reached the integrated stage.

PART B

Answer the following question.

7. What are three differences between Loevinger's lifespan theory and Erikson's psychosocial model of personality development?

Please turn to the end of this chapter to check your answers.

Lifespan Processes

In contrast to Erikson and Loevinger, many humanists believe that the steps to **self-actualization** may occur at any time during adulthood. For example, unlike Erikson, Maslow did not think that one had to wait until late adulthood to reach self-actualization. Similarly, Rogers believed that self-actualization could occur during early adulthood. Specifically, as might be expected from an American who champions individualism, Rogers felt self-actualization would be achieved once people stopped defining themselves in terms of who others wanted them to be and accepted themselves for who they really were. Presumably, becoming an adult could free people from two powerful forces that might cause them to deny their true self—the tyranny of the peer group and parents.

The humanists are not the only ones that think that the development of the self does not have to be tied to age-dependent stages. Indeed, scientists have investigated at least five basic processes that influence development of the self throughout the lifespan: underjustification, overjustification, objective self-awareness, beneffectance, and self-verification.

Underjustification and Overjustification

We will first discuss the related processes of underjustification and overjustification. The key to understanding these processes is to understand Daryl Bem's (1972) self-perception theory. According to self-perception theory, we learn about ourselves the same way we learn about others—by observing behavior. If you see that Mary, without any encouragement, practices her tennis strokes, you will conclude that she likes tennis. How do you learn that you like tennis? The same way. If you find yourself going out in the heat and practicing your serve, you realize that you must really love tennis. Thus, your decision that you love tennis is an example of the **underjustification effect,** the fact that people who voluntarily do something for no reward (justification) decide they did it because they wanted to. If, on the other hand, you are being strong-armed into playing tennis—or richly rewarded for playing—your self-perceptions will be influenced by the **overjustification effect;** when it is clear to the individual that anyone in her situation would do that behavior, she decides that she did the behavior because of the situation (being rewarded) rather than because she wanted to do it (Lepper, 1981; Bandura, 1986).

Bem's theory has some powerful implications for the development of the self. If we want our daughter to see herself as someone who likes tennis, we want to encourage her—but only enough so that she plays tennis. If we give her too much encouragement, she'll say that she's playing tennis to please her parents. If we want her to be a good student, we want to encourage her as a student, but we want her to think of herself as someone who loves learning, rather than as a person who just wants to bring home an "A" to Daddy and Mommy. Therefore, we would not emphasize the grade, but rather stress how proud she must be to have done such a wonderful project. Similarly, if we are trying to get a colleague to be more active in the community, we push, but subtly enough so that the colleague doesn't say: "They forced me into it," but instead says "I did it because I'm community-minded." Needless to say, we support and nurture this belief by saying, "I knew you'd come through because you're so community-minded. I remember last year, when you did . . ."

By not blatantly pressuring or rewarding someone for doing something, we can change their self-concept so that they see themselves as someone who likes tennis, likes learning, believes in giving blood, or likes getting involved in the community. Unfortunately, by blatantly pushing or rewarding someone for something they already like to do, they may decide that they don't really like it (Lepper, 1981). Instead, they conclude that they did it only for the rewards. For example, suppose we gave our child $10 an hour to play tennis. Then, she would lose her enthusiasm for the game. We have turned play into work. Rather than thinking she practices tennis because she likes it, she would decide that she practices only because she is paid. If our schools overemphasize grades, children may decide that they don't learn because they like to learn, but rather they learn to get grades.

The overjustification effect has been used to explain a wide variety of phenomena—from children losing curiosity to professionals "burning out." However, we should point out that rewarding people does not always dampen their internal motivation. Rewards may be necessary to get the person to work at the new task long enough to feel familiar with it. After all, familiarity often brings liking (Zajonc, 1983). Furthermore, rewards may be necessary to get the person to the point of mastering the task. For example, hours of practice are necessary before a tennis or chess player has an adequate level of competence (Ericsson & Charness, 1994). Once a person has developed competence, he is more apt to like the task (Harackeiwicz & Manderlink, 1984) and incorporate that task into his self-concept ("I am a good tennis player").

Although rewards must often be used, they should be used with care. Rather than focusing on the large "bribe" the child will get, the emphasis should always be primarily on how much the child will like the task. If the parent emphasizes the reward, internal motivation will decrease. Rewards are especially destructive in undermining the person's own motivation when the task is an interesting one. Furthermore, we now know that rewards can hinder a person's creativity (Boggiano & Ruble, 1981).

Objective Self-Awareness

Bem's self-perception theory stresses that people often lack insight into themselves and therefore must rely on their behavior to tell them what they like. Carver & Scheier (1981) have noted that people are more capable of achieving self-insight when they are made more self-conscious, a condition called **objective self-awareness.** For example, when people take a personality test with a mirror in the room or with a camera pointed at them, their test scores predict their behavior better than when no such device is present. Anecdotal evidence also supports the idea that reflection (writing in a diary, writing to a friend, explaining yourself to a therapist) can lead to self-insight.

Although increased self-awareness can occur throughout the lifespan, such awareness seems more prevalent during certain times. For example, adolescence is a time when people are reflective and are aware of how others view them. In fact, adolescents often seem to believe that everyone is watching and judging their every move. During adulthood, times of intense self-awareness may include passing a milestone such as one's 40th birthday, going to one's high school reunion, or attending one's retirement dinner. In addition, as Erikson pointed out, during late adulthood, as people try to resolve the integrity versus despair crisis, people may review their lives.

Beneffectance

As Greenwald (1980) pointed out, the self tries to make itself look good, a tendency termed **beneffectance.** Things we are not good at (whether football or algebra) are unimportant to our self-concept. Furthermore, we tend to

People can become more self-conscious in an environment that increases their self-awareness. For example, exercising in front of a mirror may make people more self-aware.

remember the positive things we did and forget the less favorable things we did. Thus, our memory, like a biased historian, makes us think that we made few mistakes.

Another way of making ourselves look good is to think of ourselves as being more logical and consistent than we are. Therefore, we tend to forget that we changed our mind on a certain issue. Young children, especially, refuse to accept that they have ever held a wrong belief (Flavell, 1993). Even if we do remember changing our position, we will tend to believe that we changed it much earlier than we did. For example, people sometimes think that they changed their position years ago when they actually changed their position only minutes ago (Greenwald, 1980). Thus, we tend to change our beliefs so that it appears that they were always consistent with what we now know actually happened (Dawes, 1994).

We also tend to change our beliefs so that they appear consistent with our actions. The most dramatic instance of our willingness to appear consistent comes from the brainwashing of POWs (prisoners of war) and of new cult members. Some POWs, for example, are induced to write a letter criticizing their country or praising the enemy for the most minimal of reward, such as an orange. After that, they have to conclude that there are problems with their country because they can't accept that they would betray their country for an orange. Cult recruits are sometimes urged to quit their jobs and give away their possessions. Once they've done that, they will convince themselves that the cult is the best thing that ever happened to them: They must have a good reason for giving away all their possessions!

Obviously, formal brainwashing isn't a common part of development. However, it could be said that we brainwash ourselves throughout adulthood as we rationalize our actions. The person who doesn't find time to register to vote decides that being a concerned, voting member of society is not important. The former hippie who now, as a yuppie, makes money working for a defense contractor changes his view of the military.

Our desire to make our self-image match our actions doesn't always lead us to change our self. Sometimes, the opposite occurs: We perform actions or rituals that help us maintain and reaffirm—rather than change—the self. For instance, someone who starts to doubt her religious faith may become more involved in her church and thereby restore her faith.

Self-Verification

Not only are we interested in feeling good about ourselves and appearing consistent, but we are also interested in feeling sure that we know who we are (Rodin, 1986; Swann, 1990). That is, we engage in **self-verification,** finding others who see us the same way we see ourselves. By interacting primarily with these people, we confirm our beliefs about ourselves. As you might expect, self-verification can complement beneffectance. For example, we may see ourselves as intelligent and kind people and then associate with people who think we are intelligent and kind. However, self-verification occurs even when it lowers our self-esteem. For instance, Swann, Stein-Seroussi, and Giesler (1992) found that "people with negative self-views preferred partners who appraised them unfavorably."

Dimensions of Self

We have discussed lifespan processes that affect the self, but we have neglected two important and related issues. First, we have not discussed which specific aspects of the self are affected by these processes. Second, we have not discussed the importance of the various parts of the self on behavior. For example, does it really matter whether a child has low self-esteem? Before we examine the importance of self-esteem, let's first examine the aspects of self that are affected by lifespan processes: self-esteem, locus of control, self-efficacy, and self-control.

Self-Esteem

After learning about beneffectance (or just thinking about your friends), you should not be surprised to learn that most people have high **self-esteem,** a feeling of self-worth. In fact, Myers (1992) found that almost all people believe that they are above average in intelligence and in getting along with other people. Having high self-esteem is healthy. People who feel good about themselves tend to be less depressed, freer of ulcers and insomnia, less prone to drug addiction, more resistant to conformity pressures, more persistent at difficult tasks (Brockner & Hulton, 1978; Greenwald & Pratkanis, 1984), and more successful (Seligman, 1990).

Low self-esteem, on the other hand, may be harmful (see figure 8.7). Hans Strupp (1982) speculated:

> *As soon as one listens to a patient's story, one encounters unhappiness, frustration, and despair which find expression in diverse forms of psychopathology, including psychosomatic symptoms, neurotic symptoms, and maladaptive character styles. . . . Basic to all these difficulties are impairments in self-acceptance and self-esteem. (pp. 64–65)*

Box 8.3

SELF-CHECK

PART A

Indicate whether each of the following statements is true or false.

1. According to Daryl Bem, we may figure out what we like by looking at our own behavior.
2. The overjustification effect suggests that giving grades for good school performance may undermine children's motivation to learn.
3. Because of the overjustification effect, we should never reward people for working on a task. For example, we should never reward young children for doing their homework or practicing on the piano.
4. Both beneffectance and self-perception theory suggest that rather than our beliefs changing our actions, our actions may sometimes change (or reaffirm) our beliefs.
5. Self-verification is almost always at odds with beneffectance.
6. When self-verification clashes with beneffectance, beneffectance usually wins out.

PART B

Answer the following question.

7. What seems to be the underlying difference between the objective self-awareness perspective and Bem's self-perception theory?

Please turn to the end of this chapter to check your answers.

The effects of low self-esteem have been demonstrated in experiments in which people's self-image is temporarily deflated (for example, by being told they did poorly on an aptitude test or by receiving a negative evaluation of their personality). Participants are, at that time, more likely to belittle other people and express heightened racial prejudice. Generally, people who feel negative about themselves also tend to be feel negative about others (Crocker & Schwarz, 1985; Wills, 1981).

In related experiments, Teresa Amabile (1983; Amabile & Glazebrook, 1982) studied an event she had noticed in everyday life. Insecure people were often excessively critical, as if to impress others with their own brilliance. In her experiments, Amabile made some students feel insecure and others to feel more secure. She then showed a videotape of a person being interviewed and had subjects evaluate the person's intelligence. Who gave the harsher evaluation? The insecure students. Insecurity also correlates with psychological and medical problems.[1] But what are the sources of self-esteem?

Rosenthal (1974) conducted several experiments that suggested one possible source of self-esteem is what others think of us. He found that when others expect us to succeed, we will succeed. Specifically, he told teachers that certain randomly selected students were "late-bloomers" who were expected to bloom that year. The students who were expected to bloom, did. Rosenthal labeled this phenomenon **self-fulfilling prophecy,** the tendency to become what others expect us to become. More recently, Harris, Milich, Corbitt, Hoover, and Brady (1992) found that if a child was told that his play partner (a normal child) had a behavior problem, then his play partner would end up misbehaving. Thus, a diagnostic label such as hyperactivity may act as a self-fulfilling prophecy to damage a child's self-esteem and impair the child's relations with others.

Correlational evidence also suggests that how others perceive us affects our self-esteem. For example, people with low self-esteem often have trouble in school, are unpopular, or act in embarrassing ways (wetting their beds). Thus, children who are held in low esteem by their teachers or classmates tend to have low self-esteem. However, this correlational evidence is not conclusive: It could be that low self-esteem is the cause—rather than the result—of these actions.

As you have seen, correlational evidence is difficult to interpret. For example, in chapter 3, you saw that identical twins reared apart had similar self-esteem (Tellegen et al., 1988). Does this mean that we inherit a level of self-esteem? Or, could it mean that our physical appearance affects how others view us and thus affects how we see ourselves (Hanna, 1994)? Therefore, the child who is born attractive and athletically gifted may be destined to be popular and thus have high self-esteem (Bean & Keller, 1994; Harter, 1989; Johnstone, Frame, & Bouman, 1992). Although we do not definitively know the cause of self-esteem, taken as a whole, the correlational evidence *suggests* that children's self-esteem is affected by how their friends view them.

Correlational studies also suggest that the family plays an important role in the child's self-esteem. For example, Felson (1989) found that children tend to evaluate themselves in part on the basis of how they believe their parents evaluate them. This finding is corroborated by recent evidence suggesting that parental praise and affection correlate with self-esteem (Bean & Keller, 1994). Correlational studies also show that children with positive self-esteem come from homes in which parents exercise control in a democratic—yet nonpermissive—manner; communicate clearly with their children; and encourage their children to display affection and other emotions (Coopersmith, 1967;

[1]However, the correlations between self-esteem and psychological problems are much smaller than might be imagined. Indeed, in many cases (such as with crime, violence, and child abuse), they are essentially zero (Dawes, 1994).

Figure 8.7

Potentially Harmful Effects of Low Self-Esteem

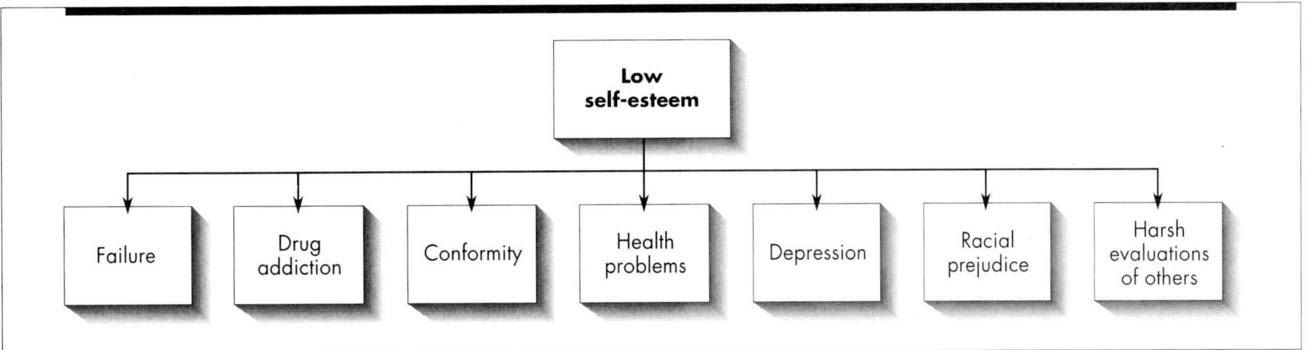

Damon, 1983; Wylie, 1961). These same parenting techniques also seem to result in having children who are independent, self-assertive, and competent.

Of course, we all know that self-esteem is not set in childhood. As children age, they start comparing themselves to others and the gap between their "real self" (who they think they are) and their "ideal self" (who they would like to be) widens (Glick & Zigler, 1985). Furthemore, as we will see in chapter 12, self-esteem tends to decline as children enter junior high (Simmons, Blyth, Van Cleave, & Bush, 1979), and math self-esteem seems to decline throughout the junior and senior high school years, probably because of the final point we want to make about the causes of self-esteem: Success boosts self-esteem, whereas failure tends to deflate it (Pulkkinen & Rönkä, 1994). Thus, academic self-esteem correlates well with academic performance (Hansfeld & Hattie, 1982) and especially with academic effort (Felson, 1984). More convincingly, experiments have shown that when college students fail a task, self-esteem often drops (Seligman, 1990). However, not everybody reacts to success and failure in the same way. For example, Jennifer Crocker and her colleagues (Crocker, Kayne, & Alloy, 1985) found that people who tended to take blame for failure and give others credit for success were most likely to become depressed. Fortunately, this self-defeating cycle can be reversed. For instance, Mary Ann Layden (1982) trained students to consider whether their failures might be due to things having nothing to do with the self (time pressures, other people, for example). After this training, students' self-esteem improved. Similarly, Judith Rodin and Ellen Langer (1980) found that the elderly felt better about themselves when they were encouraged to blame their problems on the nursing home rather than to aging. Specifically, elderly people told to blame their coordination problem on the slippery floor and their fatigue on being awakened so early felt better about themselves. (For a summary of the factors that influence self-esteem, see table 8.3.)

Table 8.3

Correlates of High Self-Esteem

People Will Probably Have High Self-Esteem IF They:

- Had parents who were democratic, yet not permissive.
- Had parents who clearly communicated with them.
- Have others who expect them to succeed.
- Succeed on tasks.
- Have been taught to attribute success to their own efforts and failure to reasons other than themselves (bad luck, other people).

Note: As Robyn Dawes (1994) points out, the goal of having a child with high self-esteem may be overrated. As you can see from this table, a child who has high self-esteem by blaming others for his failures may be antisocial.

Locus of Control and Learned Helplessness

In addition to seeing oneself as either good or bad, people see themselves as either having control over their destiny or as being at the mercy of the outside world (Rotter, 1954, 1966, 1990). Someone with an **internal locus of control** believes that she is in control of her own life. She feels she has the power to create, modify, or leave situations—she's in the driver's seat. People who feel they have mastery over themselves, their future development, and their environment feel good about themselves (Pulkkinen & Rönkä, 1994). On the other hand, people who feel that they are at the mercy of outside events and the whims of other people have an **external locus of control.** They feel helpless and powerless.

What determines one's **locus of control?** Children who have experienced a long history of nonresponsiveness from events and people in the world are clearly disadvantaged in developing an internal locus of control. They may learn to view life as a series of unsolvable problems and, in reaction, they may develop a mode of interacting with the world that Martin Seligman (1974, 1990) calls **learned helplessness,** a

If people who live in nursing homes are allowed to make decisions and take responsibility, even in small aspects, they are happier and healthier. This may be because they feel more in control over their circumstances.

belief that what happens to you does not depend on what you do. Experimental evidence shows that even normally optimistic people will become passive and depressed when continually confronted with problems beyond their control. Thus, people who have experienced many uncontrollable events may become permanently resigned to their own ineffectiveness and learn to act helpless in difficult circumstances. Thus, crises such as losing one's job, one's loved one, or being physically assaulted may result in learned helplessness.

But tragedies are not the only sources of helplessness. Ellen Langer and Judith Rodin (1976; Langer, 1989) found that if people in nursing homes were not free to make decisions and take responsibility, they were less happy, less active, and experienced poorer health than those who were given responsibility. Specifically, Langer and Rodin (1976) randomly assigned residents of a nursing home into an experimental or a control group. Those in the experimental group were encouraged to make decisions for themselves, such as choosing where to receive visitors and deciding whether to view a movie on Thursday or Friday. In addition, residents in the experimental group were given a houseplant to care for.

In contrast, residents in the control group were not encouraged to make decisions. Instead, they were told that the staff was there to help them in every way possible. Thus, if they wanted to visit with someone, they were told to ask a staff member to arrange a place for the visit. Although they were also given a houseplant, they were told that the staff would take care of it for them. Langer and Rodin found that the residents who were given more responsibility took more initiative, were more active, more vigorous, and more sociable than the control group.

Table 8.4

Risk Factors for Learned Helplessness

People Are at Risk for Learned Helplessness if:

- Average—or even good—things are happening to them, but those things are not the results of their own efforts.
- They have just experienced tragedies or crises that were beyond their control, especially if:
    - Their self-concept was very simple and undifferentiated.
    - They have rarely experienced failure before and they have little experience at working to overcome adversity.

You have seen that crises and lack of control may lead to learned helplessness. However, some people are less vulnerable to learned helplessness than others (see table 8.4).

Why are some people less affected by crises than others? One factor that may play an important role is how people organize their self-concept. Specifically, Jolley (1982), Linville (1985, 1987), and Niedenthal, Setterland, and Wherry (1992) have found that people with more differentiated self-concepts are less devastated by failure. What contributes to a more differentiated self-concept? As you might expect, the older a person is, the more roles a person assumes and more complex the self-concept is—until late adulthood, when the self-concept tends to become less complex (Jolley, 1982).

Although people can lose confidence at any age, they can also gain confidence at any age. As Bandura (1986) has shown, successful experiences can increase **self-efficacy,** confidence in one's ability to perform a particular task. Self-efficacy is like self-confidence, but it is specific to a given task or situation. For example, you might have high self-efficacy about your ability to perform competently except for when you go out on a date. However, after a few successful dates, your self-efficacy about dating will increase.

Self-Control

In addition to feeling in control of outside events (internal locus of control), people differ in their level of **self-control,** how well they can control themselves. Walter Mischel (1983) tested children's self-control by putting a single cookie in front of them and telling them that if they resisted eating it for a few minutes, they would get two cookies. By age 5, most children realized that waiting was easier if they distracted themselves from the outcomes. By sixth grade, some children were able to wait more effectively by thinking about the abstract aspects of the object rather than by focusing on how good the cookies tasted. Furthermore, even 5-year-olds who had little self-control could be taught strategies that would improve their self-control.

Figure 8.8

The Importance of Self-Control

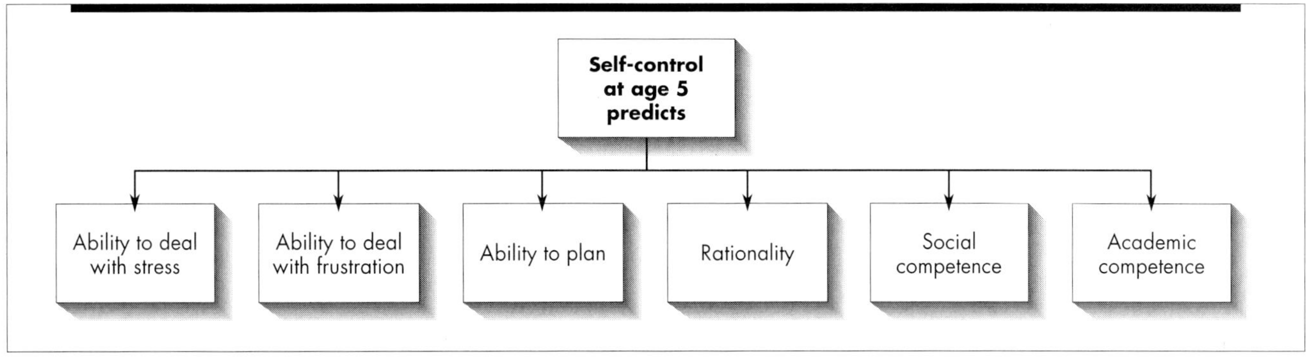

Box 8.4

SELF-CHECK

PART A

Indicate whether each of the following statements is true or false.

1. Most people suffer from low self-esteem.
2. People with high self-esteem tend to belittle others.
3. One's level of self-esteem is set during the first few years of life.
4. Low self-esteem causes children to have trouble in school.
5. Parents cause their children to have high self-esteem by encouraging their children to display affection and by exercising control in a democratic—yet nonpermissive—manner.
6. Being a permissive parent correlates with having children who have high self-esteem.
7. Learned helplessness occurs when people are rewarded for acting helpless.
8. The elderly are resistant to learned helplessness because they have a highly differentiated self.
9. The ability to delay gratification at age 5 is correlated with academic and social competence as a teenager.
10. The ability to delay gratification is almost completely inherited.

PART B

Answer the following questions.

11. How can self-esteem be increased?
12. How does locus of control differ from self-esteem?
13. What are three characteristics that would put a person at risk for learned helplessness?

Please turn to the end of this chapter to check your answers.

Perhaps such training should be an important part of our school or preschool curriculum. Why? Because Mischel and his colleagues (Mischel, Shoda, & Peake, 1988) found that how long children waited when they were 4 and 5 years old correlated with how well adjusted they were when they were in their teens. For example, the 4- and 5-year-olds who waited a long time were, as 14- and 15-year-olds, viewed as more academically and socially competent by their teachers and more rational than the children who had not been able to wait as long. The teens who had been able to wait a long time as 4-and 5-year-olds were also judged as being better than their peers at planning and at dealing with frustration and stress (see figure 8.8).

UNDERSTANDING OTHERS

As you have seen, the development of self depends, in part, on being able to understand others. Understanding others is also essential to moral development. Therefore, the next section of this chapter will be devoted to exploring how we develop the complex ability to consider the views of others.

How Infants Understand Others

Young infants lack the social skills necessary to relate to each other as social partners (see, for example, Hartup, 1983). They know very little about what other people are. What is the process by which we learn the importance of others? There are two major views of how this process occurs.

Table 8.5

One View of How Children's Interactions with Each Other Develop

Mueller and Lucas (1975): How Children Evolve from Interacting with Objects to Interacting with Others
• *Stage 1.* Treat other infants like they treat objects.
• *Stage 2.* May pay attention to the same object as the other infant is paying attention to.
• *Stage 3.* Interact directly with other children.

The first holds that social interaction emerges from interaction with objects (see table 8.5). For example, based on their study of infants participating in a play group, Mueller and Lucas (1975) proposed three stages in the development of infant peer relationships. In stage 1, late in the first year of life, infants treat one another the same way they treat toys. Over time, however, pairs of infants start to pay attention to the same object simultaneously (stage 2). Eventually, infants begin to interact directly with one another (stage 3).

The second view holds that social interaction is not solely a consequence of playing with objects. Instead, this view holds that the reason children play together is because they are naturally sociable. Thus, children play together not because they have a common interest in toys, but because they have a common interest in interacting with others (see figure 8.9). Researchers holding this second view have produced evidence that suggests that infants are more naturally disposed to play with each other than Mueller and Lucas (1975) believed. They argue that the stages described by Mueller and Lucas (1975) may depend on a coding scheme that fails to detect some subtle aspects of early peer responsiveness. Using what they considered a more sensitive coding scheme, both Hay (Hay, Pedersen, & Nash, 1982; Hay, Nash, & Pedersen, 1981a, 1981b, 1983) and Vandell, Wilson, and Buchanan (1980) demonstrated that infants engage in limited—but harmonious—social interaction with other infants as early as 6 months of age. In addition, by 12 months of age, all children show prosocial behavior (Zahn-Waxler & Radke-Yarrow, 1982). Furthermore, as early as 13 months of age, infants' peer-directed reactions are distinguishable from those directed to mothers (Fogel, 1979) and to infants' own mirror images (Field, 1979).

Regardless of which view is correct, both views suggest that direct experience with peers would improve children's social skills. Thus, as might be expected, Becker (1977) and Mueller and Brenner (1977) showed that experience with peers facilitates the growth of interaction skills in infants and toddlers, presumably by allowing interaction with many individuals who have various social styles. Children who are in regular play groups or in preschool or day care settings appear more socially competent with peers than do

Figure 8.9

Competing Views of the Factors Promoting Social Interaction

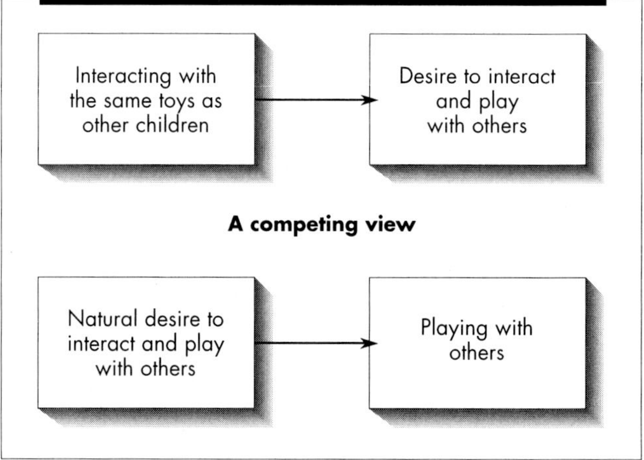

their age-mates who are cared for at home (Field & Roopnarine, 1982). Children in play groups also interact with their parents at a higher rate than do infants and toddlers raised exclusively at home (Vandell, 1979).

Childhood: The Development of Role Taking

Central to social interaction is **role taking,** the ability to understand the views of others, that is, "the ability to put yourself in someone else's shoes." Current developmental views of role taking incorporate and elaborate on the theories of George Herbert Mead (1934) and Jean Piaget (1932, 1955). Specifically, Mead's theorizing on significant symbols and role taking have influenced views on the development of social interactions, as has Piaget's construct of egocentrism. (As you may recall from chapter 6, Piaget believed that most children under age 7 were unable to understand that other people might see things differently than they do.)

George Herbert Mead's "theory of the significant symbol" emphasizes the importance of symbolic interaction for social interaction and communication (Damon, 1983). Mead defined **significant symbols** as gestures "which arouse in the individual himself the response which he is calling out in the other. . . ." For example, when you say a word, you are using a significant symbol because you expect that your interpretation of the word will be basically the same as your listener's.

This idea of symbolic interaction culminated in Mead's explanation of how shared meaning is established when we communicate. He postulated that we learn to "take the role of the other" as we interact with another. Through role taking, we achieve agreement between how our "self" and others' selves interpret actions and events. Because we learn to predict the thoughts and views of others, we can modify our "self's" gestures to enhance communication. As our self adjusts, the other's self also adapts. To Mead, this process of "mutual adjustment" is the core of human social interaction.

Although Piaget didn't use the words *role taking,* his concept of egocentrism had tremendous impact on modern role taking theory. Piaget defined egocentrism as "the confusion of the self with the non-self" (Piaget, 1955). Such a confusion occurs when we fail to recognize that others' perspectives are different from our own. In other words, egocentrism is the failure to role take. In his early work, Piaget (1932) proposed that children start in a **stage of egocentrism** in which the child "plays in an individual manner with material that is social." To illustrate this idea, Piaget pointed to the fact that young children frequently engage in **parallel play** in which they engage in a collective activity, but remain embedded in their own point of view. For example, children may be side by side in the sandbox, each playing with his own shovel and bucket. Such children may speak to one another, but they don't share ideas or communicate information. Instead, they engage in a **collective monologue,** where one child's words may cue the other's reply, but there is no reciprocal exchange. Consider the following dialogue between four children who were talking while drawing.

CHILD 1 (5 years, 11 months):

It begins with Goldilocks. I'm writing the story of the three bears. The daddy bear is dead. Only the daddy was too ill.

CHILD 2 (5 years, 11 months):

I used to live at Saleve. I lived in a little house and you had to take the funicular railway to go and buy things.

CHILD 3 (6 years, 10 months):

I can't do the bear.

CHILD 4 (6 years, 10 months):

That's not Goldilocks.

CHILD 1:

I haven't got curls. (Piaget, 1955, p. 21)

The stage of egocentrism gives way to a **stage of cooperation.** In the stage of cooperation, children can separate self from nonself. Consequently, they can truly interact and share with each other (see table 8.6).

Although Piaget's ideas about role taking are very intriguing, they are largely unsupported by research. For example, whereas Piaget originally believed that nonreciprocal speech was an inevitable consequence of egocentrism, research on two fronts has challenged this view.

First, Vygotsky (1962) discovered that children who in one situation engaged in collective monologues would, in another situation, engage in reciprocal speech. Thus, these children can role take when they want to.

Second, when Piaget's methods of coding children's speech were scrutinized, investigators realized that Piaget had underestimated children's ability to communicate. In fact, investigators learned that children as young as age 4 can engage in reciprocal, nonegocentric speech (Gottman & Parkhurst, 1980).

If Piaget's views on the developmental progression of role-taking skills are inaccurate, what is the true progression?

Table 8.6

Piaget's Stages of Role Taking

1. *Stage of egocentrism.* Piaget believed that parallel play and collective monologues revealed that children at this stage cannot interact with each other.
2. *Stage of cooperation.* Piaget believed that cooperative play and interactive discussions revealed that children at this stage can interact with others and understand each other's point of view.

One popular view of the development of role taking skills is Robert Selman's (1976, 1980). Using the same dilemmas that he developed for his studies on self, Selman derived five stages of role taking (see table 8.7).

During the preschool years most children are at stage 0, **egocentric perspective taking.** At this stage, children can make simple inferences about people's behavior. For example, if someone is screaming, children can infer that the other person is angry. However, they still may make the mistake of presuming that another person thinks and feels exactly the same way they do.

Stage 1, **social-informational role taking,** starts at about age 5. Stage 1 children understand that—because others are in different situations or have different information—others' thoughts and feelings may be different from their own.

Stage 2, **self-reflective role taking,** encompasses ages 8 through 10. Stage 2 children are able to reflect on their own thoughts and feelings. Consequently, they can anticipate what other people will think or feel by putting themselves in the other person's place. Stage 2 children are also sensitive to the ability of others to anticipate perspectives. That is, they know that other people may be able to put themselves in the child's place to predict how the child will feel in a certain situation.

Children who have reached stage 3, **mutual role taking,** can assume a third-person view, realizing that they can "step outside" a social interaction and evaluate the participants' perspectives according to criteria that none of them share. Thus, they can think about how their parents or a teacher might view an argument they are having with a friend.

By adolescence, most people have entered stage 4, **social and conventional systems role taking.** In this stage, the person realizes that the mutual perspective taking does not always result in complete understanding because we don't share identical experiences, roles, or positions. Thus, when you try to put yourself in another's shoes, what seems like a fit for you, may not actually be a fit for your friend. For this reason, we need to look at situations as our larger social group would see them so that we have a shared point of reference.

Table 8.7

Robert Selman's Stages of Role Taking

Stage	Age Range*	Child's Understanding
Stage 0: Egocentrism	3 to 6 years	Child has a sense of differentiation of self and other but fails to distinguish between the social perspective (thoughts, feelings) of other and self. Child can label other's overt feelings but does not see the cause-effect relation of reasons to social actions.
Stage 1: Social-Informational Role Taking	6 to 8 years	Child is aware that other has a social perspective based on other's own reasoning, which may or may not be similar to child's. However, child tends to focus on one perspective rather than coordinating viewpoints.
Stage 2: Self-Reflective Role Taking	8 to 10 years	Child is conscious that each individual is aware of the other's perspective and that this awareness influences self and other's view of each other. Putting self in other's place is a way of judging his intentions, purposes, and actions. Child can form a coordinated chain of perspectives, but cannot yet abstract from this process to the level of simultaneous mutuality.
Stage 3: Mutual Role Taking	10 to 12 years	Child realizes that both self and other can view each other mutually and simultaneously as subjects. Child can step outside the two-person dyad and view the interaction from a third-person perspective.
Stage 4: Social and Conventional System Role Taking	12 to 15+ years	Person realizes mutual perspective taking does not always lead to complete understanding. Social conventions are seen as necessary because they are understood by all members of the group (the generalized other) regardless of their positions, roles, or experiences.

Based on R. L. Selman, Social-Cognitive Understanding: A Guide to Educational and Clinical Practice in *Moral Development and Behavior*, edited by T. Lickona. Copyright ©1976, Holt, Rinehart & Winston, New York.

**Note.* Age ranges for all stages represent only an average approximation based on studies to date.

Box 8.5

SELF-CHECK

PART A

Indicate whether each of the following statements is true or false.

1. Most researchers believe that experience with peers at an early age will facilitate social interaction skills.
2. Nine-month-old infants who interact intensively with their mothers are also highly social with both their peers and their siblings.
3. Piaget's stages of role taking are well supported by research.

PART B

Answer the following questions.

4. Do researchers differ about the degree to which infants have the ability to interact with peers? If so, why do they disagree?
5. What two bits of evidence did Piaget use to support his belief that young children are in the stage of egocentrism?
6. What is one major similarity between Selman's views of children under 5 and Piaget's views of such children?
7. How does Selman's theory of role taking differ from Piaget's theorizing on role taking in terms of (a) number of stages and (b) research used to develop the theory?
8. What are two ways in which Selman's stage 2 is more sophisticated than his stage 1?
9. According to Selman, individuals at different ages can analyze situations from different viewpoints. What viewpoint can a stage 4 child have that a stage 3 child can't? What viewpoint can a stage 3 child have that a stage 2 child can't?

Please turn to the end of this chapter to check your answers.

In short, role taking is clearly a necessary component of mature social interaction. As we move from adolescence into the adult world of work, family, and community, our success in adapting to the demands of adult life will be mediated by our ability to understand and respect others. The need for empathy is clearly illustrated in the next section, moral development.

Moral Development

In recent years, many people have been concerned about the lack of morality in our society. Prominent politicians and television evangelists have committed immoral acts; business leaders have illegally polluted our rivers and oceans; landlords have turned dogs and knives on their tenants; sports idols have used illegal drugs; "normal" teenagers have protected the person who murdered their friends; and teenage pregnancy has reached epidemic proportions.

Furthermore, people sometimes seem unwilling to acknowledge that others hold different views from their own, and people occasionally seem unwilling to care for and aid others. People seem less and less likely to accept that they may have to subordinate their own needs and desires to the needs of others (Conger, 1988). We all know the problem; what is the solution?

We can't offer definitive solutions to the problem. We can't say that the answer is that the schools need to teach morality or that the church needs to take a larger role. However, we can discuss the basic theories of moral development. We will first describe cognitive structuralist theory, which focuses on developing the mental ability to make moral judgments. Then, we will discuss Hoffman's theory, which focuses on developing empathy and motivation to behave morally. Finally, we will discuss a comprehensive theory that tries to account for both the development of moral reasoning and moral action.

Piaget's Cognitive Structural Approach to Moral Reasoning

Piaget was the first developmental psychologist to link cognitive development to moral development. Piaget postulated two levels of moral development: heteronomous and autonomous (see table 8.8).

Table 8.8

Piaget's Stages of Morality

Heteronomous stage (ages 4 to 7).	Child does not understand where rules come from; does not understand the reasons behind rules so child does not understand that exceptions can be made; and child can judge others only in terms of whether or not they broke a rule.
Autonomous stage (ages 7 to adult).	Understands that rules are social agreements; understands the reasons behind rules so child understands when exceptions should be made; and child can judge people in terms of both their behavior and their intentions.

In the **heteronomous stage** (ages 4 to 7), rules are imposed by others ("hetero" means others). Often, children in this stage think that rules come from their own parents or from God. Although the child may claim that rules must be followed to the letter, she doesn't understand the reason behind them. Therefore, she might refuse to talk to a relative she doesn't remember because "you aren't supposed to talk to strangers."

According to Piaget, the heteronomous child's failure to understand the reason behind the rule is not the only reason such children are so literal in their interpretation of rules. Another reason is that the heteronomous child can't empathize with others. Consequently, to such a child, someone who does something that brings a bad result has done a bad thing. A person who breaks a glass trying to bring her mother some milk is no better than someone who breaks the glass trying to steal some cookies. A person who kills a cat for fun is no worse than someone who has the cat put away to relieve its misery.

After age 7, most people enter the **autonomous stage.** This stage, which coincides with the development of concrete operations, is marked by two changes. First, a person at the autonomous level understands that rules are social agreements designed to help people get along and cooperate (Maccoby, 1980). Consequently, the individual at the autonomous level not only believes that rules are good, but also realizes when exceptions should be made. Second, the autonomous person realizes that people do things for reasons. The autonomous person begins to empathize with others' intentions and feelings. As a result, before judging people who have broken a rule, the autonomous individual may want to know *why* they broke the rule. To the person at the autonomous level, the thought may count more than the deed.

Kohlberg's Cognitive Structural Approach to Moral Reasoning

As we mentioned, Piaget was the first developmental psychologist to formulate a cognitive structural theory of moral development. But he was not the last. Indeed, when most developmental psychologists think about moral development, they immediately think of Lawrence Kohlberg. Kohlberg (1963a, 1963b, 1969, 1981, 1984) proposed a theory of moral development that built on Piaget's work and that, like Piaget's theory, focused on moral reasoning.

To determine how people make moral judgments, Kohlberg asked subjects to solve moral dilemmas like the famous Heinz dilemma:

> *In Europe, a woman was near death from a very bad disease, a special kind of cancer. There was one drug that the doctors thought might save her. It was a form of radium that a druggist in the same town had recently discovered. The drug was expensive to make, but the druggist was charging ten times what the drug cost him to make. He paid $200 for the radium and charged $2,000 for a small dose of the drug. The sick woman's husband, Heinz, went to everyone he knew to borrow the money, but he could get together only about $1,000, which was half of what it cost. He told the druggist that his wife was dying and asked him to sell it cheaper or let him pay later. But the druggist said, "No, I discovered the drug and I'm going to make money from it." Heinz got desperate and broke into the man's store to steal the drug for his wife.*[2]

How would you solve this dilemma? Should Heinz have stolen the drug? Were his actions right or wrong? In evaluating people's moral reasoning, Kohlberg was not interested in *what* people thought Heinz should have done, but *why* they thought Heinz should have acted in a given way. Thus, like Piaget, Kohlberg was interested in how people reasoned.

Based on this research, Kohlberg expanded Piaget's two-level theory to three levels and he added two stages under each of these levels (see table 8.9). In the next section, we will examine Kohlberg's three levels of moral reasoning: preconventional, conventional, and postconventional.

Preconventional Level

Before age 9, most children function at the **preconventional level** in which they have a morality of self-interest. That is, they are looking out for themselves. Some adolescents and many adult criminals (as well as some pets) also function at this level.

People in stage 1, **obedience and punishment orientation,** obey rules and laws to avoid punishment. Such people might push drugs—if they were sure they wouldn't get caught. If they were to judge the morality of a person's actions, they would judge the person based on the behavior (stealing) and its consequences (getting caught), rather than on the person's intentions and motives. Thus, a stage 1 person might judge Heinz's actions just as harshly as the actions of someone who stole the drug for financial gain.

People in stage 2, **naive hedonistic and instrumental orientation,** act to gain concrete rewards, rather than solely to avoid punishment. Although there may be evidence of reciprocity and sharing, it is manipulative, self-serving reciprocity rather than one based on a true sense of justice, generosity, sympathy, or compassion. It is a kind of bartering: "I'll scratch your back, if you scratch mine" or "If you give me a piece of candy, I'll be your best friend forever."

[2]This dilemma is quoted from the appendix of a research report by Marcus Lieberman titled "Estimation of a Moral Judgment Level Using Items Whose Alternatives Form a Graded Scale," ERIC, 1971.

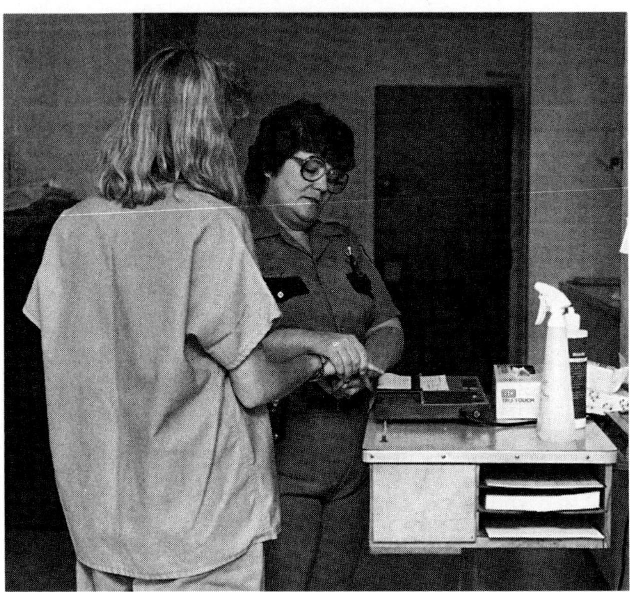

A person who is at Kohlberg's first stage of morality would obey rules only out of fear of being caught and punished.

Conventional Level: Morality of Conventional Rules and Conformity

By early adolescence, most people have matured to a conventional level of moral reasoning. People at the **conventional level** of reasoning consider someone other than just themselves. These people conform to the laws and conventions of society—not to avoid punishment or get concrete rewards—but simply because they believe that the laws and conventions of society should be obeyed. Conventional reasoning is encouraged by our need to conform in order to gain social approval. Such conformity, by definition, involves the ability to understand the perspectives of others. As Selman pointed out, neither the ability to understand others' points of view nor the ability to understand society's point of view is fully developed before age 12. Consequently, most people can't enter this stage before adolescence.

Most people will remain at the conventional level of moral reasoning for the rest of their lives. For most people, the only question is whether they will stay in stage 3 or move to stage 4.

Individuals functioning at stage three, **interpersonal concordance of "good boy—nice girl,"** perform actions that will get the acceptance and approval of others. Like people in stage 1, morality is what others dictate as being right. But unlike stage 1 people, stage 3 individuals are conforming for social acceptance, not bowing to physical power. Their concern for conformity reflects a desire to maintain goodwill with friends and family members. They may conform to avoid disapproval from others or to avoid feeling guilt. Furthermore, rather than judge another person's actions based on the physical consequences, a stage 3 person takes into consideration the person's intentions.

Table 8.9

Kohlberg's Levels and Stages of Moral Reasoning

Level/Stage	Description	Examples of Moral Reasoning in Support of Heinz's Stealing	Examples of Moral Reasoning Against Heinz's Stealing
Preconventional morality			
Stage 1: Heteronomous morality	Avoids punishment.	"If you let your wife die, you will get in trouble."	"You shouldn't steal the drug. You could get caught and sent to jail."
Stage 2: Instrumental relativist	Gains concrete rewards.	"If you do happen to get caught, you could give the drug back and you wouldn't get much of a sentence."	"He may not get much of a jail term if he steals the drug, but his wife will probably die before he gets out."
Conventional morality			
Stage 3: Interpersonal concordance of "good boy—nice girl"	Seeks approval/ avoids disapproval.	"Your family will think you're an inhuman husband if you don't."	"It isn't just the druggist who will think you're a criminal; everyone else will, too."
Stage 4: Law and order orientation	Does duty to society/ avoids dishonor or guilt.	"If you have any sense of honor, you won't let your wife die because you're afraid to do the only thing that will save her."	"You'll always feel guilty for your dishonesty and law breaking."
Postconventional morality			
Stage 5: The social-contract legalistic orientation	Affirms agreed-upon rights.	"If you let your wife die, it would be out of fear, not out of reasoning it out. Society's needs and wishes are best served by having her survive."	"You'd lose respect for yourself if you're carried away by emotion and forget the long-range point of view."
Stage 6: Universal ethical principle orientation	Affirms own ethical principles.	"If you don't steal the drug, you wouldn't have lived up to your own standards of conscience (even though you would have followed the law)."	"If you stole the drug, you'd condemn yourself because you wouldn't have lived up to your own conscience and standards of honesty (even though you wouldn't be blamed by other people)."

Based on R. L. Selman, "Social-Cognitive Understanding: A Guide to Educational and Clinical Practice" in *Moral Development and Behavior,* edited by T. Lickona, Holt, Rinehart & Winston, 1976. Reprinted by permission.

Because their behavior is so dependent on others, stage 3 individuals may engage in shocking behavior. For instance, they may not report a murder or a rape of one of their friends because they are afraid their peers will disapprove if they squeal. They cannot "just say no" to peers offering them drugs. In fact, we recently read a story of a high school senior who was president of her school's SADD (students against drunk driving) chapter. She had given speeches and coordinated activities against drunk driving. She died in a car driven by a drunk driver. Everyone in the car was legally drunk. It turned out she had succumbed to peer pressure and got them the beer that led to her death.

Instead of conforming to gain social approval, people in stage 4, **law and order orientation,** conform to authority to maintain the official social order. People in stage 4 may blindly accept social conventions and rules. To them, moral behavior is that which conforms to society's rules or laws. Ads and bumper stickers saying "55, it's the law" are appealing to this "law and order" morality that involves unquestioning acceptance of social regulations.

You may wonder why stage 4 is considered more advanced than stage 3. After all, people in stage 4 may end up being bureaucrats who are so obsessed with following procedures that they fail to help someone who needs it. Stage 3 people, on the other hand, might cut through the bureaucratic red tape, especially for friends or family members. In Kohlberg's opinion, stage 4 reasoning is more sophisticated because these people are conforming to a rule made by representatives of their society rather than to their immediate peer group. However, Kohlberg admits that stage 4 people have not reached the highest level of moral development: postconventional morality.

Postconventional: Morality of Self-Accepted Moral Principles

Most people are not at the **postconventional level** of moral reasoning. Most people cannot be at this level for at least two reasons. First, reaching postconventional morality requires experience in adult society. Consequently, Kohlberg believed that no one under age 20 reaches this level. Second, postconventional moral reasoning requires formal operational thought. As you may recall from chapter 5, only a few people achieve Piaget's stage of formal operational thought. Thus, to be able to reach postconventional thought, you must be an adult who is operating at formal operations.

Yet, even of those adults who do reach formal operations, only a few will attain postconventional levels of moral reasoning. These few do not accept rules because peers want them to or because lawmakers passed a law. Instead, they look for the reason behind the law.

Stage 5, **legalistic social-contract orientation** represents a morality based on a democratic agreement among people to conform to norms needed to maintain both social order and individual rights. As with stage 4 individuals, people at stage 5 tend to follow existing laws. However, there is a flexibility of moral beliefs in this stage that was lacking in stage 4. Thus, because stage 5 individuals realize that a law is a social contract, they realize that the law can be changed to better serve people. Indeed, the law should be changed—if people in society rationally discuss it and a majority agree that changing it would meet the needs of a larger number of people. Thus, whereas a stage 4 person would say "the law is the law," the stage 5 individual might say "that's a dumb law. It's not what we, the people, really want. Let's change it."

People in stage 6, **universal ethical principled orientation,** on the other hand, realize that what is moral is not simply what a majority of people in one society want to do. Societies have committed evil acts. Since morality is not something that can be put to a vote, stage 6 individuals look beyond society to determine what is right. Thus, rather than seek approval through conformity to a law (stage 4) or to majority opinion (stage 5), stage 6 individuals make moral decisions based on abstract principles concerned with justice, compassion, fairness, and equality. Whereas a stage 4 person might adhere rigidly to the Ten Commandments (specific guidelines for moral behavior), a stage 6 person would abide by the Golden Rule (a more abstract rule that encompasses much more than the Ten Commandments).

People who have attained stage 6 have highly individualistic moral beliefs that sometimes conflict with the social order. A greater number of nonviolent activist students who demonstrated against the Vietnam War had attained postconventional levels of moral reasoning than nonactivist students (Lickona, 1976). Put another way, stage 6 people follow their conscience, even if that means alienating friends or society. Stage 6 individuals want laws that are best for everyone, whether or not their particular society approves. Thus, white South Africans who protest their society's racist policies are placing a universal principle (equality) over acceptance from their society. However, as critics note, society might break down if everyone were stage 6.

Summary of Kohlberg's Theory

To review, Kohlberg's theory is a **stage theory.** In other words, Kohlberg makes the controversial claim that these six stages form a moral ladder that extends from the immature, preconventional morality typical of the 7-year-old to, at the top rung, a recognition of what the individual perceives to be fundamental ethical principles. The sequence is said to be unvarying and universal—everyone, regardless of culture and cognitive level, progresses through the same sequence.

This assumption that higher stages are characterized by more sophisticated reasoning has some interesting implications. First, Kohlberg found that just as people attracted to people who are slightly more sophisticated than themselves, people are attracted to moral reasoning that is one stage above their typical level of functioning. Thus, a person at stage 3 might be impressed by the reasoning of a person who was at stage 4. Second, Kohlberg found that people have trouble understanding reasoning that is more than one stage above their own. Indeed, if you are at stage 4, Kohlberg would say that you would be incapable of understanding what stage 6 really is. Thus, stage 3 thinkers would be intolerant of the civil disobedience exhibited by such leaders as Martin Luther King, Jr. and Mahatma Gandhi, who argued from a postconventional morality that human rights should take precedence over the laws of the state (Kohlberg, 1981). Consequently, Kohlberg's theory—if accurate—not only leads to insights about how individuals decide what is right or wrong, but it also explains why people may be unable to understand each other's position on moral issues (see table 8.10).

Kohlberg's theory also has several implications for society. Specifically, it has two implications for moral education. First, people can be taught higher moral reasoning without being told what to think. One can be a conservative or a liberal at any of Kohlberg's stages. Thus, teaching Kohlberg's moral reasoning sidesteps a common objection to moral education: "If you are going to teach morality in school, whose morality are you going to teach?" Second, as would be expected from someone who follows in Piaget's footsteps, Kohlberg believes that moral thinking develops as children's minds actively confront moral challenges. Rather than avoiding controversial issues and shutting out "dangerous" or "unpopular" or "different" ideas, Kohlberg believes that a person's moral consciousness is raised to a higher stage through dialogue concerning rules and moral issues. The

Table 8.10

How People at Kohlberg's Different Stages of Moral Development Might Answer the Question "Why Obey a Rule?"

"Why Obey a Rule?"
Stage 1: "So I won't get hit."
Stage 2: "Because it will pay off later on."
Stage 3: "Because my friends want me to."
Stage 4: "Because it's the law."
Stage 5: "Because obeying the rule is in the best interest of most of our society."
Stage 6: "It's an abstract, universal rule that I can live with because it is fair and just. If it wasn't, I wouldn't follow it."

implications of Kohlberg's theory can be briefly summarized as the following list:

1. A person may be unable to understand another's point of view because their own level of moral reasoning is too low.
2. People can be taught moral reasoning without being taught what to think.
3. Moral development is promoted by discussing moral dilemmas with people who have ideas that differ from one's own.

Critique of Kohlberg's Theory

If Kohlberg's theory is accurate, it has important implications. But is it accurate? The most impressive support for Kohlberg's theory comes from a 20-year longitudinal study of 58 boys (Colby, Kohlberg, Gibbs, & Lieberman, 1983). The study began when research participants were 10, 13, and 16. Each boy was individually interviewed five times at 3- or 4-year intervals. At each interview, the boys were asked to make moral judgments on nine dilemmas. With the exception of two boys, all research participants demonstrated upward movement toward higher stages, and no one skipped stages. As expected, most did not progress beyond stage 4. Indeed, only a few reached stage 5—and then only after age 20. These findings support Kohlberg's assertion that most adults reason at a conventional level of morality (stages 3 or 4). In fact, this finding led Kohlberg to doubt the practical value of scoring solutions for stage 6 responses, and this final stage has been dropped from the most recent version of his scoring system (Colby & Kohlberg, 1984).

The elimination of stage 6 from Kohlberg's most recent scoring scheme is a reminder that good theory is dynamic, not stagnant. Therefore, adjustments and improvements are made to correct flaws and increase its explanatory value. With this fact in mind, lets consider four common criticisms of Kohlberg's theory of moral reasoning:

1. *Western bias.* Postconventional reasoning is seen only in industrialized countries.
2. *Liberal bias.* Politically liberal responses tend to get higher ratings than politically conservative responses. For example, postconventional morality is assumed to be superior to conventional morality.
3. *Male bias.* "Male morality" of following rules is scored higher than "female morality" of valuing interpersonal relationships.
4. *Moral behavior.* Level of moral reasoning may have little to do with moral behavior.

First, Kohlberg's theory may be culturally biased. Although children in several cultures do progress sequentially through the first two levels of Kohlberg's stages (Edwards, 1981; Parikh, 1980; Snarey, 1985), the postconventional level is reached only by those raised in educated, middle-class families in industrialized countries such as the United States, Britain, and Israel (Edwards, 1982). However, just as with Piaget's theory, the fact that few people reach the highest stage is not a serious blow to the theory. Indeed, the fact that at least a few people reach the stage supports the theory: It's proof that the stage that the theory proposes really exists.

Second, critics question Kohlberg's assumption that there is one best way to think about moral issues—and that Kohlberg knows what that best way is. Not everyone agrees with Kohlberg's assumption that moral truths can be found by following logic and the ethic of valuing justice above all else. For example, conservatives dispute whether the lack of conformity characterized by postconventional reasoning is really morally superior to other forms of reasoning. After all, where would society be if we were all "marching to the beat of different drummers?" Feminine scholars like Carol Gilligan (1982) argue that it is rather arbitrary to say that a person who values abstract principles of justice is morally superior to someone who values taking care of others and maintaining social relationships. To Gilligan, stage 6 morality is a perspective based on studies by and of males (note that the sample used for Kohlberg's longitudinal study was all male). She argues that for women, moral maturity is less an impersonal morality of abstract ethical principles and more a morality of responsible relationships. Gilligan believes that women's moral reasoning regarding the dilemma of Heinz and the druggist reveals their concern for the whole network of human relationships and feelings among the people involved. This tends to place them at the conventional (socially concerned) level of moral reasoning rather than at the postconventional level (Blake & Cohen, 1985). Thus, measured by a male yardstick, women's moral differences become moral deficits. Actually, asserts Gilligan (1982), women's concern with rights is not inferior, but rather superior: "In the different voice of women lies the truth of an ethic of care" (p. 173).

Third, some have argued that the theory is sexist because women are more likely to be placed at stage 3, whereas men are placed in stage 4 (Rothbart et al., 1986). Again, Gilligan and her colleagues (Brown & Gilligan, 1992; Gilligan, 1982) attribute the difference to women being raised to be more concerned about relationships and caring for individual's feelings (thus scoring at stage 3) whereas men are raised to be less concerned with personal relationships and more in terms of succeeding in the system (stage 4). Feminists might also note that since laws were made by men and for men, men should have an easier time accepting them than women. The "sexism" debate may turn out to be pointless: Several studies have shown no difference between the number of men and women at stage 3 and 4 (Houston & Campbell, 1994; Pratt et al., 1991; Walker, 1984, 1989; Walker & Taylor, 1991).

Fourth, some researchers (Blasi, 1980) have found little relationship between moral reasoning (what people *say*) and moral behavior (what people *do*). Morality involves more than what people think; it involves what people do. What we do is determined by situational factors as well as attitudes (see box 8.6). Furthermore, people who are capable of thinking at one stage may, when thinking about their own life, operate at a lower stage (Krebs, Vermeulen, & Denton, 1990). Thus, if we want to develop children who act morally, we must do more than make them capable of moral reasoning.

In short, Kohlberg's critics have two basic criticisms. First, they believe the moral stages, especially the postconventional moral stages, apply primarily to liberal, middle-class, Western males. Second, although Kohlberg's critics concede that moral reasoning is linked with cognitive development, they argue that cognitive development is only one of many determinants of moral action.

Moral Motivation Theory: Hoffman's Empathy Scheme

Whereas Kohlberg views moral development in terms of moral reasoning and cognition, Martin Hoffman (1981, 1988) focuses on the role of moral affect and motivation. He asks, "What prompts people to the aid of someone at a cost to themselves? to refrain from doing something they want to do simply because it might have a harmful effect on someone? to feel bad about themselves when they realize that their actions have hurt someone?" (p. 509). Hoffman's answer—empathy.

Hoffman defines **empathy** as "a vicarious affective response that is more appropriate to someone else's situation than to one's own." In our society, it is easy to downplay the importance of emotional responses such as empathy. However, as Hoffman points out, the quality of one's empathy depends on the thoughts that are the foundation of that emotion. Therefore, as our thinking ability develops, our empathy becomes more appropriate, more sophisticated, and less focused on gut-level feelings. Specifically, Hoffman (1975) proposes four social-cognitive levels of empathy:

1. *Global empathy* (0 to 12 months).
2. *Egocentric empathy* (1 to 3 years).
3. *Empathy for another's feelings* (3 years to late childhood).
4. *Empathy for another's life condition* (late childhood on).

Global Empathy

Because young infants haven't learned to fully separate self from other, they may experience **global empathy,** mistaking another person's distress for their own distress. As a result, they may act like what happened to another person actually happened to them. For example, if one baby in a nursery cries, other babies will also cry. Similarly, Hoffman reports an 11-month-old girl who looked as if she were about to cry after viewing another child fall and cry. She then placed her thumb in her mouth and buried her head in her mother's lap—the same response she would have given if she herself had fallen.

Egocentric Empathy

As infants enter the second year of life, they outgrow global empathy. Hoffman hypothesizes that children enter a stage called **egocentric empathy** when thay are able to separate another's distress from their own. Egocentric empathy is possible because children have developed a "physical self" that is independent of others. However, the child's egocentrism is still seen in his assumption that the other's internal states are identical to his own. For example, Hoffman tells of an 18-month-old boy who had his own mother comfort a crying friend even though the friend's mother was also present.

Empathy for Another's Feelings

Once children have started role taking (at about 3 years of age), they become aware that the feelings of others may differ from their own, a stage called **empathy for another's feelings.** With this awareness comes an increasing responsiveness to cues about what the other feels. In addition, the acquisition of language helps children empathize with a broad range of emotions, and eventually with several conflicting emotions. Thus, empathy with a person's distress may include understanding a person's wish not to feel obligated, and therefore not to be helped.

Empathy for Another's Life Condition

Hoffman's final stage, **empathy for another's life condition,** begins in late childhood. A person has gained the awareness that the pleasure and pain felt by others is not always temporary. Instead, both pleasure and pain can be long-term, and both may be rooted in economic or social conditions. Thus, you do not have to see a person in

Box 8.6

RESEARCH in FOCUS

To Shock or Not to Shock

In 1963, Stanley Milgram published the shocking results of his studies on obedience. To better understand the important implications of his studies, put yourself in the shoes of one of his subjects. You agree to participate in a psychology experiment. When you arrive at the laboratory, you find another participant who is also waiting. The researcher greets you and ushers both of you into a room where he explains that you will be taking part in a learning experiment. One of you will be the "teacher," the other will be the "learner." The teacher is to read a list of word pairs and then repeat one member of each pair. The learner is to supply the missing member for each pair. You are then "randomly" assigned to either the teacher or learner condition. You end up the teacher (unknown to you, the assignment was rigged and the "learner" is a plant). You are then seated on the other side of a partition, where you can have verbal but not visual contact with the "learner." The researcher shows you a series of levers, instructing you that they are used to deliver increasingly higher levels of electrical shock to the "learner" each time an error is made. A sample shock is given to you to demonstrate what it feels like.

You read the first list of word pairs and start with the learning test. The "learner" accurately provides the missing word member for the first two word pairs, but fails on the third. You're supposed to deliver a shock—and with additional errors you are supposed to increase the dose. What will you do? If you deliver the shock, will you increase it with the next error? At what level of shock would you stop?

You look at the researcher. He looks back. You push the lever, deliver the shock. The learner yelps. You give the next word. Another error. The level of shock increases—75 volts, 105 volts . . . 210 volts. The learner is screaming with each shock, "It hurts! Please stop! Let me out of here!" Do you continue?

When questioned about whether they would deliver the maximum shock (450 volts), only 1 percent predicted they would. However, after testing more than 1,000 subjects from all walks of life, Milgram found that 65 percent will deliver the maximum shock.

Why are people so off on their predictions? Basically, because there is a difference between trying to imagine how you would behave in a certain situation and actually being in that situation. Most of us, when told by an authority to do something, will do it. That is why thousands of average people were able to brutalize and murder millions of Jews during World War II. They followed orders from their superiors. Obedience is why young American men gunned down innocent women and infants in Vietnamese jungles. The powerful lesson of Milgram's study is that we are all influenced by situational influences.

distress to feel empathy. Just being aware of the person's general level of distress or deprivation can arouse feelings of empathy in you. Such empathy may be felt toward social groups (the poor, homeless, AIDS victims) as well as toward individuals. Hoffman (1980, 1988) believed that this empathic level can motivate the creation of specific moral and political ideologies that focus on the alleviation of the plight of unfortunate groups. Thus, rather than give a hand-out to the poor, members of these political and moral organizations would try to deal with the poor's long-term problems.

Although empathy is certainly important to moral behavior, we all know it isn't enough to guarantee moral action. We have all been in a situation where we empathized with another, yet offered no aid. Thus, although moral empathy—like moral reasoning—offers us some insight into moral action and development, some pieces of the puzzle of human morality are missing.

The Dialectical Approach: Rest and Carroll's Four-Process Model

To find the missing pieces of the moral puzzle, we must ask, "Why doesn't moral reasoning correlate highly with moral action?" "Why isn't empathy enough to make you behave in a moral way?" At an intuitive level, most of us realize that when we are in a situation calling for moral action, factors other than empathy and moral conviction influence what we do. Sometimes, people buckle under to social pressure ("Come on, just one puff"). Sometimes, personal ambition, ignorance, or lack of motivation prohibit moral action. To illustrate the various influences on our moral behavior, James Carroll and James Rest (1982) propose a four-process model of morality. Specifically, they argue that every moral action involves four components:

1. *Recognition and sensitivity.* Is there a moral problem?
2. *Moral judgment.* What is the moral answer to this problem?

In Hoffman's theory, people at the final stage of development can feel empathy for others' life conditions, such as hunger.

3. *Nonmoral values and influences.* What is the best thing to do in response to the problem once practical issues and social pressures (in addition to the moral answer) are considered?
4. *Execution and implementation.* Doing the "best" thing.

The first requirement for moral behavior is **recognition and sensitivity** to the fact that a moral problem exists. To behave morally, you must translate a social situation into a moral problem. You must be sensitive enough to recognize someone's welfare is at stake. (Is the woman crying and kicking her car in need of help? What about the man being hit by the policeman? Or, the poorly dressed person sitting on the sidewalk?).

Once you are aware that a moral issue is at stake, you must make a **moral judgment.** You must determine what the moral thing to do really is. Making this judgment requires thinking about what your moral ideals call for, and deciding which moral norms apply. (Should you be charitable toward the poorly dressed man or should you refuse to encourage that kind of behavior so that others won't be bothered?) How we make this judgment depends on our level of moral reasoning.

Box 8.7

SELF-CHECK

Part A

Indicate whether each of the following statements is true or false.

1. According to Kohlberg, moral development can be promoted by teaching people traditional values and insulating them from people who have odd viewpoints.
2. Few people reach stage 6.
3. More women than men are at stage 3.
4. Stage of morality correlates well with moral behavior.

Part B

Answer the following questions.

5. How does Kohlberg's theory of moral development compare to Piaget's?
6. Why is Kohlberg's stage 4 morality considered—by some—to be more advanced than stage 3?
7. What stage of morality would people expect from a police chief? a nation's leader? the President of the UN? a seventh-grader who is heavily involved in a junior high clique?
8. According to Kohlberg, what type of morality would his program teach? According to his critics, what would be taught?

Please turn to the end of this chapter to check your answers.

Once we have made a judgment, our morals must be reconciled with **nonmoral values and influences.** We must devise a plan of action with our moral ideal in mind while taking into account nonmoral values and goals that impinge on the situation. We must balance what we think morally ought to be done against the influence of situational pressures. ("I'm going to be late if I help this woman. What if it's a setup to rob suckers like me?")

The next stage is **execution and implementation** of the moral decision. We must behave in accordance with our moral objective despite distractions, impediments, and incidental adjustments. We must organize and sustain our behavior to attain the moral objective.

Failure to act morally is due to a breakdown in any one of these processes. A stage 1 breakdown, being insensitive to the needs of others, might be caused by not noticing the problem or being confused as to whether a problem really exists. Even if a person accurately interprets the situation as a moral situation, he may experience a stage 2 breakdown

The first step toward moral action is recognizing or deciding whether a situation is a moral situation. For example, is this person stealing someone else's groceries or just wheeling their own?

(not making a moral judgment) because his level of moral reasoning is too low. For example, his moral ideas may be too limited and too simplistic to reason adequately about the situation ("That isn't really unfair, is it?" Or, "the drug user only hurts himself. He should be free to do that"). Even if a person's moral ideals are adequate, he may compromise those ideals. Personal ambition, chauvinism, the need to be liked, or other pressures may convince the person to violate his moral ideals, thereby causing a stage 3 breakdown. Finally, even though a person was sensitive, made an adequate judgment, and decided on the moral alternative, sometimes the person may fail to implement his decision. We've all run out of gas, been side-tracked, lost sight of our goal, or failed to accomplish what we wanted. Thus, not surprisingly, effective programs for treating juvenile delinquents do more than provide moral education. For example, one very successful program provides not only moral education, but also social skills training and anger management training (Gibbs, 1994).

Box 8.8

SELF-CHECK

1. Describe the development of empathy.
2. Giving a beggar $5 illustrates which kind of empathy?
3. Working to improve the social conditions in a neighborhood illustrates which kind of empathy?
4. A person decides to adopt a baby from a foreign country after seeing a news report of the plight of those children. Which type of empathy is being illustrated? Why?
5. What are the four steps of Rest and Carroll's model?
6. At what steps in Rest and Carroll's model would the following be most relevant: Kohlberg's theory, Hoffman's model of empathy, self-control, self-efficacy, and locus of control?

Please turn to the end of this chapter to check your answers.

CONCLUSIONS

This chapter has focused on the interrelated processes of developing a self- and moral development. The question some of you may have is: How can we raise a child to view herself as moral and to act in a moral way?

Theory and research in both moral development and self-development suggest that until at least age 5, there is little parents can do to encourage the child to seriously consider others' wishes. Because young children are so egocentric, moral behavior can be encouraged only through punishment and rewards. As they get older, punishment should be accompanied by an explanation (Aronfreed, 1968), but before age 5, explanations have little effect. Perhaps the best thing parents can do to enhance moral development at this stage is to follow Mischel's suggestions on how to improve a child's self-control. The key is to teach the child to resist temptation by trying to avoid temptation and by thinking about things other than the appealing aspects of the temptation.

At about age 5, moral behavior can also be encouraged through modeling. Bandura has shown that children will model bad behavior if it brings good results, and many have found that if people identify with a model who does a good behavior and gets rewarded, they will be more likely to imitate that model (Kipper & Yinon, 1978). Therefore, parents probably have more effect by what they do than what they say. Perhaps for this reason, boys whose fathers abandon the family are more likely to become delinquents than boys whose fathers stay with the family or even boys whose fathers die (Rutter, 1971). In addition, parents may have some success by encouraging children to reflect on how their actions impact others (Brody & Schaffer, 1982). That is, after a transgression, parents should ask, "How would you feel if someone did that to you?"

During the teen years, individuals want to be moral (Damon, 1988) and their moral thinking may be quite advanced. However, their moral behavior may be dictated by the peer group. Therefore, prudent parents may tactfully encourage affiliation with certain peers and discourage such affiliation with others. The easiest way to do this is to promote the desired affiliations before adolescence. Some parents manipulate associations via the proximity principle: they make sure their children live in certain neighborhoods and go to certain schools.

Parents can also encourage moral behavior by helping their child have high self-esteem. People with high self-esteem are less likely to demean others or be prejudiced and are therefore more likely to develop empathy for another's life condition. People with high self-esteem are also more sure of their ideas and less influenced by peers than people with low self-esteem. In addition, parents can also get children more committed to values by having them preach those values or sacrifice for those values. For instance, some parents encourage their children to become leaders of their church's youth group. As youth leaders, they give up their weekends to chaperone younger teens and to instruct them on values. The youth leaders, as a result of making these sacrifices, giving moral lectures, and being an example to their younger peers, become extremely committed to "their" values (see table 8.11 for a review).

To this point, we have talked about having a child conform to "conventional" morality. Parents who wish their child to reach postconventional levels can do four things:

1. They can encourage the development of formal operations (see chapter 6).
2. They can pose moral dilemmas for their child, rewarding the child for thinking through the dilemma.
3. They can discuss moral issues with their child and have their child discuss moral issues with people of different backgrounds and viewpoints.

Table 8.11

Steps Parents Can Take to Encourage the Development of Conventional Morality in Their Children

- Accompany punishment with an explanation (after age 5).
- Promote the child's ability to delay gratification.
- Model moral behavior.
- Promote moderately high self-esteem.
- Tactfully manipulate which peers the child associates with.
- Encourage the child to participate in groups or organizations in which the child will have to preach conventional values to others and make sacrifices for those values.

4. They can boost the child's self-esteem so that the child will be more resistant to what others think. However, these parents should accept the possibility that their child will not necessarily act postconventionally, even if she thinks at that level.

As Milgram's experiment showed, and as Carroll and Rest suggested, it's hard for people to act in a way that means going against authority or against the opinions of others.

Summary

1. Cognitive development is related to moral and self-development.
2. The self can be divided into the "me," which contains facts about the material, social, and psychological self, and the "I," which, like a theorist, interprets and organizes experience.
3. Not until age 2, do children evidence having a self. Not until age 5, do children view the self as a relatively stable and continuous entity.
4. Before age 5, few children show any evidence of having a social self.
5. Achieving formal operations, undergoing tremendous physical changes, and dealing with conflicting expectations from parents and peers combine to make adolescence a time when self-concept changes tremendously.
6. According to Loevinger, most people will reach the conscientious stage during adolescence and remain there the rest of their lives. In this stage, they internalize society's rules. A few adults will transcend the conscientious stage, becoming more tolerant and understanding of others' views of morality.
7. High self-esteem is associated with good mental health and a more positive view of others. Research suggests that high self-esteem can be fostered by expecting one's child to succeed; being a democratic, but nonpermissive parent; arranging successful experiences; and getting people to consider that there may be situational reasons for their failures.
8. People with an internal locus of control not only believe that they are in charge of their life, but also seem to *be* more in charge of their life. Successfully dealing with crises, being allowed independence, and having a highly differentiated self-concept all seem to be variables that allow one to have an internal locus of control and to resist learned helplessness.

9. Understanding others is essential for self- and moral development. Children go through several phases in understanding others. However, different experts propose different stages. The simplest notion is Piaget's, which argues that children start at egocentrism (where they don't understand other children and engage in parallel play rather than cooperative play, and collective monologues instead of discussion) and move to the stage of cooperation.
10. Robert Selman's view of the development of role-taking skills is more detailed and has more research support than Piaget's. Selman believes that we develop from a child who can't take anyone else's perspective to someone who can take society's perspective.
11. Kohlberg's stage theory of moral reasoning builds on Piaget's work and is extremely popular. Kohlberg proposed three levels of moral development: preconventional, conventional, and postconventional.
12. Some object to Kohlberg's assumptions that (1) postconventional reasoning is better than conventional reasoning and that (2) stage 4 reasoning is better than stage 3 reasoning. Some claim that these assumptions reflect a male bias, a Western bias, and a liberal bias in Kohlberg's theory.
13. Moral reasoning doesn't relate strongly to moral behavior. Kohlberg saw this fact as an advantage: It suggests that "value-free" moral education could be taught in the schools.
14. Hoffman believes that the development of empathy is the most important aspect of moral development. He believes that children progress from global empathy, to egocentric empathy, to empathy for another's feelings, to empathy for another's life condition.
15. Rest and Carroll's model tries to explain moral behavior. They acknowledge that moral behavior depends not merely on moral reasoning, but also on what rewards or punishments exist for behaving morally, and on having the skills to perform the moral action.

KEY TERMS

autonomous stage 261, 271
beneffectance 262
collective monologue 269
conformist stage 259
conscientious stage 259
conventional level 272
egocentric empathy 276
egocentric perspective taking 269
empathy 276
empathy for another's feelings 276
empathy for another's life condition 276
execution and implementation 278
external locus of control 265
global empathy 276
heteronomous stage 271
"I" 254
integrated stage 261
internal locus of control 265
interpersonal concordance of "good boy—nice girl" 272
law and order orientation 273
learned helplessness 265
legalistic social-contract orientation 274
locus of control 265
material self 254
"me" 254
moral judgment 278
mutual role taking 269
naive hedonistic and instrumental orientation 272
nonmoral values and influences 278
obedience and punishment orientation 272
objective self-awareness 262
overjustification effect 262
parallel play 269
physicalistic conceptions of self 256
postconventional level 274
preconventional level 272
psychological self 254
recognition and sensitivity 278
role taking 268
self 254
self-actualization 261
self-control 266
self-efficacy 266
self-esteem 263
self-fulfilling prophecy 264
self-reflective role taking 269
self-verification 263
significant symbols 268
social and conventional systems role taking 269
social-informational role taking 269
social self 254
stage of cooperation 269
stage of egocentrism 269
stage theory 259, 274
underjustification effect 262
universal ethical principled orientation 274

Self-Check Answers

Box 8.1

Part A:

1. False. Before the age of 1, the child usually does not have a sense of self. This lack of self is indicated by the mirror research, adults not having memories of themselves at that age, and from sexual reassignment research. Even at 18 months, the child's sense of self is fairly primitive.
2. False. By age 2, children have a physical self. However, they are unable to take the perspective of others so they are unable to develop a social self.
3. True. By age 3, most children can identify their gender. However, until about age 5 or 6, children do not know that their gender will stay the same throughout the lifespan.

Part B:

4. If you believe that your sense of self is simply a reflection of what other people think about you, then you need to reach a stage where you can understand what others think of you. If, on the other hand, you believe that the sense of self is a theory that you construct from your experiences, your self-theory can only be as sophisticated as your thinking process.
5. Preoperational children view the self in physical terms, believe that the self can undergo magical transformations, fail to see the self in a logically consistent manner, and fail to understand how others view them.
6. (a) Entering school; (b) developing concrete operational thought.
7. The ability to think abstractly makes them more aware of trying to integrate their present self with their future adult self; makes them realize that there are many different people they could become; and makes them capable of constructing a complex, sophisticated, and logical self-theory.

Box 8.2

Part A:

1. False.
2. False. This statement would be true of someone in the conformist stage.
3. False. A person at the conscientious stage may violate laws and then feel guilty about doing so. In addition, a person at the conscientious stage may not internalize all of society's rules.
4. False. Only a few adults will reach the autonomous stage.
5. False. Like people at the conscientious stage, these people generally follow society's rules. However, unlike people at the conscientious stage, they are more tolerant of people who have different beliefs.
6. False. This inability to define this stage hampers research on Loevinger's theory.

Part B:

7. Erikson's theory focuses on crises that he expects to occur at certain ages; Erikson's theory focuses more on early childhood events; and Loevinger's theory focuses more on morality and on evaluating others.

Box 8.3

Part A:

1. True.
2. True.
3. False. Rewards do not always hurt motivation. Rewards may be necessary to get the person to try the task and to reach a level of competence on the task (*after* which point, doing the task does become fun). Furthermore, some tasks are not intrinsically interesting.
4. True.
5. False. We usually have a good opinion of ourselves and we try to verify that opinion.
6. False. According to research by Swann, Stein-Seroussi, & Giesler (1992), self-verification often wins out. Consistent with this research, you may have noticed that people with very low self-esteem do not like to be complimented.

Part B:

7. Both theories suggest that people are often not aware of their true feelings and desires, but the theories offer different reasons and solutions for this lack of awareness. Objective self-awareness research tends to take the approach that people can be made aware of themselves—it's just that they are often too busy to listen. Thus, focusing attention on the self can lead to insight. Self-perception theory, on the other hand, tends to focus on situations where people cannot directly know their own minds.

Box 8.4

Part A:

1. False. Most people have fairly high self-esteem.
2. False. People with low self-esteem are more likely to be highly critical of others.
3. False.
4. False. Although children who do poorly in school have low self-esteem, we do not know that self-esteem *causes* the poor performance.
5. False. As with question 4, correlation does not prove causality.
6. False. Parents who were not permissive (but who were democratic) had children whose self-esteem was higher than children who were reared permissively.
7. False. Learned helplessness is an extreme form of external locus of control, where people don't believe that anything they do has an effect.
8. False. The elderly's self-concept is *not* highly differentiated.
9. True.
10. False. Strategies for delaying gratification can be taught.

Part B:

11. Self-esteem can be increased (at almost any age) by (a) being exposed to others who have faith in the person (taking advantage of the self-fulfilling prophecy research); (b) succeeding at tasks; and (c) being taught to attribute success to one's own efforts and failure to bad luck, other people, or lack of perseverance.

12. Many people argue that the two concepts are closely related. However, the main difference is that self-esteem deals with feeling whether one is a good or a bad person, whereas locus of control deals with feeling whether the person is in control of his destiny or whether things are completely out of his control. Often, a person who feels good about himself will also feel in control of his life whereas a person who feels bad about himself will feel that he has no control over anything. However, a person could have low self-esteem and an internal locus of control (a person feels bad about himself because he has done some bad things and he holds himself responsible for those). Conversely, a person could have an external locus of control and still feel good about himself. Such a person might think, "I do pretty well with the cards that life deals me."
13. They have experienced crises or other significant events that are beyond their control. Their self-concept is simple and undifferentiated. They have not had to overcome adversity before.

Box 8.5

Part A:

1. True.
2. True.
3. False. Research has shown that children are less egocentric in their interactions with others than Piaget had first assumed.

Part B:

4. Although researchers agree that young infants lack the social skills necessary for sustaining social interaction, they disagree about the rate at which children acquire these skills. Mueller and Lucas argue that, for most of the first year of life, infants treat each other like they treat other objects. Other researchers disagree and claim to observe prosocial behavior with infants as young as 6 months of age. The difference probably stems from having different ways of defining social interaction and prosocial behavior. However, the consensus seems to be that Mueller and Lucas' coding scheme overlooked some of infants' small, but measurable, steps toward social interaction.
5. Young children engaged in parallel play and in collective monologues.
6. Like Piaget, Selman believed that children under age 5 were very poor at role taking. Consequently, Selman, like Piaget, labels this early stage as a stage of egocentrism.
7. (a.) Selman breaks role taking into more stages than Piaget did. (b.) Selman's theory is based on research where children were asked to solve certain dilemmas.
8. In both stages, the child can understand another person's reaction to a certain situation. However, in stage 2, the child can anticipate how people will react to a given situation. Furthermore, the stage 2 child realizes that other people may be able to predict the child's reaction to a certain situation.
9. In stage 4, people appreciate the value of analyzing a situation from how society would view it, rather than on how they or their peer evaluate it. In stage 3, people can think about how one of their interactions could be viewed by an observer. In stage 2, people cannot step outside the interaction to see how an observer would interpret an interaction.

Box 8.7

Part A:

1. False.
2. True. And no stage 6 people have been found in non-Western societies.
3. False.
4. False.

Part B:

5. Piaget only had two stages of moral development, whereas Kohlberg has 6. Therefore, Kohlberg's theory is more detailed. It is also more explicit about proposing that, with development, people may be influenced by conceptions of morality that are progressively farther away from both their own immediate concrete experience and their own self-interest. Nevertheless, there are similarities. For example, Kohlberg's first stage corresponds fairly closely to Piaget's heteronomous stage. In addition, elements of Piaget's autonomous stage are very obvious in Kohlberg's stages 3 and 4. That is, individuals in Kohlberg's stages 2 and 4 understand that rules are social agreements and that people's motives should be considered.
6. In stage 3, people conform to others (not unlike what they did in stage 1) to avoid punishment. In stage 4, they comply with something more abstract—a rule. Put another way, in stage 4, they are considering the views of more people than just their immediate peers.
7. Stage 4; stage 5; stage 6; stage 3.
8. Kohlberg would argue that people can teach morality without teaching values. However, his critics might charge that his theory (and thus any teaching based on his theory) has a liberal, male, and Western bias.

Box 8.8

1. We progress from global empathy, where we mistake another's hurt for our own, to egocentric empathy, where we realize that another's hurt may be different from our own but we tend to assume that what would make us feel better would make them feel better. Then, we progress to empathy for another's feelings, where we realize that another may not want our help, to empathy for another's life condition, where we realize that the person's problem may extend beyond their immediate feelings.
2. Empathy for another's feelings.
3. Empathy for another's life condition.
4. It could be argued that it was egocentric empathy in that the children might be better off in their own culture. However, it could also be empathy for another's life condition, if the person realized that the unhappy children in the news report would still be unhappy tomorrow and next year because of the bad state of that country.
5. (a) Recognition and sensitivity, (b) moral judgment, (c) weighing nonmoral values and judgments, and (d) execution and implementation.
6. Hoffman's theory would deal more directly with recognition and sensitivity; Kohlberg's theory would most directly deal with making the moral judgment; and processes such as self-efficacy, locus of control, and self-control deal primarily with weighing nonmoral choices and influences, as well as with executing and implementing the decision.

9

Chapter

Attachment

Love is union with somebody or something outside oneself under the conditions of retaining the separateness and integrity of one's own self.

ERICH FROMM

CHAPTER OVERVIEW

You entered this world a helpless, noisy, and messy baby. Your only hope for survival was to have a caregiver—someone to feed, clean, hold, and teach you. Why did someone take on this arduous task?

You, in turn, became attached to this caregiver. But why? Was this attachment biologically programmed? Was it necessary for your future social development? That is, if you hadn't become attached to this person, would the lack of attachment ruin all your future relationships?

This chapter explores the answers to these intriguing questions. Specifically, this chapter explores the development of attachment behavior in both infant and caregiver and the implications of this attachment for future development. Although most theorists and researchers have focused on the relationship between children and their biological mothers, this chapter will also cover important work on the relationship between children and their fathers, children and their adoptive parents, and children and their multiple caregivers.

Why Caregivers Attach to Infants

As we mentioned, most research and theory on early parent-child attachment has focused almost exclusively on the mother. This is evident in the bonding hypothesis, which focuses on why mothers become attached to their infants.

The Bonding Hypothesis

Why do mothers become attached to their infants? One possibility is that, like some mothers in the animal kingdom, human mothers may rapidly **bond;** that is, form an instinctive emotional attachment to their children shortly after birth. Physicians Marshall Klaus and John Kennell (1976, 1982) believe that the first 6 to 12 hours after delivery are a **sensitive period** for mothers to bond to their infants. A sensitive period is a time interval in which certain conditions must occur in order to stimulate the development of a specific characteristic. If the conditions are not met within that time interval, then the characteristic will not develop properly. Thus, Klaus and Kennell hypothesize that close skin-to-skin contact during this sensitive period triggers an emotional response in the mother that helps her establish a long-lasting bond to her child. If close contact does not occur during this sensitive period, then the mother's bond to her infant will be compromised. In support of Kennell and Klaus, some researchers report that mothers who had close contact with their babies during the first few hours following birth caress their infants more and hold them closer when feeding than mothers who did not have this early close contact (Gaulin-Kremer, Shaw, & Thoman, 1977; Grossman, Thane, & Grossman, 1981).

But does bonding really occur? Many new mothers who had early contact with their newborns feel no special bond. In extreme cases, some mothers even kill their newborns. On the other hand, many mothers and fathers who were denied close contact with their infants during this hypothesized sensitive period have very strong and enduring bonds to their infants.

Research offers little support for the notion of rapid biologically based bonding (DeChateau & Wilberg, 1977) or for any permanent differences in the quality of bond formed by those mothers who had early contact and those who did not. For example, Susan Goldberg (1983) found that mothers who enjoyed early close contact were slightly more affectionate toward their infants for the first three days of life. Within nine days, however, these differences had completely disappeared. Furthermore, Michael Rutter (1979) found that parents develop close, affectionate ties to their adoptive children even though they had no contact with them during the neonatal period.

Infant Characteristics that Promote Attachment

If research does not support the idea that mothers immediately bond to their children, then why do caregivers form emotional attachments to babies? As you'll soon see, infants are born into the world with a number of characteristics and strategies designed to promote attachment.

Attachment Behaviors

Fewer than 40 years ago, most people viewed infant behavior as a series of "random, unconnected expressions of behavior and affect" (Damon, 1983, p. 29). British psychiatrist John Bowlby's (1966, 1969, 1980) work successfully challenged this notion by demonstrating that much of early infant behavior is designed to promote physical—and, in time, social—closeness to the mother. He referred to these actions as **attachment behaviors**.

Bowlby identified two kinds of attachment behaviors: signaling behaviors and approach behaviors. **Signaling behaviors** are designed to bring the mother to the baby. As a baby, your cries signaled your mother that you needed to be comforted. Your cooing, babbling, and smiles signaled that you desired her company and wanted her to stay near you. **Approach behaviors,** on the other hand, are designed to bring the baby to the mother. You approached your mother by clinging to her when she held you, sucking her fingers, and following her with your limbs or eyes.

Bowlby believed that the attachment behaviors of a baby are designed to maintain proximity to the caregiver and ensure interaction between baby and caregiver. Perhaps this close contact is reinforcing to the caregiver. If you think about it, isn't there something rewarding about a baby cooing and smiling up at you? It feels good to have a baby cling to you and nestle against your body. Even when a baby cries, you want to go near her to comfort her (or at least to stop the crying). And when the crying stops, you feel rewarded for your efforts. Thus, learning theorists might say that the baby's attachment behaviors are a built-in reward system designed to mold a dedicated caregiver. (Unfortunately, as we will see later in the chapter, the system is not perfect. For example, a caregiver who is unsuccessful in stopping the infant from crying might become frustrated and hurt or abandon the infant.)

Imitation

Signaling and approach behaviors are not the only ways babies reward us for keeping them around. Infants also reward us by using the sincerest form of flattery—imitation. Before they are even four days old, they are actively attempting to imitate our actions. We know about infants' imitation because of Tiffany Field's study of 3-day-olds. The infants were held face to face by a researcher who made a happy, surprised, or sad face. The expression was sustained until the infant looked away. The researcher then did some deep-knee bends or several tongue clicks to attract the infant's attention and made another face until the infant looked away. An observer, who could see only the baby's face, tried to guess—based solely on the infant's expression—what face the researcher had made. The observer correctly identified surprised expressions 76 percent of the time, happy expressions 58 percent of the time, and sad expressions 59 percent of the time. Since the chance of correctly guessing any one expression was only 33 percent (1 out of 3), we can be confident that the infants were attempting to imitate the researcher's expressions (reported by Trotter, 1987).

Synchronized Routines

Infant imitation not only reinforces the caregiver, but it also plays a crucial role in the child's social and language development. But imitation is not the only tool infants have that both reinforces the caregiver and aids social and language development. Infants also have the capacity for **synchronized routines**—harmonious interactions between two persons in which each adjusts his or her behaviors in response to the partner's actions (Shaffer, 1992).

Unlike imitation, which involves one person copying what the other person does, synchrony involves reacting to what the other does. If two dancers imitated each other, they would move farther and farther apart, or closer and closer together, as both stepped back at the same time, or stepped forward at the same time. Fortunately, most dancers are in synchrony. They flow together: as one dancer steps forward, the other steps back.

As with imitation, children are born with the ability to synchronize their actions to people around them. Craig Peerry (1980) found that 1-day-olds already synchronize their head movements with those of adults (see figure 9.1). If an adult moved toward them, they moved back. If the adult moved back, the infant moved forward. This simple synchrony is quickly perfected into intricate interactions, often likened to dances, in which partners alternate the lead. At first, the infant may monopolize the lead. But gradually, she learns to take turns and not to step on too many toes.

The development of synchronized routines is illustrated by Michael Rutter and Kevin Durkin's (1987) research on turn taking during mother-infant interactions. At first, the mother takes primary responsibility for coordinating vocal turn taking. The baby vocalizes at will, but mother and baby don't talk at the same time because the mother pauses when her baby interrupts. Mom begins again only when the baby has stopped. As children approach age 3, they interrupt less and start to coordinate their vocalizations around their mother's. When both mother and child coordinate their actions around the other, synchrony is achieved.

Both child and caregiver are rewarded through synchronized routines. The lessons of this early synchrony gradually evolve into the complex rules of give and take necessary to maintain mature relationships.

Appearance

We have seen that children reward us through a wide variety of behaviors: smiling when we are near, calming down when we approach them, imitating us, and interacting with us (see table 9.1). In addition to these behaviors, researchers have also discovered that we are attracted to how a baby looks. Konrad Lorenz (1943) believes that the "Kewpie doll" appearance of babies makes them cute and appealing to adults. There's just something about those chubby cheeks, large forehead, and soft rounded features that we can't resist. And, in fact, Thomas Alley (1981) found that adults judge line drawings of "babyish" faces and profiles as "cuter" than pictures that resemble 4-year-olds (see figure 9.2). Even children show a marked preference for that Kewpie doll look (Goldberg, Blumberg, & Kriger, 1982).

Figure 9.1
Synchrony

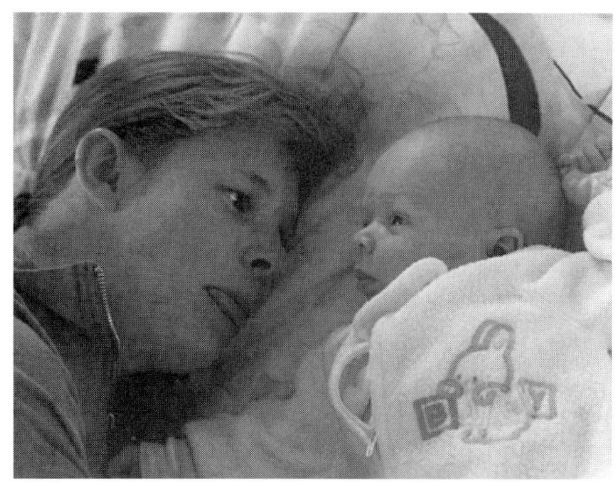

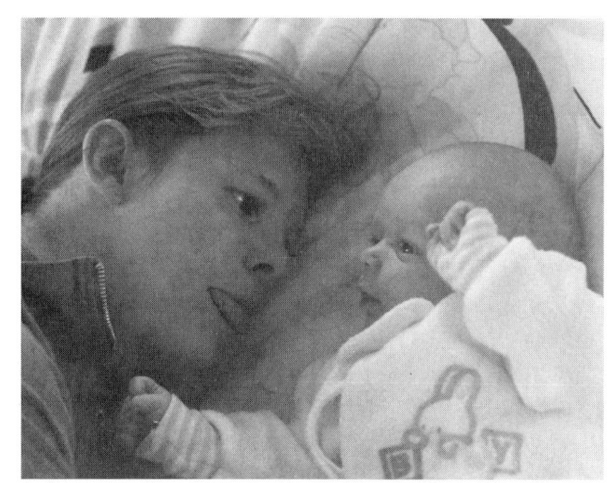

Identification

The fact that babies usually share some physical features with their parents probably also helps parents identify with their children. Even without a strong physical resemblance, parents often view children as part of their own flesh and blood—an extension of themselves. If parents view children as an extension of themselves, what's good for the child is good for the parent.

Table 9.1

Infant Behaviors that Promote Parent-Infant Attachment

Behavior	Definition/Example
Signaling behavior	Crying when caregiver is not present. Cooing, babbling, and smiling when caregiver is present and attentive.
Approach behavior	Clinging to caregiver.
Imitation	Imitating caregiver's facial expressions.
Synchronized routines	Moving head backward in response to caregiver's head moving forward, babbling when parent is quiet, being quiet when parent talks.

Figure 9.2

Kewpie Dolls

Why Parents Attach to Their Children: Conclusions

Although parents do not automatically bond to their children, the baby is not totally helpless when it comes to being popular with its parents. Not only does the baby's appearance foster identification and liking, but the baby's behaviors reward attachment (see table 9.2). Some naturists speculate that premature babies may not have fully developed the proper attachment behaviors, which would account for why premature babies are more likely to be abused than full-term infants.

But what about the nonrewarding aspects of having a child? Ironically, any problems resulting from having or caring for the baby may increase the parents' attachment to their infant. According to the theory of **cognitive dissonance,** we act to reduce discomfort (dissonance) when we feel that two of our thoughts are inconsistent (dissonance). Thus, parents may think, "Taking care of this kid is real torture. I keep changing his diapers and getting up in the middle of the night to give him a bottle. I'm either crazy or crazy in love."

Table 9.2

Explanations for Why Parents Bond to Their Children

Explanation	Status of the Explanation
Instinctive bonding	Evidence is mixed, but most does *not* support the idea of instinctive bonding.
Attachment behaviors	Accepted by most experts.
Imitation	Accepted by most experts.
Synchronized routines	Accepted by most experts.
Appearance	Some evidence that humans naturally like features characteristic of babies.
Identification	Assumed by many to be an important factor.

INFANT-CAREGIVER ATTACHMENT

Attachment is not a one-way street. Not only do caregivers attach to infants, but infants attach to caregivers. Indeed, part of the reason caregivers are attached to infants is precisely because the infant is attached to the caregiver: It's easy to like someone who likes you.

How Attachment Helps the Infant

How does this social attachment between infant and caregiver help the infant? One function of social attachment is physical survival. If the infant appears attached to its caregivers, the caregivers should be more likely to care for its physical needs than if the infant is not attached.

Furthermore, as the effects of the two world wars suggest, attachment may also be necessary for the child's emotional survival (Lamb et al., 1985). During World Wars I (1914–1918) and II (1939–1945), large numbers of children were orphaned or separated from their parents. To provide for their basic needs, these children were placed in orphanages. In the same era, isolation sanatoria were opened to care for people of all ages who had contracted infectious diseases such as tuberculosis. Many children suffering from infectious diseases were separated from their parents and placed in these sanatoria.

Although the sanatoria and orphanages were established with the best of intentions, both had tragic psychological

Box 9.1

RESEARCH in FOCUS

Anna Freud and Sophie Dann: A Study in Group Upbringing

Anna Freud and Sophie Dann studied six World War II orphans. As might be expected from 4-year-olds who had lost their parents before the age of 1, and who had lived in concentration camps most of their lives, the children were initially unruly, destructive, and hostile toward adults. If they didn't ignore an adult caregiver, they were likely to spit, bite, or swear at the poor soul.

However, the children did form attachments to each other. If getting a special treat meant leaving the others, they would go without the treat. If a child was separated from the group, all the children would experience separation anxiety. These 4-year-olds would suffer cold, hunger, and even fear to help each other. The children were so protective of one another that when a caregiver accidentally knocked over a child, two of the other children threw bricks at the caregiver.

Gradually, the children formed attachments to their caregivers. Yet, during the course of Freud and Dann's study, the children's attachments to their caregivers never reached the strength of the attachments the children had to each other. Nor did the attachments to their caregivers ever become as strong as the typical child's attachment to his or her parents.

Note: From An experiment in group upbringing by A. Freud and S. Dann, 1951. In *The psychoanalytic study of the child* (Vol. 6). International Universities Press, 1951.

consequences for the children reared in them. Providing for their basic physical needs was not enough to promote normal development. Children of all ages suffered psychological dysfunction (see box 9.1).

British psychiatrist John Bowlby and others believed that these tragic findings were the result of maternal deprivation. Alarmed by the mounting number of reports on the harmful consequences of maternal deprivation, the World Health Organization commissioned Bowlby to conduct a literature review. In his 1951 report, *Maternal Care and Mental Health*, Bowlby concluded that normal infants who suffered from any type of long-term maternal deprivation were unable to relate adequately to any person, were afraid to play, explore, and discover the world beyond their own skins, or even to discover themselves. Today, some experts believe that the child's attachment to his parents may be the cornerstone for all other relationships (Erikson, 1963; Franz & White, 1985).

Biological Explanations for Attachment

Although Bowlby's report provided valuable insights about the effects of attachment, he made some incorrect assumptions about the nature and formation of attachments. Specifically, he assumed that children would form attachment bonds only with their biological mothers—that was the way infants were instinctively programmed. This assumption proved to be false. Children can attach to anyone—mothers, stepmothers, stepfathers, single fathers, adoptive parents, nannies, aunts, uncles, and even multiple caregivers. Rather than instinctively attaching to their mothers, infants usually attach to the people who take care of them.

Need for Food

Why do children become attached to their caregivers? The simplest answer is that infants attach to their caregivers merely because caregivers provide them with food. For instance, Sigmund Freud (1920) hypothesized that, after the caregiver feeds the child numerous times, infants realize that the caregiver was the source of pleasurable and need-satisfying experiences. When infants realize this, from then on they desire the caregiver's presence. Similarly, John Dollard and Neal Miller (1950) proposed that infants attach to a caregiver because that person satisfies the baby's basic physiological needs. The evidence suggests that Freud and Dollard and Miller are probably correct: Infants are likely to attach to people who satisfy their needs.

Need for Contact Comfort

But what are those needs? Infants want and need more in a caregiver than baby food. For example, as Harry Harlow demonstrated, infants have a need for **contact comfort,** to cling to something warm and soft.

In 1958, Harry Harlow set out to test the hypothesis that attachment was linked to meeting primitive needs. Because he could not ethically test this hypothesis by experimenting on humans, he chose to experiment on the rhesus monkey. His first step was to create two **surrogate** (substitute) **mothers.** One was a "cloth mother" constructed out of a cylinder of wood covered with terry cloth. The other was a "wire mother" made out of a wire-mesh cylinder. Depending on the particular experimental condition, none, one, or both mothers would have a bottle holder so that a baby could nurse off it.

Shortly after birth, eight monkeys were separated from their natural mothers. Four were placed alone with the cloth mother, four were placed alone with the wire mother. All of their cages were constructed so that each monkey could "visit" the other mother.

Harlow's findings were startling: Even when nourishment was provided exclusively by the wire-mesh mother, infant monkeys spent most of their time clinging to the cloth mother. Apparently, having something warm and soft to cling to—what Harlow called contact comfort—was more important than food in eliciting attachment behaviors (see table 9.3 for a summary of factors that foster infant-parent attachments).

Real-life events involving human children seem to corroborate the basic finding of Harlow's experiments with infant monkeys: contact comfort is important. In fact, contact comfort may be so important that the human infant's life depends on it. The cause of death recorded on the death certificates of infants who died in orphanages in the early 1900s often read "marasmus," literally, withering away. In other words, coroners believed that the cause of death was not lack of food or warmth, but lack of contact.

Is Attachment Imprinting?

Nurturists believe babies attach to a caregiver for the environmental rewards of food and comfort. But, as naturists point out, there's another way to look at attachment. To naturists, the fact that attachment is necessary for physical survival suggests that evolution programs the infant to form attachments. Indeed, evolution has clearly programmed attachment-type behaviors in other animals. For example, baby ducks imprint, or form attachments during a critical period early in life.

But what about humans? Are we genetically programmed to attach to our caregivers? Naturists say yes. They believe that, just as a baby duck is programmed to **imprint** to the nearest moving object, baby humans are programmed to attach to any caregiver (Johnson, 1992). In support of this position, naturists point out that infants seem to exhibit reflexive, programmed attachment behaviors.

Differences Between Attachment and Imprinting

Although human attachment and a duck's imprinting share some similarities, there are differences. Ducks will imprint to anything, even a beer bottle. Humans attach only to a caregiver who meets their needs for food or contact. Baby ducks imprint almost instantly. Humans attach slowly. Social attachment, so vital to physical and emotional survival, takes most of the infant's first year to develop (Damon, 1983).

Even though nurturists and naturists agree that imprinting and attachment differ in certain ways, they disagree about the implications of these differences. To the nurturist, these differences indicate that attachment is not like imprinting; therefore, attachment is not biologically programmed. To the naturist, these differences simply mean that attachment is a more sophisticated form of imprinting (see table 9.4, for a closer look at the relationship between imprinting and attachment).

Table 9.3

Requirements for Infant-Parent Attachment

Caregiver Characteristics	Importance for Attachment
Infant's biological mother	Very little evidence to support the claim that infants instinctively attach to their biological mothers.
Person who cares for infant during first three months	Not important. Attachment bonds start to form around 6 months of age.
Food provider	Not the sole determinant of attachment, as Harlow's studies and kibbutz studies indicate (discussed later in chapter).
Person providing contact comfort	Important factor.
Person who is most often present	Not essential, as kibbutz studies show (discussed later in chapter), as well as research showing that children often attach to both parents.
Person providing meaningful social experiences	Important for developing *secure* attachments.
Person(s) with whom infants have synchronous relations	Important for developing *secure* attachments.
Caregivers who do not abuse them	Important for developing *secure* attachments.

An Intriguing Similarity: The Sequence of Attachment

If the naturists are correct and attachment is genetically programmed, we would expect that attachment would follow a predictable, programmed pattern. According to John Bowlby and Mary Ainsworth, it does (Ainsworth, 1973; Ainsworth, Blehar, Waters, & Wall, 1978; Bowlby, 1969). Specifically, Ainsworth and Bowlby claim that social attachment progresses through four distinct phases:

1. Preattachment,
2. Attachment-in-the-making,
3. Clear-cut attachment, and
4. Goal-corrected partnership (see table 9.5).

During the first two or three months of life, the **preattachment phase,** babies' attachment behaviors may be reflexively triggered by anyone—or anything. Infants promote contact with adults through such attachment behaviors as cooing, smiling, and clinging. However, these

Table 9.4

Attachment Versus Imprinting

	Imprinting	Attachment
When do imprinting and attachment start?	The infant imprints shortly after birth.	The infant doesn't form attachment bonds before six months of age.
Who is the object of imprinting and attachment?	The infant imprints to only one object.	The infant can—and usually does—attach to more than one individual.
How much time does it take?	Imprinting occurs instantly to whatever object is present during the critical hours.	Attachment develops slowly over a period of months.
How important is timing?	Timing is critical: The same object that would elicit imprinting if it had been present a few hours earlier might later elicit fear.	The timing is more flexible in attachment. However, attachment does follow a rough schedule that includes four phases.
What conditions are necessary for them to form?	The presence of an object or person is enough to elicit imprinting.	The caregiver must be responsive to the infant for attachment to occur.

behaviors are not directed toward anyone—or even anything—in particular. For instance, the baby will suck a pen, follow a yo-yo, and coo at a cat.

Around 3 months of age, babies begin the **attachment-in-the-making** phase. During this phase, infants begin to show preferences for specific people. Furthermore, they can distinguish their primary caregivers from others. Infants will even exert special effort to be close to their primary attachment figure. However, as indicated by the fact that they do not protest separation from their caregiver, they have yet to form an attachment bond.

At about the age of 6 months, the child usually forms an attachment bond to a specific caregiver, thus marking the start of the **clear-cut-attachment** phase. Infants in phase 3 often protest separation from their caregiver, clinging and crying at the first sign of impending separation. During this phase, leaving a child with a baby-sitter may be met with guilt-provoking howls of terror.

During the clear-cut attachment phase, infants learn how to crawl and then walk. These locomotion skills greatly increase the child's ability to stay close to his or her caregiver and increase the child's ability to explore the physical environment. Typically, infants use their caregivers as a base from which to explore the world. When put into a new situation, they will initially cling to their caregiver, then gradually leave the caregiver to explore the new environment, returning whenever they have a need for security and then taking off again for further exploration.

During the clear-cut attachment phase, children become goal-directed. Because they are now fairly mobile, they can go after almost anything they want. Unfortunately, because of their cognitive limitations, they are often egocentric and therefore assume that their goals are shared by everyone else. The child's inability to realize that other people may have different perspectives can be a great

Table 9.5

Phases of Attachment

Phase	Age	Characteristics
Phase 1:		
Preattachment	0 to 3 Months	Infant indiscriminately coos and clings.
Phase 2:		
Attachment-in-the-making	3 Months to 6 Months	Infant begins to show preferences for specific individuals.
Phase 3:		
Clear-cut attachment	6 Months to 4 Years	Infant forms attachment bond. Evidence: Child protests being separated from caregiver.
Phase 4:		
Goal-corrected partnership	4 Years through Adult	Child takes into account caregiver's needs as well as its own needs.

source of frustration for both caregiver and child. Many parents have experienced the rude awakening early Saturday morning, when their 2-year-old comes bounding in ready to greet the day, oblivious to his parents' wish to sleep late.

At about age 4, children begin to learn that other people do not always share their goals, feelings, or points of view. This movement away from egocentric thought marks the start of phase 4 attachment, **goal-corrected partnership.** Phase 4 children realize that parents have things to do other than maintain physical proximity to their child.

Box 9.2

SELF-CHECK

PART A

Indicate whether each of the following statements is true or false.

1. Research offers strong support for the idea that mothers bond to their children during the first few hours of the infant's life.
2. Even a 3-day-old infant may imitate adults' facial expressions.
3. Some experts believe that the child's attachment to his or her parents may be the cornerstone of all other relationships.
4. Children are instinctively programmed to form attachment bonds to their mothers—and to nobody else.
5. One reason children attach to their caregiver is that the caregiver gives them food.

PART B

Answer the following questions.

6. What are some examples of signaling and approach behaviors?
7. At what age does synchrony emerge? What is the value of synchrony in later development?
8. What did Harry Harlow's studies document?
9. How is attachment different from imprinting?
10. How does the attachment-in-the-making phase differ from the preattachment phase?
11. How does the clear-cut-attachment phase differ from the attachment-in-the-making phase?
12. How does the goal-corrected partnership differ from the clear-cut-attachment phase?

Please turn to the end of this chapter to check your answers.

Parents have their own goals, and children need to account for these parental goals when planning their own goals. Because phase 4 attachment balances the views of others against one's own position, Bowlby and Ainsworth regard phase 4 attachment as mature attachment. Ideally, this mature attachment, characterized by taking both one's partner's and one's own needs and views into account, will be the basis of all later relationships.

Quality of Attachment

The phases of attachment depict the way that "normal, typical, average" children develop clear-cut attachment to their caregivers. However, not all infants develop clear-cut attachments to their caregivers. Furthermore, even those infants who develop clear-cut attachments vary in the extent to which they attach to their caregivers. To study the differences in the *quality* of infant attachments to caregivers, Mary Ainsworth and her colleagues (1978) developed a research strategy called the **strange situation.**

In the strange situation, 1-year-olds are placed in an unfamiliar setting. In this setting, they encounter a stranger and experience the departure and reappearance of their mother. Specifically, the setting is a laboratory that contains three chairs: one for the child, one for the mother, and one for the stranger. Toys surround the child's chair (see figure 9.3).

Figure 9.3

A Few of the Situations Encountered in The "Strange Situation"

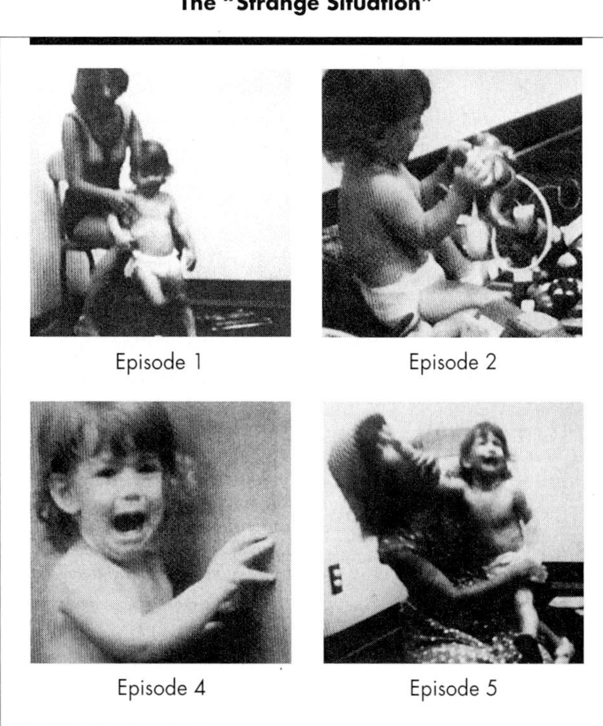

Reprinted by permission of L. Alan Sroufe/Institute of Child Development, University of Minnesota.

Table 9.6

The "Strange Situation"

Episode	Events	What Observers Watch for
Episode 1	Mother and infant enter room.	
Episode 2	Infant explores room.	Is the infant curious? Does the infant use mother as a base for exploring the environment?
Episode 3	Stranger enters, talks to mother, approaches infant.	The degree of stranger anxiety.
Episode 4	Mother leaves room, leaving infant with stranger.	The degree of separation anxiety and stranger anxiety.
Episode 5	Mother returns to room; stranger leaves.	How does the infant react to being reunited with mother? Is the infant happy? Or does the infant display attachment *and* anger? Or does the infant avoid his mother?
Episode 6	Mother leaves room; infant is now completely alone.	The degree of separation anxiety.
Episode 7	Stranger enters room.	The degree of stranger anxiety.
Episode 8	Mother returns and stranger leaves.	The infant's reaction to reunion (as in episode 5).

To be more specific, each child is exposed to eight episodes. In episode 1, the mother and baby enter the experimental room. Episode 2 offers the infant the opportunity to explore the room with the mother present. Ainsworth noted the degree to which the infant explored the room and the extent to which the infant used his mother as a base. In episode 3, the stranger enters, talks to the mother, and approaches the baby. Ainsworth noted the degree to which the baby retreated from the stranger. In episode 4, the baby and the stranger are left alone in the room together. Ainsworth noted both how the infant reacted to his mother leaving and the infant's wariness about the stranger. During episode 5, the mother returns to the room and the stranger leaves. This episode gave Ainsworth a chance to evaluate how the baby reacted when he was reunited with his mother. Then, in episode 6, the baby was left all alone in the room. This gave Ainsworth another opportunity to observe the baby's reaction to his mother's leaving. Episode 7 gives another chance to observe the infant's wariness of strangers as the stranger reenters the room. Finally, in episode 8, the mother returns and the stranger leaves, giving a final opportunity to observe how the infant reacted to being reunited with his mother (see table 9.6).

These eight episodes exposed infants to four basic events. First, each infant was placed in an unfamiliar setting—the "strange situation" lab. Second, each infant was exposed to a stranger. Third, each infant was separated from his mother. Fourth, each infant was reunited with his mother.

To determine the infant's attachment to his mother, Ainsworth assessed the child's reaction to each of these four events. Specifically, she measured:

1. The degree to which the child explored the lab,
2. How the child reacted to being reunited with his mother,
3. The degree of **stranger anxiety,** the fear that many infants feel when in the presence of strangers, and
4. The degree of **separation anxiety,** a wary reaction that infants sometimes display when separated from someone to whom they are attached (see figure 9.4).

As a result of her research, Ainsworth formulated three distinct patterns of responding to these four events. She labeled these three patterns:

1. Secure attachment,
2. Insecure/ambivalent attachment, and
3. Insecure/avoidant attachment.

Secure Attachment

Sixty to 65 percent of the infants were **securely attached.** These infants used their mothers as a base to actively explore their new environment. In addition, these infants were distressed when separated, and they warmly greeted their mothers when mom returned.

Table 9.7

Three Forms of Attachment

Characteristic	Secure	Insecure/Avoidant	Insecure/Ambivalent
Incidence	70%	20%	10%
Reaction to separation from mother	May or may not have separation anxiety. Some experience intense distress.	Little separation anxiety.	Separation anxiety.
Reaction to being reunited with mother	Joy.	If held by mother, soon tries to slip away. May try to avoid mother entirely.	Ambivalent. May combine affection with aggressive or angry behavior.
Effects on adult heterosexual relationships (according to Hazan and Shaver, 1987)	Believe in enduring love. Love characterized by trust, friendship, positive feelings.	Doubt existence of enduring love. Love characterized by fear of closeness, lack of trust.	Believe in falling in love. Love viewed as painfully exciting struggle to merge with another person.

Insecure Attachment

The remaining 35 to 40 percent were insecurely attached. Ainsworth described two basic patterns of insecure attachment. Ten to 15 percent were classified as **insecure/ambivalent attachments** because these infants were distressed when separated from their mothers, but were ambivalent when reunited. Often, these children would show their ambivalence by combining affectionate attachment behaviors with expressions of anger. About 10 percent of all the 1-year-olds were classified as insecure/ambivalent.

Ainsworth classified the remaining 20 percent of infants as **insecure/avoidant attachments.** Insecure/avoidant children were uninterested in exploring, showed little distress when separated, and avoided or ignored their mothers when reunited (see table 9.7).

In recent years, a fourth classification has been identified. Children with a **disorganized/disoriented attachment** style appear "dazed," disorganized, and disoriented when reunited with their mothers (Main & Solomon, 1989).

Causes of Insecure Attachment

What caused 30 percent of all children tested to be insecurely attached? According to attachment theorists, secure attachments result when caregivers respond appropriately to their infants' signals. Therefore, insecure attachments result when caregivers fail to respond to their infants' signals (Ainsworth et al., 1974, 1978).

Maternal Deprivation

Obviously, an absentee caregiver cannot respond to a baby's signals. For this reason, John Bowlby began his work on attachment by theorizing on the effects of repeated, long-term maternal separation on children (Bowlby, 1951). Bowlby describes three phases children may go through when separated from their mothers during the second year of life:

1. The protest phase,
2. The despair phase, and
3. The detachment phase.

In the first phase, the **protest phase,** children may protest the impending separation by crying, clinging, or calling. Once the mother has left, they protest by shouting, screaming, and running around wildly—focusing all their resources on getting her back.

After their mother has been away a week or two, the preoccupation with mother characterized by the protest phase slips into the **despair phase.** Early in the despair phase, children seem hopeless and they mope about in a listless state. Later in the despair phase, despair turns to resentment as the children attempt to fight back at their mothers for abandoning them. Children may fly into a rage at any reminder of their mother, such as at the sight of her photograph. Indeed, they may even fly into a rage at her return.

After several months, despair and resentment give way to Bowlby's third phase, the **detachment phase.** Children seemingly forget about their mothers and relate to other adults for affection. Children perk up and may *appear* quite normal.

However, Bowlby warns that the detachment phase should not be confused with healthy adjustment. Bowlby believes that a child who has learned how to get along without his or her mother may have lost the ability to sustain enduring relationships with anyone. Here you can see Bowlby's psychoanalytic orientation: an event early in our childhood, one that we may not even consciously remember, can haunt us for the rest of our lives.

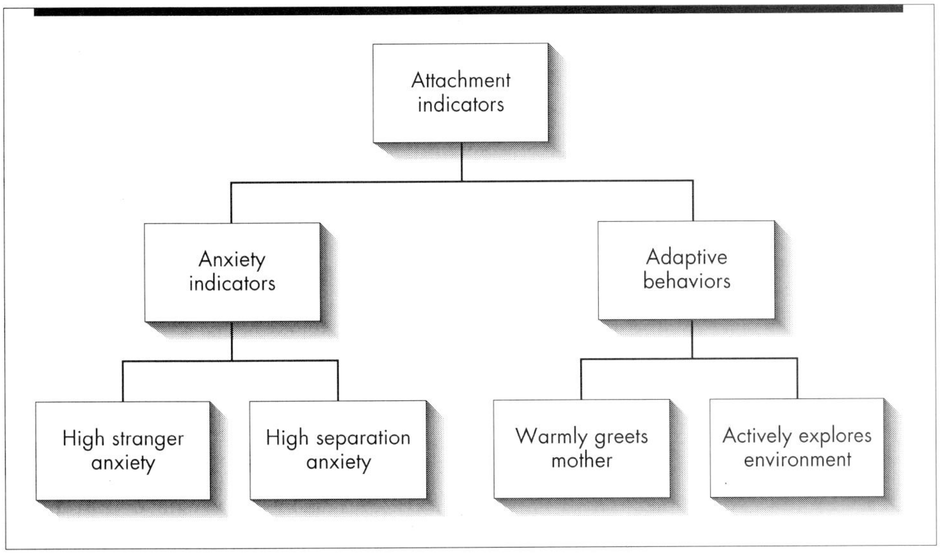

Figure 9.4

Anxieties and Behaviors Typical of the Securely Attached Child

Some people who want women to stay home and take care of the children like to cite Bowlby's theory. But before Bowlby's theory is used to tell mothers to stop working outside of the home, four questions need to be answered:

1. Does the evidence support his theory?
2. Since his theory was based on work with orphans and other institutionalized children, can his theory be applied to children who see their mothers daily, but spend a great deal of time away from them?
3. Since Bowlby looked at separation during the second year of life, do his results apply to other age groups, such as newborns and 4-year-olds?
4. Is the infant's mother the only caregiver who really matters?

Problems with the Infant-Caregiver Relationship

In 1972 and 1979, psychiatrist Michael Rutter published two reviews of the research evidence bearing on these four questions. In terms of the first question: Does the research support Bowlby? The answer is "yes" and "no." As Bowlby claimed, maternal deprivation can have long-term harmful effects on children. However, the effects are more severe than Bowlby predicted. Rather than produce subtle emotional problems in an "apparently" normal child, harmful mother-infant interactions may contribute to a number of very noticeable psychological disorders including mental retardation, disruptive behavior, and the inability to respond to others with positive emotions.

Interference in Normal Attachment Behaviors The evidence also fails to support Bowlby's notion that prolonged maternal deprivation, *by itself,* inevitably interferes with attachment. Rather, separation interferes with attachment only if problems already exist with the caregiver-infant relationship. For example, some children who have experienced repeated, long-term separations from their primary caretaker may exhibit the protest, despair, and detachment phases that characterize Bowlby's acute distress syndrome. However, these problems resulted only when the child was not securely attached *before* separation or when the child received inadequate care during the separation. Rutter notes that if children are securely attached before separation and they have positive social interactions with another caregiver during the separation, they will securely reattach to their original caretaker when they reunite. To reiterate an important conclusion from the research: For separation to interfere with attachment behaviors, some other problem needs to be present, either in the child, the caregiver, or the circumstances of the separation.

Lack of Meaningful Social Experiences Just as a mother's absence is not, *in itself,* harmful, a mother's presence is not, *in itself,* helpful. For example, consider the situation in which a present, but insensitive, caretaker rarely plays with, talks to, or listens to the child. Such a situation is rare, but is most likely to happen when a baby is unwanted, the caretaker is suffering from depression, or when the baby is the youngest of several children.

A child in this situation will lack the meaningful cognitive and verbal experiences that could aid its cognitive and social development. In one study documenting how this situation may harm social development, Harvard Medical School Researcher Karlen Lyons-Ruth and her colleagues (1987) found that mothers who were less verbally communicative with their infants at home were likely to have infants who were either anxious/resistant or anxious/avoidant. Similarly, Cox, Owen, Henderson, and Margand (1992) found that sensitivity, warmth, responsivity, and physical affection predict whether a child will be securely attached. Taken together, these findings support the argument that quantity of time spent with the infant isn't enough—the infant must also receive quality time.

Rutter notes that the long-term consequences for children who lack meaningful social experiences is some degree of intellectual retardation. Ironically, some professional women have taken comfort in this fact. They point out that, on the average, children of stay-at-home mothers do not have higher IQs than children of mothers who work outside the home. "Consequently," they argue, "on the average, children of women who work outside of the home must receive enough meaningful social experiences." Can you find a flaw in this reasoning?

Failure to Synchronize Actions Another case in which the mother's presence is not helpful is when mother and child fail to interact appropriately with one another. For instance, the mother may be too tired or too depressed to respond to the child. Or, the child may be unresponsive, as is often true with premature, "difficult," or sick children. Unresponsive children are less likely to elicit positive interaction from their parents. For example, Dymphna van den Boom and Jan Hoeksma (1994) found that mothers of irritable infants have less visual and physical contact with their infants than mothers of non-irritable infants. The mothers are also less likely to soothe their infants, are less responsive, and provide less stimulation.

Regardless of the cause, the infant-caregiver interaction needed to develop the social synchrony that characterizes a secure and happy relationship is missing. In the Ainsworth "strange situation," these children tend either to be ambivalent toward their mother or to actually avoid her when she returns to the room. Outside the lab, these children have difficulty responding to other people with positive emotions.

Disharmony Finally, a mother's presence is not helpful when there is too much disharmony or conflict between the child and the mother, such as when the mother displays overt or covert hostility toward the child (see box 9.3). Typically, mothers who tend to continually display hostility toward their child are not happily married or have anxieties about their family's economic situation (Lyons-Ruth, Connell, Zoll, & Stahl, 1987; Rutter, 1979). Thus, it could be speculated that the mother is displacing her anger toward her husband onto the child or taking out her frustrations about the family's economic situation on the child.

Whatever the causes of the maltreatment, the effects on the infant are not positive. In the short run, the effects of maltreatment can be seen in the Ainsworth strange situation. When mothers and infants were reunited, those infants whose mothers were covertly hostile were more avoidant than infants who were not maltreated (Lyons-Ruth, Connell, Zoll, & Stoll, 1987). In the long run, children whose mothers displayed frequent hostility toward them tended to behave inappropriately and aggressively in later social relationships (Rutter, 1979). Thus, the research suggests that if parents do not get along, but they do not want to harm their child, they have three options: (1) try to make sure that feelings toward the spouse do not carry over to the child; (2) put the child up for adoption; and (3) to separate or divorce "for the kid's sake." (See table 9.8 for a review of the effects of different kinds of adversity on attachment.)

Evaluating the Risks of Separation

You have seen that quality social interaction is critical for the long-term psychological development of children—and this quality interaction can come from people other than the primary caretaker. Consequently, the age at which a child can experience lengthy separation from his or her primary caregiver before suffering psychological harm depends on the availability of other suitable, responsive caregivers. The critical age also depends on security of the attachment, the developmental level of the child, the nature of the separation, the availability of alternative caregivers, and the psychological makeup of the child.

Although the critical age for separation varies tremendously depending on a wide range of factors, there are, nevertheless, some general guidelines. A child under 6-months-old usually has not attached to a specific caregiver (Ainsworth, 1970; Bowlby, 1969; Schaffer & Emerson, 1964). Separation from a child at this point is usually more traumatic for the caregiver than for the infant. Whereas the infant is not attached to the caregiver, the caregiver is not only attracted to the infant's appearance and attachment reflexes, but the caregiver is also made to feel guilty by a society that seems to think those first few months are crucial to psychological development.

Once a secure attachment has been formed, children are most sensitive to separation from the ages of 9 months to 36 months. After 36 to 48 months, Bowlby finds that children accept temporary absence from their caregiver without protest and will accept substitute attachment figures. With advancing development, the child will be able to take longer and longer periods of separation.

Does this mean that mothers should stay home with their children until the child's third or fourth birthday? Some, like Burton White (White, 1987), believe that mothers should. White believes that the first three years are the formative years and that the child needs a dedicated, ever-present mother to foster the child's intellectual, social, and personality development. But before making the decision not to work outside the home, a mother should consider at least four points.

First of all, by age 1, most children form multiple attachments (Schaffer & Emerson, 1964). There is no reason why a young child cannot divide his or her time between attachment figures. Multiple attachments provide more opportunities for meaningful social experiences. Furthermore, multiple attachments may promote quality interaction between infant and primary caregiver by reducing the amount of stress the primary caregiver experiences.

Second, there are several ways to ease a child's separation anxiety. For example, Weinraub and Lewis (1977) found that if a mother briefly explained that she was leaving and when she would return, toddlers cried less and played more constructively. With young children it is important to keep the explanation short and to the point

Type of Adversity	Causes of Adversity	Effect of Adversity
Interference with attachment behavior	Separation + poor social interactions during separation + poor relations before separation.	Acute distress syndrome described by Bowlby. Protest followed by despair followed by detachment.
Insecure early attachment	Non-interactiveness of caregiver or characteristics of the infant that may lead to lack of interaction such as passivity, bad temperament, premature birth, or illness.	Inability to feel affection toward others.
Lack of meaningful social experiences	Not enough social stimulation.	Intellectual retardation.
Conflictual interpersonal relations	Family conflict, caregiver-child disharmony.	Inappropriate and disruptive behavior.

Table 9.8

Effects of Different Types of Adversities on Caregiver-Child Relations

(Adams & Passman, 1981). Furthermore, the explanation should come just minutes before departure. If parents tell children about departure a couple of hours in advance, the warning tends to increase anxiety rather than decrease it (Adams & Passman, 1980). Separation distress may be reduced further by giving the child a sharply focused photograph of the caregiver (Passman & Longeway, 1982). Passman and Longeway speculate that the photograph reminds the child of whatever explanation the mother gave the child before departure.

Third, the mother should realize that going to work means temporarily separating from her infant; it does not mean that the infant will be permanently deprived of his mother. The child of a working mother is in a situation different from the orphans Bowlby studied. Thus, Bowlby's suggestion that young children begin to suffer after one or two weeks and that after several months permanent damage may be incurred does not apply to temporary separation. Furthermore, as Rutter cautions, the real issue is not so much separation, but whether the child's psychosocial, emotional, and physical needs are being met.

Fourth, a substantial amount of research suggests that children of mothers who work outside the home are having their needs met. In fact, Benn (1986) found that infants of mothers who returned to work earlier were more likely to be securely attached than infants of mothers who returned to work later. More directly contradictory to the "mothers should stay at home" argument, Owen, Easterbrooks, Chase-Lansdale, and Goldberg (1984) found maternal employment had no effect on infant-mother attachment. Similarly, Gottfried and Gottfried (1985) found no emotional, social, or intellectual differences between children of mothers who worked outside the home and children of mothers who stayed at home.

Alternative Caregiving Arrangements

To this point, we have discussed research and theory that focuses exclusively on attachment between an infant and its mother. Although this focus reflects the traditional Western notion that a mother should rear her children without any help or interference from anyone else, we should not assume that such child rearing is necessary for optimal psychological development. In fact, evidence suggests that children can flourish in a number of other caregiving arrangements, ranging from the communes of China and Israel to single fathers in Los Angeles. As Rutter's review suggested, what is crucial for child development is *not* who meets the child's physical and emotional needs, but that these needs are met. In this section, we will explore four alternatives to having infants reared exclusively by their mothers: multiple mothers, the kibbutz, day care, and fathers.

Multiple Mothers

In 1974, Herbert and Gloria Leiderman studied inhabitants of an agricultural region of East Africa. They found that, in some households, the biological mother was responsible for at least 75 percent of the child rearing and household chores. In other homes, other female friends and relatives also played the role of mother so that the biological mother was responsible for less than half of the child rearing and household chores. The Leidermans failed to find that these caregiving arrangements had any profound effects. Any differences that were uncovered canceled each other out. For example, although the children reared in multiple-mother households were more anxious around strangers, they earned higher scores on several cognitive tests. Perhaps the most intriguing finding was that the children who benefited the most from multiple mothers were those from less affluent homes. Apparently, the presence of several caregivers provided a rich source of social stimulation that compensated for otherwise poor living conditions.

Kibbutz

A **kibbutz** is an Israeli collective farm or settlement. In a kibbutz, children are separated from their parents at an early age and reared in communal nurseries. Parent-child interaction is limited to the afternoons and weekends. Researchers

Box 9.3

ISSUE in FOCUS

The Rescue of Mary Ellen Connolly

In the New York City of a century past, Etta Wheeler was a nurse and church worker. She made rounds through the tenement houses, helping out when and however she could.

It was in 1873 that Mrs. Wheeler began hearing the stories.

Neighbors in one tenement house were certain something terrible was going on in the Connolly apartment. Every night they heard the screams of a small child. Would Mrs. Wheeler please look into it, the neighbors asked.

The reports were too disturbing to be ignored, and so one day Mrs. Wheeler knocked on the apartment door of Mr. Francis Connolly and his wife Mary.

Yes, they had a child, they said. A 9-year-old foster daughter named Mary Ellen. What of it?

Mrs. Wheeler talked herself inside and caught a glimpse of the unimaginable truth. The Connollys had chained their little girl to her bedpost. Her body was covered with wounds and welts and bruises in various stages of healing. She was emaciated from what could not have been more than a bread-and-water diet.

Seeing this, Mrs. Wheeler demanded that the child be turned over to her. The Connollys told the nurse to mind her own business and be on her way. For months thereafter, Mrs. Wheeler returned to the Connolly apartment, hoping to rescue little Mary Ellen, and yet each time the door was slammed in her face.

Everywhere the nurse sought assistance in the matter, she was refused. Charitable organizations insisted they were helpless unless the youngster could be brought to them legally. The police and the district attorney advised that they could do nothing until evidence was furnished that a crime had been committed. And in 1873 there were no laws against child abuse—only an unwritten law that parents could rear their children in whatever way they saw fit, even if that way was unspeakably brutal.

The "meddling" Mrs. Wheeler had one last hope: a gentleman named Henry Bergh. Mr. Bergh and the men serving under him comprised a law enforcement agency. They were granted police power in New York City.

Early in 1874, Mrs. Wheeler visited this same Henry Bergh, described the ordeal of little Mary Ellen Connolly, and begged Bergh to intervene. Moved by what he had heard, Bergh immediately assigned two of his best officers to the case. They invaded the Connolly apartment and, armed with a writ of *habeas corpus,* took the cowering child into their protective custody.

Weak and hurting, whiplashed and scissor-slashed, the little girl had to be brought into the courtroom on a stretcher. Spectators, men and women alike, wept aloud. The judge himself had to turn away, so pitiful was Mary Ellen's appearance. There, in the middle of it all, was Henry Bergh, his voiced filled with emotion as he recited the law that would save Mary Ellen and send her abusing mother to the penitentiary for one year.

A warm, loving home was found for the wretched little girl. It sounds almost like a fairy tale, but she really did live happily ever after.

And so did many others like her. For it was the case of Mary Ellen Connolly that inspired this nation's movement to protect defenseless children.

Even more specifically, that movement owes Henry Bergh. For when he rescued that battered child from a New York tenement, he did so by the authority of the only extant law that applied.

Henry Bergh was founder and president of the American Society for the Prevention of Cruelty to Animals.

To save Mary Ellen's life, he had to state in court: "Your Honor, the child is an animal."

Questions

1. To what extent do you think parents should be free to rear their children as they please?
2. To what extent do we believe, even today, that abusive biological parents are better for the child than alternate caregivers?

Note: From *Destiny and 102 Other Real-Life Mysteries* by Paul Aurandt, New York: Bantam Books, 1983.

Box 9.4

SELF-CHECK

PART A

Indicate whether each of the following statements is true or false.

1. Only insecurely attached infants experience stranger anxiety and separation anxiety.
2. According to Bowlby, children who have been abandoned for so long that they enter the detachment phase may appear quite normal.
3. Bowlby's work clearly applies to the case of children of working mothers.
4. Bowlby's research clearly applies to the case of 3-month-olds who are in day care.
5. Mothers who are depressed, hostile, or uncommunicative are likely to have babies who are insecurely attached, even if the mother is around all of the time.
6. Children are most sensitive to separation between the ages of 9 months and 36 months.
7. Children cannot form attachments to multiple caregivers.
8. Several studies suggest that attachment is not hurt by having mothers work outside of the home.

PART B

Answer the following questions.

9. What four different reactions was Ainsworth looking for in the strange situation?
10. What percentage of children are securely attached, insecure/avoidant, and insecure/ambivalent?
11. What is the difference between insecure/avoidant and insecure/ambivalent children?

Please turn to the end of this chapter to check your answers.

who put kibbutz infants into Ainsworth's "strange situation" found, as the Leidermans' African study did, that children reared by multiple caregivers exhibit, on the average, more stranger anxiety than the typical American infant (Sagi et al., 1986). However, Michael Lamb and his colleagues (Lamb et al., 1985) suggest that—rather than reflect a less secure attachment—greater stranger anxiety may reflect the fact that children reared in a close-knit kibbutz have less exposure to strangers than the average American child. Thus, the stranger anxiety exhibited by kibbutz children may only show that, like most people, kibbutz children are anxious in unfamiliar situations.

Remarkably, in multiple caregiver situations, the child's primary attachment is still to his or her mother—even though the child spends more time with caregivers other than the biological mother. In short, the evidence for both child-parent and parent-child attachment in the kibbutz and in other multiple caretaker situations is very strong (Fox, 1977; Kagan et al., 1978). In fact, because such strong child-parent bonds occur in all kinds of multiple caretaker situations, Konner (1982) concludes that the development of attachment between the ages of 6 and 12 months is universal.

Day Care

These cross-cultural studies on the effects of multiple caregivers may have important implications for contemporary American culture because most mothers work. Recent statistics report that more than 50 percent of mothers with infants and toddlers are employed outside the home (Hoffman, 1989). Specifically, more than 10.5 million children under age 6 have mothers who work and 10 million children ages 6 to 13 have mothers who work (U.S. Bureau of Labor Statistics, 1988). As these numbers continue to rise, more and more children will spend at least part of their day with an alternative caregiver. Increasingly, that alternative will be day care.

Because Americans accept the idea of preschool and school, few people are worried about the effects of day care on children over age 3. However, with the increased movement of women into the labor force, a new phenomenon has emerged—the placement of infants in day care. Because day care is so widespread and its effects so controversial, people want research on multiple caregivers that goes beyond studies of other cultures suggesting that day care would not be harmful. People want research that specifically relates to Western-style day care.

Thomas Gamble and Edward Zigler (1986) reviewed several field studies that looked for specific attachment patterns and investigated out-of-home care starting in the first year of life. They concluded that although parent-child attachments are sometimes disturbed by day care, disturbances happen only in a minority of cases. Research has continued to support this claim. In fact, even the studies with the most pessimistic results still show that more than half of the infants who started day care in the first year of life were securely attached at 12 months (Belsky & Rovine, 1988). Similarly, in reviewing the literature, K. Allison Clarke-Stewart (1989) found that 64 percent of the infants of full-time working mothers were securely attached.

Since most day care children form secure attachments, Gamble and Zigler concluded that day care, by itself, does not cause insecure attachments. To explain why some day care children had insecure attachments, Gamble and Zigler speculated that personality characteristics of the child or primary caregiver, as well as the degree of family stress, may make some attachment bonds more fragile than others.

But what about Clarke-Stewart's (1989) finding that whereas 71 percent of nonemployed or part-time workers had securely attached infants, only 64 percent of the infants of full-time mothers were securely attached? Don't these data show that staying home *causes* slightly more secure attachments? No, these data do *not* tell us why there are fewer attached infants among working mothers. Admittedly, it may be, as some have argued, that infants who are left by working mothers interpret the separation as rejection or that frequent separations disrupt normal attachment (for example, Barglow et al., 1987; Belsky & Rovine, 1988). On the other hand, it may be that mothers who are insensitive to the needs of their infants or who dislike infants are more likely to work (for example, Clarke-Stewart, 1989; Hayes & Palmer, 1989). In other words, even in the minority of cases in which day care children had insecure attachments, it's careless to conclude that day care caused these poor attachments because all of the studies included in Gamble and Zigler's review were correlational. As you may recall from chapter 2, correlations tell us only that two variables are related; they don't tell us *why* the two variables are related. In the case of day care, it is possible that some other factor leads to both insecure attachments and the need for day care. For example, economic hardship, marital separation, and single parenthood are events that might require a woman to enter the labor force and subsequently place her child in day care. These events may also lead to a conflicted and stressful home environment and interfere with positive parent-child interactions.

When trying to interpret the effects of day care on attachment, not only do we need to realize that the research is not designed to describe the effects of day care, but we also need to realize that most of the research is not designed to tell us how children getting good day care differ from those getting bad day care. As Rutter (1979) has stressed, child-parent attachments do not suffer if a child's psychosocial and emotional needs are met by an alternative caregiver. In a well-controlled study, Deborah Phillips, Kathleen McCartney, and Sandra Scarr (1987) found that the overall quality of the child-care environment affects many aspects of children's social competence, as well as their language and cognitive development.

What constitutes quality day care? Several studies indicate that low child to caregiver ratios (Howes, 1983; Howes & Rubenstein, 1985) and frequent verbal interaction between child and adult caregivers (Phillips et al., 1987) are critical to quality care. Surprisingly, mixed results have been found for the effects of caregiver experience. For example, the National Day Care Study (Roupp et al., 1979) found that experienced caregivers engaged children in less social interaction and cognitive stimulation than less experienced caregivers. On the other hand, Howes (1983) found that experienced caregivers were more responsive to children. (For information about how to select a quality daycare center, consult box 9.5.)

Fathers

Like the American legal system, the attachment literature conveys a strong bias toward the mother as caregiver (for example, Main et al., 1985). After reading about the work of Bowlby and Ainsworth, you may be left with the impression that fathers and children do not form attachments. Nothing could be further from the truth. Recently, developmental psychologists have begun to focus on the role of fathers in child rearing. They have found that, contrary to popular notions, father-infant attachments have a central role in child development.

In one of the earliest studies comparing infants' attachments to both mother and father, Rudolph Schaffer and Peggy Emerson (1964) reported that infants protest separation from their mothers more than they protest separation from their fathers. However, Schaffer and Emerson's study was strongly criticized because it relied solely on mothers' claims: Critics argued that mothers' claims might be biased. The findings of subsequent research suggests that mothers' claims *were* biased. For example, subsequent research on separation protest has shown no demonstrable preference for either parent in the home or laboratory (Cohen & Campos, 1974; Kotelchuck, 1976; Lamb, 1979). Furthermore, current research clearly indicates that most infants are attached to both their mothers and fathers during the second half of the first year of life. Indeed, about the same proportion of infants are securely attached to their father as to their mother (Cox et al., 1992). Research also indicates that if a father is physically affectionate, responsive, warm, and likes the role of being a parent, the infant is very likely to form a secure attachment to the father, (Cox et al., 1992). Because infants are likely to attach to both parents, infants in distress will organize their attachment behaviors around whichever parent is present.

There are, however, differences between how infants respond to fathers and mothers. For example, if both parents are available, infants between 10 and 18 months will usually turn to their mothers (Cohen & Campos, 1974; Lamb, 1976). This preference for mom may be because the mother has been around more and thus has been present more often than the father during previous moments of distress. Are there other differences that may be the results of fathers being around less? Yes, children are more likely to smile and vocalize at fathers than at mothers.

Box 9.5

RESEARCH in FOCUS

Selecting Quality Day Care for Your Child

As you have seen, the quality of day care is very important. But how can you find quality day care? Below are some tips that will increase your chances.

1. Don't accept government licensure as a guarantee of quality.
2. Don't assume that a non-profit child-care center will provide better care than a for-profit center.
3. The smaller the children to staff ratio, the better. This is particularly true for infants because they do not profit much from peer interactions and they need extremely responsive caregivers.
4. Look for a staff that has low turnover. A stable staff allows the child to form attachments to a caregiver and vice versa.
5. Look for a dedicated, responsive staff. Infants need to believe the world is a friendly, responsive place, and they should be both held and talked to while being fed; toddlers need adults who will talk to them and name things for them; 3-year-olds need adults who will patiently answer "why" questions; and all children need caregivers who will listen to them. In short, children need caregivers who will provide meaningful social experiences, synchronize actions, and who will have harmonious interactions with the child.
6. Not only should the staff exhibit patience, empathy, concern, energy, warmth, responsiveness, and emotional stability, but it should be trained in developmental psychology. This training should be reflected in such things as:
   - Grouping the children by age so the older children don't dominate,
   - Basing activities on the child's age and developmental stage,
   - Allowing for individual differences,
   - Realizing that children need both close supervision and some freedom,
   - Providing educational programs for children above age 3, and
   - Not using physical punishment.
7. The center should allow unannounced visits.
8. The center should have outside and indoor exercise facilities.
9. The center should have a wide variety of good, safe play materials. Young children have short attention spans and do not like to wait to play with toys. Children should be taught to return toys to the proper place after they are through playing with them.
10. Centers should allow children a wide variety of opportunities for visual stimulation. There should be many mobiles, posters, and picture books. In addition, there should be windows children can easily look out of. Of course, the nap area should be dark, quiet, and relatively devoid of stimulation.
11. The center should accommodate both those who need more and those who need less nap time than others.
12. There should be places where children can keep their personal possessions.
13. Children should appear happy and involved. They should not be bored or be fighting.
14. Children should be allowed "alone time."
15. Television watching should be kept to a minimum.

This preference for vocalizing and smiling at fathers may be because fathers are more novel to the infant (Belsky, 1979; Clarke-Stewart, 1978).

Familiarity is, of course, not the only explanation for why infants respond differently to mothers than to fathers. Fathers interact with their children in ways different from mothers. Fathers are less likely to hold, tend to, and show affection toward infants (Lamb & Oppenheim, 1989). Fathers also tend to sit farther away, speak in more adult terms, and are more likely to engage in touching games (Flaste, 1976; Lamb, 1977). Fathers are usually more playful, and more likely to make abrupt shifts in the level of excitement. Typically, fathers expect and receive more heightened playful responses from their children, including brighter eyes and more vivid facial expressions (Brazelton, 1976).

The degree and kind of interaction fathers engage in with their child often depend on the child's gender. As with many primates, most fathers treat sons and daughters differently. During a child's second year, fathers usually begin to show special interest in their sons and withdraw, to some degree, from their daughters. Paralleling this heightened attention, sons may begin to show a clear preference for their father. By age 2, both boys and girls are more upset by the departure of their same-sex parent than by the departure of their opposite-sex parent (Weinraub & Frankel, 1977).

In conclusion, we can extract three lessons from the research on father-child attachment. First, since children can attach to both mothers and fathers, both parents can provide satisfactory care for their children. Second, since the father relationship tends to be different from the mother relationship, the roles of mother and father may not

Infants can become as securely attached to their fathers as to their mothers. However, they expect more play with fathers and more caretaking from mothers.

be as interchangeable as some may think; both play important and complementary roles in the lives of children (Belsky, 1979). As some have argued, mothers are the preferred caretakers, fathers are the preferred playmates (Bretherton, 1985; Yogman, 1982). Third, since the child's attachment to the mother is only moderately correlated with the child's attachment to the father, it seems reasonable to assume that attachment is not so much the result of the child's temperament, but of the parent's behavior (Fox et al., 1991; Vaughn et al., 1992). That is, if one parent is a good caregiver, the child may securely attach to that parent, whereas the child may insecurely attach to the parent who is not providing quality care.

One reason some fathers may not provide quality care is that they are not present in the home. As you'll read in chapter 11, there has been an increase in the number of single mothers and divorces over the past 30 years. In the case of divorce, mothers usually are given custody of the children. This type of separation has consequences for both child and father. Fathers frequently report feeling isolated from their children. As adults, children from divorced families are less accepting of their fathers (McCormick & Kennedy, 1994).

Promoting Attachment

You have seen that quality care is the foundation of secure attachment. But what exactly is quality care? Which parental behaviors promote secure attachment? Although more research has to be done before we can answer these questions fully and confidently, we can tentatively answer these questions by saying that several factors seem to be strong predictors of secure attachment: positive parental responding, consistency, warmth, and harmony in parent-infant interaction (Belsky & Isabella, 1988; Cox et al., 1992).

Positive parental responding means to respond to infants in a comforting, confident, and cheerful manner. Treating infants in this manner will soothe them, reduce anxiety, and teach them not to be unduly afraid of the world. Parents who are excessively anxious about taking care of their infants may unintentionally teach the child to be anxious.

Positive parental responding is especially difficult for first-time parents who do not understand infant behavior (Brazelton, 1986). For example, during the first three months of life, infants tend to end the day by crying. This crying is their way of reducing the stress of overstimulation that characterizes their initiation into the world. Parental efforts to comfort the baby rarely succeed in stopping the crying. New parents often take this crying personally, believing that it is their inadequacy as parents that both causes the crying and fails to stop it.

Once the baby's nervous system has matured to a level that can better accommodate the stresses of daily life, the nightly crying decreases or ceases. Usually, at this point new parents start to feel more confident about their parenting skills. The baby recognizes this confidence and is comforted by it.

Responding to an infant with *consistency* teaches her to trust the world and to feel she can exert control over her destiny. A consistent world is one with clear-cut rules. By mastering these rules, a child learns to trust and to feel that she can exert control over her life. An inconsistent world is much harder to understand. Without rules, a child learns to give up and retreat.

Responding to an infant with *warmth* teaches a child to love and feel valued. Warmth and affection are also potent reinforcers. A child who knows love will work to maintain that love by conforming to his parents' expectations.

Harmony in parent-infant interactions occurs when both child and caregiver exchange love. Usually, this harmony in interactions provides enjoyment for both parties. For example, it is through interaction that a child is comforted and soothed. Similarly, it is through interaction that a parent experiences the joys of parenthood.

A key element in the development of harmonious interactions between parent and child is communication (Brazelton, 1986). *Communication* involves verbal and physical interaction, as well as the ability to read each other's moods and emotions.

The parents' ability to correctly identify their baby's emotions is so important that failure to do so may be a prime culprit in child abuse, as a study done by Joseph P. Kropp and O. Maurice Haynes (1987) suggests. These investigators showed abusive and nonabusive mothers 14 slides of babies' faces. The slides showed positive emotions such as surprise, joy, and interest, and negative emotions including sadness, fear, and anger. Mothers were shown two slides of each emotion and asked, "How would you respond to this baby?" and "What is this baby feeling?" Abusive mothers were more likely to misidentify the babies' emotions. Specifically, when a baby was expressing a negative emotion, abusive mothers were much more likely

Box 9.6

SELF-CHECK

PART A

Indicate whether each of the following statements is true or false.

1. The Leidermans found that the more the child rearing was done by the biological mother, the better off the child was.
2. Children reared by multiple mothers were more anxious around strangers.
3. Children reared by multiple mothers scored higher on several intellectual ability tests, and this was especially true for children from low-income families.
4. In multiple caregiver situations, the child's primary attachment is to which caregiver happens to spend more time with the infant.
5. Virtually every study shows that most infants who go to day care are securely attached.
6. Studies showing that children who are in day care are less likely to be securely attached provide proof that day care causes, in a few instances, insecure attachment.
7. The research evidence clearly shows that infants become more strongly attached to their mothers than to their fathers.

PART B

Answer the following questions.

8. What are two explanations for why kibbutz children exhibit more stranger anxiety than the average American child?
9. In day care research, what important variable has often been overlooked (but not by Phillips, McCartney, & Scarr, 1987)?
10. What are four factors that seem to promote secure attachment?

Please turn to the end of this chapter to check your answers.

than normal mothers to think the baby was expressing a positive emotion. Kropp explains that, "It's frustrating for the mother if she's trying to help her baby but is missing the boat—not catching on to emotional signals. And, as frustration builds, so do the chances of neglect."

ATTACHMENT'S EFFECTS THROUGHOUT THE LIFESPAN

You have seen how secure attachment helps infants. From birth, "completely helpless" infants have ways to keep helpers nearby. By 10 months of age, infants are often clearly attached to their caregivers. Infants use this caregiver as a secure base from which to explore the world.

However, secure attachment is not guaranteed. You have seen two patterns of caregiver behavior that may lead to insecure attachments.

First, if the caregiver is unresponsive to the infant's desires, the infant will tend to:

- Cry more than the securely attached infant, especially when the caregiver "deserts" her,
- Explore less than the securely attached infant,
- Be more anxious than the securely attached infant, and
- Show ambivalence by combining attachment behaviors with expressions of anger.

Second, if the caregiver rejects the infant's efforts at physical contact, the infant will tend to:

- Be uninterested in exploring the environment,
- Show little distress when separated from the caregiver, and
- Avoid the caregiver.

Attachment styles predict behavior during infancy, but what about the rest of the individual's life? According to Bowlby (1973), the quality of the attachment bond has lifelong effects. Specifically, if infants do not form secure attachments, they probably will grow up to believe that:

- They are not worthy of being loved, and
- Attachment figures, whether they are one's parents or one's lover, cannot be trusted to respond to calls for protection.

Certainly, Bowlby's position seems plausible. But is there really any evidence that effects of attachment last beyond infancy?

Research on Attachment's Effects in Early Childhood

Several studies strongly suggest that attachment's effects last through early childhood. For example, Higley et al. (1992) compared two groups of monkeys. One group was separated from their mothers at birth and raised by peers. The other group was raised by their mothers for the first six months of life and then separated from their mothers. Thus, the second group had been given the opportunity to securely attach to their mothers, whereas the first group had not. Higley found that the group that had been raised for the first six months by their mothers was:

1. Less anxious,
2. More involved in exploring the environment, and
3. Had better and more secure attachment to their peers. Thus, having a good previous attachment bond improved the quality of later relationships with peers.

The human research also suggests that secure attachment has positive effects beyond infancy. For example, Matas, Arend, & Sroufe (1978) found that secure attachment was related to toddlers having better problem-solving abilities. Furthermore, Elicker et al. (1992) found that attachment style in infancy predicts social skills and self-confidence in children 10 years later. Indeed, infant attachment style also correlates with behavior problems, problems in adjusting to school, quality of relationships with peers and adults other than parents, and the quality of family relationships during the elementary school years (Bretherton, 1985; Erickson, Sroufe, & Egeland, 1985; Lewis, Feiring, McGuffog, & Jaskir, 1984; Main et al., 1985; Sroufe et al., 1990).

Research on Attachment's Effects in Adulthood

The research on the effects of infant-caregiver attachment on the middle childhood is still in its infancy. It takes time to do the longitudinal studies that follow infants through childhood. If the research on the effects of attachment on middle childhood is preliminary, you can imagine how preliminary the work on the effects of attachment on adulthood are. All the adulthood research can be criticized because it is not longitudinal. That is, this research does not assess attachment at age 1 and then look at adult behavior 20 to 50 years later. Instead, most of this research asks adults to *remember* how attached they were to their parents. Given the problems with retrospective self-report—and the well-documented "childhood amnesia" for the first two years of life—the findings of this research are open to question.

Despite the fact that the adulthood research is not conclusive, the findings suggest that attachment does affect adult relationships. To illustrate, consider a germinal study done by Phil Hazan and Cindy Shaver (1987). Their study produced two findings supporting Bowlby's belief that the quality of the attachment bond formed during infancy has lifelong implications.

First, the relative prevalence of the three attachment styles (secure, anxious/resistant, and anxious/avoidant) is roughly the same in adulthood as in infancy. This finding is consistent with Bowlby's notion that the attachment style developed in infancy lasts throughout the lifespan.

Second, the three kinds of adults (secure, anxious/resistant, and anxious/avoidant) differ in ways consistent with Bowlby's predictions. That is, these three types of adults differ in the way they view themselves, the way they view relationships, and the way they experience heterosexual love.

Secure adults find others trustworthy, believe that they themselves are likable, and believe in enduring love. For secure adults, love is characterized by trust, friendship, and positive emotions. The "Roseanne" show's Roseanne and Dan Conner are idealized forms of the securely attached adult.

Anxious/resistant adults have many self-doubts. For them, love is experienced as an almost painfully exciting struggle to merge with another person. Because love is perceived as an exciting opportunity to merge with another person, they fall in love frequently and easily. However, because of their self-doubts and their view of love as a painful struggle, they have difficulty staying in love. Because of this ambivalence about attachment, they, like some oft-married movie stars, may go from relationship to relationship.

Anxious/avoidant adults, on the other hand, do not believe that they need a love partner to be happy. Indeed, they are doubtful of the existence, let alone the durability, of romantic love. For avoidant adults, love is marked by fear of closeness and lack of trust. Many "independent" male and female television characters are stereotypes of avoidant adults.

Hazan and Shaver's basic findings have been replicated by several investigators. For example, several research teams have found that securely attached people tend to be more caring, supportive, understanding, and trusting; avoidant people tend to fear intimacy; and ambivalent adults tend to be obsessive and jealous in their romantic relationships (Collins & Read, 1990; Levy & Davis, 1988; Simpson, 1990). In addition, Mikulincer & Nachshon (1991) found that secure and ambivalent people were more likely to self-disclose than avoidant people. Similarly, Simpson, Rholes, & Nelligan (1992) found that, when one member of a dating couple was put in a stressful situation, securely attached people were more likely to be supportive of their partner than avoidant individuals.

Although the results of Hazan and Shaver's study and studies like it support Bowlby's beliefs about the long-term effects of attachment, keep two facts in mind. First, as we mentioned before, Hazan and Shaver did not know how attached their subjects were as infants. Hazan and Shaver assessed current attachment style and asked subjects questions about separation from parents during childhood and quality of childhood relationships with parents. We can't know whether subjects accurately recalled their relationship with their parents as infants.

The second thing to keep in mind about Hazan and Shaver's study is that although their findings support Bowlby's ideas about the long-term effects of attachment, their study is also consistent with other theories of how attachment unfolds. For example, Bartholomew & Horowitz (1991) argue that, rather than fitting into the model that there are three types of people (securely attached, insecure/ambivalent, and insecure/avoidant), the work of Hazan and Shaver (1987) and others could be interpreted in terms of a four-category model. According to Bartholomew & Horowitz's (1991) four-category model, the infant's relationship with the caregiver causes the infant to form two views (working models) of the social world. The first view concerns whether other people are good or bad. The second is whether the self is good or bad. From these two working models of social reality, four different types of people emerge.

First, if you think others are good and you are good, you will be *secure*. You will be comfortable with sharing yourself with others and with working by yourself. That is, you have intimate friendships but you don't lose your own identity in these friendships.

Second, if you think others are good, but that you are bad, you will be *preoccupied*. You will tend to think that others are much better than they really are. You will be obsessed with having relationships because the only way you can accept yourself is if others like you. Consequently, you tend to be very dependent.

Third, if you think others are bad and you think you are bad, you will be *fearful*. That is, you will be afraid of intimacy and you may avoid other people. You tend to be shy and unassertive. You fear others and distrust them, but you are also very insecure about yourself. The irony is that although the only way that you might like yourself is if others liked you, you don't give them the chance to like you.

Fourth, if you think others are bad, but you think you are good, you will be *dismissing*. You will want to be independent and invulnerable. You will stress self-reliance rather than friendship.

The four-category model is not the only other model that is consistent with Hazan and Shaver's (1987) research. In fact, Hazan and Shaver's data are consistent with Erik Erikson's (1963) view of the developmental course of attachment.

In Erikson's lifespan theory of psychosocial development, attachment is represented by the task of the first stage: *trust versus mistrust*. He believes that the quality of this first bond between parent and baby determines how much a person will trust the world and other people. To form a secure attachment to anyone—be it mother, father, friend, or lover—people must be able to trust. However, Erikson's theory does not actually address the role of attachment during childhood or how attachment transforms into mature bonds, such as adult intimacy (Franz & White, 1985).

Box 9.7

SELF-CHECK

PART A

Indicate whether each of the following statements is true or false.

1. Infant monkeys reared by peers will be more anxious and less likely to explore than monkeys reared by their mothers for the first six months.
2. Infant monkeys reared by peers will be more attached to their peers than infant monkeys reared by their mothers for the first six months and then left with peers.
3. An insecurely attached infant will be more likely than a securely attached infant to have behavioral problems, problems in adjusting to school, poor relationships with peers, poorer quality family relationships, and low self-confidence during the elementary school years.
4. Research definitively establishes a strong causal link between infant-caregiver attachment and problems in middle-childhood.

PART B

Answer the following questions.

5. How does Bartholomew and Horowitz's four-factor model differ from Hazan and Shaver's three-factor model?
6. What are the two basic problems with current research on infant-caregiver attachment's long-term effects?

Please turn to the end of this chapter to check your answers.

Theory about Attachment's Effects Beyond Infancy

Admittedly, part of the reason that Hazan and Shaver's data are consistent with Erikson's theory may be because Erikson's theory is not explicit about how attachment transforms into adult intimacy. However, Hazan and Shaver's data are also consistent with the most explicit theory about the effects of attachment for later life—David Ausubel's (1954) theory of satellization (Ausubel, Montemayor, & Svajian, 1977; Ausubel & Sullivan, 1970; Berzonsky, 1978, 1981). As you will see, Ausubel provides a useful framework for describing the process of attachment, separation, and reattachment to peers and partners.

First Two Years: Attachment

Like most attachment theorists, Ausubel believes that by 6 months, most infants have formed an attachment to their parents. Between the ages of about 6 months and 24 months, most babies have an inflated sense of self-importance. Some of their sense of inflated self-importance stems from their lack of cognitive development. That is, as Piaget discovered, infants are egocentric because they truly believe that the whole world revolves around them. But part of their inflated sense of importance is probably due to parents' tendency to be extremely indulgent of their babies.

Age 3: Reactions to the Devaluation Crisis

During the third year of life, however, parents start demanding more from their children. They expect their children to tolerate frustration, to delay need gratification, as well as to be both weaned and toilet-trained. At about the same time parents are making these demands, children realize that they are not the center of the universe; that, in reality, they are helpless, powerless, and must depend on others for survival. This realization is referred to as the **devaluation crisis.**

Satellization is one way of coping with this crisis. In a satellized relationship, children deal with their powerlessness by choosing to become dependent on their parents' power. A satellized child is dependent on his or her parents. That is, just as the sun provides the nucleus around which the earth orbits, parents provide the nucleus around which the child "orbits." In a satellized relationship, both parent and child are aware of and accept the child's dependence. Rather than feel threatened or resist their dependence, satellized children try to please and live up to the expectations of their parents. Similarly, parents accept their responsibility and willingly care for their children without resenting the sacrifices of parenthood. Parents love their children unconditionally and treat them with respect.

Both the child and society benefit from satellization. Satellization promotes the child's social and personal development, and society gains a conforming and responsible young member.

But if satellization is to occur, several conditions must be met:

- Children must trust their parents and feel unconditional acceptance from them;
- Parents should willingly accept responsibility for their children;
- The child must have a temperament suited for satellization; and
- The parents must not regard their child as a means of overcoming their own frustrations and achieving their own goals.

Unfortunately, meeting all the conditions of satellization is difficult. Not all children trust their parents and feel unconditional acceptance from them; not all children have a temperament suited for satellization; not all parents willingly accept responsibility for their children; and some parents do regard their child as a means of overcoming their own frustrations and meeting goals. As a result, not all children are satellized. Ausubel describes two nonsatellized statuses: undervaluation and overvaluation.

Undervalued children do not receive unconditional love and acceptance. Instead, parents treat them as a burden and resent caring for them. Parents interact with their children in a cold, rejecting manner. Children comply with parental wishes to avoid punishment rather than to please. Parents use their power to threaten and force the child into compliance, not as a means of nurturing and benefiting the child's development.

Because undervalued children are treated with hostility and rejection, they are likely to go through a more intense and earlier devaluation crisis. Furthermore, they do not resolve the crisis by satellizing because they cannot satellize: Satellization requires unconditional acceptance, and undervalued children do not get unconditional acceptance. The only acceptance they can earn is conditional. Since a child reared in a hostile home has limited opportunities and skills for earning acceptance, undervalued children tend to feel inadequate and have low self-esteem.

Despite this lack of acceptance, the undervalued child, like the satellized child, usually will develop what some psychologists call **ego strength,** the abilities to tolerate frustration, to delay need gratification, and to meet the demands of life. However, whereas the satellized child meets the demands of life out of a sense of loyalty and trust, the undervalued child meets those demands to avoid punishment.

The **overvalued** child, on the other hand, is valued—but only for what he or she can do for the parents. Often, the parents regard the child as a vehicle for fulfilling the dreams and desires the parents were never able to realize. Typically, the parents of overvalued children plan out the lives and identities of their children. For example, they may decide what type of person the child will become, what kind of career the child will have, what clubs the child will join, and whom the child will marry.

To entice the child to comply with their plans, parents often spoil and overindulge their child. Sometimes, the children are overly protected. The child who is pampered and bribed into conforming often learns to manipulate the relationship, demanding goods for action. In this sense, many overindulged children exert control over their parents. The parents are willing to give up short-term control because they value the child not for who she is, but for who she may become. Because their parents do not love them unconditionally and are using them to fulfill their dreams, the overvalued child fails to satellize.

Actually, the overvalued child probably feels little need to satellize. After all, the overvalued child is unlikely to experience a pronounced devaluation crisis. His or her parents, eager to stay in their overvalued child's good graces, indulge and cater to the child's wishes. To oversimplify, the overvalued child is spoiled and lacking in self-control, reality testing, or conscience. These children are accustomed to being the center of attention, getting their own way, and continue to have an inflated sense of self—at least until they enter school.

School Entry

Overvalued children are in for a big shock when they enter school. They soon discover that spoiled children are not highly valued or tolerated by most members of society. Their inability to cooperate with other children, inability to delay gratification, and inability to tolerate frustration will quickly alienate them from their teachers and other children.

Sometimes the situation can be partially remedied through the efforts of a perceptive teacher and open minded parents. If both cooperate in consistently exerting reasonable demands, the child may learn some self-control.

Unlike the overvalued child, satellized children usually make a smooth transition to school. At home, they wish to please their parents. At school, they wish to please their teachers. In other words, these children "resatellize" to their

David Ausubel's theory predicts that both satellized children and undervalued children will do well in school, although for different reasons.

Table 9.9

Ausubel's Satellization Theory

Age or Time Period	Critical Events
6 months to 2 years	Attachment forms.
Around age 3	Devaluation crisis, dealt with by satellizing to parents, if possible. However, if child is devalued or overvalued satellization will *not* occur.
School entry (around age 7)	Overvalued children are likely to experience rejection by teachers and peers.
Adolescence	Satellized children may *resatellize* to someone other than their parents, desatellize by *earning status*, or desatellize by adopting an *exploratory orientation*.

teacher. Resatellization will occur to the degree that their teachers' values and attitudes match their parents. The major difference between home and school is that acceptance is more conditional: Being a good boy or girl is not enough; status is contingent on earning good grades.

Nor is school an unpleasant experience for the undervalued child. On the contrary, for them, school may be a very positive experience. Spending time away from a hostile home can be a welcome respite. At school, their chances of earning status and acceptance are greater than at home. Not surprisingly, those who find that they can excel in school may compensate for their rejection at home by proving themselves academically.

Adolescence and Beyond: Desatellization

By adolescence, most undervalued and overvalued children already have assumed their basic orientation to life. As nonsatellized individuals, their orientation is toward themselves: self-enhancement and self-interest. Satellized children, on the other hand, will go through a major transformation during adolescence as they break away from their family through the process of **desatellization.** Ausubel and his colleagues (1977) describe three mechanisms involved in desatellization: resatellizing, attempting to earn status, and being exploratory.

Resatellization is the transfer of dependence from one person to another. Adolescents may resatellize their emotional dependence from their parents to others, such as their peers, other adults, or their spouse. To gain acceptance from these people, the adolescent tries to conform to their wishes and expectations. Conflict arises when these expectations are different from those of the adolescent's parents.

For some, resatellization is a permanent step. As adults, they will continue to derive self-worth by pleasing others. Although these people form attachments to other people, their emphasis on pleasing the other, rather than sharing one's inner self, may limit the level of intimacy.

Not all satellized children grow up to be adults who must continually seek approval from others. Some adolescents desatellize by **earning status**—trying to prove their worth through efforts. Because they do not yet have the skills to compete in the adult arena, these adolescents try to earn status within their peer group by being the best at something. Athletic prowess, appearance, clothes, social participation, risk taking, reputation, and popularity are all arenas where status can be earned. Later, as adults, acquiring cars, homes, jobs, spouses, and children may become the marks of status. For adults with an earning status orientation, adult attachments are more likely to be based on the status value of a particular person or object rather than on true mutual sharing.

Rather than becoming status-oriented, some adolescents desatellize by becoming task oriented. That is, they adopt an **exploratory orientation.** These adolescents feel no need to prove themselves to others or seek approval from others. They feel secure about who they are. In Erikson's terms, they have achieved their own independent, individual identity. Free of the need to be a satellite of another person, group, or status symbol, they can be themselves and can share that self with another, thereby achieving true intimacy. (For a review of Ausubel's theory, see table 9.9.)

Conclusions

Ausubel's theory epitomizes the strengths and weaknesses of work in attachment. Ausubel's theory is intriguing and intuitively appealing, but has not been tested. Whether talking about Ausubel's work or Bowlby's, we are limited by a lack of knowledge about the effects of attachment style on later development. Because of the dearth of research evidence, most theoretical predictions about the effects of attachment on later development are closer to speculation than fact.

Box 9.8

SELF-CHECK

PART A

Indicate whether each of the following statements is true or false.

1. In satellization, children accept the fact that they are dependent on their parents.
2. Parents who give their children unconditional love will not have satellized children (because the unconditional love will spoil the children and make them overlook the fact that they are dependent on the parents).
3. Ausubel claims that the undervalued child will turn out like the insecure/ambivalent child.
4. School entry is difficult for the overvalued child, but may be fairly pleasant for the undervalued child.
5. All children desatellize during adolescence.
6. Almost all satellized children will eventually develop true intimacy in adolescence or adulthood.
7. According to Ausubel, most children are securely attached between 6 months to 2 years of age.

PART B

Answer the following questions.

8. What brings on the devaluation crisis?
9. How is Ausubel's overvalued child similar to Ainsworth's securely attached child?

Please turn to the end of this chapter to check your answers.

The lack of research is unfortunate, especially since attachment theory has implications for a very emotional issue: child rearing. Because people so desperately want to know about the causes and consequences of attachment and because some feel strongly that mothers should stay home with infants, the limited research on attachment occasionally has been generalized inappropriately. Some have accepted that Bowlby's observations of the behavior of institutionalized orphans and diseased children are relevant to the working mother who leaves her child with a baby-sitter. Others have accepted the notion that all day-care situations are identical.

Fortunately, more research is being done daily, and the data we already have dispels certain myths. It is not vital that the mother stay home with the young infant because the infant does not form attachments until it is about 6 months old. In fact, Benn (1986) found that infants of working mothers who returned to work earlier were more likely to be securely attached than working mothers who returned to work later. More directly contradictory to the "mothers should stay at home" argument, Owen, Easterbrooks, Chase-Lansdale, and Goldberg (1984) found maternal employment had no effect on infant-mother attachment. Similarly, Gottfried and Gottfried (1985) found no emotional, social, or intellectual differences between children of mothers who worked outside the home and children of mothers who stayed at home.

Research even fails to support the claim that day care is necessarily harmful. Rutter's (1981) extensive review of the research reveals that day care before age 2 is not inherently harmful. Not only have researchers failed to find that nonmaternal care harms social or cognitive development, but much anecdotal evidence suggests that one form of nonmaternal care—day care—may actually improve children's cognitive abilities. In short, as both Etaugh's (1980) and Rutter's (1981) reviews of the literature show, it does not matter whether the mother is the sole or even primary caretaker. What does matter is that whoever takes care of the infant—be it a day care center, a kibbutz, or the biological mother—gives the child a warm, responsive, and predictable environment.

Although we are quickly learning about which factors promote attachment, we may have to wait for longitudinal studies to find out the effects of different types of attachment on later development. To date, we have found that many of the negative effects attributed to lack of attachment may be due to factors other than attachment, such as abuse, neglect, institutionalization, or the child's inborn temperament. Furthermore, these negative effects sometimes can be reversed by a nurturant environment later in life. Perhaps for these reasons, most research has failed to find that attachment has a significant impact on later life. For example, one area in which we would expect to find the effects of attachment is on adoptees. Yet, Singer, Brodzinksy, Ramsay, Steir, & Waters (1985) have found that the greater incidence of psychological problems found among adoptees in later childhood cannot be explained by insecure attachment relationships. Furthermore, older adoptees do not seem to have more problems than children who were adopted at a younger age.

Also on an optimistic note, infants do not have to carry the burden of insecure attachment with them throughout childhood. For example, children who have been deprived for one or more years can often recover if they are placed in homes where they receive strong doses of attention and affection from responsive caregivers. Indeed, the more developmental psychologists study the issue, the more they seem to find that children are remarkably resilient (Clarke & Clarke, 1976; Rutter, 1979). Thus, theorists who have advocated extreme stability positions, such as Burton White, John Bowlby, and Sigmund Freud, may have underestimated the ability of individuals to change.

Put another way, "If the first relationship affects future relationships by changing working models of what relationships are, can't these models be changed—at least in adulthood?" Some research suggests that supportive spousal relationships can moderate the effects of insecure attachment during infancy (Crockenberg, 1987; Quinton, Rutter, & Liddle, 1984). Furthermore, it also has been suggested that by forgiving parents, people can overcome the influence of early models (Main et al., 1985; Ricks, 1985).

On the other hand, we should be careful about dismissing the long-term effects of infant-caregiver attachment. This attachment may indeed be vital for adult development. As Sroufe and Fleeson (1986, p. 68) argue, it is "because persons select and create later social environments that early relationships are viewed as having special importance." Furthermore, studies like those of Hazan and Shaver (1987) suggest that attachment's effects are long-term.

Does attachment have subtle, long-term effects that have yet to be discovered? Or is social development less stable than some have assumed? Stay tuned—the (re)search goes on.

Summary

1. There is little support for the notion that a biological bond is formed between mothers and their babies.
2. Caregiver attachment to a baby is facilitated by infant attachment behaviors, imitation, synchronized routines, appearance, and identification.
3. Infant attachment to caregivers is facilitated by the fact that caregivers provide for basic biological needs and are the source of contact comfort.
4. **Imprinting** occurs rapidly and is indiscriminate. Attachment occurs gradually and only to a caregiver who meets the infant's needs.
5. Attachment seems to progress through four phases: **preattachment, attachment-in-the making, clear-cut attachment,** and **goal-corrected partnership.**
6. Ainsworth measures the quality of infant attachment by putting an infant in the strange situation and assessing his (1) interest in exploring his surroundings; (2) degree of stranger anxiety; (3) degree of separation anxiety; and (4) reaction to being reunited with mother.
7. According to Ainsworth, securely attached children explore their environment, are anxious around strangers, are upset when their mother leaves them, and are happy when their mother returns. **Insecure/ambivalent** children are distressed when separated from their mothers, but are ambivalent when reunited. **Insecure/avoidant** infants are uninterested in exploring, show little distress when separated from their mothers, and avoid or ignore their mothers when reunited with them.
8. Bowlby describes three phases that children may go through when separated from their mothers during the second year of life: **protest, despair,** and **detachment.**
9. Research suggests that infant separation from a caregiver interferes with normal attachment only when problems exist in the infant-caregiver bond before caregiver and child are separated.
10. Interference in normal attachment behaviors may be caused by lack of meaningful social experiences, failure to synchronize actions, and disharmony.
11. What is critical for normal attachment is **quality** social interaction. This quality interaction can be provided by people other than the biological mother.
12. The critical age when children can adjust to alternative caregivers depends on the quality of alternative caregivers, the security of attachment, the developmental level of the child, the nature of the separation, the availability of alternative caregivers, and the psychological makeup of the child.
13. Cross-cultural research suggests that children, especially environmentally disadvantaged children, benefit from the rich source of social stimulation provided by multiple caregivers.
14. In multiple caregiver situations, such as the **kibbutz,** children's primary attachment is to their parents.
15. Attachment is not adversely affected when children receive quality day care.
16. An infant can become firmly attached to both mother and father.
17. Relative to mothers, fathers tend to be more playful with their infants.
18. Research suggests that the best way to promote attachment is for the caregiver to provide **positive parental responding, consistency, warmth,** and **harmony in parent-infant interactions.**

19. The quality of the attachment bond formed during infancy is believed to have lifelong implications. For example, Hazan and Shaver (1987) found the following tendencies: (1) as adults, securely attached persons view others as trustworthy, (2) insecure/ambivalent individuals find love a painfully exciting struggle to merge with another person, and (3) avoidant men and women do not believe that they need a love partner or even that love exists.
20. Because the research on attachment's effects on adult behavior are based on questionable retrospective self-reports, this research can be challenged.
21. Satellization is the product of a secure attachment. A satellized child is one who is dependent on his or her parents.
22. Overvalued and undervalued children are both examples of insecure attachments.
23. The devaluation crisis occurs when children realize that they are helpless, powerless, and must depend on others for their survival.
24. **Desatellization** is necessary for a youth to transform into a self-governing adult.
25. The three mechanisms of desatellization are resatellization, earning status, and becoming task oriented.
26. There is little evidence that, as a result of working outside of the home, mothers cause their children to be less securely attached.
27. Problems in attachment cannot account for problems that adoptees have.
28. One promising avenue of research is on how to reverse the effects of insecure attachment—assuming that insecure attachment does produce damaging long-term effects.

Key Terms

anxious/avoidant attachment 304
anxious/resistant attachment 304
approach behaviors 286
attachment behaviors 286
attachment-in-the-making 291
bond 286
clear-cut attachment 291
cognitive dissonance 288
contact comfort 289
desatellization 307
despair phase 294
detachment phase 294
devaluation crisis 305
disorganized/disoriented attachment 294
earning status 307
ego strength 306
exploratory orientation 307
goal-corrected partnership 291
imprinting 290
insecure/ambivalent attachment 294
insecure/avoidant attachment 294
kibbutz 297
overvalued 306
positive parental responding 302
preattachment phase 290
protest phase 294
resatellization 307
satellization 306
secure attachment 293
sensitive period 286
separation anxiety 293
signaling behaviors 286
strange situation 292
stranger anxiety 293
surrogate mothers 289
synchronized routines 287
undervalued 306

Self-Check Answers

Box 9.2

Part A:

1. False.
2. True.
3. True.
4. False.
5. True.

Part B:

6. Signaling behaviors—crying, cooing, babbling, and smiles—all bring the mother to the baby. Approach behaviors—clinging, sucking, following—all bring the baby to the mother.
7. Scientists have demonstrated that even 1-day-old infants can display synchrony. Synchrony, in addition to promoting attachment, helps children learn the value of turn taking and mutual giving and taking.

8. The need for contact comfort.
9. Attachment occurs only to a caregiver who meets the infants' needs for food and contact, and attachment develops slowly over a period of months.
10. In the attachment-in-the-making phase, infants show preferences for specific people and direct their attachment behaviors toward their primary attachment figures.
11. In the clear-cut attachment phase, infants protest separation from their caretaker and use their caretaker as a base to explore the world.
12. In the goal-corrected phase, the older child is able to balance the views of others against the child's own wishes.

Box 9.4

Part A:

1. False; **2.** True; **3.** False; **4.** False; **5.** True; **6.** True; **7.** False; **8.** True.

Part B:

9. The degree to which the child uses his mother to explore the environment, the child's reaction to being reunited with his mother (was he ready to be comforted by mom? was he friendly? did the child have mixed emotions at seeing mom return? did the child try to avoid or ignore mom?); child's reaction to stranger (did he experience fear when he saw the stranger [stranger anxiety]?); and the child's distress when mom left (separation anxiety).
10. 60–70 percent were securely attached, 20 percent were insecure/avoidant; and 10 percent are insecure/ambivalent.
11. Insecure/ambivalent children have mixed feelings when reunited with their mothers; insecure/avoidant children avoid or ignore their mothers when reunited. In addition, insecure/avoidant children are less distressed when separated from mom.

Box 9.6

Part A:

1. False.
2. True.
3. True.
4. False.
5. True.
6. False. Correlational evidence does not provide proof of what causes anything.
7. False.

Part B:

8. (a) As a result of not seeing their mother very often, kibbutz children may be less securely attached than American children. (b) As a result of not seeing strangers very often, kibbutz children may show more stranger anxiety than American children.
9. The quality of the day care.
10. Positive parental responding, consistency, harmony in parent-infant interactions, and accurate communication (both verbal and nonverbal).

Box 9.7

Part A:

1. True; **2.** False; **3.** True; **4.** False.

Part B:

5. There are some similarities. In the four-factor model, the secure type matches the secure type of the three-category model, and the preoccupied type roughly corresponds to the anxious/resistant. However, whereas the three-category model has only one type of avoidant, the four-factor model has two types. One (fearful) avoids others because he fears others, the other (dismissing) avoids others because she basically holds others in contempt.
   Another way of looking at the two models is that, whereas Hazan & Shaver (1987) are looking at three types of relationships with people (like, mixed feelings, dislike), the four-factor model looks at both one's relationships with others (like/dislike) and one's feelings toward oneself (like/dislike). We should point out that both models could be viewed as consistent with Bowlby's ideas.
6. First, retrospective self-reports may be biased. A person who currently has unsatisfactory relationships may misremember childhood relationships as being unsatisfactory. Indeed, he or she may even want to blame parents for current failings. Second, the research findings are consistent with a wide range of theoretical formulations. They are consistent with the three-factor model, the four-factor model, Erikson's theory, and Ausubel's theory.

Box 9.8

Part A:

1. True.
2. False.
3. False. Even though the parents' behavior would be very similar in both cases, Ausubel thinks that the undervalued child will have good ego strength and will not necessarily try to avoid others. The child will, however, grow up being more interested in themselves than in the welfare of others.
4. True.
5. False. Only satellized children can desatellize.
6. False. Satellized children may resatellize to peers or attempt to earn status rather than achieving an independent identity that they can share with others.
7. True.

Part B:

8. The devaluation crisis is brought on by the child beginning to realize that he or she is not the center of the universe. This realization results from (a) the child's cognitive development: In Piaget's terms, the child is becoming less egocentric because the child can now consider other people's thoughts and feelings. (b) Parents are also putting more demands on the child.
9. The overvalued child, in some ways, should be like the securely attached child in that parents do try to satisfy the child's short-term needs. However, the overvalued child, unlike the securely attached child, will fail to develop true intimacy with others.

Chapter

Love and Friendships

Love is the word used to label the sexual excitement of the young, the habituation of the middle-aged, and the mutual dependence of the old.

John Ciardi

Marriage is our last, best chance to grow up.

Joseph Barth

Chapter Overview

No man or woman is an island. To a large extent, our lives revolve around our relationships. In this chapter, we will see how relationships change throughout the lifespan, why people get into relationships, and why relationships die.

Box 10.1

RESEARCH in FOCUS

Why Are People Lonely?

1. *Being shy.* Shyness hinders people from seeking new relationships. Eighty percent of people report being shy at some time in their lives; 40 percent are shy now (Zimbardo, 1977).
2. *Improper self-disclosure.* Revealing too much or too little about oneself prevents intimacy. The person who reveals too much too soon is seen as desperate, nondiscriminating (anybody can be their best friend), and someone unlikely to be able to keep a secret. The person who reveals too little is seen as cold. Consequently, the overly secretive person will soon stop receiving intimate self-disclosures.
3. *High expectations.* Loneliness is due to relationships not meeting your expectations. Since men have lower expectations than women, men are less likely to feel lonely (Borys & Perlman, 1985). Since adolescents have unrealistic expectations about both the quantity and quality of their relationships, they are lonelier than older adults.

INTIMACY

People are social animals. For example, college students spend less than 25 percent of their waking time alone (Deaux, 1978). Prisoners prefer to associate with people who might harm them rather than be in solitary confinement.

Why do we want to be around other people? One possibility is that people don't want to feel lonely. And who could blame them? Not only is loneliness unpleasant, but lonely people also feel fearful, helpless, and vulnerable (Rubenstein & Shaver, 1982).

The desire to avoid loneliness is, at best, an incomplete answer to the question of why people need to be with others. One reason this answer is incomplete is that being around others does not make loneliness disappear. People can feel alone in a crowd. In fact, lonely people are just as likely to live with someone as to live alone. Furthermore, many married people feel lonely. In short, loneliness is not the same as being alone (see box 10.1).

Why People Need Intimacy

If being with others is not enough to stop loneliness, what is? One crucial ingredient that must exist if a person is to be happy with their relationships is intimacy. For example, Wheeler, Reis, & Nezlek (1983) found that the best predictor of whether students were happy with their relationships was not the length of their interactions or the number of interactions they had, but rather the degree to which their interactions involved making intimate **self-disclosures,** that is, revealing one's thoughts, attitudes, and feelings to another person.

A cynic could argue that telling people intimate facts about yourself is stupid. After all, by revealing yourself to others, you're giving them ways to hurt you. They may unintentionally hurt you by telling others your secrets. Or, if they ever become angry with you and want to intentionally hurt you, you have told them how to hit you where it hurts. That is, they know what you are sensitive about (whether it's your body, fears about being shallow, worries about mental stability, popularity, or whatever). As Derlega (1984) notes, knowledge (of someone's vulnerabilities) is power.

Considering the risks, why do people self-disclose? Apparently, self-disclosing meets several important needs. Specifically, Derlega & Grzelak (1979) believe that self-disclosing meets three needs: (1) the need for self-expression, (2) the need for self-clarification, and (3) the need for social validation.

Self-expression is simply expressing our feelings. We often like to vent our feelings, particularly if we are angry or excited. Self-clarification occurs when, by talking about our thoughts and feelings, we reflect on them, thereby understanding them better. One reason for the popularity of humanistic therapy may be that it encourages clients to talk and reflect on their feelings, thus encouraging self-clarification (Rogers, 1961). Social validation, having others enhance our self-image, can occur in two ways. First, if a person who knows about our faults still likes us, our self-esteem will get a boost. Second, if others admit to similar beliefs or actions, we are reassured that our feelings and actions are normal (Festinger, 1954; Schachter, 1951).

But why do people want their feelings and actions to be "normal"? In part, people want to be normal because "normal is right." That is, as Festinger (1954) stated in his social comparison theory, we need to compare our beliefs with others to make sure our beliefs are "correct." In other words, since many beliefs cannot be proven correct scientifically, they are proven through "social proof": If we all agree, we must all be right (Cialdini, 1993).

In addition to needing others to confirm that our beliefs are correct, we also need others to tell us what emotional reaction we are feeling (Cottrell & Eppley, 1977; Schachter, 1959). For example, because of the human need to know what we should feel, you probably needed to talk to others right after you learned about the bombing of the Federal building in Oklahoma City.

Teenagers can use self-disclosure and friendship for social validation, that is, to discover that many of their feelings are shared by others.

Unfortunately, not everyone takes full advantage of social validation. Many teenagers would be helped by social validation, but they do not get validation because they do not self-disclose. As a result, many teenagers believe that they are "weird" or that "something is wrong" with them because they think they are the only ones who have certain feelings. If teenagers were more open with one another, some would find that many of their "unique" feelings are shared by virtually every teen in the Western world.

To recap, making intimate self-disclosures can boost self-esteem and help people form a clearer, and perhaps more accurate, picture of themselves. However, enhancing and defining self-image is not the only benefit people receive from self-disclosure. Self-disclosure paves the way for others to reveal personal things about themselves which, ultimately, paves the way for friendship (Sprecher & Duck, 1994).

People like hearing self-disclosures not merely because they are curious, but because it indicates that others trust and like them (Jones & Archer, 1976). However, intimate self-disclosures do not come endlessly and automatically. Instead, to get more self-disclosures, people must also self-disclose. If they do not self-disclose to others, others will not self-disclose to them.

Reciprocating self-disclosures is especially important in forming new relationships (Chaiken & Derlega, 1974a; Derlega, Wilson, & Chaiken, 1976). Thus, if someone self-discloses much to us, we are supposed to disclose much to them. Similarly, if someone self-discloses very little to us, we are supposed to do likewise. Unfortunately, when meeting a new person, lonely people do not reciprocate self-disclosures. Instead, they tend to disclose either too much or too little. Consequently, they are unwittingly perpetuating their loneliness (Solano, Batten, & Parish, 1982).

Once the relationship has been formed, appropriate self-disclosure remains important. In fact, if the relationship is to progress, partners must make more and more intimate disclosures (Won-Doornik, 1979).

The Development of Intimacy

The need to give and receive self-disclosures, the need to have relationships that progress, and even the need to have relationships, all change dramatically with age. Before the age of 3 months, infants exhibit very little interest in socially interacting with others. They may want others around to feed them, hold them, or comfort them, but they do not have a special relationship with anyone (LaBarba, 1981). However, by the time infants are 7 months old, they will have formed attachments to one or more people.

These early attachments will be to caregivers—not to other infants. In fact, even by the time infants are 1-year-old, they may not interact with other infants (Hartup, 1983). Perhaps because infants don't seem interested in interacting with other infants, fewer than 20 percent of firstborn, 1-year-olds are consistently given opportunity to play with another child (Lewis, Young, Brooks, & Michalson, 1975).

We do not mean that 1-year-olds are blind to other infants. They will look at other infants. Indeed, they will even cry when another infant is upset. However, a 1-year-old infant will probably *not* try to help a distressed baby. In fact, most infants have to be at least 1 1/2 years old before they will try to help a distressed infant (Radke-Yarrow & Zahn-Waxler, 1984).

When, at around age 2, children start to interact with each other regularly, these interactions often center around playing with toys. For the most part, 2-year-olds engage in **parallel play.** That is, they play beside (parallel to) each other, but not with each other.

Between the ages of 2 and 4, the child's social relationships progress tremendously. As you can see from figure 10.1, 4-year-olds are much more social than 2-year-olds. This increased interest in social activities is expressed in two ways. First, compared to 2-year-olds, 4-year-olds spend more time playing with other children. Second, 4-year-olds are also much more likely to engage in **cooperative play,** play where each child has a role and has to limit and adjust that role for the good of the group (Fagot & Leinbach, 1983; Parten, 1932).

Just as the 4-year-old's play has a different character than that of the 2-year-old, the 4-year-old's relationships have a different character than the 2-year-old's. Perhaps the sharpest difference is that the 4-year-old's friendships are more stable than the 2-year-old's. That is, the 4-year-old's friendships tend to be longer lasting. Another, more subtle clue to the different character of the 4-year-old's friendships is that these friendship attachments may, in some cases, resemble caregiver attachment. For example, when their friend leaves, 4-year-old's may feel a separation anxiety similar to that of when their parents leave them.

We should be careful, however, not to exaggerate the depth of the relationships that exist among 4-year-olds. Relative to 2-year-olds, their relationships are intimate. However, by adult standards, these relationships are not very deep. For example, many of the 4-year-olds' "friends"

Figure 10.1

How Percentage of Time Spent in Cooperative Play Increases between the Ages of 2 1/2 and 5

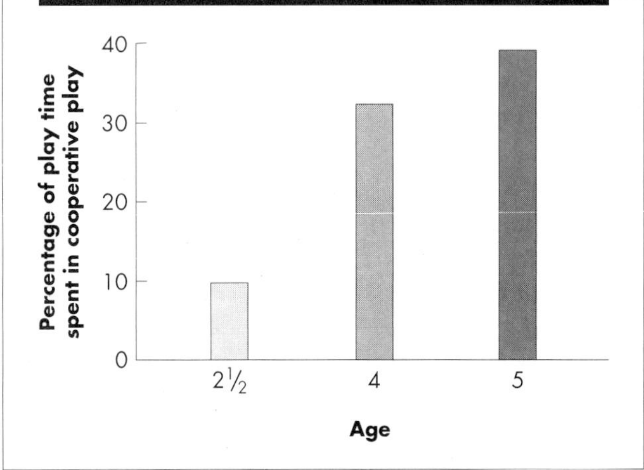

are merely the playmates who happen to be around at the moment. In fact, even a 4-year-old's "best friend" may depend on what task the child happens to be doing at the moment. That is, a 4-year-old's "best friend" while playing blocks may not be her "best friend" when playing outside.

Despite the limited depth of 4-year-old's friendships, age 4 typically marks the child's start into the world of stable, ongoing friendships. Of course, from this fairly weak starting place, there is a long way to go. Consequently, it should not surprise you that from age 4 or 5 until at least age 18, a person's friendships tend to become more stable with each passing year (Coleman, 1980; Horrocks & Baker, 1951).

One reason that later friendships can be more stable is that these later friendships—unlike the friendships of 4-year-olds—can be based on similarity of personality. The reason the 4- to 6-year-olds' friendships are not based on liking their friend's personality is because between the ages of 4 and 6, children still have little idea of other people's mental states (Barenboim, 1981; Selman, 1980).

Although the 4-year-old has little idea of other people's needs and wants, he is keenly aware of his own wants. Indeed, the 4-year-old tends to be quite egocentric. Consequently, rather than liking others for their personality or thoughts, the typical 4-year-old likes his friends for what those friends do for him.

Around age 7, the child's relationships with others changes dramatically. One indication of this change is that the 7-year-old child is now, for the first time, willing to spend as much free play time with peers as with parents (Higgins & Parsons, 1983). At least two factors are responsible for the dramatic changes in relationships that occur around age 7. First, because children at this age have reached the concrete operations stage, they are better able to see other people's viewpoints and thus are more receptive to doing things for friends. Second, because these children are

Table 10.1

Grades at Which Certain Characteristics First Become Important in Friendships

Friends Characteristic	Grade at Which It First Appears Important
Friend helps me out.	2
Friend likes the same activities I do.	2
Friend lives nearby.	3
Friend admires me.	4
Friend is loyal.	5
Friend is sincere.	6
Friend is someone I would help out.	6
Friend is someone with whom I can share my intimate feelings.	7
Friend and I share common interests, attitudes, and values.	7

Source: From B. J. Bigelow and J. J. La Gaipa, "Children's Written Descriptions of Friendship: A Multidimensional Analysis" in *Developmental Psychology*, 11:857–858, 1975.

entering school and coming into contact with more peers than they have ever previously experienced, their circle of friends widens considerably (Higgins & Parsons, 1983).

Around age 10, children start to consider psychological characteristics and make inferences about people's psychological states (Selman, 1980). For example, it is about this time when they first seem to understand why someone performed an illegal act. Thus, around this time, they start to believe that friends should have similar values and attitudes. Interestingly, around this age they also begin to believe that (1) their best friends should be same-sex friends and that (2) a person can have only one best friend.

Around age 12, children become interested in self-disclosure and intimacy (see table 10.1). They may have a very close friend, a "chum" with whom they may be inseparable. However, many will *not* have a "chum." In fact, Douvan & Adelson (1966) reported that for most girls between ages 11 and 13, friends were simply activity partners who shared little with one another and had little feeling for one another. Yet another indication that preteens are sharing little with each other is that it is not until early adolescence that children realize that peers and parents perceive the world differently (Hill, 1980).

Fortunately, intimacy with friends increases after the preteen years (Diaz & Berndt, 1982). Compared to preteens, teens are better able and better motivated to benefit from self-disclosure and friendship because of their more advanced cognitive abilities. These abilities allow them to better understand their friend's point of view. Consequently, teens can be better recipients of self-disclosure than preteens. These same, newly developed cognitive abilities also give teens the ability to experiment with new thoughts, emotions, and behaviors and they allow teens to have a more abstract sense of self. Consequently, teens can give more interesting and complex self-disclosures than preteens.

Just as newly emerged cognitive abilities give teens a greater ability to give and receive self-disclosure, newly emerging pressures give teens more motivation to appreciate self-disclosure and friendship. Specifically, in terms of motivating teens to need relationships with others, two pressures are much more powerful than they were during the preteen years: the pressure to act like an adult and the pressure to form relationships with the opposite sex.

Two pieces of evidence support the view that these pressures create a desperate need for friendship, particularly in early adolescence. First, most people feel the greatest insecurity about relationships at age 15. Second, the only thing that many 15-year-old women want from a friend is security—someone who is loyal and trustworthy, someone who can keep a secret (Douvan & Adelson, 1966).

As adolescence progresses, teenagers spend more and more of their time with fewer people. Adolescents may have fewer friends, but their friendships will involve more intimacy (Buhrmester & Furman, 1987; Douvan & Adelson, 1966; Kelly & Hanen, 1988). In addition, some of their most intimate relationships will be with the opposite sex. In fact, by the end of the high school years, many teens have paired off into heterosexual couples.

During early adulthood, the number and intimacy of friendships peak. With advancing age, friendships become fewer and less intimate—especially for men (Weiss & Lowenthal, 1976). Indeed, many adults satisfy most of their need for intimacy through one or two others.

Who will these others be? With whom will adults make enough self-disclosures to achieve **intimacy,** the sharing of thoughts, feelings, and vulnerabilities? Many people think of lovers as those with whom we become intimate. Others think first of good friends. Both are right. We may be as intimate with our good friends as we are with our lovers (Davis & Todd, 1982; Sternberg & Grajek, 1984).

Box 10.2

SELF-CHECK

PART A

Indicate whether each of the following is true or false.

1. College students spend 50 percent of their waking time alone.
2. Loneliness is due to being isolated or having a limited number of interactions with others.
3. We like to get self-disclosures from others.
4. Some lonely people self-disclose too much.
5. Babies are born wanting to interact with others.
6. Four-year-olds' friendships are based on similarity.
7. Twelve-year-olds often have a chum with whom they are extremely intimate.
8. After age 15, friendships tend to be fewer, but more intimate.

PART B

Answer the following questions.

9. What needs does self-disclosure satisfy?
10. If you wanted to get self-disclosures, what would you have to do?
11. How do friendships change from age 2 to age 4?
12. What factors might be responsible for the differences between the friendships of 7-year-olds and those of 4-year-olds?

Please turn to the end of this chapter to check your answers.

Determinants of Friendship

Who will these friends be? To an amazing extent, our friends will be determined by physical attractiveness, proximity, and similarity.

Physical Attractiveness

Although people do not like to think of themselves as superficial, most of us tend to choose our friends on the basis of the very superficial characteristic of physical attractiveness (Hatfield & Sprecher, 1986). It is not surprising that we used physical attractiveness to determine our friends when we were young. After all, 5- and 6-year-olds do not consider other people's psychological states or personalities. We could judge only their behaviors and physical appearance (Selman, 1980). But why do we persist in forming friendships on such a superficial basis?

One explanation stems from the fact that most people tend to assume that physically attractive individuals are smarter, happier, and more competent than less attractive people (Cialdini, 1993). Consequently, the attractive person's opinions and approval count more than the plain person's. Thus, if an attractive person agrees with us, we must be right (Myers, 1990b). Similarly, if they like us, we must be good.

Another explanation for why people like attractive people stems from the common belief that attractive people—because they are so popular—can be picky about who they choose to befriend. Therefore, it's flattering to be one of the chosen.

According to Zajonc, our tendency to like people we see frequently, such as our neighbors, is known as the mere exposure effect.

As we have mentioned, physical attractiveness is a key element in determining who we will befriend. We cannot overemphasize its importance. However, even among preschoolers, physical beauty is not all important. Variables such as proximity and similarity also play a role in determining who we will befriend.

Proximity

Many of our friendships are accidents of geography. Elementary school children tend to like the children who sit next to them, college students tend to like the people on their floor, and suburbanites tend to like their neighbors (Festinger, Schachter, & Back, 1950; Segal, 1974; Whyte, 1956). Obviously, one reason we befriend people who live next door or who work with us is simply that it is hard to be friends with someone we have never met.

Another reason we like familiar others is the **mere exposure effect:** under certain conditions, familiarity alone can breed liking. Specifically, if we are neutral or positive toward something to start out with, continued exposure to that thing or person (mere exposure) will make us like that person or thing even more (Zajonc, 1970; Moreland & Zajonc, 1982; Saegert, Swap, & Zajonc, 1973).

Similarity

In addition to Zajonc's mere exposure effect, we may like people we live near or work with because they tend to share our interests and concerns. Hall-mates may all want a better heating system put in the dorm or better showers; neighbors may share similar attitudes about zoning and city services; residents of a retirement community may have chosen that community for similar reasons. Thus, although attitude similarity is not important to preoperational children, much research supports the idea that adults like people who have similar attitudes (Byrne, 1971; Sprecher & Duck, 1994).

Similarity even moderates the effects of attractiveness. Rather than choosing the most attractive person (a person who might be "out of my league") as a friend, men tend to choose friends who are similar to themselves in attractiveness (Cash & Derlega, 1978; McKillip & Riedel, 1983; Stroebe, Insko, Thompson, & Layton, 1971).

As testimony to the importance of similarity, friends tend to hold similar attitudes, look and dress similarly, and share similar family backgrounds (Myers, 1990a). However, actual similarity has little effect on liking unless the people perceive this similarity. Thus, although men and women are fairly similar, they are perceived as being very different. The perception that the genders are very different may account for the fact that very few elementary school children form close friendships with the opposite sex. Similarly, race- or age-based stereotypes may prevent people who have similar interests and talents from becoming friends.

Theories Explaining Relationships

As we have seen, friendships may begin as a result of physical attractiveness, proximity, or similarity. But why do friendships deteriorate?

We all accept that some relationships decline because one person moved away, the partners grew apart, or the friends found out that they really never had much in common. When the decline of these relationships is due to one or both partners reaching a higher level of development so that superficial reasons for friendship, such as proximity, are not as important as they once were, the decline of the relationship is easy to accept. For example, we can accept the deterioration of the friendship between two former elementary school pals—if the reason for the weakening of their friendship is that, now, as adolescents, their relationships are based more on similarity of interests rather than on proximity. We can also accept the gradual fading of the friendship between a pair of 10-year-olds if the reason for dissolution is that one or both felt that friendships should now be based on mutual give and take rather than on what the other person can do for you.

What is harder for many to accept is that friendships often deteriorate because one of the partners feels that he or she can get more out of a relationship with someone else (Berg, 1984). Some of our students feel that such a cold, calculating, economic view of relationships is more appropriate for describing how we pick and stay with mutual funds rather than mutual friends. However, as we shall see, evidence strongly supports a "reward view" of relationships. Consequently, most relationship theorists don't argue about whether we are in relationships for the rewards. They argue only about how much of what kinds of rewards we demand.

Reinforcement-Affect Theory

According to the **reinforcement-affect theory** (Clore & Byrne, 1974), the rewards we are looking for in friendships are ego boosts. According to this theory, we like people who disclose to us for the same reason we like attractive people who praise us—they boost our ego.

The bigger the ego boost someone gives us, the more we will like that person. Thus, we like people who say they like us, especially if they:

- Are different from us,
- Are competent, and
- Compliment us right after we have suffered a temporary blow to our self-esteem.

If people are different from us and still like us, their liking is more flattering than if they are similar to us and like us. They like us for who we are, not merely because we agree with them. Being liked by a competent person is more flattering than being liked by a loser. Finally, if we are feeling down, we really need an ego boost.

Social Exchange Theory

According to **social exchange theory,** the rewards we are looking for are love, money, status, goods, services, and information (Foa & Foa, 1974). How happy we will be with a relationship does *not* depend on *the absolute amount of rewards* we get. Instead, our happiness with the relationship depends on how many rewards we get from the relationship *relative to* the standard amount of rewards we expect to get out of a relationship. The standard amount of rewards we expect to get out of a relationship is what social exchange theorists call our **comparison level.** If our comparison level is high, our present relationship will have to be very rewarding for us to be happy with it. If our comparison level is low, then even though our current relationship is not very rewarding, we may still be quite happy with it.

What determines how high or low our comparison level is? As you might expect, the comparison level is based on what we got out of past relationships. Thus, a good past relationship may have raised our expectations and demands, whereas a poor past relationship may have lowered our expectations. In addition, our comparison level may also depend on what our family, culture, and the media lead us to expect.

If the rewards in a relationship are falling below our comparison level, we will be unhappy with that relationship. But that doesn't mean we will leave the relationship. Nor does getting many more rewards than we expected mean that we will stay with the relationship (see figure 10.2).

Whether we leave or stay in a relationship depends on our **comparison level for alternatives,** how many rewards we think we will get from other (alternative) relationships. If we have an unsatisfying relationship, but don't feel we have any alternatives, we will stay stuck in that relationship (Drigotas & Rusbult, 1992). If we have a great relationship, but think we can have an even better one with someone else, we will spend more of our time cultivating other relationships.

Our comparison level for alternatives will be based not only on objective reality, but also on our self-concept. If we have high self-esteem, our comparison level for alternatives will be higher than if we have low self-esteem (see figure 10.3).

Figure 10.2

One Implication of Social Exchange Theory

"OK, but only until I find someone better."

HERMAN © 1989 Jim Unger. Reprinted with permission of Universal Press Syndicate. All rights reserved.

Barriers to Intimacy

Intimacy is essential to relationships. Relationships can't form or develop without progressively more intimate self-disclosures. Once the relationship is established, we continue to reward our friends, in part by making self-disclosures. If we are not making enough intimate self-disclosures, the relationship will end or weaken because people will find others who will disclose. Yet, despite the importance of self-disclosure to developing relationships, some people have trouble self-disclosing. That is, they have trouble developing intimate relationships. In the next few sections, we will explore several reasons why some people seem unable to develop intimacy.

Shyness

Shyness is a common and powerful barrier to intimacy. Shy people feel that others would not like them or be interested in them, so they avoid others. Fortunately, shyness decreases with age. Although 80 percent of Americans report being shy at some time in their life, and 50 percent of all 7th and 8th graders report being shy, only 40 percent of all adults report being currently shy (Zimbardo, 1977).

Figure 10.3

Social Exchange Theory Model of Relationships

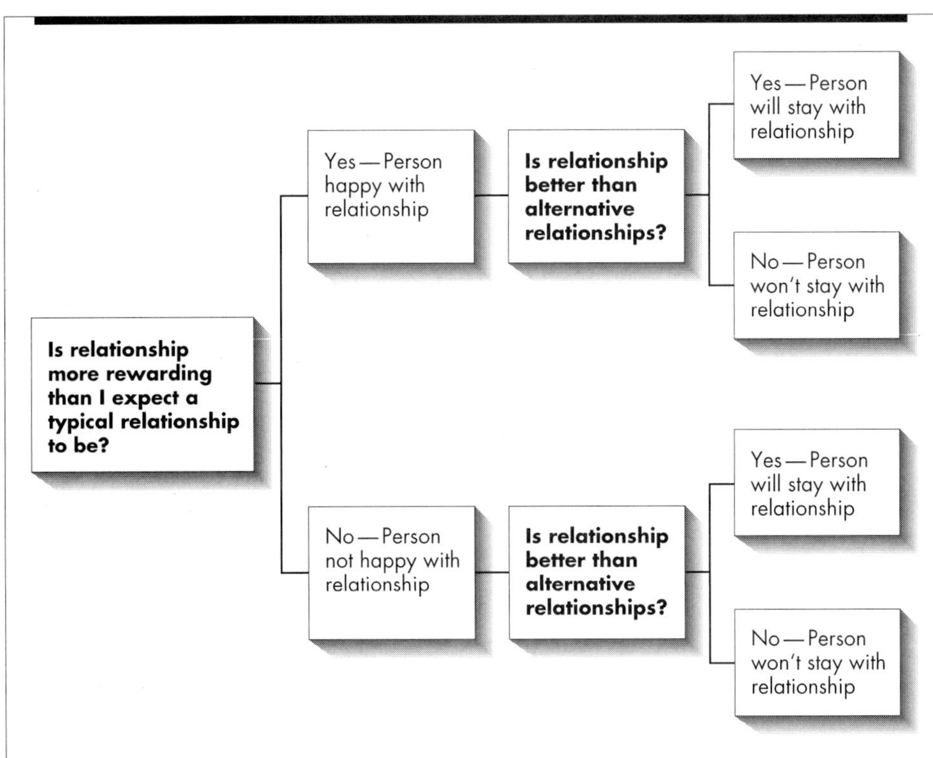

Two kinds of studies provide hope for greatly decreasing the number of shy people. The first type of study shows that "success breeds success." The second type of study suggests that "observing success may breed success."

To give shy people successful experiences, some researchers let shy people interact with younger peers. For example, in one study involving shy preschoolers, those who played with a child who was 18 months younger significantly improved their sociability (Furman, Rahe, & Hartup, 1981). This study is consistent with Harlow's finding that the effects of isolation could be reversed by having socially inept rhesus monkeys interact with younger monkeys (Suomi & Harlow, 1972). Taken together, the studies suggest that younger peers may allow children to practice both assertive and caretaking behaviors and to gain a sense of competence. Another set of studies, using college students, provides even more direct evidence that a feeling of competence can improve shyness. In these studies, men who were shy around women were helped by simply having them talk to other "subjects" in the experiment. Unknown to the men, the "subjects" were women who had been told to carry on a friendly conversation with each of the men. After 2 1/2 hours of this "conversation therapy," the men's confidence increased greatly and they dated more (Hammerlie & Montgomery, 1986).

Apparently, actually experiencing success is not always necessary. In some cases, seeing others succeed can reduce shyness. For example, in one study, extremely shy 5-year-olds were made less shy merely by watching a short film composed of 11, two-minute episodes (Cialdini, 1994). In each episode, a lonely child asked to join in a group's activities and was welcomed with open arms.

Problems in Attachment

According to Erik Erikson, it doesn't take a child long to learn whether he can trust others. In fact, Erikson thinks that the child's first relationship (usually with the mother) during the first year of life sets the tone for all future relationships. If, during the first year of life, a child can't depend on his mother to feed, clothe, and comfort him, he will not trust others. Without trust, self-disclosure is difficult. Furthermore, the person who does not trust may be reluctant to **reciprocate,** to compensate others for what they have done for you. People who are reluctant to reciprocate are viewed as unsympathetic, inconsiderate, manipulative, and unapproachable (Cotterell, Eisenberger, & Speicher, 1992).

As you saw in chapter 9, many attachment theorists agree with Erikson that developing a good relationship with a caregiver during the first year or two is vital for future relationships. Furthermore, as you also saw in chapter 9, Hazan & Shaver (1987) found evidence supporting the view that insecure attachments lead to failed relationships later in life.

Gender Roles

Not all intimacy problems are the result of less than ideal socialization. Some problems in establishing intimacy are due to "normal" gender-role socialization, a job taken very seriously in our society. Men are taught to be strong, silent, and interested in the material world; women are taught to be soft, expressive, and involved in the world of interpersonal relationships (Gilligan, 1982).

Because gender-role socialization is taken so seriously, the teaching of gender roles begins early. Even at age 2, parents reward boys for being independent and aggressive, and girls for seeking help and expressing their feelings (Huston, 1983). Children learn these lessons so well that in nursery school, children take up where parents left off by teaching and rewarding gender-role-appropriate behavior in each other (Langlois & Downs, 1980).

The result of this teaching is that men have a harder time than women in establishing intimacy. Men have a more difficult time disclosing information about themselves (Cozby, 1972; Hacker, 1981) than women and have an especially hard time disclosing intimate information (Cohn & Strassberg, 1983). Whereas women enjoy talking with their best friend, men enjoy sharing activities (Caldwell & Peplau, 1982). Consequently, Borys and Perlman (1985) estimate that most women would be very dissatisfied if they were limited to the level of disclosure and contact experienced by the typical male.

In summary, living up to the male ideal of being strong and silent does not help men develop intimacy. One measure of the problem men have with intimacy is that whereas men usually achieve greatest intimacy with their wife or mate, wives often achieve greatest intimacy with their best friend.

Gender-Role Stereotypes

Whereas gender roles limit men's intimacy, gender-role stereotypes limit the ability of both men and women to form cross-sex friendships. Cultural stereotypes tell us that men and women are so dissimilar that they could never be friends. According to these stereotypes, men and women are so different that if it weren't for sexual attraction and the desire to have children, the genders would be as sex-segregated as they are in the fourth grade. However, you know (or will know, after reading chapter 12) that these stereotypes are inaccurate. In truth, the psychological differences between men and women are small. Unfortunately, perceptions—not the truth—are what influence people. Because many people perceive the genders as being very different, many people have impoverished relationships with the opposite sex. Consequently, some still believe that the opposite sex is better suited for fulfilling physical, rather than psychological, intimacy.

Sexuality

Like psychological intimacy, physical intimacy is a human need. Also like psychological intimacy, the strength of the need for physical intimacy seems to vary tremendously from person to person.

If they stick to traditional gender roles, men prefer to share activities with their friends, while women prefer to talk. For this reason, men may find they have less intimate relationships.

Box 10.3

SELF-CHECK

Part A

Indicate whether each of the following statements is true or false.

1. Relationship theorists believe that relationships may succeed or fail based on whether both partners think they are getting enough rewards from the relationship.
2. According to social exchange theory, if people are happy with a relationship, they will stay with it.
3. For the overwhelming majority of married couples, husbands achieve the greatest degree of psychological intimacy with their wives and wives achieve the greatest degree of psychological intimacy with their husbands.

Part B

Answer the following questions.

4. What are three important determinants of friendship?
5. According to reinforcement-affect theory, how would we get someone to like us?
6. What do social exchange theorists mean by a comparison level?
7. What are four factors that may prevent intimacy?
8. Describe two general strategies for helping people overcome shyness.

Please turn to the end of this chapter to check your answers.

Biological Considerations

Despite these similarities, most people consider physical intimacy to be more biologically based than the need for psychological intimacy. In the next sections, we will focus on two salient biological factors that may play a role in sexual activity: (1) gender differences in sexual arousal and (2) the effects of aging on sex.

Gender Differences

Sexual arousal progresses through four stages: (1) excitement, (2) plateau, (3) orgasm, and (4) resolution (Masters and Johnson, 1966). Women generally take longer than men to reach **orgasm,** the climax of sexual excitement. In fact, to reach the peak of sexual arousal, men may take as few as 4 minutes, whereas women usually require 10 to 20 minutes. The difference in the rate of arousal may be due to the woman's clitoris receiving less direct and intense stimulation than the man's penis. Support for this idea comes from the fact that when masturbating, both men and women can get to the height of sexual excitement within 4 minutes.

Regardless of the cause, gender differences in speed of arousal can cause conflict. Women often see men as selfish, whereas men may see women as cold and unresponsive. Even if a man successfully delays his progression through the excitement, plateau, and orgasm stages (sometimes by concentrating on nonsexual stimuli, such as baseball scores) until his partner reaches orgasm, biology continues to create differences between the sexes. Once aroused, women stay aroused for a long time. Women can have multiple orgasms. Men, on the other hand, lose interest in sex almost immediately following orgasm.

Aging

Sexual differences between the genders extend beyond their differences in arousal. As you learned in chapter 4, aging affects men and women's sexual development differently. For example, males cannot engage in sexual intercourse until puberty. That is, although almost half of all men report preadolescent sex play, males are not physically equipped to ejaculate until puberty. They are not equipped because there is virtually no development of male sexual anatomy from birth to puberty. Thus, prior to puberty, the testes are little more than 10 percent of their adult size.

With puberty, testosterone production increases dramatically. Testosterone promotes the growth of the male sexual anatomy, especially during the first two years of puberty. Consequently, by age 21, a male's sexual structures are as large as they will be.

Starting around age 20, a male's level of testosterone declines. The decline continues until age 60, at which point the level of testosterone stays fairly constant. This decline in testosterone reduces sperm counts and sex drive. However, the main impact of the decline in testosterone is that sexual arousal takes longer. Compared to his younger counterpart, the elderly man will probably take two to three times longer to get an erection, take much longer to get a second erection (perhaps as long as 48 hours), and will probably have less reason to worry about premature ejaculation (Brecher, 1984).

Nevertheless, contrary to the visions people tend to have about their parents and grandparents being virtually sexless (Pocs & Godow, 1976), most middle-aged and elderly men are sexually active (Bretschneider & McCoy, 1988). Indeed, the frequency of sexual activity is higher among 27- to 64-year-old men than it is among 18- to 26-year-olds (Janus & Janus, 1993). Furthermore, research suggests that most men over age 70 have sex more than once a week (Brecher, 1984).

Unlike men, women can have intercourse throughout the entire lifespan (and about one-fourth report engaging in pre-adolescent sex play). However, like men, women's sexual drive increases dramatically as soon as they begin puberty. Interestingly, women have been entering puberty sooner and sooner. In fact, whereas menstruation, which marks the beginning of puberty, used to begin around age 18, it now begins around age 13—as long as the woman is well-nourished and not underweight (Warren, 1982).

Once puberty begins, there is little physiological reason—other than illness—for sexual desire to decrease. Although physiological changes do occur as women age, how these changes are interpreted is far more important than the actual changes themselves. For example, menopause decreases sex drive for some women, but increases sex drive for others (Byer & Shainberg, 1991). Why? Because women differ in how they view menopause and these different viewpoints affect their sex drives. If women believe menopause defeminizes them, their sex drive may decrease after menopause (Brecher, 1984; Schaie & Willis, 1986). If, on the other hand, women interpret menopause as freedom from fears about pregnancy, their sex drive may increase after menopause. Thus, most women are interested in sex throughout the lifespan (Brecher, 1984; Bretschneider & McCoy, 1988).

Sexual Attitudes and Behavior

Menopause is not the only instance in which the effects of a physiological change are influenced by how that change is interpreted. The effects of aging are also affected by how the individual views aging and sex. Aging decreases sex most dramatically for people who never enjoyed sex and for those who accept the stereotype that older adults are sexless (Byer & Shainberg, 1991; Schaie & Willis, 1986). Because attitudes play a large role in human sexual behavior, let's take a closer look at attitudes and their effect on premarital, marital, extramarital, and homosexual behavior.

Premarital Sex

One of the most noticeable changes in American's sexual thinking was the so-called sexual revolution of the 1960s, during which attitudes toward premarital sex changed

Table 10.2

Sex in the 70s—A Cohort Effect Linked to the Sexual Revolution: Percentage of Married Men and Women Having Ever Had Premarital Intercourse Classified According to Age Group

	Age Group				
	18–24	25–34	35–44	45–54	55+
Percentage of males	95	92	86	89	84
Percentage of females	81	65	41	36	31

Source: From M. Hunt, *Sexual Behavior in the 1970s*, Playboy Press, Chicago, 1974.

Figure 10.4

Cohort Effects: Percentage of Single White Females Having Had Premarital Intercourse by Time of Survey

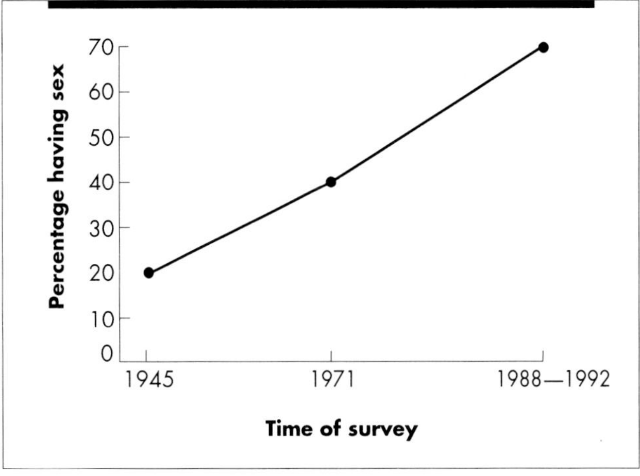

radically. According to Zelnick and Kantner (1980), the main behavioral effect of that revolution is that women become more sexually active. Whereas premarital sex had always been acceptable for men, by the 1970s, it had become slightly more acceptable for women (see table 10.2). As you can see from figure 10.4, the trend for more women to engage in premarital sex continued through the 1980s. Nevertheless, men are still more likely to lose their virginity earlier than women (Lefton, 1994).

Some people are greatly concerned by the fact that most people of both genders report losing their virginity by age 24 and that women are engaging in almost as much premarital sex as men (Curran, 1977; Dryfoos, 1985; Levin & Levin, 1975; Myers, 1992; Zelnick & Kantner, 1980). Others are not quite so concerned.

Those who are relatively unconcerned can make several arguments. First, part of the increase in *reported* incidence of premarital sex may be due to people being more honest in responding to surveys rather than to any change in actual sexual behavior. Second, much premarital sex involves engaged couples. Thus, it may be that our relatively high incidence of premarital sex is due to the fact that Americans marry later in life than natives of other countries (in some countries, most 13-year-olds are married). Third, several investigators have presented data suggesting that the effects of the sexual revolution were greatly exaggerated. Fourth, even if there was a sexual revolution in the 1960s, there is little reason to expect that premarital, sexual activity will continue to increase. AIDS should inhibit premarital sex, and some studies done in the 1990s show a slowing, and possibly even a reversal of, the sexual revolution.

Those who are extremely concerned about the high incidence of premarital sex can point to other evidence:

1. Premarital sex reported by 15- to 19-year-old women has nearly doubled since 1970 and the percentage of births to unwed mothers is five times what it was in 1960 (Myers, 1992),
2. The recent increase in the incidence of sexually transmitted diseases,
3. The high number of teenagers getting abortions, and
4. The United States having far and away the highest teenage pregnancy rate in the Western world—a rate almost twice as high as that of our Canadian neighbors (Westoff, Calot, & Foster, 1983).

Interestingly, a solution that might satisfy both the concerned and the unconcerned, and both the politically conservative and politically liberal, is sex education. Zabin and her associates (1986) found that girls who received sex education at home and at school were less likely to be sexually active, and if active, were more likely to use birth control than girls not receiving sex education.

Marital Sex

Although premarital and extramarital sex are frequently discussed, most sex occurs between married couples. One reason for this is that most Americans believe that sex and marriage go hand-in-hand. A second reason that most sex occurs between married couples is that most adults are married: 90 percent marry for some part of their lives. Even though many married people divorce, almost 70 percent of those who divorce remarry within five years (prompting jokes that divorced people really believe in marriage because they try it so many times).

A third reason that most sex takes place in marriages is that, contrary to some popular books (e.g., Hite, 1987), most marriages are happy ones and most people are satisfied with their marital sex life (Janus & Janus, 1993). Furthermore, this happiness with one's marital sex life usually continues throughout the lifespan of the marriage. Thus, although the amount of sex usually decreases over the life of the marriage (as dramatically illustrated in table 10.3), 75 percent of

Most married people are satisfied with their sex lives, according to recent reports.

Table 10.3

Sexual Activity in Married Couples as a Function of Age

Age Range	Frequency of Sexual Activity
Young marrieds	3 times per week
Middle-aged	1 time per week
Old age	Variable, depending on health, frequency of sex earlier in marriage, and acceptance of stereotypes of "sex-less" elderly.

Source: From K. W. Schaie and S. L. Willis, *Adult Development and Aging*, 2d edition, Little Brown, Boston, 1986.

elderly couples rate their sex life as the same or better than when they were younger (Starr & Weiner, 1981).

But what about elderly couples who rarely, if ever, engage in sex? These couples tend to have poor health, many worries, stereotypes of older adults as sexless, and a history of below average sexual activity throughout their marriage.

Extramarital Sex

Further evidence that most couples enjoy a happy marital sex life throughout the life of their marriages comes, ironically, from the data on extramarital affairs. More than 90 percent of married Americans have *not* cheated on their current spouse. In any given year, only 1.5 percent of married people have a sex partner other than their spouse (Myers, 1992).

But what about those who have had an extramarital affair? These people tend to have fewer than three affairs and their affairs tend to be brief. For men, affairs tend to occur primarily during the first five years of marriage. For women, affairs usually occur after 15 to 20 years of marriage. These affairs, especially for women, tend *not* to be due to an unhappy marital sex life. In fact, very few of those having affairs were unhappy with their marital sexual relations. Furthermore, most rated their marital sexual relations as more sexually pleasurable than their extramarital sexual relations (Hunt, 1974). Thus, it appears that the motivation for affairs is usually not to improve one's own sex life. Instead, these affairs probably meet other needs, such as attaining psychological intimacy or boosting self-esteem.

Homosexuality

We have discussed how attitudes influence premarital, marital, and extramarital heterosexual sex. But what about the effects of attitudes on homosexual sex? The sexual revolution appears to have brought about changes in how people view homosexuality. In the 1950s, homosexuality was considered a mental illness. In the 1970s, it was not (Wade & Tavris, 1993).

Since the 1970s, however, the sexual revolution has *not* greatly affected views toward homosexuals. In fact, whereas attitudes toward premarital sex have grown more tolerant since the 1970s, attitudes toward homosexuality have grown *less* tolerant (Byer & Shainberg, 1991).

What impact has our changing views on homosexuality had on homosexual behavior? It's hard to say. Despite all the attitudinal changes occurring between the 1950s and late 1980s, the number of male homosexuals has stayed around 2 to 5 percent and the number of female homosexuals has stayed around 1 to 3 percent (Usdansky, 1994).

But we do not mean to say that public opinion has no effect on homosexuality. Approximately 18 percent of all adult men and women have either been sexually attracted to someone of the same sex or had sex with someone of the same sex (Sell, Wells, & Wypij, 1994). If homosexuality were not so condemned by our society, more of these individuals might become and remain practicing homosexuals.

Yet, in spite of public pressure, many men remain practicing homosexuals until they die. What happens to the elderly, male homosexual? The stereotype is that he is highly sexed, always trying to associate with some young homosexual, is generally rebuffed, and is, as a result, extremely frustrated. The truth is that the elderly homosexual, like the elderly male heterosexual, is less sexed than when he was younger. Also, as with heterosexual males, some male homosexuals find their sex life more satisfying in old age. Finally, as would be expected based on the similarity effect, most older homosexual males prefer men their own age to younger men (Byer & Shainberg, 1991; Siegelman & Shaffer, 1995).

Conclusions About Sexuality

Sex is a fact of human existence. Society has become increasingly tolerant of that fact. However, society has a hard time accepting sex between homosexuals and it has a hard time accepting sex without love. Consequently, even when

Although public disapproval of homosexual relationships is high, many gay men and women find their sexual and intimate relationships satisfying throughout their adult lives.

pregnancy would lead to abortion and spontaneous sex could lead to AIDS, people don't use birth control during their first sexual experiences because using or discussing birth control before having sex would seem too planned and too unromantic (Fisher, Byrne, & White, 1983).

If you accept—as many do—the idea that "sex is okay, if you are in love," you still have to know when you're in love. To know when you're in love, you have to know what love is.

What is love? For thousands of years, people have struggled with this question. In the next section, we get our turn.

What Is "Being in Love?"

Friendship is an important component of "being in love." However, being in love is more than friendship. Specifically, being in love has an exclusivity, a fascination, a sexual intimacy, a passion that transcends mere liking.

Passionate Love

How does passion develop? According to Berscheid and Walster (1981), two things must happen for us to fall in love. First, we must be aroused while we are in the presence of another person. Then, we must interpret that arousal as **passionate love.**

This theory elegantly explains certain findings, such as the results of Dutton and Aaron's (1974) classic study. In that study, male students met a female researcher on either a 10-foot high steel bridge (low arousal condition) or on a 240-foot high, swaying bridge (high arousal). The high arousal subjects usually called the woman researcher up for a date, whereas the low arousal subjects did not. Apparently, the high arousal subjects felt they had to call up this woman who made their hearts thump, whereas the low arousal subjects were under no such compulsion. Considering this study, it is no wonder that people "fall in love" at exciting places such as rock concerts and amusement parks.

Box 10.4

SELF-CHECK

Indicate whether each of the following statements is true or false.

1. When masturbating, both men and women get to the height of sexual climax within four minutes.
2. Typically, women reach climax slower than men and stay aroused longer after climax than men.
3. Women enter puberty sooner now than they did 100 years ago.
4. Menopause decreases women's sex drive.
5. Men and women lose their virginity at the same age.
6. There is overwhelming, undebatable evidence that premarital sex and promiscuity are on the increase.
7. If there has been a change in sexual behavior, the biggest change seems to be that women are engaging in more premarital sex.
8. Sex education leads to teens being more sexually active.
9. Most married couples are happy with their sex lives.
10. Satisfaction with marital sex life increases with age.
11. Extramarital affairs are typically more sexually satisfying than marital sexual relations.
12. Attitudes toward homosexuality have become more tolerant in the last 20 years.
13. Older male homosexuals are highly sexed and seek out younger companions.

Please turn to the end of this chapter to check your answers.

Table 10.4

The Top 10 Things You Can Do to Attract a Mate

	What Men Can Do to Attract Women	What Women Can Do to Attract Men
1.	Display a good sense of humor.	Display a good sense of humor.
2.	Be sympathetic to her troubles.	Keep self well-groomed.
3.	Show good manners.	Be sympathetic to his troubles.
4.	Keep self well-groomed.	Show good manners.
5.	Spend a lot of time with the potential mate.	Shower daily.
6.	Offer to help her.	Keep physically fit to create a healthy appearance.
7.	Shower daily.	Make up jokes to make men laugh.
8.	Keep physically fit to create a healthy appearance.	Spend a lot of time with the potential mate.
9.	Exercise.	Wear attractive outfits.
10.	Wear attractive outfits.	Exercise.

Source: From D. M. Buss, "The Evolution of Human Intrasexual Competition: Tactics of Mate Attraction" in *Journal of Personality and Social Psychology,* 54: 616–628, 1988.

Figure 10.5

Two Models of Love

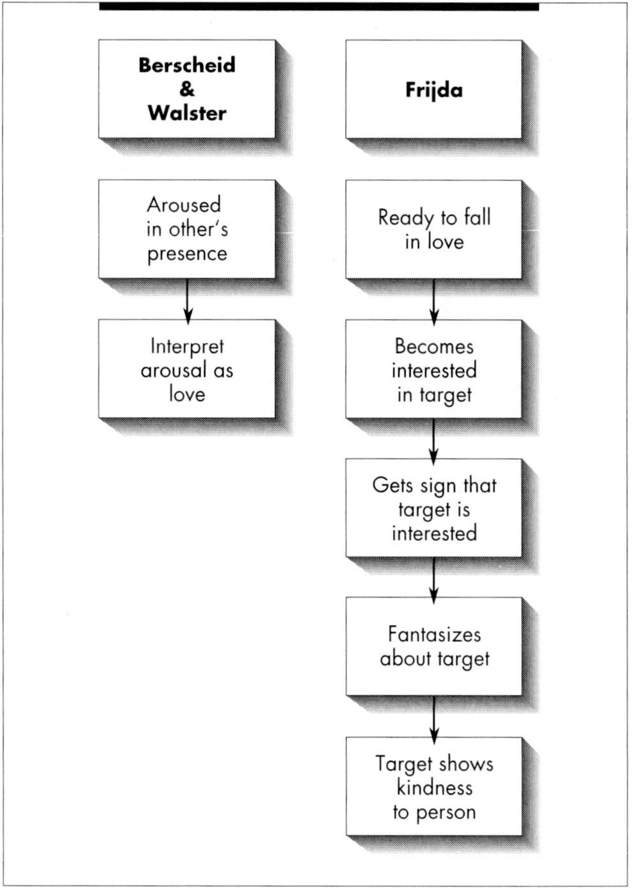

In contrast to Berscheid and Walster's two-phase model (Berscheid & Walster, 1978), Nico Frijda (1988) describes a five-step model of falling in love. First, the person is ready to fall in love because he or she is either lonely, has sexual needs, is rebounding from being "dumped," or needs variety. Second, the person becomes interested in someone, often because that someone is physically attractive or frequently encountered (see table 10.4 for more information about factors determining whether someone becomes the object of a person's affections). Third, the person receives some sign that the object of their attention reciprocates their interest. Fourth, the person is away from the target for somewhere between half an hour and half a day, during which time the individual fantasizes about the target of his or her affection. After these four phases are complete, then, if the target shows the individual any kindness, the individual will fall in love.

Which model of falling in love is correct? We don't know. Both have some research support. Perhaps both are right: Some people may fall in love the way Berscheid and Walster describe, others the way Frijda describes (see figure 10.5).

No matter how passion starts, it often fades. Why? Some theorists believe that people go through a process of **habituation:** They get so accustomed to a certain, relatively constant stimulus that it ceases to arouse them. We habituate to the noise made by our air conditioner or heater, to certain music, to electric shock (Epstein, 1973), and maybe even to loved ones.

Other theorists (Solomon, 1980) believe that passion ends as a result of **opponent processes,** every stimulus that triggers an emotional response also triggers the opposite (opponent) reaction. Over time, the opposite reaction grows so strong that it neutralizes the original response. According to opponent-process theory, when we feel passion (just as when a drug user experiences a "high"), the body rushes to subdue this feeling by producing the opposite reaction—a negative, depressing feeling. As our body gets into the habit of depressing our excitement, the passion we once felt is overwhelmed by the opposite reaction (see figure 10.6).

Some students may wonder why psychologists care whether opponent-process theory or habituation is the correct explanation for why passion fades. After all, both claim that passion declines over time. The advantage of opponent-process theory is in explaining why breaking up is hard to do. According to opponent-process theory, once the relationship breaks off, our body continues to produce the negative, depressing, "anti-love" reaction. But because we no longer have the positive stimulus (the loved one) to counteract our

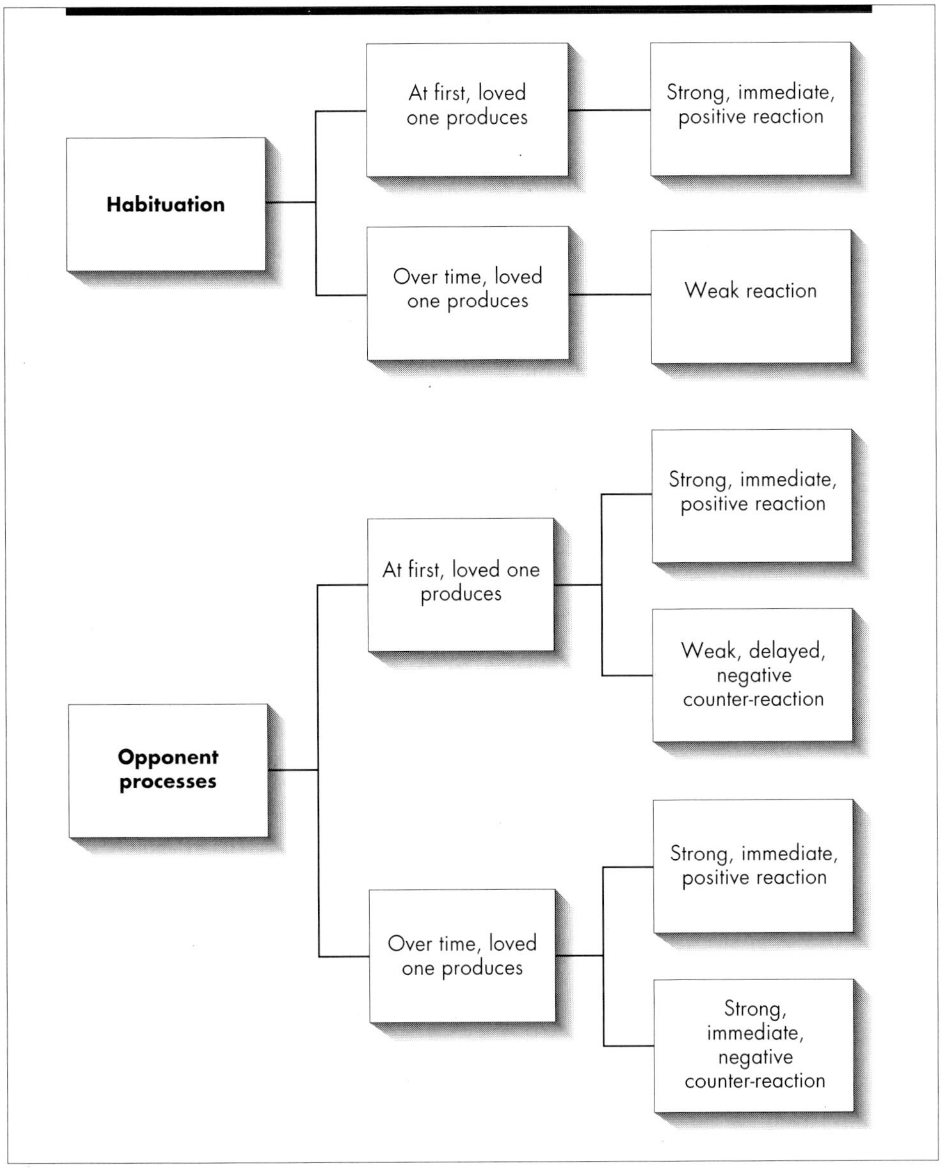

Figure 10.6

Two Models of the Decline of Passionate Love

body's negative reaction, we—like the drug addict who quits "cold turkey"—feel the emotional anguish of withdrawal.

Psychologists don't know whether habituation or opponent processes are what cause the fires of passion to dim. Psychologists do know, however, that folk wisdom is wrong in claiming that only the young feel burning passion. Widowed and divorced elderly individuals frequently report "falling passionately in love." Furthermore, the elderly often report that their passion has a strong sexual component (Bulcroft & O'Conner-Roden, 1986).

Companionate Love

Love lasts even after the sight of the loved one no longer makes our skin tingle. It endures even after we realize the loved one is not perfect. Thus, mature, lasting love is more than passionate love—and this is especially the case for women's love (Hendrik, Hendrik, & Adler, 1988).

What type of love continues to grow, even when passionate love fades? The love that keeps lovers together seems to be **companionate love** (Berscheid & Walster, 1978). That is, a couple who have companionate love are friends. They trust each other, respect each other, confide in each other, understand each other, and try to help one another (Davis & Todd, 1982).

Because companionate love (friendship) is such an important aspect of love, the factors that increase liking also increase loving. Thus, we tend not only to like, but also to love, people who live or work near us (proximity), people who are physically attractive, and people who are similar to us. Therefore, contrary to some folk wisdom, opposites do not attract. In fact, the most common reasons given for college couples breaking up deal with not having similar interests, values, or intelligence (Hill, Rubin, & Peplau, 1976). Also contrary to some folk

Box 10.5

SELF-CHECK

Part A

Answer the following questions.

1. According to Berscheid and Walster (1981), what two conditions must occur for people to fall passionately in love?
2. Passionate love inevitably fades. How do the two explanations of this fading differ in their predictions about what would happen if a couple broke up?
3. What factor increases the chances that a couple will have a high degree of companionate love?

Part B

Indicate whether each of the following statements is true or false.

4. Rather than talk about physiological arousal as a motivation for falling in love, Nico Frijda's model of falling in love focuses on being psychologically ready to fall in love.
5. Widowed and divorced elderly people frequently report "falling in love."
6. The happiest marriages are among partners who are both high on the femininity scale.
7. Passionate love is a key to a happy marriage.
8. Experts agree that commitment is a key ingredient to relationship success.

Please turn to the end of this chapter to check your answers.

Box 10.6

RESEARCH in FOCUS

Problems Encountered by Those Who Marry Young

The median age for marriage for men in the United States is 24.4; the median age for women is 22.3. About 2 1/2 times more women than men marry in their teens. Women who marry at ages 14 to 17 are three times more likely to divorce as women married between the ages of 20 and 24. Men who marry in their teens are more than twice as likely to divorce as men who marry between the ages of 25 and 29 (Gilchrist & Schinke, 1987). Gilchrist and Schinke mention several factors that seem to relate to the high divorce rate of those who marry in their teens:

- Lack of education,
- Having children soon after marriage,
- Lack of maturity,
- Inability to reconcile personal preferences, goals, and sex roles, and
- Unemployment and unstable income.

wisdom, the psychological differences between genders do not facilitate love. As both Antill (1983) and Bradbury and Fincham (1988) found, the happiest marriages were among partners who were both high on such "feminine" traits as being warm, nurturant, and sensitive.

Commitment

When friends turn into lovers, the partners enjoy a relationship that has both companionate and passionate love. But without commitment, the relationship may not last. Consequently, Sternberg (1986) claims that the ideal love relationship has passion, intimacy, and commitment. In partial support of Sternberg's model of love, happily married couples claim that friendship and commitment (*but not passion*) are the keys to a happy marriage (Lauer & Lauer, 1985).

What Is Commitment?

Like Sternberg, our society tends to value **commitment.** "Fair-weather friends" are disparaged and the words "for better or worse" are frequently incorporated into marriage vows. However, social exchange theorists, like Harold Kelley and John Thibeau (Kelley & Thibeau, 1978), claim that people are committed only to the extent that the rewards (primarily, passion and intimacy) are greater in their current relationship than in any other relationship they could currently have. To social exchange theorists, saying that a person is committed means that person doesn't have anybody better to turn to.

Although you may be offended by the view that people are committed only to getting the best deal they think they can get, social exchange theorists use this view to explain many phenomena (Drigotas & Rusbult, 1992; Rusbult, 1983). They can explain why:

- People stay married even though they claim to be unhappy with their partner (neither person has any less miserable alternatives);
- Why some people who had a happy marriage get divorced (they leave a good relationship—12 percent of all divorced people remain very good friends—for an even better one);
- Why more and more people are getting divorced (being single is a better alternative than it has been in the past, especially for women);
- Why older people suffer more when they divorce than younger adults (because youth is valued in our society, younger people feel they have more alternatives);
- Why women—despite seeming to get less out of marriage than men—suffer more when they divorce than men (because there are many more single women than men, men feel they have more alternatives [Guttentag & Secord, 1982; Tucker, 1987]);
- Why people who become successful often get divorced (they think their success gives them more attractive options than they had before); and
- Why movie stars have trouble making relationships last (too many attractive alternatives).

As you have seen, by arguing that commitment doesn't really exist, social exchange theorists are able to explain many phenomena (Rusbult, 1983; Simpson, 1987; Vaughan, 1987). But is the world really devoid of commitment? Although many people have difficulty committing themselves to another person, we all know people who seem willing to stick with a partner even though they could easily have other partners. In fact, it often seems that the people who are most desirable and most stable are the ones who have the highest level of commitment. Why do some people appear to have an easier time committing to a relationship than others? The answer to this question depends on which theorist you ask.

Social exchange theorists would say that some people appear committed because they have very low self-esteem. Once a low self-esteem person thinks they have "tricked" someone into loving them, they appear committed because they do not feel they could trick anyone else into loving them. They don't realize that they have other alternatives. What about high self-esteem people who are committed? Some high self-esteem individuals might believe that they had, in their infinite wisdom, picked the ideal mate. According to social exchange theorists, if either the low or high self-esteem "committed" individual were pursued by a clearly better alternative, "commitment" would disappear.

Barriers to Commitment

What about those who have a hard time committing to relationships? According to social exchange theorists, these people would fall into two general categories.

First, people whose "market value" (in terms of relationships) is going up should be very reluctant to commit to a relationship. For example, men and women who are rapidly becoming more attractive due to either gaining status or to physical changes (dieting, surgery, weight-lifting) won't want to sell themselves short. Thus, for the same reason a person wouldn't want to sell her home today if she thought it would double in value next year, these people don't want to invest in a relationship right away.

Second, some "hard-to-commit" people would be those who have such a good life that they could not easily improve it. For them, it makes little sense to invest in a relationship that could bring fewer rewards than they already receive.

Unlike social exchange theorists, attachment theorists trace problems in commitment back to the child's first relationship, the relationship with the caregiver. Specifically, as Hazan & Shaver (1987) suggested, if one's parents seemed uncaring, the person will fear not only intimacy, but also commitment.

According to Erik Erikson, problems in commitment are often due to a person's not having achieved his or her identity, or sense of self. Until a person knows who he is, he can't give himself to another. In a sense, Erikson agrees with people who say they are "not ready" for a relationship. However, instead of saying that these people will be ready when they graduate from college, get their first job, or reach some other milestone, Erikson would say that they will be ready when they know themselves. Only after a person knows who he is, will he be ready to share himself with another.

No evidence directly supports Erikson's claim that people have to know who they are before they can be confident in knowing whom they should commit to. However, some evidence indirectly supports his claim. People who fall in love with a dissimilar other, indicating that they do not know themselves very well, tend to have relationships that dissolve rapidly. People who have high self-esteem, indicative of finding and accepting themselves, tend to have happier relationships than people who have low self-esteem. Finally, people who marry young tend to get divorced (Myers, 1992; Spanier & Glick, 1981), possibly because they got married before they had a chance to fully achieve identity. Examining this last point shows how the evidence that supposedly supports Erikson's hypothesis is far from conclusive. After all, not forming an identity is not the only factor that could cause a high divorce rate in couples that marry young. Having less money and more children are two factors we can name. You can probably name others. (Compare your list to box 10.6.)

Figure 10.7

Gilligan's (1982) Model of the Stages to Intimacy

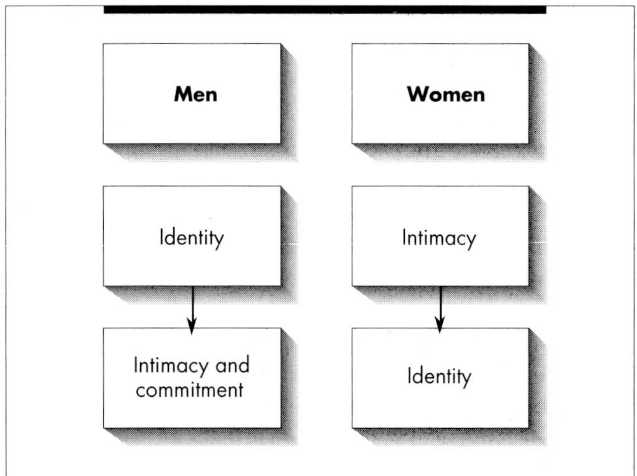

As appealing as Erikson's model is, Carol Gilligan (1982) claims Erikson's model applies only to men. Unlike men, women do not define themselves by what they have accomplished. Instead, women define themselves by their relationships. Consequently, rather than needing identity before they can achieve intimacy and commitment, women achieve identity through intimacy (see figure 10.7). Although Gilligan's arguments are persuasive, little evidence supports them (as you will see in chapter 12).

Marriage

According to our society's ideals, marriage is the epitome of both commitment and intimacy. In reality, however, marriage does not necessarily mean commitment. In the United States, the average marriage lasts 9.4 years, with about 1 million couples divorcing every year (Lauer & Lauer, 1985). Furthermore, nearly 70 percent of married men under age 40 expect to have an extramarital affair (Richardson, 1986).

Nor does marriage always promote intimacy. In fact, marriage limits opportunities for intimacy outside the relationship, especially intimacy with friends of the opposite sex. Such friends are thought to pose a threat to the marriage (Glass & Wright, 1988).

Even within the marriage itself, intimacy is not always fully achieved for several reasons. First, possibly because of gender differences in self-disclosure, women often find more intimacy with their best friend than with their husband (Sternberg & Grajek, 1984). Second, when couples have children, they have less time to spend with each other (Miller, 1976, Udry, 1974). Satisfaction with their partner declines, especially among women. Women are more dissatisfied than men because women end up doing much more of the housework and child care than they had expected (Ruble, Fleming, Hackel, & Stangor, 1988). But because children are valued in our society, having children makes people happier about being married, even though they are less happy with their partner. Fortunately, when the children finally get out of the house, the couple usually rediscovers each other and happiness with the partner rebounds to prechild levels. However, in a minority of cases, couples may discover how much they have changed and get divorced.

Happy Marriages

Although we have pointed to instances where marriage does not lead to fulfillment, we should point out that, in the United States, about 85 percent of all married couples are happy with their marriages (Janus & Janus, 1993; Myers, 1992). The most important key to a happy marriage is that spouses are also best friends. In the happiest of marriages, couples are similar to one another in terms of many variables, including level of moral reasoning (Grubb, Malatesta, & Haley, 1994), and they have committed to one another. In short, happy marriages are high on companionate love.

Passionate love, on the other hand, is not that important. Unlike people in passionate love, happily married couples do not see each other as perfect. Instead, they accept each other's faults. Furthermore, they do not place a high value on sex: Fewer than 10 percent mention that sex is an important factor in their relationship. However, most of these couples would not tolerate their partner's sexual infidelity, probably because infidelity would be a betrayal of trust (Lauer & Lauer, 1985).

We have described what happily married couples value about their relationships, but what do happily married couples actually do? They communicate, but not with complete openness. Good husbands and wives avoid displays of intensely expressed anger. They also restrain themselves from saying hurtful things during arguments. They are sure to praise more than criticize, and they are liberal in expressing affection. They also divide labor equitably. That is, both are equally satisfied that the amount of work they do (such as housework or yard work) is fair. Finally, both partners have equal voice in making decisions. One partner does not unilaterally buy a sports car or a couch (see box 10.7).

Divorce

Although there are many happy marriages, between one-third and one-half of all marriages end in divorce. That the divorce rate is higher than it was 90 years ago is not surprising since, compared to 90 years ago:

1. Attitudes and laws about divorce are much more liberal;
2. People now want more out of marriage than money, children, and respectability;
3. Living without a spouse is much more pleasant and socially acceptable (especially for women);

Box 10.7

RESEARCH in FOCUS

Five Keys to a Successful Marriage

1. Friendship and respect.
2. Similarity in values, attitudes, intelligence, background, moral reasoning, and physical attractiveness.
3. Commitment.
4. Expression of affection, especially if the ratio of affection and praise to criticism increases throughout the marriage.
5. Communication, especially positive self-disclosure. (Lauer & Lauer, 1985; Myers, 1992)

Most happily married couples share labor in a way that feels equitable. Other characteristics of happy marriages include good communication, liberal expression of affection and praise, and equal decision making.

4. There are more dual career marriages; and
5. People are living longer lives, thereby giving the couple more opportunities to grow apart, as well as making "until death do us part" a longer sentence for those who have unfulfilling marriages.

We have seen that marriage is a riskier proposition than it once was. But can we predict whether a specific marriage will be at risk? Yes—a number of researchers have been able to predict with better than 90 percent accuracy—whether a couple will divorce (Gottman, 1993).

What predicts whether a specific marriage will be at risk? Ironically, some of these predictors can be measured before the bride walks down the aisle—if the couple allows such in-depth measurement of their relationship. For example, Markman (1992) was able to predict divorce with 93 percent accuracy by looking at the couple's communication skills, especially how they handle conflict (Markman, Renick, Floyd, & Stanley, 1993). Similarly, Olson (1992) finds that communication patterns are an important predictor of divorce. Indeed, even how well each partner's parents communicated in their own marriages is a significant predictor of the couple's divorce. In addition, Olson (1992) also finds that couples who separate or divorce within three years of their engagements are those who, when surveyed around the time of their engagement, had very different views of what relationships should be like (Larsen & Olson, 1989).

Other factors that are known to predict divorce are available to anyone who attends the couple's wedding. For example, couples who marry in their teens are at high risk for divorce. These couples usually have less education and more children. The lack of education usually means the couple's income will be limited. In addition, the lack of education and the abundance of children severely restrict the woman's career. When faced with both a bleak present and a bleak future, one or both members of the couple often seek a divorce (Heaton, Albrecht, & Martin, 1985; Kurdek, 1993; Morgan & Rindfuss, 1985; Otto, 1979).

Another predictor of divorce is the speed at which the couple has gone from casual dating to formal engagement. As a general rule, couples who go from casual dating to formal engagement in less than six months are high risks for divorce (Kurdek, 1993). These couples are probably handicapped by:

- Not knowing whether they are indeed similar,
- Marrying on the basis of passionate rather than companionate love (Olson, 1992),
- Not having time to establish constructive ways of resolving conflicts (Raschke, 1987), and
- Not feeling committed to the relationship.

Although speeding from dating to engagement hurts, dawdling before getting married does not help. American couples who live together before getting married are actually less likely to have a long and happy marriage than couples who do not live together before marriage (Janis & Janis, 1993; Myers, 1992).

After the couple is married, several signs can predict marital problems. One is a lack of a social support network. Specifically, couples who do not regularly attend church and who do not have relatives living nearby are likely to divorce. Another sign is whether couples pool resources. That is, couples who do not pool their money are more likely to divorce (Greenstein, 1990; Kurdek, 1993).

Another negative sign is how spouses interpret each others actions. Distressed spouses are likely to see a partner's bad behavior as being done on purpose to hurt them, as an indication of some permanent, unchanging aspect of the partner, and as a symptom of a general defect in the partner's personality that influences many aspects of the partner's behavior (Fincham & Bradbury, 1992). This negative interpretation of the partner's behavior results in less effective problem solving, more negative behavior, and more attempts to "fight fire with fire" (Bradbury & Fincham, 1992).

You can probably figure out most of the other bad signs for a marriage by reflecting on what you know about liking and what you know about successful marriages. For example, divorce is more likely if:

- The spouses have different personality traits, different relationship values (one values freedom, the other does not) or different backgrounds (Cowan et al., 1985; Morgan & Rindfus, 1985). Thus, as you would expect from the similarity effect, dissimilarity may lead to divorce.
- One spouse, unexpectedly, achieves much greater success than the other thus giving the fortunate one more and better potential alternative relationships (Drigotas & Rusbult, 1992);
- One or both members have difficulty communicating;
- The man is extremely immersed in the traditional masculine role; and
- One member will not allow the other to share in decision making.

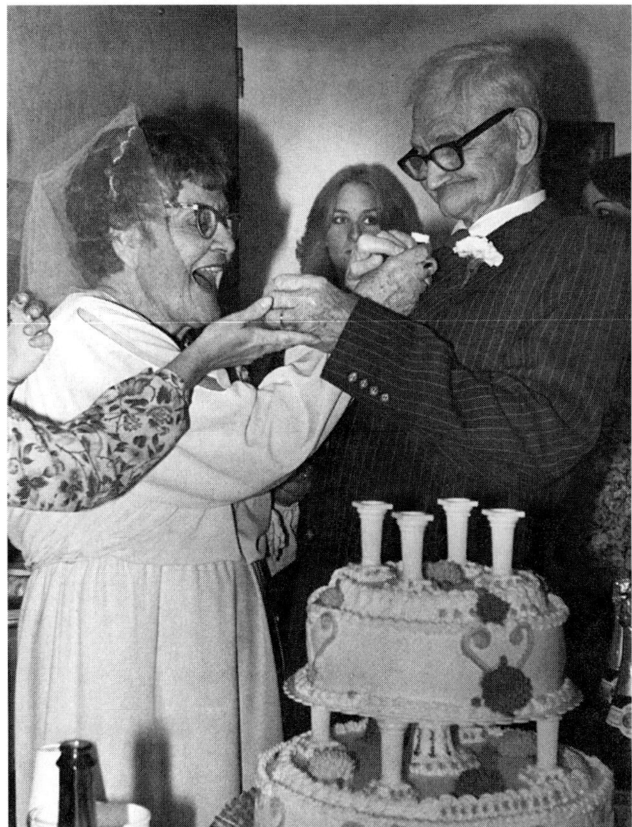

Although both men and women over 60 report falling passionately in love and being interested in sex, widowed men over 65 are about eight times more likely to remarry than widowed women the same age.

Widowhood

Even though divorce is presented as a common way for mar riage to end, the most common way is through widowhood. Widowhood is primarily a woman's role because women live longer than men and then compound the problem by marrying men who are, on the average, about four years older than they are. As a result, for men and women between the ages of 65 and 74, more than four times as many women as men are widowed (Uhlenberg & Myers, 1981).

If it is true that we cannot know the value of something until it's gone, studying widows should give us some insight into the positive and negative aspects of marriage. On the positive side, we can infer that marriage has some good aspects because many widows remain depressed long after their husbands have died, and this is true even when widows receive considerable social support from their community (Jolley, 1979). Apparently, women share an intimacy with their husband that is hard to replace. But on the negative side, marriage may have some detrimental effects for women as reflected by the fact that women often feel more independent and more competent after widowhood. Perhaps as a consequence of these newfound feelings of independence and competence, about one-third of widows have no interest whatsoever in remarrying (Gentry & Shulman, 1988).

Widowers, on the other hand, are much more likely to remarry. In fact, for people widowed after age 65, men are eight times more likely to remarry than women. Why? At least part of the reason is that, in this age range, women greatly outnumber men. However, the higher male remarriage rate probably also reflects the fact that men are happier with marriage than women (Gove, 1972) and that men do not have a confidante other than their spouse.

Conclusions

In this chapter, we have tried to explain why people form and dissolve relationships. Along the way, we hope we have demolished any misconceptions you may have had about relationships. You have seen that loneliness is not simply the result of "not being popular," but rather of not having the number or quality of intimate relationships that we expect. You have seen that who we become friends with is more a function of geography and physical attractiveness than most of us would care to admit. You saw that in love relationships,

Box 10.8

SELF-CHECK

Part A

Indicate whether each of the following statements is true or false.

1. Women suffer more from divorce than men.
2. Consistent with social exchange theory, some people who have had happy marriages get divorced.
3. Consistent with social exchange theory, some people who suddenly become very successful stay married.
4. According to Erik Erikson, people will fear commitment if their parents were uncaring, especially if the parents were uncaring during the first year of life.
5. Carol Gilligan has found convincing evidence that Erikson's model applies only to men.
6. Consistent with Erikson's view, people who marry young are more likely to get divorced.
7. Having children makes people happier about being married.
8. Having children makes people happier with their spouse.
9. Sex is an important factor in happy marriages.
10. Happily married couples communicate with complete openness.
11. Divorce is the most common way for marriage to end.
12. For people widowed after age 65, men are about eight times more likely than women to remarry.

Part B

Answer the following question.

13. According to the text, what characteristics make a couple more likely to divorce?

Please turn to the end of this chapter to check your answers.

similarity was more important than complementarity; and friendship more important than sexual pleasure. You saw that, in good marriages, both spouses tend to score high on psychological femininity (being sensitive and understanding). You saw that although popular opinion states that women want marriage and men don't, men seem to get more out of marriage than women. Thus, although psychologists don't know (and may never know) everything about the mysterious world of human relationships, you now know more than most people.

Summary

1. Before age 2, children show little interest in interacting with other children. Around age 2, children often begin parallel play.
2. Between the ages of 2 and 4, children become much more likely to interact with other children and much more likely to engage in cooperative play.
3. As children enter school and enter concrete operations, the number and quality of their friendships increase.
4. Around age 10, children start to be concerned about their friends' attitudes, gender, and exclusivity. Around age 12, intimacy may start to become important. However, research suggests that intimacy is not a vital part of friendship for most people until late adolescence.
5. Feeling lonely is not the same as being alone. Loneliness is often due to not achieving as much intimacy as one expects.
6. Self-disclosure meets our needs for self-expression, self-clarification, and social validation.
7. Three simple variables—physical attractiveness, proximity, and similarity—play a powerful role in determining who our friends are.
8. According to social exchange theory, people stay in a relationship because they do not think they have an alternative relationship that would give them more rewards.
9. Shyness, problems in attachment, sex roles, and sex-role stereotypes may hinder the development of intimate relationships.

10. Although human sexual activity is largely governed by psychological factors, conflicts between the genders may result from biological differences between the genders in speed of arousal and speed of resolution.
11. Research suggests that the sexual revolution has created cohort differences in sexual behavior.
12. Most sex occurs between husband and wife. Most couples are satisfied with their sex lives.
13. Passionate love is not just for the young. However, passionate love for a particular individual may fade over time as a result of habituation or opponent processes.
14. Companionate love is more important than passionate love for marital happiness.
15. According to Erikson, a person must first establish his or her own identity before committing to another.
16. Happy marriages are characterized by friendship, mutual praise, equitable division of labor, and equality of decision making.
17. Those most likely to divorce are couples who marry young, marry quickly, lack social support, and are dissimilar.
18. From people who have lost their spouse, we can infer that most people benefit from marriage, although men may benefit more than women.

Key Terms

commitment 328
companionate love 327
comparison level 319
comparison level for alternatives 319
cooperative play 315
habituation 326
intimacy 317
mere exposure effect 318
opponent processes 326
orgasm 322
parallel play 315
passionate love 325
reciprocate 320
reinforcement-affect theory 318
self-disclosure 314
social exchange theory 319

Self-Check Answers

Box 10.2

Part A:

1. False; **2.** False; **3.** True; **4.** True; **5.** False. Before the age of 3 months, infants are not interested in interacting with others. Indeed, not until about age 2 do children want to interact with each other; **6.** False; **7.** False; **8.** True.

Part B:

9. Self-disclosure satisfies the needs for self-expression, self-clarification, and social validation.
10. You have to reciprocate other people's self-disclosures. That is, you have to mirror the amount and the intimacy of their self-disclosures.
11. Four-year-olds are more likely to interact with other children, their interactions involve more give and take, their friendships are more stable, and they seem to be more attached to their friends.
12. As a result of entering concrete operations, 7-year-olds are less egocentric and so they can consider their friends' viewpoints. As a result of entering school, they are exposed to many more children, a factor that may account for their circle of friends widening and their increased willingness to spend free play time with peers.

Box 10.3

Part A:

1. True. **2.** False. Staying with the relationship depends on what alternatives people think they have. **3.** False.

Part B:

4. Physical attractiveness, proximity, and similarity.
5. We could boost the person's ego by acting as if we like them while emphasizing that we (a) are competent, (b) don't like just anyone, and (c) aren't saying we like them simply because they agree with us or are similar to us.
6. The comparison level is the standard amount of rewards we expect to get out of a relationship. Our self-esteem, past relationships, and culture may all play a role in determining how high or how low our comparison level is. If our present relationship gives us more rewards than our comparison level, we will be happy with the relationship; if it gives us less, we will be unhappy with the relationship.

7. (a) Shyness, (b) problems in attachment during infancy, (c) the male sex role (which does not promote intimacy), and (d) sex-role stereotypes (which cause the genders to think that they are more different from each other than they really are).
8. First, we can put shy people in situations where they will be likely to succeed. This success will breed confidence. Second, we can have shy people observe models who successfully overcome shyness.

Box 10.4

1. True; **2.** True; **3.** True; **4.** False; **5.** False; **6.** False; **7.** True; **8.** False; **9.** True; **10.** True; **11.** False; **12.** False; **13.** False.

Box 10.5

Part A:

1. People have to be physically aroused in the presence of the other person and they have to interpret this arousal as being due to the other person making their heart sing—as opposed to attributing their arousal to nervousness or an exciting environment.
2. According to the habituation explanation, the other person no longer produces a response in us, so breaking up produces very little change in our life. According to the opponent-process theory, on the other hand, the person still produces a reaction from us. Specifically, the person produces two reactions (one of positive feelings, one of negative feelings). Once a breakup is announced, however, we no longer have someone who will produce positive feelings, but the negative feelings are still being produced. Consequently, we have horrible feelings of withdrawal.
3. Similarity.

Part B:

4. True; **5.** True; **6.** True; **7.** False; **8.** False. '

Box 10.8

Part A:

1. True.
2. True.
3. False. This is not consistent with social exchange theory.
4. False. The main hurdle to commitment is not achieving identity.
5. False. She disagrees with Erikson, but the evidence for her views is not overwhelming.
6. True. Although there are other explanations for this finding.
7. True.
8. False.
9. False.
10. False.
11. False.
12. True.

Part B:

13. Inability to communicate; inability to handle conflict and disagreements in a rational, constructive way; marrying at a very young age; rushing from casual dating to formal engagement; lack of a support network; failure to pool their money; interpreting mistakes or bad behavior by the spouse as intentional and as an indication of a bad personality problem; having different values and expectations about what the relationship should be; dissimilar backgrounds; and failure to share in decision making.

Chapter

The Family

. . . the family is the principal context in which human development takes place.

URIE BRONFENBRENNER

Chapter Overview

When we ask students what the most important force in their development is, they often say "my family." Our students' sentiments are echoed by religious leaders, political leaders, and educational leaders—all of whom argue that the family plays a critical role in child development. However, few leaders emphasize the role of the family in adult development.

Is conventional wisdom right about the role of the family in development? If so, how does the family exert its influence? In this chapter, we will address these questions.

The Role of the Family in Development

Before discussing how family life *might* affect development, we will explore whether family life actually *does* affect development. Although it is tempting to say, "Of course, our family environment affects us," naturists have presented us with evidence suggesting that the influence of the family is not as strong as we might think. For example, consider cases in which two children who are unrelated are reared together in the same family. Despite living in the same family, being members of the same social class, and living in the same neighborhood, such siblings do not have similar personalities. Indeed, on many personality measures, there is almost a zero correlation between such siblings (Reiss, 1993). In other words, two unrelated people reared in the same family are, in many ways, no more similar than any two strangers picked at random. Some naturists argue that this evidence shows that family environment is not very important.

The nurturists counter that the naturists' accounts of the adoption studies are misleading. Specifically, nurturists would argue that parents may treat adopted children differently than their own children. To look at the typical effects of family, we should look at typical families. In typical families, family members do resemble each other on at least some characteristics, such as agreeableness (Plomin, 1991). (See table 11.1.) Thus, nurturists might ask, "If family is so unimportant, why are biologically related family members similar to each other?" The naturists have a two-pronged reply to that question.

First, naturists point out that biologically related family members may be similar to each other because such family members share similar genes. In support of this position, identical twins are more similar to each other than fraternal twins—and this is true even when the identical twins are reared in different households (Reiss, 1993). Furthermore, adopted children's drug use is more correlated to their biological mother's drug use than to their adopted mother's drug use (Sharma, Benson, & McGue 1993).

Second, naturists point out that even biologically related family members are not as similar as everyone likes to believe. In fact, on many dimensions of personality, biologically related family members are no more similar to each other than strangers (Loehlin, Willerman, & Horn, 1985; Plomin, 1991; Rowe & Waldman, 1993; Scarr & Weinberg, 1983).

The nurturists counter that we do have evidence of the effects of family environment. For example, enduring parental conflict hurts child development (Hetherington & Clingenpeel, 1992), and family environment seems to influence the extent to which children develop hostility (Woodall & Matthews, 1993). Furthermore, nurturists point to the fact that genes cannot explain all the similarities between family members. That is, identical twins, "genetic copies," do not have identical personalities (Reiss, 1993).

Table 11.1

Positions on the Role of the Family on Development

Position	Evidence
The family environment causes family members to resemble each other.	Family members tend to be similar on the personality trait of agreeableness. Parental conflict tends to hurt children's development.
Similarities between family members are due to shared genes rather than shared environment.	Adopted children are not similar to other family members. In many ways, they are more similar to their biological mothers than to the family that adopted them. Identical twins reared apart are more similar to each other than fraternal twins reared together.
Neither shared family genes nor shared environment cause family members to be alike.	On many dimensions of personality, biologically related family members are no more similar to each other than total strangers.

How can we reconcile these opposing findings? On the one hand, if shared family environment is most important, siblings should be much more similar than they are. On the other hand, if genes are all important, identical twins should be more similar to each other than they are. The answer to the riddle, as Judy Dunn and Robert Plomin (1991) explain in their book *Same Family, Different Lives* is that family members do not share the same environment. The life your brother had in your family was different from the life you had. Thus, family experiences may make siblings different, rather than similar. In support of this view, Tellegen et al. (1988) find some evidence that twins reared apart may be more similar in certain respects than those reared in the same family.

Why do different members of the same family experience such different environments? The three most popular explanations for this fact are that:

1. Each family member creates his or her own environment;
2. The family moderates the effect of forces outside the family, and these external forces are always changing; and
3. The family itself is a developing entity that is always changing. (See table 11.2.)

The first explanation, that children pull different behaviors out of their parents and siblings, is popular with behavior geneticists. For example, the famous behavior geneticist, Robert Plomin (1991), does not believe that children are blank slates who passively accept whatever the

View of the Family	Reason for Different Siblings Experiencing Different Environments
1. Each family member creates his or her own environment. According to behavioral geneticists, people do not passively find themselves in a certain environment or passively accept being treated a certain way. Instead, individuals try to create environments that suit their natural personalities. At the very least, a child may reward parents and siblings who treat the child in ways that are compatible with the child's personality.	Since each child has a unique personality, each child will create a different environment for him- or herself.
2. The family is not master of its fate, but it does moderate the effect of forces outside of the family.	Since societal forces are always changing—and the family reacts to those changes—the family is always changing.
3. The family naturally changes in a fairly orderly way.	As the family deals with certain, fairly predictable developmental tasks, the family changes.

Table 11.2

Three Explanations for Why Family Members Don't Share the Same Environment

family environment gives them. Instead, Plomin believes that children try to create an environment that is compatible with their personality. That is, the child's behavior influences the parents' behavior. Thus, the child who inherits an outgoing, playful, intellectually oriented personality demands—and therefore receives—more attention and stimulation than the naturally shy and reserved child (Plomin, 1993; Scarr, 1987).

The second possibility, that the family has much of its influence by moderating the effects of external systems, is popular with ecological systems theorists, such as Urie Bronfenbrenner (1986; Bronfenbrenner, 1993), and Richard and Jacqueline Lerner (1987; Lerner, 1994). (See box 11.1.) According to Bronfenbrenner, what happens inside the family is strongly affected by what happens outside the family. For example, the family unit has much of its influence on children by working with or against other systems. That is, the family may work with or against messages of peers, teachers, and television. Furthermore, the economic and social environments have roles in how the family will behave. For example, if the economic or social environment requires that both parents work, then the family dynamics will be different from a family where both parents are not required to work. In short, forces outside the family have a powerful impact on the family. Because these forces are in a constant state of flux, the family itself is constantly changing.

The third possibility is that families change in a fairly orderly way as they progress through a series of developmental tasks. To understand the pattern of these changes, many people find it useful to look at the family life-cycle approach.

The family environment is different for each child in a family. Reasons include the child's own personality, forces outside the family, and changes in the family's development.

The Family Life-Cycle Approach

The **family life-cycle approach,** an approach that focuses on how families change as their members age, is useful not only for illustrating how the family changes over time, but

Box 11.1

THEORY in FOCUS

A Goodness-of-Fit Model

Systems theorists such as Urie Bronfenbrenner and Richard and Jacqueline Lerner believe that to understand human development, we must consider the individual within the context of his or her environment. One way to conceptualize how the environment influences development is through Richard and Jacqueline Lerner's (1987; Lerner, 1994) "goodness-of-fit model." An individual comes to a situation with certain characteristics and abilities. The situation places demands on that individual. If the person's characteristics meet or exceed the demands of the situation, then the person will experience adaptive outcomes such as good personal adjustment and positive social interaction. In turn, those people whose characteristics match the demands of the setting receive supportive feedback and show evidence of positive (adaptive) behavioral functioning.

However, those who do not possess the characteristics necessary to meet the demands of the situation experience maladaptive outcomes. Thus, for optimal development, the characteristics of the individual need to "fit" the demands of the environment.

In addition to emphasizing that individuals exist within the context of an environment, systems theorists also emphasize the reciprocal interaction between individuals and their environment. Thus, how well individuals fit in their environment at one point will have implications for what kind of feedback and developmental outcomes they will receive in the future.

Temperament is one dimension that people differ on that has implications for the goodness-of-fit model. Even newborn babies differ in temperament. Although most babies engage in the same types of behaviors, such as eating, sleeping, and crying, they have temperamental differences in the regularity in which they engage in these behaviors. For example, some babies sleep in regular cycles, whereas other babies do not sleep in regular cycles.

Thomas and Chess (1981) in the New York Longitudinal Study compared babies with irregular sleep cycles—arrhythmic sleep cycles—who were born to Puerto Rican parents to arrhythmic babies born to white, middle-class parents. The Puerto Rican parents were more permissive than the white parents. The Puerto Rican parents placed few demands on their children to adhere to a regular sleep pattern, allowing their children to sleep whenever the children desired. The Puerto Rican parents adjusted their schedules to fit their children's.

In contrast, the white parents placed strong demands on their children to sleep at regular times. They did not adjust their schedules to fit their children's. While arrhythmicity in Puerto Rican infants did not predict later behavioral problems, arrhythmicity in the white middle-class infants was a good predictor of later behavioral problems.

Thus, arrhythmicity was not incongruent with the Puerto Rican parenting style, but was incongruent with the white, middle-class style. The Puerto Rican children could meet the demands of their environment and experienced positive outcomes. The white children could not meet the demands and suffered negative outcomes.

---

also for helping us understand how families affect development throughout the lifespan. Specifically, the family life-cycle approach is useful because it emphasizes that the roles we have in our family shape our own individual development and that how we execute those roles affects how the family itself develops.

Family and Roles

Before getting specific about how the family influences development, we should specify what a family is. According to Rodgers (1973), the **family** is a:

> semiclosed system of actors occupying interrelated positions defined by the society of which the family system is a part as unique to that system with respect to the role content of the positions and to ideas of kinship relatedness. The definitions of positional role content change over the history of the group. (p. 15)

Embedded in this complex definition are four ideas. First, the roles within a family are interrelated. How we play a role, or even *whether* we play that role, depends on the degree to which other family members play complementary roles. To play the role of father, for example, one needs a child. Consequently, a role change initiated by one family member will alter how, and even whether, other family members play their roles. For example, if a daughter has a child, then her parents gain the role of grandparents, and her siblings gain the roles of aunts and uncles. If a parent moves out of the family due to divorce, not only do both parents lose their roles as spouse (the husband's role cannot

Box 11.2

SELF-CHECK

Part A

Indicate whether each of the following statements is true or false.

1. Due to the impact of the family environment, children adopted into a family eventually become similar to the other family members.
2. Identical twins reared by different families are more similar to one another than fraternal twins reared in the same family.
3. According to the family life-cycle approach, fraternal twins and identical twins should share a more similar family environment than other siblings.

Part B

Answer the following questions.

4. What are three reasons individual family members might share different family environments?
5. Which model provides a picture of a more orderly and predictable pattern of changes in the family environment—Bronfenbrenner's ecological systems model or the family life-cycle approach?

Please turn to the end of this chapter to check your answers.

exist without the wife's role, the wife's role cannot exist without the husband's role), but all of the other family members must change their behavior within the family to compensate and adjust to this loss. Perhaps the mother will have to go back to school to qualify for a higher paying job. As a consequence, the oldest child must baby-sit the youngest while their mother is at school.

Second, the roles played by family members are partially defined by society. Society sets standards for how mothers, fathers, wives, husbands, grandparents, children, grandchildren, and in-laws are supposed to behave. Although people do deviate from these standards, society exerts continuous pressure for family members to conform to these external standards. However, the pressure to conform to a socially prescribed role is not all bad. As you will see, when families have roles that are not well defined by society, families often struggle.

Third, although society sets standards for roles, each family is unique in how and to what degree it implements these standards. However, most families transmit cultural norms to their children through instruction and modeling culturally appropriate behaviors. Furthermore, many families encourage individuals who have married into their family to conform to the family's cultural expectations. For example, a woman of Protestant faith may be expected to convert to Catholicism by her Catholic in-laws.

Fourth, family roles change over the family's lifespan. As you mature, the normative expectations for your roles change. For example, the role of daughter is very different for a 2-year-old than for a 65-year-old. At age 2, a child can expect her parents to support her. At age 65, she may be expected to support her parents.

Family Developmental Tasks

Family roles, such as your role in your own family, do not change simply because society commands it. Instead, your role has changed because you have changed. Family roles must change to accommodate changes in the individuals who fill those roles. According to psychologist Robert Havighurst (1953), a major reason for individual change is the completion of a **developmental task,** "a task which arises at or about a certain period in the life of an individual, the successful achievement of which leads to his [or her] happiness and to success with later tasks, while failure leads to unhappiness in the individual, disapproval by the society, and difficulty with later tasks" (p. 2). Common developmental tasks include toilet training, entering school, achieving economic independence, getting married, and retirement.

All developmental tasks either influence or are influenced by the family. In some cases, the family is the direct focus of a developmental task (for example, toilet training, marriage, parenthood, grandparenthood). In other cases, the family is affected when one of its members achieves or strives to fulfill a task related to competence in the outside world (such as entering school, striving for intimacy, or gaining economic independence).

Just as each family member struggles with his or her developmental tasks, the family as a whole must also struggle to complete developmental tasks. Sociologist Evelyn Duvall (1977) identifies eight **familial developmental tasks** that contribute to the maintenance and survival of the family. These include:

1. *Physical maintenance*—such as providing food, clothing, and housing for family members;
2. *Allocation of resources*—deciding how much money is spent on each individual, who gets a separate bedroom, who gets extra food or attention;
3. *Division of labor*—determining who does the housework, who takes care of the children, and who works outside the home;
4. *Socialization of family members*—such as teaching children manners, morals, how to dress, and how to talk;
5. *Reproduction, recruitment, and release of family members*—having children, bringing new members into the family through marriage, and losing family members through death, divorce, and marriage;

The accomplishment of a developmental task by one family member, such as starting school, changes the roles of all the family members.

6. *Maintenance of order*—establishing family rules and a hierarchy of authority;
7. *Placement of members in the larger society*—preparing children to fill roles outside the family, such as worker and citizen; and
8. *Maintenance of motivation and morale*—such as providing emotional support for family members.

How the family accomplishes these developmental tasks strongly influences the development of its individual members. That is, the performance of family developmental tasks affects the development of *both* children and adults.

As a child, you were the focus of many of your family's developmental tasks. Specifically, how your family accomplished these tasks shaped much of your existence. How you were fed, clothed, and housed permanently affected your health and physical development. The amount of family resources devoted to you determined your quality of life, what opportunities you had for personal enjoyment and growth, your concept of fairness, and your self-esteem. Your family taught you what "men's work" and "women's work" were by how it divided labor. Your family taught you how to walk, talk, and behave in public. Your family fed—or hindered—your dreams and aspirations.

Table 11.3

Key Points About Family Roles

1. The role one plays within a family depends on what roles the other members of the family are playing.
2. Society sets standards for how we are to play many of these roles—and puts pressure on individuals who deviate from society's standards.
3. Families differ in the degree to which they conform to society's standards.
4. Family roles change over the family's lifespan, often in response either to an individual's mastering a developmental task or the family's dealing with a family developmental task.
5. Changes in family roles often cause developmental changes in the affected family member.

As adults, we are often the originator of these family tasks. Indeed, many adults devote most of their energy to the maintenance of family life. That is, although it might be too strong to say that adults become their roles, adults are influenced by their family roles. Consequently, as an adult's family role changes, the adult will change (see table 11.3).

The Family Career

As we stated, families inevitably change. Some of these changes are not predictable. For example, the composition of your family may have changed over the years because of the addition of step-relatives, the birth of siblings, or the death of parents. However, many of the changes in the composition of the traditional family—what experts call the **family career**—follow a fairly regular pattern. Consequently, sociologists Duvall and Hill (1948; Duvall, 1977) developed an eight-stage model that they call the family career cycle:

1. Young, married couples without children;
2. Childbearing families (oldest child less than 2 1/2 years old);
3. Families with preschool children (oldest child between 2 1/2 and 6 years old;
4. Families with school children (oldest child between 6 and 13 years);
5. Families with teenagers (oldest child between 13 and 20 years);
6. Families launching young adults (begins when first child leaves home, ends when last child leaves home);
7. Middle-aged parents (from the time when all children have grown up and left home to retirement); and
8. Aging family members (from retirement to death of both spouses).

Table 11.4

Stage-Critical Family Developmental Tasks Through the Family Life Cycle

Stages of the Family Life Cycle	Positions in the Family	Stage-Critical Family Developmental Tasks
Married couple	Wife Husband	Establishing a mutually satisfying marriage. Adjusting to pregnancy and the promise of parenthood. Fitting into the kin network.
Childbearing	Wife-mother Husband-father Infant daughter or son or both	Having, adjusting to, and encouraging the development of infants. Establishing a satisfying home for both parents and infant(s).
Preschool-age	Wife-mother Husband-father Daughter-sister Son-brother	Adapting to the critical needs and interests of preschool children in stimulating, growth-promoting ways. Parents coping with energy depletion and lack of privacy.
School-age	Wife-mother Husband-father Daughter-sister Son-brother	Fitting into the community of school-age families in constructive ways. Encouraging children's educational achievement.
Teenage	Wife-mother Husband-father Daughter-sister Son-brother	Balancing freedom with responsibility as teenagers mature and emancipate themselves. Establishing postparental interests and careers as growing parents.
Launching center	Wife-mother-grandmother Husband-father-grandfather Daughter-sister-aunt Son-brother-uncle	Releasing young adults into work, military service, college, marriage, etc., with appropriate rituals and assistance. Maintaining a supportive home base.
Middle-age parents	Wife-mother-grandmother Husband-father-grandfather	Rebuilding the marriage relationship. Maintaining kin ties with older and younger generations.
Aging family members	Widow/widower Wife-mother-grandmother Husband-father-grandfather	Coping with bereavement and living alone. Closing the family home. Adjusting to retirement.

In the next few sections, we will summarize the major challenges facing family members during each stage of the family career. For a preview of this discussion, refer to table 11.4.

Married Young Couples

As we mentioned before, the larger society affects the family unit. This is true even at the beginning of the family life cycle. For example, in simpler times, most people married—and married early. During the early 1900s, 95 percent of U.S. citizens were married at least once by the time they turned 50. Back then, a spinster was a never-married 26-year-old woman. In recent years, however, there is a trend toward delayed marriages and avoiding marriage altogether.

Young married couples are now older than they have ever been. In biblical times, most people were married by age 16. In the early 1900s, most were married by the time they were 21. Nowadays, most 25-year-old men have not yet married (see figure 11.1). One reason for the delay in marriage is that employment opportunities for young people are limited. Consequently, more and more youths, especially those from the middle class, are going to college (Bloom, 1987). Even young people who do not go to college often have to wait several years before they can get a job that can support themselves—much less a family.

Not only are fewer people getting married at an early age, but fewer people are getting married. In 1992, almost 30 percent of households were composed of people living alone (U.S. Census, 1993). Furthermore, only slightly more than half of all households were composed of married couples (U.S. Census, 1993).

Why is marriage less common than it used to be? One explanation is that marriage is less important to personal happiness than it once was. Even 20 years ago, married people were much happier than singles. Married women in

Figure 11.1

Median Age of First Marriage from 1890 to 1988

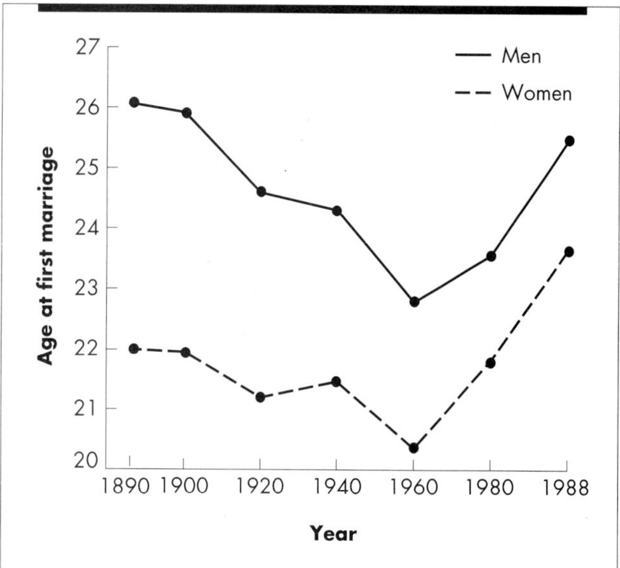

the 1990s are not as happy as they used to be and single men are happier than they used to be. As a result, although married people, on the average, are still happier than singles, the happiness gap has shrunk (Glenn, 1987; Myers, 1992). Because of the trends toward later marriages and toward less relative happiness in marriage, experts believe that, in the near future, 10 percent of the U.S. population will reach 50 without ever having been married (U.S. Census Bureau, 1989).

Those couples who do marry face the challenge of abandoning the roles of single individuals and taking on the roles of husband and wife (Nock, 1982). According to Duvall and Hill (1948), the major task of the childless young married is to establish a workable pattern of interaction. Many couples never are able to establish a stable, workable pattern of interaction, as indicated by the statistic that, internationally, divorces peak during the third and fourth year of marriage (Fisher, 1987). The fundamental problem in reaching a harmonious interaction seems to be achieving shared, realistic definitions of roles.

Some couples start married life with very different conceptions of the roles of husband and wife. Because each spouse's conception of these roles is based on his or her social class (Rainwater, 1960), ethnic background, religion, family traditions, and other life experiences, their role expectations will differ to the degree that their past histories differ. Some of these differences may seem trivial, but any difference—from which side of the bed to sleep on, to who carves the Thanksgiving turkey—may introduce conflict. Other differences lead to serious conflicts. For example, problems will certainly erupt if one spouse believes that women should hold jobs outside the home, whereas the other spouse is adamant that the home is the woman's full-time job.

However, most couples do not disagree about what the roles of husband and wife should be. As you'll see in chapter 12, society does such a thorough job of gender socialization that most men and women enter marriage with more or less traditional notions of these roles. Yet, when these traditional notions are incongruent with the demands of reality, trouble may result. For instance, both spouses may believe that the wife should stay home and raise children, but economic reality may dictate that the wife take a full-time job outside the home.

The conflict between role expectations and reality, and the inevitable adjustments necessary for two people to adapt to living together, help explain why marital relationships often deteriorate during the first few months of marriage (Huston, McHale, & Crouter, 1986; Huston & Vangelisti, 1991). For example, in a longitudinal study of 100 couples, Ted Huston and his colleagues found that during the first 3 to 15 months of marriage, couples become less satisfied with their sex lives, compliment each other less frequently, tell each other "I love you" less often, and do not self-disclose as often.

In summary, for many couples, achieving shared definitions of roles involves a complex struggle between traditional definitions of roles, the husband's personal definitions of roles, the wife's personal definitions of roles, and the demands of reality. Perhaps the difficulty in resolving this struggle accounts for the following facts:

- Spouses from different backgrounds, with divergent views of the roles of husband and wife, are most likely to divorce.
- Divorce rates are highest during the first few years of marriage (Glick & Norton, 1970). On the average, the couple has been married for seven years or less (Kitson, Babri, & Roach, 1985).
- Divorce is commonly preceded by a few years of marital distress (Gottman & Levenson, 1992; Kitson et al., 1985).
- Statistically, at least, living together before marriage increases the likelihood of divorce (DeMaris & Rao, 1992).

However, once a couple arrives at a common and workable definition of reality as a married couple, they may be able to deal effectively with the challenges of future stages.

Childbearing Families

One important challenge to a married couple is the birth of the first child. In the typical American family, the first child is usually born to a couple who are both in their twenties, and the first child is usually born during the second year of marriage (Glick, 1977; U.S. Census, 1990). However, if two recent trends continue, couples may eventually start having their first child when they are in their thirties (see figure 11.2). The first trend is

Box 11.3

SELF-CHECK

PART A

Indicate whether each of the following statements is true or false.

1. Roles within a family are interrelated.
2. Family roles change over the lifetime.
3. Virtually all developmental tasks either influence or are influenced by the family.
4. Just as individual family members have developmental tasks, the family as a whole has developmental tasks—and the performing of these tasks affects the development of both children and adults.
5. Almost all of the changes in the composition of the traditional family follow a fairly irregular pattern.
6. Employment opportunities have nothing to do with the fact that people are marrying later than they once did.
7. Because people are waiting until they are older and more mature before marrying, marriages are happier than they used to be.
8. Couples with similar backgrounds are less likely to divorce, possibly because their role expectations of husband and wife are more similar.
9. Couples who live together before marriage are less likely to divorce.

PART B

Do the following.

10. List at least two developmental tasks.

Please turn to the end of this chapter to check your answers.

Figure 11.2

First Births per 1,000 Women Between 1980 and 1990

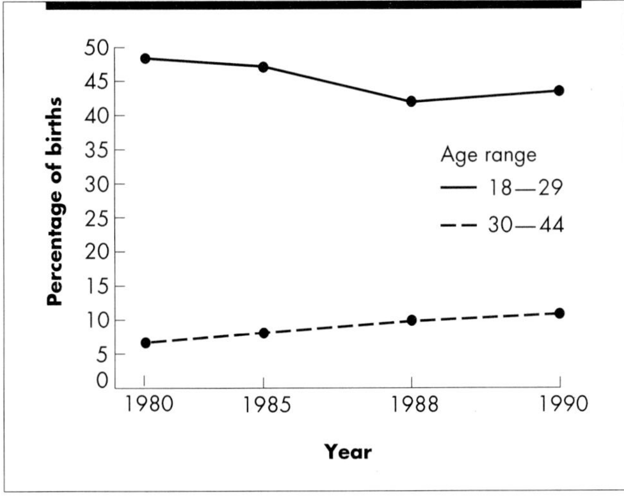

that there has been a slight decrease in the percentage of women who have their first child before they are 30. The second trend is that there has been a dramatic increase in the number of women who are having their first child after they are 39. Nevertheless, the vast majority of mothers still have their first child when they are in their twenties—and will continue to do so for the foreseeable future.

Why Couples Have Children

Now that we know when married couples have their first children, let's turn to the question of why people become parents. Before discussing reasons people decide to become parents, we should point out that many married couples do *not* decide to have children. That is, many children in this country were not deliberately conceived. For example, in a survey of adult married women, 40 percent reported that their pregnancies were unplanned (Thornburg, 1981). Furthermore, among married adolescents, 50 percent of all pregnancies are accidental (Alan Guttmacher Institute, 1981a, 1981b).

Why, in this age of contraceptives, are so many pregnancies unplanned? First of all, some people do not use contraceptives. Sometimes their religious beliefs do not permit them to, sometimes they may not know about contraceptives, and sometimes they simply prefer not to use contraceptives.

Of course, married couples are not the only ones who have unplanned pregnancies. Teenage pregnancies, in particular, are likely to occur outside of wedlock. Correlates of unplanned teenage pregnancies include alienation from parents, lack of communication with their sexual partners, preferences for risk taking, conservative opinions about abortion, low self-esteem, and an external locus of control (Bolton, 1980; Chilman, 1978; Fisher, 1984; Fischer, 1993; Herold, Goodwin, & Lero, 1979).

As you might expect, the main reason for unplanned teenage pregnancies is having sex without using birth control. Why don't sexually active teens use birth control?

One reason that female teens do not use birth control is that using birth control forces them to redefine themselves as sexual beings (Byrne & Fisher, 1983; Fisher, 1993). Probably because young women have to grapple with the notion of "nice girls don't have sex" whereas using birth control implies that one is a sexual being, the average time between becoming sexually active and using birth control for American female teenagers is one year (Harpers, 1990). Another reason that teens don't use contraception is that teens believe contraception impedes sexual pleasure. For example, Gilchirst and Schinke (1983) found that 19 percent of sexually active males agreed with the statement, "Any kind of birth control gets in the way of sex, so I wouldn't want me or my girlfriend to use it."

Even when couples intend to use contraceptives, they may have unplanned children. Their plans may be sabotaged by the heat of passion (they never get the contraceptive out of the box or wrapper) or the contraceptive may malfunction.

Although some children are "accidents," many children are planned. Why do the vast majority of people plan to have children? Researchers Warner Schaie and Sherry Willis (1986) cite four common reasons for having children.

First, in agricultural and technologically unsophisticated societies, children are needed for labor and to care for their parents when they grow older. Schultz (1985) points out that even in our modern society, the young take care of the old through the social security system. Furthermore, contrary to some popular stereotypes, when the elderly need help, they often get assistance from their children (Smolak, 1993).

Second, children can protect the family. In many cultures, it is the "older sons" who fight against enemy attack. In most modern countries, it is the young men who are drafted into military service.

Third, children can be viewed as the key to power and a better life. In our society, some groups believe that their quality of life and even survival is threatened if their numbers are reduced. For example, some white supremacists believe that unless the birth rate of whites increases relative to minorities, whites will lose their position of superiority. Although this view may seem rather extreme, there is some truth to the notion of power in numbers. In a country where each person has one vote, a large group has more power.

Fourth, children hold the hope for a better future for all of humanity. Through education, children hold the promise of a better world—a world of peace, respect, equality, and harmony.

No matter what circumstances precipitate parenthood, taking the role of parent has a major influence on each of us throughout our lifespan (Gutmann, 1975). The parental role does not stop at birth, but usually continues to dramatically affect the rest of a parent's life. As people say, "Once a parent, always a parent."

The most dramatic influence of children, however, occurs shortly after the first child is born. New parents must learn how to adapt to and encourage their infant's development. They need to understand that waking up several times in the middle of the night and crying is normal behavior for a 3-week-old infant. Parents must also realize that an infant who literally pulls out their hair is simply exploring and learning about the environment. In addition to understanding their child's behavior, parents need to encourage their child's development by providing a supportive and stimulating environment.

How supportive? How stimulating? As you saw in chapter 9, babies need more than food, clothing, and diapers. They need social interaction and opportunities to explore the world. The degree of stimulation depends on the baby. Their nervous system determines, to a degree, how much stimulation is ideal for them. Parents must learn to sense when their child is getting too much (crying is a good indicator) and when their child needs more. Parents must also learn what their baby is capable of accomplishing and adjust to changes in these capacities. For example, they must realize that walking, toilet training, language comprehension, emotional attachment to parents, and self-control cannot occur before the child is biologically ready. However, as you can see in box 11.4, parents must also impose limits from an early age.

The Impact of Children on the Marriage

Not only are parents influencing children, but children are also influencing parents. Suddenly, husbands and wives must divert much of their attention away from each other and on to the children. Not only do they have less time for each other, but they must also give up their privacy and freedom. No longer can they take off for the movies or eat out at a moment's notice. No longer can they romance in the kitchen and living room or in an unlocked bedroom. Even behind closed doors, private time will be imposed on by oblivious children. Couples must learn to carefully plan time together if they are to maintain a quality relationship. Furthermore, children take money—money that could be spent for the parents' desires and needs.

As we have discussed, having children puts a strain on new parents and on their relationship. Thus, it is not surprising that some studies indicate that marital satisfaction drops immediately after the first child is born and rebounds only after all the children have left home (Rollins & Feldman, 1970). For many individuals, the first signs of strain often appear during pregnancy (Masters & Johnson, 1966; Meyerowitz & Feldman, 1967). Restrictions on sexual activity and a woman's feelings of unattractiveness are omens of things to come. For the newlywed couple, sex is rated as one of the most important aspects of marriage, if not the most important (especially among men). After the birth of the first child, men rate sex as the second most important aspect of marriage, and women commonly rate sex as the least important (Reedy, Birren, & Schaie, 1981). Both parents complain about lack of energy and opportunity for sex. The physical toll of childbirth often leaves women feeling

Box 11.4

ISSUE in FOCUS

Civilizing Your Child

How can you avoid raising a brat? Start civilizing the child early.

"The adage 'an ounce of prevention is worth a pound of cure' is never more true than when it's applied to this topic," says Michael K. Meyerhoff, a child development expert.

"When I do talks around the country, I get many questions from mothers and fathers who had a wonderful time raising delightful infants for 24 months and then find themselves saddled with annoying, willful, totally unmanageable toddlers who are prone to throwing temper tantrums."

Meyerhoff, executive director of the Epicenter Inc., a consulting agency for parenting programs in Wellesley Hills, Massachusetts, says the "terrible twos" can be avoided if rules have been spelled out and enforced before the child reaches 2 years old. He offers guidelines for a child under 2. (Meyerhoff refers to the child as "she," but the guidelines are the same for boys.)

Birth to 3 Months

The best thing to do in the beginning is to give the infant whatever she wants whenever she wants it. When she is hungry or in pain, she cries reflexively. There is nothing intentional or manipulative about her behavior. If parents simply respond naturally by providing prompt nurturing services, there is absolutely no danger of spoiling the child.

3 to 8 Months

The child is intensely curious, but she can't get to most of the things she would like to investigate. So she gets frustrated and bored and cries.

The natural inclination of most parents is to respond in the same manner they have been responding. They come to the child immediately and do whatever they can to make her feel better. Although the infant's sense of love and trust is being reinforced, she is also learning that she will always be able to have whatever she wants whenever she wants it.

The solution: Try to eliminate the child's need to cry as much as possible. Put her in an infant seat and periodically move her around the house so she will have new scenes to observe. Place several safe objects within her reach to help keep frustration at bay.

Learn the difference between cries of hunger, pain, and frustration. Respond quickly to the first two, but with a bit of self-restraint to the frustration cry. The parent might say, "I hear you, but you'll have to wait a minute. I'm busy right now." The baby won't necessarily understand the words, but she will learn that while her desires are taken seriously by others, they are not the only factor governing the family.

8 to 15 Months

As the child learns to crawl, walk, and climb, the opportunity to explore and investigate freely is critical to a child's development. It is understandable that the parent is reluctant to interfere with it unless it is absolutely necessary.

It is not particularly pleasant to deny something to a dearly loved baby, so many parents are willing to sacrifice the good china before they start to establish and enforce restrictions. The result: The infant learns she is the only thing of importance.

The solution: Eliminate as many confrontations as possible and deal determinedly with those that occur. Safety-proof the house before the child begins to crawl and keep it that way for a couple of years.

If the child discovers a forbidden item, enters an off-limits area or engages in an undesirable activity, tell the child "no" or "stop," remove her from whatever is unacceptable and give her another activity. Your message is clear: She will be encouraged to explore and investigate the world, but there *are* limits to how far she will be able to go and rules regarding how much she will be allowed to do.

15 to 24 Months

Toward the middle of the second year, the easygoing, friendly infant gradually is replaced by a more formidable foe. She is developing a clear sense of self. Her new independence and individuality often shows itself in the tendency to say "no" to every request, test all limits, and resist any attempts at control. It is crucial for the parents to make it known that the child is still cherished but *they* are in charge. Doing this without crushing her spirit may seem difficult, but it can be done.

Continued

Box 11.4

ISSUE in FOCUS

Concluded

Some parents find the deluge of disobedience begins to wear them down, and they find themselves simply too tired to continually take a stand. So they start to relax restrictions, rely too much on verbal warnings and fail to follow up on whatever temporary victories they may achieve. The result: The baby learns it won't be easy all the time, but if she pushes hard enough and long enough, she will get her way.

The solution: Eliminate as many confrontations as possible and deal with those that occur in a determined manner.

The trick is to offer choices instead of delivering direct instructions. For instance, rather than asking, "Do you want to put on your shirt?" or stating "Please put on your shirt," you might ask, "Do you want to put your shirt or pants on first?" This gives the child a chance to exercise her personal power without having to oppose the will of her parents.

When the child does not obey a request, she should be removed promptly and physically prevented with a firm hug from doing the activity. The child will probably have to be held for a minute or two until the squirming stops. If she returns to the activity, repeat the procedure until the message sinks in.

No parent makes it through negativism without a lot of hard work and a fair amount of heartache. Setting limits requires mothers and fathers to enforce restrictions rigorously and be extremely patient.

AGE 2 AND UP

It's never too late to begin disciplining a child. But the longer parents wait to enforce rules, the more likely that confrontations with their child will be constant battles rather than occasional skirmishes. The negative behavior will become more entrenched, more difficult to correct.

Note: From "Civilizing Your Child: Enforce Rules and Be Patient," by Nanci Hellmich, *USA Today*, 7/6/89, p. D-5.

less sexually attractive. Consequently, men often complain that their wives aren't as sexually responsive as they were before parenthood.

New mothers usually find parenthood more stressful than their husbands do (Hobbs & Wimbish, 1977; Russell, 1974). This is not surprising considering that women typically provide much more of the child's care, are more likely to have given up a job to have the baby, and are physically exhausted and in poor condition from the trials of delivery and infant care. Working mothers also find parenthood stressful, especially if they have to return to work within six weeks of giving birth (Clark, 1993; Hyde, Klein, & Essex, 1993). However, fathers also find parenthood stressful. They commonly report lost sleep, and sometimes must take a second job to cope with money woes. In addition, parenthood restricts the husband's independent leisure pursuits and increases the extent to which spouses' leisure activities reflect the preferences of wives rather than husbands (Crawford & Huston, 1993).

If having one child places a stress on the marriage, what are the effects of having more than one? Are two just as easy to take care of as one? Research indicates that the more children, the more pressure on the marriage (Glenn & Weaver, 1978). Perhaps for this reason, parents with many children are more likely to divorce than parents with moderately sized families (Thornton, 1977).

Despite some of the negative influences of children on marital satisfaction, much of the crisis of parenthood can be reduced if the father takes an active parenting role. Rather than compete with his new baby for his wife's attention, the husband can share the parenting experience (Hoffman, 1983). True, there still may not be enough time for a satisfying physical relationship, but at least the husband and wife are working together. A shared goal is more likely to create parental solidarity than competing goals—and sharing the work helps families meet the ever-changing challenges that face them.

Families with Preschool Children

The primary challenges facing families with preschool children are to adapt to their children's rapid physical, cognitive, and social development in stimulating, growth-promoting ways. This is easier said than done. It is difficult to cope with a preschooler who is practicing his or her autonomy by saying "No" to every request, yet who gets very upset when left with a baby-sitter and who often appears to be upset at the prospect of being alone in the bedroom at night.

Keeping up with a preschooler as she synthesizes her new-found physical skills (such as running) with autonomy (running into the street against parental orders) can

Box 11.5

SELF-CHECK

PART A

Indicate whether each of the following statements is true or false.

1. In the United States, a married couple's first child is usually born to a couple who are both in their twenties—and this will continue to be the case for the foreseeable future.
2. For married couples, the overwhelming majority of pregnancies are planned pregnancies.
3. For U.S. female teenagers, the average time between becoming sexually active and using birth control is one year.
4. Teens who have unplanned pregnancies tend to have high self-esteem and a relationship with their sexual partners that is characterized by honesty and openness.
5. For the most part, in the United States, children do not play a significant role in taking care of their elderly parents.
6. Parents should not impose limits on a child until the child is at least age 2.
7. Marital satisfaction drops immediately after the first child is born and rebounds only after all the children have left the home.
8. New mothers usually find parenthood more stressful than their husbands do, and this is especially true of working mothers who have to return to work within six weeks of giving birth.
9. As far as marital satisfaction is concerned, two children are no more stressful than one.

PART B

Answer the following questions.

10. What are four reasons people choose to have children?
11. What is one indicator that parents have overstimulated their infant?
12. Why is it important for parents to have some sense of the child's maturational level?

Please turn to the end of this chapter to check your answers.

be a nightmare for even the most patient parent. Thus, it is not surprising that another one of the family developmental tasks of this period is coping with energy depletion.

Families with School Children

Once children enter school, families usually encourage their children to succeed academically. The impact of parents on their children's academic achievement is well publicized. For example, commentators note that:

- Some of the success of private schools is due to the parents being very involved in their children's education.
- The states that have the highest proportion of intact families tend to have students who do the best on standardized scores, perhaps because the dual-parent family has more resources to devote to their children's education than the single-parent family.

If parents are concerned about their child's education, much of the family's energy and time become focused around school and extracurricular activities. The parents' social life often becomes intertwined with their children's.

Although people commonly acknowledge the influence of parents on their child's education, people often overlook the effect of this school involvement on the parents. If parents are concerned about their children's education, much of the family's energy and time becomes focused around school activities and the friendships children form in school. PTA, homework, parent-teacher conferences, music lessons, and extracurricular activities can consume a major segment of family life. Consequently, the parents' social life often becomes intertwined with their children's, as parents form friendships with the parents of their children's friends.

Box 11.6

SELF-CHECK

Indicate whether each of the following statements is true or false.

1. One of the familial developmental tasks for families with preschool children is coping with energy depletion.
2. Parental involvement in education appears to be related to children's school achievement.
3. The child's social life may determine the parents' social life.
4. Parents of teenagers, like parents of 2-year-olds, must let their child struggle for independence, yet still be there to support the child.
5. Through skillful parenting, conflict during the teenage years can be avoided.
6. Parents become quite despondent about the fact that adolescents are changing in response to peers.

Please turn to the end of this chapter to check your answers.

Families with Teenagers

As Erikson's theory suggests, families with teenagers confront a similar challenge to families with 2-year-olds: watching their child learn to balance freedom and responsibility. Parents must let their children struggle for independence, yet always hold out an invisible safety net in case the teen falters.

Usually, teenagers try to achieve independence from their parents through peer groups. As adolescents increasingly focus on people outside the family unit, they adjust to and incorporate the expectations and norms of those outsiders. How do parents react to these changes in the teenager? Although some changes are more easily assimilated by the family than others, conflict is almost inevitable.

Fortunately, parents realize that these conflicts—and their reduced power to influence the child—mean that the child is less dependent on the parent. That is, just as the parents now have less power over their child, they also have—or soon will have—less responsibility for the child. Thus, after spending much of their young adulthood and some of their middle age serving their child, parents can see the light at the end of the tunnel. They realize that they are slowly being freed from their parental responsibilities and will soon be free to get on with their own lives.

Families Launching Young Adults: The Contracting Stage

Being free to get on with their own lives, however, takes time. Rarely will a family immediately contract from four members to two. Instead, most families contract over a multiple-year period. Specifically, the **contracting stage** begins when the eldest child first starts taking concrete steps to achieve economic and physical independence from the family and ends when the last child actually leaves the house.

In previous eras, launching children into the outside world didn't take much time. Most children went directly from high school or grade school into the workforce and independence. As a result, the contracting stage was fairly short. However, today more and more children attend college or some other post-secondary educational institution before striking out on their own.

Launching children via college can be economically stressful for many families. Furthermore, even after supporting their children through college, parents may still have to support an unemployed or underpaid college graduate. Consequently, as box 11.7 illustrates, many children remain home well into their late twenties and early thirties because the cost of living independently often exceeds their capacity to earn money (Glick & Lin, 1986; Mancini & Blieszner, 1985).

Middle-Aged Parents

Once the last child leaves the home, the postparental years begin. Because the postparental period begins with the departure of the offspring, the postparental period is often called the "empty nest." Regardless of what it is called, the period continues until retirement or the death of one of the spouses. Because there is so much variation in when the last child leaves home and when people retire or die, the length of the postparental period is extremely variable. For some couples, this period lasts only a few months; for others, it lasts for most of the family's career.

The critical tasks of the postparental period are rebuilding the marriage relationship and maintaining ties with older and younger family members. How do couples cope with these tasks? According to many pop psychologists, not very well. Indeed, pop psychologists coined the phrase the **empty-nest syndrome** to emphasize that the postparental years were a period of crisis, especially for women, because they must find a substitute for their parenting role. However, research shows that the postparental period is often a time of welcomed freedom and growth for both women and men. Few lament their diminished parental role (Deutscher, 1969; Lowenthal & Chiriboga, 1972). Indeed, many couples report this period to be one of the happiest times of their lives. Furthermore, relative to the early parental period, both men and women—but especially women—in the postparental period are much more self-confident (Wink & Helson, 1993).

Box 11.7

RESEARCH in FOCUS

The Full-Nest Syndrome

Most young people leave their parental homes during their late teens or early twenties to go to college or establish their own homes. However, recent demographic indicators show that, since the 1970s, an increasing number of young people are remaining home or returning to their parents' home because of financial or emotional hardships. Paul Glick and Sung-Ling Lin (1986) summarized Census data on living arrangements between 1940 and 1980 and found that, in 1984, 53 percent of males between 20 and 24 and 17 percent of men between 25 and 29 lived with their parents.

What toll does this living situation exact on family relations? Glick and Lin concluded that when young adults live with their parents a stressful situation is created to the degree that the children's more modern living style is incompatible with their parents. The situation may be even more stressful if a child returns with a spouse or child in tow. A time when most parents are enjoying freedom from the responsibilities of parenthood is stunted by an unexpected "full nest."

The so-called empty-nest years are often the happiest times in a couple's marriage.

Not only is the empty-nest period a positive time for the husband and the wife as individuals, but it's a positive time for them as a couple. At last, they have time for each other and for their shared interests, whims, and needs. This extra time seems to be good for most marriages, as couples almost invariably report this period as a time of increasing marital satisfaction (Miller, 1976; Orthner, 1975).

Although middle age often brings the joys of improved marital relations, advancing years are also accompanied by an increased awareness of the fact that one's death is on the horizon. That is, having aging or dying parents and experiencing one's own physical decline remind people that death is inevitable. This awareness of one's own death makes many people realize how dear their "roots" are. Consequently, people and locations from the past as well as family ties often become more important. For example, after the death of a parent, people often visit their childhood homes to reminisce and seek some connection between their present and past. Perhaps they also seek a simpler time or perhaps they wish to affirm life's central values: family and home (Duvall, 1977).

One way in which many couples affirm their family values is by enjoying grandparenthood. About half of all grandparents adopt the conventional role of friendly, active, but non-interfering grandparent. That is, they focus on having fun with their grandchild and they try to avoid disciplining or even disapproving of the grandchild. Most grandparents are able to spend time, money, and energy on their young grandchildren because the grandparents are relatively secure in their careers, have reduced expenses due to the emptying of the nest, and have the energy that one would expect from people who, for the most part, are between 38 and 58 (Cherlin & Furstberg, 1986).

For about 1 in 6 grandparents, however, grandparenting is very much like parenting. That is, in this era of single parenthood and troubled families, it is not unusual for a son or daughter to have a child, but be either incapable or unwilling to become a full-time parent. In that case, grandparents often step in and fulfill the parent role for their grandchildren. Not surprisingly, such grandparents may have mixed emotions about becoming parents again.

Aging Families

The final stage in the family career is *aging families*. This stage begins when the primary breadwinner retires and lasts until one of the spouses (usually the husband) dies. The major task of this stage, which often lasts fewer than eight years, is adjusting to the many challenges of retirement (Duvall, 1977).

One challenge of retirement is adjusting to retirement income. Many couples must survive on social security benefits and limited savings. Women who were career homemakers get little in the way of social security from this career. Furthermore, their income will decrease even more if their husband dies, since they did not pay into social security and their husbands' contributions are not fully deferred to them. A major illness may wipe out any savings, and so-called "cost of living" adjustments (COLAs) in social security rarely keep up with actual increases in the cost of living.

In addition to financial challenges, couples must meet several serious psychological challenges. They must safeguard their physical and mental health; maintain love, sex, and marital relations; keep active and involved in life; and establish a routine compatible with their new situation. Furthermore, according to Erikson, couples must work through Erikson's last crisis: the conflict between integrity and despair.

To successfully resolve the integrity versus despair conflict, people must be able to look back and see that they led meaningful lives. Perhaps because they are trying to see their lives as meaningful, people feel closer to their siblings as they age—even though this change of feeling is not accompanied by any changes in action (Cicirelli, 1985). The drive to see their lives as meaningful also accounts for why they take pride in their great grandchildren even though the elderly are typically not very involved with their great grandchildren (Smolak, 1993). However, despite having the drive to make their lives seem meaningful, not all of the elderly see their lives as meaningful. Consequently, some of the elderly fall into despair. This despair may contribute, in part, to the fact that the elderly have the highest suicide rate of all age groups.

In addition to financial and psychological challenges, the elderly also are confronted by physical challenges. They must adjust their living situation to their physical limitations. Although only 5 percent of the elderly live in a nursing home at a given time, with advanced years, most of us will eventually lose some or all of our physical independence. Moving to a retirement community, nursing home, or moving in with children can be an enormous emotional challenge. Understandably, couples do not want to say good-bye to the home they made for themselves during their more vigorous years.

With the death of one of the spouses, the original nuclear family no longer exists. The surviving spouse is faced with the challenge of finding meaning beyond his or her married family role. This challenge is primarily faced by women. Specifically, between the ages of 65 and 74, about 40 percent of women are widowed, compared with only 9 percent of men; above the age of 75, 70 percent of women are widowed (Uhlenberg & Myers, 1981).

Adjusting to the loss of a mate, a mate who may have been a companion and confidante for 50 years or more, is compounded by the loneliness of living alone. Remarkably, most women do adjust to widowhood—and the vast majority of elderly widows have no desire to get married. Men, however, don't fair as well. Indeed, from a statistical standpoint, it seems that most men do not remain unmarried widowers for very long: Within two years, most either remarry or die (Helsing, Szklo, & Comstock, 1981; McCrae & Costa, 1988). (Table 11.5 provides a summary of the challenges people face during the lifespan.)

There Is More Than One Kind of Traditional Family

To this point, we have described nuclear families as if they are all alike and as if all are basically self-contained systems that control their own destinies. However, this is not the case. The family, as a messenger of the culture, is obviously affected by the culture of its members. Furthermore, the family, as a small system, can be supported or disrupted by larger forces, such as governmental policies and adverse economic situations. In short, to this point, we have focused on commonalities among traditional families. In the next section, we will focus on differences between families that are caused by sociocultural and economic forces.

Black American and African American Families[1]

Many people believe that discrimination against Black Americans in America is a thing of the past, and that civil rights legislation has given Black Americans equality with Euro-Americans—or perhaps even an advantage. However, the statistics tell a different story. Between 1960 (a time when Black Americans weren't allowed to work or even eat in certain places) and 1991, Black American family income remained at about 57 percent of Euro-American family income (Statistical Abstracts, 1993, report No. 720). As a result, many Black American families have incomes near or below the official poverty level. Many cannot survive without public welfare. Life is unstable, with frequent job and residence changes and the constant threat of unemployment. For this reason, many Black American leaders say that the main problem now faced by Black Americans is poverty.

Queen and his associates (1985) describe the plight of being born poor and black in America:

> The impact of poverty affects blacks over the entire life-cycle. Infant mortality rates for blacks are double those for Euro-Americans; a black baby is three times as likely as a white baby to have a mother who dies in childbirth. A black child's mother is more likely to go out to work sooner, to work

[1]Although the designations *African American* and *black* are often used interchangeably, they are not synonymous. *Black* is a more inclusive term that may include people other than those of African descent. *African American* refers only to people of African descent. However, because these distinctions are recent and not universally adopted, research reports are usually unclear about whether the more inclusive groups of "blacks" was studied, or whether the blacks studied were exclusively those of African descent. For these reasons, we have chosen to use the more inclusive term *Black*, except for when we are sure that a particular study limited its scope to African Americans.

Box 11.8

SELF-CHECK

Indicate whether each of the following statements is true or false.

1. The contracting stage deals with how parents and children work out a social contract defining who should do what.
2. The age at which children are launched is strongly affected by the society's economy.
3. The postparental period may last only a few months.
4. Research shows that the empty-nest syndrome is a period of crisis and marital turbulence.
5. Grandparents are fairly strict with grandchildren.
6. Most grandparents are actively involved with their grandchildren.
7. Most first-time grandparents are over 60.
8. The aging family stage often lasts fewer than eight years.
9. A major problem in retirement years is adjusting to reduced income.
10. Perhaps as a way of achieving integrity, elderly people feel closer to their siblings as they age and they take enormous pride in their great grandchildren.
11. The elderly have the highest suicide rate of all age groups.
12. More than one-fourth of the elderly live in nursing homes.
13. Men adjust to widowhood better than women.
14. Most elderly widows wish to get remarried.

Please turn to the end of this chapter to check your answers.

Table 11.5

Review of the Eight Sets of Challenges Facing the Traditional Family Throughout Its Lifespan

Challenge 1	The married couple must learn to get along with each other. Often, because married couples fail to establish compatible roles, divorce follows the marriage ceremony by only a few years. One index of how hard it is to achieve compatible roles is that, despite fewer people getting married, people waiting longer to get married, and more people living together before getting married, the divorce rate is not going down.
Challenge 2	The parents must adjust to the newborn infant. This adjustment means adjusting to having more stress, but less sex, less time, less energy, and less money for one's own needs and the needs of one's partner. In addition, the couple must strike a balance between overstimulating and understimulating the infant.
Challenge 3	The couple must balance setting limits on the child against letting the child have some freedom. In addition, the parents themselves must either take steps to avoid becoming exhausted or find ways to cope with being exhausted.
Challenge 4	Parents encourage their child's academic success and meld into their child's social world by befriending not only their child's friends but also the parents of their child's friends.
Challenge 5	Parents must balance the adolescent's freedom versus their own responsibility for the adolescent. In addition, parents must cope with the fact that the child's peers are exerting increasingly more influence.
Challenge 6	Parents must provide the financial resources necessary to launch the child.
Challenge 7	The couple rebuild the marriage, maintain family relationships despite the fact that family members no longer live in the same house, concentrate on their own personal growth, and cope with the increased awareness of their own mortality.
Challenge 8	The couple adjust to retirement and its lower income and different role, struggle with the integrity versus despair conflict, deal with their physical decline, and deal with the death of a spouse. Women are more likely than men to experience the death of a spouse—and women are more likely than men to successfully deal with their spouse's death.

longer hours, and to make less money than a white child's mother. A black child's father is 70 percent more likely to be unemployed than a white child's father. The rate of teenage pregnancy among blacks is three times that of whites; a black child is three times more likely to live in a single-parent home; and black female household heads are the poorest in the nation. A black child is twice as likely as a white to drop out of school. Those who do remain are not rewarded for their perseverance, since a black college graduate faces about the same odds of unemployment as does a white high school dropout. In 1979, unemployment among black youths was 39 percent. A black male teenager is seven times as likely as a white youth to be arrested for violent crimes and five times as likely to be a victim of violent homicide. (pp. 288–289)

Since the days of slavery, the main source of strength for poor African American families comes from the extended-kin network, that is, the extended family. Today, the extended family remains the norm for poor African American families in rural as well as urban settings (Pearson et al., 1990; Shimkin, Shimkin, & Frate, 1975). In fact, the extended family is so central to everyday life that many researchers have concluded that it is essential for the survival of the individual as well as African American culture and tradition (Shimkin, Louie, & Frate, 1973; Sussman, 1985).

In the typical African American extended family, three generations of kin live under the same roof—grandparents, mothers, and their children or children of their close kin. The strength of the extended-kin network is in sharing: They share the responsibility of children, cooking and other household chores, and money. Thus, unlike in many Euro-American families, the grandparents take an active role in teaching values to the grandchildren.

Another strength of the extended family is that the members trade resources (Burton, 1990). The system works as long as everyone gives when they can and no one takes too much. For example, Julia Rose, a 25-year-old mother of three, critically evaluated her cousin Mae's reputation:

> If someone who takes things from me ain't giving me anything in return, she can't get nothing else. . . . Some people like my cousin don't mind borrowing from anybody, but she don't loan you no money, her clothes, nothing. . . . She don't believe in helping nobody and lots of folks gossip about her. I'll never give her nothing again. (Stack, 1974, p. 34)

Hispanic American Modified-Extended Families

The nuclear family is central to Hispanic American family life. But, for several centuries, Hispanic Americans have supplemented the nuclear family through coparenthood: a baptismal ritual that links two families. The godparents (compadres) are chosen with care from outside the kinship circle, and it is hoped that the male compadre will be well respected in the community. After the bond is established ritually, the interactions are carried on between the younger person and his or her coparent in the context of prescribed formality and mutual respect. The godparent and godchild are expected to visit each other and cultivate a close relationship. And, in the event of trouble, parents are supposed to be able to call on the godparents for both help and advice.

Differences Between African American and Euro-American Families

The different socioeconomic forces acting on Euro-American and African American families appear to affect more than the structure of the family. These economic forces affect the division of power within the family, as well as the way children are reared. However, as we shall see, economic status alone does not determine the way the family operates.

Traditionally, extended African American families have taken advantage of the strengths of sharing responsibilities and resources among three generations.

Division of Power Within the Family

In most Euro-American families, the male has more power in family decisions, contributes less time to household chores and child care, and makes more money than his wife. In comparison to traditional Caucasian and Hispanic American families, working-class and middle-class African American families are relatively egalitarian (Willie, 1985). Queen, Habenstein, and Quadagno (1985) describe the foundation and strength of working-class and middle-class African American family life as the economic cooperation of husband and wife: "They are partners, carving out a comfortable lifestyle in a discriminatory society, and this makes the relationship egalitarian." This equal partnership is seen in major, as well as everyday, decisions such as where to live, what car to buy, and how to raise their children.

Middle-Class Parents

Research shows that parental involvement in school-related activities is characteristic of African American and Euro-American parents from middle-class backgrounds. In a comparison of Euro-American and African American families, Willie (1985) reports that both types of parents are commonly involved in such activities as scouting, schools, and team sports. In terms of concern for their children's education, middle-class African American parents are often more achievement oriented than Euro-American parents. Willie reports that African Americans are more likely to urge their children on to greater achievements than their own because they visualize their family as part of a great racial movement for equality and justice. Through the achievements of the individuals in each generation, African Americans believe that the condition of minorities is improved. They believe that each generation builds on the other and that the responsibility of the parental generation is to make life better for the children, even as their mothers and fathers struggled to send them to school. To some extent, this commitment to the good of the entire race is emphasized at the expense of personal freedom.

Euro-American parents, on the other hand, don't see the children as representatives of their race. Consequently, Euro-American parents focus more on the individual and personal freedoms, self-fulfillment, and self-actualization rather than commitment to more global causes. Some people have pointed to this lack of commitment on the part of many Euro-Americans as a sign of the lack of values of the "me" generation—always focused on selfish, hedonistic desires, while ignoring the larger society. What people may not realize is that the selfishness of the "me" generation may stem from the selfishness of their parents. For example, Carol Ryff and Marilyn Essex (1992) found that parents do not want the best for their children. That is, the sentiments of most Euro-American parents seem to be, "Do well, my child, but not better than I am doing."

Working-Class Parents

This selfish view is also seen in the working class. For example, both African American and Euro-American working-class parents share the desire for their children to go to college. However, Euro-American parents are ambivalent about the outcome of education. Although they see education as an asset for their child, they also fear that education will disrupt family unity. They feel that educated offspring may no longer honor family customs and solidarity.

African American working-class parents have no such ambivalence. They regard education as a vehicle for their children to overcome racial discrimination. They focus on the opportunities that education provides, rather than on potential threats to family tradition and unity.

Poor African American and Euro-American Families

The poor usually don't value education. Not only do they feel that education is not relevant to their current life, but they also do not believe that education can help them escape poverty. Consequently, poor parents are not involved in their children's education.

If education is not seen as a way out of poverty, what is? Euro-Americans believe that they can get out of poverty if the family pulls together as a group. If all family members contribute what they can to the family income, their lives may improve. In short, the family as a whole comes first—individual family member comes last. Thus, fortifying the family takes priority over giving an individual family member a chance to succeed by paying for that member's education. Perhaps because they realize this strategy will probably not raise them from poverty, perhaps because they blame their own personal inadequacies for their condition, poor Euro-Americans commonly feel a sense of despair. That is, they doubt that things will ever get better.

Poor African Americans, on the other hand, take a very different view of the causes and solutions to their situation. Rather than blame their own personal inadequacies, they blame an unjust society. Furthermore, rather than feel a sense of despair that their situation will never change, they feel that these harmful societal forces will soon change and their lives will improve accordingly. Indeed, their attitude can be characterized by a sense of resistance—even rebellion—against those harmful societal forces they blame for their poverty. (These differences are summarized in table 11.6.)

Box 11.9

SELF-CHECK

Indicate whether each of the following statements is true or false.

1. Civil rights legislation and affirmative action have improved economic opportunities for African Americans.
2. African American college graduates face about the same odds of unemployment as does a Euro-American high school dropout.
3. Unlike in Euro-American families, African American grandparents take an active role in teaching values to grandchildren.
4. In Euro-American families, power is more evenly balanced between husband and wife than in African American and Hispanic American families.
5. According to Willie (1985), African American parents think that by helping their child succeed, they are not only helping their child, but also their race.
6. Most Euro-American parents want their children to be extremely successful.

Please turn to the end of this chapter to check your answers.

Alternatives to the Traditional Family

To this point, we have talked about traditional families. That is, we began our discussion of families by discussing the traditional family of Euro-Americans: the nuclear family. Next, we discussed the traditional family of Hispanic Americans: the modified-extended family. Finally, we discussed the traditional family of African Americans: the extended family.

Although you should know about traditional families, you should also realize that not all families are traditional. Divorce is commonplace, increasing numbers of people are choosing to remain single, and more and more couples are

Table 11.6

Key Differences Between African American and Euro-American Families

1. The African American extended family has helped African Americans survive hostile social and economic conditions.
2. Women have more power in African American families than in Euro-American families.
3. In both middle-class and working-class families, African American parents seem to be more interested in their children's academic achievement than Euro-American parents are.
4. Poor Euro-American families feel despair over their economic situation; poor African American families blame an unjust society.

deciding not to have children. Thus, the typical traditional family has become less typical. In fact, only 30 percent of all households in the United States are occupied by married couples with children (Masnick & Bane, 1980; Schaie & Willis, 1991). In this section, we will look at the 70 percent of households constituting "nontraditional" families. Specifically, we will focus on three common types: divorced families, families headed by unwed mothers, and homosexual families.

Divorce

Divorce is a reality of modern American family life. In recent years, the number of people seeking divorces has equaled nearly half the number of people marrying in that year (National Center for Health Statistics, 1985) (see figure 11.3). Based on this statistic, some experts predict that half of all marriages will end in divorce. Although the 50 percent conclusion is controversial, a reasonable projection is that 39 percent of all children will experience the marital disruption of their parents by their 15th birthday (Furstenberg, Nord, Peterson, & Zill, 1983). For African American children, the chances of living with both parents until age 16 is only one in five (Newsweek, 1993).

Divorce has consequences for the entire family. For the spouses, divorce terminates not only the roles of husband and wife, but also changes the parental roles. Usually, the mother becomes the primary caretaker of the children, and she must try to be both mother and father to her children. Many fathers must adjust to the part-time status of weekend father, trying to cram a whole week of fathering into a single day.

How do children adjust to divorce? Although research clearly shows that children are more harmed than helped by parents who "stay together for the sake of the kids," divorce is stressful on children. In a review of research on children's reasoning about divorce, Kurdek (1986) concluded that preadolescent children often interpret divorce personally, feeling

Figure 11.3

Marriage and Divorce Rates Compared

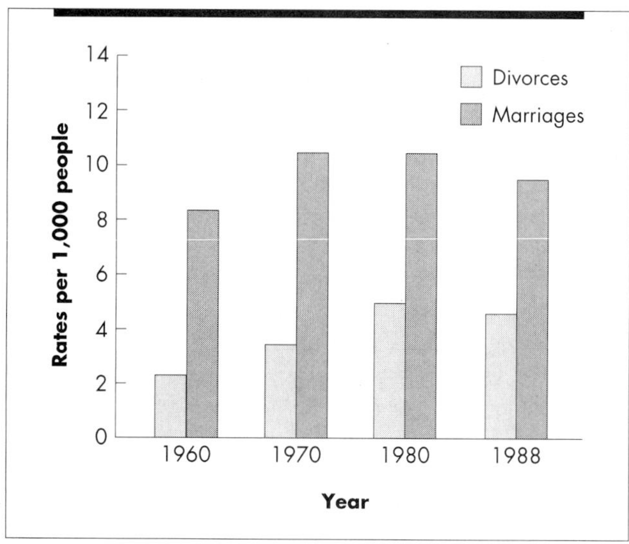

that they are somehow responsible for one of their parents moving away. Regardless of their age, children perceive divorce as stressful. In addition to experiencing the conflict that results in marital separation, the role of child changes dramatically when the family is divided. Children are shuttled back and forth between parents and are often put into the position of being a parental confidant, as each parent tries to adjust to a failed marriage and rejoin the world of single adults. Unfortunately, many parents ask their children to take sides against the other parent as a way of lashing out against their former spouse (Wallerstein, 1984).

Parents and children are not the only ones affected by divorce; grandparents and other members of the extended family (such as aunts, uncles, and cousins) experience role changes. Grandparents often feel cheated out of contact with their grandchildren. This is particularly true of paternal grandparents because visits with their grandchildren often revolve around their son's visitation rights.

Stepfamilies

In spite of the high divorce rates, people clearly believe in marriage and believe in families. In fact, 85 percent of all men and 75 percent of all women who divorce will eventually remarry (Reiss, 1980). Remarriage leads to the formation of new extended families and the addition of several roles that are not yet clearly defined by society. What is a stepparent supposed to act like? How is a stepchild supposed to behave toward a stepparent? What role do ex-spouses have in this new family, especially if their children are members of it? These are questions that society has yet to deal with.

Perhaps because society has not answered these questions, the relationships between stepparents and stepchildren are usually strained. Children often resent their stepparents, saying such things as, "She's not my real mother (or dad). I don't need a new mother, I already have one." This resentment is compounded by the child's perception that this stepparent stands in the way of her real parents' reconciliation. If there were a clear role for a stepparent, a role that did not substitute for a still living and loved parent, there might be less conflict.

The lack of societal norms not only makes it difficult for stepparents to be accepted, but also makes them unsure of how they should behave. How is a stepparent supposed to treat a stepchild relative to his or her own biological children? If he treats them the same, perhaps his children will feel betrayed. If he favors his own children, perhaps the stepchildren will feel left out and discriminated against. Once again, clear normative expectations for this role might iron out many of the wrinkles in these new extended families.

Single Adults

Although stepfamilies are a very noticeable nontraditional family form, the main reason for the decline in the number of traditional families is that more and more adults are choosing to be single. Some never marry, others return to being single through divorce, and still others do not remarry after widowhood. The trend of remaining or becoming single is so strong that there are almost as many households headed by a single person (27 percent) as there are traditional families (30 percent) (U.S. Bureau of Census, *Statistical Abstracts,* 1989; U.S. Census Internet Summary, July 15, 1991).

This large number of single people is surprising because humans need companionship and one function of marriage is companionship. Where do single people find companionship? How do they avoid social isolation? For most, kinship is the answer. Older adults who were widowed or divorced often maintain close contact with their children and grandchildren. In addition, brothers, sisters, and other blood relatives provide social support. When kinship ties fail, close friends and roommates may function as a "substitute family" (Schaie & Willis, 1991a).

In trying to avoid isolation, people are not only forming substitute families, but they are also creating new family forms. The two most common are unwed teenage mothers and homosexual couples.

There are almost as many single-person families in the United States as there are traditional families. Staying close to friends or relatives helps single people avoid isolation.

Unwed Mothers

Since 1970, there has been a dramatic increase in the percentage of births to unwed mothers. As you can see in figure 11.4, in 1990, 20 percent of Euro-American births were to unmarried women and 65 percent of Black American births were to unmarried women (*Statistical Abstracts,* 1993, No. 101). Many of these births were to teenage mothers. For the past 20 years, about 1 out of every 10 teenage females has been impregnated (Gilchrist & Schinke, 1987). Historically, about 40 percent of these pregnancies were terminated, but the remaining 60 percent resulted in babies. Not only have there been many babies born to teenage mothers, but there will continue to be even more in the future. For example, between 1986 and 1991, there was a 24 percent increase in the birth rate for girls between the ages of 15 and 19 (U.S. Bureau of Census, *Statistical Abstracts,* 1993, No. 101).

What happens to these babies? Most of them are kept by their teenage mothers, rather than put up for adoption. Unfortunately, the typical unwed teenage mother—despite her lack of skill, experience, and economic resources—ends up being the head of the family.

These young women, together with divorced mothers of dependent children, form a group called "female-headed families." About one-fourth of all families headed by someone under age 25 is a single-parent family. Of these single-parent families, over 95 percent are headed by a female (Bronfenbrenner, 1975). Since most of these female-headed families live below the poverty line, some economists have decried the "feminization of poverty" in

Figure 11.4

Births to Unmarried White and Black Women Between 1970 and 1990

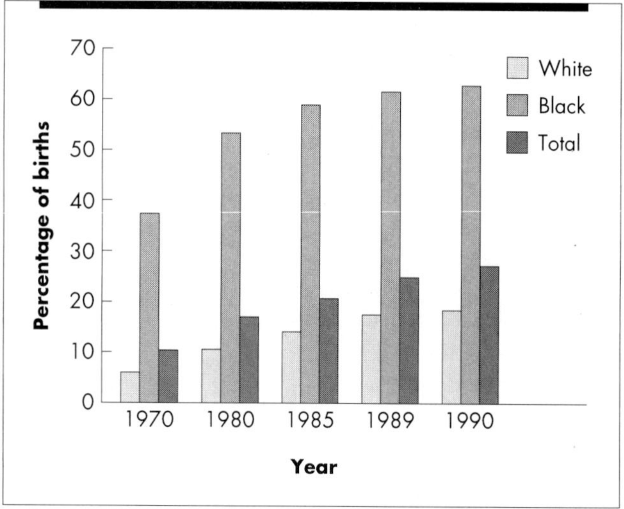

America. Unfortunately, as Mussen et al. (1979) explain, poverty exacerbates the problems confronting female-headed families:

> When one realizes that in single-parent families, the mother is likely to be working, the number of children in the family is likely to be large, and the family is likely to be faced with all the burdens of poverty, including inadequate housing and deteriorating neighborhoods, the strain in the family becomes particularly evident. (p. 389)

Homosexuals

Although less common than the single parent houschold, the homosexual family is becoming more visible. The reason for this greater visibility is increased societal acceptance and awareness, not an increase in homosexuality. According to experts, the percentage of homosexuals in the United States is about the same today as it was in the 1940s—2 to 4 percent of males and 1 percent of females (U.S. Census, 1992; Kinsey, Pomeroy, & Martin, 1948; Hyde, 1986).

In discussing homosexual family forms, it's important to distinguish between the types of relationships formed between gay men and those formed between lesbians. Generally, lesbians seek more stable monogamous relationships with women from a similar social class. Like heterosexual females, lesbians consider promiscuity offensive and immoral.

Gay men, on the other hand, often seek out strangers or men from other social classes and races. Although they may have the same roommate/lover for years, it is common for them to have relationships with other men. (However, the AIDS epidemic may encourage homosexual males to be more monogamous than they have been.) Despite their promiscuity, the gay roommate relationship may be very supportive, and in some ways is like a marriage between a man and woman. For example, division of labor often resembles that of a husband and wife.

For some homosexual couples, their relationship is so much like that of a married couple that they may even mark the beginning of their "family" by a marriage ceremony. Children from a previous heterosexual marriage may reside with the couple. Such couples even resemble married heterosexual couples on measures of psychological adjustment.

Yet, society usually refuses to accept the idea that homosexual couples are like heterosexual couples.[2] Consequently, homosexual couples face barriers that most married couples don't. Homosexual couples face rejection, scorn, revulsion, and even violence from family members and the community. Ties to parents, siblings, and children are frequently strained and may even be broken. Even when children wish to live with their homosexual parent, homosexuals have great difficulty gaining custody of their children. Furthermore, homosexuals are discriminated against when they try to adopt children. (Table 11.7 summarizes some statistics about families.)

Focus on Parents and Children: Child-Rearing Styles

As society's reaction to homosexual families illustrates, our society still believes that traditional family forms are best equipped to deal with child rearing. Although people in our society agree that traditional family forms provide the best structure for rearing children, many individuals disagree about how parents should behave. If 10 different parents are asked, "What is the best way to raise children so they become productive members of society?" they will probably give 10 different answers. Rather than providing contradictory opinions, let's look at what research has to say about this important question.

Parenting Styles

Research shows that effective parents possess several qualities. Effective parents are not permissive. They exert clear control over their children. However, they exert that control without being too restrictive. Effective parents are consistent, warm, and affectionate; they are good communicators; and they rarely use physical punishment. In this section, we will show you the research supporting these conclusions.

Degree of Control

In a classic study, Diana Baumrind (1967) observed a group of nursery school students for 14 weeks. At the

[2] However, in 1989, the state of New York ruled that gay and lesbian couples can be considered families.

Table 11.7

Statistics and the Traditional Family

Chances that a household involves a married couple with children: **less than 1 in 3**

Chances that a household involves only one person: **almost 1 in 3**

Chances that a divorced woman will remarry: **3 in 4**

Chances that a divorced man will remarry: **more than 3 in 4**

Chances that a child will go through a divorce: **about 4 in 10**

Chances that a teenager will get pregnant: **about 1 in 10**

Chances that a family headed by someone under the age of 25 is headed by only one parent: **about 1 in 4**

If a family is headed by only one parent, chances that the parent is a woman: **about 19 out of 20**

Chances that a woman is a homosexual: **about 1 in 100**

Chances that a man is a homosexual: **perhaps as high as 4 in 100**

Box 11.10

SELF-CHECK

Indicate whether each of the following statements is true or false.

1. More than half of all households in the United States are occupied by married couples with children.
2. Since about half of all marriages end in divorce, about half of all children will have parents who have divorced.
3. Research evidence suggests that parents should stay together for the sake of their children.
4. Perhaps because the roles of stepparents and stepchildren are not well defined, relationships between stepparents and stepchildren are usually strained.
5. There are almost as many households headed by a single person as there are traditional families.
6. Almost 10 percent of the U.S. population is homosexual.

Please turn to the end of this chapter to check your answers.

completion of her naturalistic observations, she classified the children into three distinct groups based on their behavior:

1. Energetic-friendly children,
2. Conflicted-irritable children, and
3. Impulsive-aggressive children.

Baumrind then studied the parents of these children and found distinct patterns of parental behavior that correspond to each type of child.

As you can see in table 11.8, **authoritarian parenting** is too restrictive and punitive. In Baumrind's study, this behavior apparently produced conflicted-irritable children. That is, children reared by an overly restrictive parent learn to conform, to fear authority, and to suppress curiosity and initiative. Such children are obedient and polite, but stifled. Indeed, some of these children are outwardly submissive, but harbor resentment and frustration. In other words, parental restrictiveness may produce outward conformity at the cost of inner turmoil. Later, as adults, restrictively reared individuals may express this turmoil and resentment by lashing out against others or by being self-aggressive (such as being involved in drug and alcohol abuse), even to the point of being suicidal. One of the common links in predicting the eating disorders anorexia nervosa (self-starving disease) and bulimia (gorging and then purging) is the presence of overly restrictive and demanding parents.

At the other extreme, **permissive parenting** is too lax and produced impulsive/aggressive children. In Baumrind's study, such children had little direction and even less concern for the rights and needs of others. As compared to other children, children reared permissively tend to be more disorderly, more aggressive, more assertive, and more uninhibited.

Baumrind (1971) thinks that both authoritarian and permissive styles are based on outdated and incorrect views of children—as creatures who are dominated by egoistic, impulsive forces. The strict, authoritarian parent believes that these tendencies must be restrained: "The little devils must be kept in line." The permissive parent glorifies these primitive expressive tendencies, justifying them as refreshing, natural, and honest. Baumrind finds that neither group takes into account their child's needs and reasoning abilities.

According to Baumrind's research, **authoritative parenting** is a democratic style of parenting that encourages children to be independent while placing realistic limits, demands, and controls on their behavior. Authoritative parents realize that neither restrictiveness nor permissiveness is the answer. Restrictiveness ignores the fact that children have certain needs, needs that vary depending on the child's developmental level. Therefore, effective parents are careful to introduce a calm, warm, supportive, and comfortable tone in their interactions and deliberations. Permissiveness, on the other hand, ignores the fact that some of

Table 11.8

Patterns of Parental Control and Corresponding Patterns of Children's Behavior

Parental Classification	Children's Behavioral Profile
Authoritative parenting	*Energetic-friendly* Self-reliant Self-controlled Cheerful and friendly Copes with stress Cooperates with adults Curious Purposive Achievement oriented
Authoritarian parenting	*Conflicted-irritable* Fearful, apprehensive Moody, unhappy Easily annoyed Passively hostile Vulnerable to stress Aimless Sulky, unfriendly
Permissive parenting	*Impulsive-aggressive* Rebellious Low in self-reliance and self-control Impulsive Aggressive Domineering Aimless Low in achievement

the child's behavior should not be glorified, but recognized for what it is—immaturity. To help children outgrow this immaturity, effective parents exert clear controls over their child's behavior and expect their child to behave as maturely as possible—given the child's developmental stage. That is, these firmly controlling parents explain the reasons for rules. Furthermore, when making new rules, these parents often let children participate in the rule making.

Children of authoritative parents have more self-confidence and self-reliance than children of other kinds of parents. As adolescents, these children are more achievement oriented, less likely to abuse drugs, and are less likely to have other behavior problems (Baumrind, 1991). In addition, these adolescents score higher on indices of psychological development and mental health including self-esteem, social integration, and the ability to make independent decisions (Dougherty, 1993). Why?

One possibility is that the child of authoritative parents feels more in control than other children because rules are consistently enforced and because children get to discuss the formation of new rules. The firm enforcement of rules helps the child feel in control (just as a rat in a Skinner box who always gets a pellet when he presses the bar probably feels in charge, even though this feeling is the result of the experimenter's consistent enforcement of a rule). Letting children in on discussions of new rules gives them some feeling of control over what rules are adopted. Thus, the authoritative parent restricts the child without destroying the child's sense of having a choice.

However, as with any correlational research, there are many other possible reasons for the relationship between authoritative parenting style and enhanced self-esteem. If authoritative parents are wealthier, better educated, or more secure in their marriage than other parents, these factors—rather than parenting style—may account for their children's high self-esteem. Yet another possibility is that the child's natural disposition may determine parenting style. If the child is born good-natured and conforming, parents may tend to develop an authoritative style. If, on the other hand, the child is born bad-natured, these same parents may adopt a different parenting style (Ambert, 1992; Lerner, 1994).

Degree of Communication

Baumrind's research not only showed that effective parents exert moderate control, but that effective parents communicate well with their children. In fact, research shows that good communication can moderate the effects of parental restrictiveness or permissiveness. For example, Baldwin (1955, 1967) found that restrictive parents with good communication skills spoke to their children at an appropriate level and explained the reasons behind rules and punishment. These parents were likely to produce a competent and self-assertive child. Restrictive parents with poor communication skills, on the other hand, did not help their children understand "why" they must behave in a certain way. Rather, they demanded "blind" obedience. Such parents were likely to produce an obedient, withdrawn, suggestible child; lacking in curiosity, originality, and affection.

How parents and children communicate changes as both age. Older children increasingly resist being externally controlled and actively negotiate. As adolescents demand more independence, most parents respond by granting their teenagers more autonomy in making their own decisions. Gradually, the parent-child relationship becomes less parent dominated and more democratic (Steinberg et al., 1981; Youniss & Smollar, 1985).

Conclusions About Parenting Styles

Although psychology has a long way to go before we can claim to understand the processes by which parental styles affect children, we can give a few words of advice to parents. First, extreme permissiveness or extreme restrictiveness is harmful. Second, both permissiveness and

Box 11.11

SELF-CHECK

PART A

Indicate whether each of the following statements is true or false.

1. Authoritative parents are too restrictive.
2. Permissive parents tend to have aggressive children.
3. According to Baumrind, children have strong, healthy, natural, honest impulses that should be expressed rather than be restrained.
4. Permissive parents have children who are more confident than the children of either authoritarian or authoritative parents.
5. Restrictive parents who have good communication skills tend to have children who are well-adjusted.
6. Children seem to like having rules when those rules are consistently enforced.
7. Using physical punishment on children appears to produce aggressive children.

PART B

Answer the following questions.

8. Who will tend to be more aggressive? (a) a child with permissive but hostile parents, (b) a child with restrictive and hostile parents, (c) a child with permissive and warm parents.
9. According to the research reviewed in this section, what should a parent do to have a well-adjusted child?

Please turn to the end of this chapter to check your answers.

physical punishment contribute to aggressiveness. Third, warmth and effective communication spiced with a moderate degree of control seem to produce a relatively happy, well-adjusted child. Finally, remember that children are resilient: They can recover from the inevitable mistakes that parents make.

EFFECTS OF FAMILY STRUCTURE

The parents' child-rearing styles are one obvious way in which the family influences the child's development. But other, less obvious, aspects also affect the child's development. In the next few sections, we'll look at two structural factors that may affect development—family size and birth order.

Family Size

The size of the average American family is shrinking because Americans are having fewer children than in the past (Dunn, 1990). This trend toward having fewer children will probably continue. In fact, a February 1985 Gallup poll found the smallest proportion of people desiring large families since Gallup began collecting information on these preferences in 1936.

Research suggests that the trend toward smaller families may pay off in smarter children. Zajonc and his associates (1979) concluded that later-born children from large families are often less intelligent than their older siblings because they receive less attention and stimulation from their parents. That is, because parents have only so much time and energy, any new arrivals must compete with existing siblings for their time. Often, older children will step in to care for their younger siblings, but the care that a child can give to another child is not of the quality that a parent can give to a child. As Zajonc (1976) writes, ". . . any infant you can subtract (from the family) raises the intellectual quality of the environment." Zajonc's work has special implications for children born to poor families because the poor are more likely to have large families. Thus, children of poor, large families face two disadvantages: starting off with less wealth than others and having less of a chance to improve their lot because of inadequate stimulation during childhood.

Birth Order

Zajonc's work also suggests that children in a given family may not be equally affected by family size. The impact of family size depends partly on the child's ordinal position within the family, for example, whether the child was the firstborn, second-born, or third-born.

If ordinal position is relevant in determining intelligence, is it relevant for personality? This is an idea that social scientists have speculated about for more than 100 years (Henderson, 1981). Some of these speculations are now popular beliefs. One such belief is that firstborn children, who initially enjoy an exclusive relationship with their parents, will remain forever closer to their parents than later-born siblings. Another popular idea is that laterborns will grow up to be more likable and popular than firstborns because they have had to acquire important social skills to deal with their older and more powerful siblings. Do these popularly accepted claims have any merit (see table 11.9)? Are firstborns different from laterborns? If so, how do they differ? And why do they differ?

Characteristics of Firstborns

In a sense, a firstborn may be regarded as a "practice baby" on which the parents learn (through trial and error) how to parent. Often, parents are more anxious with their firstborn and have stronger preconceptions about what a child is supposed to be like. Furthermore, because this firstborn initially does not have to compete with other siblings for parental attention, this child receives more attention during his or her early months. Later children often wonder why their parents took more pictures and completed the baby book on the eldest sibling, but for some reason have few records of the laterborns' early months.

What are the consequences of greater parental involvement for these firstborns? There is strong evidence that firstborns are more achievement oriented than laterborns (Schachter, 1963; Warren, 1966). For example, firstborns score higher on tests of achievement motivation and hold higher educational aspirations than laterborns (Glass, Neulinger, & Brim, 1974; Sampson & Hancock, 1967). Among college students, firstborns are overrepresented in "Who's Who" and among Rhodes scholars. In addition, firstborns are overrepresented among eminent scholars.

Firstborns also tend to have higher IQs than laterborns (Zajonc, Markus, & Markus, 1979). Furthermore, firstborns score higher on tests of English and mathematical achievement (Eysenck & Cookson, 1969; Paulus & Shaffer, 1981) and verbal reasoning (Kelleghan & MacNamara, 1972).

Perhaps because they are more achievement oriented, firstborn males also tend to be more anxious and aggressive toward their peers (Lahey, Hammer, Crumrine, & Forehand, 1980; Schachter, 1959). Firstborns also tend to be more conforming, more adult-oriented, more honest, more helpful, and more self-controlled.

What, specifically, accounts for the personality profile of firstborns? The positive characteristics of firstborns may simply be the result of firstborns getting more attention from their parents than other children. However, there are other possibilities. For example, the positive attributes of firstborns may be due to the fact that parents expect more from their firstborns and are more critical of their firstborns (Baskett, 1985).

Unfortunately, some of the same pressures that prompt the development of positive characteristics such as achievement orientation may also promote negative side effects, such as guilt, anxiety, fear, and ineffective means of coping with stress. Consequently, firstborns have higher rates of admission to child guidance clinics and are less independent, less self-confident, less socially poised, and less popular than their younger siblings.

Characteristics of Laterborns

Research on laterborns is more difficult to interpret than research on firstborns because of the variety and complexity of family roles. Whereas the firstborn was influenced by just Mom and Dad, a laterborn may be influenced by one or several siblings. The gender, age, and personality of these siblings will modify the effect of the parents. For example, Sutton-Smith and Rosenberg (1970) found that second-born sons with an older sister were more feminine than firstborn sons with an older brother. Similarly, Jolley (1989) found that firstborn daughters who had younger brothers were more masculine than firstborn daughters who had younger sisters.

In general, laterborns have better peer relationships than firstborns. For example, one study found that lastborns were the most popular with peers, middle children moderately popular, and firstborns least popular (Miller & Maruyama, 1976).

Only Children

According to popular myth, only children have little in common with firstborns. Instead, only children are commonly depicted as "spoiled brats," possessing such undesirable characteristics as dependency, egotism, lack of self-control, and emotional disorders.

This depiction is pure fiction. Research has shown that only children are no more selfish, lonely, or maladjusted than anyone else. Instead, like firstborns, only children tend to be above average in motivation to achieve and intelligence. One explanation for only children being above average in motivation is that, like firstborns, their parents demand more from them. However, Zajonc (1976) would claim that the reason only children are above average in intelligence is that, like firstborns, their parents gave them more attention.

In addition to sharing two of the firstborn's advantages, only children have two advantages over firstborns: Only children aren't displaced by later children, nor do they have to compete with other children for their parents' attention. The advantage of this sustained relationship with their parents apparently translates into only children having higher self-esteem and greater social competence than firstborns (Falbo & Polit, 1986).

Sibling Interaction

Despite the research documenting the good qualities of only children, very few of our students think it would be a good idea to have only one child. They feel that the only child will be a lonely or bored child, whereas the child with several brothers and sisters will benefit from the increased opportunities for interaction. Is there any evidence to support our students' commonsense hunches about the benefits of having several children?

As our students point out, every time you add a family member, you dramatically increase the number of interactions between family members. Thus, for couples in

Family Structure	Personality Tendency	Alternative Explanation
Large family	Slightly lower IQ.	Children from larger families may be poorer. Poverty, not family size, may cause the lower IQ.
Only child	Above average in motivation to achieve and IQ.	People who choose to have only one child may be above average in motivation and IQ, and they may pass those genes on to their child.
Firstborns	Above average in motivation to achieve and IQ. Below average in self-esteem and social skills.	Effect may be due to being born to younger parents or to seeing family's standard of living decline as siblings are added.
Laterborns	Tend to have better peer relationships than earlier borns.	Effect may be due to being born to older parents.

Table 11.9

Does Birth Order Make a Difference?

We cannot say that there is a causal relationship between the structure of your family and your personality. However, we can say that there is a relationship. We have listed some of the main relationships along with possible alternative explanations for these relationships.

the childless stage, the number of interactions is just two (husband to wife, and wife to husband). However, with the addition of just one child, the number of interactions jumps to six (mom to child, child to mom, father to child, child to father, wife to husband, husband to wife). Adding a second child produces 12 interactions, and a third produces 20 interactions.

What are the effects of additional interactions? That depends, of course, on the nature of these interactions. As Zajonc points out, increasing the number of interactions by increasing the number of children will decrease the intellectual level of the interactions. In addition, the more potential interactions there are, the more potential there is for conflict. Conflict is especially likely if children are forced to divide scarce resources, such as housing space and material possessions, if the children are similar in age, or if one of the children is highly aggressive. Unfortunately, unpleasant interactions with one's siblings can interfere with forming friendships with peers (Hartup, 1992).

Of course, children are not constantly battling their siblings and parents. They do share and cooperate—if these behaviors are modeled and encouraged by parents. Parents especially encourage and expect the oldest child to avoid conflict with and assume some responsibility for younger siblings—even though these younger siblings displaced the firstborn as the center of attention. Thus, although older children often feel jealousy and hostility toward their younger brothers and sisters, if the older child expresses this resentment, parents are likely to rebuke them for it. Parents tend to be protective of the younger children.

Despite the fact that parents tend to side with the younger siblings, the oldest child has some advantages over the younger children. Because she is the most dominant and competent child, she is more capable of bullying, assisting, and teaching her younger siblings. Consequently, older siblings have been found to show both more antagonistic (kicking, hitting, and biting) and more prosocial, nurturant behaviors toward their siblings (Abramovitch, Pepler, & Corter, 1982).

Having siblings can be an advantage or a disadvantage. There is an increased chance for conflict, but also an increased chance for positive interaction and nurturing behavior.

In summary, from a developmental psychology perspective, there are pros and cons to having a larger family. On the con side, there is the fact that only children do quite well. Only children seem to benefit from having more interaction with parents and from not being supplanted by other siblings. Peers seem to fulfill any needs that would otherwise be met by siblings. Also on the con side is the fact that children often do resent each other, and larger families have more conflict. Finally, on the con side, the more children, the less happy marriages tend to be. On the pro side, siblings do tend to like each other—even though their ambivalence toward each other often lasts a lifetime. In addition, if you are one of the very few people who would not enjoy the empty nest, having a full nest extends the time before you have to confront an empty nest. Finally, the more children, the more opportunities for grandchildren—and grandchildren are a great source of joy for many people.

Box 11.12

SELF-CHECK

Indicate whether each of the following statements is true or false.

1. The size of the average American family is shrinking.
2. According to Zajonc, children from smaller families tend to be smarter than children from larger families.
3. Firstborns are smarter and more achievement oriented than laterborns.
4. Firstborns are more conforming, more self-controlled, more adult-oriented, more honest, and more anxious than laterborns.
5. Firstborns are more self-confident and more popular than laterborns.
6. It is easier for researchers to determine the characteristics of firstborns than of laterborns because the effect of being a laterborn seems to depend on the characteristics of the older siblings.
7. Only children are not very similar to firstborns.
8. Firstborns are better adjusted than only children.
9. Unpleasant interactions with one's siblings can interfere with forming friendships with peers.
10. Older children assume responsibility for their younger siblings, even though they feel jealousy and hostility toward these siblings.
11. For only children, peers seem to fulfill any needs that would have otherwise been met by siblings.
12. Siblings feel ambivalence toward each other, an ambivalence that lasts a lifetime.

Please turn to the end of this chapter to check your answers.

Nature and Nurture Revisited

We have devoted much of this chapter to discussing a question that most of our students consider important: How does the family affect our development? Asking this question assumes, of course, that the family does affect development. Most people have no trouble with this assumption. In fact, when asked to list factors that determined their development, our students invariably put their family as the number one influence.

However, as you have seen in this chapter, two groups of researchers have questioned the importance of the family on development. One set of researchers have pointed out that many of the similarities between children and other family members may not be due to a common environment but to common genes. A second group of researchers argue that children are not as similar to other family members as we may assume. Although the two sets of researchers are looking at different kinds of data, both are suggesting that you might be basically the same person you are today if you had been born to your current parents, but reared by different parents.

What is their evidence for this position? Is this solid evidence or can it be interpreted in other ways? In the following sections, we will address these questions.

Twin Research

Years of studying twins has convinced Professor Thomas J. Bouchard Jr. that genes exert more influence on personality and intelligence than the family. He finds that, on personality and intelligence tests, identical twins reared apart resemble each other to practically the same degree as identical twins raised in the same family. This corroborates earlier evidence (Loehlin & Nichols, 1976) that twins who said their parents treated them very differently were just as much alike as twins who said their parents treated them similarly. Furthermore, Bouchard and his associates find that identical twins reared apart are more similar to one another than fraternal twins reared in the same family (Bouchard, 1983; Holden, 1987; McGue & Bouchard, 1984; Rosen, 1987; Tellegen et al., 1988).

In addition to data from personality and intelligence tests, Bouchard and his colleagues can point to the intriguing stories about identical twins raised apart who are reunited as adults. For example, Rosen describes the case of identical twins Jerry Levey and Mark Newman. They were adopted by different parents shortly after birth and grew up not knowing they were twins. An observant friend of Mark's was responsible for reuniting the twins when he noticed Jerry in a bar and couldn't get over how closely Jerry resembled Mark.

After establishing that Mark and Jerry had the same birthday, a meeting between the twins was arranged. Jerry reports his first reaction to seeing his twin for the first time, "Lop off the extra pounds and I was looking in the mirror," he says. "We had the same mustache, same sideburns, even the same glasses." They not only looked alike, but both brothers were heads of fire departments and drank only Budweiser; both held the bottle with the little finger stretched awkwardly beneath the bottom. Both were bachelors, both compulsive flirts, both raucously good-humored. "We kept making the same remarks at the same time and using the same gestures," says Jerry. "It was spooky."

On the surface, Bouchard's personality test data and anecdotes about reunited twins make a convincing case for heredity being much more important than the family. However, critics, such as Urie Bronfenbrenner (1986), urge that we look beneath the surface. The anecdotes about reunited twins could, as Bouchard would admit, be due to coincidence: If you study enough people, they are bound to find things in common.

Under closer inspection, the personality test data also lose much of their persuasiveness. Many of the twins had interacted intensively for months before visiting Bouchard's lab. Thus, similarities in attitudes might be due to their influencing one another. Furthermore, just because two people are raised in different families doesn't mean they were raised in dissimilar environments. To test this assumption, Bronfenbrenner (1975) recalculated correlations on subgroups of twins sharing common environments. He found that when separated twins were raised in the same town the correlation between their Binet IQ scores was 0.83. However, when they were raised in different towns the correlations between their IQ scores was less—only 0.67. Furthermore, when the communities were classified as similar versus dissimilar on the basis of size and economic base (for example, mining vs. agricultural), the correlation for separated twins living in similar communities was 0.86; for those residing in dissimilar localities 0.26.

Bronfenbrenner's work suggests that environment plays a significant role in intelligence. What about the specific influence of the home environment? To answer this question Betty Caldwell and Robert Bradely developed a measure called the HOME inventory that assesses the home environment on six subscales (see table 11.10). Bradely and Caldwell (1980) as well as Helen Bee et al. (1982) have found that the quality of the home environment measured when children were either 6 or 12 months old is a better predictor of their IQs at ages 3 and 4 than their infant intelligence tests scores. Both boys and girls who obtain high IQ scores had mothers who were highly involved with them, who provided an orderly environment, and provided lots of age-appropriate toys. For girls, the added factors of having a highly responsive and nonpunitive caretaker who provided them with a variety of new experiences on a regular basis was also important (Bradely & Caldwell, 1980). However, as Plomin (1991) points out, the home environment does not just magically appear—the home environment is a product of many forces, including genetics. For example, the genes of intelligent parents may be expressed not only in their children, but in the parents' own actions of producing a stimulating home environment. Furthermore, an intelligent child may reward parents for providing her with a stimulating environment (Reiss, 1993).

Adoption Studies

Looking at twins is only one way to look at the effect of family. Another tactic is to see whether an adopted child becomes like the family that adopted her. As some might have predicted, this research found that the adopted child does not resemble other family members. But the research also discovered something that no one would have predicted: Biologically related family members don't resemble one another either (Scarr, 1982; Scarr & Weinberg, 1983; Loehlin, Willerman & Horn, 1982; Loehlin, Willerman & Horn, 1985)! As Loehlin, Horn, & Willerman (1989) wrote, "Shared genes plus shared environments do not seem to make family members much alike."

How can we account for these startling results? We can't merely discount them. They have been replicated by several researchers and dovetail with some of the twin research. For example, Tellegen et al. (1988) tried to track down the effect of the family on personality by simply looking at the degree to which twins raised in the same family were more similar to one another than twins raised apart. Of 11 personality traits he looked at, only one—social closeness—was noticeably affected by the family.

Do these results mean that family experience has no influence on personality development? Not necessarily. It probably means that the effect of a family on children is not uniform: Parents who want to instill outgoingness in their children will probably not end up with an outgoing group of children. Parental efforts may end up making one child more outgoing than he would naturally be, but another less outgoing than she would naturally be (Plomin, 1989).

Why doesn't the family exert a uniform effect on their children? One possibility is that a good family environment helps the individual to fulfill her genetic potential, but that potential is different for each individual. Another possibility is suggested by the finding that fraternal twins are more similar to one another than regular siblings. This finding can't be due to genetics, because fraternal twins are no more similar genetically than regular siblings. The greater similarity of fraternal twins is probably due to sharing the same cultural environment during their formative years and sharing essentially the same basic birth order. In other words, the finding that fraternal twins resemble one another and that regular siblings don't, supports the main theme of family life-cycle approaches: To know how a child will develop, we need to know not only their parents' approach to child rearing, but also the cultural environment during their formative years, the quality of interactions with their siblings, family size, and their birth order.

Conclusions

In this chapter, we have followed the family's influence throughout the life cycle. In the process, we have stressed four themes.

First, we have emphasized that families are not as unchanging as people often think. That is, people seem to like to think that individual families don't change. Such is not the case. As the family life-cycle approach illustrates, change, rather than stability, characterizes the family. Change may also characterize the influence of the family. For example, Plomin (1991) suggests that the effects of the family on IQ are strong

Table 11.10

Subscales and Sample Items from the HOME Inventory

Subscale 1: Emotional and Verbal Responsivity of the Mother (11 items)

Sample items:

- Mother responds to child's vocalizations with a verbal response.
- Mother's speech is clear, distinct, and audible.
- Mother caresses or kisses child at least once during visit.

Subscale 2: Avoidance of Restriction and Punishment (8 items)

Sample items:

- Mother neither slaps nor spanks child during visit.
- Mother does not scold or derogate child during visit.
- Mother does not interfere with the child's actions or restrict child's movements more than three times during visit.

Subscale 3: Organization of Physical and Temporal Environment (6 items)

Sample items:

- Child gets out of house at least four times a week.
- Child's play environment appears safe and free of hazards.

Subscale 4: Provisions of Appropriate Play Materials (9 items)

Sample items:

- Child has push or pull toy.
- Parents provide learning equipment appropriate to age—mobile, table and chairs, highchair, playpen, and so on.
- Mother provides toys or interesting activities during interview.

Subscale 5: Maternal Involvement with Child (6 items)

Sample items:

- Mother "talks" to child while doing her work.
- Mother structures the child's play periods.

Subscale 6: Opportunities for Variety in Daily Stimulation (5 items)

Sample items:

- Father provides some caretaking every day.
- Mother reads stories at least three times weekly.
- Child has three or more books of his own.

Questions: Which of these "environmental" subscales are affected by the personality of the parents? If the parents inherited part of their personality, could they also have passed this personality onto their child? If that's true, then parents who provide their child with an intellectual environment may also be providing their child with intellectual genes. Finally, which of these "environmental" subscales could be affected by the child's personality? That is, could the child's genes be partly responsible for his or her environment?

Source: From R. H. Bradley and B. M. Caldwell, "The Relation of Infant's Home Environments to Mental Test Performance at Fifty-four Months: A Follow-up Study" in *Child Development*, 47:1172–1174, 1976.

when the child is living with the parents, but once the child reaches adulthood, the family's effects are negligible.

Second, we have emphasized that families are not as uniform as most people believe. That is, many people seem to believe that, with a few exceptions, all families are basically alike. However, diversity—not uniformity—characterizes U.S. families, as illustrated by the fact that fewer than 30 percent of U.S. households are comprised of "typical" families.

Third, in complex systems such as the family, it is hard to determine what causes what. One example of the difficulty of determining cause and effect is the relationship between the decline of the traditional family and the perceived decline of society. Social commentators often view the family as the cause of societal problems. However, the breakdown of the family may be the result of forces outside of the family. For example, Bronfenbrenner's systems view (1986) is consistent with the idea that the society is causing the breakdown of the family, rather than the family causing the breakdown of society. Similarly, although people may want to blame children's

Box 11.13

SELF-CHECK

Part A

Indicate whether each of the following statements is true or false.

1. Dr. Bouchard has evidence suggesting that, as far as personality is concerned, genes are more important than family environment.
2. Scores on a measure of the family environment (HOME) taken when the infant is less than 1 year old, predict the child's IQ at age 3 better than infant IQ tests.
3. The child has no effect on the type of environment parents provide for him or her.
4. Family members are similar to each other psychologically, possibly because they share common genes and a common environment.

Part B

Answer the following questions.

5. Is finding similarities between identical twins reared apart strong evidence that genes are more important than environment? Why or why not?
6. Bronfenbrenner admits that, overall, there is a strong correlation between the IQs of identical twins who are reared apart. Does he therefore agree that IQ is mostly affected by the environment? Why or why not?
7. Why doesn't a family environment exert a consistent influence on the children?

Please turn to the end of this chapter to check your answers.

behavior on their parents, some research suggests that the parents' behavior depends on the child.

Fourth, we have found that the issue of nature versus nurture is not as straightforward as some would have us believe. Already, we have made enough progress to understand that *both* nature and nurture influence development. However, to go beyond this general statement we must get more detailed descriptions of both genes and the environment. That is, just as we must learn to form detailed maps of the human DNA to pinpoint the effects of heredity, we must also learn how to create accurate and detailed descriptions of the family environment to assess its impact (Reiss, 1993). We can only go so far with vague, general measures of environment, especially those that presume that two people shared the same environment because they grew up in the same family or that two people shared a similar environment because they grew up in families who had similar incomes. Getting richer, more detailed, more microscopic, and more accurate descriptions of the family environment and its effects will be achieved once we try to take a closer look at the social and physical environment of individual family members, analyze how that environment changes through the family life cycle, and analyze how the family environment differs from culture to culture.

Unfortunately, even after we map the human environment as closely as we are trying to map the human genome, we will still not be able to understand the effect of family environment until we figure out which "environmental factors" are really due to genes. To illustrate the challenges of this task, consider the case of the child who is read to and taken to the library more than other children. Some people would say that this child is the beneficiary of a good family environment. However, the truth may be that the child was born with the genes to seek intellectual stimulation. It will be difficult to figure out whether genes or environment are responsible for the child's enriched environment. Yet, despite the difficulties involved in first accurately mapping the family environment and then disentangling which of these "environmental" factors are due to genes, the rewards should justify the efforts. For example, we may eventually be able to specify what type of environment is best for what kind of child, as well as giving detailed descriptions of what parents and society can do to create such an environment.

Summary

1. The family is important to socialization because it introduces us to our culture and society.
2. Social roles are determined by the normative expectations of one's culture, are adapted by the unique requirements of each family, and change over the family lifespan.
3. Family members experience different environments because each family member affects the way that he or she is treated by other members of the family; the family is affected by forces outside of the family (the society, the schools, peers, jobs)—that are always in flux; and the family itself evolves as it goes through a predictable series of developmental stages.

4. The social roles in a family system are interrelated.
5. The major task of married young couples is to adjust from the role of single individual to shared definitions of what a husband and wife are.
6. During the expanding stages, parents must adjust to a decrease in quality time with each other, less freedom and privacy, and greater financial strain.
7. Children detract from the quality of most marriages.
8. The primary task of families with preschool children is to adapt to their children's rapid physical, cognitive, and social development.
9. Parents of school-age children must learn to fit into the community of school-age families in constructive ways.
10. The parents of teenagers must simultaneously let their children struggle for autonomy and be ready with a safety net in case their children falter.
11. As children gain emancipation, parents also gain freedom to concentrate on their own lives and marriage.
12. The postparental years are characterized by rebuilding the marriage relationship and maintaining ties with older and younger kin.
13. The empty nest is often a time of heightened marital satisfaction.
14. Widowhood marks the beginning of the aging families stage. Concerns about finances, health, and life satisfaction are the primary concerns of this stage. Women are much more likely to experience this stage than men, and women are much more likely to adjust successfully to this stage.
15. Perhaps as a reaction to social and economic injustice, African American families have a more equal division of power between husbands and wives, have grandparents who are more active in teaching values to grandchildren, and seem more interested in helping their children succeed than white families.
16. Although there are increasing numbers of stepfamilies, the roles of stepparents and stepchildren are not well defined. Perhaps because these roles are not well defined, relationships between stepparents and stepchildren are usually strained.
17. Although increasing numbers of adults are choosing not to marry, they still have a need for family. This has lead to several alternate forms of family, including single parent and homosexual families.
18. Permissive parents typically provide few guidelines for their children's behavior, are lax with punishment, and encourage their children to freely express ideas and wishes.
19. Restrictive parents provide narrow guidelines, use punishment to coerce their children to behave in desired ways, and provide their children with little freedom.
20. Restrictive parents with good communication skills are likely to produce children who are competent and self-assertive. Those with poor communication skills are likely to produce obedient, withdrawn, and suggestible children.
21. Permissive parents who are inconsistent in their discipline often have emotionally disturbed children.
22. The most aggressive children are produced by permissive—but hostile and punitive—parents.
23. The least aggressive children have parents who are restrictive, but do not use physical punishment.
24. According to Baumrind, restrictive (authoritarian) and permissive parents have unrealistic views of children. She endorses authoritative parenting.
25. It appears that the best way to rear a child is to establish rules; enforce those rules consistently; explain the reasons for those rules; express love, caring, and concern for the child; and avoid physical punishment.
26. Children from smaller families are brighter, on the average, than children from larger families.
27. As compared to laterborns, firstborns are often more achievement oriented, more conforming, more adult oriented, more honest, more helpful, more self-controlled, and more anxious.
28. Only children share many of the positive qualities of firstborns. In addition, only children often have better self-esteem and greater social competence than firstborns.
29. The more children, the more opportunity there is for family conflict.
30. Children reared in the same family are not very similar. Research suggests that one reason for this is that siblings often experience very different family environments.
31. Families are not as unchanging as people may want to believe.
32. Families are not as similar as some people seem to believe.
33. Problems that are blamed on the family may really be the result of larger, more powerful socioeconomic forces.
34. To properly assess the impact of the family environment on children, we must first do a better job of mapping what goes on within the family. Then, we must determine which aspects of the environment are controlled by the parents rather than by the child. Finally, we must determine which types of environments are best suited for which types of children. Once we do these three things, we will be able to give clear, sound, and detailed advice about how parents should rear their children.

Key Terms

authoritarian parenting 359
authoritative parenting 359
contracting stage 350
developmental task 341
empty-nest syndrome 350
familial developmental tasks 341
family 340
family career 342
family life-cycle approach 339
permissive parenting 359

Self-Check Answers

Box 11.2

Part A:
1. False.
2. True.
3. True.

Part B:
4. Family members experience different environments because (a) each family member creates his or her own environment. The environment each creates will depend on genes; (b) the family is affected by outside forces, forces that are always changing; and (c) the family goes through a predictable series of developmental stages.
5. The family life-cycle approach.

Box 11.3

Part A:
1. True; **2.** True; **3.** True; **4.** True; **5.** False; **6.** False; **7.** False; **8.** True; **9.** False.

Part B:
10. Common developmental tasks include toilet training, entering school, achieving economic independence, getting married, and retirement.

Box 11.5

Part A:
1. True; **2.** False; **3.** True; **4.** False; **5.** False; **6.** False. See Box 11.4; **7.** True; **8.** True; **9.** False.

Part B:
10. People have children because children (a) provide cheap labor and retirement income, (b) can protect the family and the country, (c) can add to the numbers of certain groups that feel threatened if their numbers decrease, and (d) offer promise for a better future.
11. Crying. Infants often cry when overstimulated.
12. Many tasks cannot be mastered until the child is biologically mature enough to do those tasks.

Box 11.6

1. True; **2.** True; **3.** True; **4.** True; **5.** False; **6.** False.

Box 11.8

1. False; **2.** True; **3.** True; **4.** False; **5.** False; **6.** True; **7.** False; **8.** True; **9.** True; **10.** True; **11.** True; **12.** False; **13.** False; **14.** False.

Box 11.9

1. False; **2.** True; **3.** True; **4.** False; **5.** True; **6.** False.

Box 11.10

1. False.
2. False. A more reasonable projection is that 39 percent of all children may experience marital disruption before age 15. Even though half of all marriages end in divorce, some of these divorces will happen after the children have left, and some will involve people who have been married several times before.
3. False.
4. True.
5. True.
6. False.

Box 11.11

Part A:
1. False; **2.** True; **3.** False; **4.** False; **5.** True; **6.** True; **7.** True.

Part B:
8. (a) Permissive, but hostile parents will have children who tend to echo their own emotional character.
9. Establish rules and enforce them consistently; explain the reasons for the rules; don't use physical punishment; express love, caring, and concern for the child.

Box 11.12

1. True; **2.** True; **3.** True; **4.** True; **5.** False; **6.** True; **7.** False; **8.** False; **9.** True; **10.** True; **11.** True; **12.** True.

Box 11.13

Part A:
1. True; **2.** True; **3.** False; **4.** False.

Part B:
5. No. The similarities may be due to coincidence or the similarities may be due to being reared in similar environments.
6. No. When identical twins are reared in similar environments, their IQs are highly correlated. However, when twins are reared in dissimilar environments, the correlations between their IQ scores are small.
7. First, the effect of the family environment interacts with the child's genetic potential. Thus, an environment that is healthy for one child may be harmful for another. Second, there is no one unchanging family environment. The family environment changes as a result of changes in the number of children, changes in parental attitudes, and changes in the society as a whole.

Chapter

Gender Development

Anatomy is destiny.
Sigmund Freud

In our civilization, men are afraid that they will not be men enough and women are afraid that they might be considered only women.
Theodore Reik

Chapter Overview

When a baby is born in a hospital, the physician's first words aren't "It's healthy," but "It's a boy" or "It's a girl." Similarly, the sex of the child is the first thing that friends and relatives want to know about the newborn (Itons-Peterson & Reddel, 1984). Some parents can't wait for the baby's birth to find out the sex of their child. For example, some parents are willing to do prenatal testing that poses a risk to their unborn child's life merely to find out the fetus's sex. In rare cases, people have even been known to abort a fetus of the "wrong" (usually female) sex.

Why are people so concerned about the baby's biological sex? Because society assigns different gender roles to the two sexes. Biological males are supposed to act in what society considers a "masculine" way. Biological females are supposed to act in what society considers a "feminine" way. In teaching these gender roles, people believe that they are simply encouraging the natural differences between the sexes. But which differences are natural and which differences are created by society? After discussing this question, we will focus the rest of the chapter on another question: How do people learn society's gender roles?

Psychological Differences Between Males and Females

The physical differences between men and women are obvious. The reasons for these differences are also clear-cut—chromosomes and hormones. The psychological differences between men and women, on the other hand, are subtle—and the reasons for these differences are far from clear-cut.

Popular ideas about the ways men and women differ (see table 12.1) are, for the most part, misconceptions. For example, you may be surprised to know that, when Maccoby & Jacklin (1974) first reviewed over 1,600 studies looking for sex differences, they found that very few psychological differences actually existed between the sexes. Furthermore, some differences that were present at the time Maccoby and Jacklin did their review have virtually disappeared (Feingold, 1988; Hyde, 1994).

Even when popular stereotypes about the way in which men and women differ are correct, these stereotypes grossly exaggerate the extent of sex differences. For instance, people may say that all men are better than women at math; that women can't do math; or that the average male is much better than the average female at math. None of these statements are true.

In actuality, many of the differences between sexes are so tiny that they can be detected only by comparing hundreds of men to hundreds of women. Thus, although such differences may be statistically significant, they may, for practical purposes, be insignificant. For example, a researcher might find, after looking at millions of IQ scores, that right-handed people average one IQ point higher than left-handers. Such a difference would be statistically significant. Would this statistically significant result mean that if you saw a left-hander and a right-hander, that the right-hander would be the more intelligent one? Would it mean that a class of right-handers will do much better than a class of left-handers? The answer to both questions is "no."

As you can imagine, such a statistically significant difference between left-handers and right-handers would be so useless that people would probably ignore such a research finding. However, when equally small differences are found between men and women, people are fascinated. Consequently, frequent references can be found in both professional and popular literature to statistically significant—but minuscule—differences between the sexes.

In the next section, we'll take a close look at what research says about psychological differences between the sexes. As we discuss these differences, please keep two facts in mind. First, not all studies find evidence for these differences. Thus, it may be that some of these differences are very small, hold for only certain groups, or are—as a result of recent changes in how children are educated and socialized—disappearing. Second, sex differences that appear at one age may disappear or even be reversed at another age. Therefore, it is dangerous to apply the results from studies of 6-year-olds to males and females of any age.

Table 12.1

Adjectives Highly Associated with Males or Females

Which of the following characteristics do you associate with each gender?

Associated with Males	Associated with Females
Active	Affectionate
Adventurous	Appreciative
Aggressive	Attractive
Assertive	Changeable
Autocratic	Dreamy
Boastful	Excitable
Coarse	Feminine
Confident	Frivolous
Courageous	Fussy
Cruel	Gentle
Daring	High-strung
Dominant	Inventive
Enterprising	Mild
Forceful	Nagging
Handsome	Poised
Humorous	Sensitive
Lazy	Softhearted
Logical	Sophisticated
Masculine	Submissive
Rational	Sympathetic
Reckless	Talkative
Robust	Timid
Rude	Warm
Sentimental	Weak
Severe	Whiny
Stern	Worrying
Strong	
Tough	
Unemotional	
Unexcitable	

Adapted from J. Williams and D. Best, *Measuring Sex Stereotypes: A 30-Nation Study*, p. 28, copyright ©1982 by Sage Publications, Inc. Reprinted by permission of Sage Publications, Inc.

Personality Differences

We will begin by talking about the sex differences that people are most emotional about—personality differences. Specifically, most people strongly believe that men are more aggressive, whereas women are more empathic,

If you believe this child is a girl, you may interpret the child's behaviors differently than if you believe it is a boy.

nurturing, caring, fearful, anxious, and dependent. Many people strongly believe in these sex differences because they think that their opinions about sex differences are based on what they have actually observed. That is, they think their opinions are not based on unfounded speculation, but on their observations of everyday events.

But are people's observations unbiased? Apparently not. For example, Condry & Condry (1976) had people observe a videotape of an infant. Some of the observers were told that the infant was a boy, others were told that the infant was a girl. The observers who were told that the infant was a boy reported that the infant was showing "anger," but the observers who were told that the infant was a girl reported that she was showing "fear."

John Delk and his colleagues (1986) found similar results with toddlers. Specifically, observers who were told that the toddler on the videotape was a boy "saw" more masculine behaviors than observers who were told that the toddler on the tape was a girl. Because people's biases affect their perceptions, if we want to know the true extent of sex differences, we must take an open-minded look at objective, unbiased, scientific research evidence.

Empathy and Nurturance

In her ground-breaking book, *In a Different Voice,* Carol Gilligan (1982) echoes some popular sentiments about the differences between the sexes. For example, Gilligan claims that women are more cooperative and more concerned with social relations than men. In support of this claim, Gilligan argues that women are more nurturant toward the young, the weak, and the ill and that women have more **empathy,** the identification with and understanding of another's feelings, situation, and motives.

In support of this notion, the amount of empathy that women *claim* to have for others is higher than the amount of empathy that men claim to have for others. In addition, researchers observe that, in many social situations, women are more likely to nurture and care for the physical and emotional needs of others than men (Eagly, 1987; Eagly & Crowley, 1986). For example, girls are more likely than boys to write a letter to a child in a hospital and women are more likely than men to do volunteer work. Furthermore, studies have shown that women are better at reading others' nonverbal emotional cues (Eisenberg & Lennon, 1983; Malatesta, 1990).

Although we have cited evidence suggesting that women are more empathic than men, there is also evidence suggesting that women are not more empathic than men. One reason for the differences between studies is that it is difficult to measure empathy.

If we measure empathy in terms of nurturance or willingness to help another, we still need to decide what type of helping situation we are going to use. In many situations, as we mentioned earlier, women are more willing to help than men. However, men are more willing to help a stranger in distress or to help in risky situations (Eagly, 1987; Tavris & Wade, 1984). Thus, Tavris and Wade (1984) conclude that although males are more likely to help in a "masculine-appropriate" situation and females are more likely to help in a "feminine-appropriate" situation, females are not more helpful than males.

If we measure empathy in terms of self-descriptions, women are clearly more empathic than men. However, as you learned in chapter 1, we should not take self-reports at face value. To illustrate this point, consider a study by Berman (1980). Berman asked both men and women to report their responses to pictures and videos of babies. Although women reported much stronger reactions to pictures and videotapes of babies, there were no differences in the sexes' physiological reactions to these pictures and videotapes. That is, men's and women's heart rates and perspiration were equally affected by looking at babies.

In conclusion, our reading of the evidence is that females are more empathic—but not necessarily more nurturant—than males. We come to the conclusion that women are more empathic because the fact that women are better at reading people's emotions is consistent with the fact that self-report data suggests that women are higher in empathy. However, two points about this conclusion should be emphasized. First, the evidence for this conclusion is not consistent and clear-cut. The inconsistency of the findings that was evident to Eleanor Maccoby and Carol Jacklin more than 30 years ago when they reviewed 1,600 studies of sex differences (Maccoby & Jacklin, 1974) is still evident today. Second, if females are more empathic, these differences may be due to socialization rather than to any innate differences between the sexes.

Fearfulness and Anxiety

Both fearfulness and anxiety are states of arousal characterized by increased heart and respiratory rates, trembling, sweating, and muscle tension. Whereas *fearfulness* is more commonly used to describe reactions to specific objects or situations (fear of dogs, fear of being left alone), **anxiety** is more commonly used to describe a general state of arousal to nonspecific events (a vague feeling of impending disaster).

When studying children who have not yet learned to read or write, most researchers have adult observers rate how fearful or anxious each child is. These observational studies usually fail to find sex differences in fear (Maccoby & Jacklin, 1974; Tavris & Wade, 1984).

When studying children who can read and write, most researchers have children agree or disagree with statements reflecting specific types of fear-provoking situations (for example, "I am afraid of dying" or "I am afraid to be alone in the dark"). In these self-report studies, girls usually report more fears than boys (Maccoby & Jacklin, 1974; Tavris & Wade, 1984).

Why do studies on preliterate children fail to reveal sex differences, whereas studies on literate children conclude that girls are more fearful? One possibility is that sex differences in fear are tied to some maturational event. Another possibility is that girls are taught to fear and it takes time for this teaching to take hold. Hill and Sarason (1966) suggest yet another possibility: Girls and boys don't differ in actual fear, but girls score higher in reported fear because they are more willing to admit and express their fears. This "reporting bias" hypothesis might explain why:

1. There seem to be few differences between the sexes in physiological reactions to fear-provoking stimuli (Tavris & Wade, 1984); and
2. There is little relationship between physiological arousal and self-reported fear (Duffy, 1962).

Dependency

Research suggests that males and females don't differ in emotional dependency during the first few years of life. However, several studies done with older children find females score higher on measures of dependency behavior than males (Mischel, 1970). Apparently, parents expect and encourage their daughters to be dependent, whereas they encourage their sons to be independent. As learning theory would predict, the result of this differential treatment appears to be that both sexes do what they were rewarded for: males emerge as more independent and females as more dependent (Williams, 1987).

Aggression

Aggression is the intent to harm another person or oneself. A large body of research shows that males in all cultures are more aggressive than females (Eagly, 1987). Males are much more likely to commit violent crimes, engage in physical fights, and kill each other in war. The male's greater tendency to physically assault others is evident before the age of 2 (Maccoby & Jacklin, 1974).

DiPietro (1981) demonstrated the early emergence of aggression in males by putting 4-year-old nursery-school children in a room that contained a large, inflated punching doll (commonly referred to as a "Bobo doll"), a trampoline, and other toys. Boys were found to playfully assault one another, wrestle, and hit the doll. Girls were more likely to play with the toys in nonviolent ways, suggest responsible rules, and wait their turns with toys. Furthermore, boys' interactions had less verbal structuring and more unrestrained roughhousing, whereas girls' contact with one another tended to be verbal rather than physical.

Males' higher level of aggressiveness may be tied to hormones. As you learned in chapter 4, males have higher levels of male hormones (androgens), such as testosterone, than females. Furthermore, testosterone has been linked to aggressive behavior. For example, males who receive injections of testosterone become more aggressive. In addition, males who have naturally high levels of male hormones are much more likely to be aggressive (Dabbs, 1994).

Although the literature demonstrates that males are, in general, more aggressive than females, this is not to say that females aren't aggressive. In a review of 63 studies that compared males and females on aggression, Eagly and Steffen (1986) concluded that the tendency for men to aggress more than women is more pronounced for studies looking at aggression that produces pain or physical injury than for aggression that produces psychological or social harm. In other words, men were substantially more physically aggressive than women, but only slightly more verbally aggressive.

Sex differences in aggression were also larger to the extent that:

1. The aggression could seriously harm the target, and
2. The aggression might put oneself in danger.

Thus, some of the difference between the sexes in aggressiveness may be related to their differences in empathy and fearfulness. If women have more empathy for their target, they will be less likely to induce intense harm. If women are more fearful, they may be less likely to do things that would endanger themselves.

Some evidence supports the idea that differences in empathy partially account for sex differences in aggression. For example, sex differences in aggression tend to disappear under two conditions that would decrease empathy for the victim (Eagly, 1987; Hyde, 1986):

1. When men and women don't know who the victim is; and
2. When the victim has done something bad.

Differences in Cognitive Abilities

Just as you and your society have preconceived ideas about personality differences between the sexes, you and your society have preconceived ideas about sex differences in cognitive abilities. However, as you read the next sections, we hope you will keep an open mind. That is, we hope that you will be willing to critically examine popular assumptions about sex differences. For example, ask yourself such questions as: If women are worse than men at math, why do women do better in math courses than men?

Verbal Ability

It is no accident that people have beliefs about sex differences in *both* personality and cognitive domains: Some people believe that differences in mental abilities lead to personality differences. For example, some people postulate that the reason girls may be *less aggressive* than boys is that girls may be *more verbal* than boys. Recall that DiPietro's (1981) research not only demonstrated that boys are more aggressive than girls, but also suggested that girls may be more verbally skilled than boys. Could it be that girls are less likely to be frustrated—and thus less aggressive—with another person because of their superior verbal ability and superior skill at reading nonverbal cues? After all, communications skill training is often successful in making individuals less violent.

There are several problems with the argument that females are less violent than males because females have superior verbal ability. One major problem is that the evidence does not clearly and consistently support the idea that women's verbal ability is *substantially superior* to men's.

On the one hand, most early studies indicated that, during middle childhood, females surpass males in verbal ability. Consequently, Maccoby and Jacklin (1974) originally concluded that females are superior to males in such verbal skills as vocabulary, speech fluency, understanding language, and reading achievement and comprehension. On the other hand, most studies find only very small differences between men and women in verbal ability. Furthermore, this failure to find sizable differences between the sexes is especially true of studies done after 1974 (Feingold, 1988). Indeed, much of the recent research shows no difference between the sexes.

As the result of recent studies, Maccoby (1990) now claims that verbal differences between the sexes have virtually disappeared. Similarly, when Janet Hyde and Marcia Linn (1988) used a mathematical technique to combine the results of 165 studies reporting test results for approximately 1.5 million children, they found virtually no difference between the sexes in verbal ability. Furthermore, men now score higher than women on the verbal portion of the SAT (Rosser, 1989). Thus, it appears that changes in how boys and girls are educated and socialized have decreased sex differences in verbal ability.

Spatial Ability

Whereas research provides only modest support for the idea that women have greater verbal ability than men, research provides stronger support for the idea that men have greater spatial ability than women (Linn & Peterson, 1986). **Spatial ability** is commonly operationalized as the ability to see the relationships between shapes and objects or to visualize what

Figure 12.1

Rod and Frame Test

In the rod and frame task, a person is shown a box with a rod tilted to one side (*a*). The subject is asked to watch the rod as the researcher tilts it in the opposite direction and to say "stop" when the rod is perfectly horizontal (*b*). On the average, the point at which males say "stop" puts the rod closer to a perfectly horizontal position than the point at which females say "stop."

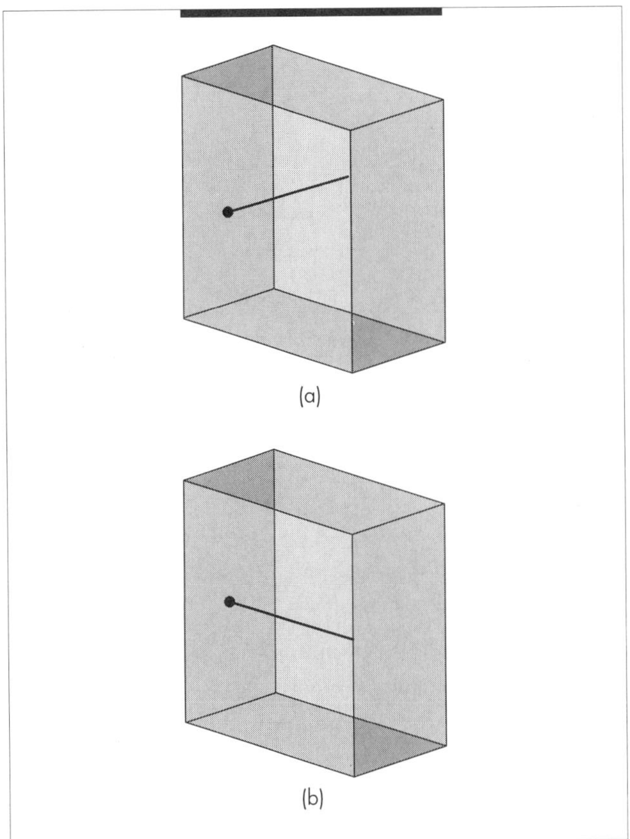

a shape should look like if its orientation in space is changed (see figure 12.1). Common tests of spatial ability include mazes, form matching, puzzles, and copying block designs.

A related concept is **field independence,** the ability to separate an element in a display from its field (background). You may be familiar with the ***Embedded-Figure Test*** (EFT), in which a person attempts to find a specific figure hidden (embedded) in an intricate background or picture (see figure 12.2). Maccoby and Jacklin (1974) found that, on spatial tasks, the average score for groups of boys begins to surpass the average score for groups of girls around age 8 or 9. This lead was maintained beyond adolescence.

Although the notion that males are superior to females on spatial tasks has been widely accepted, critics remind us that the differences are often quite small, especially on tasks like the Embedded-Figure Test (Caplan, MacPherson, & Tobin, 1985; Kimball, 1981; Foley & Cohen, 1984).

Figure 12.2

Embedded-Figure Test

In the *Embedded-Figure Test,* a person is asked to find the figure on the left in the figure on the right. Males are more likely than females to identify the correct embedded figure. (It's the figure that is second from the left.)

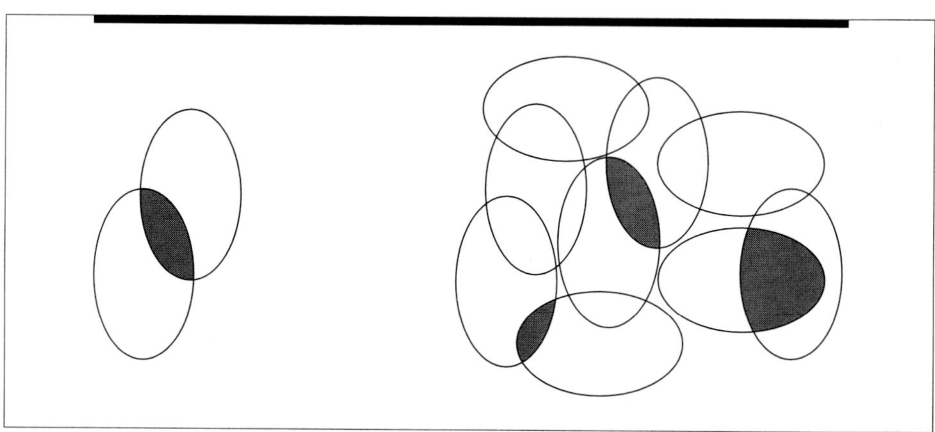

Furthermore, many studies that find sex differences for some spatial tasks don't find differences for other spatial tasks. Indeed, consistent sex differences are found only for the ability to mentally rotate objects (Linn & Petersen, 1986). Finally, as Matlin (1993) points out, there is some question about whether performing well on these artificial spatial tasks (finding hidden figures, being quick at mentally rotating an object) are related to any real-life abilities.

Mathematical Ability

In contrast to the ability to mentally rotate an object quickly, mathematical ability is clearly important to real-life functioning—especially for certain professions. Do men have higher levels of mathematical ability than women?

In the elementary school years, girls score slightly higher on math tests than boys (Hyde, Fennema, & Lamon, 1990). No differences are evident between eighth-grade boys and girls on such tasks as arithmetic operations, mathematical reasoning, and achievement in algebra and geometry.

After eighth grade, the evidence seems to suggest that boys do better than girls on mathematical tasks. However, the evidence is far from consistent. Some studies find no sex differences among 8th through 12th graders (Feingold, 1988). Furthermore, women do better than men in math classes (Brooks, 1987; Kimball, 1989) and do as well or better than men on certain standardized tests of mathematical knowledge (Smith & Walker, 1988). However, most studies, especially those conducted before 1980, suggest that, by the 11th grade, males score higher than females and continue to be superior throughout adulthood.

Why do sex differences in mathematical ability seem to emerge during adolescence? Naturists argue that males may start to do better in math because of a maturational event. For example, the surge of testosterone that males get during puberty may improve their mathematical ability (Shute et al., 1983). Nurturists argue that environmental events, such as women taking fewer math classes than men, may account for males doing better in math.

In short, the research on male superiority on mathematical tasks parallels the findings for female superiority on verbal tasks in at least two respects. First, the differences between the sexes has been decreasing, possibly as a result of decreased gender bias in schools and society. Second, the average differences are quite small, especially for recent studies.

Not only are the differences between the sexes in mathematical ability small, but they may only reflect a sex difference in another ability—spatial ability. That is, Benbow and Stanley (1980) suggest that superior spatial ability may be the only reason males do better in tests of mathematical ability. Consistent with this suggestion is the finding that male superiority in mathematics is found only in those tasks that require spatial visualization, such as geometry. For those tasks that can be figured out verbally, no sex differences are found (Fennema, 1974).

Although average differences between sexes may be small, Camilla Benbow and Julian Stanley's (1983) research also suggests that males may be more likely to have extremely high levels of mathematical ability. Benbow and Stanley's conclusions were based on their analysis of John Hopkins University's Study of Mathematically Precocious Youth (Benbow, 1988; Benbow & Stanley, 1983).

In this study, selected seventh- and eighth-graders took the SAT. Most of these students came from the Middle-Atlantic States (primarily Delaware, Maryland, Pennsylvania, Virginia, and West Virginia). Additional students were recruited as part of a nationwide talent search. Benbow and Stanley found that, for their Middle-Atlantic state sample, there were 4.1 boys to every girl who scored beyond 600 (scores range between 200 and 800) on the Math SAT. When Benbow and Stanley included the children they had recruited during a nationwide talent search, the ratio was 13 to 1 in favor of the boys. This research finding is interesting, but before we accept that men are 13 times more likely to have high levels of math ability than women, we should ask the following questions:

1. Why is the ratio for the students selected through a nationwide talent search so different from the ratio of people selected from the Middle-Atlantic states? There seems to be some kind of sampling problem here.
2. Is the ratio the same for high school students? Comparing high school students, all who would have

had courses that covered the material included in the SAT, might be fairer than looking at seventh-graders who, in many cases, have not had geometry and algebra (Matlin, 1993).

3. Is the Math SAT test biased toward men?
4. Is the difference due to men's doing better on the geometry questions (which utilize spatial reasoning)?

Despite these questions, it seems reasonable to accept the idea that there are more mathematically gifted boys than girls. Indeed, Hyde (1994) reports that it is *only among the gifted* that males outperform females in math.

Summary of Sex Differences

The research summarized in Maccoby and Jacklin's (1974, 1980; Maccoby, 1990) reports conclude that when large, randomly selected groups of females and large groups of randomly selected males are compared with each other, the average score for a group of males on aggressiveness and mathematical and spatial ability will be higher than the average score for females. A group of females will tend to have superior verbal ability, report more anxiety, and be more empathic and dependent than a group of males.

In terms of academics, girls will get better grades than boys. However, girls' grades in "masculine" academic subjects, such as math, will decline as they go from grade school to high school. Similarly, boys' grades in "feminine" academic subjects, such as English, will be lower in high school than they were in grade school (Katz & Ksansnak, 1994).

As we have mentioned before, most of these average differences tend to be small and they are getting smaller. The differences are too small to justify discriminating against either sex. Even the biggest of these differences is useless for predicting the behavior of an individual man or woman. Many women have better math and spatial abilities than the average man; many men have better verbal ability than the average woman. In short, although studies that report sex differences get people's attention, the main results of the research point to similarities (Matlin, 1993).

Accounting for Sex Differences

Despite the fact that the psychological differences between men and women are small, people are fascinated by them. Thus, although it might seem like much ado about very little, people have strong opinions about why men and women differ. Some argue vehemently that sex differences are primarily, if not solely, the result of socialization. Others argue, just as vehemently, that sex differences are primarily, if not solely, due to biology. As you'll soon see, each side can point to evidence that supports its position.

Biological Theories

Those who argue that the psychological differences between the sexes are due to biology point out that the sexes differ genetically and physiologically. Then, they try to explain how these genetic and physiological differences cause psychological differences.

Hormones

One clear physiological difference between males and females is that males have higher levels of male hormones. Consequently, some experts argue that the same hormones that cause many of the physical differences between men and women are also responsible for the psychological differences between the sexes. For instance, McEwen (1976) and Young, Goy, & Phoenix (1965) believe that hormonal differences experienced prenatally, or shortly after birth, lead to social, emotional, and cognitive differences between the sexes.

Rat Evidence Male hormones, or **androgens,** could create psychological differences between the sexes by changing the brain. The primary evidence for hormones changing the brain comes from studying the effects of hormones on the rat's hypothalamus (a part of the brain that has a role in emotion and in controlling the release of hormones). For example, injecting male hormones into a newborn female rat will permanently change how her hypothalamus works. That is, as a result of the injection, her hypothalamus will work like a male rat's. As a result of having this "masculinized" hypothalamus, the "masculinized" female rat will not be able to have children. Similarly, castrating a newborn male rat (thereby depriving him of male hormones) will result in his hypothalamus working like a female rat's (Harris, 1964).

Based on these observations, several researchers concluded that androgens have an "organizing" effect on the fetal brain, and that in the absence of these hormones, a "female" brain will develop in both males and females (Harris & Levine, 1965; Phoenix, Goy, Gerall, & Young, 1959). It wasn't long before some people not only decided that these rat results applied to humans, but also that androgens account for all the differences between the sexes. In other words, people were quick to accept the idea that male hormones "masculinize" the brain.

However, many experts think that generalizing from rat research to humans is questionable. For example, Bleier (1984) argues that, unlike the rat brain, the human brain is exposed to *both* androgens and estrogen. Furthermore, unlike rats, humans are not prisoners of biology and hormones. But the best reason for not generalizing these results to humans is that the results don't hold for primates. Studies have found that androgens don't suppress ovulation, menstruation, or pregnancy in humans or other female primates who were exposed as fetuses to high levels of circulating androgens (Goy & Resko, 1972; Valdes, del Castillo, Gutierrez, Larrea, Medina, & Perez-Palcios, 1979).

Box 12.1

SELF-CHECK

Indicate whether each of the following statements is true or false.

1. There are numerous psychological differences between the genders.
2. Most of the psychological differences between the genders are fairly large. Consequently, we can do a reasonable job of predicting the traits or abilities of an individual if we know the individual's gender.
3. Men tend to be more aggressive than women.
4. Women tend to report more anxiety than men.
5. Women are innately more empathic and responsive to babies than men are.
6. Very young girls are more afraid, more anxious, and more dependent than very young boys.
7. Males are much more aggressive than females in every way and in every situation.
8. Females are probably less aggressive than males because females' superior verbal ability allows them to better resolve difficulties and better express their ideas.
9. Men have better spatial ability than women.
10. Women do better in math classes than men.
11. Before puberty, males do not seem to do better than females in tests of mathematical ability.
12. The differences between the genders on tests of mathematical ability seem to be bigger in studies done before 1974 than they are in more recent studies.

Please turn to the end of this chapter to check your answers.

AGS Females and Social Behavior To get some human evidence that supports the claim that androgens cause a masculinization of the brain, researchers have studied women who suffer from a genetic disorder called **adrenogenital syndrome (AGS).** These women have excessive amounts of androgens, sometimes to the point that their external genitalia have been masculinized. Such women may have a penis and an empty scrotum.

Initially, John Money and his associates concluded that if androgenized girls were correctly assigned to their feminine gender role before the age of 3, the girls would experience normal psychosexual development (Money & Ehrhardt, 1972). Later, however, Money changed his mind and decided that early exposure to androgens predisposed AGS females to be tomboys.

On what did John Money base this conclusion? He found that AGS girls preferred simple, practical clothing, such as slacks and shorts, and were uninterested in cosmetics, jewelry, or hair styles. The AGS girls also showed little interest in rehearsing the maternal role through playing with dolls or baby-sitting. In addition, he found that the fantasies of these girls were more achievement and success oriented than marriage oriented. Furthermore, AGS females started dating later than the average woman.

Note, however, that, in terms of sexual preferences, AGS women didn't differ from women in general. The vast majority had sexual fantasies about men. Furthermore, AGS females were no more likely to be lesbians than females from the general population (Ehrhardt & Baker, 1974; Money & Ehrhardt, 1972; Perlman, 1971). Consequently, Hines (1982) concluded—in direct contrast to Money and Ehrhardt (1972)—that androgens do not seem to have an effect on the gender-role development of AGS women.

Perhaps Money's most controversial conclusion was that androgens might cause AGS females to have higher IQs. In support of Money's position, both males and females who were exposed to high prenatal androgen levels have above average IQs. Thus, AGS girls have above average IQs. However, the non-AGS siblings and parents of AGS girls also have above average IQs (Baker & Ehrhardt, 1974). Therefore, the high IQs of AGS girls may well be the result of genetic or social factors rather than the result of elevated levels of androgens. Of course, these same genetic and social variables may also account for AGS girls being more achievement oriented and "masculine" than the average female. Thus, scientists continue to debate whether AGS females are more "psychologically masculine" due to androgens, other hereditary variables, or the way they were socialized—and even whether AGS girls really are more psychologically masculine than other girls.

Brain Lateralization

Also open to debate is the issue of sex differences in **brain lateralization,** assigning control of specific functions to only one side of the brain. It is generally believed that the left hemisphere is responsible for language functions, and the right for nonverbal perception and spatial functions. In regard to sex differences, some evidence supports the idea that brain function may be more clearly segregated in males. For example, "women tend to use both sides of the brain in cognitive tasks such as spelling, whereas men use primarily the left side" (Lefton, 1994, p. 68). In addition, "women listen with both ears equally whereas men favor the right ear" (Lefton, 1994, p. 68).

According to some scholars, these sex differences in how brains are organized account for women's verbal superiority and men's spatial superiority: Women have devoted more of their brain to language, men to spatial tasks. Since the differences between the sexes in spatial and language ability become more evident around adolescence (Hyde, Fennema, & Lamon, 1991), naturists have argued that during adolescence the male brain is altered through exposure to massive amounts of male hormones (Kimura, 1992; Shute et al., 1983).

Nurturists attack this view on two fronts. First, the idea that males' brains are more lateralized is not a documented fact. Second, even if males' brains are more lateralized, it doesn't mean that hormones caused this lateralization. Indeed, if testosterone causes one to have a spatially gifted "male" brain, why do men seem to perform better on spatial tasks if they have low levels of testosterone (Kimura, 1987)?

Rather than looking for hormonal explanations as the cause of differences between men's and women's brains, nurturists suggest that we look at environmental explanations. That is, men may be better at spatial tasks because they are encouraged to participate in sports, build things, take shop, and do well in geometry, whereas women aren't. The differential treatment that males and females receive could thus be reflected in brain organization. In short, nurturists argue that rather than speculate about hidden, subtle brain differences that may potentially exist between the sexes, we should look at the effects of the blatantly different ways that men and women are treated.

Social Learning Theory: The Different Worlds of Males and Females

Whereas the biological view holds that differences between the genders are due to nature, people who endorse **social learning theory** maintain that these differences are learned. Social learning theorists point out that—starting at birth—males and females are treated differently. The sex of a newborn not only tells people what color to dress their child in, but traditionally dictates the kinds of toys the child will be given and the behaviors that will be encouraged and discouraged throughout that child's life.

Little girls are dressed in pink, picked up more often, and held more gently. Little boys are dressed in blue, picked up less, played with more roughly, encouraged to be more autonomous than infant girls (Lamb, 1981), and receive more positive and negative attention (Block, 1983; Matlin, 1993). Later, boys are permitted to roam over a wider area without special permission, told to be strong, encouraged to be assertive—even aggressive, and urged to control their emotions ("big boys don't cry"). Daughters, on the other hand, are given less freedom to explore their environments, encouraged to remain dependent on their parents, told that they are pretty, and that "nice girls don't fight."

In general, parents tend to encourage their sons to engage in instrumental (goal-directed) behaviors, to control their emotions, and to prepare for the world of work. Daughters, on the other hand, are encouraged toward expressive (emotion-oriented) behaviors and are socialized for a future maternal role.

Perhaps because ours is a male-oriented society, girls are less strongly sex-typed than boys (Katz & Ksansnak, 1994). Indeed, even preschoolers—who tend to rigidly hold to gender stereotypes—tolerate "masculine" behavior in girls (Smetana, 1986). Perhaps because there is little pressure for young girls to adhere to gender stereotypes, many do not. In one study, 63 percent of the junior high girls surveyed said that they were tomboys, and 51 percent of adult women surveyed recalled that they were tomboys (Hyde et al., 1977).

However, whereas our peers permit female "tomboys" to cross the barrier between dolls and trucks without much disapproval, peers are not as accepting of "tomgirls." For example, the same preschooler that would allow a girl to play with a truck would not tolerate a boy who played with dolls, wore dresses, or expressed interest in other "feminine" activities (Smetana, 1986).

Like peers, parents actively discourage boys who show "feminine" interests (Fagot, 1977; Langlois & Downs, 1980). As you might guess, fathers tend to respond more negatively to feminine behaviors in boys than mothers do (Huston, 1983). However, mothers also want to raise "manly" sons. Even feminists who had no anxieties when their daughters engaged in traditional masculine play were upset if their sons played "dress-up in frilly clothes," imitated "female" mannerisms, or played with dolls (Van Gelder & Carmichael, 1975). Apparently, many parents have a vague fear of expressive and emotional behavior in male children because parents view such behavior as effeminate (Wilson, 1975).

Box 12.2

SELF-CHECK

1. List the arguments in support of the view that hormones cause the male brain to differ from the female brain.
2. List the arguments in opposition to the view that hormones cause the male brain to differ from the female brain.

Please turn to the end of this chapter to check your answers.

Girls are less strongly sex stereotyped than boys. Peers and parents approve more of a girl doing masculine things than they approve of a boy doing feminine things.

Effects of Differential Treatment

When told that they respond differently to girls than boys, parents often explain that they are merely reacting to "natural" differences between the sexes (Wilson, 1975). Social learning theorists disagree. Social learning theorists point out that, in many cases, children who are raised male (even though their chromosomes designate them as female) act like men, whereas children who are raised female (even though their chromosomes or hormones label them as male) act like women. Furthermore, social learning theorists point out that the behavior of women has changed dramatically in the last 30 years—a rapid change that cannot be explained by changes in women's biology over that period (Matlin, 1993).

Thus far, we have made two important points in support of the social learning viewpoint. First, we have shown that males are treated differently from females. Second, we have presented evidence that this differential treatment has effects. For example, we mentioned that biological males who were labeled "female" at birth became "women." However, despite this suggestive evidence, you may be asking the question: How does differential treatment of men and women cause men and women to behave differently? According to social learning theorists, two mechanisms provide the "how" of learning gender roles.

First, males and females behave differently because they are rewarded and punished for specific kinds of sex-typed behavior (Bandura, 1977; Mischel, 1970). The Arapesh tribe (Mead, 1935) rewarded boys for being flirtatious and dependent, so their men were flirtatious and dependent; our society doesn't reward males for this behavior, so few American males are flirtatious and dependent.

Second, boys imitate male models, whereas girls imitate female models. These models may live close by (parent, sibling, peer) or be **symbolic models,** persons with whom the child does not personally interact, such as a television character.

The power of modeling is well documented (Bandura, 1977). Unfortunately for the social learning view, however, there is little support for the idea that young boys imitate primarily male models whereas young girls imitate female models (Maccoby & Jacklin, 1974; Raskin & Israel, 1981).

Although gender roles may not be learned by imitating same-sex individuals, children can learn attitudes about gender roles from models. Indeed, even symbolic models can have effects on a child's sex-typed behavior or attitudes. For example, Miller and Reaves (1976) found that children who were shown television programs in which women portrayed nontraditional roles were more willing to approve of nontraditional behaviors afterwards than children who did not watch the programs.

In a similar study, junior high school students viewed slides depicting adults as computer software designers and systems analysts. Some students saw slides in which only females were the systems analysts, while others saw slides in which only males were the analysts. Then, students were asked which career they would be more interested in pursuing. The girls who saw the slides in which only women were systems analysts preferred being a systems analyst to a software designer. However, the girls who saw the slides in which only men were systems analysts preferred being a software designer (Plost & Rosen, 1974).

These studies are consistent with reviews of the literature on the role of television. These reviews conclude that symbolic models on television do have the power to influence people's attitudes about gender roles (Perloff, Brown, & Miller, 1982). For example, the more television children watch, the more they tend to engage in gender stereotyping (McGhee & Frueh, 1980).

The social learning theorists' assertion that symbolic models in the media influence sex-role attitudes is significant because females are still presented primarily in traditional roles in today's television programs, magazine and television ads, and textbooks (Franks & Rothblum, 1983; Gerbner, 1992; Goffman, 1979; Huston et al., 1984; Welch et al., 1979). However, although it's tempting to conclude that the media's presentation of males and females will strongly influence gender-role attitudes, correlational studies show only modest association between the amount of television children watch and their sex-typed beliefs (Huston et al., 1984). Furthermore, even those small correlations don't mean that the television shows caused gender-role attitudes. It may be the other way around: Attitudes determine which programs people watch. In support of this idea, one study showed that "androgynous" girls had favorable reactions toward a popular assertive female TV character, whereas "feminine" girls disapproved of the character's behavior (Friedrich et al., 1978). Clearly, more research is needed to determine to what extent the media affect sex-typed behavior.

Summary of the Social Learning Position

Although social learning theorists have not proved that television is a strong determinant of gender roles, they

Table 12.2
Summary of Explanations for Gender Differences

Biological Explanations	Social Learning Explanations
Boys and girls differ in terms of chromosomes and hormones.	Boys and girls experience very different social worlds.
Male hormones may cause boys to be more aggressive and may lateralize the male brain, causing gender differences in mathematical ability, spatial ability, and verbal ability.	Boys and girls are rewarded for different behaviors. Live and symbolic models teach children what gender-appropriate behavior is.
Some gender differences are apparent during early infancy, suggesting a genetic component. Other gender differences may also be genetic, but emerge only as the genetic program unfolds (maturation). For example, many differences appear to emerge during puberty—a time of rapid biological maturation. Since males experience a surge of testosterone during puberty, hormones may account for the gender differences that emerge during puberty.	Few gender differences are apparent during early infancy, suggesting that most differences between genders are not inborn. Differences emerge as a result of the two genders having vastly different experiences.

have made a compelling case for the power of learning and modeling as the cause of differences between the sexes. They have shown that many differences between the sexes are not present during the first few years of life; have documented that men's and women's behavior has changed over the past few decades; have demonstrated in both lab and field studies that differential treatment can produce differences in behavior; and have documented that the genders receive differential treatment (Halpern, 1992).

As social learning theorists accumulate more evidence on the differences between how men and women are treated, they may even be able to argue convincingly that all psychological differences between men and women are due to socialization. Already, they have found shocking discrepancies between how the genders are treated. For example, teachers are three times more likely to call on a boy than on a girl. Some hints about the discrepancies that have yet to be documented are provided by case studies of people like Jan Morris. Jan, having had a gender-change operation, is in the unique position of actually experiencing firsthand what it's like to be a man and what it's like to be a woman. She claims that:

> We are told that the social gap between the sexes is narrowing, but I can only report that having, in the second half of the 20th century, experienced life in both roles, there seems to me no aspect of existence, no moment of the day, no contact, no arrangement, no response, which is not different for men and for women. . . . And if others' responses shifted, so did my own. The more I was treated as a woman, the more woman I became . . . I discovered that even now, men prefer women to be less able, less talkative and certainly less self-centered than they are themselves; so I generally obliged them. (Jan Morris, 1974, pp. 148–149)

Although the operation that transformed Jan from male to female did not diminish Jan's personal or intellectual competency, people treated *her* much worse than they had ever treated *him*. Of course, Jan shouldn't have been surprised. In our society, people don't practice (and many don't even pretend to practice) equality of the sexes. Men are assigned the role of strong, independent, unemotional breadwinners; women are assigned the role of taking care of men and children—whether as housewife, secretary, nurse, or teacher. (Table 12.2 summarizes the biological and social learning explanations for gender differences.)

Gender-Role Development

Although people may argue about whether the different gender roles are fair, people cannot dispute the fact that children of both sexes conform to these roles. In this section, we will first *describe* how gender-role development unfolds. Then, we will refer to popular theories that *explain* how gender-role development occurs.

Gender-Role Development During Infancy and Childhood

Research suggests only two common psychological differences between male and female infants (Hyde, 1985): (1) Newborn females usually have greater tactile (sense of touch) sensitivity; and (2) male infants tend to be more active (Block, 1976). The implications of these differences for later development have not been sufficiently addressed by the research. However, there may be a link between the infant male's higher activity level and his later tendency toward higher levels of aggression.

Box 12.3

SELF-CHECK

Indicate whether each of the following statements is true or false.

1. Daughters are given more freedom than sons.
2. Sons get more negative attention than daughters.
3. Sons are encouraged to control their emotions more than daughters.
4. Girls are less strongly sex-typed than boys.
5. Feminists seem to become upset if their sons display "feminine" behaviors.
6. Being a genetic male seems to be more important in becoming a "man" than does being labeled as a male from birth.
7. The fact that certain behaviors are rewarded when girls do them, but punished when boys do them, could account for some of the differences between the genders.
8. There is clear proof that televised models affect children's sex-typed behavior and attitudes.

Please turn to the end of this chapter to check your answers.

Although researchers have uncovered only two differences between male and female newborns, additional differences appear during the first three years of life. Many of these differences may be the result of children's learning gender roles. For example, by 15 months, toddlers exhibit clear preferences for gender-role-appropriate toys and play (O'Brien, Huston, & Risley, 1983). By age 2 or 3, girls sew, string beads, and play housekeeping, whereas boys play with toy guns, trucks, tractors, and fire engines, and do carpentry (Maccoby & Jacklin, 1974).

Boys and girls continue to have different interests throughout childhood, as demonstrated by findings from a national survey of more than 2,000 children between ages 7 and 11. The survey showed that boys prefer guns, boxing, wrestling, karate, team sports, and fixing and making things more than girls do. Girls, on the other hand, show a preference for dolls, sewing, cooking, dancing, and looking after younger children (Zill, 1985). These sex-typed play activities may be the source of later sex-typed social and achievement behaviors (Tittle, 1986).

Admittedly, some of these changes may be due to maturation rather than to gender-role socialization. For example, boys' preferences for aggressive toys, such as guns, may reflect their natural tendency to be more aggressive than girls (Maccoby, 1988). We say "natural" tendency for aggression not just because of the testosterone research we mentioned before, but because greater male aggressiveness is noticeable almost as soon as children begin playing with each other and persists throughout life (Maccoby & Jacklin, 1974).

In addition to sex differences in aggressiveness and toy preference, children also learn career gender stereotypes. By the time children reach kindergarten, they have learned to think that doctors, firefighters, and pilots are men, and that nurses, secretaries, and hairdressers are women (Blaske, 1984). Not only do these stereotypes influence how people view males and females in general, but they also influence how people view themselves. Consequently, these stereotypes may influence a person's career aspirations.

Not only do boys and girls play with different toys and identify with different professions, but they also play in different groups. From the preschool years until puberty, children usually gather in sex-segregated groups (Maccoby, 1988).

Although this tendency to segregate into same-sex play groups is present during preschool, it is strongest during the school-age years. Maccoby and Jacklin (1987) report that nursery school children aged 4 1/2 years spent three times as much time playing with same-sex peers as they did with opposite-sex peers. When these same children were 6 1/2 years old, they were 11 times more likely to play with same-sex playmates than opposite-sex playmates. Of special interest is the finding that sex segregation is greatest in situations that have *not* been structured by adults (Luria & Herzog, 1985; Thorne, 1986). Clearly, children *choose* to play with same-sex playmates, probably because boys play in a way that is both rougher and less polite (Maccoby, 1990).

Another common sex difference is that boys are more likely than girls to have difficulty adjusting to the requirements of school. Research shows that boys are referred for psychological evaluation and are found in remedial classes more frequently than girls (Andrews & Cappon, 1957; Werry & Quay, 1971). Boys also have more difficulty learning how to read. Some argue that the reason boys have more difficulty learning to read is that reading is often perceived by young boys as a feminine activity—and this gender-role stereotype impedes the boy's academic progress (Hyde, 1985).

Not only are boys more likely to need remedial instruction, but they are also more likely to present discipline problems in school. However, boys aren't just criticized and punished more by their teachers than girls are, boys also receive more praise (Good & Brophy, 1986; Parsons, Kaczala, & Meece, 1982). Thus, boys typically receive much more attention from teachers than girls (Matlin, 1993). Attention, whether positive or negative, can reinforce feelings of importance, and encourage autonomy and independence (Williams, 1987). Perhaps this explains why, even though girls achieve higher grades than boys throughout the educational process, boys tend to aspire toward higher status occupations.

In conclusion, boys and girls begin life acting very similarly. By age 2 or 3, they develop a gender identity and start acting in ways that are consistent with society's gender roles. Thus, young boys and girls often play with different toys and play in different groups. Sex segregation seems to intensify after age 6, at which time children realize that they will be the same sex the rest of their lives. Yet, despite differences in gender-role socialization, it is important to remember that boys and girls are more similar than they are different.

Gender-Role Development During Adolescence

There is some controversy about the path of gender development in early adolescence. According to some studies, early adolescence is a time in which males and females become less tolerant of behavior that does not conform to gender stereotypes (Sigelman, Carr, & Begley, 1986; Stoddart & Turiel, 1985). That is, eighth-graders engage in more rigid stereotyping than fifth-graders. Indeed, these studies find that eighth-graders are like kindergartners in terms of holding rigid and stereotyped attitudes about the sexes.

Other studies suggest that it is not eighth grade, but fifth grade, when children retreat to more rigid stereotypes (Signorella et al., 1993). There are at least two possibilities for these different research findings. First, children in some samples may be developing at a faster rate than children in other samples. Second, it seems the researcher's choice of measure makes a difference. In a review of studies, Margaret Signorella and her colleagues (Signorella et al., 1993) discovered that studies using rating scales or multiple-choice questions obtained results suggesting that stereotyping increased as children enter early adolescence, whereas studies asking short-answer or essay questions obtained results suggesting that stereotyping decreased in early adolescence.

Although there is some disagreement about what happens in early adolescence, the evidence is fairly consistent about what happens in later adolescence. Specifically, as adolescents get older, their gender attitudes become more flexible (Katz & Ksansnak, 1994).

We do not mean to imply that older adolescents are free from gender stereotypes. Although both young men and women want to have a family and career (Catalyst, 1987), adolescent men and women differ in their career aspirations and projected family roles. The sex-role stereotypes learned during childhood usually become more solidified during adolescence. Despite the increasing popularity of the idea that men and women should not be limited to possessing only the characteristics prescribed by traditional gender roles (Lanier & Byrne, 1981), most adolescents continue to advocate traditional gender roles. For example, one study that compared the attitudes of eleventh-graders in 1972 and in 1978 found that both cohorts equally endorsed the opinion that a man's career is more important than a woman's and that girls who compete with males are less feminine (Ditkoff, 1979).

Similarly, several studies conducted during the 1970s found that many girls believed that males disapprove of intelligent females (*Expanding adolescent sex roles,* 1978).

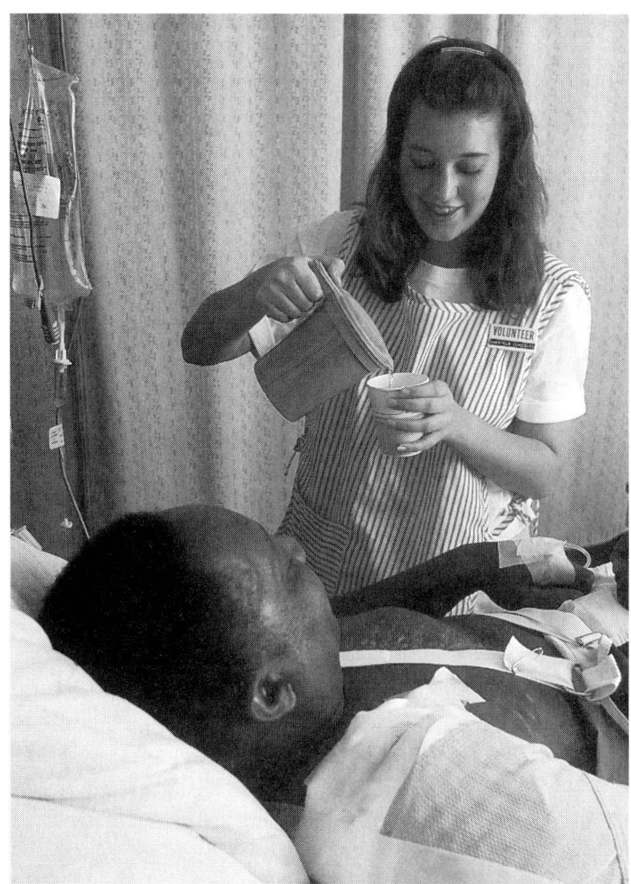

The majority of adolescent girls plan on careers in "feminine" jobs, such as nursing.

Furthermore, these studies also found that teenage girls who were not preparing themselves for any adult vocation said such preparation was unnecessary because they intended to get married. Unfortunately, many of the male and female adolescents in these surveys were unaware of the statistical fact that most married women must work to support the family.

Data from the 1980s confirm that adolescents tend to restrict their vocational options on the basis of sex-role stereotypes. Although more adolescent girls were preparing themselves for traditionally masculine vocations than in previous decades, the majority were still restricting their vocational choices to "feminine" jobs in social services, teaching, and nursing (Herzog, 1982; Jacobs, 1986). Unfortunately, these traditional feminine jobs also tend to be lower status and lower paying than traditionally male jobs.

Problems Faced by Adolescent Females

One reason adolescent girls and boys often hold gender-typed career aspirations may be their attitudes toward achievement. Research consistently portrays adolescence as a time when girls experience a decline in academic performance, intellectual self-confidence, and vocational aspirations (Douvan, 1979; Rosenberg & Simmons, 1975). According to Hyde (1985), adolescent girls begin to feel the force of the cultural rule "achievement and femininity are incompatible." The girl is caught between two conflicting value systems. On one hand, she wants a positive sense of self based on achieving and getting good grades. On the other hand, she feels pressure to conform to society's standard for a good female—one who is not intellectually competitive (Broverman et al., 1972). This double bind may cause anxiety and intellectual ambivalence.

One consequence of this anxiety and ambivalence is that many adolescent girls feel less confident about their intellectual abilities than their male peers. Furthermore, there is a tendency for girls, especially the brightest, to experience an intellectual decline, especially in math and science, during adolescence (Maccoby & Jacklin, 1974; Sherman, 1978; Tobias, 1978).

Although some scientists have tried to link male superiority in math and sciences to sex differences in brain development, recent research supports the conclusion that girls fall behind in math because they adopt the gender stereotype that only males are good at math. For example, androgynous females tend to be better in math and the sciences than females who score high in femininity (Casserly, 1979; Fitzpatrick, 1978; Rodenstein & Hughes, 1979). Furthermore, as we mentioned earlier, the gap between the sexes in intellectual abilities has narrowed significantly in recent years. For instance, when psychologist Alan Feingold (1988) compared male and female scores on standard achievement tests between the years 1940 and 1983, he found that although females still tend to score higher on verbal performance, and males higher on math and science, that these differences have *decreased* significantly since 1940. Similarly, educational psychologist Marcia Linn reports that the gap between adolescent male and female scores on national tests of science knowledge narrowed significantly between 1976 and 1985 (Adler, 1989).

Unfortunately, even when girls do excel academically, they often feel less confident about their intellectual abilities than their male peers (Evans, 1994; Sherman, 1978). Whereas high school boys who perform well have greater self-esteem than boys who earn poor grades, academically successful girls tend to feel just as anxious and depressed as girls with lower grades.

Why is academic success linked to high self-esteem for boys, but not for girls? One reason may be that the sexes differ in how they interpret success. Whereas girls often attribute their successes to effort or assistance by others, boys believe their successes are due to natural ability.

Just as the sexes differ in how they interpret success, they also differ in how they interpret failure. When a girl fails, she usually attributes it to her lack of ability or her lack of intelligence. On the other hand, when a boy fails, he typically attributes his failure to not trying hard enough or to external factors such as other people or the environmental conditions (Dweck, 1984, 1986; Parsons et al., 1982).

Another possible reason for girls' lack of academic confidence is that girls do not thrive in the competitive atmosphere that characterizes some classrooms. That is, adolescent females are most confident in situations that don't require competition with their peers (Dweck, 1984).

Finally, some believe that the reason girls are less confident about their academic abilities is that boys tend to receive more support from their teachers and parents (Sadker & Sadker, 1994). According to this reasoning, girls should be least confident when they attempt tasks for which they receive very little support, such as male sex-typed tasks. Consistent with that reasoning, girls feel least confident when they attempt a male sex-typed task, such as working on a math or science problem. In addition, if girls receive encouragement from their teachers, girls feel more confident about their ability to master the task (see box 12.4). However, the evidence for the belief that boys receive much more support than girls is questionable. For example, research suggests that the teacher bias that is supposed to exist in the classroom may be exaggerated (Evans, 1994; Heller, Puff, & Mills, 1985). Furthermore, if bias is such a problem, why do female adolescents get better grades in school than male adolescents?

Problems Faced by Adolescent Males

Although sex-role stereotypes are often blamed for harming females' academic performance, cultural sex-role stereotypes may also undermine a boy's academic success and overall happiness. For example, although boys receive more praise than girls, they also receive more criticism. In addition, internalizing these sex-role stereotypes may harm academic success. For instance, male students are more reluctant than females to ask their teachers or counselors for help and are reluctant to express anxiety about academic pressures because they fear that doing so would be "unmanly" (Glidewell, 1978). Moreover, because low grades have been found to be more highly correlated with delinquency for boys than for girls, some researchers suggest that male self-esteem is more intricately bound to academic success than female's (Gold & Petronio, 1980).

Social expectations place additional pressures on the young male. Society defines appropriate masculine behavior more narrowly than it defines feminine behavior (Gerzon, 1983; Pleck, 1981; Rubin, 1980). Males are expected to repress their emotions and "feminine" needs for dependence, nurturance, passivity, fear, affection, and self-doubt. At the same time, they are expected to act manly by being aggressive, competitive, athletic, rational, self-assured, and autonomous. Any hint of "feminine" behavior may elicit jeers (such as shouts of "sissy") from peers (Goldman & Chaillee, 1984).

Gender-Role Development During Adulthood

The gender-role stereotypes learned during childhood and adolescence will influence people throughout adulthood. Women do spend considerably more time than

Box 12.4

ISSUE in FOCUS

Helping Adolescents

Parents' and teachers' gender-role expectations and consequent behavior have been implicated in the decline of girls' academic success and lower intellectual self-confidence during adolescence. According to critics, most educators, parents, and counselors fail to encourage adolescent girls to develop their intellectual abilities to the fullest or to explore courses or vocations in masculine domains (Ahlum & Howe, 1976; Bernard, 1979; Deem, 1978; Frieze, 1978; Guttentag & Bray, 1976).

Messages about appropriate and inappropriate behavior based on sex-role stereotypes are delivered to students overtly and covertly through the curriculum, textbooks, counseling, allocation of money, and general school policies. Despite teachers' commendable intentions and their claims of treating male and female students equally, most research demonstrates that teachers' interactions with adolescents are significantly influenced by sex-role stereotypes and by students' gender (Deem, 1978; Frazier & Sadker, 1973; Good & Brophy, 1986).

In an effort to sensitize school teachers and counselors to their sexist behavior, many professional organizations are encouraging adults to examine their own conduct (see box table 12.4). The National Education Association, National Federation of Teachers, American Personnel and Guidance Association, and the American Psychological Association have all published guidelines for eliminating sexism in secondary education.

Box Table 12.4

Sexist and Nonsexist Counseling Strategies

1. Do you encourage males and females to explore the same jobs?
2. Do you inquire about boys' future marriage and parenting plans as often as you do girls?
3. Do you use sexist language and writing?
4. Do the materials in your office depict men and women with nontraditional jobs, personalities, and lifestyles?
5. Have you read about nonsexist counseling methods?
6. Do you use career or personality inventories that are biased?
7. Have you discussed stereotypes with adolescents, their parents, and teachers?
8. Do you consider certain traits "abnormal" for one sex but "acceptable" for the other (sexual activity, physical aggression, ambition, mannerisms)?
9. Do you advocate different punishment for boys and girls?
10. Do you actively encourage students to engage in positive activities that are traditionally considered appropriate only for the opposite sex?
11. Do you help textbook committees choose nonsexist materials?

A nonsexist counselor would answer "no" to questions 3, 6, 8, and 9.

Sources: From W. Fetters, *Nonsexist Counseling: Helping Men and Women Redefine Their Roles*, Kendall Hunt, Dubuque, Iowa, 1979; B. Gutik, *Enhancing Women's Career Development*, Jossey-Bass, San Francisco, 1978; and S. L. Hansen and R. S. Rapoza, *Career Development and Counseling of Women*, C. C. Thomas Publishers, Springfield, Ill., 1990.

men in child-rearing tasks (Haynes, 1993; Matlin, 1993). However, the demands of surviving in an adult world and a maturing sense of self may lead to some relaxation of gender-typed behavior (Jung, 1931/1971). For example, a longitudinal study of women from age 21 to 43 (Helson & Moane, 1987) found that women's femininity scores decreased after the age of 27. That is, women do not continue to strictly conform to the traditional role of wife-mother. Likewise, Livson (1983) found that, once free of parenting responsibilities, husbands and wives became less rigidly stereotyped. Finally, perhaps because the roles for elderly men and women are not well established, the elderly sometimes show the highest degree of gender flexibility (Neugarten, 1977; Sigelman & Shaffer, 1995).

Despite the fact that adults have some gender-role flexibility, the lives of adult men and adult women are very different. Society continues to emphasize the wife-mother role for women and the husband-provider role for men (Levinson, 1986; Roberts & Newton, 1987). For example, the dreams of most male young adults focus on the image of "independent achiever in an occupational role," (Levinson et al., 1978; Levinson, 1986), whereas the dreams of female young adults most often center on an image of "self-in-adult-world defined in relation to others," where "others" refers to husband, children, and colleagues (Roberts & Newton, 1987). That is, while most women in their twenties are most concerned with marital life and raising children, their husbands are focusing on career advancement. In light of these different priorities, it is not surprising that men achieve career success at a much earlier age than most women.

Perhaps because gender roles for elderly people are not well established, older people can be more flexible.

Even when young women dream of having a highly successful career, these dreams are often undermined by the expectation that they should marry and promote their husband's career (Roberts & Newton, 1987). That is, a young woman typically is expected to—and expects to—sacrifice career opportunities to support her husband's career. Consequently, although most women work, their career development is crippled by the belief that women's work is less important than men's work. Because she is more likely to sacrifice career opportunities than he is, she finds herself in lower paying and lower status jobs. In other words, women not only face sex discrimination in the labor force (Heilman, Martell, & Simon, 1988; Matlin, 1993), but they also face sex discrimination at home.

Sex Discrimination at Home

Sex discrimination at home is partly fueled by cultural stereotypes, such as those holding that "housework is women's work." Because of such stereotypes, the working wife usually has the major responsibility for both housework and child-rearing duties added to her career demands. Thus, it is not surprising to find that although both men and women are usually satisfied with their marital relationship, marriage seems to favor men more than women. Specifically, married women (Bradburn & Caplovitz, 1965; Gurin et al., 1960; Myers, 1992; Radloff, 1975):

1. Report more depression than married men;
2. Are only marginally less depressed than never-married women (married men, on the other hand, are substantially less depressed than never-married men); and
3. Report less satisfaction with life than single women (married men, on the other hand, report more life satisfaction than single men).

Why are married women less happy than married men? A common correlate of depression is perceived level of stress. Objective analysis of the "typical" day of a working mother versus a working father reveals that although most women work outside the home, they also perform most of the household and child-rearing duties (see figure 12.3). Thus, while the husband relaxes in front of the television after a long day at the office, the wife is busy cooking supper, doing the family's laundry, and helping the children with homework.

Interestingly, the husband who is most likely to do "his share" of the household and parenting tasks is a working-class male who wishes his wife didn't have to work. In contrast, the middle-class male who verbally supports the idea of shared household duties is likely to do only a token amount of household work, such as barbecuing on weekends (Ulbrich, 1994).

Although some people blame the labor inequity at home on "lazy men," women contribute to this imbalance by not letting men do household tasks. Often, women don't let men do household tasks because the men will "do it wrong." Thus, the impact of cultural stereotypes is seen in females' attitudes about housework, as well as men's (Haynes, 1993; Matlin, 1993).

Sex Discrimination at Work

Not only do men and women have disparate home experiences, but their experiences at work also differ. Women are regarded as less competent and less committed to their careers than men. Women are also paid less than men. Indeed, although the average female worker has at least as much schooling as her male counterpart, she makes less than three-fourths as much as he does—even when both work full-time (U.S. Department of Labor, 1989). Related to her diminished earning power is the fact that women are less likely to hold high status jobs or be promoted. Partly because of this discrimination, a woman college graduate typically makes substantially less than a male high school graduate (see table 12.3).

Insight into the psychological process of sex discrimination in the labor force comes from a classic study (Goldberg, 1968). What Goldberg showed was that even when the work of a female is identical to that of a male, the

Figure 12.3

Amount of Housework Performed Each Day by Wives and Husbands, as a Function of Whether the Wife Is Employed

woman's work is judged inferior. Specifically, Goldberg asked female college students to evaluate essays. All the women read the same essays. However, half the research participants were told that a given essay was written by a man, while the other half was told that the *same* essay was authored by a woman. When an essay was attributed to a male author, it was judged more favorably than when the same essay was attributed to a woman. Note that the research participants in this study were *women*. Also, note that this study has been repeated recently with similar results (Myers, 1992).

This belief that women are less competent may partially explain the survey finding that many people wouldn't want to work for a woman (Kanter, 1977). Consequently, it is difficult for women to be accepted in leadership roles. For example, Porter and her colleagues (1978) took advantage of the phenomenon that the person seated at the head of the table is usually accepted as the leader of the group. She showed research participants photographs of groups of people seated around a table and asked research participants to rate the leadership attributes of each group member. A man seated at the head of the table in a mixed-gender group was usually perceived as the group's leader. However, when a woman was pictured at the head of the table, she was identified as the leader only if the group was all female.

Research shows that when women hold leadership positions in real-world job situations, they are commonly viewed as lacking the qualities necessary for leadership. But do female supervisors really behave differently from their male counterparts? In general, no. Although research shows that females placed in supervisory roles are less likely to use rewarding strategies (promises of pay raises), and are more likely to use coercive strategies (pay cuts), these differences are very small (Instone et al., 1983). That is, female managers and male managers seem to have the same characteristics and use the same strategies (Baron & Paulhus, 1991).

Table 12.3

Employment Discrimination

- Women make less than three-fourths of what men make.
- Men with a high school degree make substantially more than women with a college degree.
- Women hold 14 percent of the degrees in engineering, but only 7 percent of all engineers are women.
- Women hold 80 percent of the clerical jobs, but only 20 percent of the physician jobs. (As recently as 1921, 92 percent of hospitals didn't allow women to be interns [Matlin, 1993].)
- In teaching, women hold 98 percent of the kindergarten and prekindergarten jobs, but only 51 percent of the junior and senior high jobs.
- 44 percent of the people who have four or more years of college are women, but only 15 percent of full professors are women.
- Women do better in college than men, but male college graduates make almost 150 percent more than female college graduates.
- Men with degrees in education make 26 percent more than women who have degrees in education, men with degrees in foreign language make 54 percent more than women with the same degree, males with degrees in architecture make 77 percent more than females with architecture degrees—even though men and women had the same number of years of job experience.
- In graphic design, women earn 62 cents to a man's $1.00.
- Despite having much more experience, women on staffs of the U.S. Senate earn only 78 percent of what men on those staffs earn. Men on Senate staffs are also four times more likely to have an extremely high paying staff job.
- Women hold only 3 percent of the corporate officer positions in Fortune 500 companies.

Sources: From C. Adelman, *Women at Thirtysomething: Paradoxes of Attainment*, Diane Publishers, Upland, Penn., 1993; M. W. Matlin, *Psychology of Women*, Harcourt Brace Jovanovich, Houston, Texas, 1993; U.S. Department of Labor, *Handbook of Labor Statistics*, 1989.

Gender Differences in Developmental "Crises"

Gender differences in home and work experiences persist throughout adulthood. Although both men and women may experience age-linked periods of upheaval, the age and nature of these crisis points are different for each sex. Whereas women often experience a major transition during their late twenties and early thirties (Baruch et al., 1983; Livson, 1976; Roberts & Newton, 1987), men are most likely to experience a midlife crisis at around age 40 or 50 (Levinson, 1986).

For women, the "Age Thirty Transition" (Levinson et al., 1978; Levinson, 1986) may be characterized either as:

1. A shifting in priorities from interpersonal to career, or
2. A shifting in priorities from career to interpersonal.

Levinson suggests that women experience an Age Thirty Transition when their priorities shift. For example, a woman in her thirties may place her priority on work if she's spent her twenties starting a family.

For those women who spent their twenties supporting their husbands' aspirations and starting a family, the Age Thirty Transition is when some will start to focus on their personal dreams. This period may be marked by marital upheaval as women say to their husbands, "If you cannot accept and support this part of me (my need to concentrate on my dissertation, my involvement in city politics, my desire for paid employment), then I cannot continue to be married to you" (Furst, 1983; Roberts & Newton, 1987).

For those women who spent their early twenties establishing a career, the Age Thirty Transition may be characterized by an increasing focus on the development of personal relationships (Adams, 1983). Thus, career women may decide to spend less time on their careers and more time on their relationships.

Most men spend their early thirties building their career. Rather than a time of upheaval, it is often a time of settling in. Their crisis occurs later, in their forties or fifties, when they realize that their career aspirations will not be achieved or when they decide that those aspirations no longer hold meaning. Thus, the male midlife crisis is spent reevaluating his life and developing a lifestyle that conforms to his new priorities.

Theories of Gender-Role Development

You have seen that children quickly learn gender roles and that this learning follows them throughout life. But how do children learn the appropriate gender role? In the next sections, we will evaluate the four most popular explanations: Freud's psychoanalytic view, social learning theory, cognitive developmental theory, and gender schema theory.

Freud's Psychoanalytic View

Sigmund Freud, the father of psychoanalysis, believed that male and female children assume their respective sex-typed characteristics by identifying with the same-sex parent. However, identification with the same-sex parent does not begin at birth. Instead, identification with the same-sex parent begins only after the conflicts of the phallic stage have been resolved.

Male Gender-Role Development

As you may recall from chapter 2, during the phallic stage (ages 3 to 6), the little boy wants to sexually possess his mother (i.e., the Oedipal complex). To remove his father as a rival, the young boy considers castrating his father. However, the boy soon realizes that his more powerful rival may be thinking along similar lines: "The boy's a rival, I'll have to castrate him." To reduce this castration anxiety, the boy resigns from being a rival and instead identifies with the father. ("If you can't beat 'em, join 'em.") By adopting his father's values and feelings, the small boy not only forms his superego, but also develops his male gender role.

Female Gender-Role Development

Whereas castration anxiety motivates little boys to identify with their fathers, penis envy motivates little girls to identify with their mothers. During the phallic stage, a young girl's closeness to her mother is weakened when she realizes that her mother cannot meet all her needs and when the girl becomes fascinated with her father's penis (Freud, 1965). The love once focused almost exclusively on the mother is now transferred to the father, the owner of the valued organ. However, this affection for her father is tainted by jealousy over his penis—creating penis envy.

Freud struggled with numerous explanations for how the girl eventually identifies with her mother to form her feminine gender role. He finally decided that because the girl lacked anxiety about castration, she remained in the situation of "mother-hate, father-love" for a long time. Eventually, by repressing her father-love, the girl breaks away from this bind—but not completely. The failure to

Box 12.5

SELF-CHECK

Indicate whether each of the following statements is true or false.

1. There are only two common psychological differences between male and female infants.
2. By the time children reach kindergarten, they have developed stereotypes of which careers are appropriate for men and which careers are appropriate for women.
3. The genders start to segregate around sixth grade.
4. The reason the genders segregate may be because males engage in more aggressive play than girls do.
5. Boys do better in school than girls do.
6. Teachers punish, criticize, and praise boys more than girls.
7. Female adolescents seem to buy into career-related, gender-role stereotypes such as "A man's career is more important than a woman's" and "Women are best off working in nursing, teaching, and social service professions."
8. In adolescence, girls (especially those who score high in "femininity") seem to sense that there is a conflict between achievement (especially in "masculine" fields like math) and being "feminine."
9. Sex-role stereotypes do not hinder males' academic achievement.
10. With age, men and women become even more locked into conventional gender roles.
11. Marriage seems to favor men more than women.
12. Women often prevent men from doing more of the housework.
13. There is very little evidence of sex discrimination in the workplace.
14. Both men and women seem to be biased against women managers.
15. Consistent with the theme that there are more gender similarities than gender differences, research finds that both men and women experience developmental crises at about the same time.

Please turn to the end of this chapter to check your answers.

completely identify with the mother would account for why girls like "boy" toys and may adopt "masculine" traits, whereas few boys like dolls and other "girl toys" and few boys try to emulate "feminine" characteristics.

Critique of Freud's Psychoanalytic View

Many people object to Freud's theory. Feminists argue that Freud ignored the fact that males have many more advantages than females. Thus, penis envy might be "power envy" or "freedom envy." Scientists are disturbed by the lack of empirical evidence to support the theory. Unfortunately, neither Freud nor his followers were interested in doing controlled studies to test the theory.

Much of the research that has been done provides more criticism than support for Freud's notions (see Mischel, 1970). For example, a massive study conducted over three decades ago by Robert Sears and his colleagues (Sears, Rau, & Alpert, 1965) failed to support Freud's principal contentions. Even Freud's view that the male child should identify with the "powerful" father is not fully supported by the evidence. For instance, experimental attempts to document the ability of a strong model to induce identification have not always been successful (Bryan & Walbeck, 1970). Furthermore, the evidence does not provide overwhelming support for the idea that boys model their fathers more than their mothers (Matlin, 1993).

Cross-cultural research has challenged Freud's belief that boys must have a rivalry with their fathers for possession of the mother. That is, the traditional Oedipal theory was called into question many years ago when anthropologist Bronislaw Malinowski (1927) showed that a boy doesn't have to rival his father. Malinowski found that, in the Trobriand Islands, the rivalry was between nephew and maternal uncle; relationships with the father were casual and friendly throughout childhood.

There is, admittedly, support for some of Freud's ideas. For example, boys under 5 whose father is absent seem to be less sex-typed (Stevenson & Black, 1988). In addition, as Freud would predict, children don't know that their current gender is a permanent part of them until age 5 or 6 (the end of the phallic stage). However, that indirect support for Freud's position is more than offset by the finding that children are strongly identifying with their gender role long before the Oedipal or Electra complex allegedly occurs. Specifically, 3-year-olds know which types of objects (such as overalls or dresses) belong with each sex, and they don't want to play with or wear the "wrong"-sexed object (see Kuhn, Nash, & Brucken, 1978; Mussen, 1969; Perry & Bussey, 1979).

Social Learning Theory

Although Freud's theory has not been supported, people do accept the idea that children model their behavior after others. Indeed, not only do children learn gender roles by imitating parents and peers, but they also learn from other models, such as from books and television shows. To appreciate the power of televised models to influence children's views about how the two sexes should behave, we will describe a study that is representative of the research in this area.

In the study, 4- to 6-year-olds were shown a film that resembled the "Sesame Street" television show. In one version of the film, Muppet-like characters said that a set of toys belonged to a boy. In another version of the film, the characters said that the same toys belonged to a girl (Cobb et al., 1982). As social learning theorists would predict, children played with the toys that had been described as gender appropriate to them.

In addition to modeling, social learning theory asserts that we learn gender roles by being rewarded for "gender-correct" behavior and punished for "gender-incorrect" behavior. Obviously, some of this rewarding and punishing is done by parents. Interestingly, there are only minute differences in how parents treat very young boys and girls: Major differences do not emerge until school age (Hyde, 1985).

After children enter school, many parents do treat girls and boys very differently. For example, a girl may be expected to help out with housework, whereas the boy may be expected to do yard work. However, there is considerable variation from one family to another. Very "liberated" parents may resist gender-typing their children. Indeed, such parents may give dolls to their sons and trucks to their daughters. Such parents may even try to divide child care equally and take other steps to avoid being models of gender-stereotyped roles. A traditional family, on the other hand, will encourage gender-stereotyped behavior in their children. For instance, such parents may give their sons guns, while giving their daughters dolls.

What makes some families more likely than others to put pressure on the children to rigidly conform to conventional gender roles? Within a family, the pressure put on a child to conform to a conventional gender role will typically differ depending on whether the child was firstborn, second-born, and so on. Specifically, the most pressure to conform to conventional gender roles is put on firstborns (Sutton-Smith & Rosenberg, 1970). Another factor may be the mix of genders in the family. For example, girls with sisters are more feminine than girls with brothers (Jolley, 1989; Rosenberg, 1970).

In addition to the family, schools are transmitters of gender stereotypes (Chafetz, 1974). Although there has been some improvement in recent years, school books often depict girls and women in restrictive, boring, passive, and supportive, or "down-right stupid" roles (Matlin, 1993; Weitzman et al., 1972). Boys and men, on the other hand, are depicted in independent, active, and exciting roles. Teachers tend to be much more responsive to male students and often reinforce gender-stereotyped behaviors (Matlin, 1993). However, teachers and parents put very little pressure on a child to conform to gender roles compared to the enormous pressures that peers put on a child. Peers are enthusiastically aggressive in punishing the child who doesn't conform to traditional gender-role behavior.

Some parents may resist gender stereotyping in childhood by modeling and rewarding nontraditional behavior.

Cognitive Theories

Social learning theory is accurate—as far as it goes. That is, it explains why a child might do traditional behaviors, but it does not explain how children develop attitudes about what men and women should be like, and it does not explain how children's views of male and female roles change with age. Therefore, to more fully understand gender-role development, you must also understand cognitive development.

Box 12.6

SELF-CHECK

Indicate whether each of the following statements is true or false.

1. According to Freud, identification with the same-sexed parent begins at birth.
2. According to Freud, boys are more strongly sex-typed than girls.
3. As would be predicted by Freud, boys are much more likely to model their fathers; whereas girls are much more likely to model their mothers.
4. As would be predicted by Freud, boys always have a rivalry with their fathers.
5. As would be predicted by Freud, children don't know that they will always be the same gender until they reach age 5 or 6.
6. The fact that children as young as 3 behave in gender-stereotyped ways is a problem for Freud's theory.
7. Girls with brothers are more feminine than girls with sisters.
8. Firstborns are more likely to strictly conform to conventional gender roles than laterborns.
9. There are only relatively small differences in how parents treat very young boys and girls: It is only after children reach school age that boys and girls are treated much differently.
10. Teachers pay more attention to boys than to girls.

Please turn to the end of this chapter to check your answers.

Lawrence Kohlberg's Theory of Gender-Role Development

Perhaps the best-known cognitive theory of gender-role development is that of psychologist Lawrence Kohlberg (1966). Strongly influenced by Piaget's model of cognitive development, Kohlberg thought that learning gender roles involved actively making mental deductions based on the child's knowledge of certain regularities that endure. At first, the deductions are fairly simple. For example, by age 3 or 4, most children have figured out enough about gender that they know what gender they are and can determine whether a person is male or female. By this age, they show preferences for people, things, and activities that match their own gender (Matlin, 1993). By age 6 or 7, most children realize that gender is a permanent characteristic: Whatever sex they are now, they will be for the rest of their lives.

Kohlberg (1966) collected evidence to support his idea that mental development is a prerequisite for developing gender roles. He points to the fact that children who score highest on tests of cognitive development also display the most consistently sex-appropriate identification patterns. That is, smart boys are quicker than other boys to identify with their fathers; smart girls are quicker than other girls to identify with their mothers. Even more impressive for the cognitive view is that cognitive level is more strongly related to gender-role development than chronological age. For example, in terms of gender roles, retarded children behave more like their mental-age counterparts (younger children with normal IQs) than like their chronological-age counterparts.

The idea that gender-role development is tied to cognitive development is intuitively appealing. For example, consider the 1-year-old. The 1-year-old doesn't really understand rules. If infants can't understand rules, how can they know the rules regarding gender?

Next, consider the 3-year-old. The 3-year-old is learning rules of grammar and rigidly adhering to these rules ("I goed to the store"). Doesn't it make sense that such a child will also be learning and rigidly adhering to rules regarding the genders ("Only women can be nurses")? Trying to tell 3-year-olds that they should say "Men can also be nurses" is perhaps more futile than telling them that they should say "I went to the store."

Finally, consider the older child. In middle to late childhood, children become more accepting of the fact that rules can be broken or modified. At that same age, children also become more accepting of behavior that does not fit rigid sex-role stereotypes.

Jeanne Block's Theory of Gender-Role Development

Kohlberg's theory is interesting and is based on an interesting theory—Piaget's theory of cognitive development. However, according to some psychologists, Kohlberg's theory shares two weaknesses with Piaget's theory:

1. Kohlberg focuses on the individual being *biologically able* to develop complex cognitive categories rather than on the *social* factors that influence the individual's *willingness* to conform to gender roles.
2. Kohlberg focuses on explaining child development rather than adolescent and adult development.

Consequently, some psychologists have based their theories on other models of development. For example, rather than focus on Piaget's model of cognitive development, Jeanne

Table 12.4

The Link Between Gender-Role Development and Some of Loevinger's Milestones of Ego Development

Loevinger's Stage	General Description of Individuals at This Stage	Effect on Gender Role (According to Block)
Presocial	Not aware of others.	Little or no development of gender roles.
Symbiotic	Self-assertive and individualistic.	Disregards society's gender roles.
Conformist	Wants to belong and be liked. Conformity to external rules, feels shame and guilt for breaking rules. Thinks in simplistic, stereotypical, and clichéd ways.	Strictly adheres to gender roles prescribed by society.
Autonomous	Respects individual differences, thinks in complex, sophisticated ways.	Willing to deviate from sex-typed behavior.
Integrated	Respects and cherishes individual differences. Thinks in complex, sophisticated ways.	Cherishes others who violate conventional gender roles.

Block's model is based on Jane Loevinger's theory of ego development. (We discussed Loevinger's model in chapter 8. For a review of Loevinger's theory, see table 12.4.) Specifically, Block (1976) proposes that a person's stage of ego development affects that person's willingness to adopt society's gender roles.

Block, like Loevinger, maintains that young children behave in ways that are individualistic, self-assertive, and expansive—a tendency she calls **agency.** During this period, both males and females tend to disregard society's gender roles to fulfill their ego's own tendency toward agency.

As children age, Block and Loevinger also maintain that children's behavior is guided by what Block calls **communion,** a need to conform to the group and to seek group approval. Thus, as children age, Block believes that they start to adhere more strictly to the gender roles prescribed by society.

During adolescence, both Loevinger and Block believe that many individuals become less willing to conform to norms. Thus, according to Block, individuals should become less willing to conform to norms about sex roles. Consequently, individuals who, during childhood, were unwilling to risk nonconformity may, as adolescents, begin to deviate from sex-typed behavior. According to Block the final outcome of an adolescent ego's maturation in regard to sex-role development is **androgyny,** a gender-role orientation in which individuals incorporate both male and female aspects into their character.

Block's general conclusion that androgyny increases with maturation (although at a later age than she indicated) is supported by the findings of a large-scale series of investigations known collectively as the Kansas City Studies of Adult Life (Neugarten, 1977; Neugarten & Gutmann, 1968). Research participants ranging in age from 40 to 70 were asked to tell a story about a picture that depicted a young man and woman and an old man and woman, the four apparently in conversation. Research participants over age 55 were much more likely than younger research participants to describe the old man as passive rather than authoritative and the old woman as assertive rather than submissive or under the control of her husband and children. From this and other studies, one reviewer concluded that "older men seemed more receptive than younger men of their affiliative, nurturant, and sensual promptings; older women, more receptive than younger women of aggressive and egocentric impulses" (Neugarten, 1973, p. 320).

Gender Schema Theories

We have examined several theories of gender-role development. Each has provided a useful way of understanding phenomena. However, none explain all the facts.

Social learning theory, for example, gives us some insight into why men and women behave differently. In addition, it gives us some useful ideas about how to raise children who will be less locked into conventional gender roles. However, by itself, social learning theory doesn't explain how the child whose own mother is a physician can develop the stereotyped view that women can't be physicians. Furthermore, social learning theory doesn't explain discontinuity in gender-role development. That is, social learning theory can't answer the question: Why do children, around age 5, become much more interested in same-sex models than they were at an early age (Ruble et al., 1981)?

Kohlberg's cognitive developmental theory, on the other hand, can explain why children at age 5 become more interested in same-sex models (they have just developed the ability to understand gender as a permanent characteristic), and Kohlberg can explain changes in children's views about the genders (these views become more complex, paralleling changes in the child's general level of cognitive development). Thus, Kohlberg is to be applauded for both

Box 12.7

SELF-CHECK

Indicate whether each of the following statements is true or false.

1. Kohlberg's theory of gender development is strongly influenced by Piaget's theory of cognitive development.
2. Kohlberg's theory can, unlike social learning theory, explain apparent discontinuities in gender-role development. That is, the theory can explain why a child's view of gender roles could change dramatically.
3. The fact that children develop gender-appropriate behavior before age 3 causes problems for Kohlberg's theory.
4. Kohlberg's theory does a better job than Block's at explaining how gender-role development proceeds through adolescence and adulthood.
5. Gender schema theory can explain discontinuity in gender-role development.
6. According to gender schema theory, people naturally divide the world into "us" and "not us."
7. According to gender schema theory, people naturally divide the world into "masculine" and "feminine."

Please turn to the end of this chapter to check your answers.

showing that children actively seek out information about gender roles and for tying gender-role development to cognitive development. However, Kohlberg has difficulty explaining why children as young as 15 months (nearly two years before they have a gender identity) prefer "gender-appropriate" toys (Levy & Carter, 1989)—whereas social learning theory can.

Perhaps, as we suggested earlier, the key to understanding gender development is to see the phenomena through the viewpoint of both social learning theory and cognitive developmental theories. Perhaps, the solution is to do more research on Block's theory. But perhaps the solution is to develop a new theory. One relatively new set of theories that have excited some interest are the gender schema theories (Bem, 1981, 1983, 1985; Levy & Carter, 1989; Martin & Halverson, 1981).

Like cognitive developmental theories, **gender schema theories** stress that we naturally want to form cognitive categories to classify people and things. We also want to develop a view of who we are. That is, we naturally divide the world into "me" and "not me," and into "us" and "them." Like social learning theory, gender schema theories posit that society tells us who "they are" and how "they" differ from "us."

Gender schema theories predict that boys will pay more attention to and remember more about stereotypically male activities like football.

Once children know what their gender is and are taught that gender is the most important way of categorizing people and that there are "vital psychological differences" between the genders, then children will develop gender schemas. These gender schemas will affect the way they view themselves. Thus, their self-esteem may depend on how well they conform to their schema of what a "real woman" or "real man" should be.

Their gender schema will also affect the way they view the world. Children will ignore information and activities that are irrelevant to their gender schema while seeking out information and activities that are relevant to their gender schema. Thus, a girl may ignore football, but learn how to sew, whereas a boy may do the reverse. Consistent with gender schema theory, boys remember more about male characters and about stereotypically male actions than girls do, whereas girls are better than boys at remembering female characters and stereotypically female actions (Signorella, Bigler, & Liben, 1994).

Gender schema theories are interesting. They explain why people are so reluctant to give up gender-role stereotypes (the stereotypes are part of people's personal identities) and why people are biased in perceiving both their own and others' gender role-relevant behavior (because the schemas change how we see the world). Furthermore, gender schema theories suggest solutions to gender inequality. For example, gender schema theory would suggest that we avoid making gender such an important category. That is, if we want to promote gender equality, we should not have "boys against the girls" games in schools; and we should not have television shows or books that indicate that there are different toys, occupations, and activities for boys than there are for girls. However, before wholeheartedly adopting gender schema theories, more research must be done. We need to know whether the theory is accurate and whether its recommendations would work.

CONCLUSIONS

In conclusion, much more research must be done in the area of sex differences. With a highly politicized topic that has implication for individuals' ways of life, we need the unbiased information that only sound research can provide. As we saw earlier in this chapter, we cannot rely on people's opinions about what the sexes are like. That is, biases cause people to incorrectly observe behavior. Thus, when told that a child is a boy, people will "see" the child's behavior very differently from what they will perceive when told the child is a girl.

Not only do we need more scientific research, but we need to understand what that research means. For example, in chapter 1, you learned that psychologists usually try to find **statistically significant differences,** differences between groups that are probably not due to chance. In reading research and in reading newspapers, you will come across many statistically significant results. When interpreting that research, it is important to realize four things about statistical significance.

First, statistical significance can only be used to find differences between groups. It cannot be used to find similarities. Thus, gender research will focus on finding differences rather than similarities.

Second, statistical significance is not the same thing as practical significance. Even a small, practically insignificant difference may be statistically significant. That is, most of the sex differences that are statistically significant are also quite small.

Third, statistical significance indicates only that the *average* for one group is higher than the average for another group. It doesn't mean that *all* the people in one group score higher than all the people in the other group. For example, take the statistically significant difference between students with different SAT scores: Students with high SATs do better in college than students with lower SAT scores. However, this significant difference does not mean that the students with high SAT scores will all do better than students with average SAT scores. There will be students in both groups who do well in school and there will be students in both groups who do poorly in school. If we misinterpret an average difference as meaning that everybody in one group is superior to another group, we are stereotyping. We must avoid trying to see things in black and white terms. We must avoid overgeneralizing. Thus, even if we see that, on the average, men are substantially faster than women at mentally rotating objects, we should realize that there are many women who are faster at that task than most men. In other words, we should remind ourselves that deciding what type of person someone is based on their gender would make as much sense as a professor assigning grades based on SAT scores.

Fourth, statistical significance does not mean that the difference observed in a particular study could not possibly be due to chance. It means only that the difference observed in a particular study is unlikely to be due to chance. Typically, it means that, if there really is no difference between the groups, there is a less than 5 in 100 chance that the difference observed in that one study was due to chance. However, if there really is no sex difference, but 100 people do basically the same study, 5 of those studies could obtain statistically significant results due to chance alone—and those 5 may be the studies that will get published. Few journals will publish studies that failed to find significant differences.

When considering research findings, not only should we be aware of the limitations of statistical significance, but we should also take a critical look at the study's measures. As we saw in this chapter, speed of mentally rotating an object was considered a measure of spatial ability. We should ask ourselves "Is this a valid measure of an important psychological construct or is it merely a convenient laboratory task?" Similarly, we should ask whether sex differences in scores on the SAT test reflect differences in ability or gender biases in the test.

Finally, when considering sex differences, we should also be aware of the difficulty of establishing the causes of these differences. As we discussed in chapter 1, it is very easy to mistake an effect for a cause. In this chapter, we ran into several cases in which it was hard to distinguish cause from effect. For example, some naturists believe that the natural differences between the sexes cause people to treat the sexes differently. These naturists argue that the biological differences between males and females must explain why there are psychological differences between the sexes that are remarkably consistent across a variety of cultures (Buss, 1992; Hinde, 1983; Williams & Best, 1982). Nurturists, on the other hand, can point to research suggesting that, for the most part, the vastly different treatment that the sexes receive may be the cause of sex differences. For example, boys are given more attention, more freedom, and more toys, and males are much more visible on television and in books. Thus, the nature/nurture debate rages on—despite the fact that research suggests that the differences between sexes are not all that great. Research alone will not quell the nature/nurture debate. However, future research may allow parents to rear children who are not constrained by society's gender roles and who do not try to lock others into those roles.

SUMMARY

1. Psychological similarities between the sexes are more the rule than sex differences.
2. Women report more fear, anxiety, and empathy than men, but these self-report data are not consistent with research that looks for gender differences using physiological measures of fear, anxiety, and empathy.
3. Males and females do not differ in emotional dependency during the first few years of life.
4. Men are more aggressive than women, especially when it comes to unjustified physical aggression against an acquaintance.
5. Males tend to score higher on tests of mathematical ability, whereas women tend to score higher on tests of verbal ability. However, these differences are small—and seem to be getting smaller.
6. Men do better than women on certain kinds of spatial tasks. However, the reasons for doing better on these spatial tasks and the relevance of these tasks for real-world functioning are not well understood.
7. Some evidence suggests that more men than women have extremely high levels of mathematical ability.
8. Before puberty, females seem to do as well as males in tests of mathematical ability. Even after puberty, women get better grades in math classes than men.
9. Biological explanations for sex differences, such as hormone and brain lateralization theories, may be correct. However, such theories do not currently have strong support from human research.
10. Boys receive much more attention (both praise and criticism) than girls.
11. There is more pressure on boys to conform to gender roles than on girls.
12. According to social learning theory, sex-typed behavior occurs as a result of being rewarded for the "right" (gender-appropriate) behaviors, being punished for the "wrong" (gender-inappropriate) behaviors, and modeling people of one's own gender.
13. The evidence does not provide strong support for the social learning position that very young children model the same-sexed parent more than the parent of the opposite sex. However, live and symbolic models of both sexes may teach the child what is gender-role appropriate.
14. Although researchers have uncovered only two psychological differences between male and female infants (females have more touch sensitivity, males are more active), many differences are noticeable by age 3.
15. By age 3, most children know their gender. By age 6, most children know that their gender will be a permanent part of them. By age 7, gender stereotypes are already restricting children's career aspirations.
16. Voluntary sex segregation is well established by age 4 1/2 and is very strong by age 6 1/2, possibly because boys are rougher than girls.
17. At adolescence, gender roles seem to hurt women's intellectual self-confidence, academic achievement, and career aspirations.
18. The idea that women's academic achievements are being harmed by gender-role stereotypes is supported by (1) the fact that androgynous women do better in math and sciences than "feminine" women and (2) the fact that, as gender roles have become less restrictive, the differences between the genders on tests of cognitive abilities have decreased.
19. Some adolescent males may be harmed by trying to fit into a gender role that does not permit asking for help, expressing feelings, and nurturing others.
20. Most women believe that the man's work is more important. Women sometimes do prevent men from doing housework.
21. Both men and women tend to be biased against women bosses.
22. According to Levinson, women are more likely to experience a developmental crisis in their thirties. Men experience such crises in their forties or fifties.
23. Adult women seem more concerned with interpersonal relationships than men.
24. Freud's theory of sex-role development does explain why girls are less sex-typed than boys. However, the theory has very little research support.
25. Social learning theory can account for much of gender-role development. However, it does not explain why children's views of the genders undergo qualitative shifts.
26. Kohlberg's theory of sex-role development ties sex-role development to cognitive development. There is some support for the theory. However, the theory does not explain gender-role development before age 3 or after age 12. In addition, Kohlberg's theory does not explain why children want to conform to gender roles.
27. According to some, Jeanne Block's theory of sex-role development fills many of the holes in Kohlberg's theory.

28. Gender schema theories may offer a way of synthesizing social learning theory and cognitive theories.
29. Scientific research can give us a less biased look at gender differences and similarities. However, to benefit from scientific research, we must (a) understand the limitations of statistical significance; (b) critically examine the measures used in the research; and (c) be aware that correlational research cannot establish that gender has a certain effect.
30. Statistical significance tests are designed to find differences. Such tests cannot be used to find similarities.
31. Statistical significance does not mean that a difference is large or important.
32. Research that "finds" a statistically significant difference can be wrong as much as 5 percent of the time.

Key Terms

adrenogenital syndrome (AGS) 378
agency 392
aggression 374
androgens 377
androgyny 392
anxiety 374
brain lateralization 378
communion 392
Embedded-Figure Test 375
empathy 373
field independence 375
gender roles 371
gender schema theories 393
social learning theory 379
spatial ability 375
statistically significant differences 394
symbolic models 380

Self-Check Answers

Box 12.1

1. False.
2. False. Don't confuse stereotypes with fact.
3. True.
4. True.
5. False. Although self-report evidence supports the idea that women are more responsive to babies, the physiological evidence does not support the idea that women are innately more responsive to babies than men are.
6. False.
7. False. Males are only slightly more verbally aggressive than females. Furthermore, when the victim is either anonymous or deserving of punishment, research often finds that there is little or no difference between males and females in terms of physical aggression.
8. False.
9. True.
10. True.
11. True.
12. True.

Box 12.2

1. In support of the hormone theory: (a) Hormones can masculinize the rat brain. (b) AGS women, according to John Money, were more likely to be interested in "masculine" activities. (c) Around puberty, males are exposed to much higher levels of male hormones than women. Around this time, males start to exhibit superiority in certain tests of mathematical and spatial ability—and it may be around this time that male hormones make the male brain more strictly lateralized than the female brain.
2. In opposition to the hormone theory: (a) There is not conclusive evidence that hormones masculinize the primate brain. (b) AGS women do not differ from other women in terms of sexual preferences. Furthermore, according to Hines (1982), AGS women raised as females do not differ from non-AGS women in terms of gender-role development. (c) There is little evidence that hormones lateralize the human brain and little evidence that the male brain is more lateralized than the female brain. (d) Differences that emerge around puberty seem to be smaller this generation than they were in the last—a fact that is hard for hormone theory to explain. (e) The relatively small psychological differences between the sexes may reflect the effects of teachers', parents', and society's expectations rather than any biological explanation.

Box 12.3

1. False; **2.** True; **3.** True; **4.** True; **5.** True; **6.** False; **7.** True; **8.** False. The evidence is only correlational, and correlational evidence can't prove that one thing affects another.

Box 12.5

1. True.
2. True.
3. False.
4. True.
5. False.
6. True.
7. True.
8. True. As reflected by the facts that girls are more likely than boys to experience an intellectual decline during adolescence; and that two groups of women who would be less influenced by gender stereotyping—androgynous women and women from more recent cohorts—appear to be less likely to experience intellectual declines in math during adolescence.
9. False. Males may be hindered by their resistance to ask for help. Furthermore, their lower verbal ability, their problems in reading, and their lower school achievement may all be the result of sex-role stereotypes.
10. False.
11. True.
12. True.
13. False.
14. True.
15. False.

Box 12.6

1. False.
2. True. Some evidence supports this view. For example, many girls are "tomboys," but few boys try to emulate "feminine" characteristics.
3. False. The evidence doesn't provide strong support for this idea.
4. False. Cross-cultural research shows that son-father rivalry is not inevitable.
5. True.
6. True. According to Freud, children at age 3 should be imitating their opposite-sex parent.
7. False.
8. True.
9. True.
10. True.

Box 12.7

1. True.
2. True. Gender-role development depends on cognitive development. Since Piaget's theory postulates that cognitive development proceeds in stages, gender-role development could also occur in stages.
3. True. If knowing what gender you are causes you to adopt gender-appropriate behaviors (as Kohlberg's theory suggests), then how is it possible that you adopt gender-appropriate behaviors before you know your gender?
4. False.
5. True.
6. True.
7. False. People form gender schemas because society emphasizes gender differences.

Chapter

Personality Development

By the age of 30, the character has set like plaster and will never soften again.

WILLIAM JAMES

Chapter Overview

Most newborns are similar in both appearance and behavior. Two forces influence individuals to continue acting alike: maturation and socialization. Because of maturation, the way we develop many skills—such as being able to walk, talk, play, and think—conforms to an orderly and predictable pattern. Because of socialization, all of us in a given society are encouraged to conform to many rules that affect not only how we speak and act, but also what we believe.

Yet, despite all these pressures to act like everyone else, we are all different. As we develop, we become not only more social and conforming, but also more independent and unique. How do we develop our own unique personality while establishing more connections with others? In this chapter, we will examine several different "answers" to this question.

Which, if any, of these answers is correct? That is for you to decide. In evaluating each of these answers, ask yourself three questions:

1. **To what extent is this answer supported by scientific evidence? If there is evidence, is this evidence based on experimental research or is the evidence based on some weaker research technique (case study or unstructured interviews, for example)? Could evidence be collected to either support or refute the theory?**
2. **What does the answer say about the importance of nature as compared to nurture? Is this position consistent with the evidence about the relative importance of each?**
3. **What does the answer say about whether personality development continues throughout the lifespan? Is this position consistent with the facts?**

Box 13.1

ISSUE in FOCUS

How Physical Traits Influence How We Are Treated

It would be nice to be judged based on one's efforts, abilities, and personality. However, such is not the case. Despite the familiar saying "You can't judge a book by its cover," superficial physical characteristics are very important in how we are judged. For example:

- Taller people get higher salary offers than shorter people.
- Almost every study has shown that most leaders are taller than the average person.
- In presidential races, the taller candidate almost always wins.
- People of high status are perceived as taller than people of lower status.
- People have been denied jobs—and even admission to college—for being overweight.
- Attractive men are considered to be smarter and nicer than unattractive men.
- It is no accident that advertisers use attractive people in their ads: Attractive people are perceived to be more likable and more credible.
- People think they can decide how honest someone is just by looking at a person.
- When employers receive identical resumes from black and white applicants, they are more likely to pursue the white applicant.
- Teachers give boys much more attention than girls.
- In the workplace, women are not treated the same as men—especially when it comes to salary and promotion.
- When women succeed, their success is viewed as being due to either good luck or having an easy task; when women fail, their failure is usually viewed as being due to lack of ability.
- When men succeed, their success is viewed as being due to hard work or ability; when they fail, it is often perceived as being due to bad luck.

Sources: Baron & Paulhus, 1991; Matlin 1993; Myers, 1993.

Historical Views of Personality

People have always speculated about why we are the way we are. What makes one person courageous, another artistic, and still another dishonest? In the fourth century B.C., Plato proposed that individual differences in ability and psychological functioning were localized in specific parts of the body—reason was in the head, courage in the chest, and appetite in the abdomen. In *The Republic,* Plato proposed a utopian society where individual differences were assessed by measuring different parts of the body and then assigning people to tasks based on their psychological strengths. Imagine living in a society where you are designated a slave or lawyer based on your physical attributes! If this possibility outrages you or seems impossible, realize that to some extent you already live in such a society, as box 13.1 explains.

Plato's belief that specific traits are localized in the body emerged again in the eighteenth and nineteenth centuries through the work of Viennese phrenologist Franz Gall. Gall claimed that personality can be inferred from the shape and features of the skull. As a child, Gall noted that many of his friends with exceptional memories had large, bulbous eyes. Later, he speculated that other mental traits might also correspond to physical characteristics. As a man, Gall traveled to orphanages, prisons, and lunatic asylums to measure the skulls of people who lived in these institutions. His measurements were compiled in a large catalogue where specific bumps on the skull were linked to particular psychological characteristics. For example, Gall reported that pickpockets could be identified by bumps on the side of their skull just above the ear.

In addition to studying the skulls of the living, Gall collected the skulls of the dead. He so enthusiastically pursued skulls that many Viennese specified in their wills that their heads be protected from Gall (Hothersall, 1990, p. 73).

Inherent in both Plato's and Gall's belief that psychological differences between people could be assessed by measuring differences in physical characteristics is the assumption of **biological determinism,** the idea that genes completely determine one's personality and behavior. This extreme nature position seems absurd to most contemporary developmental psychologists. Yet, throughout history, the dominant view has been that nature is all important. Not until the twentieth century did the majority of people accept the idea that personality is the product of both nature and nurture. In other words, only recently have people accepted the idea that through the process of socialization, one's inherited predispositions are molded, augmented, or diminished.

Sigmund Freud and the Birth of Psychoanalytic Theory

At the dawn of the twentieth century, a theory emerged that dealt with the struggle between nature and socialization. As with most personality theories, this theory was strongly influenced by the upbringing of its parent—Sigmund Freud.

As a child, Freud both loved and feared his strict, authoritarian father. In contrast to how he felt toward his father, Freud felt a strong attachment to his loving and protective mother. As you will soon see, Freud's fear of his father and attraction to his mother sounds remarkably like his description of the most controversial concept in his theory—the Oedipal complex.

Throughout his childhood and adolescence, Freud was a brilliant but aimless student until, at age 17, he became fascinated with Darwin's theory of evolution. Eventually, this theory was to become the pillar (or Achilles' heel, depending on your point of view) of Freud's theory of psychoanalysis. But the immediate impact of Freud's infatuation with Darwin's theory was that he developed a keen interest in using the scientific method to understand life. To pursue this interest, Freud decided to study medicine at the University of Vienna.

After receiving his degree in neurology, Freud wanted to continue pursuing his scientific interests by conducting research in a university setting. However, he was too poor to support himself over the several years it would take to earn one of the few professorships available. Reluctantly, he entered private practice as a clinical neurologist.

The Story of Bertha Pappenheim

Professionally, Freud's first big break resulted from his friendship with Josef Breuer, a successful general practitioner. Breuer told Freud about one of his patients, Bertha Pappenheim (referred to in published case studies as Anna O.), a young, wealthy, bright, and attractive woman. Bertha displayed several hysterical symptoms, including a nervous cough, memory lapses, a double personality, paralysis, nausea, hearing disorders, and a speech disorder (an inability to speak her native German, although she could speak English fluently).

Breuer began treating Bertha with hypnosis. Under hypnosis, Bertha was able to recall specific experiences that precipitated many of her symptoms. Several of these memories centered on her father's final illness and the profound emotions she experienced while caring for him. For example, one day her father asked her the time. Through her tears, the hands of the watch were blurred. From then on, she had blurred vision. Soon after recalling this incident, Bertha's vision cleared up.

Breuer attempted to remove all of Bertha's symptoms, one by one, through daily sessions. He reported that after these intense recollections, Anna became cheerful and calm. Often her symptoms would decrease in severity or actually disappear. Breuer referred to this treatment as the "talking cure."

These intense sessions continued for over a year. During one session, Bertha declared her love for Breuer. Breuer immediately concluded that the treatment was dangerous and terminated it. Bertha's response to this news was hysterical childbirth, implicating Breuer as the father. (Reportedly, Breuer's response to this was to go on a long vacation with his wife.) The physician who took over Bertha's care prescribed morphine to calm her. She became an addict and had to be institutionalized.

Fortunately, Bertha's story has a happy ending. She recovered from her hysteria and became one of Europe's first social workers and an early feminist (Freeman, 1972; Kimble, Garnezy, & Zigler, 1984).

The Birth of Psychoanalysis

In 1895, Breuer and Freud described the case of "Anna O." in *Studies in Hysteria*. Although the two men agreed on Bertha's symptoms, their disagreement over the causes was so great that it eventually led to the breakup of their friendship. Whereas Breuer attributed Bertha symptoms to something called the "hypnoidal state" of the neurotic, Freud was convinced that her problems stemmed from sexual factors.

The "talking cure" and the insights Freud gained from his experience with Bertha and Breuer eventually evolved into psychoanalysis. Sigmund Freud's construction of psychoanalytic theory marked the first systematic theory of personality development. For this reason, Freudian theory should be regarded as the most influential psychological theory—the yardstick by which all other theories are compared and contrasted (Hall & Lindzey, 1978).

The Structure of Personality

As you learned in chapter 2, Freud divided the personality into three structures: id, ego, and superego. The id, the inheritance from our animal ancestors, is present at birth. The id is an unconscious store of instinctual energy, consisting of all of our basic, primitive biological needs. For example, the primitive, animalistic needs for food, water, warmth, sex, aggression, and elimination all reside in the id. Although the id is the source of all human motivation, it has no idea how to gratify its brutish desires because it has no concept of reality.

As you can imagine, the id is in for disappointments. On the one hand, it is ruled by the pleasure principle: immediate gratification through reducing tension from internal excitation or external stimulation. On the other hand, the id, being blind to reality, can't do anything to satisfy these needs except to fantasize. Fantasizing is a poor substitute for the real thing. (Compare imagining eating food when you're starving versus really eating food.)

To deal with reality, the id creates a slave called the ego. Basically, the ego is the conscious, rational part of the personality that perceives, learns, reasons, and remembers. Rather than operating on the pleasure principle (immediate pleasure is the only thing), the ego operates on the reality principle: trying to gratify the id's demands as much as possible while considering the constraints of the real world and the long-term consequences of actions. Freud thought the ego emerged from the id during the second six months of life, as evidenced by infants beginning to know that there is a "me" who is different from the rest of the world.

Between the ages of 3 and 6, the id and ego have to start dealing with rules imposed by other people, usually parents. Because neither the id nor the ego are well-equipped to deal with social realities such as moral and ethical standards, the superego is formed. The superego governs moral and ethical conduct through its two parts: the conscience and the ego-ideal. The first part, the conscience, tells us what we shouldn't do. If we do what it considers bad, it punishes us by making us feel guilty. In addition to being punished for immoral acts by our conscience, we are rewarded for moral acts by our **ego-ideal:** our image of who we should ideally be. Like the id, the superego is unrealistic: If it had its way, all sexual and aggressive impulses would be eliminated.

The ego has the formidable task of trying to deal with reality while finding a compromise between the unrealistic desires of both the selfish id and the puritanical superego. When the ego fails to reconcile these competing desires, the person experiences anxiety.

Defense Mechanisms

To relieve anxiety, the ego may use **defense mechanisms,** unconscious ways of distorting, denying, or falsifying reality. Defense mechanisms are adaptive because, at least in the short term, they reduce anxiety. If we couldn't reduce anxiety through defense mechanisms, we might be too anxious to function. However, the reduction of anxiety has its costs. First, when we use a defense mechanism, we haven't changed reality; we've only modified the way we see or think about reality. It's like the aspirin commercials where a poor housewife is being annoyed by the family pets, the children, and her husband until she explodes. She takes an aspirin and is now smiling. Certainly, she needed relief from the headache, but the sources of the headache—the misbehaving pets, children, and husband—are still there. If she doesn't deal with these problems, she'll become an aspirin addict. Second, because we've fooled ourselves, we may be unable to see the problem clearly and thus be unable to deal with it.

The number one defense mechanism is **repression,** the pushing of unacceptable thoughts and impulses back into the unconscious. Traumatic experiences (such as a car accident), and unacceptable thoughts (such as sexual feelings toward a relative) are likely to be repressed.

Repressing unwanted thoughts or memories, however, does not eliminate them. They have simply been temporarily pushed out of the conscious mind and into the unconscious. While in the unconscious, they will try to fight their way back into consciousness. As these memories and impulses threaten to penetrate the surface of consciousness, the person experiences anxiety. To fight the anxiety, the ego calls in additional defense mechanisms, such as compensation, rationalization, sublimation, projection, reaction formation, displacement, denial, and regression. The defense mechanism that is used will depend on the person's personality and the reason for the anxiety.

If a person is anxious because of his real or perceived deficiencies, the ego may call on one of the most constructive defense mechanisms—**compensation,** making up for deficiencies by excelling in other areas. Some people may compensate for feelings of intellectual inferiority by "acting tough" or by excelling in sports. Conversely, some may compensate for feelings of physical inferiority by excelling academically. For better or worse, parents often compensate for their own unrealized desires by pushing their children to achieve those unfulfilled dreams. Thus, it's not unusual to see an unattractive woman entering her 4-year-old in numerous beauty contests.

If a person is anxious because she is ashamed of either her actions or her motives for those actions, she may engage in **rationalization,** justifying her actions, ignoring her true unconscious motivations. She makes an excuse for her behavior that she believes (and she may be the only one who believes the excuse). For example, a parent may rationalize that he beats his children because he "loves" them (It shows that he cares; it's for their own good, "you only hurt the ones you love", etc.). Or, a person who fails to get a certain job may claim, "I didn't want the job anyway."

If a person is anxious because he has natural, sexual urges, but these urges conflict with society (he is considered too young to be having sex), then he may engage in **sublimation,** converting this sexual energy (a productive and creative force) into a more socially appropriate form of productive and creative energy. For example, late in the nineteenth century, a group referred to as the "Muscular Christians" took vows of celibacy, spending most of their day involved in vigorous physical exercise. Freud would say that these people were sublimating their sexual impulses through physical exercise. Similarly, a young teenager may sublimate her sexual desires by expressing her creative urges through painting or creative writing.

If a person is anxious because he has impulses of which he is truly ashamed, the ego may call on any number of defense mechanisms. If the ego calls on **projection,** the person will attribute his own taboo impulses to someone else. For example, one student justified his cheating by saying everyone else in the class was cheating. If a person calls up **reaction formation,** the person will think and act in a manner that is the opposite of his or her unconscious impulse. One of our students reported an intriguing instance of reaction formation. Her former husband divorced her shortly after the birth of their third child, a severely retarded boy. Before the birth, their marriage seemed solid. Now, although he never visits the child, he periodically calls her telling her, "I really love that kid, and if anything ever happens to him, I'll kill you." Is this love for the child real or is it reaction formation?

The case of our student's ex-husband illustrates how several defense mechanisms may work together. You may suspect that the hostility he expresses towards his wife ("I'll kill you") may be hostility that he feels toward the retarded son, but has redirected toward a safer target. In other words, you may suspect the husband of using **displacement,** transferring or redirecting unacceptable feelings about a person or a situation from their actual target to a safer target. Often, after a frustrating encounter with her boss, a woman might "blow up" at her husband. As the song goes, "You always hurt the ones you love"—perhaps because they're a safer target.

If the source of the anxiety comes from the outside world, the ego might rely on **denial,** dealing with an unacceptable reality by denying its existance. Denial is a common initial reaction in people who have been told they have a terminal illness such as AIDS or cancer. When denial persists, however, it can lead to serious problems. For example, a mother may deny the death of a child and pretend that the child is still alive.

Alternatively, the ego might deal with a threat from the outside world by using **regression,** a return to a more immature state. Following a failed marriage, some people regress into a period of irresponsible sex and self-indulgence; following severe trauma, an adult may regress to a very childlike state. As a student of developmental psychology, you may find that regression is perhaps the most fascinating defense mechanism because, by using it, a person reverses development. But before you consider how a person's personality might regress, let's look at Freud's view of how personality progresses.

Box 13.2

SELF-CHECK

PART A

Indicate whether each of the following statements is true or false.

1. People believe that a person's appearance gives clues to the person's personality—and people have believed this since ancient times.
2. Freud's theory is based on the theory of evolution.
3. The case of Bertha Pappenheim suggested that talking about forgotten memories could cure mental symptoms.
4. According to Freud, the ego is the moral part of the personality.
5. The ego, being the rational and realistic part of the personality, governs the id.
6. According to Freud, the conscience is the part of our personality that tells us what we should and shouldn't do.
7. Defense mechanisms are not adaptive.
8. When we use a defense mechanism, we don't know that we are using it.
9. Repression involves erasing unpleasant memories.

PART B

Answer the following questions.

10. What are the differences between compensation, sublimation, and displacement?
11. What is the difference between rationalization and denial?

Please turn to the end of this chapter to check your answers.

The Development of Personality

Freud concluded that the bulk of personality development occurred during the first five years of life. He reached this conclusion as a result of noticing an interesting pattern with his adult patients: Their personality problems rarely stemmed from events that happened during adulthood; instead, their problems invariably stemmed from childhood experiences. Since the personalities of the adults he analyzed were primarily shaped by things that happened to them before the age of 5 (and rarely by events thereafter), Freud concluded that our basic personality structures were formed by the end of the fifth year (Hall & Lindzey, 1978).

What causes us to develop? According to Freud, we develop when we are forced to learn new ways of adapting to tension. In other words, we can think of common sources of tension—maturation, frustration, conflicts, and threats—as forces for development.

Since we have to adapt to tension from the day we are born, development begins at birth. Before birth (the good old days), we were protected in a warm, soundproofed, padded, and darkened environment. Then, suddenly, we were bombarded with stimulation and anxiety as we were thrust into a world full of light, noise, temperature changes, and more. Taxed beyond our adaptive capacity, we responded with fear and anxiety: crying, wiggling, gasping, and heart pounding (Freud, 1923/1963).

To protect themselves from this flood of overstimulation, people quickly learn two techniques that allow them to ignore what is happening around them: (1) sleeping and (2) focusing intensely on a single specific task, such as nursing, to the exclusion of everything else. Eventually, people get used to the stimuli around them. Unfortunately, some infants don't. These infants will be constantly threatened by overstimulation throughout their entire lives. If their defense mechanisms can't effectively deal with the anxiety resulting from this constant overstimulation, they will develop severe psychopathologies such as schizophrenia. If, on the other hand, their defense mechanisms can successfully deflect this anxiety, they may become overly dependent on (addicted to) these defense mechanisms. For

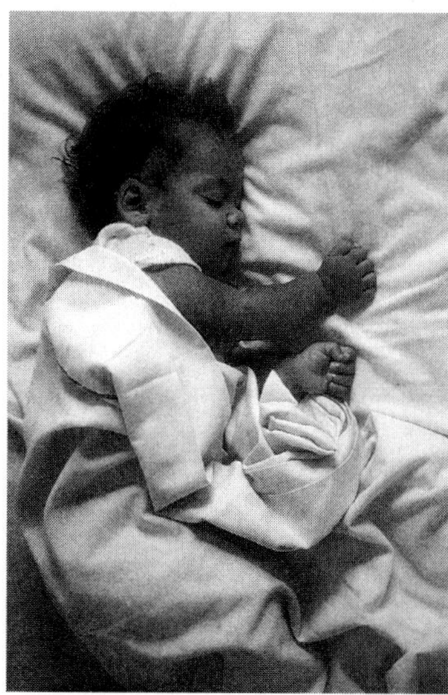

Sleeping is one of the first techniques we develop to adapt to the world.

example, such an individual might spend much of his life fleeing to a warm closet and huddling against a soft coat—a symbolic return to the womb.

Of course, birth is just the beginning of tension. It seems that once we adapt to one source of tension, we are exposed to tension from a new source. Specifically, if all goes well, we are exposed to four different sets of tensions as we progress through the four stages—and one period—of personality development: the oral stage, the anal stage, the phallic stage, the latency period, and the genital stage.

The Oral Stage

Almost immediately following birth, infants enter the first psychosexual stage of development—the **oral stage.** By forming a connection between nursing and being fed, they receive libidinal gratification (erotic pleasure) through oral activities such as eating, sucking, and putting things into their mouth. When they are hungry, they become restless and cry. When a nipple is placed in their mouth, they suck it, grow quiet, and eventually fall asleep.

As infants, they implicitly trust that they will be provided for. When they feel hunger, they cry and expect food. Although they are totally helpless and dependent on others, they don't see it that way. Instead, they have a "sense of omnipotence."

Why do they feel so all powerful? One reason is that their needs are almost always met. They expect food and then they get food. Another reason they feel omnipotent is that they have no concept of the external world. Sure, they have sensations, but how are they to know that some of these sensations came from the outside world—rather than from their tummy? Since they fail to see any connection between what they feel and what they see (or hear or smell), they have little reason to postulate an outside world.

Clearly, the unrealistic id is at the helm during the oral stage. It is the source of desires, but it can gratify infants' desires and goals only through fantasy. Therefore, when infants desire a "love object" (such as food), they hallucinate its gratification. The hallucination is maintained until the need is actually gratified, then it vanishes.

To the id, objects exist only when they are desired. An infant's rude treatment of his baby bottle showed that his love for objects lasts only as long as his need to consume them. The child loved and adored his bottle when he was hungry, but the moment his hunger subsided, he threw it aside. This same tendency to reject love objects once they have been used is sometimes expressed in the adult personality. For example, some women discard men after they have made love to them (the "black widow" syndrome). What these people experience as "love," quickly subsides once their need has been met.

Several other features of adult behavior can be tied to the oral stage. If an infant's oral needs are unsatisfied or overindulged, the infant may develop an oral personality—searching for trust and relatedness through oral cravings. These cravings may take a literal form, such as in smoking, kissing, eating, drinking, talking, and nail biting. (Many adults claim their weight problems were due to mothers who compulsively overfed them as children, teaching them to associate food with love and security). Alternatively, the oral cravings may be expressed metaphorically, such as by gullibility (a person who will swallow any story) or biting sarcasm.

The Anal Stage

During the second year of life, libidinal energy usually shifts from the mouth to the anal region. As children now enter the **anal stage,** they receive gratification by eliminating and retaining feces.

Why children receive gratification is a matter of debate. Freud believed that around age 2, the body matures so that both retaining and eliminating feces is a source of libidinal pleasure. Other psychoanalysts disagree. They argue that the shift of libidinal energy to the anus is due to toilet training. By definition, toilet training focuses attention on anal functioning, and this region becomes the source of frustration and rewards. Parents reward their children for bowel movements that occur at the appropriate time and place, and they punish children for movements that occur at the wrong time or place. Although psychoanalysts disagree about whether the trials and tribulations of the anal period are purely maturational in origin or can be explained by the experience of toilet training, almost all psychoanalysts agree that the anal stage has enormous implications for later adult personality. (To see how different theorists view toilet training, read box 13.3.)

The tasks of retaining and expelling feces place several demands on a child. The mechanics of defecating in a toilet, wiping, and then washing one's hands requires a child to be clean, orderly, obedient, and autonomous.

Box 13.3

THEORY in FOCUS

Toilet Training

Although not everyone believes that toilet training may shape the child's life, many parents agree that toilet training can be an ordeal. There are a variety of perspectives on how to toilet train. Ironically, both psychoanalysts and behaviorists agree on the basics of toilet training. That is, according to both behaviorists and psychoanalysts, toilet training should:

1. Not start until the child is ready (around 30 months); and
2. Use reinforcement rather than punishment.

However, there are subtle differences between the behavioristic and psychoanalytic approaches. Behaviorists focus more on gradually introducing the child to the toilet seat before working on rewarding full-blown toilet training. That is, they place more emphasis on shaping. Behaviorists also emphasize modeling more than the psychoanalysts. Psychoanalysts, on the other hand, emphasize not letting the child see the feces being flushed down the toilet. Some psychoanalysts believe that the child could be traumatized by seeing something the child had created (indeed, a former part of the child) disappear. Although this psychoanalytic idea may seem extreme to you, we should point out that (1) this idea did not always seem absurd—it was presented as fact in Dr. Spock's best-selling guide to taking care of babies (Spock, 1970) and (2) children do have an irrational fear of being flushed down the toilet.

In contrast to both psychoanalysts and behaviorists, humanists focus on letting the child decide about toilet training. Once the child decides to be toilet-trained, the child will learn quickly. If the child is a 2-year-old who doesn't want to be toilet-trained, toilet training can be a very frustrating event.

Which of these approaches is correct? It is hard to say. Although successful strategies for toilet training borrow heavily from the behaviorists, such strategies usually incorporate some ideas from the Freudian and humanistic viewpoints. Since successful techniques for teaching children how to use the toilet usually incorporate ideas from all three theoretical perspectives, it is hard to say which approach has more merit. It is even harder to say which approach has more merit when we consider the argument that success in toilet training should not be measured by how quickly the child conforms to toilet training, but by the long-term effects of the training process on the individual's personality.

If the parent is too strict and overbearing, problems result. Children have difficulty mastering these unreasonable demands. Consequently, they experience shame and self-doubt. This shame can cause a child to withdraw or to develop an **anal fixation,** that is, to remain focused on seeking pleasure through anal activities. This anal fixation can show itself in one of two ways: being an anal retentive or being an anal expulsive.

The **anal retentive** unconsciously rebels against the demand to expel feces on cue by holding onto feces. In some cases, the anal retentive may actually become constipated. Usually, the anal retentive symbolically refuses to let feces go by becoming stingy (holding on to money), stubborn (holding on to ideas), orderly, and compulsively neat.

The **anal expulsive,** on the other hand, rebels against the demand to hold onto feces until the right time by symbolically expelling feces. For example, the anal expulsive may throw tantrums (letting everything out), be messy (symbolically throwing their stuff around), or be very extravagant (throwing their money around).

Of course, not all parents approach toilet training in an oppressive fashion. Parents who strongly encourage their child to defecate and then make a big deal about positive results may teach their child that the process of producing things and giving them to others is very important. Thus, creativity, productivity, and generosity may be the products of patient toilet training.

Regardless of how parents deal with toilet training, the child undergoes a cognitive shift during the anal stage. Whereas the oral child desires only love objects that he or she is consuming, the anal child cherishes love objects. According to Freud, the anal child, rather then discard a love object once it has been consumed, wishes to possess it indefinitely. Since the anal child treats human love objects the same way as inanimate love objects, a child at this stage expects her parents to constantly respond to her. By adulthood, this anal possessiveness will be reflected in both jealousy and in the wish to exclusively love and copulate with another. Thus, anal possessiveness could be regarded as a defining characteristic of a monogamous relationship, such as marriage.

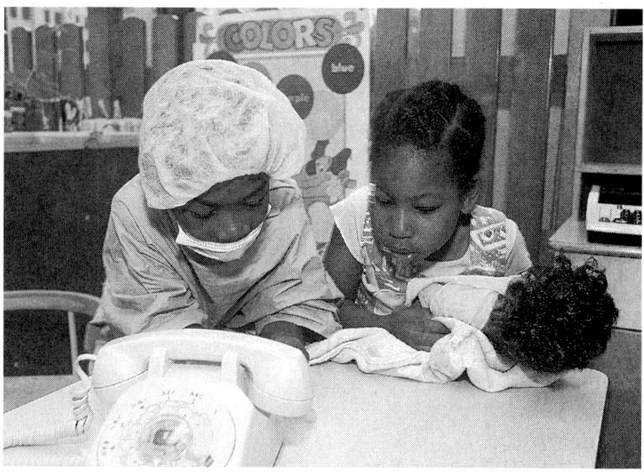

Freud believed that during the phallic stage of development children become extremely interested in their own and others' genitals.

Phallic Stage

During the fourth year of life, the beginning of the **phallic stage,** libidinal energy shifts from the anal region to the genitals. Children become fascinated with their sex organs and the pleasure they receive through sexual stimulation. Boys and girls become preoccupied about how babies are made, about the sexual activities of their parents, and about anatomical differences between the sexes (as shown by spying on others and playing "doctor"). This shift in libidinal energy combined with increasing ego maturity opens up a Pandora's box of potential conflicts in interpersonal relations. For boys, the most serious of these conflicts is the Oedipus complex; for girls, the most serious is the Electra complex.

The **Oedipus complex,** named for the Greek king who killed his father and married his mother, represents a young boy's wish to possess his mother and rival his father. The boy's strong affection and attachment to his mother is not surprising. As Alfred Baldwin (1967, pp. 364–366) explains, the mother is usually the primary caretaker, the child's constant companion, and source of security. Often, the mother's interaction with her child is physically more intimate and sensuous than the father's. When a young boy becomes interested in sexual matters, this physical sensuousness takes on a sexual tone. He wants to have sex with his mother. Of course, a 4-year-old's idea of sex is usually quite different from an adult's. Common boyhood ideas include physical closeness, voyeurism, exhibitionism, and perhaps mutual touching of the genitals (as is common among preschool children). Often, he may envision marrying his mother and replacing his father.

Of course, the boy's fantasy is doomed to failure. Even the boy realizes that his hostility toward and rivalry with his father has a potential cost: his father may castrate him. This castration anxiety is central to the boy's development during the phallic stage. To reduce his castration anxiety, the boy turns to two defense mechanisms. First, he represses his desire to sexually possess his mother. Second, rather than fighting his father, he identifies with his father. As a result, he internalizes his father's values, ideals, and interests. This identification with his former enemy not only reduces anxiety, but also marks the birth of both the superego and a masculine sex role. By becoming like his father, the young boy hopes to win his mother's sexual love vicariously. Thus, he converts his erotic feelings toward her into tender affection.

Freud was never as clear about female development during the phallic stage, but believed that it was roughly analogous to the male's. Instead of resolving the Oedipal complex, the young girl must resolve the **Electra complex** (named after Electra, who, according to a famous Greek myth, helped her brother avenge their father's murder by slaying their mother and their mother's lover).

The little girl enters the phallic stage retaining her closeness to her mother. However, she becomes fascinated with her father when she discovers he has a penis. She wants one too! She reasons that she once had one, but her mother castrated her (mom was jealous that the little girl had something that mom didn't). She transfers her love to her father because he has the valued organ and she wishes to share it with him. This love for her father is tainted with feelings of envy, manifested as penis envy. Thus rather than fear castration, she yearns for that which she has already lost. In other words, the boy's castration complex is castration anxiety, whereas the girl's castration complex is merely penis envy.

Penis envy is strong enough to partially resolve the young girl's Electra complex by weakening her affinity for her father and increasing her attachment to her mother. However, because the girl believes that she has already been castrated, her anxiety about castration is not as great as the boy's. Consequently, her need to repress her desire for the opposite sex parent and identify with the same-sex parent is not as compelling as the boy's. Thus, unlike boys, girls never fully resolve their castration complex. Since resolving the castration complex is essential to developing a superego (identifying with values of same-sex parent, accepting that social rules make acting on penis envy morally impossible), Freud believed that the female's superego was never fully developed. Because females failed to develop a strong superego, Freud believed that females were morally inferior to males.

Latency Period

To resolve the Oedipal or Electra complex, children repress their sexuality. According to Freud, this sexual **latency period** usually starts at age 7 and ends at puberty.

During the period of sexual latency, Freud believed that sexual desires were still present, but had been kept under wraps by defense mechanisms. In Freud's view, several pieces of evidence strongly supported the idea that sexual desires were merely driven underground rather than disappearing completely.

First, that children repress their sexuality is evidenced by their strategy of avoiding the opposite sex. During the latency stage, children associate almost exclusively with same-sex peers. In addition, they strongly identify with and take great pains to associate with the same-sexed parent. In the short run, this repression may not be bad: By avoiding the opposite sex, the child avoids sexual temptations and by staying with one's own sex, the child may learn sex-role appropriate behavior.

Second, that these children are using sublimation to complement repression is evidenced by their tendency to be apparently unconcerned with their bodies while focusing enormous amounts of energy developing social and cognitive skills. Again, since they have so much to learn, this use of defense mechanisms may be healthy.

Although latency is a period of sexual repression, it is not necessarily a period of calm. Rather than center on close interpersonal relationships, the problems of latency often center on rebellion against authority and father-son conflicts. For this reason, fourth, fifth, and sixth grades are commonly regarded as the most difficult to teach (Baldwin, 1967, p. 369).

Genital Stage

The sexual calm of latency ends at puberty. Puberty marks the onset of adolescence and children's entry into the **genital stage.** In previous stages, children found gratification through stimulating and manipulating their own bodies. Other people were loved only because they provided pleasure and gratified one's narcissistic needs. In the genital stage, some of this self-love is redirected in less selfish ways. The adolescent begins to love others for more altruistic reasons. Consequently, the adolescent becomes capable of mature love.

In the genital stage, the child is transformed, both physically and psychologically, into an adult. The adolescent's interests shift from childish concerns to interests necessary to assume a mature role in society. Therefore, the genital stage is characterized by socialization, group activities, vocational planning, sexual attraction, and preparations for marriage and children.

Evaluation of Freud's Theory

Whether or not you agree with Freud's view of personality development, there is no denying his invaluable contribution to psychology and society. His revolutionary ideas about the relevance of childhood in determining adult personality, and his insights into the role of defense mechanisms, unconscious processes, ego development, and anxiety mark a milestone in the history of human thought. Despite these contributions, his theory has been attacked on many fronts.

From a lifespan developmental viewpoint, his theory is extremely limited because it places too much attention on personality development during childhood and too little attention on personality development during adulthood. From a scientific point of view, the most serious problem with the theory is its lack of solid empirical support. Among the most serious of these problems are:

- Freud's concept of normal development was based on a biased sample of upper-middle-class neurotic Viennese women who lived during the late nineteenth and early twentieth centuries.
- These women's memories of their childhood may be inaccurate.
- Freud used unstructured interviews that may have biased what these women said to him.
- Freud's memory of what these women said may be inaccurate.
- Freud's interpretation of what these women said may be inaccurate.
- Freud did not use statistics to decide whether most of his sample had certain experiences. Instead, he just decided, on the basis of his intuition, that something happened regularly enough to be a pattern. But his intuition might have been wrong. If he had kept records and counted to see what percentage of the time a certain event happened, we might be more confident that his rules really held.
- Many of Freud's concepts are vague, hard to define, or virtually impossible to observe. That is, many of his concepts are hard to measure. For example, how do you measure castration anxiety, much less the unconscious? Without the ability to measure concepts scientifically, it is hard to know whether Freud is right or wrong.

In some cases, however, it appears that Freud was clearly wrong. For example, critics have viciously attacked Freud's notion that females are morally inferior. (Recall that Freud thought women were morally inferior because their lack of a penis results in an incomplete resolution of the castration complex.) There is no empirical evidence supporting the idea that women are morally inferior. Nor, as critics point out, is there any evidence that a substantial number of women want to have a penis. If women were really so envious of penises, why aren't more of them going for sex-change operations? In fact, it seems that more men want to have sex changes than women.

Even when aspects of Freud's theory are not refuted by evidence, the theory's lack of empirical support makes it vulnerable to attacks from people who simply don't like some of its ideas. For example, consider the idea that has inspired considerable wrath and mirth—Freud's notion of infantile sexuality. Although most people will admit that young children masturbate, like to be caressed by their parents, and grow very attached to their parents, few agree that children wish to sexually possess their parents. Instead, people would prefer to believe that children identify with their parents because their parents are a source of warmth, nourishment, and security. Such statements as, "I want to marry you mommy (or daddy)" may merely reflect children's desires to imitate and be like their parents, rather than to sexually possess them.

Infantile sexuality and the castration complexes are just two of the ideas that upset people. For example, some people believe that Freud overemphasizes both the role of biology and the role of the irrational side of human nature.

Many people feel that Freud's theory is too biological because it fails to emphasize the importance of culture and family in personality development. For instance, Freud says women behave differently than men because they lack a certain part of the male anatomy rather than because they are discriminated against and treated differently than men.

Numerous people argue that Freud portrays us as being more irrational and more selfish than we really are. That is, people object to Freud's portrayal of the weak, embattled ego being overwhelmed by the irrational id and superego. Although we can all think of instances of irrational behavior, we like to think that most of our behavior is rational.

Given these criticisms, why is Freud so important? Why haven't psychologists rejected his theory as utter nonsense? First, Freud had a remarkable intellect that was able to soar above traditional Victorian notions of behavior and pave the way for modern psychological thought. He produced an enormously rich theory full of hypotheses and insights. And he was constantly revising his theory as he discovered and struggled with inconsistencies and flaws. Had he lived beyond 83 years, who knows what his theories would look like. Fortunately, instead of throwing the baby out with the bath water, his followers and critics have kept his legacy alive by refining, expanding, and perfecting the theory. Indeed, all modern theories of personality and social development are indebted to Sigmund Freud.

In the next section, you will survey some of the most prominent revisionists of psychoanalytic theory, notably Erik Erikson, Alfred Adler, and Karen Horney.

Ego Psychology

Most people revising Freud's theory thought that Freud underestimated the ego. As you may recall, Freud viewed the ego as merely the faithful slave to its parent, the brutish id. The ego was relegated to satisfying the basic primitive needs of its master (the id) and mediating conflicts between the id and the superego. To expand the role of the ego, **ego psychologists** revised the traditional Freudian view in three major ways: (1) emphasizing the social side of human nature as opposed to the selfish, instinctive, animal side; (2) asserting that the ego does not emerge from the id, but has its own origins; and (3) giving the ego an expanded role beyond dealing with anxiety and unconscious conflicts. Specifically, ego psychologists claim that the ego has its own interests. For example, they believe that the ego is interested in exploration, manipulation, and competency. In the next few sections, we will discuss three of these ego psychologists: Alfred Adler, Karen Horney, and Erik Erikson.

Alfred Adler

Freud's fame and importance attracted many followers. Beginning in 1902, a small group of his most ardent disciples met on Wednesday evenings in Freud's waiting room. This Wednesday Society grew into the Vienna branch of the International Psychoanalytical Association (Hothersal, 1990). Among its four original members was Alfred Adler, then a young Viennese physician.

Alfred Adler (1870–1937) was born in a middle-class suburb of Vienna on February 7, 1870, the son of a Jewish merchant. As a child, Adler suffered from many illnesses, including rickets and a bout with pneumonia so severe that the family doctor declared the case hopeless. This illness initiated Adler's decision to become a physician.

Adler loved to play outdoors and, because he was interested in others, was very popular with other children. However, due to his poor health, Adler's childhood was marked by a constant struggle to overcome physical weakness. When we discuss Adler's theory, you won't have to be a psychoanalyst to see that these two aspects of his early experience—being concerned about others and struggling to compensate for physical weaknesses—strongly influenced his personality theory.

At age 18, Adler entered the University of Vienna to study medicine. After graduating in 1895, he became an eye doctor but eventually shifted to neurology and psychiatry. This shift lead him to Freud.

At first, Adler and Freud got along very well. Adler was the most active member of the Wednesday Society and, in 1910, Freud recommended him as the first president of the Viennese Psychoanalytic Society. However, by 1911, Freud and Adler had a major falling out over theoretical differences. Adler resigned the presidency and left the society along with nine other members. He founded his own organization, the Association for Individual Psychology.

Adler's Theory

What were these theoretical differences that lead to Adler's personal and professional estrangement from Freud? The main difference was that Adler did not believe that the root cause of maladjustment was repressed sexuality. Instead, Adler believed that the cause of maladjustment was a sense of inferiority.

Inferiority Complex Adler reasoned that because children are small, weak, and dependent on adults for their survival, they inevitably develop an **inferiority complex,** a deep sense of inferiority. According to Adler, this sense

Box 13.4

SELF-CHECK

Part A

Indicate whether each of the following statements is true or false.

1. According to Freud, most of personality development is shaped by events that occur before age 5.
2. According to Freud, the young infant feels helpless.
3. According to Freud, the young infant has object permanence: objects continue to exist even when out of sight or out of mind.
4. According to Freud, toilet training can have profound effects on the individual's later development—and these effects can be either positive or negative.
5. According to Freud, young boys have a very clear idea of what sex is.
6. According to Freud, the boy wants to replace his father, but the boy gives up this dream out of fear that the father will castrate him.
7. According to Freud, resolving the Oedipus complex results in the child's developing a male gender identity and a superego.
8. Freud believed that women were morally inferior to men.
9. The latency stage is a period of calm before the stormy period of adolescent rebellion.
10. The evidence supports Freud's theory.

Part B

Respond to the following questions.

11. List Freud's stages of development—in order.
12. Compare and contrast the anal retentive and the anal compulsive.
13. Compare and contrast the oral and the anal character's reaction to a love object.
14. Give two reasons why Freud believed that sexual urges were repressed during the latency stage.
15. How does love in the genital stage differ from love in previous stages?
16. What criticisms can be made about the data on which Freud's theory of personality was based?
17. On what philosophical positions do many people think that Freud has gone too far?

Please turn to the end of this chapter to check your answers.

of inferiority leads children to, at times, resent their stronger and more powerful parents. Adler believed that Freud had correctly noticed this resentment, but had incorrectly interpreted it as being due to some sexual cause (such as castration anxiety or penis envy).

Although the inferiority complex may cause temporary feelings of resentment toward the parents, the primary effect of the inferiority complex is to make children want to overcome these feelings of inferiority. Specifically, to overcome these feelings of inferiority, children try to become superior by reaching self-perfection. This early striving for superiority has long-term effects. That is, an adult's personality and lifestyle may be a reflection of how she, as a child, defined self-perfection and how she went about trying to achieve it.

Life Goal The way we define self-perfection and the way we go about attaining it is reflected in our life goal. The **life goal** is not a precise and consciously chosen aim, but it does guide and motivate behavior, life choices, daily routines, social activities, and relationships.

To grow, we must change our life goal. We must shift from being self-centered and focusing on being better than others to being interested in others. Whereas neurotic people are interested in perfecting themselves to attain selfish goals such as being able to compete against others, healthy individuals want to improve their abilities to better cooperate with others. According to Adler, the tendency toward being concerned with social welfare is inherited. Presumably, humans who lived in groups in which people did not help each other died out, whereas tribes who worked together survived. However, even though evolution has predisposed us to be concerned with helping others, this concern may be encouraged or discouraged by life experiences.

Schema of Apperception Thus far, we have seen several differences between Adler and Freud. We have seen that Adler believed in unconscious inferiority complexes rather than in castration complexes. We have seen that Adler, rather than postulating a selfish id, postulates that we inherit a selfless interest in helping others. We have seen that Adler, rather than focusing on psychological disorders, stresses the need to grow by revising one's life goals. However, perhaps the most important difference between Freud and Adler is that Adler emphasizes conscious, rather than unconscious, experiences. To stress the importance of conscious experience, Adler coined two phrases.

The first phrase is **schema of apperception,** our own subjective perception of ourselves and the world. Adler coined this phrase to emphasize the power of conscious experience to affect our present behavior. According to Adler, our schema of apperception determines our behavior. If we believe that a coil of rope in a dark corner is a snake, our fear will be just as intense as if the rope were actually a snake. Adler points out that "our senses do not receive actual facts, but merely a subjective image of them, a reflection of the external world" (Adler, 1956, p. 182).

The second phrase is the **creative self,** a fully conscious part of us that strives to realize our potential and overcome obstacles. Adler coined this phrase to emphasize the power of the conscious mind to change our future perceptions and behavior. According to Adler, the creative self, not sexuality, is the source of personality development.

Evaluation of Adler's Theory Unfortunately, like Freud's theory, Adler's theory has not been scientifically tested. Therefore, there is little evidence that Adler was right. Nevertheless, Adler's ideas have had a tremendous impact on many theories—from many so-called neo-Freudian theories to most humanistic theories. For example, humanistic psychologists, such as Abraham Maslow and Carl Rogers, borrowed Adler's emphasis on the importance of the following ideas:

- Being interested in others,
- How a person views the world,
- The creative self,
- Psychological growth, and
- Our ability to be rational.

Furthermore, as you will soon see, one could argue that some of the psychoanalysts commonly referred to as neo-Freudians, such as Karen Horney, are actually neo-Adlerians.

Box 13.5

SELF-CHECK

PART A

Answer the following questions.

1. In what two important ways do ego psychologists differ from Freud?
2. What problem in Adler's life is reflected in his theory?
3. How does Adler emphasize the importance of conscious experience?
4. How could Adler be considered a humanist?

PART B

Indicate whether each of the following statements is true or false.

5. Whereas Freud thought there was an evolutionary basis for violence toward others, Adler proposed that there was an evolutionary basis for caring about others.
6. According to Adler, striving to overcome one's weaknesses by achieving self-perfection was a very good thing.

Please turn to the end of this chapter to check your answers.

Karen Horney

Karen Horney (pronounced Horn-eye) was born to an upper-middle-class Protestant family in Hamburg, Germany in 1885. Her father was commodore of the North German Lloyds shipping company, and young Karen often accompanied him on long sea voyages. However, most of her time was spent with her mother, a highly intelligent, dynamic, and beautiful woman who encouraged Karen to enter medical school.

Karen excelled in medical school. When she graduated in 1913, she was one of the first women to earn a medical degree in Germany. During the next four years, she studied psychiatry at Berlin-Lankwitz where she underwent Freudian psychoanalysis. From 1918 to 1932, she taught in the Berlin Institute. In 1932, she moved to the United States where she served as the director of the Psychoanalytic Institute of Chicago. In 1934, she moved to New York where she taught at the Psychoanalytic Institute until 1941, when the psychoanalytic traditionalists forced her to leave. Horney and her supporters then founded the Association for the Advancement of Psychoanalysis and their own training institute, the American Institute of Psychoanalysis. Horney was Dean at the Institute until her death in 1952 at the age of 67.

Horney's Theory

During her career, Horney (1885–1952) proved herself to be a brilliant clinician and pioneered a new field: the psychology of women. She is best known for being a Freudian revisionist whose challenges to many of the basic tenets of Freudian theory found enthusiastic supporters and vehement foes. Horney rejected Freud's ideas about libido, death instinct, and penis envy. Most significantly, she reinterpreted the Oedipal and Electra complexes as sociocultural in origin, not biological.

Self-Realization Like all neo-Adlerians, Horney emphasized personal growth and the fulfillment of potential. Whereas Freud emphasized the negative implications of Darwin's theory of evolution (we inherit a brutal, selfish nature from our animal ancestors), Horney stressed the positive implications of evolutionary theory. Specifically, since evolution meant passing on characteristics that were adaptive, she believed that we inherited constructive forces that move us toward **self-realization,** being truthful to oneself, being active and productive, and relating to others in a spirit of mutuality. Furthermore, Horney considered the healthy person to be guided by a "morality of evolution" that fosters attitudes and orients the person to encourage rather than obstruct personal development. Working to outgrow self-destructive forces is our prime moral obligation and privilege. Horney espoused "the liberation and cultivation of the forces which lead to self-realization" (1950, p. 16) as the ideal for all persons.

Basic Anxiety Unfortunately, not all people reach this ideal. Instead, some people are detoured by neurosis. Like Adler, Horney believed that insecurity was the source of neurosis. However, unlike Adler, Horney did *not* attribute this insecurity to physical weakness, but rather to environmental events that disturb the child's sense of security. These events could lead to **basic anxiety,** the feeling a child has of being isolated and helpless in a potentially hostile world.

What environmental factors could lead to basic anxiety? A wide range of adverse factors in the environment can produce this insecurity in a child:

> direct or indirect domination, indifference, erratic behavior, lack of respect for the child's individual needs, lack of real guidance, disparaging attitudes, too much admiration or the absence of it, lack of reliable warmth, having too little responsibility, overprotection, isolation from other children, injustice, discrimination, unkept promises, hostile atmosphere, and so on and so on. (1945, p. 41)

How do these unpleasant events lead to basic anxiety? Suppose a child has been mistreated by her parents (being unfairly punished or ignored, for example). The child would be justified in protesting or criticizing. But, the child doesn't protest. Instead, whether due to feeling helpless, being intimidated, fearing the loss of love, or even feeling guilty about making trouble, the child represses this hostility. Unfortunately, the side effect of using repression is that the child now feels anxiety. Instead of realizing that this anxiety is due to repressed hostility, the child mistakenly explains the anxiety as a rational response to living in a cruel and unpredictable world. In Horney's terms, the child now feels basic anxiety: "a feeling of being small, insignificant, helpless, deserted, endangered, in a world that is out to abuse, cheat, attack, humiliate, betray, envy" (1937, p. 79).

Neurotic Needs If people feel helpless in a hostile world, what do they do? According to Horney, they develop one of 10 strategies described in table 13.1.

These strategies are called **neurotic needs** because they are irrational needs that can never be met. Trying to satisfy these needs is doomed to fail because these needs are insatiable (one can never get enough love) or are impossible to reach (perfection, pleasing everyone). Furthermore, even if these needs could be met, people would probably still be unhappy because they don't directly address the source of dissatisfaction: basic anxiety.

This person may be working late into the night because he feels a neurotic need for achievement. However, according to Horney, no matter how much they achieve, they'll still be bothered by basic anxiety.

Table 13.1

Horney's List of 10 Neurotic Needs

1. Neurotic need for a "partner" who will take over one's life.
2. Neurotic need for affection and approval from everyone.
3. Neurotic need to restrict one's life within narrow borders.
4. Neurotic need for power.
5. Neurotic need to exploit others.
6. Neurotic need for prestige.
7. Neurotic need for personal admiration.
8. Neurotic need for personal achievement.
9. Neurotic need for self-sufficiency and independence.
10. Neurotic need for perfection and unassailability.

Sadly, trying to fulfill these neurotic needs usually ends up increasing rather than decreasing anxiety. For example, to combat basic anxiety, a person might turn to a partner who will take over her life. She clings to this person, always fearing that her partner may desert her and leave her alone in this hostile world. Unfortunately, because she clings to her partner like a parasite, doesn't give him room to breathe, and is irrationally jealous, the partner starts to resent her. She senses this resentment and clings even harder, which leads to even more resentment by the partner and, in turn, stimulates even more neurotic behavior. This self-defeating cycle is what Horney calls a **vicious circle.** Each of the 10 neurotic needs listed in table 13.1 can lead to a vicious circle.

Penis Envy Reinterpreted Although Horney's concepts of neurotic needs and vicious circles are intriguing, she is perhaps best known for her challenge to Freud's notion of penis envy. Unlike Freud, Horney believed that the sources of women's feelings of envy and inferiority were not biological, but were instead sociological. When Freud developed his theory, males had more freedom and power than women. Not surprisingly, women envied men's power and freedom. Consequently, Horney argued that a concept like penis envy is unnecessary to explain females' feelings of inferiority. When young girls are punished for their sexual curiosity, stifled by the favoritism shown their brothers, rewarded for being dependent, and devalued by society, girls understandably feel inferior and have low self-esteem.

Evaluation of Horney's Theory As was the case with Adler's theory, little research has been done on Horney's theory. As with Adler's theory, this dearth of research has had two consequences. First, we do not know to what extent the theory is correct. Second, the theory has not been developed and revised.

Unlike Adler's theory, there are signs that Horney's theory may be experiencing a revival. This resurgence seems to stem from at least two sources. First, this resurgence may be due, in part, to the fact that many of the findings from the attachment research (see chapter 9) are consistent with Horney's theory. Second, this resurgence is also undoubtedly due, in part, to an increased interest in the psychology of women. Regardless of whether this resurgence of interest validates Horney's theory, this resurgence should pay off for developmental psychology by:

- Getting more psychologists to look at development through a woman's perspective,
- Doing more research examining the effect of child rearing on later relationships, and
- Looking for better ways to classify and trace the development of different kinds of relationship patterns (from being a highly dependent individual to being a hermit).

Box 13.6

SELF-CHECK

1. How does Horney's term *basic anxiety* differ from Adler's *inferiority complex?*
2. How does a person develop basic anxiety?
3. According to Horney, what is wrong with neurotic needs?
4. How do Horney and Freud differ on the issue of penis envy?
5. Is there a substantial body of research that strongly supports Horney's theory?

Please turn to the end of this chapter to check your answers.

Erik Erikson

Like Horney, Erik Erikson was also interested in what causes people to develop different ways of relating to others. Unlike Horney, however, Erikson holds to many traditionally Freudian notions. Nevertheless, he is considered an ego psychologist. Indeed, he is the best-known ego psychologist.

Erikson is considered an ego psychologist because he differs from Freud in three major ways: (1) he contends that the ego is of prime importance in development; (2) he argues that social forces must be considered if we are to understand the process of personality development, and (3) he sees development as occurring throughout the lifespan.

As you may recall from chapter 8, Erikson proposes eight stages of psychosocial development (see table 13.2 for a review). At each stage, a different conflict takes center stage.

Epigenesis

What determines whether a conflict takes center stage? That is, what determines when a person goes through each stage? Like Freud, Erikson believed that the beginning of each stage was established by biological maturation. To explain how maturation starts each stage, Erikson borrowed a concept from biology: epigenesis (literally, "upon emergence"). **Epigenesis** refers to the idea that each event during fetal development has a unique time of dominance as determined by the organism's genetic plan. Erikson believed that just as maturation lays the ground plan for fetal development, it also lays the ground plan for psychological development. As Erikson explains, "Anything that grows has a ground plan, and . . . out of this ground plan the parts arise, each having its time of special ascendancy, until all parts have arisen to form a functioning whole" (Erikson, 1959, p. 52).

Although Erikson asserts that maturation lays the ground plan for each stage of psychological development, he acknowledges that the conflicts at each stage of

Table 13.2

Erikson's Psychosocial Model of Personality Development

Age	Stage	Task
0 to 1	Oral-Sensory	Trust versus Mistrust
1 to 3	Muscular-Anal	Autonomy versus Shame or Doubt
3 to 6	Locomotor-Genital	Initiative versus Guilt
6 to 11	Latency	Industry versus Inferiority
11 to 18	Puberty and Adolescence	Identity versus Role Confusion
18 to 45	Young Adulthood	Intimacy versus Isolation
45 to 65	Adulthood	Generativity versus Stagnation
65+	Maturity	Ego-integrity versus Despair

This son may have foreclosed his identity crisis by simply accepting his father's profession and beliefs, or he may have achieved an identity in the same field as his father after much thought and a period of moratorium, according to Marcia.

development are not solely due to maturation. Rather, these conflicts result from the struggle between maturational forces and social demands. These conflicts are mediated by the ego.

Identity

Of all the conflicts proposed by Erikson, perhaps the most famous is his description of the adolescent's struggle between identity and identity diffusion. In fact, Erikson is sometimes referred to as the man who invented the identity crisis. Although many philosophers and some psychologists had recognized the tumultuous nature of adolescence, Erikson was the first to popularize the actual process of identity development.

Erikson defines identity as a relatively stable sense of our own uniqueness. In other words, in spite of changing behaviors, thoughts, and feelings, we are "familiar" to ourselves in a fundamental way. This sense of "who we are" must incorporate how others view us, as well as our relationship with society in general.

Erikson believed that identity formation was the basic task of adolescence. Specifically, adolescence is a period of psychosocial moratorium, a time to answer the question "Who am I?" and "What do I want to do with my life?"

David Marcia's Identity Statuses

David Marcia has used research to refine Erikson's basic notions of identity. For example, Marcia (1976) has found that resolution of the identity crisis is not an either-or (identity or identity diffusion) situation. Rather, to successfully resolve the crisis, we must make a compromise between identity and identity diffusion, albeit a compromise that favors identity. As Marcia (1976, p. 6) says, "The ideal resolution of any psychosocial crisis involves the individual's particular style of achieving a kind of creative tension between the polar alternatives, with an emphasis on the more positive pole."

In addition to realizing that the identity crisis isn't an either-or situation, Marcia recognizes that it is not restricted to adolescence. Admittedly, most individuals don't begin to confront the identity crisis until late adolescence. Before then, most people don't have the tools needed to confront the identity crisis: physical and sexual maturity, abstract reasoning ability, and emotional stability. But after late adolescence, the potential for growth is always present. That is, people can continue to struggle with identity after adolescence. When—or whether—individuals grow is a matter of individual choice.

Apparently, many people don't choose to grow. You probably know many adults who haven't reached identity achievement, a commitment to a vocational goal and to political and personal ideology.

But how do most people deal with the struggle for identity? Marcia's research revealed that most people used one of four strategies: identity foreclosure, moratorium, diffusion, and achievement (See table 13.3).

Identity foreclosed individuals have unquestionably accepted the expectations of their parents. They haven't explored and developed their own set of beliefs and vocational choices. Such blind acceptance lacks the commitment and understanding that characterizes self-chosen values and goals. Although society often embraces such conformity, society can thrive only when its members are capable of independent thought and informed commitment.

Table 13.3
Marcia's Identity Statuses

Identity Status	Characteristics	Commitment to Ideology and Vocation?	Role of Crisis in Identity Achievement
Foreclosure	Adoption of parental or societal values.	Yes	No independent decision making. Crisis is bypassed.
Moratorium	Active struggle for sense of identity.	No	In process of decision making. In a state of crisis (which may lead to psychological difficulties in a few adolescents).
Diffusion	Absence of struggling for identity or questioning of values, with no particular concern about this.	No	No current decision making. Not in a state of crisis (although crisis may have been experienced in the past).
Achievement	Successful attainment of a sense of identity.	Yes	Successful decision making and passage through crisis.

Moratorium individuals are actively struggling for identity. Parents often describe their child's moratorium by saying, "She is trying to find herself." Psychologists define moratorium somewhat more formally, saying it is characterized by trying out different roles, beliefs, and behaviors in order to evolve a personally satisfying identity. For most people, moratorium leads to identity achievement, but for an unfortunate few, it leads to identity diffusion.

Identity diffusion is marked by the failure to achieve an identity. As you might expect, the identity-diffused person is plagued by self-doubt. However, contrary to what you might expect, identity-diffused individuals don't seem to do anything to change their circumstances. When they were in moratorium, they were—like all individuals who are in moratorium—actively struggling with determining who they were. Now, however, they have given up the fight for self-definition. Without an identity, the identity-diffused are unfocused and incapable of making commitments. If they are to ever achieve an identity, they must return to a state of moratorium.

The ideal status is **identity achievement.** This status can be attained only by going through an identity crisis, that is, moratorium. Such individuals are able to make commitments to a vocation and to both a political and personal ideology.

Marcia regards both identity achievement and foreclosure as possible resolutions of the identity crisis because both involve commitments. The foreclosed person is committed to the ideology and goals of his or her parents, the identity achieved to his or her personal convictions. Only the moratorium and diffused statuses involve no commitment.

Evaluation of Erikson's Theory

Erikson's theory is very similar to Freud's. However, Erikson has filled in what some consider to be two major holes in Freud's original theory. First, whereas Freud has been criticized for emphasizing biological forces on development to the virtual exclusion of any other cause of development, Erikson acknowledges that social forces play a role in development. Second, whereas Freud has been chastised for emphasizing only developmental changes that occur before adulthood, Erikson discusses several conflicts dealt with during adulthood.

The remaining hole in Erikson's theory, the lack of research support, is starting to be filled in. We mentioned earlier how Marcia's research suggests that Erikson was too simplistic about how the crisis between identity achievement and identity diffusion is resolved. Other investigators have found that developmental tasks are not as restricted to age stages as Erikson's theory implies. For example, Susan Whitbourne and her colleagues (Whitbourne & Tesch, 1985; Whitbourne & Waterman, 1979) found that in the years after college, individuals develop a greater degree of industry and identity.

For the most part, however, research supports the theory. For example, achieving an identity does seem to be a prerequisite for staying happily married (Kahn, 1985). Similarly, several studies (Haan, 1981; Mortimer, Finch, & Kumka, 1982; Ochse & Plug, 1986; Ryff & Heinecke, 1983; Vaillant, 1983) have found support for the idea that there is growth (generativity) during middle age. Specifically, middle-aged people seem to be more nurturing and more mature than adolescents.

Box 13.7

SELF-CHECK

PART A

Indicate whether each of the following statements is true or false.

1. Erikson holds to many traditional Freudian notions.
2. Erikson believes that maturation lays the ground plan for each stage of psychological development and that conflicts come at each stage as a result of these maturational forces struggling with social forces.
3. As Erikson's theory predicts, identity does seem to be a prerequisite for true intimacy.
4. As Erikson's theory would predict, generativity often occurs during middle age.
5. Erikson's theory has been rigorously tested.
6. Some have criticized Erikson for focusing so much on the development of autonomy that he ignores the development of intimacy.

PART B

Answer the following questions.

7. What are the main ways in which Erikson differs from Freud?
8. How have people challenged or revised Erikson's view of the identity crisis?

Please turn to the end of this chapter to check your answers.

Despite this research support, Erikson's theory is still attacked for lacking research support—and justifiably so. Erikson used scientific terms such as *epigenesis* and said that psychological development paralleled certain types of physical development. However, Erikson was not a scientist—he did not bother to see if the analogies he made between biology and psychology had any basis in fact. Not until about 20 years after the theory's publication was any serious research done on the theory. Even now, many parts of the theory, such as the integrity versus despair stage, have been virtually unstudied. To get a better sense of the degree to which the theory has not been studied, realize that numerous lifespan stages could also fit the data.

Although most of the criticisms leveled against Erikson's theory could be leveled against almost any psychoanalytic theory, one serious criticism pertains only to Erikson's theory: its emphasis on autonomy, almost to the exclusion of intimacy and attachment. As Carol Franz and Kathleen White (1985) point out, although

> . . . Erikson views identity and intimacy (the psychosocial "virtues" emerging from his stages 5 and 6) as equal in value, his emphasis on the antecedents and consequences of identity to the neglect of the antecedents and consequences of intimacy means that his theory fails to do justice to the coherence and interrelatedness of both sets of processes in both sexes. (pp. 224–225)

Because society has traditionally reinforced men for autonomy, and women for maintaining relationships, many feminists argue that Erikson depicts a male model of development (for example, see Gilligan, 1982). However, Franz and White believe that Erikson's theory isn't inherently sexist. Instead, they believe that his theory fails to adequately account for the processes of interpersonal attachment that are essential to the development of both men and women.

Psychoanalytic Theories: A Brief Summary

Psychoanalytic theories have shaped and continue to shape the views of the general public and the views of many developmental psychologists. But despite the ability of psychoanalytic theories to capture people's imaginations, there is little evidence that these theories are valid.

Without evidence to support them, these "theories" are really only philosophies. As such, we must be cautious about blindly accepting or rejecting them. Because there is little evidence to support any of these theories, to strongly believe in any one of these theories is to put blind faith in the theorist or in your intuition. On the other hand, because there is little evidence to completely reject any of these theories, at least one of these theories may be fairly accurate. Thus, to completely reject any of them is to put blind faith in either your own gut feelings or in a person who has an opposing philosophy.

HUMANISTIC PSYCHOLOGY

Finding a person who has an opposing philosophy is not difficult. By the late 1950s, a set of these anti-psychoanalytic philosophies called **humanism** came to the fore. Humanism, describing itself as "The Third Force," emerged as a rebellion against the two dominant forces in psychology: Freud's psychoanalysis, which humanists regarded as being too pessimistic about human nature; and behaviorism, which, according to humanists, looked at people as machines, ignoring people's humanity.

In addition to opposing the two major forces in psychology, most humanists share four premises: (1) subjective experience is important; (2) free will and creativity are important determinants of one's personality; (3) all people inherit a tendency to be the best they can be; and (4) psychological research should be relevant to human experience (Buhler & Allen, 1972, pp. 1–2).

As you can see, despite their objections to psychoanalysis, humanists owe a great debt to at least one psychoanalyst—Alfred Adler. That is, Adler emphasized the importance of subjective experience, the importance of the "creative self," and people's strivings to be the best they can be. However, Adler is not generally recognized as the father of humanism (probably because he was once a Freudian, a "sin" that some humanists find hard to forgive). Instead, most people bestow the honor of fatherhood to two remarkable individuals—Abraham Maslow and Carl Ransom Rogers.

Abraham Maslow

Abraham Maslow (1908–1970) is often called the spiritual father of humanistic psychology because he promoted it to the public and helped it gain academic respectability. Maslow coined the term *Third Force* to describe the movement and introduced the general public to the concept of **self-actualization,** the inborn tendency to strive to be the best you can be.

Ironically, when Maslow was growing up, he spent little time thinking about being the best he could be. He had more pressing concerns—such as where the next meal was coming from. His parents were poor Russian-Jewish immigrants, and his father barely supported the family as a barrel maker. During adolescence, Maslow was so shy and so insecure that, despite his enormous intellect, he did poorly in school. Fortunately, Maslow entered the University of Wisconsin on scholarship as part of a special outreach program for impoverished youth. There, he studied under three great psychologists: Harry Harlow (remember his studies with monkeys and wire mothers in chapter 10), Clark Hull (a learning theorist, who, in his time was as well known and as influential as Skinner), and L. L. Thurstone (a pioneer in the fields of attitude measurement and intelligence testing).

After leaving Wisconsin, Maslow conducted extensive research on human sexual behavior. His research was guided by Freud's notion that sexuality is central to all human behavior. Through this research, Maslow hoped to improve human adjustment through increasing our understanding of sexuality. During World War II, Maslow became disillusioned by how little psychology contributed to solving world problems. His interests shifted to social and personality psychology in a quest to discover "a psychology for the peace table" (Hall, 1968, p. 54).

How could he go about finding such a psychology when so many great minds had failed? Maslow decided that others, most notably psychoanalysts, had gone about the problem in the wrong way. Whereas the psychoanalyst's view of personality was based on the problems and faults of neurotic and average individuals, Maslow argued that it was more appropriate to generalize about human nature by looking at the best examples—only then can we explore the limits of human potential. This lead to his discovery of, and fascination with, self-actualization.

Table 13.4

Maslow's 15 Characteristics of Self-Actualized Individuals

1. "more efficient perception of reality and more comfortable relations with it,"
2. "acceptance (self, others, nature),"
3. "spontaneity; simplicity; naturalness,"
4. "problem centering," as opposed to being ego-centered,
5. "the quality of detachment; the need for privacy,"
6. "autonomy; independence of culture and environment,"
7. "continued freshness of appreciation,"
8. mystic and peak experiences,
9. "gemeinschaftsgefuhl" (the feeling of kinship with others),
10. "deeper and more profound interpersonal relations,"
11. "the democratic character structure,"
12. "discrimination between means and ends, between good and evil,"
13. "philosophical, unhostile sense of humor,"
14. "self-actualizing creativeness," and
15. "resistance to enculturation; transcendence of any particular culture."

Source: From A. H. Maslow, *Motivation and Personality,* 2d edition, Harper & Row, New York, 1970.

Self-Actualization

Maslow defined self-actualization as "the full use and exploitation of talents, capacities, potentials, etc." (1970, p. 150). He studied self-actualization by looking at the lives, values, and attitudes of people he considered to be healthy and creative. By carefully examining the lives of 18 of these people (9 contemporaries and 9 historical figures, including Abraham Lincoln, Thomas Jefferson, Albert Einstein, Eleanor Roosevelt, and Jane Addams), he arrived at 15 basic characteristics possessed by self-actualizers. These characteristics are listed in table 13.4.

Maslow stressed that, despite having these 15 characteristics, the self-actualizers he studied were far from perfect. Their commitment to their chosen work and values sometimes lead them to be ruthless and they often put their work before the needs and feelings of friends and family. Thus, not surprisingly, self-actualizers, like other mortals, suffer guilt, anxiety, sadness, and conflict. As imperfect as self-actualizers are, Maslow thought that they come as

Box 13.8

ISSUES in FOCUS

Eight Ways Toward Self-Actualization

1. "First, self-actualization means experiencing fully, vividly, selflessly, with full concentration and total absorption" (p. 45).
2. Life is a process of choices. Self-actualization means to make each decision a choice for growth.
3. Become in tune with your own inner nature.
4. Be honest and take responsibility for your actions.
5. Act in accordance with your own judgment and instincts.
6. Develop your potential.
7. "Peak experiences are transient moments of self-actualization" (p. 48).
8. Recognize your defenses and work toward giving them up.

Source: From A.H. Maslow, *Motivation and Personality*, 2d edition, Harper & Row, New York, 1970.

According to Maslow's theory, until basic needs for food and safe shelter are met, a person won't be psychologically able to strive for higher-level needs.

Figure 13.1

Maslow's Hierarchy of Needs

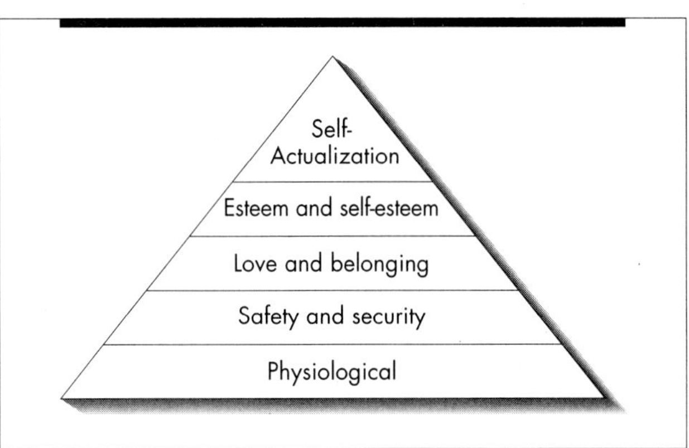

close as humans can come to perfection. If you believe Maslow and you want to get as close to perfection as humanly possible, box 13.8 lists eight actions you can take that may lead to self-actualization (Maslow, 1971).

Peak Experiences

Although very few people will become self-actualized, most people will get a glimpse of self-actualization by having what Maslow called **peak experiences,** an especially joyous and exciting moment. Peak experiences are often triggered by intense feelings of love, exposure to art or music, or experiencing the overwhelming beauty of nature (Frager & Fadiman, 1990). Although most of us have had peak experiences on a number of occasions, the most powerful peak experiences are rare. These are the magic moments of ecstasy portrayed by poets, or the religious rapture of deep mystical experiences. The highest peaks are described by Maslow as "feelings of limitless horizons opening up the vision, the feeling of being simultaneously more powerful and also more helpless than one ever was before, the feeling of great ecstasy and wonder and awe, the loss of placing in time and space . . ." (Maslow, 1970, p. 164). Maslow describes such an experience when he kissed his soon-to-be wife for the first time.

Hierarchy of Needs

If most people have both peak experiences and an inborn tendency toward self-actualization, why are so few people self-actualized? Maslow explained the dearth of self-actualized people by saying that self-actualization is but one human need. For this one need to drive the individual, other, more basic needs must be met first. If basic needs, such as the need for food, safety, love, and self-respect are not met, the person will not strive for self-actualization. In fact, severe deprivation of these needs (absence of food or warmth) can lead to death or to neurosis and psychological maladjustment. Once these basic needs are met, people will strive to meet their growth needs, their need to develop their potential, to self-actualize. But until lower needs are met, people will not aspire to growth: The starving person doesn't think of writing a symphony, she thinks of food.

You now understand the basic idea behind Maslow's hierarchy of needs: Higher level needs aren't influential until lower level needs have been met. To get a more detailed understanding of the need hierarchy, look at figure 13.1. After viewing figure 13.1, you can imagine that labor unions might start by requesting enough money so that workers can afford adequate food and shelter. Once those needs are met, unions might start negotiating for safer working conditions and for job security. Once those needs are met, the union's main job might be making workers become a cohesive group, where members like each other and feel like family. Once belongingness needs are met, the union might fight for status and self-esteem, trying to get workers more respect and narrowing the difference in status between managers and workers. Finally, if the union meets all of these needs, then workers will want the union to negotiate so that workers will get more fulfilling work that will allow them to fully use their abilities.

Evaluation of Maslow's Theory

Maslow's greatest asset is that he is one of the few psychologists to explore positive dimensions of human experience. However, his research was "exploratory" and should not be accepted as fact. He was the first to acknowledge this:

> It's just that I haven't got the time to do careful experiments myself. They take too long, in view of the years that I have left and the extent of what I want to do. So I myself do only "quick-and-dirty" little pilot explorations, mostly with a few subjects only, inadequate to publish but enough to convince myself that they are probably true and will be confirmed one day. (Maslow, 1972, pp. 66–67)

Therefore, like psychoanalysis, Maslow's theory lacks empirical support. Thus, like psychoanalysis, it should be regarded as a philosophy, rather than a serious scientific theory. As a philosophy of human development, it has obvious appeal. But do not accept it as documented fact because it isn't.

Carl Rogers

Like Maslow, Carl Rogers (1902–1987) was a leader and pioneer in the field of humanistic psychology. Like Maslow, Rogers emphasized the importance of self-actualization. But perhaps Rogers' most significant contribution to developmental personality theory is his work on self-concept. As you'll see, Rogers' ideas about the self-concept stem directly from his own childhood.

Carl Rogers was born on January 8, 1902, in Oak Park, Illinois, the son of prosperous, but narrowly fundamentalist parents. Rogers was a lonely child who was prohibited from playing with his peers because their behavior did not conform to the narrow guidelines set by his parents: Other people weren't moral enough to associate with the Rogers family. To illustrate, read how Carl summarized his family's attitudes toward nonfamily members:

> Other persons behave in dubious ways which we do not approve of in our family. Many of them play cards, go to movies, smoke, dance, drink, and engage in other activities—some unmentionable. The best thing to do is be tolerant of them, since they may not know better, and to keep away from any close communication with them and live your life with your family. (1973, p. 3)

In high school, Carl was an excellent student with a special interest in science. "I realized by now that I was peculiar, a loner, with very little place or opportunity for a place in the world of persons. I was socially incompetent. . . . My fantasies during this period were definitely bizarre, and probably would be classified as schizoid by a diagnostician, but fortunately I never came in contact with a psychologist" (1972, p. 4).

Rogers enrolled in the University of Wisconsin with the intention of becoming a minister. In college, Rogers found psychological intimacy outside of his family: He discovered that other people weren't so terrible after all. During his junior year, he achieved psychological liberation from his parents while attending a World Student Christian Federation conference in Peking, China. As Rogers wrote, "From the date of this trip, my goals, values, aims, and philosophy have been my own and very divergent from the views which my parents held and which I had held up to this point" (Rogers, 1967, p. 351).

Rogers continued to examine his views, which eventually led him to conclude that he was not sure enough about his faith to become a minister. Instead of becoming a minister, Rogers became a psychologist, receiving a Ph.D. in clinical psychology from Columbia.

The strong research background he received at Columbia made him keenly aware of how little was actually known about clinical psychology. He realized that existing ideas about the causes of unhappiness and what treatments to use were not based on fact, but on speculation. Therefore, instead of relying on existing preconceptions about patients, Rogers set out to be openminded about what his patients told him.

The Self

Rogers found that his clients talked about the world—not as it was—but as they perceived it. But much to his surprise, he found that people also talked about the "self" to a great degree. They wanted to be their "true self" or their "real self." Consequently, Rogers began investigating the

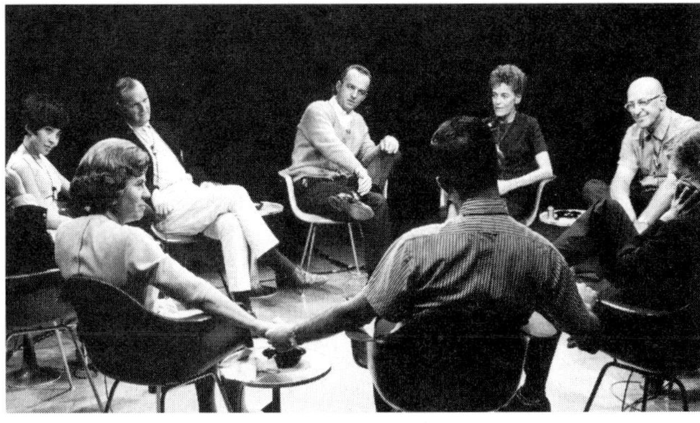

Carl Rogers (top right) recommended an environment of unconditional, positive regard to help people discover their true selves. Once the true self is found, people can work at reducing the incongruence between the way they act and the way their true self would act.

self, our beliefs about who we are. The self enables us to answer such questions as: What do I stand for? What do I believe in? Am I good or bad? industrious or lazy?

Rogers felt that the answers to these questions were established in childhood. Whether we feel we are good or bad probably depends on how our parents treated us. The same goes for whether we think we are industrious or lazy: If our parents always called us lazy, we probably think we are lazy. In essence, if our parents emphasized that there is a big difference between who we are and who we ought to be, we will have a poor self-image.

Incongruence

What we think we believe in is also influenced by our parents. How? As children, parents put **"conditions of worth"** on us: We were of worth when we did things they approved of and worthless when we did things they disapproved of. Because we valued our parents' approval so much, we disowned thoughts and feelings that our parents disapproved of. For example, after receiving strong disapproval for saying "Sometimes, I wish Grandma were dead," a child might disown that thought. As we disown more and more of our own thoughts, we become what others want us to be rather than who we are. Eventually, by trying to live up to what others want us to be, we lose touch with who we really are. In Rogers' terminology, by denying our thoughts and feelings, our self-image becomes **incongruent,** not in agreement with who we really are.

According to Rogers, the person who becomes estranged from herself by denying her true feelings is doomed to be unhappy. Specifically, incongruence leads to confusion, tension, anxiety, maladjustment, vulnerability, defensiveness, and threats. As you may have noted from the description of Carl's life, Carl Rogers felt incongruency during his early years.

Box 13.9

SELF-CHECK

PART A

Answer the following questions.

1. Why was humanism called "The Third Force?"
2. According to Maslow, what would help one reach self-actualization?
3. According to a follower of Carl Rogers, what would be wrong with rewarding children for doing what you want them to do?
4. According to Rogers, how can an adult develop a more self-actualized personality?

PART B

Indicate whether each of the following statements is true or false.

5. At least three of the four basic principles shared by all humanists are principles that were promoted by Alfred Adler.
6. Freud and Maslow would both agree that the best way to understand personality development would be to look at the development of neurotic individuals.
7. Self-actualized people can sometimes be ruthless.
8. Maslow clearly articulated how peak experiences could lead to personality development and growth.
9. According to Maslow, self-actualization is the strongest human need.
10. Maslow's theory is strongly supported by solid research.
11. Both Maslow and Rogers believed in self-actualization.
12. Unlike Freud, Rogers focused on conscious experience, especially on how one thinks about oneself.
13. Like Freud, Rogers believed that one's self-perception was often distorted and inaccurate.
14. Research evidence strongly suggests that Rogers' ideas about how to rear children are essentially correct.

Please turn to the end of this chapter to check your answers.

Unconditional Positive Regard

What can be done to reduce incongruence? One solution is to place a person in a nonthreatening relationship with a therapist. The therapist, rather than putting conditions of worth on the person, gives the person **unconditional**

positive regard; that is, accepts the person, regardless of what the person thinks or feels. Thus, the warm and accepting counselor provides an atmosphere where one's true self is free to come out and congruence may be achieved. It seems that Rogers first experienced such an atmosphere at the World Student Christian Federation Conference. In that warm, supportive, accepting environment, he was able to discover his true beliefs. Technically, he became **congruent;** his self concept was in harmony with his experiences and feelings.

Once a therapist has helped a person achieve congruence, she can maintain congruence by staying open to her own thoughts and experiences. If she continues to accept herself for who she is, she will be free to follow her inborn tendency to self-actualize. Because she is making decisions that are right for her, rather than decisions that are right for the imaginary person that some people want her to be, her continued growth as a person will be guaranteed.

Evaluation of Rogers' Theory

Like Maslow, Rogers' ideas are also intuitively appealing: Most people would agree with Rogers' position that it's important to know what people think of themselves and what they think of the world. Rogers has also provided considerably more empirical support for his position than Maslow. However, there is little evidence to support Rogers' ideas about using unconditional regard to rear children. Furthermore, like all humanistic psychologists, Rogers has failed to prove that we have an inborn desire to strive toward self-actualization. But, despite these failings, therapy based on Rogers' theory has proven to be quite useful.

Learning Theories

Thus far, we have discussed two general types of personality theories: psychoanalytic theories and humanistic theories. Both of these kinds of theories have their supporters. However, from the viewpoint of a lifespan developmental psychologist, both theories are inadequate because they lack research evidence to support them. Furthermore, both theories do a poor job of explaining normal adult development. Some of the psychoanalytic theories almost completely ignore the possibility that adults develop (Looft, 1973), and none of the humanistic or psychoanalytic theories are very specific about how normal adult development occurs.

Partly because of these weaknesses, some developmental psychologists have turned to learning theories to explain development. Two aspects of learning theories are particularly appealing to lifespan developmental psychologists. First, learning theorists have a scientific, fact-supported, approach to understanding personality development. Second, learning theories, from their inception, have emphasized specific mechanisms that permit positive changes to occur throughout the lifespan. In the next sections, you will see how these two aspects dominate the approaches of the two most influential learning theorists: B. F. Skinner and Alfred Bandura.

Skinner's Radical Behaviorism

B. F. (Burrhus Frederic) Skinner (1904–1990) was the purest example of an objective behaviorist. Skinner wanted us to report only observable behaviors and to do so with a detached, objective, scientific attitude. This attitude apparently came naturally to Skinner, as the following story from Skinner's childhood reveals. Skinner and his brother were eating. Suddenly, his brother reported not feeling well. Ten minutes later, his brother was dead. When the physician arrived on the scene, he was shocked not only by the sudden death of a previously healthy child, but also by Skinner's detached, objective report of exactly what behaviors his older brother performed while dying.

According to Skinner, we should study only what we can see. Thus, our personality is not some set of drives or unconscious forces; instead, it is our observable behaviors. Why do we regularly repeat certain behaviors? Skinner would argue that the answer is because we have been reinforced for doing these behaviors and punished for doing other behaviors. As you can see, the core of psychoanalysis, unobservable events (like unconscious forces), have no place in Skinner's theory. To highlight the differences between Skinner and Freud, compare how the two men look at Freud's childhood.

Freud attributed his own problems in interpersonal relationships to the death of an infant brother and to a later conflict with his playmate and rival, a nephew who was older and stronger. Skinner asserts that rather than concentrate on that rivalry, Freud should have looked at how his earlier behavior was rewarded and punished. Skinner argues that "What has survived through the years is not aggression and guilt, later to be manifested in behavior, but rather patterns of behavior themselves" (Skinner, 1972, pp. 244–245).

Skinnerians try to understand personality processes through systematic analysis of situations, behavior, and relationships between performance and reinforcement. Through carefully controlled laboratory studies, Skinner has demonstrated that controlling reinforcement gives us control over, not only the specific responses we will make, but also over how frequently and how vigorously we will make them.

Skinnerians agree that an individual's personality is more complicated than one kind of simple behavior, but only because personality involves more than one response. Personality is nothing more than the collection, the sum total, of all the different (simple) reinforced operant responses we produce.

If personality is simply a collection of reinforced responses, then why are we all so different? According to Skinnerians, individual differences in personality are merely the result of differences in:

- Which particular behaviors have been reinforced,
- How frequently these behaviors have been reinforced,

Imitation is frequent among children. Social learning theorists explain that by watching others' behavior, you can develop expectations about whether you would be rewarded for the same behavior.

- How consistently these behaviors have been reinforced,
- How large the reinforcements have been,
- The length of time between the behavior and the reinforcement,
- Which particular behaviors have been punished, and
- Inherited differences between people.

Thus, suppose that one child has been consistently, frequently, immediately, and richly rewarded for aggressive behaviors. Then, imagine a second child who has received only a few, very small rewards for being aggressive, and these rewards were received well after the aggression occurred. The first child will be more aggressive than the second. Furthermore, both will be more aggressive than a child who has always been punished for aggressive behaviors and has always been rewarded for finding nonaggressive ways of dealing with conflict.

Bandura's Social Learning Theory

As you can imagine, many people criticize Skinnerians for dismissing the importance of thoughts in affecting personality and behavior. An approach that is less vulnerable to such criticisms is Albert Bandura's **social learning theory.**

Expectations

Like Skinner, Bandura maintains that learning plays an important role in personality development. Also like Skinner, Bandura acknowledges that the consequences of our actions affect whether we will do that action in the future. Specifically, we will be likely to repeat actions that were rewarded and less likely to repeat actions that were not rewarded. However, Bandura claims that consequences affect behavior by changing our expectations: If we've been rewarded in the past for a certain behavior, we'll repeat the behavior because we expect to be rewarded again. Thus, unlike Skinner, Bandura admits that thoughts, such as expectations, affect behavior.

Imitation

Obviously, expectations can be changed without actually experiencing rewards and punishments. We can learn by watching others and seeing which of their behaviors are rewarded and which are punished. If we see that other people are rewarded for doing certain behaviors, then we will tend to imitate (model) those behaviors. For example, as a child, you were most likely to imitate your parents and children whom you respected. You were especially responsive to people you perceived as enthusiastic (Waxler & Radke-Yarrow, 1975).

Attention and Rehearsal

Expectations are not the only mental characteristics that Bandura discusses. For years, he has acknowledged that how well a person pays attention and the extent to which a person mentally rehearses what she has seen plays a role in whether a response will be modeled. Obviously, if a child fails to notice a model's behavior, the child will not be influenced by the model's behavior. Similarly, if the child notices the behavior, but doesn't reflect on that episode, the event will be soon forgotten.

Goals and Competence

In addition to talking about basic processes of attention and memory, Bandura also talks about beliefs and attitudes. For example, he acknowledges that people reward themselves (by praising themselves) and punish themselves (through self-criticism). Furthermore, Bandura believes that two additional mental characteristics are extremely important—the individual's goals and the individual's **self-efficacy,** the individual's feelings of competence (Bandura, 1982a, 1985).

Obviously, people set goals. The extent to which people work toward these goals depends largely on self-efficacy. If a person has low self-efficacy, he probably won't work toward his goals. If he can't achieve them, why try? Fortunately, Bandura has found that self-efficacy can often be increased in a short period of time by simply getting the person to experience success. Increasing self-efficacy (often achieved in less than three hours) has produced dramatic results—from converting male "wall-flowers" into social butterflies (Hammerlie & Montgomery, 1982, 1984, 1986) to curing people of their phobias (Bandura, 1985).

Evaluation of Learning Theories

The research data supporting learning theories is impressive. Furthermore, their assumption that we can learn and develop throughout the lifespan is appealing. Yet, not everyone loves learning theories. In fact, some even argue that the alleged strengths of learning theories—being research-based and emphasizing learning throughout the lifespan—are actually weaknesses.

According to some critics, learning theorists, by limiting their theories to include only those principles documented by research, have created theories that are as overly simplistic and sterile as some of the lab experiments on which these theories are based. More to the point, these critics complain that learning theories fail to capture the magic, the complexity, and the richness of the human personality.

Other critics believe that learning theorists overemphasize learning but underestimate the impact of genes and early experiences on development. They point out that a great deal of recent research supports the idea that heredity plays an important role in personality.

Furthermore, some critics argue that personality is much more stable than the learning theory would predict. These critics ask, "If personality is determined by learning and the environment, and if personality can change throughout one's life, then why is personality so stable?"

How would learning theorists rebut these arguments? Learning theorists would counter the objection that learning theories paint too simple a picture of humans by saying that the reverse is true: We humans like to have exaggerated opinions of ourselves and our complexity. We didn't like it when Galileo discovered that we weren't in the center of the universe; we didn't like it when we found that computers could beat humans in chess; and we don't like it when learning theory simply and accurately explains our behavior.

To address the objections that learning theory takes the wrong position on the nature versus nurture issue (overemphasizing nurture) and on the stability versus change issue (overlooking the degree of stability in human personality), learning theorists use two approaches.

The first approach is to say that learning theories can account for both nature and stability. Learning theories could account for stability by saying that expectations are set at an early age. Learning theorists would say that they account for nature; they just don't emphasize it. For example, learning theorists concede that some people are born to be faster learners than others. Similarly, many learning theorists concede that what is rewarding for a naturally active and outgoing child may not be rewarding for a naturally inactive and quiet child. Likewise, some learning theorists concede that many traits may be inherited. However, such learning theorists would also say that understanding the impact of such biological differences is irrelevant. It's irrelevant because we can't use such understanding to help people grow. That is, if you learn that someone has inherited a bad disposition, you can't do gene surgery to fix it.

The second approach is to argue that the positions attributed to learning theorists on both the nature-nurture and stability-change issues are correct: Nurture is more important than nature; change occurs more often than stability.

Issues in Personality Development

Are learning theory's positions on the nature-nurture and stability-change issues correct? This is an important question to ask of all the theories we have discussed. As you have seen, the theories disagree on these issues. But what do the facts say? In the next few sections, you'll find out.

Nature Versus Nurture

Is personality learned or is it inherited? An answer to this question determines or reflects one's theoretical orientation. If you lean toward behaviorism, you probably believe that, for the most part, personality is learned. If you tend toward the psychoanalytic view, you probably believe that personality development depends on the interaction between maturational forces and the environment. If you're a humanist, you may believe that you were born to develop a wonderful personality—but that the environment could derail your personality development.

Which position on the nature-nurture issue is correct? Because the answer to this question is extremely complex, we have dealt with it in virtually every chapter. Yet, even with our extensive discussion of nature-nurture, we have not been able to give you the final word on this issue. Indeed, almost every week, research sheds more light—and raises more questions—about this issue. Some of this research provides evidence for nature, some for nurture, and most of it provides evidence for both nature and nurture. To illustrate this, Robert Plomin (1992) points to the work on identical twins and schizophrenia. The research shows that if one identical twin has schizophrenia, the chances of the other having schizophrenia is 50 percent. On the one hand, this is very strong evidence for the role of genetics in schizophrenia—sharing the same genes as a schizophrenic means that one is 50 times more likely to have schizophrenia than a person who doesn't share those genes. On the other hand, this is also very strong evidence for the role of nurture. That is, nurture must play a role—if schizophrenia were completely inherited, 100 percent of the identical twins of schizophrenics would be schizophrenics.

Box 13.10

SELF-CHECK

PART A

Answer the following questions.

1. What two aspects of learning theories are particularly appealing to lifespan developmental psychologists?
2. How did Freud and Skinner differ in interpreting the underlying causes for Freud's problems with personal relationships?
3. According to Bandura, how could an adult's personality be changed?
4. What criticisms would a humanist have of learning theory?
5. How would Bandura's prescription for increasing self-efficacy differ from a humanist's prescription for increasing self-esteem?
6. What criticisms would a Freudian psychoanalyst have about behaviorism?

PART B

Indicate whether each of the following statements is true or false.

7. Skinner believes in the importance of unconscious processes.
8. Skinner does not believe that heredity has any role in personality.
9. Bandura acknowledges that thoughts affect behavior.
10. Bandura believes that the presence of people modeling the correct behavior will always lead the child to imitate that behavior.
11. Solid research evidence supports key aspects of learning theory.

Please turn to the end of this chapter to check your answers.

Thus, to some extent, the answer to the nature-nurture question depends on how we interpret the data (Loehlin, 1992). However, the answer also depends on which aspects of personality we are talking about.

Temperament

If we are talking about basic temperament, then most people would agree that nature plays a strong role. In other words, many experts believe that how emotional we are, how active we are, and how social we are was determined before birth (Braungart, Plomin, DeFries, & Fulker, 1992). There are three main reasons why people believe that basic temperament is inherited.

First, people believe that basic temperament is inherited because researchers have linked many differences in basic temperament to differences in the nervous system (Kagan, 1989; Kagan, Snidman, & Arcus, 1992). Some people assume that if a difference can be traced to the nervous system, it must be due to genetics. But this isn't necessarily the case. As you learned in chapter 2, the development of the nervous system is governed by both genetic and environmental factors. Thus, a non-cuddler may be that way because she inherited an easily aroused nervous system, but she may also be that way because her nervous system was altered through teratogens. Similarly, child abuse, understimulation, overstimulation, and malnutrition could also affect the development of the nervous system.

Second, studies of identical twins reared apart find that the twins are often similar in terms of temperament. However, since these twins do not always have identical temperaments, this research also shows that nurture plays a role in temperament.

Third, some people believe that temperament is inherited because one's temperament as a 5-year-old correlates with one's temperament as an adult. As with the nervous system evidence for inherited temperament, this evidence is suggestive of the importance of nature, but not conclusive. One's mood and activity level during infancy will strongly affect nurture. A warm, cuddly, baby who sleeps much of the time is more likely to encounter a more positive and supportive environment than the child who is born irritable, unresponsive, and unpredictable. The difference in the two children's environments may account for their different temperaments as adults.

To see that nurture rather than nature could be responsible for the relationship between child and adult temperament, imagine a baby who is irritable because of a minor, undiagnosed illness. After a few months of living with this irritable child, her parents expect her to be irritable. Consequently, they tend to be irritable when dealing with her. Their irritability, in turn, causes the child to be more irritable. A vicious cycle has begun, a cycle from which there is little hope of escape. Even after the child recovers from her illness, the irritability may continue because the parents expect her to be irritable and cold, because her parents treat her in an aloof manner, and because she expects her parents to be irritable and cold.

Nurturists also have data to support their view that temperament is not established at birth. First, they point to the fact that although infant temperament correlates with adult temperament, this correlation is very small—so small that it is virtually worthless for predicting adult behavior. Only after the child reaches about age 4 can we predict what the child's temperament will be at adulthood. Nurturists argue that if temperament were inherited, we could predict adult temperament from infant temperament. The reason we can't predict adult temperament until around age 4 is that, until age 4, nurture has not had time to have an effect. In support of this position, evidence suggests that behavioral problems can be made worse if the parenting style is impatient, inconsistent, and demanding. Similarly, Mischel's work (Mischel, Shoda, & McPeek, 1988) indicates that a child's later adjustment to life depends on what cognitive strategies the child uses—and these cognitive strategies can be taught.

Self-Esteem

Despite the arguments of the nurturists, most experts believe that temperament is largely—but not exclusively—the result of heredity. However, most psychologists do not think that every aspect of personality is due to nature. Indeed, psychologists have traditionally assumed that self-esteem is mostly a product of environment.

According to most theorists, self-esteem probably has a lot to do with how our parents and others treated us. If we felt love and support, we probably feel good about who we are. In support of this position, parents who are warm, nurturing, and have a democratic parenting style tend to have children who have high self-esteem (Coopersmith, 1967; Lamborn, Mounts, Steinberg, & Dornbusch, 1991; Scott, Scott, & McCabe, 1991).

Other environmental influences also have a strong effect on self-esteem. For example, successful experiences can boost self-esteem (Hammerlie & Montgomery, 1986). In addition, optimism can be learned (Nolen-Hoeksema, Girgus, & Seligman, 1992).

However, the final word on the role of nature in self-esteem has not been written. Naturists point out that how our parents and peers treated us may depend on such inherited qualities as physical appearance, gender, and cognitive capacity. Similarly, the extent to which we experience success may depend on our temperament and on our physical and mental abilities. Since temperament, physical appearance, and intelligence are largely inherited, perhaps it is not so surprising that Tellegen et al. (1988) have found that identical twins raised apart have remarkably similar self-esteem.

Conclusions about Nature and Nurture

Clearly, personality is a product of both nature and nurture. People develop within both a biological and environmental context. Which is more important? It's hard to say. Ten years ago, most psychologists would have said that nurture is more important. Today, the pendulum is swinging back toward nature. But what is the truth? We may never know. However, thanks to research like that done by Richard Lerner and his colleagues (Lerner, 1994; Lerner, Nitz, Talwar, & Lerner, 1989), we are starting to learn how nature and nurture combine to affect personality. For example, we now know that the parenting style that would be appropriate with an "easy temperament" baby will actually make a "difficult temperament" baby worse.

Psychologists who advocate a theory of personality stability over the lifespan point out that the drastic changes of the stereotyped male midlife crisis are more of a myth than reality.

Stability Versus Change

Like the nature-nurture issue, the stability-change issue is a difficult one to resolve. Like the nature-nurture issue, the stability-change issue is one about which theorists hold strong positions. For example, Freud said that "the child is the father of the man." In other words, early socialization and biological differences determine adult personality: Personality is relatively unchanging after childhood. Although some theorists support this position, many others emphasize the ever-present capacity for change due to the experiences of grade school, adolescence, and later life. We will now take a brief look at these two positions.

The Stability Position

Stability advocates point out that personality traits are, by definition, relatively enduring and stable characteristics. More importantly, there is widespread evidence that personality is stable. For example, as we just discussed, one's temperament at age 4 correlates well with one's temperament as an adult. In addition, how one scores on a personality test as a young adult will correlate well with how that person will score on the same test 25 years later (Costa & McCrae, 1988). Furthermore, research shows that the one event often assumed to cause change during adulthood—the infamous midlife crisis—is more a myth than a reality (Vaillant, 1977).

Table 13.5

What Selected Longitudinal Studies Have to Say About the Stability-Change Debate

Study	Findings
Fels longitudinal study, following infants through adulthood (Moss & Sussman, 1980).	Stability for socially valued traits, such as sex-role appropriate behavior, and need for achievement. However, very little stability in general attitude.
McCrae and Costa's (1984) study of 2,000 men between the ages of 20 to 80 for a 10-year period.	For three important personality traits: neuroticism, extroversion, and openness to experience, stability was the rule.
Guttman (1977).	Found that men and women age in different ways. With age, men become more interested in the expressive, interpersonal world. Women, on the other hand, become more interested in the outer world.
Neugarten (1977) Studied Kansas City residents who were between 40 to 80 years of age for 10 years.	Found evidence of both stability and change. People were stable in terms of their coping strategies, their life satisfaction, and their goal-directedness. People exhibited considerable change in terms of becoming less tied to traditional sex roles (indeed, often exhibiting a sex-role reversal with age, with women becoming more directive, men becoming more interested in social relationships); becoming more self-reflective; and taking a more passive view of life.
California Longitudinal Study, looking at 2-year-olds and their parents over a 40-year period.	Found stability for some traits, but not for others. Indeed, for some traits, making predictions from people's personality scores at age 18 about their personality at age 30, would mean making wrong predictions two-thirds of the time. Also, found that mothers tended to show more stability in personality than fathers.
Thomas & Chess (1986) conducted a study	Found that temperament during the first five years of life were not good predictors of temperament in later life.
Mischel, Shoda, & Peake (1988).	Found that ability to delay gratification at age 4 predicts adjustment at adolescence.

The Change Position

Change advocates point out that personality definitely does change with age. Indeed, in the extreme, the stability position is ridiculous. For example, because personality does change with age, an adult who behaved like a 2-year-old would be considered mentally ill; a 2-year-old who behaved like an 80-year-old would be considered sluggish and withdrawn.

In the extreme, a stability position is hopeless. For example, a child who had a problem would be saddled with that problem for life. However, we know that's not the case. Shyness is a problem for up to 70 percent of children, but only 30 percent of adults (Zimbardo, 1990). Similarly, anxiety and phobias in childhood are virtually useless predictors of having those same problems in adulthood (Eron, 1987).

The extreme stability position also seems to avoid the fact that different behavior problems are more prevalent at different points in life. For example, crime and eating disorders are most likely to be problems during adolescence, whereas suicide is more likely to be a problem in late adulthood.

The extreme stability position also ignores some of the challenges of adolescence. For example, we know that self-esteem falls upon entering junior high. Furthermore, we know that from adolescence to middle adulthood, people become more intellectual, more self-aware, more giving, and more self-confident (Haan, 1981; Helson & Wink, 1992).

The stability position also ignores the growth reported by many people between their twenties and their fifties (Finn, 1986). For example, middle-aged people are more likely to reach generativity than younger adults (Whitbourne et al., 1992). Similarly, as we discussed in chapter 10, many men and women experience tremendous growth in their forties. For example, Florence Livson (1976, 1981) found that people who were not gender-role stereotyped felt better as they got older and were freer of the restrictive bonds of gender roles.

Thus far, you have seen that supporters of the change position have some good arguments against the extreme stability position. But what can they say about the less extreme stability position that personality is, for the most part, stable? For example, what can change advocates say about the studies showing that children's personality test scores predict adult personality test scores? Basically, change advocates have three basic responses to such personality test studies.

First, they point out that even when we accept the data at face value, the data suggest stability only for certain traits. For example, Kagan (Brim & Kagan, 1980, Kagan & Moss, 1962) finds that the correlations between the child and the adult's level of dependency, anger arousal, and sexual behavior are very low. According to Brim and Kagan (1980), the only behaviors that show evidence of stability are the ones that are public and are valued by society—such as achievement-oriented behavior and sex-typed behavior.

Second, change advocates note that even for the traits that appear to be stable, the evidence could be interpreted to

Box 13.11

SELF-CHECK

Indicate whether each of the following statements is true or false.

1. A behaviorist would take a nurture position.
2. The research on identical twins and schizophrenia provides very strong support for the role of nurture in personality development.
3. The research on identical twins and schizophrenia provides very strong support for the role of nature in personality development.
4. Nature seems to play a stronger role in the development of temperament than in the development of self-esteem.
5. Basic temperament seems to be established at birth.
6. Entering junior high seems to coincide with a decrease in one's self-esteem.
7. Identical twins reared apart have very different levels of self-esteem, probably because nurture plays such an important role in self-esteem.
8. Freud was on the change side of the stability-change debate.
9. Midlife crises often result in dramatic personality changes during adulthood.
10. Temperament at age 5 correlates fairly well with adult temperament.
11. If someone has anxieties or fears during childhood, they will probably have problems with anxiety or fear during adulthood.
12. From adolescence to middle adulthood, people tend to become more intellectual, more self-aware, more generous, and more self-confident.
13. Suicide is most likely to be a problem during late adulthood.
14. The research clearly rejects both the extreme stability and the extreme change position.
15. A .70 correlation between childhood and adulthood personality scores indicates that 70 percent of the variation in adult scores can be predicted from childhood scores.
16. Researchers who use in-depth measures of personality tend to find more evidence of change than researchers who use multiple-choice measures of personality.

Please turn to the end of this chapter to check your answers.

show that there is considerable change. For example, stability advocates like to point to .70 correlations between childhood and adult behavior. However, a .70 correlation is not as high as most people may think. Actually, in terms of the change versus stability issue, a .70 correlation means that only half of the variation in people's later scores can be predicted from earlier scores. If only half of the variability in personality tests can be predicted, then half of the variability *can't* be predicted. According to Jack Block (1977), this unpredicted variability reflects change.

Third, change advocates attack the methodology of these studies. Indeed, Jack Block (1977), has such a low opinion of many of these studies that he refers to them as the "litter-ature." In support of Block's position, we should point out that personality tests are devised to get consistent results. If people don't respond the same way to an item, the item is usually thrown out. Thus, stability is built into the measure. Furthermore, if everyone changes to approximately the same degree, then one's score relative to everyone else's during childhood will correlate with one's score relative to everyone else's in adulthood. Thus, a stability bias is built into the standard methodology for assessing stability. Thus, researchers who use richer, more in-depth measures of personality tend to find more evidence of change than people who use multiple-choice tests of personality. For example, Vaillant (1983), using in-depth interviews, found that young adults were more likely to use immature coping strategies (escaping reality and blaming others) whereas middle-aged adults were more likely to cope with problems by making realistic plans and by using their sense of humor.

Conclusions about Stability-Change

As you can see from our discussion and from table 13.5, the stability-change debate is far from settled. However, we can reach at least three conclusions. First, any theory holding an extreme stability position is certainly not consistent with the facts. Second, because there is change, we must study the whole lifespan rather than focusing only on childhood. Third, we need to devote more energy to finding out why some people change throughout the lifespan—and why some people don't.

Conclusions

As you have seen, early attempts to explain personality development were not very successful. Without having facts to guide them, researchers developed explanations that were often inaccurate and vague.

Now, theorists are using scientific evidence to test and revise old theories and to build new ones. The result is theories that acknowledge our capacity for change as well as the fact that we are influenced by both our genes and our environment. In short, thanks to scientific research, theories are providing richer and more accurate views of how personality develops.

Summary

1. As shown in the theories of Plato and Gall, the naturist position has dominated our views of personality development for most of recorded history.
2. Freud's theory focuses on the struggle between nature and socialization.
3. Through his observations of Breuer's patient Bertha Pappenheim, Freud developed the basic principles of psychoanalysis.
4. According to Freud, the id, ego, and superego comprise the basic elements of personality.
5. The ego uses unconscious defense mechanisms to deal with conflicts between the id and superego.
6. Freud believed that during the first five years of life the foundation of adult personality was forged. Freud traced personality development through four biologically determined psychosexual stages and one psychosexual period: oral, anal, and phallic stages, the latency period, and the genital stage.
7. Common criticisms of Freud's theory are that the theory places too much emphasis on personality development during childhood, that it lacks empirical support, that it relies on a male standard of development, and that its notions of infantile sexuality are offensive.
8. Modern psychology is indebted to Freud for his wealth of hypotheses and insights. All modern theories of personality and social development are either an extension of Freud's theory or a reaction against his views.
9. Erikson's views differed from traditional Freudian theory in four ways: (a) he emphasized our social needs rather than our sexual needs; (b) he asserted that the ego had its own origins and thus did not originate from the id; (c) he theorized that the ego is concerned with exploration, manipulation, and competency, as well as mediating unconscious conflicts; and (d) he presented a lifespan view of development.
10. According to Erikson, epigenesis is the mechanism by which maturation lays the ground plan for our progress through eight psychosocial conflicts.
11. Erikson's conflict of identity versus identity diffusion was expanded by James Marcia into four identity statuses: foreclosed, diffused, moratorium, and achieved.
12. Common criticisms of Erikson's theory include (a) his failure to do research to test and refine the theory; (b) the fact that the conflicts do not end when Erikson's theory suggests that they would end; and (c) that Erikson overemphasized autonomy to the near exclusion of intimacy.
13. Adler believed that the root of all maladjustment was a sense of inferiority. People avoid maladjustment through self-perfection. How we define self-perfection is reflected in our life goal.
14. Adler stressed our inherited selflessness (social interest), and our ability to consciously choose to develop (the creative self).
15. Karen Horney rejected Freud's notions of penis envy. Furthermore, she reinterpreted the Oedipal and Electra complexes as sociocultural in origin, rather than biological.
16. Horney stressed personal growth (self-realization), basic anxiety, and neurotic needs as the source of development or maladjustment.
17. The major criticism of all psychoanalytic theories is their lack of empirical support.
18. Humanistic theory ("The Third Force") emerged as a rebellion against the two existing forces in psychology: the overly pessimistic psychoanalytic view and the overly mechanistic behavioristic view.
19. All humanists share four beliefs in common: (a) subjective experience is important, (b) free will and creativity help determine personality, (c) all people inherit a tendency to be the best they can be, and (d) psychological research should be relevant to human experience.

20. Maslow is the spiritual father of humanism and introduced the public to the concept of self-actualization. Maslow also emphasized the role of peak experiences and his hierarchy of needs in the individual's quest toward perfection.
21. Carl Rogers is best known for his work on self-concept. The major cause of psychological problems is incongruence between one's true feelings and their perception of who they should be. Unconditional positive regard is a critical ingredient for the development of congruence.
22. Learning theory is distinguished by its strong basis in research and its assumption that personality development depends on learning.
23. According to Skinner, differences in personality are due not only to biology, but to differences in (a) which behaviors are reinforced, (b) how frequently and consistently those behaviors are reinforced, (c) the magnitude of reinforcement, (d) the length of the interval between the behavior and reinforcement, and (e) which behaviors are punished or ignored.
24. Social learning theorists, such as Albert Bandura, include the role of thought in learning. They focus on the roles of imitation, attention, rehearsal, goals, and self-efficacy.
25. Personality is a product of both nature and nurture. However, some research suggests that nature has more of a role in temperament than in self-esteem.
26. There is evidence for both stability and change in personality. The relative degree of change depends on (a) what traits we are looking at, (b) whether we use in-depth measures (which favor change) or traditional, multiple-choice measures (which favor stability), and (c) what group of people we are looking at (some groups change more than others).

Key Terms

anal expulsive 405
anal fixation 405
anal retentive 405
anal stage 404
basic anxiety 411
biological determinism 400
compensation 402
conditions of worth 419
congruent 420
creative self 410
defense mechanisms 402
denial 403
displacement 403
ego-ideal 402
ego psychologists 408
Electra complex 406
epigenesis 412
genital stage 407
humanism 415
identity achievement 414
identity diffusion 414
identity foreclosed 413
incongruent 419
inferiority complex 408
latency period 406
life goal 409
moratorium 414
neurotic needs 411
Oedipus complex 406
oral stage 404
peak experiences 417
phallic stage 406
projection 402
rationalization 402
reaction formation 402
regression 403
repression 402
schema of apperception 410
self 419
self-actualization 416
self-efficacy 421
self-realization 411
social learning theory 421
sublimation 402
unconditional positive regard 419
vicious circle 412

SELF-CHECK ANSWERS

BOX 13.2

Part A:

1. True.
2. True.
3. True.
4. False.
5. False.
6. False. The conscience is the part of the superego that tells us what we *shouldn't* do. The part of the superego that tells us what we should do is the ego-ideal.
7. False. They reduce anxiety, thus allowing us to function.
8. True. Defense mechanisms are unconscious. They work by fooling our conscious mind. The only way we can fool our own conscious mind is to keep the conscious mind in the dark about the trick.
9. False. Repressed thoughts are banished to the unconscious. However, while in the unconscious, they may fight their way back to consciousness.

Part B:

10. *Compensation* involves trying to make up for weaknesses by excelling in another area; *sublimation* involves converting sexual energy into a more socially appropriate form of energy; *displacement* involves transferring negative drives to a safer target.
11. *Rationalization* involves making excuses for our actions that we believe. *Denial* involves refusing to accept that a real-life event has occurred.

BOX 13.4

Part A:

1. True.
2. False.
3. False.
4. True.
5. False.
6. True.
7. True.
8. True.
9. False.
10. False.

Part B:

11. Oral, anal, phallic, and genital
12. *Anal retentives* rebel by trying to hold onto possessions; *anal expulsives* rebel by expelling things in an uncontrolled way.
13. The *oral character* is interested only in the love object during the moments that the object is meeting an immediate need; the *anal character* is interested in permanently possessing the love object.
14. Children seem to avoid opposite-sex peers and concentrate heavily on developing social and cognitive skills.
15. The genital stage is characterized by more mature and selfless love.
16. The theory was based on Freud's admittedly subjective interpretations of his memories of what clients said to him (in unstructured interviews) about what they claimed to remember about their childhood. In addition, Freud's observations were based on a biased sample. Finally, Freud made causal inferences from correlational data.
17. Many people think Freud overemphasizes biology (especially sex), stability, and the irrational side of human nature.

BOX 13.5

Part A:

1. Ego psychologists place more emphasis on the ego as an independent, powerful force in development. In addition, they place more importance on the role of social needs and influences on development.
2. Adler was helpless against the health problems that afflicted him. To try to overcome these physical limitations, he decided to become a physician. Thus, his early experiences are quite consistent with his view that children have an inferiority complex that they strive to overcome—and that this striving is often reflected in the adult's life goals.
3. Adler points out that how we consciously interpret a situation affects how we react to it, and he believes that our conscious mind has the power to help us change our personality and even reach our potential.
4. Adler could be considered a humanist because he thinks that we are born basically good (we inherit social interest), he thinks understanding conscious experience is very important to understanding the individual (remember the schema of apperception), and he thinks that we have the ability, as adults, to choose to do whatever is necessary to reach our potential.

Part B:

5. True.
6. False. Such striving could lead to selfishness.

BOX 13.6

1. Basic anxiety differs from the inferiority complex in that basic anxiety is due to poor parenting, whereas the inferiority complex is an inevitable consequence of children not having the skills and abilities that adults have.
2. The child first feels hostility toward the parent because the parent has wronged the child. However, the child is unable to acknowledge her hostility and consequently represses it. The repressed thoughts cause anxiety, which the child interprets as a rational response to being relatively alone and helpless in a hostile world.

3. Neurotic needs are usually impossible to satisfy and they don't lead to solving the underlying reasons for the unhappiness—basic anxiety.
4. Horney thinks that women resented men for having more freedom and status than women, not for men having more prominently displayed sex organs.
5. Like most psychoanalysts, Horney and her followers did very little research. Consequently, there is little research to directly support or refute her theory. However, some of the attachment research is consistent with parts of her theory.

Box 13.7

Part A:
1. True.
2. True.
3. True.
4. True.
5. False.
6. True.

Part B:
7. Erikson believes that the conscious ego can play a role in development and that development occurs during adulthood. In addition, Erikson gives social forces a larger role in development.
8. Whereas Erikson portrayed only two resolutions to the identity crisis (identity or identity confusion), Marcia pointed out that there are at least four different outcomes of the identity crisis: identity foreclosed, moratorium, diffusion, and achievement. Furthermore, whereas Erikson portrayed the search for identity as being an activity of adolescence, researchers have found that the struggle for identity can occur throughout adulthood.

Box 13.9

Part A:
1. Humanism was called the "Third Force" because it rebelled against the two dominant forces in psychology at the time: psychoanalysis and behaviorism.
2. Realizing one's full potential will be aided by having peak experiences and by having one's needs for food, security, belongingness, and self-esteem met.
3. A disciple of Rogers might prefer using unconditional positive regard rather than rewarding the desired behavior. A disciple might be concerned that—by putting conditions of worth on the child—the parent would get the child to do what the parent wanted, but that this could lead to incongruence. That is, a disciple of Rogers would think that the child should decide who he is and who he will become rather than having the parents control the child's destiny.
4. Personality development can occur—even in adulthood—by exploring and accepting one's own thoughts and experiences.

Part B:
5. True.
6. False. Maslow thought that we should look at exceptionally good human beings.
7. True.
8. False. The vagueness of the theory is a real problem.
9. False. Self-actualization is the least pressing need. It is a need that will influence our behavior only after all other needs have been met.
10. False.
11. True.
12. True.
13. True.
14. False.

Box 13.10

Part A:
1. Learning theories have research support and focus on lifelong development.
2. Skinner would say that, through rewards and punishments, Freud learned certain patterns of behavior. On the other hand, Freud interpreted his own problems as being due to unconscious forces, such as repressed guilt and anger.
3. One way to change a person's personality would be to increase the person's self-efficacy. The person's self-efficacy would be increased if she experiences tremendous success in a situation where she had previously felt inept. For example, by arranging for shy men to have pleasant conversations with women, the men's self-efficacy about talking to women increases, and, consequently, they date more and act less shy around women.
4. A humanist might say that learning theory was too simplistic and hadn't focused enough on the more positive, mysterious, and magical aspects of human nature.
5. Bandura thinks that the way to increase self-efficacy is to get the person to experience success. That is, nothing succeeds (in boosting self-efficacy) like success. Put another way, success breeds confidence. According to humanists, self-esteem is not increased by changing behavior. Instead, increased self-esteem is achieved when the person reevaluates what he has done and who he is. Specifically, self-esteem can be increased by having other people offer support (by listening and by giving unconditional positive regard) and by simply accepting oneself for who he is.
6. A Freudian would argue that learning theories fail to capture the complexity of human personality and that learning theories also fail to account for stability of personality throughout the lifespan.

Part B:
7. False.
8. False.
9. True.
10. False. The child must attend to the model and rehearse what the model did.
11. True.

Box 13.11

1. True.
2. True.
3. True.
4. True.
5. False. Infant temperament does not predict adult temperament very well.
6. True.
7. False. Identical twins reared apart have fairly similar levels of self-esteem. This similarity could mean that there is a genetic component to self-esteem.
8. False. Freud believed that personality was stable during adulthood. As you will recall, the periods of change (Freud's psychosexual changes) end before adulthood.
9. False. Midlife crises are fairly rare.
10. True.
11. False. Change, rather than stability, seems to be the rule for childhood fears and anxieties.
12. True.
13. True.
14. True.
15. False. As change advocates point out, a .70 correlation between personality test scores at age 40 and personality test scores at age 50 is not as large as a naive person might think. A .70 correlation does not mean that we can predict scores with 70 percent accuracy. If we want to know the precise degree to which we can predict personality test scores at 50 from personality test scores at age 40, we must square the correlation coefficient. Thus, if we have a correlation of .70, we square it and get 49 percent. Consequently, a correlation of .70 means that personality tests scores at age 40 can account for only about half—not 70 percent—of the variation among scores of 50-year-old's.
16. True.

Chapter

Death and Bereavement

To everything there is a season, and a time to every purpose under the heaven: A time to be born, and a time to die—A time to weep and a time to laugh; a time to mourn, and a time to dance—

ECCLESIASTES 3: 1, 2, 4

Chapter Overview

We will all die. Of all developmental experiences, none is as overwhelming as this final event—the end of life as we know it. To better understand the implications of death for human development, psychologists focus on four questions: What is death? What are people's attitudes toward death? What developmental stages do people go through as they die? and How do people grieve? In this chapter, we will explore these four questions.

Box 14.1

ISSUE in FOCUS

Life-Extending Technologies

At a major Midwest hospital not long ago, a patient appeared at the emergency room in the middle of the night. He was hiccupping violently, sixty times a minute. The patient, it turned out, was an early pacemaker wearer. A fast-thinking resident realized what had happened: a pacemaker wire, instead of stimulating the heart, had broken loose and become lodged in the diaphragm. Its jolts of electricity were causing the hiccupping. Acting swiftly, the resident inserted a needle into the patient's chest near the pacemaker, ran a wire out from the needle and grounded it to the hospital plumbing. The hiccupping stopped, giving doctors a chance to operate and reposition the faulty wire. A foretaste of tomorrow's medicine? (Alvin Toffler, *Future Shock,* p. 184)

You are gravely ill. Your physician has informed you that without medical intervention you will die in weeks, possibly days. To ensure your survival, which and how many of the following procedures would you be willing to live with? Are there any circumstances under which you would refuse treatment?

kidney dialysis	liver transplant
kidney transplant	respirator
pacemaker	iron lung
artificial heart	lung transplant
heart transplant	multiple organ transplant

Types of Death

On the surface, death may seem like a simple concept. However, in recent years, we have become increasingly aware of death's complexity. For example, how should we determine when a person is dead? Consider the case of Philadelphia Flyer's hockey star, Pelle Lindbergh (Veatch, 1988). On November 10, 1985, Lindbergh slammed his Porsche into a cement wall. The newspaper headline blared "Flyers' Goalie Declared Brain Dead." The newspaper went on to explain that he was listed in critical condition and his family was flying to the states from Sweden to be with him at the hospital. How could someone be brain dead (the absence of neuronal activity in the brain), but in critical condition? Doesn't brain dead mean the person is dead? Yes and no.

Although **brain death** is the accepted criterion for clinical death, modern technology has blurred this criterion. Before medical technology introduced its myriad of life-preserving machines (see box 14.1), if a person were brain dead, other bodily functions (such as respiration and pulse) would also cease. Brain death was as good as dead. But then, we invented life-support machines that could breathe for us, oxygenate our heart, and keep the body alive even if our brains were "dead." Initially, medical practice tended to support the idea of keeping people alive as long as possible, even if there were no possibility that they would regain brain function. However, when physicians started to transplant organs, medical views about prolonging life changed. To increase the chances that an organ will be accepted by a recipient, the organ needs to be fresh. To ensure freshness, patients need to die at the "right time"—when a compatible and needy recipient has been identified and is ready to receive the organ. A potential donor's right to die in dignity may compete with a potential organ recipient's chance to survive. Physicians and public policy makers are currently confronted with a moral dilemma, "Is it acceptable to prolong the life of a brain dead patient merely for the purpose of harvesting the patient's organs?" The debate still rages.

In the case of Pelle Lindbergh, if brain death were enough to declare him dead, then he was a perfect organ donor, because his liver, lungs, and corneas were undamaged. Here was an opportunity to help another person live. However, if brain death were not enough to declare Pelle dead, then he would have to remain on a respirator indefinitely and no one would benefit from his organs. Was Pelle dead? Should the "plug be pulled" and his organs used to help others live? Once again, "when is a person dead?" If you were his family, what would you do?

As you will see in this section, your answer to this question not only depends on your philosophical position, but on what type of death you're talking about: biological death, psychological death, social death, or legal death (Aiken, 1994).

Biological Death

Biological death occurs when vital functions such as respiration and heart beat stop. When the respiratory center of the brain stem fails, oxygen is no longer inhaled and diffused by the lungs into the blood. When the heart fails, the

Box 14.2

ISSUE in FOCUS

Social Death Sometimes Occurs Well After Biological Death

WORCESTER, Mass. (AP) 10/27/93

One neighbor had Adele A. Gaboury's lawn mowed for her. Another took care of a pile of mail. A utility company was called to tend to her broken pipes.

All the while, the recluse lay dead, probably for four years, in trash on the kitchen floor. . . .

Neighbors had inquired about Gaboury about four years ago after they noticed she was missing. But one of her brothers, with whom she wasn't close, told police she had gone into a nursing home. Police say a formal missing person report was never filed, so there was no full-scale investigation.

Once the search for Gaboury ended, neighbors began to tend to her two-story house that stood out in its decay in a middle-class neighborhood of the central Massachusetts city. The mailman kept delivering her mail through a slot in the door until neighbor Michael Crowley noticed a pileup. He opened the door and hundreds of pieces of mail fluttered into the yard. Crowley notified police, who got the deliveries stopped. Next-door neighbor Eileen Dugan started paying her own grandson $10 twice a month to mow Gaboury's lawn.

No one could imagine Gaboury was inside. Even when the police searched the home Friday, after a neighbor complained about it as a health hazard, they missed her badly decomposed body in 6 feet of trash, which police say Gaboury probably had allowed to pile up in her home before she died.

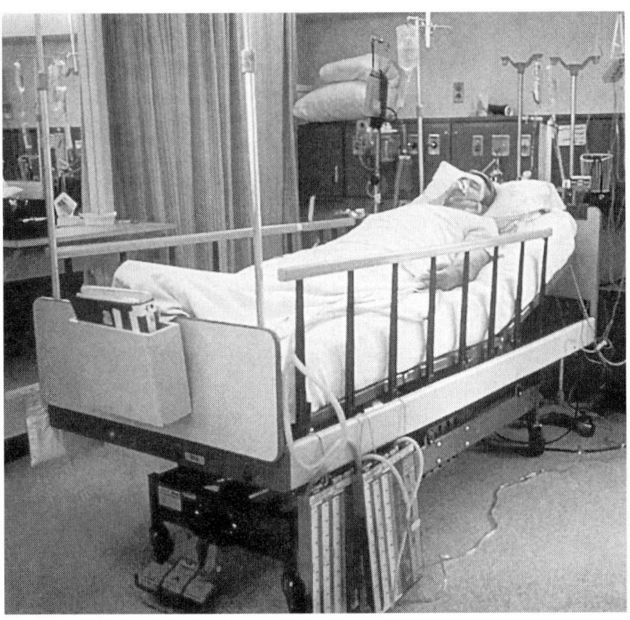

The many definitions of death and advances in medical technology have made determining when a person is dead difficult.

oxygenated blood is not pumped through the blood vessels. The body starts to die. We say "starts" to die because different cells die at different rates. Higher brain cells die first, 5 to 8 minutes after respiration ceases. Lower brain cells die next; then kidney cells after one hour; striated muscle cells after several hours; and epithelial cells (hair and nails) after several days.

Psychological and Social Death

Biological death is not the only type of death. **Psychological death** occurs when a person's mind (the seat of conscious experiences) ceases to function. A person with severe brain damage may be able to breath and maintain cell life, but not be able to think, consciously experience, or know anything. People with degenerative brain disorders such as Korsakoff's syndrome, Alzheimer's disease, and Huntington's chorea die psychologically before they die biologically.

A person may be biologically and psychologically alive, but socially dead when others treat her as if she were dead. As you may have read in the classic novel, *The Scarlet Letter*, a form of **social death** occurred when the Puritans shunned a young woman who had violated their moral code by committing adultery. In the novel, *Clan of the Cave Bear* (Auel, 1980), a prehistoric young woman who did not conform to the expectations of her clan was declared "dead" by them and treated as if she didn't exist.

Just as a person may be biologically alive and socially dead, a person may be biologically dead, but socially alive. Alfred Hitchcock took advantage of this fact to create fear and suspense in his 1960 movie *Psycho*. In that movie, Norman Bates treated his biologically and psychologically dead mother as if she were alive. In the real world, people who treat a biologically dead person as if that person were alive do so to reduce anxiety. For example, some parents cannot accept their child's death. Therefore, they maintain the child's room and set a place at the dinner table just as if the child were alive. Perhaps just as sad, but much less dramatic, is the case of elderly people who are actually dead, but thought to be alive (see box 14.2).

Box 14.3

ISSUE in FOCUS

Premature Burial

The wife of one of the most respectable citizens—a lawyer of eminence and a member of congress—was seized with a sudden and unaccountable illness, which completely baffled the skill of her physician. After much suffering, she died, or was supposed to die. No one suspected, indeed, or had reason to suspect, that she was not actually dead. She presented all the ordinary appearances of death. The face assumed the usual pinched and sunken outline. The lips were of the usual marble pallor. The eyes were lusterless. There was no warmth. Pulsation had ceased. For three days, the body was preserved unburied, during which it had acquired a stony rigidity. The funeral, in short, was hastened, on account of the rapid advance of what was supposed to be decomposition.

The lady was deposited in her family vault, which, for three subsequent years, was undisturbed. At the expiration of this term it was opened for the reception of a sarcophagus—but, alas! how fearful a shock awaited the husband, who, personally, opened the door! As its portals swung outwardly back, some white-appareled object fell rattling within his arms. It was the skeleton of his wife in her yet unmolded shroud.

A careful investigation rendered it evident that she had revived within two days after her entombment; that her struggles within the coffin had caused it to fall from a ledge, or shelf to the floor, where it was broken as to permit her escape. A lamp that had been accidentally left, full of oil, within the tomb, was found empty; it might have been exhausted, however, by evaporation. On the uttermost of the steps, which led down into the dread chamber was a large fragment of the coffin, with which, it seemed, that she had endeavored to arrest attention by striking the iron door. While thus occupied, she probably swooned, or possibly died, through sheer terror; and in falling, her shroud became entangled in some iron-work which projected her interiorly. Thus she remained, and thus she rotted, erect.

Note: From *The Complete Poems and Stories of Edgar Allan Poe* (Vol. 1, p. 532) by A. H. Quinn and E. H. O'Neill (Eds.), 1976, New York: Alfred A. Knopf, Inc.

Legal Death

In addition to biological, psychological, and social death, there is **legal death.** Legal death occurs when a person is declared dead by a legal authority and his or her possessions are distributed. In such cases, a person may or may not be biologically dead. For example, a person who is missing in action may not be biologically dead, but may be declared legally dead.

Determination of Death

As we have seen, death is more than a biological event. Indeed, even in a hospital, the decision to "pull the plug" is affected by many nonbiological considerations, such as ethical, economic, and legal issues. But, once the plug has been pulled or the person stops breathing and responding to stimulation in spite of the machines, how is it determined that he or she is actually dead? That is, what are the biological indicators of death?

The Indicators of Biological Death

Aiken (1994) lists the clinical indicators of death as cessation of heartbeat (and peripheral pulse) and respiration; unresponsiveness of the eyes to light and of the other sense organs to sound, touch, and pain; and bluing of the mouth and lips. As biological death advances, the skin turns purplish-red **(livor mortis),** the muscles stiffen **(rigor mortis),** and the body temperature gradually declines until it reaches the temperature of the environment **(algor mortis).**

But, how do you know the person is dead for sure? Any student of late-night horror movies or Edgar Allan Poe's fictional account "The Premature Burial" (see box 14.3) is familiar with the fear of premature burial. Fortunately, modern techniques for determining death combined with current funeral practices can assure that only the dead are buried. However, in years past, imprecise methods for determining death (such as no fogging of a mirror when placed near the mouth, lack of response to tickling the nose with a feather, and no constriction of the pupils to light), resulted in occasional premature burials. In fact, my mother was almost buried prematurely.

In 1932, she was declared dead. Her appendix had burst and infected her entire abdominal cavity—a condition called peritonitis. Her temperature soared above the thermometer's scale for two days, then suddenly plunged. At the same time, her breathing and heart rate slowed to such an extent that it couldn't be detected. On the basis of these criteria, she was declared dead. After her family was notified of her death, she awakened to find a sheet pulled over her head. Her family thought she had come back from the dead. However, as we know today, her death had been misdiagnosed by using imperfect criteria. Fortunately, she awakened before she had been removed to the funeral home for embalming. I was born 24 years later.

Today, termination of heartbeat and respiratory movements are not sufficient for a clinical diagnosis of death. Emergency techniques such as CPR (cardiopulmonary resuscitation) and countershock may restore both functions. In other words, modern technology has made it possible to revive some people who have died. How long do we attempt to revive people before we give up and declare them dead? In most cases, death is declared when brain death has been established. When a person's heartbeat stops, the oxygen supply to the brain also stops and the neurons begin to die. If the brain has been deprived of oxygen for more than 5 to 10 minutes, it is likely that the brain has been severely and permanently damaged. If the damage is so severe that the brain no longer functions, the person is declared brain dead.

Determining brain death may seem straightforward. However, it is not. For example, if someone had been deprived of oxygen for 10 minutes and is then taken to the hospital where 10 minutes of physiological testing reveal no evidence of brain functioning, it would seem clear that the person is brain dead. However, as you can see from table 14.1, such a person may not be brain dead. That is, whereas showing no sign of brain activity for 10 minutes would signal brain death for adults, some children actually recover brain functioning after such long periods of physiological unresponsiveness. Similarly, small children may survive oxygen deprivation for longer than 10 minutes. Children are most likely to recover from long periods of oxygen deprivation when hypothermia (low body temperature) is involved because the body's cells use less oxygen when body temperature is reduced. Thus, you may have heard of cases where children have been trapped under ice for more than 10 minutes and survived.

Although children may survive such experiences, they often suffer brain damage. If the brain damage is severe, the electrical activity in the brain stem (the center for respiratory and heart reflexes) may not be sufficient to meet the psychological definition of life (Veatch, 1981, as cited in Rybash, Roodin, & Hoyer, 1995).

What happens when a child is psychologically dead, but still (with the help of machines) breathing? That will depend on the parents'—and the physicians'—attitudes about death. For example, people in the United States are more likely to use life-extending technologies than people in other developed countries, perhaps because Americans are less accepting of death (*Newsweek*, 1993). Indeed, some believe that a large part of our health care crisis is due to elderly people racking up enormous medical expenses on care that prolongs the dying process by a few days.

Table 14.1

Current Brain Death Criteria

Statement: An individual with irreversible cessation of all functions at the entire brain including the brain stem is dead. The determination at death must follow accepted medical standards.

1. Cessation is determined by evaluation of a and b
   a. *Cerebral functions are absent*—Deep coma with no receptivity and unresponsivity; confirmation by flat EEG (no electrical activity) or blood flow analysis/angiography showing no circulating blood to brain for at least ten minutes may be done to confirm evaluation.

   b. *Brain stem functions are absent*—No pupillary reflex to bright light in either eye; no extraocular movements (no eye movements when head turned from side to side or when ear canals are irrigated with ice water); no corneal reflex when the cornea is lightly touched; no gag reflex when a tongue depressor is touched against the back of the pharynx; no cough reflex; no respiratory (apnea) reflexes. Note that some primitive spinal cord reflexes may persist after brain death.
2. Irreversibility of death is determined when evaluation discloses a and b and c
   a. The cause of coma is determined and is sufficient to account for the loss of brain functions.

   b. The possibility of recovery of any brain function is excluded.

   c. The cessation of all brain functions persists during a reasonable period of observation and/or trial of therapy; and confirmation at this clinical judgment, when appropriate, is made with EEG or blood flow data (cessation of blood flow for at least ten minutes).
3. Conditions Limiting the Reliable Application of the Above-Mentioned Criteria:
   a. *Drug and metabolic conditions*—If any sedative is suspected to be present, there must be toxicology screening to identify the drug.

   b. *Hypothermia-temperature below 32.2 degrees C/ 90 degrees F.*

   c. *Developmental immaturity*—Infants and young children under the age of five have increased resistance to damage and greater potential for recovery despite showing neurologic unresponsiveness for longer periods of time than adults.

   d. *Shock*—Produces significant reduction in cerebral blood flow.

Source: "Guidelines for the Determination of Death" in *Journal of the American Medical Association*, 246 (19): 2184–2186 (November 13, 1981).

What Are People's Attitudes Toward Death?

Why would people in some countries be more accepting of death than people in other countries? Like all attitudes, our fears and attitudes about death are largely learned from the

Box 14.4

SELF-CHECK

Part A

Indicate whether each of the following statements is true or false.

1. If a person is brain dead, the rest of the body will die.
2. When the heart stops beating, oxygen is no longer pumped through the body and so virtually all the cells in the body die within a few minutes.
3. People with degenerative brain disorders such as Alzheimer's disease die psychologically before they die biologically.
4. If a person goes without oxygen for 10 minutes, she will be brain dead.

Part B

Answer the following questions.

5. Some children are born with only one part of their brain—the brain stem. If these children are viewed as being alive by their parents, what is their status in terms of biological, social, and psychological death?
6. What is algor mortis and why do detectives like to reach a murder victim before the victim has achieved algor mortis?
7. In television shows and movies, a corpse is sometimes referred to as a "stiff." What clinical indicator of death might be responsible for this slang term?
8. What is one possible explanation for stories about people who "came back from the dead?"

Please turn to the end of this chapter to check your answers.

experiences we have had with our culture and family (Aiken, 1994; Huyck & Hoyer, 1982; Kastenbaum, 1985).

Just as our views of death reflect the experiences we have had, our culture's views reflect the experiences that our country has had. For example, in less developed countries such as India, Ethiopia, and Mexico, death is more prevalent. Plagues, famines, and natural disasters are more likely to exact a toll. For example, compare the death statistics of the October, 1989, San Francisco earthquake with the September 30, 1993, earthquake in southern India. The earthquake in San Francisco was 7.5 on the Richter scale, and about 4,000 people died. In contrast, the India earthquake measured 6.4 on the Richter scale and over 30,000 people died! Similarly, very few people died in the great floods that struck the Midwestern United States during the summer of 1993. A similar level of flooding would have killed thousands in a less developed country. Even without natural disasters, the rigors of everyday life in these less developed countries result in higher infant and child mortality rates, as well as lower life expectancies. Indeed, in some underdeveloped countries, parents typically bury as many children as they raise to adulthood. Death is common and the people accept it as a normal part of living. In contrast to most parents in the United States, parents in these countries commonly educate their young about death and dying, even providing them with guidelines on how to die (Rybash, Roodin, & Hoyer, 1995). Thus, the fact that many people in developed countries like the United States have infrequent contact with death may explain why people raised in developed countries are more likely to deny death (DeSpelder & Strickland, 1992).

In many countries outside the United States, death is more easily accepted. Here, families in South Korea visit the national cemetery in Seoul for family memorial day.

Not only do people from different countries hold different views of death, but there can be major differences within the same country. For example, in a landmark study by Kalish and Reynolds (1981) African Americans, Euro-Americans, Japanese Americans, and Mexican Americans were surveyed about their attitudes and beliefs concerning death and dying. African and Euro-Americans were more likely to believe that dying patients should be told that they are dying than Japanese and Mexican Americans. Relative to the other three groups, Mexican Americans were (1) less likely to let a person die if the person wanted to, (2) less likely to want to know if they were mortally ill, and (3) less likely to try to control their emotions in public if someone close to them died.

Kalish and Reynolds report that a greater percentage of Euro-Americans indicated that slow death is more tragic than sudden death and death in childhood is most tragic of all. Euro-Americans were also more likely to avoid funerals as well as to report having had less contact with people who were dying.

Mexican and African Americans were the most likely to report that they wanted to live past 90. They were also most likely to admit having experienced or felt the presence of someone who had died.

Despite these cultural differences, we should point out two facts. First, many of these cultural differences were diminished when the responses of older participants were compared. Second, most cultures do share some common attitudes about death. For example, most cultures do not view death as the end of a person's existence. Most people, regardless of their culture, believe that an individualized consciousness survives and goes on to some kind of afterlife (Grof & Halifax, 1977). For example, some people believe that God has called their loved one home. This belief in an afterlife may be common to most cultures because it seems to help people get over the loss of a loved one (McIntosh, Silver, & Wortman, 1993).

Historical Views of Death

We have tried to stress that a person's view of death depends on one's culture. If you were part of another culture, for example, your view of death would be different. It may be hard to fathom that your views of death would be different if you were raised in a different culture. Even if you accept that, you may feel that Western culture's notions of death are more sophisticated and accurate than those of other cultures.

To help you question your assumptions about the accuracy of Western culture's views of death, let's look at how Western views of death have changed over the past few centuries. To do this, we will rely on the work of Philippe Aries (1981), who analyzed historical documents and artifacts from the European Middle Ages and traced the evolution of attitudes toward death from 1,000 years ago up to the twentieth century.

During most of the Middle Ages, death was accepted and expected as a terrible but necessary human misfortune. The dead were thought merely to be sleeping until the Second Coming of Christ. Death itself was not feared so much as the method and timing of death because the dead were believed to be judged at the moment of death. Of greatest concern was a sudden death because it provided no opportunity for confession and absolution. Understandably, deathbed confessions were common, because it was believed that such confessions could determine whether the immortal soul would be seized by an angel or a devil.

Later, in the seventeenth and eighteenth centuries, people began to perceive death as a sorrowful—but remote—event. Mortality was accepted, but thoughts of personal death still made people anxious. It was also a time of romantic or macabre eroticism in which death was intermingled with sex in art and literature.

The dominant attitude toward death had changed again by the beginning of the nineteenth century. The belief that death was ugly, including the belief in hell, began to diminish. During this period, death was considered to be a beautiful event leading to a happy reunion in paradise.

Aries is most critical of the next era, that of the denial of death beginning in the late nineteenth century. This was the start of what he calls "the lie" and a time when death became less visible. Dying people were hidden away in hospitals, children were "spared" the unpleasantness of viewing and knowing about death and dying, the deceased was efficiently prepared and interred by a team of professionals, and public mourning was essentially eliminated. Death was likely to be seen as either an accident or a medical failure, and in contrast to the belief of the Middle Ages, the best way to die was during sleep.

Aries believes that there are indications that the denial of death, which has been so characteristic of twentieth-century Western society, has eroded somewhat in the past two or three decades. According to Aries, adults and children are learning once again that death is a part of what it means to be human, and that it is inhuman for people to die all alone attached to tubes and life-sustaining machines without being given a chance to make their peace and say their good-byes.

Death Today

There is evidence to support Aries' belief that death is becoming more visible in our everyday life. In recent years, for example, university courses in death and dying have become common (Association for Gerontology in Higher Education, 1989). A walk through your local bookstore will yield several volumes on death and dying, including manuals on how to die. The media displays pictures of corpses on its screens and pages so that everyone is familiar with the look of death. People in our inner cities have a more personal experience with death, as violence takes its toll on their families and friends. For those dying of terminal illness, hospice programs have tried increasingly to move the dying out of the hospitals and back into their homes.

Despite our increased familiarity with death, the actual process of dying remains impersonal. Most people in the United States do not die at home in their own bed. Rather, 80 percent die in a medical institution or enroute to one (Benoliel, 1988). As early as the nineteenth century, our bodies were washed and prepared by our families and then placed in a handmade coffin (DeSpelder & Strickland, 1992). Today, our bodies are washed by a nurse and then whisked away by a funeral director's assistant, embalmed,

Box 14.5

SELF-CHECK

Indicate whether each of the following statements is true or false.

1. Because death (especially of children) is more likely in underdeveloped countries, people in underdeveloped countries fear death more than Americans do.
2. Euro-Americans are more likely than other Americans to avoid funerals.
3. Mexican Americans and African Americans were more likely than other Americans to report that they wanted to live past 90.
4. African Americans were least likely to try to control their emotions in public if someone close to them died.
5. Differences between African Americans, Euro-Americans, Japanese Americans, and Mexican Americans in terms of attitudes about death are most pronounced among older Americans.
6. Most cultures share some common attitudes about death, such as believing that death is not the end of a person's existence.
7. In the Middle Ages, people feared a sudden death because such a death might not allow one to confess one's sins and be forgiven prior to death.
8. In the early 1800s, death was considered to be a beautiful event, leading to a happy reunion in paradise.
9. Aries thinks that, starting in the late 1800s, Westerners started trying to deny the existence of death.
10. Aries thinks that the worst period of Western history, in terms of our views of death, is the present.

Please turn to the end of this chapter to check your answers.

cosmetically restored, dressed, and placed in an ornate coffin lined with satin. In earlier times, our bodies were placed in the family parlor for friends and relatives to keep vigil during that final night before they buried us. Today, our bodies are viewed in a slumber room at the funeral home for a few hours one evening. The next day, a closed casket funeral is held, and perhaps a graveside ceremony will be observed. Then, after the people have left, the body will be lowered into the grave and dirt filled in by strangers employed for that purpose.

Whereas our ancestors participated in the burial of their friends and family members (see box 14.6), we are only reluctant observers. In fact, we are such reluctant observers that we try to shield our children from the reality of death. Thus, children are often excluded from the unpleasantness of attending a funeral. Death is removed from normal experience. Instead, death is something for late-night horror movies and impersonal obituaries.

Life Expectancy and Mortality Rates

Why have our attitudes and rituals shifted so dramatically? Both technological and social variables have altered our view of death. Advances in medical technology mean that more people live longer. Since the turn of the century, average life expectancy in the United States has increased from 47 to 73 years. In 1900, over half (53 percent) of reported deaths involved people age 15 and younger. Today, only about 5 percent of the total reported deaths occur in this age group (Kain, 1988; U.S. Bureau of the Census, 1993). Today, Americans view early death as premature, often assuming that a newborn will live into his or her seventh decade. Death before 60 is regarded as a tragic exception—"She was struck down in her prime."

To further contribute to our infrequent exposure to death, our circle of family and close friends has shrunk as the extended family has been increasingly replaced by a smaller and highly mobile nuclear family. Few people live in the same town as their parents and grown siblings. Cousins meet infrequently, and having everyone home for the holidays can be a logistical nightmare. Furthermore, friendships are more likely to be transient, a function of who we live near or work with at a particular point in our career. Fewer close ties mean fewer opportunities to experience personally the death of someone close to us.

Although death may be an infrequent visitor in our personal lives, it is a frequent visitor to our homes. As stated earlier, we view death at a distance through media pictures and reports of violence, disease, and deterioration. But death in the media, however vivid, is also death once removed from experience. It is impersonal. It can be turned off with a flick of the remote control.

Developmental Level and Attitude Toward Death

Of course death *does* happen to people we love and know—approximately 50 million people die worldwide every year and 1 million people in the United States are now in the process of dying (Aiken, 1994; Kain, 1988). How we come to grips with these experiences depends on our level of development.

Box 14.6

RESEARCH in FOCUS

Small Town America

Death brought the community into play for the last time: the food discreetly left in the kitchen; the condolence calls; the preparation of the corpse in the beds in which [the person] had died—and perhaps slept in for many years—without benefit of the mortician's cosmetics; the laying out in the parlor; a stream of people filing softly by throughout the day paying respects to the family; the old friends who sat up with the body through the long lonely night; and then the funeral the next day, with family, friends, numerous townspeople, members of the husband's lodge, and ladies of the burial society who had decorated the grave site. Funerals were long and doleful; the minister droned on interminably about the virtues of the deceased and hymns were sung; then the black hearse with white-gloved pallbearers in attendance and a black-plumed horse drawing it made its slow progress to the cemetery. It was not unusual for town businesses to close down completely for a funeral, and nearly everyone joined the procession to the burying-place, where at graveside a few last words were said, before the finality of the earth raining down on the coffin. Back at home, neighbors had cleaned and dusted, leaving a neat—and empty—home for the grieving family to return to. There they sank down wearily and talked in numbed voices and at last went to bed, to try to get some rest in preparation for the new day.

Note: From *Small Town America* (p. 316) by R. R. Lingeman, 1980, New York: G. P. Putnam.

Children

American children in general are not personally familiar with death. Not only is death less common in society at large, but children rarely witness death because adults exclude them from hospital rooms (where people die) and funerals. Furthermore, adults avoid talking about death with children. Yet, children do think about death. Parents cannot shield their children from death forever. Eventually a pet, a grandparent, or a friend will die. Children will see death on the television, witness it on the highways or in the woods. Death is a normal part of development and cannot be avoided. Parents should help children understand death in a manner appropriate for the child's cognitive and emotional level (see box 14.7).

Stage Theories of Death How do children view death? Over 40 years ago, Maria Nagy (1948) conducted a classic study on how children view death. In her investigation, she questioned 378 Hungarian children ages 3 through 10 on their ideas on death and had children ages 6 through 10 write and draw their ideas. Nagy then developed a model of death that was based on these interviews as well as on Piaget's stages of cognitive development. For example, because Piaget's theory postulates that the 2-year-old is capable only of sensorimotor thought, Nagy did not question 2-year-olds and does not think they are capable of having a conception of death. Similarly, because Piaget's theory postulates qualitative shifts as children progress from preoperational, to concrete operational, to formal operational thought, Nagy believes that children's understanding of death progresses through three qualitatively different stages.

In Nagy's first stage, children (typically, 3- to 5-year-olds) relate to death in egocentric ways. In her study, these children did not distinguish between death and separation. Death was regarded as a temporary state from which the dead person would soon become alive again. The dead were simply asleep or on a trip, from which they would eventually return. Although dead people were viewed as less alive than alive people, they could still eat, breathe, and drink in a coffin—as Tommy tells us:

Tommy (age 4):
It can't move because it's in the coffin.

Interviewer: If it weren't in the coffin, could it?

Tommy:
It can eat and drink.

In Nagy's second stage, children (typically, 4- to 9-year-olds) viewed death as something that happened to old people. Children viewed death as irreversible, but avoidable. Certainly, bad people or those who had accidents would die. However, death could be outwitted if you were good, quick, and careful: One must be careful not to eat or drink too much, catch a disease, or get hurt.

Children at this stage personified death in their drawings. Thus, in some cases, death was an angel. In other cases, death was a monster or a "death man." But in almost all cases, death was an individual.

Given this crude understanding of death, it is not surprising that these children had trouble distinguishing

Box 14.7

ISSUE in FOCUS

Educating Children About Death

Children often learn about death in an informal and unplanned way. Parents and teachers usually discuss death only when a child asks questions about it or when a pet or person they know dies (Leviton & Forman, 1974). However, experts recommend that parents talk to children about death before children encounter it. DeSpelder and Strikland (1983) point out that if parents put off talking about death until a family member or friend dies, the parents' ability to provide a clear explanation of death may be impeded by the parents' experience of intense grief.

Parents should be honest and straightforward when they talk about death with their children. Parents should directly respond to children's questions, yet gear their responses to the child's developmental level. For example, when explaining the specifics of death to a preschooler parents should use simple physical and biological terms. Avoid abstractions and elaborate explanations. Perhaps more important than an accurate description of death is a preschooler's need to be reassured that she is loved and will not be abandoned.

Older children should be encouraged to go beyond simple notions and think more abstractly about the meaning of life and death (Stein, 1974). No matter the child's age, adults should be honest, sensitive, and sympathetic. They should encourage children to express their feelings and ideas. Furthermore, children should be informed when family members or other people they know are dying. Children should be encouraged, not forced, to be with dying family and friends and to attend the funeral. If children want to attend the funeral, they should be told what will happen during the service. Finally, when answering children's questions about life after death, you should explain your views, but tell them you don't have all the answers.

---

between life and death. For example, stage 2 children often classified moving things as alive and unmoving things as dead. The following transcripts may give you a better feel for the primitive view of death that is typical of stage 2 children.

MARTA (age 6):

Carries off bad children. Catches them and takes them away.

INTERVIEWER: What is he like?

MARTA:

White as snow. Death is white everywhere. It's wicked. It doesn't like children.

INTERVIEWER: Why?

MARTA:

Because it is bad-hearted. Death even takes away men and women too.

LACI (age 8):

What is death?

INTERVIEWER: A being, dead of old age or illness.

Children in Nagy's third stage (aged 10+) believe that death can happen to anyone, even if they are careful. Death is the real, inevitable, and irreversible destruction of the body. As you can see from the following statements by Guyla, children at this stage hold a fairly realistic, adult view of death. That is, unlike statements made by the children at earlier stages, you may find yourself agreeing with Guyla's statements.

GUYLA (age 9):

Death is the termination of life. Death is destiny. Then we finish our earthly life. Death is the end of life on earth.

Note that Guyla is expressing a stage 3 view, even though Guyla is not yet 10. Thus, as with Piaget's stages, there are no hard and fast age boundaries to a stage. Cultural factors have a tremendous impact on how children view death. For example, in the United States children do not personify death to the same extent as Nagy's children. Furthermore, U.S. children understand the biological basis of death earlier than Nagy's children (Childers & Wimmer, 1971; Melear, 1973). Yet, regardless of the culture, it is not until relatively late in childhood that children understand that death is a permanent event that happens to everyone (White, Elson, & Prawat, 1978).

Although Nagy's theory has been widely cited in discussions of children's death, it has also been widely criticized. For example, some attack the theory for not taking into account how the environment affects children's understanding of death. That is, Nagy's theory is relatively silent about what impact children's culture or experiences have on their understanding of death. Furthermore, some argue that the research evidence that forms the basis for Nagy's theory is weak.

Critics feel the evidence is weak because it was based on a small sample of Hungarian children and because Nagy's interpretations of what the children's drawings really meant could be wrong. Some ammunition for Nagy's critics comes from the fact that subsequent research has failed to corroborate Nagy's findings. For example, Kane (1979) studied 122 middle-class American children, aged 3 through 12. She found no evidence for Nagy's personification stage (stage 2). As a result of this study, Kane decided to develop a theory that fit the facts better than Nagy's.

In some ways, Kane's theory is like Nagy's. Like Nagy, Kane based her theory on Piaget's theory of cognitive development. As a result, Kane, like Nagy, proposed that children's understanding of death progressed through three stages. However, as you will see, Kane's three stages differ from Nagy's.

Stage 1 As we mentioned, Kane's theory is strongly influenced by Piaget's theory of cognitive development. Piaget's influence on Kane's theory is especially strong in Kane's first stage. Kane's first stage starts at age 2, the age at which Piaget proposed that children began to think verbally. This thinking, however, is egocentric and illogical. Therefore, in Kane's first stage, Kane postulates that young children (aged 2 through 5) think about death in primitive, egocentric, and illogical ways.

Consistent with Piaget's view that young children's thinking is egocentric, the stage 1 child understands that the death of another person means that the child will never again get help or hugs from the dead person. That is, children understand what happens to them when someone else dies.

Consistent with Piaget's view that young children's thinking is illogical, Kane postulates that the young child's views about what the dead person experiences and about what causes death are quite primitive. Thus, recognizing that the dead person is immobile, the child may rely on certain magical and animistic mental processes to understand the way dead people "live." In the same way, the child may be prone to believe that magical thinking can cause death. For example, if a relative died shortly after the child had yelled "I wish you were dead," the child might think she had killed the relative.

Stage 2 Kane's second stage corresponds to Piaget's concrete operations stage (6 through 12 years). At this stage, children appreciate that death has two essential sources: one that is internal (disease, old age) and another that is external (murder, accident). These "causes" produce an irreversible result.

Stage 3 Kane's third stage corresponds to Piaget's formal operations stage. The child at this stage has a very accurate understanding of the causes of death. Like adults, children of this age can think about death in very abstract and speculative ways.

Children's understanding of death changes as they develop cognitively, either in stages or continuously.

Non-Stage Theories of Death As you have seen, the stage views of both Nagy and Kane assume that the child's general level of cognitive development limits the child's ability to understand death. Not everyone accepts these stage views. For example, in her book describing the private world of terminally ill children (ages 3 through 9), Bluebond-Langer (1978) states that each of these children came to an adult's understanding of death. These children described death as a "mutilating experience" that causes final separation from family and things. She argued that achieving this level of understanding did not depend on the child's overall level of cognitive development, but on the experience of being ill. As the terminally ill child comes closer to death, the child's understanding of death increases. Thus, dying children go through the same changes in understanding death, regardless of their age.

Dying is not the only experience that can affect a child's understanding of death. For example, a child's social class seems to affect how a child will perceive death. Specifically, lower-class children are more likely to associate death with violence, whereas middle-class children tend to associate death with disease (Tallmer, Formaneck, & Tallmer, 1974). This finding makes sense when we remember that the poor are more likely to see violence and violent deaths, whereas the middle class are more likely to experience the death of the old.

Adolescents

We have discussed young children's views of death, but what about the views of adolescents and adults? As loyal followers of Piaget, neither Nagy or Kane believed that

Adolescents may engage in life-threatening behavior, such as drinking and driving because they believe death to be "a long way off" and that they are invulnerable.

Table 14.2

The Meaning of Death

What Does Death Mean to You?	Percentage Agreeing
The end, the final process of life.	35%
Termination of this life but with survival of the spirit.	17%
The beginning of a life after death; a transition; a new beginning.	13%
A joining of the spirit with a universal cosmic consciousness.	12%
A kind of endless sleep; rest and peace.	9%
Don't know, or other answers.	14%

Source: From E. Schneidman, *Deaths of Man*, Quadrangle, New York, 1973.

conceptions of death changed after age 12. Therefore, they didn't study adolescents or adults. However, other investigators have questioned adolescents and adults.

Adolescents usually view death as something that happens only to the elderly. Death is a distant, abstract event, although sometimes tinged with romance. Adolescents learn to accept death as something that, in time, will happen to everyone. However, in regard to themselves, they think death could occur only as a result of violence or because it was "meant to be" (Ambron & Brodzinsky, 1979). Interestingly, one survey (McIntyre, Angle, & Struempler, 1972) found that adolescents do not necessarily accept the finality of death. In fact, in that survey, McIntyre, Angle, & Struempler (1972) found that 7- to 9-year-olds accepted death more readily than adolescents.

In terms of believing in an afterlife, adolescents with a religious background are more likely than others to think about heaven, hell, and an afterlife. However, for most people, adolescence is a time where religious doubts are strong. Consequently, many youth are uncertain about their beliefs in a supreme being, much less in heaven and hell (Hogan, 1970).

Adults

Children and young adults usually spend little time contemplating their mortality. To the young and energetic, death seems far away. Rather than fear old age and dying, young people are usually in a hurry to grow up so they can start living on their own and enjoying the benefits and privileges of adulthood.

Around the age of 30 for women and age 40 for men, most people begin to consider aging and death. Perhaps stimulated by observing their parents age, and experiencing subtle changes in their own bodies indicative of aging, people begin counting the number of years left to live, rather than the number of years lived. One indicator of this is the reluctance to give one's true age as one enters their fourth decade of life. One popular comedienne gives her age by adding a number to 20. Thus, when she was 35 she said her age was "20—15."

As a person grows older and physical deterioration becomes undeniable, the psychological distance from death diminishes. With each passing year, people view themselves as getting closer and closer to the end of life. The personal past—the time of one's major successes and failures—is seen as being relatively long and the personal future as relatively short. People begin to reminisce more and more about the "good ol' days." The aging process also prompts people to think more and more about death and perhaps to feel more anxious about dying. However, the fear of death and dying is not directly related to age.

Personal Attitudes Toward Death

In this section, we will explore the fear of death. To get started, look at table 14.2, which summarizes the responses to a survey in which Shneidman (1973) asked a national sample of people "What does death mean to you?"

Fear of Death

What does death mean to you? If you have some apprehension about death, you are not alone. Most of us have some apprehension about it. Indeed, as you can see from table 14.3, because so many people fear death, a death anxiety scale has been developed. Why are so many people afraid of death? Is it the process of dying and the associated pain and suffering that cause fear? Is it fear of abandonment, aloneness, and separation from loved ones or from life in general? Is it a fear of dying before accomplishing one's goals or a fear of not knowing what will happen after death? Is it what the existentialists refer to as the state of nonbeing or nothingness—the loss of identity—that is feared?

Box 14.8

SELF-CHECK

Indicate whether each of the following statements is true or false.

1. Despite Aries' belief that death is becoming more visible in everyday life, our society still tries to remove death from normal experience.
2. According to both Nagy and Kane, a child's understanding of death progresses through three stages—stages that roughly correspond to Piaget's preoperational, concrete, and formal operations stages.
3. In Nagy's first stage, children seem to think of a dead person as someone who is asleep.
4. In Nagy's second stage, children thought that death could be avoided, especially if you weren't old.
5. Nagy thought that 4- to 9-year-olds saw death as an individual.
6. Children in Nagy's third stage still have very unrealistic views of death.
7. Nagy's findings seem to hold pretty well for children in the United States.
8. In some cultures, fairly young children understand that death is a permanent, irreversible event that happens to everyone.
9. According to Kane, a 5-year-old child might think that he had killed his grandmother by wishing her to be dead.
10. According to Kane's model, an 8-year-old would understand that hitting another person repeatedly with a brick could lead to the other being permanently dead.
11. Bluebond-Langer agrees with both Nagy and Kane that the child's general level of cognitive development limits the child's ability to understand death. For example, no 3-year-old can understand death the way an adult can.
12. Adolescents' views of death are more sophisticated in every way than those of 7-year-olds.
13. After age 12, people's understandings of death usually do not change significantly.

Please turn to the end of this chapter to check your answers.

There is no single standard answer to these questions. Not only are different people afraid of death for different reasons, but the intensity and direction of the fear vary with the person and external circumstances. That is, fears and attitudes toward death and dying change with culture, chronological age, sex, education level, familial and other social supports, personal mishaps, the sense of purpose or meaning in a person's life, and other conditions. Thus, like all emotional responses, attitudes and fears concerning death are shaped by the sociocultural context in which a person develops and particularly the family situation (Huyck & Hoyer, 1982).

Not all people admit to being afraid of death. For many of the same reasons some people fear death, others want to die. Pain, loneliness, shame, guilt, depression, and the feeling that there is nothing worthwhile to live for may culminate in a wish to die. In fact, among the elderly, only a minority report fearing death (Kalish & Reynolds, 1981; Kinsey, Roberts, & Logan, 1972).

Table 14.3

Death Anxiety Scale

1. I am very much afraid to die. (T)
2. The thought of death seldom enters my mind. (F)
3. It doesn't make me nervous when people talk about death. (F)
4. I dread to think about having to have an operation. (T)
5. I am not at all afraid to die. (F)
6. I am not particularly afraid of getting cancer. (F)
7. The thought of death never bothers me. (F)
8. I am often distressed by the way time flies so very rapidly. (T)
9. I fear dying a painful death. (T)
10. The subject of life after death troubles me greatly. (T)
11. I am really scared of having a heart attack. (T)
12. I often think about how short life really is. (T)
13. I shudder when I hear people talking about a World War III. (T)
14. The sight of a dead body is horrifying to me. (T)
15. I feel that the future holds nothing for me to fear. (F)

From D. Templer, "The Construction and Validation of a Death Anxiety Scale" in *Journal of General Psychology*, 82:176, 1972. Reprinted with permission of the Helen Dwight Reid Educational Foundation. Published by Heldref Publications, 1319 Eighteenth St., N.W., Washington, D.C. 20036-1802. Copyright © 1972

The keyed answers (in parentheses) indicate high death anxiety.

THE PROCESS OF DYING

To this point, we have explored people's feelings about death. You have seen that although many people fear death, some people welcome it. However, we have not explored how people feel during the process of dying.

People are becoming increasingly interested in what happens during the dying process because advances in medical technology have made it so that more and more people go through a prolonged dying process. For example, as you can see from table 14.4, we are less likely than our grandparents to die of short-term illnesses such as the flu and more likely to die from long-term illnesses such as cancer.

Table 14.4

Ten Leading Causes of Death in the United States in 1900, 1940, and 1985

Rank	1900	1940	1985
1	Influenza and pneumonia	Heart diseases	Heart diseases
2	Tuberculosis	Cancer	Cancer
3	Gastroenteritis	Stroke	Stroke
4	Heart diseases	Accidents	Accidents
5	Stroke	Kidney diseases	Pulmonary diseases
6	Kidney diseases	Influenza and pneumonia	Influenza and pneumonia
7	Accidents	Tuberculosis	Diabetes
8	Cancer	Diabetes	Suicide
9	Early infancy diseases	Artherosclerosis	Liver diseases
10	Diphtheria	Syphilis	Artherosclerosis

Sources: *Major Causes of Death in the United States, 1900–1975,* Population Reference Bureau, n.d.; *Monthly Vital Statistics Report* 31 (13), 1983, National Center for Health Statistics; *Monthly Vital Statistics Report* 35 (117), 1987, National Center for Health Statistics.

As a response to the increased interest in the dying process, more colleges are offering courses in **thanatology,** the study of death and dying. One issue of concern to thanatologists is whether there are certain common experiences that are shared by everyone who is dying.

Elisabeth Kübler-Ross's Stage Theory of Dying

According to the world's most famous thanatologist, Elisabeth Kübler-Ross (1969, 1971, 1975), there are certain universal reactions to the dying process. Specifically, Kübler-Ross proposed five stages of dying. Kübler-Ross notes that people differ in how quickly they pass through each stage and that some never reach the final stage. Keep in mind, that like all developmental stage theorists, Kübler-Ross states that once a stage is attained, a person cannot regress to previous stages, nor can one be at two stages at the same time.

Denial

Her first stage, **denial,** is what happens when people first receive the news that they are going to die. As you learned in the chapter on personality, denial is an important defense mechanism that protects us from being overwhelmed by frightening and depressing events. Clearly, accepting that we are going to die may be a frightening event. By refusing to accept the fact of imminent death, we protect ourselves from this fear.

Denial is not always maladaptive. In fact, upon receiving a fatal prognosis, people may be well advised to have some denial. Enough diagnostic errors are made to warrant a second opinion. Denial becomes maladaptive only when a patient invests valuable time and resources looking for a miracle cure when death is imminent.

Denial is expressed in many ways. A patient in the final stages of cancer might send out resumes for a job he will never be able to hold, some refuse to write a will (see box 14.9), others may apply masses of makeup in an unsuccessful attempt to camouflage their disease-ravaged faces. Some even deny being told that they are gravely ill (Aitken-Swan & Easson, 1959; Bennett, 1976).

Denial is not limited to a dying patient. Family, friends, and medical personnel also tend to deny the unavoidable. All too often such denial is a disservice to the dying. People deserve the opportunity to prepare for death. To withhold such news may rob them of this last dignity.

Anger

Eventually, a patient's health and feelings of well-being deteriorate to such a point that death is not easily denied. As the patient begins to partially accept death, denial is replaced by **anger** and bitterness about how "unfair it is" "Why me?" "What did I ever do to deserve this?" or "Why not someone else?" Angry feelings are often nondiscriminating and are vented on family, medical staff, and the environment. Even God is a ready target for wrath: "Father, why have you forsaken me?" Frustration, feelings of betrayal, and anger would seem a predictable response from a person fond of life.

Bargaining

Next comes hope, as the person enters the **bargaining** stage in which he tries to negotiate for his life. Kübler-Ross compares this stage to the child whose request for an overnight visit with a friend has been turned down. After stamping her foot in anger and shouting "No!" the child eventually tries to strike a bargain, "If I am very good all week and wash the dishes every evening, then will you let me go?" (Kübler-Ross, 1969, p. 72). A terminally ill patient attempts to bargain for an extension of life, a postponement of death. Much of the bargaining is likely to occur covertly between the patient and God, but the process sometimes can be seen in interactions with others.

Depression

Once it becomes evident that life can't be bargained for, a terminal patient gives up. **Depression** sets in "when the terminally ill patient can no longer deny his illness, when he is forced to undergo more surgery or hospitalization, when he begins to have more symptoms or becomes weaker and thinner, he cannot smile it off anymore. His numbness or stoicism, his anger and rage will soon be replaced with a sense of guilt and loss" (Kübler-Ross, 1969, p. 75).

Box 14.9

ISSUE in FOCUS

Death Denial in the Personal Advice Columns

Dear Abby: I have been married to a wonderful man for more than 50 years. My problem is that he will not face the fact that he is not going to live forever. He has made no provisions for a cemetery lot. He won't even discuss it. I know nothing about his business, or his wishes in the event of his sudden demise. We are both in fairly good health, but now that we are approaching our later 70s we need to discuss these matters, but he refuses. To make matters even ridiculous, he is a lawyer. Abby, what is wrong with my husband? What can I do about it? —BEWILDERED IN BIRMINGHAM

DEAR BEWILDERED: Nothing is wrong with your husband; like most of us, he doesn't want to face his own mortality. And this is what you should do about it: When you both have plenty of time, put your hand in his and say: "Darling, we have been blessed with many years together, but nothing is forever, and one day, one of us must leave the other. Should you go first, do you realize how helpless, confused and utterly bewildered I will be? I know nothing about your wishes. Do you want to be buried in a family plot—perhaps near your parents? And do you want me to be buried beside you when my time comes? Perhaps you prefer cremation. Many do these days."

"We need to talk to our clergy person (if you have one) and mortician who will explain all the options. Have you made a will? Probably not, because you've never asked me to make one, and that is something we both should do."

"If you love me, you will not leave me with a mess of unfinished business. As a lawyer, you surely are aware of how important it is to have all these things settled now while we are both of sound mind and body."

"I may go first. And if I do, I should have a will. So let's discuss what shall be done with our property, our personal possessions or whatever we have to leave behind. Even if we have little, there may be debts and obligations that will have to be honored."

"So, darling, before my time or yours is up, let's make our plans. I love you and hope these plans will not be needed for a long time, but just as sure as we were put on this earth, we are going to depart from it."

Acceptance

According to Kübler-Ross, the final stage of death, **acceptance,** is the healthiest stage. It is characterized by an attitude of "quiet acceptance." The struggle is over. Although tired and physically weak, the patient nevertheless has risen above the anguish and depression. The dying person sees positive aspects of dying such as being released from agony and anxiety. Although reminiscing and coming to terms with one's life are common features of this stage, people in this final stage usually limit their concerns to a select group of friends, family, and health care providers. "Acceptance should not be mistaken for a happy stage. It is almost void of feelings. It is as if the pain had gone, the struggle is over, and there comes a time for 'the final rest before the long journey' as one patient phrased it" (Kübler-Ross, 1969, p. 100).

Critique of Kübler-Ross's Stage Theory

Kübler-Ross was one of the first to propose a theory of dying. Her dedication to the anguish of the dying and her willingness to address a subject many are too repelled to address is admirable. Perhaps her greatest contribution was to awaken and legitimize interest in death among both professionals and lay people (Feifel, 1959). Her book, *On Death and Dying*, presented a comprehensive, systematic, and intuitively appealing model of death that was easily understood by professional and layperson alike. Kübler-Ross's work is credited with stimulating a nationwide death education movement (Kastenbaum, 1975; Wilcox & Sutton, 1985), and it provided a basis for health professionals to communicate about the death process.

Kübler-Ross's contribution to the field of death and dying is undeniable. However, this is not to say that her theory should be embraced as the truth. Several legitimate criticisms have been leveled at her stage theory, indicating that much work remains in the field of thanatology before we have an accurate understanding of dying and death. (See table 14.5.)

The thrust behind most criticisms of her theory is that it has not been empirically supported. Although based on several hundred dying patients, no effort was made to quantify and analyze the information. Kastenbaum (1975) notes:

> virtually every operation that might be performed on clinical information for conversion into research data has been neglected. The sample has not been described. Terms have not been defined. Transcripts have not been subjected to analysis and interrater reliability procedures that might demonstrate the existence of the five stages have not been performed. The interaction between the method of data

Table 14.5

Criticisms of Kübler-Ross's Theory of Dying

- It has not been empirically tested.
- No effort has been made to quantify and analyze the information gathered in her interviews of dying patients.
- The sample has not been described.
- Terms have not been defined.
- Transcripts have not been subjected to analysis and interrater reliability procedures that might demonstrate the existence of the five stages were not followed.
- The interaction between the method of data gathering and the results has not been discussed.
- No statistical information has been provided to support the five-stage model.
- The theory does not address sources of individual differences in the dying process.

> gathering and the results has not been discussed. The most basic types of statistical information have not been provided. (How many patients, for example, were seen for what periods of time? How many, in fact, did die while the interview series was in process? How many were interviewed only on a single occasion?) (p. 41)

Furthermore, the theory does not address sources of individual difference in the dying process. Kastenbaum lists several possible sources of variation in the death process, including the nature of the illness, sex differences, ethnicity, personality, and developmental level.

Even though Kübler-Ross has not presented empirical evidence to support her case and has not addressed the issue of individual differences, this does not mean her theory should be discarded. Her theory provides a rich source of hypotheses for researchers to test. And, in fact, researchers have found some credence in some of her ideas. For example, although there is considerable movement back and forth between denial and acceptance, denial is more common during the early part and acceptance more common during the later part of the dying trajectory (Kalish, 1988).

The fact that Kübler-Ross's theory has been accepted by many professionals and lay people is evidence of the wide appeal and usefulness of a stage theory of dying. However, this blind acceptance of an untested theory is misguided. Empirical support and refinement of her theory are clearly needed.

Such a theory could be responsibly used in training health professionals how to help and understand dying clients. Medical personnel are busy people who are receptive to understandable and easily applicable suggestions for dealing with terminal patients—and the terminal patient's relatives and close friends. As a result of the training, health professionals may also be more accepting of the full range of emotions expressed by dying people, emotions that otherwise might be viewed as inappropriate.

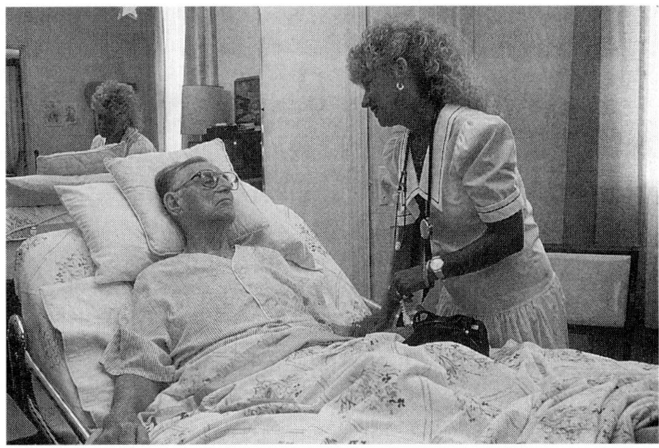

Despite a lack of research support, Kübler-Ross's stage theory of dying has been helpful for medical professionals working with dying patients.

Other Views of the Dying Process

Several other theorists have offered their views on the dying process, including Weisman and Kastenbaum (1968), Shneidman (1976), and Pattison (1977). Weisman and Kastenbaum (1968) report two broad patterns of response in dying persons. One group became less and less active as the time of death approached. A second, contrasting group of people remained active in hospital life up until the day they died.

Referring to the dying person's task as "death work," Shneidman (1976) asserts that people first deal with their impending death at a psychological level by preparing to meet the end. Dying people then ready themselves for death in a way that assists loved ones to be survivors. Shneidman (1976) recognized, however, that there is a great deal of variability in how people face death. As with any life crisis, the manner in which a person approaches death is a reflection of his or her total personality and the kind of life that person led. One person sees death as a punishment for wrongdoing; another as a reward for leading a charitable life; still another as an opportunity to be reunited with loved ones.

A variety of emotions and concerns are expressed by people who are dying—fear of the unknown, loneliness and sorrow, pain and suffering, loss of body, loss of self-control, and loss of identity. Pattison (1977) proposed a three-phase model to describe these reactions and other psychological responses during the "living-dying interval."

The first phase, the **acute phase,** corresponds to Kübler-Ross's denial, anger, and bargaining stages. During the acute phase, anxiety and fear are at a peak. The high level of anxiety experienced during the acute phase is reduced by defense mechanisms and other cognitive and affective resources.

During the second phase, the **chronic living-dying phase,** anxiety is reduced. Consequently, the dying person starts to ask questions about the unknown: "What will happen to my body, my 'self,' and my family and friends while I am dying and afterward? Considering my present

SELF-CHECK

Indicate whether each of the following statements is true or false.

1. Most of the elderly, perhaps because death is relatively imminent, report fearing death.
2. A major reason more people are living to old age is that fewer people are dying from bronchitis, pneumonia, and the flu.
3. Thanatology is the study of grieving.
4. Elisabeth Kübler-Ross believes that there are five stages of dying.
5. According to Kübler-Ross, you can experience both denial and anger at the same time.
6. Denial is always maladaptive.
7. According to Kübler-Ross, people go from depression to bargaining.
8. In the acceptance stage, the patient is happy.
9. Kübler-Ross's work has been extremely influential.
10. Kübler-Ross's work is supported by the research evidence.
11. Denial is more common during the early part of the dying process whereas acceptance is more common during the latter part.
12. The first and last phases of Pattison's model roughly correspond to four of the five stages of Kübler-Ross's theory.
13. Other, less well-known models of the dying process are superior to Kübler-Ross's model.

Please turn to the end of this chapter to check your answers.

situation, what realistic future plans can I make?" It is also during the chronic living-dying phase that the person begins to accept death gracefully.

The final phase is aptly named the **terminal phase.** During the terminal phase, the dying person still wants to live but now accepts the fact that death is imminent. Physically drained, and desiring mainly comfort and caring, the person begins a final social and emotional withdrawal from the living.

We have discussed several views that compete with Kübler-Ross' theory of the dying process. Are any of these competing views superior to Kübler-Ross's theory? No. As with Kübler-Ross's theory, these competing views lack sufficient empirical support. Furthermore, most of the ideas presented in these theories are less comprehensive than Kübler-Ross's and thus may be subsumed under Kübler-Ross's stage theory.

GRIEF

As theories of people's adjustment to the dying process are refined, we will be better able to understand what the dying person is going through and we will be better able to help the dying person. But what about the survivors? How will they feel? What can we do for them?

These are important questions because we are all survivors. All of us have experienced a loss. Even if you haven't experienced the death of a friend or family member, you have lost a friend, a pet, a job, or something that you loved. Because each of us has lost something that we loved, each of us has experienced **grief,** an emotional response to loss.

The Experience of Grief

Grief is common, natural, and universal. According to Peter Metcalf and Richard Huntington (1991), there are four basic reasons why we grieve another's death:

1. Sometimes, we grieve because we are separated from someone we love.
2. Sometimes, we grieve because we know the person will no longer enjoy the fruits of life (as is the case when someone dies young).
3. Sometimes, we grieve the suddenness of death and regret that we weren't prepared for the person to die.
4. Sometimes, grief may represent fear for our own life, or the fear of death in general.

One of the most obvious ways that we grieve is through mourning: the way we show others our sense of loss. The way we publicly express our feelings of loss is strongly affected by culture. Thus, different cultures will express loss differently. In the United States, wearing black clothes, flying the flag at half-mast, and driving in a funeral procession are all forms of mourning. In some Middle Eastern cultures, wailing and self-mutilation (pulling hair out, scratching one's face) are normal forms of mourning.

Duration of Grief

In some cultures, custom dictates the duration of mourning. For example, in Egypt, a widow wears black for one year following her husband's death (Sadat, 1987). However, in the United States, social definitions of appropriate grief behavior vary. In fact, lack of agreement over what is appropriate is a common source of conflict. To one person,

Public expressions of grief feelings through mourning are highly determined by cultural traditions. In Euro-American cultures, a funeral home "viewing" is an appropriate opportunity for mourning.

mourning means carrying on as if nothing happened; to another, it means throwing a party in memory of the deceased; to yet another, it means spending time in somber reflection. Furthermore, in the United States, there is no standard for how long grief should last. Thus, many of us have no idea of what *normal* grief is.

The emotions associated with grief are varied. Grief is usually most intense during the first four to six weeks following a death (Glick, Weiss, & Parkes, 1974; Parkes, 1972; Stephenson, 1985). However, during the first year of bereavement, survivors commonly experience intense grief on anniversaries, birthdays, and holidays.

Gradually, survivors learn to accept their loss and adjust to life without the deceased. Although some feeling of loss may remain indefinitely, healthy adjustment requires survivors to get on with their lives. If grief causes such problems as sleeplessness and loss of appetite for over six months, then the survivor probably has a problem in coping (Bugen, 1977). Medical complaints may also signal problems in coping. For example, ulcerative colitis, rheumatoid arthritis, and asthma are sometimes symptoms of prolonged grief. Survivors showing any of these psychological or medical symptoms should see a trained counselor to help them cope with the death.

Symptoms of Normal Grief

Like the symptoms and behaviors that characterized prolonged grief, the symptoms and behaviors that characterize normal grief are broad. How any given person experiences grief will depend on his or her personality, previous experience with grief, the circumstances of the loss, the culture, and the environment where mourning must occur.

The Effects of Culture

Although it is safe to assume that grief is normally associated with strong emotions, it is important to recognize that custom may dictate what emotions should be expressed and when. For example, Metcalf and Huntington (1991) report that there are few cultural universals governing reactions to grief. Whereas we might expect that weeping would be a natural and normal way to mourn a friend, Rosenblatt et al. (1976) found some cultures where crying was not a common response to grief. For example, in response to grief, it would be unusual for someone from Java to cry and it would be unheard of for a Balinese to cry.

In contrast to both American and the Balinese reactions, Radcliffe-Brown (1964) reports a very structured ritual of crying that is expected of mourners from the Andaman Island. After suffering the death of a loved one, an Andamanese "sits down and wails and howls and tears stream down his or her face" (p. 117). An Andamanese does this on exactly seven different occasions. This crying is not a spontaneous expression of feeling. Rather, it is mandatory, and the person has complete control.

Other cultural differences include how to behave at a funeral. For example, in a classic study of the Nyakyusa, an African tribe, Godfrey Wilson (1939) described the two main activities of their burial ceremony: the women wailed and the men danced. In a traditional Euro-American funeral, wailing and dancing would most likely produce condemnation.

Grief Work

Although there are tremendous cultural differences in what is accepted, there may be certain commonalties in how we learn to cope, at least in Euro-American culture. These are clearly described in Erich Lindemann's (1944) landmark study, "The symptomatology and management of acute grief," where he identified three central tasks necessary for managing grief:

- First, the survivor must let go of the deceased and accept the loss.
- Second, the survivor must adjust to a life without the deceased.
- Third, the survivor must form new relationships.

Lindemann's research, when combined with the findings of other studies (for example, Brewster, 1950; Maddison, 1968; Parkes & Brown, 1972; Stephenson, 1985), provides a detailed description of the range of physical symptoms that accompany normal grief. Physical symptoms may include tightness of the throat, shortness of breath, frequent sighing, an empty feeling in the abdomen, muscle weakness, chills, and tremors. These physical sensations are often accompanied by severe mental distress such as tension, loneliness, and anguish.

Frequently, a survivor's perceptions are disorganized. The experience is not unlike the feeling that one has after almost any traumatic experience—things seem a little "unreal," as if you are seeing them in a dream. In some cases, perceptions may even include periods of hallucination, where the survivor sees visions of the deceased (Neale, 1973). Sometimes, there are periods of euphoria when a survivor experiences heightened perceptual and emotional sensitivity to people and events in his or her environment. Some survivors may be restless and irritable, even hostile. Some may talk constantly about the deceased, whereas others will talk about everything but the deceased.

Grief is frequently accompanied by feelings of sadness, aloneness, and sorrow. Survivor's frequently experience guilt about things they "should have done" and said. In addition, survivors often feel anger toward an "unjust world," or even toward the deceased for leaving them.

Stages of Grief

No matter which symptoms we express, when loss occurs, our usual patterns of behavior are altered. Several theorists (for example, Glick, Weiss, & Parkes 1974; Gorer, 1967) have described stages of grieving that are similar to Kübler-Ross's stages of dying. Most of these theorists incorporate elements analogous to Stephenson's (1985) three stages of grieving.

In Stephenson's model, the **reaction stage** marks the initial period of shock when one first learns of the death. Shock is followed by numbness and a dazed lack of feeling. This numbness permits the survivor to accomplish such necessary tasks as notifying friends and relatives, as well as planning and participating in the funeral. This initial lack of feeling is probably very adaptive in emergencies or crises where some die and the survivors must act to stay alive (such as casualties during a war, fire, or plane crash). In short, the reaction stage allows the person time to reach safety before being overwhelmed by the reality of the situation.

Another normal response during the reaction stage is bewilderment. It can be hard to make sense of a loss, especially one that wasn't anticipated. Once the griever understands the loss, the griever has the desire—sometimes conscious, but often unconscious—to bring the deceased back to life. Crying out in sorrow over the deceased is not uncommon. The tension builds and the survivor gives in to the emotional overload of grief.

Anger and hostility are also common in the reaction stage. Anger may be directed at the deceased, another person, or at God. The survivor needs to blame someone to help reduce the guilt that there must have been "something I could have done to prevent this."

In the second stage—**disorganization and reorganization**—reality sets in, and the bereaved is disappointed that the loss cannot be recovered. Incapacitating despair may leave the person with unfocused thoughts and inability to make sense out of old activities. Reasons or satisfaction for former actions may no longer exist, and actions must be examined in light of their lack of meaning or painful association with the dead person. The bereaved may not be able to maintain organized patterns of activity and feel unsure of what to do with themselves.

The need to reevaluate actions and former patterns of living involves a process of internal reorganization. The characteristic helplessness, uncertainty, and loss of meaningful focus is often the result of feeling stripped of a part of the self. The bereaved may wish someone to come and organize their lives. They may develop dependencies on those who offer help. The process of reorganization that emerges from such a painful and desperate emotional response is especially difficult because the grief-stricken person must dismantle the sense of former structure provided by the connectedness and activities surrounding the loved one. The feelings associated with this stage are complicated and often conflicting. To grieve is to pay respect to the dead. To give up grieving is to lose that respect and possibly feel guilty. To grieve is to live a tragic role. To give up grieving is to give up a position that offers us the respect of others. The bereaved may be especially overwhelmed by fearful feelings that one is losing either a sense of identity or one's mind.

In the final stage, **reorientation and recovery,** the survivor reorganizes the symbolic world and gives the deceased a new identity outside the world of the survivor. In giving the dead a new status, often in a new place such as heaven, the griever is enabled to continue in the old world. Funeral ceremonies are among those rites of passage that announce status changes of individuals. The bereaved see the ceremony as being both for themselves as well as for the dead because it signals changes in both their statuses.

According to Stephenson, acceptance of the changes and the new perspectives on the world built during this stage are crucial to successful recovery.[1] Grief becomes resolved when a person is able to reintegrate with the world, interact openly with others, find new avenues for creative living, and take charge of life in an independent fashion.

Variables Influencing Grief

Although it is normal to grieve when we experience the loss of someone close to us, there are wide variations in how people grieve. Robert Fulton (1978) describes a **high-grief** death as an intense emotional and physical reaction to loss and a **low-grief** death as emotionally taxing, but not

[1]Stroebe, Gergen, Gergen, & Stroebe (1992) disagree, arguing that, in the 1800s—and even for many people today, breaking the bonds with the deceased would destroy one's identity and make life meaningless.

Box 14.11

SELF-CHECK

Indicate whether each of the following statements is true or false.

1. Grief is an emotional response to loss, and this loss is not limited to the death of another—losses of pets, jobs, and friendships can all trigger grief.
2. We may grieve another person's death because we fear for our own life.
3. The way in which we mourn and the duration of mourning may be dictated by one's culture.
4. Rheumatoid arthritis can be a symptom of prolonged grief.
5. In all cultures, crying is a common response to grief.
6. When people cry in response to the death of a loved one, the crying always represents a spontaneous reaction that they can't really help.
7. Someone who has suffered the death of a loved one may have disturbances of perception.
8. It is relatively common for survivors to feel anger at the deceased.
9. During Stephenson's second stage of grieving, the survivors cope by losing themselves in familiar habits, rituals, and routines.

Please turn to the end of this chapter to check your answers.

Survivors of an unexpected death, such as an auto accident, often have a more intense grief reaction. A possible explanation is that survivors who knew a loved one was dying had the opportunity to experience anticipatory grief, working through grieving before the actual death.

devastating. Thus, in a low-grief death, the reaction is less severe and the bereaved is more able to cope. Although a child's death is more likely to be experienced as a high-grief death, and the death of an elderly person as a low-grief death, it is the context of a particular death and its effect on a specific survivor that determines whether the response is high- or low-grief. A survivor's level of attachment to the deceased, as well as his or her feelings about the appropriateness of the death, determines the level of grief (Bugen, 1977). More specifically, individual differences in the intensity and duration of bereavement are influenced by many factors, including developmental level, gender, personality, culture, the relationship to the deceased, and how expected the death was.

Expectedness

Arlene Sheskin and Samuel Wallace (1976) have found that the more unexpected the death, the more intense the grief response. For example, families who have lost someone to a suicide usually have more difficulty coping than families of someone who died of natural causes. This conclusion is further supported by research comparing young widows (often survivors of an unexpected death) versus older widows (often survivors of an expected death). For instance, Ball (1977) found that younger widows, those in the 18- to 46-year age bracket, grieved more intensely than older widows, those who were over the age of 46. A possible explanation for this age difference is that older women are more likely to have expected their husband's death than the younger widows. In other words, **anticipatory grief** (grieving prior to the death of a loved one) may provide an opportunity for survivors to work through some of their grief before the actual death and, hence, recover faster (Parkes, 1975, Berardo, 1988).

The effectiveness of anticipatory grief is questionable. On the one hand, we have seen some evidence that anticipatory grief may be helpful. For example, perhaps because of anticipatory grief, older widows may be better able to cope than younger widows. Similarly, families who have lost a member to an unexpected death usually have a difficult time coping, perhaps partly because there was no opportunity for anticipatory grief. On the other hand, research indicates that prolonged periods of anticipatory grieving (as is the case when a loved one dies from a prolonged chronic illness) is often predictive of poorer recuperation by the survivors than when the dying trajectory and the anticipatory grieving period is shorter (Gerber et al., 1975).

Developmental Level

A person's reaction to a death depends not only on the expectedness of the death, but on the person's developmental level. As you might expect, children react to death differently than adults.

We are not saying that children do not experience grief. They do. Children who have experienced the loss of a close relative or friend do experience grief. Every year, over 3 million children in the United States under the age of 19 lose one or both parents (Bernstein, 1977). Not surprisingly, many of these children have adjustment problems. In general, children experience greater difficulty adjusting to the loss of a family member when intrafamilial relationships are strained (Hilgard & Newman, 1959). However, children tend to work through their problems and get on with their lives more quickly than adults (Cohen, 1980).

Sex Differences

Cultural stereotypes have a strong influence on sex differences in bereavement. In the United States, as in most countries, men are expected to be less emotional than women when they grieve. Glick, Weiss, and Parkes (1974) report that the death of a loved one means different things to men and women. Women tend to feel abandoned, but men feel dismembered.

Personality

If personality influences how we relate to most life experiences, then personality should affect how we react to death. Thus, personality differences might, in part, account for the wide range of grief reactions across people. In support of this idea, there is little consistency in the grief responses among different people, but there is great consistency within an individual (Bornstein et al., 1973).

The question researchers need to address is which personality traits affect one's reaction to grief. It seems likely that neuroticism and attachment style would be related to grief. However, the relationship of these variables to grief reactions has not been intensively studied. One of the few people to seriously discuss the role of any personality variable on grief reaction was Jackson. Jackson (1957) emphasizes the importance of self-concept in how a person responds to a death. According to Jackson, an immature, dependent personality is most vulnerable to the death of a person in whom they have invested emotionally. Jackson explains that a person with a dependent personality is attempting to compensate for feelings of personal inadequacy by projecting part of his or her identity onto the other person. When death occurs, the survivor not only loses the deceased, they lose the projected identity. In contrast, people with greater self-esteem and a stronger self concept usually cope better because they have not lost their identity.

Relationship to the Deceased

The experience of bereavement is profoundly affected by the relationship the survivor had to the deceased. The most common experience of death is the death of a parent.

The Death of a Parent For adults, the death of a parent forces them to accept their adult status. Because parents are often associated with unconditional acceptance and love, the death of a parent often leaves an adult offspring feeling alone and without the unconditional emotional support to which they are accustomed. Without that feeling of support, many people experience insecurity, feelings of isolation, aloneness, and anxiety (DeSpelder & Strickland, 1983).

The Death of a Child As you know, the death of a child is very difficult. Such a death is unexpected and means the loss of part of one's identity (parent). The bonds to the child are very strong. And for some couples, it is their only joint project. No wonder that recent research suggests that parents never fully recover from the death of their child (Lehman, Wortman, & Williams, 1987).

The Death of a Fetus Like the death of a child, the death of a fetus is unexpected. Part of the reason such deaths are unexpected is that technological advances have decreased the percentage of stillbirths. However, technological advances have not completely eliminated stillbirths. Thus, even today, 1 to 2 percent of pregnancies end in a stillbirth.

Parents are not prepared for this crisis and our society does not help these parents. Our society does not help because it does not recognize the loss that these parents feel. This refusal to recognize the loss is evident in the language we use. For example, a stillborn, or late fetal death (after the 28th week of gestation), may be defined as "the failure of the product of conception to show evidence of respiration, heartbeat, or definite movement of voluntary muscle after expulsion from the uterus, with no possibility of resuscitation" (*Dorland's Pocket Medical Dictionary*, 1991, p. 348). In practice, some physicians avoid even using the word *dead* in conjunction with a stillborn baby. Instead they will say "gestationally nonviable infant" (p. 5). However, regardless of the language that other people use, parents do experience loss, and the grief resulting from fetal death increases in proportion to the length of the pregnancy.

Although parents do form attachments to the fetus, medical personnel are often insensitive to this fact. Thus, medical personnel and others may try to comfort parents by saying "It's merciful that he died; he would have had serious brain damage had he survived." Regardless of the possible truth contained in these comments, most parents are not comforted by such remarks. Instead, parents would be comforted most by someone who would let them express

Box 14.12

SELF-CHECK

Indicate whether each of the following statements is true or false.

1. The more expected the death, the more intense the grief response.
2. There is clear evidence that long periods of anticipatory grief make survivors able to recover more quickly after the actual death of a loved one.
3. Children do not experience grief.
4. After the death of a loved one, children tend to get on with their lives more quickly than adults.
5. For adults, the death of a parent often leads to feelings of isolation and aloneness.
6. With time, most parents fully recover from the death of their child.
7. Fewer than 1 in 1,000 pregnancies end in a stillbirth.
8. The longer the pregnancy, the more the parents grieve a fetal death.
9. Parents should name their stillborn baby.
10. Parents should be encouraged to see their stillborn baby and to make funeral arrangements for it.
11. The death of a spouse is more devastating if the relationship between the spouses was intense and unhealthy.
12. Widowhood seems to be bad for one's physical health.

Please turn to the end of this chapter to check your answers.

their profound sense of loss and acknowledge that feeling of loss as legitimate—as well as letting them express their confusing and ambivalent feelings (Smith, 1985). It is important to remember that, for many parents, prenatal death is the first important death that the couple has experienced together. Parents need help in realizing that their subjective reactions to the loss of their baby are normal for people in their circumstances.

Fortunately, in recent years, some health professionals have developed a more humane attitude toward the survivors of fetal death and stillbirth. For those concerned individuals, Smith (1985) makes the following recommendations:

- *Establish the personal identity of the infant.* Many parents have formed an emotional bond with their fetus. It was a living entity and they had a personal relationship. This needs to be acknowledged.
- *Have parents name the baby.* This can be one of the most important steps in establishing the identity of the dead baby. Although there is no legal requirement that a stillborn be named, the parents should be encouraged to name their baby and staff should use this name in talking about the child. Some parents may wish to christen the baby.
- *Let parents see the baby.* Of all the issues concerning the care of the parents of stillborn children, none has stirred more controversy than that of whether parents should be encouraged or permitted to view and hold the body (Smith, 1985). Kennell, Slyter, and Klaus (1970), in a classic discussion of the mourning response to stillbirths, see viewing as part of the full expression of grief. The overwhelming consensus among those who have worked with parents of stillborns is that viewing is one of the most important variables affecting the course of bereavement.
- *Photograph the baby.* Sometimes viewing the body may be inadvisable. In that case, Smith recommends photographing the deceased. Months down the road, these photographs may be the only evidence the parents have that the child existed. Thus, the photographs may be important in their grief resolution.
- *Let parents arrange for the burial of the baby.* Current research suggests that parents should be involved in funeral arrangements to help them work through the grief process. This recommendation is opposed to the once common practice of hospitals arranging for the disposal of stillborns through cremation or burial in unmarked graves. For example, Jolly (1976) recalls the case of a mother who had delivered a stillborn child. On the day after the delivery, when she had recovered enough to plan in her own mind the funeral arrangements she desired, she discovered that the hospital had already cremated her baby.

The Death of a Spouse The stronger the emotional bond between a married couple, the more difficult the recovery (Berardo, 1988; Lopata, 1973). Ironically, this is especially true for relationships characterized by extreme dependency or persisting conflict. Thus, when the relationship is built on mutual trust and fulfillment, the bereaved person can more easily get on with the process of readjustment and self-renewal.

The elderly are especially vulnerable to feelings of loneliness and isolation when their spouse dies. Even when social contact outside the home is the same for elderly widowed and married peers, widows are more likely to feel depressed and alienated (Jolley, 1979).

Widowhood often has a negative impact on health. The impact of bereavement on health includes higher mortality rates from cardiovascular disease or suicide, especially for older males, and increased incidences of accidents and infectious diseases. Widowhood changes both an individual's perceived and real health status. Deaths following the demise of an especially dear other, usually a spouse, have been attributed to the **broken heart syndrome.**

Death of a loved one not only alters an already poor health condition, but may, in fact, decrease the body's defenses against diseases, thereby making grief-stricken survivors particularly at risk. However, supporting social factors—such as living with others or remarriage—diminish the widow's vulnerability to disease.

Conclusions

Despite the fact that everyone will die, people don't think about death, and limited research has been done on death. Instead, we rely on technology to cheat death.

Technology allows us to sustain people who would otherwise have died; allows us to detect deaths (miscarriages in early weeks of pregnancy) that we would never have known about; and allows us to predict deaths well in advance (AIDS detection). However, our sophisticated technology also causes problems, especially since our thinking about death has not kept up with our death-delaying technology. For example, people are not sure whether a brain dead person is indeed dead.

Moreover, technology can't rid us of death. Technology has not increased our maximum lifespan. It has only allowed more people to live to old age. We will all die. The sooner we accept this, the sooner we can institute research and treatment that will help the living better survive the loss of their loved ones.

Summary

1. Death is the unavoidable final step in our developmental experience.
2. The question of "what is dead?" has led to the categorization of specific types of death.
3. Biological, psychological, social, and legal death are each variations of the concept of death.
4. Among Aiken's list of indicators of biological death are termination of pulse and respiration and failure to respond to sensory stimulation.
5. Livor mortis, rigor mortis, and algor mortis occur as death progresses.
6. The shrinking of the family has caused a decline in personal experiences with death. Attitudes and fears towards death are shaped through experience, cultural background, and developmental level.
7. Society's views on death have changed throughout history. Death has moved from a common and highly visible event to a less common and more hidden event.
8. Life expectancy has increased significantly over the last few decades. In the early 1900s, over half of the reported deaths were of children age 15 and younger. Today, only 5 percent of reported deaths are in this age group.
9. Research shows that our attitudes toward death change as we grow older. Whereas younger adults rarely think about death, middle-aged and elderly adults often think about death.
10. Maria Nagy believes that children's attitudes toward death progress through three stages. First, children view death as temporary. Second, they view death as irreversible, but avoidable. Finally, they hold realistic and adult-like views.
11. Nagy's theory has been criticized. Some believe the theory is flawed because it fails to consider the role of culture and experience on how a child understands death. Some believe that the evidence that served as the foundation for the theory is faulty because it was based on a small sample and because we have to trust Nagy's interpretation of what the children's drawings and comments revealed about their understanding of death.
12. Like Nagy, Kane believes that children's understanding of death progresses through three stages. Like Nagy, Kane's theory is based on Piaget's stages of development. The big difference is that in Kane's second stage, children are thought to have a better understanding of the causes of death and do not see death as avoidable.
13. Adolescents are more likely than children to question death because they are uncertain about their beliefs and the finality of death.
14. In this century, medical technology has changed the causes of death. Currently, the most common causes of death are heart disease, cancer, and stroke.
15. Elisabeth Kübler-Ross developed a five-stage model of dying. Her stages are denial, anger, bargaining, depression, and acceptance.

16. Although Kübler-Ross's stage theory has stimulated interest in the dying process, it is not empirically supported.
17. Grief is a person's emotional response to loss.
18. Bereavement is the actual event of loss.
19. Mourning is the process of incorporating the experience of loss into our everyday lives.
20. Cultures differ in how they define "normal grieving."
21. Stephenson defines three stages of grieving: the reaction stage, the disorganization and reorganization stage, and the reorientation and recovery stage.
22. How a person grieves is affected by many variables. In addition to the expectedness of the death, the extent of grieving is affected by the person's gender, personality, developmental level, and their relationship to the deceased.

KEY TERMS

acceptance 447
acute phase 448
algor mortis 436
anger 446
anticipatory grief 452
bargaining 446
biological death 434
brain death 434
broken heart syndrome 455
chronic living-dying phase 448
denial 446
depression 446
disorganization and reorganization 451
grief 449
high-grief 451
legal death 436
livor mortis 436
low-grief 451
psychological death 435
reaction stage 451
reorientation and recovery 451
rigor mortis 436
social death 435
terminal phase 449
thanatology 446

SELF-CHECK ANSWERS

Box 14.4

Part A:
1. False. Because of modern medical technology, life-support machines can keep the rest of the body alive. **2.** False. **3.** True. **4.** False.

Part B:
5. They would be socially alive, biologically alive, but psychologically dead. Note that if the parents viewed them as being dead, they would be biologically alive, but psychologically and socially dead. **6.** Algor mortis is when the dead person's body temperature reaches the temperature of the environment. Detectives may wish to establish the time of death by how much the body has cooled off. If the body has already reached the temperature of the environment, it would be hard to pinpoint (from temperature alone) the time of death. That is, you would know that the person had been dead for some time, but whether that some time was 12 hours or 6 days, you wouldn't know. If, on the other hand, the body is discovered before it reaches algor mortis, time of death can be established within an hour or two. **7.** Rigor mortis. **8.** The people were not really dead. Faulty ways of detecting biological death were responsible. Reportedly, some of these false indicators led to "proof" of the existence of vampires. In fourteenth-century Asia and Europe, people were sometimes buried alive during the black plague. Some would revive and try to get out of their coffin. Later, if the coffin were opened, there was blood where the victims had cut themselves trying to get out.

Box 14.5

1. False; **2.** True; **3.** True; **4.** False; **5.** False; **6.** True; **7.** True; **8.** True; **9.** True; **10.** False.

Box 14.8

1. True; **2.** True; **3.** True; **4.** True; **5.** True; **6.** False; **7.** False; **8.** False; **9.** True; **10.** True; **11.** False; **12.** False; **13.** False.

Box 14.10

1. False; **2.** True; **3.** False; **4.** True; **5.** False; **6.** False; **7.** False; **8.** False; **9.** True; **10.** False; **11.** True; **12.** True; **13.** False.

Box 14.11

1. True; **2.** True; **3.** True; **4.** True; **5.** False; **6.** False; **7.** True; **8.** True; **9.** False.

Box 14.12

1. False; **2.** False; **3.** False; **4.** True; **5.** True; **6.** False; **7.** False; **8.** True; **9.** True; **10.** True; **11.** True; **12.** True.

GLOSSARY

A

absolute threshold The lowest level of stimulation that can be consciously detected. 156

acceptance The fifth and final stage in Kübler-Ross's theory of dying during which the dying person experiences a sense of peace and an acceptance of his or her fate. 447

accommodate The adjustments the lens of the eye makes in order to focus on objects at different distances. 135

accommodation According to Jean Piaget, the process by which new concepts and experiences modify existing structures and behaviors. 55, 195

acromegaly A condition in which the body starts producing too much growth hormone during adulthood. The person suffering from acromegaly will experience thickening of the tissues of the skin, nose, eyelids, lips, and tongue and will usually die young. 124

acute phase According to Pattison, the first phase during the living-dying interval. The person experiences intense anxiety and fear. This anxiety may be reduced by defense mechanisms and other cognitive and affective resources. 448

adrenogenital syndrome (AGS) A genetic disorder in which women have excessive amounts of androgens, sometimes to the point that their external genitalia become masculinized. 378

adulthood The seventh stage in Erikson's theory, between ages 45 and 65, during which a person resolves issues pertaining to generativity versus stagnation. 45

afterbirth The placenta and fetal membranes that are expelled after delivery. 116

age grading Basing scores on what is typical for a certain age.

age of viability The point when the organs and physiological systems of most fetuses are mature enough for the fetus to survive outside the womb. 115

agency Block's term to describe the observation that young children behave in ways that are individualistic, self-assertive, and expansive. 392

age-specific designs Research designs that are used to study age-related changes. 26

aggression The intent to harm another person or oneself. 374

aging The progressive cellular and bodily deterioration that culminates in death. 137

algor mortis Following cessation of bodily functions, the body temperature gradually declines until it reaches the temperature of the environment. 436

allele Each member of a pair of genes that occupies the same genetic location. 74

Alzheimer's disease A chronic and progressive disorder of the brain that is a major cause of degenerative dementia. 140, 176

amniocentesis A prenatal diagnostic procedure in which a needle is inserted into the amniotic sac, which surrounds the fetus, and fluid is removed. This fluid contains cells that have been sloughed off by the fetus and when examined may reveal abnormalities. 80

amniotic sac A watertight bag that surrounds and protects the embryo and contains amniotic fluid. 114

anal expulsive A form of anal fixation characterized by sloppiness, rudeness, and a tendency to throw tantrums. 41, 405

anal fixation In Freud's theory, being stuck at the anal stage due to improper toilet training. Anal fixation takes two forms, anal retentiveness and anal expulsiveness. 41, 405

anal retentive A form of anal fixation characterized by stinginess and a preoccupation with cleanliness and orderliness. 41, 405

anal stage Freud's second stage of personality development, from about age 1 to about 3 years of age, during which children learn to control the immediate gratification they obtain through defecation and to become responsive to the demands of society. 41, 404

androgens Hormones that promote the development of male or male-like sexual structures and characteristics. 128, 377

androgyny A gender-role orientation in which the individual incorporates both male and female aspects into his or her character. 392

anger In Kübler-Ross's theory, the second stage of dying during which the dying person realizes that denial cannot be maintained. Denial gives way to rage, resentment, and anger. 446

animistic thought The belief that inanimate objects have thoughts, feelings, and life. 199

anorexia nervosa A severe eating disorder in which the person diets to the point of starvation. 131

anticipatory grief Grieving prior to the death of a loved one. 452

anxiety A sense of apprehension and fear. 374

anxious/avoidant attachment According to Ainsworth, a form of insecure attachment in which children are distressed (anxious) when separated from their mothers, but ambivalent when reunited. These children show their ambivalence by combining affectionate attachment behaviors with expressions of anger. 304

anxious/resistant attachment According to Ainsworth, a form of insecure attachment in which children are uninterested in exploring, show little distress when separated, and avoid or ignore their mothers when reunited. 304

Apgar scale A scale that assesses the condition of an infant after birth and 5 minutes later. 117

aphasia A language disorder involving damage to the language centers of the brain. 236

approach behaviors Infant attachment behaviors that are designed to bring the infant to the mother. 286

arteriosclerosis Hardening of the arteries. 140

assimilation In Piaget's theory, the process by which new concepts and experiences are incorporated into existing mental frameworks (schemes). 54, 195

association The assumption that events occurring in sequence are related to each other. 48

attachment behaviors Early infant behaviors that promote physical proximity. 286

attachment-in-the-making According to Ainsworth and Bowlby, the second phase of attachment during which infants begin to show preferences for specific people and can distinguish their primary caregivers from others. 291

attention To focus one's thoughts on a specific idea or object. 155

attrition Research participants dropping out due to death, loss of interest, or loss of contact. 28

authoritarian parenting According to Baumrind, a style of parenting having a restrictive and punitive orientation with little communication between parent and child. 359

authoritative parenting According to Baumrind, a democratic style of parenting that encourages children to be independent while placing realistic limits, demands, and controls on their behavior. 359

autism A disorder originating in childhood in which the individual is noncommunicative and withdrawn. 27

autoimmune theory of aging A theory of aging based on the finding that because of age-related genetic changes in cells, the immune system begins to perceive the body's own cells as "foreign" and tries to destroy these cells. This makes older adults more vulnerable to disease and stress. 137

automatization How a process that is, at first, consciously controlled (such as driving a stick-shift car) becomes automatic. 210

autonomous stage According to Loevinger, a stage of ego development characteristic of a minority of adults, where people are fully aware of the range of choices available and can tolerate—rather than condemn—people whose choices differ from their own. 261, 271

autonomy versus shame and doubt The psychosocial crisis corresponding with Erikson's muscular-anal stage during which the young child experiences a struggle between the drive for self-control, or a feeling of shame and doubt about oneself and one's ability. 44

B

babbling Strings of consonants and vowel phonemes put together and produced by babies beginning around age 3 months to 6 months. Babbling exercises the vocal tract and helps develop the skills necessary to produce words. 225

Babinski reflex A reflex in which an infant projects its toes outward and up when the soles of its feet are touched. 115

bargaining The third stage in Kübler-Ross's theory of dying during which the dying person develops the hope that death can be postponed or delayed. The person may try to bargain with God or try "miracle cures." 446

basic anxiety According to Horney, the feeling a child has of being isolated and helpless in a potentially hostile world. 411

Bayley Scales of Infant Development A series of tests designed to evaluate a child's motor, mental, and behavioral development. 188

behavioral genetics A discipline concerned with the influence of heredity on behavior and development. 12

behaviorism The school of psychological thought that focuses on describing and measuring only what is directly observable. 47

behaviorists Psychologists who endorse behaviorism; the school of psychological thought that focuses on describing and measuring only what is directly observable. 47

beneffectance The tendency to see oneself in a favorable light. 262

biological death When vital functions such as respiration and heartbeat stop. 434

biological determinism The belief that genes completely determine our personality and actions. 400

biological model The school of psychological thought that examines psychological issues based on how heredity and biological structures affect mental processes and behavior and development. 243

biological motion The patterns of human locomotion. 136

blastocyst A 100- to 150-cell, ball-like structure formed during the period of the zygote that consists of two layers, the embryoblast and the trophoblast. 112

bodily-kinesthetic intelligence The ability to skillfully coordinate the body's movements to achieve a given objective. 211

bonding A hypothesis that mothers instinctively attach to their children shortly after birth. 286

brain death The absence of neuronal activity in the brain. 434

brain lateralization Assigning control of specific functions to only one side of the brain. 378

Broca's aphasia A form of aphasia characterized by a break in neural transmission between the frontal lobes and the vocal musculature. Broca aphasics know what they want to say but, when they try to speak, their words come out in the wrong order. 236

broken heart syndrome When a person dies shortly after a loved one, presumably because they miss the deceased. 455

C

canalization The degree to which genes limit actual behavior or expressed potential. 93

case study An in-depth study of a single person. 21

castration anxiety Occurring during the phallic stage, a young boy's fear that his father will castrate him. 41

cataracts A condition of the eye, often associated with aging, in which the lenses become clouded so that light entering the eye is blocked before it can reach the retina. 142

cephalocaudal Gesell's maturational principle that development occurs from head to tail (toe). 114

cervix The pathway between a woman's vagina and her uterus. 130

Cesarean section Birth through the walls of the abdomen and uterus. 117

chorion A membrane that provides nourishment to the fetus. 82

chorionic villi biopsy A prenatal diagnostic procedure in which a catheter is inserted through the mother's cervix into the chorion and sloughed off fetal cells are extracted. These cells can be tested for abnormalities. 82

chromosomes Strands of DNA in the nuclei of cells that occur in pairs and carry genetic information. 70

chronic living-dying phase According to Pattison, the second phase during the living-dying interval. Anxiety is less than during the acute phase. The person starts to ask questions about the unknown and begins to accept death gracefully. 448

chronological age Age since birth. 183

chunk Manageable and meaningful unit of information that permits groupings of information to be easily encoded, stored, and retrieved. 157

chunking The process of putting together pieces of information to form or increase the size of a memory chunk. 158

circular reactions The process of fitting two previously unrelated schemes into a common schema. 198

classic aging pattern A common pattern found on intelligence test performance; age-related declines are typically small on the verbal scale and more pronounced on the performance scale. 190

classical conditioning A conditioning process in which an originally neutral stimulus, by repeated pairings with a stimulus that normally elicits a response, comes to elicit a similar or even identical response. 48, 150

class inclusion problems A problem that requires the understanding that a specific set of objects is also a subset of a more general category. 202

clear-cut attachment phase According to Ainsworth and Bowlby, the third phase of attachment during which the child forms an attachment bond to a specific caregiver and will protest separation from that caregiver. 291

clitoris A female's primary sexual organ. 130

cochlea The primary neural receptor of hearing. 142

cognitive developmental theory A theoretical approach that focuses on how cognitive development unfolds in a stage-like sequence that is uniform for all people. 181

cognitive dissonance A state in which individuals feel uncomfortable because they hold two or more thoughts, attitudes, or behaviors that are inconsistent with one another. 288

cognitive structuralism A theoretical orientation that views people as active agents in constructing their knowledge of the world. Cognitive structuralists focus on rules and patterns governing the physical world and believe development consists of a set of discrete stages. 54

cohort A group of people who are born at about the same time and who share common historical experiences. 6

cohort effect Confounding true age changes with differences between generations due to being exposed to different historical events. 26

cohort or historical events Events that affect a specific group of people who share a common time in history. 6

collective monologue According to Piaget, a dialogue among children where one child's words may cue another's reply, but there is no reciprocal exchange. 269

commitment Sticking with a relationship or situation. 328

communion Block's term to describe a child's need to conform to the group and to seek group approval. 392

companionate love Love based on trust and understanding. 327

comparison level The standard amount of rewards a person expects to get out of a relationship. 319

comparison level for alternatives The amount of rewards a person thinks he or she will get from other (alternative) relationships. 319

compensation A defense mechanism in which a person tries to make up for deficiencies by excelling in other areas. 402

componential intelligence In Sternberg's triarchic theory of intelligence, analytic intelligence. 209

concrete operations stage Piaget's third stage of cognitive development (lasting from approximately age 6 to 12), during which the child develops the ability to understand constant factors in the environment, rules, and higher-order symbolism. 56, 200

conditioned response The response elicited by a conditioned stimulus. 48

conditioned stimulus A neutral stimulus that, through repeated association with an unconditioned stimulus, becomes capable of eliciting a conditioned response. 48

conditions of worth According to Carl Rogers, what a person must do to gain approval from others. 60, 419

conformist stage According to Loevinger, a stage of ego development characteristic of most junior high students and some adults in which people are concerned with obeying rules, maintaining appearances, and conforming to their group's (clique's) standards. 259

confound In regard to experimental designs, a factor that is unintentionally manipulated and that might account for effects attributed to the independent variable. 30

congenital defect Birth defect. 76

congruent According to Rogers, when a person's self-concept is in harmony with his or her experiences and feelings. 420

connotation The emotional meaning of a word. 222

conscientious stage According to Loevinger, a stage of ego development characteristic of many adolescents and most adults, during which people follow certain rules because they believe and accept those rules. 259

conservation The ability to recognize that something that changed in some way (such as "shape") still has the same weight, substance, or volume. 200

contact comfort A need to cling to something warm and soft. 289

contextual intelligence In Sternberg's triarchic theory of intelligence, practical intelligence. 210

continuity versus discontinuity The argument over whether development occurs in a gradual, step by step fashion or in abrupt spurts followed by plateaus. 9

contracting stage The stage in family development that begins when the eldest child first starts taking concrete steps to achieve economic and physical independence from the family and ends when the last child actually leaves the house. 350

convenience sampling A research technique in which people are haphazardly surveyed because the researcher has easy access to them, such as those who call in with their opinions or who shop at a particular mall. 22

conventional level According to Kohlberg, the second level of moral reasoning, during which people adhere to society's rules and conventions. Contains stages 3 and 4. 272

cooing An array of vowel-like sounds, produced by repeating over and over again such vowels sounds as "aaaah" and "ooo." 225

cooperative play A form of play in which each child plays a role and has to limit and adjust that role for the good of the group. 315

cornea A transparent membrane that covers and protects the eyeball. 134

corpus callosum A bridge of neurons that allows the two cerebral hemispheres to communicate freely. 123

correlational designs Designs that provide data that can be used to compute correlation coefficients. 26

correlation coefficient A number that expresses the degree and direction of a relationship between two variables, ranging from –1 (a perfect negative correlation) to +1 (a perfect positive correlation). 25

creative self According to Adler, a fully conscious part of a person that strives to realize the person's potentials and overcome obstacles. 410

cross-sectional design An age-specific design that compares people of one age group with people of at least one other age group. 26

crying A state in which an individual has crying vocalizations associated with vigorous diffuse motor activity. 224

crystallized intelligence Intelligence that includes verbal skills and mechanical knowledge and reflects the ability to handle well-learned information in familiar situations. 192

D

declarative knowledge Facts that a person can state (declare). 149

defense mechanism Unconscious ways of distorting, denying, or falsifying reality. 402

dementia Impairment of mental function and global cognitive abilities of long-standing duration in otherwise alert individuals, resulting in memory loss and related symptoms. 140, 176

denial A defense mechanism in which a person deals with an unacceptable reality by denying it exists. This is seen in the first stage of Kübler-Ross's view of dying. 403, 446

denotation The concrete, dictionary meaning of a word. 222

dependent variable The behavior or characteristic that the researcher predicts will be influenced by the independent variable. 30

depression The fourth stage in Kübler-Ross's theory of dying during which the dying person comes to accept the inevitability of death and enters a period of depression. 446

depth perception The ability to perceive distance. 135

desatellization According to Ausubel, the process of becoming independent from one's parents and becoming a self-governing adult. 307

descriptive designs Research designs that reveal whether two or more variables are related. Data from these designs permit developmental psychologists to describe and predict development. 21

despair phase According to Bowlby, the second phase children may go through when separated from their mothers. Initially, children may seem hopeless and listless. Later, they exhibit resentment and rage at their mother's leaving. 294

detachment phase According to Bowlby, the third and final phase children go through when separated from their mothers. Children may appear normal; however, Bowlby believed their ability to form future attachments may be permanently impaired. 294

devaluation crisis According to Ausubel, the child's realization that he or she is helpless and powerless and must rely on others to survive. 305

developmental quotient (DQ) An index of developmental level used for infants and young children. 187

developmental task According to Havighurst, a characteristic of a certain period in an individual's life, the successful achievement of which leads to happiness and to success with later tasks, while failure leads to unhappiness in the individual, disapproval by the society, and difficulty with later tasks. 341

difference threshold The smallest difference between two stimuli that can be detected. 156

discourse The ability to communicate thoughts verbally. 238

disorganization and reorganization According to Stephenson, the second stage of grief during which reality sets in and the bereaved is disappointed that the loss cannot be recovered. Despair may leave the person with unfocused thoughts and an inability to make sense out of old activities. 451

disorganized/disoriented attachment A form of insecure attachment in which children appear "dazed," disorganized, and disoriented when reunited with their mothers. 294

displaced reference The ability to refer to objects and events that are not physically present. 218

displacement A defense mechanism in which a person transfers or redirects unacceptable feelings about a person or a situation from the actual target to a safer target (place). 403

dizygotic Twins who come from two different zygotes. 70

DNA (deoxyribonucleic acid) A complex molecule running the length of each chromosome that forms the genetic code. 70

dominant allele An allele that will be expressed phenotypically when paired with another allele. 75

double-blind technique Both the person collecting the data and the research participant are uninformed (blind) as to whether the research participant is in the control or the experimental group. 31

Down syndrome A human genetic defect in which more than two whole chromosomes are present for the 21st pair; usually accompanied by characteristic physical abnormalities and mental retardation. 82

dyslexia A reading disorder unrelated to intelligence, caused by a defect in the development of laterality. 123

E

earning status According to Ausubel, a step toward desatellization during which individuals try to prove their worth and earn status through individual effort. 307

echoic memory A sensory memory for sound. 157

ecological systems approach Bronfenbrenner's view that development is a dynamic process involving an interaction between the individual and several, interconnected environmental systems. 95

effacement and dilation The first and longest phase of birth marked by the thinning (effacement) and enlargement (dilation) of the cervix. 116

ego According to Freud, the rational component of personality. 40

egocentric empathy According to Hoffman, the second stage of empathy, during which children are able to separate another's distress from their own. However, they assume that the other's internal states are identical to their own. 276

ego instincts According to Freud, all impulses that serve self-preservation of the individual. 40

egocentric perspective taking According to Selman, the first stage of role taking during which children make simple inferences about people's behavior, but make the mistake of presuming that another person thinks and feels exactly the way they do. 269

egocentric thought The inability to separate one's own perspective from the perspective of others. 200

ego-ideal One's image of who one should ideally be. 402

ego instincts In Freud's view, instincts related to the preservation of the individual. 40

ego psychologists Psychologists who revised traditional Freudian theory by emphasizing the social side of humans, asserting that the ego has its own origins, and asserting that the ego has a role beyond dealing with anxiety and unconscious conflicts. 408

ego strength The abilities to tolerate frustration, to delay need gratification, and to meet the demands of life. 306

elaborative rehearsal A method of getting information from short-term memory into long-term memory by making information meaningful by thinking about it and relating it to other things that you know. 159

Electra complex The female version of the Oedipus complex, in which a girl is believed to envy her father because he has a penis and decides to focus on him as a sex object in the hope of sharing this valuable organ that the girl lacks. 42

Embedded-Figure Test A test of field independence that requires a person to identify a specific shape or object that is embedded in a field of other shapes or objects. 375

embryoblast The inner layer of the blastocyst that will develop into the embryo. 112
empathy The identification with and understanding of another's feelings, situation, and motives. 276, 373
empathy for another's feelings According to Hoffman, the third stage in the development of empathy, during which children become aware that the feelings of others may differ from their own. With this awareness comes an increasing responsiveness to cues about what others feel. 276
empathy for another's life condition According to Hoffman, the fourth and final stage of empathy during which a person has gained the awareness that the pleasure and pain felt by others is not always temporary. 276
empty-nest syndrome A largely unsupported view that parents feel a sense of emptiness when their children leave home. 350
encoding The process by which information is put into memory, through transduction of an experience into electrochemical energy for neural representations. 159
epigenesis According to Erikson, each event during fetal development has a unique time of dominance as determined by the organism's genetic plan. 412
episodic memory Memory for specific events, objects, and situations. 161
equilibration Our need to resolve contradiction; cognitive balance. 55, 197
eros instincts In Freud's view, instincts related to the survival of the species. 39
estrogens A group of hormones that promote the development of the female reproductive tract and female physical characteristics. 130
eugenics The selective breeding of humans for desired traits. 182
execution and implementation According to Carroll and Rest's four-process model, one must organize and sustain one's behavior to attain one's moral objective. 278
executive components Higher-order processes used in planning, monitoring, and evaluating performance of a task. (Same as a metacomponent). 209
exosystem According to Bronfenbrenner, an environmental system that affects a person, but is not affected by that person. 97
experiential intelligence In Sternberg's triarchic theory of intelligence, creative intelligence. 209
experimental design Research designs that reveal causal relationships between variables. Causal inferences are possible because research participants were randomly assigned to control and experimental groups, and the researcher was able to manipulate the independent variable. 29
exploratory orientation According to Ausubel, the final step in desatellization and the attainment of self-governance. The individuals are task-oriented and feel no need to prove themselves to others or seek approval from others. 307
expulsion of the afterbirth The third and final phase of birth marked by the expulsion of the placenta and other fetal membranes. 116
expulsion of the fetus The second phase of birth during which the baby is expelled from the mother's body. 116
external locus of control The belief that one is at the mercy of outside events and the whims of other people. 265
extinction In classical conditioning, the process of reducing the likelihood of a conditioned response to a conditioned stimulus by withholding the unconditioned stimulus. 48, 152

F

fallopian tube The tube that the ovum travels through in its journey from the ovary to the uterus. 130
familial developmental tasks Tasks that families are expected to master during specific times in their developmental careers. 341
family A group of people often living in the same household who are connected by ancestral or legal ties. 340
family career The changes in the composition of the traditional family. 342
family life-cycle approach The sequence of changes in family composition, roles, and relationships that unfold in the course of a family's existence. 339
field experiments Studies in which research participants are randomly assigned to either the experimental or the control group in a real-world setting, rather than a laboratory setting. 30
field independence The ability to separate an element in a display from its field. 375
fixation An excessive attachment to a person or object.
fluid intelligence A type of intelligence that includes abstract, nonverbal reasoning, and problem-solving skills, and reflects the ability to deal with novel situations. 191
follicles The fluid-filled cavity that encloses an ova. 130
follicle-stimulating hormone (FSH) A hormone secreted by the pituitary gland that stimulates the development of an ovarian follicle in a female or the production of sperm in a male. 130
forebrain The newest part of the brain, in an evolutionary sense, comprised of two cerebral hemispheres. The cerebral hemispheres are responsible for our highest intellectual functions. 122
forethought The ability to predict likely outcomes of actions. 51
formal operational stage Piaget's fourth and final stage of cognitive development (beginning at about age 12), during which the person can think hypothetically, can consider future possibilities, and is capable of deductive logic. 56, 202
formal universals General rules that relate to linguistic forms. 243
fragile X syndrome A sex chromosome abnormality in which individuals have an X chromosome that appears to be pinched or narrowed in some areas. These chromosomes are so fragile that the pinched areas may break off. The syndrome has been associated with mild to profound retardation in males and occasionally mild retardation in women. 79
free will versus determinism The argument over whether people actively create their own environments (free will), or whether they passively and predictably react to events that happen to them (determinism). 11
functional properties Aspects of communication unique to human language, including displaced reference, productivity, and prevarication. 218

G

gametes Sex cells. 71
gender roles Culturally defined sex-appropriate behaviors. 371
gender schema theory A theory of development that states that children are taught by society that gender is the most important way of categorizing people and are taught the "vital psychological differences" between the genders. 393

generalizability The degree to which a study's results can be applied to people and settings other than those in the study. 20

generalization In classical and operant conditioning, the fact that a response learned in one setting may be elicited in a similar setting. 153

generativity versus stagnation The seventh conflict in Erikson's theory of development, corresponding with the stage of adulthood. The crisis is positively resolved if an adult feels that he has produced something that will outlive him and feels he has assisted the younger generation in developing and leading useful lives. 45

genes The units of heredity transmission carried in chromosomes and consisting of DNA and protein. 70

genetic reshuffling The exchange of genes between members of a chromosome pair. Genetic reshuffling occurs as the pair splits apart early in meiosis. 71

genital stage Freud's last stage of psychosexual development, from the onset of puberty through adulthood, during which the sexual conflicts of childhood resurface at puberty. 42, 407

genocide The deliberate and systematic destruction of a racial, political, or cultural group to get rid of certain genes. 99

genotype An organism's genetic makeup. 74

Gesell's Developmental Schedules A series of tests designed to evaluate a child's progress in four areas: (1) motor development, (2) adaptive behavior, (3) language development, and (4) personal-social behavior. 187

gestation The time between conception and delivery. 112

giantism A condition resulting from too much growth hormone in which the person's body proportions appear normal, but their stature is enormous. 124

glaucoma High pressure in the eye causing hardening of the eye and damage to the internal structures of the eye. 142

glial cell Cells that nurture and protect the neurons. 121

global empathy According to Hoffman, the first stage of empathy during which a child mistakes another person's distress for his or her own distress. 276

goal-corrected partnership The fourth and final phase of attachment during which children realize that parents have things to do other than maintain physical proximity to their child. Bowlby and Ainsworth regard phase four attachment as mature attachment. 291

grammar The structural rules of language. 221

grammatical morphemes Modifiers that allow language to more specifically and accurately represent what the person really means. 228

grasping reflex A reflex in which an infant grasps anything placed in its hand. 132

grief An emotional response to loss. 449

growth hormone (GH) A hormone that brings about physical growth by stimulating protein synthesis and causing the body's cells to divide. 124

H

habituation The decrease in responsiveness as a result of repeated presentation of a stimulus. 166, 326

heritability quotient A number expressing the degree to which differences between people in a population are due to genes. 98

heteronomous stage Piaget's first stage of moral development during which a child views the rules of authority figures as sacred and unalterable. 271

heterozygous Two differing alleles in an individual at a particular locus. 74

heuristic value The extent to which a scientific theory is a source of hypotheses. 38

hierarchy of needs Maslow's pyramid of human needs, beginning at the base with physiological needs that must first be satisfied before higher level safety needs and psychological needs become active. 59

high-grief An intense emotional and physical reaction to loss. 451

hindbrain The most primitive part of the brain that is also the most necessary for survival. 121

historical events Events shared by members of a particular cohort that make that cohort different from other cohorts. 6

holophrastic speech The use of one word to convey the information usually contained in a whole phrase or sentence. 227

homeostasis The body's need to maintain an internal balance. 55, 197

homozygous Two identical alleles in an individual at a particular locus. 74

hormones Powerful and highly specialized chemicals that are usually produced by glands and circulate in the blood. Hormones interact with cells capable of receiving and responding to the hormonal message. 124

humanism A theoretical approach that stresses the importance of individual uniqueness. Perception is stressed over actual behavior, and the self-concept is the core of personality. Deemphasizes science. 415

Huntington's chorea An inherited disorder in which the nervous system gradually deteriorates, resulting in the progressive decline of physical and mental abilities. 76

hypothesis An idea that can be objectively tested to see if it is right or wrong. 14

I

"I" According to James, one's self-theory. 254

iconic memory A visual sensory memory. 157

id The instinctual component from our animal (evolutionary) past that operates on the pleasure principle. 40

identity achievement According to Marcia, the final step in identity development during which a person has a commitment to a self-chosen vocational goal and to a political and personal ideology. 414

identity diffusion According to Marcia, an identity status in which the adolescent has not experienced a crisis or made commitments to self-chosen vocational goals, or political and ideological systems. 414

identity foreclosed According to Marcia, an identity status in which individuals have unquestionably accepted the expectations of their parents. They haven't explored and developed their own set of beliefs and vocational choices. 413

identity versus role confusion The psychosocial crisis corresponding with Erikson's puberty and adolescence stage during which the adolescent struggles to achieve an identity or else becomes identity diffused. 45

immediate constituent analysis A linguistic technique that captures the hierarchical organization of sentences. 223

imprinting The tendency of young animals to learn to approach and associate with a parent or other role model. 92, 290

incongruent According to Carl Rogers, incongruency occurs when one's real self is not compatible with the conditions of worth that person believes others have placed on him. 60, 419

independent variable The variable in an experiment that is directly and purposefully manipulated by the experimenter to see if it causes a change in the dependent variable. 29

individuality versus universality The argument over whether developmental psychologists should focus on the study of individual differences or on uncovering universal principles that apply to all people. 12

industry versus inferiority The psychosocial crisis corresponding with Erikson's latency period during which the child masters many skills or develops a sense of incompetence. 44

infantile amnesia An inability to remember events from one's early childhood. 171

inferiority complex According to Adler, a deep sense of inferiority. 408

information-processing approach An approach that emphasizes that learning and remembering declarative knowledge involves several stages of information processing. 150

initiative versus guilt The psychosocial crisis corresponding with Erikson's locomotor-genital stage during which the child begins, or initiates, new activites—and feels guilty when his efforts result in failure or criticism. 44

inner speech Words that are thought instead of spoken. Usually inner speech is highly abbreviated and consists mostly of predicates rather than subjects. Vygotsky believed that inner speech helps us reason. 196, 246

instinctual drives Inborn, primitive drives related to the survival of the species. 39

integrated stage According to Loevinger, the last stage in ego development. Almost no one reaches this stage, which is characterized by the ability to create an environment that allows people to express their individuality and fulfill their potential. 261

integrity versus despair The crisis corresponding to Erikson's eighth and final stage of development, maturity. To successfully resolve the crisis, elderly individuals must have a sense of meaning in their lives and accept the inevitability of death. 46

intelligence quotient (IQ) An index of an individual's performance on a standardized test of intelligence relative to the performance of others his or her age. 183

internal consistency The extent to which a scientific theory doesn't contradict itself. 38

internal locus of control The belief that one is in control of one's own life. 265

interpersonal concordance orientation Kohlberg's third stage of moral reasoning in which people perform actions that will gain them the acceptance and approval of others. 272

interpersonal intelligence The ability to understand other people. 211

intimacy The sharing of thoughts, feelings, and vulnerabilities. 317

intimacy versus isolation The crisis corresponding to Erikson's sixth stage of development, adulthood. To successfully resolve this crisis, individuals must commit themselves to a shared identity with another person. 45

intrapersonal intelligence The ability to understand one's self. 212

iris The colored part of the eye that blocks light from entering the pupil. 134

K

kibbutz An Israeli collective farm or settlement. 297

kinship study An investigation in which the researcher compares similarities and differences among family members. 99

knowledge acquisition components Processes used in learning new things. 209

L

lab experiment An experiment conducted in a laboratory setting, characterized by the random assignment of research participants to control or experimental groups. 29

labia In a woman, folds of tissue protecting the genital area. 130

laboratory observation An observational study conducted in a laboratory setting. Although the study occurs in a laboratory, it is not an experiment because research participants were not randomly assigned to condition. 24

language A structured system of symbols that have socially agreed upon meanings. 218

language acquisition device (LAD) A hypothetical structure in the brain believed to be responsible for a child's natural ability to learn language. 243

lanugo A soft, down-like hair that covers the bodies of premature infants. 115

latency period A period between Freud's phallic and genital stages when sexual urges are inactive. 42, 406

latency stage The fourth stage in Erikson's theory, between ages 6 and 11, during which a child resolves issues pertaining to industry versus inferiority. 44

lateralization The localization of a particular brain function primarily in one hemisphere. 123

law and order orientation Kohlberg's fourth stage of moral reasoning during which people conform to authority to maintain the official social order. 273

learned helplessness A belief that what happens to us does not depend on what we do. 265

learning theory In language acquisition, the belief that language, like any other behavior, is learned through association, imitation, and reinforcement. 240

legal death When a person is declared dead by a legal authority. 436

legalistic social-contract orientation Kohlberg's fifth stage of moral reasoning during which people base their moral decisions on a democratic agreement among people to conform to norms needed to maintain both social order as well as individual rights. 274

lens The disc-like structure of the eye that focuses light onto the retina. 134

lexical meaning The meaning of individual words. 222

lexicon The individual dictionary that each of us uses. 237

libido Sexual energy. 39

life goal According to Adler, the way a person defines self-perfection. 409

lifespan developmental psychology The scientific study of how people grow and change from conception to the moment of death. 4

limbic system The part of the midbrain that plays a major role in emotions and primitive urges like hunger, thirst, lust, and aggression. 122

limited division potential In reference to Hayflick's finding that cells can divide only about 50 times. This limit may be a reason for aging and eventual death. 137

linguistic determinism The belief that the structure of language determines all other forms of perception and thinking. 246

linguistic intelligence The ability to use words. 211

linguistic period The period of language acquisition, from age 1 onward, that begins with the use of patterned speech and continues throughout the rest of a person's life. 226

linguistic relativity hypothesis Also called the Whorfian hypothesis, this hypothesis states that the structures of a particular language influence the thinking process of the native speakers of that language. 246

linguistics The field devoted to the study of language. 217

livor mortis Following cessation of bodily function, the skin turns purplish-red. 436

locomotor-genital stage The third stage in Erikson's theory, between ages 4 and 5, during which a child resolves issues pertaining to initiative versus guilt. 44

locus A specific location or place on a specific chromosome. 74

locus of control Whether we see ourselves as having control over our destiny or are at the mercy of the outside world. 265

logical-mathematical intelligence Logical and mathematical thinking. 211

longitudinal design An age-specific design that studies one group of people over a period of time. 27

longitudinal sequence design A design that combines aspects of longitudinal and cross-sectional designs, permitting researchers to separate the cohort effects from age effects. 28

long-term memory (LTM) The memory storage system that keeps a relatively permanent record of information. 159

low birth-weight Infants who weigh less than 5 pounds at birth. 118

low-grief A relatively mild reaction to loss. 451

M

macrosystem According to Bronfenbrenner, an environmental system representing the values, beliefs, opportunities, and resources of one's culture. 98

magical thought According to Piaget, children's failure to distinguish between the concrete world and the world of imagination. 199

maintenance rehearsal Information is repeated for the purpose of being maintained in short-term memory. Once repetition ceases, the information is forgotten. 158

masking conditions Situations where a sound may be hidden (masked) by surrounding sounds. 142

material self According to James, the aspect of the "me" composed of all one's physical possessions. 254

maturation The process of becoming biologically mature. 195

maturation versus learning The argument over whether development is the result of biological changes (maturation) or the result of learning from the environment. 10

maturity The eighth and final stage in Erikson's theory, age 65 and older, during which a person resolves issues pertaining to ego-integrity versus despair. 46

"me" According to James, all that can be known about the self. It has three parts: the material self, the social self, and the psychological self. 254

mean length of utterance (MLU) A measure of language development obtained by taking a sample of a child's statements and then calculating the average number of morphemes in those statements. 227

meiosis The process by which reproductive, or germ, cells divide. It is a process of reduction division in which a cell divides in such a way that the daughter cells include only one member of each pair of chromosomes. 71

menarche The onset of menstruation. 131

menopause Cessation of a women's menstrual cycle and the end of female fertility. 141

mental age An index of a child's absolute performance on a test of intelligence. If a child's performance is the same as that of the average 6-year-old, the child is said to have the mental age of 6 years. 183

mere exposure effect If a person is neutral or positive toward something to start out with, continued exposure to that thing or person will make one like that person or thing even more. 318

mesosystem According to Bronfenbrenner, the environmental level that comprises the interrelationships among contexts of the microsystems in which a person actively participates, such as those between home and work. 95

metalinguistic skill The ability to think and talk about language. 231

metamemory Personal knowledge of how one's own memory works. 168

metathought Thinking about thinking. 202

microgenetic method Intensively observing individuals throughout an entire period of change. 10

microsystem According to Bronfenbrenner, the actual setting in which a person lives and interacts with other people. 95

midbrain The part of the brain that serves as a relay station for almost all the information coming in and out of the cerebral hemispheres. Contains the limbic system. 122

mitosis A process of cell division in body cells in which each of the 46 chromosomes in the parent cell duplicates itself before division. Each of the two daughter cells includes 46 chromosomes. 70

modeling Imitating another person's behavior. 51, 154

monozygotic Twins who developed from a single zygote. 70

moral judgment In Carroll and Rest's four-process model, one must determine what one's moral ideals call for, and decide which moral norms apply. 278

moratorium According to Marcia, an identity status in which adolescents experience an identity crisis. The individual does not have firm commitments to a personal ideology, vocational goal, or belief system. 414

Moro reflex A reflex in response to a loud sound or jarring, or to a sudden head or body drop of a few inches. The arms are thrown out in extension and then toward each other in a convulsive manner; hands are fanned out at first and then clenched tightly. 132

morphemes Modifiers and qualifiers that make the meaning of a word more precise. For example, the suffix *-est* in the word tall*est*. 221

morphological rules Rules governing whether a group of sounds is a word (vocabulary rules). 221

motherese The simplified dialect used by caretakers and others when addressing a young child. 242

muscular-anal stage The second stage in Erikson's theory of personality development, occurring during the second year of life, during which a child resolves issues pertaining to autonomy versus shame and doubt. 44

musical intelligence The ability to produce and appreciate music. 211

mutations Chemical changes in the genetic code leading to changes in the genotype. 85

mutual role taking According to Selman, the fourth stage in role taking. People in this stage can assume a third-person view, realizing that they can "step outside" a social interaction and evaluate the participants' perspectives according to criteria that none of them share. 269

myelin A waxy substance that forms a sheath around some of the neurons. Myelin protects the neuron and speeds up the rate of neuronal transmission. 121

myelination The process by which neurons become covered with myelin. 121

N

naive hedonistic and instrumental orientation Kohlberg's second stage of moral reasoning during which people act to gain concrete rewards rather than solely to avoid punishment. 272

naturalistic observation Observing organisms in their natural environment. 24

nature versus nurture The argument about whether heredity or environment is more important. 10

negation The use of negative morphemes in language. 228

negative correlation Two variables that change in the opposite direction. Thus, when one variable increases, the other decreases. 25

negative reinforcement Removal of an aversive stimulus after a desired response to increase the likelihood that that response will occur again. 50, 151

neonate A newborn. 117

neurofibrilary tangles Tiny twisted tubes found in the brains of people suffering from senile dementia. 140

neuron A nerve cell. 121

neurotic needs According to Horney, irrational needs that can never be met. 411

neutral stimulus The stimulus that initially does not produce the conditioned response. Once paired with the unconditioned stimulus, the neutral stimulus becomes associated with the unconditioned stimulus. The neutral stimulus then becomes a conditioned stimulus and produces a conditioned response that is similar to the unconditioned response. 48

nominal realism The belief that an object's name is a real part or characteristic of the object. 199

nondisjunction The most common form of Down syndrome in which the person has an extra 21st chromosome. 82

nonmoral values and influences In Carroll and Rest's four-process model, one must devise a plan of action with one's moral ideal in mind while taking into account nonmoral values and goals that impinge on the situation. 278

nonnormative events Unexpected events that either don't happen to most people or that happen at an atypical age. 6

normative age-graded events Events that most people (normally) experience at about the same age. 5

normative maturational events Biological events that most people experience at about the same age. 5

normative social events Nonbiological events that most people in a given culture experience at about the same age. 6

nucleotides Molecules that make up the genetic code. 72

O

obedience and punishment orientation Kohlberg's first stage of moral reasoning during which people obey rules and laws to avoid punishment. 272

objectively scored A person's score should not be affected by who does the scoring. 15

objective self-awareness The fact that people are more self-aware when they are made self-conscious. 262

objectivity The extent to which science research is unbiased and free of personal interpretations. 14

object permanence The belief that objects continue to exist even when one can't see them. 56, 199

observation A research measurement technique in which research participants' behaviors are systematically and objectively observed and recorded. 25

Oedipus complex Occurring during the phallic stage, feelings of rivalry with the parent of the same sex and love of the parent of the opposite sex, ultimately resolved through identification with the same-sex parent. 41, 406

operant conditioning A conditioning procedure in which the probability that an organism will emit a response is increased or decreased by the subsequent delivery of a reinforcer or punisher. 49, 151

operations An action performed mentally, rather than physically. 56, 199

opponent processes Every stimulus that triggers an emotional response also triggers the opposite (opponent) reaction. Over time, the opposite reaction grows so strong that it neutralizes the original response. 326

oral fixation Preoccupation with oral traits such as excessive eating, drinking, talking, or biting sarcasm. 41

oral-sensory stage The first stage in Erikson's theory, between birth and about age 1, when an infant resolves the issue of basic trust versus mistrust. 44

oral stage Freud's first stage of personality development, from birth to about age 1, during which infants obtain gratification primarily through the mouth. 41, 404

organization A memory strategy in which one groups or classifies information into meaningful chunks or clusters. 155

orgasm Intense pleasure caused by sexual stimulation. 130, 322

osteoporosis Decalcification of the bones resulting in a collapse of the skeletal system. 137

ovaries The pair of female reproductive glands in which the ova and female sexual hormones are produced. 130

overextension A common error in children's early word use in which a single word is used to mean many things. 227

overjustification effect When it is clear to an individual that anyone in his situation would do a specific behavior, the person decides that he did the behavior because of the situation (being rewarded) rather than because he wanted to do it. 154, 262

overregularization A common error made by young children in which the child ignores irregularities and exceptions and applies grammatical rules to all cases. 228

overvalued According to Ausubel, children who are valued—but only for what they can do for their parents. 306

ovum Mature female sex cell. 70, 130

P

parallel play According to Piaget, when children engage in a collective activity, but remain embedded in their own point of view. When children play beside (parallel to) each other, but not with each other. 269, 315

parsimonious The extent to which a scientific theory, uses very few principles. 38

passionate love Intense positive absorption in another, usually at the beginning of a relationship. 325

patterned speech Meaningful speech. 226

peak experiences An especially joyous and exciting moment. 58, 417

perception The process of organizing and interpreting sensory information, enabling us to recognize meaningful objects and events. 155

performance components According to Sternberg, the ability to quickly and accurately solve simple mathematical and reasoning tasks. 209

period of the embryo The period of development during which differentiation of the most important organs and systems occurs. In humans it occurs from the beginning of the third week to the eighth week after conception. 113

period of the fetus The period of development marked by the growth of existing systems, rather than the establishment of new systems. In humans it lasts from the eighth week after conception until birth. 115

period of the zygote The period of development between fertilization of the ovum and implantation. 112

permissive parenting A parenting practice in which few restrictions are placed on children. 359

phallic stage Freud's third stage of personality development, from age 3 to about age 6, during which children obtain gratification primarily through the genitals. 41, 406

phenomenalistic causality The belief that if two things occur together, one caused the other. 199

phenotype The way an individual's genotype is expressed in observable or measurable characteristics. 74

phoneme The shortest speech unit in which a change produces a change in meaning. 221

phonological rules Rules governing which sounds are part of the language and which sounds can be put together. 221

physicalistic conceptions of self According to Selman, a child's failure to distinguish between inner psychological experience and outward behavior. 256

physical salience How intense or noticeable a stimuli is. 166

pituitary dwarfism A condition resulting from insufficient growth hormone in which the person's body proportions appear normal, but the person is extremely small in stature. 124

pituitary gland The master gland, that in conjunction with the hypothalamus regulates the activity of all other glands. 124

placenta A fleshy disc attached to the uterus through which nutrients and waste products are exchanged between the maternal and infant systems. 113

plaques Rust-like patches found on the brains of people suffering from senile dementia. 140

plasticity The capacity of brain cells to work on a variety of tasks. 123

plasticity theory The belief that declines in test performance associated with age can be largely reversed. 191

pleasure principle Seeks pleasure through the immediate gratification of instinctual desires regardless of the long-term consequences. 40

polygenic Influenced by many genes. 76

positive correlation Two variables that vary in the same direction. Thus, when one increases, the other increases too. 25

positive parental responding Responding to an infant in a comforting, confident, and cheerful manner. 302

positive reinforcement Presentation of a rewarding or pleasant stimulus after a desired response to increase the likelihood that the response will recur. 49, 151

postconventional level According to Kohlberg, the third and last level of moral reasoning, during which people make moral decisions based on self-chosen, universal principles. Contains stages 5 and 6. 274

pragmatics The use of language to affect the behavior, knowledge, or attitude of another. 218

preattachment phase According to Ainsworth and Bowlby, the first phase of attachment during which babies' attachment behaviors may be reflexively triggered by anyone—or anything. 290

preconventional level According to Kohlberg, the first level of moral reasoning, during which people make moral decisions based on their own self-interests. Contains stages 1 and 2. 272

prelinguistic period Begins at birth and ends at about age 1 with the onset of patterned speech. 223

preoperational stage The second of Piaget's four stages of cognitive development, occurring from about age 2 to about 7 years, during which the child constructs the world of symbols. 56, 199

preterm A baby having a gestation period of less than 38 weeks. 118

prevarication The ability to lie. 218

primary sex characteristics The male and female genital tracts. 128

proactive interference Information learned in the past interferes with one's memory for something recently learned. 160

problem-finding stage According to Arlin, a stage beyond Piaget's formal operations, during which people rethink and reorganize existing knowledge and then ask crucial questions and define new problems. 208

procedural knowledge Knowing how to do things (what procedures to follow) and learning how events are connected. 149

productive function Productive function of language. 223

productivity (also called generativity) The capacity to produce novel messages. 218

projection A defense mechanism in which a person attributes his own taboo impulses to someone else. 402

propositional logic Forming a logical conclusion based on combining two or more hypothetical statements. 202

protest phase According to Bowlby, the first phase children may go through when separated from their mothers. Children may protest the impending separation by crying, clinging, or calling. Once the mother has left, they protest by shouting, screaming, and running around wildly—focusing all their resources on getting her back. 294

proximodistal Gesell's maturational principle that development proceeds from the center of the body and then radiates outward toward the extremities. 114

psychoanalytic theory Based on Freud's view that behavior arises from unconscious drives and conflicts, many of which may stem from childhood experiences. 39

psychological death When a person's mind (the seat of conscious experiences) ceases to function. 435

psychological self According to James, the aspect of the "me" comprised of one's beliefs, ambitions, and goals that are independent of the material and social self. 254

psychological test A more formalized version of the questionnaire, often designed to measure mental abilities and personality traits. 18

psychometric approach An approach to psychology that is concerned with measuring psychological phenomena. 181

psychosexual stages According to Freud, the developmental stages (oral, anal, phallic, latency, genital) during which the id's pleasure-seeking energies are focused on different erogenous zones.

psychosocial stages Erikson's theory that emphasizes social and cultural effects on the individual. 44

puberty (1) The time of sexual maturation; (2) The fifth stage in Erikson's theory, between ages 11 and 18, during which a person resolves issues pertaining to identity versus role confusion. 45, 125

punishment The process of presenting an undesirable stimulus after an undesired behavior to decrease the likelihood that the response will recur. 50

pupil The dark area in the center of the eye that dilates and constricts to control the amount of light that enters your eye. 134

Q

questionnaire method A research measurement technique in which the participants are given a list of written questions (a questionnaire) to which they respond in writing. 17

R

random assignment A way of assigning research participants to experimental or control groups so that each research participant has an equal chance of being put in either group. 29
random sampling A research technique whereby everyone in the designated group has an equal chance of being surveyed. 22
range of reaction Genetically based variations of an individual's responsiveness to the environment. 93
rationalization A defense mechanism in which people justify their actions by ignoring their true unconscious motivations. 402
reaction formation A defense mechanism in which a person thinks and acts in a manner that is the opposite of his or her unconscious impulse. 402
reaction stage According to Stephenson, the initial period of shock when one first learns about the death of someone. Shock is followed by numbness and a dazed lack of feeling. 451
receptive function Language comprehension. 223
recessive allele An allele that will not be expressed phenotypically when paired with a dominant allele. Recessive alleles are expressed only when they are paired with similar recessive alleles. 75
reciprocate To compensate others for what they have done for you. 320
recognition and sensitivity In Carroll and Rest's four-process model, a person must translate a social situation into a moral problem. 278
recognition tests Methods of determining whether people recognize what they have seen before. 167
regression A defense mechanism in which a person returns to a more immature state. 40, 403
reinforcement-affect theory The theory of friendship that hypothesizes that we like people who boost our ego. 318
reliability The ability of a measure to produce the same results from one day to the next. 15
reorientation and recovery According to Stephenson, the third and final stage of grief during which the survivor reorganizes the symbolic world and gives the deceased a new identity outside the world of the survivor. 451
replicability The extent to which a research study can be repeated under similar conditions to produce the same results. 14
repression In Freud's theory, pushing unacceptable thoughts and impulses into the unconscious. 40, 402
resatellization According to Ausubel, when a person becomes dependent on someone other than one's parents. 307
research design The researcher's general strategy about who to test under what conditions. 19
respiratory distress syndrome A leading cause of mortality in infants in which the air sacs in the infants' lungs collapse. 116
reticular formation The part of the brain responsible for attention. 121
retina The part of the eye containing the rods and cones and that converts light into neuronal impulses. 134
retrieval Transferring information from long-term memory to short-term memory. 160
retroactive interference Information recently learned interferes with memories for information learned in the past. 160
rigor mortis The stiffening of the muscles following cessation of bodily function. 436
role taking According to Mead, the ability to understand the views of others as we interact with them. 268
rooting reflex (or response) A reflex in which the head is turned toward a nipple or other object touched lightly to the infant's cheek. The infant opens its mouth and tries to suck the object (sucking reflex). 132

S

satellization According to Ausubel, the process by which a child becomes dependent on his or her parent. 306
schema (pl. is *schemata*) A mental representation of an event. 54, 195
schema of apperception According to Adler, our subjective perception of ourselves and the world. 410
schemata (sing. of *schema*) Organized, coherent categories of information. 195
scrotum The skin sack housing the testicles. 128
secondary sex characteristics Nonreproductive sex traits such as breasts and pubic hair. 128
second-order operations The ability to perform mental operations on operations. 56, 202
secular trends Systematic changes in a culture that may influence a person's development. For example, improved nutrition and medical care have increased the size of people in industrialized countries. 132
secure attachment As determined by Ainsworth, an attachment to the mother in which the child occasionally seeks to be close to her mother and is actively curious about exploring new objects in unfamiliar situations when her mother is present. After separation, she exhibits an increase in contact-maintaining behavior. 293
selective breeding A systematic method of breeding animals for a specific trait. 99
selective encoding The skill of attending to relevant information and ignoring irrelevant information. 166
self According to Carl Rogers, our beliefs about who we are. 60, 254, 419
self-actualization The full use and exploitation of talents, capacities, potentials. 58, 261, 416
self-control The degree to which we can control ourselves. 266
self-disclosure Revealing one's thoughts, attitudes, and feelings to another person. 314
self-efficacy The degree to which we think we can be effective in a given situation. 53, 266, 421
self-esteem A feeling of self-worth. 263
self-fulfilling prophecy The tendency to become what others expect us to become. 264
self-realization According to Horney, being truthful to oneself, being active and productive, and relating oneself to others in a spirit of mutuality. 411
self-reflective role taking The third stage in Selman's theory of role taking, during which children are able to reflect on their own thoughts and feelings. Consequently, they can anticipate what other people will think or feel by putting themselves in the other person's place. 269
self-regulatory mechanisms Internal processes that give feedback and help sustain behaviors necessary to meet internal goals. 52
self-verification Finding others who see us the same way we see ourselves. 263
semantic memory A memory of concepts and meanings. 155
semantic rules Rules determining what a statement means. 222

semen A grayish-white, sticky mixture discharged from the urethra of the male during ejaculation; contains the sperm and seminal fluid. 128

senile dementia A general loss of intellectual abilities associated with aging. 176

sensation The raw sensory information received through our sense organs. 156

sensitive period A period during which a certain skill or characteristic is most influenced by environmental events. 84, 286

sensorimotor stage The first of Piaget's four stages of cognitive development, occurring from birth to about 2 years, during which the child constructs the world of objects by interacting with the environment. 55, 198

sensory level The first level of learning in which a person senses the information to be learned. 155

sensory memory The mechanism that performs initial encoding and brief storage of stimuli. 156

sensory stable factors Things in the environment that all members of the species encounter. 92

sensory variable factors Anything in the environment that is not universal to all members of a species. 93

separation anxiety A wary reaction that infants sometimes display when separated from someone to whom they are attached. 293

sequential designs A series of hybrid designs that attempt to disentangle cohort, age, and history effects. 28

seriation Arranging objects in a logical order. 200

sex-linked defects Defects that are the result of genes that appear on the X chromosome, but not on the Y. 78

short-term memory (STM) The memory storage system that temporarily holds information for immediate short-term use. Information may be recently acquired or retrieved from long-term memory. Also called working memory. 157

SIDS Sudden infant death syndrome is the leading cause of death in infants between the age of 2 weeks and 1 year. Caused by an immature brain stem, the infant stops breathing. 122

signaling behaviors An infant attachment behavior that brings the mother to the infant. 286

significant symbols Gestures which arouse in the individual the response which the individual is calling out in the other. 268

small for date Infants who are small for their gestational age. 118

social and conventional systems role taking Selman's fifth stage of role taking, during which people realize that mutual perspective taking does not always result in complete understanding because people don't share identical experiences, roles, or positions. 269

social death When others treat a person as if he or she is dead. 435

social exchange theory Theory that the rewards one seeks are love, money, status, goods, services, and information. 319

social-informational role taking The second stage in Selman's theory of role taking, during which children understand that others' thoughts and feelings may be different from their own. 259

social learning theory Bandura's scientific theory that accounts for our ability to learn from personal experience and from the experiences of models. 51, 379, 421

social self According to James, the aspect of the "me" comprised of one's social identity, social behavior, and reputation. 254

spatial ability See spatial intelligence. 375

spatial intelligence The ability to form a mental model of a spatial world and to be able to maneuver and operate using that model. 211

spontaneous recovery In reference to classical and operant conditioning, a response reappears after it has been extinguished. 153

spreading activation The process in which a specific concept is activated in a person's memory and the other related concepts are also activated. 237

stability versus change The argument over the extent to which we change as we age. 8

stage of cooperation According to Piaget, the second stage of role taking during which children can separate self from nonself. Consequently, they can truly interact and share with each other. 269

stage of egocentrism According to Piaget, the first stage of role taking during which the child "plays in an individual manner with material that is social." 269

stage theory A theory emphasizing qualitative changes in development that occur in sequential phases that are age-related. 9, 259, 274

standardized Administered in the same way every time. 15

Stanford-Binet An intelligence test originally developed by Lewis Terman at Stanford University. 183

statistically significant Research results that are unlikely to be due to chance. 30, 394

stranger anxiety The fear that many infants feel when in the presence of strangers. 292

strange situation A research situation developed by Ainsworth to assess a child's attachment to his or her mother. 292

Stroop Task A complex task that requires subjects to label the ink colors of 100 designs and label the ink colors of 100 words. The task is challenging because the ink colors are different from the color described by the word. 239

structuralists In regard to language acquisition, nativists such as Chomsky who believe children are born to learn the underlying structural rules that govern language. 243

structural properties Complex rules that govern the way sounds and words can be put together. 218

structured interview A research measurement technique in which a questionnaire is prepared and the researcher reads the questionnaire to the research participants. Thus, each participant is asked exactly the same questions. 17

sublimation A defense mechanism in which a person converts sexual energy (a productive and creative force) into a more socially appropriate form of productive and creative energy. 402

substantive universals Language rules that relate to a specific element, such as rules related to the use of nouns or verbs. 243

sucking reflex An infant's reflex to suck anything placed in its mouth. 132

Sudden Infant Death Syndrome See **SIDS.** 122

superego In Freud's theory, the moral aspect of mental functioning taught by parents and society. 40

surfactin A liquid that allows the lungs to transfer oxygen from the air into the blood. 116

surrogate mother Substitute mother. 289

survey A research method employing a questionnaire or interview about people attitudes, behaviors, or beliefs. 22

symbolic models A person with whom a child does not personally interact, such as a television character. 51, 380

symbolic thought Using mental symbols such as words to refer to objects. 56, 199

synchronized routines Harmonious interactions between two persons in which each adjusts his or her behaviors in response to the partner's actions. 287

syntactic meanings (also called propositional meanings) The meanings that words and phrases take on when they become parts of sentences. 222

syntactic rules Rules governing the order in which words can be put together to make meaningful sentences. 221

syntax The rules governing how words can be put together to form meaningful sentences. 222

system In Bronfenbrenner's model, the interplay between two or more environments. 95

systematic When observing and recording research participants' behaviors, the researcher looks for specific behaviors and immediately records them. 16

systems approach A multidimensional approach to intelligence. 181

T

tacit knowledge The unspoken rules that help us adapt or get ahead. 210

telegraphic speech Speech that includes content words, such as nouns and verbs, but omits the extra words that serve a grammatical function, such as prepositions and articles. 227

teratogens Agents that increase the incidence of genetic defects or produce malformations in the course of prenatal development. 85

terminal phase According to Pattison, the third and final phase during the living-dying interval. The dying person accepts that death is imminent and begins a final social and emotional withdrawal from the living. 449

testicles The male reproductive organs responsible for the production of sperm. 128

testosterone A class of male hormones. 127

thanatology The study of death and dying. 446

thanatos In Freud's view, instincts related to destruction and death. 40

theory A set of rules that explains a broad range of findings and suggests other hypotheses that could be tested. 15

threshold The level of stimulation required before a person can detect that a stimulus is present. 156

translocation A form of Down syndrome in which a part or all of one of the 21st chromosomes is in the wrong location. Instead of pairing off with the other 21st chromosome, it has attached to another chromosome pair (usually to chromosome 14). 82

triarchic theory Sternberg's theory of three types of intelligence: experiential (creative), contextual (practical intelligence), and componential (analytical intelligence). 209

trophoblast The outer layer of the blastocyst that will become the placenta, umbilical cord, and amnion. 112

trust versus mistrust The psychosocial crisis corresponding with Erikson's oral-sensory stage during which the infant's basic experience of the world is either of a good and comfortable environment or of a threatening and uncomfortable one. 44

U

umbilical cord A structure containing two arteries and one vein that transport blood between the embryo and placenta. 113

unconditional positive regard In Rogers' client centered therapy, the therapist accepts the person, regardless of what the client thinks or feels. 60, 419

unconditioned response The unlearned or involuntary response to an unconditioned stimulus. 48

unconditioned stimulus A stimulus that normally produces an involuntary, measurable response. 48

unconscious motivation Freud's premise that much of human behavior is determined by desires, goals, and internal states buried within the unconscious. 40

underextension The use of a single word in a highly restricted and individualistic way. 227

underjustification effect The fact that people who voluntarily do something for no reward (justification) decide they did it because they wanted to. 262

undervalued According to Ausubel, children who do not receive unconditional love and acceptance. 306

universal ethical principled orientation Kohlberg's sixth and final stage of moral reasoning during which people realize that what is moral is not simply what a majority of people in one society want to do. Thus, stage 6 individuals make moral decisions based on abstract principles concerned with justice, compassion, fairness, and equality. 274

unstructured interview Asking a research participant whatever questions come to mind. 17

uterus The female organ for containing and nourishing the embryo and fetus from implantation to birth. 130

urethra In a woman, the tube that carries urine from the bladder. 130

V

vagina The pathway through which a baby passes from the uterus to the outside world, and the opening in which a man normally inserts his penis during intercourse. 130

validity In testing, the extent to which a test measures what it is claimed it measures. 15

vas deferens The small, muscular tube that carries sperm upward from each epididymis to the ejaculatory duct. 128

vernix A lanolin-like substance on the faces and bodies of newborns. 118

vicious circle According to Horney, trying to reduce basic anxiety through neurotic needs increases basic anxiety, which increases the desire to fulfill neurotic needs, which increases basic anxiety. 412

vocabulary spurt The rapid growth in spoken vocabulary that occurs when a child is about two years old. 230

W

wear and tear theory of aging A theory proposed by Wilson that aging is the result of genetic damage caused by the accumulation of environmental insults. 137

Wechsler Adult Intelligence Scale (WAIS) An individually administered test of general intelligence for adults that consists of five verbal scales and five performance scales. 186

Wechsler Intelligence Scale for Children (WISC) An individually administered test of general intelligence for children that consists of five verbal scales and five performance scales. 186

Wechsler Preschool and Primary Scale of Intelligence (WPPSI) An individually administered test of general intelligence for preschoolers. 186

Wernicke's-type aphasia A type of aphasia in which victims are able to speak fluently, and at times grammatically, but don't understand the words they produce. 236

Whorfian hypothesis The hypothesis that the structures of a particular language influence the thinking process of the native speakers of that language. 246

***Wh*- questions** Questions used by children entering their third year. Includes the interrogatives, *what, where, who,* and *why*. 229

working memory Another name for short-term memory because short-term memory is where we think about information and do our mental "work." 157

Y

young adulthood The sixth stage in Erikson's theory, between ages 18 and 45, during which a person resolves issues pertaining to intimacy versus isolation. 45

Z

zone of proximal development According to Vygotsky, the gap between a child's current level of skills and what the child's level could be if he or she received proper instruction. 196

zygote (1) A cell formed when an ovum is fertilized by sperm; and (2) the developing individual produced from the division of such a cell. 70

REFERENCES

A

Aaronson, L. S., & MacNee, C. L. (1989). Tobacco, alcohol, and caffeine use during pregnancy. *Journal of Obstetrics, Gynecology and Neonatal Nursing, 18,* 279–287.

Abramovitch, R., Pepler, D., & Corter, C. (1982). Patterns of sibling interaction among preschool-age children. In M. E. Lamb & B. Sutton-Smith (Eds.), *Sibling relationships.* Hillsdale, NJ: Erlbaum.

Ackerman, B. P. (1982). Contextual integration and utterance interpretation: The ability of children and adults to interpret sarcastic utterances. *Child Development, 53,* 1075–1083.

Ackerman, B. P. (1986). Children's sensitivity to comprehension failure in interpreting a nonliteral use of an utterance. *Child Development, 57,* 485–497.

Acredolo, L. P., & Hake, J. L. (1982). Infant perception. In B. B. Wolman (Ed.), *Handbook of developmental psychology.* Englewood Cliffs, NJ: Prentice Hall.

Adams, D. (1983). *The psychosocial development of professional Black women's lives and the consequences of career for their personal happiness.* Unpublished doctoral dissertation, Wright Institute, Berkeley, CA.

Adams, R. E., & Passman, R. H. (1980). *The effects of advance preparation upon children's behavior during brief separation from their mother.* Paper presented at the annual meeting of the Southeastern Psychological Association, Washington, DC.

Adams, R. E., & Passman, R. H. (1981). The effects of preparing two-year-olds for brief separations from their mothers. *Child Development, 52,* 1068–1070.

Adelman, C. (1993). *Women at thirtysomething: Paradoxes of attainment.* Upland, PA: Diane Publishers.

Adler, A. (1956). *The individual psychology of Alfred Adler: A systematic presentation in selections from his writings* (H. L. Ansbacher & R. R. Ansbacher, Eds.). New York: Harper.

Adler, T. (1989, March). Sex-based differences declining, study shows. *APA Monitor,* American Psychological Association, p. 6.

Adler, T. (1990, May). Military fails to help low-aptitude recruits. *APA Monitor,* pp. 12–13.

Adler, J., & Carey, J. (1982, January 11). But is it a person? *Newsweek,* p. 44.

Ahlum, A., & Howes, F. (Eds.). (1976). *High school feminist studies.* Old Westbury, NY: Feminist Press.

Aiken, L. R. (1985). *Dying, death, and bereavement.* Boston: Allyn & Bacon.

Aiken, L. R. (1989). *Later life* (2nd ed.). Hillsdale, NJ: Erlbaum.

Aiken, L. R. (1994). *Dying, death, and bereavement* (3rd ed.). Boston: Allyn & Bacon.

Ainsworth, M. D. (1973). The development of infant-mother attachment. In B. M. Caldwell & H. Ricciuti (Eds.), *Review of child development research* (Vol. 3). Chicago: University of Chicago Press.

Ainsworth, M. D. S., & Bell, S. M. (1970). Attachment, exploration, and separation: Illustrated by the behavior of one-year-olds in a strange situation. *Child Development, 41,* 49–67.

Ainsworth, M. D. S., Bell, S. M., & Stayton, D. J. (1974). Infant-mother attachment and social development: Socialization as a product of reciprocal responsiveness to signals. In M. O. Richards (Ed.), *The integration of a child into a social world.* Cambridge: Cambridge University Press.

Ainsworth, M. D. S., Blehar, M. C., Waters, E., & Wall, S. N. (1978). *Patterns of attachment.* Hillsdale, NJ: Erlbaum.

Aitken-Swan, J., & Easson, E. C. (1959). Reactions of cancer patients on being told their diagnosis. *British Medical Journal, 1,* 770–783.

Alan Guttmacher Institute. (1981a). *Factbook on teenage pregnancy.* New York: Author.

Alan Guttmacher Institute. (1981b). *Teenage pregnancy: The problem that hasn't gone away.* New York: Author.

Alderfer, C. (1972). *Existence, relatedness, and growth: Human needs in organizational settings.* New York: Free Press.

Allen, P. A., & Crozier, L. C. (1992). Age and ideal chunk size. *Journal of Gerontology: Psychological Sciences, 47,* 47–51.

Alley, T. R. (1981). Head shape and the perception of cuteness. *Developmental Psychology, 17,* 650–654.

Altmann, S. (Ed.). (1967). *Social communication among primates.* Chicago: University of Chicago Press.

Amabile, T. M. (1983). *The social psychology of creativity.* New York: Springer-Verlag.

Amabile, T. M., & Glazebrook, A. H. (1982). A negativity bias in interpersonal evaluation. *Journal of Experimental and Social Psychology, 18,* 1–22.

Ambert, A. (1992). *The effect of children on the family.* New York: Haworth.

Ambron, S. R., & Brodzinsky, D. (1979). *Lifespan human development.* New York: Holt, Rinehart & Winston.

Anders, K. A., & Charness, N. (1994). Expert performance: Its structure and acquisition. *American Psychologist, 49,* 725–747.

Anderson, L. D. (1939). The predictive value of infant tests in relation to intelligence at 5 years. *Child Development, 10,* 202–212.

Andrews, S. E., & Cappon, D. (1957). Autism and schizophrenia in a child guidance clinic. *Canadian Psychiatric Association Journal, 2,* 1–25.

Angoff, W. H. (1988). The nature-nurture debate, aptitudes, and group differences. *American Psychologist, 43,* 713–720.

Antill, J. K. (1983). Sex-role complementarity versus similarity in married couples. *Journal of Personality and Social Psychology, 45,* 145–155.

Apgar, V., & Beck, J. (1974). *Is my baby alright?* New York: Pocket Books.

Applebaum, M. I., & Hogarty, P. S. (1973). Developmental changes in mental performance. *Monographs of the Society for Research in Child Development, 38* (No. 150).

Aries, P. (1962). *Centuries of childhood.* London: Jonathan Cape.

Aries, P. (1974). *Western attitudes toward death: From the Middle Ages to the present.* Baltimore: Johns Hopkins University Press.

Aries, P. (1981). *The hour of death* (H. Weaver, Trans.). New York: Knopf.

Arlin, P. K. (1975). Cognitive development in adulthood: A fifth stage? *Developmental Psychology, 11,* 602–606.

Arlin, P. K. (1977). Piagetian operations in problem finding. *Developmental Psychology, 13,* 297–298.

Arlin, P. K. (1983). Adolescent and adult thought: A structural interpretation. In N. Commons & S. Benack (Eds.), *Post-formal operations.* New York: Praeger.

Armstrong, J. M. (1981). Achievement and participation of women in mathematics: Results of two national surveys. *Journal for Research in Mathematics Education, 12*(5), 356–372.

Aronfreed, J. (1968). The concept of internalization. In D. A. Goslin & D. C. Glass (Eds.), *Handbook of socialization theory.* New York: Rand-McNally.

Aslin, R. N. (1987). Visual and auditory development in infancy. In J. D. Osofsky (Ed.), *Handbook of infant development* (2nd ed.). New York: Wiley.

Aslin, R. N., & Smith, L. B. (1988). Perceptual development. *Annual Review of Psychology, 39,* 435–473.

Association for Gerontology in Higher Education. (1989). *Standards and guidelines for gerontology programs.* Washington, DC: Author.

Atkinson, K., McWhinney, B., & Stoel, C. (1970). *An experiment on the recognition of babbling.* Papers and reports on child language development, Committee on Linguistics, Stanford University (No. 1).

Auel, J. M. (1980). *Clan of the cave bear.* New York: Crown Publishers.

Aurandt, P. (1983). *Destiny and 102 other real-life mysteries.* New York: Bantam Books.

Austin, J. (1962). *How to do things with words.* London: Oxford University Press.

Ausubel, D. P. (1952). *Ego development and the personality disorders.* New York: Grune & Stratton.

Ausubel, D. P. (1954). *Theory and problems of adolescent development.* New York: Grune & Stratton.

Ausubel, D. P., Montemayor, R., & Svajian, P. (1977). *Theory and problems of adolescent development* (2nd ed.). New York: Grune & Stratton.

Ausubel, D. P., & Sullivan, E. V. (1970). *Theory and problems in child development* (2nd ed.). New York: Grune & Stratton.

B

Bacon, M. K., & Ashmore, R. D. (1986). A consideration of the activities of parents and their role in the socialization process. In R. D. Ashmore & D. M. Brodzinsky (Eds.), *Thinking about the family: Views of parents and children.* Hillsdale, NJ: Erlbaum.

Bahrick, H. P. (1984). Semantic memory content in permastore: Fifty years of memory for language learned in high school. *Journal of Experimental Psychology: General, 113,* 1–29.

Bahrick, H. P., Bahrick, P. O., & Wittlinger, R. P. (1975). Fifty years of memory for names and faces: A cross-sectional approach. *Journal of Experimental Psychology: General, 104,* 54–75.

Baillargeon, R. (1993). The object concept revisited: New directions in the investigation of infants' physical knowledge. In C. E. Granrud (Ed.), *Visual perception and cognition in infancy.* Hillsdale, NJ: Erlbaum.

Baillargeon, R. (1994). How do infants learn about the world? *Current Directions, 3,* 133–140.

Baillargeon, R., & Graber, M. (1988). Evidence of location memory in 8-month-old infants in a non-search AB task. *Developmental Psychology, 24,* 502–511.

Baker, L. A., & Daniels, D. (1990). Nonshared environmental influences and personality differences in adult twins. *Journal of Personality and Social Psychology, 58,* 103–110.

Baker, S. W., & Ehrhardt, A. A. (1974). Prenatal androgen, intelligence, and cognitive sex differences. In E. C. Friedman, R. M. Richart, & R. L. VandeWiele (Eds.), *Sex differences in behavior.* New York: Wiley.

Baldwin, A. L. (1947). Changes in parent behavior during childhood. *American Psychologist, 2,* 425–430.

Baldwin, A. L. (1955). *Behavior and development in childhood.* New York: Dryden.

Baldwin, A. L. (1967). *Theories of child development.* New York: Wiley.

Ball, J. F. (1977). Widow's grief: The impact of age and mode of death. *Omega, 7,* 307–333.

Balota, D. A., & Duchek, J. M. (1988). Age-related differences in lexical access, spreading activation, and simple pronunciation. *Psychology and Aging, 3,* 84–93.

Baltes, P. B. (1987). Theoretical propositions of life-span developmental psychology: On the dynamics between growth and decline. *Developmental Psychology, 23,* 611–626.

Baltes, P. B. (1993). The aging mind: Potential and limits. *The Gerontologist, 33,* 580–594.

Baltes, P. B., Dittmann-Kohli, F., & Kliegl, R. (1986). Reserve capacity of the elderly in aging-sensitive tests of fluid intelligence: Replication and extension. *Psychology and Aging, 2,* 172–177.

Baltes, P. B., & Schaie, K. W. (1976). On the plasticity of intelligence in adulthood and old age: Where Horn and Donaldson fail. *American Psychologist, 31,* 720–725.

Baltes, P., & Reese, H. W. (1984). The life-span perspective in developmental psychology. In M. H. Bornstein & M. E. Lamb (Eds.), *Developmental psychology: An advanced textbook.* (pp. 493–532). Hillsdale, NJ: Erlbaum.

Baltes, P. B., Reese, H. W., & Nesselroade, J. R. (1988). *Introduction to research methods: Life-span developmental psychology.* Hillsboro, NJ: Erlbaum.

Baltes, P. B., & Staudinger, U. M. (1993). The search for a psychology of wisdom. *Current Directions in Psychological Science, 2,* 75–80.

Banaji, M. R., & Crowder, R. G. (1989). The bankruptcy of everyday memory. *American Psychologist, 44,* 1185–1193.

Bandura, A. (1977). *Social learning theory.* Englewood Cliffs, NJ: Prentice Hall.

Bandura, A. (1982a). Self-efficacy: Mechanism in human agency. *American Psychologist, 37,* 122–147.

Bandura, A. (1982b). The self and mechanisms of agency. In J. Suls (Ed.), *Psychological perspectives on the self* (Vol. 1, pp. 3–39). Hillsdale, NJ: Erlbaum.

Bandura, A. (1986). *Social foundations of thought and action: A social-cognitive theory.* Englewood Cliffs, NJ: Prentice Hall.

Bandura, A. (1989a). Human agency in social cognitive theory. *American Psychologist, 44,* 1175–1184.

Bandura, A. (1989b). Social cognitive theory. In R. Vasta (Ed.), *Six theories of child development: Revised formulations and current issues.* Greenwich, CT: JAI Press, Inc.

Bandura, A., Ross, D., & Ross, S. A. (1961). Transmission of aggression through imitation of aggressive models. *Journal of Abnormal and Social Psychology, 63,* 575–582.

Bandura, A. L. (1962). Social learning through imitation. In M. R. Jones (Ed.), *Nebraska Symposium on Motivation.* Lincoln: University of Nebraska Press.

Banks, M. S., & Salapatek, P. (1983). Infant visual perception. In P. H. Mussen (Ed.), *Handbook of child psychology* (Vol. 2). New York: Wiley.

Barclay, A., & Cusumano, D. C. (1967). Father absence, cross-sex identity, and field dependent behavior in male adolescents. *Child Development, 38,* 243–250.

Barenboim, C. (1981). The development of person perception in childhood and adolescence: From behavioral comparisons to psychological constructs to psychological comparisons. *Child Development, 52,* 129–144.

Barglow, P., Vaughn, B. E., & Molitor, N. (1987). Effects of maternal absence due to employment on the quality of infant-mother attachment in a low-risk sample. *Child Development, 58,* 945–954.

Bargones, J. Y., & Werner, L. A. (1994). Adults listen selectively; infants do not. *Psychological Science, 5,* 170–174.

Barnes, D. M. (1989). "Fragile X" syndrome and its puzzling genetics. *Science, 243,* 171–172.

Baron, R. A., & Paulhus, P. B. (1991). *Understanding human relations: A practical guide to people at work* (2nd ed.). Needham Heights, MA: Allyn & Bacon.

Barr, H. M., Streissguth, A. P., Darby, B. L., & Sampson, P. D. (1990). Prenatal exposure to alcohol, caffeine, tobacco, and aspirin: Effects on fine and gross motor performance in 4-year-old children. *Developmental Psychology, 26,* 339–348.

Bartholomew, K., & Horowitz, L. M. (1991). Attachment styles among young adults: A test of a four-category model. *Journal of Personality and Social Psychology, 61,* 226–244.

Bartlett, F. C. (1932). *Remembering.* Cambridge: Cambridge University Press.

Baruch, G. K., Barnett, R. C., & Rivers, C. (1983). *Lifeprints.* New York: McGraw-Hill.

Baskett, L. (1985). Sibling status effects: Adult expectations. *Developmental Psychology, 21,* 441–445.

Bates, E. (1976). *Language and context: The acquisition of pragmatics.* New York: Academic Press.

Bates, E., Bretherton, I., & Snyder, L. (1988). *From first words to grammar.* Cambridge, England: Cambridge University Press.

Batson, C. D., Batson, J. G., Griffith, C. A., Barrientos, S., Brandt, J. R., Sprengelmeyer, P., & Bayly, M. J. (1989). Negative-state relief and the empathy-altruism hypothesis. *Journal of Personality and Social Psychology, 56,* 922–933.

Baumrind, D. (1967). Child care practices anteceding three patterns of preschool behavior. *Genetic Psychology Monographs, 75,* 43–88.

Baumrind, D. (1971). Current patterns of parental authority. *Developmental Psychology Monographs, 1,* 1–103.

Baumrind, D. (1991). Effective parenting during early adolescent transitions. In P. A. Cowan & E. M. Hetherington (Eds.), *Family transitions* (pp. 111–164). Hillsdale, NJ: Erlbaum.

Bayley, N. (1969). *Bayley scales of infant development.* New York: Psychological Corporation.

Beall, A. E., & Sternberg, R. J. (1993). *The psychology of gender.* New York: The Guilford Press.

Bean, J. R., & Keller, L. (1994, July). *Psychosocial correlates of male and female self-esteem in college students: Is there a stable trait called "self-esteem?"* Paper presented at the Sixth Annual Convention of the American Psychological Society, Washington, DC.

Beasom, L. A., & Krauss, I. K. (1992, June). *Affect, helping behavior, and the Persian Gulf War.* Paper presented at the annual meeting of the American Psychological Society, San Diego, CA.

Beck, I. L., & McKeown, M. G. (1984). Application of theories of reading to instruction. *American Journal of Education, 93,* 61–81.

Becker, J. N. T. (1977). A learning analysis of the development of peer-orientation behavior in nine-month-old infants. *Developmental Psychology, 13,* 481–491.

Becker, W. C. (1964). Consequences of different kinds of parental discipline. In M. L. Hoffman & L. W. Hoffman (Eds.), *Review of child development research* (Vol. 1). New York: Sage.

Beckwith, L., & Parmelee, A. H. (1986). EEG patterns of preterm infants, home environment, and later IQ. *Child Development, 57,* 777–789.

Bédard, J., & Chi, M. T. H. (1992). Expertise. *Current Directions in Psychological Science, 1,* 135–139.

Bee, H., Barnard, K., Eyeres, S., Gray, C., Hammond, M., Speitz, A., Snyder, C., & Clark, B. (1982). Prediction of IQ and language skill from perinatal status, child performance, family characteristics, and mother-infant interaction. *Child Development, 53,* 1134–1156.

Begley, S., Carey, J., & Katz, S. (1984, March 5). The genetic counselors. *Newsweek,* p. 69.

Behrman, R. E., & Vaughan, V. C. (1983). *Pediatrics.* New York: Saunders.

Beilin, H. (1989). Piagetian theory. In R. Vasta (Ed.), *Six theories of child development: Revised formulations and current issues.* Greenwich, CT: JAI Press, Inc.

Beilin, H. (1992). Piaget's enduring contribution to developmental psychology. *Developmental Psychology, 28,* 191–204.

Bellugi, U. (1967). *The acquisition of language.* Unpublished doctoral dissertation, Harvard University.

Belsky, J. (1979). Mother-father-infant interaction: A naturalistic observational study. *Developmental Psychology, 15,* 601–607.

Belsky, J., & Rovine, M. (1988). Nonmaternal care in the first year of life and infant-parent attachment security. *Child Development, 57,* 1224–1231.

Bem, D. (1972). Self-perception theory. *Advances in Experimental Social Psychology, 6,* 1–62.

Bem, S. L. (1981). Gender schema theory: A cognitive account of sex typing. *Psychological Review, 88,* 354–364.

Bem, S. L. (1983). Gender schema theory and its implications for child development: Raising gender-aschematic children in a gender-schematic society. *Signs, 8,* 598–616.

Bem, S. L. (1985). Androgyny and gender schema theory: A conceptual and empirical integration. In R. Dienstbier & T. B. Sonderegger (Eds.), *Psychology and gender, Nebraska Symposium on Motivation* (Vol. 32, pp. 179–226). Lincoln: University of Nebraska Press.

Benbow, C. P. (1988). Sex differences in mathematical reasoning ability in intellectually talented preadolescents: Their nature, effects, and possible causes. *Behavioral and Brain Sciences, 11,* 169–232.

Benbow, C. P., & Stanley, J. C. (1980). Sex differences in mathematical ability: Fact or artifact? *Science, 210,* 1262–1264.

Benbow, C. P., & Stanley, J. C. (1983). Sex differences in mathematical reasoning: More facts. *Science, 222,* 1029–1031.

Benedict, H. (1979). Early lexical development: Comprehension and production. *Journal of Child Language, 6,* 183–200.

Bengtson, V. L. (1975). Generation and family effects in value socialization. *American Sociological Review, 40,* 358–371.

Benn, R. K. (1986). Factors promoting secure attachment relationships between employed mothers and their sons. *Child Development, 57,* 1224–1231.

Bennett, R. (1976). Attitudes of the young toward the old: A review of research. *Personnel and Guidance Journal, 55,* 136–139.

Benoliel, J. Q. (1988). Institutional dying: A convergence of cultural values, technology, and social organization. In H. Hannelore, F. M. Berardo, & R. A. Neimeyer (Eds.), *Dying: Facing the facts* (2nd ed.). Washington, DC: Hemisphere Publishing Corporation.

Berardo, D. H. (1988). Bereavement and mourning. In H. Hannelore, F. M. Berardo, & R. A. Neimeyer (Eds.), *Dying: Facing the facts* (2nd ed.). Washington, DC: Hemisphere Publishing Corporation.

Berg, J. H. (1984). Development of friendship between roommates. *Journal of Personality and Social Psychology, 46,* 346–356.

Berko Gleason, J. B. (1985). *The development of language.* Columbus, OH: Merrill.

Berman, P. W. (1980). Are women more responsive than men to the young? A review of developmental and situational variables. *Psychological Bulletin, 12,* 365–695.

Bernard, M. (1979). Does sex-role behavior influence the way teachers evaluate students? *Journal of Educational Psychology, 71,* 553–562.

Berndt, T. (1979). Developmental changes in conformity to peers and parents. *Developmental Psychology, 15,* 608–616.

Bernstein, B. E. (1977, Fall). Lawyer and therapist as an interdisciplinary team: Interfacing for the terminally ill. *Death Education, 1,* 277–291.

Berscheid, E., & Walster, E. H. (1978). *Interpersonal attraction* (2nd ed.). Reading, MA: Addison-Wesley.

Bertenthal, B. I., & Fischer, K. W. (1978). Development of self-recognition in the infant. *Developmental Psychology, 14,* 44–50.

Berzonsky, M. D. (1978). Ausubel's satellization theory: Applications to some research on adolescents. *Adolescence, 13,* 167–180.

Berzonsky, M. D. (1981). *Adolescent development.* New York: Macmillan.

Bettelheim, B. (1987). *A good enough parent.* New York: Knopf.

Bhatt, R. S., Rovee-Collier, C., & Weiner, S. (1994). Developmental changes in the interface between perception and memory retrieval. *Developmental Psychology, 30,* 151–162.

Bigelow, B. J., & LaGaipan, J. J. (1975). Children's written descriptions of friendship: A multidimensional analysis. *Developmental Psychology, 11,* 857–858.

Bijou, S. W. (1989). Behavior analysis. In R. Vista (Ed.), *Six theories of child development: Revised formulations and current issues.* Greenwich, CT: Jai Press, Inc.

Bjorksten, J. (1974). Cross-linkage and the aging process. In M. Rockstein, M. L. Sussman, & J. Chesky (Eds.), *Theoretical aspects of aging.* New York: Academic Press.

Blackburn, S. T., & Loper, D. L. (1992). *Maternal, fetal, and neonatal physiology: A clinical perspective.* Philadelphia: W. B. Saunders.

Blair, S. N., Kohl, H. W., Paffenbarger, R. S., Clark, D. G., Cooper, K. H., & Gibbons, L. W. (1989). Physical fitness and all-cause mortality. *New England Journal of Medicine, 262,* 2395–2401.

Blake, C., & Cohen, H. (1985, May). A meta-analysis of sex differences in moral development. *Resources in Education,* Document ED251749, Quebec, Canada.

Blasi, A. (1980). Bridging moral cognition and moral action: A critical review of literature. *Psychological Bulletin, 88,* 1–45.

Blaske, D. M. (1984). Occupational sex typing by kindergarten and fourth grade children. *Psychological Reports, 54,* 795–801.

Bleier, R. (1984). *Science and gender.* New York: Pergamon.

Block, J. H. (1973). Conceptions of sex role: Some cross-cultural and longitudinal perspectives. *American Psychologist, 28,* 512–536.

Block, J. H. (1976). Issues, problems, and pitfalls in assessing sex differences: A critical review of "The psychology of sex differences." *Merrill-Palmer Quarterly, 22,* 283–308.

Block, J. H. (1977). Advancing the psychology of personality: Paradigmatic shift or improving the quality of research. In D. Magnusson & N. S. Endler (Eds.), *Personality at the crossroads: Current issues in interactional psychology* (pp. 37–63). Hillsdale, NJ: Erlbaum.

Block, J. H. (1978). Another look at sex differentiation in the socialization of mothers and fathers. In J. Sherman & F. L. Denmark (Eds.), *Psychology of women: Future directions of research* (pp. 29–87). New York: Psychological Dimensions.

Block, J. H. (1983). Differential premises arising from differential socialization of the sexes: Some conjectures. *Child Development, 54,* 1335–1354.

Bloom, A. D. (1987). *The closing of the American mind.* New York: Simon & Schuster.

Bloom, B. S. (1964). *Stability and change in human characteristics.* New York: Wiley.

Bloom, B. S. (Ed.). (1985). *Developing talent in young people.* New York: Ballantine.

Bloom, F. E., Lazerson, A., & Hofstadter, L. (1985). *Brain, mind, and behavior.* New York: W. H. Freeman.

Bloom, L. (1970). *Language development: Form and function in emerging grammar.* Cambridge, MA: MIT Press.

Bloom, L. (1973). *One word at a time: The use of single-word utterances before syntax.* The Hague, The Netherlands: Mouton.

Bloom, L. (1976). *An interactive perspective on language development.* Keynote address, Child Language Research Forum, Stanford University.

Bloom, M. (1984). *Configurations of human behavior: Life span development in social environments.* New York: Macmillan.

Bloomfield, L. (1933). *Language.* New York: Holt.

Bluebond-Langner, M. (1978). *The private world of dying children.* Princeton, NJ: Princeton University Press.

Boggiano, A. K., & Ruble, D. N. (1981). *Self-perception vs. cued expectancy: Analyses of the effects of reward on task interest.* Paper presented at the American Psychological Convention.

Bohannon, J., & Marquis, A. (1977). Children's control of adult speech. *Child Development, 48,* 1002–1008.

Bohannon, J. N., & Stanowicz, L. (1988). The issue of negative evidence: Adult responses to children's language errors. *Developmental Psychology, 24,* 684–689.

Bolton, F. (1980). *The pregnant adolescent: Problems of premature parenthood.* Beverly Hills: Sage.

Bondareff, W. (1985). The neural basis of aging. In J. E. Birren & K. W. Schaie (Eds.), *Handbook of the psychology of aging* (2nd ed.). New York: Van Nostrand Reinhold.

Boneau, A. (1994). Psychology's world views: General approaches to understanding human behavior. *The General Psychologist, 30,* 12–30.

Bornstein, M. H. (1985). How infant and mother jointly contribute to developing cognitive competence in the child. *Proceedings of the National Academy of Sciences of the U.S.A., 82,* 7470–7473.

Bornstein, P. E., Clayton, P. J., Halikas, J. A., Maurice, W. L., & Robins, E. (1973). The depression of widowhood after thirteen months. *British Journal of Psychiatry, 122,* 561–566.

Borod, J., Goodglass, H., & Kaplan, E. (1980). Normative data on the Boston diagnostic aphasia examination, parietal lobe battery, and the Boston Naming Test. *Journal of Clinical Neuropsychology, 2,* 209–215.

Borys, S., & Perlman, D. (1985). Gender differences in loneliness. *Personality and Social Psychology Bulletin, 11,* 63–74.

Botwinick, J. (1978). *Cognitive processes in maturity and old age* (2nd ed.). New York: Springer-Verlag.

Botwinick, J. (1984). *Cognitive processes in maturity and old age* (3rd ed.). New York: Springer-Verlag.

Botwinick, J., & Siegler, I. C. (1980). Intellectual ability among the elderly: Simultaneous cross-sectional and longitudinal comparisons. *Developmental Psychology, 16,* 49–53.

Botwinick, J., & Storandt, M. (1974a). *Memory, related functions, and age.* Springfield, IL: Charles C. Thomas.

Botwinick, J., & Storandt, M. (1974b). Vocabulary ability in later life. *Journal of Genetic Psychology, 125,* 303–308.

Bouchard, T. J. (1983). Do environmental similarities explain the similarity in intelligence of identical twins reared apart? *Intelligence, 7,* 175–184.

Bouchard, T. J., & McGue, M. (1981). Familial studies of intelligence: A review. *Science, 250,* 223–238.

Bouchard, T. J., Jr., Lykken, D. T., McGue, M., Segal, N. L., & Tellegen, A. (1990). Sources of human psychological differences: The Minnesota study of twins reared apart. *Science, 250,* 223–228.

Bouchard, T. T., Lykken, D. T., Segal, N. L., & Wilcox, K. J. (1986). Development in twins reared apart: A test of the chronogenetic hypothesis. In A. Demirijian (Ed.), *Human growth: A multidiciplinary review* (pp. 299–310). London: Taylor & Francis.

Bouton, M. E. (1994). Context, ambiguity, and classical conditioning. *Current Directions in Psychological Science, 3,* 49–53.

Bower, B. (1992, February 29). Reading the code, reading the whole: Researchers wrangle over the nature and teaching of reading. *Science News, 42,* 138–140.

Bower, B. (1994, October 8). Images of the intellect: Brain scans may colorize intelligence. *Science News, 46,* 236–237.

Bower, G. H. (1981). Mood and memory. *American Psychologist, 36,* 129–149.

Bower, G. H., & Mayer, J. D. (1989). In search of mood-dependent retrieval. *Journal of Personality and Social Psychology, 4,* 121–156.

Bower, T. G. R. (1982). *Development in infancy.* San Francisco, CA: W. H. Freeman.

Bowlby, J. (1951). *Maternal care and mental health.* Geneva: WHO.

Bowlby, J. (1958). Psychoanalysis and child care. In J. D. Sutherland (Ed.), *Psychoanalysis and contemporary theory.* London: Hogarth.

Bowlby, J. (1966). *Maternal care and mental health.* New York: Schocken.

Bowlby, J. (1969). *Attachment and loss: Vol. 1. Attachment.* New York: Basic Books.

Bowlby, J. (1973). *Attachment and loss: Vol. 2. Separation: Anxiety and anger.* New York: Basic Books.

Bowlby, J. (1980). *Attachment and loss: Vol. 3. Loss.* New York: Basic Books.

Bowlby, J. (1992). *Charles Darwin: A new life.* New York: Norton.

Bowles, N. L., & Poon, L. W. (1985). Aging and the retrieval of words in semantic memory. *Journal of Gerontology, 40,* 71–77.

Boxer, M. E., Barron, K. L., & Farrar, M. J. (1994, April). *Three-year-olds remember a novel event: Evidence for memory one to two years later?* Paper presented at the Conference on Human Development, Pittsburgh, PA.

Boyer, M. E., Barron, K. L., & Farrar, M. J. (1994, April). *Three-year-olds remember a novel event: Evidence for memory one to two years later?* Paper presented at the Conference on Human Development, Pittsburgh, PA.

Bradburn, W., & Caplovitz, D. (1965). *Reports on happiness.* Chicago: Aldine.

Bradbury, T. N., & Fincham, F. D. (1988). Individual differences in close relationships: A contextual model of marriage as an integrative framework. *Journal of Personality and Social Psychology, 54,* 713–721.

Bradbury, T. N., & Fincham, F. D. (1992). Attributions and behavior in marital interaction. *Journal of Personality and Social Psychology, 63,* 613–628.

Bradely, R. H., & Caldwell, B. M. (1980). The relation of home environment to cognitive competence and IQ among males and females. *Child Development, 51,* 1140–1148.

Brainerd, C. J. (1978). The stage question in cognitive-developmental theory. *Behavioral and Brain Sciences, 2,* 173–213.

Bransford, J., & Johnson, M. (1972). Contextual prerequisites for understanding some investigations of comprehension and recall. *Journal of Verbal Learning and Verbal Behavior, 11,* 717–726.

Braungert, J. M., Plomin, R., DeFries, J. C., & Fulker, D. W. (1992). Genetic influence on tester-rated infant temperament as assessed by Bayley's Infant Behavior Record: Nonadoptive and adoptive siblings and twins. *Developmental Psychology, 28,* 40–47.

Bray, N. W., Saarino, D. A., & Hawk, L. W. (1994). Context for understanding intellectual and developmental differences in strategy competencies. *American Journal of Mental Retardation, 99,* 44–49.

Brazelton, T. B. (1973). *Neonatal behavioral assessment scale.* London: Heinemann Medical Books.

Brazelton, T. B. (1976). Early parent-infant reciprocity. In V. C. Vaughn III & T. B. Brazelton (Eds.), *The family—can it be spared?* Chicago: Year Book Medical Publishers, Inc.

Brazelton, T. B. (1984). *Neonatal behavioral assessment scale* (2nd ed.). Philadelphia: Lippincott.

Brazelton, T. B. (1986). Infant day care: Issues for working parents. *American Journal of Orthopsychiatry, 56,* 14–25.

Brazelton, T. B. (1987, August). *Opportunities for intervention with infants at risk.* Paper presented at the meeting of the American Psychological Association, New York City.

Brazelton, T. B. (1988, November). *Family stresses and emotional issues of parents during NICU hospitalization.* Paper presented at Developmental Interventions in Neonatal Care Conference, San Diego, CA.

Brazelton, T. B., & Als, H. (1979). Four early stages in the development of mother-infant interaction. *Psychoanalytic Study of the Child, 34,* 349–369.

Brazelton, T. B., Nugent, J. K., & Lester, B. M. (1987). Neonatal behavioral assessment scale. In J. D. Osofsky (Ed.), *Handbook of infant development* (2nd ed.). New York: Wiley.

Brecher, E. (1974). *Love, sex, & aging.* Boston: Little, Brown.

Breitmayer, B. J., & Ramey, C. T. (1986). Biological nonoptimality and quality of postnatal environments as codeterminants of intellectual development. *Child Development, 57,* 1151–1165.

Bretherton, I. (1985). Attachment theory: Retrospect and prospect. In I. Bretherton & E. Waters (Eds.), Growing points of attachment theory and research. *Monographs of the Society for Research in Child Development, 50* (Serial No. 209).

Bretschneider, J. G., & McCoy, N. L. (1988). Sexual interest and behavior in healthy 80- to 102-year-olds. *Archives of Sexual Behavior, 17,* 109–129.

Brewster, H. H. (1950). Grief: A disrupted human relationship. *Human Organization, 9,* 19–22.

Brim, O. G., Jr., & Kagan, J. (Eds.). (1980). *Constancy and change in human development.* Cambridge, MA: Harvard University Press.

Brockner, J., & Hulton, A. J. B. (1978). How to reverse the vicious cycle of low self-esteem: The importance of attentional focus. *Journal of Experimental Social Psychology, 14,* 564–578.
Brodt, S. E., & Zimbardo, P. G. (1981). Modifying shyness-related social behavior through symptom misattribution. *Journal of Personality and Social Psychology, 41,* 437–449.
Brody, G. H., & Schaffer, D. R. (1982). Contributions of parents and peers to children's moral socialization. *Developmental Review, 2,* 31–75.
Brody, N. (1994). .5 + or – .5: Continuity and change in personal dispositions. In T. F. Heatherton & J. L. Weinberger (Eds.), *Can personality change?* (pp. 59–77). Washington, DC: American Psychological Association.
Bronfenbrenner, U. (1975). Nature with nurture: A reinterpretation of the evidence. In A. A. Montague (Ed.), *Race and IQ* (pp. 114–144). New York: Oxford University Press.
Bronfenbrenner, U. (1979). *The ecology of human development.* Cambridge, MA: Harvard University Press.
Bronfenbrenner, U. (1986). Ecology of the family as a context for human development: Research perspectives. *Developmental Psychology, 22,* 723–742.
Bronfenbrenner, U. (1989). Ecological systems theory. In R. Vasta (Ed.), *Six theories of child development: Revised formulations and current issues.* Greenwich, CT: JAI Press.
Bronfenbrenner, U. (1993). The ecology of cognitive development: Research models and fugitive findings. In R. H. Wozniak & K. Fischer (Eds.), *Thinking in context* (pp. 3–24). Hillsdale, NJ: Erlbaum.
Bronfenbrenner, U., Kessel, F., & White, S. (1986). Toward a critical social history of developmental psychology: A propaedeutic discussion. *American Psychologist, 41,* 1218–1230.
Brooks, C. I. (1987). Superiority of women in statistics achievement. *Teaching of Psychology, 14,* 45.
Brooks-Gunn, J., & Lewis, M. (1982). The development of self-knowledge. In C. B. Kopp & J. B. Krakow (Eds.), *The child: Development in a social context.* Reading, MA: Addison-Wesley.
Broughton, J. (1978). Development of concepts of self, mind, reality, and knowledge. *New Directions for Child Development, 1,* 75–100.
Broughton, J. M. (1984). Not beyond formal operations but beyond Piaget. In M. L. Commons, F. A. Richards, & C. Armon (Eds.), *Beyond formal operations: Late adolescent and adult cognitive development* (pp. 395–411). New York: Praeger.
Broverman, I. K., Vogel, S. R., Broverman, D. M., Clarkson, F. E., & Rosenkrantz, P. S. (1972). Sex-role stereotypes: A current appraisal. *Journal of Social Issues, 28,* 59–78.
Brown, A. L., Armbruster, B., & Baker, L. (1986). The role of metacognition in reading and studying. In J. Orasanu (Ed.), *Reading comprehension: From research to practice.* Hillsdale, NJ: Erlbaum.
Brown, A. L., & Scott, M. S. (1971). Recognition memory for pictures in preschool children. *Journal of Experimental Child Psychology, 11,* 401–412.
Brown, J., & Jaffe, J. (1975). Hypothesis on cerebral dominance. *Neuropsychologia, 13,* 107–110.
Brown, L. N., & Gilligan, C. (1992). *Meeting at the crossroads.* Cambridge, MA: Harvard University Press.
Brown, R. (1973). *A first language: The early stages.* Cambridge, MA: Harvard University Press.
Brown, R. (1986). *Social psychology* (2nd ed.). New York: Free Press.
Brown, R. W. (1965). *Social psychology.* New York: Free Press.
Bryan, J. H., & Walbeck, N. H. (1970). Preaching and practicing generosity: Children's actions and reactions. *Child Development, 41,* 329–353.
Buckley, K. W. (1982). The selling of a psychologist: John Broadus Watson and the application of behavioral techniques to advertising. *Journal of the History of the Behavioral Sciences, 18,* 207–221.
Buckmaster, L., & Brownell, K. D. (1988). The social and psychological world of the obese child. In V. A. Krasnagor, G. D. Grave, & N. Kretchmer (Eds.), *Childhood obesity: A biobehavioral perspective* (pp. 9–28). Caldwell, NJ: Telford Press.
Bugen, L. A. (1977). Human grief: A model for prediction and intervention. *American Journal of Orthopsychiatry, 47,* 196–206.
Buhler, C., & Allen, M. (1972). *Introduction to humanistic psychology.* Pacific Grove, CA: Brooks/Cole.
Buhrmester, D., & Furman, W. (1987). The development of companionship and intimacy. *Child Development, 58,* 1101–1113.
Bulcroft, K., & O'Conner-Roden, M. (1986, June). Never too late. *Psychology Today,* pp. 66–69.
Bullinger, A., & Chatillon, J. (1983). Recent theory and research of the Genevan school. In P. H. Mussen (Ed.), *Handbook of child psychology* (Vol. 3). New York: Wiley.
Burke, D. M., MacKay, D. G., Worthley, J., & Wade, E. (1991). On the tip of the tongue: What causes word finding failures in young and older adults? *Journal of Memory and Language, 30,* 542–579.
Burke, D. M., White, H., & Diaz, D. L. (1987). Semantic priming in young and older adults: Evidence for age constancy in automatic and attentional processes. *Journal of Experimental Psychology: Human Perception and Performance, 13,* 79–88.
Burling, R. (1986). The selective advantage of complex language. *Ethology and Sociobiology, 7,* 1–16.
Burns, B., Schlewit, L., & Terrell, T. (1994, April). *Attention and meta-attention in reflective and impulsive children.* Paper presented at the Conference on Human Development, Pittsburgh, PA.
Burton, L. (1990). Teenage childrearing as an alternative life-course strategy in multigenerational Black families. *Human Nature, 1,* 123–143.
Buss, D. M. (1988). The evolution of human intrasexual competition: Tactics of mate attraction. *Journal of Personality and Social Psychology, 54,* 616–628.
Buss, D. M. (1991). Evolutionary personality psychology. *Annual Reviews of Psychology, 42,* 459–491.
Buss, D. M. (1992, August). *Sociobiology.* Paper presented at the 100th Annual Convention of the American Psychological Association, Washington, DC.
Buss, D. M. (1994). Personality evoked: The evolutionary psychology of stability and change. In T. F. Heatherton & J. L. Weinberger (Eds.), *Can personality change?* Washington, DC: American Psychological Association.
Butter, I. (1993). Premature adoption and routinization of medical technology: Illustrations from childbirth technology. *Journal of Social Issues, 49,* 11–34.
Byer, C. O., & Shainberg, L. W. (1991). *Dimensions of human sexuality* (3rd ed.). Dubuque, IA: Wm. C. Brown.
Byrne, D. (1971). *The attraction paradigm.* New York: Academic Press.
Byrne, D., & Fisher, W. A. (1983). *Adolescents, sex, and contraception.* Hillsdale, NJ: Erlbaum.

C

Caldwell, M. A., & Peplau, L. A. (1982). Sex differences in same-sex friendship. *Sex Roles, 8,* 721–732.

Campbell, F. A., & Ramey, C. T. (1994). Effects of early intervention on intellectual and academic achievement: A follow-up study of children from low-income families. *Child Development, 65,* 684–698.

Campos, J., Hiatt, S., Ramsey, D., Henderson, C., & Svejda, M. (1978). The emergence of fear on the visual cliff. In M. Lewis & L. Rosenblum (Eds.), *Infancy and developmental psychobiology.* New York: Wiley.

Caplan, F. (Ed.). (1973). *The first twelve months of life.* Princeton Center for Infancy and Early Childhood, Princeton, NJ.

Caplan, P. J., MacPherson, G. M., & Tobin, P. (1985). Do sex-related differences in spatial abilities exist? A multilevel critique with new data. *American Psychologist, 40,* 786–799.

Caporael, L. (1981). The paralanguage of caregiving: Baby talk to the institutionalized aged. *Journal of Personality and Social Psychology, 40,* 876–884.

Caporael, L. R., & Culbertson, G. H. (1986). Verbal response modes of baby talk and other speech institutions for the aged. *Language and Communication, 6,* 99–112.

Caporael, L. R., Lucasazewski, M. P., & Culbertson, G. H. (1983). Secondary babytalk: Judgments of institutionalized elderly and their caregivers. *Journal of Personality and Social Psychology, 44,* 746–754.

Carey, S., & Bartlett, E. (1978). *Acquiring a single new word.* (Papers and reports on child language development, Vol. 15, pp. 17–29). Stanford, CA: Stanford University, Department of Linguistics.

Carroll, J. C., & Rest, J. R. (1982). Moral development. In B. B. Wolman et al. (Eds.), *Handbook of developmental psychology.* Englewood Cliffs, NJ: Prentice Hall.

Carver, C. S., & Scheier, M. F. (1981). *Attention and self-regulation: A control-theory approach to human behavior.* New York: Springer-Verlag.

Case, R. (1972). Learning and development: A neo-Piagetian interpretation. *Human Development, 15,* 339–358.

Case, R. (1985). *Intellectual development: Birth to adulthood.* New York: Academic Press.

Case, R., Kurland, D. M., & Goldberg, J. (1982). Operational efficiency and the growth of short-term memory span. *Journal of Experimental Child Psychology, 33,* 386–404.

Cash, T. F., & Derlega, V. J. (1978). The matching hypothesis: Physical attractiveness among same-sexed friends. *Personality and Social Psychology Bulletin, 4,* 240–243.

Caspi, A., & Herbener, E. (1990). Continuity and change: Assortative marriage and the consistency of personality in adulthood. *Journal of Personality and Social Psychology, 58,* 250–258.

Casserly, P. (1979). Helping able young women take math and science seriously in school. In N. Colangelo & R. Zaffrann (Eds.), *New voices in counseling the gifted* (pp. 346–369). Dubuque, IA: Kendall Hunt.

Cassidy, J. (1986). The ability to negotiate the environment: An aspect of infant competence as related to quality of attachment. *Child Development, 57,* 331–337.

Catalyst. (1987). *New roles for men and women: A report on an educational intervention with college students.* New York: Author.

Cavanaugh, J. C., Grady, J. G., & Perlmutter, M. (1983). Forgetting and use of memory aid in 20 to 70 year olds' everyday life. *International Journal of Aging and Human Development, 17,* 113–122.

Ceci, S. J. (1994, May). *Children's testimony: How reliable is it?* Invited address given at the annual meeting of the Midwestern Psychological Association, Chicago, IL.

Cerella, J., & Fozard, J. L. (1984). Lexical access and age. *Developmental Psychology, 20,* 235–243.

Chafetz, J. S. (1974). *Masculine/feminine or human? An overview of the sociology of sex roles.* Itasca, IL: F. E. Peacock.

Chaiken, A. L., & Derlega, V. J. (1974a). Liking for the norm breaker in self-disclosure. *Journal of Personality, 42,* 117–129.

Chaiken, A. L., & Derlega, V. J. (1974b). Variables affecting the appropriateness of self-disclosure. *Journal of Consulting and Clinical Psychology, 42,* 588–593.

Chall, J. (1967). *Learning to read: The great debate.* New York: McGraw-Hill.

Chall, J. S. (1983). *Stages of reading development.* New York: McGraw-Hill.

Chance, P. (1987, April). Master of mastery. *Psychology Today,* pp. 43–46.

Chapman, M. (1988). *Constructive evolution: Origins and development of Piaget's thought.* Cambridge, England: Cambridge University Press.

Chasnoff, I. J., Griffith, D. R., MacGregor, S., Dirkes, K., & Burns, K. A. (1989, March 24/31). Temporal patterns of cocaine use in pregnancy. *Journal of the American Medical Association, 261,* 1741–1744.

Cherlin, A., & Furstberg, F. F., Jr. (1986). *The new American grandparent: A place in the family, a life apart.* New York: Basic Books.

Chess, S., & Thomas, A. (1984). *Origins and evolution of behavior disorders: From infancy to early adult life.* New York: Brunner/Mazel.

Chi, M. T. H. (1978). Knowledge structures and memory development. In R. S. Siegler (Ed.), *Children's thinking: What develops?* (pp. 73–96). Hillsdale, NJ: Erlbaum.

Chiesi, H. L., Spilich, G. J., & Voss, J. F. (1979). Acquisition of domain-related information in relation to high and low domain knowledge. *Journal of Verbal Learning and Verbal Behavior, 18,* 257–273.

Childers, P., & Wimmer, M. (1971). The concept of death in early childhood. *Child Development, 42,* 1299–1301.

Chilman, C. (1978). *Adolescent sexuality in a changing American society: Social and psychological perspectives.* Washington, DC: U.S. Government Printing Office.

Chomsky, N. (1957). *Syntatic structures.* The Hague: Mouton.

Chomsky, N. (1959). Review of Skinner's *Verbal behavior. Language, 3,* 25–58.

Chomsky, N. (1968). *Language and mind.* New York: Harcourt Brace & World.

Chomsky, N. (1972). *Language and mind.* New York: Harcourt Brace Jovanovich.

Chomsky, N. (1975). *Reflections on language.* New York: Pantheon.

Chomsky, N. (1980). *Rules and representation.* New York: Columbia University Press.

Cialdini, R. (1984). *Influence.* New York: Quill.

Cialdini, R. (1993). *Influence: Science and practice* (3rd ed.). New York: HarperCollins.

Cicirelli, V. G. (1985). The role of siblings as family caregivers. In W. J. Saver & R. T. Coward (Eds.), *Social support networks and the care of the elderly* (pp. 93–107). New York: Springer.

Clark, E. V. (1978). Awareness of language: Some evidence from what children say and do. In A. Sinclair, R. Jarvella, & W. Levelt (Eds.), *The child's conception of language.* New York: Springer-Verlag.

Clark, H. H., & Clark, E. V. (1977). *Psychology and language: An introduction to psycholinguistics*. New York: Harcourt Brace Jovanovich.

Clark, R. (1993, August). *Length of maternity leave and quality of mother-infant interaction*. Paper presented at the 101st Annual Convention of the American Psychological Association, Toronto, Ontario, Canada.

Clarke, A. M., & Clarke, A. D. B. (1976). *Early experience: Myth and evidence*. New York: Free Press.

Clarke-Stewart, K. (1973). Interactions between mothers and their children: Characteristics and consequences. *Monographs of the Society for Research in Child Development, 38(6–7, Serial No. 153, 1–109)*.

Clarke-Stewart, K. A. (1978). And daddy makes three: The father's impact on mother and young child. *Child Development, 49*, 466–478.

Clarke-Stewart, K. A. (1989). Infant day care: Maligned or malignant? *American Psychologist, 44*, 266–273.

Clausen, J. A. (1975). The social meaning of differential physical and sexual maturation. In S. E. Elder (Ed.), *Adolescence in the life-cycle: Psychological change and social context* (pp. 25–47). Washington, DC: Hemisphere.

Clore, G. L., & Byrne, D. (1974). A reinforcement-affect model of attraction. In T. L. Huston (Ed.), *Foundations of interpersonal attraction*. New York: Academic Press.

Cobb, N. J., Stevens-Long, J., & Goldstein, S. (1982). The influence of televised models on toy preference in children. *Sex Roles, 8*, 1080–1087.

Cohen, D. (1983). *Piaget: Critique and reassessment*. New York: St. Martin's Press.

Cohen, L. J., & Campos, J. J. (1974). Father, mother, and stranger as elicitors of attachment behaviors in infancy. *Developmental Psychology, 10*, 146–154.

Cohen, S. (1980, November 15). She turned grief into help for others. *Los Angeles Times*, p. IA-4.

Cohen, S. E., & Parmelee, A. H. (1983). Prediction of five-year Stanford-Binet scores in preterm infants. *Child Development, 54*, 1242–1253.

Cohn, N. B., & Strassberg, D. S. (1983). Self-disclosure among preadolescents. *Personality and Social Psychology Bulletin, 9*, 97–102.

Colby, A., & Kohlberg, L. (1984). Invariant sequence and internal consistency in moral judgment stages. In W. M. Kurtines & J. L. Gewirtz (Eds.), *Morality, moral behavior and moral development*. New York: Wiley.

Colby, A., Kohlberg, L., Gibbs, J., & Lieberman, M. (1983). A longitudinal study of moral judgment. *Monographs of the Society for Research in Child Development, 48*(Serial No. 200).

Cole, M., & Scribner, S. (1974). *Culture and thought*. New York: Wiley.

Coleman, J. C. (1980). Friendship and the peer group in adolescence. In J. Adelson (Ed.), *The handbook of adolescent psychology*. New York: Wiley.

Coleman, P. D. (1986, August). *Regulation of dendritic extent: Human aging brain and Alzheimer's disease*. Paper presented at the 94th annual meeting of the American Psychological Association, Washington, DC.

Collins, N. L., & Read, S. J. (1990). Adult attachment, working models, and relationship quality in dating couples. *Journal of Personality and Social Psychology, 58*, 644–663.

Commons, M. L., Richards, F. A., & Kuhn, D. (1982). Systematic and metasystematic reasoning: A case for levels of reasoning beyond Piaget's stage of formal operations. *Child Development, 53*, 1058–1069.

Condry, J. C. (1984). Gender identity and social competence. *Sex Roles, 11*, 485–511.

Condry, J. C., & Condry, S. (1976). Sex differences: A study in the eye of the beholder. *Child Development, 47*, 812–819.

Conger, J. J. (1988, August). *Hostages to fortune: Youth, values, and the public interest*. Invited address presented at the annual meeting of the American Psychological Association, New York.

Connelly, S. L., & Hasher, L. (1993). Aging and the inhibition of spatial location. *Journal of Experimental Psychology, Human Perception and Performance, 19*, 1238–1250.

Conrad, R. (1972). Cognitive economy in semantic memory. *Journal of Experimental Psychology, 92*, 149–154.

Cook, G. L., & Odom, R. D. (1992). Perception of multidimensional stimuli: A differential-sensitivity account of cognitive processing and development. *Journal of Experimental Child Psychology, 54*, 213–249.

Cook, K. (1987, June 9). Cancer legacy: Risks for DES granddaughters. *USA Today*, p. 1D.

Cooke, B. (1991). Thinking and knowledge underlying expertise in parenting: Comparisons between expert and novice mothers. *Family Relations, 40*, 3–13.

Cooley, C. H. (1902). *Human nature and the social order*. New York: Scribner's.

Coopersmith, S. (1967). *The antecedents of self-esteem*. San Francisco: W. H. Freeman.

Corballis, M. C. (1983). *Human laterality*. New York: Academic Press.

Cornell, T. L., Fromkin, V. A., & Mauner, G. (1993). A linguistic approach to language processing in Broca's aphasia: A paradox resolved. *Current Directions in Psychological Science, 2*, 47–52.

Corso, J. F. (1977). Presbycusis, hearing aids and aging. *Audiology, 16*, 146–163.

Corso, J. F. (1981). *Aging sensory systems and perceptions*. New York: Praeger.

Costa, P., & McCrae, R. (1980). Still stable after all these years: Personality as a key to some issues in adulthood and old age? In P. B. Baltes & O. Brim, Jr. (Eds.), *Life-span development and behavior*. New York: Academic Press.

Costa, P., & McCrae, R. (1990). *Personality in adulthood*. New York: Guilford Press.

Costa, P. T., Jr., & McCrae, R. R. (1988). Personality in adulthood: A six-year longitudinal study of self-reports and spouse ratings on the NEO Personality Inventory. *Journal of Personality and Social Psychology, 54*, 853–863.

Costa, P. T., & McCrae, R. R. (1994). Set like plaster? Evidence for the stability of adult personality. In T. F. Heatherton & J. L. Weinberger (Eds.), *Can personality change?* Washington, DC: American Psychological Association.

Cotterell, N., Eisenberger, R., & Speicher, H. (1992). Inhibiting effects of reciprocation wariness on interpersonal relationships. *Journal of Personality and Social Psychology, 62*, 658–668.

Cottrell, N. B., & Epley, S. W. (1977). Affiliation, social comparison, and socially mediated stress reduction. In J. Suls & R. L. Miller (Eds.), *Social comparison processes*. Washington, DC: Hemisphere/Halsted.

Coupland, N., & Coupland, J. (1990). Language and later life: The diachrony and decrement predicament. In H. Giles & P. Robinson (Eds.), *Handbook of language and social psychology*. London: Wiley.

Cowan, C. P., Cowan, P. A., Heming, G., Garret, E., Coysh, W. S., Curtis-Boles, H., & Boles, A. J. (1985). Transitions to parenthood: His, hers, and theirs. *Journal of Family Issues, 6*, 451–481.

Cowan, M. W. (1979). The development of the brain. *Scientific American, 241,* 112–133.

Cowan, N., Wood, N. L., & Borne, D. N. (1994). Reconfirmation of the short-term storage concept. *Psychological Science, 5,* 103–106.

Cox, M. J., Owen, M. T., Henderson, V. K., & Margand, N. A. (1992). Prediction of infant-father and infant-mother attachment. *Developmental Psychology, 28,* 474–483.

Cozby, P. C. (1972). Self-disclosure and liking. *Sociometry, 35,* 151–160.

Craik, F. I. M. (1977). Age differences in human memory. In J. E. Birren & K. W. Schaie (Eds.), *Handbook of the psychology of aging.* New York: Van Nostrand Reinhold.

Craik, F. I. M., & Watkins, M. J. (1973). The role of rehearsal in short-term memory. *Journal of Verbal Learning and Verbal Behavior, 12,* 599–607.

Crain, W. C. (1992). *Theories of development: Concepts and applications* (2nd ed.). Englewood Cliffs, NJ: Prentice Hall.

Crandall, C. S. (1994). Prejudice against fat people: Ideology and self-interest. *Journal of Personality and Social Psychology, 66,* 882–894.

Crawford, D. W., & Huston, T. L. (1993). The impact of the transition to parenthood on marital leisure. *Personality and Social Psychology Bulletin, 19,* 39–46.

Crockenberg, S. B. (1987). Predictors and correlates of anger toward and punitive control of toddlers by adolescent mothers. *Child Development, 58,* 964–975.

Crocker, J., Kayne, N. T., & Alloy, L. B. (1985). Comparing the self with others in depressed and nondepressed college students: Reply to McCauley. *Journal of Personality and Social Psychology, 48,* 1579–1583.

Crocker, J., & Schwarz, I. (1985). Effects of self-esteem on prejudice and ingroup favoritism in a minimal intergroup situation. *Personality and Social Psychology Bulletin, 11*(4).

Cromer, R. F. (1974). The development of language and cognition. In B. M. Foss (Ed.), *New perspectives in child development.* Baltimore: Penguin.

Cromer, R. F. (1981). Reconceptualizing language acquisition and cognitive development. In R. L. Schiefelbusch & D. Bricker (Eds.), *Early language: Acquisition and intervention* (pp. 51–137). Baltimore, MD: University Park Press.

Crooks, T. H., III, & Larrabee, G. L. (1992). Changes in facial recognition memory across the adult life span. *Journal of Gerontology: Psychological Sciences, 47,* 138–141.

Cunningham, W. R., Clayton, V., & Overton, W. (1975). Fluid and crystallized intelligence in young adulthood and old age. *Journal of Gerontology, 30,* 53–55.

Cunningham, W. R., & Owens, W. A. (1983). The Iowa State Study of the adult development of intellectual abilities. In K. W. Schaie (Ed.), *Longitudinal studies of adult psychological development.* New York: Guilford Press.

Curcio, C. A., Buell, S. J., & Coleman, B. D. (1982). Morphology of the aging central nervous system: Not all downhill. In J. A. Mortimer, F. J. Pizzola, & G. L. Maletta (Eds.), *Advances in neurogerontology: The aging motor system.* New York: Praeger.

Curran, J. (1977). Convergence toward a single sexual standard? In D. Byrne & L. Byrne (Eds.), *Exploring human sexuality.* New York: Thomas Y. Crowell.

Curtiss, S. (1977). *Genie: A psycholinguistic study of a modern-day "wild child."* New York: Academic Press.

Cyrus, V. (1993). *Experiencing race, class, and gender in the United States.* Mountain View, CA: Mayfield.

D

Dabbs, J. (1994, August). *Aggression.* Paper presented at the 104th Annual Convention of the American Psychological Association, Los Angeles. Reported in *USA Today,* August 11, 1994 by Marilyn Elias.

Dale, P. S. (1976). *Language development: Structure and function* (2nd ed.). New York: Holt.

Damasio, A. R., & Damasio, H. (1992, September). Brain and language. *Scientific American, 267,* 88–95.

Damasio, A. R., & Geschwind, N. (1984). The neural basis of language. *Annual Review of Neuroscience, 7,* 127–147.

Damon, W. (1983). *Social and personality development.* New York: Norton.

Damon, W. (1984). Self-understanding and moral development from childhood to adolescence. In W. M. Kurtines & J. L. Gewirtz (Eds.), *Morality, moral behavior, and moral development.* New York: Wiley.

Damon, W. (1988). Self-understanding and moral development from childhood to adolescence. In J. Gewirtz & W. Kurtines (Eds.), *Morality, moral development, and moral behavior: Basic issues in theory and research.* New York: Wiley.

Damon, W., & Hart, D. (1982). The development of self-understanding from infancy through adolescence. *Child Development, 53,* 831–857.

Daniels, D., & Plomin, R. (1985). Origins of individual differences in infant shyness. *Developmental Psychology, 21,* 118–121.

Dasen, P., & Heron, A. (1981). Cross-cultural tests of Piaget's theory. In H. C. Triandis & A. Heron (Eds.), *Handbook of cross-cultural psychology: Vol. 4. Developmental psychology.* Boston: Allyn & Bacon.

Dasen, P. R. (Ed.), (1977). *Piagetian psychology: Cross-cultural contributions.* New York: Gardner.

Davis, K. E., & Todd, M. J. (1982). Friendship and love relationships. *Advances in Descriptive Psychology, 2,* 79–122.

Dawes, R. M. (1994). *House of cards: Psychology and psychotherapy built on myth.* New York: Free Press.

Deaux, K. (1978, May). *Sex-related patterns of social interaction.* Paper presented at the meeting of the Midwestern Psychological Association, Chicago.

Deaux, K. (1985). Sex and gender. *Annual Review of Psychology, 36,* 49–81.

Deaux, K., & Lewis, L. L. (1984). Structure of gender stereotypes: Interrelationships among components and gender label. *Journal of Personality and Social Psychology, 46,* 991–1004.

DeCasper, A. (1990, August). *Prenatal influences on newborn perception and learning.* Presented at the 98th Annual Convention of the American Psychological Association, Boston, MA.

DeCasper, A. J., & Spence, M. J. (1986). Prenatal maternal speech influences on newborn's perceptions of speech sounds. *Infant Behavior and Development, 9,* 133–150.

DeCasper, A. J., & Spence, M. J. (1991). Auditorily mediated behavior during the prenatal period: A cognitive view. In M. J. S. Weiss & P. R. Zelazo (Eds.), *Newborn attention: Biological constraints and the influences of experience.* Norwood, NJ: Ablex.

De Chateau, P., & Wilberg, B. (1977). Long-term effect on mother-infant behavior of extra contact duration at 36 hours. *Acta Paediatrica Scandinavia, 66,* 137–143.

Deem, R. (1978). *Women and schooling.* London: Routledge & Kegan Paul.

Delack, J. B. (1976). Aspects of infant speech development in the first year of life. *Canadian Journal of Linguistics, 21,* 17–37.

DeLisi, R., & Staudt, J. (1980). Individual differences in college student's performance on formal operational tasks. *Journal of Applied Developmental Psychology, 1,* 201–208.

Delk, J. L., Madden, R. B., Livingston, M., & Ryan, T. T. (1986). Adult perceptions of the infant as a function of gender labeling and observer gender. *Sex Roles, 15,* 527–534.

DeLoache, J. (1994, April). *Symbolic representation and reasoning.* Invited symposium. 13th biennial meeting of the Conference on Human Development, Pittsburgh, PA.

DeMarie-Dreblow, D., & Miller, P. H. (1988). The development of children's strategies for selective attention: Evidence for a transitional period. *Child Development, 59,* 1504–1513.

DeMaris, A., & Rao, K. V. (1992). Premarital co-habitation and subsequent marital stability in the United States: A reassessment. *Journal of Marriage and the Family, 54,* 178–190.

Dennis, W. (1940). The effect of cradling practices upon the onset of walking in Hopi children. *Journal of Genetic Psychology, 56,* 77–86.

Dennis, W. (1960). Causes of mental retardation among institutionalized children: Iran. *Journal of Genetic Psychology, 96,* 47–59.

Denton, K., & Krebs, D. (1990). From the scene to the crime: The effect of alcohol and social context on moral judgment. *Journal of Personality and Social Psychology, 59*(2), 242–248.

Derlega, V. J. (1984). Self-disclosure and intimate relationships. In V. J. Derlega (Ed.), *Communication, intimacy, and close relationships.* New York: Academic Press.

Derlega, V. J., & Grzelak, A. L. (1979). Appropriate self-disclosure. In G. J. Chelune (Ed.), *Self-disclosure: Origins, patterns, and implications of openness in interpersonal relationships.* San Francisco, CA: Jossey-Bass.

Derlega, V. J., Wilson, M., & Chaikin, A. L. (1976). Friendship and disclosure reciprocity. *Journal of Personality and Social Psychology, 34,* 578–582.

DeSpelder, L. A., & Strickland, A. L. (1983). *The last dance: Encountering death and dying.* Palo Alto, CA: Mayfield Publishing.

DeSpelder, L. A., & Strickland, A. L. (1992). *The last dance* (3rd ed.). Mountain View, CA: Mayfield.

Deutscher, I. (1969). From parental to post parental life. *Sociological Symposium, 3,* 47–60.

deVilliers, P. A., & deVilliers, J. G. (1972). Early judgments of semantic and syntactic acceptability by children. *Journal of Psycholinguistic Research, 1,* 299–310.

deVilliers, P. A., & deVilliers, J. G. (1979). *Early language.* Cambridge, MA: Harvard University Press.

deVilliers, P. A., & deVilliers, J. G. (1992). Language development. In M. E. Lamb & M. H. Bornstein (Eds.), *Developmental psychology: An advanced textbook* (3rd ed.). Hillsdale, NJ: Erlbaum.

Diamond, A. M. (1986). The life-cycle research productivity of mathematicians and scientists. *Journal of Gerontology, 41,* 520–525.

Diaz, R. M., & Berndt, T. J. (1982). Children's knowledge of a best friend: Fact or fancy? *Developmental Psychology, 18,* 787–794.

DiLalla, L. F., Thompson, L. A., Plomin, R., Phillips, K., Fagan, J. K., III, Haith, M. M., Cyphers, L. H., & Fulker, D. W. (1990). Infant predictors of preschool and adult IQ: A study of infant twins and their parents. *Developmental Psychology, 26,* 759–764.

DiPietro, J. A. (1981). Rough and tumble play: A function of gender. *Developmental Psychology, 17,* 50–58.

Ditkoff, G. S. (1979). Stereotypes of adolescents towards the working woman. *Adolescence, 14,* 277–282.

Dollard, J., & Miller, N. E. (1950). *Personality and psychotherapy.* New York: McGraw-Hill.

Donovan, P. (1992, July). Sex education in American schools: Progress and obstacles. *USA Today Magazine,* pp. 28–30.

Dorland, W. A. (1991). *Dorland's pocket medical dictionary* (26th ed.). Philadelphia: Saunders.

Dougherty, D. (1993). Major policy options from a report to Congress on adolescent health. 120th Annual Meeting of the American Public Health Association: Symposium on improving adolescent health: A time for action. *Journal of Adolescent Health, 14,* 499–504.

Douvan, E. (1979). Differing views on marriage 1957–1976. *Newsletter of the Center for Continuing Education of Women* (University of Wisconsin), *12,* 1–2.

Douvan, E., & Adelson, J. (1966). *The adolescent experience.* New York: Wiley.

Doyle, J. A., & Paludi, M. A. (1989). *Sex and gender: The human experience* (2nd ed.). Dubuque, IA: Wm. C. Brown.

Drachman, D. A. (1978). Central cholinergic system and memory. In M. A. Lipton, A. DiMascio, & K. F. Killam (Eds.), *Psychopharmacology: A generation of progress.* Englewood Cliffs, NJ: Prentice Hall.

Drigotas, S. M., & Rusbult, C. E. (1992). Should I stay or should I go? A dependency model of breakups. *Journal of Personality and Social Psychology, 62,* 62–87.

Dror, I. E., & Kosslyn, S. M. (1994). Mental imagery and aging. *Psychology and Aging, 9,* 90–102.

Dryfoos, J. G. (1985). A time for new thinking about teenage pregnancy. *American Journal of Public Health, 75,* 13–14.

Dubois, N. F. (1987, April). *Training students to be autonomous learners.* Paper presented at the annual meeting of the American Educational Research Association, Washington, DC.

Duffy, E. (1962). *Activation and behavior.* New York: Wiley.

Dunn, J., & Plomin, R. (1991). Why are siblings so different? The significance of differences in sibling experiences within the family. *Family Process, 30,* 271–283.

Dunn, W. (1990, May 8). Families grow to 2.0 kids. *USA Today,* p. 1D.

Dunn, W., & Henderson, J. (1987, September 14). Futurists take a look at the way we will be. *USA Today,* p. 6E.

Dutton, D. G., & Aron, A. P. (1974). Some evidence for heightened sexual attraction under conditions of high anxiety. *Journal of Personality and Social Psychology, 30,* 510–517.

Duvall, E. M. (1977). *Family development* (5th ed.). Philadelphia: Lippincott.

Duvall, E. M., & Hill, R. (1948). *Report of the committee on the dynamics of family interaction.* Prepared at the request of the National Conference on Family Life, Washington, DC.

Dweck, C. S. (1984). Attribution theory. In P. Mussen & M. Hetherington (Eds.), *Child development handbook* (pp. 210–285). New York: Wiley.

Dweck, C. S. (1986). Motivational processes affecting learning. *American Psychologist, 41,* 1040–1048.

Dworetzky, T. (1987, March). Opening new frontiers in molecular biology. *Discover,* pp. 14–15.

E

Eagly, A. H. (1987). *Sex differences in social behavior: A social-role interpretation.* Hillsdale, NJ: Erlbaum.

Eagly, A. H., & Crowley, M. (1986). Gender and helping behavior: A meta-analytic review of the social psychological literature. *Psychological Bulletin, 100,* 203–220.

Eagly, A. H., & Steffen, V. J. (1986). Gender and aggressive behavior: A meta-analytic review of the social psychological literature. *Psychological Bulletin, 100,* 309–330.

Edwards, C. P. (1981). The comparative study of the development of moral judgment and reasoning. In R. H. Munroe, R. L. Munroe, & B. B. Whiting (Eds.), *Handbook of cross-cultural human development.* New York: Garland Press.

Edwards, C. P. (1982). Moral development in comparative cultural perspective. In D. A. Wagner & H. W. Stevenson (Eds.), *Cultural perspectives on child development.* San Francisco: W. H. Freeman.

Ehrhardt, A. A., & Baker, S. W. (1974). Fetal androgens, human central nervous system differentiation, and behavioral sex differences. In E. C. Friedman, R. M. Richart, & R. L. VandeWiele (Eds.), *Sex differences in behavior.* New York: Wiley.

Eilers, R., Wilson, W., & Moore, J. (1977). Developmental changes in speech discrimination in infants. *Journal of Speech and Hearing Research, 20,* 766–780.

Eimas, P. D. (1976). Developmental aspects of speech perception. In R. Held, H. Leibowitz, & H. Teuber (Eds.), *Handbook of sensory physiology: Perception.* New York: Springer-Verlag.

Eimas, P. D. (1982). Speech perception: A view of the initial state and perceptual mechanisms. In J. Mehler, M. Garrett, & E. Walker (Eds.), *Perspective on mental representation.* Hillsdale, NJ: Erlbaum.

Eisenberg, N. (Ed.). (1986). *Altruistic emotion, cognition, and behavior.* Hillsdale, NJ: Erlbaum.

Eisenberg, N., & Lennon, R. (1983). Sex differences in empathy and related capacities. *Psychological Bulletin, 94,* 100–131.

Eisenberg-Berg, N. (1979). Development of children's prosocial moral judgment. *Developmental Psychology, 15,* 128–137.

Elias, M. (1990, July 16). Menopausal stress may be a myth. *USA Today,* p. 1D.

Elicker, J., Englund, M., & Sroufe, L. A. (1992). Predicting peer competence and peer relationships in childhood from early parent-child relationships. In R. D. Parke & G. W. Ladd (Eds.), *Family-peer relationships: Modes of linkage.* Hillsdale, NJ: Erlbaum.

Elkind, D. (1961). Children's discovery of mass, weight, and volume: Piaget Replication Study II. *Journal of Genetic Psychology, 98,* 219–227.

Elkind, D. (1982). Jean Piaget (1896–1980). *American Psychologist, 36,* 911–913.

Elkind, D. (1987, May). Superkids and super problems. *Psychology Today,* pp. 60–61.

Elkind, D., & Bower, R. (1979). Imaginary audience behavior in children and adolescents. *Developmental Psychology, 15,* 38–44.

Elseth, G. D., & Baumgardner, K. D. (1984). *Genetics.* Reading, MA: Addison-Wesley.

English, H. B., & English, A. C. (1958). *A comprehensive dictionary of psychological and psychoanalytical terms.* New York: David McKay Company, Inc.

Enns, J. T. (1990). *The development of attention: Research and theory.* New York: Elsevier.

Epstein, S. (1973). The self concept revisited: Or a theory of a theory. *American Psychologist, 28,* 404–416.

Epstein, S. (1983). The stability of behavior across time and situations. In R. Zucker, J. Aronoff, & A. I. Rabin (Eds.), *Personality and the prediction of behavior.* San Diego, CA: Academic Press.

Erber, J. T. (1981). Remote memory and age: A review. *Experimental Aging Research, 1,* 189–199.

Ericksson, M. F., Sroufe, L. A., & Egeland, B. (1985). The relationship between quality of attachment and behavior problems in preschool in a high risk sample. In I. Bretherton & E. Waters (Eds.), Growing points of attachment theory and research. *Monographs of the Society for Research in Child Development, 50,* (1–2, Serial No. 109).

Ericsson, K. A., & Charness, N. (1994). Expert performance: Its structure and acquisition. *American Psychologist, 49,* 725–747.

Erikson, E. H. (1950/1963). *Childhood and society.* New York: Norton.

Erikson, E. H. (1959). Identity and the life cycle: Selected papers. *Psychological Issue Monograph Series, I* (No. 1). New York: Academic Press.

Erikson, E. H. (1963). *Childhood and society* (2nd ed.). New York: Norton. (Original work published 1950)

Erikson, E. H. (1968). *Identity: Youth and crisis.* New York: Norton.

Erikson, E. H. (1983, June). A conversation with Erikson (by E. Hall). *Psychology Today,* pp. 22–30.

Erlenmeyer-Kimling, L., & Jarvik, L. F. (1963). Genetics and intelligence: A review. *Science, 142,* 1479.

Eron, L. D. (1982). Parent-child interaction, television violence, and aggression in children. *American Psychologist, 37,* 197–211.

Eron, L. D. (1987). The development of aggressive behavior from the perspective of a developing behaviorism. *American Psychologist, 42,* 435–422.

Eron, L. D., & Huesmann, L. R. (1987). Television as a source of maltreatment of children. *School Psychology Review, 16,* 195–200.

Escalona, S. (1968). *The roots of individuality: Normal patterns of individuals.* Chicago: Aldine.

Etaugh, C. (1980). Effects of nonmaternal care on children. *American Psychologist, 35,* 309–319.

Evans, L. M. (1994, July). *A reassessment of "the chilly classroom climate": Evidence of a warming trend.* Poster presented at the Sixth Annual Convention of the American Psychological Society, Washington, DC.

Evans, W., & Rosenberg, I. H. (1991). *Biomarkers: The ten determinants of aging you can control.* New York: Simon & Schuster.

Expanding adolescent sex roles. (1978). Ithaca, NY: Cornell University.

Eysenck, H. J., & Cookson, D. (1969). Personality in primary school children I: Ability and achievement. *British Journal of Educational Psychology, 39,* 109–122.

Eysenck, M. W. (1974). Age differences in incidental learning. *Developmental Psychology, 10,* 936–941.

Eysenck, M. W. (1977). *Human memory: Theory, research and individual differences.* Oxford: Pergamon.

F

Fagan, J. F., III. (1992). Intelligence: A theoretical viewpoint. *Current Directions in Psychological Science, 1,* 82–86.

Fagan, J. F., III, & Singer, J. T. (1983). Infant recognition memory as a measure of intelligence. In L. P. Lipsitt & C. K. Rovee-Collier (Eds.), *Advances in infancy research* (Vol. 2). Norwood, NJ: Ablex.

Fagot, B. I. (1977). Consequences of moderate cross-gender behavior in preschool children. *Child Development, 48,* 902–907.

Fagot, B. I., & Leinbach, M. D. (1983). Play styles in early childhood: Social consequences for boys and girls. In M. B. Liss (Ed.), *Social and cognitive skills: Sex roles and children's play*. New York: Academic Press.

Falbo, T., & Polit, D. F. (1986). Quantitative review of the only child literature: Research evidence and theory development. *Psychological Bulletin, 100,* 176–189.

Fancher, R. E. (1979). *Pioneers of psychology*. New York: Norton.

Fancher, R. E. (1993). Francis Galton and the Darwins. *The General Psychologist, 29,* 1–5.

Fantz, R. L. (1958). Pattern vision in young infants. *Psychological Review, 8,* 43–47.

Fantz, R. L. (1961). The origins of form perception. *Scientific American, 204,* 66–72.

Farb, P. (1975). *Word play: What happens when people talk*. New York: Knopf.

Faust, M. S. (1977). Somatic development of adolescent girls. *Monographs of the Society for Research in Child Development, 42*(Whole No. 169).

Feather, N. T. (1980). Values in adolescence. In J. Adelson (Ed.), *Handbook of adolescent psychology*. New York: Wiley.

Feather, W. T. (1985). Attitudes, values and attributions: Explanations of unemployment. *Journal of Personality and Social Psychology, 48,* 876–889.

Fehr, L. (1976). J. Piaget and S. Claus: Psychology makes strange bedfellows. *Psychological Reports, 39,* 740–742.

Feifel, H. (Ed.) 1959. *The meaning of life*. New York: Macmillan.

Feingold, A. (1988). Cognitive gender differences are disappearing. *American Psychologist, 43,* 95–103.

Feldman, D. H. (1986). *Nature's gambit: Child prodigies and the development of human potential*. New York: Basic Books.

Feldman, H., Goldin-Meadow, S., & Gleitman, L. (1978). Beyond Herodotus, The creation of language by linguistically deprived deaf children. In A. Lock (Ed.), *Action, symbol, and gesture: The emergence of language*. New York: Academic Press.

Felson, R. B. (1984). The effects of self-appraisal of ability on academic performance. *Journal of Personality and Social Psychology, 47,* 944–952.

Felson, R. B. (1989). Parents and the reflected appraisal process: A longitudinal analysis. *Journal of Personality and Social Psychology, 56,* 965–971.

Fennema, E. (1974). *Mathematics, spatial ability and the sexes*. Paper presented at the American Educational Research Association's Annual Meeting, Chicago.

Festinger, L. (1950). Informal social communication. *Psychological Review, 57,* 271–282.

Festinger, L. (1954). A theory of social comparison processes. *Human Relations, 7,* 117–140.

Festinger, L., Schachter, S., & Back, K. (1950). *Social pressures in informal groups: A study of a housing community*. New York: Harper.

Fetters, W. (1979). *Nonsexist counseling: Helping men and women redefine their roles*. Dubuque, IA: Kendall Hunt.

Feuerstein, R. (1980). *Instrumental enrichment: An intervention program for cognitive modifiability*. Baltimore, MD: University Park Press.

Fiatarone, M. A., Marks, E. C., Ryan, N. D., Meredith, C. N., Lipsitz, L. A., & Evans, W. J. (1990). High-intensity strength training in nonagenarians: Effects on skeletal muscles. *Journal of the American Medical Association, 263,* 3029–3034.

Field, D., & Millsap, R. E. (1991). Personality in advanced old age: Continuity or change. *Journal of Gerontology: Psychological Sciences, 46,* 299–308.

Field, T. M. (1979). Infant behaviors directed towards peers and adults in the presence and absence of mother. *Infant Behavior and Development, 2,* 47–54.

Field, T. M., & Roopnarine, J. L. (1982). Infant-peer interactions. In T. M. Field, A. Huston, H. C. Quay, L. Troll, & G. E. Finley (Eds.), *Review of human development*. New York: Wiley.

Fighting poverty. (1983, July 22). *USA Today,* p. 8A.

Finckenauer, J. O. (1979, August). Scared crooked. *Psychology Today,* pp. 6–11.

Finn, S. E. (1986). Stability of personality self-ratings over 30 years: Evidence for an age/cohort interaction. *Journal of Personality and Social Psychology, 50,* 813–818.

Fisher, H. F. (1987, October). The four-year itch. *Natural History, 96,* 353–376.

Fisher, W. A. (1984). Predicting contraceptive behavior among university men: The role of emotions and behavioral intentions. *Journal of Applied Social Psychology, 14,* 104–123.

Fisher, W. A. (1993). Confessions of a sexual scientist. In G. C. Brannigan & M. R. Matthews (Eds.), *The undaunted psychologist: Adventures in research* (pp. 13–29). New York: McGraw-Hill.

Fisher, W. A., Byrne, D., & White, L. A. (1983). Emotional barriers to contraception. In D. Byrne & W. A. Fisher (Eds.), *Adolescents, sex, and contraception* (pp. 207–239). Hillsdale, NJ: Erlbaum.

Fitzpatrick, J. L. (1978). Academic underachievement, other-direction, and attitudes toward women's roles in bright adolescent females. *Journal of Educational Psychology, 70,* 645–650.

Fivush, R. (1994, April). *Language, autobiography, gender and self: How individual representations are socially constructed.* Invited symposium presented at the Conference on Human Development, Pittsburgh, PA.

Flaste, R. (1976, August). Scientists wonder what's on a baby's mind. *The New York Times,* p. 18.

Flavell, J. H. (1963). *The developmental psychology of Jean Piaget*. Princeton, NJ: Van Nostrand.

Flavell, J. H. (1970). Developmental studies of mediated memory. In H. W. Reese & L. P. Lipsitt (Eds.), *Advances in child development and child behavior* (Vol. 5). New York: Academic Press.

Flavell, J. H. (1981). Cognitive monitoring. In W. P. Dickson (Ed.), *Children's oral communication skills*. New York: Academic Press.

Flavell, J. H. (1982). On cognitive development. *Child Development, 53,* 1–10.

Flavell, J. H. (1985). *Cognitive development* (2nd ed.). Englewood Cliffs, NJ: Prentice Hall.

Flavell, J. H. (1986). The development of children's knowledge about the appearance-reality distinction. *American Psychologist, 41,* 418–425.

Flavell, J. H. (1993). Young children's understanding of thinking and consciousness. *Current Directions, 2,* 40–43.

Flavell, J. H., Everett, B. H., Croft, K., & Flavell, E. R. (1981). Young children's knowledge about visual perception: Further evidence for the level 1–level 2 distinction. *Developmental Psychology, 17,* 99–103.

Flavell, J. H., Friedrichs, A. G., & Hoyt, J. D. (1970). Developmental changes in memorization processes. *Cognitive Psychology, 1,* 324–340.

Flavell, J. H., & Ross, L. (Eds.), (1981). *Social cognitive development: Frontiers and possible futures*. Cambridge, England: Cambridge University Press.

Flavell, J. H., Speer, J. R., Green, F. L., & August, D. L. (1981). The development of comprehension monitoring and knowledge about communication. *Monographs of the Society for Research in Child Development, 46*(5, Serial No. 192).

Fletcher, P., & Garman, M. (Eds.). (1986). *Language acquisition: Studies in first language development.* London: Cambridge University Press.

Foa, U. G., & Foa, E. B. (1974). *Social structures of the mind.* Springfield, IL: Charles C Thomas.

Fogel, A. (1979). Peer vs. mother directed behavior in 1- to 3-month-old infants. *Infant Behavior and Development, 2,* 215–226.

Foley, J. E., & Cohen, A. J. (1984, March). *Gender differences in cognitive mapping.* Paper presented at the Toronto Area Women's Research Colloquium, Toronto, Canada.

Fowler, W., & Swenson, A. (1979). The influence of early language stimulation on development: Four studies. *Genetic Monographs, 100,* 73–109.

Fox, N. (1977). Attachment of kibbutz infants to mother and metapelet. *Child Development, 48,* 1228–1239.

Fox, N. A., Kimmerly, N. L., & Schaffer, W. D. (1991). Attachment to mother/attachment to father: A meta-analysis. *Child Development, 62,* 210–225.

Fox, R., & McDaniel, C. (1982). The perception of biological motion by human infants. *Science, 218,* 486–487.

Frager, R., & Fadiman, J. (1990). *Maslow's motivation and personality* (3rd ed.). New York: Harper College.

Franks, V., & Rothblum, E. S. (Eds.). (1983). *The stereotyping of women: Its effects on mental health.* New York: Springer.

Frantz, R. L., Fagan, R. F., & Miranda, S. (1975). Early visual selectivity. In L. B. Cohen & P. Salapatek (Eds.), *Infant perception: From sensation to cognition.* New York: Academic Press.

Franz, C. E., & White, K. M. (1985). Individuation and attachment in personality development: Extending Erikson's theory. *Journal of Personality, 53,* 224–256.

Frazier, N., & Sadker, M. (1973). *Sexism in school and society.* New York: Harper & Row.

Frederiksen, N. (1986). Toward a broader conception of human intelligence. *American Psychologist, 41,* 445–452.

Freeman, L. (1972). *The story of Anna O.* New York: Walker.

Freud, A., & Dann, S. (1951). *The psychoanalytic study of the child* (Vol. 6, pp. 127–168). Independence, MO: International Universities Press.

Freud, S. (1915). *Instincts and their vicissitudes.* London: Hogarth Press.

Freud, S. (1920/1963). *Beyond the pleasure principle* (J. Strachey, Trans. and Ed.). New York: W. W. Norton.

Freud, S. (1923). *The ego and the id.* New York: Norton.

Freud, S. (1935). The sexual life of man (Lecture XX). In J. Riviere (Trans.), *A general introduction to psychoanalysis.* New York: Liveright. (Original work published 1916–1917)

Freud, S. (1938). *An outline of psychoanalysis.* New York: Norton.

Freud, S. (1940). *An outline of psychoanalysis* (J. Strachey, Trans.). New York: Norton.

Freud, S. (1963). *The ego and the id.* New York: Norton. (Original work published 1923)

Freud, S. (1965). *New introductory lectures on psychoanalysis.* New York: Norton. (Original work published 1933)

Freud, S., & Breuer, J. (1895). *Studies on hysteria.* In J. Strachey (Ed.), *The standard edition of the complete psychological works of Sigmund Freud* (Vol. 2). London: Hogarth, 1953–1974.

Friedman-Erickson, S., Hamilton, R., Hawkins, J., Rudisill, M., & Lorence, J. (1994, July). *Adult age differences in the relationship between memory and expertise.* Paper presented at the meeting of the American Psychological Society, Washington, DC.

Friedrich, L., Tucker, C., Norris, C., Farnsworth, J., Fisher, D., Hannington, D., & Hoxie, K. (1978). *Perceptions by adolescents of television heroines.* Paper presented at the meeting of the Southeastern Psychological Association, New Orleans.

Frieze, I. (1978). *Women and sex roles.* New York: Norton.

Frijda, N. H. (1988). The laws of emotion. *American Psychologist, 43,* 349–358.

Fromkin, V., & Rodman, R. (1983). *An introduction to language* (3rd ed.). New York: Holt, Rinehart & Winston.

Frueh, T., & McGhee, P. H. (1975). Traditional sex-role development and the amount of time spent watching television. *Developmental Psychology, 11,* 109.

Fuchs, F., & Cederquist, L. L. (1978). Use of amniotic fluid in prenatal diagnosis. In D. V. I. Fairweather & T. K. A. B. Eskes (Eds.), *Amniotic fluid: Research and clinical application.* Amsterdam: Elsevier.

Fulker, D. W., DeFries, J. C., & Plomin, R. (1988). Genetic influence on general mental ability increases between infancy and middle childhood. *Nature, 336,* 767–769.

Fulton, R. (1978). The sacred and the secular attitudes of the American public toward death, funerals, and funeral directors. In R. Fulton & R. Bendiksen (Eds.), *Death and identity* (rev. ed.). Bowie, MD: Charles Press.

Furman, W., Rahe, D., & Hartup, W. (1979). Rehabilitation of socially withdrawn preschool children through mixed-age and same-age socialization. *Child Development, 50,* 915–922.

Furman, W., Rahe, D. F., & Hartup, W. W. (1981). Rehabilitation of socially withdrawn preschool children through mixed-age and same-age socialization. In E. M. Hetherington & R. D. Parke (Eds.), *Contemporary readings in child psychology* (2nd ed.). New York: McGraw-Hill.

Furst, K. (1983). *Origins and evolution of women's dreams in early adulthood.* Unpublished doctoral dissertation, California School of Professional Psychology, Berkeley, CA.

Furstenberg, F. F., Nord, C. W., Peterson, J. L., & Zill, N. (1983). The life course of children of divorce: Marital disruption and parental contact. *American Sociological Review, 48,* 656–668.

Furth, H. (1966). *Thinking about language.* New York: Free Press.

G

Galanter, E. (1962). Contemporary psychophysics. In *New directions in psychology: Vol. 1* (pp. 87–156). New York: Holt, Rinehart & Winston.

Galler, J. R. (1984). *Human nutrition: A comprehensive treatise: Vol. 5. Nutrition and behavior.* New York: Plenum.

Galton, F. (1962). *Hereditary genius: An enquiry into its laws and consequences.* Cleveland, OH: World Publishing. (Original work published in 1869)

Gamble, T. J., & Zigler, E. (1986). Effects of infant day care: Another look at the evidence. *American Journal of Orthopsychiatry, 56,* 26–42.

Garbarino, J. (1982). *Children and families in the social environment.* New York: Aldine.

Gardner, H. (1982). *Developmental psychology.* Boston: Little Brown.

Gardner, H. (1983). *Frames of mind.* New York: Basic Books.
Gardner, H. (1993). *Multiple intelligences: The theory in practice.* New York: Basic Books.
Gaulin-Kremer, E., Shaw, J. L., & Thoman, E. B. (1977, March). *Mother-infant interaction at first encounter: Effects of variation in delay after delivery.* Paper presented at biennial meeting of the Society for Research in Child Development, New Orleans.
Gelman, R. (1972). Logical capacity of very young children: Number invariance rules. *Child Development, 43,* 75–90.
Gelman, R. (1978). Cognitive development. *Annual Review of Psychology, 29,* 297–332.
Gelman, R. (1982). Basic numerical abilities. In R. J. Sternberg (Ed.), *Advances in the psychology of human intelligence* (Vol. 1). Hillsdale, NJ: Erlbaum.
Gelman, R., & Greeno, J. (1988). On the nature of competence: Principles for understanding in a domain. In L. B. Resnick (Ed.), *Knowing, learning, and instruction: Essays in honor of Robert Glaser.* Hillsdale, NJ: Erlbaum.
Gelman, R., & Shatz, M. (1977). Appropriate speech adjustments: The operation of conversational constraints on talk to 2-year-old. In M. Lewis & L. Rosenblum (Eds.), *Interaction, conversation, and the development of language.* New York: Academic Press.
Gentry, M., & Shulman, A. D. (1988). Remarriage as a coping for widowhood. *Psychology and Aging, 3,* 191–196.
Gerber, I., Rusalem, R., Hannon, N., Battin, D., & Arkin, A. (1975). Anticipatory grief and aged widows and widowers. *Journal of Gerontology, 30,* 225–229.
Gerbner, G. (1992). Society's storyteller: How television creates the myths by which we live. *Media and Values, 60,* 8–9.
Gerzon, M. (1983, Fall). Let's have some new horses: Thoughts on sexuality and masculinity. *Television and Children, 6,* 33–36.
Gesell, A. (1945). *The embryology of behavior.* New York: Harper & Row.
Gesell, A. (1952). *Infant development: The embryology of early human behavior.* Westport, CT: Greenwood Press.
Gesell, A., & Amatruda, C. S. (1947). *Developmental diagnosis* (2nd ed.). New York: Hoeber-Harper.
Gesell, A., & Ilg, F. L. (1946). The child from five to ten. In A. Gessell & F. L. Ilg, *Child development.* New York: Harper & Row.
Gibbs, J. (1994, Winter). New program for delinquents cuts repeat offenses. Cited in *Quest, 4.* Columbus, OH: The Ohio State University.
Gibson, E. J., & Walk, R. D. (1960). The visual cliff. *Scientific American, 202,* 2–9.
Gilbert, J. G., & Levee, R. F. (1971). Patterns of declining memory. *Journal of Gerontology, 26,* 70–75.
Gilchrist, L. D., & Schinke, S. P. (1983). Coping with contraception: Cognitive and behavioral methods with adolescents. *Cognitive Therapy and Research, 7,* 379–388.
Gilchrist, L. D., & Schinke, S. P. (1987). Adolescent pregnancy and marriage. In V. B. Van Hasselt & M. Hersen (Eds.), *Handbook of adolescent psychology.* Great Britain: Pergamon Press.
Gilligan, C. (1982). *In a different voice.* Cambridge, MA: Harvard University Press.
Gilligan, C., Lyons, N. P., & Hanmer, T. (1990). *Making connections: The relational worlds of adolescent girls at Emma Willard School.* Cambridge, MA: Harvard University Press.
Ginsburg, H. P., & Opper, S. (1988). *Piaget's theory of intellectual development.* Englewood Cliffs, NJ: Prentice Hall.
Glaser, G., & Bassok, M. (1989). Learning theory and the study of instruction. *Annual Review of Psychology, 40,* 631–666.
Glass, D. C., Neulinger, J., & Brim, O. G. (1974). Birth order, verbal intelligence, and educational aspiration. *Child Development, 45,* 807–811.
Glass, S., & Wright, T. (1988). Emotional affairs. In R. A. Brown & J. R. Field (Eds.), *Treatment of sexual problems in individual and couples therapy.* New York: PMA.
Gleason, J. B. (1985). Studying language development. In J. B. Gleason (Ed.), *The development of language.* Columbus, OH: Merrill.
Gleitman, H. (1987). *Basic psychology* (2nd ed.). New York: Norton.
Gleitman, L. R., Newport, E. L., & Gleitman, H. (1984). The current status of the motherese hypothesis. *Journal of Child Language, 11,* 43–79.
Glenberg, A., Smith, S. M., & Green, C. (1977). Type 1 rehearsal: Maintenance and more. *Journal of Verbal Learning and Verbal Behavior, 16,* 339–352.
Glenn, N. (1986, June). Children of divorce. *Psychology Today,* pp. 68–69.
Glenn, N. D. (1987, October). Marriage on the rocks. *Psychology Today,* pp. 21–22.
Glenn, N. D., & Weaver, C. N. (1978). The marital happiness of remarried and divorced persons. *Journal of Marriage and the Family, 40,* 269–282.
Glick, I. O., Weiss, R., & Parkes, C. M. (1974). *The first year of bereavement.* New York: Wiley.
Glick, M., & Zeigler, E. (1985). Self-image: A cognitive-developmental approach. In R. L. Leahy (Ed.), *The development of the self.* Orlando, FL: Academic Press.
Glick, P. C. (1977). Updating the life cycle of the family. *Journal of Marriage and the Family, 38,* 5–13.
Glick, P. C., & Lin, S. (1986). More young adults are living with their parents: Who are they? *Journal of Marriage and the Family, 48,* 107–112.
Glick, P. C., & Norton, A. J. (1970, April). *Probabilities of marriage, divorce, widowhood, and remarriage.* Paper presented at the annual meeting of the Population Association of America, Atlanta, GA.
Glick, P. C., & Spanier, G. B. (1980). Married and unmarried cohabitation in the United States. *Journal of Marriage and the Family, 42,*19–30.
Glidewell, J. (1978). The psychological context of distress in school. In D. Bartal & L. Saxe (Eds.), *Social psychology of education* (pp. 167–188). New York: Halsted.
Goffman, E. (1979). *Gender advertisements.* Cambridge, MA: Harvard University Press.
Gold, M., & Petronio, R. (1980). Delinquent behavior in adolescence. In J. Adelson (Ed.), *Handbook of adolescent psychology.* New York: Wiley.
Goldberg, P. A. (1968). Are women prejudiced against women? *Transactions, 5,* 28–30.
Goldberg, S. (1983). Parent-infant bonding: Another look. *Child Development, 54,* 1355–1382.
Goldberg, S., Blumberg, S. L., & Kriger, A. (1982). Menarche and interest in infants: Biological and social influences. *Child Development, 53,* 1544–1550.
Goldman, J. A., & Chaillee, C. (1984). A comparison of same- and cross-age interactions in mixed age groups. *Journal of Abnormal Child Psychology, 5,* 23–33.
Good, T., & Brophy, J. (1986). School effects. In M. Wittrock (Ed.), *Third handbook of research on teaching* (pp. 570–602). New York: Macmillan.
Gorer, G. (1967). *Death, grief, and mourning.* Garden City, NY: Doubleday.

Gottesman, I. I. (1963). Genetic aspects of intelligent behavior. In N. Ellis (Ed.), *Handbook of mental deficiency: Psychological theory and research.* New York: McGraw-Hill.

Gottfried, A. E., & Gottfried, A. N. (1985, August). *Maternal employment and young children's development: A longitudinal investigation.* Paper presented at the 93rd Annual Convention of the American Psychological Association, Los Angeles, CA.

Gottman, J., & Parkhurst, J. (1980). A developmental theory of friendship and acquaintance processes. In W. A. Collins (Ed.), *Development of cognition, affect, and social relations* (Minnesota Symposium on Child Psychology, Vol. 13). Hillsdale, NJ: Erlbaum.

Gottman, J. M. (1993). *What predicts divorce? The relationship between marital processes and marital outcomes.* Hillsdale, NJ: Erlbaum.

Gottman, J. M., & Levenson, R. W. (1992). Marital processes predictive of later dissolution: Behavior, physiology, and health. *Journal of Personality and Social Psychology, 63,* 221–233.

Gould, J. L. (1982). *Ethology.* New York: Norton.

Gould, S. J. (1981). *The mismeasure of man.* New York: Norton.

Gould, S. J. (1983, June 30). Genes on the brain. *New York Review of Books,* pp. 5, 6, 8, 10.

Gove, W. R. (1972). The relationship between sex roles, mental illness and marital status. *Social Forces, 51,* 34–44.

Goy, R., & Resko, J. A. (1972). Gonadal hormones and behavior of normal and pseudohermaphroditic nonhuman female primates. In E. B. Astwood (Ed.), *Recent progress in hormone research, 28.* New York: Academic Press.

Green, M. (1989). *Theories of human development.* Englewood Cliffs, NJ: Prentice Hall.

Greenstein, T. N. (1990). Marital disruption and the employment of married women. *Journal of Marriage and the Family, 51,* 657–675.

Greenwald, A. G. (1980). The totalitarian ego: Fabrication and revision of personal history. *American Psychologist, 35,* 603–618.

Greenwald, A. G., & Pratkanis, A. R. (1984). The self. In R. S. Wyer & T. K. Srull (Eds.), *Handbook of social cognition.* Hillsdale, NJ: Erlbaum.

Greif, E. B., & Ulman, K. J. (1982). The psychological impact of menarche on early adolescent females: A review of the literature. *Child Development, 53,* 1413–1430.

Grof, S., & Halifax, J. (1977). *The human encounter with death.* New York: Dutton.

Grossman, K., Thane, K., & Grossman, K. E. (1981). Maternal tactile contact of the newborn after various postpartum conditions of mother-infant contact. *Developmental Psychology, 17,* 158–169.

Grubb, D. D., Malatesta, T., & Haley, T. M. (1994, July). *Moral reasoning impacts on satisfaction in romantic relationships.* Poster presented at the Sixth Annual Convention of the American Psychological Society, Washington, DC.

Gruber, H. E., & Voneche, J. J. (Eds.). (1977). *The essential Piaget: An interpretive reference and guide.* New York: Basic Books.

Guidelines for the determination of death: Report of the medical consultants on the diagnosis of death to the President's Commission for the Ethical Problems of Medicine and Biomedical and Behavioral Research. (1981). *Journal of the American Medical Association, 246,* 2184–2186.

Gurin, G., Veroff, J., & Feld, S. (1960). *Americans view their mental health.* New York: Basic Books.

Gutik, B. (1978). *Enhancing women's career development.* San Francisco: Jossey-Bass.

Gutmann, D. L. (1975). Parenthood, key to comparative study of the life cycle. In N. Datan & L. Ginsberg (Eds.), *Life-span developmental psychology: Normative life crises.* New York: Academic Press.

Gutmann, D. (1977). The cross-cultural perspective: Notes toward a comparative psychology of aging. In J. Birren & K. W. Schaie (Eds.), *Handbook of the psychology of aging.* New York: Van Nostrand Reinhold.

Guttentag, M., & Bray, H. (1976). *Undoing sex stereotypes.* New York: McGraw-Hill.

Guttentag, M., & Secord, P. F. (1982). *Too many women: The sex ratio question.* Beverly Hills, CA: Sage Publications.

H

Haan, N. (1981). Common dimensions of personality development: Early adolescence to middle life. In D. H. Eichorn, J. A. Clausen, N. Haan, M. P. Honzik, & P. H. Mussen (Eds.), *Present and past in middle life.* New York: Academic Press.

Hacker, H. (1981). Blabbermouths and clams: Sex differences in self-disclosure in same-sex and cross-sex friendship dyads. *Psychology of Women Quarterly, 5,* 385–401.

Hainline, L. (1978). Developmental changes in visual scanning of face and nonface patterns by infants. *Journal of Experimental Child Psychology, 25,* 90–115.

Haith, M. M., Berman, T., & Moore, M. J. (1977). Eye contact and face scanning in early infancy. *Science, 198,* 853–854.

Hall, C. S., & Lindzey, G. (1978). *Theories of personality* (3rd ed.). New York: Wiley.

Hall, G. S. (1904). *Adolescence: Its psychology and its relations to physiology, anthropology, sociology, sex, crime, religion, and education* (2 vols.). New York: D. Appleton.

Hall, M. H. (1968, February). A conversation with Abraham H. Maslow. *Psychology Today,* pp. 34–37.

Halpern, D. F. (1986). *Sex differences in cognitive abilities.* Hillsdale, NJ: Erlbaum.

Halpern, D. F. (1992). *Sex differences in cognitive abilities* (2nd ed.). Hillsdale, NJ: Erlbaum.

Hamill, P., Johnston, F., & Lemeshow, S. (1973). Height and weight of youths, 12–17 years. *Vital and Health Statistics* (Serial 11, No. 124).

Hammerlie, F. M., & Montgomery, R. L. (1982). Self-perception theory and unobtrusively biased interactions: A treatment for heterosexual anxiety. *Journal of Counseling Psychology, 29,* 362–370.

Hammerlie, F. M., & Montgomery, R. L. (1984). Purposefully biased interventions: Reducing heterosexual anxiety through self-perception theory. *Journal of Personality and Social Psychology, 47,* 900–908.

Hammerlie, F. M., & Montgomery, R. L. (1986). Self-perception theory and the treatment of shyness. In W. H. Jones, J. M. Cheek, & S. R. Briggs (Eds.), *A sourcebook on shyness: Research and treatment.* New York: Plenum.

Hanna, N. A. (1994, April). *Predictors of friendship and peer acceptance at summer camp.* Poster presented at the Conference on Human Development, Pittsburgh, PA.

Hansfeld, B. C., & Hattie, J. A. (1982). The relationship between self-achievement/performance measures. *Review of Educational Research, 52,* 123–142.

Hanson, S. L., & Rapoza, R. S. (1990). *Career development and counseling of women.* Springfield, IL: Charles C Thomas Publishers.

Harackeiwicz, J. M., & Manderlink, G. (1984). A process analysis of the effects of performance-contingent rewards on intrinsic emotions. *Journal of Experimental Social Psychology, 20,* 531–551.

Harlow, H. (1973). "Harry, you are going to go down in history as the father of the cloth mother." *Psychology Today, 8,* 65–77.

Harlow, H. F. (1958). The nature of love. *American Psychologist, 13,* 637–685.

Harlow, H. F. (1971). *Learning to love.* New York: Ballantine Books.

Harlow, H. F., & Zimmerman, M. K. (1959). Affectional responses in the infant monkey. *Science, 130,* 421–432.

Harman, D. (1968). Free theory of aging. *Journal of Gerontology, 23,* 476–482.

Harman, D. (1993). Free radical involvement in aging. Pathophysiology and therapeutic implications. *Drugs and Aging, 3,* 60–80.

Harman, S. M., & Talbert, G. B. (1985). Reproductive aging. In C. E. Finch & E. L. Schneider (Eds.), *Handbook of the biology of aging* (2nd ed.). New York: Van Nostrand.

Harper's index. (1990, March). *Harper's,* p. 17.

Harris, G. (1964). Sex hormones, brain development and brain function. *Endocrinology, 75,* 627–648.

Harris, G., & Levine, S. (1965). Sexual differentiation of the brain and its experimental control. *Journal of Physiology, 181,* 379–400.

Harris, J. (1986). *Stranger in two worlds.* New York: Macmillan.

Harris, M., Jones, D., Brookes, S., & Grant, J. (1986). Relations between the non-verbal context of maternal speech and rate of language development. *British Journal of Developmental Psychology, 4,* 261–268.

Harris, M. J., Milich, R., Corbitt, E. M., Hoover, D. W., & Brady, M. (1992). Self-fulfilling effects of stigmatizing information on children's social interactions. *Journal of Personality and Social Psychology, 63,* 41–50.

Harter, S. (1983). Developmental perspectives on the self-system. In P. H. Mussen (Ed.), *Handbook of child psychology: Vol. 4. Socialization, personality, and social development.* New York: Wiley.

Harter, S. (1989). Causes, correlates and the functional role of global self-worth: A life span perspective. In J. Kolligan & R. Sternberg (Eds.), *Perceptions of competence and incompetence across the life span.* New Haven, CT: Yale University Press.

Hartup, W. W. (1983). Peer relations. In P. H. Mussen (Ed.), *Handbook of child psychology: Vol. 4. Socialization, personality, and social development* (4th ed.). New York: Wiley.

Hartup, W. W. (1992). Adolescents and their families. In B. Lauresen (Ed.), *Close friendships in adolescence.* San Francisco: Jossey-Bass.

Hartup, W. W. (1992, August). *Friendships and their developmental significance.* Invited address, American Psychological Association Annual Meeting, Washington, DC.

Harvard Medical School. (1968). Criteria for brain death. *Journal of the American Medical Association, 205,* 307–340.

Hastie, R. (1980). Memory for information which confirms or contradicts a general impression. In R. Hastie, T. Ostrom, E. Ebbesson, R. Wyer, D. Hamilton, & D. Carlston (Eds.), *Person memory: Cognitive basis of social perception.* Hillsdale, NJ: Erlbaum.

Hatfield, E., & Sprecher, S. (1986). Measuring passionate love in intimate relationships. *Journal of Adolescence, 9,* 383–410.

Havighurst, R. J. (1953). *Human development and education.* New York: Longman.

Hay, D. F., Nash, A., & Pedersen, J. (1981a, March). *Reciprocal contact between six-month-old-peers.* Paper presented at the International Conference on Infant Studies, Austin, TX.

Hay, D. F., Nash, A., & Pedersen, J. (1981b). Responses of six-month-olds to the distress of their peers. *Child Development, 52,* 1071–1075.

Hay, D. F., Nash, A., & Pedersen, J. (1983). Interaction between six-month-old peers. *Child Development, 54,* 557–562.

Hay, D. F., Pedersen, J., & Nash, A. (1982). Dyadic interactions in the first years of life. In R. H. Rubin & H. S. Ross (Eds.), *Peer relationships and social skills in childhood.* New York: Springer-Verlag.

Hayes, C. D., & Palmer, J. L. (Eds.). (1989). *Who cares for America's children? Child care policy for the 1990's.* Washington, DC: National Academy Press.

Hayflick, L. (1977). The cellular basis for biological aging. In C. E. Finch & L. Hayflick (Eds.), *Handbook of the biology of aging.* New York: Van Nostrand.

Hayflick, L. (1987). The cell biology and theoretical basis of aging. In L. Carstensen & B. A. Edelstein (Eds.), *Handbook of clinical gerontology.* New York: Pergamon.

Hayflick, L. (1992). Aging, longevity, and immortality in vitro. *Experimental Gerontology, 27,* 363–368.

Haynes, V. (1993, March). *Women and men and child-rearing.* Colloquium presented at Clarion University, Clarion, PA.

Hayslip, B., & Sterns, H. L. (1979). Age differences in relationships between crystallized and fluid intelligences and problem solving. *Journal of Gerontology, 34,* 404–414.

Hazan, C., & Shaver, P. (1987). Romantic love conceptualized as an attachment process. *Journal of Personality and Social Psychology, 52,* 511–524.

Headey, B., & Wearing, A. (1989). Personality, life events, and subjective well-being: Toward a dynamic equilibrium model. *Journal of Personality and Social Psychology, 57,* 731–739.

Heath, S. B. (1982). What no bedtime story means: Narrative skills at home and school. *Language and Society, 11,* 49–76.

Heatherton, T. F., & Nichols, P. A. (1994). Conceptual issues in assessing whether personality can change. In T. F. Heatherton & J. L. Weinberger (Eds.), *Can personality change?* Washington, DC: American Psychological Association.

Heatherton, T. F., & Weinberger, J. L. (Eds.). (1994). *Can personality change?* Washington, DC: American Psychological Association.

Heaton, T. B., Albrecht, S. L., & Martin, A. (1985). The timing of divorce. *Journal of Marriage and the Family, 47,* 631–639.

Hebb, D. (1978). On watching myself get old. *Psychology Today, 12,* 15, 20–23.

Hebb, D. O. (1966). *A textbook of psychology* (2nd ed.). Philadelphia: Saunders.

Heilman, M. E., Martell, R. F., & Simon, M. C. (1988). The variables of sex bias: Conditions regulating the undervaluation, and overvaluation of female job applicants. *Organizational Behavior and Human Decision Processes, 41,* 98–110.

Heller, J. F., Puff, C. R., & Mills, C. J. (1985). Assessment of the chilly college climate for women. *Journal of Higher Education, 56,* 446–461.

Hellmich, N. (1992, March 30). Midlife middles are prime for reducing. *USA Today,* 3D.

Helsing, M., Szklo, M., & Comstock, G. (1981). Factors associated with mortality after widowhood. *American Journal of Public Health, 71,* 802–809.

Helson, R., & Moane, G. (1987). Personality change in women from college to midlife. *Journal of Personality and Social Psychology, 53,* 176–186.

Helson, R., & Stewart, A. (1994). Personality change in adulthood. In T. F. Heatherton & J. L. Weinberger (Eds.), *Can personality change?* Washington, DC: American Psychological Association.

Helson, R., & Wink, P. (1992). Personality change in women from the early 40s to the early 50s. *Psychology and Aging, 7,* 46–55.

Henderson, R. W. (1981). Home environment and intellectual performance. In R. W. Henderson (Ed.), *Parent-child interaction: Theory, research, and prospects.* New York: Academic Press.

Hendrick, S. S., Hendrick, C., & Adler, N. (1988). Romantic relationships: Love, satisfaction, and staying together. *Journal of Personality and Social Psychology, 54,* 980–988.

Herold, E., Goodwin, M., & Lero, D. (1979). Self-esteem, locus of control and adolescent contraception. *Journal of Personality, 28,* 190–191.

Herstein, J. A. (1981). Keeping the voter's limits in mind: A cognitive process analysis of decision making. *Journal of Personality and Social Psychology, 40,* 843–861.

Hertzog, C., & Schaie, K. W. (1988). Stability and change in adult intelligence: 2. Simultaneous analysis of longitudinal means and covariance structures. *Psychology and Aging, 3,* 122–130.

Herzog, R. (1982). High school seniors' occupational plans and values: Trends in sex differences, 1976 through 1980. *Sociology of Education, 55,* 1–13.

Hetherington, E. M., & Climgenpeel, W. G. (1992). Coping with marital transitions: A family systems perspective. *Monographs of the Society for Research in Child Development, 57*(2 and 3, Serial No. 227).

Hetherington, E. M., & Parke, R. D. (1993). *Child psychology: A contemporary viewpoint* (4th ed.). New York: McGraw-Hill.

Higgins, E. T., & Parsons, J. E. (1983). Social cognition and the social life of the child: Stages as subcultures. In E. T. Higgins, D. N. Ruble, & W. W. Hartup (Eds.), *Social cognition and social development* (pp. 15–62). Cambridge, England: Cambridge University Press.

Higley, J. D., Hopkins, W. D., Thompson, W. W., Bryne, E. A., Hirsh, R. M., & Suomi, S. J. (1992). Peers as primary attachment sources in yearling rhesus monkeys. *Developmental Psychology, 28,* 1163–1171.

Hilgard, J. R., & Newman, M. F. (1959). Anniversaries in mental illness. *Psychiatry, 22,* 113–121.

Hill, C. T., Rubin, Z., & Peplau, L. A. (1976). Breakups before marriage: The end of 103 affairs. *Journal of Social Issues, 32,* 168.

Hill, J. P. (1980). *Understanding early adolescence: A framework.* Carrboro, NC: Center for Early Adolescence.

Hill, J. P., & Lynch, M. E. (1983). The intensification of gender-related role expectations during early adolescence. In J. Brooks-Gunn & A. C. Petersen (Eds.), *Girls at puberty: Biological and psychosocial perspectives.* New York: Plenum.

Hill, K. T., & Sarason, S. B. (1966). The relation of test anxiety and defensiveness to test and school performance over the elementary school years. *Monographs of the Society for Research in Child Development, 31*(No. 104).

Hill, W. L., Borovsky, D., & Rovee-Collier, C. (1988). Continuities in infant memory development. *Developmental Psychobiology, 21,* 43–62.

Hilts, P. J. (1991, April 6). U.S. reports drop in infant deaths. *New York Times,* pp. 1, 8.

Hinde, R. A. (1983). Ethology and child development. In P. H. Mussen (Ed.), *Handbook of child psychology: Vol. 2. Infancy and developmental psychobiology* (4th ed.). New York: Wiley.

Hindley, C. B., & Owen, C. F. (1978). The extent of individual changes in I.Q. for ages between 6 months and 17 years, in a British longitudinal sample. *Journal of Child Psychology and Psychiatry and Allied Disciplines, 19,* 329–350.

Hines, M. (1982). Prenatal gonadal hormones and sex differences in human behavior. *Psychological Bulletin, 92,* 56–80.

Hite, S. H. (1987). *The Hite report, women in love: A cultural revolution in progress.* New York: Macmillan.

Hobbes, T. (1968). *Leviathan.* Baltimore: Penguin Books. (Original work published 1651)

Hobbs, D. F., Jr., & Wimbish, J. M. (1977). Transition to parenthood by black couples. *Journal of Marriage and the Family, 38,* 677–689.

Hockett, C. (1960). The origin of speech. *Scientific American, 203,* 88–95.

Hoffman, E. (1988). *The right to be human: A biography of Abraham Maslow.* Los Angeles: Tarcher.

Hoffman, L. W. (1983). Increased fathering effects on the mother. In M. Lamb & A. Sagi (Eds.), *Social politics and legal issues pertaining to fatherhood.* Hillsdale, NJ: Erlbaum.

Hoffman, L. W. (1989). Effects of maternal employment in the two-parent family. *American Psychologist, 44,* 283–292.

Hoffman, M. L. (1975). Developmental synthesis of affect and cognition and its implications for altruistic motivation. *Developmental Psychology, 11,* 607–622.

Hoffman, M. L. (1980). Adolescent morality in developmental perspective. In J. Adelson (Ed.), *Handbook of adolescent psychology.* New York: Wiley Interscience.

Hoffman, M. L. (1981). Is altruism part of human nature? *Journal of Personality and Social Psychology, 40,* 121–137.

Hoffman, M. L. (1982). Development of prosocial motivation empathy and guilt. In N. Eisenberg-Berg (Ed.), *Development of prosocial behavior.* Hillsdale, NJ: Erlbaum.

Hoffman, M. L. (1988). Moral development. In M. H. Bornstein & M. E. Lamb (Eds.), *Developmental psychology: An advanced textbook* (2nd ed.). Hillsdale, NJ: Erlbaum.

Hogan, R. A. (1970). Adolescent views of death. *Adolescence, 5,* 55–56.

Holden, C. (1987). The genetics of personality. *Science, 237,* 598–601.

Holland, C. A., & Rabbitt, P. M. A. (1992). Effects of age-related reductions in processing resources on text recall. *Journal of Gerontology: Psychological Sciences, 47,* 129–137.

Honzik, M. P. (1976). Value and limitations of infant tests: An overview. In M. Lewis (Ed.), *Origins of intelligence: Infancy and early childhood.* New York: Plenum Press.

Honzik, M. P. (1983). Measuring mental abilities in infancy: The value and limitations. In M. Lewis (Ed.), *Origins of intelligence* (2nd ed.). New York: Plenum.

Honzik, M. P., Macfarlane, J. W., & Allen, L. (1948). Stability of mental test performance between 2 and 18 years. *Journal of Experimental Education, 17,* 309–324.

Horbar, J. D., Wright, L. L., Soll, R. F., Wright, E. C., Fanaroff, A. A., & Korones, S. B. (1993). A multicenter randomized trial comparing two surfactants for the treatment of neonatal respiratory distress syndrome. *Journal of Pediatrics, 123,* 757–766.

Horn, J. L., & Cattel, R. B. (1967). Age differences in fluid and crystallized intelligence. *Acta Psychologica, 26,* 107–129.

Horn, J. L., & Donaldson, G. (1976). On the myth of intellectual decline in adulthood. *American Psychologist, 31,* 701–709.

Horn, J. L., & Donaldson, G. (1980). Cognitive development in adulthood. In O. G. Brim, Jr., & J. Kagan (Eds.), *Constancy and change in human development.* Cambridge, MA: Harvard University Press.

Horney, K. (1937). *The neurotic personality of our time.* New York: Norton.

Horney, K. (1945). *Our inner conflicts.* New York: Norton.

Horney, K. (1950). *Neurosis and human growth.* New York: Norton.

Horrocks, J. E., & Baker, M. E. (1951). A study of the friendship fluctuations of preadolescents. *Journal of Genetic Psychology, 78,* 131–144.

Hothersall, D. (1990). *History of psychology* (2nd ed.). New York: McGraw-Hill.

Houston, S. E., & Campbell, J. B. (1994, June). *Interactive effects of gender and sex on moral reasoning scores.* Poster presented at the 6th Annual Convention of the American Psychological Society, Washington, DC.

Hoving, K. L., Spencer, T., Robb, K. Y., & Schulte, D. (1978). Developmental changes in visual information processing. In P. A. Ornstein (Ed.), *Memory development in children.* Hillsdale, NJ: Erlbaum.

Howard, D. V., Shaw, R. J., & Heisey, J. G. (1986). Aging and time course of semantic activation. *Journal of Gerontology, 41,* 195–203.

Howes, C. (1983). Caregiver behavior in center and family day-care. *Journal of Applied Developmental Psychology, 4,* 99–107.

Howes, C., & Rubenstein, J. (1985). Determinants of toddlers' experiences in daycare: Age of entry and quality of setting. *Child Care Quarterly, 14,* 140–151.

Hsu, L. K. G. (1990). *Eating disorders.* New York: Guilford Press.

Hubel, D. H. (1979). The brain. *Scientific American, 241,* 44–53.

Hudson, J., & Nelson, K. (1983). Effects of script structure on children's story recall. *Developmental Psychology, 19,* 625–635.

Hudson, J. A., Fivush, R., & Kuebli, J. (1992). Scripts and episodes: The development of event memory: Special Issue. *Applied Cognitive Psychology, 6,* 483–505.

Hultsch, D. F. (1975). Adult age differences in retrieval: Trace-dependent and cue-dependent forgetting. *Developmental Psychology, 11,* 197–201.

Hultsch, D. F., & Dixon, R. A. (1983). The role of preexperimental knowledge in text processing in adulthood. *Experimental Aging Research, 9,* 17–22.

Hultsch, D. F., Hertzog, C., & Dixon, R. A. (1987). Age differences in metamemory: Resolving the inconsistencies. *Canadian Journal of Psychology, 41,* 193–208.

Humphrey, T. (1978). Function of the nervous system during prenatal life. In U. Stave (Ed.), *Perinatal physiology.* New York: Plenum.

Hunt, M. (1974). *Sexual behavior in the 1970s.* Chicago: Playboy Press.

Hunt, M. (1982). *The universe within: A new science explores the human mind.* New York: Simon & Schuster.

Hunt, M. (1993). *The story of psychology.* New York: Anchor Books.

Huston, A. C. (1983). Sex typing. In P. H. Mussen (Ed.), *Handbook of child psychology: Vol. 4. Socialization, personality, and social development* (4th ed.). New York: Wiley.

Huston, A. C. (1985). The development of sex-typing: Themes from recent research. *Developmental Review, 5,* 1–17.

Huston, A. C., Greer, D., Wright, J. C., Welch, R., & Ross, R. (1984). Children's comprehension of televised formal features with masculine and feminine connotations. *Developmental Psychology, 20,* 707–716.

Huston, T. L., McHale, S. M., & Crouter, A. C. (1986). When the honeymoon's over: Changes in the marriage relationship over the first year. In R. Gilmour & S. Duck (Eds.), *The emerging field of personality relationships.* Hillsdale, NJ: Erlbaum.

Huston, T. L., & Vangelisti, A. L. (1991). Socioemotional behavior and satisfaction in marital relationships: A longitudinal study. *Journal of Personality and Social Psychology, 61,* 721–733.

Hutt, S. J., Hutt, C., Leonard, H. C., Benuth, H. V., & Muntjeweff, W. J. (1968). Auditory responsivity in the human newborn. *Nature, 218,* 888–890.

Huyck, M. H., & Hoyer, W. J. (1982). *Adult development and aging.* Belmont, CA: Wadsworth.

Hyde, J. S. (1981). How large are cognitive gender differences? A meta-analysis using w^2 and d. *American Psychologist, 36,* 892–901.

Hyde, J. S. (1985). *Half the human experience: The psychology of women* (3rd ed.). Lexington, MA: D. C. Heath.

Hyde, J. S. (1986). *Understanding sexuality* (3rd ed.). New York: McGraw Hill.

Hyde, J. S. (1994). Meta-analysis and the psychology of women. In F. L. Denmark & M. A. Paludi (Eds.), *Handbook on the psychology of women.* Dubuque, IA: Wm. C. Brown.

Hyde, J. S., Fennema, E., & Lamon, S. J. (1990). Gender differences in mathematics performance: A meta-analysis. *Psychological Bulletin, 107*(2), 139–155.

Hyde, J. S., Klein, M. H., & Essex, M. J. (1993, August). *Patterns of maternity leave and women's mental and physical health.* Paper presented at the 101st Annual Convention of the American Psychological Association, Toronto, Ontario, Canada.

Hyde, J. S., & Linn, M. C. (1988). Gender differences in verbal ability: A meta-analysis. *Psychological Bulletin, 104,* 53–69.

Hyde, J. S., & Linn, M. C. (Eds.). (1986). *The psychology of gender: Advances through meta-analysis.* Baltimore, MD: John Hopkins University Press.

Hyde, J. S., Rosenberg, B. G., & Behram, J. (1977). Tomboyism. *Psychology of Women Quarterly, 2,* 73–75.

Hymes, D. (1972). Introduction. In C. Cazden, V. John, & D. Hymes (Eds.), *Functions of language in the classrooms.* New York: Teachers College, Columbia University.

I

Ingram, D. (1989). *First language acquisition: Method, description, and explanation.* London: Cambridge University Press.

Institute of Medicine. (1985). *Preventing low birthweight.* Washington, DC: National Academy Press.

Instone, D., Major, B., & Bunker, B. B. (1983). Gender, self-confidence, and social influence strategies: An organizational simulation. *Journal of Personality and Social Psychology, 44,* 322–333.

Itons-Peterson, M. J., & Reddel, M. (1984). What do people ask about a neonate? *Developmental Psychology, 20,* 358–359.

Izard, C. E. (1978). On the ontogenesis of emotions and cognition in infancy. In M. Lewis & L. Rosenblum (Eds.), *The development of affect.* New York: Plenum.

J

Jackson, E. N. (1957). *Understanding grief: Its roots, dynamics, and treatment.* Nashville, TN: Abingdon Press.

Jacobs, J. A. (1986). The sex-segregation of fields of study: Trends during the college years. *Journal of Higher Education, 57,* 134–154.

Jakobson, R., & Halle, M. (1956). *Fundamentals of language.* The Hague: Mouton.

James, E. (1961). *Psychology.* New York: Harper Torch Books.

James, M. E., & Coles, C. D. (1991). Cocaine abuse during pregnancy: Psychiatric considerations. *General Hospital Psychiatry, 13,* 399–409.

James, W. (1892). *The principles of psychology: The briefer course.* New York: Henry Holt.

James, W. (1981). *The principles of psychology* (Vol. 1). Cambridge, MA: Harvard University Press. (Original work published 1890)

Janus, S. S., & Janus, C. L. (1993). *The Janus report on sexual behavior.* New York: Wiley.

Jenkins, T. M. (1978, July/August). Don't take it easy: You'll live longer. *Aging,* pp. 285–286.

Johnson, H., & Smith, L. B. (1981). Children's inferential abilities in the context of reading to understand. *Child Development, 52,* 1216–1223.

Johnson, J. S., & Newport, E. L. (1989). Critical period effects in second language learning: The influence of maturational state on the acquisition of English as a second language. *Cognitive Psychology, 21,* 60–99.

Johnson, M. H. (1992). Imprinting and the development of face recognition: From chick to men. *Current Directions in Psychological Science, 1,* 52–55.

Johnstone, B., Frame, C. L., & Bouman, D. (1992). Physical attractiveness and athletic and academic ability in controversial-aggressive and rejected-aggressive children. *Journal of Social and Clinical Psychology, 11,* 71–79.

Jolley, J. (1989). *Birth order and sibling relationships.* Unpublished manuscript, Clarion University.

Jolley, J. M. (1979). *Psychological disengagement: A study of alienation and depression in the small town widow.* Unpublished master's thesis, The Ohio State University, Columbus, OH.

Jolley, J. M. (1982). *The relationship of self to age and susceptibility to learned helplessness.* Unpublished doctoral dissertation, The Ohio State University, Columbus, OH.

Jolly, H. (1976). Family reactions to stillbirth. *Proceedings of the Royal Society of Medicine, 69,* 835–837.

Jonaitis, M. A. (1988). Nutrition during pregnancy. In W. D. Todd, D. F. Tapley, G. J. Subak-Sharpe, & D. M. Goetz (Eds.). *The Columbia University College of Physicians and Surgeons complete guide to pregnancy.* New York: Crown.

Jones, E. E., & Archer, R. L. (1976). Are there special effects of personalistic self-disclosure? *Journal of Experimental Social Psychology, 12,* 180–193.

Jones, M. C. (1924). A laboratory study of fear: The case of Peter. *Pedagogical Seminary, 31,* 308–315.

Jones, M. C., & Mussen, P. H. (1958). Self-conceptions, motivations, and interpersonal attitudes of early- and late-maturing girls. *Child Development, 29,* 491–501.

Jung, C. G. (1971). The stages of life. In J. Campbell (Ed.), *The portable Jung* (pp. 3–22). New York: Viking. (Original work published 1931)

K

Kagan, J. (1989a). Temperamental contributions to social behavior. *American Psychologist, 44,* 668–674.

Kagan, J. (1989b). [William James address.] Annual meeting of the American Psychological Association, New Orleans.

Kagan, J., Kearsley, R., & Zelazo, P. (1978). *Infancy: Its place in human development.* Cambridge, MA: Harvard University Press.

Kagan, J., & Moss, H. A. (1962). *Birth to maturity.* New York: Wiley.

Kagan, J., Snidman, N., & Arcus, D. M. (1992). Initial reactions to unfamiliarity. *Current Directions in Psychological Science, 1,* 171–174.

Kahn, S., Zimmerman, G., Csikszentmihalyi, M., & Getzels, J. W. (1985). Relations between identity in young adulthood and intimacy in midlife. *Journal of Personality and Social Psychology, 49,* 1316–1322.

Kail, R. (1988). Developmental functions for speeds of cognitive processes. *Journal of Experimental Child Psychology, 45,* 339–364.

Kain, E. L. (1988). Trends in the demography of death. In H. Hannelore, F. M. Berardo, & R. A. Neimeyer (Eds.), *Dying: Facing the facts* (2nd ed.). Washington, DC: Hemisphere Publishing Corporation.

Kalish, R. A. (1988). The study of death: A psychosocial perspective. In H. Hannelore, F. M. Berardo, & R. A. Neimeyer (Eds.), *Dying: Facing the facts* (2nd ed.). Washington, DC: Hemisphere Publishing Corporation.

Kalish, R. A., & Reynolds, D. K. (1981). *Death and ethnicity: A psychocultural study.* Farmingdale, NY: Baywood. (Original work published by University of Southern California Press 1976)

Kamin, L. (1981a). Separated identical twins. In H. J. Eysenck versus L. Kamin, *The intelligence controversy.* New York: Wiley.

Kamin, L. (1981b). Studies of adopted children. In H. J. Eysenck versus L. Kamin, *The intelligence controversy.* New York: Wiley.

Kandel, E. R. (1981). Calcium and the control of synaptic strength by learning. *Nature, 293,* 697–700.

Kane, B. (1979). Children's concepts of death. *Journal of Genetic Psychology, 134,* 141–153.

Kane, M. J., Hasher, L., Stolzfus, E. R., Zacks, R. T., & Connelly, S. L. (1994). Inhibitory attentional mechanisms and aging. *Psychology and Aging, 9,* 103–112.

Kanter, R. M. (1977). *Men and women of the corporation.* New York: Basic Books.

Kaplan, E., Goodglass, H., & Weintraub, S. (1976). *Boston Naming Test.* Experimental Edition. Philadelphia: Lea & Febiger.

Kaplan, E., & Kaplan, G. (1971). The prelinguistic child. In J. Elliot (Ed.), *Human development and cognitive process.* New York: Holt, Rinehart, & Winston.

Kasser, T., & Ryan, R. M. (1993). A dark side of the American dream: Correlates of financial success as a central life aspiration. *Journal of Personality and Social Psychology, 65*(2), 410–422.

Kastenbaum, R. (1975). Is death a life crisis? In N. Datan & L. H. Ginsberg (Eds.), *Life-span developmental psychology: Normative life crises.* New York: Academic Press.

Kastenbaum, R. J. (1985). Dying and death: A life-span approach. In J. E. Birren & W. Schaie (Eds.), *Handbook of the psychology of aging* (2nd ed., pp. 619–643). New York: Van Nostrand Reinhold.

Katchadorian, H. (1977). *The biology of adolescence.* San Francisco: W. H. Freeman.

Katz, P. A., & Ksansnak, K. R. (1994). Developmental aspects of gender-role flexibility and traditionality in middle childhood and adolescence. *Developmental Psychology, 30*(2), 272–282.

Kausler, D. H., & Puckett, J. M. (1980). Frequency judgments and correlated cognitive abilities in young and elderly adults. *Journal of Gerontology, 35,* 376–382.

Keating, D. (1980). Thinking processes in adolescence. In J. Adelson (Ed.), *Handbook of adolescent psychology* (pp. 211–246). New York: Wiley.

Keating, D. P., & Bobbitt, B. L. (1978). Individual and developmental differences in cognitive-processing components of mental ability. *Child Development, 49,* 155–167.

Kelleghan, T., & MacNamara, J. (1972). Family correlates of verbal reasoning ability. *Developmental Psychology, 7,* 49–53.

Kelley, H. H., & Thibaut, J. W. (1978). *Interpersonal relations: A theory of independence.* New York: Wiley-Interscience.

Kelley, J. H., & Hanen, M. P. (1987). *Archaeology and the methodology of science.* Albuquerque: University of New Mexico Press.

Kelly, G. A. (1955). *The psychology of personal constructs.* New York: Norton.

Kemper, S. (1987). Life-span changes in syntactic complexity. *Journal of Gerontology, 42,* 323–328.

Kemper, S. (1988). Geriatric psycholinguistics: Syntactic limitations of oral and written language. In L. L. Light & D. M. Burke (Eds.), *Language, memory, and aging.* New York: Cambridge University Press.

Kemper, S. (1992). *Language and aging.* In F. I. M. Craik & T. Salthouse (Eds.), *The handbook of aging and cognition.* Hillsdale, NJ: Erlbaum.

Kennedy, B. A., & Miller, D. J. (1976). Persistent use of verbal rehearsal as a function of information about its value. *Child Development, 47,* 566–569.

Kennel, J. H., Slyter, H., & Klaus, M. H. (1970). The mourning response of parents to the death of a newborn infant. *New England Journal of Medicine, 283,* 344–349.

Kent, C. W. (Ed.). (1965). *The poems of Edgar Allan Poe.* New York: AMS Press Inc.

Kessler, R. C., Foster, C., Webster, P. S., & House, J. S. (1992). The relationship between age and depressive symptoms in two national surveys. *Psychology and Aging, 7,* 119–126.

Kihlstrom, J. F. (1994, June/July). *The social construction of memory.* Presidential symposium. American Psychological Society, Washington, DC.

Kilmartin, C. T. (1994). *The masculine self.* New York: Macmillan.

Kimball, M. M. (1981). Women and science: A critique of biological theories. *International Journal of Women's Studies, 4,* 318–388.

Kimball, M. M. (1989). A new perspective on women's math achievement. *Psychological Bulletin, 105*(2), 198–214.

Kimble, G. A. (1992). A new formula for behaviorism. *The General Psychologist, 28,* 3–9.

Kimble, G. A., Garmezy, N., & Zigler, E. (1984). *Principles of psychology* (6th ed.). New York: Wiley.

Kimura, D. (1987). Are men's and women's brains really different? *Canadian Psychology, 28,* 133–147.

Kimura, D. (1992, September). Sex differences in the brain. *Scientific American,* pp. 119–125.

Kinsey, A. C., Pomeroy, W. B., & Martin, C. (1948). *Sexual behavior in the human male.* Philadelphia, PA: Saunders.

Kinsey, L. R., Roberts, J. L., & Logan, D. L. (1972). Death, dying, and denial in the aged. *American Journal of Psychiatry, 129,* 75–80.

Kipper, D. A., & Yinon, Y. (1978). The effect of modeling with expressed conflict on children's generosity. *Journal of Social Psychology, 106,* 277–278.

Kitson, G. C., Babri, K. B., & Roach, M. J. (1985). Who divorces and why: A review. *Journal of Family Issues, 6,* 255–293.

Klahr, D. (1982). Non monotone assessment of monotone development: An information processing analysis. In S. Strauss (Ed.), *U-shaped behavioral growth* (pp. 63–99). New York: Academic Press.

Klahr, D. (1984). Transition processes in quantitative development. In R. J. Sternberg (Ed.), *Mechanisms of cognitive development.* New York: Freeman.

Klatzky, R. L., & Forrest, F. H. (1984). Recognizing familiar and unfamiliar faces. *Memory and Cognition, 12,* 60–70.

Klaus, M. H., Jerauld, R., Kreger, N. C., McAlpine, W., Steffa, M., & Kennell, J. H. (1972). Maternal attachment: Importance of the first post-partum days. *New England Journal of Medicine, 286,* 460–463.

Klaus, M. H., & Kennel, J. H. (1976). *Maternal infant bonding.* St. Louis: CV Mosby Co.

Klaus, M. H., & Kennel, J. H. (1982). *Parent-infant bonding.* St. Louis: Mosby.

Klesges, R., Malott, J., Boschee, P., & Weber, J. (1986). The effects of parental influences on children's food intake, physical activity and relative weight. *International Journal of Eating Disorders, 5,* 335–345.

Kligman, A. M., Grove, G., & Balin, A. K. (1985). Aging of human skin. In C. E. Finch & E. L. Schneider (Eds.), *Handbook of the biology of aging* (2nd ed.). New York: Van Nostrand.

Klima, E., & Bellugi, U. (1966). Syntactic regularities in the speech of children. In J. Lyons & R. Wales (Eds.), *Psycholinguistic papers.* Edinburgh: Edinburgh University Press.

Kline, D. W., & Schieber, F. (1985). Vision and aging. In J. E. Birren & K. W. Schaie (Eds.), *Handbook of the psychology of aging* (2nd ed.). New York: Van Nostrand.

Kohlberg, L. (1963a). Moral development and identification. In H. W. Stevenson (Ed.), *Child psychology.* 62nd Yearbook of the National Society for the Study of Education. Chicago: University of Chicago Press.

Kohlberg, L. (1963b). The development of children's orientations towards a moral order. 1. Sequence in the development of moral thought. *Vita Humana, 6,* 11–33.

Kohlberg, L. (1966). A cognitive-developmental analysis of children's sex-role concepts and attitudes. In E. E. Maccoby (Ed.), *The development of sex differences* (pp. 82–173). Stanford, CA: Stanford University Press.

Kohlberg, L. (1969). *Stages in the development of moral thought and action.* New York: Holt.

Kohlberg, L. (1981). *The philosophy of moral development* (Vol. 1). San Francisco: Harper & Row.

Kohlberg, L. (1984). *Essay on moral development: Vol. 11. The psychology of moral development.* New York: Harper & Row.

Kohlberg, L. (1985). *The psychology of moral development.* San Francisco: Harper & Row.

Kohlberg, L., & Candee, D. (1984). The relationship of moral judgment to moral action. In W. M. Kurtines & J. L. Gewirtz (Eds.), *Morality, moral behavior and moral development.* New York: Wiley.

Konner, M. (1982). Biological aspects of the mother-infant bond. In C. Parks & J. Stevenson-Hinde (Eds.), *The place of attachment in human behavior.* New York: Basic Books.

Konopka, G. (1976). *Young girls: A portrait of adolescence.* Englewood Cliffs, NJ: Prentice Hall.

Kopp, C. B. (1983). Risk factors in development. In M. M. Haith & J. Campos (Eds.), *Infancy and developmental psychobiology: Vol 2. Handbook of child psychology.* New York: Wiley.

Kopp, C. B. (1987). The growth of self-regulation: Caregivers and children. In N. Eisenberg (Ed.), *Contemporary topics in developmental psychology.* New York: Wiley.

Kopp, C. B., & Kaler, S. R. (1989). Risk in infancy. *American Psychologist, 44,* 224–230.

Korbin, F. E., & Hendershot, G. E. (1977). Do family ties reduce mortality? Evidence from the United States 1966–1968. *Journal of Marriage and the Family, 38,* 737–745.

Kotelchuck, M. (1976). The infant's relationship to the father. In M. E. Lamb (Ed.), *The role of father in child development*. New York: Wiley.

Kramer, M. S. (1987). Intrauterine growth and gestational duration determinants. *Pediatrics, 80,* 502–511.

Krebs, D. L., Vermeulen, S. C., & Denton, K. L. (1990, November). *The corruption of moral judgment in everyday life*. Paper presented at the 15th Annual Conference of the Association of Moral Education, Notre Dame, Indiana.

Kreutzer, M. A., Leonard, C., & Flavell, J. H. (1975). An interview study of children's knowledge about memory. *Monographs of the Society for Research in Child Development, 40*(Serial No. 159, 1–60).

Kropp, J. P., & Haynes, O. M. (1987). Abusive and nonabusive mothers' ability to identify general and specific emotion signals of infants. *Child Development, 58,* pp. 187–190.

Krosnick, J. A., & Schuman, H. (1988). Attitude intensity, importance, and certainty and susceptibility to response effects. *Journal of Personality and Social Psychology, 54,* 940–952.

Kübler-Ross, E. (1969). *On death and dying*. New York: Macmillan.

Kübler-Ross, E. (1971, January). What is it like to be dying? *The American Journal of Nursing, 71,* 54–62.

Kübler-Ross, E. (1975). *Death: The final stage of growth*. Englewood Cliffs, NJ: Prentice Hall.

Kuczaj, S. A., II. (1986). Discussion: On social interaction as a type of explanation of language development. *British Journal of Developmental Psychology, 4,* 289–299.

Kuhn, D. (1988). Cognitive development. In M. H. Bornstein & M. E. Lamb (Eds.), *Developmental psychology: An advanced textbook of developmental psychology* (2nd ed.). Hillsdale, NJ: Erlbaum.

Kuhn, D., Nash, S. C., & Brucken, L. (1978). Sex role concepts of two- and three-year olds. *Child Development, 49,* 445–451.

Kurdek, L. A. (1986). Children's reasoning about parental divorce. In R. D. Ashmore & D. M. Brodzinsky (Eds.), *Thinking about the family*. Hillsdale, NJ: Erlbaum.

Kurdek, L. A. (1993). Predicting marital dissolution: A 5-year prospective longitudinal study of newlywed couples. *Journal of Personality and Social Psychology, 64,* 221–242.

Kussin, S. A., & Wrightsman, L. (Eds.). (1985). *The psychology of evidence and trial procedure*. Beverly Hills, CA: Sage.

L

LaBarba, R. C. (1981). *Foundations of developmental psychology*. New York: Academic Press.

Labouvie-Vief, G. (1985). Intelligence and cognition. In J. E. Birren & K. W. Schaie (Eds.), *Handbook of the psychology of aging* (2nd ed.). New York: Van Nostrand Reinhold.

LaBuda, M. C., DeFries, J. C., Plomin, R., & Fulker, D. W. (1986). Longitudinal stability of cognitive ability from infancy to early childhood: Genetic and environmental etiologies. *Child Development, 57,* 1142–1150.

Lahey, B. B., Hammer, D., Crumrine, R. L., & Forehand, R. L. (1980). Birth order × sex interactions in child behavior problems. *Child Psychology, 16,* 608–615.

Lamb, M. E. (1976). Twelve-month-olds and their parents: Interaction in a laboratory playroom. *Developmental Psychology, 12,* 237–246.

Lamb, M. E. (1977). The development of mother-infant and father-infant attachments in the second year of life. *Developmental Psychology, 13,* 637–648.

Lamb, M. E. (1979). Parental influences and the father's role: A personal perspective. *American Psychologist, 34,* 938–943.

Lamb, M. E. (1981). *The role of the father in child development* (2nd ed.). New York: Wiley.

Lamb, M. E. (1984). Social and emotional development. In M. H. Bornstein & M. E. Lamb (Eds.), *Developmental psychology: An advanced textbook* (pp. 241–277). Hillsdale, NJ: Erlbaum.

Lamb, M. E. (1988). Social and emotional development in infancy. In M. H. Bornstein & M. E. Lamb (Eds.), *Developmental psychology: An advanced textbook* (2nd ed.). Hillsdale, NJ: Erlbaum.

Lamb, M. E., & Oppenheim, D. (1989). Fatherhood and father-child relations: Five years of research. In S. H. Cath, A. Gurwitt, & L. Gunsberg (Eds.), *Fathers and their families* (pp. 11–26). Hillsdale, NJ: Erlbaum.

Lamb, M. E., Thompson, R. A., Gardner, W., & Charnov, E. L. (1985). *Infant-mother attachment: The origins and developmental significance of individual differences in strange situation behavior*. Hillsdale, NJ: Erlbaum.

Lamborn, S. D., Mounts, N. S., Steinberg, L., & Dornbusch, S. M. (1991). Patterns of competence and adjustment among adolescents from authoritative, authoritarian, indulgent, and neglectful families. *Child Development, 62,* 1049–1065.

Landers, S. (1987, June). Autism turns a corner. *APA Monitor*, p. 24.

Langer, E. J. (1983). *The psychology of control*. Beverly Hills, CA: Sage.

Langer, E. J. (1989). *Mindfulness*. Reading, MA: Addison-Wesley.

Langer, E. J., & Rodin, J. (1976). The effects of choice and enhanced personal responsibility for the aged: A field experiment in an institutional setting. *Journal of Personality and Social Psychology, 34,* 191–198.

Langer, J. (1981, June). *The structural development of concept and symbol formation*. Paper presented at the First Biennial Conference of the Heinz Werner Institute of Developmental Psychology, Worcester, MA.

Langlois, J. H. (1985). In the eye of the beholder: The development of social behaviors and social relations as a function of physical attractiveness. In C. P. Herman (Ed.), *Physical appearance, stigma and social behavior*. Hillsdale, NJ: Erlbaum.

Langlois, J. H., & Downs, A. C. (1980). Mothers, fathers, and peers as socialization of agents of sex-typed play behaviors in young children. *Child Development, 51,* 1237–1247.

Langlois, J. H., Roggman, L. A., Casey, R. J., Ritter, J. M., & Rieser-Danner, L. A. (1987). Infant preferences for attractive faces: Rudiments of a stereotype? *Developmental Psychology, 23,* 363–369.

Langlois, J. H., Roggman, L. A., & Rieser-Danner, L. A. (1990). Infants' differential social responses to attractive and unattractive faces. *Developmental Psychology, 26,* 153–159.

Lanier, H. B., & Byrne, J. (1981). How high school students view women: The relationship between perceived attractiveness, occupation, and education. *Sex Roles, 7,* 145–148.

Larsen, A. S., & Olson, D. H. (1989). Predicting marital satisfaction using PREPARE: A replication study. *Journal of Marital and Family Therapy, 15,* 311–322.

Lauer, J., & Lauer, R. (1985, December). Marriages made to last. *Psychology Today*, pp. 22–26.

Layden, M. A. (1982). Attributional therapy. In C. Autaki & C. Brewin (Eds.), *Attributions and psychological change: Applications of attributional theories to clinical and educational practice*. London: Academic Press.

Layng, A. (1994). Why don't we act like the opposite sex? In K. G. Duffy (Ed.), *Annual Edition: Psychology* (24th ed., pp. 203–205.) Guilford, CT: Dushkin.

Leach, E. (1989). Anthropological aspects of language: Animal categories and verbal abuse. *Anthrozoos, 2,* 151–165.

Lecci, L., Okun, M. A., & Karoly, P. (1994). Life regrets and current goals as predictors of psychological adjustment. *Journal of Personality and Social Psychology, 66,* 731–741.

Lefton, L. A. (1994). *Psychology* (5th ed.). Needham Heights, MA: Allyn & Bacon.

Lehman, D. R., Wortman, C. B., & Williams, A. F. (1987). The long-term effects of losing a spouse or child in a motor vehicle crash. *Journal of Personality and Social Psychology, 52,* 218–231.

Leiderman, P. H., & Leiderman, G. F. (1974). Affective and cognitive consequences of polymatric infant care in the East African highlands. In A. Pick (Ed.), *Minnesota Symposium on Child Development* (Vol. 8). Minneapolis: University of Minnesota Press.

Lenneberg, E. H. (1967). *Biological foundations of language.* New York: Wiley.

Lenneberg, E. H., Rebelsky, F. G., & Nichols, I. A. (1965). The vocalizations of infants born to deaf and hearing parents. *Human Development, 8,* 23–37.

Leopold, W. F. (1953). Patterning in children's language learning. *Language Learning, 5,* 1–14.

Lepper, M. R. (1981). Intrinsic and extrinsic motivation in children: Detrimental effects of superfluous social controls. In W. A. Collins (Ed.), *Minnesota Symposium on Child Psychology* (Vol. 14, pp. 155–214). Hillsdale, NJ: Erlbaum.

Lepper, M. R., & Greene, D. (Eds.). (1979). *The hidden costs of rewards.* Hillsdale, NJ: Erlbaum.

Lerner, J. V., Nitz, K., Talwar, R., & Lerner, R. M. (1989). On the functional significance of temperamental individuality: A developmental contextual view of the concept of goodness of fit. In G. A. Kohnstamm, J. E. Bates, & M. K. Rothbart (Eds.), *Temperamental in childhood.* Chichester, England: Wiley.

Lerner, R. M. (1984). *On the nature of human plasticity.* New York: Cambridge University Press.

Lerner, R. M. (1994, June/July). *Developmental determinants.* Address given at the Sixth Annual Convention of the American Psychological Society, Washington, DC.

Lerner, R. M., & Lerner, J. V. (1987). Children in their contexts: A goodness-of-fit model. In J. B. Lancaster, J. Altmann, A. S. Rossi, & L. R. Sherrod (Eds.), *Parenting across the life span: Biosocial dimensions* (pp. 377–404). New York: Aldine de Gruyter.

Lester, B. M., & Boukydis, C. F. Z. (Eds.). (1985). *Infant crying: Theoretical and research perspectives.* New York: Plenum Press.

Lester, B. M., & Brazelton, T. B. (1982). Cross-cultural assessment of neonatal behavior. In D. A. Wagner & H. V. Stevenson (Eds.), *Cultural perspectives in child development.* San Francisco: W. H. Freeman.

Levin, R. J., & Levin, A. (1975, September). Sexual pleasure: The surprising preference of 100,000 women. *Redbook,* p. 51.

Levinson, D. (1986). A conception of adult development. *American Psychologist, 41,* 3–13.

Levinson, D. J. (1978). *The seasons of a man's life.* New York: Ballantine.

Levinson, D., Darrow, C., Klein, E., Levinson, M., & McKee, B. (1978). *The seasons of a man's life.* New York: Knopf.

Leviton, D., & Forman, E. C. (1974). Death education for children and youth. *Journal of Clinical Psychology, 3,* 8–10.

Levy, B., & Langer, E. (1994). Aging free from negative stereotypes: Successful memory in China and among the American deaf. *Journal of Personality and Social Psychology, 66,* 989–997.

Levy, G. D., & Carter, D. B. (1989). Gender schema, gender constancy, and gender-role knowledge: The roles of cognitive factors in preschoolers' gender-role stereotype attributions. *Developmental Psychology, 25,* 444–449.

Levy, J. (1985, May). Right brain, left brain: Fact or fiction. *Psychology Today,* pp. 38–44.

Levy, M. B., & Davis, K. E. (1988). Lovestyles and attachment styles compared: Their relations to each other and to various relationship characteristics. *Journal of Social and Personal Relationships, 5,* 439–471.

Lewis, M., & Brooks-Gunn, J. (1979). *Social cognition and the acquisition of self.* New York: Plenum Press.

Lewis, M., Feiring, C., McGuffog, C., & Jaskir, J. (1984). Predicting psychopathology in six-year-olds from early social relations. *Child Development, 55,* 123–136.

Lewis, M., Young, G., Brooks, J., & Michalson, L. (1975). The beginning of friendship. In M. Lewis & L. A. Rosenblum (Eds.), *Friendship and peer relations* (pp. 27–66). New York: Wiley.

Lezak, M. (1976). *Neurological assessment.* New York: Oxford University Press.

Liben, L. S. (1975). Long-term memory for pictures related to seriation, horizontality, and verticality concepts. *Developmental Psychology, 11,* 795–806.

Liben, L. S., & Signorella, M. L. (Eds.). (1987). *Children's gender schemata: New directions for child development* (No. 38). San Francisco: Jossey-Bass.

Lickona, T. (1976). *Moral development and behavior: Theory, research, and social issues.* New York: Holt, Rinehart & Winston.

Lieberman, M. (1971, February). *Estimation of a moral judgment level using items whose alternatives form a graded scale.* Paper presented at the annual meeting of the American Educational Research Association, New York.

Lindberg, M. A. (1980). Is knowledge base development a necessary and sufficient condition for memory development? *Journal of Experimental Child Psychology, 30,* 401–410.

Lindemann, E. (1944). Symptomatology and management of acute grief. *American Journal of Psychiatry, 101,* 141–148.

Lingeman, R. R. (1980). *Small Town America: A narrative history, 1620–present.* New York: G. P. Putnam.

Linn, M. C., & Peterson, A. C. (1986). A meta-analysis of gender differences in spatial ability: Implications for mathematics and science achievement. In J. S. Hyde & M. C. Linn (Eds.), *The psychology of gender: Advances through meta-analysis.* Baltimore: Johns Hopkins University Press.

Linville, P. W. (1985). Self-complexity and affective extremity: Don't put all your eggs in one cognitive basket. *Social Cognition, 3,* 94–120.

Linville, P. W. (1987). Self-complexity as a cognitive buffer against stress-related depression and illness. *Journal of Personality and Social Psychology, 52,* 663–676.

Lipsitt, L. P. (1979). Critical conditions in infancy. *American Psychologist, 34,* 973–980.

Lipsitt, L. P. (1982). Infancy and life-span development. *Human Development, 25,* 41–48.

Livson, F. B. (1976, October). *Sex differences in personality development in the middle adult years: A longitudinal study.* Paper presented at the 28th Annual Scientific Meeting of the Gerontological Society, Louisville, KY.

Livson, F. B. (1981). Paths to psychological health in middle years: Sex differences. In D. H. Eichorn, J. A. Clausen, N. Haan, M. P. Honzik, & P. H. Mussen (Eds.), *Present and past in middle life.* New York: Academic Press.

Livson, F. B. (1983). Gender identity: A life-span view of sex-role development. In R. B. Weg (Ed.), *Sexuality in the later years: Roles and behavior.* New York: Academic Press.

Localio, A. R., Lawthers, A. G., Bengtson, J. M., Herbert, L. E., Weaver, S. L., Brennan, T. A., & Landis, R. (1993). Relationship between malpractice claims and Cesarean delivery. *Journal of the American Medical Association, 269,* 366–373.

Loehlin, J. C. (1992). *Genes and environment in personality development.* Newbury Park, CA: Sage.

Loehlin, J. C., Horn, H. M., & Willerman, L. (1989). Modeling IQ change: Evidence from the Texas Adoption Project. *Child Development, 60,* 993–1004.

Loehlin, J. C., & Nichols, R. (1976). *Heredity, environment and personality: A study of 850 sets of twins.* Austin: University of Texas Press.

Loehlin, J. C., Willerman, L., & Horn, J. M. (1982). Personality resemblances between unwed mothers and their adopted-away offspring. *Journal of Personality and Social Psychology, 42,* 1089–1099.

Loehlin, J. C., Willerman, L., & Horn, J. M. (1985). Personality resemblances in adoptive families when the children are late-adolescent or adult. *Journal of Personality and Social Psychology, 48,* 376–392.

Loehlin, J. C., Willerman, L., & Horn, J. M. (1988). Human behavior genetics. *Annual Review of Psychology, 39,* 101–133.

Loevinger, J. (1966). The meaning and measurement of ego development. *American Psychologist, 21,* 195–206.

Loevinger, J. (1976). *Ego development: Conceptions and theories.* San Francisco: Jossey-Bass.

Loftus, E. F. (1979). *Eyewitness testimony.* Cambridge, MA: Harvard University Press.

Loftus, E. F. (1992). When a lie becomes memory's truth: Memory distortion after exposure to misinformation. *Current Directions in Psychological Science, 1,* 121–123.

Loftus, E. F. (1993). The reality of repressed memories. *American Psychologist, 48,* 15–25.

Loftus, E. F. (1994, July). *The repressed memory mystery.* Closing Plenary given at the meeting of the American Psychological Society, Washington, DC.

Looft, W. R. (1973). Socialization and personality throughout the life span: An examination of contemporary psychological approaches. In P. B. Baltes & K. W. Schaie (Eds.), *Life-span developmental psychology: Personality and socialization.* New York: Academic Press.

Lopata, H. Z. (1973). *Widowhood in an American city.* Cambridge, MA: Schenckman.

Lopata, H. Z. (1975). Widowhood: Societal factors in life-span disruptions and alternatives. In N. Datan & L. H. Ginsberg (Eds.), *Life-span developmental psychology: Normative life crises.* New York: Academic Press.

Lopata, H. Z. (1988). Support systems of American urban widowhood. *Journal of Social Issues, 44,* 113–128.

Lorenz, K. (1935). Companions as factors in the bird's environment. In K. Lorenz, (Ed.), *Studies in animal and human behavior* (Vol. I). (R. Martin, trans.). Cambridge, MA: Harvard University Press, 1971.

Lorenz, K. Z. (1937). The companion in the bird's world. *Auk, 54,* 245–273.

Lorenz, K. Z. (1943). Die angebornen Formen moglicher Erfahrung. *Zeitgeist fur Tierpsychologie, 5,* 233–409.

Lovaas, O. I. (1987). Behavioral treatment and normal educational and intellectual functioning in young autistic children. *Journal of Consulting Clinical Psychology, 55,* 3–9.

Lowenthal, M. F., & Chiriboga, D. (1972). Transition to the empty nest. *Archives of General Psychiatry, 26,* 8–14.

Lowenthal, M. F., & Weiss, L. (1976). Intimacy and crises in adulthood. *Counseling-Psychologist, 6,* 10–15.

Lozoff, B. (1989). Nutrition and behavior. *American Psychologist, 44,* 231–236.

Lubin, B., Larsen, R. M., & Matarazzo, J. D. (1984). Patterns of psychological test usage in the United States: 1935–1982. *American Psychologist, 39,* 451–454.

Lummis, M., & Stevenson, H. W. (1990). Gender differences in beliefs and achievement: A cross-cultural study. *Developmental Psychology, 26,* 252–263.

Luong, H. V. (1986). Language, cognition and ontogenic development: A reexamination of Piaget's premises. *Ethos, 14,* 7–46.

Luria, Z., & Herzog, E. (1985, April). *Gender segregation across and within settings.* Paper presented at the biennial meeting of the Society for Research in Child Development, Toronto, Ontario, Canada.

Lyons-Ruth, K., Connell, D. B., Zoll, D., & Stahl, J. (1987). Infants at social risk: Relations among infant maltreatment, maternal behavior, and infant attachment behavior. *Developmental Psychology, 23,* 223–232.

Lytton, L., & Romney, D. M. (1991). Parents' differential socialization of boys and girls: A meta-analysis. *Psychological Bulletin, 109,* 267–296.

M

Maccoby, E. E. (1980). *Social development: Psychological growth and the parent-child relationship.* New York: Harcourt Brace Jovanovich.

Maccoby, E. E. (1988). Gender as a social category. *Developmental Psychology, 24,* 755–765.

Maccoby, E. E. (1990). Gender and relationships: A developmental account. *American Psychologist, 45,* 513–520.

Maccoby, E. E., & Jacklin, C. N. (1974). *The psychology of sex differences.* Stanford, CA: Stanford University Press.

Maccoby, E. E., & Jacklin, C. N. (1980). Sex differences in aggression: A rejoinder and reprise. *Child Development, 51,* 964–980.

Maccoby, E. E., & Jacklin, C. N. (1987). Gender segregation in childhood. In H. W. Reese (Ed.), *Advances in child development and behavior* (Vol. 20, pp. 239–288). New York: Academic Press.

Maccoby, E. E., & Martin, J. A. (1983). Socialization in the context of the family: Parent-child interaction. In P. H. Mussen (Ed.), *Handbook of child psychology: Vol. 4. Socialization, personality, and social development.* New York: Wiley.

MacLeod, C. M. (1992). The Stroop task. *Journal of Experimental Psychology General, 121,* 12–14.

MacNamara, J. (1972). Cognitive basis of language learning in infants. *Psychological Review, 79,* 1–14.

MacNamara, J. T. (1987). Review of language development in the preschool years. *Canadian Psychology, 28,* 304–305.

Maddison, D. G. (1968). The relevance of conjugal bereavement for preventative psychiatry. *British Journal of Medical Psychology, 41,* 223–233.

Maddux, J. E. (1994). The social cognitive theories: General principles and implications for psychological adjustment. *The General Psychologist, 30,* 13–17.

Magenis, R. E., Overton, K. M., Chamberlin, J., Brady, T., & Lorrien, E. (1977). Prenatal origin of the extra chromosome in Down syndrome. *Human Genetics, 37,* 7–16.

Mahler, M. S. (1968). *On human symbiosis and the vicissitudes of individualism: Vol. 1. Infantile psychosis.* New York: International Universities Press.

Maidman, J. (1988). What is safe? In W. D. Todd, D. F. Tapley, G. J. Subak-Sharpe, and D. M. Goetz (Eds.). *The Columbia University College of Physicians and Surgeons complete guide to pregnancy.* New York: Crown.

Main, M., Kaplan, N., & Cassidy, J. (1985). Security in infancy, childhood, and adulthood: A move to the level of representation. *Monographs of the Society for Research in Child Development, 50*(1–2, Serial No. 209).

Main, M., & Solomon, J. (1989). Procedures for identifying infants as disorganized/disoriented during Ainsworth strange situation. In M. Greenberg, D. Cichetti, & M. Cummings (Eds.), *Attachment in the preschool years.* Chicago: University of Chicago Press.

Malatesta, C. (1990, May 28). Commentary. *Newsweek,* p. 61.

Malina, R. M. (1979). Secular changes in size and maturity. *Monographs of the Society for Research in Child Development, 44*(3–4, Serial No. 179).

Malinowski, B. (1927). *Sex and repression in a savage society.* New York: Harcourt Brace Jovanovich.

Mancini, J. A., & Blieszner, R. (1985). Return of middle-aged children to the parental home. *Medical Aspects of Human Sexuality, 19,* 192–194.

Maratsos, M., & Chalkley, M. A. (1980). The internal language of children's syntax: The ontogenesis and representation of syntactic categories. In K. E. Nelson (Eds.), *Children's language* (Vol. 2). New York: Gardner Press.

Marchalonis, J. J., Schluter, S. F., Wilson, L., Yocum, D. E., Boyer, J. T., & Kay, M. M. (1993). Natural human antibodies to synthetic peptide autoantigens: Correlations with age and autoimmune disease. *Gerontology, 39,* 65–79.

Marcia, J. (1976). Identity six years later: A follow-up study. *Journal of Youth and Adolescence, 5,* 145–160.

Marcia, J. E. (1976). *Studies in ego identity.* Unpublished monograph, Simon Fraser University, Burnaby, British Columbia.

Marcus, D. E., & Overton, W. F. (1978). The development of cognitive gender constancy and sex-role preferences. *Child Development, 49,* 434–444.

Markman, H. J. (1979). Application of a behavioral model of marriage in predicting relationship satisfaction of couples planning marriage. *Journal of Consulting and Clinical Psychology, 47,* 743–749.

Markman, H. J. (1992). Marital and family psychology: Burning issues [Special issue: Diversity in contemporary family psychology]. *Journal of Family Psychology, 5,* 264–275.

Markman, H. J., Renick, M. J., Floyd, F. J., Stanley, S. M., et al. (1993). Preventing marital distress through communication and conflict management training: A 4- and 5-year follow up [Special section: Couples and couple therapy]. *Journal of Consulting and Clinical Psychology, 61,* 70–77.

Marshall, W. A. (1977). *Human growth and its disorders.* New York: Academic Press.

Martin, C. L., & Halverson, C. F., Jr. (1981). A schematic processing model of sex typing and stereotyping in children. *Child Development, 52,* 1119–1134.

Martin, C. L., & Little, J. K. (1990). The relation of gender understanding to children's sex-typed preferences and gender stereotypes. *Child Development, 61,* 1427–1439.

Martorano, C. S. (1977). A developmental analysis of performance on Piaget's formal operation tasks. *Developmental Psychology, 13,* 666–672.

Masangkay, Z. S., McCluskey, K. A., McIntyre, C. W., Sims-Knight, J., Vaughn, B. E., & Flavell, J. H. (1974). The early development of inferences about the visual percepts of others. *Child Development, 45,* 357–366.

Maslow, A. H. (1954). *Motivation and personality.* New York: Harper.

Maslow, A. H. (1962). *Toward a psychology of being.* Princeton: Van Nostrand.

Maslow, A. H. (1970). *Motivation and personality* (2nd ed.). New York: Harper & Row.

Maslow, A. H. (1971). *The farther reaches of human nature.* New York: Viking Press.

Maslow, A. H. (1972). *Abraham Maslow: A memorial volume.* Monterey, CA: Brooks/Cole.

Masnick, G., & Bane, M. J. (1980). *The nation's families: 1960–1990.* Joint Center for Urban Studies of MIT and Harvard.

Masters, W. H., & Johnson, V. E. (1966). *Human sexual response.* Boston: Little, Brown.

Masters, W. H., Johnson, V. E., & Kolodny, R. C. (1985). *Human sexuality* (2nd ed.). Boston: Little, Brown.

Matas, L., Arend, R., & Sroufe, L. A. (1978). Continuity of adaptation in the second year: The relationship between quality of attachment and later competence. *Child Development, 49,* 547–556.

Matlin, M. W. (1993). *The psychology of women.* Fort Worth, TX: Harcourt Brace Jovanovich.

Matthews, K. A., & Wing, R. R. (1990). Influences of natural menopause on psychological characteristics and symptoms of middle-aged healthy women. *Journal of Consulting and Clinical Psychology, 58,* 345–351.

Maurer, D., & Barrera, M. (1981). Infants' perception of natural and distorted arrangements of schematic faces. *Child Development, 52,* 196–202.

Maurer, D., & Salapatek, P. (1976). Developmental changes in the scanning of faces by young infants. *Child Development, 47,* 523–537.

Mayer, R. E. (1984). Aids to text comprehension. *Educational Psychologist, 19,* 30–42.

Mayer, R. E. (1992). *Thinking, problem solving, cognition* (2nd ed.). New York: W. H. Freeman.

McAuliffe, K. (1985, October). Making of a mind. *Omni,* pp. 62–74.

McCall, R. B. (1983). Environmental effects on intelligence: The forgotten realm of discontinuous nonshared with-family factors. *Child Development, 54,* 408–415.

McCall, R. B., Applebaum, M. I., & Hogarty, P. S. (1973). Developmental changes in mental performance. *Monographs of the Society for Research in Child Development, 38*(3, 1–84. Serial No. 150).

McCay, C. M., Maynard, L. A., Sperling, G., & Barnes, L. L. (1939). Retarded growth, life span, ultimate body size and age changes in the albino rat after feeding diets restricted in calories. *Journal of Nutrition, 18* 1–18.

McClearn, G. E. (1993). Behavioral genetics: The last century and the next. In R. Plomin & G. E. McClearn (Eds.), *Nature nurture & psychology.* Washington, DC: American Psychological Association.

McCormick, C. B., & Kennedy, J. H. (1994, June/July). *Father-child separation and attachment working models in adulthood.* Poster presented at the annual meeting of the American Psychological Society, Washington, DC.

McCrae, R., & Costa, P. (1984). *Emerging lives, enduring dispositions.* Boston: Little, Brown.

McCrae, R., & Costa, P. (1988). Psychological resilience among widowed men and women: A 10-year follow-up of a national sample. *Journal of Social Issues, 44,* 129–142.

McDade, H. L., & Varnedoe, D. R. (1987). Training parents to be language facilitators. *Topical Language Disorders, 7,* 19–20.

McEwen, B. S. (1976). Interactions between hormones and nerve tissue. *Scientific American, 235,* 48–58.

McFarland, C., Ross, M., & Giltrow, M. (1992). Biased recollections in older adults: The role of implicit theories of aging. *Journal of Personality and Social Psychology, 62,* 837–850.

McGhee, P. H., & Frueh, T. (1980). Television viewing and the learning of sex-role stereotypes. *Sex Roles, 6,* 179–188.

McGue, M., & Bouchard, T. J. (1984). Adjustment of twin data for the effects of age and sex. *Behavior Genetics, 14,* 325–343.

McGue, M., Bouchard, T. J., Iacono, W. G., & Lykken, D. T. (1993). Behavioral genetics of cognitive ability: A life-span perspective. In R. Plomin & G. E. McClearn (Eds.), *Nature nurture & psychology.* Washington, DC: American Psychological Association.

McGuire, W. J., & Padawer-Singer, A. (1976). Trait salience in the spontaneous self-concept. *Journal of Personality and Social Psychology, 33,* 743–754.

McIntosh, D. N., Silver, R. C., & Wortman, C. B. (1993). Religion's role in adjustment to a negative life event: Coping with the loss of a child. *Journal of Personality and Social Psychology, 65,* 812–821.

McIntyre, M. S., Angle, C. R., & Struempler, L. J. (1972). The concept of death in midwestern children and youth. *American Journal of Diseases of Children, 123,* 527–532.

McKillip, J., & Riedell, S. L. (1983). External validity of matching on physical attractiveness for same and opposite sex couples. *Journal of Applied Social Psychology, 13,* 328–337.

McKinnon, J. W. (1976). The college student and formal operations. In J. W. Renner, D. G. Stafford, A. E. Lawson, J. W. McKinnon, F. E. Friot, & D. H. Kellog (Eds.), *Research training and learning with the Piaget model* (pp. 110–129). Norman: University of Oklahoma Press.

McKinnon, J. W., & Renner, J. W. (1971). Are colleges concerned with intellectual development? *American Journal of Psychology, 39,* 1047–1052.

McNeill, D. (1970). *The acquisition of language.* New York: Harper & Row.

Mead, G. H. (1934). *Mind, self, and society.* Chicago: University of Chicago Press.

Mead, M. (1935). *Sex and temperament in three primitive societies.* New York: William Morrow.

Melear, J. D. (1973). Children's conceptions of death. *Journal of Genetic Psychology, 123,* 527–532.

Mendel, G. (1959). Experiments in plant-hybridization, 1865. Reprinted in J. A. Peters (Ed.), *Classic papers in genetics.* Englewood Cliffs, NJ: Prentice Hall.

Menyuk, P. (1971). *The acquisition and development of language.* New York: Prentice Hall.

Menyuk, P. (1977). *Language and maturation.* Cambridge, MA: MIT Press.

Meredith, D. (1986, June). Mom, dad and the kids. *Psychology Today,* pp. 62–67.

Metcalf, P., & Huntington, R. (1991). *Celebrations of death: The anthropology of mortuary ritual* (2nd ed.). New York: Cambridge University Press.

Meyer, B. J. F., Rice, G. E., Knight, C. C., & Jensen, J. L. (1979). *Differences in the type of information remembered from prose by young, middle, and old adults* (Research report No. 5, Prose Learning Series). Tempe: Arizona State University.

Meyerowitz, J., & Feldman, H. (1967). Transitions to parenthood. In I. Cohn (Ed.), *Family structure, dynamics, and therapy.* New York: American Psychiatric Association.

Mikulincer, M., & Nachshon, O. (1991). Attachment styles and patterns of self-disclosure. *Journal of Personality and Social Psychology, 61,* 321–331.

Milham, J., Widmayer, S., Bauer, C. R., & Peterson, L. (1983, April). *Predicting cognitive deficits for preterm, low birthweight infants.* Paper presented at the biennial meeting of the Society for Research in Child Development, Detroit.

Miller, B. C. (1976). A multivariate developmental model of marital satisfaction. *Journal of Marriage and the Family, 38,* 643–657.

Miller, G. A. (1956). The magical number seven, plus or minus two: Some limits on our capacity for processing information. *Psychological Review, 63,* 81–87.

Miller, J. (1981). *Assessing language production in children.* Baltimore: University Park Press.

Miller, M., & Reaves, B. (1976). Children's occupational sex-role stereotypes. *Journal of Broadcasting, 20,* 35–50.

Miller, N., & Maruyama, G. (1976). Ordinal position and peer popularity. *Journal of Personality and Social Psychology, 33,* 123–131.

Miller, P. H., & Weiss, M. G. (1981). Children's attention allocation, understanding of attention, and performance on the incidental learning task. *Child Development, 52,* 1183–1190.

Miller, P. H., Woody-Ramsey, J., & Aloise, P. A. (1991). The role of strategy effortfulness in strategy effectiveness. *Developmental Psychology, 27,* 738–745.

Miller, R. (1976). Mere exposure, psychological reactance and attitude change. *Public Opinion Quarterly, 40,* 229–233.

Miller, R. G. (1987, November). Athletes and steroids: Playing a deadly game. *FDA Consumer,* 17–22.

Miller, W. R., & C'deBaca, J. (1994). Quantum change: Toward a psychology of transformation. In T. F. Heatherton & J. L. Weinberger (Eds.), *Can personality change?* Washington, DC: American Psychological Association.

Milstein, R. M. (1980). Responsiveness in newborn infants of overweight and normal weight parents. *Appetite, 1,* 65–74.

Mischel, W. (1970). Sex-typing and socialization. In. P. H. Mussen (Ed.), *Carmichael's manual of child psychology* (Vol. 2). New York: Wiley.

Mischel, W. (1983). Delay of gratification as process and as person variable in development. In D. Magnusson & V. P. Allen (Eds.), *Human development: An interactional perspective* (pp. 149–165). New York: Academic Press.

Mischel, W., Shoda, Y., & Peake, P. K. (1988). The nature of adolescent competencies predicted by preschool delay of gratification. *Journal of Personality and Social Psychology, 54,* 687–696.

Moely, B. E. (1977). Organizational factors in the development of memory. In R. V. Kail & J. W. Hagen (Eds.), *Perspectives on the development of memory and cognition* (pp. 203–236). Hillsdale, NJ: Erlbaum.

Moely, B. E., Olson, F. A., Halwes, T. G., & Flavell, J. H. (1969). Production deficiency in young children's clustered recall. *Developmental Psychology, 1,* 26–34.

Molfese, D. L. (1985, November). When is a word a word? *Psychology Today,* pp. 10–11.

Money, J., & Annecillo, C. (1987). Body image pathology: Koro, the shrinking penis syndrome in transcultural sexology. *Sexual and Marriage Therapy, 2,* 91–100.

Money, J., & Ehrhardt, A. A. (1973). *Man and woman, boy and girl.* Baltimore and London: John Hopkins Press.

Montagna, W., & Carlisle, K. (1979). Structural changes in aging human skin. *Journal of Investigations in Dermatology, 73,* 47–53.

Moore, K. L. (1982). *The developing human: Clinically oriented embryology* (3rd ed.). Philadelphia: Saunders.

Moreland, R. L., & Zajonc, R. B. (1979). Exposure effects may not depend on stimulus recognition. *Journal of Personality and Social Psychology, 37,* 1085–1089.

Moreland, R. L., & Zajonc, R. B. (1982). Exposure effects in person perception: Familiarity, similarity, and attraction. *Journal of Experimental Social Psychology, 18,* 395–415.

Morgan, S. P., & Rindfus, R. R. (1985). Marital disruption: Structural and temporal dimensions. *American Journal of Sociology, 90,* 1055–1077.

Morris, J. (1974). *Conundrum, from James to Jan.* New York: Harcourt Brace Jovanovich.

Morrison, F. J., Holmes, D. L., & Haith, M. M. (1974). A developmental study of the effect of familiarity on short-term visual memory. *Journal of Experimental Child Psychology, 18,* 412–425.

Mortimer, J. T., Finch, M. D., & Kumka, D. (1982). Persistence and change in development: The multi-dimensional self-concept. In P. B. Baltes & O. G. Brim, Jr. (Eds.), *Lifespan development and behavior* (Vol. 4). New York: Academic Press.

Morycz, R. K. (1992). Widowhood and bereavement in later life. In V. B. Van Hasselt & M. Heresen (Eds.), *Handbook of social development: A lifespan perspective.* New York: Plenum Press.

Moss, H. A., & Sussman, E. J. (1980). Longitudinal study of personality development. In O. G. Brim, Jr., & J. Kagan (Eds.), *Constancy and change in human development.* Cambridge, MA: Harvard University Press.

Mueller, E., & Brenner, J. (1977). The growth of social interaction in a toddler playgroup: The role of peer experience. *Child Development, 48,* 854–861.

Mueller, E., & Lucas, T. (1975). A developmental analysis of peer interaction among toddlers. In M. Lewis & L. Rosenblum (Eds.), *Friendship and peer relations.* New York: Wiley.

Muir, J. J., & Kennedy, J. H. (1994, July). *Intellectually active older adults have no age-related decline in naming abilities.* Paper presented at the meeting of the American Psychological Society, Washington, DC.

Mussen, P. H. (1969). Early sex-role development. In D. A. Goslin (Eds.), *Handbook of socialization theory and research.* Skokie, IL: Rand McNally.

Mussen, P. H., Conger, J. J., Kagan, J., & Geiwitz, J. (1979). *Psychological development: A life-span approach.* New York: Harper & Row.

Myers, D. G. (1990a). *Exploring psychology.* New York: Worth.

Myers, D. G. (1990b). *Social psychology (3rd ed.).* New York: McGraw-Hill.

Myers, D. G. (1992). *The pursuit of happiness.* New York: William Morrow & Co.

Myers, D. G. (1993). *The pursuit of happiness: Who is happy—and why.* New York: William Morrow.

N

Nagy, M. H. (1948). The child's theories concerning death. *Journal of Genetic Psychology, 73,* 3–27.

National Center for Health Statistics. (1983). *Monthly Vital Statistics, 31* (13). Washington, DC: U.S. Department of Health and Human Services.

National Center for Health Statistics. (1985). *Health: United States 1985.* Washington, DC: U.S. Department of Health and Human Services.

National Center for Health Statistics. (1987). *Monthly Vital Statistics, 35* (117). Washington, DC: U.S. Department of Health and Human Services.

Neale, R. E. (1973). *The art of dying.* New York: Harper & Row.

Neel, J. V., & Schull, W. J. (1956). Studies on the potential genetic effects of the atomic bombs. *Acta Genetica, 6,* 183–189.

Neimark, E. D. (1975). Longitudinal development of formal operations thought. *Genetic Psychology Monographs, 91,* 171–225.

Neimark, E. D. (1979). Current status of formal operations research. *Human Development, 22,* 60–67.

Neisser, U. (1984, August). *Discussant: Autobiographical memory.* Symposium presented at the annual meeting of the American Psychological Association, Toronto.

Nelson, K. (1973). Structure and strategy in learning to talk. *Monographs of the Society for Research in Child Development, 38*(1 & 2, Serial No. 149).

Nelson, K. (1981). Individual differences in language development: Implications for development and language. *Developmental Psychology, 17,* 170–187.

Nelson, K. E., & Nelson, K. (1978). Cognitive pendulums and their linguistic realization. In K. Nelson (Ed.), *Children's language.* New York: Gardner.

Nelson, K. E., & Ross, G. (1980). The generalities and specifics of long-term memory in infants and young children. In M. Perlmutter (Guest Ed.), *New directions for child development* (No. 10). San Francisco: Jossey-Bass.

Nesselroade, J. R. (1994, April). *Intraindividual variability and stability: Some reflections on adult development and aging.* Invited address, Conference on Human Development, Pittsburgh, PA.

Nesselroade, J. R., & Boker, S. M. (1994). Assessing constancy and change. In T. F. Heatherton & J. L. Weinberger (Eds.), *Can personality change?* Washington, DC: American Psychological Association.

Neugarten, B. (1973). A new look at menopause. In C. Tavris (Ed.), *The female experience.* Del Mar, CA: Communications/Research/Machines.

Neugarten, B. L. (1977). Personality and aging. In J. E. Birren & K. W. Schaie (Eds.), *Handbook of the psychology of aging.* New York: Van Nostrand Reinhold.

Neugarten, B. L., & Gutmann, D. L. (1968). Age-sex roles and personality in middle age. In B. L. Neugarten (Ed.), *Middle age and aging.* Chicago: University of Chicago Press.

Newman, E. (1974). *Strictly speaking.* New York: Bobbs-Merrill.

Newmeyer, F. J. (1986). *Linguistic theory in America.* New York: Academic Press.

Newport, E. L., Gleitman, H., & Gleitman, L. R. (1977). Mother, I'd rather do it myself: Some effects and non-effects of maternal speech style. In C. A. Ferguson & C. E. Snow (Eds.), *Talking to children: Language input and acquisition.* New York: Cambridge University Press.

Newsweek. (1993, October 5). The Clinton Health Plan and what it means for you.

Nicholas, M., Obler, L., Albert, M., & Goodglass, H. (1985). Lexical retrieval in healthy aging. *Cortex, 21,* 595–606.

Nicholls, J. G., Patashnick, M., & Mettetal, G. (1986). Conceptions of ability and intelligence. *Child Development, 57,* 636–645.

Nichols, R. C. (1978). Twins studies of ability, personality and interests. *Homo, 29,* 158–173.

Nickerson, R., Green, D., Stevens, K., & Kalikow, D. (1975). Some experimental tasks for the study of effects of aging on cognitive performance. In L. Poon & J. Fozard (Eds.), *Design conference on decision making and aging.* (Technical reports 76-01 of the Normative Aging Study, pp. 136–175).

Nickerson, R. S., & Adams, M. J. (1979). Long-term memory for a common object. *Cognitive Psychology, 11,* 287–307.

Niedenthal, P. M., Setterland, M. B., & Wherry, M. B. (1992). Possible self-complexity and affective reactions to goal relevant evaluation. *Journal of Personality and Social Psychology, 63,* 5–16.

Nisbett, R. E., & Wilson, F. D. (1977). Telling more than we can know: Verbal reports on mental processes. *Psychological Review, 84,* 231–259.

Nock, S. L. (1982). The life-cycle approach to family analysis. In B. B. Wolman (Ed.), *Handbook of developmental psychology.* Englewood Cliffs, NJ: Prentice Hall.

Nolen-Hoeksema, S., Girgus, J. S., & Seligman, M. E. P. (1986). Predictors and consequences of childhood depressive symptoms: A longitudinal study of depression, achievement, and explanatory style. *Journal of Personality and Social Psychology, 51,* 435–442.

Norman-Jackson, J. (1982). Family interactions, language development, and primary reading achievement of Black children in families of low income. *Child Development, 53,* 349–358.

Nuland, S. B. (1994). *How we die: Reflections on life's final chapter.* New York: Knopf.

Nussbaum, R. L., & Ledbetter, D. H. (1986). Fragile X syndrome, A unique mutation in man. *Annual Review of Genetics, 20,* 109–145.

Nye, R. D. (1992). *The legacy of B. F. Skinner.* Pacific Grove, CA: Brooks/Cole.

O

Obler, L., Albert, M., Goodglass, H., & Berson, D. F. (1978). Aging and aphasia type. *Brain and Language, 6,* 318–322.

Obler, L. K. (1980). Narrative discourse style in the elderly. In L. K. Obler & M. L. Albert (Eds.), *Language and communication in the elderly.* Lexington, MA: Heath.

Obler, L. K., Albert, M., & Goodglass, H. (1981, November). *The word finding difficulties of aging and dementia.* Annual Meeting of the Gerontological Society of America, Toronto, Canada.

Obler, L. K., & Albert, M. L. (1985). Language skills across adulthood. In J. E. Birren & K. W. Schaie (Eds.), *Handbook of the psychology of aging.* New York: Van Nostrand Reinhold.

O'Brien, M., Huston, A. C., & Risley, T. R. (1983). Sex-typed play of toddlers in a day care center. *Journal of Applied Developmental Psychology, 4,* 1–9.

Obusek, C., & Warren, R. (1973). A comparison of speech perception in senile and well-preserved aged by means of the verbal transformation effect. *Journal of Gerontology, 28,* 184–188.

Ochse, R., & Plug, C. (1986). Cross-cultural investigation of the validity of Erikson's theory of personality development. *Journal of Personality and Social Psychology, 50,* 1240–1252.

Odom, R. D., Astor, E. C., & Cunningham, J. G. (1975). Effects of perceptual salience in the matrix task performance of four- and six-year-old children. *Child Development, 46,* 758–762.

Olson, G. M. (1981). The recognition of specific persons. In M. E. Lamb & L. R. Sherrod (Eds.), *Infant social cognition: Empirical and theoretical considerations.* Hillsdale, NJ: Erlbaum.

Olson, J. A. (1992). "The centrality of relationship: What's not being said": Response. *Dissociation Progress in the Dissociative Disorders, 5,* 174–175.

Opitz, J. M., & Sutherland, G. R. (1984). Conference report: International workshop on the fragile x and x-linked mental retardation. *American Journal of Medical Genetics, 17,* 5–94.

Ornstein, P. A., Naus, M. J., & Liberty, C. (1975). Rehearsal and organizational processes in children's memory. *Child Development, 46,* 818–830.

Orthner, D. K. (1975). Leisure activity patterns and marital satisfaction over the marital career. *Journal of Marriage and the Family, 37,* 91–102.

Ortman, P. E. (1993). A feminist approach to teaching learning theory with educational applications. *Teaching of Psychology, 20,* 38–40.

Osgood, C. (1963). On understanding and creating sentences. *American Psychologist, 18,* 735–751.

Otto, L. B. (1979). Antecedents and consequences of marital timing. In W. R. Burr, R. Hill, F. I. Nye, & I. L. Reiss (Eds.), *Contemporary theories about family* (Vol. 1). New York: Free Press.

Owen, M. T., Easterbrooks, M. A., Chase-Lansdale, L., Goldberg, W. A. (1984). The relation between maternal employment status and the stability of attachments to mother and to father. *Child Development, 55,* 1894–1901.

Owens, R. E., Jr. (1984). *Language development: An introduction.* Columbus, OH: Merrill.

Owens, W. A., Jr. (1953). Age and mental abilities: A longitudinal study. *Genetic Psychology Monographs, 48,* 3–54.

P

Page, D. C., et al. (1987). The sex determining region of the human Y chromosome encodes a finger protein. *Cell, 51,* 1091–1104.

Paikoff, R. L., & Brooks-Gunn, J. (1991). Do parent-child relationships change during puberty? *Psychological Bulletin, 110,* 47–66.

Palmore, E. B. (1981). The facts on aging quiz: Part two. *The Gerontologist, 21,* 431–437.

Parikh, B. (1980). Development of moral judgment and its relation to family environmental factors in Indian and American families. *Child Development, 51,* 1030–1039.

Paris, S. G. (1978). Coordination of means and goals in the development of mnemonic skills. In P. A. Ornstein (Ed.), *Memory development in children* (pp. 259–273). Hillsdale, NJ: Erlbaum.

Parkes, C. M. (1972). *Bereavement: Studies of grief in adult life.* New York: Basic Books.

Parkes, C. M. (1975). Determinants of outcome following bereavement. *Omega, 6,* 303–323.

Parkes, C. M., & Brown, R. (1972). Health after bereavement: A controlled study of young Boston widows and widowers. *Psychosomatic Medicine, 34,* 449–461.

Parsons, J. E., Adler, T. F., & Kaczala, C. M. (1982). Socialization of achievement attitudes and beliefs: Parental influences. *Child Development, 53,* 310–321.

Parsons, J. E., Kaczala, C. M., & Meece, J. L. (1982). Socialization of achievement attitudes and beliefs: Classroom influences. *Child Development, 53,* 322–339.

Parsons, T. (1949). *The structure of social action.* Glencoe, IL: Free Press.

Parten, M. B. (1932). Social play among pre-school children. *Journal of Abnormal and Social Psychology, 27,* 243–269.

Pascual-Leone, J. (1970). A mathematical model for the transition rule in Piaget's developmental stages. *Acta Psychologia, 32,* 301–345.

Pascual-Leone, J. (1988). Affirmations and negations, disturbances and contradictions, in understanding Piaget: Is his later theory causal? *Contemporary Psychology, 33,* 420–421.

Passman, R. H., & Longeway, K. P. (1982). The role of vision in maternal attachment: Giving 2-year-olds a photograph of their mother during separation. *Developmental Psychology, 18,* 530–533.

Pattison, E. M. (1969, Spring). Help in the dying process. *Voices,* pp. 6–14.

Pattison, E. M. (1977). Death throughout the life cycle. In E. M. Pattison (Ed.), *The experience of dying.* Englewood Cliffs, NJ: Prentice Hall.

Paulus, D., & Shaffer, D. R. (1981). Sex differences in the impact of number of older and number of younger siblings on scholastic aptitude. *Social Psychology Quarterly, 44,* 363–368.

Pavlov, I. (1960). *Conditioned reflexes: An investigation of the physiological activity of the cerebral cortex.* (G. V. Anrep, Trans. and Ed.). New York: Dover. (Original work published 1927)

Pavlov, I. P. (1929). *Conditioned reflexes.* Cambridge: Oxford University Press.

Pearson, J. L., Hunter, A. G., Ensminger, M. E., & Kellam, S. G. (1990). Black grandmothers in multigenerational households. *Child Development, 61,* 434–442.

Pederson, N. L., Plomin, R., Nesselroade, J. R., & McClearn, G. E. (1992). A quantitative genetic analysis of cognitive abilities during the second half of the life span. *Psychological Sciences, 3,* 346–353.

Peery, J. C. (1980). Neonate and adult head movements: No and yes revisited. *Developmental Psychology, 16,* 245–250.

Pennebaker, J. W., Colder, M., & Sharp, L. K. (1990). Accelerating the coping process. *Journal of Personality and Social Psychology, 58,* 528–537.

Perfetti, C. A., & Roth, L. R. (1981). Some of the interactive processes in reading and their role in reading skill. In A. M. Lesgold & C. A. Perfetti (Eds.), *Interactive processes in reading* (pp. 269–297). Hillsdale, NJ: Erlbaum.

Perl, D. P., Gajducek, D. C., & Garruto, R. M. (1982). Intraneuronal aluminum accumulation in amyotrophic lateral sclerosis and parkinsonism-dementia in Guam. *Science, 217,* 1053–1055.

Perlman, S. M. (1971). *Cognitive function in children with hormone abnormalities.* Unpublished doctoral dissertation, Northwestern University.

Perlmutter, M., & Lange, G. (1978). A developmental analysis of recall-recognition distinctions. In P. A. Ornstein (Ed.), *Memory development in children.* Hillsdale, NJ: Erlbaum.

Perloff, R. M., Brown, J. D., & Miller, M. M. (1982). Mass media and sex-typing: Research perspectives and policy implications. *International Journal of Women's Studies, 5,* 265–272.

Perry, D. G., & Bussey, K. (1979). The social learning theory of sex differences: Imitation is alive and well. *Journal of Personality and Social Psychology, 37,* 1699–1712.

Peterson, L. R., & Peterson, M. J. (1959). Short-term retention of individual verbal items. *Journal of Experimental Psychology, 58,* 193–198.

Petri, H. L., & Mishkin, M. (1994). Behaviorism, cognitivism and the neuropsychology of memory. *American Scientist, 82,* 30–37.

Petros, T. V., Zehr, H. D., & Chabot, R. J. (1983). Adult age differences in accessing and retrieving information from long-term memory. *Journal of Gerontology, 38,* 589–592.

Phillips, D., McCartney, K., & Scarr, S. (1987). Child-care quality and children's social development. *Developmental Psychology, 23,* 537–543.

Phillips, J. (1973). Syntax and vocabulary of mother's speech to young children: Age and sex comparisons. *Child Development, 44,* 182–185.

Phoenix, C. H., Goy, R. W., Gerall, A. A., & Young, W. C. (1959). Organizing action of prenatally administered testosterone propionate on the tissues mediating mating behavior in female guinea pigs. *Endocrinology, 65,* 369–382.

Piaget, J. (1932). *The moral judgment of the child.* London: Routledge & Kegan Paul.

Piaget, J. (1936). *La naissance de l'intelligence chez l'enfant* [The origins of intelligence in the child]. Neuchâtel: Delachaux and Niestlë.

Piaget, J. (1950). *Introduction to genetic epistemology.* Paris: University Presses.

Piaget, J. (1952). *The origins of intelligence in children.* New York: Norton.

Piaget, J. (1955). *The language and thought of the child.* Cleveland, OH: World Publishing.

Piaget, J. (1967). *Six psychological studies* (A. Tenzer, Trans.). New York: Vintage. (Original work published 1964)

Piaget, J. (1970a). Piaget's theory. In P. H. Mussen (Ed.), *Carmichael's manual of child psychology* (Vol. 1). New York: Wiley.

Piaget, J. (1970b). *Science and education and the psychology of the child.* New York: Orion.

Piaget, J., & Inhelder, B. (1973). *Memory and intelligence.* New York: Basic Books.

Piatelli-Palmarini, M. (Ed.). (1980). *Learning and language.* Cambridge, MA: Harvard University Press.

Pines, M. (1981, September). The civilizing of Genie. *Psychology Today,* pp. 28–34.

Pinker, S. (1994). *The language instinct: How the mind creates language.* New York: Morrow.

Plato. (1902). *The republic,* (J. Adam, Ed.). Cambridge, England: Cambridge University Press.

Pleck, J. H. (1981). *The myth of masculinity.* Cambridge, MA: The MIT Press.

Pleck, J. H. (1985). *Working wives/working husbands.* Beverly Hills, CA: Sage.

Plomin, R. (1986). *Development, genetics and psychology.* Hillsdale, NJ: Erlbaum.

Plomin, R. (1989). Environment and genes: Determinants of behavior. *American Psychologist, 44,* 105–111.

Plomin, R. (1990). *Nature and nurture.* Pacific Grove, CA: Brooks/Cole.

Plomin, R. (1991). Why children in the same family are so different from one another. *Behavioral and Brain Sciences, 14,* 336–338.

Plomin, R. (1992, March). *Nature and nurture.* Colloquium presented at Clarion University, Clarion, PA.

Plomin, R. (1993). Nature and nurture: Perspective and prospective. In R. Plomin, R. McClearn, & G. E. McClearn (Eds.), *Nature Nurture & Psychology.* Washington, DC: American Psychological Association.

Plost, M., & Rosen, M. (1974). Effects of sex of career models on adolescents' occupational preferences. *AV Communication, 22,* 41–50.

Pocs, O., & Godow, A. (1976). Can student view parents as sexual beings? *Family Coordinator, 26,* 31–36.

Pomerleau, A., Bolduc, D., Malcuit, G., & Cossette, L. (1990). Pink or blue: Environmental gender stereotypes in the first two years of life. *Sex Roles, 22,* 359–367.

Poon, L. W. (1985). Differences in human memory with aging: Nature, causes, and clinical implications. In J. E. Birren & K. W. Schaie (Eds.), *Handbook of the psychology of aging* (2nd ed.). New York: Van Nostrand Reinhold.

Poon, L. W., & Fozard, J. L. (1980). Age and word frequency effects in continuous recognition memory. *Journal of Gerontology, 35,* 77–86.

Poon, L. W., Fozard, J. L., Paulshock, D. R., & Thomas, J. C. (1979). A questionnaire assessment of age differences in retention of recent and remote events. *Experimental Aging Research, 5,* 401–411.

Poon, L. W., & Schaffer, G. (1982). *Prospective memory in young and elderly adults.* Paper presented at the Annual Meeting of the American Psychological Association, Washington, D.C.

Popkin, S. J., Schaie, K. W., & Krauss, I. K. (1983). Age-fair assessment of psychometric intelligence. *Educational Gerontology, 9,* 47–55.

Population Reference Bureau. (n.d.). *Major causes of death in the United States, 1900–1975.* Washington, DC: U.S. Department of Health and Human Services.

Porter, N. P., Geis, F. L., & Walstedt, J. J. (1978, August). *Are women invisible as leaders?* Paper presented at the Annual Meeting of the American Psychological Association, Toronto, Canada.

Powell, D. H., & Whitla, D. K. (1994). Normal cognitive aging: Toward empirical perspectives. *Current Directions, 3,* 27–31.

Power, T. G. (1985). Mother- and father-infant play: A developmental analysis. *Child Development, 56,* 1514–1524.

Prather, E., Hedrick, D., & Kern, C. (1975). Articulation development in children aged two to four years. *Journal of Speech and Hearing Disorders, 40,* 179–191.

Pratt, M. W., Diessner, R., Hunsberger, B., Pancer, S. M., & Savoy, K. (1991). Four pathways in the analysis of adult development and aging: Comparing analyses of reasoning about personal-life dilemmas. *Psychology and Aging, 4,* 666–675.

Pressley, M., Forest-Pressley, D. L., Elliot-Faust, D., & Miller, G. (1985). Children's use of cognitive strategies, how to teach strategies, and what to do if they can't be taught. In M. Pressley & C. J. Brainerd (Eds.), *Cognitive learning and memory in children: Progress in cognitive development research.* New York: Springer-Verlag.

Pressley, M., & Levin, J. R. (1977). Developmental differences in subjects' associative-learning strategies and performance: Assessing a hypothesis. *Journal of Experimental Child Psychology, 24,* 431–439.

Preston, S. H. (1976). *Mortality patterns in national populations: With special reference to recorded causes of death.* New York: Academic Press.

Price, G. G., Hess, R. D., & Dickson, W. P. (1981). Processes by which verbal-educational abilities are affected when mothers encourage preschool children to verbalize. *Developmental Psychology, 17,* 554–564.

Pulkkinen, L., & Rönkä, A. (1994). Personal control over development, identity formation, and future orientation as components of life orientation: A developmental approach. *Developmental Psychology, 30,* 260–271.

Q

Queen, S. A., Habenstein, R. W., & Quadagno, J. S. (1985). *The family in various cultures* (5th ed.). New York: Harper & Row.

Quinn, A. H., & O'Neill, E. H. (1976). *The complete poems and stories of Edgar Allan Poe* (Vol. 1, p. 532). New York: Knopf.

Quinton, D., Rutter, M., & Liddle, C. (1984). Institutional rearing, parenting difficulties and marital support. *Psychological Medicine, 14,* 107–124.

R

Rabinowitz, M., & Chi, M. T. H. (1987). An interactive model of strategic processing. In S. J. Ceci (Ed.), *Handbook of cognitive, social, and neuro-psychological aspects of learning disabilities.* Hillsdale, NJ: Erlbaum.

Radcliffe-Brown, A. R. (1964). *The Andaman Islanders.* New York: Free Press.

Radke-Yarrow, M., & Zahn-Waxler, C. (1984). Roots, motives, and patterns in children's prosocial behavior. In J. Reykowski, J. Karylowski, D. Bar-Tal, & E. Staub (Eds.), *Origins and maintenance of prosocial behaviors.* New York: Plenum.

Radloff, L. S. (1975). Sex differences in depression: The effects of occupation and marital status. *Sex Roles, 1,* 249–265.

Rainey, L. C. (1988). The experience of dying. In H. Hannelore, F. M. Berardo, & R. A. Neimeyer (Eds.), *Dying: Facing the facts* (2nd ed.). Washington, DC: Hemisphere Publishing Corporation.

Rainwater, L. (1960). *And the poor get children.* New York: Quadrangle/The New York Times Book Co.

Ramey, C. T., & Haskins, R. (1981). The modification of intelligence through early experiences. *Intelligence, 5,* 43–57.

Raschke, H. J. (1987). Divorce. In M. B. Sussman & S. K. Seinmetz (Eds.), *Handbook of marriage and the family.* New York: Plenum.

Raskin, P. A., & Israel, A. C. (1981). Sex-role imitation in children: Effects of sex of child, sex of model, and sex-role appropriateness of modeled behavior. *Sex Roles, 7,* 1067–1076.

Ratner, H. H. (1984). Memory demands and the development of young children's memory. *Child Development, 55,* 2173–2191.

Ratner, H. H., Schell, D. A., Crimmins, A., Mittelman, D., & et al. (1987). Changes in adults' prose recall: Aging or cognitive demands? *Developmental Psychology, 23,* 521–525.

Raudenbush, B., & Zellner, D. A. (1994, June/July). *Effects of abnormal eating behaviors and actual and perceived weight status on body image satisfaction in males and females.* Presented at the annual meeting of the American Psychological Society, Washington, DC.

Rayner, K., & Pollastsek, A. (1989). *The psychology of reading.* Englewood Cliffs, NJ: Prentice Hall.

Ree, M. J., & Earles, J. A. (1993). g is to psychology what carbon is to chemistry: 1. A reply to Sternberg and Wagner, McClelland, and Calfee. *Current Directions in Psychological Science, 2,* 11–12.

Reedy, M. N., Birren, J. E., & Schaie, K. W. (1981). Age differences in the life span. *Human Development, 24,* 62–66.

Reese, H. W. (1977). Imagery and associative memory. In R. V. Kail & J. W. Hagan (Eds.), *Perspectives on the development of memory and cognition* (pp. 113–116). Hillsdale, NJ: Erlbaum.

Reich, P. A. (1986). *Language development.* Englewood Cliffs, NJ: Prentice Hall.

Reiss, D. (1993). Genes and environment: Siblings and synthesis. In R. Plomin & G. McClearn (Eds.), *Nature, nurture, and psychology* (pp. 417–432). Washington, DC: American Psychological Association.

Reiss, I. (1980). *Family systems in America.* New York: Holt, Rinehart & Winston.

Remafedi, G., Resnick, M., Blum, R., & Harris, L. (1992). Demography of sexual orientation in adolescents. *Pediatrics, 89,* 714–721.

Renner, J. S. (1976). What this research says to schools. In J. W. Renner, D. G. Stafford, A. E. Lawson, J. W. McKinnon, F. E. Friot, & D. H. Kellog (Eds.), *Research training and learning with the Piaget model* (pp. 174–191). Norman: University of Oklahoma Press.

Rescorla, R. A. (1988). Behavioral studies of Pavlovian conditioning. *Annual Review of Neuroscience, 11,* 329–352.

Rest, J., Power, C., & Brabeck, M. (1988). Lawrence Kohlberg (1927–1987). *American Psychologist, 43,* 399–400.

Rice, M. L. (1982). Child language: What children know and how. In T. Field, A. Huston, H. C. Quay, L. Troll, & G. E. Finley (Eds.), *Review of human development.* New York: Wiley.

Rice, M. L., & Schiefelbusch, R. L. (Eds.). (1989). *Teachability of language.* Baltimore: Brookes.

Richardson, L. (1986). Another world. *Psychology Today, 20,* 22–27.

Ricks, S. S. (1985). Father-infant interactions: A review of empirical research. *Family Relations, 34,* 505–511.

Riegel, K. F. (1975). Toward a dialectical theory of development. *Human Development, 18,* 50–64.

Riegel, K. F. (1976). The dialectics of human development. *American Psychologist, 31,* 689–701.

Riegel, K. F., & Meacham, J. A. (Eds.). (1976). *The developing individual in a changing world* (2 vols.). Chicago: Aldine.

Riley, M. W., & Foner, A. (1968). *Aging and society: An inventory of research findings.* New York: Russell Sage Foundation.

Roberts, C. J., & Lowe, C. R. (1975). Where have all the conceptions gone? *Lancet, 1,* 498–499.

Roberts, M. (1987, June). No language but a cry. *Psychology Today,* pp. 57–59.

Roberts, P., & Newton, P. M. (1987). Levinsonian Studies of Women's Adult Development. *Psychology and Aging, 2,* 154–163.

Rodenstein, J., & Hughes, C. (1979). Career and lifestyle determinants of gifted women. In N. Colangelo & R. Zaffrann (Eds.), *New voices in counseling the gifted* (pp. 346–369). Dubuque, IA: Kendall Hunt.

Rodgers, R. H. (1973). *Family interaction and transaction: The developmental approach.* Englewood Cliffs, NJ: Prentice Hall.

Rodin, J. (1976). Density, perceived choice, and response to controllable and uncontrollable outcomes. *Journal of Experimental Social Psychology, 12,* 564–578.

Rodin, J. (1986). Aging and health: Effects of the sense of control. *Science, 233,* 1271–1275.

Rodin, J., & Langer, E. J. (1980). Aging labels: The decline of control and fall of self-esteem. *Journal of Social Issues, 36,* 12–29.

Rogers, C. R. (1951). *Client-centered therapy.* Boston: Houghton Mifflin.

Rogers, C. R. (1961). *On becoming a person.* Boston: Houghton Mifflin.

Rogers, C. R. (1967). The conditions of change from a client-centered viewpoint. In B. Berson & R. Carkhuff (Eds.), *Sources of gain in counseling and psychotherapy.* New York: Holt, Rinehart & Winston.

Rogers, C. R. (1972). Autobiography. In E. G. Boring & G. Lindzey (Eds.), *A history of psychology in autobiography* (Vol. 5, pp. 343–384). New York: Appleton-Century-Crofts.

Rogers, C. R. (1973). Some new challenges. *American Psychologist, 28,* 379–387.

Rogers, W. A. (1993, July/August). Age-related differences in learning. *Psychological Science Agenda,* pp. 9–10.

Rollins, B. C., & Feldman, H. (1970). Marital satisfaction over the life cycle. *Journal of Marriage and the Family, 32,* 20–28.

Rorvick, D. M., & Shettles, L. (1970, April). You can choose your baby's sex. *Look,* pp. 88–94.

Rosch, E. (1973). On the internal structure of perceptual and semantic categories. In T. Moore (Ed.), *Cognitive development and the acquisition of language.* New York: Academic Press.

Rose, S. A. (1981). Developmental changes in infants' retention of visual stimuli. *Child Development, 52,* 227–233.

Rose, S. A., Feldman, J. F., McCarton, C. M., & Wolfson, J. (1988). Information processing in seven-month-old infants as a function of risk status. *Child Development, 59,* 589–603.

Rosen, C. M. (1987, September). The eerie world of reunited twins. *Discover,* pp. 36–46.

Rosenberg, F. R., & Simmons, R. G. (1975). Sex differences in the self-concept in adolescence. *Sex Roles, 1,* 147–159.

Rosenberg, M. (1965). *Society and adolescent self-image.* Princeton, NJ: Princeton University Press.

Rosenblatt, P. C., Walsh, P. R., & Jackson, D. A. (1976). *Grief and mourning in cross-cultural perspective.* New Haven, CT: HRAF Press.

Rosenfeld, A. (1985). *Prolongevity II.* New York: Knopf.

Rosenthal, R. (1974). *On the social psychology of the self-fulfilling prophecy: Further evidence for Pygmalion effects and their mediating mechanisms (Module 53).* New York: MSS Modular Publications.

Roses, A. D. (1990, July). *Alzheimer's gene located.* Paper presented at the annual meeting of the American Academy of Neurology, Bar Harbor, Maine.

Ross, M. H. (1972). Length of life and caloric intake. *American Journal of Clinical Nutrition, 25,* 834–838.

Ross, M. H. (1978). Nutritional regulation of longevity. In J. A. Behnke, C. E. Finch, & G. B. Moment (Eds.), *The biology of aging.* New York: Plenum.

Rosser, P. (1989). *The SAT gender gap.* Washington, DC: Center for Women Policy Studies.

Rossman, I. (1977). Anatomic and body-composition changes with aging. In C. E. Finch & L. Hayflick (Eds.), *Handbook of the biology of aging.* New York: Van Nostrand.

Rothbart, M. K., Hanley, D., & Albert, M. (1986). Gender differences in moral reasoning. *Sex Roles, 15,* 645–653.

Rotter, J. B. (1954). *Social learning and clinical psychology.* New York: Prentice Hall.

Rotter, J. B. (1966). Generalized expectancies for internal versus external control of reinforcement. *Psychological Monographs, 80* (whole No. 609).

Rotter, J. B. (1990). Internal versus external control of reinforcement: A case history of a variable. *American Psychologist, 45,* 489–493.

Roupp, R., Tavers, J., Glantz, F., & Coelen, C. (1979). *Children at the center: Final results of the National Day Care Study.* Boston: Abt Associates.

Rowe, D. C., & Waldman, I. D. (1993). The question "how?" reconsidered. In R. Plomin & G. E. McClearn (Eds.), *Nature & nurture & psychology.* Washington, DC: American Psychological Association.

Rubenstein, C., Shaver, P., & Peplau, L. A. (1979, February). Loneliness. *Human Nature,* pp. 58–65.

Rubenstein, C. M., & Shaver, P. (1982). The experience of loneliness. In L. A. Peplau & D. Perlman (Eds.), *Loneliness: A sourcebook of current theory, research, and therapy.* New York: Wiley—Interscience.

Rubin, R., & Balow, B. (1979). Measures of infant development and socioeconomic status as predictors of later intelligence and school achievement. *Developmental Psychology, 15,* 225–227.

Rubin, S., & Wolf, D. (1979). The development of maybe: The evolution of social roles into narrative roles. *New Directions for Child Development, 6,* 15–28.

Rubin, Z. (1980). *Children's friendships.* Cambridge, MA: Harvard University Press.

Ruble, D., Balaban, T., & Cooper, J. (1981). Loving and leaving: Sex differences in romantic attachments. *Sex Roles, 7,* 821–835.

Ruble, D. N. (1983). The development of comparison processes and their role in achievement-related self-socialization. In E. T. Higgins, D. N. Ruble, & W. W. Hartup (Eds.), *Social cognition and social development: A sociocultural perspective.* New York: Cambridge University Press.

Ruble, D. N. (1988). Sex-role development. In M. H. Bornstein & M. E. Lamb (Eds.), *Developmental psychology: An advanced textbook* (pp. 441–460). Hillsdale, NJ: Erlbaum.

Ruble, D. N., Fleming, A. S., Hackel, L. S., & Stangor, C. (1988). Changes in the marital relationship during the transition to first time motherhood: Effects of violated expectations concerning division of household labor. *Journal of Personality and Social Psychology, 55,* 78–87.

Ruble, D. N., & Stangor, C. (1986). Stalking the elusive schema: Insights from developmental and social-psychological analyses of gender schemas. *Social Cognition, 4,* 397–402.

Rusbult, C. E. (1983). A longitudinal test of the investment model: The development (and deterioration) of satisfaction and commitment in heterosexual involvements. *Journal of Personality and Social Psychology, 45,* 101–117.

Russell, C. S. (1974). Transition to parenthood: Problems and gratifications. *Journal of Marriage and the Family, 36,* 294–301.

Rutter, D. R., & Durkin, K. (1987). Turn-taking in mother-infant interaction: An examination of vocalizations and gaze. *Developmental Psychology, 23,* 54–61.

Rutter, M. (1971). Parent-child separation: Psychological effects on the children. *Journal of Child Psychology and Psychiatry, 12,* 233–256.

Rutter, M. (1972). *Maternal deprivation reassessed.* Harmondsworth, Middlesex: Penguin.

Rutter, M. (1979). Maternal deprivation, 1972–1978: New findings, new concepts, new approaches. *Child Development, 50,* 283–305.

Rutter, M. (1981). Social-emotional consequences of day care for preschool children. *American Journal of Orthopsychiatry, 51,* 4–28.

Ryan, E. B., Giles, H., & Henwood, K. (1986). Psycholinguistic and social psychological components of communication by and with the elderly. *Language and Communication, 6,* 1–24.

Rybash, J. M., Roodin, P. A., & Hoyer, W. J. (1995). *Adult development and aging* (3rd ed.). Dubuque, IA: Brown & Benchmark.

Ryff, C. D. (1991). Possible selves in adulthood and old age: A tale of shifting horizons. *Psychology and Aging, 6,* 286–295.

Ryff, C. D., & Essex, M. J. (1992, August). *Midlife parents' well being: Influence of grown children's accomplishments and adjustment.* Symposium presented at the 100th Annual Meeting of the American Psychological Association, Washington, DC.

Ryff, C. D., & Heinecke, S. G. (1983). The subjective organization of personality in adulthood and aging. *Journal of Personality and Social Psychology, 44,* 807–816.

Rymer, R. (1993). *Genie: An abused child's flight from silence.* New York: HarperCollins.

S

Sadat, J. (1987). *A woman of Egypt.* New York: Simon & Schuster.

Sadker, M., & Sadker, D. (1986). Sexism in the classroom from grade school to graduate school. *Phi Delta Kappan, 67,* 512–515.

Sadker, M., & Sadker, D. (1994). *Failing at fairness: How America's schools cheat girls.* New York: Charles Scribner's Sons.

Saegert, S., Swap, W., & Zajonc, R. B. (1973). Exposure, context, and interpersonal attraction. *Journal of Personality and Social Psychology, 25,* 234–252.

Sagi, A., Lamb, M. E., Lewkowicz, K., Shoham, R., & Estes, D. (1986). Security of mother-infant, -father, -metapelet attachments among Kibbutz-reared Israeli children. In I. Bretherton & E. Waters (Eds.), *Growing points in attachment theory and research. Monographs of the Society for Research in Child Development 50(1–1 Serial No. 209, 257–275).*

Sahler, O. J. Z., & McAnamey, E. R. (1981). *The child between 3 to 18.* St. Louis: Mosby.

Salkind, N. J. (1985). *Theories of human development* (2nd ed.). New York: Wiley.

Salthouse, T. (1985). *A theory of cognitive aging.* Amsterdam: North Holland Press.

Salthouse, T. M., & Skovronek, E. (1992). Within-context assessment of age differences in working memory. *Journal of Gerontology: Psychological Sciences, 47,* 110–120.

Sameroff, A. J. (1968). The components of sucking in the human newborn. *Journal of Experimental Child Psychology, 6,* 607–623.

Sampson, E. E., & Hancock, F. T. (1967). An examination of the relationship between ordinal position, personality, and conformity: An extension, replication, and partial verification. *Journal of Personality and Social Psychology, 23,* 398–407.

Samuelson, R. J. (1993, September 13). Should we think the unthinkable? Time to abolish welfare for teen mothers. *Newsweek,* p. 43.

Sapir, E. (1921). *Language.* New York: Harcourt, Brace, and World.

Scarr, S. (1982). Development is internally guided, not determined. *Contemporary Psychology, 27,* 852–853.

Scarr, S. (1987). Distinctive environments depend on genotypes. *Behavioral and Brain Science, 10,* 38–39.

Scarr, S. (1992). Developmental theories for the 1990s: Development and individual differences. *Child Development, 63,* 1–19.

Scarr, S., & McCartney, K. (1983). How people make their own environments: A theory of genotype-environment effects. *Child Development, 54,* 424–435.

Scarr, S., Webber, P. L., Weinberg, R. A., & Wittig, M. A. (1981). Personality resemblance among adolescents and their parents in biologically related and adoptive families. *Journal of Personality and Social Psychology, 40,* 885–898.

Scarr, S., & Weinberg, R. A. (1976). IQ test performance of black children adopted by white families. *American Psychologist, 31,* 726–739.

Scarr, S., & Weinberg, R. A. (1983). The Minnesota adoption studies: Genetic differences and malleability. *Child Development, 54,* 260–267.

Schachter, S. (1951). Deviation, rejection, and communication. *Journal of Abnormal and Social Psychology, 46,* 190–207.

Schachter, S. (1959). *The psychology of affiliation.* Stanford, CA: Stanford University Press.

Schachter, S. (1963). Birth order, eminence, and higher education. *American Sociological Review, 28,* 757–767.

Schacter, D. L., Osowiecki, D., Kazniak, A. W., Kihlstrom, J. F., & Valdiserri, M. (1994). Source memory: Extending the boundaries of age-related deficits. *Psychology and Aging, 9,* 81–89.

Schaffer, H. R., & Emerson, P. E. (1964). The development of social attachments in infancy. *Monographs of the Society for Research in Child Development, 29*(3, Serial No. 94).

Schaie, K. W. (1958). Rigidity-flexibility and intelligence. A cross-sectional study of the adult life-span from 20 to 70. *Psychological Monographs, 72* (462, Whole no. 9).

Schaie, K. W. (1965). A general model for the study of developmental change. *Psychological Bulletin, 64,* 92–107.

Schaie, K. W. (1977). Quasi-experimental research designs in the psychology of aging. In J. E. Birren & K. W. Schaie (Eds.), *Handbook of the psychology of aging.* New York: Van Nostrand Reinhold.

Schaie, K. W. (1979). The primary mental abilities in adulthood: An exploration in the development of psychometric intelligence. In P. Baltes & O. Brim (Eds.), *Life-span development and behavior* (Vol. 2). New York: Academic Press.

Schaie, K. W. (1982). Toward a stage theory of adult cognitive development. In K. W. Schaie & J. Geiwitz (Eds.), *Readings in adult development and aging.* Boston: Little Brown. (Original work published in *Journal of Aging and Human Development,* 1977–1978)

Schaie, K. W. (1983). The Seattle Longitudinal Study: A twenty-one-year exploration of psychometric intelligence in adulthood. In K. W. Schaie (Ed.), *Longitudinal studies of adult psychological development.* New York: Guilford Press.

Schaie, K. W. (1986). Beyond calendar definitions of age, time, and cohort: The general developmental model revisited. *Developmental Review, 6,* 252–277.
Schaie, K. W. (1988). Internal validity threats in studies of adult cognitive development. In M. L. Howe & C. J. Brainard (Eds.), *Cognitive development in adulthood: Progress in cognitive development research,* (pp. 241–272). New York: Springer-Verlag.
Schaie, K. W. (1994). The course of adult intellectual development. *American Psychologist, 49,* 304–313.
Schaie, K. W., & Baltes, P. B. (1977). Some faith helps to see the forest: A final comment on the Horn and Donaldson myth of the Baltes-Schaie position on adult intelligence. *American Psychologist, 32,* 1118–1120.
Schaie, K. W., & Parham, I. A. (1976). Stability of adult personality traits: Fact or fable? *Journal of Personality and Social Psychology, 34,* 146–158.
Schaie, K. W., & Willis, S. L. (1986). *Adult development and aging* (2nd ed.). Boston: Little, Brown.
Schaie, K. W., & Willis, S. L. (1991a). *Adult development and aging* (3rd ed.). New York: HarperCollins.
Schaie, K. W., & Willis, S. L. (1991b). Adult personality and psychomotor performance: Cross-sectional and longitudinal analyses. *Journal of Gerontology, 46,* 275–284.
Schiff, M., Duyme, M., Dumaret, A., & Tomkiewicz, S. (1982). How much could we boost scholastic achievement and IQ scores? A direct answer from a French adoption study. *Cognition, 12,* 165–196.
Schull, W. J., & Neel, J. V. (1958). Radiation and the sex ratio in man. *Science, 128,* 343–348.
Schultz, D. P., & Schultz, S. E. (1990). *Psychology and industry today: An introduction to industrial and organizational psychology* (5th ed.). New York: Macmillan.
Schultz, J. H. (1985). *The economics of aging* (3rd ed.). New York: Van Nostrand Reinhold.
Schwartzman, A. E., Gold, D., Auders, D., Arbuckle, T. Y., & Chaikelson, J. (1987). Stability of intelligence: A 40-year follow-up. *Canadian Journal of Psychology, 41,* 244–256.
Scollon, R., & Scollon, S. B. K. (1979). *Linguistic convergence: An ethnography of speaking at Fort Chipewyan, Alberta.* New York: Academic Press.
Scott, W. A., Scott, R., & McCabe, M. (1991). Family relationships and children's personality: A cross-cultural, cross-source comparison. *British Journal of Social Psychology, 30,* 1–20.
Scribner, S. (1977). Modes of thinking and ways of speaking: Culture and logic reconsidered. In P. N. Johnson-Laird & P. C. Wason (Eds.), *Thinking: Readings in cognitive science.* New York: Cambridge University Press.
Seagert, S. C., Swap, W., & Zajonc, R. B. (1973). Exposure, context, and interpersonal attraction. *Journal of Personality and Social Psychology, 25,* 234–242.
Searle, J. R. (1969). *Speech acts: An essay in the philosophy of language.* London: Cambridge University Press.
Searle, J. R. (1975). Indirect speech acts. In P. Cole & J. Morgan (Eds.), *Syntax and semantics: Vol. 3. Speech acts.* New York: Academic Press.
Sears, R. R., Maccoby, E. E., & Levin, H. (1957). *Patterns of child rearing.* New York: Harper & Row.
Sears, R. R., Raul, L., & Alpert, R. (1965). *Identification and child-rearing.* Stanford, CA: Stanford University Press.
Secord, P., & Peevers, B. H. (1974). The development and attribution of person concepts. In T. Mischel (Ed.), *Understanding other persons.* Totowa, NJ: Rowman & Littlefield.
Segal, M. W. (1974). Alphabet and attraction: An unobtrusive measure of the effect of propinquity in a field setting. *Journal of Personality and Social Psychology, 30,* 654–657.
Seligman, M. E. P. (1974). Depression and learned helplessness. In R. J. Friedman & M. M. Katz (Eds.), *The psychology of depression: Contemporary theory and research.* Washington, DC: Winston-Wiley.
Seligman, M. E. P. (1975). *Helplessness.* San Francisco: W. H. Freeman.
Seligman, M. E. P. (1990). *Learned optimism: How to change your mind and your life.* New York: Pocket Books.
Selman, R. L. (1976). Social-cognitive understanding. In T. Lickona (Ed.), *Moral development and behavior.* New York: Holt, Rinehart & Winston.
Selman, R. L. (1980). *The growth of interpersonal understanding.* New York: Academic Press.
Semin, G. R., & Fiedler, K. (1988). The cognitive functions of linguistic categories in describing persons: Social cognition and language. *Journal of Personality and Social Psychology, 54,* 558–568.
Shaffer, D. R. (1992). *Developmental psychology: Theory, research, and applications* (2nd ed.). Monterey, CA: Brooks/Cole.
Sharma, A. R., Benson, P. L., & McGue, M. (1993, August). *Comparing adopted and nonadopted adolescents on emotional and behavioral adjustment.* Poster presented at the 101st Annual Convention of the American Psychological Association, Toronto, Canada.
Sheffield, E. G., & Hudson, J. A. (1994, April). *Reactivation of toddler's event memory.* Paper presented at the Conference on Human Development, Pittsburgh, PA.
Sherman, J. (1978). *Sex-related cognitive differences.* Springfield, IL: Charles C. Thomas.
Sheskin, A., & Wallace, S. (1976). Differing bereavements: Suicide, natural, and accidental death. *Omega, 7,* 229–242.
Shimkin, D. B., Louie, G. J., & Frate, D. (1973). *The black extended family: A basic rural institution and a mechanism of urban adaptation.* Paper presented at the 9th International Congress of Anthropological and Ethnological Sciences, Chicago.
Shimkin, D. B., Shimkin, E. M., & Frate, D. A. (Eds.). (1975). *The extended family in black societies.* The Hague: Mouton.
Shirley, M. M. (1933). *The first two years: A study of 25 babies: Vol. 1. Postural and locomotor development.* Minneapolis: University of Minnesota Press.
Shneidman, E. S. (1973). *Deaths of man.* New York: Quadrangle.
Shneidman, E. S. (1976). Death work and stages of dying. In E. S. Shneidman (Ed.), *Death: Current perspectives.* Palo Alto, CA: Mayfield.
Shorter, E. (1975). *The making of the modern family.* New York: Basic Books.
Shum, P. C., Morton, N. E., & Rice, J. P. (1992). Segregation analysis of the NIMA collaborative study: Family data on bipolar disorder. *Psychiatric Genetics, 2,* 175–184.
Shute, V. J., Pellegrino, J. W., Hubert, I., & Reynolds, R. W. (1983). The relationship between androgen levels and human spatial abilities. *Bulletin of the Psychonomic Society, 21,* 465–468.
Siegel, L. S. (1981). Infant tests as predictors of cognitive and language development at two years. *Child Development, 52,* 545–557.
Siegler, R., & Richards, D. (1982). The development of intelligence. In R. Sternberg (Ed.), *Handbook of human intelligence* (pp. 493–559). New York: Cambridge University Press.
Siegler, R. S. (1986). *Children's thinking.* Englewood Cliffs, NJ: Prentice Hall.
Siegler, R. S. (1992). The other Alfred Binet. *Developmental Psychology, 28,* 179–190.
Siegler, R. S. (1994, April). *Recent advances in understanding cognitive developmental change.* Invited address, Conference on Human Development, Pittsburgh, PA.

Siegler, R. S., & Crowley, K. (1991). The microgenetic method: A direct means of studying cognitive development. *American Psychologist, 46,* 606–620.

Sigel, I. E. (1986). Reflections on the belief-behavior connection: Lessons learned from a research program on parental belief systems and teaching strategies. In R. D. Ashmore & D. M. Brodzinsky (Eds.), *Thinking about the family: Views of parents and children.* Hillsdale, NJ: Erlbaum.

Sigelman, C. K., Carr, M. B., & Begley, N. L. (1986). Developmental changes in the influence of sex-role stereotypes on person perception. *Child Study Journal, 16,* 191–205.

Sigelman, C. K., & Shaffer, D. R. (1995). *Life-span human development* (2nd ed.). Pacific Grove, CA: Brooks/Cole.

Signorella, M. L., Bigler, R. S., & Liben, L. S. (1993). Developmental differences in children's gender schemata about others: A meta-analysis. *Developmental Review, 13,* 147–183.

Signorella, M. L., Bigler, R. S., & Liben, L. S. (1994, May). *A meta-analysis of children's memories for own-sex and other-sex information.* Paper presented at the 13th Biennial Conference on Human Development, Pittsburgh, PA.

Sih, R. C. (1994, May). *Testosterone and its effects on cholesterol.* Paper presented at the annual meeting of American Geriatric Society, Los Angeles.

Simmons, R. G., Blyth, D. A., Van Cleave, E. F., & Bush, D. M. (1979). Entry into adolescence: The impact of school structure, puberty, and early dating on self-esteem. *American Sociological Review, 44,* 948–967.

Simon, H. A. (1980). Problem solving and education. In D. T. Tuma & F. Reif (Eds.), *Problem solving and education: Issues in teaching and learning.* Hillsdale, NJ: Erlbaum.

Simpson, J. A. (1987). The dissolution of romantic relationships: Factors involved in relationship stability and emotional distress. *Journal of Personality and Social Psychology, 53,* 683–692.

Simpson, J. A. (1990). Influence of attachment styles on romantic relationships. *Journal of Personality and Social Psychology, 59,* 971–980.

Simpson, J. A., Rholes, W. S., & Nelligan, J. S. (1992). Support seeking and support giving within couples in an anxiety-provoking situation: The role of attachment styles. *Journal of Personality and Social Psychology, 62,* 434–446.

Sinclair, H. (1971). Sensorimotor action patterns as a condition of the acquisition of syntax. In R. Huxley & E. Ingram (Eds.), *Language acquisition: Models and methods.* London: Academic Press.

Sinclair-DeZwart, H. (1969). Developmental psycholinguistics. In D. Elkind & J. Flavell (Eds.), *Studies in cognitive development: Essays in honor of Jean Piaget.* New York: Oxford University Press.

Singer, L. M., Brodzinsky, D. M., Ramsay, D., Steir, M., & Waters, E. (1985). Mother-infant attachment in adoptive families. *Child Development, 56,* 1543–1551.

Singer, M. (1990). *Psychology and language.* Hillsdale, NJ: Erlbaum.

Skinner, B. F. (1938). *The behavior of organisms: An experimental analysis.* New York: Appleton-Century-Crofts.

Skinner, B. F. (1948). Superstition in the pigeon. *Journal of Experimental Psychology, 38,* 168–172.

Skinner, B. F. (1950). Are theories of learning necessary? *Psychological Review, 57,* 193–216.

Skinner, B. F. (1957). *Verbal behavior.* New York: Appleton-Century-Crofts.

Skinner, B. F. (1972). *Beyond freedom and dignity.* New York: Knopf.

Skinner, B. F. (1974). *About behaviorism.* New York: Knopf.

Skinner, B. F. (1983). *A matter of consequences.* New York: Knopf.

Slaby, R. G., & Frey, K. S. (1975). Development of gender constancy and selective attention to same-sex-models. *Child Development, 46,* 849–856.

Slobin, D. I. (1973). Cognitive prerequisites for the acquisition of grammar. In C. A. Ferguson & D. I. Slobin (Eds.), *Studies of child language development.* New York: Holt, Rinehart, & Winston.

Smetana, J. G. (1986). Preschool children's conceptions of sex-role transgressions. *Child Development, 57,* 862–871.

Smith, S. (1980, October). The mnemonic cues of familiar rooms. *Psychology Today,* pp. 30, 107.

Smith, S. E., & Walker, W. J. (1988). Sex differences on New York state regents examinations: Support for the differential course-taking hypothesis. *Journal of Research in Mathematics Education, 19,* 81–85.

Smith, W. J. (1985). *Dying in the human life cycle.* New York: Holt, Rinehart & Winston.

Smolak, L. (1993). *Adult development.* Englewood Cliffs, NJ: Prentice Hall.

Snarey, J. R. (1985). Cross-cultural universality of social-moral development: A critical review of Kohlbergian research. *Psychological Bulletin, 97,* 202–232.

Snow, C. E., & Ferguson, C. A. (1977). *Talking to children: Language input and acquisition.* New York: Cambridge University Press.

Snyder, M., & Uranowitz, S. W. (1978). Reconstructing the past: Some cognitive consequences of person perception. *Journal of Personality and Social Psychology, 36,* 941–950.

Solano, C. H., Batten, P. G., & Parish, E. A. (1982). Loneliness and patterns of self-disclosure. *Journal of Personality and Social Psychology, 43,* 524–531.

Solomon, R. L. (1980). The opponent-process theory of acquired motivation. *American Psychologist, 35,* 691–712.

Spanier, G., & Glick, P. (1981). Marital instability in the United States: Some correlates and recent changes. *Family Relations, 30,* 329–338.

Spear, N. E. (1984). Behaviours that indicate memory: Levels of expression. *Canadian Journal of Psychology, 38,* 348–367.

Spearman, C. (1927). *The abilities of man: Their nature and measurement.* New York: Macmillan.

Spence, S. L. (1994, April 18). Memoirs of a Virgin Prom Queen. [Letter to the editor.] *USA Today.*

Sperling, D. (1990, July 20). Cesarean rate levels, but still high. *USA Today,* p. 5D.

Sperling, G. (1960). The information available in brief visual presentations. *Psychological Monographs, 74*(Whole No. 498).

Spilich, G. J., Vesonder, G. T., Chiesi, H. L., & Voss, J. F. (1979). Text processing of domain-related information for individuals with high and low domain knowledge. *Journal of Verbal Learning and Verbal Behavior, 18,* 275–290.

Spirduso, W. W., & Clifford, P. (1978). Replication of age and physical activity effects on reaction and movement time. *Journal of Gerontology, 33,* 26–30.

Spiro, R. J. (1980). Accommodative reconstruction in prose recall. *Journal of Verbal Learning and Verbal Behavior, 19,* 84–95.

Spock, B. M. (1970). *Dr. Spock's baby and child care.* New York: Dutton.

Sprecher, S., & Duck, S. (1994). Sweet talk: The importance of perceived communication for romantic and friendship attraction experiences during a get-acquainted date. *Personality and Social Psychology Bulletin, 20,* 391–400.

Sprecher, S., & Hatfield, E. (1982). Self-esteem and romantic attraction: Four experiments. *Recherches de Psychologie Sociale, 4,* 61–81.

Sroufe, L. A. (1979). Socioemotional development. In J. Osofsky (Ed.), *Handbook of infant development.* New York: Wiley.

Sroufe, L. A., Carlson, E., & Shulman, S. (1993). The development of individuals in relationships: From infancy through adolescence. In D. C. Funder, R. D. Parke, C. Tomlinson-Keasey, & K. Widman (Eds.), *Studying lives through time: Approaches to personality and development.* Washington, DC: American Psychological Association.

Sroufe, L. A., Cooper, R. G., & Marshall, M. E. (1988). *Child development: Its nature and course.* New York: Knopf.

Sroufe, L. A., Egeland, B., & Kreutzer, T. (1990). The fate of early experience following developmental change: Longitudinal approaches to individual adaption in childhood. *Child Development, 61,* 1363–1373.

Sroufe, L. A., & Fleeson, J. (1986). Attachment and the construction of relationships. In W. W. Hartup & Z. Rubin (Eds.), *Relationships and development.* Hillsdale, NJ: Erlbaum.

Stabu, E. (1978). *Positive social behavior and morality: Vol I. Social and personal influences.* New York: Academic Press.

Stack, C. (1974). *All our kin.* New York: Harper & Row.

Stamps, L. E., & Porges, S. W. (1975). Heart rate conditioning in newborn infants: Relationships among conditionability, heart rate variability, and sex. *Developmental Psychology, 11,* 424–431.

Stankov, L. (1988). Aging, attention, and intelligence. *Psychology and Aging, 3,* 59–74.

Stanovich, K. E. (1980). Toward an interactive compensatory model of individual differences in the development of reading fluency. *Reading Research Quarterly, 16,* 32–71.

Starr, B. D., & Weiner, M. B. (1981). *The Starr-Weiner report on sex and sexuality in the later years.* New York: Stein & Day.

Staub, E. (1979). Understanding and predicting social behavior—with emphasis on prosocial behavior. In E. Staub (Ed.), *Personality: Basic issues and current research.* Englewood Cliffs, NJ: Prentice Hall.

Stein, S. B. (1974). *About dying, an open family book for parents and children together.* New York: Walker.

Steinberg, L., Dornbusch, S. M., & Brown, B. B. (1992). Ethnic differences in adolescent achievement: An ecological perspective. *American Psychologist, 47,* 723–729.

Steinberg, L. D., Catalano, R., & Dooley, D. (1981). Economic antecedents of child abuse and neglect. *Child Development, 52,* 975–985.

Steiner, J. E. (1979). Human facial expressions in response to taste and smell stimulation. In H. E. Reese & L. Lipsitt (Eds.), *Advances in child development and behavior* (Vol. 13). New York: Academic Press.

Stephenson, J. S. (1985). *Death, grief, and mourning.* New York: Free Press.

Stern, Y., Gurland, B., Tatemichi, T. K., Tang, M. X., Wilder, D., & Mayeux, R. (1994, April 6). Influence of education and occupation on the incidence of Alzheimer's disease. *Journal of the American Medical Association,* 1004–1010.

Sternberg, R. J. (1982, April). Who's intelligent? *Psychology Today, 16,* 30–34.

Sternberg, R. J. (1985). *Beyond IQ.* Cambridge, England: Cambridge University Press.

Sternberg, R. J. (1986). A triangular theory of love. *Psychological Review, 93,* 119–135.

Sternberg, R. J. (1988). Intellectual development: Psychometric and information-processing approaches. In M. H. Bornstein & M. E. Lamb (Eds.), *Developmental psychology: An advanced textbook* (2nd ed.). Hillsdale, NJ: Erlbaum.

Sternberg, R. J. (1988, Spring). Beyond IQ testing. *PHI KAPPA PHI Journal,* pp. 8–11.

Sternberg, R. J. (Ed.). (1986). *Advances in the psychology of human intelligence* (Vol. 3). Hillsdale, NJ: Erlbaum.

Sternberg, R. J., & Grajek, S. (1984). The nature of love. *Journal of Personality and Social Psychology, 47,* 312–329.

Sternberg, R. J., & Kerton, J. L. (1982). Selection and implementation of strategies in reasoning by analogy. *Journal of Educational Psychology, 74,* 399–413.

Stevenson, M. R., & Black, K. N. (1988). Paternal absence and sex-role development: A meta-analysis. *Child Development, 59,* 793–814.

Stoddart, T., & Turiel, E. (1985). Children's concepts of cross-gender activities. *Child Development, 56,* 1241–1252.

Streissguth, A. P., Barr, H. M., Sampson, P. D., Darby, B. L., & Martin, D. C. (1989). IQ at age 4 in relation to maternal alcohol use and smoking during pregnancy. *Developmental Psychology, 25,* 3–11.

Streissguth, A. P., Landesman-Dwyer, S., Martin, J. C., & Smith, D. W. (1980). Teratogenic effects of alcohol in human and laboratory animals. *Science, 209,* 353–361.

Streissguth, M. (1976). Maternal alcoholism and the outcome of pregnancy. In M. Greenblatt & M. A. Schuckut (Eds.), *Alcoholism problems in women and children.* New York: Grune & Stratton.

Streitfeld, D. (1988). Shere Hite and the trouble with numbers. *Chance, 1,* 26–31.

Stricker, G. (1994). The psychodynamic approach. *The General Psychologist, 30,* 17–20.

Stroebe, M., Gergen, M. M., Gergen, K. J., & Stroebe, W. (1992). Broken hearts or broken bonds: Love and death in historical perspective. *American Psychologist, 47,* 1205–1212.

Stroebe, W., Insko, C. A., Thompson, V. D., & Layton, B. D. (1971). Effects of physical attractiveness, attitude similarity, and sex on various aspects of interpersonal attraction. *Journal of Personality and Social Psychology, 18,* 79–91.

Stroop, J. (1935). Studies of inference in serial verbal reactions. *Journal of Experimental Psychology, 18,* 643–662.

Strupp, H. H. (1982). The outcome problem in psychotherapy: Contemporary perspectives. In J. H. Harvey & M. M. Parks (Eds.), *The master lecture series: Vol. 1. Psychotherapy research and behavior change.* Washington, DC: American Psychological Association.

Stunkard, A. J., Foch, T. T., & Hrubeck, C. (1986). A twin study of human obesity. *Journal of the American Medical Association, 256,* 51–54.

Stunkard, A. J., Sorrenson, T. I., Hanis, C., Teasdale, T. W., Chakraborty, R., Schull, W. J., & Schulsinger, F. (1986). An adoption study of obesity. *New England Journal of Medicine, 314,* 193–198.

Sudman, S., & Bradburn, W. M. (1982). *Asking questions: A practical guide to questionnaire design.* San Francisco: Jossey-Bass.

Sujan, H., Sujan, M., & Bettman, J. R. (1988). Knowledge structure differences between more effective and less effective salespeople. *Journal of Marketing Research, 25,* 81–86.

Sulzby, E. (1982). Oral and written language mode adaptations in stories of kindergarten children. *Journal of Reading Behavior, 14,* 51–59.

Suomi, S. J. (1987). Genetic and maternal contributions to individual differences in rhesus monkey biobehavioral development. In N. A. Krasnegor, E. M. Blass, M. A. Hofer, & W. P. Smotherman (Eds.), *Parental development: A psychobiological perspective* (pp. 397–420). San Diego, CA: Academic Press.

Suomi, S. J., & Harlow, H. F. (1972). Social rehabilitation of isolate reared monkeys. *Developmental Psychology, 6,* 487–496.

Sussman, M. B. (1985). The family life of old people. In R. H. Binstock & E. Shanas (Eds.), *Handbook of aging in the social sciences* (2nd ed.). New York: Van Nostrand.

Sutton-Smith, B., & Rosenberg, B. G. (1970). *The sibling*. New York: Holt, Rinehart & Winston.

Swann, W. B. (1990). To be adored or to be known: The interplay of self-enhancement and self-verification. In R. M. Sorrentino & E. T. Higgins (Eds.), *Handbook of motivation and cognition*. New York: Guilford.

Swann, W. B., Jr., Stein-Seroussi, A., & Geisler, R. B. (1992). Why people self-verify. *Journal of Personality and Social Psychology, 62,* 392–401.

T

Taffel, S. M., Placek, P. J., Moien, M., & Kosary, C. L. (1991). U.S. cesarean section rate studies—VBAC rate rises to nearly one in five. *Birth, 18,* 73–77.

Tallmer, M., Formaneck, R., & Tallmer, J. (1974). Factors influencing children's concepts of death. *Journal of Clinical Child Psychology, 3,* 17–19.

Tanner, J. M. (1970). Physical growth. In P. H. Mussen (Ed.), *Carmichael's manual of child psychology* (Vol. 1, pp. 77–155). New York: Wiley.

Tanner, J. M. (1978). *Fetus into man: Physical growth from conception to maturity*. Cambridge, MA: Harvard University Press.

Tanner, J. M. (1981). Growth and maturation during adolescence. *Nutrition Review, 39,* 43–55.

Taub, H. A. (1979). Comprehension and memory of prose materials by young and old adults. *Experimental Aging Research, 5,* 3–13.

Tavris, C., & Wade, C. (1984). *The longest war*. New York: Harcourt Brace Jovanovich.

Taylor, S. E. (1989). *Positive illusions: Creative self-deception and the healthy mind*. New York: Basic Books.

Tellegen, A., Lykken, D. T., Bouchard, T. J., Wilcox, K., Segal, N., & Rowe, S. (1988). Personality similarity in twins reared apart and together. *Journal of Personality and Social Psychology, 54,* 1031–1039.

Temerlin, L. M. (1975). *Lucy: Growing up human*. Palo Alto, CA: Science and Behavior Books.

Templer, D. (1972). The construction and validation of a death anxiety scale. *Journal of General Psychology, 82,* 176.

Terman, L. M. (1916). *The measurement of intelligence*. Boston: Houghton Mifflin.

Terry, R. D., & Wisneiowski, H. M. (1975). Structural and chemical changes in the aged human brain. In S. Gershon & A. Raskind (Eds.), *Aging* (Vol. 2). New York: Raven Press.

Thatcher, R. W., Walker, R. A., & Giudice, S. (1987). Human cerebral hemispheres develop at different rates and ages. *Science, 236,* 1110–1113.

Thelen, E., & Fisher, D. M. (1982). Newborn stepping: An explanation for a "disappearing" reflex. *Developmental Psychology, 18,* 760–775.

Thomas, A., & Chess, C. S. (1986). The New York longitudinal study: From infancy to early life. In R. Plomin & J. Dunn (Eds.), *The study of temperament: Changes, continuities, and challenges*. Hillsdale, NJ: Erlbaum.

Thomas, A., & Chess, S. (1981). The role of temperament in the contributions of individuals to their development. In R. M. Lerner & N. A. Busch-Rossnagel (Eds.), *Individuals as producers of their own development: A life-span perspective*. New York: Academic Press.

Thomas, D. G., Lykins, M. S., Letterman, M., Whitaker, E., Martin, S., Graham, S., & Pittman, R. (1994, April). *Infant memory: A new electrophysiological measure*. Paper presented at the Conference on Human Development, Pittsburgh, PA.

Thompson, J. S., & Thompson, M. W. (1986). *Genetics in medicine* (4th ed.). Philadelphia: W. B. Saunders.

Thornburg, H. (1981). The amount of sex information learning obtained during adolescence. *Journal of Early Adolescence, 1,* 171–183.

Thorndike, R. L., Hagen, E. P., & Sattler, J. M. (1986). *The Stanford-Binet intelligence scale: Guide for administering and scoring* (4th ed.). Chicago: Riverside.

Thorne, B. (1986). Girls and boys together, not mostly apart. In W. W. Hartup & Z. Rubin (Eds.), *Relationship and development* (pp. 167–184). Hillsdale, NJ: Erlbaum.

Thornton, A. (1977). Children and marital stability. *Journal of Marriage and the Family, 38,* 531–540.

Thornton, A., Alwin, D. F., & Camburn, D. (1983). Causes and consequences of sex-role attitudes and attitude change. *American Sociological Review, 48,* 211–227.

Thurstone, L. L. (1938). *Primary mental abilities: Psychometric monographs* (No. 1). Chicago, IL: University of Chicago Press.

Tittle, G. K. (1986). Gender research and education. *American Psychologist, 41,* 1161–1168.

Tkacz, S., Kincaid, K., & Latimore, R. R. (1994, July). *Knowledge representation for psychology concepts: Expert-novice comparisons*. Paper presented at the meeting of the American Psychological Society, Washington, DC.

Tobias, S. (1978). *Overcoming math anxiety*. New York: Norton.

Toffler, A. (1971). *Future shock*. New York: Bantam Books.

Tomilson-Keasey, C., Eisert, D. C., Kahle, L. R., Hardy-Brown, K., & Keasey, B. (1979). The structure of concrete-operational thought. *Child Development, 50,* 1153–1163.

Tonkova-Yampol'skaya, R. (1969). Development of speech intonation in infants in the first two years of life. *Soviet Psychology, 7,* 48–54.

Topousis, T. (1987, July 10). From birth trauma to suicide. *USA Today,* p. 1D.

Torgeson, J., & Goldman, T. (1977). Verbal rehearsal and short-term memory in reading-disabled children. *Child Development, 48,* 56–60.

Treloar, A. E. (1981). Menstrual activity and the pre-menopause. *Maturita, 3,* 249–264.

Trotter, R. J. (1985, November). Lefty means larger. *Psychology Today,* p. 24.

Trotter, R. J. (1986, August). Three heads are better than one. *Psychology Today,* pp. 56–62.

Trotter, R. J. (1987, January). The play's the thing. *Psychology Today,* pp. 26–34.

Tryon, R. C. (1940). Genetic differences in maze-learning abilities in rats. In Thirty-ninth yearbook of the National Society for the Study of Education. *Intelligence: Its nature and nurture. Part I. Comparative and critical exposition*. Bloomington, IL: Public School Publishing.

Tucker, M. B. (1987). The black male shortage in Los Angeles *Sociology and Social Research, 71,* 221–227.

Tulving, E. (1972). Episodic and semantic memory. In E. Tulving & W. Donaldson (Eds.), *Organization and memory*. New York: Academic Press.

Tulving, E. (1985). How many memory systems are there? *American Psychologist, 40,* 385–398.

Tulving, E. (1993). What is episodic memory? *Current Directions in Psychological Science, 2,* 67–70.

Tulving, E., & Thomson, D. M. (1973). Encoding specificity and retrieval processes in episodic memory. *Psychological Review, 80,* 352–373.

Turkington, C. (1987, September). Special talents. *Psychology Today,* pp. 42–46.

Turkington, C. (1992, May 21). Getting kids to eat vegetables. *USA Today,* p. 1A.

Turnure, J., Buium, N., & Thurlow, M. (1976). The effectiveness of interrogatives for promoting verbal elaboration productivity in young children. *Child Development, 47,* 851–855.

U

U.S. Bureau of the Census. Internet Summary. July 15, 1991.

U.S. Bureau of the Census. (1970). Total midyear population for the world: 1950–2050. Washington, DC: U.S. Government Printing Office, No. A 158–159.

U.S. Bureau of the Census. (1987, March). *Marital status and living arrangements.* Washington, DC: U.S. Government Printing Office.

U.S. Bureau of the Census. (1990, June). Marital status and living arrangements: March 1989. *Current population reports: Population characteristics.* Washington, DC: U.S. Government Printing Office, Series P-20, No. 445.

U.S. Bureau of the Census. *Statistical Abstracts of the United States: 1989* (109th ed.). Washington, DC: U.S. Government Printing Office, No. 127.

U.S. Bureau of the Census. *Statistical Abstracts of the United States: 1992* (112th ed.). Washington, DC: U.S. Government Printing Office, No. 91.

U. S. Bureau of the Census. *Statistical Abstracts of the United States: 1993* (113th ed.). Washington, DC: U.S. Government Printing Office, No. 101, 117, 140, 143, 270.

U.S. Bureau of Labor Statistics. (1988, March). *Marital and family characteristics of the labor force.* Washington, DC: U.S. Government Printing Office.

U.S. Department of Labor Statistics. (1989). *Handbook of labor statistics.* Washington, DC: U.S. Government Printing Office.

Udry, J. R. (1974). *The social context of marriage.* Philadelphia: Lippincott.

Udry, J. R. (1977). The importance of being beautiful: A re-examination and racial comparison. *American Journal of Sociology, 83,* 154–160.

Uhlenberg, P., & Myers, M. (1981). Divorce and the elderly. *Gerontologist, 21,* 276–282.

Ulbrich, P. (1994, August). Paper presented at annual convention of the American Sociological Society. Reported in *USA Today,* "White men don't jump into chores" by Margaret I. Usdansky, August 8, 1994.

Ullian, D. Z. (1976). The development of conceptions of masculinity and femininity. In B. Lloyd & J. Aicker (Eds.), *Exploring sex differences* (pp. 25–47). San Diego, CA: Academic Press.

Ullman, M. (1994, March). *The use of verb forms and plurals by Alzheimer's patients.* Paper presented at the meeting of the Cognitive Neuroscience Society, Pittsburgh, PA.

Urban Institute. (1982). *The subtle revolution: Women at work.* Washington, DC: Author.

Urberg, K. A. (1979). Sex-role conceptualization in adolescents and adults. *Developmental Psychology, 15,* 90–92.

Usdansky, M. L. (1994, August 17). Study fuels homosexuality debate. *USA Today,* p. 8A.

V

Valdës, E., del Castillo, C., Gutiërrez, R., Larrea, F., Medina, M., & Përez-Palcios, G. (1979). Endocrine studies and successful treatment in a patient with true hermaphroditism. *Acta Endocrinologica, 91,* 184–192.

Valliant, G. E. (1977). *Adaptation to life.* Boston: Little, Brown.

Valliant, G. E. (1983). Childhood environment and maturity of defense mechanisms. In D. Magnusson & V. L. Allen (Eds.), *Human development: An interactional perspective.* New York: Academic Press.

Vandell, D. L. (1979). The effect of playgroup experience on mother—son and father—son interaction. *Developmental Psychology, 15,* 379–385.

Vandell, D. L., & Wilson, K. S. (1987). Infants' interactions with mother, sibling, and peer: Contrasts and relations between interaction systems. *Child Development, 58,* 176–186.

Vandell, D. L., Wilson, K. S., & Buchanan, N. R. (1980). Peer interaction in the first year of life: An examination of its structure, content, and sensitivity to toys. *Child Development, 51,* 481–488.

van den Boom, D. C., & Hoeksma, J. B. (1994). The effect of infant irritability on mother-infant interaction: A growth-curve analysis. *Developmental Psychology, 30,* 581–590.

Vandershaf, V. (1987, March). Dyslexia: Recognizing shapes, not sounds. *Psychology Today,* p. 12.

Van Dusen, R. A., & Sheldon, E. B. (1976). The changing status of American women. *American Psychologist, 31,* 106–116.

Van Gelder, L., & Carmichael, C. (1975, October). But what about our sons? *Ms. Magazine.*

Vaughn, B. E., Stevenson-Hinde, J., Waters, E., Kotsaftis, A., Lefever, G. B., Shouldice, A., Trudel, M., & Belsky, J. (1992). Attachment security and temperament in infancy and early childhood: Some conceptual clarifications. *Developmental Psychology, 28,* 463–473.

Vaughan, D. (1987 July). The long goodbye. *Psychology Today, 21,* 36–42.

Veatch, R. M. (1988). The definitions of death: Problems for public policy. In H. Hannelore, F. M. Berardo, & R. A. Neimeyer (Eds.), *Dying: Facing the facts* (2nd ed.). Washington, DC: Hemisphere Publishing Corporation.

Versaci, C., Gholami, G. H., Panci, C., & Caffa, B. (1993). Oocyte donation in menopausal women. *Human Reproduction, 8,* 1487–1490.

Viken, R. J., Rose, R. J., Kaprio, J., & Koskenvuo, M. (1994). A developmental genetic analysis of adult personality: Extraversion and neuroticism from 18 to 59 years of age. *Journal of Personality and Social Psychology, 66,* 722–730.

Volpe, E. P. (1971). *Human heredity and birth defects.* New York: Pegasus.

Vygotsky, L. (1986). *Thought and language.* Cambridge, MA: M.I.T. Press. (Original work published 1934)

Vygotsky, L. S. (1956). *Selected psychological investigations.* Moscow: Izdstelsto Akademii Pedagogicheskikh Nack SSR.

Vygotsky, L. S. (1978). *The mind in society: The development of higher psychological processes.* Cambridge, MA: Harvard University Press.

Vygotsky, L. S. (1992). *Thought and language.* Cambridge, MA: Harvard University Press.

W

Waber, D. P. (1977). Sex differences in mental abilities, hemispheric lateralization, and rate of physical growth at adolescence. *Developmental Psychology, 13,* 29–38.

Wada, J. A., Clark, R., & Hamm, A. (1975). Cerebral hemisphere asymmetry in humans. *Archives of Neurology, 32,* 239–246.

Waddington, C. H. (1966). *Principles of development and differentiation.* New York: Macmillan.

Wade, C. (1993). The impact of gender and culture on our conception of psychology. *The General Psychologist, 29,* 78–91.

Wade, C., & Tavris, C. (1993). *Psychology* (3rd ed.). New York: HarperCollins.

Waldfogel, S. (1948). The frequency and affective character of childhood memories. *Psychological Monographs, 62*(Whole No. 291).
Walford, R. L. (1969). *The immunological theory of aging.* Baltimore: Williams & Wilkins.
Walker, L. J. (1984). Sex differences in the development of moral reasoning: A critical review. *Child Development, 55,* 131–139.
Walker, L. J. (1989). A longitudinal study of moral reasoning. *Child Development, 60,* 157–166.
Walker, L. J., & Taylor, J. H. (1991). Family interactions and the development of moral reasoning. *Child Development, 62,* 264–283.
Walker, V. G., Hardiman, C. J., Hedrick, D. L., & Holbrook, A. (1981). Speech and language characteristics of an aging population. In J. J. Lass (Ed.), *Advances in basic research and practice* (Vol. 6, pp. 143–202). New York: Academic Press.
Walker, V. G., Roberts, P. M., & Hedrick, D. L. (1988). Linguistic analyses of the discourse narratives of young and aged women. *Folia Phoniatica, 40,* 58–64.
Wallerstein, J. S. (1984). Children of divorce. *American Journal of Orthopsychiatry, 54,* 444–458.
Walsh, M. R. (1987). *The psychology of women: Ongoing debates.* New Haven, CT: Yale University Press.
Walton, G. E., & Bower, T. G. R. (1993). Newborns form "prototypes" in less than 1 minute. *Psychological Science, 4,* 203–205.
Warren, J. R. (1966). Birth order and social behavior. *Psychological Bulletin, 65,* 38–49.
Warren, M. (1982, April). Onset of puberty later in athletic girls. *Medical Aspects of Human Sexuality,* 77–78.
Warren, R. M. (1961). Illusory changes in repeated words: Differences between young adults and the aged. *American Journal of Psychology, 74,* 506–516.
Warren, R. M., & Warren, R. P. (1966). A comparison of speech perception in childhood, maturity, and old age by means of the verbal transformation effect. *Journal of Verbal Learning and Verbal Behavior, 5,* 142–146.
Wass, H., & Stillion, J. M. (1988). Deaths in the lives of children and adolescents. In H. Hannelore, F. M. Berardo, & R. A. Neimeyer (Eds.), *Dying: Facing the facts* (2nd ed.). Washington, DC: Hemisphere Publishing Corporation.
Watson, J. B. (1913). Psychology as the behaviorist views it. *Psychological Reviews, 20,* 158–177.
Watson, J. B. (1925). *Behaviorism.* New York: Norton.
Watson, J. B. (1928). *Psychological care of infant and child.* New York: Norton.
Watson, J. B., & Rayner, R. (1920). Conditioned emotional reactions. *Journal of Experimental Psychology, 3,* 1–14.
Waxler, C. Z., & Radke-Yarrow, M. (1975). An observational study of maternal models. *Developmental Psychology, 11,* 485–494.
Wechsler, D. (1972). "Hold" and "Don't Hold" tests. In S. M. Chown (Ed.), *Human aging.* New York: Penguin.
Wechsler, D. (1981). *WAIS-R manual.* New York: The Psychological Corporation.
Weinberg, R. A. (1989). Intelligence and IQ: Landmark issues and great debates. *American Psychologist, 44,* 98–104.
Weinraub, M., & Frankel, J. (1977). Sex differences in parent-infant interaction during free play, departure, and separation. *Child Development, 48,* 1240–1249.
Weinraub, M., & Lewis, M. (1977). The determinates of children's responses to separation. *Monographs of the Society for Research in Child Development, 42*(4, Serial No. 172).
Weisman, A. D., & Kastenbaum, R. (1968). The psychological autopsy: A study of the terminal phase of life. *Community Mental Health* (Monograph No. 4).
Weitzman, L. J., Eifler, D., Hokada, E., & Ross, C. (1972). Sex-role socialization in picture books for preschool children. *American Journal of Sociology, 77,* 1125–1150.
Welch, R. L., Huston-Stein, A., Wright, J. C., & Plehal, R. (1979). Subtle sex-role cues in children's commercials. *Journal of Communication, 29,* 202–209.
Werner, H. (1957). The concept of development from a comparative and organismic point of view. In D. Harris (Ed.), *The concept of development.* Minneapolis: University of Minnesota Press.
Werner, J. S., & Siqueland, E. R. (1978). Visual recognition memory in the preterm infant. *Infant Behavior and Development, 1,* 79–94.
Werry, J. S., & Quay, H. C. (1971). The prevalence of behavior symptoms in younger elementary school children. *American Journal of Orthopsychiatry, 41,* 136–143.
Wertsch, J. V., & Tulviste, P. (1992). L. S. Vygotsky and contemporary developmental psychology. *Developmental Psychology, 28,* 548–557.
Westoff, C. F., Calot, G., & Foster, A. D. (1983). Teenage fertility in developed nations. *Family Planning Perspectives, 15,* 105.
Wheeler, L., Reis, H., & Nezlek, J. (1983). Loneliness, social interaction, and sex roles. *Journal of Personality and Social Psychology, 45,* 943–953.
Wheelock, J. H. (1963). A true poem is a way of knowing. *What is poetry?* New York: Scribner.
Whinfield, E. H. (1975). *The teachings of the Rumi.* New York: E. P. Dutton.
Whitaker, H. (1980). *Neurofunctional approach to second language acquisition.* Paper presented at Neurolinguistics of Second Language Learning Symposium, Rio de Janeiro.
Whitbourne, S. K., & Tesch, S. A. (1985). A comparison of identity and intimacy statuses in college students and alumni. *Developmental Psychology, 21,* 1039–1044.
Whitbourne, S. K., & Waterman, A. S. (1979). Psychosocial development during the adult years: Age and cohort comparisons. *Developmental Psychology, 15,* 373–378.
Whitbourne, S. K., Zuschlag, M. K., Elliot, L. B., & Waterman, A. S. (1992). Psychosocial development in adulthood: A 22-year sequential study. *Journal of Personality and Social Psychology, 63,* 260–271.
White, B. L. (1985). *The first three years of life.* Englewood Cliffs, NJ: Prentice Hall.
White, E., Elson, B., & Prawat, R. (1978). Children's conceptions of death. *Child Development, 49,* 307–310.
White, P. L. (1971). *Human infants: Experience and psychological development.* Englewood Cliffs, NJ: Prentice Hall.
White, S. H., & Pillemer, D. B. (1979). Childhood amnesia and the development of a socially accessible memory system. In J. F. Kihlstrom & F. J. Evans (Eds.), *Functional disorders of memory* (pp. 29–73). Hillsdale, NJ: Erlbaum.
Whorf, B. (1956). *Language, thought, and reality.* New York: Wiley.
Whyte, W. W., Jr. (1956). *The organization man.* New York: Simon & Schuster.
Wilcox, S., & Sutton, M. (Eds.). (1985). *Understanding death and dying* (3rd ed.). Palo Alto, CA: Mayfield.
Wilcox, S. G., & Sutton, M. (Eds.). (1981). *Understanding death and dying* (2nd ed.). Palo Alto, CA: Mayfield Publishing.
Williams, J. E., & Best, D. L. (1982). *Measuring sex stereotypes.* Beverly Hills, CA: Sage.
Williams, J. H. (1987). *Psychology of women: Behavior in a biosocial context* (3rd ed.). New York: Norton.

Williamson, D. F., Madams, J., Ada, R. F., Kleinman, J. C., Giovino, G. A., & Byers, T. (1991). Smoking cessation and severity of weight gain in a national cohort. *New England Journal of Medicine, 324,* 739–745.

Willie, C. V. (1985). *Black and white families: A study in complementarity.* Bayside, NY: General Hall, Inc.

Wills, T. A. (1981). Downward comparison principles in social psychology. *Psychology Bulletin, 90,* 245–259.

Wilson, D. L. (1974). The programmed theory of aging. In M. Rockstein, M. L. Sussman, & J. Chesky (Eds.), *Theoretical aspects of aging.* New York: Academic Press.

Wilson, E. O. (1975). *Sociobiology: A new synthesis.* Cambridge, MA: Harvard University Press.

Wilson, G. (1939). Nyakyusa conceptions of burial. *Bantu Studies, 13,* 1–31.

Wink, P., & Helson, R. (1993). Personality change in women and their partners. *Journal of Personality and Social Psychology, 65,* 597–606.

Winnick, M. (1974). Childhood obesity. *Nutrition Today, 9,* 6–12.

Wolf, M., & Dickerson, D. (1985). From oral to written language: Transitions in the school years. In J. B. Gleason (Ed.), *The development of language.* Columbus, OH: Merrill.

Won-Doornik, M. J. (1979). On getting to know you: The association between the stage of a relationship and the reciprocity of self-disclosure. *Journal of Experimental Social Psychology, 15,* 229–241.

Woodall, K. L., & Matthews, K. A. (1993). Changes in and stability of hostile characteristics: Results from a 4-year longitudinal study of children. *Journal of Personality and Social Psychology, 64,* 491–499.

Woods, N. F., Dery, G. K., & Most, A. (1983). Recollections of menarche, current menstrual attitudes, and premenstrual symptoms. In S. Golub (Ed.), *Menarche: The transition from girl to woman.* Lexington, MA: Lexington Books.

Woodward, A. L., Markman, E. M., & Fitzsimmons, C. M. (1994). Rapid word learning in 13- and 18-month-olds. *Developmental Psychology, 30,* 553–566.

Woody-Ramsey, J., & Miller, P. H. (1988). The facilitation of selective attention in preschoolers. *Child Development, 59,* 1497–1503.

Wozniak, R. H. (1975a). A dialectical paradigm for psychological research: Implications drawn from the history of psychology in the Soviet Union. *Human Development, 18,* 18–34.

Wozniak, R. H. (1975b). Dialectics and structuralism: The philosophical foundations of Soviet psychology and Piagetian cognitive developmental theory. In K. F. Riegel & G. Rosenwald (Eds.), *Structure and transformation: Developmental aspects.* New York: Wiley.

Wylie, R. C. (1961). *The self concept* (Vol.2). Lincoln: University of Nebraska Press.

Y

Yeates, K. O., & Selman, R. L. (1989). Social competence in the schools: Toward an integrative developmental model for intervention. *Developmental Review, 9,* 64–100.

Yogman, M. W. (1981). Development of the father-infant relationship. In H. Fitzgerald, B. Lester, & M. W. Yogman (Eds.), *Theory and research in behavioral pediatrics* (Vol. 1). New York: Plenum.

Yogman, M. W. (1982). Observations on the father-infant relationship. In S. Cath, A. Gurwitt, & J. M. Ross (Eds.), *Father and child: Development and clinical perspectives* (pp. 101–122). Boston: Little Brown.

Young, E. W., & Stevenson, D. K. (1990). Limiting treatment for extremely premature, low-birth-weight infants (500 to 750 g). *American Journal of Diseases of Children, 144,* 549–552.

Young, W. C., Goy, R. W., & Phoenix, C. H. (1965). Hormones and sexual behavior. In J. Money (Ed.), *Sex research: New developments.* New York: Holt, Rinehart & Winston.

Youniss, J., & Smollar, J. (1985). *Adolescent relations with mothers, fathers, and friends.* Chicago: University of Chicago Press.

Z

Zabin, L. S., Hirsch, M. B., Smith, E. A., Strett, R., & Hardy, J. B. (1986). Evaluation of a pregnancy prevention program for urban teenagers. *Family Planning Perspectives, 18,* 119–126.

Zahn-Waxler, C., & Radke-Yarrow, M. (1982). The development of altruism: Alternative research strategies. In N. Eisenberg (Ed.), *The development of prosocial behavior.* New York: Academic Press.

Zajonc, R. B. (1970, February). Brainwash: Familiarity breeds comfort. *Psychology Today,* pp. 32–35, 60–62.

Zajonc, R. B. (1976). Family configuration and intelligence. *Science, 192,* 227–236.

Zajonc, R. B. (1980). Feeling and thinking: Preferences need no inferences. *American Psychologist, 35,* 151–175.

Zajonc, R. B. (1983). Validating the confluence model. *Psychological Bulletin, 93,* 457–480.

Zajonc, R. B., Markus, H., & Markus, G. B. (1979). The birth order puzzle. *Journal of Personality and Social Psychology, 37,* 1325–1341.

Zarit, S. H., Cole, K. D., & Guider, R. L. (1981). Memory training strategies and subjective complaints of memory in aged. *The Gerontologist, 21,* 158–164.

Zelazo, P. R. (1976). From reflexive to instrumental behavior. In L. P. Lipsitt (Ed.), Developmental psychobiology: The significance of infancy. Hillsdale, NJ: Erlbaum.

Zelinski, E. M., Gilewski, M. J., & Thompson, L. W. (1980). Do laboratory memory tests relate to everyday remembering and forgetting? In L. W. Poon, J. I. Fozzard, L. S. Cremak, D. Arenberg, & L. W. Thompson (Eds.), *New directions in memory and aging: Proceedings of the George A. Talland Memorial Conference.* Hillsdale, NJ: Erlbaum.

Zelnik, M., & Kantner, J. (1977). Sexual and contraceptive experience of young, unmarried women in the United States, 1976 and 1971. *Family Planning Perspectives, 9,* 55–71.

Zelnik, M., & Kantner, J. F. (1980). Sexual activity, contraceptive use, and pregnancy among metropolitan-area teenagers: 1971–1979. *Family Planning Perspectives, 12,* 230–237.

Zigler, E., & Styfco, S. J. (1994). Head Start: Criticisms in a constructive context. *American Psychologist, 49,* 127–132.

Zigler, E. F., Lamb, M. E., & Child, I. L. (1982). *Socialization and personality development.* New York: Oxford University Press.

Zill, N. (1985). *Happy, healthy, and insecure: A portrait of middle childhood in the United States.* New York: Cambridge University Press.

Zimbardo, P. G. (1977). *Shyness: What it is, what you can do about it.* Reading, MA: Addison-Wesley.

Zimbardo, P. G. (1990). *Shyness: What it is, what to do about it* (rev. ed.). Reading, MA: Addison-Wesley.

Zinchenko, V. P. (1983). The problem of involuntary memory. *Soviet Psychology, 22,* 55–111.

Zivian, M., & Darjes, R. (1983). Free recall by in-school and out-of-school adults: Performance and metamemory. *Developmental Psychology, 19,* 513–520.

CREDITS

PHOTOGRAPHS

Chapter 1

Opener: © Bachmann/The Image Works; **p. 5:** © James L. Shaffer; **p. 10:** © David Frazier Photo CD; **p. 16:** © Richard T. Nowitz/Photo Researchers, Inc.; **p. 25:** © James L. Shaffer; **p. 29:** © Llewellyn/Uniphoto Picture Agency

Chapter 2

Opener: © Yves DeBraine/Black Star; **p. 40:** © 1994 Laura Dwight; **p. 41:** © Sharon Dague; **p. 46:** © Arthur Gurmankin/Unicorn Stock Photos; **p. 52:** © Uniphoto Picture Agency; **p. 55:** © David J. Deluhery; **p. 59:** Digital Stock Photo CD

Chapter 3

Opener: © Frank Pedrick/The Image Works; **p. 78:** Bettmann Archive; **fig. 3.2:** © 1994 Laura Dwight; **fig. 3.3:** Dr. Gail Stetten, Johns Hopkins University Prenatal Diagnostic Center; **fig. 3.5:** Courtesy of A. P. Streissguth, H. M. Barr, and D. C. Martin; **p. 92:** © Art Stein/Photo Researchers, Inc.; **p. 93:** © 1994 Laura Dwight; **p. 97:** © Billy E. Barnes/PhotoEdit; **p. 100:** © David Frazier Photo CD

Chapter 4

Opener: © Jean-Claude Lejeune; **fig. 4.1A:** © D. W. Fawcett/D. Phillips/Photo Researchers, Inc.; **fig. 4.1B:** © Petit Format/Nestle/Science Source/Photo Researchers, Inc.; **fig. 4.1C:** © Russ Kinne/Comstock; **fig. 4.1D:** © Dr. C. Reather/Photo Researchers, Inc.; **fig. 4.1E:** © Petit Format/Nestle/Science Source/Photo Researchers, Inc.; **fig. 4.1F:** © Tom McCarthy/PhotoEdit; **figs. 4.11A–D:** Clinical Pathological Conference on Acromegaly, Diabetes, Hypermetabolism, Protein Use and Heart Failure. *American Journal of Medicine*, 20: 133, (1956). © Cahners Publishing Co., Inc.; **fig. 4.18:** © David Linton; **fig. 4.19:** William Vandivert, *Scientific American*, April 1960; **p. 140:** Courtesy Ronald Reagan Library

Chapter 5

Opener: © Nita Winter/The Image Works; **p. 151:** © Bob Daemmrich/The Image Works; **p. 156:** © Comstock, Inc.; **p. 160:** © James L. Shaffer; **p. 163:** © Kathi Corder/Unicorn Stock Photos; **p. 168:** © Sandra Johnson/The Picture Cube; **p. 173:** © Uniphoto Picture Agency

Chapter 6

Opener: © Jeff Greenberg/PhotoEdit; **p. 185:** © Brown Brothers; **p. 190:** © H. Armstrong Roberts; **p. 192:** © George E. Goodwin/The Picture Cube; **p. 194:** © Linda Benedict-Jones/The Picture Cube; **p. 203:** © James L. Shaffer; **p. 207:** © Uniphoto Picture Agency; **p. 210:** Digital Stock Photo CD; **p. 211:** © Daniel Grogan/Uniphoto Picture Agency

Chapter 7

Opener: © Arni Katz/Unicorn Stock Photos; **p. 225:** Digital Stock Photo CD; **p. 229:** © 1994 Laura Dwight; **p. 231:** © Joel Dexter/Unicorn Stock Photos; **p. 233:** © Steve Niedorf/The Image Bank, Texas; **p. 237:** © Michael Siluk; **p. 242:** © Elizabeth Crews/The Image Works

Chapter 8

Opener: © Dion Ogust/The Image Works; **p. 255:** © Elizabeth Crews/The Image Works; **p. 258:** © Michael Siluk; **p. 263:** © Ursula Markus/Photo Researchers, Inc.; **p. 266:** © Michael Siluk; **p. 272:** © James L. Shaffer; **p. 278:** © Jeff Greenberg/Unicorn Stock Photos; **p. 279:** © James L. Shaffer

Chapter 9

Opener: © 1994 Laura Dwight; **fig. 9.1:** © Jeff Storm; **fig. 9.2:** Bettmann Archive; **fig. 9.3:** Reprinted with permission of L. Alan Sroufe/Institute of Child Development, University of Minnesota; **p. 302:** © Alan Carey/The Image Works; **p. 307:** © David Young-Wolff/PhotoEdit

Chapter 10

Opener: © Michael Siluk; **p. 315:** © Jeff Greenberg/Unicorn Stock Photos; **p. 318:** Digital Stock Photo CD; **p. 321:** Uniphoto Picture Agency; **p. 324:** © 1994 Laura Dwight; **p. 325:** © Jean Higgins/Unicorn Stock Photos; **p. 331:** Skjold Stock Photographs; **p. 332:** © David Strickler/The Image Works

Chapter 11

Opener: Skjold Stock Photographs; **p. 339:** © Erika Stone/Photo Researchers, Inc.; **p. 342:** © Chuck Savage/Uniphoto Picture Agency; **p. 349:** © V. E. Horne/Unicorn Stock Photos; **p. 351:** James Kay/Uniphoto Picture Agency; **p. 354:** © Henley & Savage/Uniphoto Picture Agency; **p. 357:** © 1994 Laura Dwight; **p. 363:** © 1994 Laura Dwight

Chapter 12

Opener: © Chester Higgins/Photo Researchers, Inc.; **p. 373:** © 1994 Laura Dwight; **p. 380:** © 1994 Laura Dwight; **p. 383:** © Charles Gupron/Uniphoto Picture Agency; **p. 386:** © David Brownell/The Image Bank; **p. 388:** © 1994 Laura Dwight; **p. 390:** © Bob Daemmrich/Uniphoto Picture Agency; **p. 393:** Courtesy Green Bay Packers

Chapter 13

Opener: © Bachmann/Uniphoto Picture Agency; **p. 404:** © Gary Chapman/The Image Bank–Texas; **p. 406:** © 1994 Laura Dwight; **p. 411:** © 1994 Laura Dwight; **p. 413:** © Karen Holsinger Mullen/Unicorn Stock Photos; **p. 417:** Skjold Stock Photography; **p. 419:** Michael Rougier/Life Magazine, © Time Warner, Inc.; **p. 421:** © William Thompson/The Picture Cube; **p. 424:** Uniphoto Picture Agency

Chapter 14

Opener: © James L. Shaffer; **p. 435:** © Herb Snitzer/Stock Boston; **p. 438:** © David Burnett/Stock Boston; **p. 443:** © Dennis MacDonald/PhotoEdit; **p. 444:** © Robert Brenner/PhotoEdit; **p. 448:** © Blair Seitz/Photo Researchers, Inc.; **p. 450:** © James L. Shaffer; **p. 452:** © James L. Shaffer

LINE ART

Chapter 2

Fig. 2.2: Source: Data from A. H. Maslow, *Motivation and Personality*, 2d edition, Harper & Row, New York, 1970.

Chapter 3

Fig. 3.4: From K. L. Moore and T. V. N. Persaud, *The Developing Human: Clinically Oriented Embryology*, 5th edition. Copyright © 1993 W. B. Saunders, Orlando, Fla. Reprinted by permission.

Chapter 4

Figs. 4.3 and 4.6: From Kent M. Van De Graaff and Stuart Ira Fox, *Concepts of Human Anatomy*, 4th edition. Copyright © 1995 Wm. C. Brown Communications, Inc., Dubuque, Iowa. Reprinted by permission of Times Mirror Higher Education Group, Inc., Dubuque, Iowa. All Rights Reserved; **fig. 4.4:** From Donald B. Irwin and Janet A. Simons, *Lifespan Developmental*

Psychology, 1st edition. Copyright © 1994 Wm. C. Brown Communications, Inc., Dubuque, Iowa. Reprinted by permission of Times Mirror Higher Education Group, Inc., Dubuque, Iowa. All Rights Reserved; **fig. 4.5:** Source: Data from M. C. Allen, P. K. Donohue, and A. E. Dusman, "The Limit of Viability—Neonatal Outcome of Infants Born at 22 to 25 Weeks Gestation" in *New England Journal of Medicine,* November 26, 1993, pages 1597–1601; **figs. 4.12 and 4.13:** Source: Data from J. M. Tanner, *Fetus Into Man: Physical Growth from Conception to Maturity,* Harvard University Press, Cambridge, Mass., 1978; **fig. 4.16:** From M. M. Shirley, *The First Two Years.* Institute of Child Welfare Monograph No. 7, University of Minnesota Press. Copyright © 1933 by the University of Minnesota, renewed 1961.

Chapter 5

Fig. 5.9: Source: Data from J. Botwinick, *Cognitive Processes in Maturity and Old Age,* 3d edition, Springer-Verlag, New York, 1984.

Chapter 6

Fig. 6.2: Sources: From H. E. Jones, "Intelligence and Problem-Solving" in *Handbook of Aging and the Individual,* edited by J. E. Birren, University of Chicago Press, Chicago, 1959, pages 700–738; and from D. H. Kausler, *Experimental Psychology and Human Aging,* John Wiley & Sons, New York, 1982, page 574.

Chapter 7

Fig. 7.5: Source: Data from L. K. Obler and M. L. Albert, "Language Skills Across Adulthood" in *Handbook of the Psychology of Aging* edited by J. E. Birren and K. W. Schaie, Van Nostrand Reinhold, New York, 1985.

Chapter 10

Fig. 10.1: Source: From B. I. Fagot and M. D. Leinbach, "Play Styles in Early Childhood: Social Consequences for Boys and Girls" in *Social and Cognitive Skills: Sex Roles and Children's Play,* edited by M. B. Liss, Academic Press, New York, 1983; **fig. 10.4:** Source: From M. Hunt, *Sexual Behavior in the 1970s,* Playboy Press, Chicago, 1974.

Chapter 11

Fig. 11.1: Sources: *Statistical Abstracts of the United States,* No. 143, 1993; and U.S. Census Report, No. A 158–159, 1970; **fig. 11.2:** Source: *Statistical Abstracts of the United States,* No. 91, 1992; **fig. 11.3:** Sources: *Statistical Abstracts of the United States,* No. 127, 1989; and *Statistical Abstracts of the United States,* No. 140, 1993; **fig. 11.4:** Source: *Statistical Abstracts of the United States,* No. 101, 1993.

Chapter 12

Fig. 12.3: Source: From J. H. Pleck, *Working Wives/Working Husbands,* Sage, Thousand Oaks, Calif., 1985.

Chapter 13

Fig. 13.1: Source: Data from A. H. Maslow, *Motivation and Personality,* 2d edition, Harper & Row, New York, 1970.

NAME INDEX

C

D

E

F

G

H

I

J

K

L

Q

R

S

SUBJECT INDEX

G

H

I

K

L

M

S

T

U

V

W

Z